Alice M. G

P9-DCZ-426

THE ROOTS OF NATIONAL CULTURE

AMERICAN LITERATURE: A PERIOD ANTHOLOGY

OSCAR CARGILL, *General Editor*

THE ROOTS OF NATIONAL CULTURE: TO 1830

ROBERT E. SPILLER
Swarthmore College

THE ROMANTIC TRIUMPH: 1830-1860

TREMAINE MCDOWELL
University of Minnesota

THE RISE OF REALISM: 1860-1888

LOUIS WANN
University of Southern California

THE SOCIAL REVOLT: 1888-1914

OSCAR CARGILL
New York University

CONTEMPORARY TRENDS: SINCE 1914

JOHN HERBERT NELSON
University of Kansas

THE ROOTS OF NATIONAL CULTURE

American Literature

TO 1830

EDITED BY
ROBERT E. SPILLER
ASSOCIATE PROFESSOR OF ENGLISH
SWARTHMORE COLLEGE

NEW YORK
THE MACMILLAN COMPANY
1933

GreerCrest Library
Millbrook, N.Y.

COPYRIGHT, 1933,
BY THE MACMILLAN COMPANY

All rights reserved—no part of this book may be reproduced in any form without permission in writing from the publisher, except by a reviewer who wishes to quote brief passages in connection with a review written for inclusion in magazine or newspaper.

—Set up and electrotyped by Kingsport Press, Inc.—
—Printed in the United States of America—

PREFACE

The two centuries of American literary history which are illustrated by the selections in this volume may claim for themselves the greatest of all pioneer scholars in the field, Moses Coit Tyler. But in spite of the exhaustive detail of his work and that of his successors, this period as yet seems to lack the critical patterns and standards which have recently defined a romantic movement in the first half of the nineteenth century and charted the course of our later literary development in terms of realism and the frontier.

The problem was first confused by "belles lettristic" anthologists like Duyckinck and Griswold, who indiscriminately listed all the writers known to them, and then attempted, somewhat apologetically, to apply æsthetic judgment to their work. More recently, social and economic historians like Parrington and Beard have provided some useful organic principles of criticism, but the material under consideration sinks, in their hands, to the level of mere evidence, and loses much of its claim to the modest literary excellence which it unquestionably possesses.

The selection and arrangement of the material in this volume have been determined by factors in literary rather than in other forms of history. It would be impossible to apply a single term of criticism to all of it, or even to a part. It is not "romantic," "classic," or "realistic." In the work of individual authors, we do not hesitate to speak of early production as "apprentice" or "experimental" work, and some such term may well be applied to early American literature. But there could not be an American literature before there was an American race or nation in something more than a political sense. Our study, therefore, divides itself into two parts which are clearly demarked by a date somewhere in the neighborhood of 1760 to 1785. The first is concerned with an organic process of social and economic evolution, the transfer of matured civilizations to a primitive environment; the second with an organic process of literary evolution, the earliest expression in art forms of the new civilization which emerged. American writing of the period of settlement and of adjustment to the new environment is more interesting and important for its bearing upon the process of constructing a new civilization than it is for its artistic excellences or defects. With the awakening of a literary consciousness in the periods of imitation and of national self-assertion, emphasis must shift to the study of literary forms and modes, and of works which, in their authors' own minds, were literature.

There are certain traditions as to which authors and works may be considered American and which may not. Certain of the writings of John Smith and Thomas Paine are usually included in our literature, whereas all those of William Penn are excluded; and yet Penn left as deep an impress upon our thought, and wrote as much in the spirit of America, as either of the others. It has also been customary, in these doubtful cases, to include only those works which were written in America or which deal with American themes. Yet it is difficult to judge of Smith without reading the lusty account of his combats with the Turks, of Paine without considering his later and more philosophical works as well as his political tracts, and of Penn without reading his *Fruits of Solitude*. For the same reasons, the writings of the early explorers and the legends of the Indians must be considered in any broad study of our literary origins.

The texts in this volume are based upon printed rather than manuscript sources; and they have been reprinted from these sources without editorial changes other than the elimination of certain typographical archaisms, such as the long ſ and the interchanged *v* and *u*. Changes have also been made in the type style of captions and notes in order to make them conform to the style of the series. The sources are either the final printed text that presumably met the approval of the author, the contemporary text that modern criticism has preferred, or a modern edition prepared according to conservative principles and accurate workmanship, and based upon a manuscript or acceptable early printed version. In accepting the work of other editors, three tests have been applied: the known reliability of the editor concerned; a check of representative passages against manuscripts or early editions in order to determine the editorial principles used; and prefatory statements of editorial policy. Even in cases where such policy is slightly more liberal than is perhaps desirable, the text has been faithfully reproduced. For each selection, the date of first publication is given at the foot of the passage; that of composition is given in parentheses when much earlier than that of printing. Omissions in the text are indicated by three asterisks.

The editor gratefully recognizes his debt to those who have advised and assisted him: Randolph G. Adams, Nelson F. Adkins, Philip C. Blackburn, Edward S. Bradley, Frederic Ives Carpenter, Arthur Christy, Harry Hayden Clark, S. Foster Damon, John B. Foster, James Thayer Gerould, Thomas O. Mabbott, Tremaine McDowell, Stewart Mitchell, S. E. Morison, Albert Cook Myers, Arthur H. Nason, John H. Nelson, V. V. Parma, Arthur Hobson Quinn, Ralp L. Rusk, Townsend Scudder III, Rufus Suter, Louis Wann, Harry R. Warfel, George Parker Winship, and Theodore A. Zunder. To Oscar Cargill must go a large share of credit for the volume as a whole.

ROBERT E. SPILLER

ACKNOWLEDGMENTS

For permission to reprint copyright texts, acknowledgment is hereby made:

To D. Appleton and Company: for selections from the prose and poetry of W. C. Bryant.

To The Century Company, and Arthur H. Quinn: for Royall Tyler's *The Contrast.*

To The Champlain Society: for the selection from Champlain's *Les Voyages.*

To Columbia University Press: for the selection from Samuel Johnson's *Raphael,* edited by H. and C. Schneider.

To Mr. Bridgham Curtis: for selections from *The Indians' Book,* by Natalie Curtis, published by Harper and Brothers.

To Dodd, Mead and Company: for the Winthrop letters from *Some Old Puritan Love Letters,* edited by J. H. Twichell.

To Doubleday, Doran and Company: for the selection from *The Writings of Col. William Byrd,* edited by J. S. Bassett.

To Harcourt, Brace and Company: for selections from volumes in the "American Authors' Series": *Poems of Freneau,* edited by H. H. Clark; *Selections from the Works of Cotton Mather,* edited by K. B. Murdock; and Irving's *A History of New York by Diedrich Knickerbocker,* edited by S. T. Williams and T. McDowell.

To The Harvard University Press: for selections from Anne Hulton's *Letters of a Loyalist Lady.*

To Henry Holt and Company: for Letter XXIII from Hamilton's *The Federalist,* edited by P. L. Ford.

To Houghton Mifflin Company: for selections from the edition of Bradford's *History of Plymouth Plantation,* edited by Worthington C. Ford for the Massachusetts Historical Society.

To J. B. Lippincott Company: for "Home, Sweet Home," from Gabriel Harrison's *Life of John Howard Payne.*

To Thomas O. Mabbott and F. L. Pleadwell: for selections from the poetry of E. C. Pinkney, published by The Macmillan Company.

To The Macmillan Company: for selections from *The Journal of John Woolman,* edited by A. M. Gummere; and from *The Writings of Benjamin Franklin,* edited by A. H. Smyth.

To Arthur H. Nason and The Andiron Club: for selections from the poetry of John Trumbull.

To The New York Public Library: for the translation of the Columbus letter, by Wilberforce Eames.

To The Oxford University Press, New York: for the selection from Cooper's *Gleanings in Europe,* edited by R. E. Spiller.

To The Prince Society: for the selection from Morton's *The New English Canaan,* edited by C. F. Adams.

To George Parker Winship: for selections from the journal of Sarah Kemble Knight, published by The Harvard University Press.

To Yale University Press: for the selection from Crèvecœur's *Sketches of Eighteenth Century America,* edited by H. L. Bourdin, R. H. Gabriel, and S. T. Williams.

CONTENTS

PAGE

THE ROOTS OF NATIONAL CULTURE

I. THE FIRST FRONTIER 1

II. THE AWAKENING OF LITERARY CONSCIOUSNESS . 10

PROLOGUE

I. CHRISTOPHER COLUMBUS

The Discovered Islands 23

II. THOMAS HARIOT

From Hakluyt's *The Principal Navigations, Voyages, &c.* . 28

III. SAMUEL DE CHAMPLAIN

Les Voyages, Book II, Chapter IX 33

THE SETTLEMENT

I. JOHN SMITH

From *The True Travels &c.* 40

The Generall Historie of Virginia &c., Book III, Chapter II 41

II. WILLAM BRADFORD

From *Of Plimmoth Plantation* 46

III. JOHN WINTHROP

Letters 52

From *A Journal* 58

THE COLONIAL MIND: NEW ENGLAND

I. THOMAS MORTON

The New English Canaan, Book III, Chapter XIV . . . 62

II. ROGER WILLIAMS

From *The Bloudy Tenent &c.* 64

III. RICHARD MATHER

From *"The Bay Psalm Book"* 67

IV. ANNE BRADSTREET

To My Dear Children 68

The Prologue 68

To My Dear and Loving Husband 69

The Four Seasons of the Year 69

PAGE

Contemplations 71
The Author to Her Book 75

V. MICHAEL WIGGLESWORTH
From *The Day of Doom* 75

VI. NATHANIEL WARD
From *The Simple Cobler of Aggawamm* 82

VII. INCREASE MATHER
From *An Essay for the Recording of Illustrious Providences* 83

VIII. COTTON MATHER
From *Magnalia Christi Americana* 89
From *The Wonders of the Invisible World* 90
From *Political Fables* 95

IX. SAMUEL SEWALL
From *Diary* 97

X. MARY ROWLANDSON
Narrative of Captivity 105

XI. SARAH KEMBLE KNIGHT
From *The Private Journal on a Journey from Boston to New-York* 111

THE COLONIAL MIND: MIDDLE STATES AND SOUTH

I. WILLIAM PENN
From *A General Description of Pennsylvania* 119
From *Fruits of Solitude* 124

II. WILLIAM BYRD
From *History of the Dividing Line* 130

III. JOHN WOOLMAN
From *The Journal* 137

THE PROGRESS OF REASON

I. JOHN WISE
From *A Vindication of the Government of New England Churches* 149

II. ETHAN ALLEN
From *Reason the Only Oracle of Man* 157

III. SAMUEL JOHNSON
From *Raphael, or the Genius of English America* . . . 162

PAGE

JONATHAN EDWARDS
The Flying Spider 168
Personal Narrative 171
Sarah Pierrepont 178
Resolutions 178
The Great Awakening at Northampton 179
From *Freedom of the Will* 186

BENJAMIN FRANKLIN
From *The Autobiography* 192
Dogood Papers No. IV 217
The Way to Wealth 220
An Edict by the King of Prussia 226
Rules by Which a Great Empire May Be Reduced to a Small One 229
The Whistle 235
The Ephemera 236

THE REVOLUTIONARY ISSUE: REBEL *vs.* TORY
I. JOHN DICKINSON
Letters from a Farmer in Pennsylvania 238
A Liberty Song 244

II. THOMAS PAINE
From Common Sense 245
The American Crisis, Letter I 256
Liberty Tree 262
From *The Age of Reason* 263

III. ANNE HULTON
Letters 264

IV. JONATHAN BOUCHER
A View of the Causes and Consequences of the American Revolution, Discourse XII 269

THE NATIONAL ISSUE: DEMOCRACY *vs.* FEDERALISM
I. THOMAS JEFFERSON
From *Autobiography* 276
From *Notes on Virginia* 280

II. ALEXANDER HAMILTON
The Federalist, Number XXIII 285

PAGE

THE AWAKENING OF LITERARY CONSCIOUSNESS: POETRY AND ESSAY

I. TIMOTHY DWIGHT
From *Greenfield Hill* 289

II. JOHN TRUMBULL
From *The Progress of Dulness* 296
M'Fingal, Canto III 299

III. JOEL BARLOW
The Hasty-Pudding, Cantos I, II, III 307

IV. FRANCIS HOPKINSON
To Myrtilla 316
The Battle of the Kegs 316
The New Roof: a Song for Federal Mechanics . . . 317
On White-Washing 318

V. THOMAS GODFREY
Song 324

VI. JOSEPH DENNIE
From *The Lay Preacher,* The Man of Understanding . . 324
On the Sabbath 325
Of Precipitation 327

VII. BENJAMIN RUSH
From *Essays* 329

PHILIP FRENEAU
The British Prison Ship, Canto III 335
On the Memorable Victory 339
To the Memory 341
To Shylock Ap-Shenkin 342
Ode 342
On the Anniversary 343
The House of Night 344
The Pyramids of Egypt 348
The Indian Burying Ground 351
The Dying Indian 352
The Indian Student 353
The Deserted Farm-House 354
The Wild Honey Suckle 355
On a Honey Bee 356
To a Caty-did 356
Man of Ninety 357

PAGE

The Vanity of Existence 358
On the Religion of Nature 358
Advice to Authors 359
The Sailor's Relief 362

THE AWAKENING OF LITERARY CONSCIOUSNESS: DRAMA AND NOVEL

I. ROYALL TYLER
The Contrast 366

II. HUGH HENRY BRACKENRIDGE
From *Modern Chivalry* 404

III. SUSANNA HASWELL ROWSON
Charlotte Temple, Chapters I, IX, XI, XII 416

IV. CHARLES BROCKDEN BROWN
From *Arthur Mervyn* 423
Wieland, Chapters I, II 426
Edgar Huntly, Chapter XV 435

THE NATURALISTS

I. WILLIAM BARTRAM
Travels, Part II, Chapter V 445

II. ST. JOHN DE CRÈVECŒUR
Letters from an American Farmer, Letters III, VI . . . 451
Ant-Hill Town 457

III. JOHN JAMES AUDUBON
A Flood 463
The Florida Keys 467

WILLIAM CULLEN BRYANT
American Poetry 470
From *Lectures on Poetry* 475
Thanatopsis 482
Inscription for the Entrance to a Wood 484
To a Waterfowl 484
Green River 485
A Winter Piece 486
The Yellow Violet 489
Monument Mountain 489
A Forest Hymn 492
June 494
I Cannot Forget with What Fervid Devotion 495

PAGE

The Past 495
The Evening Wind 496
Song of Marion's Men 497
Oh Fairest of the Rural Maids 498
To the Fringed Gentian 498
The Prairies 498
Oh Mother of a Mighty Race 501
Robert of Lincoln 502
The Death of Lincoln 503

THE PROGRESS OF ROMANTICISM

I. JAMES GATES PERCIVAL
New-England 504

II. CARLOS WILCOX
From *The Age of Benevolence* 504
From The Religion of Taste 506

III. EDWARD COOTE PINKNEY
The Voyager's Song 507
A Serenade 508
A Health 508

IV. RICHARD HENRY WILDE
My Life Is Like the Summer Rose 509
To the Mocking Bird 509

V. JOHN HOWARD PAYNE
Home, Sweet Home 509

VI. FITZ-GREENE HALLECK
Marco Bozzaris 510
On the Death of Joseph Rodman Drake 512
From *Fanny* 512

VII. JOSEPH RODMAN DRAKE
The Culprit Fay 515
To a Friend 525
The American Flag 528

VIII. JAMES KIRKE PAULDING
The Dutchman's Fireside, Book II, Chapters II, III, VIII . 529
The Diverting History of John Bull and Brother Jonathan,
Chapters I, XVIII 537

PAGE

WILLIAM ELLERY CHANNING
The Moral Argument against Calvinism 542
Remarks on the Character and Writings of John Milton . 548
Remarks on National Literature 556

WASHINGTON IRVING
Knickerbocker's History of New York,
Book II, Chapter II 570
Book IV, Chapter IV 572
Book VI, Chapter VII 577

The Sketch Book of Geoffrey Crayon, Gent^{n}.,
The Author's Account of Himself 584
Christmas Eve 586
Rip Van Winkle 593
Bracebridge Hall, The Stout Gentleman 606
The Alhambra, Legend of the Rose of the Alhambra . . . 613
From *Abbotsford and Newsted Abbey* 623

JAMES FENIMORE COOPER
The Pioneers, Chapter XXII 630
The Last of the Mohicans, Chapter III 636
From *A History of the Navy* 643
From *Satanstoe* 652
Notions of the Americans, Letter XXIII 662
From *Gleanings in Europe* [France] 669
From *The American Democrat* 673

FOLK LITERATURE
INDIAN SONGS AND LEGENDS
I. Hiawatha, or, the Origin of the Onondaga Council-Fire 680
II. Hunting the Moose 683
III. T'Äpk'o Daagya, Song of the Antelope Ceremony . . 684
IV. The Story of Wakiash and the First Totem Pole . . 686
V. Mountain-Songs. 688

NOTES 691
INDEX 755

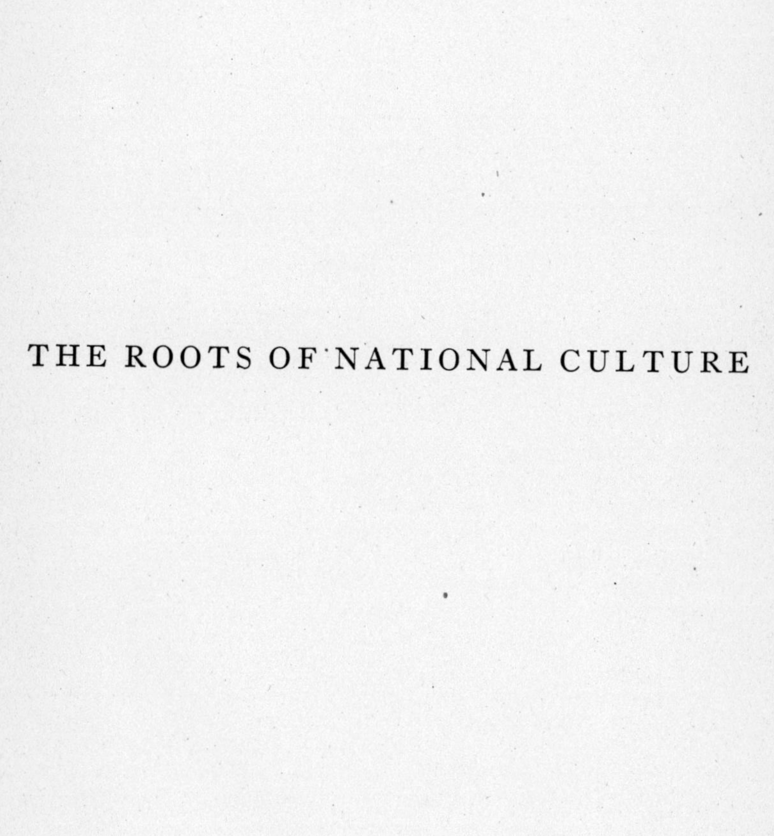

THE ROOTS OF NATIONAL CULTURE

THE ROOTS OF NATIONAL CULTURE

I. THE FIRST FRONTIER
(1492–1760)

American literature was as cosmopolitan in its origins as it has been in its mature developments. Most of its distinguishing characteristics may be traced by one channel or another to European tradition. Our national culture, with the exception of the Indian, Negro, and Mongol strains in it, is a product of the movement of the Aryan race in its later westward migrations. The substratum of folksong, legend, and dance, which is present in all literatures, occurs in that of America chiefly among the Indians, and, in a transplanted form, among the Negroes, and the pioneers. Our literature of conscious art is largely derivative, or is a product of the impact of older cultures on a new environment.

The importance of the frontier movement in the later periods of American literature has recently received a deserved emphasis, but the larger meaning of that movement as a phase in the westward progress of European civilization does not always receive the attention it deserves. In this larger view, the settlement of the eastern seaboard is the first chapter in the history of the American frontier, and the explorers are the earliest pioneers. The first mature literary culture in America, the romantic movement which culminated in the writings of Emerson and his contemporaries, grew in the soil of the thirteen original colonies. There is some doubt as to whether the literature of the larger nation, as it was heralded by Walt Whitman, has as yet reached its maturity.

The first stage of literary culture in any primitive environment is the initial impact of the old upon the new. The pioneer blazes his trail and the settler follows with his ax. If these men write, their eyes are turned westward and they record first impressions and primitive emotional responses. They write narratives of discovery and settlement, and songs and ballads of the trail and camp.

The second stage of literary growth on the frontier results from the effort of men to make homes for themselves in the new environment. With group settlements of a more or less temporary nature, men begin to exchange their ideas and impressions among themselves. They discuss political, social, and religious problems. The local news sheet prints stories and verse copied from journals the pioneer has brought with him from his former home, and each community soon produces its own story-teller and its own bard. Eyes have already begun to look eastward, and there is a curious and crude mingling of the old with the new. The back-trail movement is already suggested, and with it, conscious literary production begins. The crude materials of the new environment are rough-hewn into the traditional forms.

The third stage in the progress toward culture is a sudden revulsion from the crudities of the new environment. The settler has become homesick for his racial past and he goes back to the eastern sources of wisdom and beauty in order to improve his condition. Physically he remains the man of the frontier; mentally he has become the complete back-trailer. Whether he be Brockden Brown with his eyes on England, or William Dean Howells with his eyes on Boston, his mind and heart are those of the back-trailer.

The final stage is that in which civilization strikes root in new soil and sends out its own branches. The materials of the new environment are no longer rough-hewn into old forms. Life has matured and its expression is complete—both old and new at once, and in harmony. The new environment is understood for itself and finds its own expression in accord with tradition.

If we apply this process to American literary history, we find all four stages represented in the period which we are here studying. The explorers and settlers of the eastern seaboard mark the first stage with their narratives of adventure. The process of settlement continued in these terms until the wall of the Appalachian Mountains and the resentful Indians together arrested the pioneer and brought about a permanent settlement along the coast from Boston to Charleston. Without too arbitrary an insistence upon dates, we may fix this period as extending from 1492 to about 1700. The second stage extends from 1700 to about 1760. During this time the settlers were developing their communities, establishing their first schools, printing their first newspapers, debating their political, social, and religious ideals, collecting their libraries by importation from Europe, and in general adjusting their desire for a civilized life to an environment which was not yet ready to supply all the amenities of civilization. The third stage extends from 1760 to the close of the century and beyond. The Revolutionary War was the result and not the cause of adolescent pride in awakening powers and knowledge. The desire for independence is the first sign of manhood. In literary history, the characteristic production of this period is not so much the controversial writing of patriots and Tories as a sudden torrent of novels, verse, plays, and essays in imitation of English and continental classics and best-sellers. The back-trailer movement was the determining factor in spite of a strong and growing spirit of nationalism. In the terms of literary criticism, this was predominantly a period of convention because even romantic writings were imitative and therefore in the spirit of convention. The final stage is marked by the beginning of an American romantic movement in the work of Channing, Bryant, Cooper, Irving, and their contemporaries. These men were divided in their cultural loyalties between a growing comprehension of the meaning of the American environment and a romantic interest in European culture. Put Cooper's *The Pioneers* beside his *The Bravo* and the conflict in their minds is vividly illustrated. The essay in exhortation for a national literature was invariably written by a man who respected and feared Europe while he loved and overrated America.

American literature reached its first maturity in the Concord and Cambridge groups, and in the work of Poe, Melville, Whittier, and Simms, between 1820 and 1850. The evolutionary development was thus allowed to complete its cycle on the Atlantic seaboard at the same time that the process was being repeated in the first of its four stages, but this time against the background of the whole nation, with the narratives of pioneers like Daniel Boone and Davy Crockett.

The only native literature with which the white settlers came into direct contact was that of the Indians. These races, originally nomadic, had developed a settled habit of life by the end of the fifteenth century when the mistake of calling them Indians was first made by the searchers for a Western trade route to the source of spices. In the Southwest and in Mexico they had built up a civilization which was comparable in its level of culture to many of those of Europe and Asia. The tribes of the Atlantic seacoast had developed a less complex civilization, but they had nevertheless a sense of tribal unity, of political, economic, and social organization and at least an oral literature of their own. Indians figure in the works of Freneau, Paulding, Cooper, and even Longfellow, not so much for what they were as for what the white man believed them to be. Only recently has their culture been at all understood for itself and absorbed into our literary tradition.

The Indian provides the first element in the cosmopolitan origins of our literature; the explorers and early settlers, the second. America was discovered and settled first by Spaniards; the French were as active as the English during the seventeenth century; and the Dutch, the Swedes, and almost all the other races of Europe made their contributions to the westward migration which established the white man on our shores. Even today a cursory study of the Atlantic seaboard will reveal cultural survivals of the Spaniards in Florida, of the Dutch in New York, and of the French in southeastern Canada. The Mississippi valley has not entirely forgotten its French origins; and the Southwest and far West are still proud of their Spanish traditions. To forget Columbus, Cortes, Champlain, and their fellows is to ignore vital factors in the story of America's cultural origins. But like that of the Indians, the part which these early adventurers contributed to the ground work of our literary history has only recently been recognized as our heritage in the writings of Willa Cather, Archibald MacLeish, and historians like James Truslow Adams.

Our principal attention must therefore still be directed to the small band of English settlers on the Atlantic seaboard. The dogged perseverance of the Puritans and the serene confidence of the Quakers in the face of appalling obstacles leaves the modern mind aghast. Less unified perhaps, but none the less enduring were the motives for settlement in the South. The Catholic cavaliers of Maryland and the Virginia gentlemen shaped the destinies of these colonies in the early days, but the middle-class pioneer and small farmer did the actual work of clearing the forests and of laying the foundations for an agricultural society in the South as they did in the North. The progress of these English tradesmen and farmers from the bare conquest of a wilderness to a state stable enough for the luxuries of culture was slow. The Spaniards, the French, and the Elizabethan seamen gayly transplanted their cultures and went home again, leaving them to decay and to survive only in memory and in written record. The English middle class were less concerned with the amenities; they laid the foundations of a new state in religious, economic, and social adjustment to a primitive environment, and left the development of culture to their descendants of later generations.

With such origins, the Colonial mind could hardly be unified. Its predominant characteristic is diversity rather than unanimity of opinion on questions of first importance to man on this earth. No men could be more at odds in their readings of life than John Smith and John Winthrop, Cotton Mather and William Byrd. Puritanism was only one, even though probably the most enduring, of many elements in seventeenth and eighteenth century thought in America. Even within Puritanism itself the strict Calvinism of the Massachusetts Bay Colony is offset by a liberalism among the Plymouth colonists, which recent historians have traced back to John Wyclif and his Lollard priests of Chaucerian England.

The four colonies which did most to determine colonial thought were Massachusetts, Virginia, Pennsylvania, and New York. The other nine were either offshoots from these four, or were strongly influenced by them. New York and Virginia were basically cavalier and aristocratic; Pennsylvania and Massachusetts, middle class and democratic. The Church of England had its greatest following in the first pair; the dissenting sects in the second. New York was distinguished from Virginia in that its social organization was created by the Dutch patroons, whereas that in the South was modeled on an English pattern. Pennsylvania's differences from Massachusetts were not social. Penn, himself a landed proprietor at home, attracted to his following the same classes of tradesmen and farmers that came over in the *Mayflower* and the *Arbella.* Difference in religious beliefs, however, shaped their social attitudes and made the resultant colonies very different in character.

Virginia and Massachusetts have retained their distinctive characters even to the present; and at least one cause of the Civil War seems to have been the clash between their sectional interests and ideals. Paulding recognized this situation as early as 1812 when he likened the "Southland" to the ticklish toes and the "Down East" to the ticklish nose of the nation. But by his time the New York proprietors had lost their influence because of their Tory sympathies, and the "Middlelands" could be characterized as "steady, sober-minded farmers." The "Far West" was to him a vague region of little character at all. The colonial writers of Massachusetts and of Virginia each strongly reflect their respective backgrounds of religious, social, and economic ideals. New York and Pennsylvania writers reveal backgrounds almost as narrowly determined in the early days, but by the end of the eighteenth century the sharper lines in their thought had been softened; and it was they who first attempted an orderly expression of their lives in literary and other art forms. The so-called "Philadelphia" and "Knickerbocker" groups were the first to take literature seriously and for its own sake.

The story of the New England church-state is told in the rise and fall of the Mather dynasty through four generations. The dogmatism of Richard Mather and John Cotton, the founders of the family, is mild when compared to that of their grandson and namesake, Cotton Mather. They and their contemporaries, however, accepted fully the doctrine that the Puritans were a second chosen people and that Massachusetts was a new Canaan. Life in this world was shaped in terms of rewards and punishments in the next, meted out by a God who was just in the old Judaic sense, and whose praise was sung by Michael Wigglesworth. From the Mayflower Compact to the Half-Way Covenant of 1662, the progress of American Puritanism is marked by an increasing determination on the part of a few strong-willed leaders to establish a Holy Commonwealth in fact as well as in theory. The wars with the Indians without and Satan within were holy wars which culminated in the witchcraft trials at the end of the century, an example of religious fanaticism that can only be explained by a zeal born of desperation and fear. The greatest of the Captains of the Lord was Increase Mather, of the second generation. His was a war with heresy which had become organized in the defiance of the Brattle Street Group and the Stoddardeans during the final decade of the century; but with the revocation of the Massachusetts charter in 1692 the temporal authority of the church came to an end. The zeal of its leaders was vainly intensified in Cotton Mather, of the third generation, who lived his best years during this period of loss of power. His history and defense of the movement, the *Magnalia,* has aptly been termed by Schneider to have been, "even at the time of its publication in 1702, little more than a ponderous monument erected over a dead cause." Increase Mather died in 1723, Cotton in 1728. Samuel Mather, of the fourth generation, carried on the war with his *Apology for the Liberties of the Churches in New England* (1738), but temporal power was gone.

The fall of the church-state in New England may be interpreted, in political terms, as the failure of an oligarchic dictatorship to master a people of independent spirit. But the deeper causes of its failure lie buried in the creed upon which it was founded. The desire for liberty of conscience which brought the Pilgrims to America was the seed of that critical independence of mind which flowered in the rationalism of Franklin and Paine, and not in the determinism of the Mathers. The Puritans were better organized in the early days than were their antagonists, but the latter were none the less vocal and persistent, and the end of the Colonial period is marked by their complete triumph.

The first step in the destruction of Puritan dogma came from within the Massachusetts Bay Colony itself in the persons of the early radicals and in the political liberalism which grew out of their attacks on church government. Thomas Hooker was a mild liberal, but Roger Williams, the most influential of these early radicals, attacked both the dogma and the organization of the church-state. In the "Bloudy Tenent" controversy with John Cotton, he assailed the root of that dogma, the doctrine of "persecution for cause of conscience." But Williams was primarily a political and social rather than a religious thinker. The enduring significance of his revolt lies rather in his substitution of the social compact for the divine right theory of the state, whereby he laid the foundations for Jeffersonian democracy. Like Williams, John Wise began his revolt on theological grounds, but his real interest was in the institutional rather than the doctrinal problems of the church, and his thought led to similar conclusions. In the revolt of these two men, and in the broad tolerance of William Penn, may readily be discovered the roots of the political idealism which brought about the Revolutionary War and determined the character of our government.

A more philosophical form of reasoning, the analytical study of science and natural phenomena, disturbed the Calvinistic integrity of the two ablest defenders of the faith, Cotton Mather and Jonathan Edwards, the former in his age and the latter in his youth. More serious, however, was the call to reason as opposed to authoritarian dogma which was early heard outside the fold of the elect. Robert Calef made a direct attack upon the witchcraft fanaticism of the Mathers, but his mind was not sufficiently orderly to produce a positive philosophy as a substitute for that which he scorned. It was Benjamin Franklin who first accomplished a satisfactory transition from dogma to reason.

Although the term "philosopher" was perhaps applied more frequently to Franklin, both at home and abroad, than to any other American of his day, he was not a metaphysician in the strict sense. His was a natural philosophy, the product of an objective curiosity about nature and a belief in man. Although his earlier essays contain a clear statement of a Deistic creed, he was more utilitarian than contemplative in his habit of mind. He formulated a creed and a philosophy in order to use rather than to enjoy them. Having established an objective nature, he proceeded to devote his attention to its scientific analysis, an impulse which Mather and Edwards had felt before him, but without the same philosophical justification. After convincing himself of the free will of man, he turned the moral zeal of his ancestors toward teaching him how to live happily and profitably in this world rather than to prepare for the next. His belief in a benevolent God of limited powers allowed him to take that personage for granted in his interesting and active daily life; while his spirit of inquiry stimulated an intense activity in the sciences of botany and medicine, particularly in Philadelphia in the work of men like John Bartram and Benjamin Rush, during the years immediately before and after the war.

The Deism of Ethan Allen in his *Oracles of Reason* (1784), and Tom Paine, in his *Age of Reason* (1793–95), was of a more metaphysical nature than was that of Franklin. During his sojourn in America, Paine thought more about politics than religion or philosophy, but his *Age of Reason* is so logical a climax to his earlier radicalism that it must be claimed for American literature if the political pamphlets on the Revolutionary War are included. Entirely unoriginal as it was, this tract carried the thought of French and English rationalists to the banks of the Ohio and the mountains of Kentucky.

Similar in its inquiring spirit and its emphasis on common sense was the philosophy which found congenial soil at Princeton after the advent of President Witherspoon in 1768. It must be remembered that Brackenridge, Freneau, and Madison were among the students who came under this influence, just as Godfrey and Hopkinson came under a similar influence at the infant University of Pennsylvania; and the seething political activity of these undergraduates bears testimony to the absence of other-worldliness in their intellectual life. Calvinism had little power in the states of Pennsylvania and New Jersey when the minds of Franklin, Jefferson, Adams, Hamilton, and their fellows were transmuting these "common sense" philosophies into the system of government and the social organization which gave first form to the national character.

The philosophical idealism which early developed, both within and without the fold of Calvinism, has even more place in American literary history than have these more materialistic schools of thought because, in its late development in the minds of Emerson and the Concord transcendentalists, it became one of the most vital factors in the romantic movement in this country. Its influence had already been clearly felt in New England before Bishop Berkeley came to Newport, Rhode Island, in 1729 and discussed with his American friends the theory that matter does not exist. His threat to the dogmatic and authoritarian position of the New England Calvinists lay rather in the incentive he gave to free and speculative thought than in any fundamental heresy in his system. But there was no holy war; the danger was too far-reaching to be immediately alarming. Berkeley made few American friends or disciples except Samuel Johnson, tutor at Yale and later president of King's College (Columbia). Franklin revealed his sympathy with the movement by assuming the expense of printing the latter's *Elementa Philosophica,* which was used as a text at both Columbia and the College in Philadelphia.

As an undergraduate at Yale, Jonathan Edwards expressed, in his paper *Of Being,* an idealism almost identical with that of Berkeley, but investigation has failed to prove that there was any direct influence of the English philosopher upon him. Rather, we may attribute the early liberalism, which later hardened into a dogmatic Calvinism, to his reading of Locke and others. His youthful experiences during a personal religious awakening led him to a mysticism not unlike that of Woolman and the Quakers. The "sense of divine things" of which he writes in his personal narrative brought to him a humility that was intense and immediate. There was no intermediary authority, either of Bible or minister, between his own soul and the spirit of beauty which was his God. The Judaism of the Mathers broke down before the intensity of this personal experience, and the last of the great Puritan divines prostrated his spirit before the "fresh Visitations of Heavenly Love," of which the Quaker Woolman wrote with such singleness of heart. That early evangelical revival at Northampton, which has been termed the "Great Awakening," was the result, when Edwards himself became the authority that administered justice, and the spirit of the Mathers returned. But his mysticism never entirely left him, and it prepared the way, a century later, for the intensely personal religion of William Ellery Channing and the Unitarians, and later for the revolt of Emerson, an arch-rebel among rebels, who finally declared that self-reliance rather than reliance upon book and dogma was the only key to salvation.

During the century between Edwards and Channing there was little development of idealism as a metaphysical system. The issues which led up to the Revolutionary War, and the problems of reconstruction, turned men's minds from abstractions to more materialistic habits of thought. There was, however, one counter-movement, in spirit akin to Edwards' most extreme mysticism. Between 1738 and 1769, George Whitefield, one of the most enthusiastic and compelling followers of Wesley, made seven trips to America in order to preach the Evangelical revival. An enemy to common sense and dogma alike, Whitefield made many converts to the faith which comes from emotional conviction. The movement took firmest root in the South, but its influence was felt throughout the colonies, and at least a slight connection may be traced between it and the more temperate liberalism of Channing.

Channing's attack on Calvinism was direct and vigorous. Slight in body, but silver-tongued, his persuasive eloquence carried the younger elements in New England with him when, in his Baltimore sermon of 1819, he gave the Unitarian revolt its first clear definition. Abroad, his name was linked with those of Irving and Cooper in the first group of writers in that national literature for which he plead so earnestly. As a literary critic, his work was limited to a few reviews in the *Christian Examiner,* and it all was colored by his religious convictions. But his thought gave courage to the fearful and provided a metaphysical reason for independence, a valuable supplement to the political independence derived from the common sense rationalism of Franklin.

The political events that caused the Revolutionary War focused all of Colonial thought on an immediate and practical issue. It was not difficult to lead the various types of individualism developed by Roger Williams, Jonathan Edwards, and Benjamin Franklin up to Tom Paine's succinct conclusion: " 'Tis repugnant to reason, to the universal order of things; to all examples from former ages, to suppose, that this continent can long remain subject to any external power." He cut the issue clearly: "Should the colonies remain a part of the British Empire, or should they not?" His answer was that they should not, and this he called common sense; but not all his intelligent compatriots saw the problem in so white a light. John Dickinson, temperamentally a conservative, was whipped into the rebel position by what he believed to be unjust taxation. Franklin made up his mind slowly and gave his love of conciliation full play. Jefferson, the wisest political philosopher in the rebel camp, reasoned himself to a firm conviction in democracy and wrote arguments similar to Payne's into the Declaration of Independence. Samuel Adams and Patrick Henry were born agitators, and rebellion came easily to them. But lawyers and statesmen like Alexander Hamilton, John Adams, and James Wilson reached a similar point of view less hastily; for not all political radicals favored a break with England, not all conservatives were Tories. The revolutionary issue was less one of reasoned political philosophy than an indignation against tyranny in a specific case. Rebels were not all Democrats, nor were all Federalists Tories, when the later issue, the best form for the new government to take, shaped itself into a clash between liberal and conservative thinkers.

The Loyalists fell into such extreme disfavor after the break with England that their writings have received less emphasis than they deserve. Samuel Seabury, the first American bishop of the Protestant Episcopal Church, was a man of cultivated mind and the author of a number of vigorous sermons and political tracts. William Smith, the first Provost of the College in Philadelphia, was a thorough liberal in his thought on religion, education, and politics, but his oath of personal allegiance to the King made it impossible for him, as it was for Seabury, to indorse absolute separation. Jonathan Boucher, also an Anglican clergyman, gave perhaps the most vigorous expression to Toryism in sober prose, as did Jonathan Odell in satire. Nor were the Loyalists without their verse apologists, as the ballads of the Revolutionary War will bear witness.

The poetry of the so-called "Hartford Wits" reveals clearly the distinction which must be made between the revolutionary and the national issues. Conservative as Dwight was in theology, he joined with Trumbull, Barlow, and their lesser associates in patriotic zeal and the spirit of rebellion. But Barlow alone of the group was a Democrat in the post-Revolutionary days. His later poems and pamphlets are as radical as his earlier, and his visit to France made him follow in the tracks of Paine's thought in most matters of importance to government and religion.

The literary groups of New Jersey and Pennsylvania were similarly divided upon the two issues. Francis Hopkinson was a Loyalist up to the eve of the war, devoted his poetry to the cause of revolution, and served the Federalists with his prose satire after the peace. Philip Freneau was, however, a rebel and later a Jeffersonian Democrat, as was his college mate, Brackenridge.

Although there were many shades of opinion on the national issue between Democracy and Federalism, the extreme spokesmen of the two groups were respectively Thomas Jefferson and Alexander Hamilton. John Adams was a Federalist of milder stamp than Hamilton, and James Madison joined with the latter in the series of papers which took its name from that of the party in whose support it was published.

Jeffersonian Democracy in its purest form rests upon faith in the integrity, idealism, and capacity for self-government of the average man. It was suggested in the thought of Williams, Wise, Penn, and other early radicals, but it came to America, in 1775, in an almost unpolluted stream from the French radicals. This political philosophy in its application to the immediate situation in America found perhaps its briefest statement in the Declaration of Independence. Hamilton's *The Federalist* served a similar purpose for the opposing belief that man is fundamentally selfish and ignorant, and that he requires a strong and arbitrary government to regulate his actions. The war between these two political philosophies shaped the early and influenced all the later years of our national life. Their effect upon our literature was indirect, as most of our early literary men were not active in politics after the turn of the century, but Cooper, Irving, Bryant, and many others were strongly influenced by their political sympathies.

By the middle of the eighteenth century, therefore, the men of our first frontier had marked out the geographical and mental boundaries of a new civilization and had laid foundations in political, social, economic, religious, and philosophical thought upon which we as a nation have been building ever since. The time was ripe for the later generations to turn to the amenities of a more settled and cultured life.

II. THE AWAKENING OF LITERARY CONSCIOUSNESS (1760–1830)

The development of a conscious literary culture is the natural consequence of the action of civilization upon frontier conditions. The colonies were slow in reaching this stage in evolution, but by 1760 there were sufficient schools, colleges, literary societies, libraries, printing presses, and theatres to create a public taste for literature and a means of subsistence for literary men. George Sandys, English treasurer of the Jamestown colony, published in 1626 a translation of Ovid's *Metamorphoses,* a part of which he had made during his short residence in Virginia, and Benjamin Tompson (1642–1714) deliberately elected the life of a poet and suffered the natural consequences in the uncongenial New England cultural climate. Even Benjamin Franklin, who perhaps did more than anyone else to prepare the way for an American literature, both in his own work and in his reprints of English novels, was himself primarily a man of affairs and not of books. Charles Brockden Brown (1771–1810) was the first American to succeed in the profession of literature. The six novels, the dialogue, and the monthly magazine which he produced between 1798 and 1804 were offered to a reasonably large public which had been educated in American schools and nurtured on American reprints of English literary works. The foundations of a national literature were firm enough to make the erection of a superstructure practicable. The architecture of that building was English.

In 1764, when Brown University was founded at Providence, Rhode Island, there were already five other colleges in the colonies. Harvard, which was authorized by the general court of Massachusetts in 1636 and graduated its first class in 1642, and William and Mary, established in Virginia in 1693, are the only colleges which date from the seventeenth century. In 1700, however, the more liberal Calvinists withdrew from Harvard and made their contribution to the decline of Puritan authority by the founding of Yale the following year. The University of Pennsylvania (1740), Princeton (1746), and Columbia (1754) complete the list. The University of Pennsylvania was the only one of them which was non-sectarian, and religious training was almost as large a part of their early curricula as was education in the seven liberal arts. Latin, Greek, philosophy, and mathematics provided the secular training which had long been the rule in English secondary schools, and the standards of attainment were approximately those of Eton, Harrow, or Westminister. There was little study of English or other modern literatures, almost none of history or geography, and comparatively little of natural science. Nevertheless, these eighteenth century colleges provided the Hellenic attitude toward culture which was necessary before other than theological and practical ideals for the mental life could be openly accepted.

The founding of literary societies and circulating libraries had an even more immediate effect than the colleges in arousing colonial interest in cultural ideals and problems. The plantation aristocrats of the South like William Byrd of Westover, and Massachusetts theologians like Cotton Mather, who confesses to "a mighty Thirst after the Sight of Books," had large private collections which contained works of "belles lettres," as well as of philosophy and history, but their influence did not extend far beyond their owners. Boston had a short-lived public library in 1656, but Franklin seems to have been the first to have developed the plan of collecting books for even a limited public circulation. Between 1730 and 1760 his Junto society for the discussion of science, literature, morals, and religion led to the establishment of the Library Company of Philadelphia (1731), the Redwood Library of Newport (1747), the Library Society of Charleston (1748), and that of New York (1754). The libraries of Harvard and Yale were large enough by the middle of the century to issue catalogues, and that of the New York Society Library (1793) listed five thousand titles. Boston, Salem, and other cities had literary clubs or libraries early in the century, one result of which was the incorporation of the Boston Athenæum in 1807. The national government had a library as early as 1800, but it was not until after its destruction by fire in 1814 and the subsequent purchase of Jefferson's books that the Library of Congress was more than a reference collection for the use of members. By 1829 it ranked fourth in the country.

The groups which founded these libraries were invariably composed of the moneyed classes who seem suddenly to have awakened to the intellectual and cultural poverty of the country. Their interests were chiefly theological, political, and scientific, but volumes of Shakespeare, Milton, Richardson, Goldsmith, Johnson, and other English authors, both classic and contemporary, frequently found their places on shelves weighted down by collections of travels, ancient history, and moral philosophy. The shelves grew lighter with works of contemporary novelists and poets as the century advanced, but such strictly literary clubs as Brockden Brown's Belles Lettres Club and the Authors' Club of New York, which was founded in 1837 with Irving as president, did not appear in great numbers until well after 1800. Nor must we forget the traditional lure of light fiction for the weaker sex, which, late in the century, broke the bonds of the stern colonial ideals of womanhood and flooded the country with imported and reprinted novels and fireside journals. It was Cooper's habit of reading such books to his wife and daughters that suggested the career of a novelist to him.

In spite of strict censorship and discouraging economic conditions, printing was among the first of the arts to be practiced by the colonists. Stephen Day set up a press at Cambridge in 1639 and printed, among other things, *The Bay Psalm Book* and a translation of the Bible into the language of the Indians. In the century which followed, presses were set up in Boston, New York, New London, Philadelphia, and Ephrata, Pennsylvania. When Franklin first arrived in Philadelphia in 1723, he had a choice of at least two established printers to whom he might apply for employment.

The product of these colonial presses consisted chiefly of broadsides and pamphlets. An attempt to print a newspaper in Boston in 1690 was suppressed, and it was not until 1704 that the first successful paper, *The Boston News-Letter,* appeared. Seven other newspapers had at least survived their infancy when Franklin established *The Pennsylvania Gazette* in 1729, and there were successful ventures of the kind in Boston, New York, Philadelphia, Annapolis, Williamsburg, and Charleston by 1836.

These newspapers did little to encourage literature except by increasing the reading public and thus preparing the way for the monthly journals. The first of these, *The American Magazine,* published in 1741 by Andrew Bradford, was quickly followed in the same year by Franklin's *The General Magazine and Historical Chronicle.* Both had ceased publication by the end of the year, but the experiment attracted attention, and by 1760 ten other journals had at least continued through short runs in Boston, New York, and Philadelphia. By 1800, the total had swelled to over eighty. The figure is, however, somewhat misleading, for the term of their average life was so brief that there was seldom any alarming competition between them. Among their editors we may count Tom Paine, Mathew Carey, Noah Webster, Philip Freneau, and Brockden Brown. In the encouragement of literature Joseph Dennie was the most successful of them all in his conduct of *The Port Folio* (1801–1811). Irving edited *The Analectic Magazine* from 1813 to 1814, and the first of the successful reviews, *The North American,* made its appearance in 1815. The great age of *The Knickerbocker, Graham's, Godey's Lady's*

Book, and *The New York Mirror* was yet to come, when original contributions were in such demand that Poe, Paulding, Willis, and even Cooper turned from books to the periodical press for a chief means of support. The vogues of sentimental poetry and the short story between 1825 and 1850 undoubtedly owe much to this influence.

As we turn the musty pages of the earlier journals, we may wonder how they could have encouraged literature. Even in their own day the small type in double columns, and the lack of artistic quality in their borrowed contents must have done little to stimulate reading. No wonder their lives were short; but their influence was far reaching. Although interested chiefly in politics, the editors summoned the ghosts of Addison and Pope to stalk their pages; and dramatic criticism began to appear as soon as there were plays to criticize. The ideal of almost all of them was the establishment of an American *Gentleman's Magazine,* and men and women who could still recall the hardship of breaking a wilderness were summoned to the enjoyment of relaxed indolence in a London club. Flowers of literature may be transplanted from another's garden, but they will be somewhat wilted when they first dig their roots into a strange soil. Borrowing—imitation—creation—these are the normal stages of growth in a transplanted as contrasted with an indigenous national literature. By 1760 the magazines had prepared our reading and writing public for the second of them.

Although a trifle later in maturing, the American theatre had a strikingly parallel growth. Plays had been written or acted in the colonies, chiefly by college students, before 1767. Recorded dramatic performances of one kind or another date from 1713, and Governor Richard Hunter published in 1714 a play which was never acted. Lewis Hallam and his English company arrived in 1752 and produced old plays in the principal cities for six years, when his company was reorganized under Douglass. Thomas Godfrey, a college student, doubtless saw them in 1754 when they went to Philadelphia, and was stimulated to write a play of his own. His friend, Francis Hopkinson, adapted *The Masque of Alfred* and produced it with his fellow students in the old English fashion during the Christmas holidays of 1756–57. The first original play to be presented by a professional company was Thomas Godfrey's tragedy of blood, *The Prince of Parthia,* performed "by the American Company, at the New Theatre in Southwark [Philadelphia], on Friday, the twenty-fourth of April [1767]." Williamsburg and Charleston were also early theatrical centers, but censorship in Boston practically excluded dramatic activity from that city during the greater part of the eighteenth century. Even in Philadelphia, a city ordinance caused history to repeat itself by banishing the earliest performance to a new-world Southwark which, like Shakespeare's, was just outside the city limits. From 1774 to 1784 the Continental Congress discouraged all dramatic performances, although the officers of both armies occasionally amused themselves with such diversions. The real history of the American theatre begins in 1784 when the younger Hallam returned with his company, and Royall Tyler's *The Contrast,* the first dramatic treatment of an American theme, was produced three years later. Before 1830, William Dunlap, James Nelson Barker, John Howard Payne, Washington Irving, and Robert Montgomery Bird had written plays which were produced by Hallam, Forrest, and others, and which are worthy of inclusion in literary history.

Although not strictly a part of this history, the development of the art of painting by Benjamin West and his followers so nearly coincides in date with these other movements that it may be considered a part of the same story. Nor is the sudden increase, about 1760, in the emigration of American students of law and medicine to England for training an unrelated fact. American eyes were at last turned eastward to the traditional homes of wisdom and culture.

With the establishment of these means for culture, the early stages in the development of American literature on our first frontier may be declared at an end. Two decades before they united as an independent nation, the colonies had laid the foundation for a national literature and art. American writers were at last conscious of literary ideals and were eager in their experimentation in literary forms. The Revolutionary War is an incident which first delayed and afterwards stimulated this progress. From the point of view of literary history, it should not be regarded as the pivotal fact of the half-century after 1760.

This period produced a body of essays, poems, novels, short stories, and plays which bear the unifying stamp of a purely literary movement. Sectional divisions may be considered at least as of secondary importance; political social, economic, and philosophical movements may be examined as background rather than for themselves.

The distinguishing characteristics of this movement are: that in mode and form it was almost completely imitative of classical and contemporary English and, to a far lesser extent, continental literatures; that it showed a marked interest in tradition, which was balanced by a growing curiosity about the literary possibilities of native materials and ideas; that it developed in the various colonies literary groups of surprisingly similar tastes and ideals; and that it laid the foundations for a romantic movement of primarily native origin and growth. The search for a satisfactory critical term to apply to this movement presents insurmountable difficulties. It might be called a classical period if by that term we mean only a search for standards, a concern with form, and an effort to imitate and adapt rather than to explore and experiment. Certainly its motivating impulses were those of convention rather than of revolt, but so many of the favorite models of these writers were romantic that the traditional uses of these terms could lead only to paradox and confusion. It is probably safer to characterize the period as one of an awakening of literary consciousness through imitation.

English literature in 1760 was at the beginning of a half-century of transition from the most classical to the most romantic period it has ever known. In the distant background were the masters of the past, notably Shakespeare, Milton, and Dryden, the fame of Chaucer and Spenser being for the moment under clouds. In the nearer distance were the masters of the formal essay and poem, of criticism and of satire, Defoe, Pope, Addison, Swift, and their fellows. Among elder contemporaries or recent masters were Samuel Johnson, Goldsmith, and the novelists Richardson, Fielding, Sterne, and the blue-stocking ladies. The romantic impulse had already been felt in the poetry of Thomson, Gray, and Cowper, and was soon to become more pronounced in that of Blake, Burns, and Wordsworth. In the novel it was taking the mode of Gothic horror in the work of Horace Walpole, Mrs. Radcliffe, and "Monk" Lewis, and of manners in Jane Austen. Practically all of these planets had their satellites in the western sky. If we can be satisfied with a division of English writers of the century into neo-classical and romantic schools, we may connect the Hartford Wits and the periodical essayist like Dennie with the former, and Freneau and Brockden Brown with the latter. About the proper classification of the sentimental or picaresque novel, the social comedy, and the political and social satire in prose or verse, we may perhaps be allowed to reserve judgment.

Doubtless the most satisfactory approach to a study of this literature is in terms of forms. The essay, poetry, the novel, the short story, and the drama each had its brief evolution from anarchy of form and purpose to definition of aims, standards, materials, and structure. The short story alone was in its infancy when Irving began to write during the first decade of the nineteenth century.

Benjamin Franklin was the first notable American apprentice in the art of the essay. A professed student of Addison, he experimented with the periodical essay in his *Dogood* and *Busy-Body* papers, with the Swiftian essay in his political satires like his "An Edict by the King of Prussia," and with the informal essay in his letters like that on "The Whistle." As early as 1736, however, *The Virginia Gazette* had its "Monitor" who, like the "Spectator," commented on the events, morals, and manners of the day, the current drama, and how to give the fair Letitia Tattle a view of his long nose. Letters from Caleb Tenderheart to his friend, Nahab Din, appeared in *The New York Weekly Journal* for April 16, 1739, and a decade earlier Will Pedant was writing saucy letters in *The New England Weekly Journal*. When the weekly, monthly, and quarterly journals were established, they had innumerable Timothy Timbertoes to contribute essays upon characters, manners, fashions, religion, politics, and "The Character and Effects of Modern Novels." Timothy Dwight contributed essays in the "Spectator" manner to Boston and New Haven papers in 1769–1770, and Brockden Brown became "The Rhapsodist" in the August to November numbers of *The Columbian Magazine* in 1789. Innumerable as these essays were, the most important of them are probably Joseph Dennie's "The Lay Preacher," "The Farrago," and "An Author's Evenings," in the various journals which he edited. These essays were serious in tone although lightened by an occasional whimsy. Their subjects were frequently American; their pattern and point of view English. It remained for Washington Irving, his brother William, and his friend, James Kirke

Paulding, to develop the type into something more characteristically American in *Salmagundi; or the Whimwhams and Opinions of Lancelot Langstaff, Esq.* (1807–08), an independent humorous journal that may almost be taken as the beginning of a national American literature.

The novel and the short story were closely linked to the essay in eighteenth century England, and they remained so in America. Many of our early periodicals essays have as much narrative interest as the de Coverley papers or Goldsmith's *Citizen of the World.* Irving is usually credited with being the "father of the short story," but there was a whole literature of narrative essays before the appearance of *The Sketch Book* with its "Rip Van Winkle" in 1819. The definition of the short story as an independent literary form belongs, however, to the period 1830–1850.

The novel, on the other hand, reached a comparative maturity in the earlier period. Most works of this class bear testimony to the popularity which English stories of sentiment and of assailed virtue must have enjoyed on this as well as on the other side of the water. *The Power of Sympathy* (1789), now believed to have been written by William Hill Brown, is in the epistolary form which had been so popular since Richardson adopted it for his *Pamela,* and it reflected the Richardsonian influence in its theme and mood as well. Mrs. Susannah Haswell Rowson's *Charlotte Temple* (1790) explained its moral purpose most carefully in a preface and then proceeded to a well-constructed tale of seduction that retained its popularity for half a century and suggests many a modern movie story of virtue at war with alluring and cruel vice. The picaresque, or rogue, story, which came to Defoe, Fielding, and Smollet from the Spanish, was transplanted again to America by H. H. Brackenridge in his *Modern Chivalry* (1793–1815) and turned to the purposes of political and social satire, as was *The Algerine Captive* (1797) of Royall Tyler. But perhaps most important of all was the novel of Gothic horror, represented in America by Brockden Brown's *Wieland* (1798) and *Edgar Huntly* (1799). The influence of Godwin's *Caleb Williams* is also to be discovered in Brown's interest in social problems. Practically all other contemporary English vogues, including those of Scott and of Maria Edgeworth, found reflection in one or another of the American novels published prior to 1830.

A similar echo is to be found in the drama of the period. It is not difficult to hear the cry of Lear, first muffled and then shouted through a loud-speaker, when Vardanes, of *The Prince of Parthia,* exclaims:

> "Why rage the elements, they are not curs'd
> Like me?"

but it is the voice of the "improved" Shakespeare of the eighteenth century rather than of that of the Elizabethan stage. And Charlotte of *The Contrast,* similarly recalls the eighteenth century comedy of manners when she extols the virtues of the bell-hoop for swimming in a minuet before the eyes of fifty well-dressed beaux. Hallam's repertory had included plays by Cibber, Addison, Lillo, Otway, and Steele. The romantic tragedy and the sentimental comedy of the English stage were moved bodily to the American stage, as was the historical tragedy in Dunlap's *André* and the historical comedy in Payne's collaboration with Irving on *Charles the Second.* The scenes and themes of these plays, like those of the novels, were often aggressively American, but their forms, manners, and modes were English.

American poetry of the period provides an even more accurate index to the change in English literary fashions. The objects of the satirical verse of Barlow, Dwight, and Trumbull were American political and theological problems, but its form was usually the rimed couplet and its vocabulary the poetic diction of Pope. Dwight's mild contemplation of nature in the blank verse of *Greenfield Hill* suggests Cowper's *The Task,* even though its fantastic scheme and imagery lends it originality, and the churchyard mood of Freneau's *The House of Night* sounds echoes from the work of Gray and Young. The transition from the classic to the romantic mode was telescoped, in New England and New Jersey, to the compass of a few years.

Philip Freneau rises above the other poets of this time in both originality and distinction. His verse forms are imitative and far from perfect in technique, but they are varied and usually successful. His diction adds to the formal vocabulary of English neo-classical writers a freshness which comes from his immediate contact with the life of nature and man. But Freneau was far ahead of his times in poetic understanding, a fact which was recognized by Coleridge and other English poets. His naturalism was not imitative; it came to him from an awareness of natural beauty, a keen perception, and a habit of contemplation. His patriotism has a fervor which carries it above the controversial issues that prompted it. His emotions are deeply stirred and his expression of them is sincere in the best of his poetry. Until the time of Poe, America could boast no poet of greater power.

In spite of imitation, by 1815 American literature was already sending out new roots into the new soil. The romantic movement was born in this country of a strong national pride, an immediate contemplation of nature, an appreciation of the simple elements in the lives of living men, and a search of the past and the present for new forms and themes. These are the elements of romanticism in any age or country.

National pride became vocal soon after 1800 and was belligerent by 1830. America's declarations of cultural and intellectual independence were many during the early years of the century. Challenged by the aspersions of British critics, intelligent Americans suddenly became conscious of the cultural crudity of their countrymen. Indignant protest was one form of their admission of the truth of these criticisms; exhortation to improvement, another. James Nelson Barker, in the Prologue to *Tears and Smiles* (1807), cried,

> But, if some humble beauties catch your sight,
> Behold them in their proper, native light;
> Not peering through discol'ring foreign prisms,
> Find them but hideous, rank Columbianisms.

The campaign was continued by Royall Tyler in his mock travel record *A Yankey in London* (1809), and Charles J. Ingersoll in his *Inchiquin Letters* (1810) made a frontal attack on the worst offender, *The Quarterly Review.* The fight raged merrily for two decades and more, in spite of Bryant's judicious essay on American poetry in *The North American Review* (1818), and Irving's efforts to calm his excited countrymen by his essay "English Writers on America" in *The Sketch Book* (1819–20).

Paulding was perhaps the most bitter of the warriors. In his *Salmagundi* paper on "National Literature," he urged rather mildly that "real life is fraught with adventures" and that the American writer could find in his own country the best material for romantic fiction. His acerbity is marked, however, in his John Bull satires of the preceding years. Ingersoll's speech before the American Philosophical Society in 1823 was moderate, but it urged the same point: "In the literature of imagination, our standard is considerably below that of England, France, and Germany, and perhaps of Italy. . . . In the literature of fact, of education, of politics, and perhaps even science, European preëminence is by no means so decided." This literature Cooper reviewed briefly in his *Notions of the Americans* (1828), another mock travel record; and Samuel Knapp, author of our first literary history, *Lectures on American Literature* (1829), pleaded for the indulgence of his hearers on the ground that he was "nothing more than one of the pioneers in the great work of redeeming our fame from the foul aspersions of our enemies."

These were a few of the direct answers to Sydney Smith's famous question of 1818: "Who reads an American book?" but William Ellery Channing, in his belated review of Ingersoll's lecture, wrote a more constructive exhortation for a national literature in *The Christian Examiner* (1830). His text was a definition of literature as "the expression of a nation's mind in writing," a conception which departed from the limitations of the conventional "belles lettres" ideal of the eighteenth century and prepared for Emerson's plea for the "man thinking" seven years later.

The conflict between the spirit of nationalism and the sense of value in tradition became most acute in Irving and Cooper. Both started their careers as authors with a feeling of intense Americanism; both felt the lure of Europe and its past; and both, after residences abroad, returned to an incomplete reconciliation with their land and the ideals and manners of its people. In Irving the issue was less acute because he had the milder temperament. He became more completely absorbed than did Cooper in the romantic traditions of Old England and the continent, and when he returned to Sunnyside to write the *Life of Washington,* he was content to be apart from, rather than in conflict with, the hurried and practical activities of his countrymen. Cooper, on the other hand, reacted violently against all things with which he could not be in accord. The aristocratic social tradition of New York, with its landed patroons and Tory memories, early turned his mind against the leveling forces of democracy. He insisted upon values without realizing that their permanent incorporation in a social pattern inevitably leads to an aristocracy of worth. Like Jefferson, he believed that gentlemen in the old English sense could survive under a popular government, and he took upon himself that rôle. Critical of the corruptions of European government and society, he was equally annoyed by American crudities and haste. In *The American Democrat* (1838) he defined his social and political ideals; in his *Gleanings* and his European novels he applied them to French, German, and English life and found the old world civilization wanting in vitality; in his later social novels he applied them to American life and found the new world culture lacking in sturdy roots. In Cooper the spirit of nationalism lost some of its youthful confidence, and gained in return the imperfect adjustment of adolescence.

A steady increase of interest in American scenes, people, and problems was the first literary result of this growth of the spirit of nationalism. Although adopting borrowed forms and modes, even Dwight wrote of the "Afric infant . . . to slavery born," Trumbull of "the country clown" at college, and Barlow of a corn husking. The problems of theology and patriotism which occupied most of the poetry of the time were immediate fruits of American social and political history. An election in *Modern Chivalry* was an American election and the Irishman Teague O'Regan is not unlike the braggard Yankee of later years. A Jonathan who spoke a Connecticut dialect had paced the boards in Tyler's *The Contrast* and Brown's Indians supplied the traditional horrors necessary to the Gothic novel by the sort of unromantic atrocities described by the early chroniclers.

The Indians and the Dutch were the first Americans of alien stock who appeared in our literature. Brown looked at his primitive neighbors realistically and saw a race driven to extremity by defeat at the hand of the whites, while Freneau meditated philosophically upon their method of burying their dead. Irving wrote of them in *The Sketch Book* with the feeling of the historian he was to become. It was Cooper, however, who first threw over them a romantic glamour. Of the second generation on the frontier, he saw only the remnants of the race and drew upon the missionary Heckewelder for his facts. The result was the glamorous red man who has superseded the actuality in the popular imagination of French, German, English, and American readers of both his day and ours.

The situation was reversed, however, in the case of the Dutch. Cooper knew and admired them as the rightful landed aristocrats of his state, Paulding wrote of them realistically, and Irving, who began by burlesquing them in his *Knickerbocker's History* (1809), turned to their legends for his more mature writing and added them to the American folk tradition.

National pride found its principal source of gratification, however, in the contemplation of the grandeur of American scenery and in the habits and peculiarities in forms of life characteristic of this hemisphere. With the calm of a philosophic mind, Crèvecoeur observed the bees and the ants that set up their establishments at his door; but the Bartrams, both father and son, traveled far into the wilderness, the one toward Canada, the other toward Florida, and described the wonders of tree and animal life. Freneau wrote of the "caty-did," the honey bee, and the wild honeysuckle, and Bryant of the fringed gentian, the yellow violet, and, less explicitly, a waterfowl. It is to Audubon, however, that we owe our matured and scientific interest in the wild life of the new country. He devoted his life to the observation of the birds and quadrupeds of America, drew them with the hand of an artist, and wrote of them with the feeling of a poet.

The romantic feeling of a Byron was grafted upon this love of native soil in Cooper. He was the first of any race or nation to put the sea into the novel with the passion of the sailor, and he carried with him even to the Alps a mental picture of his beloved Hudson valley, his inland wooded hills and stretches of primitive wilderness, and the natural marvel of Niagara Falls. His Indians may have been products of his romantic imagination, but the forest trails through which they went were drawn from his childhood memory. A similar love of the soil motivated and colored the work of his contemporaries, Irving, Bryant, and their lesser fellows. The Hudson valley was the first American scene to provide a native background for the romantic imaginations of our early writers.

Another characteristic of romantic writing which was early evident in the American movement is a concern with the near distance. English writers of the late eighteenth century turned from the classics of Greece and Rome to the middle ages and to Elizabethan times. Early American history provided Barlow and Freneau with themes for patriotic poetry, and the Revolutionary War was scarcely over before it became the subject of historical as well as patriotic poems like Freneau's celebration of the "memorable victory" of the *Bon Homme Richard,* and Cooper's "tale of the neutral ground," *The Spy* (1821). Irving and Prescott turned, however, to Spain when they became seriously interested in history, and even Cooper was lured from his American themes, in his European novels of 1831–33, only to return to them as social historian in the Littlepage and related novels of his later years.

The commanding positions of Halleck and Bryant—particularly the former —among their contemporaries have not stood the test of time. Halleck was soon overshadowed by his less conspicuous friend Joseph Rodman Drake, and the romantic glamour of *Alnwick Castle* and *Marco Bozzaris* now appears rather as a symptom of the age than a sign of genius, whereas the wit of *Fanny* expresses, in less lofty mood, a gift for social satire in verse. Bryant's early verse brought him almost instant recognition, both because America needed him and because he was a truer poet than any of his immediate contemporaries. In authentic interpretation of nature, in technical maturity, and in moral earnestness, it revealed the steady hand of the master. His essay in *The North American Review* (1818) was the wisest criticism of American literature that had as yet appeared; and his *Lectures on Poetry* (1825) defined an acceptable code: poetry must express not only imagination and passion, but practical understanding, moral purpose, and eloquence as well. This statement of aim, so well illustrated by Bryant's own work, gave authoritative expression to the temper of the times; and under his leadership as editor of

The New York Evening Post for a half-century, the profession of letters gained in dignity and assurance. Between Freneau and Poe there is no more authentic American poet than this spokesman for the religion of nature; but his importance as a liberal critic, always and intelligently in accord with the better spirit of his day, has perhaps not yet been adequately estimated.

Except that they tried almost every possibility, the American writers of the early romantic movement show little originality in their choice and development of literary forms. The power of their writers' personalities did much to shape Irving's Addisonian essays, Bryant's blank-verse meditation in *Thanatopsis,* and Cooper's treatment of the long chase and capture, into forms which bear some stamp of novelty. The short story alone seems to have developed from the peculiar needs of the American materials and the circumstances of periodical publication, and its maturing must be left to Poe and Hawthorne. For the rest, the second group of American authors was as imitative in the forms which it chose as was the first. Irving had his Addison, Cooper his Scott, and Bryant his Wordsworth.

By 1830, when these three writers had a decade of work behind them and others of greater literary value, like Poe and Hawthorne, had already published their first work, the seat of American literature was ready to move from New York and Philadelphia to Concord and Cambridge, and to proclaim the romantic triumph of the early 30's. The national mind of the united colonies had ripened to a state at which the first frontier had begun to produce a culture and a literature distinctively its own.

ROBERT E. SPILLER

PROLOGUE

I. CHRISTOPHER COLUMBUS
(*c.* 1451–1506)

THE DISCOVERED ISLANDS

Letter of Christopher Columbus, to whom our age owes much, concerning the islands recently discovered in the Indian sea. For the search of which, eight months before, he was sent under the auspices and at the cost of the most invincible Ferdinand, king of Spain. Addressed to the magnificent lord Raphael Sanxis, treasurer of the same most illustrious king, and which the noble and learned man Leander de Cosco has translated from the Spanish language into Latin, on the third of the kalends of May, 1493, the first year of the pontificate of Alexander the Sixth.

Because my undertakings have attained success, I know that it will be pleasing to you: these I have determined to relate, so that you may be made acquainted with everything done and discovered in this our voyage. On the thirty-third day after I departed from Cadiz, I came to the Indian sea, where I found many islands inhabited by men without number, of all which I took possession for our most fortunate king, with proclaiming heralds and flying standards, no one objecting. To the first of these I gave the name of the blessed Saviour, on whose aid relying I had reached this as well as the other islands. But the Indians call it Guanahany. I also called each one of the others by a new name. For I ordered one island to be called Santa Maria of the Conception, another Fernandina, another Isabella, another Juana, and so on with the rest. As soon as we had arrived at that island which I have just now said was called Juana, I proceeded along its coast towards the west for some distance; I found it so large and without perceptible end, that I believed it to be not an island, but the continental country of Cathay; seeing, however, no towns or cities situated on the seacoast, but only some villages and rude farms, with whose inhabitants I was unable to converse, because as soon as they saw us they took flight. I proceeded farther, thinking that I would discover some city or large residences. At length, perceiving that we had gone far enough, that nothing new appeared, and that this way was leading us to the north, which I wished to avoid, because it was winter on the land, and it was my intention to go to the south, moreover the winds were becoming violent, I therefore determined that no other plans were practicable, and so, going back, I returned to a certain bay that I had noticed, from which I sent two of our men to the land, that they might find out whether there was a king in this country, or any cities. These men traveled for three days, and they found people and houses without number, but they were small, and without any government, therefore they returned. Now in the meantime I had learned from certain Indians, whom I had seized there, that this country was indeed an island, and therefore I proceeded towards the east, keeping all the time near the coast, for 322 miles, to the extreme ends of this island. From this place I saw another island to the east, distant from this Juana 54 miles, which I called forthwith Hispana; and I sailed to it; and I steered along the northern coast, as at Juana, towards the east, 564 miles. And the said Juana and the other islands there appear very fertile. This island is surrounded by many very safe and wide harbors, not excelled by any others that I have ever seen. Many great and salubrious rivers flow through it. There are also many very high mountains there. All these islands are very beautiful, and distinguished by various qualities; they are accessible, and full of a great variety of trees stretching up to the stars; the leaves of which I believe are never shed, for I saw them as green and flourishing as they are usually in Spain in the month of May; some of them were blossoming, some were bearing fruit, some were in other conditions; each one was thriving in its own way. The nightingale and various other birds without number were singing, in the month of November, when I was exploring them. There are besides in the said island Juana seven or eight kinds of palm trees, which far excel ours in height and beauty, just as all the other trees, herbs, and fruits do. There are also excellent pine trees, vast plains and meadows, a variety of birds, a variety of honey, and a variety of metals, excepting iron. In the one which was called Hispana, as we said above, there are great and beautiful mountains, vast fields, groves, fertile plains, very suitable for planting and cultivating, and for the building of houses. The convenience of the harbors in this island, and the remarkable number of rivers contributing to the healthfulness of man, exceed belief, unless one has seen them. The trees, pasturage, and fruits of this island differ greatly from those of Juana. This Hispana, moreover, abounds in different kinds of spices, in gold, and in metals. On this island, indeed, and on all the others which I have seen, and of which I have knowledge, the inhabitants of both sexes go always naked, just as they came into the world, except some of the women, who use a covering of a leaf or some foliage, or a cotton cloth, which they make themselves for that purpose. All these people lack, as I said above, every kind of iron; they are also without weapons, which indeed are unknown; nor are they competent to use them, not on account of deformity of body, for they are well formed, but because they are timid and full of fear. They carry for weapons, however, reeds baked in the sun, on the lower ends of which they fasten some shafts of dried wood rubbed down to a point; and indeed they do not venture to use these always; for it frequently happened when I sent two or three of my men to some of the villages, that they might speak with the natives, a compact troop of the Indians would march out, and as soon as they saw our men approaching, they would quickly take flight, children being pushed aside by their fathers, and fathers by their children. And this was not because any hurt or injury had been inflicted on any one of them, for to every one whom I visited and with whom I was able to converse, I distributed whatever I had, cloth and many other things, no return being made to me; but they are by nature fearful and timid. Yet when they perceive that they are safe, putting aside all fear, they are of simple manners and trustworthy, and very liberal with everything they have, refusing no one who asks for anything they may possess, and even themselves inviting us to ask for things. They show greater love for all others than for themselves; they give valuable things for trifles, being satisfied even with a very small return, or with nothing; however, I forbade that things so small and of no value should be given to them, such as pieces of plates, dishes and glass, likewise keys and shoe-straps; although if they were able to obtain these, it seemed to them like getting the most beautiful jewels in the world. It happened, indeed, that a certain sailor obtained in exchange for a shoe-strap as much worth of gold as would equal three golden coins; and likewise other things for articles of very little value, especially for new silver coins, and for some gold coins, to obtain which they gave whatever the seller desired, as for instance an ounce and a half and two ounces of gold, or thirty and forty pounds of cotton, with which they were already acquainted. They also traded cotton and gold for pieces of bows, bottles, jugs and jars, like persons without reason, which I forbade because it was very wrong; and I gave to them many beautiful and pleasing things that I had brought with me, no value being taken in exchange, in order that I might the more easily make them friendly to me, that they might be made worshippers of Christ, and that they might be full of love towards our king, queen, and prince, and the whole Spanish nation; also that they might be zealous to search out and collect, and deliver to us those things of which they had plenty, and which we greatly needed. These people practice no kind of idolatry; on the contrary they firmly believe that all strength and power, and in fact all good things are in heaven, and that I had come down from thence with these ships and sailors; and in this belief I was received there after they had put aside fear, Nor are they slow or unskilled, but of excellent and acute understanding; and the men who have navigated that sea give an account of everything in an admirable manner; but they never saw people clothed, nor these kind of ships. As soon as I reached that sea, I seized by force several Indians on the first island, in order that they might learn from us, and in like manner tell us about those things in these lands of which they themselves had knowledge; and the plan succeeded, for in a short time we understood them and they us, sometimes by gestures and signs, sometimes by words; and it was a great advantage to us. They are coming with me now, yet always believing that I descended from heaven, although they have been living with us for a long time, and are living with us to-day. And these men were the first who announced it wherever we landed, continually proclaiming to the others in a loud voice, "Come, come, and you will see the celestial people." Whereupon both women and men, both children and adults, both young men and old men, laying aside the fear caused a little before, visited us eagerly, filling the road with a great crowd, some bringing food, and some drink, with great love and extraordinary goodwill. On every island there are many canoes of a single piece of wood; and though narrow, yet in length and shape similar to our row-boats, but swifter in movement. They steer only by oars. Some of these boats are large, some small, some of medium size. Yet they row many of the larger row-boats with eighteen cross-benches, with which they cross to all those islands, which are innumerable, and with these boats they perform their trading, and carry on commerce among them. I saw some of these row-boats or canoes which were carrying seventy and eighty rowers. In all these islands there is no difference in the appearance of the people, nor in the manners and language, but all understand each other mutually; a fact that is very important for the end which I suppose to be earnestly desired by our most illustrious king, that is, their conversion to the holy religion of Christ, to which in truth, as far as I can perceive, they are very ready and favorably inclined. I said before how I proceeded along the island Juana in a straight line from west to east 322 miles, according to which course and the length of the way, I am able to say that this Juana is larger than England and Scotland together; for besides the said 322 thousand paces, there are two more provinces in that part which lies towards the west, which I did not visit; one of these the Indians call Anan, whose inhabitants are born with tails. They extend to 180 miles in length, as I have learned from those Indians I have with me, who are all acquainted with these islands. But the circumference of Hispana is greater than all Spain from Colonia to Fontarabia. This is easily proved because its fourth side, which I myself passed along in a straight line from west to east, extends 540 miles. This island is to be desired and is very desirable, and not to be despised; in which, although as I have said, I solemnly took possession of all the others for our most invincible king, and their government is entirely committed to the said king, yet I especially took possession of a certain large town, in a very convenient location, and adapted to all kinds of gain and commerce, to which we give the name of our Lord of the Nativity. And I commanded a fort to be built there forthwith, which must be completed by this time; in which I left as many men as seemed necessary, with all kinds of arms, and plenty of food for more than a year. Likewise one caravel, and for the construction of others men skilled in this trade and in other professions; and also the extraordinary good will and friendship of the king of this island toward us. For those people are very amiable and kind, and to such a degree that the said king gloried in calling me his brother. And if they should change their minds, and should wish to hurt those who remained in the fort, they would not be able, because they lack weapons, they go naked, and are too cowardly. For that reason those who hold the said fort are at least able to resist easily this whole island, without any imminent danger to themselves, so long as they do not transgress the regulations and command which we gave. In all these islands, as I have understood, each man is content with only one wife, except the princes or kings, who are permitted to have twenty. The women appear to work more than the men. I was not able to find out surely whether they have individual property, for I saw that one man had the duty of distributing to the others, especially refreshments, food, and things of that kind. I found no monstrosities among them, as very many supposed, but men of great reverence, and friendly. Nor are they black like the Ethiopians. They have straight hair, hanging down. They do not remain where the solar rays send out the heat, for the strength of the sun is very great here, because it is distant from the equinoctial line, as it seems, only twenty-six degrees. On the tops of the mountains too the cold is severe, but the Indians, however, moderate it, partly by being accustomed to the place and partly by the help of very hot victuals, of which they eat frequently and immoderately. And so I did not see any monstrosity, nor did I have knowledge of them any where, excepting a certain island named Charis, which is the second in passing from Hispana to India. This island is inhabited by a certain people who are considered very warlike by their neighbors. These eat human flesh. The said people have many kinds of row-boats, in which they cross over to all the other Indian islands, and seize and carry away every thing that they can. They differ in no way from the others, only that they wear long hair like the women. They use bows and darts made of reeds, with sharpened shafts fastened to the larger end, as we have described. On this account they are considered warlike, wherefore the other Indians are afflicted with continual fear, but I regard them as of no more account than the others. These are the people who visit certain women, who alone inhabit the island Mateunin, which is the first in passing from Hispana to India. These women, moreover, perform no kind of work of their sex, for they use bows and darts, like those I have described of their husbands; they protect themselves with sheets of copper, of which there is great abundance among them. They tell me of another island greater than the aforesaid Hispana, whose inhabitants are without hair, and which abounds in gold above all the others. I am bringing with me men of this island and of the others that I have seen, who give proof of the things that I have described. Finally, that I may compress in few words the brief account of our departure and quick return, and the gain, I promise this, that if I am supported by our most invincible sovereigns with a little of their help, as much gold can be supplied as they will need, indeed as much of spices, of cotton, of chewing gum (which is only found in Chios), also as much of aloes wood, and as many slaves for the navy, as their majesties will wish to demand. Likewise rhubarb and other kinds of spices, which I suppose these men whom I left in the said fort have already found, and will continue to find; since I remained in no place longer than the winds forced me, except in the town of the Nativity, while I provided for the building of the fort, and for the safety of all. Which things, although they are very great and remarkable, yet they would have been much greater, if I had been aided by as many ships as the occasion required. Truly great and wonderful is this, and not corresponding to our merits, but to the holy Christian religion, and to the piety and religion of our sovereigns, because what the human understanding could not attain, that the divine will has granted to human efforts. For God is wont to listen to his servants who love his precepts, even in impossibilities, as has happened to us on the present occasion, who have attained that which hitherto mortal men have never reached. For if any one has written or said any thing about these islands, it was all with obscurities and conjectures; no one claims that he had seen them; from which they seem like fables. Therefore let the king and queen, the princes and their most fortunate kingdoms, and all other countries of Christendom give thanks to our Lord and Saviour Jesus Christ, who has bestowed upon us so great a victory and gift. Let religious processions be solemnized; let sacred festivals be given; let the churches be covered with festive garlands. Let Christ rejoice on earth, as he rejoices in heaven, when he foresees coming to salvation so many souls of people hitherto lost. Let us be glad also, as well on account of the exaltation of our faith, as on account of the increase of our temporal affairs, of which not only Spain, but universal Christendom will be partaker. These things that have been done are thus briefly related. Farewell. Lisbon, the day before the ides of March.

Christopher Columbus, admiral of the Ocean Fleet.

EPIGRAM OF R. L. DE CORBARIA,
BISHOP OF MONTE PELOSO.

To the Most Invincible King of Spain.

No region now can add to Spain's great deeds:
To such men all the world is yet too small.
An Orient land, found far beyond the waves,
Will add, great Betica, to thy renown.
Then to Columbus, the true finder, give
Due thanks; but greater still to God on high;
Who makes new kingdoms for himself and thee:
Both firm and pious let thy conduct be.

1493

II. THOMAS HARIOT
(1560–1621)

From *THE PRINCIPAL NAVIGATIONS, VOYAGES* [*&c.*]

BY RICHARD HAKLUYT

THE NEW FOUND LAND OF VIRGINIA

To the Adventurers, Favorers, and Welwillers of the enterprise for the inhabiting and planting in Virginia.

Since the first undertaking by Sir Walter Ralegh to deale in the action of discovering of that countrey which is now called and knowen by the name of Virginia, many voyages having beene thither made at sundry times to his great charge; as first in the yere 1584, and afterwards in the yeres 1585, 1586, and now of late this last yeere 1587: there have bene divers and variable reports, with some slanderous and shamefull speeches bruted abroad by many that returned from thence: especially of that discovery which was made by the Colony transported by Sir Richard Grinvile in the yere 1585, being of all others the most principall, and as yet of most effect, the time of their abode in the countrey being a whole yere, when as in the other voyage before they stayed but sixe weeks, and the others after were onely for supply and transportation, nothing more being discovered then had bene before. Which reports have not done a little wrong to many that otherwise would have also favoured and adventured in the action, to the honour and benefit of our nation, besides the particular profit and credit which would redound to themselves the dealers therein, as I hope by the sequel of events, to the shame of those that have avouched the contrary, shall be manifest, if you the adventurers, favourers and welwillers doe but either increase in number, or in opinion continue, or having beene doubtfull, renew your good liking and furtherance to deale therein according to the woorthinesse thereof already found, and as you shall understand hereafter to be requisit. Touching which woorthinesse through cause of the diversity of relations and reports, many of your opinions could not be firme, nor the minds of some that are well disposed be setled in any certaintie.

I have therefore thought it good, being one that have beene in the discoverie, and in dealing with the naturall inhabitants specially imployed: and having therefore seene and knowen more then the ordinary, to impart so much unto you of the fruits of our labours, as that you may know how injuriously the enterprise is slandered, and that in publique maner at this present, chiefly for two respects.

First, that some of you which are yet ignorant or doubtfull of the state thereof, may see that there is sufficient cause why the chiefe enterpriser with the favour of her Maiesty, notwithstanding such reports, hath not onely since continued the action by sending into the countrey againe, and replanting this last yeere a new Colony, but is also ready, according as the times and meanes will affourd, to follow and prosecute the same.

Secondly, that you seeing and knowing the continuance of the action, by the view hereof you may generally know and learne what the countrey is, and thereupon consider how your dealing therein, if it proceed, may returne you profit and gaine, be it either by inhabiting and planting, or otherwise in furthering thereof.

And least that the substance of my relation should be doubtfull unto you, as of others by reason of their diversitie, I will first open the cause in a few words, wherefore they are so different, referring my selfe to your favourable constructions, and to be adiudged of, as by good consideration you shall finde cause.

Of our company that returned, some for their misdemeanour and ill dealing in the countrey have bene there worthily punished, who by reason of their bad natures, have maliciously not onely spoken ill of their Governours, but for their sakes slandered the countrey it selfe. The like also have those done which were of their consort.

Some being ignorant of the state thereof, notwithstanding since their returne amongst their friends & acquaintance, and also others, especially if they were in company where they might not be gainsayd, would seeme to know so much as no men more and make no men as great travellers as themselves. They stood so much as it may seeme, upon their credit and reputation, that having bene a twelvemoneth in the countrey, it would have bene a great disgrace unto them, as they thought, if they could not have sayd much, whether it were true or false. Of which some have spoken of more then ever they saw, or otherwise knew to be there. Other some have not bene ashamed to make absolute deniall of that, which although not by them, yet by others is most certainly and there plentifully knowen, & other some make difficulties of those things they have no skill of.

The cause of their ignorance was, in that they were of that many that were never out of the Island where we were seated, or not farre, or at the leastwise in few places els, during the time of our abode in the countrey: or of that many, that after gold & silver was not so soone found, as it was by them looked for, had litle or no care of any other thing but to pamper their bellies: or of that many which had litle understanding, lesse discretion, and more tongue than was needfull or requisite.

Some also were of a nice bringing up, only in cities or townes, or such as never (as I may say) had seene the world before. Because there were not to be found any English cities, nor such faire houses, nor at their owne wish any of their old accustomed dainty food, nor any soft beds of downe or feathers, the countrey was to them miserable, and their reports thereof according.

Because my purpose was but in briefe to open the cause of the variety of such speeches, the particularities of them, and of many envious, malicious, and slanderous reports and devices els, by our owne countreymen besides, as trifles that are not worthy of wise men to be thought upon, I meane not to trouble you withall, but will passe to the commodities, the substance of that which I have to make relation of unto you.

The Treatise whereof, for your more ready view and easier understanding, I will divide into three speciall parts. In the first I will make declaration of such commodities there already found or to be raised, which will not onely serve the ordinary turnes of you which are and shall be the planters and inhabitants, but such an overplus sufficiently to be yeelded, or by men of skill to be provided, as by way of traffique and exchange with our owne nation of England, will inrich yourselves the providers: those that shall deale with you, the enterprisers in generall, and greatly profit our owne countreymen, to supply them with most things which heretofore they have bene faine to provide either of strangers or of our enemies, which commodities, for distinction sake, I call Merchantable.

In the second I will set downe all the commodities which we know the countrey by our experience doth yeeld of it selfe for victuall and sustenance of mans life, such as are usually fed upon by the inhabitants of the countrey, as also by us during the time we were there.

In the last part I will make mention generally of such other commodities besides, as I am able to remember, and as I shall thinke behoovefull for those that shall inhabit, and plant there to know of, which specially concerne building, as also some other necessary uses: with a briefe description of the nature and maners of the people of the countrey. * * *

The second part of such commodities as Virginia is knowen to yeeld for victuall and sustenance of mans life, usually fed upon by the naturall inhabitants; as also by us, during the time of our abode: and first of such as are sowed and husbanded.

Pagatowr, a kinde of graine so called by the inhabitants: the same in the West Indies is called Mayz: English men call it Guiny-wheat or Turkey-wheat, according to the names of the countreys from whence the like hath beene brought. The graine is about the bignesse of our ordinary English peaze, and not much different in forme and shape: but of divers colours: some white, some red, some yellow, and some blew. All of them yeeld a very white and sweet flowre: being used according to his kinde, it maketh a very good bread. We made of the same in the countrey some Mault, whereof was brewed as good Ale as was to be desired. So likewise by the helpe of Hops, therof be made as good Beere. It is a graine of marvellous great increase: of a thousand, fifteene hundred, and some two thousand folde. There are three sorts, of which two are ripe in eleven & twelve weeks at the most, sometimes in tenne, after the time they are set, and are then of height in stalke about sixe or seven foot. The other sort is ripe in foureteene, and is about tenne foot high, of the stalks some beare foure heads, some three, some one, and some two: every head conteining five, sixe, or seven hundred graines, within a few more or lesse. Of these graines, besides bread, the inhabitants make victuall, either by parching them, or seething them whole untill they be broken: or biling the flowre with water into a pap.

Okingier, called by us Beanes, because in greatnesse and partly in shape they are like to the Beanes in England, saving that they are flatter, of more divers colors, and some pide. The leafe also of the stemme is much different. In taste they are altogether as good as our English peaze. * * *

There is also another great herbe, in forme of a Marigolde, about sixe foot in height, the head with the floure is a spanne in breadth. Some take it to be Planta Solis: of the seeds hereof they make both a kinde of bread and broth.

All the aforesayd commodities for victuall are set or sowed, sometimes in grounds apart and severally by themselves, but for the most part together in one ground mixtly: the maner thereof, with the dressing and preparing of the ground, because I will note unto you the fertility of the soile, I thinke good briefly to describe.

The ground they never fatten with mucke, dung, or any other thing, neither plow nor digge it as we in England, but onely prepare it in sort as followeth. A few dayes before they sowe or set, the men with woodden instruments made almost in forme of mattocks or hoes with long handles: the women with short peckers or parers, because they use them sitting, of a foot long, and about five inches in breadth, doe onely breake the upper part of the ground to raise up the weeds, grasse, and olde stubbes of corne stalks with their roots. The which after a day or two dayes drying in the Sunne, being scrapt up into many small heaps, to save them labour for carying them away, they burne into ashes. And whereas some may thinke that they use the ashes for to better the ground, I say that then they would either disperse the ashes abroad, which wee observed they do not, except the heaps be too great, or els would take speciall care to set their corne where the ashes lie, which also wee finde they are carelesse of. And this is all the husbanding of their ground that they use.

Then their setting or sowing is after this maner. First for their corne, beginning in one corner of the plot, with a pecker they make a hole, wherein they put foure graines, with care that they touch not one another (about an inch asunder) & cover them with the molde againe: and so thorowout the whole plot making such holes, and using them after such maner, but with this regard, that they be made in ranks, every ranke differing from other halfe a fadome or a yard, and the holes also in every ranke as much. By this meanes there is a yard spare ground betweene every hole: where according to discretion here and there, they set as many Beanes and Peaze; in divers places also among the seeds of Macocquer, Melden, and Planta solis. * * *

I thought also good to note this unto you, that you which shall inhabit, and plant there, may know how specially that countrey corne is there to be preferred before ours: besides, the manifold wayes in applying it to victual, the increase is so much, that small labor & paines is needful in respect of that which must be used for ours. For this I can assure you that according to the rate we have made proofe of, one man may prepare and husband so much ground (having once borne corne before) with less then foure and twenty houres labour, as shall yeeld him victual in a large proportion for a twelvemoneth, if he have nothing els but that which the same ground will yeeld, and of that kinde onely which I have before spoken of: the sayd ground being also but of five and twenty yards square. And if need require, but that there is ground enough, there might be raised out of one and the selfesame ground two harvests or ofcomes: for they sow or set, and may at any time when they thinke good, from the midst of March untill the end of June: so that they also set when they have eaten of their first croppe. In some places of the countrey notwithstanding they have two harvest, as we have heard, out of one and the same ground.

For English corne neverthelesse, whether to use or not to use it, you that inhabit may doe as you shall have further cause to thinke best. Of the growth you need not to doubt: for Barley, Oats, and Peaze, we have seene proofe of, not being purposely sowen, but fallen casually in the woorst sort of ground, and yet to be as faire as any we have ever seene heere in England. But of Wheat, because it was musty, and had taken salt water, we could make no triall: and of Rie we had none. Thus much have I digressed, and I hope not unnessarily: now will I returne againe to my course, and intreat of that which yet remaineth, apperteining to this chapter.

There is an herbe which is sowed apart by it selfe, and is called by the inhabitants Uppowoc: in the West Indies it hath divers names, according to the severall places and countreys where it groweth and is used: the Spanyards generally call it Tabacco. The leaves thereof being dried and brought into pouder, they use to take the fume or smoake thereof, by sucking it thorow pipes made of clay, into their stomacke and head; from whence it purgeth superfluous fleame and other grosse humours, and openeth all the pores and passages of the body; by which meanes the use thereof not onely preserveth the body from obstructions, but also (if any be, so that they have not bene of too long continuance) in short time breaketh them; whereby their bodies are notably preserved in health, and know not many grievous diseases, wherewithall we in England are often times afflicted.

This Uppowoc is of so precious estimation amongst them, that they thinke their gods are marvellously delighted therewith: whereupon sometime they make hallowed fires, and cast some of the pouder therin for a sacrifice: being in a storme upon the waters, to pacifie their gods, they cast some up into the aire, and into the water: so a weare for fish being newly set up, they cast some therein and into the aire: also after an escape of danger, they cast some into the aire likewise: but all done with strange gestures, stamping, sometime dancing, clapping of hands, holding up of hands, and staring up into the heavens, uttering therewithall, and chattering strange words and noises.

We our selves, during the time we were there, used to sucke it after their maner, as also since our returne, and have found many rare and woonderfull experiments of the vertues thereof: of which the relation would require a volume by it selfe: the use of it by so many of late men and women of great calling, as els, and some learned Physicians also, is sufficient witnesse.

And these are all the commodities for sustenance of life, that I know and can remember, they use to husband: all els that follow, are found growing naturally or wilde. * * *

1588

III. SAMUEL DE CHAMPLAIN (1567–1635)

LES VOYAGES

BOOK II, CHAPTER IX

[A BATTLE WITH THE IROQUOIS]

Departure from the Rapids of the river of the Iroquois. Description of a great lake. Our meeting with the enemy at the aforesaid lake and of the manner in which our Indians attack the Iroquois.

I set out then from the rapid of the river of the Iroquois on the second of July. All the Indians began to carry their canoes, arms and baggage about half a league by land, to avoid the swiftness and force of the rapid. This they soon accomplished.

Then they put all the canoes into the water and two men with their baggage into each; but they made one of the men of each canoe go by land some three leagues which is about the length of the rapids, but the water is here less impetuous than at the entrance, except in certain places where rocks block the river, which is only some three or four hundred yards wide. After we had passed the rapids, which was not without difficulty, all the Indians who had gone overland, by a rather pleasant path through level country, although there were many trees, again got into their canoes. The men whom I had with me also went by land, but I went by water in a canoe. The Indians held a review of all their people and there were sixty men in twenty-four canoes. After holding the review we kept on our way as far as an island, three leagues long, which was covered with the most beautiful pines I had ever seen. There the Indians hunted and took some game. Continuing some three leagues farther, we encamped to take rest during the following night.

Immediately each began, some to cut down trees, others to strip bark from the trees to cover their wigwams in which to take shelter, others to fell big trees for a barricade on the bank of the river round their wigwams. They know how to do this so quickly that after less than two hours' work, five hundred of their enemies would have had difficulty in driving them out, without losing many men. They do not barricade the river bank where their boats are drawn up, in order to embark in case of need. After their wigwams had been set up, according to their custom each time they camp, they sent three canoes with nine good men, to reconnoitre two or three leagues ahead, whether they could perceive anything; and afterwards these retired. All night long they rely upon the explorations of these scouts, and it is a very bad custom; for sometimes they are surprised in their sleep by their enemies, who club them before they have time to rise and defend themselves. Realizing this, I pointed out to them the mistake they were making and said that they ought to keep watch as they had seen us do every night, and have men posted to listen and see whether they might perceive anything, and not live as they were doing like silly creatures. They told me that they could not stay awake, and that they worked enough during the day when hunting. Besides when they go to war they divide their men into three troops, that is, one troop for hunting, scattered in various directions, another troop which forms the bulk of their men is always under arms, and the other troop of scouts to reconnoitre along the rivers and see whether there is any mark or sign to show where their enemies or their friends have gone. This they know by certain marks by which the chiefs of one nation designate those of another, notifying one another from time to time of any variations of these. In this way they recognise whether enemies or friends have passed that way. The hunters never hunt in advance of the main body, nor of the scouts, in order not to give alarm or to cause confusion, but only when these have retired and in a direction from which they do not expect the enemy. They go on in this way until they are within two or three days' march of their enemy, when they proceed stealthily by night, all in a body, except the scouts. In the day time they retire into the thick of the woods, where they rest without any straggling, or making a noise, or making a fire even for the purpose of cooking. And this they do so as not to be noticed, if by chance their enemy should pass that way. The only light they make is for the purpose of smoking which is almost nothing. They eat baked Indian meal, steeped in water, which becomes like porridge. They keep these meal cakes for their needs, when they are near the enemy or when they are retiring after an attack; for then they do not waste time in hunting but retire quickly.

Each time they encamp they have their *Pilotois* or *Ostemoy* who are people who play the part of wizards, in whom these tribes have confidence. One of these wizards will set up a tent, surround it with small trees, and cover it with his beaver-skin. When it is made, he gets inside so that he is completely hidden; then he seizes one of the poles of his tent and shakes it whilst he mumbles between his teeth certain words, with which he declares he is invoking the devil, who appears to him in the form of a stone and tells him whether his friends will come upon their enemies and kill many of them. This *Pilotois* will lie flat on the ground, without moving, merely speaking to the devil, and suddenly he will rise to his feet, speaking and writhing so that he is all in a perspiration, although stark naked. The whole tribe will be about the tent sitting on their buttocks like monkeys. They often told me that the shaking of the tent which I saw, was caused by the devil and not by the man inside, although I saw the contrary; for, as I have said above, it was the *Pilotois* who would seize one of the poles of the tent, and make it move in this way. They told me also that I should see fire coming out of the top, but I never saw any. These scamps also counterfeit a loud, distinct voice, and speak a language unknown to the other Indians. And when they speak in an old man's voice, the rest think that the devil is speaking, and is telling them what is going to happen in their war, and what they must do.

Yet out of a hundred words all these scoundrels, who pretend to be wizards, do not speak two that are true, and go on deceiving these poor people to get things from them, as do many others in this world who resemble these gentry. I often pointed out to them that what they did was pure folly, and that they ought not to believe in such things.

Having learned from their wizards what is to happen to them, the chiefs take sticks a foot long, one for each man, and indicate by others somewhat longer, their leaders. Then they go into the wood, and level off a place five or six feet square, where the headman, as sergeant-major, arranges all these sticks as to him seems best. Then he calls all his companions, who approach fully armed, and he shows them the rank and order which they are to observe when they fight with the enemy. This all these Indians regard attentively, and notice the figure made with these sticks by their chief. And afterwards they retire from that place and begin to arrange themselves in the order in which they have seen these sticks. Then they mix themselves up and again put themselves in proper order, repeating this two or three times, and go back to their camp, without any need of a sergeant to make them keep their ranks, which they are quite able to maintain without getting into confusion. Such is the method they observe on the war-path.

We departed on the following day, pursuing our way up the river as far as the entrance to the lake. In it are many beautiful low islands covered with very fine woods and meadows with much wild fowl and animals to hunt, such as stags, fallow deer, fawns, roebucks, bears, and other kinds of animals which come from the mainland to these islands. We caught there a great many of them. There are also many beavers, both in that river and in several small streams which fall into it. This region although pleasant is not inhabited by Indians, on account of their wars; for they withdraw from the rivers as far as they can into the interior, in order not to be easily surprised.

On the following day we entered the lake which is some 80 or 100 leagues in length, in which I saw four beautiful islands about ten, twelve and fifteen leagues in length, which, like the Iroquois river, were formerly inhabited by Indians: but have been abandoned, since they have been at war with one another. There are also several rivers flowing into the lake, on whose banks are many fine trees of the same varieties we have in France, with many of the finest vines I had seen anywhere. There are many chestnut trees which I had only seen on the shore of this lake, in which there is also a great abundance of many species of fish. Amongst others there is one called by the natives *Chaousarou,* which is of various lengths; but the largest of them, as these tribes have told me, are from eight to ten feet long. I have seen some five feet long, which were as big as my thigh, and had a head as large as my two fists, with a snout two feet and a half long, and a double row of very sharp, dangerous teeth. Its body has a good deal the shape of the pike; but it is protected by scales of a silvery gray colour and so strong that a dagger could not pierce them. The end of its snout is like a pig's. This fish makes war on all the other fish which are in these lakes and rivers. And, according to what these tribes have told me, it shows marvellous ingenuity in that, when it wishes to catch birds, it goes in amongst the rushes or reeds which lie along the shores of the lake in several places, and puts its snout out of the water without moving. The result is that when the birds come and light on its snout, mistaking it for a stump of wood, the fish is so cunning that, shutting its half-open mouth, it pulls them by their feet under the water. The natives gave me the head of one of them, a thing they prize highly, saying that when they have a headache, they bleed themselves with the teeth of this fish at the spot where the pain is and it eases them at once.

Continuing our way along this lake in a westerly direction and viewing the country, I saw towards the east very high mountains on the tops of which there was snow. I enquired of the natives whether these parts were inhabited. They said they were, and by the Iroquois, and that in those parts there were beautiful valleys and fields rich in corn such as I have eaten in that country, along with other products in abundance. And they said that the lake went close to the mountains, which, as I judged, might be some twenty-five leagues away from us. Towards the south I saw others which were not less lofty than the first-mentioned, but there was no snow on these. The Indians told me that it was there that we were to meet their enemies, that the mountains were thickly populated, and that we had to pass a rapid which I saw afterwards. Thence they said we had to enter another lake which is some nine or ten leagues in length, and that on reaching the end of it we had to go by land some two leagues and cross a river which descends to the coast of Norumbega, adjoining that of Florida. They could go there in their canoes in two days, as I learned afterwards from some prisoners we took, who conversed with me very particularly regarding all they knew, with the help of some Algonquin interpreters who knew the Iroquois language.

Now as we began to get within two or three days' journey of the home of their enemy, we proceeded only by night, and during the day we rested. Nevertheless, they kept up their usual superstitious ceremonies in order to know what was to happen to them in their undertakings, and often would come and ask me whether I had had dreams and had seen their enemies. I would tell them that I had not, but nevertheless continued to inspire them with courage and good hope. When night came on, we set off on our way until the next morning. Then we retired into the thick woods where we spent the rest of the day. Towards ten or eleven o'clock, after walking around our camp, I went to take a rest, and while asleep I dreamed that I saw in the lake near a mountain our enemies, the Iroquois, drowning before our eyes. I wanted to succour them, but our Indian allies said to me that we should let them all perish; for they were bad men. When I awoke they did not fail to ask me as usual whether I had dreamed anything. I told them what I had seen in my dream. This gave them such confidence that they no longer had any doubts as to the good fortune awaiting them.

Evening having come, we embarked in our canoes in order to proceed on our way, and as we were paddling along very quietly, and without making any noise, about ten o'clock at night on the twenty-ninth of the month, at the extremity of a cape which projects into the lake on the west side, we met the Iroquois on the war-path. Both they and we began to utter loud shouts and each got his arms ready. We drew out into the lake and the Iroquois landed and arranged all their canoes near one another. Then they began to fell trees with the poor axes which they sometimes win in war, or with stone axes; and they barricaded themselves well.

Our Indians all night long also kept their canoes close to one another and tied to poles in order not to get separated, but to fight all together in case of need. We were on the water within bowshot of their barricades. And when they were armed, and everything in order, they sent two canoes which they had separated from the rest, to learn from their enemies whether they wished to fight, and these replied that they had no other desire, but that for the moment nothing could be seen and that it was necessary to wait for daylight in order to distinguish one another. They said that as soon as the sun should rise, they would attack us, and to this our Indians agreed. Meanwhile the whole night was spent in dances and songs on both sides, with many insults and other remarks, such as the lack of courage of our side, how little we could resist or do against them, and that when daylight came our people would learn all this to their ruin. Our side too was not lacking in retort, telling the enemy that they would see such deeds of arms as they had never seen, and a great deal of other talk, such as is usual at the siege of a city. Having sung, danced, and flung words at one another for some time, when daylight came, my companions and I were still hidden, lest the enemy should see us, getting our fire-arms ready as best we could, being however still separated, each in a canoe of the Montagnais Indians. After we were armed with light weapons, we took, each of us, an arquebus and went ashore. I saw the enemy come out of their barricade to the number of two hundred, in appearance strong, robust men. They came slowly to meet us with a gravity and calm which I admired; and at their head were three chiefs. Our Indians likewise advanced in similar order, and told me that those who had the three big plumes were the chiefs, and that there were only these three, whom you could recognize by these plumes, which were larger than those of their companions; and I was to do what I could to kill them. I promised them to do all in my power, and told them that I was very sorry they could not understand me, so that I might direct their method of attacking the enemy, all of whom undoubtedly we should thus defeat; but that there was no help for it, and that I was very glad to show them, as soon as the engagement began, the courage and readiness which were in me.

As soon as we landed, our Indians began to run some two hundred yards towards their enemies, who stood firm and had not yet noticed my white companions who went off into the woods with some Indians. Our Indians began to call to me with loud cries; and to make way for me they divided into two groups, and put me ahead some twenty yards, and I marched on until I was within some thirty yards of the enemy, who as soon as they caught sight of me halted and gazed at me and I at them. When I saw them make a move to draw their bows upon us, I took aim with my arquebus and shot straight at one of the three chiefs, and with this shot two fell to the ground and one of their companions was wounded who died thereof a little later. I had put four bullets into my arquebus. As soon as our people saw this shot so favourable for them, they began to shout so loudly that one could not have heard it thunder, and meanwhile the arrows flew thick on both sides. The Iroquois were much astonished that two men should have been killed so quickly, although they were provided with shields made of cotton thread woven together and wood, which were proof against their arrows. This frightened them greatly. As I was reloading my arquebus, one of my companions fired a shot from within the woods, which astonished them again so much that, seeing their chiefs dead, they lost courage and took to flight, abandoning the field and their fort, and fleeing into the depth of the forest, whither I pursued them and laid low still more of them. Our Indians also killed several and took ten or twelve prisoners. The remainder fled with the wounded. Of our Indians fifteen or sixteen were wounded with arrows, but these were quickly healed.

After we had gained the victory, our Indians wasted time in taking a large quantity of Indian corn and meal belonging to the enemy, as well as their shields, which they had left behind, the better to run. Having feasted, danced, and sung, we three hours later set off for home with the prisoners. The place where this attack took place is in 43° and some minutes of latitude, and was named Lake Champlain.

1613

THE SETTLEMENT

I. JOHN SMITH
(*c.* 1580–1631)

From *THE TRUE TRAVELS* [*&c.*]

CHAPTER VII

[COMBATS WITH THE TURKS]

* * * Which slow proceedings the *Turkes* oft derided, that the Ordnance were at pawne, and how they grew fat for want of exercise; and fearing lest they should depart ere they could assault their Citie, sent this Challenge to any Captaine in the Armie.

> That to delight the Ladies, who did long to see some court-like pastime, the Lord *Turbashaw* did defie any Captaine, that had the command of a Company, who durst combate with him for his head.

The matter being discussed, it was accepted; but so many questions grew for the undertaking, it was decided by lots: which fell upon Captaine *Smith,* before spoken of.

(*Three single Combates.*) Truce being made for that time, the Rampiers all beset with faire Dames, and men in Armes, the *Christians* in *Battalio; Turbashaw* with a noise of Howboyes entred the fields well mounted and armed; on his shoulders were fixed a paire of great wings, compacted of Eagles feathers within a ridge of silver, richly garnished with gold and precious stones; a *Ianizary* before him, bearing his Lance; on each side, another leading his horse: where long hee stayed not, ere *Smith* with a noise of Trumpets, only a Page bearing his Lance, passing by him with a courteous salute, tooke his ground with such good successe, that at the sound of the charge, he passed the *Turke* throw the sight of his Beaver, face, head, and all, that he fell dead to the ground; where alighting and unbracing his Helmet, [he] cut off his head, and the Turkes tooke his body; and so returned without any hurt at all.

The head hee presented to the Lord *Moses,* the Generall, who kindly accepted it; and with joy to the whole armie he was generally welcomed.

The death of this Captaine so swelled in the heart of one *Grualgo,* his vowed friend, as, rather inraged with madnesse than choller, he directed a particular challenge to the Conquerour, to regaine his friends head, or lose his owne, with his horse and Armour for advantage: which according to his desire, was the next day undertaken.

As before, upon the sound of the Trumpets, their Lances flew in peeces upon a cleare passage; but the *Turke* was neere unhorsed. Their Pistolls was the next, which marked *Smith* upon the placard; but the next shot the *Turke* was so wounded in the left arme, that being not able to rule his horse, and defend himselfe, he was throwne to the ground; and so bruised with the fall, that he lost his head, as his friend before him;

with his horse and Armour: but his body and his rich apparell was sent backe to the Towne.

Every day the *Turkes* made some sallies, but few skirmishes would they endure to any purpose. Our workes and approaches being not yet advanced to that height and effect which was of necessitie to be performed; to delude time, *Smith,* with so many incontradictible perswading reasons, obtained leave that the Ladies might know he was not so

> much enamoured of their servants heads, but if any *Turke* of their ranke would come to the place of combate to redeeme them, [he] should have his also upon the like conditions, if he could winne it.

The challenge presently was accepted by *Bonny Mulgro.*

The next day both the Champions entring the field as before, each discharging their Pistoll (having no Lances, but such martiall weapons as the defendant appointed), no hurt was done; their Battle-axes was the next, whose piercing bils made sometime the one, sometime the other to have scarce sense to keepe their saddles: specially the *Christian* received such a blow that he lost his Battle-axe, and failed not much to have fallen after it; whereat the supposing conquering *Turk,* had a great shout from the Rampiers. The *Turk* prosecuted his advantage to the uttermost of his power; yet the other, what by the readinesse of his horse, and his judgement and dexterity in such a businesse, beyond all mens expectation, by Gods assistance, not onely avoided the *Turks* violence, but having drawne his Faulchion, pierced the *Turke* so under the Culets thorow backe and body, that although he alighted from his horse, he stood not long ere hee lost his head, as the rest had done.

1630

THE GENERALL HISTORIE OF VIRGINIA [*&c.*]

BOOK III, CHAPTER II

[CAPTIVITY]

* * * But our *Comœdies* never endured long without a *Tragedie;* some idle exceptions being muttered against Captaine *Smith,* for not discovering the head of *Chickahamania* river, and [being] taxed by the Councell, to be too slow in so worthy an attempt. The next voyage hee proceeded so farre that with much labour by cutting of trees insunder he made his passage; but when his Barge could passe no farther, he left her in a broad bay out of danger of shot, commanding none should goe a shore till his returne: himselfe with two English and two Salvages went up higher in a Canowe; but hee was not long absent, but his men went a shore, whose want of government gave both occasion and opportunity to the Salvages to surprise one *George Cassen,* whom they slew, and much failed not to have cut of[f] the boat and all the rest.

(*Iehu Robinson* and *Thomas Emry* slaine.) *Smith* little dreaming of that accident, being got to the marshes at the rivers head, twentie myles in the desert, had his two men slaine (as is supposed) sleeping by the Canowe, whilst himselfe by fowling sought them victuall: who finding he was beset with 200. Salvages, two of them hee slew, still defending himselfe with the ayd of a Salvage his guid, whom he bound to his arme with his garters, and used him as a buckler, yet he was shot in his thigh a little, and had many arrowes that stucke in his cloathes but no great hurt, till at last they tooke him prisoner.

When this newes came to *Iames* towne, much was their sorrow for his losse, fewe expecting what ensued.

Sixe or seven weekes those Barbarians kept him prisoner, many strange triumphes and coniurations they made of him, yet hee so demeaned himselfe amongst them, as he not onely diverted them from surprising the Fort, but procured his owne libertie, and got himselfe and his company such estimation amongst them, that those Salvages admired him more then their owne *Quiyouckosucks.*

The manner how they used and delivered him, is as followeth.

(Captaine *Smith* taken prisoner.) The Salvages having drawne from *George Cassen* whether Captaine *Smith* was gone, prosecuting that oportunity they followed him with 300. bowmen, conducted by the King of *Pamaunkee,* who in divisions searching the turnings of the river, found *Robinson* and *Emry* by the fire side: those they shot full of arrowes and slew. Then finding the Captaine, as is said, that used the Salvage that was his guide as his shield (three of them being slaine and divers other so gauld) all the rest would not come neere him. Thinking thus to have returned to his boat, regarding them, as he marched, more then his way, [he] slipped up to the middle in an oasie creeke and his Salvage with him; yet durst they not come to him til being neere dead with cold, he threw away his armes. Then according to their composition they drew him forth and led him to the fire, where his men were slaine. Diligently they chafed his benummed limbs.

He demanding for their Captaine, they shewed him *Opechankanough,* King of *Pamaunkee,* to whom he gave a round Ivory double compass Dyall. Much they marvailed at the playing of the Fly and Needle, which they could see so plainely, and yet not touch it, because of the glasse that covered them. But when he demonstrated by that Globe-like Iewell, the roundnesse of the earth, and skies, the spheare of the Sunne, Moone, and Starres, and how the Sunne did chase the night round about the world continually; the greatnesse of the Land and Sea, the diversitie of Nations, varietie of complexions, and how we were to them *Antipodes,* and many other such like matters, they all stood as amazed with admiration.

Notwithstanding, within an houre after they tyed him to a tree, and as many as could stand about him prepared to shoot him: but the King holding up the Compass in his hand, they all laid downe their Bowes and Arrowes, and in a triumphant manner led him to *Orapaks,* where he was after their manner kindly feasted, and well used.

(The order they observed in their triumph.) Their order in conducting him was thus; Drawing themselves all in fyle, the King in the middest had all their Peeces and Swords borne before him. Captaine *Smith* was led after him by three great Salvages, holding him fast by each arme: and on each side six went in fyle with their Arrowes nocked. But arriving at the Towne [*Orapaks*] (which was but onely thirtie or fortie hunting houses made of Mats, which they remove as they please, as we our tents) all the women and children staring to behold him, the souldiers first all in fyle performed the forme of a *Bissone* so well as could be; and on each flanke, officers as Serieants to see them keepe their orders. A good time they continued this exercise, and then cast themselves in a ring, dauncing in such severall Postures, and singing and yelling out such hellish notes and screeches; being strangely painted, every one his quiver of Arrowes, and at his backe a club; on his arme a Foxe or an Otters skinne, or some such matter for his umbrace; their heads and shoulders painted red, with Oyle and *Pocones* mingled together, which Scarlet-like colour made an exceeding handsome shew; his Bow in his hand, and the skinne of a Bird with her wings abroad dryed, tyed on his head, a peece of copper, a white shell, a long feather, with a small rattle growing at the tayles of their snak[e]s tyed to it, or some such like toy. All this while *Smith* and the King stood in the middest guarded, as before is said: and after three dances they all departed. *Smith* they conducted to a long house, where thirtie or fortie tall fellowes did guard him; and ere long more bread and venison was brought him then would have served twentie men. I thinke his stomacke at that time was not very good; what he left they put in baskets and tyed over his head. About midnight they set the meate againe before him, all this time not one of them would eate a bit with him, till the next morning they brought him as much more; and then did they eate all the old, and reserved the new as they had done the other, which made him thinke they would fat him to eat him. Yet in this desperate estate to defend him from the cold, one *Maocassater* brought him his gowne, in requitall of some beads and toyes *Smith* had given him at his first arrivall in *Virginia*.

(How he should have beene slaine at *Orapacks*.) Two dayes after a man would have slaine him (but that the guard prevented it) for the death of his sonne, to whom they conducted him to recover the poore man then breathing his last. *Smith* told them that at *Iames* towne he had a water would doe it, if they would let him fetch it, but they would not permit that: but made all the preparations they could to assault *Iames* towne, craving his advice; and for recompence he should have life, libertie, land, and women. In part of a Table booke he writ his minde to them at the Fort, what was intended, how they should follow that direction to affright the messengers, and without fayle send him such things as he writ for. And an Inventory with them. The difficultie and danger, he told the Salvages, of the Mines, great gunnes, and other Engins exceedingly affrighted them, yet according to his request they went to *Iames* towne, in as bitter weather as could be of frost and snow, and within three dayes returned with an answer.

(How he saved *Iames* towne from

being surprised.) But when they came to *Iame*[*s*] towne, seeing men sally out as he had told them they would, they fled; yet in the night they came againe to the same place where he had told them they should receive an answer, and such things as he had promised them: which they found accordingly, and with which they returned with no small expedition, to the wonder of them all that heard it, that he could either divine, or the paper could speake.

(How they did Coniure him at *Pamaunkee.*) Then they led him to the *Youthtanunds,* the *Mattapanients,* the *Payankatanks,* the *Nantaughtacunds,* and *Onawmanients* upon the rivers of *Rapahanock,* and *Patawomek;* over all those rivers, and backe againe by divers other severall Nations, to the Kings habitation at *Pamaunkee:* where they entertained him with most strange and fearefull Coniurations;

As if neare led to hell,
Amongst the Devils to dwell.

Not long after, early in a morning a great fire was made in a long house, and a mat spread on the one side, as on the other; on the one they caused him to sit, and all the guard went out of the house, and presently came skipping in a great grim fellow, all painted over with coale, mingled with oyle; and many Snakes and Wesels skins stuffed with mosse, and all their tayles tyed together, so as they met on the crowne of his head in a tassell; and round about the tassell was as a Coronet of feathers, the skins hanging round about his head, backe, and shoulders, and in a manner covered his face; with a hellish voyce, and a rattle in his hand. With most strange gestures and passions he began his invocation, and environed the fire with a circle of meale; which done, three more such like devils came rushing in with the like antique tricks, painted halfe blacke, halfe red: but all their eyes were painted white, and some red stroakes like Mutchato's, along their cheekes: round about him those fiends daunced a pretty while, and then came in three more as ugly as the rest; with red eyes, and white stroakes over their blacke faces, at last they all sat downe right against him; three of them on the one hand of the chiefe Priest, and three on the other. Then all with their rattles began a song, which ended, the chiefe Priest layd downe five wheat cornes: then strayning his armes and hands with such violence that he sweat, and his veynes swelled, he began a short Oration: at the conclusion they all gave a short groane; and then layd down three graines more. After that, began their song againe, and then another Oration, ever laying downe so many cornes as before, till they had twice incirculed the fire; that done, they tooke a bunch of little stickes prepared for that purpose, continuing still their devotion, and at the end of every song and Oration, they layd downe a sticke betwixt the divisions of Corne. Til night, neither he nor they did either eate or drinke; and then they feasted merrily, with the best provisions they could make. Three dayes they used this Ceremony; the meaning whereof they told him, was to know if he intended them well or no. The circle of meale signified their Country, the circles of corne the bounds of the Sea, and the stickes his

Country. They imagined the world to be flat and round, like a trencher; and they in the middest.

After this they brought him a bagge of gunpowder, which they carefully preserved til the next spring, to plant as they did their corne; because they would be acquainted with the nature of that seede.

Opitchapam the Kings brother invited him to his house, where, with as many platters of bread, foule, and wild beasts, as did environ him, he bid him wellcome; but not any of them would eate a bit with him, but put up all the remainder in Baskets.

At his returne to *Opechancanoughs,* all the Kings women, and their children, flocked about him for their parts; as a due by Custome, to be merry with such fragments.

But his waking mind in hydeous dreames
did oft see wondrous shapes,
Of bodies strange, and huge in growth,
and of stupendious makes.

(How *Powhatan* entertained him.) At last they brought him to *Meronocomoco,* where was *Powhatan* their Emperor. Here more than two hundred of those grim Courtiers stood wondering at him, as he had beene a monster; till *Powhatan* and his trayne had put themselves in their greatest braveries. Before a fire upon a seat like a bedsted, he sat covered with a great robe, made of *Rarowcun* skinnes, and all the tayles hanging by. On either hand did sit a young wench of 16 or 18 yeares, and along on each side the house, two rowes of men, and behind them as many women, with all their heads and shoulders painted red: many of their heads bedecked with the white downe of Birds; but every one with something: and a great chayne of white beads about their necks.

At his entrance before the King, all the people gave a great shout. The Queene of *Appamatuck* was appointed to bring him water to wash his hands, and another brought him a bunch of feathers, in stead of a Towell to dry them: having feasted him after their best barbarous manner they could, a long consultation was held, but the conclusion was, two great stones were brought before *Powhatan:* then as many as could layd hands on him, dragged him to them, and thereon laid his head, and being ready with their clubs, to beate out his braines, *Pocahontas* the Kings dearest daughter, when no intreaty could prevaile, got his head in her armes, and laid her owne upon his to save him from death: whereat the Emperour was contented he should live to make him hatchets, and her bells, beads, and copper; for they thought him as well of all occupations as themselves. For the King himselfe will make his owne robes, shooes, bowes, arrows, pots; plant, hunt, or doe any thing so well as the rest.

They say he bore a pleasant shew,
But sure his heart was sad.
For who can pleasant be, and rest,
That lives in feare and dread:
And having life suspected, doth
It still suspected lead.

(How *Powhatan* sent him to *James* Towne.) Two days after, *Powhatan* having disguised himselfe in the most fearefullest manner he could, caused Captain *Smith* to be brought forth to a great house in the woods, and there upon a mat by the fire to be left alone. Not long after from behinde a mat that divided the house, was made the most dolefullest noyse he ever heard; then *Powhatan* more like a devill then a man, with some two hundred more as blacke as himselfe, came unto him and told him now they were friends, and presently he should goe to *Iames* towne, to send him two great gunnes, and a gryndstone, for which he would give him the Country of *Capahowosick,* and for ever esteeme him as his sonne *Nantaquoud.*

So to *Iames* towne with 12 guides *Powhatan* sent him. That night they quarterd in the woods, he still expecting (as he had done all this long time of his imprisonment) every houre to be put to one death or other: for all their feasting. But almightie God (by his divine providence) had mollified the hearts of those sterne *Barbarians* with compassion. The next morning betimes they came to the Fort, where *Smith* having used the Salvages with what kindnesse he could, he shewed *Rawhunt, Powhatans* trusty servant, two demi-Culverings and a millstone to carry *Powhatan:* they found them somewhat too heavie; but when they did see him discharge them, being loaded with stones, among the boughs of a great tree loaded with Isickles, the yce and branches came so tumbling downe, that the poore Salvages ran away halfe dead with feare. But at last we regained some conference with them, and gave them such toyes; and sent to *Powhatan,* his women, and children such presents, as gave them in generall full content. * * *

1624

II. WILLIAM BRADFORD
(1590–1657)

From *OF PLIMMOTH PLANTATION*

[THE MAYFLOWER COMPACT]

1620. I shall a litle returne backe and begine with a combination made by them before they came a shore, being the first foundation of their govermente in this place; occasioned partly by the discontented and mutinous speeches that some of the strangers amongst them had let fall from them in the ship; That when they came a shore they would use their owne libertie; for none had power to command them, the patente they had being for Virginia, and not for New england, which belonged to an other Government, with which the Virginia Company had nothing to doe. And partly that shuch an acte by them done (this their condition considered) might be as firme as any patent, and in some respects more sure.

The forme was as followeth.

In the name of God, Amen. We whose names are underwriten, the loyall subjects of our dread soveraigne Lord, King James, by the grace of God, of Great Britaine, Franc, and Ireland king, defender of the faith, etc.

Haveing undertaken, for the glorie of God, and advancemente of the Christian faith, and honour of our king and countrie, a voyage to plant the first colonie in the Northerne parts of Virginia, doe by these presents solemnly and mutualy in the presence of God, and one of another, covenant and combine our selves togeather into a civill body politick, for our better ordering and preservation and furtherance of the ends aforesaid; and by vertue hearof to enacte, constitute, and frame shuch just and equall lawes, ordinances, acts, constitutions, and offices, from time to time, as shall be thought most meete and convenient for the generall good of the Colonie, unto which we promise all due submission and obedience. In witnes wherof we have hereunder subscribed our names at Cap-Codd the ·11· of November, in the year of the raigne of our soveraigne lord, King James, of England, France, and Ireland, the eighteenth, and of Scotland the fiftie fourth. Anno Dom. 1620.

After this they chose, or rather confirmed, Mr. John Carver (a man godly and well approved amongst them) their Governour for that year. And after they had provided a place for their goods, or comone store, (which were long in unlading for want of boats, foulnes of the winter weather, and sicknes of diverce,) and begune some small cottages for their habitation, as time would admitte, they mette and consulted of lawes and orders, both for their civill and military Govermente, as the necessitie of their condition did require, still adding therunto as urgent occasion in severall times, and as cases did require.

In these hard and difficulte beginings they found some discontents and murmurings arise amongst some, and mutinous speeches and carriages in other; but they were soone quelled and overcome by the wisdome, patience, and just and equall carrage of things by the Gov[erno]r and better part, which clave faithfully togeather in the maine. But that which was most sadd and lamentable was, that in ·2· or ·3· moneths time halfe of their company dyed, espetialy in Jan: and February, being the depth of winter, and wanting houses and other comforts; being infected with the scurvie and other diseases, which this long voiage and their inacomodate condition had brought upon them; so as ther dyed some times ·2· or ·3· of a day, in the aforesaid time; that of ·100· and odd persons, scarce ·50· remained. And of these in the time of most distres, ther was but ·6· or ·7· sound persons, who, to their great comendations be it spoken, spared no pains, night nor day, but with abundance of toyle and hazard of their owne health, fetched them woode, made them fires, drest them meat, made their beads, washed their lothsome cloaths, cloathed and uncloathed them; in a word, did all the homly and necessarie offices for them which dainty and quesie stomacks cannot endure to hear named; and all this willingly and cherfully, without any grudging in the least, shewing herein their true love unto their freinds and bretheren. A rare example and worthy to be remembred. Tow of these ·7· were Mr. William Brewster, ther reverend Elder, and Myles Standish, ther Captein and Military comander, unto whom my selfe, and many others, were much beholden in our low and sicke condition. And yet the Lord so upheld these persons, as in this generall calamity they were not at all infected either with sicknes, or lamnes. And what I have said of these, I may say of many others who dyed in this generall visitation, and others yet living, that whilst they had health, yea, or any strength continuing, they were not wanting to any that had need of them. And I doute not but their recompence is with the Lord.

But I may not hear pass by an other remarkable passage not to be forgotten. As this calamitie fell among the passengers that were to be left here to plant, and were hasted a shore and made to drinke water, that the sea-men might have the more bear, and one in his sickness desiring but a small cann of beere, it was answered, that if he were their owne father he should have none; the disease begane to fall amongst them also, so as allmost halfe of their company dyed before they went away, and many of their officers and lustyest men, as the boatson, gunner, ·3· quarter-maisters, the cooke, and others. At which the m[aste]r was something strucken and sent to the sick a shore and tould the Gov[erno]r he should send for beer for them that had need of it, though he drunke water homward bound. But now amongst his company ther was farr another kind of carriage in this miserie then amongst the passengers; for they that before had been boone companions in drinking and joyllity in the time of their health and wellfare, begane now to deserte one another in this calamitie saing, they would not hasard ther lives for them, they should be infected by coming to help them in their cabins, and so, after they came to lye by it, would doe litle or nothing for them, but if they dyed let them dye. But shuch of the passengers as were yet abord shewed them what mercy they could, which made some of their harts relente, as the boatson (and some others), who was a prowd yonge man, and would often curse and scofe at the passengers; but when he grew weak, they had compasion on him, and helped him; then he confessed he did not deserve it at their hands, he had abused them in word and deed. O! saith he, you, I now see, shew your love like Christians indeed one to another, but we let one another lye and dye like doggs. Another lay cursing his wife, saing if it had not ben for her he had never come this unlucky viage, and anone cursing his felows, saing he had done this and that, for some of them, he had spente so much, and so much, amongst them, and they were now weary of him, and did not help him, having need. Another gave his companion all he had, if he died, to help him in his weaknes; he went and got a little spise and made him a mess of meat once or twise, and because he dyed not so soone as he expected, he went amongst his fellows, and swore the rogue would cousen him, he would see him chooked before he made him any more meate; and yet the pore fellow dyed before morning.

All this while the Indians came skulking about them, and would sometimes show them selves aloofe of, but when any aproached near them, they would rune away. And once they stoale away their tools wher they had been at worke, and were gone to diner. But about the *·16· of March* a certaine Indian came bouldly amongst them, and spoke to them in broken English, which they could well understand, but marvelled at it. At length they understood by discourse with him, that he was not of these parts, but belonged to the eastrene parts, wher some English-ships came to fhish, with whom he was acquainted, and could name sundrie of them by their names, amongst whom he had gott his language. He became prof[i]table to them in aquainting them with many things concerning the state of the cuntry in the east-parts wher he lived, which was afterwards profitable unto them; as also of the people hear, of their names, number, and strength; of their situation and distance from this place, and who was cheefe amongst them. His name was *Samasett;* he tould them also of another Indian whose name was *Squanto,* a native of this place, who had been in England and could speake better English then him selfe. Being, after some time of entertainmente and gifts, dismist, a while after he came againe, and ·5· more with him, and they brought againe all the tooles that were stolen away before, and made way for the coming of their great Sachem, called *Massasoyt;* who, about *·4· or ·5· days after,* came with the cheefe of his freinds and other attendance, with the aforesaid *Squanto.* With whom, after frendly entertainment, and some gifts given him, they made a peace with him (which hath now continued this ·24· years) in these terms.

·1· That neither he nor any of his, should injurie or doe hurte to any of their peopl[e].

·2· That if any of his did any hurte to any of theirs, he should send the offender, that they might punish him.

·3· That if any thing were taken away from any of theirs, he should cause it to be restored; and they should doe the like to his.

·4· If any did unjustly warr against him, they would aide him; if any did warr against them, he should aide them.

·5· He should send to his neighbours confederates, to certifie them of this, that they might not wrong them, but might be likewise comprised in the conditions of peace.

·6· That when ther men came to them, they should leave their bows and arrows behind them.

(1630) 1856

[HARDSHIPS OF THE WILDERNESS]

* * * Mr. Roger Williams (a man godly and zealous, having many precious parts, but very unsettled in judgmente) came over first to the Massachusets, but upon some discontente left that place, and came hither, (wher he was friendly entertained, according to their poore abilitie,) and exercised his gifts amongst them, and after some time was admitted a member of the church; and his teaching well approoved, for the benefite wherof I still blese God, and am thankfull to him, even for his sharpest admonitions and reproufs, so farr as they agreed with truth. He this year begane to fall into some strang opinions, and from opinion to practise; which caused some controversie betweene the church and him, and in the end some discontente on his parte, by occasion wherof he left them some thing abruptly. Yet after wards sued for his dismission to the church of Salem, which was granted, with some caution to them concerning him, and what care they ought to have of him. But he soone fell into more things ther, both to their and the goverments

troble and disturbance. I shall not need to name perticulers, they are too well knowen now to all, though for a time the church here wente under some hard scensure by his occassion, from some that afterwards smarted them selves. But he is to be pitied, and prayed for, and so I shall leave the matter, and desire the Lord to shew him his errors, and reduce him into the way of truth, and give him a setled judgment and constancie in the same; for I hope he belongs to the Lord, and that he will shew him mercie.

Having had formerly converse and fam[i]liarity with the Dutch, (as is before remembred,) they, seeing them seated here in a barren quarter, tould them of a river called by them the Fresh River, but now is known by the name of Conightecute-River, which they often comended unto them for a fine place both for plantation and trade, and wished them to make use of it. But their hands being full otherwise, they let it pass. But afterwards ther coming a company of banishte Indeans into these parts, that were drivene out from thence by the potencie of the Pequents, which usurped upon them, and drive them from thence, they often sollicited them to goe thither, and they should have much trade, espetially if they would keep a house ther. And having now good store of comodities, and allso need to looke out wher they could advantage them selves to help them out of their great ingagments, they now begane to send that way to discover the same, and trade with the natives. They found it to be a fine place, but had no great store of trade; but the Indeans excused the same in regard of the season, and the fear the Ind[e]ans were in of their enemise. So they tried diverce times, not with out profite, but saw the most certainty would be by keeping a house ther, to receive the trad when it came down out of the inland. These Indeans, not seeing them very forward to build ther, solisited them of the Massachusets in like sorte (for their end was to be restored to their countrie againe); but they in the Bay being but latly come, were not fitte for the same; but some of their cheefe made a motion to joyne with the partners here, to trade joyntly with them in that river, the which they were willing to imbrace, and so they should have builte, and put in equall stock togeather. A time of meeting was appointed at the Massachusets, and some of the cheefe here was appointed to treat with them, and went accordingly; but they cast many fears of deanger and loss and the like, which was perceived to be the maine obstacles, though they alledged they were not provided of trading goods. But those hear offered at presente to put in sufficente for both, provided they would become ingaged for the halfe, and prepare against the nexte year. They conffessed more could not be offered, but thanked them, and tould them they had no mind to it. They then answered, they hoped it would be no offence unto them, if them sellves wente on without them, if they saw it meete. They said there was no reason they should; and thus this treaty broake of, and those here tooke conveniente time to make a begining ther; and were the first English that both discovered that place, and built in the same, though they were litle better then thrust out of it afterward as may appeare.

But the Dutch begane now to repente, and hearing of their purpose and preparation, inde[v]oured to prevente them, and gott in a litle before them, and made a slight forte, and planted ·2· peeces of ordnance, thretening to stopp their passage. But they having made a smale frame of a house ready, and haveing a great new-barke, they stowed their frame in her hold, and bords to cover and finishe it, having nayles and all other provisions fitting for their use. This they did the rather that they might have a presente defence against the Indeans, who weare much offended that they brought home and restored the right Sachem of the place (called Natawanute); so as they were to incounter with a duble danger in this attempte, both the Dutch and the Indeans. When they came up the river, the Dutch demanded what they intended, and whither they would goe; they answered, up the river to trade (now their order was to goe and seat above them). They bid them strike, and stay, or els they would shoote them; and stood by ther ordnance ready fitted. They answered they had commission from the Gov[erno]r of Plimoth to goe up the river to shuch a place, and if they did shoote, they must obey their order and proceede; they would not molest them, but would goe one. So they passed along, and though the Dutch threatened them hard, yet they shoot not. Comming to their place, they clapt up their house quickly, and landed their provissions, and left the companie appoynted, and sent the barke home; and afterwards palisadoed their house aboute, and fortified them selves better. The Dutch sent word home to the Monhatas what was done; and in proces of time, they sent a band of aboute ·70· men, in warrlike maner, with collours displayed, to assaulte them; but seeing them strengt[h]ened, and that it would cost blood, they came to parley, and returned in peace. And this was their enterance ther, who deserved to have held it, and not by friends to have been thrust out, as in a sorte they were, as will after appere. They did the Dutch no wrong, for they took not a foote of any land they bought, but went to the place above them, and bought that tracte of land which belonged to these Indeans which they carried with them, and their friends, with whom the Dutch had nothing to doe. But of these matters more in another place.

It pleased the Lord to visite them this year with an infectious fevoure, of which many fell very sicke, and upward of ·20· persons dyed, men and women, besides children, and sundry of them of their anciente friends which had lived in Holand; as Thomas Blossome, Richard Masterson, with sundry others, and in the end (after he had much helped others) Samuell Fuller, who was their surgeon and phisition, and had been a great help and comforte unto them; as in his facultie, so otherwise, being a deacon of the church, a man godly, and forward to doe good, being much missed after his death; and he and the rest of their brethren much lamented by them, and caused much sadnes and mourning amongst them; which caused them to humble them selves, and seeke the Lord; and towards winter it pleased the Lord the sicknes ceased. This disease allso swept away many of the Indeans from all the places near adjoyning; and the spring before, espetially all the *month of May,* ther was shuch a quantitie of a great sorte of flies, like (for bignes) to wasps, or bumble-bees, which came out of holes in the ground, and replenished all the woods, and eate the green-things, and made shuch a constante yelling noyes, as made all the woods ring of them, and ready to deafe the hearers. They have not by the English been heard or seen before or since. But the Indeans tould them that sicknes would follow, and so it did in *June, July, August,* and the cheefe heat of sommer.

It pleased the Lord to inable them this year to send home a great quantity of beaver, besides paing all their charges, and debts at home, which good returne did much incourage their freinds in England. They sent in beaver *3366li.* waight, and much of it coat beaver which yeeled *20s.* per pound, and some of it above; and of otter-skines ·346· sould also at a good prise. And thus much of the affairs of this year.

(1633) 1856

III. JOHN WINTHROP
(1588–1649)

LETTERS

II

To my best beloved Mrs. Margaret Tyndall at Great Maplested, Essex.

Grace mercie & peace, &c:

My onely beloved Spouse, my most sweet freind, & faithfull companion of my pilgrimage, the happye & hopefull supplie (next Christ Jesus) of my greatest losses, I wishe thee a most plentifull increase of all true comfort in the love of Christ, w*th* a large & prosperous addition of whatsoever happynesse the sweet estate of holy wedlocke, in the kindest societye of a lovinge husbande, may afford thee. Beinge filled w*th* the ioye of thy love, & wantinge opportunitye of more familiar com̄union w*th* thee, w*ch* my heart fervently desires, I am constrained to ease the burthen of my minde by this poore helpe of my scriblinge penne, beinge sufficiently assured that, although my presence is that w*ch* thou desirest, yet in the want thereof, these lines shall not be unfruitfull of comfort unto thee. And now, my sweet Love, lett me a whyle solace my selfe in the remembrance of our love, of w*ch* this springe tyme of o*r* acquaintance can putt forthe as yet no more but the leaves & blossomes, whilest the fruit lyes wrapped up in the tender budde of hope; a little more patience will disclose this good fruit, & bringe it to some maturitye: let it be o*r* care & labour to preserve these hopefull budds from the beasts of the fielde, & from frosts & other iniuryes of the ayre, least o*r* fruit fall off ere it be ripe, or lose ought in the beautye & pleasantnesse of it: Lett us pluck up suche nettles & thornes as would defraud o*r* plants of their due nourishment; let us pruine off superfluous branches; let us not sticke at some labour in wateringe & manuringe them:—the plentye & goodnesse of o*r* fruit shall recompense us abundantly: O*r* trees are planted in a fruitfull soyle; the grounde, & patterne of *or* love, is no other but that betweene Christe & his deare spouse, of whom she speakes as she finds him, My welbeloved is mine & I am his: Love was their banquetting house, love was their wine, love was their ensigne; love was his invitinges, love was hir fayntinges; love was his apples, love was hir comforts; love was his embracinges, love was hir refreshinge: love made him see hir, love made her seeke him: love made him wedde hir, love made hir followe him: love made him hir saviour, love makes hir his servant. Love bredd of fellowshippe, let love continue it, & love shall increase it, untill deathe dissolve it. The prime fruit of the Spirit is love; truethe of Spirit & true love: abounde w*th* the spirit, & abounde w*th* love: continue in the spirit & continue in love: Christ in his love so fill *or* hearts w*th* holy hunger & true appetite, to eate & drinke w*th* him & of him in this his sweet Love feast, w*ch* we are now preparinge unto, that when *or* love feast shall come, Christ Jesus himselfe may come in unto us, & suppe w*th* us, & we w*th* him: * so shall we be merrye indeed. (O my sweet Spouse) can we esteeme eache others love, as worthy the recompence of *or* best mutuall affections, & can we not discerne so muche of Christs exceedinge & undeserved love, as may cheerfully allure us to love him above all? He loved us & gave himselfe for us; & to helpe the weaknesse of the eyes & hande & mouthe of *or* faithe, w*ch* must seeke him in heaven where he is, he offers himselfe to the eyes, hands & mouthe of *or* bodye, heere on earthe where he once was. The Lord increace *or* faithe.

Nowe my deare heart let me parlye a little *wth* thee about trifles, for when I am present w*th* thee my speeche is preiudiced by thy prescence, w*ch* drawes my minde from it selfe: I suppose nowe, upon thy unkle's com̄inge, there wilbe advisinge & counsellinge of all hands; & amongst many I knowe there wilbe some, that wilbe provokinge thee, in these indifferent things, as matter of apparell, fashions & other circumstances, rather to give contente to their vaine minds savouringe too muche of the fleshe &c, then to be guided by the rule of Gods worde, w*ch* must be the light & the Rule; for allthoughe I doe easyly grant that the Kingdome of heaven is not meat & drinke, apparell &c, but Righteousnesse, peace &c: yet beinge forbidden to fashion *or*selves like unto this world, & to avoyde not onely evill but all appearance of it must be avoyded, & allso what soever may breed offence to the weake (for w*ch* I praye thee reade for thy direction the xiiij*th* to the Rom:) & for that Christians are rather to seeke to edifie then to please, I hould it a rule of Christian wisdome in all these things to followe the soberest examples: I confesse that there be some ornaments w*ch* for Virgins & Knights daughters, &c, may be comly & tollerable, w*ch* yet in so great a change as thine is, may well admitt a change allso: I will medle w*th* no particulars, neither doe I thinke it shalbe needfull; thine owne wisdome & godlinesse shall teache thee sufficeintly what to doe in suche things: & the good assurance w*ch* I have of thy unfained love towards me, makes me

* Cant: 2; Jer.: 2, 2; Ezek.: 16; Jo.: 3:16; Deut.: 10:12; Gal.: 5:22. [Author's marginal citations.]

perswaded that thou wilt have care of my contentment, seeing it must be a cheife staye to thy comfort: & w*th* all the great & sincere desire w*ch* I have that there might be no discouragement to daunt the edge of my affections, whyle they are truly labouring to settle & repose themselves in thee, makes me thus watchfull & iealous of the least occasion that Satham might stirre up to o*r* discomfort. He that is faithfull in the least wilbe faithfull in the greatest, but I am too fearfull I doe thee wronge, I knowe thou wilt not grieve me for trifles. Let me intreat thee (my sweet Love) to take all in good parte, for it is all of my love to thee, & in my love I shall requite thee: I acknowledge, indeed, thou maist iustly say to me as Christ to the Pharisies, Hypocrite, first cast out the beame that is in thine owne eye &c, for whatsoever I may be in thy opinion, yet mine owne guiltie heart tells me of farre greater things to be reformed in my selfe, & yet I feare there is muche more than in mine owne partiall iudgement I can discerne; iust cause I have to complaine of my pride, unbeleefe, hardnesse of heart & impenitencie, vanitye of minde, unrulinesse of my affections, stubbornesse of my will, ingratitude, & unfaithfullnesse in the Covenant of my God, &c. therefore (by Gods assistance) I will endeavour that in myselfe, w*ch* I will allso desire in thee. Let us search & trye o*r* hearts & turne to the Lord: for this is o*r* safetye, not o*r* owne innocencye, but his mercie: If when we were enemies he loved us to reconciliatiō; much more, beinge reconciled will he save us from destructiō.

Lastly for my farewell (for thou seest my lothenesse to parte w*th* thee makes me to be teadious) take courage unto thee, & cheare up thy heart in the Lorde, for thou knowest that Christ thy best husbande can never faile thee: he never dies, so as there can be no greife at partinge; he never changes, so as once beloved & ever the same: his abilitye is ever infinite, so as the dowrye & inheritance of his sonnes & daughters can never be diminished. As for me a poore worme, dust & ashes, a man full of infirmityes, subiect to all sinnes, changes & chances, w*ch* befall the sonnes of men, how should I promise thee any thinge of my selfe, or if I should, what credence couldst thou give thereto, seeinge God only is true & every man a lyar. Yet so farre as a man may presume upon some experience, I may tell thee, that my hope is, that suche comfort as thou hast allreadye conceived of my love towards thee, shall (throughe Gods blessinge) be happily continued; his grace shalbe sufficient for me, & his power shalbe made perfect in my greatest weaknesse: onely let thy godly, kinde, & sweet carriage towards me, be as fuell to the fire, to minister a constant supplie of meet matter to the confirminge & quickninge of my dull affections: This is one ende why I write so muche unto thee, that if there should be any decaye in kindnesse &c, throughe my default & slacknesse heerafter, thou mightest have some patternes of o*r* first love by thee, to helpe the recoverye of suche diseases: yet let o*r* trust be wholly in God, & let us constantlye followe him by o*r* prayers, complaininge & moaninge unto him o*r* owne povertye, imperfections & unworthynesse, untill his fatherly affectiō breake forthe upon us, & he speake kindly to the hearts of his poore servant & handmayd, for the full assurance of Grace & peace through Christ Jesus, to whom I nowe leave thee (my sweet Spouse & onely beloved). God send us a safe & comfortable meetinge on Mondaye morninge. Farewell. Remember my love & dutye to my Ladye thy good mother, w*th* all kinde & due salutations to thy unkle E: & all thy brothers & sisters.

Thy husband by promise

JOHN WINTHROP.

Groton where I wish thee. Aprill 4. 1618.

XXII

To my very loving Husband John Winthrop Esq. at Mr. Downings.

MY MOST DEARE AND LOVEINGE HUSBAND: I doe blesse and prayse God for the continuance of your health, and for the safe delivery of my good sister Downinge; it was very welcom Nuse to us. I thanke the Lord wee are all heare reasonably well. My pore Stephen is up to day. Amye hath had a very sore ague but is well againe. I hope the Lord will heare our prayers and be pleased to stay his hand in this visitation, w*ch* if he please to doe we shall have great cause of thankfulnesse: but I desire in this and all other things to submit unto his holy will; it is the Lord, let him doe what semeth good in his owne eyse. He will doe nothinge but that shall be for our good if we had harts to trust in him, & all shall be for the best what so ever it shall please him to exercise us withall. He wounds & he can heale. He hath never fayled to doe us good, & now he will not shake us off, but continue the same God still that he hath bin heare to fore. The Lord sanctify unto us what soever it shall please him to send unto us, that we may be the better for it & furthered in our corce to heaven. I am sorye for the hard condishtion of Rochell: the Lord helpe them & fite for them & then none shall prevayle against them or overcome them. In vaine they fite that fite against the Lorde, who is a myty god & will destroye all his enimyes. And now my deare husband I have nothinge but my dearest affections to send thee—with many thankes for thy kinde letters, prayinge you to except a little for a great deale: my will is good but that I want abilite how to show & expresse it to thee as I desire. I pray remember me to my brothers & sisters, & tel my brother Foones I thanke him for the thinges he sent, & so I bid my good husband farewell & commite him to God.

Your lovinge & obedient wife,

MARGARET WINTHROPE.

I send up a turkey & 2 capons & a cheese: the carier is payde.

(1628)

XLVII

To My verye loving wife Mrs Winthrop the Elder at Groton in Suffolk.

MY LOVE, MY JOY, MY FAITHFULL ONE,—I suppose thou didest not expects to have any more Lrēs from me till the returne of o*r* shippes; but so is the good pleasure of God, that the windes should not serve yet to carrye us hence. He will doe all thinges in his own tyme & that shalbe for the best in the ende. We acknowledge it a great mercye to us, that we went not out to sea on mondaye when the winde was fair for one daye, for we had been exposed ever since to sore tempestes & contrarye windes: I prayse God, we are all in good health, & want nothinge. For my selfe I was never at more liberty of bodye & minde these many yeares. The Lord make me thankfull & wise to improve his blessinges for the furtherance of his owne worke. I desire to resigne my selfe wholly to his gratious disposinge. O, that I had an heart so to doe, & to trust perfectly in him, for his assistance in all o*r* wayes. We finde him still goeinge alonge w*th* us. He hath brought in the heart of the master of o*r* shippe to afforde us all good respect, & to joyne w*th* us in everye good action. Yesterday he caused his seamen to keepe a fast with us, wherein the Lorde assisted us & o*r* minister very comfortably; & when 5: of the clocke came, I had respitt to remember thee, (it being frydaye) & to parlye w*th* thee, & to meet thee in spiritt before the Lord. After supper we discovered some notorious lewd psons of o*r* owne company, who in tyme of o*r* fast had committed thefte, & done other vilanies, for w*ch* we have caused them to be severely punished.

I am uncertaine whither I shall have opportunitye to sende these to thee; for, if the winde turne we shall soone be gone. Therefore I will not write much. I knowe it wilbe sufficient for thy present comfort to heare of o*r* wellfare; & this is the third lrē I have written to thee since I came to Hampton, in requitall of those 2: I received from thee, w*ch* I doe often read w*th* much delight, apprehend*g* so much love & sweet Affection in them, as I am never satisfied w*th* readinge, nor can reade them w*th* out teares; but whither they proceed from joy sorrowe or desire, or from that consent of Affection w*ch* I allwayes holde w*th* thee, I cañot conceive. Ah, my deare heart, I ever holde thee in high esteeme as thy Love & goodnesse hath well deserved; but (if it be possible) I shall yet prize thy vertue at a greater rate, & longe more to enjoye thy sweet society then ever before. I am sure thou art not shorte of me in this desire. Let us pray harde & pray in faith, & o*r* God, in his good tyme will accomplish o*r* desire. O, how loth am I to bedd thee farewell, but since it must be, farewell, my sweet Love, farewell. Farewell my deare children & familye. The Lord blesse you all, & grant me to see y*r* faces once againe. Come (my deare) take him & let him rest in thine armes, who will ever remaine

Thy faithfull husband

JO: WINTHROP

From abord the Arbella ryding before Yarmouth in the Isle of Wight. April 3, 1630.

XLVIII

To my verye lovinge wife Mrs Winthrop the elder at Groton in Suff neere Sudbury.

Charleton in N: England.
July 16. 1630.

MY DEARE WIFE,—Blessed be the Lord o*r* good God & mercifull father, that yet hath preserved me in life & health to salute thee, & to comforte thy longe longinge heart, w*th* the joyfull newes of my wellfare, & the wellfare of thy beloved children.

We had a longe & troublesome passage, but the Lord made it safe & easye to us: & though we have mett w*th* many & great troubles (as this bearer can certifie thee) yet he hath pleased to uphold us, & to give us hope of a happye issue.

I am so overpressed w*th* businesse, as I have no tyme for these or other mine owne private occasions. I onely write now, that thou mayest knowe that yet I live & am mindfull of thee, in all my affairs. The larger discourse of all thinges thou shalt receive from my brother Dowinge, w*ch* I must sende by some of the last shippes. We have mett w*th* many sadd & discomfortable thinges, as thou shalt heare after: & the Lords hande hath been heavy upon my selfe in some verye neare to me: My sonne Henry, my sonne Henrye, ah, poore child! Yet it greives me much more for my deare daughter. The Lord strengthen & comfort her heart, to beare this crosse patiently. I knowe thou wilt not be wanting to her in this distresse: yet for all these thinges (I prayse my God) I am not discouraged, nor doe I see cause to repent, or dispaire of those good dayes here, w*ch* will make amends for all.

I shall expect thee next somer (if the Lord please) & by that tyme I hope to be provided for thy comfortable entertainment. My most sweet wife, be not disheartened; trust in the Lord, & thou shalt see his faithfullnesse.

Commende me heartyly to all o*r* kinde friends, at Castleins, Groton hall, M*r* Leigh & his wife my neighb*r* Cole & all the rest of my neighb*rs* & their wives, both rich & poore.

Rember me to them at Assington hall & Codenham hall, M*r* Brande M*r* Alston M*r* Mott & their wives, Goodm̄ Ponde, Charles Neale &c etc. The good Lord be w*th* thee & blesse thee & all o*r* children & servants.

Com̄end my Love to them all, I kisse & embrace thee, my deare wife, & all my children, & leave thee in his armes who is able to preserve you all, & to fulfill o*r* joye in o*r* happye meeting in his good tyme. Amen.

Thy faithfull husband

Jo: Winthrop

I shall write to my sonne John by London.

LII

My Deare Wife,—I have small hope that this should come to thy hands, in regard of the longe staye of the shippe heer, so as thou maiest be well onward of thy waye hether before these can come to England. Therefore I write little to thy selfe & my sonne & those whom I expect to see heer shortly, if it shall so please the Lorde. And blessed be his holy & glorious name that he hath so far magnified his mercy towards us, that when so many have been layd in their graves since we parted, yet he hath pleased to preserve us unto this hope of a joyfull meetinge, that we may see the faces of each other againe, the faces of o*r* children & sweet babes. These thinges I durst scarce thinke off heertofore, but now I embrace them ofte & delight my heart in them, because I trust, that the Lord o*r* God, who hath kept me & so many of my Company in health & safety amonge so many dead corps, through the heat of the sūmer & the cold of winter & hath also preserved thee in the perill of childbirth, & upheld thy heart in the midst of so many discouragements, w*th* the life of all thy companye, will of his owne goodnesse & free mercye preserve us & ours still that we shall meet in joye & peace, w*ch* I dayly pray for, & shall expect in the Lords good tyme: who still continue his favour & blessinge upon thee & o*r* sweet babes & all thy company. For o*r* little daughter, doe as thou thinkest best, the Lord direct thee in it. If thou bringest her, she wilbe more trouble to thee in the shipp then all the rest. I knowe my sister wilbe tender of her till I may send for her. Bring Amy & Anne Goslin w*th* thee if thou canst. If they come not, they will much wronge themselves. They need feare no want heer, if they wilbe guided by Gods word: otherwise they can looke to prosper no where. I prayse God I want nothinge but thee & the rest of my family: Commend my Love & blessinge to them all: & to all my neighb*rs* & frends, but I have desired my brother Gostlin to performe that. Remember to bringe juice of lemons to sea w*th* thee, for thee & thy company to eat w*th* y*or* meate as sauce. But of these thinges my sonne hath direct'*on:* so again I Kisse thee my sweet wife & commend thee & all o*rs* to the Lord, & rest, thine,

Jo: Winthrop

March 28, 1631.

From *A JOURNAL*

[ON LIBERTY]

* * * Two of the magistrates and many of the deputies were of opinion that the magistrates exercised too much power, and that the people's liberty was thereby in danger; and other of the deputies (being about half) and all the rest of the magistrates were of a different judgment, and that authority was overmuch slighted, which, if not timely remedied, would endanger the commonwealth, and bring us to a mere democracy. By occasion of this difference, there was not so orderly carriage at the hearing, as was meet, each side striving unseasonably to enforce the evidence, and declaring their judgments thereupon, which should have been reserved to a more private debate, (as after it was,) so as the best part of two days was spent in this publick agitation and examination of witnesses &c. This being ended, a committee was chosen of magistrates and deputies, who stated the case, as it appeared upon the whole pleading and evidence, though it cost much time, and with great difficulty did the committee come to accord upon it.

The case being stated and agreed, the magistrates and deputies considered it apart, first the deputies, having spent a whole day, and not attaining to any issue, sent up to the magistrates to have their thoughts about it, who taking it into consideration, (the deputy always withdrawing when that matter came into debate,) agreed upon these four points chiefly; 1. that the petition was false and scandalous, 2. that those who were bound over &c. and others that were parties to the disturbance at Hingham, were all offenders, though in different degrees, 3. that they and the petitioners were to be censured, 4. that the deputy governour ought to be acquit and righted &c. This being sent down to the deputies, they spent divers days about it, and made two or three returns to the magistrates, and though they found the petition false and scandalous, and so voted it, yet they would not agree to any censure. The magistrates, on the other side, were resolved for censure, and for the deputy's full acquittal. * * *

According to this agreement [the acquittal of Winthrop and the fining of his accusers], presently after the lecture the magistrates and deputies took their places in the meeting house, and the people being come together, and the deputy governour placing himself within the bar, as at the time of the hearing &c. the governour read the sentence of the court, without speaking any more, for the deputies had (by importunity) obtained a promise of silence from the magistrates. Then was the deputy governour desired by the court to go up and take his place again upon the bench, which he did accordingly, and the court being about to arise, he desired leave for a little speech, which was to this effect.

I suppose something may be expected from me, upon this charge that is befallen me, which moves me to speak now to you; yet I intend not to intermeddle in the proceedings of the court, or with any of the persons concerned therein. Only I bless God, that I see an issue of this troublesome business. I also acknowledge the justice of the court, and, for mine own part, I am well satisfied, I was publickly charged, and I am publickly and legally acquitted, which is all I did expect or desire. And though this be sufficient for my justification before men, yet not so before the God, who hath seen so much amiss in my dispensations (and even in this affair) as calls me to be humble. For to be publickly and criminally charged in this court, is matter of humiliation, (and I desire to make a right use of it,) notwithstanding I be thus acquitted. If her father had spit in her face, (saith the Lord concerning Miriam,) should she not have been ashamed seven days? Shame had lien upon her, whatever the occasion had been. I am unwilling to stay you from your urgent affairs, yet give me leave (upon this special occasion) to speak a little more to this assembly. It may be of some good use, to inform and rectify the judgments of some of the people, and may prevent such distempers as have arisen amongst us. The great questions that have troubled the country, are about the authority of the magistrates and the liberty of the people. It is yourselves who have called us to this office, and being called by you, we have our authority from God, in way of an ordinance, such as hath the image of God eminently stamped upon it, the contempt and violation whereof hath been vindicated with examples of divine vengeance. I entreat you to consider, that when you choose magistrates, you take them from among yourselves, men subject to like passions as you are. Therefore when you see infirmities in us, you should reflect upon your own, and that would make you bear the more with us, and not be severe censurers of the failings of your magistrates, when you have continual experience of the like infirmities in yourselves and others. We account him a good servant, who breaks not his covenant. The covenant between you and us is the oath you have taken of us, which is to this purpose, that we shall govern you and judge your causes by the rules of God's laws and our own, according to our best skill. When you agree with a workman to build you a ship or house &c. he undertakes as well for his skill as for his faithfulness, for it is his profession, and you pay him for both. But when you call one to be a magistrate, he doth not profess nor undertake to have sufficient skill for that office, nor can you furnish him with gifts &c. therefore you must run the hazard of his skill and ability. But if he fail in faithfulness, which by his oath he is bound unto, that he must answer for. If it fall out that the case be clear to common apprehension, and the rule clear also, if he transgress here, the errour is not in the skill, but in the evil of the will: it must be required of him. But if the cause be doubtful, or the rule doubtful, to men of such understanding and parts as your magistrates are, if your magistrates should err here, yourselves must bear it.

For the other point concerning liberty, I observe a great mistake in the country about that. There is a twofold liberty, natural (I mean as our nature is now corrupt) and civil or federal. The first is common to man with beasts and other creatures. By this, man, as he stands in relation to man simply, hath liberty to do what he lists; it is a liberty to evil as well as to good. This liberty is incompatible and inconsistent with authority, and cannot endure the least restraint of the most just authority. The exercise and maintaining of this liberty makes men grow more evil, and in time to be worse than brute beasts: omnes sumus licentia deteriores. This is that great enemy of truth and peace, that wild beast, which all the ordinances of God are bent against, to restrain and subdue it. The other kind of liberty I call civil or federal, it may also be termed moral, in reference to the covenant between God and man, in the moral law, and the politic covenants and constitutions, amongst men themselves. This liberty is the proper end and object of authority, and cannot subsist without it; and it is a liberty to that only which is good, just and honest. This liberty you are to stand for, with the hazard (not only of your goods, but) of your lives, if need be. Whatsoever crosseth this, is not authority, but a distemper thereof. This liberty is maintained and exercised in a way of subjection to authority; it is of the same kind of liberty wherewith Christ hath made us free. The woman's own choice makes such a man her husband; yet being so chosen, he is her lord, and she is to be subject to him, yet in a way of liberty, not of bondage; and a true wife accounts her subjection her honour and freedom, and would not think her condition safe and free, but in her subjection to her husband's authority. Such is the liberty of the church under the authority of Christ, her king and husband; his yoke is so easy and sweet to her as a bride's ornaments; and if through frowardness or wantonness &c. she shake it off, at any time, she is at no rest in her spirit, until she take it up again; and whether her lord smiles upon her, and embraceth her in his arms, or whether he frowns, or rebukes, or smites her, she apprehends the sweetness of his love in all, and is refreshed, supported and instructed by every such dispensation of his authority over her. On the other side, ye know who they are that complain of this yoke and say, let us break their bands &c. we will not have this man to rule over us. Even so, brethren, it will be between you and your magistrates. If you stand for your natural corrupt liberties, and will do what is good in your own eyes, you will not endure the least weight of authority, but will murmur, and oppose, and be always striving to shake off that yoke; but if you will be satisfied to enjoy such civil and lawful liberties, such as Christ allows you, then will you quietly and cheerfully submit unto that authority which is set over you, in all the administrations of it, for your good. Wherein, if we fail at any time, we hope we shall be willing (by God's assistance) to hearken to good advice from any of you, or in any other way of God; so shall your liberties be preserved, in upholding the honour and power of authority amongst you.

The deputy governour having ended his speech, the court arose, and the magistrates and deputies retired to attend their other affairs. Many things were observable in the agitation and proceedings about this case. It may be of use to leave a memorial of some of the most material, that our posterity and others may behold the workings of satan to ruin the colonies and churches of Christ in New England, and into what distempers a wise and godly people may fall in times of temptation; and when such have entertained some false and plausible principles, what deformed superstructures they will raise thereupon, and with what unreasonable obstinacy they will maintain them. * * *

(1645) 1825–26

THE COLONIAL MIND: NEW ENGLAND

I. THOMAS MORTON
(*c.* 1590–1646)

THE NEW ENGLISH CANAAN

BOOK III, CHAPTER XIV

OF THE REVELLS OF NEW CANAAN

The Inhabitants of Pasonagessit, (having translated the name of their habitation from that ancient Salvage name to Ma-re Mount, and being resolved to have the new name confirmed for a memorial to after ages,) did devise amongst themselves to have it performed in a solemne manner, with Revels and merriment after the old English custome; [they] prepared to sett up a Maypole upon the festivall day of Philip and Iacob, and therefore brewed a barrell of excellent beare and provided a case of bottles, to be spent, with other good cheare, for all commers of that day. And because they would have it in a compleat forme, they had prepared a song fitting to the time and present occasion. And upon Mayday they brought the Maypole to the place appointed, with drumes, gunnes, pistols and other fitting instruments, for that purpose; and there erected it with the help of Salvages, that came thether of purpose to see the manner of our Revels. A goodly pine tree of 80. foote longe was reared up, with a peare of buckshornes nayled one somewhat neare unto the top of it: where it stood, as a faire sea marke for directions how to finde out the way to mine Hoste of Ma-re Mount.

And because it should more fully appeare to what end it was placed there, they had a poem in readines made, which was fixed to the Maypole, to shew the new name confirmed upon that plantation; which, allthough it were made according to the occurrents of the time, it, being Enigmatically composed, pusselled the Seperatists most pittifully to expound it, which, (for the better information of the reader,) I have here inserted.

THE POEM

Rise Oedipeus, and, if thou canst, unfould
What meanes Caribdis underneath the mould,
When Scilla sollitary on the ground
(Sitting in forme of Niobe,) was found,
Till Amphitrites Darling did acquaint
Grim Neptune with the Tenor of her plaint,
And causd him send forth Triton with the sound
Of Trumpet lowd, at which the Seas were found
So full of Protean formes that the bold shore
Presented Scilla a new parramore
So stronge as Sampson and so patient
As Job himselfe, directed thus, by fate,
To comfort Scilla so unfortunate.
I doe professe, by Cupids beautious mother,
Heres Scogans choise for Scilla, and none other;
Though Scilla's sick with greife, because no signe
Can there be found of vertue masculine.
Esculapius come; I know right well
His laboure's lost when you may ring her Knell.

The fatall sisters doome none can withstand,
Nor Cithareas powre, who poynts to land
With proclamation that the first of May
At Ma-re Mount shall be kept hollyday.

The setting up of this Maypole was a lamentable spectacle to the precise seperatists, that lived at new Plimmouth. They termed it an Idoll; yea, they called it the Calfe of Horeb, and stood at defiance with the place, naming it Mount Dagon; threatning to make it a woefull mount and not a merry mount.

The Riddle, for want of Oedipus, they could not expound; onely they made some explication of part of it, and sayd it was meant by Sampson Iob, the carpenter of the shipp that brought over a woman to her husband, that had bin there longe before and thrived so well that hee sent for her and her children to come to him; where shortly after hee died: having no reason, but because of the sound of those two words; when as, (the truth is,) the man they applyed it to was altogether unknowne to the Author.

There was likewise a merry song made, which, (to make their Revells more fashionable,) was sung with a Corus, every man bearing his part; which they performed in a daunce, hand in hand about the Maypole, whiles one of the Company sung and filled out the good liquor, like gammedes and Iupiter.

THE SONGE

Cor.
Drinke and be merry, merry, merry boyes;
Let all your delight be in the Hymens ioyes;
Iô to Hymen, now the day is come,
About the merry Maypole take a Roome.
Make greene garlons, bring bottles out
And fill sweet Nectar freely about.
Uncover thy head and feare no harme,
For hers good liquor to keepe it warme.
Then drinke and be merry, &c.
Iô to Hymen, &c.
Nectar is a thing assign'd
By the Deities owne minde
To cure the hart opprest with greife,
And of good liquors is the cheife.
Then drinke, &c.
Iô to Hymen, &c.
Give to the Mellancolly man
A cup or two of 't now and than;
This physick will soone revive his bloud,
And made him be of a merrier moode.
Then drinke, &c.
Iô to Hymen, &c.
Give to the Nymphe thats free from scorne
No Irish stuff nor Scotch over worne.
Lasses in beaver coats come away,
Yee shall be welcome to us night and day.
To drinke and be merry &c.
Iô to Hymen, &c.

This harmeles mirth made by younge men, (that lived in hope to have wifes brought over to them, that would save them a laboure to make a voyage to fetch any over,) was much distasted of the precise Seperatists, that keepe much a doe about the tyth of Muit and Cummin, troubling their braines more then reason would require about things that are indifferent: and from that time sought occasion against my honest Host of Ma-re Mount, to overthrow his ondertakings and to destroy his plantation quite and cleane. But because they presumed with their imaginary gifts, (which they have out of Phaos box,) they could expound hidden misteries, to convince them of blindnes, as well in this as in other matters of more consequence, I will illustrate the poem, according to the true intent of the authors of these Revells, so much distasted by those Moles.

Oedipus is generally receaved for the absolute reader of riddles, who is invoaked: Silla and Caribdis are two dangerous places for seamen to incounter, neere unto Vennice; and have bin by poets formerly resembled to man and wife. The like licence the author challenged for a paire of his nomination, the one lamenting for the losse of the other as Niobe for her children. Amphitrite is an arme of the Sea, by which the newes was carried up and downe of a rich widow, now to be tane up or laid downe. By Triton is the fame spread that caused the Suters to muster, (as it had bin to Penellope of Greece;) and, the Coast lying circuler, all our passage to and froe is made more convenient by Sea then Land. Many aimed at this marke; but hee that played Proteus best and could comply with her humor must be the man that would carry her; and hee had need have Sampsons strenght to deale with a Dallila, and as much patience as Iob that should come there, for a thing that I did observe in the life-time of the former.

But marriage and hanging, (they say,) comes by desteny and Scogans choise tis better [than] none at all. Hee that playd Proteus, (with the helpe of Priapus,) put their noses out of joynt, as the Proverbe is.

And this the whole company of the Revellers at Ma-re Mount knew to be the true sence and exposition of the riddle that was fixed to the Maypole, which the Seperatists were at defiance with. Some of them affirmed that the first institution thereof was in memory of a whore; not knowing that it was a Trophe erected at first in honor of Maja, the Lady of learning which they despise, vilifying the two universities with uncivile termes, accounting what is there obtained by studdy is but unnecessary learning; not considering that learninge does inable mens mindes to converse with eliments of a higher nature then is to be found within the habitation of the Mole.

1637

II. ROGER WILLIAMS
(*c.* 1604–1683)

THE BLOUDY TENENT [*&c*]

CHAPTER II

[ON PERSECUTION]

[Peace]: Deare *Truth,* I have two sad *Complaints:*

First, the most sober of thy *Witnesses,* that dare to *plead* thy *Cause,* how are they charged to be *mine Enemies, contentious, turbulent, seditious?*

Secondly, Thine *Enemies,* though they speake and raile against thee, though they outragiously *pursue, imprison, banish, kill* thy faithfull *Witnesses,* yet how is all vermillion'd o're for *Justice* 'gainst the *Hereticks?* Yea, if they kindle coales, and blow the flames of *devouring Warres,* that leave neither *Spirituall* nor *Civill State,* but burns up *Branch* and *Root,* yet how doe all pretend an *holy War?* He that *kills,* and hee that's *killed,* they both cry out, It is for *God,* and for their *conscience.*

Tis true, nor one nor other seldome dare to plead the mighty Prince *Christ Jesus* for their *Authour,* yet both (both *Protestant* and *Papist*) pretend they have spoke with *Moses* and the *Prophets,* who all, say they (before *Christ* came) allowed such *holy persecutions, holy Warres* against the enemies of holy *Church.*

Truth. *Deare Peace* (to ease thy first *complaint*) tis true, thy dearest *Sons,* most like their mother, *Peace-keeping, Peace-making* Sons of *God,* have borne and still must beare the *blurs* of *troublers* of *Israel,* and turners of the *World* upside downe. And tis true againe, what *Salomon* once spake: The *beginning* of *strife* is as when one letteth out *Water,* therefore (saith he) leave off *contention* before it be medled with. This *Caveat* should keepe the *bankes* and *sluces* firme and strong, that *strife,* like a *breach of waters,* breake not in upon the sons of men.

Yet *strife* must be distinguished: It is *necessary* or *unnecessary, godly* or *ungodly, Christian* or *unchristian,* &c.

It is *unnecessary, unlawfull, dishonourable, ungodly, unchristian,* in most cases in the world, for there is a *possibility* of keeping *sweet Peace* in most cases, and if it be *possible,* it is the expresse command of *God* that *Peace* be kept, *Rom.* 13.

Againe, it is *necessary, honourable, godly,* &c. with *civill* and earthly *weapons* to *defend* the *innocent,* and to *rescue* the oppressed from the violent *pawes* and *jaws* of oppressing persecuting *Nimrods, Psal.* 73. *Job* 29.

It is as *necessary,* yea more *honourable, godly,* and *Christian,* to *fight* the *fight* of *faith,* with *religious* and *spirituall Artillery,* and to *contend earnestly* for the *faith* of *Jesus, once* delivered to the *Saints* against all *opposers,* and the *gates* of *earth* and *hell, men* or *devils,* yea against *Paul* himselfe, or an *Angell* from *heaven,* if he bring any other *faith* or *doctrine, Jude vers.* 4. *Gal.* 1. 8.

Peace. With the *clashing* of such *Armes* am I never *wakened.* Speake once againe (deare Truth) to my second *complaint* of bloody *persecution,* and devouring *wars,* marching under the colours of upright *Justice,* and holy *Zeale,* &c.

Truth. Mine eares have long beene filled with a threefold dolefull *Outcry.*

First, of one hundred forty foure thousand *Virgins* (*Rev.* 14.) forc'd and ravisht by *Emperours, Kings,* and *Governours* to their beds of *worship* and *Religion,* set up (like *Absaloms*) on high in their severall *States* and *Countries.*

Secondly, the cry of those precious *soules* under the *Altar* (*Rev.* 6) the *soules* of such as have been persecuted and slaine for the testimony and *witnesse* of *Jesus,* whose *bloud* hath been spilt like *water* upon the *earth,* and that because they have held fast the *truth* and *witnesse* of *Jesus,* against the *worship* of the *States* and *Times,* compelling to an *uniformity* of *State Religion.*

These *cries* of *murthered Virgins* who can sit still and heare? Who can but run with zeale inflamed to prevent the *deflowring* of *chaste soules,* and spilling of the *bloud* of the *innocent? Humanity* stirs up and prompts the *Sonnes* of men to draw *materiall swords* for a *Virgins chastity* and *life,* against a *ravishing murtherer?* And *Piety* and *Christianity* must needs awaken the *Sons of God* to draw the *spiritual sword* (the Word of *God*) to preserve the *chastity* and *life* of *spirituall Virgins,* who abhorre the spirituall *defilements* of *false worship, Rev.* 14.

Thirdly, the *cry* of the *whole earth,* made *drunke* with the *bloud* of its *inhabitants,* slaughtering each other in their *blinded zeale,* for *Conscience,* for *Religion,* against the *Catholickes,* against the *Lutherans,* &c.

What fearful *cries* within these twenty years of hundred *thousands* men, women, children, fathers, mothers, husbands, wives, brethren, sisters, old and young, high and low, *plundred, ravished, slaughtered, murthered, famished?* And hence these cries, that men fling away the *spiritual sword and spiritual artillery* (in *spiritual* and *religious* causes) and rather trust for the suppressing of each others *God, Conscience,* and *Religion* (as they suppose) to an *arme* of *flesh,* and *sword* of *steele?*

TRUTH. *Sweet Peace,* what hast thou there?

PEACE. *Arguments* against *persecution* for cause of *Conscience.*

TRUTH. And what there?

PEACE. An *Answer* to such *Arguments,* contrarily maintaining such *persecution* for *cause* of *Conscience.*

TRUTH. These *Arguments* against such *persecution,* and the *Answer* pleading for it, written (as *Love* hopes) from godly *intentions, hearts,* and *hands,* yet in a marvellous different *stile* and *manner.* The *Arguments* against *persecution* in *milke,* the *Answer* for it (as I may say) in *bloud.*

The *Authour* of these *Arguments* (against *persecution*) (as I have beene informed) being committed by *some* then in power, *close prisoner* to *Newgate,* for the witnesse of some *truths* of *Jesus,* and having not the use of *Pen* and *Inke,* wrote these *Arguments* in *Milke,* in sheets of Paper, brought to him by the *Woman* his *Keeper,* from a friend in *London,* as the *stopples* of his *Milk bottle.*

In such Paper written with *Milk* nothing will appeare, but the way of reading it by *fire* being knowne to this *friend* who received the Papers, he transcribed and kept together the Papers, although the *Author* himselfe could not correct, nor view what himselfe had written.

It was in *milke,* tending to soule *nourishment,* even for *Babes* and Sucklings in *Christ.*

It was in *milke,* spiritually *white,* pure and innocent, like those *white horses* of the *Word of truth* and *meeknesse,* and the *white Linnen* or *Armour* of *righteousness,* in the *Army* of *Jesus. Rev.* 6. & 19.

It was in *milke,* soft, meeke, peaceable and gentle, tending both to the *peace* of *soules,* and the *peace* of *States* and Kingdomes.

PEACE. The *Answer* (though I hope out of milkie pure intentions) is returned in *bloud: bloudy* & slaughterous *conclusions; bloudy* to the *souls* of all men, forc'd to the *Religion* and *Worship* which every civil State or Common-weale agrees on, and compells all subjects to in a dissembled *uniformitie.*

Bloudy to the *bodies,* first of the holy *witnesses* of *Christ Jesus,* who testifie against such invented worships.

Secondly, of the *Nations* and Peoples slaughtering each other for their severall respective Religions and Consciences.

1644

III. [RICHARD MATHER]
(1596–1669)

From *"THE BAY PSALM BOOK"*

PREFACE

* * * The psalmes are penned in such verses as are sutable to the poetry of the hebrew language, and not in the common style of such other bookes of the old Testament as are not poeticall; now no protestant doubteth but that all the bookes of the scripture should by Gods ordinance be extant in the mother tongue of each nation, that they may be understood of all, hence the psalmes are to be translated into our english tongue: and if in our english tongue wee are to sing them, then as all our english songs (according to the course of our english poetry) do run in metre, soe ought Davids psalmes to be translated into meeter, that soe wee may sing the Lords songs, as in our English tongue soe in such verses as are familiar to an english eare which are commonly metricall: and as it can be no just offence to any good conscience, to sing David's hebrew songs in english words, soe neither to sing his poeticall verses in english poeticall metre: men might as well stumble at singing the hebrew psalmes in our english tunes (and not in the hebrew tunes) as at singing them in english meeter, (which are our verses) and not in such verses as are generally used by David according to the poetry of the hebrew language: but the truth is, as the Lord hath hid from us the hebrew tunes, lest wee should think our selves bound to imitate them; soe also the course and frame (for the most part) of their hebrew poetry, that wee might not think our selves bound to imitate that, but that every nation without scruple might follow as the grave sort of tunes of their owne country songs, soe the graver sort of verses of their owne country poetry.

Neither let any think, that for the meetre sake wee have taken liberty or poeticall license to depart from the true and proper sence of Davids words in the hebrew verses, noe; but it hath beene one part of our religious care and faithfull indeavour, to keepe close to the originall text. * * *

1640

PSALME I

O Blessed man, that in th' advice
 of wicked doeth not walk:
nor stand in sinners way, nor sit
 in chayre of scornful folk,
2 But in the law of Jehovah,
 is his longing delight:
and in his law doth meditate,
 by day and eke by night.
3 And he shall be like to a tree
 planted by water-rivers:
that in his season yeilds his fruit,
 and his leafe never withers.
4 And all he doth, shall prosper well,
 the wicked are not so:

but they are like unto the chaffe,
which winde drives to and fro.
5 Therefore shall not ungodly men,
rise to stand in the doome,
nor shall the sinners with the just,
in their assemblie *come.*
6 For of the righteous men, the Lord
acknowledgeth the way:
but the way of ungodly men,
shall utterly decay.

1640

23. A PSALME OF DAVID

The Lord to mee a shepheard is,
want therefore shall not I.
2 Hee in the folds of tender-grasse,
doth cause mee downe to lie:
To waters calme me gently leads
3 Restore my soule doth he:
he doth in paths of righteousness:
for his names sake leade mee.
4 Yea though in valley of death shade
I walk, none ill I'le feare:
because thou are with mee, thy rod,
and staffe my comfort are.
5 For mee a table thou hast spread,
in presence of my foes:
thou dost annoynt my head with oyle,
my cup it over-flowes.
6 Goodness & mercy surely shall
all my dayes follow me:
and in the Lords house I shall dwell
so long as dayes shall bee.

1640

IV. ANNE BRADSTREET
(*c.* 1612–1672)

TO MY DEAR CHILDREN

This Book by Any yet unread,
I leave for you when I am dead,
That, being gone, here you may find
What was your liveing mother's mind.
Make use of what I leave in Love
And God shall blesse you from above.

A. B.

(*c.* 1670) 1867

THE PROLOGUE

1

To sing of Wars, of Captains, and of Kings,
Of Cities founded, Commonwealths begun,
For my mean pen are too superior things:
Or how they all, or each their dates have run
Let Poets and Historians set these forth,
My obscure Lines shall not so dim their worth.

2

But when my wondring eyes and envious heart
Great *Bartas* sugar'd lines, do but read o're
Fool I do grudg the Muses did not part
'Twixt him and me that overfluent store;
A *Bartas* can, do what a *Bartas* will
But simple I according to my skill.

3

From school-boyes tongue no rhet'rick we expect
Nor yet a sweet Consort from broken strings,
Nor perfect beauty, where's a main defect:
My foolish, broken, blemish'd Muse so sings
And this to mend, alas, no Art is able,
'Cause nature, made it so irreparable.

4

Nor can I, like that fluent sweet tongu'd Greek,
Who lisp'd at first, in future times speak plain
By Art he gladly found what he did seek
A full requital of his, striving pain
Art can do much, but this maxime's most sure

A weak or wounded brain admits no cure.

5

I am obnoxious to each carping tongue
Who says my hand a needle better fits,
A Poets pen all scorn I should thus wrong,
For such despite they cast on Female wits:
If what I do prove well, it won't advance,
They'l say it's stoln, or else it was by chance.

6

But sure the Antique Greeks were far more mild
Else of our Sexe, why feigned they those Nine
And Poesy made, *Calliope's* own Child;
So 'mongst the rest they placed the Arts Divine,
But this weak knot, they will full soon untie,
The Greeks did nought, but play the fools & lye.

7

Let Greeks be Greeks, and women what they are
Men have precedency and still excell,
It is but vain unjustly to wage warre;
Men can do best, and women know it well
Preheminence in all and each is yours;
Yet grant some small acknowledgement of ours.

8

And oh ye high flown quills that soar the Skies,
And ever with your prey still catch your praise,
If e're you daigne these lowly lines your eyes
Give Thyme or Parsley wreath, I ask no bayes,
This mean and unrefined ure of mine
Will make you glistring gold, but more to shine.

1650

TO MY DEAR AND LOVING HUSBAND

If ever two were one, then surely we.
If ever man were lov'd by wife, then thee;
If ever wife was happy in a man,
Compare with me ye women if you can.
I prize thy love more then whole Mines of gold,
Or all the riches that the East doth hold.
My love is such that Rivers cannot quench,
Nor ought but love from thee, give recompence.
Thy love is such I can no way repay,
The heavens reward thee manifold I pray.
Then while we live, in love lets so persever,
That when we live no more, we may live ever.

1678

THE FOUR SEASONS OF THE YEAR

SPRING

Another four I've left yet to bring on,
Of four times four the last *Quaternion*,
The Winter, Summer, Autumn & the Spring,
In season all these Seasons I shall bring:
Sweet Spring like man in his Minority,
At present claim'd, and had priority.
With smiling face and garments somewhat green,

She trim'd her locks, which late had frosted been,
Nor hot nor cold, she spake, but with a breath,
Fit to revive, the nummed earth from death.
Three months (quoth she) are 'lotted to my share
March, April, May of all the rest most fair.
Tenth of the first, *Sol* into *Aries* enters,
And bids defiance to all tedious winters,
Crosseth the Line, and equals night and day,
(Stil adds to th' last til after pleasant *May*)
And now makes glad the darkned northern wights
Who for some months have seen but starry lights.
Now goes the Plow-man to his merry toyle,
He might unloose his winter locked soyl:
The Seeds-man too, doth lavish out his grain,
In hope the more he casts, the more to gain:
The Gardner now superflouous branches lops,
And poles erects for his young clambring hops.
Now digs then sowes his herbs, his flowers & roots
And carefully manures his trees of fruits.
The *Pleiades their influence* now give,
And all that seem'd as dead afresh doth live.
The croaking frogs, whom nipping winter kil'd
Like birds now chirp, and hop about the field,
The Nightingale, the black-bird and the Thrush
Now tune their layes, on sprayes of every bush.
The wanton frisking Kid, and soft-fleec'd Lambs
Do jump and play before their feeding Dams,
The tender tops of budding grass they crop,
They joy in what they have, but more in hope:
For though the frost hath lost his binding power,
Yet many a fleece of snow and stormy shower
Doth darken *Sol's* bright eye, makes us remember
The pinching North-west wind of cold *December*.
My second moneth is *April*, green and fair,
Of longer dayes, and a more temperate Air:
The Sun in *Taurus* keeps his residence,
And with his warmer beams glanceth from thence
This is the month whose fruitful showrs produces
All set and sown for all delights and uses:
The Pear, the Plum, and Apple-tree now flourish
The grass grows long the hungry beast to nourish.
The Primrose pale and azure violet
Among the virduous grass hath nature set,
That when the Sun on's Love (the earth) doth shine
These might as lace set out her garment fine.
The fearfull bird his little house now builds
In trees and walls, in Cities and in fields.
The outside strong, the inside warm and neat;
A natural Artificer compleat.
The clocking hen her chirping chickins leads
With wings & beak defends them from the gleads

My next and last is fruitfull pleasant *May*,
Wherein the earth is clad in rich aray,
The Sun now enters loving *Gemini*,
And heats us with the glances of his eye,
Our thicker rayment makes us lay aside
Lest by his fervor we be torrifi'd.
All flowers the Sun now with his beams discloses,
Except the double pinks and matchless Roses.
Now swarms the busy, witty, honey-Bee,
Whose praise deserves a page from more then me
The cleanly Huswifes Dary's now in th' prime,
Her shelves and firkins fill'd for winter time.
The meads with Cowslips, Honey-suckles dight,
One hangs his head, the other stands upright:
But both rejoyce at th' heavens clear smiling face,
More at her showers, which water them a space.
For fruits my Season yields the early Cherry,
The hasty Peas, and wholsome cool Strawberry.
More solid fruits require a longer time,
Each Season hath his fruit, so hath each Clime:
Each man his own peculiar excellence,
But none in all that hath prehemi-nence.
Sweet fragrant Spring, with thy short pittance fly
Let some describe thee better then can I.
Yet above all this priviledg is thine,
Thy dayes still lengthen without least decline.

1650

CONTEMPLATIONS

1

Some time now past in the Autumnal Tide,
When *Phœbus* wanted but one hour to bed,
The trees all richly clad, yet void of pride,
Where gilded o're by his rich golden head.
Their leaves & fruits seem'd painted, but was true
Of green, of red, of yellow, mixed hew,
Rapt were my sences at this delectable view.

2

I wist not what to wish, yet sure thought I,
If so much excellence abide below;
How excellent is he that dwells on high?
Whose power and beauty by his works we know.
Sure he is goodness, wisdome, glory, light,
That hath this under world so richly dight:
More Heaven then Earth was here no winter & no night.

3

Then on a stately Oak I cast mine Eye,
Whose ruffling top the clouds seem'd to aspire;
How long since thou wast in thine Infancy?
Thy strength, and stature, more thy years admire,
Hath hundred winters past since thou wast born?
Or thousand since thou brakest thy shell of horn,
If so, all these as nought, Eternity doth scorn.

4

Then higher on the glistering Sun I gaz'd,
Whose beams was shaded by the leavie Tree,
The more I look'd, the more I grew amaz'd,
And softly said, what glory's like to thee?
Soul of this world, this Universes Eye,
No wonder, some made thee a Deity:
Had I not better known, (alas) the same had I.

5

Thou as a Bridegroom from thy Chamber rushes,
And as a strong man, joyes to run a race,
The morn doth usher thee, with smiles & blushes,
The Earth reflects her glances in thy face.
Birds, insects, Animals with Vegative,
Thy heart from death and dulness doth revive:
And in the darksome womb of fruitful nature dive.

6

Thy swift Annual, and diurnal Course,
Thy daily streight, and yearly oblique path,
Thy pleasing fervor, and thy scorching force,
All mortals here the feeling knowledg hath.
Thy presence makes it day, thy absence night,
Quaternal Seasons caused by thy might;
Hail Creature, full of sweetness, beauty & delight.

7

Art thou so full of glory, that no Eye
Hath strength, thy shining Rayes once to behold?
And is thy splendid Throne erect so high?
As to approach it, can no earthly mould.
How full of glory then must thy Creator be?
Who gave this bright light luster unto thee:
Admir'd, ador'd for ever, be that Majesty.

8

Silent alone, where none or saw, or heard,
In pathless paths I lead my wandring feet,
My humble Eyes to lofty Skyes I rear'd
To sing some Song, my mazed Muse thought meet.
My great Creator I would magnifie,
That nature had, thus decked liberally:
But Ah, and Ah, again, my imbecility!

9

I heard the merry grashopper then sing,
The black clad Cricket, bear a second part,
They kept one tune, and plaid on the same string,
Seeming to glory in their little Art.
Shall Creatures abject, thus their voices raise?
And in their kind resound their makers praise:
Whilst I as mute, can warble forth no higher layes.

10

When present times look back to Ages past,
And men in being fancy those are dead,
It makes things gone perpetually to last,

And calls back moneths and years that long since fled
It makes a man more aged in conceit,
Then was *Methuselah,* or's grand-sire great:
While of their persons & their acts his mind doth treat.

11

Sometimes in *Eden* fair, he seems to be,
Sees glorious *Adam* there made Lord of all,
Fancyes the Apple, dangle on the Tree,
That turn'd his Sovereign to a naked thral.
Who like a miscreant's driven from that place,
To get his bread with pain, and sweat of face:
A penalty impos'd on his backsliding Race.

12

Here sits our Grandame in retired place,
And in her lap, her bloody *Cain* new born,
The weeping Imp oft looks her in the face,
Bewails his unknown hap, and fate forlorn;
His Mother sighs, to think of Paradise,
And how she lost her bliss, to be more wise,
Believing him that was, and is, Father of lyes.

13

Here *Cain* and *Abel* come to sacrifice,
Fruits of the Earth, and Fatlings each do bring,
On *Abels* gift the fire descends from Skies,
But no such sign on false *Cain's* offering;
With sullen hateful looks he goes his wayes.
Hath thousand thoughts to end his brothers dayes,
Upon whose blood his future good he hopes to raise.

14

There *Abel* keeps his sheep, no ill he thinks,
His brother comes, then acts his fratricide,
The Virgin Earth, of blood her first draught drinks
But since that time she often hath been cloy'd;
The wretch with gastly face and dreadful mind,
Thinks each he sees will serve him in his kind,
Though none on Earth but kindred near then could he find.

15

Who fancyes not his looks now at the Barr,
His face like death, his heart with horror fraught,
Nor Male-factor ever felt like warr,
When deep dispair, with wish of life hath sought,
Branded with guilt, and crusht with treble woes,
A Vagabond to Land of *Nod* he goes,
A City builds, that wals might him secure from foes.

16

Who thinks not oft upon the Fathers ages.
Their long descent, how nephews sons they saw,
The starry observations of those Sages,
And how their precepts to their sons were law,
How Adam sigh'd to see his Progeny,

Cloath'd all in his black sinfull Livery,
Who neither guilt, nor yet the punishment could fly.

17

Our Life compare we with their length of dayes
Who to the tenth of theirs doth now arrive?
And though thus short, we shorten many wayes,
Living so little while we are alive;
In eating, drinking, sleeping, vain delight
So unawares comes on perpetual night,
And puts all pleasures vain unto eternal flight.

18

When I behold the heavens as in their prime,
And then the earth (though old) stil clad in green,
The stones and trees, insensible of time,
Nor age nor wrinkle on their front are seen;
If winter come, and greeness then do fade,
A Spring returns, and they more youthfull made;
But Man grows old, lies down, remains where once he's laid.

[19]20

By birth more noble then those creatures all,
Yet seems by nature and by custome curs'd
No sooner born, but grief and care makes fall
That state obliterate he had at first:
Nor youth, nor strength, nor wisdom spring again
Nor habitations long their names retain,
But in oblivion to the final day remain.

20

Shall I then praise the heavens, the trees, the earth
Because their beauty and their strength last longer
Shall I wish there, or never to had birth,
Because they're bigger, & their bodyes stronger?
Nay, they shall darken, perish, fade and dye,
And when unmade, so ever shall they lye,
But man was made for endless immortality.

21

Under the cooling shadow of a stately Elm
Close sate I by a goodly Rivers side,
Where gliding streams the Rocks did overwhelm;
A lonely place, with pleasures dignifi'd.
I once that lov'd the shady woods so well,
Now thought the rivers did the trees excel,
And if the sun would ever shine, there would I dwell.

22

While on the stealing stream I fixt mine eye,
Which to the long'd for Ocean held its course,
I markt, nor crooks, nor rubs that there did lye
Could hinder ought, but still augment its force:
O happy Flood, quoth I, that holds thy race
Till thou arrive at thy beloved place,
Nor is it rocks or shoals that can obstruct thy pace

23

Nor is't enough, that thou alone may'st slide,
But hundred brooks in thy cleer waves do meet,
So hand in hand along with thee they glide
To *Thetis* house, where all imbrace and greet:
Thou Emblem true, of what I count the best,
O could I lead my Rivolets to rest,
So may we press to that vast mansion, ever blest. * * *

1678

THE AUTHOR TO HER BOOK

Thou ill-form'd offspring of my feeble brain,
Who after birth did'st by my side remain,
Till snatcht from thence by friends, less wise then true
Who thee abroad, expos'd to publick view,
Made thee in raggs, halting to th' press to trudg,
Where errors were not lessened (all may judg)
At thy return my blushing was not small,
My rambling brat (in print) should mother call,
I cast thee by as one unfit for light,
Thy Visage was so irksome in my sight;
Yet being mine own, at length affection would
Thy blemishes amend, if so I could:
I wash'd thy face, but more defects I saw,
And rubbing off a spot, still made a flaw.
I stretched thy joynts to make thee even feet,
Yet still thou run'st more hobling then is meet;
In better dress to trim thee was my mind,
But nought save home-spun Cloth, i' th' house I find
In this array, 'mongst Vulgars mayst thou roam
In Criticks hands, beware thou dost not come;
And take thy way where yet thou art not known,
If for thy Father askt, say, thou hadst none:
And for thy Mother, she alas is poor,
Which caus'd her thus to send thee out of door.

1678

V. MICHAEL WIGGLESWORTH
(1631–1705)

From *THE DAY OF DOOM*

TO THE CHRISTIAN READER

Reader, I am a fool,
And have adventured
To play the fool this once for Christ,
The more his fame to spread.
If this my foolishness
Help thee to be more wise,
I have attainéd what I seek,
And what I only prize.

Thou wonderest perhaps,
That I in Print appear,
Who to the Pulpit dwell so nigh,
Yet come so seldome there.
The God of Heaven knows
What grief to me it is,
To be with-held from serving Christ:
No sorrow like to this. * * *

Or who of all my Friends
That have my tryals seen,
Can tell the time in seven years,
When I have dumpish been?
Some think my voice is strong,

Most times when I do Preach:
But ten days after what I feel
And suffer, few can reach.

My prison'd thoughts break forth,
When open'd is the door,
With greater force and violence,
And strain my voice the more.
But vainly do they tell,
That I am growing stronger,
Who hear me speak in half an hour,
Till I can speak no longer.

Some for because they see not
My chearfulness to fail,
Nor that I am disconsolate,
Do think I nothing ail.
If they had born my griefs,
Their courage might have fail'd them,
And all the Town (perhaps) have known
(Once and again) what ail'd them.

But why should I complain
That have so good a God,
That doth mine heart with comfort fill,
Ev'n whilst I feel his Rod?
In God I have been strong,
But wearied and worn out,
And joy'd in him, when twenty woes
Assail'd me round about.

Nor speak I this to boast,
But make Apology
For mine own self, and answer those
That fail in Charity.
I am (alas!) as frail,
Impatiént a Creature,
As most that tread upon the ground,
And have as bad a nature.

Let God be magnify'd,
Whose everlasting strength
Upholds me under sufferings
Of more than ten years length.
Through whose Almighty pow'r
Although I am surrounded
With sorrows more than can be told,
Yet I am not confounded.

For his dear sake have I
This service undertaken,
For I am bound to honour Him
Who hath not me forsaken.
I am a Debtor too,
Unto the sons of Men;
Whom, wanting other means, I would
Advantage with my Pen.

I would, But (ah!) my strength,
When triéd, proves so small,
That to the ground without effect,
My wishes often fall.
Weak heads, and hands, and states,
Great things cannot produce:
And therefore I this little Piece
Have publish'd for thine use. * * *

1662

[THE APPEARANCE OF CHRIST] *

I

The security of the World before Christ's coming to judgment. Luke 12:19.

Still was the night, Serene and Bright,
  when all Men sleeping lay;
Calm was the season, and carnal reason
  thought so 'twould last for ay.
Soul, take thine ease, let sorrow cease,
  much good thou hast in store.
This was their Song, their Cups among,
  the Evening before.

* This text is numbered by half-lines since the poem was originally set in this form.

II

Wallowing in all kind of sin,
vile wretches lay secure:
The best of men had scarcely then
their Lamps kept in good ure.
Virgins unwise, who through disguise
amongst the best were number'd, Mat. 25:5.
Had clos'd their eyes; yea, and the wise
through sloth and frailty slumber'd.

III

Like as of old, when Men grew bold
Gods' threat'nings to contemn,
Who stopt their Ear, and would not hear Mat. 24:37, 38.
when Mercy warnéd them,
But took their course, without remorse,
til God began to powre
Destruction the World upon
in a tempestuous showre.

IV

They put away the evil day,
and drown'd their cares and fears, 1 Thes. 5:3.
Till drown'd were they, and swept away
by vengeance unawares;
So at the last, whilst men sleep fast
in their security,
Surprized they are in such a snare
as cometh suddenly.

V

The suddenness, Majesty, and Terror of Christ's appearing.

For at midnight brake forth a Light,
which turn'd the night to day,
And speedily an hideous cry,
did all the world dismay.
Sinners awake, their hearts do ake, Mat. 25:6.
trembling their loyns surprizeth; 2 Pet. 3:10.
Amaz'd with fear, by what they hear,
each one of them ariseth.

VI

They rush from Beds with giddy heads,
and to their windows run,
Viewing this light, which shines more bright
than doth the Noon-day Sun. Mat. 24:29, 30.
Straightway appears (they see't with tears)
the Son of God most dread;

Who with his Train comes on amain
to Judge both Quick and Dead.

VII

Before his face the Heav'ns gave place,
and Skies are rent asunder,
With mighty voice, and hideous noise,
more terrible than Thunder.
His brightness damps heav'ns glorious lamps
and makes them hide their heads, 2 Pet. 3:10.
As if afraid and quite dismay'd,
they quit their wonted steads. * * *

[THE JUDGMENT]

CLXVI

Then to the Bar, all they drew near
Who dy'd in infancy,
And never had or good or bad
effected pers'nally,
But from the womb unto the tomb
were straightway carried,
(Or at the last e're they transgrest)
who thus began to plead:

Rom. 2:12, 15 & 1:32. Mat. 12:41. Reprobate Infants plead for themselves. Rev. 20:12, 15, compared with Rom. 5:12, 14, & 9:11, 13. Ezek. 18:2.

CLXVII

If for our own transgression, Ezek. 18:2.
or disobedience,
We here did stand at thy left-hand
just were the Recompence:
But *Adam's* guilt our souls hath spilt,
his fault is charg'd on us;
And that alone hath overthrown
and utterly undone us.

CLXVIII

Not we, but he, ate of the Tree,
whose fruit was interdicted:
Yet on us all of his sad Fall,
the punishment's inflicted.
How could we sin that had not been,
or how is his sin our,
Without consent, which to prevent,
we never had a pow'r?

CLXIX

O great Creator, why was our Nature
depraved and forlorn?

Why so defil'd and made so vild
  whilst we were yet unborn?
If it be just, and needs we must
  transgressors reck'ned be,
Thy Mercy, Lord, to us afford, Psal. 51:5.
  which sinners hath set free.

CLXX

Behold we see *Adam* set free,
  and sav'd from his trespass,
Whose sinful Fall hath spilt us all,
  and brought us to this pass.
Canst thou deny us once to try,
  or Grace to us to tender,
When he finds grace before thy face,
  that was the chief offender?

CLXXI

Then answered the Judge most dread, Their arguments taken off. Ezek. 18:20. Rom. 5:12, 19.
  God doth such doom forbid,
That men should die eternally
  for what they never did.
But what you call old *Adam's* Fall,
  and only his Trespass,
You call amiss to call it his,
  both his and yours it was.

CLXXII

He was design'd of all Mankind
  to be a publick Head,
A common Root, whence all should shoot, 1 Cor. 15:48, 49.
  and stood in all their stead.
He stood and fell, did ill or well,
  not for himself alone,
But for you all, who now his Fall
  and trespass would disown.

CLXXIII

If he had stood, then all his brood
  had been establishéd
In Gods true love, never to move,
  nor once awry to tread:
Then all his Race my Father's Grace,
  should have enjoy'd for ever,
And wicked Sprites by subtile sleights
  could them have harmed never.

CLXXIV

Would you have griev'd to have receiv'd
  through *Adam* so much good,
As had been your for evermore,
  if he at first had stood?
Would you have said, We ne'r obey'd,
  nor did thy Laws regard;
It ill befits with benefits,
  us, Lord, to so reward? * * *

CLXXX

You sinners are, and such a share
  as sinners may expect;
Such you shall have; for I do save
  none but mine own Elect.
Yet to compare your sin with their
  who liv'd a longer time,
I do confess yours is much less,
  though every sin's a crime.

Psal. 58:8.
Rom. 6:23.
Gal. 3:10.
Rom. 8:29, 30, & 11:7.
Rev. 21:27.
Luke 12:48.

CLXXXI

A crime it is, therefore in bliss
  you may not hope to dwell,
But unto you I shall allow
  the easiest room in Hell.
The glorious King thus answering,
  they cease, and plead no longer:
Their Consciences must needs confess
  his Reasons are the stronger.

Mat. 11:22.
The wicked all convinced and put to silence.
Ro. 3:19.
Mat. 22:12.

CLXXXII

Thus all mens Pleas the Judge with ease
  doth answer and confute,
Until that all, both great and small,
  are silenced and mute.
Vain hopes are cropt, all mouths are stopt,
  sinners have nought to say,
But that 'tis just, and equal most
  they should be damn'd for ay.

Behold the formidable estate of all the ungodly, as they stand hopeless & helpless before an impartial judge, expecting their final Sentence.
Rev. 6:16, 17.

CLXXXIII

Now what remains, but that to pains
  and everlasting smart,
Christ should condemn the sons of men,
  which is their just desert;
Oh, rueful plights of sinful wights!
  Oh wretches all forlorn:

'T had happy been they ne're had seen
the Sun, or not been born. * * *

CXCVI

Where tender love mens hearts did move
unto a sympathy,
And bearing part of others smart
in their anxiety; 1 Cor. 6:2.
Now such compassion is out of fashion,
and wholly laid aside:
No Friends so near, but Saints to hear
their Sentence can abide.

CXCVII

One natural Brother beholds another
in his astonied fit,
Yet sorrows not thereat a jot, Compare Prov. 1:26, with 1 Job 3:2, & 2 Cor. 5:16.
nor pitties him a whit.
The godly wife conceives no grief,
nor can she shed a tear
For the sad state of her dear Mate,
when she his doom doth hear.

CXCVIII

He that was erst a Husband pierc't
with sense of Wives distress,
Whose tender heart did bear a part
of all her grievances,
Shall mourn no more as heretofore
because of her ill plight;
Although he see her now to be
a damn'd forsaken wight.

CXCIX

The tender Mother will own no other
of all her numerous brood,
But such as stand at Christ's right hand
acquitted through his Blood. Luk. 16:25.
The pious Father had now much rather
his graceless Son should ly
In Hell with Devils, for all his evils,
burning eternally,

CC

Then God most High should injury,
by sparing him sustain;
And doth rejoyce to hear Christ's voice, Psal. 58:10.
adjudging him to pain;

Who having all, both great and small,
  convinc'd and silenced,
Did then proceed their Doom to read,
  and thus it uttered:

CCI

Ye sinful wights, and cursed sprights,
  that work Iniquity,
Depart together from me for ever
  to endless Misery;
Your portion take in yonder Lake,
  where Fire and Brimstone flameth:
Suffer the smart, which your desert
  as it's due wages claimeth. * * *

The judge pronounceth the Sentence of condemnation. Mat. 25:41.

1662

VI. NATHANIEL WARD
(*c.* 1579–*c.* 1652)

From *THE SIMPLE COBLER OF AGGAWAMM*

[ON TOLERANCE]

Either I am in an Appoplexie, or that man is in a Lethargie, who doth not now sensibly feele God shaking the heavens over his head, and the earth under his feet: The Heavens so, as the Sun begins to turne into darknesse, the Moon into blood, the Starres to fall down to the ground; So that little Light of Comfort or Counsell is left to the sonnes of men: The Earth so, as the foundations are failing, the righteous scarce know where to finde rest, the inhabitants stagger like drunken men: it is in a manner dissolved both in Religions and Relations: And no marvell; for, they have defiled it by transgressing the Lawes, changing the Ordinances, and breaking the Everlasting Covenant. The Truths of God are the Pillars of the world, whereon States and Churches may stand quiet if they will; if they will not, Hee can easily shake them off into delusions, and distractions enough.

Sathan is now in his passions, he feeles his passion approaching; hee loves to fish in royled waters. Though that Dragon cannot sting the vitals of the Elect mortally, yet that Beelzebub can fly-blow their Intellectuals miserably: The finer Religion grows, the finer hee spins his Cobwebs, hee will hold pace with Christ so long as his wits will serve him. Hee sees himselfe beaten out of grosse Idolatries, Heresies, Ceremonies, where the Light breakes forth with power; he will therefore bestirre him to prevaricate Evangelicall Truths, and Ordinances, that if they will needs be walking, yet they shall *laborare varicibus,* and not keep their path, he will put them out of time and place; Assassinating for his Engineers, men of Paracelsian parts; well complexioned for honesty; for, such are fittest to Mountebanke his Chimistry into sicke Churches and weake Judgements.

Nor shall hee need to stretch his

strength overmuch in this worke: Too many men having not laid their foundations sure, nor ballasted their Spirits deepe with humility and feare, are prest enough of themselves to evaporate their owne apprehensions. Those that are acquainted with Story know, it hath ever beene so in new Editions of Churches: Such as are least able, are most busie to pudder in the rubbish, and to raise dust in the eyes of more steady Repayrers. Civill Commotions made roome for uncivill practises: Religious mutations, for irreligious opinions: Change of Aire, discovers corrupt bodies; Reformation of Religion, unsound mindes. Hee that hath any well-faced phansy in his Crowne, and doth not vent it now, fears the pride of his owne heart will dub him dunce for ever. Such a one will trouble the whole *Israel* of God with his most untimely births, though he makes the bones of his vanity stick up, to the view and griefe of all that are godly wise. The devill desiers no better sport then to see light heads handle their heels, and fetch their carreers in a time, when the Roofe of Liberty stands open.

The next perplexed Question, with pious and ponderous men, will be: What should bee done for the healing of these comfortlesse exulcerations. I am the unablest adviser of a thousand, the unworthiest of ten thousand; yet I hope I may presume to assert what follows without just offence.

First, such as have given or taken any unfriendly reports of us *New-English,* should doe well to recollect themselves. Wee have beene reputed a Colluvies of wild Opinionists, swarmed into a remote wilderness to find elbow-roome for our phanatick Doctrines and practises: I trust our diligence past, and constant sedulity against such persons and courses, will plead better things for us. I dare take upon me, to bee the Herauld of *New-England* so farre, as to proclaime to the world, in the name of our Colony, that all Familists, Antinomians, Anabaptists, and other Enthusiasts shall have free Liberty to keepe away from us, and such as will come to be gone as fast as they can, the sooner the better.

Secondly, I dare averre, that God doth no where in his word tolerate Christian States, to give Tolerations to such adversaries of his Truth, if they have power in their hands to suppresse them.

1647

VII. INCREASE MATHER
(1639–1723)

From *AN ESSAY FOR THE RECORDING OF ILLUSTRIOUS PROVIDENCES*

[THE HOUSE OF WILLIAM MORSE]

As there have been several Persons vexed with evil Spirits, so divers Houses have been wofully Haunted by them. In the Year 1679, the House of *William Morse* in *Newberry* in *New-England,* was strangely disquieted by a *Dæmon.* After those troubles began, he did by the Advice of Friends write down the particulars of those unusual Accidents. And the Account which he giveth thereof is as followeth;

On *December* 3. in the night time,

he and his Wife heard a noise upon the roof of their House, as if Sticks and Stones had been thrown against it with great violence; whereupon he rose out of his Bed, but could see nothing. Locking the Doors fast, he returned to Bed again. About midnight they heard an Hog making a great noise in the House, so that the Man rose again, and found a great Hog in the house, the door being shut, but upon the opening of the door it ran out.

On *December* 8. in the Morning, there were five great Stones and Bricks by an *invisible hand* thrown in at the west end of the house while the Mans Wife was making the Bed, the Bedstead was lifted up from the floor, and the Bedstaff flung out of the Window, and a Cat was hurled at her; a long Staff danced up and down in the Chimney; a burnt Brick, and a piece of a weatherboard were thrown in at the Window: The Man at his going to Bed put out his Lamp, but in the Morning found that the Saveall of it was taken away, and yet it was unaccountably brought into its former place. On the same day, the long Staff but now spoken of, was hang'd up by a line, and swung to and fro, the Man's Wife laid it in the fire, but she could not hold it there, inasmuch as it would forcibly fly out; yet after much ado with joynt strength they made it to burn. A shingle flew from the Window, though no body near it, many sticks came in at the same place, only one of these was so scragged that it could enter the hole but a little way, whereupon the Man pusht it out, a great Rail likewise was thrust in at the Window, so as to break the Glass.

At another time an Iron Crook that was hanged on a Nail, violently flew up and down, also a Chair flew about, and at last lighted on the Table where Victuals stood ready for them to eat, and was likely to spoil all, only by a nimble catching they saved some of their Meal with the loss of the rest, and the overturning of their Table.

People were sometimes Barricado'd out of doors, when as yet there was no body to do it: and a Chest was removed from place to place, no hand touching it. Their Keys being tied together, one was taken from the rest, & the remaining two would fly about making a loud noise by knocking against each other. But the greatest part of this *Devils* feats were his mischievous ones, wherein indeed he was sometimes Antick enough too, and therein the chief sufferers were, the Man and his Wife, and his Grand-Son. The Man especially had his share in these *Diabolical* Molestations. For one while they could not eat their Suppers quietly, but had the Ashes on the Hearth before their eyes thrown into their Victuals; yea, and upon their heads and Clothes, insomuch that they were forced up into their Chamber, and yet they had no rest there; for one of the Man's Shoes being left below, 'twas filled with Ashes and Coals, and thrown up after them. Their Light was beaten out, and they being laid in their Bed with their little Boy between them, a great stone (from the Floor of the Loft) weighing above three pounds was thrown upon the mans stomach, and he turning it down upon the floor, it was once more thrown upon him. A Box, and a Board were likewise thrown upon them all. And a Bag of Hops was taken out of their Chest, wherewith they were beaten, till some of the Hops were scattered on the floor, where the Bag was then laid, and left.

In another Evening, when they sat by the fire, the Ashes were so whirled at them, that they could neither eat their Meat, nor endure the House. A Peel struck the Man in the face. An Apron hanging by the fire, was flung upon it, and singed before they could snatch it off. The Man being at Prayer with his Family, a Beesom gave him a blow on his head behind, and fell down before his face.

On another day, when they were Winnowing of Barley, some hard dirt was thrown in, hitting the Man on the Head and both the Man and his Wife on the back; and when they had made themselves clean, they essayed to fill their half Bushel but the foul Corn was in spite of them often cast in amongst the clean, and the Man being divers times thus abused was forced to give over what he was about.

On *January* 23 (in particular) the Man had an iron Pin twice thrown at him, and his Inkhorn was taken away from him while he was writing, and when by all his seeking it he could not find it, at last he saw it drop out of the Air, down by the fire: a piece of Leather was twice thrown at him; and a shoe was laid upon his shoulder, which he catching at, was suddenly rapt from him. An handful of Ashes was thrown at his face, and upon his clothes: and the shoe was then clapt upon his head, and upon it he clapt his hand, holding it so fast, that somewhat unseen pulled him with it backward on the floor.

On the next day at night, as they were going to Bed, a lost Ladder was thrown against the Door, and their Light put out; and when the Man was a bed, he was beaten with an heavy pair of Leather Breeches, and pull'd by the Hair of his Head and Beard, *P*inched and Scratched, and his Bed-board was taken away from him; yet more in the next night, when the Man was likewise a Bed; his Bed-board did rise out of its place, notwithstanding his putting forth all his strength to keep it in; one of his Awls wa[s] brought out of the next room into his Bed, and did prick him; the clothes wherewith he hoped to save his head from blows were violently pluckt from thence. Within a night or two after, the Man and his Wife received both of them a blow upon their heads, but it was so dark that they could not see the stone which gave it; the Man had his Cap pulled off from his head while he sat by the fire.

The night following, they went to bed undressed, because of their late disturbances, and the Man, Wife, Boy, presently felt themselves pricked, and upon search found in the Bed a Bodkin, a knitting Needle, and two sticks picked at both ends. He received also a great blow, as on his Thigh, so on his Face, which fetched blood: and while he was writing a Candlestick was twice thrown at him, and a great piece of Bark fiercely smote him, and a pail of Water turned up without hands. On the 28 of the mentioned Moneth, frozen clods of Cow-dung were divers times thrown at the man out of the house in which they were; his Wife went to milk the Cow, and received a blow on her head, and sitting down at her Milking-work had Cow-dung divers times thrown into her Pail, the Man tried to save the Milk, by holding a Piggin side-wayes under the Cowes belly, but the Dung would in for all, and the Milk was only made fit for Hogs. On that night ashes were thrown into the porridge which they had made ready for their Supper, so as that they could not eat it; Ashes were likewise often thrown into the Man's Eyes, as he sat by the fire. And an iron Hammer flying at him, gave him a great blow on his back; the Man's Wife going into the Cellar for Beer, a great iron Peel flew and fell after her through the trapdoor of the Cellar; and going afterwards on the same Errand to the same place, the door shut down upon her, and the Table came and lay upon the door, and the man was forced to remove it e're his Wife could be released from where she was; on the following day while he was Writing, a dish went out of its place, leapt into the pale, and cast Water upon the Man, his Paper, his Table, and disappointed his procedure in what he was about; his Cap jumpt off from his head, and on again, and the Pot-lid leapt off from the Pot into the Kettle on the fire.

February 2. While he and his Boy were eating of Cheese, the pieces which he cut were wrested from them, but they were afterwards found upon the Table under an Apron, and a pair of Breeches: And also from the fire arose little sticks and Ashes, which flying upon the Man and his Boy, brought them into an uncomfortable pickle; But as for the Boy, which the last passage spoke of, there remains much to be said concerning him, and a principal sufferer in these afflictions: For on the 18. of *December*, he sitting by his Grandfather, was hurried into great motions and the Man thereupon took him, and made him stand between his Legs, but the Chair danced up and down, and had like to have cast both Man and Boy into the fire: and the Child was afterwards flung about in such a manner, as that they feared that his Brains would have been beaten out; and in the evening he was tossed as afore, and the Man tried the project of holding him, but ineffectually. The Lad was soon put to Bed, and they presently heard an huge noise, and demanded what was the matter? and he answered that his Bed-stead leaped up and down: and they (*i.e.* the Man and his Wife) went up, and at first found all quiet, but before they had been there long, they saw the Board by his Bed trembling by him, and the Bed-clothes flying off him, the latter they laid on immediately, but they were no sooner on than off; so they took him out of his Bed for quietness.

December 29. The Boy was violently thrown to and fro, only they carried him to the house of a Doctor in the Town, and there he was free from disturbances, but returning home at night, his former trouble began, and the Man taking him by the hand, they were both of them almost tript into the fire. They put him to bed, and he was attended with the same iterated loss of his clothes, shaking off his Bed-board, and Noises, that he had in his last conflict; they took him up, designing to sit by the fire, but the doors clattered, and the Chair was thrown at him, wherefore they carried him to the Doctors house, and so for that night all was well. The next morning he came home quiet, but as they were doing somewhat, he cried out that he was prickt on the back, they looked, and found a three-tin'd Fork sticking strangely there; which being carried to the Doctors house, not only the Doctor himself said that it was his, but also the Doctors Servant affirmed it was seen at home after the Boy was gone. The Boys vexations continuing they left him at the Doctors, where he remained well till awhile after, and then he complained he was pricked, they looked and found an iron Spindle sticking below his back; he complained he was pricked still, they looked, and found Pins in a Paper sticking to his skin; he once more complained of his Back, they looked, and found there a long Iron, a bowl of a Spoon, and a piece of a Pansheard. They lay down by him on the Bed, with the Light burning, but he was twice thrown from them, and the second time thrown quite under the Bed; in the Morning the Bed was tossed about with such a creaking noise, as was heard to the Neighbours; in the afternoon their knives were one after another brought, and put into his back, but pulled out by the Spectators; only one knife which was missing seemed to the standers by to come out of his Mouth: he was bidden to read his Book, was taken and thrown about several times, at last hitting the Boys Grandmother on the head. Another time he was thrust out of his Chair and rolled up and down with out cries, that all things were on fire; yea, he was three times very dangerously thrown into the fire, and preserved by his Friends with much ado. The Boy also made for a long time together a noise like a Dog, and like an Hen with her Chickens, and could not speak rationally.

Particularly, on *December* 26. He barked like a Dog, and clock't like an Hen, and after long distraining to speak, said, there's *Powel,* I am pinched; his Tongue likewise hung out of his mouth, so as that it could by no means be forced in till his Fit was over, and then he said 'twas forced out by *Powel.* He & the house also after this had rest till the ninth of *January*: at which time the Child, because of his intolerable ravings, lying between the Man and his Wife, was pulled out of Bed, and knockt vehemently against the Bed-stead Boards, in a manner very perillous and amazing. In the Day time he was carried away beyond all possibility of their finding him. His Grandmother at last saw him creeping on one side, and drag'd him in, where he lay miserable lame, but recovering his speech, he said, that he was carried above the Doctors house, and that *Powel* carried him, and that the said *Powel* had him into the Barn, throwing him against the Cart-wheel there, and then thrusting him out at an hole; and accordingly they found some of the Remainders of the Threshed Barley which was on the Barn-floor hanging to his Clothes.

At another time he fell into a Swoon, they forced somewhat Refreshing into his mouth, and it was turned out as fast as they put it in; e're long he came to himself, and expressed some willingness to eat, but the Meat would forcibly fly out of his mouth; and when he was able to speak, he said *Powel* would not let him eat: Having found the *B*oy to be best at a Neighbours house, the Man carried him to his Daughters, three miles from his own. The Boy was growing antick as he was on the Journey, but before the end of it he made a grievous hollowing, and when he lighted, he threw a great stone at a Maid in the house, and fell on eating of Ashes. Being at home afterwards, they had rest awhile, but on the 19 of *January* in the Morning he swooned, and coming to himself, he roared terribly, and did eat Ashes, Sticks, Rug-yarn. The Morning following, there was such a racket with the Boy, that the Man and his Wife took him to Bed to them. A Bed-staff was thereupon thrown at them, and a Chamber pot with its Contents was thrown upon them, and they were severely pinched. The Man being about to rise, his Clothes were divers times pulled from them, himself thrust out of his Bed, and his Pillow thrown after him. The Lad also would have his clothes plucked off from him in these Winter Nights, and was wofully dogg'd with such fruits of Devilish spite, till it pleased God to shorten the Chain of the wicked *Dæmon.*

All this while the Devil did not use to appear in any visible shape, only they would think they had hold of the Hand that sometimes scratched them; but it would give them the slip. And once the Man was discernably beaten by a Fist, and an Hand got hold of his Wrist which he saw, but could not catch; and the likeness of a *Blackmore* Child did appear from under the Rugg and Blanket, where the Man lay, and it would rise up, fall down, nod & slip under the clothes when they endeavoured to clasp it, never speaking any thing.

Neither were there many Words spoken by Satan all this time, only once having put out their Light, they heard a scraping on the Boards, and then a Piping and Drumming on them, which was followed with a Voice, singing *Revenge! Revenge! Sweet is Revenge!* And they being well terrified with it, called upon God; the issue of which was, that suddenly with a mournful Note, there were six times over uttered such expressions as *Alas! Alas! me knock no more! me knock no more!* and now all ceased.

The Man does moreover affirm, that a Seaman (being a Mate of a Ship) coming often to visit him, told him that they wronged his Wife who suspected her to be guilty of Witchcraft; and that the Boy (his Grandchild) was the cause of this trouble; and that if he would let him have the Boy one day, he would warrant him his house should be no more troubled as it had been; to which motion he consented. The Mate came the next day betimes, and the Boy was with him until night; after which his house he saith was not for some time molested with evil Spirits.

Thus far is the Relation concerning the *Dæmon* at *William Morse* his House in *Newbery*. The true Reason of these strange disturbances is as yet not certainly known: some (as has been hinted) did suspect *Morse's* Wife to be guilty of Witchcraft.

One of the Neighbours took Apples which were brought out of that house and put them into the fire; upon which they say, their houses were much disturbed. Another of the Neighbours, caused an Horse-shoe to be nailed before the doors, & as long as it remained so, they could not perswade the suspected person to go into the house; but when the Horse-shoe was gone, she presently visited them. I shall not here inlarge upon the vanity and superstition of those Experiments, reserving that for another place: All that I shall say at present is, that the *Dæmons* whom the blind Gentiles of old worshipped, told their Servants, that such things as these would very much affect them; yea, and that certain Characters, Signs and Charms would render their power ineffectual; and accordingly they would become subject, when their own directions were obeyed. It is sport to the Devils when they see silly Men thus deluded and made fools of by them. Others were apt to think that a Seaman by some suspected to be a Conjurer, set the Devil on work thus to disquiet *Morse's* family. Or it may be some other thing as yet kept hid in the secrets of providence might be the true original of all this Trouble.* * *

1684

VIII. COTTON MATHER (1663–1728)

From *MAGNALIA CHRISTI AMERICANA*

A GENERAL INTRODUCTION

'Ερῶ δὲ τοῦτο, τῆς τῶν ἐντευξαμένων 'ωφελείας ἕνεκα.

Dicam hoc propter utilitatem eorum qui Lecturi sunt hoc opus.
—Theodorit.[1]

§ I. I WRITE the *Wonders* of the CHRISTIAN RELIGION, flying from the Depravations of *Europe*, to the *American Strand:* And, assisted by the Holy Author of that *Religion*, I do, with all Conscience of *Truth*, required therein by Him, who is the *Truth* itself, Report the *Wonderful Displays* of His Infinite Power, Wisdom, Goodness, and Faithfulness, wherewith His Divine Providence hath *Irradiated* an *Indian Wilderness*.

I Relate the *Considerable Matters*, that produced and attended the First Settlement of COLONIES, which have been Renowned for the Degree of REFORMATION, Professed and Attained by *Evangelical Churches*, erected in those *Ends of the Earth:* And a *Field* being thus prepared, I proceed unto a Relation of the *Considerable Matters* which have been acted thereupon.

I first introduce the Actors, that have, in a more exemplary manner served those *Colonies;* and give *Remarkable Occurrences*, in the exemplary LIVES of many *Magistrates*, and of more *Ministers*, who so *Lived*, as to leave unto Posterity, *Examples* worthy of *Everlasting Remembrance*.

I add hereunto, the *Notables* of the only *Protestant University*, that ever *shone* in that Hemisphere of the *New World;* with particular Instances of *Criolians*, in our *Biography*, provoking the *whole World*, with vertuous Objects of Emulation.

I introduce then, the *Actions* of a more Eminent Importance, that have signalized those *Colonies;* Whether the *Establishments*, directed by their *Synods;* with a Rich Variety of *Synodical* and *Ecclesiastical* Determinations; or, the *Disturbances*, with which they have been from all sorts of *Temptations* and *Enemies* Tempestuated; and the *Methods* by which they have still weathered out each *Horrible Tempest*.

[1] "I say this for the benefit of those who are readers of this book." Theodoret was one of the early fathers of the Church, *c.* 393–457.

And into the midst of these *Actions,* I interpose an entire *Book,* wherein there is, with all possible Veracity, a *Collection* made, of *Memorable Occurrences,* and amazing *Judgments* and *Mercies,* befalling many *particular Persons* among the People of *New-England.*

Let my Readers expect all that I have promised them, in this *Bill of Fare;* and it may be they will find themselves entertained with yet many other Passages, above and beyond their Expectation, deserving likewise a room in *History:* In all which, there will be nothing, but the *Author's* too mean way of preparing so great Entertainments, to Reproach the Invitation.

1702

From *THE WONDERS OF THE INVISIBLE WORLD*

ENCHANTMENTS ENCOUNTRED

§*II.* The *New-Englanders* are a People of God settled in those, which were once the *Devils* Territories; and it may easily be supposed that the *Devil* was Exceedingly disturbed, when he perceived such a People here accomplishing the Promise of old made unto our Blessed Jesus, *That He should have the Utmost parts of the Earth for his Possession.* There was not a greater Uproar among the *Ephesians,* when the Gospel was first brought among them, than there was among, *The Powers of the Air* (after whom those *Ephesians* walked) when first the *Silver Trumpets* of the Gospel here made the *Joyful Sound.* The Devil thus Irritated, immediately try'd all sorts of Methods to overturn this poor Plantation: and so much of the Church, as was *Fled into this Wilderness,* immediately found, *The Serpent cast out of his Mouth a Flood for the carrying of it away.* I believe, that never were more *Satanical Devices* used for the Unsetling of any People under the Sun, than what have been Employ'd for the Extirpation of the *Vine* which God has here *Planted, Casting out the Heathen, and preparing a Room before it, and causing it to take deep Root, and fill the Land; so that it sent its Boughs unto the* Attlantic *Sea* Eastward, *and its Branches unto the* Connecticut *River* Westward, *and the Hills were covered with the Shadow thereof.* But, All those Attempts of Hell, have hitherto been Abortive, many an *Ebenezer* has been Erected unto the Praise of God, by his Poor People here; and, *Having obtained Help from God, we continue to this Day.* Wherefore the Devil is now making one Attempt more upon us; an Attempt more Difficult, more Surprizing, more snarl'd with unintelligible Circumstances than any that we have hitherto Encountred; an Attempt so *Critical,* that if we get well through, we shall soon Enjoy *Halcyon* Days with all the *Vultures* of Hell, *Trodden under our Feet.* He has wanted his *Incarnate Legions* to Persecute us, as the People of God have in the other Hemisphere been Persecuted: he has therefore drawn forth his more *Spiritual* ones to make an Attacque upon us. We have been advised by some Credible Christians yet alive, that a Malefactor, accused of *Witchcraft* as well as *Murder,* and Executed in this place more than Forty Years ago, did then give Notice, of, *An Horrible PLOT against the Country by* WITCHCRAFT, *and a Foundation of* WITCHCRAFT *then Laid, which if it were not seasonably Discovered, would probably Blow up, and pull down all the Churches in the Country.* And we have now with Horror seen the *Discovery* of such a *Witchcraft!* An Army of *Devils* is horribly broke in upon the place which is the *Center,* and after a sort, the *First-born* of our *English* Settlements: and the Houses of the Good People there, are fill'd with the doleful Shrieks of their Children and Servants, Tormented by Invisible Hands, with Tortures altogether preternatural. After the Mischiefs there Endeavoured, and since in part Conquered, the terrible Plague, of *Evil Angels,* hath made its Progress into some other places, where other Persons have been in like manner Diabolically handled. These our poor Afflicted Neighbours, quickly after they become *Infected* and *Infested* with these *Dæmons,* arrive to a Capacity of Discerning those which they conceive the *Shapes* of their Troublers; and notwithstanding the Great and Just Suspicion, that the *Dæmons* might Impose the *Shapes* of Innocent Persons in their *Spectral Exhibitions* upon the Sufferers, (which may perhaps prove no small part of the *Witch-Plot* in the issue) yet many of the Persons thus Represented, being Examined, several of them have been Convicted of a very Damnable *Witchcraft:* yea, more than One *Twenty* have *Confessed,* that they have Signed unto a *Book,* which the Devil show'd them, and Engaged in his Hellish Design of *Bewitching,* and *Ruining* our Land. *We* know not, at least *I* know not, how far the *Delusions* of Satan may be Interwoven into some Circumstances of the *Confessions;* but one would think, all the Rules of Understanding Humane Affayrs are at an end, if after so many most Voluntary Harmonious *Confessions,* made by Intelligent Persons of all Ages, in sundry Towns, at several Times, we must not Believe the *main strokes* wherein those *Confessions* all agree: especially when we have a thousand preternatural Things every day before our eyes, wherein the *Confessors* do acknowledge their Concernment, and give Demonstration of their being so Concerned. If the Devils now can strike the minds of men, with any *Poisons* of so fine a Composition and Operation, that Scores of Innocent People shall Unite, in *Confessions* of a Crime, which we see actually committed, it is a thing prodigious, beyond the Wonders of the former Ages, and it threatens no less than a sort of a Dissolution upon the World. Now, by these *Confessions* 'tis Agreed, *That* the Devil has made a dreadful Knot of *Witches* in the Country, and by the help of *Witches* has dreadfully increased that Knot: *That* these *Witches* have driven a Trade of Commissioning their *Confederate Spirits,* to do all sorts of Mischiefs to the Neighbours, whereupon there have ensued such Mischievous consequences upon the Bodies and Estates of the Neighbourhood, as could not otherwise be accounted for: yea, *That* at prodigious *Witch-Meetings,* the Wretches have proceeded so far, as to Concert and Consult the Methods of Rooting out the Christian Religion from this Country, and setting up instead of it, perhaps a more gross *Diabolism,* than ever the World saw before. And yet it will be a thing little short of *Miracle,* if in so *spread* a Business, as this, the Devil should not get in some of his Juggles, to confound the Discovery of all the rest.

1693

THE TRYAL OF BRIDGET BISHOP

ALIAS OLIVER, AT THE COURT OF OYER AND TERMINER, HELD AT SALEM, JUNE 2, 1692

I. She was Indicted for Bewitching of several Persons in the Neighbourhood, the Indictment being drawn up, according to the *Form* in such Cases usual. And pleading, *Not Guilty,* there were brought in several persons, who had long undergone many kinds of Miseries, which were preternaturally inflicted, and generally ascribed unto an *horrible Witchcraft,* There was little occasion to prove the *Witchcraft;* it being Evident and Notorious to all Beholders. Now to fix the *Witchcraft* on the Prisoner at the Bar, the first thing used was, the Testimony of the *Bewitched;* whereof several Testifi'd, That the *Shape* of the Prisoner did oftentimes very grievously pinch them, choak them, Bite them, and Afflict them; urging them to write their Names in a *Book,* which the said Spectre called, *Ours.* One of them did further Testify, that it was the *Shape* of this Prisoner, with another, which one day took her from her Wheel, and carrying her to the River side, threatened there to Drown her, if she did not Sign to the *Book* mentioned: which yet she refused. Others of them did also Testify, that the said *Shape* did in her Threats brag to them that she had been the Death of sundry persons, then by her Named; that she had *Ridden* a Man then likewise named. Another testify'd, the Apparition of *Ghosts* unto the Spectre of *Bishop,* crying out, *You Murdered us!* About the Truth whereof, there was in the Matter of Fact, but too much suspicion.

II. It was testifi'd, That at the Examination of the Prisoner before the Magistrates, the Bewitched were extreamly Tortured. If she did but cast her Eyes on them, they were presently struck down; and this in such a manner as there could be no Collusion in the Business. But upon the Touch of her Hand upon them, when they lay in their Swoons, they would immediately Revive; and not upon the Touch of any ones else. Moreover, upon some Special Actions of her Body, as the shaking of her Head, or the Turning of her Eyes, they presently and painfully fell into the like postures. And many of the like Accidents now fell out, while she was at the Bar. One at the same time testifying, That she said, *She could not be Troubled to see the Afflicted thus Tormented.* * * *

V. To render it further Unquestionable, that the prisoner at the Bar, was the Person truly charged in THIS *Witchcraft,* there were produced many Evidences of OTHER *Witchcrafts,* by her perpetrated. For Instance, *John Cook* testify'd, That about five or six Years ago, one Morning, about Sun-Rise, he was in his Chamber assaulted by the *Shape* of this prisoner: which Look'd on him, grin'd at him, and very much hurt him with a Blow on the side of the Head: and that on the same day, about Noon, the same *Shape* walked in the Room where he was, and an Apple strangely flew out of his Hand, into the Lap of his mother, six or eight Foot from him.

VI. *Samuel Gray* testify'd, That about fourteen Years ago, he wak'd on a Night, & saw the Room where he lay, full of Light; & that he then saw plainly a Woman between the Cradle, and the Bed-side, which look'd upon him. He Rose, and it vanished; tho' he found the Doors all fast. Looking out at the Entry-Door, he saw the same Woman, in the same Garb again; and said, *In Gods Name, what do you come for?* He went to Bed, and had the same Woman again assaulting him. The Child in the Cradle gave a great screech, and the Woman Disappeared. It was long before the Child could be quieted; and tho' it were a very likely thriving Child, yet from this time it pined away, and, after divers Months, dy'd in a sad Condition. He knew not *Bishop,* nor her Name; but when he saw her after this, he knew by her Countenance, and Apparrel, and all Circumstances, that it was the Apparition of this *Bishop,* which had thus troubled him. * * *

IX. *Samuel Shattock* testify'd, That in the Year, 1680, this *Bridget Bishop,* often came to his House upon such frivolous and foolish errands, that they suspected she came indeed with a purpose of mischief. Presently, whereupon, his eldest child, which was of as promising Health & Sense, as any child of its Age, began to droop exceedingly, & the oftner that *Bishop* came to the House, the worse grew the Child. As the Child would be standing at the Door, he would be thrown and bruised against the Stones, by an Invisible Hand, and in like sort knock his Face against the sides of the House, and bruise it after a miserable manner. Afterwards this *Bishop* would bring him things to Dy, whereof he could not Imagine any use; and when she paid him a piece of Money, the Purse and Money were unaccountably conveyed out of a Lock'd box, and never seen more. The Child was immediately, hereupon, taken with terrible fits, whereof his Friends thought he would have dyed: indeed he did almost nothing but cry and Sleep for several Months together: and at length his understanding was utterly taken away. Among other Symptoms of an Inchantment upon him, one was, that there was a Board in the Garden, whereon he would walk; and all the invitations in the world could never fetch him off. About Seventeen or Eighteen years after, there came a Stranger to *Shattocks* House, who seeing the Child, said, *This poor Child is Bewitched; and you have a Neighbour living not far off, who is a Witch.* He added, *Your Neighbour has had a falling out with your Wife; and she said in her Heart, your Wife is a proud Woman, and she would bring down her Pride in this Child.* He then Remembred, that *Bishop* had parted from his Wife in muttering and menacing Terms, a little before the Child was taken Ill. The abovesaid Stranger would needs carry the Bewitched Boy with him, to *Bishop's* House, on pretence of buying a pot of Cyder. The Woman entertained him in furious manner; and flew also upon the Boy, scratching his Face till the Blood came; and saying, *Thou Rogue, what? dost thou bring this Fellow here to plague me?* Now it seems the Man had said before he went, that he would fetch Blood of *her*. Ever after the Boy was follow'd with grievous Fits, which the Doctors themselves generally ascribed unto *Witchcraft;* and wherein he would be thrown still into the *Fire* or the *Water,* if he were not constantly look'd after; and it was verily believed that *Bishop* was the cause of it.

X. *John Louder* testify'd, That upon some little Controversy with *Bishop* about her fowles, going well to Bed, he did awake in the Night by moonlight, and did see clearly the likeness of this woman grievously oppressing him; in which miserable condition she held him unable to help himself, till near Day. He told *Bishop* of this; but she deny'd it, and threatned him, very much. Quickly after this, being at home on a Lords Day, with the doors shutt about him, he saw a Black Pig approach him; at which, he going to kick, it vanished away. Immediately after, sitting down, he saw a Black thing jump in at the Window, & come & stand before him. The Body, was like that of a Monkey, the Feet like a Cocks, but the Face much like a mans. He being so extreemely affrighted, that he could not speak; this Monster spoke to him, and said, *I am a Messenger sent unto you, for I understand that you are in some Trouble of Mind, and if you will be ruled by me, you shalll want for nothing in this World.* Whereupon he endeavoured to clap his hands upon it; but he could feel no substance; and it jumped out of the window again; but immediately came in by the Porch, tho' the Doors were shut, and said, *You had better take my Counsel!* He then struck at it with a stick, but struck only the Ground-sel, and broke the Stick: The Arm with which he struck was presently Disenabled, and it vanished away. He presently went out at the Back-Door, and spyed this *Bishop,* in her Orchard, going toward her House; but he had not power to set one foot forward unto her. Whereupon, returning into the House, he was immediately accosted by the Monster he had seen before; which Goblin was now going to Fly at him; whereat he cry'd out, *The whole Armour of God, be between me and you!* So it sprang back, and flew over the Apple Tree; shaking many Apples off the Tree, in its flying over. At its leap, it flung Dirt with its Feet, against the Stomach of the Man; whereon he was then struck Dumb, and so continued for three *Days* together. Upon the producing of this Testimony, *Bishop* deny'd that she knew this *D*eponent: Yet their two Orchards joined; and they had often had their little Quarrels for some years together. * * *

XIII. One thing that made against the Prisoner was, her being evidently convicted of *Gross Lying,* in the Court, several Times, while she was making her Plea; but besides this, a Jury of Women found a preternatural Teat upon her Body: but upon a second search, within Three or four hours, there was no such thing to be seen. There was also an account of other people whom this woman had afflicted. And there might have been many more, if they had been enquired for. But there was no need of them.

XIV. There was one very strange thing more, with which the Court was newly Entertained. As this Woman was under a Guard, passing by the Great and Spacious Meeting-House of *Salem,* she gave a *L*ook towards the House: And immediately a *Dæmon* Invisibly Entring the Meeting-house, Tore down a part of it; so that tho' there was no person to be seen there, yet the people, at the Noise running in, found a Board, which was strongly fastned with several Nails, transported unto another quarter of the House.

1693

From *POLITICAL FABLES*

MERCURY'S NEGOTIATION

Mercury had been long diverted from his desired employment of carrying messages between earth and heaven, by his agency in Jupiter's palace on the behalf of the sheep, for whom he was willing to do the kindness of a shepherd. It grieved his heart within him to see the beasts of prey breaking in upon the sheep, after their folds had been by the foxes broken down.

2. He laboured with an assiduous diligence to get the sheep accommodated in all their expectations: but after long waiting and seeking to get their folds rebuilt after the old fashion, he found it necessary to comply with such directions as Jupiter, by the advice of Janus, had given for the new shaping of the folds; otherwise he saw the poor sheep had been left without any folds at all; and he could not but confess, the new modelling of the folds would more effectually defend them, in these days of common danger, from the wolves, though some inconveniences in it had caused him always to use all means for the sheep's better satisfaction.

3. When Mercury returned to the sheep, he found them strangely metamorphosed from what they were, and miserably discontented. He found that such things as the sheep would have given three quarters of the fleece on their backs to have purchased, when he first went from them, they were now scarce willing to accept of. He found that there were, (though a few,) which had the skins of sheep on them, and yet, by their claws and growls, were indeed, he knew not what. He was ready to inquire, whether no mad dogs had let fall their slaver upon the honest sheep, since he found here and there one begun to bark like them, and he feared whether these distempers might not hinder their ever being folded more.

4. Orpheus had an harp, which sometimes formerly had reduced the beasts unto a temper little short of reason, and being jealous lest the hard censures bleated out against Mercury (as if he had been the cause of their new forms now brought upon the folds) might produce ill effects, he improved his harp upon this occasion. I don't remember the rhythm of his notes, but the reason was to this purpose: "Pray, all you friends, which of Mercury's administrations is it whereat you are so much offended? Are you angry because he evidently ventured the ruin of his person and family by the circumstances of his first appearance in Saturn's palace for

you? Are you angry because, for divers years together, he did, with an industry indefatigable to a prodigy, solicit for the restoration of your old folds; but with a vexation like that of Sysiphus, who was to roll a great stone up an high hill, from whence he was presently kicked down, so that the labour was all to begin again? Are you angry because he has employed all the interest which God has wonderfully given him with persons of the greatest quality, to increase the number of your powerful friends: addressing the king and queen, the nobility, the convention and the parliaments, until the resettling of your old folds was most favourably voted for you? Is your anger because the signal hand of heaven overruled all these endeavours? Or is your displeasure that he hath cost you a little money to support his negotiations? I am to tell you, that he spent two hundred pounds of his own personal estate in your service—never like to be repaid. He made over all his own American estate, that he might borrow more to serve you. At length he has obtained in boon for your college, and in the bounty, which he lately begged of the royal Juno, (a bounty worth more than fourteen or sixteen hundred pounds sterling,) got more for you than he has yet expended for your agency. Had you not starved your own cause, you had never missed so much as you say you have of your own expectations. Besides, how came you to have your title to all your lands and properties confirmed for ever? Not one of you doth own one foot of land, but what you are now beholden to Mercury for your being undisturbed in it. Are you displeased because you have not a reversion of the judgment against your folds? It was none of his fault; and had such a thing happened, you had then been far more miserable than you are now like to be: for both Plymouth and the eastern provinces had been most certainly put under a commission government; so likewise had Hampshire; and if they should have a Brellin, yet his government would have reached as far south as Salem itself. How finely had your flock been deprived of your trade by this, and squeezed into an atom! Nor could you have proceeded again, as formerly, upon your charter, without being quo-warrantoed. Are you displeased because he did accept of Jupiter's offers? I say he did not accept, and the way is left open for you to recover all the liberties you would have, when you see a time to move in a legal way for it. Yea, he did absolutely reject as many of the offers as he could, and procured them to be altered. The rest he did not refuse, because you had infallibly been left open to a western condition, if he had gone on to protest. Moreover, you yourselves had forbidden him to refuse. Are you troubled because your liberties, whether as Christians or as Englishmen, are fully secured? Are you troubled because you have privileges above any part of the English nation whatsoever, either abroad or at home? Are you troubled that your officers are to be for ever your own; so that, if you please, you may always have your judges as at the first, and the counsellors as at the beginning? Is it your trouble that, by being without your charter, you are put into a condition to do greater and better things for yourselves than the charter did contain, or could have done? Did any man living more zealously oppose those one or two things that you account undesirable, than this faithful Mercury, at whom you fret for those things? Or must very much good be frowardly thrown away, because 'tis not all? If you would have more, don't blame your Mercury that you have so much."—So sang Orpheus, and, for the better harmony of the musick, eleven more of the celestial choristers joined with him in it.

5. The sound of those things caused the sheep to be a little better satisfied; but Mercury was not much concerned whether they were or no, for he looked elsewhere for all the reward of his charitable undertakings; and he knows, he that would do froward sheep a kindness must do it them against their wills; only he wished the sheep would have a care of all snakes in the grass, who did mischief by insinuating, and employed their hisses to sow discord.

(*c.* 1692) 1825

IX. SAMUEL SEWALL
(1652–1730)

From *DIARY*

[THE COURTSHIP OF MADAM WINTHROP]

[May 26, 1720]. Din'd with the Churches at the Dragon. Between 4 and 5. the Govr adjourn'd to Ten a-clock Satterday morning, and presently rose up and went away. NB. Went to Bed after Ten: about 11 or before, my dear Wife was op̄ress'd with a rising of Flegm that obstructed her Breathing. I arose and lighted a Candle, made Scipio give me a Bason of Water (he was asleep by the fire) Call'd Philadelphia, Mr. Cooper, Mayhew. About midnight my dear wife expired to our great astonishment, especially mine. May the Sovereign Lord pardon my Sin, and Sanctify to me this very Extraordinary, awfull Dispensation. Major Epes, Dr. Cotton Mather, Mr. Williams of Hatfield, of Derefield, Mr. Prince, Mr. Whiting of Concord, visit me in a very friendly and Christian manner. Before Sup̄er I sung the 130th Psalm, and a staff out of the 46. Mr. Williams of Hatfield, sympathising with me, said twas what befell the Prophet Ezekiel. * * *

May, 29. God having in his holy Sovereignty put my Wife out of the Fore-Seat, I ap̄rehended I had Cause to be asham̄'d of my Sin, and to loath my self for it; and retired into my Pue. Mr. Williams of Derefield preach'd in the morning from Rom. 5. Christ died for Sin̄ers. Mr. Sewall administered the Lords Sup̄er. I put up a Note to this purpose; Samuel Sewall, depriv'd of his dear Wife by a very sudden and awfull Stroke, desires Prayers that God would sanctify the same to himself, and Children, and family. Writ and sent three; to the South, Old, and Mr. Colman's. Mr. Prince preaches p. m. Mat. 25. At midnight behold a Cry was made. * * *

Tuesday, May, 31. Buried my dear Wife. Bearers, Col. Tailer, Bromfield; Stoddard, Davenport; Dudley, Mr. Danl Oliver. Govr and Lt Govr had Scarvs and Rings. Bro^{r} heard the Funeral was not over, by the Post, came away after 2. and was timely at the Funeral: had a Comfortable day; though threatened with Rain. *Laus Deo.* I went into the Tomb: The good Lord prepare for me a House not made with Hands, eternal in the Heavens, and the Consideration of that will make the Grave a Lightsom place. My Son prays in his Sister's Chamber very pertinently, affectionatly.

June, 1. Brother goes home; gave him a Scarf: prov'd the will of Jno Loring of Hull. Eat a good Dish of Strawberries, part of Sister Stoddard's present. * * *

Septr. 5. Mary Hirst goes to Board with Madam Oliver and her Mother Loyd. Going to Son Sewall's I there meet with Madam Winthrop, told her I was glad to meet her there, had not seen her a great while; gave her Mr. Homes's Sermon. * * *

7^{r} 30. Mr. Colman's Lecture: Daughter Sewall acquaints Madam Winthrop that if she pleas'd to be within at 3 p. m̄. I would wait on her. She answer'd she would be at home.

8^{r} 1. Satterday, I dine at Mr. Stoddard's: from thence I went to Madam Winthrop's just at 3. Spake to her, saying, my loving wife died so soon and suddenly, 'twas hardly convenient for me to think of Marrying again; however I came to this Resolution, that I would not make my Court to any person without first Consulting with her. Had a pleasant discourse about 7 Single persons sitting in the Fore-seat 7^{r} *29th,* viz. Mad^{m} Rebekah Dudley, Catherine Winthrop, Bridget Usher, Deliverance Legg, Rebekah Loyd, Lydia Colman, Elizabeth Bellingham. She propounded one and another for me; but none would do, said Mrs. Loyd was about her Age.

Octob^{r} 3. 2. Waited on Madam Winthrop again; 'twas a little while before she came in. Her daughter Noyes being there alone with me, I said, I hoped my Waiting on her Mother would not be disagreeable to her. She answer'd she should not be against that that might be for her Comfort. I Saluted her, and told her I perceiv'd I must shortly wish her a good Time; (her mother had told me, she was with Child, and within a Moneth or two of her Time). By and by in came Mr. Airs, Chaplain of the Castle, and hang'd up his Hat, which I was a little startled at, it seeming as if he was to lodge there. At last Madam Winthrop came too. After a considerable time, I went up to her and said, if it might not be inconvenient I desired to speak with her. She assented, and spake of going into another Room; but Mr. Airs and Mrs. Noyes presently rose up, and went out, leaving us there alone. Then I usher'd in Discourse from the names in the Fore-seat; at last I pray'd that Katherine [Mrs. Winthrop] might be the person assign'd for me. She instantly took it up in the way of Denyal, as if she had catch'd at an Opportunity to do it, saying she could not do it before she was asked. Said that was her mind unless she should Change it, which she believed she should not; could not leave her Children. I express'd my Sorrow that she should do it so Speedily, pray'd her Consideration, and ask'd her when I should wait on her agen. She setting no time, I mention'd that day Sennight. Gave her Mr. Willard's Fountain open'd with the little print and verses; saying, I hop'd if we did well read that book, we should meet together hereafter, if we did not now. She took the Book, and put it in her Pocket. Took Leave.

8^{r} 5. Midnight, I din'd with the Court; from thence went and visited Cousin Jonathan's wife, Lying in with her little Betty. Gave the Nurse 2^{s}. Although I had ap̄ointed to wait upon her, M^{m} Winthrop, next Monday, yet I went from my Cousin Sewall's thither about 3. p. m̄. The Nurse told me Madam dined abroad at her daughter Noyes's, they were to go out together. I ask'd for the Maid, who was not within. Gave Katee a pen̄y and a Kiss, and came away. Accompanyed my Son and dâter Cooper in their Remove to their New House. * * *

[8^{r} 6th.] A little after 6. p. m. I went to Madam Winthrop's. She was not within. I gave Sarah Chickering the Maid 2^{s}, Juno, who brought in wood, 1^{s}. Afterward the Nurse came in, I gave her 18^{d}, having no other small Bill. After awhile Dr. Noyes came in with his Mother; and quickly after his wife came in: They sat talking, I think, till eight a-clock. I said I fear'd I might be some Interruption to their Business: Dr. Noyes reply'd pleasantly: He fear'd they might be an Interruption to me, and went away. Madam seem'd to harp upon the same string. Must take care of her Children; could not leave that House and Neighbourhood where she had dwelt so long. I told her she might doe her children as much or more good by bestowing what she laid out in Hous-keeping, upon them. Said her Son would be of Age the 7th of August. I said it might be inconvenient for her to dwell with her Daughter-in-law, who must be Mistress of the House. I gave her a piece of Mr. Belcher's Cake and Ginger-Bread wrapped up in a clean sheet of Paper; told her of her Father's kindness to me when Treasurer, and I Constable. My Daughter Judith was gon from me and I was more lonesom—might help to forward one another in our Journey to Canaan. —Mr. Eyre came within the door; I saluted him, ask'd how Mr. Clark did, and he went away. I took leave about 9 aclock. I told [her] I came now to refresh her Memory as to Monday-night; said she had not forgot it. In discourse with her, I ask'd leave to speak with her Sister; I meant to gain Mad^{m} Mico's favour to persuade her Sister. She seem'd surpris'd and displeas'd, and said she was in the same condition! * * *

[10th.] * * * In the Evening I visited Madam Winthrop, who treated me with a great deal of Curtesy; Wine, Marmalade. I gave her a News-Letter about the Thanksgiving; Proposals, for sale of the verses for David Jeffries. She tells me Dr. Increase Mather visited her this day, in Mr. Hutchinson's Coach. * * *

8^{r} 11th I writ a few Lines to Madam Winthrop to this purpose: "Madam, These wait on you with Mr. Mayhew's Sermon, and Account of the state of the Indians on Martha's Vinyard. I thank you for your Unmerited Favours of yesterday; and hope to have the Hap̄iness of Waiting on you to-morrow before Eight a-clock after Noon. I pray God to keep you, and give you a joyfull entrance upon the Two Hundred and twenty ninth year of Christopher Columbus his Discovery; and take Leave, who am, Madam, your humble Servt.

S. S."

Sent this by Deacon Green, who deliver'd it to Sarah Chickering, her Mistress not being at home. * * *

[8^{r}. 12th.] * * * Mrs. Anne Cotton came to door (twas before 8.) said Madam Winthrop was within, directed me into the little Room, where she was full of work behind a Stand; Mrs. Cotton came in and stood. Madam Winthrop pointed to her to set me a Chair. Madam Winthrop's Countenance was much changed from what 'twas on Monday, look'd dark and lowering. At last, the work, (black stuff or Silk) was taken away, I got my Chair in place, had some Converse, but very Cold and indifferent to what 'twas before. Ask'd her to acquit me of Rudeness if I drew off her Glove. Enquiring the reason, I told her twas great odds between handling a dead Goat, and a living Lady. Got it off. I told her I had one Petition to ask of her, that was, that she would take off the Negative she laid on me the third of October; She readily answer'd she could not, and enlarg'd upon it; She told me of it so soon as she could; could not leave her house, children, neighbours, business. I told her she might do som Good to help and sup̄ort me. Mentioning Mrs. Gookin, Nath, the widow Weld was spoken of; said I had visited Mrs. Denison. I told her Yes! Afterward I said, If after a first and second Vagary she would Accept of me returning, Her Victorious Kindness and Good Will would be very Obliging. She thank'd me for my Book, (Mr. Mayhew's Sermon), But said not a word of the Letter. When she insisted on the Negative, I pray'd there might be no more Thunder and Lightening, I should not sleep all night. I gave her Dr. Preston, The Church's Marriage and the Church's Carriage, which cost me 6^{s} at the Sale. The door standing open, Mr. Airs came in, hung up his Hat, and sat down. After awhile, Madam Winthrop moving, he went out. Jno Eyre look'd in, I said How do ye, or, your servant Mr. Eyre: but heard no word from him. Sarah fill'd a Glass of Wine, she drank to me, I to her, She sent Juno home with me with a good Lantern, I gave her 6^{d} and bid her thank her Mistress. In some of our Discourse, I told her I had rather go to the Stone-House adjoining to her, than to come to her against her mind. Told her the reason why I came every other night was lest I should drink too deep draughts of Pleasure. She had talk'd of Canary, her Kisses were to me better than the best Canary. Explain'd the expression Concerning Columbus. * * *

8^{r} 15. I dine on Fish and Oyle at Mr. Stoddard's. Capt. Hill wish'd me Joy of my proceedings i.e. with M—— Winthrop; Sister Cooper ap̄lauded it, spake of Visiting her: I said her Complaisance of her Visit would be obliging to me.

8^{r} 16. L. Day, I upbraided my self that could be so solicitous about Earthly things; and so cold and indifferent as to the Love of Christ, who is altogether Lovely. * * *

[8^{r} 17.] * * * In the Evening I visited Madam Winthrop, who Treated me Courteously, but not in Clean Linen as sometimes. She said, she did not know whether I would come again, or no. I ask'd her how she could so impute inconstancy to me. (I had not visited her since Wednesday night being unable to get over the Indisposition received by the Treatment received that night, and I *must* in it seem'd to sound like a made piece of Formality.) Gave her this day's Gazett. * * *

8^r 18. Visited Madam Mico, who came to me in a splendid Dress. I said, It may be you have heard of my Visiting Madam Winthrop, her Sister. She answered, Her Sister had told her of it. I ask'd her good Will in the Affair. She answer'd, If her Sister were for it, she should not hinder it. I gave her Mr. Homes's Sermon. She gave me a Glass of Canary, entertain'd me with good Discourse, and a Respectfull Remembrance of my first Wife. I took Leave.

8^r 19. Midweek, Visited Madam Winthrop; Sarah told me she was at Mr. Walley's, would not come home till late. I gave her Hañah 3 oranges with her Duty, not knowing whether I should find her or no. Was ready to go home: but said if I knew she was there, I would go thither. Sarah seem'd to speak with pretty good Courage, She would be there. I went and found her there, with Mr. Walley and his wife in the little Room below. At 7 a-clock I mentioned going home; at 8. I put on my Coat, and quickly waited on her home. She found occasion to speak loud to the servant, as if she had a mind to be known. Was Courteous to me; but took occasion to speak pretty earnestly about my keeping a Coach: I said 'twould cost £100. per añum: she said 'twould cost but £40. Spake much against John Winthrop, his false-heartedness. Mr. Eyre came in and sat awhile; I offer'd him Dr. Incr. Mather's Sermons, whereof Mr. Ap̄leton's Ordination Sermon was one; said he had them already. I said I would give him another. Exit. Came away somewhat late. * * *

[8^r 20.] At Council, Col. Townsend spake to me of my Hood: Should get a Wigg. I said twas my chief ornament: I wore it for sake of the Day. Bro^r Odlin, and Sam, Mary, and Jane Hirst dine with us. Promis'd to wait on the Govr about 7. Madam Winthrop not being at Lecture, I went thither first; found her very Serene with her dâter Noyes, Mrs. Dering, and the widow Shipreev sitting at a little Table, she in her arm'd Chair. She drank to me, and I to Mrs. Noyes. After awhile pray'd the favour to speak with her. She took one of the Candles, and went into the best Room, clos'd the shutters, sat down upon the Couch. She told me Madam Usher had been there, and said the Coach must be set on Wheels, and not by Rusting. She spake somthing of my needing a Wigg. Ask'd me what her Sister said to me. I told her, She said, If her Sister were for it, She would not hinder it. But I told her, she did say she would be glad to have me for her Brother. Said, I shall keep you in the Cold, and asked her if she would be within to morrow night, for we had had but a running Feat. She said she could not tell whether she should, or no. I took Leave. As were drinking at the Governour's, he said: In England the Ladies minded little more than that they might have Money, and Coaches to ride in. I said, And New-England brooks its Name. At which Mr. Dudley smiled. Govr said they were not quite so bad here.

8^{r} 21. Friday, My Son, the Minister, came to me p. m̄ by ap̄ointment and we pray one for another in the Old Chamber; more especially respecting my Courtship. About 6. a-clock I go to Madam Winthrop's; Sarah told me her Mistress was gon out, but did not tell me whither she went. She presently order'd me a Fire; so I went in, having Dr. Sibb's Bowels with me to read. I read the two first Sermons, still no body came in: at last about 9. a-clock Mr. Jno Eyre came in; I took the op̄ortunity to say to him as I had done to Mrs. Noyes before, that I hoped my Visiting his Mother would not be disagreeable to him; He answered me with much Respect. When twas after 9. a-clock He of himself said he would go and call her, she was but at one of his Brothers: A while after I heard Madam Winthrop's voice, enquiring somthing about John. After a good while and Clap̄ing the Garden door twice or thrice, she came in. I mention'd somthing of the lateness; she banter'd me, and said I was later. She receiv'd me Courteously. I ask'd when our proceedings should be made publick: She said They were like to be no more publick than they were already. Offer'd me no Wine that I remember. I rose up at 11 a-clock to come away, saying I would put on my Coat. She offer'd not to help me. I pray'd her that Juno might light me home, she open'd the Shutter, and said twas pretty light abroad; Juno was weary and gon to bed. So I came hôm by Star-light as well as I could. At my first coming in, I gave Sarah five Shillings. I writ Mr. Eyre his Name in his book with the date Octob^{r} 21. 1720. It cost me 8^{s}. Jehovah jireh! Madam told me she had visited M. Mico, Wendell, and Wm Clark of the South [Church].

Octob^{r} 22. Dâter Cooper visited me before my going out of Town, staid till about Sun set. I brought her going near as far as the Orange Tree. Coming back, near Leg's Corner, Little David Jeffries saw me, and looking upon me very lovingly, ask'd me if I was going to see his Grandmother? I said, Not to-night. Gave him a peny, and bid him present my Service to his Grandmother.

Octob^{r} 24. I went in the Hackny Coach through the Com̄on, stop'd at Madam Winthrop's (had told her I would take my departure from thence). Sarah came to the door with Katee in her Arms: but I did not think to take notice of the Child. Call'd her Mistress. I told her, being encourag'd by David Jeffries loving eyes, and sweet Words, I was come to enquire whether she could find in her heart to leave that House and Neighbourhood, and go and dwell with me at the South-end; I think she said softly, Not yet. I told her It did not ly in my Lands to keep a Coach. If I should, I should be in danger to be brought to keep company with her Neighbour Brooker, (he was a little before sent to prison for Debt). Told her I had an Antipathy against those who would pretend to give themselves; but nothing of their Estate. I would a proportion of my Estate with my self. And I sup̄os'd she would do so. As to a Perriwig, My best and greatest Friend, I could not possibly have a greater, began to find me with Hair before I was born, and had continued to do so ever since; and I could not find in my heart to go to another. She com̄ended the book I gave her, Dr. Preston, the Church Marriage; quoted him saying 'twas inconvenient keeping out of a Fashion com̄only used. I said the Time and Tide did circumscribe my Visit. She gave me a Dram of Black-Cherry Brandy, and gave me a lump of the Sugar that was in it. She wish'd me a good Journy. I pray'd God to keep her, and came away. Had a very pleasant Journy to Salem.

8^{r} 25. Sent a Letter of it to my Son by Wakefield, who delivered it not till Wednesday; so he visited her not till Friday p. m̄. and then presented my Service to her. * * *

31. 2. She proves her Husband's Will. At night I visited Madam Winthrop about 6. p. m̄. They told me she was gon to Madam Mico's. I went thither and found she was gon; so return'd to her house, read the Epistles to the Galatians, Ephesians in Mr. Eyre's Latin Bible. After the Clock struck 8. I began to read the 103. Psalm. Mr. Wendell came in from his Warehouse. Ask'd me if I were alone? Spake very kindly to me, offer'd me to call Madam Winthrop. I told him, She would be angry, had been at Mrs. Mico's; he help'd me on with my Coat and I came home: left the Gazett in the Bible, which told Sarah of, bid her present my Service to Mrs. Winthrop, and tell her I had been to wait on her if she had been at home.

Novr 1. I was so taken up that I could not go if I would.

Novr 2. Midweek, went again, and found Mrs. Alden there, who quickly went out. Gave her about ½ pound of Sugar Almonds, cost 3^{s} per £. Carried them on Monday. She seem'd pleas'd with them, ask'd what they cost. Spake of giving her a Hundred pounds per an̄um if I dy'd before her. Ask'd her what sum she would give me, if she should dy first? Said I would give her time to Consider of it. She said she heard as if I had given all to my Children by Deeds of Gift. I told her 'twas a mistake, Point-Judith was mine &c. That in England, I own'd, my Father's desire was that it should go to my eldest Son; 'twas 20£ per an̄um; she thought 'twas forty. I think when I seem'd to excuse pressing this, she seem'd to think twas best to speak of it; a long winter was coming on. Gave me a Glass or two of Canary.

Novr 4th. Friday, Went again about 7. a-clock; found there Mr. John Walley and his wife: sat discoursing pleasantly. I shew'd them Isaac Moses's [an Indian] Writing. Madam W. serv'd Comfeits to us. After a-while a Table was spread, and Sup̄er was set. I urg'd Mr. Walley to Crave a Blessing; but he put it upon me. About 9. they went away. I ask'd Madam what fashioned Neck-lace I should present her with, She said, None at all. I ask'd her Whereabout we left off last time; mention'd what I had offer'd to give her; Ask'd her what she would give me; She said she could not Change her Condition: She had said so from the beginning; could not be so far from her Children, the Lecture. Quoted the Apostle Paul affirming that a single Life was better than a Married. I answer'd That was for the present Distress. Said she had not pleasure in things of that nature as formerly: I said, you are the fitter to make me a Wife. If she held in that mind, I must go home and bewail my Rashness in making more haste than good Speed. However, considering the Sup̄er, I desired her to be within next Monday night, if we liv'd so long. Assented. She charg'd me with saying, that she must put away Juno, if she came to me: I utterly deny'd it, it never came in my heart; yet she insisted upon it; saying it came in upon Discourse about the Indian woman that obtained her Freedom this Court. About 10. I said I would not disturb the good orders of her House, and came away. She not seeming pleas'd with my Coming away. Spake to her about David Jeffries, had not seen him.

Monday, Novr 7th. My Son pray'd in the Old Chamber. Our time had been taken up by Son and Daughter Cooper's Visit; so that I only read the 130th and 143. Psalm. Twas on the Account of my Courtship. I went to Mad. Winthrop; found her rocking her little Katee in the Cradle. I excus'd my Coming so late (near Eight). She set me an arm'd Chair and Cusheon; and so the Cradle was between her arm'd Chair and mine. Gave her the remnant of my Almonds; She did not eat of them as before; but laid them away; I said I came to enquire whether she had alter'd her mind since Friday, or remained of the same mind still. She said, Thereabouts. I told her I loved her, and was so fond as to think that she loved me: She said had a great respect for me. I told her, I had made her an offer, without asking any advice; she had so many to advise with, that twas a hindrance. The Fire was come to one short Brand besides the Block, which Brand was set up in end; at last it fell to pieces, and no Recruit was made: She gave me a Glass of Wine. I think I repeated again that I would go home and bewail my Rashness in making more haste than good Speed. I would endeavour to contain myself, and not go on to sollicit her to do that which she could not Consent to. Took leave of her. As came down the steps she bid me have a Care. Treated me Courteously. Told her she had enter'd the 4th year of her Widowhood. I had given her the News-Letter before: I did not bid her draw off her glove as sometime I had done. Her Dress was not so clean as somtime it had been. Jehovah jireh!

Midweek, 9^{r} 9th. Dine at Bro^{r} Stoddard's: were so kind as to enquire of me if they should invite M'm Winthrop; I answer'd No. Thank'd my Sister Stoddard for her Courtesie; sat down at the Table Simeon Stoddard esqr, Mad. Stoddard, Samuel Sewall, Mr. Colman, M^{m} Colman, Mr. Cooper, Mrs. Cooper, Mrs. Hañah Cooper, Mr. Samuel Sewall of Brooklin, Mrs. Sewall, Mr. Joseph Sewall, Mrs. Lydia Walley, Mr. William Stoddard. Had a noble Treat. At night our Meeting was at the Widow Belknap's. Gave each one of the Meeting One of Mr. Homes's Sermons, 12 in all; She sent her servant home with me with a Lantern. Madam Winthrop's Shutters were open as I pass'd by. * * *

Novr 11th. Went not to M^{m} Winthrop's. This is the 2^{d} Withdraw.

(1720) 1878–82

X. MARY ROWLANDSON
(*c.* 1636–1678)

NARRATIVE OF CAPTIVITY

On the tenth of *February* 1675, Came the Indians with great numbers upon *Lancaster:* Their first coming was about Sun-rising; hearing the noise of some Guns, we looked out; several Houses were burning, and the Smoke ascending to Heaven. There were five persons taken in one house, the Father, and the Mother and a sucking Child they knockt on the head; the other two they took and carried away alive. Their were two others, who being out of their Garison upon some occasion were set upon; one was knockt on the head, the other escaped: Another their was who running away was shot and wounded, and fell down; he begged of them his life, promising them Money (as they told me) but they would not hearken to him but knockt him in head, and stript him naked, and split open his Bowels. Another seeing many of the *Indians* about his Barn, ventured and went out, but was quickly shot down. There were three others belonging to the same Garison who were killed; the *Indians* getting up upon the roof of the Barn, had advantage to shoot down upon them over their Fortification. Thus these murtherous wretches went on, burning, and destroying before them,

At length they came and beset our own house, and quickly it was the dolefullest day that ever mine eyes saw. The House stood upon the edg of a hill; some of the *Indians* got behind the hill, others into the Barn, and others behind any thing that could shelter them; from all which places they shot against the House, so that the Bullets seemed to fly like hail; and quickly they wounded one man among us, then another, and then a third, About two hours (according to my observation, in that amazing time) they had been about the house before they prevailed to fire it (which they did with Flax and Hemp, which they brought out of the Barn, and there being no defence about the House, only two Flankers at two opposite corners and one of them not finished) they fired it once and one ventured out and quenched it, but they quickly fired it again, and that took. Now is the dreadful hour come, that I have often heard of (in time of War, as it was the case of others) but now mine eyes see it. Some in our house were fighting for their lives, others wallowing in their blood, the House on fire over our heads, and the bloody Heathen ready to knock us on the head, if we stirred out. Now might we hear Mothers & Children crying out for themselves, and one another, *Lord, what shall we do?* Then I took my Children (and one of my sisters, hers) to go forth and leave the house: but as soon as we came to the dore and appeared, the *Indians* shot so thick that the bulletts rattled against the House, as if one had taken an handfull of stones and threw them, so that we were fain to give back. We had six stout Dogs belonging to our Garrison, but none of them would stir, though another time, if any *Indian* had come to the door, they were ready to fly upon him and tear him down. The Lord hereby would make us the more to acknowledge his hand, and to see that our help is alwayes in him. But out we must go, the fire increasing, and coming along behind us, roaring, and the *Indians* gaping before us with their Guns, Spears and Hatchets to devour us. No sooner were we out of the House, but my Brother in Law (being before wounded, in defending the house, in or near the throat) fell down dead, wherat the *Indians* scornfully shouted, and hallowed, and were presently upon him, stripping off his cloaths, the bulletts flying thick, one went through my side, and the same (as would seem) through the bowels and hand of my dear Child in my arms. One of my elder Sisters Children, named *William,* had then his Leg broken, which the *Indians* perceiving, they knockt him on head. Thus were we butchered by those merciless Heathen, standing amazed, with the blood running down to our heels. My eldest Sister being yet in the House, and seeing those wofull sights, the Infidels haling Mothers one way, and Children another, and some wallowing in their blood: and her elder Son telling her that her Son *William* was dead, and my self was wounded, she said, And, *Lord let me dy with them;* which was no sooner said, but she was struck with a Bullet, and fell down dead over the threshold. I hope she is reaping the fruit of her good labours, being faithfull to the service of God in her place. In her younger years she lay under much trouble upon spiritual accounts, till it pleased God to make that precious Scripture take hold of her heart, 2 *Cor.* 12. 9. *And he said unto me my Grace is sufficient for thee.* More than twenty years after I have heard her tell how sweet and comfortable that place was to her, But to return: The *Indians* laid hold of us, pulling me on way, and the Children another, and said, *Come go along with us;* I told them they would kill me: they answered, *If I were willing to go along with them, they would not hurt me.*

Oh the dolefull sight that now was to behold at this House! *Come, behold the works of the Lord, what dissolations he has made in the Earth.* Of thirty seven persons who were in this one House, none escaped either present death, or a bitter captivity, save only one, who might say as he. *Job* 1. 15. *And I only am escaped alone to tell the News.* There were twelve killed, some shot, some stab'd with their Spears, some knock'd down with their Hatchets. When we are in prosperity, Oh the little that we think of such dreadfull sights, and to see our dear Friends, and Relations ly bleeding out their heart-blood upon the ground. There was one who was chopt into the head with a Hatchet, and stript naked, and yet was crawling up and down. It is a solemn sight to see so many Christians lying in their blood, some here, and some there, like a company of Sheep torn by wolves. All of them stript naked by a company of hell-hounds, roaring, singing, ranting and insulting, as if they would have torn our very hearts out; yet the Lord by his Almighty power preserved a number of us from death, for there were twenty-four of us taken alive and carried Captive.

I had often before this said, that if the Indians should come, I should chuse rather to be killed by them then taken alive but when it came to the tryal my mind changed; their glittering weapons so daunted my spirit, that I chose rather to go along with those (as I may say) ravenous Bears, then that moment to end my dayes; and that I may the better declare what happened to me during that grievous Captivity I shall particularly speak of the severall Removes we had up and down the Wilderness.

The first Remove.

Now away we must go with those Barbarous Creatures, with our bodies wounded and bleeding, and our hearts no less than our bodies. About a mile we went that night, up upon a hill within sight of the Town where they intended to lodge, There was hard by a vacant house (deserted by the English before, for fear of the *Indians*) I asked them whither I might not lodge in the house that night to which they answered, what will you you love *English men* still? this was the dolefullest night that ever my eyes saw. Oh the roaring, and singing and danceing, and yelling of those black creatures in the night, which made the peace a lively resemblance of hell. And as miserable was the wast that was there made, of Horses, Cattle, Sheep, Swine, Calves, Lambs, Roasting Pigs, and Fowl (which they had plundered in the Town) some roasting, some lying and burning, and some boyling to feed our merciless Enemies; who were joyful enough though we were disconsolate. To add to the dolefulness of the former day, and the dismalness of the present night: my thoughts ran up on my losses and sad bereaved condicion. All was gone, my Husband gone (at least separated from me, he being in the Bay; and to add to my grief, the *Indians* told me they would kill him as he came homeward) my children gone, my Relations and Friends gone, our House and home and all our comforts within door, and without, all was gone, (except my life) and I knew not but the next moment that might go too. There remained nothing to me but one poor wounded Babe, and it seemed at present worse than death that it was in such a pitiful condition, bespeaking, Compassion, and I had no refreshing for it, nor suitable things to revive it, Little do many think what is the savageness and bruitishness of this barbarous Enemy: even those that seem to profess more than others among them, when the *English* have fallen into their hands.

Those seven that were killed at *Lancaster* the summer before upon a Sabbath day, and the one that was afterward killed upon a week day, were slain and mangled in a barbarous manner, by one-ey'd *John,* and *Marlborough's* Praying *Indians,* which Capt. *Mosely* brought to *Boston,* as the *Indians* told me.

The second Remove.

But now, the next morning, I must turn my back upon the Town, and travel with them into the vast and desolate Wilderness, I knew not whither. It is not my tongue, or pen can express the sorrows of my heart, and bitterness of my spirit, that I had at this departure: but God was with me, in a wonderfull manner, carrying me along, and bearing up my spirit, that it did not quite fail.

One of the Indians carried my poor wounded Babe upon a horse, it went moaning all along, I shall dy, I shall dy. I went on foot after it, with sorrow that cannot be exprest. At length I took it off the horse, and carried it in my armes till my strength failed, and I fell down with it: Then they set me upon a horse with my wounded Child in my lap, and there being no furnituure upon the horse back; as we were going down a steep hill, we both fell over the horses head, at which they like inhumane creatures laught, and rejoyced to see it, though I thought we should there have ended our dayes, as overcome with so many difficulties. But the Lord renewed my strength still, and carried me along, that I might see more of his Power; yea, so much that I could never have thought of, had I not experienced it.

After this it quickly began to snow, and when night came on, they stopt: and now down I must sit in the snow, by a little fire, and a few boughs behind me, with my sick Child in my lap; and calling much for water, being now (through the wound) fallen into a violent Fever. My own wound also growing so stiff, that I could scarce sit down or rise up; yet so it must be, that I must sit all this cold winter night upon the cold snowy ground, with my sick Child in my armes, looking that every hour would be the last of its life; and having no Christian friend near me, either to comfort or help me. *Oh, I may see the wonderfull power of God, that my Spirit did not utterly sink under my affliction: still the Lord upheld me with his gracious and mercifull Spirit, and we were both alive to see the light of the next morning.* * * *

The eight Remove.

On the morrow morning we must go over the River, i.e. *Connecticot,* to meet with King *Philip,* two *Cannoos* full, they had carried over, the next Turn i myself was to go; but as my foot was upon the *Cannoo* to step in, there was a sudden outcry among them, and j must step back; and instead of going over the River j must go four or five miles up the River farther Northward. Some of the *jndians* ran one way, and some another. The cause of this rout was, as j thought, their espying some *English Scouts,* who were thereabout. *In* this travel up the River; about noon the Company made a stop, and sate down; some to eat, and others to rest them. As I sate amongst them, musing of things past, my Son *Joseph* unexpectedly came to me: we asked of each others welfare, bemoaning our dolefull condition, and the change that had come upon uss. We had Husbands and Father, and Children, and Sisters, and Friends, and Relations, and House, and Home, and many Comforts of this Life: but now we may say, as Job, *Naked came I out of my Mothers Womb, and naked shall I return: The Lord gave, and the Lord hath taken away, Blessed be the Name of the Lord.* I asked him whither he would read; he told me, he earnestly disired it, J gave him my Bible, and he lighted upon that comfortable Scripture, *Psal.* 18. 17, 18. *I shall not dy but live, and declare the works of the Lord: the Lord hath chastened me sore, yet he hath not given me over to death.* Look here, *Mother* (sayes he) did you read this? And here I may take occasion to mention one principall ground of my setting forth these Lines: even as the Psalmist sayes, *To declare the Works of the Lord,* and his wonderfull Power in carrying us along, preserving us in the *Wilderness*, while under the Enemies band, and returning of us in safety again. And His goodness in bringing to my hand so many comfortable and suitable Scriptures in my distress. But to Return, We travelled on till night; and in the morning, we must go over the River to *Philip's* Crew. When I was in the Cannoo, I could not but be amazed at the numerous crew of Pagans that were on the Bank on the other side. When J came ashore, they gathered all about me, I sitting alone in the midst: I observed they asked one another questions, and laughed, and rejoyced over their Gains and Victories. Then my heart began to fail: and I fell a weeping which was the first time to my remembrance, that J wept before them. Although J had met with so much Affliction, and my heart was many times ready to break, yet could J not shed one tear in their sight: but rather had been all this while in a maze, and like one astonished: but now J may say as, *Psal.* 137. 1. By *the Rivers of* Babylon, *there we sate down: yea, we wept when we remembred Zion.* There one of them asked me, why J wept, J could hardly tell what to say: yet J answered, they would kill me: No, said he, none will hurt you. Then came one of them and gave me two spoon-fulls of Meal to comfort me, and another gave me half a pint of Pease; which was more worth than many Bushels at another time. Then J went to see King *Philip*, he bade me come in and sit down, and asked me whether J would smoke it (a usual Complement now adayes amongst Saints and Sinners) but this no way suited me. For though I had formerly used Tobacco, yet I had left it ever since I was first taken. *It seems to be a Bait, the Devil layes to make men loose their precious time:* J remember with shame, how formerly, when J had taken two or three pipes, J was presently ready for another, such a bewitching thing it is: But J thank God, he has now given me power over it: surely there are many who may be better imployed than to ly sucking a stinking Tobacco-pipe.

Now the *Indians* gather their Forces to go against *North-Hampton:* over-night one went about yelling and hooting to give notice of the design. Whereupon they fell to boyling of Ground-nuts, and parching of Corn (as many as had it) for their Provision: and in the morning away they went. *During my abode in this place,* Philip *spake to me to make a shirt for his boy, which I did, for which he gave me a shilling: I offered the money to my master, but he bade me keep it: and with it J bought a piece of Horse flesh.* Afterwards he asked me to make a Cap for his boy, for which he invited me to Dinner. J went, and he gave me a Pancake, about as big as two fingers; it was made of parched wheat, beaten, and fryed in Bears grease, but I thought I never tasted pleasanter meat in my life. There was a *Squaw* who spake to me to make a shirt for her *Sannup*, for which she gave me a piece of Bear. Another asked me to knit a pair of Stockins, for which she gave me a quart of Pease: I boyled my Pease and Bear together, and invited my master and mistress to dinner, but the proud Gossip, because J served them both in one Dish, would eat nothing, except one bit that he gave her upon the point of his knife. Hearing that my son was come to this place, J went to see him, and found him lying flat upon the ground: I asked him how he could sleep so & he answered me, *That he was not asleep, but at Prayer;* and lay so that they might not observe what he was doing. J pray God he may remember these things now he is returned in safety. At this Place (the Sun now getting higher) what with the beams and heat of the Sun, and the smoak of the *Wigwams,* J thought I should have been blind, I could scarce discern one *Wigwam* from another. There was here one *Mary Thurston* of *Medfield,* who seeing how it was with me, lent me a Hat to wear: but as soon as I was gone, the *Squaw* who owned that *Mary Thurston* came running after me, and got it away again. *Here was the* Squaw *that gave me one spoonfull of Meal.* I put it in my Pocket to keep it safe: yet notwithstanding some body stole it, but put five *Indian* Corns in the room of it: which Corns were the greatest Provisions I had in my travel for one day.

The *Indians* returning from *North-Hampton,* brought with them some Horses, and Sheep, and other things which they had taken: J desired them, that they would carry me to *Albany,* upon one of those Horses, and sell me for Powder: for so they had sometimes discoursed. J was utterly hopeless of getting home on foot, the way that I came. J could hardly bear to think of the many weary steps I had taken, to come to this place. * * *

I can remember the time, when I used to sleep quietly without workings in my thoughts, whole nights together, but now it is otherwayes with me. When all are fast about me, and no eye open, but his who ever waketh, my thoughts are upon things past, upon the awfull dispensation of the Lord towards us; upon his wonderfull power and might, in carrying of us through so many difficulties, in returning us in safety, and suffering none to hurt us. I remember in the night season, how the other day I was in the midst of thousands of enemies, & nothing but death before me: It [was] then hard work to perswade my self, that ever I should be satisfied with bread again. But now we are fed with the finest of the Wheat, and, as I may say, *With honey out of the rock:* In stead of the Husk, we have the fatted Calf: The thoughts of these things in the particulars of them, and of the love and goodness of God toward us, make it true of me, what *David* said of himself, *Psal.* 6. 5. *I watered my Couch with my tears.* Oh! the wonderfull power of God that mine eyes have seen, affording matter enough for my thoughts to run in, that when others are sleeping mine eyes are weeping.

J have seen the extrem vanity of this World: One hour I have been in health, and wealth, wanting nothing: But the next hour in sickness and wounds, and death, having nothing but sorrow and affliction.

Before I knew what affliction means, I was ready sometimes to wish for it. When I lived in prosperity; having the comforts of the World about me, my relations by me, my Heart chearfull: and taking little care for any thing; and yet seeing many, whom I preferred before my self, under many tryals and afflictions, in sickness, weakness, poverty, losses, crosses, and cares of the World, I should be sometimes jealous least I should have my portion in this life, and that Scripture would come to my mind, *Heb.* 12. 6. *For whom the Lord loveth he chasteneth, and scourgeth every Son whom he receivith.* But now I see the Lord had his time to scourge and chasten me. The portion of some is to have their afflictions by drops, now one drop and then another; but the dregs of the Cup, the Wine of astonishment: like a sweeping rain that leaveth no food, did the Lord prepare to be my portion. Affliction I wanted, and affliction I had, full measure (I thought) pressed down and running over; yet I see, when God calls a Persen to anything, and through never so many difficulties, yet he is fully able to carry them through and make them see, and say they have been gainers thereby. And I hope I can say in some measure, As *David* did, *It is good for me That I have been afflicted.* The Lord hath shewed me the vanity of these outward things. That they are the *Vanity of vanities, and vexation of spirit;* that they are but a shadow, a blast, a bubble, and things of no continuance. That we must rely on God himself, and our whole dependance must be upon him. If trouble from smallar matters begin to arise in me, I have found something at hand to check my self with, and say, why am I troubled? It was but the other day that if I had had the world, I would have given it for my freedom, or to have been a Servant to a Christian. I have learned to look beyond present and smaller troubles, and to be quieted under them, as *Moses* said, *Exod.* 14. 13. *Stand still and see the salvation of the Lord.*

*c.*1682

XI. SARAH KEMBLE KNIGHT
(1666–1727)

From *THE PRIVATE JOURNAL ON A JOURNEY FROM BOSTON TO NEW-YORK*

[SETTING OUT]

Monday, Octb'r. *ye* second, 1704.

About three o'clock afternoon, I begun my Journey from Boston to New-Haven; being about two Hundred Mile. My Kinsman, Capt. Robert Luist, waited on me as farr as Dedham, where I was to meet *ye* Western post. * * *

Wedensday, Octobr 4th.

About four in the morning, we set out for Kingston (for so was the Town called) with a french Doctor in our company. Hee and *ye* Post put on very furiously, so that I could not keep up with them, only as now and then they'd stop till they see mee. This Rode was poorly furnished w*th* accommodations for Travellers, so that we were forced to ride 22 miles by the post's account, but neerer thirty by mine, before wee could bait so much as our Horses, w*ch* I exceedingly complained of. But the post encourag'd mee, by saying wee should be well accommodated anon at mr. Devills, a few miles further. But I questioned whether we ought to go to the Devil to be helpt out of affliction. However, like the rest of Deluded souls that post to y*e* Infernal denn, Wee made all posible speed to this Devil's Habitation; where alliting, in full assurance of good accommodation, wee were going in. But meeting his two daughters, as I suposed twins, they so neerly resembled each other, both in features and habit, and look't as old as the Divel himselfe, and quite as Ugly, We desired entertainm't, but could hardly get a word out of 'um, till with our Importunity, telling them our necesity, &c. they call'd the old Sophister, who was as sparing of his words as his daughters had bin, and no, or none, was the reply's hee made us to our demands. Hee differed only in this from the old fellow in to'ther Country: hee let us depart. However, I thought it proper to warn poor Travailers to endeavor to Avoid falling into circumstances like ours, w*ch* at our next Stage I sat down and did as followeth:

May all that dread the cruel feind of night
Keep on, and not at this curs't Mansion light.
'Tis Hell; 'tis Hell! and Devills here do dwell:
Here dwells the Devill—surely this's Hell.
Nothing but Wants: a drop to cool yo'r Tongue
Cant be procur'd these cruel Feinds among.
Plenty of horrid Grins and looks sevear,
Hunger and thirst, But pitty's bannish'd here—
The Right hand keep, if Hell on Earth you fear!

Thus leaving this habitation of cruelty, we went forward; and arriving at an Ordinary about two mile further, found tollerable accommodation. But our Hostes, being a pretty full mouth'd old creature, entertain'd our fellow travailer, y*e* french Doctor w*th* Inumirable complaints of her bodily infirmities; and whispered to him so lou'd, that all y*e* House had as full a hearing as hee: which was very divirting to y*e* company, (of which there was a great many,) as one might see by their sneering. But poor weary I slipt out to enter my mind in my Jornal, and left my Great Landly with her Talkative Guests to themselves.

From hence we proceeded (about ten forenoon) through the Narragansett country, pretty Leisurely; and about one afternoon come to Paukataug River, w*ch* was about two hundred paces over, and now very high, and no way over to to'ther side but this. I darid not venture to Ride thro, my courage at best in such cases but small, And now at the Lowest Ebb, by reason of my weary, very weary, hungry and uneasy Circumstances. So takeing leave of my company, tho, w*th* no little Reluctance, that I could not proceed w*th* them on my Jorny, Stop at a little cottage Just by the River, to wait the Waters falling, w*ch* the old man that lived there said would be in a little time, and he would conduct me safe over. This little Hutt was one of the wretchedest I ever saw a habitation for human creatures. It was suported with shores enclosed with Clapbords, laid on Lengthways, and so much asunder, that the Light come throu' every where; the doore tyed on w*th* a cord in *ye* place of hinges; The floor the bear earth; no windows but such as the thin covering afforded, nor any furniture but a Bedd w*th* a glass Bottle hanging as *ye* head on't; an earthan cupp, a small pewter Bason, A Bord w*th* sticks to stand on, instead of a table, and a block or two in *ye* corner instead of chairs. The family were the old man, his wife and two Children; all and every part being the picture of poverty. Notwithstanding both the Hutt and its Inhabitance were very clean and tydee: to the crossing the Old Proverb, that bare walls make giddy howswifes.

I Blest myselfe that I was not one of this misserable crew; and the Impressions their wretchedness formed in me caused mee on the very Spott to say:

Tho' Ill at ease, A stranger and alone,
All my fatigu's shall not extort a grone.
These Indigents have hunger with their ease;
Their best is wors behalfe then my disease.
Their Misirable hutt w*ch* Heat and Cold
Alternately without Repulse do hold;
Their Lodgings thyn and hard, their Indian fare,
The mean Apparel which the wretches wear,
And their ten thousand ills w*ch* can't be told,
Makes nature er'e 'tis midle age'd look old.
When I reflect, my late fatigues do seem
Only a notion or forgotten Dreem.

I had scarce done thinking, when an Indian-like Animal come to the door, on a creature very much like himselfe, in mien and feature, as well as Ragged cloathing; and having 'litt, makes an Awkerd Scratch w*th* his Indian shoo, and a Nodd, sitts on *ye* block, fumbles out his black Junk, dipps it in *ye* Ashes, and presents it piping hott to his muscheeto's, and fell to sucking like a calf, without speaking, for near a quarter of an hower. At length the old man said how do's Sarah do? who I understood was the wretches wife, and Daughter to *ye* old man: he Replyed—as well as can be expected, &c. So I remembred the old say, and suposed I knew Sarah's case. Butt hee being, as I understood, going over the River, as ugly as hee was, I was glad to ask him to show me *ye* way to Saxtons, at Stoningtown; w*ch* he promising, I ventur'd over w*th* the old mans assistance; who having rewarded to content, with my Tattertailed guide, I Ridd on very slowly thro' Stoningtown, where the Rode was very Stony and uneven. I asked the fellow, as we went, divers questions of the place and way, &c. I being arrived at my country Saxtons, at Stonington, was very well accommodated both as to victuals and Lodging, the only Good of both I had found since my setting out. Here I heard there was an old man and his Daughter to come that way, bound to N. London; and being now destitute of a Guide, gladly waited for them, being in so good a harbour. * * *

[THE PEOPLE OF CONNECTICUT]

[Saturday, Oct. 7th.]

* * * About two a clock afternoon we arrived at New Haven, where I was received with all Posible Respects and civility. Here I discharged Mr. Wheeler with a reward to his satisfac-

tion, and took some time to rest after so long and toilsome a Journey; and Inform'd myselfe of the manners and customs of the place, and at the same time employed myselfe in the afair I went there upon.

They are Govern'd by the same Laws as wee in Boston, (or little differing,) thr'out this whole Colony of Connecticot, And much the same way of Church Government, and many of them good, Sociable people, and I hope Religious too: but a little too much Independent in their principalls, and, as I have been told, were formerly in their Zeal very Riggid in their Administrations towards such as their Lawes made Offenders, even to a harmless Kiss or Innocent merriment among Young people. Whipping being a frequent and counted an easy Punishment, about w*ch* as other Crimes, the Judges were absolute in their Sentances. They told mee a pleasant story about a pair of Justices in those parts, w*ch* I may not omit the relation of.

A negro Slave belonging to a man in y*e* Town, stole a hogs head from his master, and gave or sold it to an Indian, native of the place. The Indian sold it in the neighbourhood, and so the theft was found out. Thereupon the Heathen was Seized, and carried to the Justices House to be Examined. But his worship (it seems) was gone into the feild, with a Brother in office, to gather in his Pompions. Whither the malefactor is hurried, And Complaint made, and satisfaction in the name of Justice demanded. Their Worships cann't proceed in form without a Bench: whereupon they Order one to be Imediately erected, which, for want of fitter materials, they made with pompions—which being finished, down setts their Worships, and the Malefactor call'd, and by the Senior Justice Interrogated after the following manner. You Indian why did You steal from this man? You sho'dn't do so—it's a Grandy wicked thing to steal. Hol't Hol't cryes Justice Junr. Brother, You speak negro to him. I'le ask him. You sirrah, why did You steal this man's Hoggshead? Hoggshead? (replys the Indian,) me no stomany. No? says his Worship; and pulling off his hatt, Patted his own head with his hand, sais, Tatapa—You, Tatapa—you; all one this. Hoggshead all one this. Hah! says Netop, now me stomany that. Whereupon the Company fell into a great fitt of Laughter, even to Roreing. Silence is comanded, but to no effect: for they continued perfectly Shouting. Nay, sais his worship, in an angry tone, if it be so, *take mee off the Bench.*

Their Diversions in this part of the Country are on Lecture days and Training days mostly: on the former there is Riding from town to town.

And on training dayes The Youth divert themselves by Shooting at the Target, as they call it, (but it very much resembles a pillory,) where hee that hitts neerest the white has some yards of Red Ribbin presented him w*ch* being tied to his hattband, the two ends streeming down his back, he is Led away in Triumph, w*th* great applause, as the winners of the Olympiack Games. They generally marry very young: the males oftener as I am told under twentie than above; they generally make public wedings, and have a way something singular (as they say) in some of them, *viz.* Just before Joyning hands the Bridegroom quitts the place, who is soon followed by the Bridesmen, and as it were, dragg'd back to duty—being the reverse to y*e* former practice among us, to steal his Bride.

There are great plenty of Oysters all along by the sea side, as farr as I Rode in the Collony, and those very good. And they Generally lived very well and comfortably in their famelies. But too Indulgent (especially the farmers) to their slaves: sufering too great familiarity from them, permitting them to sit at Table and eat with them, (as they say to save time,) and into the dish goes the black hoof as freely as the white hand. They told me there was a farmer lived nere the Town where I lodgd who had some difference w*th* his slave, concerning something the master had promised him and did not punctualy perform; w*ch* caused some hard words between them; But at length they put the matter to Arbitration and Bound themselves to stand to the award of such as they named —w*ch* done, the Arbitrators Having heard the Allegations of both parties, Order the master to pay 40^{s} to black face, and acknowledge his fault. And so the matter ended: the poor master very honestly standing to the award.

There are every where in the Towns as I passed, a Number of Indians the Natives of the Country, and are the most salvage of all the salvages of that kind that I had ever Seen: little or no care taken (as I heard upon enquiry) to make them otherwise. They have in some places Landes of their owne, and Govern'd by Law's of their own making;—they marry many wives and at pleasure put them away, and on the least dislike or fickle humour, on either side, saying *stand away* to one another is a sufficient Divorce. And indeed those uncomely *Stand aways* are too much in Vougue among the English in this (Indulgent Colony) as their Records plentifully prove, and that on very trivial matters, of which some have been told me, but are not proper to be Related by a Female pen, tho some of that foolish sex have had too large a share in the story.

If the natives committ any crime on their own precincts among themselves, Y*e* English takes no Cognezens of. But if on the English ground, they are punishable by our Laws. They mourn for their Dead by blackening their faces, and cutting their hair, after an Awkerd and frightfull manner; But can't bear You should mention the names of their dead Relations to them: they trade most for Rum, for w*ch* they*d* hazzard their very lives; and the English fit them Generally as well, by seasoning it plentifully with water.

They give the title of merchant to every trader; who Rate their Goods according to the time and spetia they pay in: *viz.* Pay, mony, Pay as mony, and trusting. *Pay* is Grain, Pork, Beef, &c. at the prices sett by the General Court that Year; *mony* is pieces of Eight, Ryalls, or Boston or Bay shillings (as they call them,) or Good hard money, as sometimes silver coin is termed by them; also Wampom, *vizt.* Indian beads w*ch* serves for change. *Pay as mony* is provisions, as afores*d* one Third cheaper then as the Assembly or Gene*l* Court sets it; and *Trust* as they and the merch*t* agree for time.

Now, when the buyer comes to ask for a comodity, sometimes before the merchant answers that he has it, he sais, *is Your pay redy?* Perhaps the Chap Reply's Yes: what do You pay in? say's the merchant. The buyer having answered, then the price is set; as suppose he wants a sixpenny knife, in pay it is 12d—in pay as money eight pence, and hard money its own price, *viz.* 6d. It seems a very Intricate way of trade and what *Lex Mercatoria* had not thought of.

Being at a merchants house, in comes a tall country fellow, w*th* his alfogeos full of Tobacco; for they seldom Loose their Cudd, but keep Chewing and Spitting as long as they'r eyes are open,—he advanc't to the midle of the Room, makes an Awkward Nodd, and spitting a Large deal of Aromatick Tincture, he gave a scrape with his shovel like shoo, leaving a small shovel full of dirt on the floor, made a full stop, Hugging his own pretty Body with his hands under his arms, Stood staring rown'd him, like a Catt let out of a Baskett. At last, like the creature Balaam Rode on, he opened his mouth and said: have You any Ribinen for Hatbands to sell I pray? The Questions and Answers about the pay being past, the Ribin is bro't and opened. Bumpkin Simpers, cryes its confounded Gay I vow; and beckning to the door, in comes Jone Tawdry, dropping about 50 curtsees, and stands by him: hee shows her the Ribin. *Law You,* sais shee, *its right Gent,* do You, take it, *tis dreadfull pretty.* Then she enquires, *have You any hood silk I pray?* w*ch* being brought and bought, Have You any *thred silk to sew it wth* says shee, w*ch* being accomodated w*th* they Departed. They Generaly stand after they come in a great while speachless and sometimes dont say a word till they are askt what they want, which I Impute to the Awe they stand in of the merchants, who they are constantly almost Indebted too; and must take what they bring without Liberty to choose for themselves; but they serve them as well, making the merchants stay long enough for their pay.

We may Observe here the great necessity and bennefitt both of Education and Conversation; for these people have as Large a portion of mother witt, and sometimes a Larger, than those who have bin brought up in Citties; But for want of emprovements, Render themselves almost Ridiculos, as above. I should be glad if they would leave such follies, and am sure all that Love Clean Houses (at least) would be glad on't too.

They are generaly very plain in their dress, throuout all ye Colony, as I saw, and follow one another in their modes; that You may know where they belong, especially the women, meet them where you will.

Their Cheif Red Letter day is St. Election, w*ch* is annualy Observed according to Charter, to choose their Goven*r*: a blessing they can never be thankfull enough for, as they will find, if ever it be their hard fortune to loose it. The present Govenor in Conecticott is the Hon*ble* John Winthrop Esq. A Gentleman of an Ancient and Honourable Family, whose Father was Govenor here sometime before, and his Grandfather had bin Gov*r* of the Massachusetts. This gentleman is a very curteous and afable person, much Given to Hospitality, and has by his Good services Gain'd the affection of the people as much as any who had bin before him in that post.

[NEW YORK]

[Dec. 6.] * * * The Cittie of New York is a pleasant, well compacted place, situated on a Commodius River w*ch* is a fine harbour for shipping. The Buildings Brick Generaly, very stately and high, though not altogether like ours in Boston. The Bricks in some of the Houses are of divers Coullers and laid in Checkers, being glazed look very agreeable. The inside of them are neat to admiration, the wooden work, for only the walls are plasterd, and the Sumers and Gist are plained and kept very white scowr'd as so is all the partitions if made of Bords. The fire places have no Jambs (as ours have) But the Backs run flush with the walls, and the Hearth is of Tyles and is as farr out into the Room at the Ends as before the fire, w*ch* is Generally Five foot in the Low'r rooms, and the peice over where the mantle tree should be is made as ours with Joyners work, and as I suppose is fasten'd to iron rodds inside. The House where the Vendue was, had Chimney Corners like ours, and they and the hearths were laid w*th* the finest tile that I ever see, and the stair cases laid all with white tile which is ever clean, and so are the walls of the Kitchen w*ch* had a Brick floor. They were making Great preparations to Receive their Governor, Lord Cornbury from the Jerseys, and for that End raised the militia to Gard him on shore to the fort.

They are Generaly of the Church of England and have a New England Gentleman for their minister, and a very fine church set out with all Customary requisites. There are also a Dutch and Divers Conventicles as they call them, *viz.* Baptist, Quakers, &c. They are not strict in keeping the Sabbath as in Boston and other places where I had bin, But seem to deal with great exactness as farr as I see or Deall with. They are sociable to one another and Curteos and Civill to strangers and fare well in their houses. The English go very fasheonable in their dress. But the Dutch, especially the middling sort, differ from our women, in their habitt go loose, were French muches w*ch* are like a Capp and a head band in one, leaving their ears bare, which are sett out w*th* Jewells of a large size and many in number. And their fingers hoop't with Rings, some with large stones in them of many Coullers as were their pendants in their ears, which You should see very old women wear as well as Young.

They have Vendues very frequently and make their Earnings very well by them, for they treat with good Liquor Liberally, and the Customers Drink as Liberally and Generally pay for't as well, by paying for that which they Bidd up Briskly for, after the sack has gone plentifully about, tho' sometimes good penny worths are got there. Their Diversions in the Winter is Riding Sleys about three or four Miles out of Town, where they have Houses of entertainment at a place called the Bowery, and some go to friends Houses who handsomely treat them. * * *

[THE RETURN]

* * * The next day being March 3d wee got safe home to Boston, where I found my aged and tender mother and my Dear and only Child in good health with open arms redy to receive me, and my Kind relations and friends flocking in to welcome mee and hear the story of my transactions and travails I having this day bin five months from home and now I cannot fully express my Joy and Satisfaction. But desire sincearly to adore my Great Benefactor for thus graciously carying forth and returning in safety his unworthy handmaid.

1825

THE COLONIAL MIND: MIDDLE STATES AND SOUTH

I. WILLIAM PENN
(1644–1718)

From [*A GENERAL DESCRIPTION OF PENNSYLVANIA*]

[THE INDIANS]

A Letter from William Penn Proprietary and Governor of Pennsylvania In America, To the Committee of the Free Society of Traders of that Province, residing in *London*, containing A General Description of the said *Province*, [&c.]

XI. The *NATIVES* I shall consider in their *Persons, Language, Manners, Religion* and *Government,* with my sence of their *Original.* For their *Persons,* they are generally tall, streight, well-built, and of singular Proportion; they tread strong and clever, and mostly walk with a lofty Chin: Of Complexion, *Black,* but by design, as the *Gypsies* in *England:* They grease themselves with Bears-fat clarified, and using no defence against *Sun* or *Weather,* their skins must needs be swarthy: Their *Eye* is little and black, not unlike a straight-look't *Jew:* The *thick Lip* and *flat Nose,* so frequent with the *East-Indians* and *Blacks,* are not common to them; for I have seen as comely *European-like faces* among them of both, as on your side the Sea; and truly an *Italian Complexion* hath not much more of the *White,* and the *Noses* of several of them have as much of the *Roman.*

XII. Their *Language* is lofty, yet narrow, but like the *Hebrew;* in Signification full; like *Short-hand* in writing; *one* word serveth in the place of *three,* and the rest are supplied by the understanding of the Hearer: Imperfect in their *Tenses,* wanting in their *Moods, Participles, Adverbs, Conjunctions, Interjections:* I have made it my business to understand it, that I might not want an interpreter on any occasion: And I must say, that I know not a Language spoken in *Europe,* that hath words of more sweetness or greatness, in *Accent* and *Emphasis,* than theirs; for Instance, Octorockon, Rancocas, Oricton, Shakamaxon, Poquessin, all which are names of Places, and have Grandeur in them: Of words of Sweetness, Anna, is *Mother,* Issimus, a *Brother,* Netap, *Friend,* usque oret, *very good;* pone, *Bread,* metse, *eat,* matta, *no,* hatta, *to have,* payo, *to come;* Sepassen, Passijon, the Names of Places; Tamane, Secane, Menanse, Secatereus, are the Names of Persons. If one ask them for any thing they have not, they will answer, mattá ne hattá, which to translate is, *not I have,* instead of *I have not.*

XIII. Of their *Customs* and *Manners* there is much to be said; I will begin with *Children.* So soon as they are born, they wash them in *Water,* and while very young, and in cold Weather to chuse, they *Plunge* them in the Rivers to harden and embolden them. Having wrapt them in a Clout, they lay them on a straight thin Board, a little more than the length and breadth of the Child, and swadle it fast upon the Board to make it straight; wherefore all *Indians* have flat Heads; and thus they carry them at their Backs. The Children will go very *young,* at *nine Moneths* commonly; they wear only a small Clout round their Waste, till they are big; if *Boys,* they go a Fishing till ripe for the Woods, which is about *Fifteen;* then they Hunt, and after having given some Proofs of their Manhood, by a good return of *Skins,* they may *Marry,* else it is a shame to think of a *Wife.* The *Girls* stay with their Mothers, and help to hoe the Ground, plant Corn and carry Burthens; and they do well to use them to that *Young,* they must do when they are *Old;* for the *Wives* are the true *Servants* of their *Husbands:* otherwise the Men are very affectionate to them.

XIV. When the *Young Women* are fit for *Marriage,* they wear something upon their Heads for an Advertisement, but so as their Faces are hardly to be seen, but when they please: The *Age* they *Marry* at, if *Women,* is about *thirteen* and *fourteen;* if Men, *seventeen* and *eighteen;* they are rarely elder.

XV. Their *Houses* are *Mats,* or *Barks of Trees* set on Poles, in the fashion of an *English Barn,* but out of the power of the Winds, for they are hardly higher than a Man; they lie on *Reeds* or *Grass.* In *Travel* they lodge in the *Woods* about a great Fire, with the Mantle of *Duffills* they wear by day, wrapt about them, and a few Boughs stuck round them.

XVI. Their *Diet* is *Maze,* or *Indian Corn,* divers ways prepared; sometimes Roasted in the Ashes, sometimes beaten and *Boyled* with Water, which they call *Homine;* they also make *Cakes,* not unpleasant to eat: They have likewise several sorts of *Beans* and *Pease* that are good Nourishment; and the *Woods* and *Rivers* are their *Larder.*

XVII. If an *European* comes to see them, or calls for Lodging at their House or *Wigwam,* they give him the best place and first cut. If they come to visit us, they salute us with an ITAH, which is as much as to say, *Good be to you,* and set them down, which is mostly on the Ground, close to their Heels, their Legs upright; may be they speak not a word more, but observe all Passages: If you give them any thing to eat or drink, well, for they will not ask; and be it little or much, if it be with Kindness, they are well pleased, else they go away sullen, but say nothing.

XVIII. They are great *Concealers* of their own *Resentments,* brought to it, I believe, by the *Revenge* that hath been practised among them; in either of these, they are not exceeded by the *Italians.* A *Tragical* Instance fell out since I came into the Country; A *King's Daughter* thinking her self slighted by her Husband, in suffering another *Woman* to lie down between them, rose up, went out, pluck't a Root out of the Ground, and ate it, upon which she immediately dyed; and for which last Week he made an *Offering* to her Kindred for *Attone-*

ment and liberty of Marriage; as two others did to the Kindred of their Wives, that dyed a natural Death: For till *Widdowers* have done so, they must not *marry* again. Some of the *young Women* are said to take undue liberty before Marriage for a Portion; but when *marryed,* chaste; when with Child, they know their Husbands no more, till delivered; and during their Moneth, they touch no *Meat;* they eat, but with a *Stick,* least they should defile it; nor do their Husbands frequent them, till that time be expired.

XIX. But in *Liberality* they excell, nothing is too good for their friend; give them a *fine Gun, Coat,* or other thing, it may pass *twenty hands,* before it sticks; *light* of Heart, *strong* Affections, but soon spent; the most *merry* Creatures that live, *Feast* and *Dance* perpetually; they never have much, nor want much: *Wealth* circulateth like the *Blood,* all parts partake; and though none shall want what another hath, yet exact Observers of *Property.* Some *Kings* have sold, others presented me with several *parcels* of *Land;* the Pay or Presents I made them, were *not hoarded* by the particular Owners, but the *neighbouring Kings* and their *Clans* being present when the Goods were brought out, the Parties chiefly concerned consulted, what and to whom they should give them? To every *King* then, by the hands of a Person for that work appointed, is a proportion sent, so sorted and folded, and with that *Gravity,* that is admirable. Then that *King* sub-divideth it in like manner among his Dependents, they hardly leaving themselves an *Equal share* with one of their *Subjects:* and be it on such occasions, at *Festivals,* or at their *common Meals,* the *Kings* distribute, and to themselves *last.* They care for *little,* because they want but *little;* and the Reason is, a *little* contents them: In this they are sufficiently revenged on us; if they are ignorant of our *Pleasures,* they are also free from our *Pains.* They are not disquieted with *Bills of Lading* and *Exchange,* nor perplexed with *Chancery-Suits* and *Exchequer-Reckonings.* We *sweat* and *toil* to live; their *pleasure* feeds them, I mean, their *Hunting, Fishing* and *Fowling,* and this Table is spread every where; they *eat twice a day,* Morning and Evening; their *Seats* and *Table* are the *Ground.* Since the *Europeans* came into these parts, they are grown great lovers of *strong Liquors, Rum* especially, and for it exchange the richest of their *Skins* and *Furs:* If they are heated with *Liquors,* they are restless till they have enough to *sleep;* that is their cry, *Some more, and I will go to sleep;* but when *Drunk,* one of the *most wretchedst Spectacles in the World.*

XX. In *Sickness* impatient to be cured, and for it give any thing, especially for their *Children,* to whom they are extreamly natural; they drink at those times a *Teran* or Decoction of some Roots in spring Water; and if they eat any *flesh,* it must be of the *Female* of any Creature: If they dye, they bury them with their *Apparel,* be they *Men* or *Women,* and the nearest of *Kin* fling in something precious with them, as a token of their Love: Their *Mourning* is *blacking* of their *faces,* which they continue for a *year:* They are choice of the *Graves* of their *Dead;* for least they should be lost by time, and fall to common use, they *pick off the Grass* that grows upon them, and heap up the fallen Earth with great care and exactness.

XXI. These poor *People* are under a dark Night in things relating to *Religion,* to be sure, the *Tradition* of it; yet they believe a *God* and *Immortality,* without the help of *Metaphysicks;* for they say, *There is a great King that made them, who dwells in a glorious Country to the Southward of them,* and *that the Souls of the good shall go thither, where they shall live again.* Their *Worship* consists of two parts, *Sacrifice* and *Cantico.* Their *Sacrifice* is their *first Fruits;* the first and fattest *Buck* they kill, goeth to the *fire,* where he is all burnt with a *Mournful Ditty* of him that performeth the *Ceremony,* but with such *marvelous Fervency* and *Labour of Body,* that he will even *sweat* to a *foam.* The other part is their *Cantico,* performed by round-*Dances,* sometimes *Words,* sometimes *Songs,* then *Shouts,* two being in the middle that begin, and by *Singing* and *Drumming* on a *Board* direct the *Chorus:* Their Postures in the *Dance* are very *Antick* and differing, but all *keep measure.* This is done with equal Earnestness and Labour, but great appearance of *Joy.* In the *Fall,* when the *Corn* cometh in, they begin to *feast* one another; there have been two great *Festivals* already, to which all come that will: I was at one my self; their Entertainment was a *green Seat* by a *Spring,* under some *shady Trees,* and *twenty Bucks,* with *hot Cakes* of *new Corn,* both *Wheat* and *Beans,* which they make up in a square form, in the leaves of the Stem, and bake them in the Ashes: And after that they fell to *Dance.* But they that go, must carry a small *Present* in *their Money,* it may be *six Pence,* which is made of the *Bone* of a *Fish;* the *black* is with them as *Gold,* the *white, Silver;* they call it all *Wampum.*

XXII. Their *Government* is by *Kings,* which they call *Sachema,* and those by *Succession,* but always of the *Mothers side;* for Instance, the *Children* of him that is now *King,* will not succeed, but his *Brother* by the *Mother,* or the *Children* of his *Sister,* whose *Sons* (and after them the *Children* of her *Daughters*) will reighn; for no *Woman* inherits; the Reason they render for this way of Descent, is, that their Issue may not be spurious.

XXIII. Every *King* hath his *Council,* and that consists of all the *Old* and *Wise men* of his *Nation,* which perhaps is *two hundred People:* nothing of Moment is undertaken, be it *War, Peace, Selling* of *Land* or *Traffick,* without advising with them; and which is more, with the *Young Men* too. 'Tis admirable to consider, how *Powerful* the *Kings* are, and yet how they move by the *Breath* of their *People.* I have had occasion to be in *Council* with them upon *Treaties* for *Land,* and to adjust the terms of *Trade;* their Order is thus: The *King* fits in the middle of an half Moon, and hath his *Council,* the *Old* and *Wise* on each hand; behind them, or at a little distance, sit the younger *Fry,* in the same figure. Having consulted and resolved their business, the *King* ordered one of them to speak to me; he stood up, came to me, and in the Name of his *King* saluted me, then took me by the hand, and told me, *That he was ordered by his* King *to speak to me, and that now it was not he, but the* King *that spoke, because what he should say, was the* King's *mind.* He first pray'd me, *To excuse them that they had not complyed with me the last time; he feared, there might be some fault in the Interpreter, being neither* Indian *nor* English; *besides, it was the* Indian *Custom to deliberate, and take up much time in Council, before they resolve; and that if the Young People and Owners of the Land had been as ready as he, I had not met with so much delay.* Having thus introduced his matter, he fell to the Bounds of the Land they had agreed to dispose of, and the Price, (which now is little and dear, that which would have bought *twenty Miles,* not buying now *two.*) During the time that this Person spoke, not a man of them was observed to *whisper* or *smile;* the *Old Grave,* the *Young Reverend* in their *Deportment;* they do speak *little,* but *fervently,* and with *Elegancy:* I have never seen more *natural Sagacity,* considering them without the help, (I was a going to say, the *spoil*) of *Tradition;* and he will deserve the Name of *Wise,* that *Out-wits* them in any *Treaty* about a thing they understand. When the Purchase was agreed, great Promises past between us *of Kindness and good Neighbourhood, and that the* Indians *and* English *must live in Love, as long as the Sun gave light.* Which done, another made a Speech to the *Indians,* in the Name of all the *Sachamakers* or *Kings,* first to tell them what was done; next, to charge and command them, *To Love the* Christians, *and particularly live in Peace with* me, *and the People under my Government: That many Governours had been in the River, but that no Governour had come himself to live and stay here before; and having now such a one that had treated them well, they should never do him or his any wrong.* At every sentence of which they shouted, and said, *Amen,* in their way.

XXIV. The *Justice* they have is *Pecuniary:* In case of any *Wrong* or *evil Fact,* be it *Murther* it self, they Attone by *Feasts* and *Presents* of their *Wampon,* which is proportioned to the quality of the *Offence* or *Person injured,* or of the *Sex* they are of: for in case they *kill a Woman,* they pay *double,* and the Reason they render, is, *That she breedeth Children, which Men cannot do.* 'Tis rare that they fall out, if *Sober;* and if *Drunk,* they forgive it, saying, *It was the Drink, and not the Man, that abused them.*

XXV. We have agreed, that in all *Differences* between us, *Six* of each side shall end the matter: Don't *abuse* them, but let them have *Justice,* and you win them: The worst is, that they are the *worse* for the *Christians,* who have propagated their *Vices,* and yielded them *Tradition* for *ill,* and not for *good things.* But as *low* an *Ebb* as they are at, and as *glorious* as their Condition looks, the *Christians* have not *out-liv'd* their *sight* with all their *Pretensions* to an *higher Manifestation:* What *good* then might not a *good People* graft, where there is so *distinct a Knowledge* left between *Good* and *Evil?* I beseech God to incline the *Hearts* of all that come Into these parts, to *out-live* the *Knowledge* of the *Natives,* by a *fixt Obedience* to their *greater Knowledge* of the *Will of God;* for it were *miserable* indeed for us to fall under the just *censure* of the poor *Indian Con-*

science, while we make profession of things so far *transcending.*

XXVI. For their *Original,* I am ready to believe them of the *Jewish Race,* I mean, of the stock of the *Ten Tribes,* and that for the following Reasons; *first,* They were to go to a *Land not planted or known,* which to be sure *Asia* and *Africa* were, if not *Europe;* and he that intended that extra-ordinary Judgment upon them, might make the Passage not uneasie to them, as it is not impossible in it self, from the *Easter-most* parts of *Asia,* to the *Wester-most* of *America.* In the *next* place, I find them of like *Countenance,* and their Children of *so lively Resemblance,* that a man would think himself in *Dukes-place* or *Berry-street* in *London,* when he seeth them. But this is not all, they agree in *Rites,* they reckon by *Moons;* they *offer* their *first Fruits,* they have a kind of *Feast* of *Tabernacles;* they are said to lay their *Altar* upon *twelve Stones;* their *Mourning a year, Customs of Women,* with many things that do not now occur. * * *

1683

From *FRUITS OF SOLITUDE*

[MEDITATIONS]

EDUCATION

5. The first thing obvious to Children is what is sensible; and that we make no Part of their Rudiments.

6. We press their Memory too soon, and puzzle, strain and load them with Words and Rules; to know *Grammer* and *Rhetorick,* and a strange Tongue or two, that it is ten to one may never be useful to them; leaving their natural *Genius* to *Mechanical* and *Physical* or natural Knowledge uncultivated and neglected; which would be of exceeding Use and Pleasure to them through the whole Course of their Life.

7. To be sure, Languages are not to be despised or neglected. But Things are still to be preferred.

8. Children had rather be making of *Tools* and *Instruments* of Play; *Shaping, Drawing, Framing,* and *Building,* &c. than getting some Rules of Propriety of Speech by heart: And those also would follow with more Judgment, and less Trouble and Time.

9. It were happy if we studied Nature more in natural things; and acted according to Nature; whose Rules are *few, plain* and *most reasonable.*

10. Let us begin where she begins, go her Pace, and close always where she ends, and we cannot miss of being good *Naturalists.*

11. The Creation would not be longer a Riddle to us: The *Heavens, Earth,* and *Waters,* with their respective, various and numerous Inhabitants: Their Productions, Natures, Seasons, Sympathies and Antipathies; their Use, Benefit and Pleasure, would be better understood by us: And an *eternal Wisdom, Power, Majesty* and *Goodness,* very *conspicuous* to us; through those sensible and passing Forms: The World wearing the *Mark* of it's Maker, whose Stamp is every where *visible,* and the *Characters* very *legible* to the Children of Wisdom.

12. And it would go a great Way to caution and direct People in their Use of the World, that they were better studied and knowing in the Creation of it.

13. For how could Men find the Confidence to abuse it, while they

should see the Great Creator stare them in the Face, in all and every Part thereof?

14. Their Ignorance makes them insensible, and that Insensibility hardy in misusing this noble Creation, that has the Stamp and Voice of a *Deity* every where, and in every Thing to the Observing.

15. It is Pity therefore that Books have not been composed for *Youth,* by some curious and careful *Naturalists,* and also *Mechanicks,* in the *Latin* Tongue, to be used in Schools, that they might learn Things with Words: Things *obvious* and *familiar* to them, and which would make the Tongue easier to be attained by them.

16. Many able *Gardiners* and *Husbandmen* are yet ignorant of the *Reason* of their Calling; as most *Artificers* are of the Reason of their own Rules that govern their excellent Workmanship. But a Naturalist and Mechanick of this Sort, is Master of the Reason of both, and might be of the Practice too, if his Industry kept Pace with his Speculation; which were very commendable; and without which he cannot be said to be a *compleat* Naturalist or Mechanick.

17. Finally, if Man be the *Index* or *Epitomy* of the World, as *Philosophers* tell us, we have only to read our *selves* well to be *learn'd* in it. But because there is nothing we less regard than the *Characters* of the Power that made us, which are so clearly written upon us and the World he has given us, and can best tell us what we are and should be, we are even Strangers to our own *Genius:* The *Glass* in which we should see that true instructing and agreeable Variety, which is to be observed in Nature, to the Admiration of that Wisdom and Adoration of that Power which made us all.

CENSORIOUSNESS

41. We are apt to be very pert at *censuring others,* where we will not endure Advice our selves. And nothing, shews our *Weakness* more than to be so sharp-sighted at spying other Men's Faults, and so *purblind* about our own.

42. When the Actions of a Neighbour are upon the Stage, we can have all our Wits about us, are so quick and critical we can split an Hair, and find out every Failure and Infirmity: *But are without feeling, or have but very little Sense of our own.*

43. Much of this comes from *ill Nature,* as well as from an inordinate Value of our selves: For we love rambling better than Home, and blaming the unhappy, rather than covering and relieving them.

44. In such Occasions some shew their Malice and are witty upon *Misfortunes;* others their Justice, they can reflect a pace: but few or none their *Charity;* especially if it be about Money Matters.

45. You shall see an *old Miser* come forth with a set Gravity, and so much Severity against the *Distressed,* to *excuse his Purse,* that he will, 'ere he has done, put it out of all Question, That RICHES is *Righteousness* with him. *This,* says he, *is the Fruit of your Prodigality* (as if, poor Man, *Covetousness* were no Fault) Or, *of your Projects, or grasping after a great Trade:* While he himself would have done the same thing, but that he had not the *Courage* to venture so much ready Money *out of his own trusty Hands,* though it

had been to have brought him back the *Indies* in Return. But the Proverb is just, *Vice should not correct Sin.*

46. They have a Right to censure, that have an *Heart* to help: The rest is Cruelty, not Justice.

TEMPERANCE

59. To this a *spare* Dyet contributes much. Eat therefore to *live,* and do not live to eat. That's like a Man, but this below a *Beast.*

60. Have wholesome, but not *costly* Food, and be rather cleanly than *dainty* in ordering it.

61. The *Receipts* of Cookery are *swell'd* to a Volume, but a *good Stomack* excels them all; to which nothing contributes more than *Industry* and *Temperance.*

62. It is a cruel Folly to offer up to *Ostentation* so many Lives of Creatures, as make up the State of our Treats; as it is a prodigal one to spend more in Sauce than in Meat.

63. The Proverb says, *That enough is as good as a Feast:* But it is certainly better, if Superfluity be a Fault, which never fails to be at Festivals.

64. If thou rise with an Appetite thou art sure never to sit down without one.

65. Rarely drink but when thou art dry; nor then, between Meals, if it can be avoided.

66. The *smaller* the Drink, the *clearer* the Head, and the *cooler* the *Blood;* which are great Benefits in Temper and Business.

67. Strong Liquors are good at some times, and in small Proportions; being better for *Physick* than Food, for *Cordials* than common Use.

68. The most *Common* things are the most *useful;* which shews both the *Wisdom* and *Goodness* of the great Lord of the Family of the World.

69. What therefore he has made *rare,* don't thou use *too commonly:* Lest thou shouldest invert the Use and Order of Things; become Wanton and Voluptuous; and thy *Blessings* prove a *Curse.*

70. *Let nothing be lost,* said our Saviour: But that is *lost* that is *misused.*

71. Neither urge another to that thou wouldst be unwilling to do thy self; nor do thy self what looks to thee *unseemly,* and intemperate in another.

72. All Excess is ill: but *Drunkenness* is of the worst Sort: It *spoils* Health, *dismounts* the Mind, and unmans Men: It *reveals Secrets,* is *Quarrelsome, Lascivious, Impudent, Dangerous* and *mad:* In fine, he that is Drunk is not a Man; because he is so long void of *Reason,* that distinguishes a Man from a Beast.

APPAREL

73. Excess in *Apparel* is another *costly* Folly: The very Trimming of the vain World would *cloath* all the *naked* one.

74. Chuse thy Cloaths by thine owne Eyes, not anothers. The more plain and simple they are, the better. Neither unshapely nor Fantistical; and for Use and Decency, and not for Pride.

75. If thou art clean and warm, it is sufficient; for more doth but rob the *Poor,* and please the *Wanton.*

76. It is said of the true Church, *The King's Daughter is all glorious* **within.** Let our Care therefore be of our Minds more than of our *Bodies,* if we would be of her Communion.

77. We are told with Truth, that *Meekness* and *Modesty* are the Rich

and Charming Attire of the Soul: And the plainer the Dress, the more distinctly, and with greater Lustre, their Beauty shines.

78. It is a great Pity such Beauties are so *rare,* and those of *Jezebel's* Forehead are so *common:* Whose Dresses are Incentives to Lust; but *Bars* instead of Motives, to *Love* or *Vertue.*

RIGHT MARRIAGE

79. Never Marry but *for Love;* but see that thou lov'st what is *lovely.*

80. If Love be not thy *chiefest* Motive, thou wilt soon grow *weary* of a Married State, and *stray* from thy Promise, to search out thy Pleasures in *forbidden* Places.

81. Let not Enjoyment *lessen,* but augment Affection; it being the basest of Passions *to like when we have not, what we slight when we possess.*

82. It is the Difference betwixt *Lust* and *Love,* that this is fix't, that Volatile. Love grows, Lust wasts by Enjoyment: And the Reason is, that one springs from an *Union of Souls, and the other from an Union of Sense.*

83. They have divers Originals, and so are of different Families: That *inward* and *deep,* this superficial; this transient, and that permanent.

84. They that Marry for *Money,* cannot have the true Satisfaction of Marriage; the requisite Means being wanting.

85. Men are generally more careful of the *Breed* of their *Horses* and *Dogs* than of their Children.

86. Those must be of the best Sort, for *Shape, Strength, Courage* and *good Conditions:* But as for these, their own Posterity, *Money shall answer all Things.* With such, it makes the *Crooked Streight, sets Squint-Eyes right, cures Madness, covers Folly, changes ill Conditions, mends the Skin, gives a sweet Breath, repairs Honours, makes Young, works Wonders.*

87. O how *sordid* is *Man* grown! *Man,* the Noblest Creature of the World, as a *God* on *Earth,* and the *Image* of him that made it; thus to *mistake* Earth for Heaven, and *Worship Gold* for God!

FRIENDSHIP

106. *Friendship* is the next Pleasure we may hope for: And where we find it not at Home, or have no home to find it in, we may seek it abroad. It is an Union of *Spirits,* a Marriage of *Hearts,* and the Bond thereof *Virtue.*

107. There can be no Friendship where there is no *Freedom.* Friendship loves a *free* Air, and will not be penned up in streight and narrow Enclosures. It will speak *freely,* and *act* so too; and take nothing ill, where no Ill is meant; nay where it is, 'twill *easily* forgive, and forget too, upon small Acknowledgments.

108. Friends are true *Twins* in Soul; they Sympathize in every thing, and have the same Love and Aversion.

109. One is not happy without the other, nor can either of them be miserable *alone.* As if they could change *Bodies,* they take their *Turns* in Pain as well as in Pleasure; *relieving* one another in their most adverse Conditions.

110. What one enjoys, the other cannot Want. Like the Primitive Christians, they have all things in common, and no *Property but in one another.*

QUALITIES OF A FRIEND

111. A true Friend unbosomes *freely,* advises *justly,* assists *readily,*

adventures *boldly,* takes all *patiently,* defends *couragiously,* and continues a Friend *unchangeably.*

112. These being the Qualities of a Friend, we are to find them before we chuse one.

113. The *Covetous,* the *Angry,* the *Proud,* the *Jealous,* the *Talkative,* cannot but make ill Friends, as well as the *False.*

114. In short, chuse a Friend as thou dost a Wife, *till Death separate you.*

115. Yet be not a Friend beyond the *Alter:* But let *Virtue* bound thy *Friendship:* Else it is not Friendship, but an evil Confederacy.

116. If my *Brother* or *Kinsman* will be my Friend, I ought to prefer him before a Stranger, or I shew little Duty or *Nature* to my *Parents.*

117. And as we ought to prefer our *Kindred* in Point of Affection, so too in Point of *Charity,* if *equally* needing and deserving.

KNOWLEDGE

162. *Knowledge* is the *Treasure,* but *Judgment* the Treasurer of a *wise* Man.

163. He that has more Knowledge than Judgment, is made for *another Man's* Use more than his own.

164. It cannot be a good Constitution, where the Appetite is great and the Digestion weak.

165. There are some Men like *Dictionaries;* to be lookd into upon Occasion, but have no Connection, and are little entertaining.

166. Less Knowledge than Judgment will always have the Advantage upon the *Injudicious* knowing Man.

167. A wise Man makes what he learns his *own,* 'tother shews he's but a *Copy,* or a Collection at most.

WIT

168. *Wit* is an happy and striking Way of expressing a Thought.

169. 'Tis not often tho' it be lively and mantling, that it carries a great Body with it.

170. Wit therefore is fitter for Diversion than Business, being more grateful to Fancy than Judgment.

171. Less Judgment than Wit, is *more Sail than Ballast.*

172. Yet it must be confest, that Wit gives an *Edge* to Sense, and recommends it extreamly.

173. Where Judgment has Wit to express it, there's the *best* Orator.

ART AND PROJECT

227. *Art,* is Good, where it is beneficial. *Socrates* wisely bounded his Knowledge and Instruction by *Practice.*

228. Have a Care therefore of *Projects:* And yet despise nothing rashly, or in the *Lump.*

229. *Ingenuity,* as well as Religion, sometimes suffers between two *Thieves; Pretenders* and *Despisers.*

230. Though injudicious and dishonest Projecters often discredit Art, yet the most *useful* and *extraordinary* Inventions have not, at first, escap'd the Scorn of *Ignorance;* as their Authors, rarely, have cracking of their Heads, or breaking of their Backs.

231. Undertake no Experiment, in Speculation, that appears not *true in Art;* nor then, at thine *own* Cost, if costly or hazardous in making.

232. As many Hands make light Work, so *several Purses* make *cheap* Experiments.

INDUSTRY

233. *Industry* is certainly very com-

mendable, and *supplies* the Want of Parts.

234. *Patience* and *Diligence,* like Faith, *remove Mountains.*

235. Never give out while there is *Hope;* but hope not beyond Reason, for that shews more Desire than Judgment.

236. It is a profitable Wisdom to know when we have done enough: Much Time and Pains are spared, in not flattering our selves against Probabilities.

BALLANCE

309. We must not be concern'd above the Value of the Thing that engages us; nor raised *above* Reason, in maintaining what we think reasonable.

310. It is too common an Error, to invert the Order of Things; by making an *End* of that which is a *Means,* and a *Means* of that which is an *End.*

311. *Religion* and *Government* escape not this *Mischief:* The first is too often made a *Means* instead of an End; the other an End instead of a Means.

312. Thus Men seek Wealth rather than Subsistence; and the End of Cloaths is the least Reason of their Use. Nor is the satisfying of our Appetite our End in Eating, so much as the pleasing of our Pallate. The like may also be said of Building, Furniture, *&c.* where the Man rules not the Beast, and Appetite submits not to Reason.

313. It is great Wisdom to proportion our Esteem to the Nature of the Thing: For as that way things will not be undervalued, so neither will they engage us *above* their intrinsick *Worth.*

314. If we suffer little Things to have great Hold upon us, we shall be as *much* transported for them, as if they deserved it.

315. It is an old Proverb, *Maxima Bella ex levissimis Causis:* The greatest Feuds have had the smallest Beginnings.

316. No matter what the Subject of the Dispute be, but what Place we give it in our Minds: For that governs our Concern and Resentment.

317. It is one of the fatalest Errors of our Lives, when we spoil a good Cause by an ill Management: And it is not impossible but we may *mean well* in an *ill* Business; but that will not defend it.

318. If we are but sure the End is Right, we are too apt to gallop over all Bounds to compass it; not considering that lawful Ends may be very *unlawfully* attained.

319. Let us be careful to take *just ways* to compass just Things; that they may *last* in their Benefits to us.

320. There is a troublesome Humor some Men have, that if they may not lead, *they will not follow;* but had rather a thing were never done, than not done their own way, tho' other ways very desirable.

321. This comes of an *over-fulness* of our selves, and shews we are more concern'd for *Praise,* than the *Success* of what we think a good Thing.

RELIGION

* * * 550. I find all Sorts of People *agree,* whatsoever were their Animosities, when *humbled* by the Approaches of Death: *Then they forgive, then they pray for, and love one another:* Which shews us, that it is not our Reason, but our *Passion,* that

makes and holds up the *Feuds* that reign among Men in their Health and Fulness. They, therefore, that live *nearest* to that which they should die, must certainly live *best.*

551. Did we *believe* a Final Reckoning and Judgment, or did we think *enough* of what we do *believe,* we would allow *more Love* in Religion than we do; since *Religion* it self is nothing else but *Love to God and Man.*

552. *He that lives in Love lives in God,* says the Beloved Disciple: And to be sure a Man can live *no where better.*

553. It is more reasonable Men should value that Benefit, which is most *durable.* Now Tongues shall cease, and Prophecy fail, and *Faith* shall be *consummated* in Sight, and Hope in Enjoyment; but *Love remains.*

554. Love is indeed Heaven upon Earth; since Heaven above would not be Heaven without it: For where there is not Love; there is Fear: But *perfect Love casts out Fear.* And yet we naturally *fear most* to offend what we *most Love.*

555. What we Love, we'll Hear; and what we love, we'll trust; and what we love we'll serve, ay, and suffer for too. *If you love me* (says our Blessed Redeemer) *keep my Commandments.* Why? Why then he'll *Love us;* then we shall be his *Friends;* then he'll send us the *Comforter;* then whatever we ask, we shall receive; and then where he is *we shall be also and that for ever.* Behold the Fruits of *Love;* the *Power, Vertue, Benefit,* and *Beauty* of *Love!*

556. *Love* is above all; and when it prevails in us all, we shall all be *Lovely,* and in *Love* with *God* and *one* with *another. Amen.*

1693

II. WILLIAM BYRD
(1674–1744)

From *HISTORY OF THE DIVIDING LINE*

[THE DISMAL SWAMP]

14 March, [1728]. Before nine of the Clock this Morning, the Provisions, Bedding and other Necessaries, were made up into Packs for the Men to carry on their Shoulders into the Dismal. They were victuall'd for 8 days at full Allowance, Nobody doubting but that wou'd be abundantly Sufficient to carry them thro' that Inhospitable Place; nor Indeed was it possible for the Poor Fellows to Stagger under more. As it was, their Loads weigh'd from 60 to 70 Pounds, in just Proportion to the Strength of those who were to bear them.

Twou'd have been unconscionable to have Saddled them with Burthens heavier than that, when they were to lugg them thro' a filthy Bogg, which was hardly practicable with no Burthen at all.

Besides this Luggage at their Backs, they were oblig'd to measure the distance, mark the Trees, and clear the way for the Surveyors every Step they went. It was really a Pleasure to see with how much Cheerfulness they undertook, and with how much Spirit they went thro' all this Drudgery. For their Greater Safety, the Commissioners took care to furnish them with Peruvian-Bark, Rhubarb and Hipocoacanah, in case they might happen, in that wet Journey, to be taken with fevers or Fluxes.

Altho' there was no need of Example to inflame Persons already so cheerful, yet to enter the People with better grace, the Author and two more of the Commissioners accompanied them half a Mile into the Dismal. The Skirts of it were thinly Planted with Dwarf Reeds and Gall-Bushes, but when we got into the Dismal itself, we found the Reeds grew there much taller and closer, and, to mend the matter was so interlac'd with bamboe-briars, that there was no scuffling thro' them without the help of Pioneers. At the same time, we found the Ground moist and trembling under our feet like a Quagmire, insomuch that it was an easy Matter to run a Ten-Foot-Pole up to the Head in it, without exerting any uncommon Strength to do it.

Two of the Men, whose Burthens were the least cumbersome, had orders to march before, with their Tomahawks, and clear the way, in order to make an Opening for the Surveyors. By their Assistance we made a Shift to push the Line half a Mile in 3 Hours, and then reacht a small piece of firm Land, about 100 Yards wide, Standing up above the rest like an Island. Here the people were glad to lay down their Loads and take a little refreshment, while the happy man, whose lot it was to carry the Jugg of Rum, began already, like Aesop's Bread-Carriers, to find it grow a good deal lighter.

After reposing about an Hour, the Commissioners recommended Vigour and Constancy to their Fellow-Travellers, by whom they were answer'd with 3 Cheerful Huzzas, in Token of Obedience. This Ceremony was no sooner over but they took up their Burthens and attended the Motion of the Surveyors, who, tho' they workt with all their might, could reach but one Mile farther, the same obstacles still attending them which they had met with in the Morning.

However small this distance may seem to such as are us'd to travel at their Ease, yet our Poor Men, who were oblig'd to work with an unwieldy Load at their Backs, had reason to think it a long way; Especially in a Bogg where they had no firm Footing, but every Step made a deep Impression, which was instantly fill'd with Water. At the same time they were labouring with their Hands to cut down the Reeds, which were Ten-feet high, their Legs were hampered with the Bryars. Besides, the Weather happen'd to be very warm, and the tallness of the Reeds kept off every Friendly Breeze from coming to refresh them. And, indeed, it was a little provoking to hear the Wind whistling among the Branches of the White Cedars, which grew here and there amongst the Reeds, and at the same time not have the Comfort to feel the least Breath of it.

In the mean time the 3 Commissioners return'd out of the Dismal the same way they went in, and, having join'd their Brethren, proceeded that Night as far as Mr. Wilson's.

This worthy Person lives within sight of the Dismal, in the Skirts whereof his Stocks range and Maintain themselves all the Winter, and yet he knew as little of it as he did of Terra Australis Incognita. He told us a Canterbury Tale of a North Briton, whose Curiosity spurr'd him a long way into this great Desart, as he call'd it, near 20 Years ago, but he having no Compass, nor seeing the Sun for several Days Together, wander'd about till he was almost famisht; but at last he bethought himself of a Secret his Countrymen make use of to Pilot themselves in a Dark day.

He took a fat Louse out of his Collar, and expos'd it to the open day on a Piece of White Paper, which he brought along with him for his Journal. The poor Insect having no Eyelids, turn'd himself about till he found the Darkest Part of the Heavens, and so made the best of his way toward the North. By this Direction he Steer'd himself Safe out, and gave such a frightful account of the Monsters he saw, and the Distresses he underwent, that no mortall Since has been hardy enough to go upon the like dangerous Discovery. * * *

24 [March]. This being Sunday, we had a Numerous congregation, which flockt to our Quarters from all the adjacent Country. The News that our Surveyors were come out of the Dismal, increas'd the Number very much, because it wou'd give them an Opportunity of guessing, at least, whereabouts the Line wou'd cut, whereby they might form Some Judgment whether they belong'd to Virginia or Carolina. Those who had taken up Land within the Disputed Bounds were in great pain lest it should be found to ly in Virginia; because this being done contrary to an Express Order of that government, the Patentees had great reason to fear they should in that case have lost their land. But their Apprehensions were now at an end, when they understood that all the Territory which had been controverted was like to be left in Carolina.

In the afternoon, those who were to re-enter the Dismal were furnisht with the Necessary Provisions, and Order'd to repair the Over-Night to their Landlord, Peter Brinkley's, that they might be ready to begin their Business early on Monday Morning. Mr. Irvin was excus'd from the Fatigue, in complement to his Lungs; but Mr. Mayo and Mr. Swan were Robust enough to return upon that painful Service, and, to do them Justice, they went with great Alacrity. The Truth was, they now knew the worst of it; and cou'd guess pretty near at the time when they might hope to return to Land again.

25 [March]. The Air was chill'd this Morning with a Smart North-west Wind, which favour'd the Dismalites in their Dirty March. They return'd by the Path they had made in coming out, and with great Industry arriv'd in the Evening at the Spot where the Line had been discontinued.

After so long and laborious a Journey, they were glad to repose themselves on their couches of Cypress-bark, where their sleep was as sweet as it wou'd have been on a Bed of Finland Down.

In the mean time, we who stay'd behind had nothing to do, but to make the best observations we cou'd upon that Part of the Country. The Soil of our Landlord's Plantation, tho' none of the best, seem'd more fertile than any thereabouts, where the Ground is near as Sandy as the Desarts of Affrica, and consequently barren. The Road leading from thence to Edenton, being in distance about 27 Miles, lies upon a Ridge call'd Sandy-Ridge, which is so wretchedly Poor that it will not bring Potatoes.

The Pines in this Part of the country are of a different Species from those that grow in Virginia: their bearded Leaves are much longer and their Cones much larger. Each Cell contains a Seed of the Size and Figure of a black-ey'd Pea, which, Shedding in November, is very good Mast for Hogs, and fattens them in a Short time.

The Smallest of these Pines are full of Cones, which are 8 or 9 Inches long, and each affords commonly 60 or 70 Seeds. This Kind of Mast has the Advantage of all other, by being more constant, and less liable to be nippt by the Frost, or Eaten by the Caterpillars. The Trees also abound more with Turpentine, and consequently yield more Tarr, than either the Yellow or the White Pine; And for the same reason make more durable Timber for building. The Inhabitants hereabouts pick up Knots of Lightwood in Abundance, which they burn into tar, and then carry it to Norfolk or Nansimond for a Market. The Tar made in this method is the less Valuable, because it is said to burn the Cordage, tho' it is full as good for all other uses, as that made in Sweden and Muscovy.

Surely there is no place in the World where the Inhabitants live with less labour than in N. Carolina. It approaches nearer to the Description of Lubberland than any other, by the great felicity of the Climate, the easiness of raising Provisions, and the Slothfulness of the People.

Indian Corn is of so great increase, that a little Pains will Subsist a very large Family with Bread, and then they may have meat without any pains at all, by the Help of the Low Grounds, and the great Variety of Mast that grows on the High-land. The Men, for their Parts, just like the Indians, impose all the Work upon the poor Women. They make their Wives rise out of their Beds early in the Morning, at the same time that they lye and Snore, till the Sun has run one third of his course, and disperst all the unwholesome Damps. Then, after Stretching and Yawning for half an Hour, they light their Pipes, and, under the Protection of a cloud of Smoak, venture out into the open Air; tho', if it happens to be never so little cold, they quickly return Shivering into the Chimney corner. When the Weather is mild, they stand leaning with both their arms upon the corn-field fence, and gravely consider whether they had best go and take a Small Heat at the Hough: but generally find reasons to put it off till another time.

Thus they loiter away their Lives, like Solomon's Sluggard, with their Arms across, and at the Winding up of the Year Scarcely have Bread to Eat.

To speak the Truth, tis a thorough Aversion to Labor that makes People file off to N Carolina, where Plenty and a Warm Sun confirm them in their Disposition to Laziness for their whole Lives.

26 [March]. Since we were like to be confin'd to this place, till the People return'd out of the Dismal, twas agreed that our Chaplain might Safely take a turn to Edenton, to preach the Gospel to the Infidels there, and Christen their Children. He was accompany'd thither by Mr. Little, One of the Carolina Commissioners, who, to shew his regard for the Church, offer'd to treat Him on the Road with a Fricassee of Rum. They fry'd half

a Dozen Rashers of very fat Bacon in a Pint of Rum, both which being disht up together, serv'd the Company at once for meat and Drink.

Most of the Rum they get in this Country comes from New England, and is so bad and unwholesome, that it is not improperly call'd "Kill-Devil." It is distill'd there from foreign molosses, which, if Skilfully manag'd, yields near Gallon for Gallon. Their molosses comes from the same country, and has the name of "Long Sugar" in Carolina, I suppose from the Ropiness of it, and Serves all the purposes of Sugar, both in their Eating and Drinking.

When they entertain their Friends bountifully, they fail not to set before them a Capacious Bowl of Bombo, so call'd from the Admiral of that name. This is a Compound of Rum and Water in Equal Parts, made palatable with the said long Sugar. As good Humour begins to flow, and the Bowl to Ebb, they take Care to replenish it with Shear Rum, of which there always is a Reserve under the Table. But such Generous doings happen only when that Balsam of life is plenty; for they have often such Melancholy times, that neither Landgraves nor Cassicks can procure one drop for their Wives, when they ly in, or are troubled with the Colick or Vapours. Very few in this Country have the Industry to plant Orchards, which, in a Dearth of Rum, might supply them with much better Liquor.

The Truth is, there is one Inconvenience that easily discourages lazy People from making This improvement: very often, in Autumn, when the Apples begin to ripen, they are visited with Numerous Flights of paraqueets, that bite all the Fruit to Pieces in a moment, for the sake of the Kernels. The Havock they make is Sometimes so great, that whole Orchards are laid waste in Spite of all the Noises that can be made, or Mawkins that can be dresst up, to fright 'em away. These Ravenous Birds visit North Carolina only during the warm Season, and so soon as the Cold begins to come on, retire back towards the Sun. They rarely Venture so far North as Virginia, except in a very hot Summer, when they visit the most Southern Parts of it. They are very Beautiful; but like some other pretty Creatures, are apt to be loud and mischievous.

27 [March]. Betwixt this and Edenton there are many thuckleberry Slashes, which afford a convenient Harbour for Wolves and Foxes. The first of these wild Beasts is not so large and fierce as they are in other countries more Northerly. He will not attack a Man in the keenest of his Hunger, but run away from him, as from an Animal more mischievous than himself.

The Foxes are much bolder, and will Sometimes not only make a Stand, but likewise assault any one that would balk them of their Prey. The Inhabitants hereabouts take the trouble to dig abundance of Wolf-Pits, so deep and perpendicular, that when a Wolf is once tempted into them, he can no more Scramble out again, than a Husband who has taken the Leap can Scramble out of Matrimony.

Most of the Houses in this Part of the Country are Log-houses, covered with Pine or Cypress Shingles, 3 feet long, and one broad. They are hung upon Laths with Peggs, and their doors too turn upon Wooden Hinges, and have wooden Locks to Secure them, so that the Building is finisht without Nails or other Iron-Work. They also set up their Pales without any Nails at all, and indeed more Securely than those that are nail'd. There are 3 Rails mortised into the Posts, the lowest of which serves as a Sill with a Groove in the Middle, big enough to receive the End of the Pales: the middle Part of the Pale rests against the Inside of the Next Rail, and the Top of it is brought forward to the outside of the uppermost. Such Wreathing of Pales in and out makes them stand firm, and much harder to unfix than when nail'd in the Ordinary way.

Within 3 or 4 Miles of Edenton, the Soil appears to be a little more fertile, tho' it is much cut with Slashes, which seem all to have a tendency towards the Dismal.

This Town is Situate on the North side of Albemarle Sound, which is there about 5 miles over. A Dirty Slash runs all along the Back of it, which in the Summer is a foul annoyance, and furnishes abundance of that Carolina plague, musquetas. There may be 40 or 50 Houses, most of them Small, and built without Expense. A Citizen here is counted Extravagant, if he has Ambition enough to aspire to a Brick-chimney. Justice herself is but indifferently Lodged, the Court-House having much the Air of a Common Tobacco-House. I believe this is the only Metropolis in the Christian or Mahometan World, where there is neither Church, Chappel, Mosque, Synagogue, or any other place of Publick Worship of any Sect or Religion whatsoever.

What little Devotion there may happen to be is much more private than their vices. The People seem easy without a Minister, as long as they are exempted from paying Him. Sometimes the Society for propagating the Gospel has had the Charity to send over Missionaries to this Country; but unfortunately the Priest has been too Lewd for the people, or, which oftener happens, they too lewd for the Priest. For these Reasons these Reverend Gentlemen have always left their Flocks as arrant Heathen as they found them. Thus much however may be said for the Inhabitants of Edenton, that not a Soul has the least taint of Hypocrisy, or Superstition, acting very Frankly and above-board in all their Excesses.

Provisions here are extremely cheap, and extremely good, so that People may live plentifully at a triffleing expense. Nothing is dear but Law, Physick, and Strong Drink, which are all bad in their Kind, and the last they get with so much Difficulty, that they are never guilty of the Sin of Suffering it to Sour upon their Hands. Their Vanity generally lies not so much in having a handsome Dining-Room, as a Handsome House of Office: in this Kind of Structure they are really extravagant.

They are rarely guilty of Flattering or making any Court to their governors, but treat them with all the Excesses of Freedom and Familiarity. They are of Opinion their rulers wou'd be apt to grow insolent, if they grew Rich, and for that reason take care to keep them poorer, and more dependent, if possible, than the Saints in New England used to do their Governors. They have very little coin, so they are forced to carry on their Home-Traffick with Paper-Money. This is the only Cash that will tarry in the Country, and for that reason the Discount goes on increasing between that and real Money, and will do so to the End of the Chapter.

28 [March]. Our Time passt heavily in our Quarters, where we were quite cloy'd with the Carolina Felicity of having nothing to do. It was really more insupportable than the greatest Fatigue, and made us even envy the Drudgery of our Friends in the Dismal. Besides, tho' the Men we had with us were kept in Exact Discipline, and behav'd without Reproach, yet our Landlord began to be tired of them, fearing they would breed a Famine in his Family.

Indeed, so many keen Stomachs made great Havock amongst the Beef and Bacon, which he had laid in for his Summer Provision, nor cou'd he easily purchase More at that time of the Year, with the Money we paid him, because the People having no certain Market seldom provide any more of these Commodities than will barely supply their own Occasions. Besides the Weather was now grown too warm to lay in a fresh Stock so late in the Spring. These Considerations abated somewhat of that chearfulness with which he bidd us Welcome in the Beginning, and made him think the time quite as long as we did till the Surveyors return'd.

While we were thus all Hands uneasy, we were comforted with the News that this Afternoon the Line was finisht through the Dismal. The Messenger told us it had been the hard work of three days to measure the Length of only 5 Miles, and mark the Trees as they past along, and by the most exact Survey they found the Breadth of the Dismal in this Place to be completely 15 Miles.

How wide it may be in other Parts, we can give no Account, but believe it grows narrower towards the North; possibly towards Albemarle Sound it may be something broader, where so many Rivers issue out of it. All we know for certain is, that from the Place where the Line enter'd the Dismal, to where it came out, we found the Road round that Portion of it which belongs to Virginia to be about 65 Miles. How great the Distance may be from each of those Points, round that Part that falls within the Bounds of Carolina, we had no certain Information: tho' tis conjectur'd it cannot be so little as 30 Miles. At which rate the whole Circuit must be about an Hundred. What a Mass of Mud and Dirt is treasur'd up within this filthy circumference, and what a Quantity of Water must perpetually drain into it from the riseing ground that Surrounds it on every Side?

Without taking the Exact level of the Dismal, we may be sure that it declines towards the Places where the Several Rivers take their Rise, in order to carrying off the constant Supplies of Water. Were it not for such Discharges, the whole Swamp would long Since have been converted into a Lake. On the other Side this Declension must be very gentle, else it would be laid perfectly dry by so many continual drains; Whereas, on the contrary, the Ground seems every where to be thoroughly drencht even in the dryest Season of the Year.

The Surveyors concluded this day's

Work with running 25 chains up into the Firm Land, where they waited further Orders from the Commissioners.

(1728) 1841

III. JOHN WOOLMAN
(1720–1772)

From *THE JOURNAL*

[EARLY LIFE]

I have often felt a motion of Love to leave some hints of my experience of the Goodness of God: and pursuant thereto, in the 36 year of my age, I begin this work.

I was Born in Northampton, in Burlington county, in West Jersey, in the year of our Lord 1720 & before I was seven years old, I began to be acquainted with the operations of Divine Love. Through the care of my Parents, I was taught to Read near as soon as I was capable of it, and as I went from School one seventh-day, I remember, while my companions went to play by the way, I went forward out of sight, and seting down, I read the twenty second chapter of the Revelations: "He showed me a pure River of Water of Life, clear as Crystal, proceeding out of the Throne of God and of the Lamb," &c. and in the reading of it, my mind was drawn to seek after that Pure Habitation, which I then believed God had prepared for his servants. The place where I sat, and the sweetness that attended my mind, remain fresh in my memory.

This and the like Gracious Visitations, had that effect upon me, that when boys used ill language, it troubled me, & through the continued Mercies of God, I was preserved from it. The pious instructions of my Parents were often fresh in my mind when I happened to be among wicked children, and were of use to me.

My Parents haveing a large family of children, used frequently on first-days after meeting, to put us to read in the Holy Scriptures, or some religious books, one after another, the rest sitting by without much conversation, which I have since often thought was a good practice. From what I had read, I believed there had been in past ages, people who Walked in Uprightness before God in a degree exceeding any that I knew, or heard of, now living: & the Apprehension of their being less Steadiness and firmness amongst people in this age than in past ages, often Troubled me while I was still young.

I had a Dream about the ninth year of my age as follows: I saw the Moon rise near the West, & run a regular course Eastward, so swift that in about a quarter of an hour, she reached our Meridian, when there descended from her a small Cloud on a Direct line to the Earth, which lighted on a pleasant Green about twenty yards from the Door of my Father's House (in which I thought I stood) and was immediately turned into a Beautiful green Tree. The Moon appeared to run on with Equal swiftness, and soon set in the East, at which time the Sun arose at the place where it com̄only doth in the Sumer, and Shineing with full Radiance in a Serene air, it appeared as pleasant a morning as ever I saw.

All this time I stood still in the door, in an Awfull frame of mind, and I observed that as heat increased by the Riseing Sun, it wrought so powerfully on the little green Tree, that the leaves gradually withered, and before Noon it appear'd dry & dead. There then appeared a Being, Small of Size, moving Swift from the North Southward, called a *"Sun Worm."*

[Tho' I was A Child, this dream was instructive to me.]

Another thing remarkable in my childhood was, that once as I went to a neighbour's house, I saw, on the way, a Robbin sitting on to her nest, and as I came near she went off, but having young ones, flew about, and with many cries expressed her Concern for them. I stood and threw stones at her, till one striking her, she fell down dead. At first I was pleas'd with the Exploit, but after a few minutes was seized with Horror, as haveing in a sportive way kild an Innocent Creature while she was carefull for her young. I beheld her lying dead, & thought those young ones for which she was so carefull must now perish for want of their dam to nourish them; and after some painfull considerations on the subject, I climbed up the Tree, took all the young birds, and killed them supposing that better than to leave them to pine away and die miserably: and believ'd in this case, that scripture proverb was fulfilled, "The tender mercies of the wicked are Cruel." I then went on my errand, but, for some hours, could think of little else but [the Cruelties I had committed, and was much troubled.]

Thus He whose tender Mercies are over all his works, hath placed that in the Human mind which incites to exercise goodness towards every liveing creature and This being singly attended to, people become tenderhearted and sympathizing; but being frequently & totally rejected, the mind shuts itself up in a Contrary disposition.

About the twelfth year of my age, my Father being abroad, my Mother reproved me for some misconduct, to which I made an Undutifull reply & the next first-day, as I was with my Father returning from Meeting, He told me he understood I had behaved amis to my Mother, and Advised me to be more carefull in future. I knew myself blameable, and in shame and confusion remained silent. Being thus awakened to a sense of my Wickedness, I felt remorse in my mind, and geting home, I retired and prayed to the Lord to forgive me; and I do not remember that I ever after that, spoke unhandsomely to either of my Parents, however foolish in some other things.

Having attained the age of Sixteen, I began to love wanton company: and though I was preserved from profane language or Scandalous conduct, Still I perceived a plant in me which produced much wild grapes. Yet my Merciful Father forsook me not utterly, but at times through his grace I was brought seriously to consider my ways, and the sight of my backsliding affected me with sorrow: but for want of rightly attending to the reproofs of Instruction, Vanity was added to Vanity, and Repentance. Upon the whole my mind was more and more Alienated from the Truth, and I hastened towards Destruction. While I meditate on the Gulf towards which I traveled, and reflect on my youthful Disobedience, my heart is affected with Sorrow.

Advancing in age, the number of

my Acquaintance increased, and thereby my way grew more difficult. Though I had heretofore found comfort in reading the Holy Scriptures, and thinking on heavenly things, I was now Estranged therefrom. I knew I was going from the flock of Christ, and had no resolution to return, hence serious reflections were uneasie to me, and Youthfull Vanities and Diversions my greatest pleasure. Runing in this Road I found many like myself, and we associated in that which is reverse to true Friendship: but in this swift race it pleased God to Visit me with Sickness, so that I doubted of recovering: and then did Darkness, Horror and Amazement, with full force seize me, even when my pain and distress of body was verry great: I thought it would have been better for me never to have had a being, than to see the day which I now saw. I was filled with Confusion, & in great affliction both of mind & body, I lay and bewailed myself. [I had not confidence to lift up my cries to God, whom I had thus offended; but in a deep sense of my great folly I was humbled before Him,] & at length that Word which is as a Fire and a Hamer, broke and dissolved my rebellious heart, and then my Cries were put up in contrition, and in the multitude of His mercies I found inward relief, and felt a close Engagement, that if he was pleased to Restore my health, I might walk Humbly before Him.

After my Recovery, this Exercise remained with me a considerable time, but, by degrees, giving way to youthfull vanities, they gained strength, and geting with wanton young people I lost ground. The Lord had been verry Gracious, and Spoke peace to me in the time of my distress, and I now most ungratefully turned again to folly, on which account, at times, I felt sharp reproof, but did not get low enough to Cry for help. I was not so hardy as to commit things scandalous, but to Exceed in Vanity, and promote myrth, was my chief study. Still I retained a love and esteem for pious people, and their company brought an Awe upon me. My Dear Parents several times Admonished me in the fear of the Lord, and their admonition entered into my heart, & had a good effect for a season, but not geting deep enough to pray rightly, the tempter when he came found entrance. I remember once having spent a part of a day in wantonness, as I went to bed at night, there lay in a window near my bed a Bible, which I opened, and first cast my eye on the Text, "we lie down in our shame, and our confusion covers us." This I knew to be my case, and meeting with so unexpected a reproof, I was somewhat Affected with it, and went to bed under remorse of conscience, which I soon cast off again.

Thus time passed on, my heart was replenished with myrth and wantonness, while pleasing scenes of Vanity were presented to my Imagination, till I attain'd the age of Eighteen years, near which time I felt the Judgments of God in my soul like a consuming fire, and looking over my past life, the prospect was moveing. I was often sad, and longed to be deliver'd from those vanities; then again my heart was Strongly Inclined to them, and there was in me a sore conflict. At times I turned to folly, and then again sorrow and confusion took hold of me. In a while I resolved totally to leave off some of my vanities, but there was a secret reserve in my heart, of the more refined part of them, and I was not low enough to find true peace. Thus for some months, I had great troubles and disquiet, there remaining in me an unsubjected will, which rendered my labours fruitless, till at length, through the Mercifull continuance of Heavenly Visitations, I was made to bow down in Spirit before the Most High. I remember one evening I had spent some time in reading a pious author, and walking out a lone, I humbly prayed to the Lord for his help, that I might be delivered from those vanities which so ensnared me. . . . Thus being brought low he helped me, and as I learned to bear the Cross, I felt refreshment to come from his Presence: but not keeping in that Strength which gave victory I lost ground again, The sense of which greatly afflicted me and I sought Desarts and lonely places, and there with tears did confess my Sins to God, and humbly craved help of Him, and I may say with Reverence he was near to me in my troubles, and in those times of Humiliation opened my ear to Discipline.

I was now led to look seriously at the means by which I was drawn from the pure Truth, and I learned this. That if I would live in the life which the Faithful servants of God lived in, I must not go into company as heretofore in my own will, but all the cravings of Sense must be governed by a Divine principle. In times of sorrow and abasement these Instructions were sealed upon me, and I felt the power of Christ prevail over all selfish desires, so that I was preserved in a good degree of steadiness, and being young and believing at that time that a single life was best for me, I was strengthened to keep from such company as had often been a snare to me.

I kept steady to meetings, spent first-days in the afternoon chiefly in reading the scriptures and other good Books, and was early convinced in my mind that true Religion consisted in an inward life, wherein the Heart doth Love and Reverence God the Creator, and learn to Exercise true Justice and Goodness, not only toward all men, but allso toward the Brute Creatures. That as the mind was moved by an inward Principle to Love God as an invisible, Incomprehensible Being, by the same principle it was moved to love him in all his manifestations in the Visible world. That as by his breath the flame of life was kindled in all Animal and Sensible creatures, to say we Love God as unseen, and at the same time Exercise cruelty toward the least creature moving by his life, or by life derived from Him, was a Contradiction in itself.

I found no narrowness respecting Sects and Opinions, but believe that sincere upright-hearted people, in Every society who truly love God were accepted of Him.

As I lived under the Cross, and simply followed the openings of Truth, my mind from day to day was more Enlightened, my former acquaintance were left to judge of me as they would, for I found it safest for me to live in private and keep these things sealed up in my own breast. While I silently ponder on that change which was wrought in me, I find no language equal to it, nor any means to convey to another a clear idea of it. I looked upon the works of God in this Visible Creation, and an awfullness covered me: my heart was tender and often contrite, and a universal Love to my fellow Creatures increased in me. This will be understood by such who have troden in the same path. * * *

(1756) 1775

[LOVE OF MAN]

From an inward purifying, and stedfast abideing under it, springs a lively operative desire for the good of others. All faithful people are not called to the publick ministry but whoever are called to it, are called to minister of that which they have taisted and handled spiritually. The outward modes of worship are various, but wheresoever [men] are true Ministers of Jesus Christ, it is from the operation of his Spirit upon their hearts, first purifying them, and thus giving them a [feeling] sense of the conditions of others. This truth was early fixed in my mind, and I was taught to watch the pure opening, and to take heed least while I was standing to speak, my own will should get upermost, and cause me to utter words from worldly wisdom, and depart from the Chanel of the true Gospel Ministry.

In the management of my outward affiairs, I may say with thankfulness I found Truth to be my Support, and I was respected in my Masters Family who came to live in Mountholly within two years after my going there [1742]. . . .

About the twenty third year of my age I had many fresh and heavenly openings, in respect to the care and providence of the Almighty over his creatures in general, and over man as the most noble amongst those which are visible, and Being clearly convinced in my Judgmt that to place my whole trust in God was best for me, I felt renewed engagements that in all things I might act on an inward principle of Virtue, and pursue worldly business no further than as Truth open'd my way therein.

About the time called Christmas I observed many people from the Country, and dwellers in Town, who resorting to publick houses, spent their time in drinking and vain sports, tending to corrupt one another, on which account I was much troubled. At one house in particular there was [much disorder,] and I believed it was a duty laid on me to go and speak to the master of that house. I considered I was young, and that several Elderly friends in Town had opportunity to See these things, and though I would [gladly] have been excused, yet I could not feel my mind clear. The Exercise was heavy, and as I was Reading what the Almighty Said to Ezekiel, respecting his duty as a watchman, the matter was set home more clearly, and then with prayer and tears, I besought the Lord for his Assistance, who in loving kindness gave me a Resigned heart. Then at a sutable Oportunity, I went to the publick house, and Seeing the man amongst a company, I went to him and told him I wanted to speak with him, so we went aside, and there in the Fear and dread of the Almighty I Exprest to him what rested on my mind, which he took kindly, and afterward showed more regard to me than before. In a few years after he died, midle-aged, and I often thought that had I neglected my duty in that case, it would have given me great trouble and I was humbly thankfull to my Gracious Father, [who had supported me therein.]

My Employer having a Negro woman sold her, and directed me to write a bill of Sale, The man being waiting who had bought her. The thing was Sudden, and though the thoughts of writing an Instrument of Slavery for one of my fellow creatures felt uneasie, yet I remembered I was hired by the year; that it was my master who [directed] me to do it, and that it was an Elderly man, a member of our society who bought her, so through weakness I gave way, and wrote it, but at the Executing it I was so Afflicted in my mind, that I said before my Master and the friend, that I believed Slavekeeping to be a practice inconsistent with the Christian Religion: this in some degree abated my uneasiness, yet as often as I reflected seriously upon it I thought I should have been clearer, if I had desired to be Excused from it, as a thing against my conscience, for such it was. [And] Some time after this a young man of our Society, spake to me to write [an instrument of Slavery], he having lately taken a Negro into his house. I told him I was not easie to write it, for though many [people] kept slaves in our society as in others, I still believed the practice was not right, and desired to be excused from doing the writing. I spoke to him in good will, and he told me that keeping slaves was not altogether agreeable to his mind, but that the slave being a gift made to his wife, he had accepted of her. . . .

(1743) 1774

[THE INDIAN MISSION]

18da. 6mo. We rested ourselves this forenoon, & the Indians knowing that the Moravian and I were of different Religious Societies, and as some of their people had encouraged him to come & Stay a while with them were I believe concern'd that no jarring or discord might be in their meetings, & they I suppose having conferred together acquainted me that the People at my request would at any time come together & hold meetings, & allso told me that they Expected the Moravian would speak in their setled meetings which are commonly held morning and near evening. So I found liberty in my heart to Speak to the Moravian, & told him of the care I felt on my mind for the good of these people, & that I believed no ill Effects would follow it, if I sometimes Spake in their meetings when love engaged me thereto, without calling them together at times when they did not meet of course: whereupon he expresst his good-will toward my Speaking at any time, all that I found in my heart to say. So near evening I was at their meeting where the pure Gospel love was felt, to the tendering Some of our Hearts, and the Interpreters endeavouring to Acquaint the people with what I said in Short Sentences found some difficulty as none of them were quite perfect in the English and

Delaware Tongues; So they helped one another, and we Laboured along, Divine Love attending, and afterwards, feeling my mind covered with the Spirit of Prayer, I told [those who] Interpreted that I found it in my heart to pray to God, & believed if I prayed Aright he whould hear me, & Expresst my willingness for them to Omit Interpreting. So our meeting ended with a degree of Divine Love, & before the people went out, I observed [Papoonal] the man who had been Zealous in Labouring for a Reformation in that Town being then very tender Spoke to one of the Interpreters, and I was afterwards told that he said in substance as follows, "I Love to Feel where words come from." * * *

19$^{da.}$ 6$^{mo.}$ 1$^{st.}$ of the week. This morning in the meeting the Indian who came up with the Moravian being allso a member of that Society prayed, and then the Moravian Spake a Short time to the people. And in the afternoon, they coming together, and my heart being filled with a Heavenly care for their good, I spake to them awhile by Interpreters, but none of them being perfect in the work, & I feeling the Current of Love run Strong, told the Interpreters that I believed Some of the people would understand me, & so proceeded: In which exercise I believe the Holy [Ghost] wrought on Some hearts to Edification where all the words were not understood. I looked upon it as a time of Divine Favour, & my Heart was tendered and truly thankfull before the Lord: and after I Sat down one of the Interpreters Seemed Spirited up to give the Indians the Substance of what I said.

Before our first meeting this morning, [my mind] was led to meditate on the manifold difficulties of these Indians, who by permission of the Six Nations dwell in these parts, and a Near Sympathy with them was raised in me, And my Heart being enlarged in the Love of [Christ] I thought that the Affectionate care of a good man for his only Brother in Affliction, does not exceed what I then felt for that people.

I came to this place through much trouble, & though through the Mercies of God, I believed that if I died in the Journey it would be well with me, yet the thoughts of falling into the hands of [those] Indian warriors, was in times of weakness afflicting to me. And being of a Tender Constitution of Body the thoughts of captivity amongst them was at times grievous, as Supposing that they being strong & hardy might demand service of me beyound what I could well bear; but the Lord alone was my helper, and I believed if I went into captivity it would be for Some good end, and thus from time to time my mind was centered in Resignation in which I always found quietness. And now this day, though I had the Same Dangerous Wilderness between me & home, was inwardly Joyfull that the Lord had Strengthened me to come on this Visit, and Manifested a Fatherly care over me in my poor lowly condition, when in mine own eyes I appear'd inferior to many amongst the Indians.

When the last mentioned meeting

was ended it being night, [Papoonal] went to Bed, and one of the Interpreters Seting by me, I observed [Papoonal] Spoke with an harmonious voice I suppose a minute or two and I asking the Interpreter, was told that he was Expressing "his Thankfullness to God for the favours he had received that day, and Prayed that he would continue to favour him with that same which he had experienced in that meeting." [That though Papoonal] had before agreed to receive the Moravian, and to join with them, he still appeared kind & Loving to us.

20da. 6mo. was at two meetings, & Silent in [both]. 21da. This morning in Meeting my heart was Enlarged in pure love amongst them, and in Short plain Sentences Expresst several things that rested upon me; which one of the Interpreters gave the people pretty readily after which the meeting ended in Supplication, and I had cause humbly to acknowledge the Loving kindness of the Lord toward us; And then I believed that a Door remained open for the Faithfull disciples of Jesus Christ to Labour amongst these people.

I feeling my mind at Liberty to return, took my leave of them in general at the Conclusion of what I said in meeting, and so we prepared to go homeward, but some of their most active men told us, that when we were ready to move the people would choose to come & shake hands with us; which those who usually came to meeting [generally] did, & from a secret [draft] in my mind I went amongst some who did not use to go to meetings & took my leave of them allso, and the Moravian and his Indian Interpreter appeared respectful to us at parting. This Town stands on the bank of Susquehannah & consists I believe of about forty Houses mostly compact together; Some about thirty feet long, & Eighteen wide, some biger, & some less, mostly built of Split plank, one end set in the ground & the other piñed to a plate, [and then] Rafters, and covered with Bark. I understand a great Flood last winter overflowed the Chief part of the ground where the Town Stands, and some were now about moveing their Houses to higher ground.

We Expected only two Indians to be our Company, but when we were ready to go we found many of them were going to Bethlehem with Skins and Furs, who chose to go in company with us: So they loaded two Canows, which they desired us to go in, telling us that the Waters were so raised with the Rains that the Horses should be taken by Such who were better Acquainted with the fording places. So we with several Indians went in the Canows, and others went on Horses, there being Seven besides ours, and we met with the Horsemen once on the way by Appointment, and then near night, a little below A Branch called Tankhannah we lodged there, and some of the young men going out a little before dusk with their Guns brought in a Deer.

22da. 6mo. Through diligence we reached Wioming before Night, and understood the Indians were mostly gone from this place; here we went up a Small Creek into the woods with our Canows, and pitching our Tent, carried out our Baggage, and before dark our Horses came to us.

23da 6mo In the morning their Horses were loaded, & we prepar'd our Baggage and so Set forward being in all fourteen, and with diligent Traveling were favoured to get near half way to Fort Allen. The Land on this Road from Wioming to Our Frontier being mostly poor, & good grass Scarce, they chose a piece of low ground to lodge on, as the best for graseing; and I having Swet much in Traveling, and being weary Slept sound. I perceiv'd in the Night that I had taken cold; of which I was favoured to get better soon.

24da 6mo We passed fort Allen, & lodged near it in the woods; having forded the westerly branch of Delaware three times, and thereby had a shorter way, & mist going over the highest part of the Blue Mountains, called the Second Ridge. In the Second time fording where the River cuts through the Mountain, the waters being Rapid and pretty deep, And my companion's mare being a tall & Tractable Animal, He Sundry times drove her back through the River, & they loaded her with the Burthens of some Small Horses, which they thought not Sufficient to [venture] through with their Loads.

The Troubles Westward and the difficulty for Indians to pass through our Frontier, I apprehend was one Reason why so many came as Expecting that our being in Company would prevent the outside Inhabitants from being Surprised.

25da 6mo We reached Bethlehem takeing care on the way to keep foremost, and to Acquaint people on & near the Road who these Indians were. This we found very needfull for the Frontier Inhabitants were often alarmed at the Report of English being killed by Indians Westward.

Amongst our Company were Some who did I not remember to have Seen at Meeting, and some of these at first were very reserved; But we being several days together, and behaving friendly toward them, & making them sutable returns for the Services they did us, they became more free and Sociable.

26da 6mo & 1da of the week. Having carefully endeavoured to Settle all Affairs with the Indians relative to our Journey, we took leave of them and I thought they generally parted with us Affectionately. So we geting to Richland had a very Comfortable Meeting amongst our Friends: here I parted with my kind [& Beloved] Companion Benjamin Parvin, and accompanied by my Friend Samuel Foulke we rode to John Cadwaladers, from whence I reached home the Next day, where I found my Family midling well, and they & my Friends all along appear'd glad to see me return from a Journey which they apprehended Dangerous, but my mind while I was out, had been Employed in Striving for a perfect Resignation; I had often been confirmed in a Belief that whatever the Lord might be pleased to allot for me would work for good. [And] I was now carefull lest I should admit any degree of Selfishness in being glad overmuch; And Laboured to Improve by those Tryals in Such a maner as my Gracious Father & Protector [may] intend for me.

Between the English Inhabitants and Wahalowsing, we had only a narrow path, which in many places is much grown up with Bushes, and Interrupted by abundance of Trees lying across it; which together with the Mountains, Swamps, and rough Stones, it is a difficult road to Travel, and the more so for that Rattle-Snakes abound there, of which we killed four. That people who have never been in such places, have but an Imperfect Idea of them. But I was not only taught patience, but also made thankful to God who thus led me about and instructed me, that I might have a quick and lively feeling of the Afflictions of my fellow-Creatures, whose Scituation in life is difficult.

(1756) 1775

[EXPERIENCES IN ENGLAND]

8$^{da.}$ 6$^{mo.}$ 1772. Landed at London & went Straitway to the yearly meeting of Ministers and Elders, which had been gathered (I suppose) half an hour.

In this meeting, my mind was humbly contrite. Afternoon meeting of business opened, which by adjournments, held near a week. In these meetings, I often felt a living concern for the Establishment of Friends in the pure life of Truth and my heart was Enlarged in the meeting of Ministers, Meeting of business, and in Several meetings for publick worship, & I felt my mind united in true love to the faithful labourers, now gathered [from the several parts of] this Yearly Meeting. * * *

[16$^{da.}$ 8$^{mo.}$] Stage Coaches frequently go upwards of a hundred miles in 24 hours, and I have heard friends say, in several places that it is common for horses to be killed with hard driving, and many others are driven till they grow blind. [These Coaches runing chief part of the Night, do often run over & hurt people in the dark.]

Post boys pursue their business, each one to his Stage, all night through the winter. Some boys who ride long Stages suffer greatly in winter nights and at several places I have heard of their being froze to death. So great is the hurry in the Spirit of this world, that in aiming to do business quick, and to gain wealth, the Creation at this day doth loudly groan!

As my journey hath been without a horse I have had several offers of being assisted on my way in these Stage Coaches but have not been in them nor have I had freedom to send letters by these posts, in the present way of their riding, the stages being so fixed and one body dependant on another as to time, that they commonly go upward of 100 miles in 24 hours, and in the cold long winter nights, the poor boys suffer much.

I heard in America of the way of these posts, and cautioned friends in the general meeting of Ministers and Elders at philada and in the yearly meeting of Ministers and Elders at London, not to send letters to me on any common occasion by post. And though on this account I may be likely to hear Seldomer from the family I left behind, yet for Righteousness Sake I am through Divine favour made content.

I have felt great distress of mind since I came on this Island on account of the members of our Society being mixed with the world in various Sorts of business and traffick carried on in impure Channels. Great is the trade to Africa for Slaves! and in loading these Ships, abundance of people are employed in the factories amongst whom are many of our Society! Friends in Early times refused on a religious principle to make or trade in Superfluities, of which we have many large testimonies on record, but for want of faithfulness some gave way; even some whose examples were of note in Society, and from thence others took more liberty. Members of our society worked in Superfluities, and bought and Sold them, and thus dimness of sight came over many. At length friends got into the use of Some Superfluities in dress, and in the furniture of their houses, and this hath spread from less to more, till Superfluity of some kinds is common amongst us.

In this declining State many look at the examples one of another, and too much neglect the pure feeling of Truth. Of late years [this increasing,] a deep exercise hath attended my mind, that friends may dig deep, may carefully cast forth the loose matter, and get down to the Rock, the Sure foundation, and there hearken to that divine voice which gives a Clear & certain Sound, and I have felt in that which doth not deceive, that if friends who have known the Truth, keep in that tenderness of heart, where all views of outward gain are given up, and their trust is only in the Lord, He will graciously lead some to be patterns of deep Self denial in things relating to trade and handicraft labour, and that some who have plenty of the treasures of this world, will example in a plain, frugal life, and pay wages to such whom they may hire, more liberally than is now customary in some places. * * *

[26$^{da.}$ 8mo 1772.] In a time of Sickness with the plurisie, a little upward of two years and a half ago I was brought so Near the gates of death, that I forgot my name. Being then desirous to know who I was, I saw a mass of matter of a dull gloomy collour, between the South and the East, and was informed that this mass was human beings, in as great misery as they could be, & live, and that I was mixed in with them, & henceforth I might not consider myself as a distinct or Separate being. In this state I remained several hours. I then heard a soft melodious voice, more pure and harmonious than any voice I had heard with my ears before, and I believed it was the voice of an angel who spake to the other angels. The words were *John Woolman is dead.* I soon remembered that I once was John Woolman, and being assured that I was alive in the body, I greatly wondered what that heavenly voice could mean.

I believed beyond doubting that it was the voice of an holy Angel, but as yet it was a mystery to me.

I was then carried in Spirit to the mines, where poor Oppressed people were digging rich treasures for those called Christians, and heard them blaspheme the name of Christ, at which I was grieved for his Name to me was precious.

Then I was informed that these heathen were told that those who oppressed them were the followers of Christ; and they said amongst themselves, If Christ directed them to use us in this Sort then Christ is a cruel tyrant.

All this time the Song of the Angel remained a Mystery, and in the morning my dear wife and some others coming to my bedside I asked them if they knew who I was, and they telling me I was John Woolman, thought I was only light-headed, for I told them not what the Angel said, nor was I disposed to talk much to any one; but was very desirous to get so deep that I might understand this Mystery.

My tongue was often so dry that I could not speak till I had moved it about and gathered some moisture, and as I lay still for a time, at length I felt divine power prepare my mouth that I could speak, and then I said, "I am crucified with Christ, nevertheless I live yet not I, but Christ, [that] liveth in me, and the life I now live in the flesh is by faith [in] the Son of God who loved me and gave himself for me."

Then the Mystery was opened and I perceived there was Joy in heaven over a Sinner who had repented, and that that language, *John Woolman is dead,* meant no more than the death of my own will.

(1772) 1775

THE PROGRESS OF REASON

I. JOHN WISE
(1652–1725)

From *A VINDICATION OF THE GOVERNMENT OF NEW ENGLAND CHURCHES*

CHAPTER II

[THE FREEDOM OF MAN]

1. I Shall disclose several Principles of Natural Knowledge; plainly discovering the Law of Nature; or the true sentiments of Natural Reason, with Respect to Mans Being and Government. And in this Essay I shall peculiarly confine the discourse to two heads, *viz*

1. Of the Natural [in distinction to the Civil] and then,

2. Of the Civil Being of Man. And I shall Principally take Baron *Puffendorff* for my Chief Guide and Spokesman. * * *

But to proceed under the head of a State of Natural Being, I shall more distinctly Explain the State of Humane Nature in its Original Capacity, as Man is placed on Earth by his Maker, and Cloathed with many Investitures, and Immunities which properly belong to Man separately considered. As,

1. The Prime Immunity in Mans State, is that he is most properly the Subject of the Law of Nature. He is the Favourite Animal on Earth; in that this Part of Gods Image, *viz.* Reason is Congenate with his Nature, wherein by a Law Immutable, Instampt upon his Frame, God has provided a Rule for Men in all their Actions, obliging each one to the performance of that which is Right, not only as to Justice, but likewise as to all other Moral Vertues, the which is nothing but the Dictate of Right Reason founded in the Soul of Man. *Motloy, De Mao, Præf.* That which is to be drawn from Man's Reason, flowing from the true Current of that Faculty, when unperverted, may be said to be the Law of Nature; on which account, the Holy Scriptures declare it written on Mens hearts. For being indowed with a Soul, you may know from your self, how, and what you ought to act, Rom. 2. 14. *These having not a Law, are a Law to themselves.* So that the meaning is, when we acknowledge the Law of Nature to be the dictate of Right Reason, we must mean that the Understanding of Man is Endowed with such a power, as to be able, from the Contemplation of humane Condition to discover a necessity of Living agreeably with this Law: And likewise to find out some Principle, by which the Precepts of it, may be clearly and solidly Demonstrated. The way to discover the Law of Nature in our own state, is by a narrow Watch, and accurate Contemplation of our Natural Condition, and propensions. Others say this is the way to find out the Law of Nature. *scil.* If a Man any ways doubts, whether what he is going to do to another Man be agreeable to the Law of Nature, then let him suppose himself

to be in that other Mans Room; And by this Rule effectually Executed. A Man must be a very dull Scholar to Nature not to make Proficiency in the Knowledge of her Laws. But more Particularly in pursuing our Condition for the discovery of the Law of Nature, this is very obvious to view, *viz.*

1. A Principle of Self-Love, & Self-Preservation, is very predominant in every Mans Being.

2. A Sociable Disposition.

3. An Affection or Love to Mankind in General. And to give such Sentiments the force of a Law, we must suppose a God who takes care of all Mankind, and has thus obliged each one, as a Subject of higher Principles of Being, then meer Instincts. For that all Law properly considered, supposes a capable Subject, and a Superiour Power; And the Law of God which is Binding, is published by the Dictates of Right Reason as other ways: Therefore says *Plutarch, To follow God and obey Reason is the same thing.* But moreover that God has Established the Law of Nature, as the General Rule of Government, is further Illustrable from the many Sanctions in Providence, and from the Peace and Guilt of Conscience in them that either obey, or violate the Law of Nature. But moreover, the foundation of the Law of Nature with relation to Government, may be thus Discovered. *scil.* Man is a Creature extreamly desirous of his own Preservation; of himself he is plainly Exposed to many Wants, unable to secure his own safety, and Maintenance without the Assistance of his fellows; and he is also able of returning Kindness by the furtherance of mutual Good; But yet Man is often found to be Malicious, Insolent, and easily Provoked, and as powerful in effecting mischief, as he is ready in designing it. Now that such a Creature may be Preserved, it is necessary that he be Sociable; that is, that he be capable and disposed to unite himself to those of his own species, and to Regulate himself towards them, that they may have no fair Reason to do him harm; but rather incline to promote his Interests, and secure his Rights and Concerns. This then is a Fundamental Law of Nature, that every Man as far as in him lies, do maintain a Sociableness with others, agreeable with the main end and disposition of humane Nature in general. For this is very apparent, that Reason and Society render Man the most potent of all Creatures. And Finally, from the Principles of Sociableness it follows as a fundamental Law of Nature, that Man is not so Wedded to his own Interest, but that he can make the Common good the mark of his Aim: And hence he becomes Capacitated to enter into a Civil State by the Law of Nature; for without this property in Nature, *viz.* Sociableness, which is for Cementing of parts, every Government would soon moulder and dissolve.

2. The Second Great Immunity of Man is an Original Liberty Instampt upon his Rational Nature. He that intrudes upon this Liberty, Violates the Law of Nature. In this Discourse I shall wave the Consideration of Mans Moral Turpitude, but shall view him Physically as a Creature which God has made and furnished essentially with many Enobling Immunities, which render him the most August Animal in the World, and still, what-

ever has happened since his Creation, he remains at the upper-end of Nature, and as such is a Creature of a very Noble Character. For as to his Dominion, the whole frame of the Lower Part of the Universe is devoted to his use, and at his Command; and his Liberty under the Conduct of Right Reason, is equal with his trust. Which Liberty may be briefly Considered, Internally as to his Mind, and externally as to his Person.

1. The Internal Native Liberty of Mans Nature in general implies, a faculty of Doing or Omitting things according to the Direction of his Judgment. But in a more special meaning, this Liberty does not consist in a loose and ungovernable Freedom, or in an unbounded Licence of Acting. Such Licence is disagreeing with the condition and dignity of Man, and would make Man of a lower and meaner Constitution then Bruit Creatures; who in all their Liberties are kept under a better and more Rational Government, by their Instincts. Therefore as *Plutarch* says, *Those Persons only who live in Obedience to Reason, are worthy to be accounted free: They alone live as they Will, who have Learnt what they ought to Will.* So that the true Natural Liberty of Man, such as really and truely agrees to him, must be understood, as he is Guided and Restrained by the Tyes of Reason, and Laws of Nature; all the rest is Brutal, if not worse.

2. Mans External Personal, Natural Liberty, Antecedent to all Humane parts, or Alliances must also be considered. And so every Man must be conceived to be perfectly in his own Power and disposal, and not to be controuled by the Authority of any other. And thus every Man, must be acknowledged equal to every Man, since all Subjection and all Command are equally banished on both sides; and considering all Men thus at Liberty, every Man has a Prerogative to Judge for himself, *viz.* What shall be most for his Behoof, Happiness and Well-being.

3. The Third Capital Immunity belonging to Mans Nature, is an equality amongst Men; Which is not to be denyed by the Law of Nature, till Man has Resigned himself with all his Rights for the sake of a Civil State; and then his Personal Liberty and Equality is to be cherished, and preserved to the highest degree, as will consist with all just distinctions amongst Men of Honour, and shall be agreeable with the publick Good. For Man has a high valuation of himself, and the passion seems to lay its first foundation [not in Pride, but] really in the high and admirable Frame and Constitution of Humane Nature. The Word Man, says my Author, is thought to carry somewhat of Dignity in its sound; and we commonly make use of this as the most proper and prevailing Argument against a rude Insulter, *viz. I am not a Beast or a Dog, but am a Man as well as your self.* Since then Humane Nature agrees equally with all persons; and since no one can live a Sociable Life with another that does not own or Respect him as a Man; It follows as a Command of the Law of Nature, that every Man Esteem and treat another as one who is naturally his Equal, or who is a Man as well as he. There be many popular, or plausible Reasons that greatly Illustrate this Equality, *viz.* that we all Derive our

Being from one stock, the same Common Father of humane Race. On this Consideration *Bœthius* checks the pride of the Insulting Nobility.

Quid Genus et Proavos Strepitis?
Si Primordia Vestra,
Auteremque Deum Spectas,
Nullus Degener Extat
Nisi vitiis Perjura fovens,
Proprium Deserat Orturn.

Fondly our first Descent we Boast;
If whence at first our Breath we Drew
The common springs of Life we view,
The Airy Notion soon is Lost.

The Almighty made us equal all;
But he that slavishly complyes
To do the Drudgery of Vice,
Denyes his high Original.

And also that our Bodies are Composed of matter, frail, brittle, and lyable to be destroyed by thousand Accidents; we all owe our Existence to the same Method of propagation. The Noblest Mortal in his Entrance on to the Stage of Life, is not distinguished by any pomp or of passage from the lowest of Mankind; and our Life hastens to the same General Mark: Death observes no Ceremony, but Knocks as loud at the Barriers of the Court, as at the Door of the Cottage. This Equality being admitted, bears a very great force in maintaining Peace and Friendship amongst Men. For that he who would use the Assistance of others, in promoting his own Advantage, ought as freely to be at their service, when they want his help on the like Occasions. *One Good turn Requires another,* is the Common Proverb; for otherwise he must need esteem others unequal to himself, who constantly demands their Aid, and as constantly denies his own. And whoever is of this Insolent Temper, cannot but highly displease those about him, and soon give Occasion of the Breach of the Common Peace. It was a Manly Reproof which *Charactacus* gave the *Romans. Num Si vos Omnibus* &c. What! because you desire to be Masters of all Men, does it follow therefore that all Men should desire to be your Slaves, for that it is a Command of Natures Law, that no Man that has not obtained a particular and special Right, shall arrogate to himself a Larger share then his fellows, but shall admit others to equal Priviledges with himself. So that the Principle of Equality in a Natural State, is peculiarly transgressed by Pride, which is when a Man without sufficient reason prefers himself to others. And though as *Hensius,* Paraphrases upon *Aristotle's* Politicks to this Purpose. *viz. Nothing is more suitable to Nature, then that those who Excel in Understanding and Prudence, should Rule and Controul those who are less happy in those Advantages,* &c. Yet we must note, that there is room for an Answer, *scil.* That it would be the Greatest absurdity to believe, that Nature actually Invests the Wise with a Sovereignity over the weak; or with a Right of forcing them against their Wills; for that no Sovereignty can be established, unless some Humane Deed, or Covenant Precede: Nor does Natural fitness for Government make a Man presently Governour over another; for that as *Ulpian* says, *by a Natural Right all Men are born free;* and Nature having set all Men upon a Level and made them Equals, no Servitude or Subjection can be conceived without Inequality; and this cannot be made without Usurpation or Force in others, or Voluntary Compliance in those who Resign their freedom, and give away their degree of Natural Being And thus we come,

2. To consider Man in a Civil State of Being; wherein we shall observe the great difference betwen a Natural, and Political State; for in the Latter State many Great disproportions appear, or at least many obvious distinctions are soon made amongst Men; which Doctrine is to be laid open under a few heads.

1. Every Man considered in a Natural State, must be allowed to be Free, and at his own dispose; yet to suit Mans Inclinations to Society; And in a peculiar manner to gratify the necessity he is in of publick Rule and Order, he is Impelled to enter into a Civil Community; and Divests himself of his Natural Freedom, and puts himself under Government; which amongst other things Comprehends the Power of Life and Death over Him; together with Authority to Injoyn him some things to which he has an utter Aversation, and to prohibit him other things, for which he may have as strong an Inclination; so that he may be often under this Authority, obliged to Sacrifice his Private, for the Publick Good. So that though Man is inclined to Society, yet he is driven to a Combination by great necessity. For that the true and leading Cause of forming Governments, and yielding up Natural Liberty, and throwing Mans Equality into a Common Pile to be new Cast by the Rules of fellowship; was really and truly to guard themselves against the Injuries Men were lyable to Interchangeably; for none so Good to Man, as Man, and yet none a greater Enemy. So that,

2. The first Humane Subject and Original of Civil Power is the People. For as they have a Power every Man over himself in a Natural State, so upon a Combination they can and do bequeath this Power unto others; and settle it according as their united discretion shall Determine. For that this is very plain, that when the Subject of Sovereign Power is quite Extinct, that Power returns to the People again. And when they are free, they may set up what species of Government they please; or if they rather incline to it, they may subside into a State of Natural Being, if it be plainly for the best. In the *Eastern* Country of the *Mogul,* we have some resemblance of the Case; for upon the Death of an absolute Monarch, they live so many days without a Civil Head; but in that *Interregnum,* those who survive the Vacancy, are glad to get into a Civil State again; and usually they are in a very Bloody Condition when they return under the Covert of a new Monarch; this project is to indear the People to a Tyranny, from the Experience they have so lately had of an Anarchy.

3. The formal Reason of Government is the Will of a Community, yielded up and surrendered to some other Subject, either of one particular Person, or more, Conveyed in the following manner.

Let us conceive in our Mind a multitude of Men, all Naturally Free & Equal; going about voluntarily, to Erect themselves into a new Common-Wealth. Now their Condition being such, to bring themselves into a Politick Body, they must needs Enter into divers Covenants.

1. They must Interchangeably each Man Covenant to joyn in one lasting Society, that they may be capable to concert the measures of their safety, by a Publick Vote.

2. A Vote or Decree must then nextly pass to set up some Particular species of Government over them. And if they are joyned in their first Compact upon absolute Terms to stand to the Decision of the first Vote concerning the Species of Government: Then all are bound by the Majority to acquiesce in that particular Form thereby settled, though their own private Opinion, incline them to some other Model.

3. After a Decree has specified the Particular form of Government, then there will be need of a New Covenant, whereby those on whom Sovereignty is conferred, engage to take care of the Common Peace, and Welfare. And the Subjects on the other hand, to yield them faithful Obedience. In which Covenant is Included that Submission and Union of Wills, by which a State may be conceived to be but one Person. So that the most proper Definition of a Civil State, is this, *viz.* A Civil State is a Compound Moral Person. whose Will [United by those Covenants before passed] is the Will of all; to the end it may Use, and Apply the strength and riches of Private Persons towards maintaining the Common Peace, Security, and Well-being of all. Which may be conceived as tho' the whole State was now become but one Man; in which the aforesaid Covenants may be supposed under Gods Providence, to be the Divine *Fiat*, Pronounced by God, let us make Man. And by way of resemblance the aforesaid Being may be thus Anatomized.

1. The Sovereign Power is the Soul infused, giving Life and Motion to the whole Body.

2. Subordinate Officers are the Joynts by which the Body moves.

3. Wealth and Riches are the Strength.

4. Equity and Laws are the Reason.

5. Councellors the Memory.

6. *Salus Populi,* or the Happiness of the People, is the End of its Being; or main Business to be attended and done.

7. Concord amongst the Members, and all Estates, is the Health.

8. Sedition is Sickness, and Civil War Death.

4. The Parts of Sovereignty may be considered: So,

1. As it Prescribes the Rule of Action: It is rightly termed *Legislative Power.*

2. As it determines the Controversies of Subjects by the Standard of those Rules. So is it justly Termed Judiciary Power.

3. As it Arms the Subjects against Foreigners, or forbids Hostility, so its called the Power of Peace and War.

4. As it takes in Ministers for the discharge of Business, so it is called the Right of Appointing Magistrates. So that all great officers and Publick Servants, must needs owe their Original to the Creating Power of Sovereignty. So that those whose Right it is to Create, may Dissolve the being of those who are Created, unless they cast them into an Immortal Frame. And yet must needs be dissoluble if they justly forfeit their being to their Creators.

5. The Chief End of Civil Communities, is, that Men thus conjoyned,

may be secured against the Injuries, they are lyable to from their own Kind. For if every Man could secure himself singly; It would be great folly for him, to Renounce his Natural Liberty, in which every Man is his own King and Protector.

6. The Sovereign Authority besides that it inheres in every State as in a Common and General Subject. So farther according as it resides in some One Person, or in a Council [consisting of some Select Persons, or of all the Members of a Community] as in a proper and particular Subject, so it produceth different Forms of Common-wealths, *viz.* Such as are either simple and regular, or mixt.

1. The Forms of a Regular State are three only, which Forms arise from the proper and particular Subject, in which the Supream Power Resides. As,

1. A Democracy, which is when the Sovereign Power is Lodged in a Council consisting of all the Members, and where every Member has the Priviledge of a Vote. This Form of Government, appears in the greatest part of the World to have been the most Ancient. For that Reason seems to shew it to be most probable, that when Men [being Originally in a condition of Natural Freedom and Equality] had thoughts of joyning in a Civil Body, would without question be inclined to Administer their common Affairs, by their common Judgment, and so must necessarily to gratifie that Inclination establish a Democracy; neither can it be rationally imagined, that Fathers of Families being yet Free and Independent, should in a moment, or little time take off their long delight in governing their own Affairs, & Devolve all upon some single Sovereign Commander; for that it seems to have been thought more Equitable, that what belonged to all, should be managed by all, when all had entered by Compact into one Community. The Original of our Government, says *Plato,* [speaking of the *Athenian* Common-wealth] *was taken from the Equality of our Race. Other States there are composed of different Blood, and of unequal Lines, the Consequence of which are disproportionable Soveraignty, Tyrannical or Oligarchycal Sway; under which men live in such a manner, as to Esteem themselves partly Lords, and partly Slaves to each other. But we and our Country men, being all Born Brethren of the same Mother, do not look upon our selves, to stand under so hard a Relation, as that of Lords, and Slaves; but the Parity of our Descent incline us to keep up the like Parity by our Laws, and so yield the precedency to nothing but to Superiour Vertue and Wisdom.* And moreover it seems very manifest that most Civil Communities arose at first from the Union of Families, that were nearly allyed in Race and Blood. And though Ancient Story make frequent mention of Kings, yet it appears that most of them were such that had an Influence rather in perswading, then in any Power of Commanding. So *Justin* discribes that Kind of Government, as the most Primitive, which *Aristotle* stiles an Heroical Kingdom. *viz.* Such as is no ways Inconsistent with a Democratical State. *De Princip. Reru.* 1. *L.* 1. *C.*

A democracy is then Erected, when a Number of Free Persons, do Assemble together, in Order to enter into a Covenant for Uniting themselves in a Body: And such a Preparative Assembly hath some appearance already of a Democracy; it is a Democracy in *Embrio* properly in this Respect, that every Man hath the Priviledge freely to deliver his Opinion concerning the Common Affairs. Yet he who dissents from the Vote of the Majority, is not in the least obliged by what they determine, till by a second Covenant, a Popular Form be actually Established; for not before then can we call it a Democratical Government, *viz.* Till the Right of Determining all matters relating to the publick Safety, is actually placed in a General Assembly of the whole People; or by their own Compact and Mutual Agreement, Determine themselves the proper Subject for the Exercise of Sovereign Power. And to compleat this State, and render it capable to Exert its Power to answer the End of a Civil State: These Conditions are necessary.

1. That a certain Time and Place be Assigned for Assembling.

2. That when the Assembly be Orderly met, as to Time and Place, that then the Vote of the Majority must pass for the Vote of the whole Body.

3. That Magistrates be appointed to Exercise the Authority of the whole for the better dispatch of Business, of every days Occurrence; who also may with more Mature diligence, search into more Important Affairs; and if in case any thing happens of greater Consequence, may report it to the Assembly; and be peculiarly Serviceable in putting all Publick Decrees into Execution. Because a large Body of People is almost useless in Respect of the last Service, and of many others, as to the more Particular Application and Exercise of Power. Therefore it is most agreeable with the Law of Nature, that they Institute their Officers to act in their Name, and Stead.

2. The Second Species of Regular Government, is an Aristocracy; and this is said then to be Constituted when the People, or Assembly United by a first Covenant, and having thereby cast themselves into the first Rudiments of a State; do then by Common Decree, Devolve the Sovereign Power, on a Council consisting of some Select Members; and these having accepted of the Designation, are then properly invested with Sovereign Command; and then an Aristocracy is formed.

3. The Third Species of a Regular Government, is a Monarchy which is settled when the Sovereign Power is confered on some one worthy Person. It differs from the former, because a Monarch who is but one Person in Natural, as well as in Moral account, & so is furnished with an Immediate Power of Exercising Sovereign Command in all Instances of Government; but the fore named must needs have Particular Time and Place assigned; but the Power and Authority is Equal in each.

2. Mixt Governments, which are various and of divers kinds [not now to be Enumerated] yet possibly the fairest in the World is that which has a Regular Monarchy; [in Distinction to what is Dispotick] settled upon a Noble Democracy as its Basis. And each part of the Government is so adjusted by Pacts and Laws that renders the whole Constitution an *Elisium.* It is said of the *British* Empire, *That it is such a Monarchy, as that by the necessary subordinate*

Concurrence of the Lords and Commons, in the Making and Repealing all Statutes or Acts of Parliament; it hath the main advantages of an Aristocracy, and of a Democracy, and yet free from the Disadvantages and Evils of either. It is such a Monarchy, as by most Admirable Temperament affords very much to the Industry, Liberty, and Happiness of the Subject, and reserves enough for the Majesty and Prerogative of any King, who will own his People as Subjects, not as Slaves. It is a Kingdom, that of all the Kingdoms of the World, is most like to the Kingdom of Jesus Christ, whose Yoke is easie, and Burden light. Present State of *England* 1st Part 64 *p* * * *

1717

II. ETHAN ALLEN
(1738–1789)

From *REASON THE ONLY ORACLE OF MAN*

[SUPERSTITION *vs.* REASON]

Chapter I. Section I. The Duty of reforming Mankind from Superstition and Error and the good Consequences of it.

THE desire of knowledge has engaged the attention of the wise and curious among mankind in all ages, which has been productive of extending the arts and sciences far and wide in the several quarters of the globe, and excited the contemplative to explore nature's laws in a gradual series of improvement, 'till philosophy, astronomy, geography and history, with many other branches of science, have arrived to a great degree of perfection.

IT is nevertheless to be regreted, that the bulk of mankind, even in those nations which are most celebrated for learning and wisdom, are still carried down the torrent of superstition, and entertain very unworthy apprehensions of the BEING, PERFECTIONS, CREATION and PROVIDENCE of GOD, and their duty to him, which lays an indispensible obligation on the philosophic friends of human nature, unanimously to exert themselves in every lawful, wise and prudent method, to endeavour to reclaim mankind from their ignorance and delusion, by enlightening their minds in those great and sublime truths concerning God and his providence, and their obligations to moral rectitude, which in this world, and that which is to come, cannot fail greatly to affect their happiness and well being.

THOUGH *"None by searching can find out God, or the Almighty to perfection;"* yet I am persuaded, that if mankind would dare to exercise their reason as freely on those divine topics, as they do in the common concerns of life, they would, in a great measure rid themselves of their blindness and superstition, gain more exalted ideas of God and their obligations to him and one another, and be proportionably delighted and blessed with the views of his moral government, make better members of society, and acquire many powerful incentives to the practice of morality, which is the last and greatest perfection that human nature is capable of.

Section II. Of *the* BEING *of a* GOD.

THE Laws of Nature having subjected mankind to a state of absolute dependence on something out of, and manifestly beyond themselves, or the compound exertion of their natural powers, gave them the first conception of a superior principle existing; otherwise they could have had no possible conception of a superintending power. But this sense of dependency, which results from experience and reasoning on the facts, which every day cannot fail to produce, has uniformly established the knowledge of our dependence to every of the species who are rational, which necessarily involves or contains in it the idea of a ruling power, or that there is a GOD, which ideas are synonimous.

THIS is the first glimpse of a Deity, and powerfully attracts the rational mind to make farther discoveries, which, through the weakness of human reasonings opens a door for errors and mistakes respecting the divine essence, though there is no possibility of our being deceived in our first conceptions of a superintending power. Of which more will be observed in its order.

THE globe with its productions, the planets in their motions, and the starry heavens in their magnitudes, surprize our senses, and confound our reason, in their munificent lessons of instruction concerning GOD, by means whereof we are apt to be more or less lost in our ideas of the object of divine adoration, though at the same time every one is truly sensible that their being and preservation is from GOD. We are too apt to confound our ideas of GOD with his works, and take the latter for the former. Thus barbarous and unlearned nations have imagined, that inasmuch as the sun in its influence is beneficial to them in bringing forward the spring of the year, causing the production of vegetation, and food for their subsistence, that therefore it is their GOD: while others have located other parts of creation, and ascribe to them the prerogatives of God; and mere creatures and images have been substituted to be Gods by the wickedness or weakness of man, or both together. It seems that mankind in most ages and parts of the world have been fond of corporeal Deities with whom their outward senses might be gratified, or as fantastically diverted from the just apprehension of the true God, by a supposed supernatural intercourse with invisible and mere spiritual beings, to whom they ascribe divinity, so that through one means or other, the character of the true God has been much neglected, to the great detriment of truth, justice and morality in the world; nor is it possible, that mankind can be uniform in their religious opinions, or worship God according to knowledge, except they can form a consistent arrangment of ideas of the Divine character. This therefore shall be the great object of the following pages, to which all others are only subordinate; for the superstructure of our religion will be proportionate to the notions we entertain of the divinity whom we adore. A sensibility of mere dependence includes an idea of something, on which we depend (call it by what name we will) which has a real existence, in as much as a dependency on nonentity is inadmissib[l]e, for that the absence or nonexistence of all being could not have caused an existence to be. But should we attempt to trace the succession of the causes of our dependence, they would exceed our comprehension, though every of them, which we could understand, would be so many evidences (of the displays) of a God. Although a sense of dependency discloses to our minds the certainty of a Supreme Being, yet it does not point out to us the object, nature or perfections of that being; this belongs to the province of reason, and in our course of ratiocination on the succession of causes and events. Although we extend our ideas retrospectively ever so far upon the succession, yet no one cause in the extended order of succession, which depends upon another prior to itself, can be the independent cause of all things: nor is it possible to trace the order of the succession of causes back to that self-existent cause, inasmuch as it is eternal and infinite, and therefore cannot be traced out by succession, which operates according to the order of time, consequently can bear no more proportion to the eternity of God, than time itself may be supposed to do, which has no proportion at all; as the succeeding arguments respecting the eternity and infinity of God will evince. But notwithstanding the series of the succession of causes cannot be followed in a retrospective succession up to the self-existent or eternal cause, it is nevertheless a perpetual and conclusive evidence of a God. For a succession of causes, considered collectively, can be nothing more than effects of the independent cause, and as much dependent on it, as those dependent causes are upon one another; so that we may with certainty conclude that the system of nature, which we call by the name of natural causes, is as much dependent on a self-existent cause, as an individual of the species in the order of generation is dependent on its progenitors for existence. Such part of the series of nature's operations, which we understand, has a regular and necessary connection with, and dependence on its parts, which we denominate by the names of cause and effect. From hence we are authorised from reason to conclude, that the vast system of causes and effects are thus necessarily connected, (speaking of the natural world only) and the whole regularly and necessarily dependent on a self-existent cause; so that we are obliged to admit an independent cause, and ascribe self-existence to it, otherwise it could not be independent, and consequently not a God. But the eternity or manner of the existence of a self-existent and independent being is to all finite capacities utterly incomprehensible; yet this is so far from an objection against the reality of such a being, that it is essentially necessary to support the evidence of it; for if we could comprehend that being, whom we call God, he would not be God, but must have been finite, and that in the same degree as those may be supposed to be, who could comprehend him; therefore so certain as God is, we cannot comprehend his essence, eternity or manner of existence. This should always be premised, when we assay to reason on the being, perfection, eternity and infinity of God, or of his creation and providence. As far as we understand nature, we are become acquainted with the character of God; for the knowledge of nature is the revelation of God. If we form in our imagination a compeduous idea of the harmony of the universe, it is the same as calling God by the name of harmony, for there could be no harmony without regulation, and no regulation without a regulator, which is expressive of the idea of a God. Nor could it be possible, that there could be order or disorder, except we admit of such a thing as creation, and creation contains in it the idea of a creator, which is another appellation for the Divine Being, distinguishing God from his creation. Furthermore there could be no proportion, figure or motion without wisdom and power; wisdom to plan, and power to execute, and these are perfections, when applied to the works of nature, which signify the agency or superintendency of God. If we consider nature to be matter, figure and motion, we include the idea of God in that of motion; for motion implies a mover, as much as creation does a creator. If from the composition, texture, and tendency of the universe in general, we form a complex idea of general good resulting therefrom to mankind, we implicitly admit a God by the name of good, including the idea of his providence to man. And from hence arises our obligation to love and adore God, because he provides for, and is benificent to us: abstract the idea of goodness from the character of God, and it would cancel all our obligations to him, and excite us to hate and detest him as a tyrant; hence it is, that ignorant people are superstitiously misled into a conceit that they hate God, when at the same time it is only the idol of their own imagination, which they truly ought to hate and be ashamed of; but were such persons to connect the ideas of power, wisdom, goodness and all possible perfection in the character of God, their hatred toward him would be turned into love and adoration.

For mankind to hate truth as it may bring their evil deeds to light and punishment, is very easy and common; but to hate truth as truth, or God as God, which is the same as to hate goodness for its own sake, unconnected with any other consequences, is impossible even to a (premised) diabolical nature itself. If we advert to the series of the causes of our being and preservation in the world, we shall commence a retrospective examination from son to father, grand-father and great-grandfather, and so on to the supreme and self-existent father of all: and as to the means of our preservation or succeeding causes of it, we may begin with parental kindness in nourishing, succouring and providing for us in our helpless age, always remembering it to have originated from our eternal father, who implanted that powerful and sympathetic paternal affection in them.

By extending our ideas in a larger circle, we shall perceive our dependence on the earth and waters of the globe, which we inhabit, and from which we are bountifully fed and gorgeously arrayed, and nextly extend our ideas to the sun, whose fiery mass darts its brilliant rays of light to our terraqueous ball with amazing velocity, and whose region of inexhaustible fire supplies it with fervent heat, which causes vegetation and guilds the various seasons of the year with ten thousand charms: this is not the atchievement of man, but the workmanship and providence of God. But how the sun is supplied with materials thus to perpetuate its kind influences, we know not. But will any one deny the reality of those beneficial influences, because we do not understand the manner of the perpetuality of that fiery world, or how it became such a body of fire; or will any one deny the reality of nutrition by food, because we do not understand the secret operation of the digesting powers of animal nature, or the minute particulars of its cherishing influence, none will be so stupid as to do it. Equally absurd would it be for us to deny the providence of God, by "whom we live, move, and have our being," because we cannot comprehend it.

We know that earth, water, fire and air in their various compositions subserve us, and we also know that these elements are devoid of reflection, reason or design; from whence we may easily infer, that a wise, understanding, and designing being has ordained them to be thus subservient. Could blind chance constitute order and decorum, and consequently a providence? That wisdom, order, and design should be the production of nonentity, or of chaos, confusion and old night, is too absurd to deserve a serious confutation, for it supposeth that there may be effects without a cause, viz. produced by non-entity, or that chaos and confusion could produce the effects of power, wisdom and goodness; such absurdities as these we must assent to, or subscribe to the doctrine of a self-existent and providential being. Chaos itself would necessarily include the idea of a creator, inasmuch as it supposes a positive existence, though it precludes the idea of a Providence, which cannot exist without order, tendency and design.

But Chaos could no more exist independent of a Creator than the present aptly disposed system of nature. For there could be no fortuitious jumble, or chaos of original atoms, independent of or previous to creation, as nonentity could not produce the materials. *Nothing from nothing and there remains nothing, but something from nothing is contradictory and impossible.* The evidence of the being and providence of a God, is so full and compleat, that we cannot miss of discerning it, if we but open our eyes and reflect on the visible creation. The display of God's providence is that by which the evidence of his being is evinced to us, for though mere Chaos would evince the certainty of a Creator, yet that abstracted method of argument could not have been conceived of, or known by us, was it not for the exercise of God's Providence, (by whom we have our being;) though that argument in itself would have been true whether it had been used by us or not: for the reason of propositions and just inferrences in themselves, are in truth the same, independent of our conceptions of them, abstractedly considered from our existence.

The benefit accruing to us from reasoning and argument, as it respects our knowledge and practice, is to explore the truth of things, as they are in their own nature, this is our wisdom. All other conceptions of things are false and imaginary. We cannot exercise a thought on any thing whatever, that has a positive existence, but if we trace it thoroughly it will center in an independent cause, and be evidential of a God. Thus it is from the works of nature that we explore its great author; but all inquisitive minds are lost in their searches and researches into the immensity of the divine fullness, from whence our beings and all our blessings flow.

1784

III. SAMUEL JOHNSON
(1696–1772)

From *RAPHAEL, OR THE GENIUS OF ENGLISH AMERICA*

A RHAPSODY

[THE LOVE OF TRUTH]

PART I

Aristocles to *Crito*

1. I should be wanting (dear Crito) in that friendship which has many years subsisted between us, if I should neglect to give you an account of a most important conversation which happened to me not long since. I was invited one evening by a pleasant setting sun and a serene fragrant air to take a walk in a delightful neighboring field, amidst a most beautiful grove of trees of various sorts, where Nature had plentifully poured out her verdure and bounty. It is under a gradually rising hill, at the foot of which runs rushing down among the rocks, and sometimes with sudden rapid falls, a most delicious rivulet of pure water; on the one hand, taking its rise from a thicket of trees, and on the other hand, losing itself in a gentle winding stream amidst grass and flowers of various hue, in a pleasant meadow below; beyond which, on one side, the sea at a distance, with two or three small islands, terminates the prospect, and on the other, a beautiful landscape of pleasant pastures, flocks, and herds, and a delightful country village with mighty hills and vales beyond them, of various heights and distances.

In this place I delight sometimes solitary, and sometimes in company with a philosophical friend to spend an hour or two of vacant time, and being at this time alone, I was deeply musing on the weakness of human nature, and the many empty debates in philosophy, religion and politics that obtain among the inhabitants of this our mansion, and considering how easily they might most of them be accommodated, did men but give themselves leave calmly to think and reflect and consider things as being what they really are, without suffering themselves to be imposed on by empty names and sounds, without prejudice and partiality and with that temper wherewith it becomes them to treat one another, and duly disengaged from every consideration besides the pure disinterested love of truth and right. This led me to think what a contemptible figure they must needs make in the eyes of those superior intelligences who are the immediate attendants of the Almighty, and are said to be by Him appointed the guardians of human affairs. Surely, thought I, if they know what passes among us, they must think as despicably of our low way of thinking, and of the trifling controversies that subsist among us, as we do of the low imaginations and little squabbles and debates that pass among children.

2. While I was thus entertaining my thoughts, I was surprised upon casting my eyes among the trees towards the top of the hill, with the

sight of a seemingly extraordinary person coming towards me in the habit of the remotest antiquity, with a most venerable but pleasant and benign aspect, of a beautiful countenance and agreeable air, mixed with seriousness, sweetness, and benevolence. As he approached me I soon discovered in myself signs of awe and surprise because his habit and manner were such as bespoke him an appearance certainly very extraordinary, and as he came up, I addressed him with ceremonies of the profoundest respect and veneration; whereupon with an air of the greatest tenderness and compassion for my surprise, he spoke to me and said: Be not surprised, O Aristocles, or in the least concerned at my making this sudden and extraordinary appearance to you in this solitary place; for I am your friend and the friend of mankind, and am neither a stranger to your name nor condition in the world, nor to the affairs of the rest of your species, and come to you with no other views than those of benevolence towards you and that race of intelligent beings to which you belong, and to suggest to you several things in the course of a few hours conversation which it may be of use to you and your country to consider in order to promote their good and happiness.

May I then, said I, presume upon your great benignity and condescension so far as to express my desire of knowing who it is I have the honor to speak to and that thus deigns to converse with me in this retired place? Be not, said he, in the least surprised if I let you know that I am indeed one of an order of intelligences superior to you, not clothed with flesh and blood, nor confined to the same laws and limitations of being and acting to which you are tied in this your state of probation. But know, however, that by how much greater the dignity is to which the rational nature is advanced in the intelligent and moral system, by so much the more it abounds in what you call humanity, candor, and benevolence; and therefore you are at liberty without reserve or distance and without fear or diffidence to ask me any questions you shall think proper, and to converse with me with the same openness, freedom and ease and with as little ceremony as you would with any of your friends or such as you have a respectful regard for among your own species; and for this present intercourse you may call me Raphael.

This, I said, is an instance of unspeakable goodness and condescension, and which I am not able to express sufficient thankfulness for; and I shall endeavor to use the liberty you have given me with that deference and veneration which is due to your superior nature and character. May I know then, continued I, the occasion of this your unexpected appearance and condescending intercourse with one of our inferior order of rational beings in this lower world?—In order to this, said he, you must know (what indeed you are not altogether ignorant of) that of us who are continually employed on the greatest and important behests of the most high God, father of spirits, the almighty creator and supreme king and lord of all things and his great Son and vicegerent, the visible creator, lord and governor of the whole natural and moral world, and whose business it is to minister to Him in the moral government of the whole rational creation, I say, of us some there are who are destined to inspect the affairs of particular kingdoms, countries, and provinces, and to promote the general good and welfare of the nations or people assigned to our charge; and the business allotted to me is to be the guardian or genius of New England. In this quality it is that I now appear to you with a design, as I said, to communicate a few things which, if duly attended to, may have some tendency to render you a flourishing and happy people. And the reason why I appear to you in this solitary retreat, is because I know you are extremely solicitous for the public good of mankind and your country, and at leisure to attend to what may be suggested to you on this subject, and would willingly communicate it to others.

3. This, said I, O venerable Raphael, I should gladly do, and nothing could give me greater satisfaction than to be instructed in what may contribute to the good of my species, and particularly my dear country; for nothing so much distresses me as to behold mankind by their own folly and perverseness (as by their conduct one would be tempted to imagine), contriving to make themselves miserable; as on the other hand nothing could give me a more exquisite pleasure than to discover, if it were possible, what might recover them from their madness and waywardness, and put them in a way to prosecute their true and genuine happiness. This earnest concern of yours for the public good, O Aristocles (said he, with a most benign smiling aspect), is truly a noble and divine passion, and could everyone be in some good measure possessed of it, this one thing would lay an effectual foundation for public weal: for did every one consider himself but as a part of the moral system so related to the whole that his own private weal and happiness is bound up in, and depends on the general weal of mankind, and especially of the community he belongs to, he would then even from the principle of self love, find himself necessitated to love and study the general good of mankind and his country, and be always ready to promote every thing that contributes to it, as a necessary means and indeed the only course he can take to promote and secure his own welfare. Necessary therefore it is that he should consider mankind as being what they really are, the creatures of God, and all children of the same common parent, made by Him for society and so constituted as that by the necessity of their nature they depend not only on Him their common Father, but even on oneanother for their happiness in such a manner that every one must necessarily seek his own good in that of the whole community of his fellow creatures, and especially those that are about him, as being all partakers of the same nature, liable to the same wants and necessities, and exposed to the same dangers and difficulties, and all being made for the same kind of happiness, they must therefore be considered to have one common interest. He would then look on every one of his race with a brother's eye and a brother's kindness, tenderness and compassion, and contribute all he could to the general weal of the whole

great family of that heavenly parent on whom they all equally depend, and to whom they are alike allied.

Alas! said I, instead of this, we are apt every one to consider himself alone as the center of all his views and pursuits, and to sacrifice not only every particular person's interest to his own, but even that of the whole community to which he belongs. This, replied Raphael, is owing to a certain abject meanness of soul, and can be derived from nothing else but a most despicable narrowness of mind. In short it flows from such a contemptible, grovelling temper that one would think, whoever should look inward on himself and find this to be the case with him, would be so much ashamed as even to abhor himself as one of a most odious character, as one of a most wretched, contracted, unthinking soul, uncapable of reflection and therefore of a brutish disposition, nay, indeed of a temper worse than brutish, for there are many kinds of brute animals which are remarkable for a joint tendency among the individuals in their whole economy towards the general good of each of their several tribes, and should be looked on as so many noble examples or emblems by which the God of nature would teach this divine lesson to the human race. Necessary therefore it is, if men would in earnest contrive to be happy, that they should awaken their attention to the consideration of things as being what they really are and enlarge their views taking into their thoughts the whole system at once of which each one is but a part, and so a part, that he can no more subsist happily without regard to the whole and earnestly contributing to the weal of it, than his leg or arm without the health of his whole body, or the branch of a tree without the life and good order of its trunk, or the tree itself without the earth and the sun and rain.

4. I could not forbear breaking out here in a piteous lamentation on the wretched condition of that poor unhappy race of mortals to which I belong: O miserable species of animals this, which is called human kind! (Said I, with a deep sigh.) We seem made for thinking and reflection, but it is the least of what we really do; we suffer appetite, passion, interest, anything to bear sway in us, and prevail with us rather than reason, consideration and truth! We are easily carried down the stream of a senseless, untoward, impetuous humor, and have not resolution to muster up force of mind and thought sufficient to stem the current. 'Tis not reason or a sense of what is right that generally governs or has the least influence in that affair, but it is education, 'tis custom, 'tis interest, 'tis prejudice, 'tis empty names and sounds, 'tis fondness for a party or some great name or chief manager, 'tis everything besides what it should be that possesses, biasses and determines us on all occasions. Such poor weak despicable creatures we are, that I protest I am sometimes tempted to think we are beneath the Almighty's care, some blasted race that He has abandoned to themselves without designing to concern himself any further about them! —You are very right, said he, O dear Aristocles, in having such a tender, compassionate sense of the unhappy condition of your species, but would be as much in the wrong to go into

such a conclusion about them. Weak, low and untoward as they are, they are rational and immortal spirits, and as such they are natures of very great dignity, and ought to be dearly loved and their weal solicitously sought and tendered. You must be content to take them as they are and endeavor to make the best of them. You must deal tenderly with them, pity their weakness and patiently bear with their forwardness. Let therefore all your conduct one towards another be animated with benevolence and breathe nothing but compassion and love. O divine charity! Could that but reign in the hearts of men and banish the sour, ill-natured, censorious, hard-hearted passions, it would be the greatest means of recovering them from their degeneracy, for they would then indeed do all that they could to recover both each one himself and one another. This truly noble temper, therefore, you must possess yourself of, and endeavor all that you can to propagate and cultivate among others; for you can in nothing more imitate and resemble God, the great Father of Spirits, who, weak, perverse, despicable as they are, is so far from neglecting . . . and attention, for the sake of mere shadows to gild over any empty and uncertain and sometimes false and pernicious opinions with the sacred name of truth. For, what is truth but the knowledge of things as being what they really are? And what is right but a conduct conformable thereto? And what can be happier than these united when all the powers of the soul enjoy their proper objects without diffidence, distrust or anxiety, and everything in the soul is order, harmony, stability, peace and joy? Whereas on the other hand, a mind not utterly lost to all sense of itself and its true interest must needs be continually worried in endless mazes of anxiety, that is ever fluctuating in doubt, scepticism and uncertainty, or under a perpetual delusion,—mistaking sounds for things, and grasping at shadows instead of substance. If such an one conceits himself happy, it must be only an imaginary happiness like a golden dream or the empty enjoyments which a child values itself upon, but are mean, trifling and contemptible in the eyes of a man.

He therefore that would be really happy must set down this as the only unshaken foundation whereon to build his happiness, that he lay aside and even trample upon every other consideration besides the mere love of truth for its own sake, and that he defy and spurn at everything that stands in competition with it; that anxiously pursuing that alone, he readily and candidly lend his ear without prejudice or partiality to everything that can be offered on each side of a question; that in order to [do] this, he be scrupulously careful not to be misled by names and sounds, but diligently attend to the things themselves and the true intent and meaning of the language he uses about them; that he apply himself to consider them with the utmost force of attention he is capable of, animated with a most solicitous care not to be deceived or led into error; that he diligently and exactly examine the truth and certainty of his principles and see to it that the consequences he draws from them be really in the nature of things connected with them, and do certainly flow from them; and finally, that embracing the truth in the love of it he act up to it and govern all his appetites and passions, and form his whole conduct and behavior according to its sacred dictates, being honestly and resolutely engaged to follow whithersoever that leads. It is indeed necessary that he set out on every inquiry with this resolution or otherwise he will be in danger of being biassed and misled in the several steps he takes. He must therefore be prepared with that resigned temper that will make him sincerely willing to sacrifice every interest, houses, land, wife, children, every lust and every passion to the love of truth and right, and then he may depend upon this that he will not fail of being possessed of them, nor of being infinitely happier in the enjoyment of them than he could possibly be in anything that he sacrifices to this sacred interest. * * *

(*c.* 1763) 1929

JONATHAN EDWARDS
(1703–1758)

[THE FLYING SPIDER]

May it please your Honour,

There are some things that I have happily seen of the wondrous way of the working of the spider. Although every thing belonging to this insect is admirable, there are some phenomena relating to them more particularly wonderful. Every body that is used to the country, knows their marching in the air from one tree to another, sometimes at the distance of five or six rods. Nor can one go out in a dewy morning, at the latter end of August and the beginning of September, but he shall see multitudes of webs, made visible by the dew that hangs on them, reaching from one tree, branch and shrub, to another: which webs are commonly thought to be made in the night, because they appear only in the morning; whereas none of them are made in the night, for these spiders never come out in the night when it is dark, as the dew is then falling. But these webs may be seen well enough in the day time by an observing eye, by their reflection in the sun-beams. Especially late in the afternoon, may these webs, that are between the eye and that part of the horizon that is under the sun, be seen very plainly, being advantageously posited to reflect the rays. And the spiders themselves may be very often seen travelling in the air, from one stage to another amongst the trees, in a very unaccountable manner. But I have often seen that, which is much more astonishing. In very calm and serene days in the forementioned time of year, standing at some distance behind the end of an house or some other opake body, so as just to hide the disk of the sun and keep off his dazzling rays, and looking along close by the side of it, I have seen a vast multitude of little shining webs, and glistening strings, brightly reflecting the sunbeams, and some of them of great length, and of such a height, that one would think they were tacked to the vault of the heavens, and would be burnt like tow in the sun, and make a very beautiful, pleasing, as well as surprising appearance. It is wonderful at what a distance, these webs may plainly be seen. Some that are at a great distance appear (it cannot be less than) several thousand times as big as they ought. I believe they appear under as great an angle, as a body of a foot diameter ought to do at such a distance; so greatly doth brightness increase the apparent bigness of bodies at a distance, as is observed of the fixed stars.

But that which is most astonishing, is, that very often appears at the end of these webs, spiders sailing in the air with them; which I have often beheld with wonderment and pleasure, and showed to others. And since I have seen these things, I have been very conversant with spiders; resolving if possible, to find out the mysteries of these their astonishing works. And I have been so happy as very frequently to see their manner of working; that when a spider would go from one tree to another, or would fly in the air, he first lets himself down a little way from the twig he stands on by a web, as in Fig. 1; and then, laying hold of it by his fore feet,

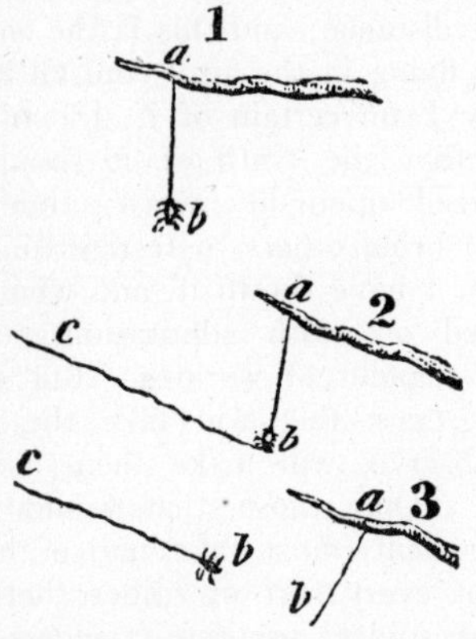

and bearing himself by that, puts out a web, as in Fig 2, which is drawn out of his tail with infinite ease, in the gently moving air, to what length the spider pleases; and if the farther end happens to catch by a shrub or the branch of a tree, the spider immediately feels it, and fixes the hither end of it to the web by which he let himself down, and goes over by that web which he put out of his tail as in Fig 3. And this, my eyes have innumerable times made me sure of.

Now, Sir, it is certain that these webs, when they first proceed from the spider, are so rare a substance, that they are lighter than the air, because they will ascend in it, as they will immediately in a calm air, and never descend except driven by a wind; wherefore 'tis certain. And 'tis as certain, that what swims and ascends in the air is lighter than the air, as that what ascends and swims in water is lighter than water. So that if we should suppose any such time, wherein the air is perfectly calm, this web is so easily drawn out of the spider's tail, that if the end of it be once out, barely the levity of it is sufficient to draw it out to any length; wherefore if it don't happen that the end of this web, *b c,* catches by a tree or some other body, 'till there is so long a web drawn out, that its levity shall be so great as more than to counterbalance the gravity of the spider, or so that the web and the spider, taken together, shall be lighter than such a quantity of air as takes up equal space, then according to the universally acknowledged laws of nature, the web and the spider together will ascend, and not descend, in the air: as when a man is at the bottom of the water, if he has hold of a piece of timber so great, that the wood's tendency upwards is greater than the man's tendency downwards, he together with the wood will ascend to the surface of the water. And therefore, when the spider perceives that the web *b c* is long enough to bear him up by its ascending force, he lets go his hold of the web *a b,* Fig. 3, and ascends in the air with the web *b c.* If there be not web more than enough, just to counterbalance the gravity of the spider, the spider together with the web will hang in equilibrio, neither ascending nor descending, otherwise than as the air moves. But if there is so much web, that its greater levity shall more than equal the greater density of the spider, they will ascend till the air is so thin, that the spider and web together are just of an equal weight with so much air. And in this way, Sir, I have multitudes of times seen spiders mount away into the air, from a stick in my hands, with a vast train of this silver web before them; for, if the spider be disturbed upon the stick by shaking of it, he will presently in this manner leave it. And their way of working may very distinctly be seen, if they are held up in the sun, or against a dark door, or any thing that is black.

Now, Sir, the only remaining difficulty is, how they first put out the end of the web *b c,* Fig. 3, out of their tails. If once the web is out, it is easy to conceive how the levity of it, together with the motion of the air, may draw it out to a great length. But how should they first let out of their tails, the end of so fine and even a string; seeing that the web, while it is in the spider, is a certain cloudy liquor, with which that great bottle tail of theirs is filled; which immediately, upon its being exposed to the air, turns to a dry substance, and exceedingly rarifies and extends itself. Now if it be a liquor, it is hard to conceive how they should let out a fine even thread, without expelling a little drop at the end of it; but none such can be discerned. But there is no need of this; for it is only separating that part of the web *b c,* Fig. 2, from *a b,* and the end of the web is already out. Indeed, Sir, I never could distinctly see them do this: so small a piece of web being imperceptible among the spider's legs. But I cannot doubt but that it is so, because there is a necessity that they should some way or other separate the web *a b,* Fig. 3, from their tails, before they can let out the web *b c.* And then I know they do have ways of dividing their webs by biting them off, or in some other way. Otherwise they could not separate themselves from the web *a b,* Fig. 3.

And this, Sir, is the way of spiders going from one tree to another, at a great distance; and this is the way of their flying in the air. And, although I say I am certain of it, I don't desire that the truth of it should be received upon my word; though I could bring others to testify to it, to whom I have shown it, and who have looked on, with admiration, to see their manner of working. But every one's eyes, that will take the pains to observe, will make them as sure of it. Only those, that would make experiment, must take notice that it is not every sort of spider that is a flying spider, for those spiders that keep in houses are a quite different sort, as also those that keep in the ground, and those that keep in swamps, in hollow trees, and rotten logs; but those spiders, that keep on branches of trees and shrubs, are the flying spiders. They delight most in walnut trees, and are that sort of spiders that make those curious network polygonal webs, that are so frequently to be seen in the latter end of the year. There are more of this sort of spiders by far than of any other.

But yet, Sir, I am assured that the chief end of this faculty, that is given them, is not their recreation, but their destruction; because their destruction is unavoidably the effect of it; and we shall find nothing, that is the continual effect of nature, but what is of the means by which it is brought to pass. But it is impossible, but that the greatest part of the spiders upon the land should, every year, be swept into the ocean. For these spiders never fly, except the weather is fair and the atmosphere dry; but the atmosphere is never clear, neither in this nor any other continent, only when the wind blows from the midland parts, and consequently towards the sea. As here in New-England, the fair weather is only when the wind is westerly, the land being on that side, and the ocean on the easterly. And I never have seen any of these spiders flying, but when they have been hastening directly towards the sea. And the time of their flying being so long, even from about the middle of August every sunshiny day, until about the end of October; (though their chief time, as I observed before, is the latter end of August, and beginning of September;) and they never flying from the sea, but always towards it; must needs get there at last; for its unreasonable to suppose that they have sense enough to stop themselves when they come near the sea; for then they would have hundreds of times as many spiders upon the sea-shore, as any where else.

The same also holds true of other sorts of flying insects; for at these times, that I have viewed the spiders with their webs in the air, there has also appeared vast multitudes of flies, and all flying the same way with the spiders and webs directly to the ocean; and even such as butterflies, millers and moths, which keep in the grass at this time of year, I have seen vastly higher than the tops of the highest trees, all going the same way. These I have seen towards evening, without such a screen to defend my eyes from the sunbeams; which I used to think were seeking a warmer climate.

The reason of their flying at that time of year, I take to be because then the ground and trees, the places of their residence in summer, begin to be chilly and uncomfortable. Therefore when the sun shines pretty warm they leave them, and mount up in the air, and expand their wings to the sun, and flying for nothing but their own ease and comfort, they suffer themselves to go that way, that they find they can go with the greatest ease, and so where the wind pleases; and it being warmth they fly for, they find it cold and laborious flying against the wind. They therefore seem to use their wings, but just so much as to bear them up, and suffer them to go with the wind. So that without doubt almost all aerial insects, and also spiders which live upon trees and are made up of them, are at the end of the year swept away into the sea, and buried in the ocean, and leave nothing behind them but their eggs, for a new stock the next year.

(*c.* 1715) 1829

[PERSONAL NARRATIVE]

I had a variety of concerns and exercises about my soul, from my childhood; but I had two more remarkable seasons of awakening, before I met with that change, by which I was brought to those new dispositions, and that new sense of things, that I have since had. The first time was when I was a boy, some years before I went to college, at a time of remarkable awakening in my father's congregation. I was then very much affected for many months, and concerned about the things of religion, and my soul's salvation; and was abundant in religious duties. I used to pray five times a day in secret, and to spend much time in religious conversation with other boys; and used to meet with them to pray together. I experienced I know not what kind of delight in religion. My mind was much engaged in it, and had much self-righteous pleasure; and it was my delight to abound in religious duties. I, with some of my school-mates, joined together, and built a booth in a swamp, in a very retired spot, for a place of prayer.—And besides, I had particular secret places of my own in the woods, where I used to retire by myself; and was from time to time much affected. My affections seemed to be lively and easily moved, and I seemed to be in my element, when engaged in religious duties. And I am ready to think, many are deceived with such affections, and such a kind of delight as I then had in religion, and mistake it for grace.

But, in process of time, my convictions and affections wore off; and I entirely lost all those affections and delights, and left off secret prayer, at least as to any constant preference of it; and returned like a dog to his vomit, and went on in the ways of sin. Indeed, I was at times very uneasy, especially towards the latter part of my time at college; when it pleased God, to seize me with a pleurisy; in which he brought me nigh to the grave, and shook me over the pit of hell. And yet, it was not long after my recovery, before I fell again into my old ways of sin. But God would not suffer me to go on with any quietness; I had great and violent inward struggles, till, after many conflicts with wicked inclinations, repeated resolutions, and bonds that I laid myself under by a kind of vows to God, I was brought wholly to break off all former wicked ways, and all ways of known outward sin; and to apply myself to seek salvation, and practise many religious duties; but without that kind of affection and delight which I had formerly experienced. My concern now wrought more, by inward struggles, and conflicts, and self-reflections. I made seeking my salvation, the main business of my life. But yet, it seems to me, I sought it after a miserable manner; which has made me sometimes since to question, whether ever it issued in that which was saving; being ready to doubt, whether such miserable seeking ever succeeded. I was indeed brought to seek salvation, in a manner that I never was before; I felt a spirit to part with all things in the world, for an interest in Christ. My concern continued and prevailed, with many exercising thoughts and inward struggles; but yet it never seemed to be proper, to express that concern by the name of terror.

From my childhood up, my mind had been full of objections against the doctrine of God's sovereignty, in choosing whom he would to eternal life, and rejecting whom he pleased; leaving them eternally to perish, and be everlastingly tormented in hell. It used to appear like a horrible doctrine to me. But I remember the time very well, when I seemed to be convinced, and fully satisfied, as to this sovereignty of God, and his justice in thus eternally disposing of men, according to his sovereign pleasure. But never could give an account, how, or by what means, I was thus convinced, not in the least imagining at the time, nor a long time after, that there was any extraordinary influence of God's Spirit in it; but only that now I saw further, and my reason apprehended the justice and reasonableness of it. However, my mind rested in it; and it put an end to all those cavils and objections. And there has been a wonderful alteration in my mind, with respect to the doctrine of God's sovereignty, from that day to this; so that I scarce ever have found so much as the rising of an objection against it, in the most absolute sense, in God shewing mercy to whom he will shew mercy, and hardening whom he will. God's absolute sovereignty and justice, with respect to salvation and damnation, is what my mind seems to rest assured of, as much as of any thing that I see with my eyes; at least it is so at times. But I have often, since that first conviction, had quite another kind of sense of God's sovereignty than I had then. I have often since had not only a conviction, but a *delightful* conviction. The doctrine has very often appeared exceedingly pleasant, bright, and sweet. Absolute sovereignty is what I love to ascribe to God. But my first conviction was not so.

The first instance, that I remember, of that sort of inward, sweet delight in God and divine things, that I have lived much in since, was on reading those words, 1 Tim. i. 17. *Now unto the King eternal, immortal, invisible, the only wise God, be honour and glory for ever and ever, Amen.* As I read the words, there came into my soul, and was as it were diffused through it, a sense of the glory of the Divine Being; a new sense, quite different from any thing I ever experienced before. Never any words of Scripture seemed to me as these words did. I thought with myself, how excellent a Being that was, and how happy I should be, if I might enjoy that God, and be rapt up to him in heaven, and be as it were swallowed up in him for ever! I kept saying, and as it were singing, over these words of scripture to myself; and went to pray to God that I might enjoy him, and prayed in a manner quite different from what I used to do; with a new sort of affection. But it never came into my thought, that there was any thing spiritual, or of a saving nature in this.

From about that time, I began to have a new kind of apprehensions and ideas of Christ, and the work of redemption, and the glorious way of salvation by him. An inward, sweet sense of these things, at times, came into my heart; and my soul was led away in pleasant views and contemplations of them. And my mind was greatly engaged to spend my time in reading and meditating on Christ, on the beauty and excellency of his person, and the lovely way of salvation by free grace in him. I found no books so delightful to me, as those that treated of these subjects. Those words Cant. ii. 1. used to be abundantly with me, *I am the Rose of Sharon, and the Lily of the valleys.* The words seemed to me, sweetly to represent the loveliness and beauty of Jesus Christ. The whole book of Canticles used to be pleasant to me, and I used to be much in reading it, about that time; and found, from time to time, an inward sweetness, that would carry me away, in my contemplations. This I know not how to express otherwise, than by a calm, sweet abstraction of soul from all the concerns of this world; and sometimes a kind of vision, or fixed ideas and imaginations, of being alone in the mountains, or some solitary wilderness, far from all mankind, sweetly conversing with Christ, and wrapt and swallowed up in God. The sense I had of divine things, would often of a sudden kindle up, as it were, a sweet burning in my heart; an ardour of soul, that I know not how to express.

Not long after I first began to experience these things, I gave an account to my father of some things that had passed in my mind. I was pretty much affected by the discourse we had together; and when the discourse was ended, I walked abroad alone, in a solitary place in my father's pasture, for contemplation. And as I was walking there, and looking upon the sky and clouds, there came into my mind so sweet a sense of the glorious *majesty* and *grace* of God, as I know not how to express.—I seemed to see them both in a sweet conjunction; majesty and meekness joined together: it was a sweet, and gentle, and holy majesty; and also a majestic meekness; an awful sweetness; a high, and great, and holy gentleness.

After this my sense of divine things gradually increased, and became more and more lively, and had more of that inward sweetness. The appearance of every thing was altered; there seemed to be, as it were, a calm, sweet, cast, or appearance of divine glory, in almost every thing. God's excellency, his wisdom, his purity and love, seemed to appear in every thing; in the sun, moon and stars; in the clouds and blue sky; in the grass, flowers, trees; in the water and all nature; which used greatly to fix my mind. I often used to sit and view the moon for a long time; and in the day, spent much time in viewing the clouds and sky, to behold the sweet glory of God in these things: in the meantime, singing forth, with a low voice, my contemplations of the Creator and Redeemer. And scarce any thing, among all the works of nature, was so sweet to me as thunder and lightning; formerly nothing had been so terrible to me. Before, I used to be uncommonly terrified with thunder, and to be struck with terror when I saw a thunder-storm rising; but now, on the contrary, it rejoiced me. I felt God, if I may so speak, at the first appearance of a thunder-storm; and used to take the opportunity, at such times, to fix myself in order to view the clouds, and see the lightnings play, and hear the majestic and awful voice of God's thunder, which oftentimes was exceedingly entertaining, leading me to sweet contemplations of my great and glorious God. While thus engaged, it always seemed natural for me to sing, or chant forth my meditations; or, to speak my thoughts in soliloquies with a singing voice.

I felt then great satisfaction, as to my good estate; but that did not content me. I had vehement longings of soul after God and Christ, and after more holiness, wherewith my heart seemed to be full, and ready to break; which often brought to my mind the words of the Psalmist, Psal. cxix. 28. *My soul breaketh for the longing it hath.* I often felt a mourning and lamenting in my heart, that I had not turned to God sooner, that I might have had more time to grow in grace. My mind was greatly fixed on divine things; almost perpetually in the contemplation of them. I spent most of my time in thinking of divine things, year after year; often walking alone in the woods, and solitary places, for meditation, soliloquy, and prayer, and converse with God; and it was always my manner, at such times, to sing forth my contemplations. I was almost constantly in ejaculatory prayer, wherever I was. Prayer seemed to be natural to me, as the breath by which the inward burnings of my heart had vent. The delights which I now felt in the things of religion, were of an exceedingly different kind from those before-mentioned, that I had when a boy; and what then I had no more notion of, than one born blind has of pleasant and beautiful colours. They were of a more inward, pure, soul-animating and refreshing nature. Those former delights never reached the heart; and did not arise from any sight of the divine excellency of the things of God; or any taste of the soul-satisfying and life-giving good there is in them.

My sense of divine things seemed gradually to increase, till I went to preach at New-York; which was about a year and a half after they began; and while I was there, I felt them very sensibly, in a much higher degree, than I had done before. My longings after God, and holiness, were much increased. Pure and humble, holy and heavenly, christianity appeared exceedingly amiable to me. I felt a burning desire to be, in every thing, a complete christian; and, conformed to the blessed image of Christ; and that I might live, in all things, according to the pure, sweet and blessed rules of the gospel. I had an eager thirsting after progress in these things; which put me upon pursuing and pressing after them. It was my continual strife day and night, and constant inquiry, how I should *be* more holy, and *live* more holily, and more becoming a child of God, and a disciple of Christ. I now sought an increase of grace and holiness, and a holy life, with much more earnestness, than ever I sought grace before I had it. I used to be continually examining myself, and studying and contriving for likely ways and means, how I should live holily, with far greater diligence and earnestness, than ever I pursued any thing in my life; but yet with too great a dependence on my own strength; which afterwards proved a great damage to me. My experience had not then taught me, as it has done since, my extreme feebleness and impotence, every manner of way; and the bottomless depths of secret corruption and deceit, there was in my heart. However, I went on with my eager pursuit after more holiness, and conformity to Christ.

The heaven I desired was a heaven

of holiness; to be with God, and to spend my eternity in divine love, and holy communion with Christ. My mind was very much taken up with contemplations on heaven, and the enjoyments there; and living there in perfect holiness, humility and love: and it used at that time to appear a great part of the happiness of heaven, that there the saints could express their love to Christ. It appeared to me a great clog and burden, that what I felt within, I could not express as I desired. The inward ardour of my soul, seemed to be hindered and pent up, and could not freely flame out as it would. I used often to think, how in heaven this principle should freely and fully vent and express itself. Heaven appeared exceedingly delightful, as a world of love; and that all happiness consisted in living in pure, humble, heavenly, divine love.

I remember the thoughts I used then to have of holiness; and said sometimes to myself, "I do certainly know that I love holiness, such as the gospel prescribes." It appeared to me, that there was nothing in it but what was ravishingly lovely; the highest beauty and amiableness—a *divine* beauty; far purer than any thing here upon earth; and that every thing else was like mire and defilement, in comparison of it.

Holiness, as I then wrote down some of my contemplations on it, appeared to me to be of a sweet, pleasant, charming, serene, calm nature; which brought an inexpressible purity, brightness, peacefulness and ravishment to the soul. In other words, that it made the soul like a field or garden of God, with all manner of pleasant flowers; enjoying a sweet calm, and the gently vivifying beams of the sun. The soul of a true christian, as I then wrote my meditations, appeared like such a little white flower as we see in the spring of the year; low and humble on the ground, opening its bosom, to receive the pleasant beams of the sun's glory; rejoicing, as it were, in a calm rapture; diffusing around a sweet fragrancy; standing peacefully and lovingly, in the amidst of other flowers round about; all in like manner opening their bosoms, to drink in the light of the sun. There was no part of creature-holiness, that I had so [great a] sense of its loveliness, as humility, brokenness of heart and poverty of spirit; and there was nothing that I so earnestly longed for. My heart panted after this—to lie low before God, as in the dust; that I might be nothing, and that God, might be ALL, that I might become as a little child.

While at New York, I sometimes was much affected with reflections on my past life, considering how late it was before I began to be truly religious; and how wickedly I had lived till then: and once so as to weep abundantly, and for a considerable time together.

On *January* 12, 1723, I made a solemn dedication of myself to God, and wrote it down; giving up myself, and all that I had to God; to be for the future, in no respect, my own; to act as one that had no right to himself, in any respect. And solemnly vowed, to take God for my whole portion and felicity; looking on nothing else, as any part of my happiness, nor acting as if it were; and his law for the constant rule of my obedience: engaging to fight, with all my might, against the world, the flesh, and the devil, to the end of my life. But I have reason to be infinitely humbled, when I consider, how much I have failed, of answering my obligation.

I had, then, abundance of sweet, religious conversation, in the family where I lived, with Mr. John Smith, and his pious mother. My heart was knit in affection, to those, in whom were appearances of true piety; and I could bear the thoughts of no other companions, but such as were holy, and the disciples of the blessed Jesus. I had great longings, for the advancement of Christ's kingdom in the world; and my secret prayer used to be, in great part, taken up in praying for it. If I heard the least hint, of any thing that happened, in any part of the world, that appeared, in some respect or other, to have a favourable aspect, on the interests of Christ's kingdom, my soul eagerly catched at it; and it would much animate and refresh me. I used to be eager to read public news-letters, mainly for that end; to see if I could not find some news, favourable to the interest of religion in the world.

I very frequently used to retire into a solitary place, on the banks of Hudson's River, at some distance from the city, for contemplation on divine things and secret converse with God: and had many sweet hours there. Sometimes Mr. Smith and I walked there together, to converse on the things of God; and our conversation used to turn much on the advancement of Christ's kingdom in the world, and the glorious things that God would accomplish for his church in the latter days. I had then, and at other times, the greatest delight in the holy scriptures, of any book whatsoever. Oftentimes in reading it, every word seemed to touch my heart. I felt a harmony between something in my heart, and those sweet and powerful words. I seemed often to see so much light exhibited by every sentence, and such a refreshing food communicated, that I could not get along in reading; often dwelling long on one sentence, to see the wonders contained in it; and yet almost every sentence seemed to be full of wonders.

I came away from New York in the month of *April*, 1723, and had a most bitter parting with Madam Smith and her son. My heart seemed to sink within me, at leaving the family and city, where I had enjoyed so many sweet and pleasant days. I went from New York to Wethersfield, by water; and as I sailed away, I kept sight of the city as long as I could. However, that night after this sorrowful parting, I was greatly comforted in God at Westchester, where we went ashore to lodge: and had a pleasant time of it all the voyage to Saybrook. It was sweet to me to think of meeting dear christians in heaven, where we should never part more. At Saybrook we went ashore to lodge on Saturday, and there kept the Sabbath; where I had a sweet and refreshing season, walking alone in the fields.

After I came home to Windsor, I remained much in a like frame of mind, as when at New York; only sometimes I felt my heart ready to sink, with the thoughts of my friends at New York. My support was in contemplations on the heavenly state; as I find in my Diary of May 1, 1723. It was a comfort to think of that state, where there is fulness of joy; where reigns heavenly, calm, and delightful love, without alloy; where there are continually the dearest expressions of this love; where is the enjoyment of the persons loved, without ever parting; where those persons who appear so lovely in this world, will really be inexpressibly more lovely, and full of love to us. And how sweetly will the mutual lovers join together, to sing the praises of God and the Lamb! How will it fill us with joy to think, that this enjoyment, these sweet exercises, will never cease, but will last to all eternity. * * *

(*c.* 1740) 1808

[SARAH PIERREPONT]

They say there is a young lady in [New Haven] who is beloved of that Great Being, who made and rules the world, and that there are certain seasons in which this Great Being, in some way or other invisible, comes to her and fills her mind with exceeding sweet delight, and that she hardly cares for any thing, except to meditate on him—that she expects after a while to be received up where he is, to be raised up out of the world and caught up into heaven; being assured that he loves her too well to let her remain at a distance from him always. There she is to dwell with him, and to be ravished with his love and delight forever. Therefore, if you present all the world before her, with the richest of its treasures, she disregards it and cares not for it, and is unmindful of any pain or affliction. She has a strange sweetness in her mind, and singular purity in her affections; is most just and conscientious in all her conduct; and you could not persuade her to do any thing wrong or sinful, if you would give her all the world, lest she should offend this Great Being. She is of a wonderful sweetness, calmness and universal benevolence of mind; especially after this Great God has manifested himself to her mind. She will sometimes go about from place to place, singing sweetly; and seems to be always full of joy and pleasure; and no one knows for what. She loves to be alone, walking in the fields and groves, and seems to have some one invisible always conversing with her.

(1723) 1829

RESOLUTIONS

Being sensible that I am unable to do any thing without God's help, I do humbly entreat him by his grace, to enable me to keep these Resolutions, so far as they are agreeable to his will, for Christ's sake.

Remember to read over these Resolutions once a week.

1. *Resolved,* That *I will do whatsoever* I think to be most to the glory of God and my own good, profit and pleasure, in the whole of my duration; without any consideration of the time, whether now, or never so many myriads of ages hence. Resolved to do whatever I think to be my *duty,* and most for the good and advantage of mankind in general. Resolved, so

to do, whatever *difficulties* I meet with, how many soever, and how great soever.

2. *Resolved,* To be continually endeavouring to find out some *new contrivance,* and invention, to promote the forementioned things.

3. *Resolved,* If ever I shall fall and grow dull, so as to neglect to keep any part of these Resolutions, to repent of all I can remember, when I come to myself again.

4. *Resolved,* Never *to do* any manner of thing, whether in soul or body, less or more, but what tends to the glory of God, nor *be,* nor *suffer* it, if I can possibly avoid it.

5. *Resolved,* Never to lose one moment of time, but to improve it in the most profitable way I possibly can.

6. *Resolved,* To live with all my might, while I do live.

7. *Resolved,* Never to do any thing, which I should be afraid to do, if it were the last hour of my life.

8. *Resolved,* To act, in all respects, both speaking and doing, as if nobody had been so vile as I, and as if I had committed the same sins, or had the same infirmities or failings as others; and that I will let the knowledge of their failings promote nothing but shame in myself, and prove only an occasion of my confessing my own sins and misery to God. *Vid. July* 30.

9. *Resolved,* To think much, on all occasions, of my own dying, and of the common circumstances which attend death. * * *

47. *Resolved,* To endeavour, to my utmost, to deny whatever is not most agreeable to a good and universally sweet and benevolent, quiet, peaceable, contented and easy, compassionate and generous, humble and meek, submissive and obliging, diligent and industrious, charitable and even, patient, moderate, forgiving and sincere, temper; and to do, at all times, what such a temper would lead me to; and to examine strictly, at the end of every week, whether I have so done. *Sabbath Morning, May* 5, 1723. * * *

69. *Resolved,* Always to do that, which I shall wish I had done when I see others do it. *Aug.* 11, 1723.

70. Let there be something of benevolence, in all that I speak. *Aug.* 17, 1723.

1808, 1829

[THE GREAT AWAKENING AT NORTHAMPTON]

I

Northampton, March 19, 1737.

We in this town were, the last Lord's day, (March 13th) the spectators, and many of us the subjects, of one of the most amazing instances of Divine preservation, that perhaps was ever known in the world. Our meeting-house is old and decayed, so that we have been for some time building a new one, which is yet unfinished. It has been observed of late, that the house we have hitherto met in, has gradually spread at the bottom; the sills and walls giving way, especially in the foreside, by reason of the weight of timber at top pressing on the braces, that are inserted into the posts and beams of the house. It has done so more than ordinarily this spring: which seems to have been occasioned by the heaving of the ground, through the extreme frosts of the winter past, and its now settling again on that side which is next the sun, by the spring thaws. By this means, the underpinning has been considerably disordered, which people were not sensible of, till the ends of the joists, which bore up the front gallery, were drawn off from the girts on which they rested, by the walls giving way. So that in the midst of the public exercise in the forenoon, soon after the beginning of the sermon, the whole gallery—full of people, with all the seats and timbers, suddenly and without any warning—sunk, and fell down, with the most amazing noise, upon the heads of those that sat under, to the astonishment of the congregation. The house was filled with dolorous shrieking and crying; and nothing else was expected than to find many people dead, or dashed to pieces.

The gallery, in falling, seemed to break and sink first in the middle; so that those who were upon it were thrown together in heaps before the front door. But the whole was so sudden, that many of those who fell, knew nothing what it was, at the time, that had befallen them. Others in the congregation, thought it had been an amazing clap of thunder. The falling gallery seemed to be broken all to pieces, before it got down; so that some who fell with it, as well as those who were under, were buried in the ruins; and were found pressed under heavy loads of timber, and could do nothing to help themselves.

But so mysteriously and wonderfully did it come to pass, that every life was preserved; and though many were greatly bruised, and their flesh torn, yet there is not, as I can understand, one bone broken, or so much as put out of joint, among them all. Some, who were thought to be almost dead at first, are greatly recovered; and but one young woman, seems yet to remain in dangerous circumstances, by an inward hurt in her breast: but of late there appears more hope of her recovery.

None can give an account, or conceive, by what means people's lives and limbs should be thus preserved, when so great a multitude were thus imminently exposed. It looked as though it was impossible, but that great numbers must instantly be crushed to death, or dashed in pieces. It seems unreasonable to ascribe it to any thing else but the care of Providence, in disposing the motions of every piece of timber, and the precise place of safety where every one should sit and fall, when none were in any capacity to care for their own preservation. The preservation seems to be most wonderful, with respect to the women and children in the middle alley, under the gallery where it came down first, and with greatest force, and where there was nothing to break the force of the falling weight.

Such an event, may be a sufficient argument of a Divine providence over the lives of men. We thought ourselves called on to set apart a day to be spent in the solemn worship of God, to humble ourselves under such a rebuke of God upon us, in time of public service in his house, by so dangerous and surprising an accident; and to praise his name for so wonderful, and as it were miraculous, a preservation. The last Wednesday was kept by us to that end; and a mercy, in which the hand of God is so remarkably evident, may be well worthy to affect the hearts of all who hear it. * * *

(1737) 1829

II

Northampton, Dec. 12, 1743.

REV AND DEAR SIR,

Ever since the great work of God, that was wrought here about nine years ago, there has been a great and abiding alteration in this town, in many respects. There has been vastly more religion kept up in the town, among all sorts of persons, in religious exercises, and in common conversation; there has been a great alteration among the youth of the town, with respect to revelry, frolicking, profane and licentious conversation, and lewd songs; and there has also been a great alteration, amongst both old and young, with regard to tavern-haunting. I suppose the town has been in no measure, so free of vice in these respects, for any long time together for sixty years, as it has been these nine years past. There has also been an evident alteration, with respect to a charitable spirit to the poor: though I think with regard to this, we in this town, as well as the land in general, come far short of gospel rules. And though after that great work nine years ago, there has been a very lamentable decay of religious affections, and the engagedness of people's spirit in religion; yet many societies for prayer and social worship, were all along kept up, and there were some few instances of awakening, and deep concern about the things of another world, even in the most dead time.

In the year 1740, in the spring, before Mr. Whitefield came to this town, there was a visible alteration: there was more seriousness and religious conversation; especially among young people: those things that were of ill tendency among them, were foreborne; and it was a very frequent thing for persons to consult their minister upon the salvation of their souls; and in some particular persons, there appeared a great attention, about that time. And thus it continued, until Mr. Whitefield came to town, which was about the middle of October following: he preached here four sermons in the meeting-house, (besides a private lecture at my house,) one on Friday, another on Saturday, and two upon the Sabbath. The congregation was extraordinarily melted by every sermon; almost the whole assembly being in tears for a great part of sermon time. Mr. Whitefield's sermons were suitable to the circumstances of the town; containing a just reproof of our backslidings, and in a most moving and affecting manner, making use of our great professions, and great mercies, as arguments with us to return to God, from whom we had departed. Immediately after this, the minds of the people in general appeared more engaged in religion, shewing a greater forwardness to make religion the subject of their conversation, and to meet frequently for religious purposes, and to embrace all opportunities to hear the word preached. The revival at first, appeared chiefly among professors, and those that had entertained hope that they were in a state of salvation, to whom Mr. Whitefield chiefly addressed himself; but in a very short time, there appeared an awakening and deep concern among some young persons, that looked upon themselves in a christless state; and there were some hopeful appearances of conversion, and some professors were greatly revived. In about a month or six weeks, there was a great attention in the town, both as to the revival of professors and the awakening of others. By the middle of December, a considerable work of God appeared among those that were very young; and the revival of religion continued to increase, so that in the spring an engagedness of spirit, about the things of religion, was become very general amongst young people and children, and religious subjects almost wholly took up their conversation, when they were together.

In the month of May, 1741, a sermon was preached to a company, at a private house: Near the conclusion of the discourse, one or two persons, that were professors, were so greatly affected with a sense of the greatness and glory of divine things, and the infinite importance of the things of eternity, that they were not able to conceal it—the affection of their minds overcoming their strength, and having a very visible effect upon their bodies. When the exercises were over, the young people that were present, removed into the other room for religious conference; and particularly that they might have opportunity to enquire of those, that were thus affected, what apprehensions they had: and what things they were, that thus deeply impressed their minds; and there soon appeared a very great effect of their conversation; the affection was quickly propagated throughout the room; many of the young people and children, that were professors, appeared to be overcome with a sense of the greatness and glory of divine things, and with admiration, love, joy, and praise, and compassion to others, that looked upon themselves as in a state of nature; and many others at the same time were overcome with distress, about their sinful and miserable estate and condition; so that the whole room was full of nothing but outcries, faintings, and the like. Others soon heard of it in several parts of the town, and came to them; and what they saw and heard there, was greatly affecting to them, so that many of them were overpowered in like manner, and it continued thus for some hours; the time being spent in prayer, singing, counselling and conferring. There seemed to be a consequent happy effect of that meeting, to several particular persons, and on the state of religion in the town in general. After this, were meetings from time to time, attended with like appearances. But a little after it, at the conclusion of the public exercises on the Sabbath, I appointed the children that were under seventeen years of age, to go from the meeting-house to a neighbouring house, that I might there further enforce what they had heard in public, and might give in some counsels proper for their age. The children were there very generally and greatly affected with the warnings and counsels that were given them, and many exceedingly overcome; and the room was filled with cries; and when they were dismissed, they almost all of them went home crying aloud through the streets, to all parts of the town. The like appearances attended several such meetings of children, that were appointed. But their affections appeared by what followed, to be of a very different nature: in many, they appeared indeed but childish affections, and in a day or two would leave them as they were before: others were deeply impressed; their convictions took fast hold of them, and abode by them: and there were some that, from one meeting to another, seemed extraordinarily affected for some time, to but little purpose, their affections presently vanishing from time to time; but yet afterwards, were seized with abiding convictions, and their affections became durable.

About the middle of the summer, I called together the young people that were communicants, from sixteen to twenty-six years of age, to my house; which proved to be a most happy meeting: many seemed to be very greatly and most agreeably affected with those views, which excited humility, self-condemnation, self-abhorrence, love and joy: many fainted under these affections. We had several meetings that summer, of young people, attended with like appearances. It was about that time, that there first began to be cryings out in the meeting house; which several times occasioned many of the congregation to stay in the house after the public exercises were over, to confer with those who seemed to be overcome with religious convictions and affections, which was found to tend much to the propagation of their impressions, with lasting effect upon many; conference being, at these times, commonly joined with prayer and singing. In the summer and autumn, the children in various parts of the town, had religious meetings by themselves, for prayer, sometimes joined with fasting; wherein many of them seemed to be greatly and properly affected, and I hope some of them savingly wrought upon.

The months of August and September, were the most remarkable of any this year, for appearances of the conviction and conversion of sinners, and great revivings, quickenings, and comforts of professors, and for extraordinary external effects of these things. It was a very frequent thing, to see an house full of out-cries, faintings, convulsions, and such like, both with distress, and also with admiration and joy. It was not the manner here, to hold meetings all night, as in some places, nor was it common to continue them till very late in the night: but it was pretty often so, that there were some that were so affected, and their bodies so overcome, that they could not go home, but were obliged to stay all night where they were. There was no difference, that I know of here, with regard to these extraordinary effects, in meetings in the night and in the day time: the meetings in which these effects appeared in the evening, being commonly begun, and their extraordinary effects, in the day, and continued in the evening; and some meetings have been very remarkable for such extraordinary effects, that were both begun and finished in the day time. There was an appearance of a glorious progress of the work of God upon the hearts of sinners, in conviction and conversion, this summer and autumn, and great numbers, I think we have reason to hope, were brought savingly home to Christ. But this was remarkable: the work of God in his influences of this nature, seemed to be almost wholly upon a new generation—those that were not come to years of discretion in that wonderful season, nine years ago, children, or those that were then children: Others, who had enjoyed that former glorious opportunity, without any appearance of saving benefit, seemed now to be almost wholly passed over and let alone. But now we had the most wonderful work among children, that ever was in Northampton. The former outpouring of the Spirit, was remarkable for influences upon the minds of children, beyond all that ever been before; but this far exceeded that. Indeed, as to influences on the minds of professors, this work was by no means confined to a new generation. Many, of all ages, partook of it: but yet in this respect, it was more general on those that were of the young sort. Many, who had been formerly wrought upon, and in the time of our declension had fallen into decays, and had in a great measure left God, and gone after the world, now passed under a very remarkable new work of the Spirit of God, as if they had been the subjects of a second conversion. They were first led into the wilderness, and had a work of conviction; having much deeper convictions of the sins of both nature and practice, than ever before; though with some new circumstances, and something new in the kind of conviction in some, with great distress, beyond what they had felt before their first conversion. Under these convictions, they were excited to strive for salvation, and the kingdom of heaven suffered violence from some of them, in a far more remarkable manner than before; and after great convictions and humblings, and agonizing with God, they had Christ discovered to them anew, as an all sufficient Saviour, and in the glories of his grace, and in a far more clear manner than before; and with greater humility, self-emptiness and brokenness of heart, and a purer, a higher joy, and greater desires after holiness of life; but with greater self-diffidence and distrust of their treacherous hearts. One circumstance, wherein this work differed from that, which had been in the towns five or six years before, was, that conversions were frequently wrought more sensibly and visibly; the impressions stronger, and more manifest by their external effects; the progress of the Spirit of God in conviction, from step to step, more apparent; and the transition from one state to another, more sensible and plain; so that it might, in many instances, be as it were seen by bystanders. The preceding season had been very remarkable on this account, beyond what had been before; but this more remarkable than that. And in this season, these apparent or visible conversions, (if I may so call them,) were more frequently in the presence of others, at religious meetings, where the appearances of what was wrought on the heart, fell under public observation. * * *

With respect to the late season of revival of religion amongst us, for three or four years past, it has been observable, that in the former part of it, in the years 1740 and 1741, the work seemed to be much more pure, having less of a corrupt mixture, than in the former great outpouring of the Spirit, in 1735 and 1736. Persons seemed to be sensible of their former errors, and had learned more of their own hearts, and experience had taught them more of the tendency and consequences of things. They were now better guarded, and their affections were not only stronger, but attended with greater solemnity, and greater humility and self distrust, and greater engagedness after holy living and perseverance; and there were fewer errors in conduct. But in the latter part of it, in the year 1742, it was otherwise: the work continued more pure till we were infected from abroad: Our people hearing of, and some of them seeing, the work in other places, where there was a greater visible commotion than here, and the outward appearances were more extraordinary, were ready to think that the work in those places far excelled what was amongst us, and their eyes were dazzled with the high profession and great show that some made, who came hither from other places.

That those people went so far beyond them in raptures and violent emotions of the affections, and a vehement zeal, and what they called *boldness for Christ,* our people were ready to think was owing to far greater attainments in grace, and intimacy with heaven: they looked little in their own eyes, in comparison with them, and were ready to submit themselves to them, and yield themselves up to their conduct, taking it for granted, that every thing was right that they said and did. These things had a strange influence on the people, and gave many of them a deep and unhappy tincture from which it was a hard and long labour to deliver them, and from which some of them are not fully delivered, to this day.

The *effects* and *consequences* of things among us plainly show the following things, viz. That the degree of *grace* is by no means to be judged of by the degree of *joy,* or the degree of *zeal;* and that indeed we cannot at all determine by these things, who are gracious and who are not; and that it is not the *degree* of religious affections, but the *nature* of them, that is chiefly to be looked at. *Some* that have had very great raptures of joy, and have been extraordinarily *filled,* (as the vulgar phrase is,) and have had their bodies overcome, and that very often, have manifested far less of the temper of christians in their conduct since, than some others that have been still, and have made no great outward show. But then again, there are *many others,* that have had extraordinary joys and emotions of mind, with frequent great effects upon their bodies, that behave themselves stedfastly, as humble, amiable, eminent christians.

'Tis evident that there may be great religious affections in individuals, which may, in show and appearance, resemble gracious affections, and have the same effects upon their bodies, but are far from having the same effect on the temper of their minds and the course of their lives. And likewise, there is nothing more manifest, by what appears amongst us, than that the good estate of individuals is not chiefly to be judged of by any exactness of steps, and method of experiences, in what is supposed to be the first conversion; but that we must judge by the spirit that breathes, the effect wrought upon the temper of the soul in the time of the work and remaining afterwards. Though there have been very few instances among professors, amongst us, of what is ordinarily called scandalous sins, known to me; yet the temper that some of them show, and the behaviour they have been of, together with some things in the nature and circumstances of their experiences, make me much afraid least there be a considerable number, that have wofully deceived themselves. Though, on the other hand, there is a great number, whose temper and conversation is such, as justly confirms the charity of others towards them; and not a few, in whose disposition and walk, there are amiable appearances of eminent grace. And notwithstanding all the corrupt mixtures that have been in the late work here, there are not only many blessed fruits of it, in particular persons that yet remain, but some good effects of it upon the town in general. A spirit of party has more extensively subsided. I suppose there has been less appearance, these three or four years past, of that division of the town into two parties, which has long been our bane, than has been, at any time during the preceding thirty years; and the people have apparently had much more caution, and a greater guard on their spirit and their tongues, to avoid contention and unchristian heats, in town-meetings, and on other occasions. And 'tis a thing greatly to be rejoiced in, that the people very lately came to an agreement and final issue, with respect to their grand controversy relating to their common lands; which has been, above any other particular thing, a source of mutual prejudices, jealousies and debates, for fifteen or sixteen years past. The people also seem to be much more sensible of the danger of resting in old experiences, or what they were subjects of at their supposed first conversion; and to be more fully convinced of the necessity of forgetting the things that are behind, and pressing forward and maintaining earnest labour, watchfulness and prayerfulness, as long as they live.

I am, Rev. Sir,

Your friend and brother,

JONATHAN EDWARDS.

(1743) 1829

From *FREEDOM OF THE WILL*

[A DEFINITION OF THE WILL]

PART I

SECT. I. *Concerning the Nature of the Will.*

It may possibly be thought, that there is no great need of going about to define or describe the *Will;* this word being generally as well understood as any other words we can use to explain it: and so perhaps it would be, had not philosophers, meta-physicians and polemic divines brought the matter into obscurity by the things they have said of it. But since it is so, I think it may be of some use, and will tend to greater clearness in the following discourse, to say a few things concerning it.

And therefore I observe, that the

Will (without any metaphysical refining) is, *That by which the mind chooses any thing.* The faculty of the *Will,* is that power, or principle of mind, by which it is capable of *choosing:* an act of the *Will* is the same as an act of *choosing* or *choice.*

If any think it is a more perfect definition of the Will, to say, that it is that by which the soul either *chooses* or *refuses;* I am content with it: though I think it enough to say, It is that by which the soul chooses: for in every act of Will whatsoever, the mind chooses one thing rather than another; it chooses something rather than the contrary, or rather than the want or non-existence of that thing. So in every act of refusal, the mind chooses the absence of the thing refused; the positive and the negative are set before the mind for its choice, and it chooses the negative; and the mind's making its choice in that case is properly the act of the Will: the Will's determining between the two, is a voluntary determination; but that is the same thing as making a choice. So that by whatever names we call the act of the Will, choosing, refusing, approving, disapproving, liking, disliking, embracing, rejecting, determining, directing, commanding forbidding, inclining or *being* averse, *being* pleased or displeased *with;* all may be reduced to this act of *choosing.* For the soul to act *voluntarily* is evermore to act *electively.* * * *

SECT. II. *Concerning the Determination of the Will.*

By *determining* the Will, if the phrase be used with any meaning, must be intended, *causing* that the act of the Will or Choice should be thus, and not otherwise: and the Will is said to be determined, when, in consequence of some action, or influence, its choice is directed to, and fixed upon, a particular object. As when we speak of the determination of motion, we mean causing the motion of the body to be in such a direction, rather than another.

The Determination of the Will, supposes an effect, which must have a cause. If the Will be determined, there is a Determiner. This must be supposed to be intended even by them that say the Will determines itself. If it be so, the Will is both Determiner and determined; it is a cause that acts and produces effects upon itself, and is the object of its own influence and action.

With respect to that grand enquiry, "What determines the Will?" it would be very tedious and unnecessary, at present, to examine all the various opinions, which have been advanced concerning this matter; nor is it needful that I should enter into a particular discussion of all points debated in disputes on that other question, "Whether the Will always follows the last dictate of the understanding?" It is sufficient to my present purpose to say, *It is that motive, which, as it stands in the view of the mind, is the strongest, that determines the Will.* But it may be necessary that I should a little explain my meaning.

By *motive,* I mean the whole of that which moves, excites, or invites the mind to volition, whether that be one thing singly, or many things conjunctly. Many particular things may concur, and unite their strength, to induce the mind; and when it is so, all together are as one complex motive. And when I speak of the *strongest* motive, I have respect to the strength of the whole that operates to induce a particular act of volition, whether that be the strength of one thing alone, or of many together.

Whatever is objectively a motive, in this sense, must be something that is *extant in the view or apprehension of the understanding,* or perceiving faculty. Nothing can induce or invite the mind to will or act any thing, any further than it is perceived, or is some way or other in the mind's view; for what is wholly unperceived and perfectly out of the mind's view, cannot affect the mind at all. It is most evident, that nothing is in the mind, or reaches it, or takes any hold of it, any otherwise than as it is perceived or thought of.

And I think it must also be allowed by all, that every thing that is properly called a motive, excitement, or inducement to a perceiving, willing agent, has some sort and degree of *tendency,* or *advantage* to move or excite the Will, previous to the effect, or to the act of the Will excited. This previous tendency of the motive is what I call the *strength* of the motive. That motive which has a less degree of previous advantage, or tendency to move the will, or which appears less inviting, as it stands in the view of the mind, is what I call a *weaker* motive. On the contrary, that which appears most inviting, and has, by what appears concerning it to the understanding or apprehension, the greatest degree of previous tendency to excite and induce the choice, is what I call the *strongest* motive. And in this sense, I suppose the Will is always determined by the strongest motive.

Things that exist in the view of the mind have their strength, tendency, or advantage to move, or excite its Will, from many things appertaining to the nature and circumstances of the *thing viewed,* the nature and circumstances of the *mind that views,* and the degree and manner of its *view;* of which it would perhaps be hard to make a perfect enumeration. But so much I think may be determined in general, without room for controversy, that whatever is perceived or apprehended by an intelligent and voluntary agent, which has the nature and influence of a motive to volition or choice, is considered or viewed *as good;* nor has it any tendency to engage the election of the soul in any further degree than it appears such. For to say otherwise, would be to say, that things that appear, have a tendency, by the appearance they make, to engage the mind to elect them, some other way than by their appearing eligible to it; which is absurd. And therefore it must be true, in some sense, that *the Will always is, as the greatest apparent good is.* * * *

SECT. V. *Concerning the Notion of Liberty, and of Moral Agency.*

The plain and obvious meaning of the words *Freedom* and *Liberty,* in common speech, is *The power, opportunity, or advantage that any one has, to do as he pleases.* Or in other words, his being free from hinderance or impediment in the way of doing, or conducting in any respect as he wills.

And the contrary to Liberty, whatever name we call that by, is a person's being hindered or unable to conduct as he will, or being necessitated to do otherwise.

If this which I have mentioned be the meaning of the word Liberty, in the ordinary use of language; as I trust that none that has ever learned to talk, and is unprejudiced, will deny; then it will follow, that in propriety of speech, neither Liberty, nor its contrary, can properly be ascribed to any being or thing, but that which has such a faculty, power, or property, as is called will. For that which is possessed of no *will,* cannot have any *power* or *opportunity* of doing *according to its will,* nor be necessitated to act *contrary to its will,* nor be restrained from acting agreeably to it. And therefore to talk of Liberty, or the contrary, as belonging to the *very will itself,* is not to speak good sense; if we judge of sense, and nonsense, by the original and proper signification of words.—For the *will itself* is not an Agent that *has a will:* the power of choosing, itself, has not a power of choosing. That which has the power of volition is the man, or the soul, and not the power of volition itself. And he that has the Liberty of doing according to his will, is the Agent who is possessed of the will; and not the will which he is possessed of. We say with propriety, that a bird let loose has power and liberty to fly; but not that the bird's power of flying has a power and Liberty of flying. To be free is the property of an agent, who is possessed of powers and faculties, as much as to be cunning, valiant, bountiful, or zealous. But these qualities are the properties of persons; and not the properties of properties.

There are two things contrary to what is called Liberty in common speech. One is *constraint;* otherwise called *force, compulsion,* and *coaction;* which is a person's being necessitated to do a thing *contrary* to his will. The other is *restraint;* which is, his being hindered, and not having power to do *according* to his will. But that which has no will cannot be the subject of these things.—I need say the less on this head, Mr. LOCKE having set the same thing forth, with so great clearness, in his *Essay on the Human Understanding.*

But one thing more I would observe concerning what is vulgarly called *Liberty;* namely, that power and opportunity for one to do and conduct as he will, or according to his choice, is all that is meant by it; without taking into the meaning of the word, any thing of the *cause* of that choice; or at all considering how the person came to have such a volition; whether it was caused by some external motive, or internal habitual bias; whether it was determined by some internal antecedent volition, or whether it happened without a cause; whether it was necessarily connected with something foregoing, or not connected. Let the person come by his choice any how, yet, if he is able, and there is nothing in the way to hinder his pursuing and executing his will, the man is perfectly free, according to the primary and common notion of freedom.

What has been said may be sufficient to shew what is meant by *Liberty,* according to the common notions of mankind, and in the usual and primary acceptation of the word: but the word, as used by *Arminians, Pelagians* and others, who oppose the *Calvinists,* has an entirely different signification.—These several things belong to their notion of Liberty. 1. That it consists in a *self-determining power* in the will, of a certain sovereignty the will has over itself, and its own acts, whereby it determines its own volitions; so as not to be dependent in its determinations, on any cause without itself, nor determined by any thing prior to its own acts. 2. *Indifference* belongs to Liberty in their notion of it, or that the mind, previous to the act of volition, be *in equilibrio.* 3. *Contingence* is another thing that belongs and is essential to it; not in the common acceptation of the word, as that has been already explained, but as opposed to all *necessity,* or any fixed and certain connection with some previous ground or reason of its existence. They suppose the essence of Liberty so much to consist in these things, that unless the will of man be free in this sense, he has no real freedom, how much soever he may be at Liberty to act according to his will.

A *moral Agent* is a being that is capable of those actions that have a *moral* quality, and which can properly be denominated good or evil in a moral sense, virtuous or vicious, commendable or faulty. To moral Agency belongs a *moral faculty,* or sense of moral good and evil, or of such a thing as desert or worthiness, of praise or blame, reward or punishment; and a capacity which an Agent has of being influenced in his actions by moral inducements or motives, exhibited to the view of understanding and reason, to engage to a conduct agreeable to the moral faculty.

The sun is very excellent and beneficial in its actions and influence on the earth, in warming and causing it to bring forth its fruits; but it is not a moral Agent: its action, though good, is not virtuous or meritorious. Fire that breaks out in a city, and consumes great part of it, is very mischievous in its operation; but it is not a moral Agent: what it does is not faulty or sinful, or deserving of any punishment. The brute creatures are not moral Agents: the actions of some of them are very profitable and pleasant; others are very hurtful: yet seeing they have no moral faculty, or sense of desert, and do not act from choice guided by understanding, or with a capacity of reasoning and reflecting, but only from instinct, and are not capable of being influenced by moral inducements, their actions are not properly sinful or virtuous; nor are they properly the subjects of any such moral treatment for what they do, as moral Agents are for their faults or good deeds.

Here it may be noted, that there is a circumstantial difference between the moral Agency of a *ruler* and a *subject.* I call it *circumstantial,* because it lies only in the difference of moral inducements, by which they are capable of being influenced, arising from the difference of *circumstances.* A *ruler* acting in that capacity only, is not capable of being influenced by a moral law, and its sanctions of threatenings and promises, rewards and punishments, as the *subject* is; though both may be influenced by a knowledge of moral good and evil. And therefore the moral Agency of the

Supreme Being, who acts only in the capacity of a *ruler* towards his creatures, and never as a *subject,* differs in that respect from the moral Agency of created intelligent beings. God's actions, and particularly those which he exerts as a moral governor, have moral qualifications, and are morally good in the highest degree. They are most perfectly holy and righteous; and we must conceive of Him as influenced in the highest degree, by that which, above all others, is properly a moral inducement; viz. the moral good which He sees in such and such things: and therefore He is, in the most proper sense, a moral Agent, the source of all moral ability and Agency, the fountain and rule of all virtue and moral good; though by reason of his being supreme over all, it is not possible He should be under the influence of law or command, promises or threatenings, rewards or punishments, counsels or warnings. The essential qualities of a moral Agent are in God, in the greatest possible perfection; such as understanding, to perceive the difference between moral good and evil; a capacity of discerning that moral worthiness and demerit, by which some things are praiseworthy, others deserving of blame and punishment; and also a capacity of choice, and choice guided by understanding, and a power of acting according to his choice or pleasure, and being capable of doing those things which are in the highest sense praiseworthy. And herein does very much consist that image of God wherein he made man, (which we read of *Gen.* i. 26, 27, and *chap.* ix. 6.) by which God distinguished man from the beasts, *viz.* in those faculties and principles of nature, whereby He is capable of moral Agency. Herein very much consists the *natural* image of God; whereas the *spiritual* and *moral* image, wherein man was made at first, consisted in that moral excellency with which he was endowed.

1754

BENJAMIN FRANKLIN
(1706–1790)

From *THE AUTOBIOGRAPHY*

[BOYHOOD]

Twyford, *at the Bishop of St. Asaph's,* 1771.

DEAR SON: I have ever had pleasure in obtaining any little anecdotes of my ancestors. You may remember the inquiries I made among the remains of my relations when you were with me in England, and the journey I undertook for that purpose. Imagining it may be equally agreeable to you to know the circumstances of my life, many of which you are yet unacquainted with, and expecting the enjoyment of a week's uninterrupted leisure in my present country retirement, I sit down to write them for you. To which I have besides some other inducements. Having emerged from the poverty and obscurity in which I was born and bred, to a state of affluence and some degree of reputation in the world, and having gone so far through life with a considerable share of felicity, the conducing means I made use of, which with the blessing of God so well succeeded, my posterity may like to know, as they may find some of them suitable to their own situations, and therefore fit to be imitated.

That felicity, when I reflected on it, has induced me sometimes to say, that were it offered to my choice, I should have no objection to a repetition of the same life from its beginning, only asking the advantages authors have in a second edition to correct some faults of the first. So I might, besides correcting the faults, change some sinister accidents and events of it for others more favourable. But though this were denied, I should still accept the offer. Since such a repetition is not to be expected, the next thing most like living one's life over again seems to be a recollection of that life, and to make that recollection as durable as possible by putting it down in writing.

Hereby, too, I shall indulge the inclination so natural in old men, to be talking of themselves and their own past actions; and I shall indulge it without being tiresome to others, who, through respect to age, might conceive themselves obliged to give me a hearing, since this may be read or not as any one pleases. And, lastly (I may as well confess it, since my denial of it will be believed by nobody), perhaps I shall a good deal gratify my own *vanity.* Indeed, I scarce ever heard or saw the introductory words, "*Without vanity I may say,*" etc., but some vain thing immediately followed. Most people dislike vanity in others, whatever share they have of it themselves; but I give it fair quarter wherever I meet with it, being persuaded that it is often productive of good to the possessor, and to others that are within his sphere of action; and therefore, in many cases, it would not be altogether absurd if a man were to thank God for his vanity among the other comforts of life.

And now I speak of thanking God, I desire with all humility to acknowledge that I owe the mentioned happiness of my past life to His kind providence, which lead me to the means I used and gave them success. My belief of this induces me to *hope,* though I must not *presume,* that the same goodness will still be exercised toward me, in continuing that happiness, or enabling me to bear a fatal reverse, which I may experience as others have done; the complexion of my future fortune being known to Him only in whose power it is to bless to us even our afflictions. * * *

Josiah, my father, married young, and carried his wife with three children into New England, about 1682. The conventicles having been forbidden by law, and frequently disturbed, induced some considerable men of his acquaintance to remove to that country, and he was prevailed with to accompany them thither, where they expected to enjoy their mode of religion with freedom. By the same wife he had four children more born there, and by a second wife ten more, in all seventeen; of which I remember thirteen sitting at one time at his table, who all grew up to be men and women, and married; I was the youngest son, and the youngest child but two, and was born in Boston, New England. My mother, the second wife, was Abiah Folger, daughter of Peter Folger, one of the first settlers of New England, of whom honorable mention is made by Cotton Mather, in his church history of that country, entitled *Magnalia Christi Americana,* as *"a godly, learned Englishman,"* if I remember the words rightly. I have heard that he wrote sundry small occasional pieces, but only one of them was printed, which I saw now many years since. It was written in 1675, in the home-spun verse of that time and people, and addressed to those then concerned in the government there. It was in favour of liberty of conscience, and in behalf of the Baptists, Quakers, and other sectaries that had been under persecution, ascribing the Indian wars, and other distresses that had befallen the country, to that persecution, as so many judgments of God to punish so heinous an offense, and exhorting a repeal of those uncharitable laws. The whole appeared to me as written with a good deal of decent plainness and manly freedom. The six concluding lines I remember, though I have forgotten the two first of the stanza; but the purport of them was, that his censures proceeded from good-will, and, therefore, he would be known to be the author.

"Because to be a libeller (says he)
  I hate it with my heart;
From Sherburne town, where now I dwell
  My name I do put here;
Without offense your real friend,
  It is Peter Folgier."

My elder brothers were all put apprentices to different trades. I was put to the grammar-school at eight years of age, my father intending to devote me, as the tithe of his sons, to the service of the Church. My early readiness in learning to read (which must have been very early, as I do not remember when I could not read), and the opinion of all his friends, that I should certainly make a good scholar, encouraged him in this purpose of his. My uncle Benjamin, too, approved of it, and proposed to give me all his short-hand volumes of sermons, I suppose as a stock to set up with, if I would learn his character. I continued, however, at the grammar-school not quite one year, though in that time I had risen gradually from the middle of the class of that year to be the head of it, and farther was removed into the next class above it, in order to go with that into the third at the end of the year. But my father, in the meantime, from a view of the expense of a college education, which having so large a family he could not well afford, and the mean living many so educated were afterwards able to obtain—reasons that he gave to his friends in my hearing—altered his first intention, took me from the grammar-school, and sent me to a school for writing and arithmetic, kept by a then famous man, Mr. George Brownell, very successful in his profession generally, and that by mild, encouraging methods. Under him I acquired fair writing pretty soon, but I failed in the arithmetic, and made no progress in it. At ten years old I was taken home to assist my father in his business, which was that of a tallow-chandler and sope-boiler; a business he was not bred to, but had assumed on his arrival in New England, and on finding his dying trade would not maintain his family, being in little request. Accordingly, I was employed in cutting wick for the candles, filling the dipping mold and the molds for cast candles, attending the shop, going of errands, etc.

I disliked the trade, and had a strong inclination for the sea, but my father declared against it; however, living near the water, I was much in and about it, learnt early to swim well, and to manage boats; and when in a boat or canoe with other boys, I was commonly allowed to govern, especially in any case of difficulty; and upon other occasions I was generally a leader among the boys, and sometimes led them into scrapes, of which I will mention one instance, as it shows an early projecting public spirit, tho' not then justly conducted.

There was a salt-marsh that bounded part of the mill-pond, on the edge of which, at high water, we used to stand to fish for minnows. By much trampling, we had made it a mere quagmire. My proposal was to build a wharff there fit for us to stand upon, and I showed my comrades a large heap of stones, which were intended for a new house near the marsh, and which would very well suit our purpose. Accordingly, in the evening, when the workmen were gone, I assembled a number of my playfellows, and working with them diligently like so many emmets, sometimes two or three to a stone, we brought them all away and built our little wharff. The next morning the workmen were surprised at missing the stones, which were found in our wharff. Inquiry was made after the removers; we were discovered and complained of; several of us were corrected by our fathers; and, though I pleaded the usefulness of the work, mine convinced me that nothing was useful which was not honest. * * *

To return: I continued thus employed in my father's business for two years, that is, till I was twelve years old; and my brother John, who was bred to that business, having left my father, married, and set up for himself at Rhode Island, there was all appearance that I was destined to supply his place, and become a tallow-chandler. But my dislike to the trade continuing, my father was under apprehensions that if he did not find one for me more agreeable, I should break away and get to sea, as his son Josiah had done, to his great vexation. He therefore sometimes took me to walk with him, and see joiners, bricklayers, turners, braziers, etc., at their work, that he might observe my inclination, and endeavour to fix it on some trade or other on land. It has ever since been a pleasure to me to see good workmen handle their tools; and it has been useful to me, having learnt so much by it as to be able to do little jobs myself in my house when a workman could not readily be got, and to construct little machines for my experiments, while the intention of making the experiment was fresh and warm in my mind. My father at last fixed upon the cutler's trade, and my uncle Benjamin's son Samuel, who was bred to that business in London, being about that time established in Boston, I was sent to be with him some time on liking. But his expectations of a fee with me displeasing my father, I was taken home again.

From a child I was fond of reading, and all the little money that came into my hands was ever laid out in books. Pleased with the Pilgrim's Progress, my first collection was of John Bunyan's works in separate little volumes. I afterward sold them to enable me to buy R. Burton's Historical Collections; they were small chapmen's books, and cheap, 40 or 50 in all. My father's little library consisted chiefly of books in polemic divinity, most of which I read, and have since often regretted that, at a time when I had such a thirst for knowledge, more proper books had not fallen in my way, since it was now resolved I should not be a clergyman. Plutarch's *Lives* there was in which I read abundantly, and I still think that time spent to great advantage. There was also a book of De Foe's, called an Essay on Projects, and another of Dr. Mather's, called Essays to do Good, which perhaps gave me a turn of thinking that had an influence on some of the principal future events of my life.

This bookish inclination at length determined my father to make me a printer, though he had already one son (James) of that profession. In 1717 my brother James returned from England with a press and letters to set up his business in Boston. I liked it much better than that of my father, but still had a hankering for the sea. To prevent the apprehended effect of such an inclination, my father was impatient to have me bound to my brother. I stood out some time, but at last was persuaded, and signed the indentures when I was yet but twelve years old. I was to serve as an apprentice till I was twenty-one years of age, only I was to be allowed journeyman's wages during the last year. In a little time I made great proficiency in the business, and became a useful hand to my brother. I now had access to better books. An acquaintance with the apprentices of booksellers enabled me sometimes to borrow a small one, which I was careful to return soon and clean. Often I sat up in my room reading the greatest part of the night, when the book was borrowed in the evening and to be returned early in the morning, lest it should be missed or wanted.

And after some time an ingenious tradesman, Mr. Matthew Adams, who had a pretty collection of books, and who frequented our printing-house, took notice of me, invited me to his library, and very kindly lent me such books as I chose to read. I now took a fancy to poetry, and made some little pieces; my brother, thinking it might turn to account, encouraged me and put me on composing occasional ballads. One was called *The Lighthouse Tragedy,* and contained an account of the drowning of Captain Worthilake, with his two daughters: the other was a sailor's song, on the taking of *Teach* (or Blackbeard) the pirate. They were wretched stuff, in the Grub-street-ballad style; and when they were printed he sent me about the town to sell them. The first sold wonderfully, the event being recent, having made a great noise. This flattered my vanity; but my father discouraged me by ridiculing my performances, and telling me verse-makers were generally beggars. So I escaped being a poet, most probably a very bad one; but as prose writing has been of great use to me in the course of my life, and was a principal means of my advancement, I shall tell you how, in such a situation, I acquired what little ability I have in that way.

There was another bookish lad in the town, John Collins by name, with whom I was intimately acquainted. We sometimes disputed, and very fond we were of argument, and very desirous of confuting one another, which disputatious turn, by the way, is apt to become a very bad habit, making people often extremely disagreeable in company by the contradiction that is necessary to bring it into practice; and thence, besides souring and spoiling the conversation, is productive of disgusts and, perhaps enmities where you may have occasion for friendship. I had caught it by reading my father's books of dispute about religion. Persons of good sense, I have since observed, seldom fall into it, except lawyers, university men, and men of all sorts that have been bred at Edinborough.

A question was once, somehow or other, started between Collins and me, of the propriety of educating the female sex in learning, and their abilities for study. He was of opinion that it was improper, and that they were naturally unequal to it. I took the contrary side, perhaps a little for dispute's sake. He was naturally more eloquent, had ready plenty of words; and sometimes, as I thought, bore me down more by his fluency than by the strength of his reasons. As we parted without settling the point, and were not to see one another again for some time, I sat down to put by arguments in writing, which I copied fair and sent to him. He answered, and I replied. Three or four letters of a side had passed, when my father happened to find my papers and read them. Without entering into the discussion, he took occasion to talk to me about the manner of my writing; observed that, though I had the advantage of my antagonist in correct spelling and pointing (which I ow'd to the printing-house), I fell far short in elegance of expression, in method and in perspicuity, of which he convinced me by several instances. I saw the justice of his remarks, and thence grew more attentive to the manner in writing, and determined to endeavour at improvement.

About this time I met with an odd volume of the *Spectator*. It was the third. I had never before seen any of them. I bought it, read it over and over, and was much delighted with it. I thought the writing excellent, and wished, if possible, to imitate it. With this view I took some of the papers, and, making short hints of the sentiment in each sentence, laid them by a few days, and then, without looking at the book, try'd to compleat the papers again, by expressing each hinted sentiment at length, and as fully as it had been expressed before, in any suitable words that should come to hand. Then I compared my *Spectator* with the original, discovered some of my faults, and corrected them. But I found I wanted a stock of words, or a readiness in recollecting and using them, which I thought I should have acquired before that time if I had gone on making verses; since the continual occasion for words of the same import, but of different length, to suit the measure, or of different sound for the rhyme, would have laid me under a constant necessity of searching for variety, and also have tended to fix that variety in my mind, and make me master of it. Therefore I took some of the tales and turned them into verse; and, after a time, when I had pretty well forgotten the prose, turned them back again. I also sometimes jumbled my collections of hints into confusion, and after some weeks endeavoured to reduce them into the best order, before I began to form the full sentences and compleat the paper. This was to teach me method in the arrangement of thoughts. By comparing my work afterwards with the original, I discovered many faults and amended them; but I sometimes had the pleasure of fancying that, in certain particulars of small import, I had been lucky enough to improve the method or the language, and this encouraged me to think I might possibly in time come to be a tolerable English writer, of which I was extreamly ambitious. My time for these exercises and for reading was at night, after work or before it began in the morning, or on Sundays, when I contrived to be in the printing-house alone, evading as much as I could the common attendance on public worship which my father used to exact of me when I was under his care, and which indeed I still thought a duty, though I could not, as it seemed to me, afford time to practise it.

When about 16 years of age I happened to meet with a book, written by one Tryon, recommending a vegetable diet. I determined to go into it. My brother, being yet unmarried, did not keep house, but boarded himself and his apprentices in another family. My refusing to eat flesh occasioned an inconveniency, and I was frequently chid for my singularity. I made myself acquainted with Tryon's manner of preparing some of his dishes, such as boiling potatoes or rice, making hasty pudding, and a few others, and then proposed to my brother, that if he would give me, weekly, half the money he paid for my board, I would board myself. He instantly agreed to it, and I presently found that I could save half what he paid me. This was an additional fund for buying books. But I had another advantage in it. My brother and the rest going from the printing-house to their meals, I remained there alone, and, despatching presently my light repast, which often was no more than a bisket or a slice of bread, a handful of raisins or a tart from the pastry-cook's, and a glass of water, had the rest of the time till their return for study, in which I made the greater progress, from that greater clearness of head and quicker apprehension which usually attend temperance in eating and drinking.

And now it was that, being on some occasion made asham'd of my ignorance in figures, which I had twice failed in learning when at school, I took Cocker's book of Arithmetick, and went through the whole by myself with great ease. I also read Seller's and Shermy's books of Navigation, and became acquainted with the little geometry they contain; but never proceeded far in that science. And I read about this time Locke *on Human Understanding,* and the *Art of Thinking,* by Messrs. du Port Royal.

While I was intent on improving my language, I met with an English grammar (I think it was Greenwood's), at the end of which there were two little sketches of the arts of rhetoric and logic, the latter finishing with a specimen of a dispute in the Socratic method; and soon after I procur'd Xenophon's Memorable Things of Socrates, wherein there are many instances of the same method. I was charm'd with it, adopted it, dropt my abrupt contradiction and positive argumentation, and put on the humble inquirer and doubter. And being then, from reading Shaftesbury and Collins, became a real doubter in many points of our religious doctrine, I found this method safest for myself and very embarrassing to those against whom I used it; therefore I took a delight in it, practis'd it continually, and grew very artful and expert in drawing people, even of superior knowledge, into concessions, the consequences of which they did not foresee, entangling them in difficulties out of which they could not extricate themselves, and so obtaining victories that neither myself nor my cause always deserved. I continu'd this method some few years, but gradually left it, retaining only the habit of expressing myself in terms of modest diffidence; never using, when I advanced anything that may possibly be disputed, the words *certainly, undoubtedly,* or any others that give the air of positiveness to an opinion; but rather say, I conceive or apprehend a thing to be so and so; it appears to me, or *I should think it so or so,* for such and such reasons; or *I imagine it to be so;* or *it is so, if I am not mistaken.* This habit, I believe, has been of great advantage to me when I have had occasion to inculcate my opinions, and persuade men into measures that I have been from time to time engag'd in promoting; and, as the chief ends of conversation are to *inform* or to be *informed,* to *please* or to *persuade,* I wish well-meaning, sensible men would not lessen their power of doing good by a positive, assuming manner, that seldom fails to disgust, tends to create opposition, and to defeat everyone of those purposes for which speech was given to us, to wit, giving or receiving information or pleasure. For, if you would inform, a positive and dogmatical manner in advancing your sentiments may provoke contradiction and prevent a candid attention. If you wish information and improvement from the knowledge of others, and yet at the same time express yourself as firmly fix'd in your present opinions, modest, sensible men, who do not love disputation, will probably leave you undisturbed in the possession of your error. And by such a manner, you can seldom hope to recommend yourself in *pleasing* your hearers, or to persuade those whose concurrence you desire. Pope says, judiciously:

"Men should be taught as if you taught them not,
And things unknown propos'd as things forgot;"

farther recommending to us

"To speak, tho' sure, with seeming diffidence."

And he might have coupled with this line that which he has coupled with another, I think, less properly,

"For want of modesty is want of sense."

If you ask, Why less properly? I must repeat the lines,

"Immodest words admit of no defense,
For want of modesty is want of sense."

Now, is not *want of sense* (where a man is so unfortunate as to want it) some apology for his *want of modesty?* and would not the lines stand more justly thus?

"Immodest words admit *but* this defense,
That want of modesty is want of sense."

This, however, I should submit to better judgments.

My brother had, in 1720 or 1721, begun to print a newspaper. It was the second that appeared in America, and was called the New England Courant. The only one before it was the Boston News-Letter. I remember his being dissuaded by some of his friends from the undertaking, as not likely to succeed, one newspaper being, in their judgment, enough for America. At this time (1771) there are not less than five-and-twenty. He went on, however, with the undertaking, and after having worked in composing the types and printing off the sheets, I was employed to carry the papers thro' the streets to the customers.

He had some ingenious men among his friends, who amus'd themselves by writing little pieces for this paper, which gain'd it credit and made it more in demand, and these gentlemen often visited us. Hearing their conversations, and their accounts of the approbation their papers were received with, I was excited to try my hand among them; but, being still a boy, and suspecting that my brother would object to printing anything of mine in his paper if he knew it to be mine, I contrived to disguise my hand, and, writing an anonymous paper, I put it in at night under the door of the printing-house. It was found in the morning, and communicated to his writing friends when they call'd in as usual. They read it, commented on it in my hearing, and I had the exquisite pleasure of finding it met with their approbation, and that, in their different guesses at the author, none were named but men of some character among us for learning and ingenuity. I suppose now that I was rather lucky in my judges, and that perhaps they were not really so very good ones as I then esteem'd them.

Encourag'd, however, by this, I wrote and convey'd in the same way to the press several more papers which were equally approv'd; and I kept my secret till my small fund of sense for such performances was pretty well exhausted, and then I discovered it, when I began to be considered a little more by my brother's acquaintance, and in a manner that did not quite please him, as he thought, probably with reason, that it tended to make me too vain. And, perhaps, this might be one occasion of the differences that we began to have about this time. Though a brother, he considered himself as my master, and me as his apprentice, and, accordingly, expected the same services from me as he would from another, while I thought he demean'd me too much in some he requir'd of me, who from a brother expected more indulgence. Our disputes were often brought before our father, and I fancy I was either generally in the right, or else a better pleader, because the judgment was generally in my favour. But my brother was passionate, and had often beaten me, which I took extreamly amiss; and, thinking my apprenticeship very tedious, I was continually wishing for some opportunity of shortening it, which at length offered in a manner unexpected.

One of the pieces in our newspaper on some political point, which I have now forgotten, gave offense to the Assembly. He was taken up, censur'd, and imprison'd for a month, by the speaker's warrant, I suppose, because he would not discover his author. I too was taken up and examin'd before the council; but, tho' I did not give them any satisfaction, they content'd themselves with admonishing me, and dismissed me, considering me, perhaps, as an apprentice, who was bound to keep his master's secrets.

During my brother's confinement, which I resented a good deal, notwithstanding our private differences, I had the management of the paper; and I made bold to give our rulers some rubs in it, which my brother took very kindly, while others began to consider me in an unfavourable light, as a young genius that had a turn for libelling and satyr. My brother's discharge was accompany'd with an order of the House (a very odd one), that "*James Franklin should no longer print the paper called the New England Courant.*"

There was a consultation held in our printing-house among his friends, what he should do in this case. Some proposed to evade the order by changing the name of the paper; but my brother, seeing inconveniences in that, it was finally concluded on as a better way, to let it be printed for the future under the name of BENJAMIN FRANKLIN; and to avoid the censure of the Assembly, that might fall on him as still printing it by his apprentice, the contrivance was that my old indenture should be return'd to me, with a full discharge on the back of it, to be shown on occasion, but to secure to him the benefit of my service, I was to sign new indentures for the remainder of the term, which were to be kept private. A very flimsy scheme it was; however, it was immediately executed, and the paper went on accordingly, under my name for several months.

At length, a fresh difference arising between my brother and me, I took upon me to assert my freedom, presuming that he would not venture to produce the new indentures. It was not fair in me to take this advantage, and this I therefore reckon one of the first errata of my life; but the unfairness of it weighed little with me, when under the impressions of resentment for the blows his passion too often urged him to bestow upon me, though he was otherwise not an ill-natur'd man: perhaps I was too saucy and provoking. * * *

(1771) 1791

[ENTERING PHILADELPHIA]

I have been the more particular in this description of my journey, and shall be so of my first entry into that city, that you may in your mind compare such unlikely beginnings with the figure I have since made there. I was in my working dress, my best clothes being to come round by sea. I was dirty from my journey; my pockets were stuff'd out with shirts and stockings, and I knew no soul nor where to look for lodging. I was fatigued with travelling, rowing, and want of rest, I was very hungry; and my whole stock of cash consisted of a Dutch dollar, and about a shilling in copper. The latter I gave the people of the boat for my passage, who at first refus'd it, on account of my rowing; but I insisted on their taking it. A man being sometimes more generous when he has but a little money than when he has plenty, perhaps thro' fear of being thought to have but little.

Then I walked up the street, gazing about till near the market-house I met a boy with bread. I had made many a meal on bread, and, inquiring where he got it, I went immediately to the baker's he directed me to, in Second-street, and ask'd for bisket, intending such as we had in Boston; but they, it seems, were not made in Philadelphia. Then I asked for a three-penny loaf, and was told they had none such. So not considering or knowing the difference of money, and the greater cheapness nor the names of his bread, I bad him give me three-penny worth of any sort. He gave me, accordingly, three great puffy rolls. I was surpriz'd at the quantity, but took it, and, having no room in my pockets, walk'd off with a roll under each arm, and eating the other. Thus I went up Market-street as far as Fourth-street, passing by the door of Mr. Read, my future wife's father; when she, standing at the door, saw me, and thought I made, as I certainly did, a most awkward, ridiculous appearance. Then I turned and went down Chestnut-street and part of Walnut-street, eating my roll all the way, and, coming round, found myself again at Market-street wharf, near the boat I came in, to which I went for a draught of the river water; and, being filled with one of my rolls, gave the other two to a woman and her child that came down the river in the boat with us, and were waiting to go farther.

Thus refreshed, I walked again up the street, which by this time had many clean-dressed people in it, who were all walking the same way. I joined them, and thereby was led into the great meeting-house of the Quakers near the market. I sat down among them, and, after looking round awhile and hearing nothing said, being very drowsy thro' labour and want of rest the preceding night, I fell fast asleep, and continu'd so till the meeting broke up, when one was kind enough to rouse me. This was, therefore, the first house I was in, or slept in, in Philadelphia.

Walking down again toward the river, and, looking in the faces of people, I met a young Quaker man, whose countenance I lik'd, and, accosting him, requested he would tell me where a stranger could get lodging. We were then near the sign of the Three Mariners. "Here," says he, "is one place that entertains strangers, but it is not a reputable house; if thee wilt walk with me, I'll show thee a better." He brought me to the Crooked Billet in Water-street. Here I got a dinner; and, while I was eating it, several sly questions were asked me, as it seemed to be suspected from my youth and appearance, that I might be some runaway.

After dinner, my sleepiness return'd, and being shown to a bed, I lay down without undressing, and slept till six in the evening, was call'd to supper, went to bed again very early, and slept soundly till next morning. Then I made myself as tidy as I could, and went to Andrew Bradford the printer's. I found in the shop the old man his father, whom I had seen at New York, and who, travelling on horseback, had got to Philadelphia before me. He introduc'd me to his son, who receiv'd me civilly, gave me a breakfast, but told me he did not at present want a hand, being lately suppli'd with one; but there was another printer in town, lately set up, one Keimer, who, perhaps, might employ me; if not, I should be welcome to lodge at his house, and he would give me a little work to do now and then till fuller business should offer.

The old gentleman said he would go with me to the new printer; and when we found him, "Neighbour," says Bradford, "I have brought to see you a young man of your business; perhaps you may want such a one." He ask'd me a few questions, put a composing stick in my hand to see how I work'd, and then said he would employ me soon, though he had just then nothing for me to do; and, taking old Bradford, whom he had never seen before, to be one of the town's people that had a good will for him, enter'd into a conversation on his present undertaking and prospects; while Bradford, not discovering that he was the other printer's father, on Keimer's saying he expected soon to get the greatest part of the business into his own hands, drew him on by artful questions, and starting little doubts, to explain all his views, what interest he reli'd on, and in what manner he intended to proceed. I, who stood by and heard all, saw immediately that one of them was a crafty old sophister, and the other a mere novice. Bradford left me with Keimer, who was greatly surpris'd when I told him who the old man was.

Keimer's printing-house, I found, consisted of an old shatter'd press, and one small, worn-out font of English, which he was then using himself, composing an Elegy on Aquila Rose, before mentioned, an ingenious young man, of excellent character, much respected in the town, clerk of the Assembly, and a pretty poet. Keimer made verses too, but very indifferently. He could not be said to write them, for his manner was to compose them in the types directly out of his head. So there being no copy, but one pair of cases, and the Elegy likely to require all the letter, no one could help him. I endeavour'd to put his press (which he had not yet us'd, and of which he understood nothing) into order fit to be work'd with; and, promising to come and print off his Elegy as soon as he should have got it ready, I return'd to Bradford's, who gave me a little job to do for the present, and there I lodged and dieted. A few days after, Keimer sent for me to print off the Elegy. And now he had got another pair of cases, and a pamphlet to reprint, on which he set me to work.

These two printers I found poorly qualified for their business. Bradford had not been bred to it, and was very illiterate; and Keimer, tho' something of a scholar, was a mere compositor, knowing nothing of presswork. He had been one of the French prophets, and could act their enthusiastic agitations. At this time he did not profess any particular religion, but something of all on occasion; was very ignorant of the world, and had, as I afterward found, a good deal of the knave in his composition. He did not like my lodging at Bradford's while I work'd with him. He had a house, indeed, but without furniture, so he could not lodge me; but he got me a lodging at Mr. Read's before mentioned, who was the owner of his house; and, my chest and clothes being come by this time, I made rather a more respectable appearance in the eyes of Miss Read than I had done when she first happen'd to see me eating my roll in the street. * * *

(1771) 1791

[FIRST VISIT TO ENGLAND]

The governor, seeming to like my company, had me frequently to his house, and his setting me up was always mention'd as a fixed thing. I was to take with me letters recommendatory to a number of his friends, besides the letter of credit to furnish me with the necessary money for purchasing the press and types, paper, etc. For these letters I was appointed to call at different times, when they were to be ready; but a future time was still named. Thus he went on till the ship, whose departure too had been several times postponed, was on the point of sailing. Then, when I call'd to take my leave and receive the letters, his secretary, Dr. Bard, came out to me, and said the governor was extremely busy in writing, but would be down at Newcastle before the ship, and there the letters would be delivered to me.

Ralph, though married, and having one child, had determined to accompany me in this voyage. It was thought he intended to establish a correspondence, and obtain goods to sell on commission; but I found afterwards, that, thro' some discontent with his wife's relations, he purposed to leave her on their hands, and never return again. Having taken leave of my friends, and interchang'd some promises with Miss Read, I left Philadelphia in the ship, which anchor'd at Newcastle. The governor was there; but when I went to his lodging, the secretary came to me from him with the civillest message in the world, that he could not then see me, being engaged in business of the utmost importance, but should send the letters to me on board, wished me heartily a good voyage and a speedy return, etc. I returned on board a little puzzled, but still not doubting. * * *

Ralph and I were inseparable companions. We took lodgings together in Little Britain at three shillings and sixpence a week—as much as we could then afford. He found some relations, but they were poor, and unable to assist him. He now let me know his intentions of remaining in London, and that he never meant to return to Philadelphia. He had brought no money with him, the whole he could muster having been expended in paying his passage. I had fifteen pistoles; so he borrowed occasionally of me to subsist, while he was looking out for business. He first endeavoured to get into the playhouse, believing himself qualify'd for an actor; but Wilkes, to whom he apply'd, advis'd him candidly not to think of that employment, as it was impossible he should succeed in it. Then he propos'd to Roberts, a publisher in Paternoster Row, to write for him a weekly paper like the Spectator, on certain conditions, which Roberts did not approve. Then he endeavoured to get employment as a hackney writer, to copy for the stationers and lawyers about the Temple, but could find no vacancy.

I immediately got into work at Palmer's, then a famous printing-house in Bartholomew Close, and here I continu'd near a year. I was pretty diligent, but spent with Ralph a good deal of my earnings in going to plays and other places of amusement. We had together consumed all my pistoles, and now just rubbed on from hand to mouth. He seem'd quite to forget his wife and child, and I, by degrees, my engagements with Miss Read, to whom I never wrote more than one letter, and that was to let her know I was not likely soon to return. This was another of the great errata of my life, which I should wish to correct if I were to live it over again. In fact, by our expenses, I was constantly kept unable to pay my passage.

At Palmer's I was employed in composing for the second edition of Wollaston's "Religion of Nature." Some of his reasonings not appearing to me well founded, I wrote a little metaphysical piece in which I made remarks on them. It was entitled "A Dissertation on Liberty and Necessity, Pleasure and Pain." I inscribed it to my friend Ralph; I printed a small number. It occasion'd my being more consider'd by Mr. Palmer as a young man of some ingenuity, tho' he seriously expostulated with me upon the principles of my pamphlet, which to him appear'd abominable. My printing this pamphlet was another erratum. While I lodg'd in Little Britain, I made an acquaintance with one Wilcox, a bookseller, whose shop was at the next door. He had an immense collection of second-hand books. Circulating libraries were not then in use; but we agreed that, on certain reasonable terms, which I have now forgotten, I might take, read, and return any of his books. This I esteem'd a great advantage, and I made as much use of it as I could.

My pamphlet by some means falling into the hands of one Lyons, a surgeon, author of a book entitled "The Infallibility of Human Judgment," it occasioned an acquaintance between us. He took great notice of me, called on me often to converse on these subjects, carried me to the Horns, a pale alehouse in —— Lane, Cheapside, and introduced me to Dr. Mandeville, author of the "Fable of the Bees," who had a club there, of which he was the soul, being a most facetious, entertaining companion. Lyons, too, introduced me to Dr. Pemberton, at Batson's Coffee-house, who promis'd to give me an opportunity, some time or other, of seeing Sir Isaac Newton, of which I was extreamly desirous; but this never happened.

I had brought over a few curiosities, among which the principal was a purse made of the asbestos, which purifies by fire. Sir Hans Sloane heard of it, came to see me, and invited me to his house in Bloomsbury Square, where he show'd me all his curiosities, and persuaded me to let him add that to the number, for which he paid me handsomely.

In our house there lodg'd a young woman, a milliner, who, I think, had a shop in the Cloisters. She had been genteelly bred, was sensible and lively, and of most pleasing conversation. Ralph read plays to her in the evenings, they grew intimate, she took another lodging, and he followed her. They liv'd together some time; but, he being still out of business, and her income not sufficient to maintain them with her child, he took a resolution of going from London, to try for a country school, which he thought himself well qualified to undertake, as he wrote an excellent hand, and was a master of arithmetic and accounts. This, however, he deemed a business below him, and confident of future better fortune, when he should be unwilling to have it known that he once was so meanly employed, he changed his name, and did me the honour to assume mine; for I soon after had a letter from him, acquainting me that he was settled in a small village (in Berkshire, I think it was, where he taught reading and writing to ten or a dozen boys, at sixpence each per week), recommending Mrs. T—— to my care, and desiring me to write to him, directing for Mr. Franklin, schoolmaster, at such a place.

He continued to write frequently, sending me large specimens of an epic poem which he was then composing, and desiring my remarks and corrections. These I gave him from time to time, but endeavour'd rather to discourage his proceeding. One of Young's Satires was then just published. I copy'd and sent him a great part of it, which set in a strong light the folly of pursuing the Muses with any hope of advancement by them. All was in vain; sheets of the poem continued to come by every post. In the mean time, Mrs. T——, having on his account lost her friends and business, was often in distresses, and us'd to send for me, and borrow what I could spare to help her out of them. I grew fond of her company, and, being at that time under no religious restraint, and presuming upon my importance to her, I attempted familiarities (another erratum) which she repuls'd with a proper resentment, and acquainted him with my behaviour. This made a breach between us; and, when he returned again to London, he let me know he thought I had cancell'd all the obligations he had been under to me. So I found I was never to expect his repaying me what I lent to him, or advanc'd for him. This, however, was not then of much consequence, as he was totally unable; and in the loss of his friendship I found myself relieved from a burthen. I now began to think of getting a little money beforehand, and, expecting better work, I left Palmer's to work at Watts's, near Lincoln's Inn Fields, a still greater printing-house. Here I continued all the rest of my stay in London. * * *

Thus I spent about eighteen months in London; most part of the time I work'd hard at my business, and spent but little upon myself except in seeing plays and in books. My friend Ralph had kept me poor; he owed me about twenty-seven pounds, which I was now never likely to receive; a great sum out of my small earnings! I lov'd him, notwithstanding, for he had many amiable qualities. I had by no means improv'd my fortune; but I had picked up some very ingenious acquaintance, whose conversation was of great advantage to me; and I had read considerably. * * *

We landed in Philadelphia on the 11th of October, where I found sundry alterations. * * *

(1771) 1791

[MORAL REFLECTIONS]

My brother-in-law, Holmes, being now at Philadelphia, advised my return to my business; and Keimer tempted me, with an offer of large wages by the year, to come and take the management of his printing-house, that he might better attend his stationer's shop. I had heard a bad character of him in London from his wife and her friends, and was not fond of having any more to do with him. I tri'd for farther employment as a merchant's clerk; but, not readily meeting with any, I clos'd again with Keimer. * * *

Before I enter upon my public appearance in business, it may be well to let you know the then state of my mind with regard to my principles and morals, that you may see how far those influenc'd the future events of my life. My parents had early given me religious impressions, and brought me through my childhood piously in the Dissenting way. But I was scarce fifteen, when, after doubting by turns of several points, as I found them disputed in the different books I read, I began to doubt of Revelation itself. Some books against Deism fell into my hands; they were said to be the substance of sermons preached at Boyle's Lectures. It happened that they wrought an effect on me quite contrary to what was intended by them; for the arguments of the

Deists, which were quoted to be refuted, appeared to me much stronger than the refutations; in short, I soon became a thorough Deist. My arguments perverted some others, particularly Collins and Ralph; but, each of them having afterwards wrong'd me greatly without the least compunction, and recollecting Keith's conduct towards me (who was another freethinker), and my own towards Vernon and Miss Read, which at times gave me great trouble, I began to suspect that this doctrine, tho' it might be true, was not very useful. My London pamphlet, which had for its motto these lines of Dryden:

"Whatever is, is right. Though purblind man
Sees but a part o' the chain, the nearest link:
His eyes not carrying to the equal beam,
That poises all above;"

and from the attributes of God, his infinite wisdom, goodness and power, concluded that nothing could possibly be wrong in the world, and that vice and virtue were empty distinctions, no such things existing, appear'd now not so clever a performance as I once thought it; and I doubted whether some error had not insinuated itself unperceiv'd into my argument, so as to infect all that follow'd, as is common in metaphysical reasonings.

I grew convinc'd that *truth, sincerity* and *integrity* in dealings between man and man were of the utmost importance to the felicity of life; and I form'd written resolutions, which still remain in my journal book, to practice them ever while I lived. Revelation had indeed no weight with me, as such; but I entertain'd an opinion that, though certain actions might not be bad *because* they were forbidden by it, or good *because* it commanded them, yet probably these actions might be forbidden *because* they were bad for us, or commanded *because* they were beneficial to us, in their own natures, all the circumstances of things considered. And this persuasion, with the kind hand of Providence, or some guardian angel, or accidental favourable circumstances and situations, or all together, preserved me, thro' this dangerous time of youth, and the hazardous situations I was sometimes in among strangers, remote from the eye and advice of my father, without any willful gross immorality or injustice, that might have been expected from my want of religion. I say willful, because the instances I have mentioned had something of *necessity* in them, from my youth, inexperience, and the knavery of others. I had therefore a tolerable character to begin the world with; I valued it properly, and determin'd to preserve it. * * *

I should have mentioned before, that, in the autumn of the preceding year, I had form'd most of my ingenious acquaintance into a club of mutual improvement, which we called the JUNTO; we met on Friday evenings. The rules that I drew up required that every member, in his turn, should produce one or more queries on any point of Morals, Politics, or Natural Philosophy, to be discuss'd by the company; and once in three months produce and read an essay of his own writing, on any subject he pleased. Our debates were to be under the direction of a president, and to be conducted in the sincere spirit of inquiry after truth, without fondness for dispute, or desire of victory; and, to prevent warmth, all expressions of positiveness in opinions, or direct contradiction, were after some time made contraband, and prohibited under small pecuniary penalties. * * *

(1771) 1791

[A RULE OF LIFE]

At the time I establish'd myself in Pennsylvania, there was not a good bookseller's shop in any of the colonies to the southward of Boston. In New York and Philad'a the printers were indeed stationers; they sold only paper, etc., almanacs, ballads, and a few common school-books. Those who lov'd reading were oblig'd to send for their books from England; the members of the Junto had each a few. We had left the alehouse, where we first met, and hired a room to hold our club in. I propos'd that we should all of us bring our books to that room, where they would not only be ready to consult in our conferences, but become a common benefit, each of us being at liberty to borrow such as he wish'd to read at home. This was accordingly done, and for some time contented us.

Finding the advantage of this little collection, I propos'd to render the benefit from books more common, by commencing a public subscription library. I drew a sketch of the plan and rules that would be necessary, and got a skilful conveyancer, Mr. Charles Brockden, to put the whole in form of articles of agreement to be subscribed, by which each subscriber engag'd to pay a certain sum down for the first purchase of books, and an annual contribution for increasing them. So few were the readers at that time in Philadelphia, and the majority of us so poor, that I was not able, with great industry, to find more than fifty persons, mostly young tradesmen, willing to pay down for this purpose forty shillings each, and ten shillings per annum. On this little fund we began. The books were imported; the library was opened one day in the week for lending to the subscribers, on their promissory notes to pay double the value if not duly returned. The institution soon manifested its utility, was imitated by other towns, and in other provinces. The libraries were augmented by donations; reading became fashionable; and our people, having no publick amusements to divert their attention from study, became better acquainted with books, and in a few years were observ'd by strangers to be better instructed and more intelligent than people of the same rank generally are in other countries.

When we were about to sign the above-mentioned articles, which were to be binding to us, our heirs, etc., for fifty years, Mr. Brockden, the scrivener, said to us, "You are young men, but it is scarcely probable that any of you will live to see the expiration of the term fix'd in the instrument." A number of us, however, are yet living; but the instrument was after a few years rendered null by a charter that incorporated and gave perpetuity to the company.

The objections and reluctances I met with in soliciting the subscriptions, made me soon feel the impropriety of presenting one's self as the proposer of any useful project, that might be suppos'd to raise one's reputation in the smallest degree above that of one's neighbours, when one has need of their assistance to accomplish that project. I therefore put myself as much as I could out of sight, and stated it as a scheme of a *number of friends,* who had requested me to go about and propose it to such as they thought lovers of reading. In this way my affair went on more smoothly, and I ever after practis'd it on such occasions; and, from my frequent successes, can heartily recommend it. The present little sacrifice of your vanity will afterwards be amply repaid. If it remains a while uncertain to whom the merit belongs, some one more vain than yourself will be encouraged to claim it, and then even envy will be disposed to do you justice by plucking those assumed feathers, and restoring them to their right owner.

This library afforded me the means of improvement by constant study, for which I set apart an hour or two each day, and thus repair'd in some degree the loss of the learned education my father once intended for me. Reading was the only amusement I allow'd myself. I spent no time in taverns, games, or frolicks of any kind; and my industry in my business continu'd as indefatigable as it was necessary. I was indebted for my printing-house; I had a young family coming on to be educated, and I had to contend with for business two printers, who were established in the place before me. My circumstances, however, grew daily easier. My original habits of frugality continuing, and my father having, among his instructions to me when a boy, frequently repeated a proverb of Solomon, "Seest thou a man diligent in his calling, he shall stand before kings, he shall not stand before mean men," I from thence considered industry as a means of obtaining wealth and distinction, which encourag'd me, tho' I did not think that I should ever literally *stand before kings,* which, however, has since happened; for I have stood before *five,* and even had the honour of sitting down with one, the King of Denmark, to dinner.

We have an English proverb that says, *"He that would thrive, must ask his wife."* It was lucky for me that I had one as much dispos'd to industry and frugality as myself. She assisted me chearfully in my business, folding and stitching pamphlets, tending shop, purchasing old linen rags for the paper-makers, etc., etc. We kept no idle servants, our table was plain and simple, our furniture of the cheapest. For instance, my breakfast was a long time bread and milk (no tea), and I ate it out of a twopenny earthen porringer, with a pewter spoon. But mark how luxury will enter families, and make a progress, in spite of principle: being call'd one morning to breakfast, I found it in a China bowl, with a spoon of silver! They had been bought for me without my knowledge by my wife, and had cost her the enormous sum of three-and-twenty shillings, for which she had no other excuse or apology to make, but that she thought *her* husband deserv'd a silver spoon and China bowl as well as any of his neighbors. This was the first appearance of plate and China in our house, which afterward, in a course of years, as our wealth increas'd, augmented gradually to several hundred pounds in value.

I had been religiously educated as a Presbyterian; and tho' some of the dogmas of that persuasion, such as *the eternal decrees of God, election, reprobation, etc.,* appeared to me unintelligible, others doubtful, and I early absented myself from the public assemblies of the sect, Sunday being my studying day, I never was without some religious principles. I never doubted, for instance, the existence of the Deity; that he made the world, and govern'd it by his Providence; that the most acceptable service of God was the doing good to man; that our souls are immortal; and that all crime will be punished, and virtue rewarded, either here or hereafter. These I esteem'd the essentials of every religion; and, being to be found in all the religions we had in our country, I respected them all, tho' with different degrees of respect, as I found them more or less mix'd with other articles, which, without any tendency to inspire, promote, or confirm morality, serv'd principally to divide us, and make us unfriendly to one another. This respect to all, with an opinion that the worst had some good effects, induc'd me to avoid all discourse that might tend to lessen the good opinion another might have of his own religion; and as our province increas'd in people, and new places of worship were continually wanted, and generally erected by voluntary contribution, my mite for such purpose, whatever might be the sect, was never refused.

Tho' I seldom attended any public worship, I had still an opinion of its propriety, and of its utility when rightly conducted, and I regularly paid my annual subscription for the support of the only Presbyterian minister or meeting we had in Philadelphia. He us'd to visit me sometimes as a friend, and admonish me to attend his administrations, and I was now and then prevail'd on to do so, once for five Sundays successively. Had he been in my opinion a good preacher, perhaps I might have continued, notwithstanding the occasion I had for the Sunday's leisure in my course of study; but his discourses were chiefly either polemic arguments, or explications of the peculiar doctrines of our sect, and were all to me very dry, uninteresting, and unedifying, since not a single moral principle was inculcated or enforc'd, their aim seeming to be rather to make us Presbyterians than good citizens.

At length he took for his text that verse of the fourth chapter of Philippians, *"Finally, brethren, whatsoever things are true, honest, just, pure, lovely, or of good report, if there be any virtue, or any praise, think on these things."* And I imagin'd, in a sermon on such a text, we could not miss of having some morality. But he confin'd himself to five points only, as meant by the apostle, viz.: 1. Keeping holy the Sabbath day. 2. Being diligent in reading the holy Scriptures. 3. Attending duly the publick worship. 4. Partaking of the Sacrament. 5. Paying a due respect to God's ministers. These might be all good things; but, as they were not the kind of good things that I expected from that text, I despaired of ever meeting with them from any other, was disgusted, and attended his preaching no more. I had some years before compos'd a little Liturgy, or form of prayer, for my own private use (viz., in 1728), entitled, *Articles of Belief and Acts of Religion.* I return'd to the use of this, and went no more to the public assemblies. My conduct might be blameable, but I leave it, without attempting further to excuse it; my present purpose being to relate facts, and not to make apologies for them.

It was about this time I conceiv'd the bold and arduous project of arriving at moral perfection. I wish'd to live without committing any fault at any time; I would conquer all that either natural inclination, custom, or company might lead me into. As I knew, or thought I knew, what was right and wrong, I did not see why I might not always do the one and avoid the other. But I soon found I had undertaken a task of more difficulty than I had imagined. While my care was employ'd in guarding against one fault, I was often surprised by another; habit took the advantage of inattention; inclination was sometimes too strong for reason. I concluded, at length, that the mere speculative conviction that it was our interest to be completely virtuous, was not sufficient to prevent our slipping; and that the contrary habits must be broken, and good ones acquired and established, before we can have any dependence on a steady, uniform rectitude of conduct. For this purpose I therefore contrived the following method.

In the various enumerations of the moral virtues I had met with in my reading, I found the catalogue more or less numerous, as different writers included more or fewer ideas under the same name. Temperance, for example, was by some confined to eating and drinking, while by others it was extended to mean the moderating every other pleasure, appetite, inclination, or passion, bodily or mental, even to our avarice and ambition. I propos'd to myself, for the sake of clearness, to use rather more names, with fewer ideas annex'd to each, than a few names with more ideas; and I included under thirteen names of virtues all that at that time occurr'd to me as necessary or desirable, and annexed to each a short precept, which fully express'd the extent I gave to its meaning.

These names of virtues, with their precepts, were:

1. Temperance.

Eat not to dullness; drink not to elevation.

2. Silence.

Speak not but what may benefit others or yourself; avoid trifling conversation.

3. Order.

Let all your things have their places; let each part of your business have its time.

4. Resolution.

Resolve to perform what you ought; perform without fail what you resolve.

5. Frugality.

Make no expense but to do good to others or yourself; *i.e.,* waste nothing.

6. Industry.

Lose no time; be always employ'd

in something useful; cut off all unnecessary actions.

7. Sincerity.

Use no hurtful deceit; think innocently and justly, and, if you speak, speak accordingly.

8. Justice.

Wrong none by doing injuries, or omitting the benefits that are your duty.

9. Moderation.

Avoid extreams; forbear resenting injuries so much as you think they deserve.

10. Cleanliness.

Tolerate no uncleanliness in body, cloaths, or habitation.

11. Tranquillity.

Be not disturbed at trifles, or at accidents common or unavoidable.

12. Chastity.

Rarely use venery but for health or offspring, never to dulness, weakness, or the injury of your own or another's peace or reputation.

13. Humility.

Imitate Jesus and Socrates.

My intention being to acquire the *habitude* of all these virtues, I judg'd it would be well not to distract my attention by attempting the whole at once, but to fix it on one of them at a time; and, when I should be master of that, then to proceed to another, and so on, till I should have gone thro' the thirteen; and, as the previous acquisition of some might facilitate the acquisition of certain others, I arrang'd them with that view, as they stand above. Temperance first, as it tends to procure that coolness and clearness of head, which is so necessary where constant vigilance was to be kept up, and guard maintained against the unremitting attraction of ancient habits, and the force of perpetual temptations. This being acquir'd and establish'd, Silence would be more easy; and my desire being to gain knowledge at the same time that I improv'd in virtue, and considering that in conversation it was obtain'd rather by the use of the ears than of the tongue, and therefore wishing to break a habit I was getting into of prattling, punning, and joking, which only made me acceptable to trifling company, I gave *Silence* the second place. This and the next, *Order,* I expected would allow me more time for attending to my project and my studies. *Resolution,* once become habitual, would keep me firm in my endeavours to obtain all the subsequent virtues; *Frugality* and Industry freeing me from my remaining debt, and producing affluence and independence, would make more easy the practice of Sincerity and Justice, etc., etc. Conceiving then, that, agreeably to the advice of Pythagoras in his Golden Verses, daily examination would be necessary, I contrived the following method for conducting that examination.

I made a little book, in which I allotted a page for each of the virtues. I rul'd each page with red ink, so as to have seven columns, one for each day of the week, marking each column with a letter for the day. I cross'd these columns with thirteen red lines, marking the beginning of each line with the first letter of one of the virtues, on which line, and in its proper column, I might mark, by a little black spot, every fault I found upon examination to have been committed respecting that virtue upon that day. * * *

I determined to give a week's strict attention to each of the virtues successively. Thus, in the first week, my great guard was to avoid every the least offence against *Temperance,* leaving the other virtues to their ordinary chance, only marking every evening the faults of the day. Thus, if in the first week I could keep my first line, marked T, clear of spots, I suppos'd the habit of that virtue so much strengthen'd, and its opposite weaken'd, that I might venture extending my attention to include the next, and for the following week keep both lines clear of spots. Proceeding thus to the last, I could go thro' a course compleat in thirteen weeks, and four courses in a year. And like him who, having a garden to weed, does not attempt to eradicate all the bad herbs at once, which would exceed his reach and his strength, but works on one of the beds at a time, and, having accomplish'd the first, proceeds to a second, so I should have, I hoped, the encouraging pleasure of seeing on my pages the progress I made in virtue, by clearing successively my lines of their spots, till in the end, by a number of courses, I should be happy in viewing a clean book, after a thirteen weeks' daily examination.

This my little book had for its motto these lines from Addison's *Cato:*

"Here will I hold. If there's a power above us
(And that there is, all nature cries aloud
Thro' all her works), He must delight in virtue;
And that which he delights in must be happy."

Another from Cicero,

"O vitæ Philosophia dux! O virtutum indagatrix expultrixque vitiorum! Unus dies, bene et ex præceptis tuis actus, peccanti immortalitati est anteponendus."

Another from the Proverbs of Solomon, speaking of wisdom or virtue:

"Length of days is in her right hand, and in her left hand riches and honour. Her ways are ways of pleasantness, and all her paths are peace."

iii. 16, 17.

And conceiving God to be the fountain of wisdom, I thought it right and necessary to solicit his assistance for obtaining it; to this end I formed the following little prayer, which was prefix'd to my tables of examination, for daily use.

"O powerful Goodness! bountiful Father! merciful Guide! Increase in me that wisdom which discovers my truest interest. Strengthen my resolutions to perform what that wisdom dictates. Accept my kind offices to thy other children as the only return in my power for thy continual favours to me."

I used also sometimes a little prayer which I took from Thomson's Poems, viz.:

"Father of light and life, thou Good Supreme!
O teach me what is good; teach me Thyself!
Save me from folly, vanity, and vice,

From every low pursuit; and fill my soul
With knowledge, conscious peace, and virtue pure;
Sacred, substantial, never-fading bliss!"

The precept of *Order* requiring that *every part of my business should have its allotted time,* one page in my little book contain'd the following scheme of employment for the twenty-four hours of a natural day.

	Hours	
THE MORNING. *Question.* What good shall I do this day?	5, 6, 7	Rise, wash, and address *Powerful Goodness!* Contrive day's business, and take the resolution of the day; prosecute the present study, and breakfast.
	8, 9, 10, 11	Work.
NOON.	12, 1	Read, or overlook my accounts, and dine.
	2, 3, 4, 5	Work.
EVENING. *Question.* What good have I done to-day?	6, 7, 8, 9	Put things in their places. Supper. Music or diversion, or conversation. Examination of the day.
NIGHT.	10, 11, 12, 1, 2, 3, 4	Sleep.

I enter'd upon the execution of this plan for self-examination, and continu'd it with occasional intermissions for some time. I was surpris'd to find myself so much fuller of faults than I had imagined; but I had the satisfaction of seeing them diminish. To avoid the trouble of renewing now and then my little book, which, by scraping out the marks on the paper of old faults to make room for new ones in a new course, became full of holes, I transferr'd my tables and precepts to the ivory leaves of a memorandum book, on which the lines were drawn with red ink, that made a durable stain, and on those lines I mark'd my faults with a black-lead pencil, which marks I could easily wipe out with a wet sponge. After a while I went thro' one course only in a year, and afterward only one in several years, till at length I omitted them entirely, being employ'd in voyages and business abroad, with a multiplicity of affairs that interfered; but I always carried my little book with me.

My scheme of ORDER gave me the most trouble; and I found that, tho' it might be practicable where a man's business was such as to leave him the disposition of his time, that of a journeyman printer, for instance, it was not possible to be exactly observed by a master, who must mix with the world, and often receive people of business at their own hours. *Order,* too, with regard to places for things, papers, etc., I found extreamly difficult to acquire. I had not been early accustomed to it, and, having an exceeding good memory, I was not so sensible of the inconvenience attending want of method. This article, therefore, cost me so much painful attention, and my faults in it vexed me so much, and I made so little progress in amendment, and had such frequent relapses, that I was almost ready to give up the attempt, and content myself with a faulty character in that respect, like the man who, in buying an ax of a smith, my neighbour, desired to have the whole of its surface as bright as the edge. The smith consented to grind it bright for him if he would turn the wheel; he turn'd, while the smith press'd the broad face of the ax hard and heavily on the stone, which made the turning of it very fatiguing. The man came every now and then from the wheel to see how the work went on, and at length would take his ax as it was, without farther grinding. "No," said the smith, "turn on, turn on; we shall have it bright by-and-by; as yet, it is only speckled." "Yes," says the man, *"but I think I like a speckled ax best."* And I believe this may have been the case with many, who, having, for want of some such means as I employ'd, found the difficulty of obtaining good and breaking bad habits in other points of vice and virtue, have given up the struggle, and concluded that *"a speckled ax was best"*; for something, that pretended to be reason, was every now and then suggesting to me that such extream nicety as I exacted of myself might be a kind of foppery in morals, which, if it were known, would make me ridiculous; that a perfect character might be attended with the inconvenience of being envied and hated; and that a benevolent man should allow a few faults in himself, to keep his friends in countenance.

In truth, I found myself incorrigible with respect to Order; and now I am grown old, and my memory bad, I feel very sensibly the want of it. But, on the whole, tho' I never arrived at the perfection I had been so ambitious of obtaining, but fell far short of it, yet I was, by the endeavour, a better and a happier man than I otherwise should have been if I had not attempted it; as those who aim at perfect writing by imitating the engraved copies, tho' they never reach the wish'd-for excellence of those copies, their hand is mended by the endeavour, and is tolerable while it continues fair and legible.

It may be well my posterity should be informed that to this little artifice, with the blessing of God, their ancestor ow'd the constant felicity of his life, down to his 79th year in which this is written. What reverses may attend the remainder is in the hand of Providence; but, if they arrive, the reflection on past happiness enjoy'd ought to help his bearing them with more resignation. To Temperance he ascribes his long-continued health, and what is still left to him of a good constitution; to Industry and Frugality, the early easiness of his circumstances and acquisition of his fortune, with all that knowledge that enabled him to be a useful citizen, and obtained for him some degree of reputation among the learned; to Sincerity and Justice, the confidence of his country, and the honorable employs it conferred upon him; and to the joint influence of the whole mass of the virtues, even in the imperfect state he was able to acquire them, all that evenness of temper, and that cheerfulness in conversation, which makes his company still sought for, and agreeable even to his younger acquaintance. I hope, therefore, that some of my descendants may follow the example and reap the benefit.

It will be remark'd that, tho' my scheme was not wholly without religion, there was in it no mark of any of the distinguishing tenets of any particular sect. I had purposely avoided them; for, being fully persuaded of the utility and excellency of my method, and that it might be serviceable to people in all religions, and intending some time or other to publish it, I would not have any thing in it that should prejudice any one, of any sect, against it. I purposed writing a little comment on each virtue, in which I would have shown the advantages of possessing it, and the mischiefs attending its opposite vice; and I should have called my book The Art of Virtue, because it would have shown the means and manner of obtaining virtue, which would have distinguished it from the mere exhortation to be good, that does not instruct and indicate the means, but is like the apostle's man of verbal charity, who only without showing to the naked and hungry how or where they might get clothes or victuals, exhorted them to be fed and clothed.—James ii. 15, 16.

But it so happened that my intention of writing and publishing this comment was never fulfilled. I did, indeed, from time to time, put down short hints of the sentiments, reasonings, etc., to be made use of in it, some of which I have still by me; but the necessary close attention to private business in the earlier part of my life, and public business since, have occasioned my postponing it; for, it being connected in my mind with *a great and extensive project*, that required the whole man to execute, and which an unforeseen succession of employs prevented my attending to, it has hitherto remain'd unfinish'd.

In this piece it was my design to explain and enforce this doctrine, that vicious actions are not hurtful because they are forbidden, but forbidden because they are hurtful, the nature of man alone considered; that it was, therefore, every one's interest to be virtuous who wish'd to be happy even in this world; and I should, from this circumstance (there being always in the world a number of rich merchants, nobility, states, and princes, who have need of honest instruments for the management of their affairs, and such being so rare), have endeavoured to convince young persons that no qualities were so likely to make a poor man's fortune as those of probity and integrity.

My list of virtues contain'd at first but twelve; but a Quaker friend having kindly informed me that I was generally thought proud; that my pride show'd itself frequently in conversation; that I was not content with being in the right when discussing any point, but was overbearing, and rather insolent, of which he convinc'd me by mentioning several instances; I determined endeavouring to cure myself, if I could, of this vice or folly among the rest, and I added *Humility* to my list, giving an extensive meaning to the word.

I cannot boast of much success in acquiring the *reality* of this virtue, but I had a good deal with regard to the *appearance* of it. I made it a rule to forbear all direct contradiction to the sentiments of others, and all positive assertion of my own. I even forbid myself, agreeably to the old laws of our Junto, the use of every word or expression in the language that imported a fix'd opinion, such as *certainly, undoubtedly,* etc., and I adopted, instead of them, *I conceive, I apprehend,* or *I imagine* a thing to be so or so; or it *so appears to me at present.* When another asserted something that I thought an error, I deny'd myself the pleasure of contradicting him abruptly, and of showing immediately some absurdity in his proposition; and in answering I began by observing that in certain cases or circumstances his opinion would be right, but in the present case there *appear'd* or *seem'd* to me some difference, etc. I soon found the advantage of this change in my manner; the conversations I engag'd in went on more pleasantly. The modest way in which I propos'd my opinions procur'd them a readier reception and less contradiction; I had less mortification when I was found to be in the wrong, and I more easily prevail'd with others to give up their mistakes and join with me when I happened to be in the right.

And this mode, which I at first put on with some violence to natural inclination, became at length so easy, and so habitual to me, that perhaps for these fifty years past no one has ever heard a dogmatical expression escape me. And to this habit (after my character of integrity) I think it principally owing that I had early so much weight with my fellow-citizens when I proposed new institutions, or alterations in the old, and so much influence in public councils when I became a member; for I was but a bad speaker, never eloquent, subject to much hesitation in my choice of words, hardly correct in language, and yet I generally carried my points.

In reality, there is, perhaps, no one of our natural passions so hard to subdue as *pride.* Disguise it, struggle with it, beat it down, stifle it, mortify it as much as one pleases, it is still alive, and will every now and then peep out and show itself; you will see it, perhaps, often in this history; for, even if I could conceive that I had compleatly overcome it, I should probably be proud of my humility. * * *

(1784) 1798

DOGOOD PAPERS No. IV

[ON EDUCATION]

An sum etiam nunc vel Græcè loqui vel Latinè docendus?

—Cicero.

To the Author of the New-England Courant

Sir,

Discoursing the other Day at Dinner with my Reverend Boarder, formerly mention'd, (whom for Distinction sake we will call by the Name of *Clericus,*) concerning the Education of Children, I ask'd his Advice about my young Son *William,* whether or no I had best bestow upon him Academical Learning, or (as our Phrase is) *bring him up at our College:* He perswaded me to do it by all Means, using many weighty Arguments with me, and answering all the Objections that I could form against it; telling me withal, that he did not doubt but that the Lad would take his Learning very well, and not idle away his Time as too many there now-a-days do. These words of *Clericus* gave me a Curiosity to inquire a little more strictly into the present Circumstances of that famous Seminary of Learning; but the Information which he gave me, was neither pleasant, nor such as I expected.

As soon as Dinner was over, I took a solitary Walk into my Orchard, still ruminating on *Clericus's* Discourse with much Consideration, until I came to my usual Place of Retirement under the *Great Apple-Tree;* where having seated my self, and carelesly laid my Head on a verdant Bank, I fell by Degrees into a soft and undisturbed Slumber. My waking Thoughts remained with me in my Sleep, and before I awak'd again, I dreamt the following Dream.

I fancy'd I was travelling over pleasant and delightful Fields and Meadows, and thro' many small Country Towns and Villages; and as I pass'd along, all Places resounded with the Fame of the Temple of Learning: Every Peasant, who had wherewithal, was preparing to send one of his Children at least to this famous Place; and in this Case most of them consulted their own Purses instead of their Childrens Capacities: So that I observed, a great many, yea, the most part of those who were travelling thither, were little better than Dunces and Blockheads. Alas! Alas!

At length I entred upon a spacious Plain, in the Midst of which was erected a large and stately Edifice: It was to this that a great Company of Youths from all Parts of the Country were going; so stepping in among the Crowd, I passed on with them, and presently arrived at the Gate.

The Passage was Kept by two sturdy Porters named *Riches* and *Poverty,* and the latter obstinately refused to give Entrance to any who had not first gain'd the Favour of the former; so that I observed, many who came even to the very Gate, were obliged to travel back again as ignorant as they came, for want of this necessary Qualification. However, as a Spectator I gain'd Admittance, and with the rest entred directly into the Temple.

In the Middle of the great Hall stood a stately and magnificent Throne, which was ascended to by two high and difficult Steps. On the Top of it sat Learning in awful State; she was apparelled wholly in Black, and surrounded almost on every Side with innumerable Volumes in all Languages. She seem'd very busily employ'd in writing something on half a Sheet of Paper, and upon Enquiry, I understood she was preparing a Paper, call'd, *The New-England Courant.* On her Right Hand sat *English,* with a pleasant smiling Countenance, and handsomely attir'd; and on her left were seated several *Antique Figures* with their Faces vail'd. I was considerably puzzl'd to guess who they were, until one informed me, (who stood beside me,) that those Figures on her left Hand were *Latin, Greek, Hebrew,* &c. and that they were very much reserv'd, and seldom or never unvail'd their Faces here, and then to few or none, tho' most of those who have in this Place acquir'd so much Learning as to distinguish them from *English,* pretended to an intimate Acquaintance with them. I then enquir'd of him, what could be the Reason why they continued vail'd, in this Place especially: He pointed to the Foot of the Throne, where I saw *Idleness,* attended with *Ignorance,* and these (he informed me) were they, who first vail'd them, and still kept them so.

Now I observed, that the whole Tribe who entred into the Temple with me, began to climb the Throne; but the Work proving troublesome and difficult to most of them, they withdrew their Hands from the Plow, and contented themselves to sit at the Foot, with Madame *Idleness* and her Maid *Ignorance,* until those who were assisted by Diligence and a docible Temper, had well nigh got up the first Step: But the Time drawing nigh in which they could no way avoid ascending, they were fain to crave the Assistance of those who had got up before them, and who, for the Reward perhaps of a *Pint of Milk,* or a *Piece of Plumb-Cake,* lent the Lubbers a helping Hand, and sat them in the Eye of the World, upon a Level with themselves.

THE other Step being in the same Manner ascended, and the usual Ceremonies at an End, every Beetle-Scull seem'd well satisfy'd with his own Portion of Learning, tho' perhaps he was *e'en just* as ignorant as ever. And now the Time of their Departure being come, they march'd out of Doors to make Room for another Company, who waited for Entrance: And I, having seen all that was to be seen, quitted the Hall likewise, and went to make my Observations on those who were just gone out before me.

SOME I perceiv'd took to Merchandizing, others to Travelling, some to one Thing, some to another, and some to Nothing; and many of them from henceforth, for want of Patrimony, liv'd as poor as church Mice, being unable to dig, and asham'd to beg, and to live by their Wits it was impossible. But the most Part of the Crowd went along a large beaten Path, which led to a Temple at the further End of the Plain, call'd, *The Temple of Theology.* The Business of those who were employ'd in this Temple being laborious and painful, I wonder'd exceedingly to see so many go towards it; but while I was pondering this Matter in my Mind, I spy'd *Pecunia* behind a Curtain, beckoning to them with her Hand, which Sight immediately satisfy'd me for whose Sake it was, that a great Part of them (I will not say all) travel'd that Road. In this Temple I saw nothing worth mentioning, except the ambitious and fraudulent Contrivances of *Plagius,* who (notwithstanding he had been severely reprehended for such Practices before) was diligently transcribing some eloquent Paragraphs out of *Tillotson's* Works, &c. to embellish his own.

Now I bethought my self in my Sleep, that it was Time to be at Home, and as I fancy'd I was travelling back thither, I reflected in my Mind on the extream Folly of those Parents, who, blind to their Childrens Dulness, and insensible of the Solidity of their Skulls, because they think their Purses can afford it, will needs send them to the Temple of Learning, where, for want of a suitable Genius, they learn little more than how to carry themselves handsomely, and enter a Room genteely, (which might as well be acquir'd at a Dancing-School,) and from whence they return, after Abundance of Trouble and Charge, as great Blockheads as ever, only more proud and self-conceited.

While I was in the midst of these unpleasant Reflections, *Clericus* (who with a Book in his Hand was walking under the Trees) accidentally awak'd me; to him I related my Dream with all its Particulars, and he, without much Study, presently interpreted it, assuring me, *That it was a lively Representation of* Harvard College, *Etcetera.*

I remain, Sir,

Your Humble Servant,

Silence Dogood.

1722

THE WAY TO WEALTH

Courteous Reader

I have heard that nothing gives an Author so great Pleasure, as to find his Works respectfully quoted by other learned Authors. This Pleasure I have seldom enjoyed; for tho' I have been, if I may say it without Vanity, an *eminent Author* of Almanacks annually now a full Quarter of a Century, my Brother Authors in the same Way, for what Reason I know not, have ever been very sparing in their Applauses, and no other Author has taken the least Notice of me, so that did not my Writings produce me some solid *Pudding,* the great Deficiency of *Praise* would have quite discouraged me.

I concluded at length, that the People were the best Judges of my Merit; for they buy my Works; and besides, in my Rambles, where I am not personally known, I have frequently heard one or other of my Adages repeated, with, *as Poor Richard says,* at the End on 't; this gave me some Satisfaction, as it showed not only that my Instructions were regarded, but discovered likewise some Respect for my Authority; and I own, that to encourage the Practice of remembering and repeating those wise Sentences, I have sometimes *quoted myself* with great Gravity.

Judge, then how much I must have been gratified by an Incident I am going to relate to you. I stopt my Horse lately where a great Number of People were collected at a Vendue of Merchant Goods. The Hour of Sale not being come, they were conversing on the Badness of the Times and one of the Company call'd to a plain clean old Man, with white Locks, "Pray, Father Abraham, what think you of the Times? Won't these heavy Taxes quite ruin the Country? How shall we be ever able to pay them? What would you advise us to?" Father *Abraham* stood up, and reply'd, "If you'd have my Advice, I'll give it to you in short, for *A Word to the Wise is enough,* and *many Words won't fill a Bushel,* as *Poor Richard* says." They join'd in desiring him to speak his Mind, and gathering round him, he proceeded as follows:

"Friends," says he, and Neighbours, "the Taxes are indeed very heavy, and if those laid on by the Government were the only Ones we had to pay, we might more easily discharge them; but we have many others, and much more grievous to some of us. We are taxed twice as much by our *Idleness,* three times as much by our *Pride,* and four times as much by our *Folly;* and from these Taxes the Commissioners cannot ease or deliver us by allowing an Abatement. However let us hearken to good Advice, and something may be done for us; *God helps them that help themselves,* as *Poor Richard* says, in his Almanack of 1733.

It would be thought a hard Government that should tax its People one-tenth Part of their *Time,* to be employed in its Service. But *Idleness* taxes many of us much more, if we reckon all that is spent in absolute Sloth, or doing of nothing, with that which is spent in idle Employments or Amusements, that amount to nothing. *Sloth,* by bringing on Diseases, absolutely shortens Life. *Sloth, like Rust, consumes faster than Labour wears; while the used Key is always bright,* as *Poor Richard* says. *But dost thou love Life, then do not squander Time, for that's the stuff Life is made of,* as *Poor Richard* says. How much more than is necessary do we spend in sleep, forgetting that *The sleeping Fox catches no Poultry,* and that *There will be sleeping enough in the Grave,* as *Poor Richard* says.

If Time be of all Things the most precious, wasting Time must be, as *Poor Richard* says, *the greatest Prodigality;* since, as he elsewhere tells us, *Lost Time is never found again; and what we call Time enough, always prooves little enough:* Let us then up and be doing, and doing to the Purpose; so by Diligence shall we do more with less Perplexity. *Sloth makes all Things difficult, but Industry all easy,* as *Poor Richard* says; and *He that riseth late must trot all Day, and shall scarce overtake his Business at Night;* while *Laziness travels so slowly, that Poverty soon overtakes him,* as we read in *Poor Richard,* who adds, *Drive thy Business, let not that drive thee;* and *Early to Bed, and early to rise, makes a Man healthy, wealthy, and wise.*

So what signifies *wishing* and *hoping* for better Times. We may make these Times better, if we bestir ourselves. *Industry need not wish,* as *Poor Richard* says, *and he that lives upon Hope will die fasting. There are no Gains without Pains; then Help Hands, for I have no Lands,* or if I have, they are smartly taxed. And, as *Poor Richard* likewise observes, *He that hath a Trade hath an Estate; and he that hath a Calling, hath an Office of Profit and Honour;* but then the *Trade* must be worked at, and the *Calling* well followed, or neither the *Estate* nor the *Office* will enable us to pay our Taxes. If we are industrious, we shall never starve; for, as *Poor Richard* says, *At the working Man's House Hunger looks in, but dares not enter.* Nor will the Bailiff or the Constable enter, for *Industry pays Debts, while Despair encreaseth them,* says *Poor Richard.* What though you have found no Treasure, nor has any rich Relation left you a Legacy, *Diligence is the Mother of Good-luck* as *Poor Richard* says *and God gives all Things to Industry. Then plough deep, while Sluggards sleep, and you shall have Corn to sell and to keep,* says *Poor Dick.* Work while it is called To-day, for you know not how much you may be hindered To-morrow, which makes *Poor Richard* say, *One to-day is worth two To-morrows,* and farther, *Have you somewhat to do To-morrow, do it To-day.* If you were a Servant, would you not be ashamed that a good Master should catch you idle? Are you then your own Master, *be ashamed to catch yourself idle,* as *Poor Dick* says. When there is so much to be done for yourself, your Family, your Country, and your gracious King, be up by Peep of Day; *Let not the Sun look down and say, Inglorious here he lies.* Handle your Tools without Mittens; remember that *The Cat in Gloves catches no Mice,* as *Poor Richard* says. 'Tis true there is much to be done, and perhaps you are weak-handed, but stick to it steadily; and you will see great Effects, for *Constant Dropping wears away Stones,* and by *Diligence and Patience the Mouse ate in two the Cable;* and *Little Strokes fell great Oaks,* as *Poor Richard* says in his Almanack, the Year I cannot just now remember.

Methinks I hear some of you say, *Must a Man afford himself no Leisure?* I will tell thee, my friend, what *Poor Richard* says, *Employ thy Time well, if thou meanest to gain Leisure; and, since thou are not sure of a Minute, throw not away an Hour.* Leisure, is Time for doing something useful; this Leisure the diligent Man will obtain, but the lazy Man never; so that, as *Poor Richard* says *A Life of Leisure and a Life of Laziness are two Things.* Do you imagine that Sloth will afford you more Comfort than Labour? No, for as *Poor Richard* says, *Trouble springs from Idleness, and grievous Toil from Needless Ease. Many without Labour, would live by their Wits only, but they break for want of Stock.* Whereas Industry gives Comfort, and Plenty, and Respect: *Fly Pleasures, and they'll follow you. The diligent Spinner has a large Shift; and now I have a Sheep and a Cow, every-Body bids me good Morrow;* all which is well said by *Poor Richard.*

But with our Industry, we must likewise be *steady, settled,* and *careful,* and oversee our own Affairs *with our own Eyes,* and not trust too much to others; for, as *Poor Richard* says

I never saw an oft-removed Tree,
Nor yet an oft-removed Family,
That throve so well as those that settled be.

And again, *Three Removes is as bad as a Fire;* and again, *Keep thy shop, and thy Shop will keep thee;* and again, *If you would have your Business done, go; if not, send.* And again,

He that by the Plough would thrive,
Himself must either hold or drive.

And again, *The Eye of a Master will do more Work than both his Hands;* and again, *Want of Care does us more Damage than Want of Knowledge;* and again, *Not to oversee Workmen, is to leave them your Purse open.* Trusting too much to others' Care is the Ruin of many; for, as the Almanack says, *In the Affairs of this World, Men are saved, not by Faith, but by the Want of it;* but a Man's own Care is profitable; for, saith *Poor Dick, Learning is to the Studious,* and *Riches to the Careful,* as well as *Power to the Bold,* and *Heaven to the Virtuous,* And farther, *If you would have a faithful Servant, and one that you like, serve yourself.* And again, he adviseth to Circumspection and Care, even in the smallest Matters, because sometimes *A little Neglect may breed great Mischief;* adding, *for want of a Nail the Shoe was lost; for want of a Shoe the Horse was lost; and for want of a Horse the Rider was lost, being overtaken and slain by the*

Enemy; all for want of Care about a Horse-shoe Nail.

So much for Industry, my Friends, and Attention to one's own Business; but to these we must add *Frugality,* if we would make our *Industry* more certainly successful. A Man may, if he knows not how to save as he gets, *keep his Nose all his Life to the Grindstone,* and die not worth a *Groat* at last. A *fat kitchen makes a lean Will,* as *Poor Richard* says, and

Many Estates are spent in the Getting,
Since Women for Tea forsook Spinning and Knitting,
And Men for Punch forsook Hewing and Splitting.

If you would be wealthy, says he, in another Almanack, *think of Saving as well as of Getting: The Indies have not made Spain rich, because her Outgoes are greater than her Incomes.*

Away then with your expensive Follies, and you will not then have so much Cause to complain of hard Times, heavy Taxes, and chargeable Families; for, as *Poor Dick* says,

Women and Wine, Game and Deceit,
Make the Wealth small and the Wants great.

And farther, *What maintains one Vice, would bring up two Children.* You may think perhaps, that a *little* Tea, or a *little* Punch now and then, Diet a *little* more costly, Clothes a *little* finer, and a *little* Entertainment now and then, can be no *great* Matter; but remember what *Poor Richard* says, *Many a Little makes a Mickle;* and farther, Beware of little *Expences; A small Leak will sink a great Ship;* and again, *Who Dainties love, shall Beggars prove;* and moreover, *Fools make Feasts, and Wise Men eat them.*

Here you are all got together at this Vendue of *Fineries* and *Knickknacks.* You call them *Goods;* but if you do not take Care, they will prove *Evils* to some of you. You expect they will be sold *cheap,* and perhaps they may for less than they cost; but if you have no Occasion for them, they must be *dear* to you. Remember what *Poor Richard* says; *Buy what thou hast no Need of, and ere long thou shalt sell thy Necessaries.* And again, *At a great Pennyworth pause a while:* He means, that perhaps the Cheapness is *apparent* only, and not *Real;* or the bargain, by straitening thee in thy Business, may do thee more Harm than Good. For in another Place he says, *Many have been ruined by buying good Pennyworths.* Again, *Poor Richard* says, 'tis *foolish to lay out Money in a Purchase of Repentance;* and yet this Folly is practised every Day at Vendues, for want of minding the Almanack. *Wise Men,* as *Poor Dick* says, *learn by others Harms, Fools scarcely by their own;* but *felix quem faciunt aliena pericula cautum.* Many a one, for the Sake of Finery on the Back, have gone with a hungry Belly, and half-starved their Families. *Silks and Sattins, Scarlet and Velvets,* as *Poor Richard* says, *put out the Kitchen Fire.*

These are not the *Necessaries* of Life; they can scarcely be called the *Conveniences;* and yet only because they look pretty, how many *want* to *have* them! The *artificial* Wants of Mankind thus become more numerous than the *Natural;* and, as *Poor Dick* says, *for one poor Person, there are an hundred indigent.* By these, and other Extravagancies, the Genteel are reduced to poverty, and forced to borrow of those whom they formerly despised, but who through Industry and Frugality have maintained their Standing; in which Case it appears plainly, that *A Ploughman on his Legs is higher than a Gentleman on his Knees,* as *Poor Richard* says. Perhaps they have had a small Estate left them, which they knew not the Getting of; they think, *'tis Day, and will never be Night;* that a little to be spent out of *so much,* is not worth minding; *a Child and a Fool,* as *Poor Richard* says, *imagine Twenty shillings and Twenty Years can never be spent* but, *always taking out of the Meal-tub, and never putting in, soon comes to the Bottom;* as *Poor Dick* says, *When the Well's dry, they know the Worth of Water.* But this they might have known before, if they had taken his Advice; *if you would know the Value of Money, go and try to borrow some; for, he that goes a borrowing goes a sorrowing;* and indeed so does he that lends to such People, when he goes *to get it in again. Poor Dick* further advises, and says,

Fond Pride of Dress is sure a very Curse;
E'er Fancy you consult, consult your Purse.

And again, *Pride is as loud a Beggar as Want, and a great deal more saucy.* When you have bought one fine Thing, you must buy ten more, that your Appearance may be all of a Piece; but *Poor Dick* says, *'Tis easier to suppress the first Desire, than to satisfy all that follow it.* And 'tis as truly Folly for the Poor to ape the Rich, as for the Frog to swell, in order to equal the ox.

Great Estates may venture more,
But little Boats should keep near Shore.

'Tis, however, a Folly soon punished; for *Pride that dines on Vanity, sups on Contempt,* as *Poor Richard* says. And in another Place, *Pride breakfasted with Plenty, dined with Poverty, and supped with Infamy.* And after all, of what Use is this *Pride of Appearance,* for which so much is risked so much is suffered? It cannot promote Health, or ease Pain; it makes no Increase of Merit in the Person, it creates Envy, it hastens Misfortune.

What is a Butterfly? At best
He's but a Caterpillar drest
The gaudy Fop's his Picture just,

as *Poor Richard* says.

But what Madness must it be to *run in Debt* for these Superfluities! We are offered, by the Terms of this Vendue, *Six Months' Credit;* and that perhaps has induced some of us to attend it, because we cannot spare the ready Money, and hope now to be fine without it. But, ah, think what you do when you run in Debt; *you give to another Power over your Liberty.* If you cannot pay at the Time, you will be ashamed to see your Creditor; you will be in Fear when you speak to him; you will make poor pitiful sneaking Excuses, and by Degrees come to lose your Veracity, and sink into base downright lying; for, as *Poor Richard* says *The second Vice is Lying, the first is running in Debt.* And again, to the same Purpose, *Lying rides upon Debt's Back.* Whereas a free-born *Englishman* ought not to be ashamed or afraid to see or speak to any Man living. But Poverty often deprives a Man of all Spirit and Virtue: *'Tis hard for an empty Bag to stand upright,* as *Poor Richard* truly says.

What would you think of that Prince, or that Government, who should issue an Edict forbidding you to dress like a Gentleman or a Gentlewoman, on Pain of Imprisonment or Servitude? Would you not say, that you were free, have a Right to dress as you please, and that such an Edict would be a Breach of your Privileges, and such a Government tyrannical? And yet you are about to put yourself under that Tyranny, when you run in Debt for such Dress! Your Creditor has Authority, at his Pleasure to deprive you of your Liberty, by confining you in [Gaol] for Life, or to sell you for a Servant, if you should not be able to pay him! When you have got your Bargain, you may, perhaps, think little of Payment; but *Creditors, Poor Richard* tells us, *have better Memories than Debtors;* and in another Place says, *Creditors are a superstitious Sect, great Observers of set Days and Times.* The Day comes round before you are aware, and the Demand is made before you are prepared to satisfy it, Or if you bear your Debt in Mind, the Term which at first seemed so long, will, as it lessens, appear extreamly short. *Time* will seem to have added Wings to his Heels as well as Shoulders. *Those have a short Lent,* saith *Poor Richard, who owe Money to be paid at Easter.* Then since, as he says, *The Borrower is a Slave to the Lender, and the Debtor to the Creditor,* disdain the Chain, preserve your Freedom; and maintain your Independency: Be *industrious* and *free;* be *frugal* and *free.* At present, perhaps, you may think yourself in thriving Circumstances, and that you can bear a little Extravagance without Injury; but,

For Age and Want, save while you may;
No Morning Sun lasts a whole Day,

as *Poor Richard* says. Gain may be temporary and uncertain, but ever while you live, Expense is constant and certain; and *'tis easier to build two Chimnies, than to keep one in Fuel,* as *Poor Richard* says. So, *Rather go to Bed supperless than rise in Debt.*

Get what you can, and what you get hold;
'Tis the Stone that will turn all your lead into Gold,

as *Poor Richard* says. And when you have got the Philosopher's Stone, sure you will no longer complain of bad Times, or the Difficulty of paying Taxes.

This Doctrine, my Friends, is *Reason* and *Wisdom;* but after all, do not depend too much upon your own *Industry,* and *Frugality,* and *Prudence,* though excellent Things, for they may all be blasted without the Blessing of Heaven; and therefore, ask that Blessing humbly, and be not uncharitable to those that at present seem to want it, but comfort and help them. Remember, *Job* suffered, and was afterwards prosperous.

And now to conclude, *Experience keeps a dear School, but Fools will learn in no other, and scarce in that;* for it is true, *we may give Advice, but we cannot give Conduct,* as *Poor Richard* says: However, remember this, *They that won't be counselled, can't be helped,* as *Poor Richard* says: and farther, That, *if you will not hear Reason, she'll surely rap your Knuckles.*"

Thus the old Gentleman ended his Harangue. The People heard it, and approved the Doctrine, and immediately practiced the contrary, just as if it had been a common Sermon; for the Vendue opened, and they began to buy extravagantly, notwithstanding, his Cautions and their own Fear of Taxes. I found the good Man had thoroughly studied my Almanacks, and digested all I had dropt on these Topicks during the Course of Five and twenty Years. The frequent Mention he made of me must have tired any one else, but my Vanity was wonderfully delighted with it, though I was conscious that not a tenth Part of the Wisdom was my own, which he ascribed to me, but rather the *Gleanings* I had made of the Sense of all Ages and Nations. However, I resolved to be the better for the Echo of it; and though I had at first determined to buy Stuff for a new Coat, I went away resolved to wear my old One a little longer. *Reader,* if thou wilt do the same, thy Profit will be as great as mine. I *am, as ever, thine to serve thee,*

RICHARD SAUNDERS.

(1757) 1758

AN EDICT BY THE KING OF PRUSSIA

Dantzic, Sept. 5, [1773].

We have long wondered here at the supineness of the English nation, under the Prussian impositions upon its trade entering our port. We did not, till lately, know the claims, ancient and modern, that hang over that nation; and therefore could not suspect that it might submit to those impositions from a sense of duty or from principles of equity. The following Edict, just made publick, may, if serious, throw some light upon this matter.

"FREDERIC, by the grace of God, King of Prussia, &c. &c. &c., to all present and to come, (*à tous présens et à venir,*) Health. The peace now enjoyed throughout our dominions, having afforded us leisure to apply ourselves to the regulation of commerce, the improvement of our finances, and at the same time the easing our domestic subjects in their taxes: For these causes, and other good considerations us thereunto moving, we hereby make known, that, after having deliberated these affairs in our council, present our dear brothers, and other great officers of the state, members of the same, we, of our certain knowledge, full power, and authority royal, have made and issued this present Edict, viz.

"Whereas it is well known to all the world, that the first German settlements made in the Island of Britain, were by colonies of people, subject to our renowned ducal ancestors, and drawn from their dominions, under the conduct of Hengist, Horsa, Hella, Uff, Cerdicus, Ida, and others; and that the said colonies have flourished under the protection of our august house for ages past; have never been emancipated therefrom; and yet have hitherto yielded little profit to the same: And whereas we ourself have in the last war fought for and defended the said colonies, against the power of France, and thereby enabled them to make conquests from the said power in America, for which we have not yet received adequate compensation: And whereas it is just and expedient that a revenue should be raised from the said colonies in Britain, towards our indemnification; and that those who are descendants of our ancient subjects, and thence still owe us due obedience, should contribute to the replenishing of our royal coffers as they must have done, had their ancestors remained in the territories now to us appertaining: We do therefore hereby ordain and command, that, from and after the date of these presents, there shall be levied and paid to our officers of the *customs,* on all goods, wares, and merchandizes, and on all grain and other produce of the earth, exported from the said Island of Britain, and on all goods of whatever kind imported into the same, a duty of four and a half per cent *ad valorem,* for the use of us and our successors. And that the said duty may more effectually be collected, we do hereby ordain, that all ships or vessels bound from Great Britain to any other part of the world, or from any other part of the world to Great Britain, shall in their respective voyages touch at our port of Koningsberg, there to be unladen, searched, and charged with the said duties.

"And whereas there hath been from time to time discovered in the said island of Great Britain, by our colonists there, many mines or beds of iron-stone; and sundry subjects, of our ancient dominion, skilful in converting the said stone into metal, have in time past transported themselves thither, carrying with them and communicating that art; and the inhabitants of the said island, presuming that they had a natural right to make the best use they could of the natural productions of their country for their own benefit, have not only built furnaces for smelting the said stone into iron, but have erected plating-forges, slitting-mills, and steel-furnaces, for the more convenient manufacturing of the same; thereby endangering a diminution of the said manufacture in our ancient dominion;—we do therefore hereby farther ordain, that, from and after the date hereof, no mill or other engine for slitting or rolling of iron, or any plating-forge to work with a tilt-hammer, or any furnace for making steel, shall be erected or continued in the said island of Great Britain: And the Lord Lieutenant of every county in the said island is hereby commanded, on information of any such erection within his county, to order and by force to cause the same to be abated and destroyed; as he shall answer the neglect thereof to us at his peril. But we are nevertheless graciously pleased to permit the inhabitants of the said island to transport their iron into Prussia, there to be manufactured, and to them returned; they paying our Prussian subjects for the workmanship, with all the costs of commission, freight, and risk, coming and returning; any thing herein contained to the contrary notwithstanding.

"We do not, however, think fit to extend this our indulgence to the article of wool; but, meaning to encourage, not only the manufacturing of woollen cloth, but also the raising of wool, in our ancient dominions, and to prevent both, as much as may be, in our said island, we do hereby absolutely forbid the transportation of wool from thence, even to the mother country, Prussia; and that those islanders may be farther and more effectually restrained in making any advantage of their own wool in the way of manufacture, we command that none shall be carried out of one county into another; nor shall any worsted, bay, or woollen yarn, cloth, says, bays, kerseys, serges, frizes, druggets, cloth-serges, shalloons, or any other drapery stuffs, or woollen manufactures whatsoever, made up or mixed with wool in any of the said counties, be carried into any other county, or be water-borne even across the smallest river or creek, on penalty of forfeiture of the same, together with the boats, carriages, horses, &c., that shall be employed in removing them. Nevertheless, our loving subjects there are hereby permitted (if they think proper) to use all their wool as manure for the improvement of their lands.

"And whereas the art and mystery of making hats hath arrived at great perfection in Prussia, and the making of hats by our remoter subjects ought to be as much as possible restrained: And forasmuch as the islanders before mentioned, being in possession of wool, beaver and other furs, have presumptuously conceived they had a right to make some advantage thereof, by manufacturing the same into hats, to the prejudice of our domestic manufacture: We do therefore hereby strictly command and ordain, that no hats or felts whatsoever, dyed or undyed, finished or unfinished, shall be loaded or put into or upon any vessel, cart, carriage, or horse, to be transported or conveyed out of one county in the said island into another county, or to any other place whatsoever, by any person or persons whatsoever; on pain of forfeiting the same, with a penalty of five hundred pounds sterling for every offence. Nor shall any hat-maker, in any of the said counties, employ more than two apprentices, on penalty of five pounds sterling per month; we intending hereby, that such hatmakers, being so restrained, both in the production and sale of their commodity, may find no advantage in continuing their business. But, lest the said islanders should suffer inconveniency by the want of hats, we are farther graciously pleased to permit them to send their beaver furs to Prussia; and we also permit hats made thereof to be exported from Prussia to Britain; the people thus favoured to pay all costs and charges of manufacturing, interest, commission to our merchants, insurance and freight going and returning, as in the case of iron.

"And, lastly, being willing farther to favour our said colonies in Britain, we do hereby also ordain and command, that all the *thieves,* highway and street robbers, housebreakers, forgerers, murderers, s-d-tes, and villains of every denomination, who have forfeited their lives to the law in Prussia; but whom we, in our great clemency, do not think fit here to hang, shall be emptied out of our gaols into the said island of Great Britain, for the better peopling of that country.

"We flatter ourselves, that these our royal regulations and commands will be thought just and reasonable by our much-favoured colonists in England; the said regulations being copied from their statutes of 10 and 11 William III. c. 10, 5 Geo. II. c. 22, 23, Geo. II. c. 29, 4 Geo. I. c. 11, and from other equitable laws made by their parliaments; or from instructions given by their Princes; or from resolutions of both Houses, entered into for the good government of their *own colonies in Ireland and America.*

"And all persons in the said island are hereby cautioned not to oppose in any wise the execution of this our Edict, or any part thereof, such opposition being high treason; of which all who are suspected shall be transported in fetters from Britain to Prussia, there to be tried and executed according to the Prussian law.

"Such is our pleasure.

"Given at Potsdam, this twenty-fifth day of the month of August, one thousand seven hundred and seventy-three, and in the thirty-third year of our reign.

"By the King, in his Council.

"RECHTMAESSIG, *Sec.*"

Some take this Edict to be merely one of the King's *Jeux d'Esprit:* others suppose it serious, and that he means a quarrel with England; but all here think the assertion it concludes with, "that these regulations are copied from acts of the English parliament respecting their colonies," a very injurious one; it being impossible to believe, that a people distinguished for their love of liberty, a nation so wise, so liberal in its sentiments, so just and equitable towards its neighbours, should, from mean and injudicious views of petty immediate profit, treat its own children in a manner so arbitrary and tyrannical!

1773

RULES BY WHICH A GREAT EMPIRE MAY BE REDUCED TO A SMALL ONE

An ancient Sage boasted, that, tho' he could not fiddle, he knew how to make a *great city* of a *little one*. The science that I, a modern simpleton, am about to communicate, is the very reverse.

I address myself to all ministers who have the management of extensive dominions, which from their very greatness are become troublesome to govern, because the multiplicity of their affairs leaves no time for *fiddling*.

I. In the first place, gentlemen, you are to consider, that a great empire, like a great cake, is most easily diminished at the edges. Turn your attention, therefore, first to your *remotest* provinces; that, as you get rid of them, the next may follow in order.

II. That the possibility of this separation may always exist, take special care the provinces are never incorporated with the mother country; that they do not enjoy the same common rights, the same privileges in commerce; and that they are governed by *severer* laws, all of *your enacting,* without allowing them any share in the choice of the legislators. By carefully making and preserving such distinctions, you will (to keep to my simile of the cake) act like a wise ginger-bread-baker, who, to facilitate a division, cuts his dough half through in those places where, when baked, he would have it *broken to pieces.*

III. Those remote provinces have perhaps been acquired, purchased, or conquered, at the *sole expence* of the settlers, or their ancestors, without the aid of the mother country. If this should happen to increase her *strength,* by their growing numbers, ready to join in her wars; her *commerce,* by their growing demand for her manufactures; or her *naval power,* by greater employment for her ships and seamen, they may probably suppose some merit in this, and that it entitles them to some favour; you are therefore to *forget it all, or resent it,* as if they had done you injury. If they happen to be zealous whigs, friends of liberty, nurtured in revolution principles, *remember all that* to their prejudice, and resolve to punish it; for such principles, after a revolution is thoroughly established, are of *no more use;* they are even *odious* and *abominable.*

IV. However peaceably your colonies have submitted to your government, shewn their affection to your interests, and patiently borne their grievances; you are to *suppose* them always inclined to revolt, and treat them accordingly. Quarter troops among them, who by their insolence may *provoke* the rising of mobs, and by their bullets and bayonets *suppress* them. By this means, like the husband who uses his wife ill *from suspicion,* you may in time convert your *suspicions* into *realities.*

V. Remote provinces must have *Governors* and *Judges,* to represent the Royal Person, and execute everywhere the delegated parts of his office and authority. You ministers know, that much of the strength of government depends on the *opinion* of the people; and much of that opinion on the *choice of rulers* placed immediately over them. If you send them wise and good men for governors, who study the interest of the colonists, and advance their prosperity, they will think their King wise and good, and that he wishes the welfare of his subjects. If you send them learned and upright men for Judges, they will think him a lover of justice. This may attach your provinces more to his government. You are therefore to be careful whom you recommend for those offices. If you can find prodigals, who have ruined their fortunes, broken gamesters or stockjobbers, these may do well as *governors;* for they will probably be rapacious, and provoke the people by their extortions. Wrangling proctors and pettifogging lawyers, too, are not amiss; for they will be for ever disputing and quarrelling with their little parliaments. If withal they should be ignorant, wrong-headed, and insolent, so much the better. Attornies' clerks and Newgate solicitors will do for *Chief Justices,* especially if they hold their places *during your pleasure;* and all will contribute to impress those ideas of your government, that are proper for a people *you would wish to renounce it.*

VI. To confirm these impressions, and strike them deeper, whenever the injured come to the capital with complaints of mal-administration, oppression, or injustice, punish such suitors with long delay, enormous expence, and a final judgment in favour of the oppressor. This will have an admirable effect every way. The trouble of future complaints will be prevented, and Governors and Judges will be encouraged to farther acts of oppression and injustice; and thence the people may become more disaffected, and at length desperate.

VII. When such Governors have crammed their coffers, and made themselves so odious to the people that they can no longer remain among them, with safety to their person, *recall and reward* them with pensions. You may make them *baronets* too, if that respectable order should not think fit to resent it. All will contribute to encourage new governors in the same practice, and make the supreme government, *detestable.*

VIII. If, when you are engaged in war, your colonies should vie in liberal aids of men and money against the common enemy, upon your simple requisition, and give far beyond their abilities, reflect that a penny taken from them by your power is more honourable to you, than a pound presented by their benevolence; despise therefore their voluntary grants, and resolve to harass them with novel taxes. They will probably complain to your parliaments, that they are taxed by a body in which they have no representative, and that this is contrary to common right. They will petition for redress. Let the Parliaments flout their claims, reject their petitions, refuse even to suffer the reading of them, and treat the petitioners with the utmost contempt. Nothing can have a better effect in producing the alienation proposed; for though many can forgive injuries, *none ever forgave contempt.*

IX. In laying these taxes, never regard the heavy burthens those remote people already undergo, in defending their own frontiers, supporting their own provincial governments, making new roads, building bridges, churches, and other public edifices, which in old countries have been done to your hands by your ancestors, but which occasion constant calls and demands on the purses of a new people. Forget the *restraints* you lay on their trade for *your own* benefit, and the advantage a *monopoly* of this trade gives your exacting merchants. Think nothing of the wealth those merchants and your manufacturers acquire by the colony commerce; their encreased ability thereby to pay taxes at home; their accumulating, in the price of their commodities, most of those taxes, and so levying them from their consuming customers; all this, and the employment and support of thousands of your poor by the colonists, you are *intirely to forget.* But remember to make your arbitrary tax more grievous to your provinces, by public declarations importing that your power of taxing them has *no limits;* so that when you take from them without their consent one shilling in the pound, you have a clear right to the other nineteen. This will probably weaken every idea of *security in their property,* and convince them, that under such a government they *have nothing they can call their own;* which can scarce fail of producing the *happiest consequences!*

X. Possibly, indeed, some of them might still comfort themselves, and say, "Though we have no property, we have yet *something* left that is valuable; we have constitutional *liberty,* both of person and of conscience. This King, these Lords, and these Commons, who it seems are too remote from us to know us, and feel for us, cannot take from us our *Habeas Corpus* right, or our right of trial *by a jury of our neighbours;* they cannot deprive us of the exercise of our religion, alter our ecclesiastical constitution, and compel us to be Papists, if they please, or Mahometans." To annihilate this comfort, begin by laws to perplex their commerce with infinite regulations, impossible to be remembered and observed; ordain seizures of their property for every failure; take away the trial of such property by Jury, and give it to arbitrary Judges of your own appointing, and of the lowest characters in the country, whose salaries and emoluments are to arise out of the duties or condemnations, and whose appointments are *during pleasure*. Then let there be a formal declaration of both Houses, that opposition to your edicts is *treason,* and that any person suspected of treason in the provinces may, according to some obsolete law, be seized and sent to the metropolis of the empire for trial; and pass an act, that those there charged with certain other offences, shall be sent away in chains from their friends and country to be tried in the same manner for felony. Then erect a new Court of Inquisition among them, accompanied by an armed force, with instructions to transport all such suspected persons; to be ruined by the expence, if they bring over evidences to prove their innocence, or be found guilty and hanged, if they cannot afford it. And, lest the people should think you cannot possibly go any farther, pass another solemn declaratory act, "that King, Lords, Commons had, hath, and of right ought to have, full power and authority to make statutes of sufficient force and validity to bind the unrepresented provinces IN ALL CASES WHATSOEVER." This will include *spiritual* with temporal, and, taken together, must operate wonderfully to your purpose; by convincing them, that they are at present under a power something like that spoken of in the scriptures, which can not only *kill their bodies,* but *damn their souls* to all eternity, by compelling them, if it pleases, *to worship the Devil.*

XI. To make your taxes more odious, and more likely to procure resistance, send from the capital a board of officers to superintend the collection, composed of the most *indiscreet, ill-bred,* and *insolent* you can find. Let these have large salaries out of the extorted revenue, and live in open, grating luxury upon the sweat and blood of the industrious; whom they are to worry continually with groundless and expensive prosecutions before the abovementioned arbitrary revenue Judges; *all at the cost of the party prosecuted,* tho' acquitted, because *the King is to pay no costs.* Let these men, *by your order,* be exempted from all the common taxes and burthens of the province, though they and their property are protected by its laws. If any revenue officers are *suspected* of the least tenderness for the people, discard them. If others are justly complained of, protect and reward them. If any of the under officers behave so as to provoke the people to drub them, promote those to better offices: this will encourage others to procure for themselves such profitable drubbings, by multiplying and enlarging such provocations, and *all will work towards the end you aim at.*

XII. Another way to make your tax odious, is to misapply the produce of it. If it was originally appropriated for the *defence* of the provinces, the better support of government, and the administration of justice, where it may be *necessary,* then apply none of it to that *defence,* but bestow it where it is *not necessary,* in augmented salaries or pensions to every governor, who had distinguished himself by his enmity to the people, and by calumniating them to their sovereign. This will make them pay it more unwillingly, and be more apt to quarrel with those that collect it and those that imposed it, who will quarrel again with them, and all shall contribute to your *main purpose,* of making them *weary of your government.*

XIII. If the people of any province have been accustomed to support their own Governors and Judges to satisfaction, you are to apprehend that such Governors and Judges may be thereby influenced to treat the people kindly, and to do them justice. This is another reason for applying part of that revenue in larger salaries to such Governors and Judges, given, as their commissions are, *during your pleasure* only; forbidding them to take any salaries from their provinces; that thus the people may no longer hope any kindness from their Governors, or (in Crown cases) any justice from their Judges. And, as the money thus misapplied in one province is extorted from all, probably *all will resent the misapplication.*

XIV. If the parliaments of your provinces should dare to claim rights, or complain of your administration, order them to be harrassed with *repeated dissolutions.* If the same men are continually returned by new elections, adjourn their meetings to some country village, where they cannot be accommodated, and there keep them *during pleasure;* for this, you know, is your PREROGATIVE; and an excellent one it is, as you may manage it to promote discontents among the people, diminish their respect, and *increase their disaffection.*

XV. Convert the brave, honest officers of your *navy* into pimping tide-waiters and colony officers of the *customs.* Let those, who in time of war fought gallantly in defence of the commerce of their countrymen, in peace be taught to prey upon it. Let them learn to be corrupted by great and real smugglers; but (to show their diligence) scour with armed boats every bay, harbour, river, creek, cove, or nook throughout the coast of your colonies; stop and detain every coaster, every wood-boat, every fisherman, tumble their cargoes and even their ballast inside out and upside down; and, if a penn'orth of pins is found un-entered, let the whole be seized and confiscated. Thus shall the trade of your colonists suffer more from their friends in time of peace, than it did from their enemies in war. Then let these boats crews land upon every farm in their way, rob the orchards, steal the pigs and the poultry, and insult the inhabitants. If the injured and exasperated farmers, unable to procure other justice, should attack the aggressors, drub them, and burn their boats; you are to call this *high treason and rebellion,* order fleets and armies into their country, and threaten to carry all the offenders three thousand miles to be hanged, drawn, and quartered. *O! this will work admirably!*

XVI. If you are told of discontents in your colonies, never believe that they are general, or that you have given occasion for them; therefore do not think of applying any remedy, or of changing any offensive measure. Redress no grievance, lest they should be encouraged to demand the redress of some other grievance. Grant no request that is just and reasonable, lest they should make another that is unreasonable. Take all your informations of the state of the colonies from your Governors and officers in enmity with them. Encourage and reward these *leasing-makers;* secrete their lying accusations, lest they should be confuted; but act upon them as the clearest evidence; and believe nothing you hear from the friends of the people: suppose all *their* complaints to be invented and promoted by a few factious demagogues, whom if you could catch and hang, all would be quiet. Catch and hang a few of them accordingly; and the *blood of the Martyrs* shall *work miracles* in favour of your purpose.

XVII. If you see *rival nations* rejoicing at the prospect of your disunion with your provinces, and endeavouring to promote it; if they translate, publish, and applaud all the complaints of your discontented colonists, at the same time privately stimulating you to severer measures, let not that *alarm* or offend you. Why should it, since you all mean *the same thing?*

XVIII. If any colony should at their own charge erect a fortress to secure their port against the fleets of a foreign enemy, get your Governor to betray that fortress into your hands. Never think of paying what it cost the country, for that would look, at least, like some regard for justice; but turn it into a citadel to awe the inhabitants and curb their commerce. If they should have lodged in such fortress the very arms they bought and used to aid you in your conquests, seize them all; it will provoke like *ingratitude* added to *robbery.* One admirable effect of these operations will be, to discourage every other colony from erecting such defences, and so your enemies may more easily invade them; to the great disgrace of your government, and of course *the furtherance of your project.*

XIX. Send armies into their country under pretence of protecting the inhabitants; but, instead of garrisoning the forts on their frontiers with those troops, to prevent incursions, demolish those forts, and order the troops into the heart of the country, that the savages may be encouraged to attack the frontiers, and that the troops may be protected by the inhabitants. This will seem to proceed from your ill will or your ignorance, and contribute farther to produce and strengthen an opinion among them, *that you are no longer fit to govern them.*

XX. Lastly, invest the General of your army in the provinces, with great and unconstitutional powers, and free him from the controul of even your own Civil Governors. Let him have troops enow under his command, with all the fortresses in his possession; and who knows but (like some provincial Generals in the Roman empire, and encouraged by the universal discontent you have produced) he may take it into his head to set up for himself? If he should, and you have carefully practised these few *excellent rules* of mine, take my word for it, all the provinces will immediately join him; and you will that day (if you have not done it sooner) get rid of the trouble of governing them, and all the *plagues* attending their *commerce* and connection from henceforth and for ever.

Q. E. D.

1773

THE WHISTLE

Passy, November 10, 1779.

I RECEIVED my dear friend's two letters, one for Wednesday and one for Saturday. This is again Wednesday. I do not deserve one for to-day, because I have not answered the former. But, indolent as I am, and averse to writing, the fear of having no more of your pleasing epistles, if I do not contribute to the correspondence, obliges me to take up my pen; and as Mr. B. has kindly sent me word, that he sets out to-morrow to see you, instead of spending this Wednesday evening as I have done its namesakes, in your delightful company, I sit down to spend it in thinking of you, in writing to you, and in reading over and over again your letters.

I am charmed with your description of Paradise, and with your plan of living there; and I approve much of your conclusion, that, in the mean time, we should draw all the good we can from this world. In my opinion, we might all draw more good from it than we do, and suffer less evil, if we would take care not to give too much for *whistles*. For to me it seems, that most of the unhappy people we meet with, are become so by neglect of that caution.

You ask what I mean? You love stories, and will excuse my telling one of myself.

When I was a child of seven years old, my friends, on a holiday, filled my pocket with coppers. I went directly to a shop where they sold toys for children; and, being charmed with the sound of a *whistle,* that I met by the way in the hands of another boy, I voluntarily offered and gave all my money for one. I then came home, and went whistling all over the house, much pleased with my *whistle,* but disturbing all the family. My brothers, and sisters, and cousins, understanding the bargain I had made, told me I had given four times as much for it as it was worth; put me in mind what good things I might have bought with the rest of the money; and laughed at me so much for my folly, that I cried with vexation; and the reflection gave me more chagrin than the *whistle* gave me pleasure.

This however was afterwards of use to me, the impression continuing on my mind; so that often, when I was tempted to buy some unnecessary thing, I said to myself, *Don't give too much for the whistle;* and I saved my money.

As I grew up, came into the world, and observed the actions of men, I thought I met with many, very many, who *gave too much for the whistle.*

When I saw one too ambitious of court favour, sacrificing his time in attendance on levees, his repose, his liberty, his virtue, and perhaps his friends, to attain it, I have said to myself, *This man gives too much for his whistle.*

When I saw another fond of popularity, constantly employing himself in political bustles, neglecting his own affairs, and ruining them by that neglect, *He pays, indeed,* said I, *too much for his whistle.*

If I knew a miser, who gave up every kind of comfortable living, all the pleasure of doing good to others, all the esteem of his fellow-citizens, and the joys of benevolent friendship, for the sake of accumulating wealth, *Poor man,* said I, *you pay too much for your whistle.*

When I met with a man of pleasure, sacrificing every laudable improvement of the mind, or of his fortune, to mere corporeal sensations, and ruining his health in their pursuit, *Mistaken man,* said I, *you are providing pain for yourself, instead of pleasure; you give too much for your whistle.*

If I see one fond of appearance, or fine clothes, fine houses, fine furniture, fine equipages, all above his fortune, for which he contracts debts, and ends his career in a prison, *Alas!* say I, *he has paid dear, very dear, for his whistle.*

When I see a beautiful, sweet-tempered girl married to an ill-natured brute of a husband, *What a pity,* say I, *that she should pay so much for a whistle!*

In short, I conceive that great part of the miseries of mankind are brought upon them by the false estimates they have made of the value of things, and by their *giving too much for their whistles.*

Yet I ought to have charity for these unhappy people, when I consider, that, with all this wisdom of which I am boasting, there are certain things in the world so tempting, for example, the apples of King John, which happily are not to be bought; for if they were put to sale by auction, I might very easily be led to ruin myself in the purchase, and find that I had once more given too much for the *whistle.*

Adieu, my dear friend, and believe me ever yours very sincerely and with unalterable affection,

B. Franklin.

(1779) 1818

THE EPHEMERA

An Emblem of Human Life

You may remember, my dear friend, that when we lately spent that happy day in the delightful garden and sweet society of the Moulin Joly, I stopt a little in one of our walks, and staid some time behind the company. We had been shown numberless skeletons of a kind of little fly, called an ephemera, whose successive generations, we were told, were bred and expired within the day. I happened to see a living company of them on a leaf, who appeared to be engaged in conversation. You know I understand all the inferior animal tongues: my too great application to the study of them is the best excuse I can give for the little progress I have made in your charming language. I listened through curiosity to the discourse of these little creatures; but as they, in their national vivacity, spoke three or four together, I could make but little of their conversation. I found, however, by some broken expressions that I heard now and then, they were disputing warmly on the merit of two foreign musicians, one a *cousin,* the other a *moscheto;* in which dispute they spent their time, seemingly as regardless of the shortness of life as if they had been sure of living a month. Happy people! thought I, you live certainly under a wise, just, and mild government, since you have no public grievances to complain of, nor any subject of contention but the perfections and imperfections of foreign music. I turned my head from them to an old grey-headed one, who was single on another leaf, and talking to himself. Being amused with his soliloquy, I put it down in writing, in hopes it will likewise amuse her to whom I am so much indebted for the most pleasing of all amusements, her delicious company and heavenly harmony.

"It was," said he, "the opinion of learned philosophers of our race, who lived and flourished long before my time, that this vast world, the Moulin Joly, could not itself subsist more than eighteen hours; and I think there was some foundation for that opinion, since, by the apparent motion of the great luminary that gives life to all nature, and which in my time has evidently declined considerably towards the ocean at the end of our earth, it must then finish its course, be extinguished in the waters that surround us, and leave the world in cold and darkness, necessarily producing universal death and destruction. I have lived seven of those hours, a great age, being no less than four hundred and twenty minutes of time. How very few of us continue so long! I have seen generations born, flourish, and expire. My present friends are the children and grandchildren of the friends of my youth, who are now, alas, no more! And I must soon follow them; for, by the course of nature, though still in health, I cannot expect to live above seven or eight minutes longer. What now avails all my toil and labor, in amassing honey-dew on this leaf, which I cannot live to enjoy! What the political struggles I have been engaged in, for the good of my compatriot inhabitants of this bush, or my philosophical studies for the benefit of our race in general! for, in politics, what can laws do without morals? Our present race of ephemeræ will in a course of minutes become corrupt, like those of other and older bushes, and consequently as wretched. And in philosophy how small our progress! Alas! art is long, and life is short! My friends would comfort me with the idea of a name, they say, I shall leave behind me; and they tell me I have lived long enough to nature and to glory. But what will fame be to an ephemera who no longer exists? And what will become of all history in the eighteenth hour, when the world itself, even the whole Moulin Joly, shall come to its end, and be buried in universal ruin?"

To me, after all my eager pursuits, no solid pleasures now remain, but the reflection of a long life spent in meaning well, the sensible conversation of a few good lady ephemeræ and now and then a kind smile and a tune from the ever amiable *Brillante*.

(1778) 1818

THE REVOLUTIONARY ISSUE: REBEL *vs.* TORY

I. JOHN DICKINSON (1732–1808)

LETTERS FROM A FARMER IN PENNSYLVANIA

LETTER I

Beloved Countrymen,

I AM a *Farmer,* settled after a variety of fortunes, near the banks of the river *Delaware,* in the province of *Pennsylvania.* I received a liberal education, and have been engaged in the busy scenes of life: But am now convinced, that a man may be as happy without bustle, as with it. My farm is small; my servants are few, and good; I have a little money at interest; I wish for no more; my employment in my own affairs is easy; and with a contented grateful mind, I am compleating the number of days allotted to me by divine goodness.

Being master of my time, I spend a good deal of it in a library, which I think the most valuable part of my small estate; and being acquainted with two or three gentlemen of abilities and learning, who honour me with their friendship, I believe, I have acquired a greater share of knowledge in history, and the laws and constitution of my country, than is generally attained by men of my class, many of them not being so fortunate as I have been in the opportunities of getting information.

From infancy I was taught to love humanity and liberty. Inquiry and experience have since confirmed my reverence for the lessons then given me, by convincing me more fully of their truth and excellence. Benevolence towards mankind excites wishes for their welfare, and such wishes endear the means of fulfilling them. Those can be found in liberty alone, and therefore her sacred cause ought to be espoused by every man, on every occasion, to the utmost of his power. As a charitable but poor person does not withhold his mite, because he cannot relieve *all* the distresses of the miserable, so let not any honest man suppress his sentiments concerning freedom, however small their influence is likely to be. Perhaps he may "touch some wheel" that will have an effect greater than he expects.

These being my sentiments, I am encouraged to offer to you, my countrymen, my thoughts on some late transactions, that in my opinion are of the utmost importance to you. Conscious of my defects, I have waited some time in expectation of seeing the subject treated by persons much better qualified for the task; but being therein disappointed, and apprehensive that longer delays will be injurious, I venture at length to request the attention of the public, praying only for one thing,—that is, that these lines may be *read* with the same zeal for the happiness of *British*

America, with which they were *wrote.*

With a good deal of surprize I have observed that little notice has been taken of an act of parliament, as injurious in its principle to the liberties of these colonies, as the *Stamp-Act* was: I mean the act for suspending the legislation of *New-York.*

The assembly of that government complied with a former act of parliament, requiring certain provisions to be made for the troops in *America,* in every particular, I think, except the articles of salt, pepper and vinegar. In my opinion they acted imprudently, considering all circumstances, in not complying so far, as would have given satisfaction, as several colonies did: But my dislike of their conduct in that instance, has not blinded me so much, that I cannot plainly perceive, that they have been punished in a manner pernicious to *American* freedom, and justly alarming to all the colonies.

If the *British* parliament has a legal authority to order, that we shall furnish a single article for the troops here, and to compel obedience to that order; they have the same right to order us to supply those troops with arms, cloaths, and every necessary, and to compel obedience to *that* order also; in short, to lay *any burdens* they please upon us. What is this but *taxing* us at a *certain sum,* and leaving to us only the *manner* of raising it? How is this mode more tolerable than the *Stamp-Act?* Would that act have appeared more pleasing to *Americans,* if being ordered thereby to raise the sum total of the taxes, the mighty privilege had been left to them, of saying how much should be paid for an instrument of writing on paper, and how much for another on parchment?

An act of parliament commanding us to do a certain thing, if it has any validity, is a tax upon us for the expence that accrues in complying with it, and for this reason, I believe, every colony on the continent, that chose to give a mark of their respect for *Great-Britain,* in complying with the act relating to the troops, cautiously avoided the mention of that act, lest their conduct should be attributed to its supposed obligation.

The matter being thus stated, the assembly of *New-York,* either had, or had not a right, to refuse submission to that act. If they had, and I imagine no *American* will say, they had not, then the parliament had no *right* to compel them to execute it. If they had not *that right,* they had *no right* to punish them for not executing it; and therefore had *no right* to suspend their legislation, which is a punishment. In fact, if the people of *New-York* cannot be legally taxed but by their own representatives, they cannot be legally deprived of the privileges of making laws, only for insisting on that exclusive privilege of taxation. If they may be legally deprived in such a case of the privilege of making laws, why may they not, with equal reason, be deprived of every other privilege? Or why may not every colony be treated in the same manner, when any of them shall dare to deny their assent to any impositions that shall be directed? Or what signifies the repeal of the *Stamp-Act,* if these colonies are to lose their *other* privileges, by not tamely surrendering that of *taxation?*

There is one consideration arising from the suspicion, which is not generally attended to, but shews its importance very clearly. It was not *necessary,* that this suspension should be caused by an act of parliament. The crown might have restrained the governor of *New-York,* even from calling the assembly together, by its prerogative in the royal governments. This step, I suppose, would have been taken, if the conduct of the assembly of *New-York* had been regarded as an act of disobedience *to the crown alone:* But it is regarded as an act of "disobedience to the authority of the BRITISH LEGISLATURE." This gives the suspension a consequence vastly more affecting. It is a parliamentary assertion of the *supreme authority* of the *British* legislature over these colonies in *the point of taxation;* and is intended to COMPEL *New-York* unto a submission to that authority. It seems therefore to me as much a violation of the liberty of the people of that province, and consequently of all these colonies, as if the parliament had sent a number of regiments to be quartered upon them, till they should comply. For it is evident, that the suspension is meant as a compulsion; and the *method* of compelling is totally indifferent. It is indeed probable, that the sight of redcoats, and the beating of drums would have been most alarming, because people are generally more influenced by their eyes and ears than by their reason: But whoever seriously considers the matter, must perceive, that a dreadful stroke is aimed at the liberty of these colonies. I say of these colonies: For the cause of *one* is the cause of *all.* If the parliament may lawfully deprive *New-York* of any of its rights, it may deprive any, or all the other colonies of their rights; and nothing can possibly so much encourage such attempts, as a mutual inattention to the interest of each other. *To divide and thus to destroy,* is the first political maxim in attacking those who are powerful by their union. He certainly is not a wise man, who folds his arms and reposeth himself at home, seeing with unconcern the flames that have invaded his neighbour's house, without any endeavours to extinguish them. When Mr. *Hampden's* ship-money cause for three shillings and four-pence was tried, all the people of *England,* with anxious expectation, interested themselves in the important decision; and when the slightest point touching the freedom of a single colony is agitated, I earnestly wish, that all the rest may with equal ardour support their sister. Very much may be said on this subject, but I hope, more at present is unnecessary.

With concern I have observed that two assemblies of this province have sat and adjourned, without taking any notice of this act. It may perhaps be asked, what would have been proper for them to do? I am by no means fond of inflammatory measures. I detest them. I should be sorry that any thing should be done which might justly displease our sovereign or our mother-country. But a firm, modest exertion of a free spirit should never be wanting on public occasions. It appears to me, that it would have been sufficient for the assembly, to have ordered our agents to represent to the King's ministers, their sense of the suspending act, and to pray for its repeal. Thus we should have borne our testimony against it; and might therefore reasonably expect that on a like occasion, we might receive the same assistance from the other colonies.

"Concordia res parvæ crescunt."

Nov. 4. [1767] A FARMER.

LETTER III

My Dear Countrymen,

I rejoice to find that my two former letters to you have been generally received with so much favour, by such of you whose sentiments I have had an opportunity of knowing. Could you look into my heart, you would instantly perceive an ardent affection for your persons, a zealous attachment to your interests, a lively resentment of every insult and injury offered to your honour or happiness; and an inflexible resolution to assert your rights, to the utmost of my weak power, to be the only motives that have engaged me to address you.

I am no farther concerned in any thing affecting *America,* than any one of you, and when liberty leaves it, I can quit it much more conveniently than most of you. But while Divine Providence that gave me existence in a land of freedom, permits my head to think, my lips to speak, and my hand to move, I shall so highly and gratefully value the blessing received, as to take care, that my silence and inactivity shall not give my implied assent to any act, degrading my brethren and myself from the birthright, wherewith Heaven itself "hath made us free."

Sorry I am to learn, that there are some few persons, who shake their heads with solemn motion, and pretend to wonder, what can be the meaning of these letters. *"Great-Britain,"* they say, "is too powerful to contend with; she is determined to oppress us; it is in vain to speak of right on one side, when there is power on the other; when we are strong enough to resist, we shall attempt it; but now we are not strong enough, and therefore we had better be quiet; it signifies nothing to convince us that our rights are invaded, when we cannot defend them; and if we should get into riots and tumults about the late act, it will only draw down heavier displeasure upon us."

What can such men design? What do their grave observations amount to, but this—"That these colonies totally regardless of their liberties, should commit them with humble resignation to *chance, time,* and the tender mercies of *ministers."*

Are these men ignorant that usurpations which might have been successfully opposed at first, acquire strength by continuance, and thus become irresistable? Do they condemn the conduct of the colonies concerning the *Stamp-Act?* Or have they forgot its successful issue? Ought the colonies at that time, instead of acting as they did, to have trusted for relief to the fortuitous events of futurity? If it is needless "to speak of *rights"* now, it was as needless then. If the behaviour of the colonies was prudent and glorious then, and successful too; it will be equally prudent and glorious to act in the same manner now, if our rights are equally invaded, and may be as successful.--Therefore it becomes necessary to enquire, whether "our rights *are* invaded." To talk of "defending" them, as if they could be no otherwise "defended" than by arms, is as much out of the way, as if a man having a choice of several roads, to reach his journey, and should prefer the worst, for no other reason but because it *is* the worst.

As to "riots and tumults," the gentlemen who are so apprehensive of them, are much mistaken if they think, that grievances cannot be redressed without such assistance.

I will now tell the gentlemen what is "the meaning of these letters." The meaning of them is, to convince the people of these colonies that they are, at this moment, exposed to the most imminent dangers; and to persuade them immediately, vigorously, unanimously to exert themselves, in the most firm, and most peaceable manner, for obtaining relief.

The cause of liberty is a "cause of too much dignity, to be sullied by turbulence and tumults." It ought to be maintained in a manner suitable to her nature. Those who engage in it, should breathe a sedate yet fervent spirit, animating them to actions of prudence, justice, modesty, bravery, humanity and magnanimity.

To such a wonderful degree were the antient *Spartans,* as brave and free a people as ever existed, inspired by this happy temperature of soul, that rejecting even in their battles the use of trumpets, and other instruments, for exciting heat and rage, they marched up to scenes of havock and horror, with the sound of flutes, to the tunes of which their steps kept pace—"exhibiting," as *Plutarch* says, "at once a terrible and delightful sight, and proceeding, with a deliberate valour, full of hope and good assurance, as if some divinity had sensibly assisted them."

I hope, my dear countrymen, that you will in every colony be upon your guard against those who may at any time endeavour to stir you up, under pretences of patriotism, to any measures disrespectful to our sovereign and our mother-country. Hot, rash, disorderly proceedings injure the reputation of a people as to wisdom, valour, and virtue, without procuring them the least benefit. I pray GOD that he may be pleased to inspire you and your posterity to the latest ages with that spirit, of which I have an idea, but find a difficulty to express: To express in the best manner I can, I mean a spirit that shall so guide you, that it will be impossible to determine whether an *American's* character is most distinguishable for his loyalty to his sovereign, his duty to his mother-country, his love of freedom, or his affection for his native soil.

Every government, at some time or other, falls into wrong measures; these may proceed from mistake or passion. But every such measure does not dissolve the obligation between the governors and the governed; the mistake may be corrected; the passion may pass over. It is the duty of the governed, to endeavour to rectify the mistake, and to appease the passion. They have not at first any other right, than to represent their grievances, and to pray for redress, unless an emergence is so pressing as not to allow time for receiving an answer to their applications, which rarely happens. If their applications are disregarded, *then* that kind of opposition becomes justifiable, which can be made without breaking the laws, or disturbing the public peace. This consists in the prevention of the oppressors reaping advantage from their oppressions, and not in their punishment. For experience may teach them what reason did not; and harsh methods cannot be proper till milder ones have failed.

If at length it becomes UNDOUBTED, that an inveterate resolution is formed to annihilate the liberties of the governed, the *English* history affords frequent examples of resistance by force. What particular circumstances will in any future case justify such resistance, can never be ascertained till they happen. Perhaps it may be allowable to say, generally, that it never can be justifiable, until the people are FULLY CONVINCED, that any further submission will be destructive to their happiness.

When the appeal is made to the sword, highly probable is it, that the punishment will exceed the offence; and the calamities attending on war outweigh those preceding it. These considerations of justice and prudence will always have great influence with good and wise men.

To these reflections on this subject, it remains to be added, and ought forever to be remembered; that resistance in the case of colonies against their mother-country, is extremely different from the resistance of a people against their prince. A nation may change their kings, or race of kings, and retaining their antient form of government, be gainers by changing. Thus *Great-Britain,* under the illustrious house of *Brunswick,* a house that seems to flourish for the happiness of mankind, has found a felicity, unknown in the reigns of the *Stuarts*. But if once *we* are separated from our mother-country, what new form of government shall we accept, or where shall we find another *Britain* to supply our loss? Torn from the body to which we are united by religion, liberty, laws, affections, relations, language and commerce, we must bleed at every vein.

In truth, the prosperity of these provinces is founded in their dependance on *Great-Britain;* and when she returns to "her old good humour, and old good nature," as Lord *Clarendon* expresses it, I hope they will always esteem it their duty and interest, as it most certainly will be, to promote her welfare by all the means in their power.

We cannot act with too much caution in our disputes. Anger produces anger; and differences that might be accommodated by kind and respectful behaviour, may by imprudence be enlarged to an incurable rage.

In quarrels between countries, as well as in those between individuals, when they have risen to a certain height, the first cause of dissention is no longer remembered, the minds of the parties being wholly engaged in recollecting and resenting the mutual expressions of their dislike. When feuds have reached that fatal point, all considerations of reason and equity vanish; and a blind fury governs, or rather confounds all things. A people no longer regards their interest, but the gratification of their wrath. The sway of the *Cleons,* and *Clodius's,* the designing and detestable flatterers of the prevailing passion, becomes confirmed. Wise and good men in vain oppose the storm, and may think themselves fortunate, if endeavouring to preserve their ungrateful fellow-citizens, they do not ruin themselves. Their *prudence* will be called *baseness;*

their *moderation, guilt;* and if their virtue does not lead them to destruction, as that of many other great and excellent persons has done, they may survive to receive from their expiring country, the mournful glory of her acknowledgement, that their councils, if regarded, would have saved her.

The *constitutional* modes of obtaining relief, are those which I would wish to see pursued on the present occasion; that is, by petitions of our Assemblies, or, where they are not permitted to meet, of the people, to the powers that can afford us relief.

We have an excellent prince, in whose good dispositions toward us we may confide. We have a generous, sensible and humane nation, to whom we may apply. They *may* be deceived: They may, by artful men, be provoked to anger against us; but I cannot yet believe they will be cruel or unjust, or that their anger will be implacable. Let us behave like dutiful children, who have received unmerited blows from a beloved parent. Let us complain to our parents; but let our complaints speak, at the same time, the language of affliction and veneration.

If, however, it shall happen by an unfortunate course of affairs, that our applications to his Majesty and the Parliament for redress prove ineffectual, let us *then* take another step, by witholding from *Great-Britain,* all the advantages she has been used to receive from us. *Then* let us try, if our ingenuity, industry and frugality, will not give weight to our remonstrances. Let us all be united with one spirit in one cause. Let us invent; let us work; let us save; let us, at the same time, keep up our claims, and unceasingly repeat our complaints; but above all, let us implore the protection of that infinitely good and gracious Being, "by whom kings reign and princes decree justice."

"Nil desperandum."

A FARMER.

1767

A [LIBERTY] SONG

To the Tune of HEART OF OAK, &C.

COME, join Hand in Hand, brave AMERICANS all,
And rouse your bold Hearts at fair LIBERTY'S Call;
No tyrannous Acts shall suppress your *just Claim,*
Or stain with *Dishonour* AMERICA'S Name.
In FREEDOM we're BORN, and in FREEDOM we'll LIVE,
Our Purses are ready,
Steady, Friends, steady,
Not as SLAVES, but as FREEMEN our Money we'll give.

Our worthy *Forefathers*—let's give them a Cheer—
To *Climates unknown* did courageously steer;
Thro' *Oceans* to *Desarts* for *Freedom* they came,
And dying bequeath'd us their *Freedom* and *Fame*—
In FREEDOM we're BORN, *&c.*

Their generous Bosoms all Dangers despis'd,
So *highly,* so *wisely,* their BIRTHRIGHTS they priz'd;
We'll keep what they gave, we will piously keep,

Nor frustrate their Toils on the Land and the Deep.
In Freedom we're Born, *&c.*

The Tree their own Hands had to Liberty rear'd,
They liv'd to behold growing strong and rever'd;
With Transport then cry'd, "now our Wishes we gain,
For our Children shall gather the Fruits of our Pain."
In Freedom we're Born, *&c.* * * *

Then join Hand in Hand brave Americans all,
By *uniting* we stand, by *dividing* we fall;
In So Righteous a Cause let us hope to succeed,
For Heaven approves of each generous Deed.
In Freedom we're born, *&c.*

All Ages shall speak with *Amaze* and *Applause,*
Of the *Courage* we'll shew in Support of Our Laws;
To Die we can *bear*—but to Serve we *disdain*
For Shame is to *Freemen* more dreadful than Pain.
In Freedom we're Born, *&c.*

This Bumper I crown for our Sovereign's Health,
And this for Britannia's Glory and Wealth;
That Wealth and that Glory immortal may be,
If *she* is but *just*—and if *we* are but *free.*
In Freedom we're Born, *&c.*

II. THOMAS PAINE
(1737–1809)

From COMMON SENSE

* * * In the following pages I offer nothing more than simple facts, plain arguments, and common sense: and have no other preliminaries to settle with the reader, than that he will divest himself of prejudice and prepossession, and suffer his reason and his feelings to determine for themselves: that he will put on or rather that he will not put off the true character of a man, and generously enlarge his views beyond the present day.

Volumes have been written on the subject of the struggle between England and America. Men of all ranks have embarked in the controversy, from different motives, and with various designs; but all have been ineffectual, and the period of debate is closed. Arms as the last resource decide the contest; the appeal was the choice of the King, and the Continent has accepted the challenge.

It hath been reported of the late Mr. Pelham (who tho' an able minister was not without his faults) that on his being attacked in the House of Commons on the score that his measures were only of a temporary kind, replied, *"they will last my time."* Should a thought so fatal and unmanly possess the Colonies in the present contest, the name of ancestors will be remembered by future generations with detestation.

The Sun never shined on a cause of greater worth. 'Tis not the affair of a City, a County, a Province, or a Kingdom; but of a Continent—of at least one eighth part of the habitable Globe. 'Tis not the concern of a day, a year, or an age; posterity are virtually involved in the contest, and will be more or less affected even to the end of time by the proceedings now. Now is the seed time of Continental union, faith, and honour. The least fracture now, will be like a name engraved with the point of a pin on the tender rind of a young oak; the wound will enlarge with the tree, and posterity read it in full grown characters.

By referring the matter from argument to arms, a new æra for politics is struck—a new method of thinking hath arisen. All plans, proposals, &c. prior to the 19th of April, *i.e.* to the commencement of hostilities, are like the almanacks of the last year; which tho' proper then, are superceded and useless now. Whatever was advanced by the advocates on either side of the question then, terminated in one and the same point, viz. a union with Great Britain; the only difference between the parties was the method of effecting it; the one proposing force the other friendship; but it hath so far happened that the first hath failed, and the second hath withdrawn her influence.

As much hath been said of the advantages of reconciliation, which like an agreeable dream, hath passed away and left us as we were, it is but right, that we should examine the contrary side of the argument, and enquire into some of the many material injuries which these Colonies sustain, and always will sustain, by being connected with and dependant on Great Britain. To examine that connection and dependance, on the principles of nature and common sense, to see what we have to trust to if separated, and what we are to expect if dependant.

I have heard it asserted by some, that as America hath flourished under her former connection with Great-Britain, the same connection is necessary towards her future happiness, and will always have the same effect—Nothing can be more fallacious than this kind of argument:—we may as well assert that because a child has thrived upon milk, that it is never to have meat, or that the first twenty years of our lives is to become a precedent for the next twenty. But even this is admitting more than is true, for I answer, roundly, that America would have flourished as much, and probably much more had no European power taken any notice of her. The commerce by which she hath enriched herself are the necessaries of life, and will always have a market while eating is the custom of Europe.

But she has protected us say some. That she hath engrossed us is true, and defended the Continent at our expense as well as her own is admitted; and she would have defended Turkey from the same motive, viz. for the sake of trade and dominion.

Alas! we have been long led away by ancient prejudices and made large sacrifices to superstition. We have boasted the protection of Great Britain, without considering, that her motive was *interest* not *attachment;* and that she did not protect us from *our enemies on our account,* but from *her enemies* on *her own account,* from those who had no quarrel with us on any *other account,* and who will always be our enemies on the *same account.* Let Britain waive her pretensions to the continent, or the continent throw off the dependance, and we should be at peace with France and Spain were they at war with Britain. The miseries of Hanover['s] last war ought to warn us against connections.

It hath lately been asserted in parliament, that the colonies have no relation to each other but through the Parent Country, *i.e.* that Pennsylvania and the Jerseys, and so on for the rest, are sister Colonies by the way of England; this is certainly a very round-about way of proving relationship, but it is the nearest and only true way of proving enemyship, if I may so call it. France and Spain never were, nor perhaps ever will be our enemies as *Americans,* but as our being the *subjects of Great Britain.*

But Britain is the parent country say some. Then the more shame upon her conduct. Even brutes do not devour their young, nor savages make war upon their families; wherefore, the assertion if true, turns to her reproach; but it happens not to be true, or only partly so, and the phrase, *parent* or *mother country,* hath been jesuitically adopted by the King and his parasites, with a low papistical design of gaining an unfair bias on the credulous weakness of our minds. Europe and not England is the parent country of America. This new World hath been the asylum for the persecuted lovers of civil and religious liberty from *every part* of Europe. Hither have they fled, not from the tender embraces of the mother, but from the cruelty of the monster; and it is so far true of England, that the same tyranny which drove the first emigrants from home, pursues their descendants still.

In this extensive quarter of the Globe, we forget the narrow limits of three hundred and sixty miles (the extent of England) and carry our friendship on a larger scale; we claim brotherhood with every European Christian, and triumph in the generosity of the sentiment.

It is pleasant to observe by what regular gradations we surmount the force of local prejudice as we enlarge our acquaintance with the World. A man born in any town in England divided into parishes, will naturally associate most with his fellow parishioners (because their interests in many cases will be common) and distinguish him by the name of *neighbour:* if he meet him but a few miles from home, he drops the narrow idea of a street, and salutes him by the name of *townsman:* if he travel out of the country and meet him in any other, he forgets the minor divisions of street and town, and calls him *countryman,* i.e. *county-man:* but if in their foreign excursions they should associate in France, or any other part of *Europe,* their local remembrance would be enlarged into that of *Englishmen.* And by a just parity of reasoning, all Europeans meeting in America, or any other quarter of the Globe, are *countrymen;* for England, Holland, Germany, or Sweden, when compared with the whole, stand in the same places on the larger scale, which the divisions of street, town, and county do on the smaller ones; Distinctions too limited for Continental minds. Not one third of the inhabitants, even of this province, [Pennsylvania], are of English descent. Wherefore, I reprobate the phrase of parent or mother country applied to England only, as being false, selfish, narrow and ungenerous.

But admitting, that we were all of English descent, what does it amount to? Nothing. Britain, being now an open enemy, extinguishes every other name and title: and to say that reconciliation is our duty, is truly farcical. The first king of England, of the present line (William the Conqueror) was a Frenchman, and half the Peers of England are descendants from the same country; wherefore, by the same method of reasoning, England ought to be governed by France.

Much hath been said of the united strength of Britain and the Colonies, that in conjunction, they might bid defiance to the world: But this is mere presumption; the fate of war is uncertain, neither do the expressions mean any thing; for this Continent would never suffer itself to be drained of inhabitants, to support the British Arms in either Asia, Africa, or Europe.

Besides, what have we to do with setting the world at defiance? Our plan is commerce, and that well attended to, will secure us the peace and friendship of Europe because it is the interest of all Europe to have America a *free port*. Her trade will always be a protection, and her barrenness of gold and silver secure her from invaders.

I challenge the warmest advocate for reconciliation, to shew, a single advantage that this Continent can reap by being connected with Great Britain. I repeat the challenge, not a single advantage is derived. Our corn will fetch its price in any market in Europe, and our imported goods must be paid for by them where we will.

But the injuries and disadvantages which we sustain by that connection, are without number, and our duty to mankind at large, as well as to ourselves, instruct us to renounce the alliance: Because, any submission to, or dependance on Great Britain, tends directly to involve this Continent in European wars and quarrels. [And sets us at variance with nations, who would otherwise seek our friendship, and against whom, we have neither anger nor complaint.] As Europe is our market for trade, we ought to form no partial connection with any part of it. 'Tis the true interest of America, to steer clear of European contentions, which she never can do, while by her dependance on Britain, she is made the make-weight in the scale of British politics.

Europe is too thickly planted with Kingdoms, to be long at peace, and whenever a war breaks out between England and any foreign power, the trade of America goes to ruin, *because, of her connection with Britain.* The next war may not turn out like the last, and should it not, the advocates for reconciliation now, will be wishing for separation then, because neutrality in that case, would be a safer convoy than a man of war. Every thing that is right or reasonable pleads for separation. The blood of the slain, the weeping voice of nature cries, 'TIS TIME TO PART. Even the distance at which the Almighty hath placed England and America, is a strong and natural proof, that the authority of the one over the other, was never the design of Heaven. The time likewise at which the Continent was discovered, adds weight to the argument, and the manner in which it was peopled encreases the force of it.—The Reformation was preceded by the discovery of America; as if the Almighty graciously meant to open a sanctuary to the persecuted in future years, when home should afford neither friendship nor safety.

The authority of Great Britain over this Continent, is a form of government which sooner or later must have an end: and a serious mind can draw no true pleasure by looking forward, under the painful and positive conviction that what he calls "the present constitution," is merely temporary. As parents, we can have no joy, knowing that *this government* is not sufficiently lasting to ensure any thing which we may bequeath to posterity: And by a plain method of argument, as we are running the next generation into debt, we ought to do the work of it, otherwise we use them meanly and pitifully. In order to discover the line of our duty rightly, we should take our children in our hand, and fix our station a few years farther into life; that eminence will present a prospect, which a few present fears and prejudices conceal from our sight.

Though I would carefully avoid giving unnecessary offence, yet I am inclined to believe, that all those who espouse the doctrine of reconciliation, may be included within the following descriptions. Interested men, who are not to be trusted, weak men who *cannot see,* prejudiced men who *will not* see, and a certain set of moderate men who think better of the European world than it deserves; and this last class, by an ill-judged deliberation, will be the cause of more calamities to this continent, than all the other three.

It is the good fortune of many to live distant from the scene of present sorrow; the evil is not sufficiently brought to *their* doors to make *them* feel the precariousness with which all American property is possessed. But let our imaginations transport us a few moments to Boston; that seat of wretchedness will teach us wisdom, and instruct us for ever to renounce a power in whom we can have no trust. The inhabitants of that unfortunate city who but a few months ago were in ease and affluence, have now no other alternative than to stay and starve, or turn out to beg. Endangered by the fire of their friends if they continue within the city, and plundered by government if they leave it. In their present condition they are prisoners without the hope of redemption, and in a general attack for their relief, they would be exposed to the fury of both armies.

Men of passive tempers look somewhat lightly over the offences of Britain, and still hoping for the best, are apt to call out, *Come, come, we shall be friends again for all this.* But examine the passions and feelings of mankind: Bring the doctrine of reconciliation to the touchstone of nature, and then tell me, whether you can hereafter love, honour, and faithfully serve the power that hath carried fire and sword into your land? If you cannot do all these, then are you only deceiving yourselves, and by your delay bringing ruin upon posterity. Your future connection with Britain whom you can neither love nor honor, will be forced and unnatural, and being formed only on the plan of present convenience, will in a little time, fall into a relapse more wretched than the first. But if you say, you can still pass the violations over, then I ask, Hath your house been burnt? Hath your property been destroyed before your face? Are your wife and children destitute of a bed to lie on, or bread to live on? Have you lost a parent or a child by their hands, and yourself the ruined and wretched survivor? If you have not, then are you not a judge of those who have. But if you have, and still can shake hands with the murderers, then are you unworthy the name of husband, father, friend, or lover, and whatever may be your rank or title in life, you have the heart of a coward, and the spirit of a sycophant.

This is not inflaming or exaggerating matters, but trying them by those feelings and affections which nature justifies, and without which, we should be incapable of discharging the social duties of life, or enjoying the felicities of it. I mean not to exhibit horror for the purpose of provoking revenge, but to awaken us from fatal and unmanly slumbers, that we may pursue determinately some fixed object. 'Tis not in the power of England or of Europe to conquer America, if she doth not conquer herself by *delay* and *timidity*. The present winter is worth an age if rightly employed, but if lost or neglected, the whole continent will partake of the misfortune; and there is no punishment which that man doth not deserve, be he, who, or what, or where he will, that may be the means of sacrificing a season so precious and useful.

'Tis repugnant to reason, to the universal order of things, to all examples from former ages, to suppose, that this continent can long remain subject to any external power. The most sanguine in Britain doth not think so. The utmost stretch of human wisdom cannot at this time, compass a plan, short of separation, which can promise the continent even a year's security. Reconciliation is *now* a fallacious dream. Nature hath deserted the connection, and art cannot supply her place. For, as Milton wisely expresses "never can true reconcilement grow where wounds of deadly hate have pierced so deep."

Every quiet method for peace hath been ineffectual. Our prayers have been rejected with disdain; and hath tended to convince us that nothing flatters vanity or confirms obstinacy in Kings more than repeated petitioning—and nothing hath contributed more, than that very measure, to make the Kings of Europe absolute. Witness Denmark and Sweden. Wherefore, since nothing but blows will do, for God's sake let us come to a final separation, and not leave the next generation to be cutting throats under the violated unmeaning names of parent and child.

To say, they will never attempt it again is idle and visionary, we thought so at the repeal of the stamp-act, yet a year or two undeceived us; as well may we suppose that nations which have been once defeated will never renew the quarrel.

As to government matters 'tis not in the power of Britain to do this continent justice: The business of it will soon be too weighty and intricate to be managed with any tolerable degree of convenience, by a power so distant from us; and so very ignorant of us; for if they cannot conquer us, they cannot govern us. To be always running three or four thousand miles with a tale or a petition, waiting four or five months for an answer, which when obtained requires five or six more to explain it in, will in a few years be looked upon as folly and childishness—There was a time when it was proper, and there is a proper time for it to cease.

Small islands not capable of protecting themselves; are the proper objects for government to take under their care: but there is something very absurd, in supposing a Continent to be perpetually governed by an island. In no instance hath nature made the satellite larger than its primary planet, and as England and America with respect to each other reverse the common order of nature, it is evident that they belong to different systems. England to Europe: America to itself.

I am not induced by motives of pride, party or resentment to espouse the doctrine of separation and independence; I am clearly positively, and conscientiously persuaded that 'tis the true interest of this continent to be so; that every thing short of that is mere patchwork, that it can afford no lasting felicity,—that it is leaving the sword to our children, and shrinking back at a time, when a little more, a little further, would have rendered this continent the glory of the earth.

As Britain hath not manifested the least inclination towards a compromise, we may be assured that no terms can be obtained worthy the acceptance of the continent, or any ways equal to the expence of blood and treasure we have been already put to.

The object contended for, ought always to bear some just proportion to the expence. The removal of North, or the whole detestable junto, is a matter unworthy the millions we have expended. A temporary stoppage of trade was an inconvenience, which would have sufficiently ballanced the repeal of all the acts complained of, had such repeals been obtained; but if the whole Continent must take up arms, if every man must be a soldier, 'tis scarcely worth our while to fight against a contemptible ministry only. Dearly, dearly, do we pay for the repeal of the acts, if that is all we fight for; for in a just estimation 'tis as great a folly to pay a Bunker-hill price for law as for land. As I have always considered the independancy of this Continent, as an event which sooner or later must arrive, so from the late rapid progress of the Continent to maturity, the event could not be far off. Wherefore on the breaking out of hostilities, it was not worth the while to have disputed a matter, which time would have finally redressed, unless we meant to be in earnest: otherwise it is like wasting an estate on a suit at law, to regulate the trespasses of a tenant, whose lease is just expiring. No man was a warmer wisher for a reconciliation than myself, before the fatal 19th of April 1775, but the moment the event of that day was made known, I rejected the hardened, sullen-tempered Pharaoh of England for ever; and disdain the wretch, that with the pretended title of FATHER OF HIS PEOPLE can unfeelingly hear of their slaughter, and composedly sleep with their blood upon his soul.

But admitting that matters were

now made up, what would be the event? I answer, the ruin of the Continent. And that for several reasons.

First. The powers of governing still remaining in the hands of the king, he will have a negative over the whole legislation of this Continent: And as he hath shewn himself such an inveterate enemy to liberty, and discovered such a thirst for arbitrary power; is he, or is he not, a proper man to say to these Colonies, *You shall make no laws but what I please!* ? And is there any inhabitant in America so ignorant, as not to know, that according to what is called the *present constitution,* that this Continent can make no laws but what the king gives leave to; and is there any man so unwise, as not to see, that (considering what has happened) he will suffer no laws to be made here, but such as suits his purpose? We may be as effectually enslaved by the want of laws in America, as by submitting to laws made for us in England. After matters are made up (as it is called) can there be any doubt, but the whole power of the crown will be exerted to keep this Continent as low and humble as possible? Instead of going forward, we shall go backward, or be perpetually quarrelling or ridiculously petitioning.—We are already greater than the King wishes us to be, and will he not hereafter endeavour to make us less. To bring the matter to one point, is the power who is jealous of our prosperity, a proper power to govern us? Whoever says *No* to this question is an *Independant* for independency means no more than whether we shall make our own laws, or, whether the King the greatest enemy this Continent hath, or can have, shall tell us, *there shall be no laws but such as I like.*

But the King you'll say, hath a negative in England; the people there can make no laws without his consent. In point of right and good order, there is something very ridiculous that a youth of twenty-one (which hath often happened) shall say to several millions of people older and wiser than himself, "I forbid this or that act of yours to be law." But in this place I decline this sort of reply, though I will never cease to expose the absurdity of it, and only answer that England being the King's residence, and America not so, makes quite another case. The King's negative here is ten times more dangerous and fatal than it can be in England, for there he will scarcely refuse his consent to a bill for putting England into as strong a state of defence as possible, and here he would never suffer such a bill to be passed.

America is only a secondary object in the system of British politics. England consults the good of this country no farther than it answers her own purpose. Wherefore her own interest leads her to suppress the growth of ours in every case which doth not promote her advantage, or in the least interferes with it. A pretty state we should soon be in, under such a second hand government, considering what has happened! Men do not change from enemies to friends by the alteration of a name: And in order to shew that reconciliation now is a dangerous doctrine, I affirm, *that it would be policy in the King at this time, to repeal the acts for the sake of reinstating himself in the govern-*

ment of the provinces; In order that HE MAY ACCOMPLISH BY CRAFT AND SUBTLETY, IN THE LONG RUN, WHAT HE CANNOT DO BY FORCE AND VIOLENCE IN THE SHORT ONE. Reconciliation and ruin are nearly related.

Secondly.—That as even the best terms which we can expect to obtain, can amount to no more than a temporary expedient, or a kind of government by guardianship, which can last no longer than till the Colonies come of age, so the general face and state of things in the interim will be unsettled and unpromising: Emigrants of property will not choose to come to a country whose form of government hangs but by a thread, and who is every day tottering on the brink of commotion and disturbance; And numbers of the present inhabitants would lay hold of the interval to dispose of their effects, and quit the Continent.

But the most powerful of all arguments is, that nothing but independance, i.e. a continental form of government, can keep the peace of the Continent, and preserve it inviolate from civil wars. I dread the event of a reconciliation with Britain now, as it is more than probable, that it will be followed by a revolt some where or other, the consequences of which may be far more fatal than all the malice of Britain.

Thousands are already ruined by British barbarity; (thousands more will probably suffer the same fate;) Those men have other feelings than us who have nothing suffered. All they now possess is liberty, what they before enjoyed is sacrificed to its service, and having nothing more to lose, they disdain submission. Besides, the general temper of the Colonies towards a British government will be like that of a youth, who is nearly out of his time; they will care very little about her: And a government which cannot preserve the peace, is no government at all, and in that case we pay our money for nothing; and pray what is it that Britain can do, whose power will be wholly on paper, should a civil tumult break out the very day after reconciliation? I have heard some men say, many of whom I believe spoke without thinking, that they dreaded an independance, fearing that it would produce civil wars: It is but seldom that our first thoughts are truly correct, and that is the case here; for there are ten times more to dread from a patched up connection, than from independance. I make the sufferers case my own, and I protest, that were I driven from house and home, my property destroyed, and my circumstances ruined, that as a man sensible of injuries, I could never relish the doctrine of reconciliation, or consider myself bound thereby.

The Colonies hath manifested such a spirit of good order and obedience to continental government, as is sufficient to make every reasonable person easy and happy on that head. No man can assign the least pretence for his fears, on any other grounds, than such as are truly childish and ridiculous, viz., that one colony will be striving for superiority over another.

Where there are no distinctions, there can be no superiority; perfect equality affords no temptation. The Republics of Europe are all, (and we may say always) in peace. Holland and Switzerland, are without wars, foreign or domestic: Monarchical governments, it is true, are never long at rest; the crown itself is a temptation to enterprising ruffians at home; and that degree of pride and insolence ever attendant on regal authority, swells into a rupture with foreign powers in instances, where a republican government by being formed on more natural principles, would negociate the mistake.

If there is any true cause for fear respecting independance, it is because no plan is yet laid down. Men do not see their way out—Wherefore, as an opening into that business I offer the following hints; at the same time modestly affirming, that I have no other opinion of them myself, than that they may be the means of giving rise to something better. Could the straggling thoughts of individuals be collected, they would frequently form materials for wise and able men to improve into useful matter.

Let the assemblies be annual with a president only. The representation more equal. Their business wholly domestic, and subject to the authority of a Continental Congress.

Let each Colony be divided into six, eight or ten convenient districts, each district to send a proper number of Delegates to Congress, so that each Colony send at least thirty. The whole number in Congress will be at least 390. Each congress to sit and to choose a president by the following method. When the Delegates are met, let a Colony be taken from the whole thirteen Colonies by lot, after which let the Congress choose (by ballot) a president from out of the Delegates of that province. In the next Congress let a Colony be taken by lot from twelve only, omitting that Colony from which the president was taken in the former Congress, and so proceeding on till the whole thirteen shall have had their proper rotation. And in order that nothing may pass into a law but what is satisfactorily just, not less than three fifths of the Congress to be called a majority—He that will promote discord under a government so equally formed as this, would have joined Lucifer in his revolt.

But as there is a peculiar delicacy from whom, or in what manner this business must first arise, and as it seems most agreeable and consistent, that it should come from some intermediate body between the governed and the governors, that is, between the Congress and the People Let a CONTINENTAL CONFERENCE be held in the following manner, and for the following purpose,

A Committee of twenty six members of congress, viz. Two for each Colony. Two Members from each House of Assembly, or Provincial convention; and five Representatives of the people at large, to be chosen in the capital city or town of each Province, for, and in behalf of the whole Province, by as many qualified voters as shall think proper to attend from all parts of the Province for that purpose: or if more convenient, the Representatives may be chosen in two or three of the most populous parts thereof. In this CONFERENCE thus assembled, will be united the two grand principles of business, *knowledge* and *power*. The members of Congress, Assemblies, or Conventions, by having had experience in national concerns, will be able and useful counsellors, and the whole, being impowered by the people, will have a truly legal authority.

The conferring members being met, let their business be to frame a CONTINENTAL CHARTER, or Charter of the United Colonies; (answering, to what is called the Magna Charta of England) fixing the number and manner of choosing Members of Congress, Members of Assembly, with their date of sitting; and drawing the line of business and jurisdiction between them: Always remembering, that our strength and happiness is Continental, not Provincial. Securing freedom and property to all men, and above all things, the free exercise of religion, according to the dictates of conscience; with such other matter as is necessary for a charter to contain. Immediately after which, the said conference to dissolve, and the bodies which shall be chosen conformable to the said charter, to be the Legislators and Governors of this Continent, for the time being: Whose peace and happiness, may GOD preserve. AMEN.

Should any body of men be hereafter delegated for this or some similar purpose, I offer them the following extracts from that wise observer on Governments, Dragonetti. "The science" says he "of the Politician consists in fixing the true point of happiness and freedom. Those men would deserve the gratitude of ages, who should discover a mode of government that contained the greatest sum of individual happiness, with the least national expense."

But where says some is the King of America? I'll tell you Friend, he reigns above; and doth not make havoc of mankind like the Royal Brute of Great Britain. Yet that we may not appear to be defective even in earthly honours, let a day be solemnly set apart for proclaiming the Charter; let it be brought forth placed on the divine law, the word of god; let a Crown be placed thereon, by which the world may know, that so far as we approve of monarchy, that in America THE LAW IS KING. For as in absolute governments the King is law, so in free countries the law *ought* to be King; and there ought to be no other. But lest any ill use should afterwards arise, let the Crown at the conclusion of the ceremony be demolished, and scattered among the People whose right it is.

A government of our own is our natural right: and when a man seriously reflects on the precariousness of human affairs, he will become convinced, that it is infinitely wiser and safer, to form a constitution of our own, in a cool deliberate manner, while we have it in our power, than to trust such an interesting event to time and chance. If we omit it now, some Massanello may hereafter arise, who laying hold of popular disquietudes, may collect together the desperate and the discontented, and by assuming to themselves the powers of government, may sweep away the liberties of the Continent like a deluge. Should the government of America return again into the hands of Britain, the tottering situation of things will be a temptation for some desperate adventurer to try his fortune; and in such a case, what relief can Britain give? Ere she could hear the news, the fatal business might be done; and ourselves suffering like the wretched Britons under the oppression of the Conqueror.

Ye that oppose independance now, ye know not what ye do: ye are opening a door to eternal tyranny, by keeping vacant the seat of government. There are thousands, and tens of thousands, who would think it glorious to expel from the Continent, that barbarous and hellish power, which hath stirred up the Indians and the Negroes to destroy us, the cruelty hath a double guilt, it is dealing brutally by us, and treacherously by them.

To talk of friendship with those in whom our reason forbids us to have faith, and our affections wounded thro' a thousand pores instruct us to detest, is madness and folly. Every day wears out the little remains of kindred between us and them, and can there be any reason to hope, that as the relationship expires, the affection will encrease, or that we shall agree better, when we have ten times more and greater concerns to quarrel over than ever?

Ye that tell us of harmony and reconciliation, can ye restore to us the time that is past? Can ye give to prostitution its former innocence? Neither can ye reconcile Britain and America. The last cord now is broken, the people of England are presenting addresses against us. There are injuries which nature cannot forgive; she would cease to be nature if she did. As well can the lover forgive the ravisher of his mistress, as the Continent forgive the murders of Britain. The Almighty hath implanted in us these unextinguishable feelings for good and wise purposes. They are the guardians of his image in our hearts. They distinguish us from the herd of common animals. The social compact would dissolve, and justice be extirpated from the earth, or have only a casual existence were we callous to the touches of affection. The robber and the murderer would often escape unpunished, did not the injuries which our tempers sustain, provoke us into justice.

O ye that love mankind! Ye that dare oppose not only the tyranny, but the tyrant, stand forth! Every spot of the old world is over-run with oppression. Freedom hath been hunted round the globe. Asia and Africa have long expelled her.—Europe regards her like a stranger, and England hath given her warning to depart. O! receive the fugitive, and prepare in time an asylum for mankind. * * *

1776

THE AMERICAN CRISIS

LETTER I

These are the times that try men's souls: The summer soldier and the sunshine patriot will, in this crisis, shrink from the service of his country; but he that stands it NOW, deserves the love and thanks of man and woman. Tyranny, like hell, is not easily conquered; yet we have this consolation with us, that the harder the conflict, the more glorious the triumph. What we obtain too cheap, we esteem too lightly:—'tis dearness only that gives every thing its value. Heaven knows how to put a proper price upon its goods; and it would be strange indeed, if so celestial an article as FREEDOM should not be highly rated. Britain, with an army to enforce her tyrrany, has declared that she has a right (*not only to* TAX) but "to BIND *us in* ALL CASES

WHATSOEVER," and if being *bound in that manner* is not slavery, then is there not such a thing as slavery upon earth. Even the expression is impious for so unlimited a power can belong only to GOD.

WHETHER the Independence of the Continent was declared too soon, or delayed too long, I will not now enter into as an argument; my own simple opinion is, that had it been eight months earlier, it would have been much better. We did not make a proper use of last winter, neither could we, while we were in a dependent state. However, the fault, if it were one, was all our own; we have none to blame but ourselves. But no great deal is lost yet; all that Howe has been doing for this month past is rather a ravage than a conquest, which the spirit of the Jerseys a year ago would have quickly repulsed, and which time and a little resolution will soon recover.

I have as little superstition in me as any man living, but my secret opinion has ever been, and still is, that GOD Almighty will not give up a people to military destruction, or leave them unsupportedly to perish, who have so earnestly and so repeatedly sought to avoid the calamities of war, by every decent method which wisdom could invent. Neither have I so much of the infidel in me, as to suppose, that He has relinquished the government of the world, and given us up to the care of devils; and as I do not, I cannot see on what grounds the king of Britain can look up to heaven for help against us: a common murderer, a highwayman, or a house breaker, has as good a pretence as he.

'TIS surprising to see how rapidly a panic will sometimes run through a country. All nations and ages have been subject to them: Britain has trembled like an ague at the report of a French fleet of flat bottomed boats; and in the fourteenth [fifteenth] century the whole English army, after ravaging the kingdom of France, was driven back like men petrified with fear; and this brave exploit was performed by a few broken forces collected and headed by a woman, Joan of Arc. Would, that heaven might inspire some Jersey maid to spirit up her countrymen, and save her fair fellow sufferers from ravage and ravishment! Yet panics, in some cases, have their uses; they produce as much good as hurt. Their duration is always short; the mind soon grows thro' them, and acquires a firmer habit than before. But their peculiar advantage is, that they are the touchstones of sincerity and hypocrisy, and bring things and men to light, which might otherwise have lain forever undiscovered. In fact, they have the same effect on secret traitors, which an imaginary apparition would have upon a private murderer. They sift out the hidden thoughts of man, and hold them up in public to the world. Many a disguised Tory has lately shewn his head, that shall penitentially solemnize with curses the day on which Howe arrived upon the Delaware.

As I was with the troops at fort Lee, and marched with them to the edge of Pennsylvania, I am well acquainted with many circumstances, which those, who live at a distance, know but little or nothing of. Our situation there was exceedingly cramped, the place being a narrow neck of land between the North river and the Hackensack. Our force was inconsiderable, being not one fourth so great as Howe could bring against us. We had no army at hand to have relieved the garrison, had we shut ourselves up and stood on the defence. Our ammunition, light artillery, and the best part of our stores, had been removed upon the apprehension that Howe would endeavour to penetrate the Jersies, in which case fort Lee could be of no use to us; for it must occur to every thinking man, whether in the army or not, that these kind of field forts are only for temporary purposes, and last in use no longer than the enemy directs his force against the particular object, which such forts are raised to defend. Such was our situation and condition at fort Lee on the morning of the 20th of November, when an officer arrived with information, that the enemy with 200 boats had landed about seven miles above: Major General [Nathaniel] Green, who commanded the garrison, immediately ordered them under arms, and sent express to his Excellency General Washington at the town of Hackensack, distant by the way of the ferry six miles. Our first object was to secure the bridge over the Hackensack, which laid up the river between the enemy and us, about six miles from us and three from them. General Washington arrived in about three quarters of an hour, and marched at the head of the troops towards the bridge, which place I expected we should have a brush for; however they did not choose to dispute it with us, and the greatest part of our troops went over the bridge, the rest over the ferry, except some which passed at a mill on a small creek, between the bridge and the ferry, and made their way through some marshy grounds up to the town of Hackensack, and there passed the river. We brought off as much baggage as the waggons could contain, the rest was lost. The simple object was to bring off the garrison, and to march them on till they could be strengthened by the Jersey or Pennsylvania militia, so as to be enabled to make a stand. We staid four days at Newark, collected our out-posts with some of the Jersey militia, and marched out twice to meet the enemy, on information of their being advancing, though our numbers were greatly inferiour to theirs. Howe, in my little opinion, committed a great error in generalship, in not throwing a body of forces off from Staaten Island through Amboy, by which means he might have seized all our stores at Brunswick, and intercepted our march into Pennsylvania: But, if we believe the power of hell to be limited, we must likewise believe that their agents are under some providential controul.

I shall not now attempt to give all the particulars of our retreat to the Delaware; suffice it for the present to say, that both officers and men, though greatly harassed and fatigued, frequently without rest, covering, or provision, the inevitable consequences of a long retreat, bore it with a manly and a martial spirit. All their wishes were one, which was, that the country would turn out and help them to drive the enemy back. Voltaire has remarked, that king William never appeared to full advantage but in difficulties and in action; the same remark may be made on General Washington, for the character fits him.

There is a natural firmness in some minds which cannot be unlocked by triffles, but which, when unlocked, discovers a cabinet of fortitude; and I reckon it among those kind of public blessings, which we do not immediately see, that God hath blessed him with uninterrupted health, and given him a mind that can even flourish upon care.

I shall conclude this paper with some miscellaneous remarks on the state of our affairs; and shall begin with asking the following question, Why is it that the enemy hath left the New-England provinces, and made these middle ones the seat of war? The answer is easy: New-England is not infested with Tories, and we are. I have been tender in raising the cry against these men, and used numberless arguments to shew them their danger, but it will not do to sacrifice a world either to their folly or their baseness. The period is now arrived, in which either they or we must change our sentiments, or one or both must fall. And what is a Tory? Good God! what is he? I should not be afraid to go with a hundred Whigs against a thousand Tories, were they to attempt to get into arms. Every Tory is a coward for servile, slavish, self-interested fear is the foundation of Toryism; and a man under such influence, though he may be cruel, never can be brave.

But, before the line of irrecoverable separation be drawn between us, let us reason the matter together: Your conduct is an invitation to the enemy, yet not one in a thousand of you has heart enough to join him. Howe is as much deceived by you as the American cause is injured by you. He expects you will all take up arms, and flock to his standard with muskets on your shoulders. Your opinions are of no use to him, unless you support him personally; for 'tis soldiers, and not Tories, that he wants.

I once felt all that kind of anger, which a man ought to feel, against the mean principles that are held by the Tories: A noted one, who kept a tavern at Amboy, was standing at his door, with as pretty a child in his hand, about eight or nine years old, as most I ever saw, and after speaking his mind as freely as he thought was prudent, finished with this unfatherly expression, *"Well! give me peace in my day."* Not a man lives on the Continent but fully believes that a separation must some time or other finally take place, and a generous parent would have said, *"If there must be trouble, let it be in my day, that my child may have peace;"* and this single reflection, well applied, is sufficient to awaken every man to duty. Not a place upon earth might be so happy as America. Her situation is remote from all the wrangling world, and she has nothing to do but to trade with them. A man may easily distinguish in himself between temper and principle, and I am as confident, as I am that God governs the world, that America will never be happy till she gets clear of foreign dominion. Wars, without ceasing, will break out till that period arrives, and the Continent must in the end be conqueror; for, though the flame of liberty may sometimes cease to shine, the coal can never expire.

America did not, nor does not, want force; but she wanted a proper application of that force. Wisdom is not the purchase of a day, and it is no wonder that we should err at the first setting off. From an excess of tenderness, we were unwilling to raise an army, and trusted our cause to the temporary defence of a well meaning militia. A summer's experience has now taught us better; yet with those troops, while they were collected, we were able to set bounds to the progress of the enemy, and, thank God! they are again assembling. I always considered a militia as the best troops in the world for a sudden exertion, but they will not do for a long campaign. Howe, it is probable, will make an attempt on this city; should he fail on this side the Delaware, he is ruined: if he succeeds, our cause is not ruined. He stakes all on his side against a part on ours; admitting he succeeds, the consequence will be, that armies from both ends of the Continent will march to assist their suffering friends in the middle States; for he cannot go every where, it is impossible. I consider Howe as the greatest enemy the Tories have; he is bringing a war into their country, which, had it not been for him and partly for themselves, they had been clear of. Should he now be expelled, I wish, with all the devotion of a Christian, that the names of Whig and Tory may never more be mentioned; but should the Tories give him encouragement to come, or assistance if he come, I as sincerely wish that our next year's arms may expell them from the Continent, and the Congress appropriate their possessions to the relief of those who have suffered in well doing. A single successful battle next year will settle the whole. America could carry on a two years war by the confiscation of the property of disaffected persons, and be made happy by their expulsion. Say not that this is revenge, call it rather the soft resentment of a suffering people, who, having no object in view but the GOOD of ALL, have staked their OWN ALL upon a seemingly doubtful event. Yet it is folly to argue against determined hardness; eloquence may strike the ear, and the language of sorrow draw forth the tear of compassion, but nothing can reach the heart that is steeled with prejudice.

Quitting this class of men, I turn with the warm ardour of a friend to those who have nobly stood, and are yet determined to stand the matter out: I call not upon a few, but upon all; not on THIS State or THAT State, but on EVERY State; up and help us; lay your shoulders to the wheel; better have too much force than too little, when so great an object is at stake. Let it be told to the future world, that in the depth of winter, when nothing but hope and virtue could survive, that the city and the country, alarmed at one common danger, came forth to meet and repulse it. Say not, that thousands are gone, turn out your tens of thousands; throw not the burthen of the day upon Providence, but *"shew your faith by your works,"* that God may bless you. It matters not where you live, or what rank of life you hold, the evil or the blessing will reach you all. The far and the near, the home counties and the back, the rich and the poor, shall suffer or rejoice alike. The heart that feels not now, is dead: The blood of his children will curse his cowardice, who shrinks back at a time when a little might have saved the whole, and made *them* happy. I love the man that can smile in trouble, that can gather strength from distress, and grow brave by reflection. 'Tis the business of little minds to shrink; but he whose heart is firm, and whose conscience approves his conduct, will pursue his principles unto death. My own line of reasoning is to myself as strait and clear as a ray of light. Not all the treasures of the world, so far as I believe, could have induced me to support an offensive war, for I think it murder; but if a thief break into my house, burn and destroy my property, and kill or threaten to kill me, or those that are in it, and to *"bind me in all cases whatsoever,"* to his absolute will, am I to suffer it? What signifies it to me, whether he who does it, is a king or a common man; my countryman or not my countryman? whether it be done by an individual villain, or an army of them? If we reason to the root of things we shall find no difference; neither can any just cause be assigned why we should punish in the one case, and pardon in the other. Let them call me rebel, and welcome, I feel no concern from it; but I should suffer the misery of devils, were I to make a whore of my soul by swearing allegiance to one, whose character is that of a sottish, stuped, stubborn, worthless, brutish man. I conceive likewise a horrid idea in receiving mercy from a being, who at the last day shall be shrieking to the rocks and mountains to cover him, and fleeing with terror from the orphan, the widow and the slain of America.

THERE are cases which cannot be overdone by language, and this is one. There are persons too who see not the full extent of the evil which threatens them; they solace themselves with hopes that the enemy, if they succeed, will be merciful. It is the madness of folly to expect mercy from those who have refused to do justice; and even mercy, where conquest is the object, is only a trick of war: The cunning of the fox is as murderous as the violence of the wolfe; and we ought to guard equally against both. Howe's first object is partly by threats and partly by promises, to terrify or seduce the people to deliver up their arms, and receive mercy. The ministry recommended the same plan to Gage, and this is what the Tories call making their peace; *"a peace which passeth all understanding" indeed!* A peace which would be the immediate forerunner of a worse ruin than any we have yet thought of. Ye men of Pennsylvania, do reason upon those things! Were the back countries to give up their arms, they would fall an easy prey to the Indians, who are all armed: This perhaps is what some Tories would not be sorry for. Were the home counties to deliver up their arms, they would be exposed to the resentment of the back counties, who would then have it in their power to chastise their defection at pleasure. And were any one state to give up its arms, THAT state must be garrisoned by all Howe's army of Britons and Hessians to preserve it from the anger of the rest. Mutual fear is the principal link in the chain of mutual love, and woe be to that state that breaks the compact. Howe is mercifully inviting you to barbarous destruction, and men must be either rogues or fools that will not see it. I dwell not upon the vapours of imagination; I bring reason to your ears; and in language as plain as A, B, C, hold up truth to your eyes.

I thank God, that I fear not. I see no real cause for fear. I know our situation well, and can see the way of it. While our army was collected, Howe dared not risk a battle, and it is no credit to him that he decamped from the White Plains, and waited a mean opportunity to ravage the defenceless Jersies; but it is great credit to us, that, with an handful of men, we sustained an orderly retreat for near an hundred miles, brought off our ammunition, all our field pieces, the greatest part of our stores, and had four rivers to pass. None can say that our retreat was precipitate, for we were near three weeks in performing it, that the country might have time to come in. Twice we marched back to meet the enemy and remained out till dark. The sign of fear was not seen in our camp, and had not some of the cowardly and disaffected inhabitants spread false alarms thro' the country, the Jersies had never been ravaged. Once more we are again collected and collecting; our new army at both ends of the Continent is recruiting fast, and we shall be able to open the next campaign with sixty thousand men, well armed and cloathed. This is our situation, and who will may know it. By perseverance and fortitude we have the prospect of a glorious issue; by cowardice and submission, the sad choice of a variety of evils—a ravaged country—a depopulated city—habitations without safety, and slavery without hope—our homes turned into barracks and baudy-houses for Hessians, and a future race to provide for whose fathers we shall doubt of. Look on this picture, and weep over it!—and if there yet remains one thoughtless wretch who believes it not, let him suffer it unlamented.

Common Sense.
1776

LIBERTY TREE

I

In a chariot of light from the regions of day,
The Goddess of Liberty came;
Ten thousand celestials directed the way,
And hither conducted the dame.
A fair budding branch from the gardens above,
Where millions with millions agree,
She brought in her hand as a pledge of her love,
And the plant she named, *Liberty Tree.*

II

The celestial exotic struck deep in the ground,
Like a native it flourish'd and bore;
The fame of its fruit drew the nations around,
To seek out this peaceable shore.
Unmindful of names or distinctions they came,
For freemen like brothers agree;
With one spirit endued, they one friendship pursued,
And their temple was *Liberty tree.*

III

Beneath this fair tree, like the patriarchs of old,
Their bread in contentment they eat
Unvex'd with the troubles of silver and gold,
The cares of the grand and the great.

With timber and tar they Old England supply'd,
And supported her pow'r on the sea;
Her battles they fought, without getting a groat,
For the honor of *Liberty tree*.

IV

But hear, O ye swains, ('tis a tale most profane,)
How all the tyrannical powers,
Kings, Commons, and Lords, are uniting amain,
To cut down this guardian of ours;
From the east to the west, blow the trumpet to arms,
Thro' the land let the sound of it flee,
Let the far and the near,—all unite with a cheer,
In defense of our *Liberty tree*.

ATLANTICUS
1775

From *THE AGE OF REASON*

[A CREED]

It has been my intention, for several years past, to publish my thoughts upon religion. I am well aware of the difficulties that attend the subject; and from that consideration, had reserved it to a more advanced period of life. I intended it to be the last offering I should make to my fellow-citizens of all nations; and that at a time when the purity of the motive that induced me to it, could not admit of a question, even by those who might disapprove the work.

The circumstance that has now taken place in France, of the total abolition of the whole national order of priesthood, and of every thing appertaining to compulsive systems of religion, and compulsive articles of faith, has not only precipitated my intention, but rendered a work of this kind exceedingly necessary; lest, in the general wreck of superstition, of false systems of government, and false theology, we lose sight of morality, of humanity, and of the theology that is true.

As several of my colleagues, and others of my fellow-citizens of France, have given me the example of making their voluntary and individual profession of faith, I also will make mine; and I do this with all that sincerity and frankness with which the mind of man communicates with itself.

I believe in one God, and no more; and I hope for happiness beyond this life.

I believe the equality of man, and I believe that religious duties consist in doing justice, loving mercy, and endeavouring to make our fellow-creatures happy.

But lest it should be supposed that I believe many other things in addition to these, I shall in the progress of this work, declare the things I do not believe, and my reasons for not believing them.

I do not believe in the creed professed by the Jewish church, by the Roman church, by the Greek church, by the Turkish church, by the Protestant church, nor by any church that I know of. My own mind is my own church.

All national institutions of churches, whether Jewish, Christian, or Turkish, appear to me no other than human inventions set up to terrify and enslave mankind, and monopolize power and profit.

I do not mean by this declaration to condemn those who believe otherwise. They have the same right to their belief as I have to mine. But it is necessary to the happiness of man, that he be mentally faithful to himself. Infidelity does not consist in believing or in disbelieving; it consists in professing to believe what he does not believe.

It is impossible to calculate the moral mischief, if I may so express it, that mental lying has produced in society. When a man has so far corrupted and prostituted the chastity of his mind, as to subscribe his professional belief to things he does not believe, he has prepared himself for the commission of every other crime. He takes up the trade of a priest for the sake of gain, and, in order to *qualify* himself for that trade, he begins with a perjury. Can we conceive anything more destructive to morality than this?

Soon after I had published the pamphlet, "*Common Sense,*" in America, I saw the exceeding probability that a Revolution in the System of Government would be followed by a revolution in the system of religion. The adulterous connection of church and state, wherever it had taken place, whether Jewish, Christian, or Turkish, had so effectually prohibited, by pains and penalties, every discussion upon established creeds, and upon first principles of religion, that until the system of government should be changed, those subjects could not be brought fairly and openly before the world: but that whenever this should be done, a revolution in the system of religion would follow. Human inventions and priest craft would be detected; and man would return to the pure, unmixed, and unadulterated belief of one God, and no more.

1794

III. ANNE HULTON
(?–1779)

LETTERS

[THE CONSEQUENCES OF THE TEA PARTY]

Jan*y* 31*st,* 1774.

You will perhaps expect me to give you some Acc*t* of the State of B—— & late proceedings here but really the times are too bad & the Scenes too shocking for me to describe. I suppose you will have heard long before this arrives of the fate of the Tea—Whilst this was in suspence. The Commiss*rs* of the Customs & the Tea Consignees were obliged to seek refuge at the Castle. My Bro*r* happen*d* to be there on a vissit of a long engagement to Col Lessley when those other Gentlemen came over. He continue*d* there about twenty days, in the mean time vissiting his own House (about 8 Miles from the Castle) several times. The Col*o* & the Gentlemen of his Choir render*d* the retreat as agreeable as possible by their polite Attention to every Refugee. After the destruction of the Tea. my Bro*r* returnd Home & the other Commiss*rs* Left the Castle. the violent fury of the People having subsided a little. One woud have tho*t* before that all the Malice that Earth & Hell coud raise were pointed against the Governor. Mr. Paxton (one of the Commiss*rs*) & the Tea Consignees, two of whom are the Govern*rs* Sons, the others are M*r* Clark a respecta [ble] Old Gentleman & his Sons, with two other Merchants M*r*. Haliwell another Commiss*r* & likewise of this Country was an object of their threats.

The Tea Consignees remain Still at the Castle. Six weeks since the Tea was destroyd, and there is no prospect of thier ever returning & residing in Boston with Safety. This place, & all the Towns about enterd into a written agrement not to afford them any Shelter or protection, so that they are not only banishd from their families & homes, but their retreat is cut off, & their interest greatly injured by ruining their Trade.

It is indeed a severe case, & can hardly be credited, I think, that the Gov*rs* Sons sho'd be treated as fugitives & outlaws in their own Country. One of them lately went from the Castle, & with his Wife to her Fathers house, a Gentleman at Plymouth 40 Miles from Boston They had no sooner arrived there, but the Bells toll*d* and the Town Assemble*g* instantly went to the House, demanded that M*r*. Hutchinson shoud depart immediately out of the Town. Col*o* Watson his father in law, spoke to them, saying that it was so late at Night, & the Weather so severe, that M*r* H. & his wife cou'd not without great inconvenience remove from his house that night, but promised them, they shoud go in the Morning by 9 o'Clock. The time came, and they were not gone, when the Town bells tolld again, & the people gatherd about the house. Upon which the Young Couple Sett off in a great snow storm. & nobody knows since where they are.

But the most shocking cruelty was exercised a few Nights ago, upon a poor Old Man a Tidesman one Malcolm he is reckond creasy, a quarrel was pickd w*th* him, he was afterward taken, & Tarrd, & featherd. Theres no Law that knows a punishment for the greatest Crimes beyond what this is, of cruel torture. And this instance exceeds any other before it he was stript Stark naked, one of the severest cold nights this Winter, his body coverd all over with Tar, then with feathers, his arm dislocated in tearing off his cloaths, he was drag*d* in a Cart with thousands attending, some beating him w*th* clubs and Knocking him out of the Cart, then in again. They gave him several severe whipings, at different parts of the Town. This Spectacle of horror & sportive cruelty was exhibited for about five hours.

The unhappy wretch they say behaved with the greatest intrepidity, & fortitude all the while. before he was taken, defended himself a long time against Numbers, & afterw*ds* when under Torture they demanded of him to curse his Masters The K: Gov*r* &c which they coud not make him do, but he still cried, Curse all Traitors. They bro*t* him to the Gallows & put a rope about his neck say*g* they woud hang him he said he wishd they woud, but that they coud not for God was above the Devil. The Doctors say that it is imposible this poor creature can live They say his flesh comes off his back in Stakes

It is the second time he has been

Tarrd & featherd & this is look*d* upon more to intimidate the Judges & others than a spite to the unhappy Victim tho' they owe him a Grudge for some things, particul*y* he was with Gov*r* Tryon in the Battle with the Regulators & the Governor has declared that he was of great servise to him in that Affair, by his undaunted Spirit encountering the greatest dangers

Gov*r* Tryon had sent him a gift of ten Guineas just before this inhuman treatment. he has a Wife & family & an Aged Father & Mother who they say saw the Spectacle w*ch* no indiffer*t* person can mention without horror.

These few instances amongst many serve to shew the abject State of Governm*t* & the licentiousness & barbarism of the times. There's no Majestrate that dare or will act to suppress the Outrages. No person is secure there are many Objects pointed at, at this time & when once mark'd out for Vengence, their ruin is certain.

The Judges have only a weeks time allow'd them to consider, whether they will take the Salaries from the Crown or no. Gov*r* Hutchinson is going to England as soon as the Season will permit.

We are under no apprehension at present on our own Acc*t* but we can't look upon our Safety, secure for Long

[July 8, 1774.]

* * * The concern you express for your friends in these troublesome times here, deserved an immediate acknowledgment, but indeed I've waited some weeks for the oportunity of a Liverp*l* Vessil which I heard was expected, yet none has arriv'd this Spring, & I can't delay it longer, tho' as I understand Letters by Lond*n* Ships are generaly put in at Portsmouth—a long way to travel by Land.

I imagine you will be desirous to Know how the New Acts of Parliam*t* operate here, & how y*r* friends are affected by the Commotions, & disturbances of the Publick. I am sorry to say there appears no disposition yet in the People towards complying with the Port Bill,—They carry thier Melasses & other Goods easily by Land from Salem, & find little inconvenience at present from its operation, The distress it will bring on the Town will not be felt very sever'ly before Winter, when the Roads will be impassible. There's little prospect of Boston Port being Opend this Year. The Leaders of the Faction are only more unwearied, & are pursuing every measure to draw the People onto resistance, & to irritate Governm*t* more, & more and which probably will end in the total ruin of the Town & the Individuals

It is now a very gloomy place, the Streets almost empty, many families have removed from it, & the Inhabitants are divided into several parties, at variance, & quarreling with each other, some appear desponding, others full of rage. The People of Property of best sense & Characters feel the Tyrrany of the Leaders, & foresee the Consequences of their proceedings, woud gladly extricate themselves from the difficulties, & distress they are involv*d* in by makeing their peace with G: Britain, & speedily submitting to the Conditions & penalties required.

Those who are well disposed towards Governm*t* (more from interest than principle it's to be feard, as there are few will*g* to acknowledge the Authority of Parliam*t*) are termd Tories. they daily increase, & have made some efforts to take the power out of the hands of the Patriots, but they are intimidated & overpowered by Numbers, & the Arts, & Machinations of the Leader, who Governs absolutly, the Minds & the Passions of the People—by publishing numberless falshoods to impose on their credulity, & various artifices to influence or terrify. The Ministers from the Pulpit & the Committee of Correspond*ce* by writing inflame the Minds of the ignorant Country People. Their endeavors to engage the Other Colonies to shut up their Ports, & the Merch*ts* here to joyn in a Nonimportation Agrement, proving without effect. The next plan is in opposition to the Merch*ts* & which if it spreads must be attended w*th* the ruin of most of 'em here 'tis a Solemn League & Covenant, not to use any British Manufactures, till the Port is opend, & the New Acts repeald. This is a deep & diabolical scheme, & some people are taken into the Snare, but it's to be hoped the progress of it will be stopd. Gen*l* Gage who conducts himself with great good sense & spirit, issues a Proclaimation Against it to warn 'em of its Consequences, They are startled in general, however, the little town of Marlborough has had the Audacity to burn the Gen*l* in effigy w*th* the Proclaimation.

There are four Regiments & a Train of Artillery now encamped on the Common at Boston, & several Men of War [in] y*e* Harbor. Tho' as yet we are in no wise humbled. We [expect] support from the other Colonies, & build much on a general Congress to be held in Sept*r* or Octo*r* of Deputies from all the [Colonies] We are told that Blocking up the Port is the best thing that can be for Americans, that it will unite the Colonies against G: B:, distress ther Manufactorers and raise our friends, a numerous body as we have been informed by D*r* Frankland, viz the Dissenters, & the Commercial part of the Nation, to exert themselves in our favor, & that we may expect a Rebellion there, which will answer our purpose, & we shall become intirely free & Independant. But if we now submit—Our Lands will be taxd—Popery introduced & we shall be Slaves for ever. I mention these as Some of the Artifices & Arguments which Keep up the spirit of opposition [by] w*ch* the People are inflamed to the highest degree.

However I don't despair of seeing Peace & tranquility in America, tho' they talk very high & furious at present. They are all preparing their Arms & Amunition & say if any of the Leaders are seizd, they will make reprizals on the friends of Gover'ment. Three weeks will bring on the Crises. * * *

(1774) 1927

[CONCORD AND LEXINGTON]

* * * On the 18*th* ins*t* at 11 at Night, about 800 Grenadiers & light Infantry were ferry'd across the Bay to Cambridge, from whence they march*d* to Concord, about 20 Miles.

The Congress had been lately assembled at that place, & it was imagined that the General had intelligence of a Magazine being formed there & that they were going to destroy it.

The People in the Country (who are all furnished with Arms & have what they call Minute Companys in every Town ready to march on any alarm), had a signal it's supposed by a light from one of the Steeples in Town, Upon the Troops embarkg. The alarm spread thro' the Country, so that before daybreak the people in general were in Arms & on their March to Concord. About Daybreak a number of the People appeard before the Troops near Lexington. They were called to, to disperse, when they fired on the Troops & ran off, Upon which the Light Infantry pursued them & brought down about fifteen of them. The Troops went on to Concord & executed the business they were sent on, & on their return found two or three of their people Lying in the Agonies of Death, scalp'd & their Noses & ears cut off & Eyes bored out—Which exasperated the Soldiers exceedingly—a prodigious number of People now occupying the Hills, woods, & Stone Walls along the road. The Light Troops drove some parties from the hills, but all the road being inclosed with Stone Walls Served as a cover to the Rebels, from whence they fired on the Troops still running off whenever they had fired, but still supplied by fresh Numbers who came from many parts of the Country. In this manner were the Troops harrased in their return for Seven or eight Miles they were almost exhausted & had expended near the whole of their Ammunition when to their great joy they were releived by a Brigade of Troops under the command of Lord Percy with two pieces of Artillery. The Troops now combated with fresh Ardour, & marched in their return with undaunted countenances, recieving Sheets of fire all the way for many Miles, yet having no visible Enemy to combat with, for they never woud face 'em in an open field, but always skulked & fired from behind Walls, & trees, & out of Windows of Houses, but this cost them dear for the Soldiers enterd those dwellings, & put all the Men to death. Lord Percy has gained great honor by his conduct thro' this day of severe Servise he was exposed to the hottest of the fire & animated the Troops with great coolness & spirit. Several officers are wounded & about 100 Soldiers. The killed amount to near 50, as to the Enemy we can have no exact acc*t* but it is said there was about ten times the Number of them engaged, & that near 1000 of 'em have fallen.

The Troops returned to Charlestown about Sunset after having some of 'em marched near fifty miles, & being engaged from Daybreak in Action, without respite, or refreshment, & about ten in the Evening they were brought back to Boston. The next day the Country pourd down its Thousands, and at this time from the entrance of Boston Neck at Roxbury round by Cambridge to Charlestown is surrounded by at least 20,000 Men, who are raising batteries on three or four different Hills. We are now cut off from all communication with the

Country & many people must soon perish with famine in this place. Some families have laid in store of Provisions against a Siege. We are threatned that whilst the Out Lines are attacked *wth* a rising of the Inhabitants within, & fire & sword, a dreadful prospect before us, and you know how many & how dear are the objects of our care. The Lord preserve us all & grant us an happy issue out of these troubles.

For several nights past, I have expected to be roused by the firing of Cannon. Tomorrow is Sunday, & we may hope for one day of rest, at present a Solemn dead silence reigns in the Streets, numbers have packed up their effects, & quited the Town, but the General has put a Stop to any more removing, & here remains in Town about 9000 Souls (besides the Servants of the Crown) These are the greatest Security, the General declared that if a Gun is fired within the Town the inhabitants shall fall a Sacrifice. Amidst our distress & apprehension, I am rejoyced our British Hero was preserved, My Lord Percy had a great many & miraculous escapes in the late Action. This amiable Young Nobleman with the Graces which attracts Admiration, possesses the virtues of the heart, & all those qualities that form the great Soldier —Vigilent, Active, temperate, humane, great Command of temper, fortitude in enduring hardships & fatigue, & Intrepidity in dangers. His Lordships behavior in the day of trial has done honor to the Percys. indeed all the Officers & Soldiers behaved with the greatest bravery it is said * * *

(1775) 1927

IV. JONATHAN BOUCHER (1738–1804)

A VIEW OF THE CAUSES AND CONSEQUENCES OF THE AMERICAN REVOLUTION

ON CIVIL LIBERTY, &c.

Discourse XII. On Civil Liberty; Passive Obedience, and Non-Resistance. Galatians, ch. v. ver. 1. Stand fast, therefore, in the liberty wherewith Christ hath made us free.

* * * "Civil liberty (says an excellent writer) is a severe and a restrained thing; implies, in the notion of it, authority, settled subordinations, subjection, and obedience; and is altogether as much hurt by too little of this kind, as by too much it. And the love of liberty, when it is indeed the love of liberty, which carries us to withstand tyranny, will as much carry us to reverence authority, and to support it; for this most obvious reason, that one is as necessary to the being of liberty, as the other is destructive of it. And, therefore, the love of liberty which does not produce this effect, the love of liberty which is not a real principle of dutiful behaviour towards authority, is as hypocritical as the religion which is not productive of a good life. Licentiousness is, in truth, such an excess of liberty as is of the same nature with tyranny. For, what is the difference betwixt them, but that one is lawless power exercised under pretence of authority, or by persons vested with it; the other, lawless power exercised under pretence of liberty, or without any

pretence at all? A people, then, must always be less free in proportion as they are more licentious; licentiousness being not only different from liberty, but directly contrary to it—a direct breach upon it."

True liberty, then, is a liberty to do every thing that is right, and the being restrained from doing any thing that is wrong. So far from our having a right to do every thing that we please, under a notion of liberty, liberty itself is limited and confined—but limited and confined only by laws which are at the same time both it's foundation and it's support. It can, however, hardly be necessary to inform you, that ideas and notions respecting liberty, very different from these, are daily suggested in the speeches and the writings of the times; and also that some opinions on the subject of government at large, which appear to me to be particularly loose and dangerous, are advanced in the sermon now under consideration; and that, therefore, you will acknowledge the propriety of my bestowing some farther notice on them both.

It is laid down in this sermon, as a settled maxim, that the end of government is "the common good of mankind." I am not sure that the position itself is indisputable; but, if it were, it would by no means follow that, "this common good being matter of common feeling, government must therefore have been instituted by common consent." There is an appearance of logical accuracy and precision in this statement; but it is only an appearance. The position is vague and loose; and the assertion is made without an attempt to prove it. If by men's "common feelings" we are to understand that principle in the human mind called common sense, the assertion is either unmeaning and insignificant, or it is false. In no instance have mankind ever yet agreed as to what is, or is not, "the common good." A form or mode of government cannot be named, which these "common feelings" and "common consent," the sole arbiters, as it seems, of "common good," have not, at one time or another, set up and established, and again pulled down and reprobated. What one people in one age have concurred in establishing as the "common good," another in another age have voted to be mischievous and big with ruin. The premises, therefore, that "the common good is matter of common feeling," being false, the consequence drawn from it, viz. that government was instituted by "common consent," is of course equally false.

This popular notion, that government was originally formed by the consent or by a compact of the people, rests on, and is supported by, another similar notion, not less popular, nor better founded. This other notion is, that the whole human race is born equal; and that no man is naturally inferior, or, in any respect, subjected to another; and that he can be made subject to another only by his own consent. The position is equally ill-founded and false both in it's premises and conclusions. In hardly any sense that can be imagined is the position strictly true; but, as applied to the case under consideration, it is demonstrably not true. Man differs from man in every thing that can be supposed to lead to supremacy and subjection, *as one star differs from another star in glory.* It was the purpose of the Creator, that man should be social: but, without government, there can be no society; nor, without some relative inferiority and superiority, can there be any government. A musical instrument composed of chords, keys, or pipes, all perfectly equal in size and power, might as well be expected to produce harmony, as a society composed of members all perfectly equal to be productive of order and peace. If (according to the idea of the advocates of this chimerical scheme of equality) no man could rightfully *be compelled to come in* and be a member even of a government to be formed by a regular compact, but by his own individual consent; it clearly follows, from the same principles, that neither could he rightfully be made or compelled to submit to the ordinances of any government already formed, to which he has not individually or actually consented. On the principle of equality, neither his parents, nor even the vote of a majority of the society, (however virtuously and honourably that vote might be obtained,) can have any such authority over any man. Neither can it be maintained that acquiescence implies consent; because acquiescence may have been extorted from impotence or incapacity. Even an explicit consent can bind a man no longer than he chooses to be bound. The same principle of equality that exempts him from being governed without his own consent, clearly entitles him to recall and resume that consent whenever he sees fit; and he alone has a right to judge when and for what reasons it may be resumed.

Any attempt, therefore, to introduce this fantastic system into practice, would reduce the whole business of social life to the wearisome, confused, and useless talk of mankind's first expressing, and then withdrawing, their consent to an endless succession of schemes of government. Governments, though always forming, would never be completely formed: for, the majority to-day, might be the minority to-morrow; and, of course, that which is now fixed might and would be soon unfixed. Mr. Locke indeed says, that, "by consenting with others to make one body-politic under government, a man puts himself under an obligation to every one of that society to submit to the determination of the majority, and to be concluded by it." For the sake of the peace of society, it is undoubtedly reasonable and necessary that this should be the case: but, on the principles of the system now under consideration, before Mr. Locke or any of his followers can have authority to say that it actually is the case, it must be stated and proved that every individual man, on entering into the social compact, did first consent, and declare his consent, to be concluded and bound in all cases by the vote of the majority. In making such a declaration, he would certainly consult both his interest and his duty; but at the same time he would also completely relinquish the principle of equality, and eventually subject himself to the possibility of being governed by ignorant and corrupt tyrants. Mr. Locke himself afterwards disproves his own position respecting this supposed obligation to submit to the "determination of the majority," when he argues that a right of resistance still exists in the governed: for, what is resistance but a recalling and resuming the consent heretofore supposed to have been given, and in fact refusing to submit to the "determination of the majority?" It does not clearly appear what Mr. Locke exactly meant by what he calls "the determination of the majority:" but the only rational and practical public manner of declaring "the determination of the majority," is by law: the laws, therefore, in all countries, even in those that are despotically governed, are to be regarded as the declared "determination of a majority" of the members of that community; because, in such cases, even acquiescence only must be looked upon as equivalent to a declaration. A right of resistance, therefore, for which Mr. Locke contends, is incompatible with the duty of submitting to the determination of "the majority," for which he also contends.

It is indeed impossible to carry into effect any government which, even by compact, might be framed with this reserved right of resistance. Accordingly there is no record that any such government ever was so formed. If there had, it must have carried the seeds of it's decay in it's very constitution. For, as those men who make a government (certain that they have the power) can have no hesitation to vote that they also have the right to unmake it; and as the people, in all circumstances, but more especially when trained to make and unmake governments, are at least as well disposed to do the latter as the former, it is morally impossible that there should be any thing like permanency or stability in a government so formed. Such a system, therefore, can produce only perpetual dissensions and contests, and bring back mankind to a supposed state of nature; arming every man's hand, like Ishmael's, against every man, and rendering the world an *aceldama,* or field of blood.—Such theories of government seem to give something like plausibility to the notions of those other modern theorists, who regard all governments as invasions of the natural rights of men, usurpations, and tyranny. On this principle it would follow, and could not be denied, that government was indeed fundamentally, as our people are sedulously taught it still is, an evil. Yet it is to government that mankind owe their having, after their fall and corruption, been again reclaimed, from a state of barbarity and war, to the conveniency and the safety of the social state: and it is by means of government that society is still preserved, the weak protected from the strong, and the artless and innocent from the wrongs of proud oppressors. It was not without reason, then, that Mr. Locke asserted, that a greater wrong cannot be done to prince and people, than is done by "propagating wrong notions concerning government."

Ashamed of this shallow device, that government originated in superior strength and violence, another party, hardly less numerous, and certainly not less confident than the former, fondly deduce it from some imaginary compact. They suppose that, in the decline perhaps of some fabulous age of gold, a multitude of human beings, who, like their brother beasts, had hitherto ranged the forests, *without guide, overseer, or ruler*—at length convinced, by experience, of the impossibility of living either alone with any degree of comfort or security, or together in society, with peace, without government, had (in some lucid interval of reason and reflection) met together in a spacious plain, for the express purpose of framing a government. Their first step must have been the transferring to some individual, or individuals, some of those rights which are supposed to have been inherent in each of them: of these it is essential to government that they should be divested; yet can they not, rightfully, be deprived of them, otherwise than by their own consent. Now, admitting this whole supposed assembly to be perfectly equal as to rights, yet all agreed as to the propriety of ceding some of them, on what principles of equality is it possible to determine, either who shall relinquish such a portion of his rights, or who shall be invested with such new accessory rights? By asking another to exercise jurisdiction over me, I clearly confess that I do not think myself his equal; and by his consenting to exercise such authority, he also virtually declares that he thinks himself superior. And, to establish this hypothesis of a compact, it is farther necessary that the whole assembly should concur in this opinion —a concurrence so extremely improbable, that it seems to be barely possible. The supposition that a large concourse of people, in a rude and imperfect state of society, or even a majority of them, should thus rationally and unanimously concur to subject themselves to various restrictions, many of them irksome and unpleasant, and all of them contrary to all their former habits, is to suppose them possessed of more wisdom and virtue than multitudes in any instance in real life have ever shewn. Another difficulty respecting this notion may yet be mentioned. Without a power of life and death, it will, I presume, be readily admitted that there could be no government. Now, admitting it to be possible that men, from motives of public and private utility, may be induced to submit to many heavy penalties, and even to corporal punishment, inflicted by the sentence of the law, there is an insuperable objection to any man's giving to another a power over his life: this objection is, that no man has such a power over his own life; and cannot therefore transfer to another, or to others, be they few or many, on any conditions, a right which he does not himself possess. He only who gave life, can give the authority to take it away: and as such authority is essential to government, this argument seems very decidedly to prove, not only that government did not originate in any compact, but also that it was originally from God.

This visionary idea of a government by compact was, as Filmer says, "first hatched in the schools; and hath, ever since, been fostered by Papists, for good divinity." For some time, the world seemed to regard it merely as another Utopian fiction; and it was long confined to the disciples of Rome and Geneva, who, agreeing in nothing else, yet agreed in this. In an evil hour it gained admittance into the Church of England; being first patronized by her during the civil wars, by "a few miscreants, who were as far from being true

Protestants, as true Subjects." Mankind have listened, and continue to listen to it with a predilection and partiality, just as they do to various other exceptionable notions, which are unfavourable to true religion and sound morals; merely from imagining, that if such doctrines be true, they shall no longer be subjected to sundry restraints, which, however wholsome and proper, are too often unpalatable to our corrupt natures. What we wish to be true, we easily persuade ourselves is true. On this principle it is not difficult to account for our thus eagerly following these *ignes fatui* of our own fancies or "feelings," rather than the sober steady light of the word of God; which (in this instance as well as in others) lies under this single disadvantage, that it proposes no doctrines which may conciliate our regards by flattering our pride.

If, however, we can even resolve no longer to be bewildered by these vain imaginations, still the interesting question presses on us, "Where," in the words of Plato, "where shall we look for the origin of government?" Let Plato himself instruct us. Taught then by this oracle of Heathen wisdom, "we will take our stations there, where the prospect of it is most easy and most beautiful." Of all the theories respecting the origin of government with which the world has ever been either puzzled, amused, or instructed, that of the Scriptures alone is accompanied by no insuperable difficulties.

It was not to be expected from an all-wise and all-merciful Creator, that, having formed creatures capable of order and rule, he should turn them loose into the world under the guidance only of their own unruly wills; that, like so many wild beasts, they might tear and worry one another in their mad contests for preeminence. His purpose from the first, no doubt, was, that men should *live godly and sober lives*. But, such is the sad estate of our corrupted nature, that, ever since the Fall, we have been averse from good, and prone to evil. We are, indeed, so disorderly and unmanageable, that, were it not for the restraints and the terrors of human laws, it would not be possible for us to dwell together. But as men were clearly formed for society, and to dwell together, which yet they cannot do without the restraints of law, or, in other words, without government, it is fair to infer that government was also the original intention of God, who never decrees the end, without also decreeing the means. Accordingly, when man was made, his Maker did not turn him adrift into a shoreless ocean, without star or compass to steer by. As soon as there were some to be governed, there were also some to govern: and the first man, by virtue of that paternal claim, on which all subsequent governments have been founded, was first invested with the power of government. For, we are not to judge of the Scriptures of God, as we do of some other writings; and so, where no express precept appears, hastily to conclude that none was given. On the contrary, in commenting on the Scriptures, we are frequently called upon to find out the precept from the practice. Taking this rule, then, for our direction in the present instance, we find, that, copying after the fair model of heaven itself, wherein there was government even among the angels, the families of the earth were subjected to rulers, at first set over them by God: *for, there is no power, but of God; the powers that be are ordained of God.* The first father was the first king: and if (according to the rule just laid down) the law may be inferred from the practice, it was thus that all government originated; and monarchy is it's most ancient form.

Little risque is run in affirming, that this idea of the patriarchal origin of government has not only the most and best authority of history, as far as history goes, to support it; but that it is also by far the most natural, most consistent, and most rational idea. Had it pleased God not to have interfered at all in the case, neither directly nor indirectly, and to have left mankind to be guided only by their own uninfluenced judgments, they would naturally have been led to the government of a community, or a nation, from the natural and obvious precedent of the government of a family. In confirmation of this opinion, it may be observed; that the patriarchal scheme is that which always has prevailed, and still does prevail, among the most enlightened people: and (what is no slight attestation of it's truth) it has also prevailed, and still does prevail, among the most unenlightened. According to Vitruvius, the rudiments of architecture are to be found in the cottage: and, according to Aristotle, the first principles of government are to be traced to private families. Kingdoms and empires are but so many larger families: and hence it is that our Church, in perfect conformity with the doctrine here inculcated, in her explication of the fifth commandment, from the obedience due to parents, wisely derives the congenial duty of *honouring the king and all that are put in authority under him.*

(1775) 1797

THE NATIONAL ISSUE: DEMOCRACY *vs.* FEDERALISM

I. THOMAS JEFFERSON (1743–1826)

From *AUTOBIOGRAPHY*

[THE DECLARATION OF INDEPENDENCE]

Congress proceeded the same day to consider the declaration of Independence which had been reported & lain on the table the Friday preceding, and on Monday referred to a commee of the whole. The pusillanimous idea that we had friends in England worth keeping terms with, still haunted the minds of many. For this reason those passages which conveyed censures on the people of England were struck out, lest they should give them offence. The clause too, reprobating the enslaving the inhabitants of Africa, was struck out in complaisance to South Carolina and Georgia, who had never attempted to restrain the importation of slaves, and who, on the contrary, still wished to continue it. Our northern brethren also I believe felt a little tender under those censures; for tho' their people had very few slaves themselves, yet they had been pretty considerable carriers of them to others. The debates, having taken up the greater parts of the 2d 3d & 4th days of July were in the evening of the last, closed; the Declaration was reported by the commee, agreed to by the house and signed by every member present, except Mr. Dickinson. As the sentiments of men are known not only by what they receive, but what they reject also, I will state the form of the declaration as originally reported. The parts struck out by Congress shall be distinguished by a black line drawn under them; & those inserted by them shall be placed in the margin, or in a concurrent column.

A DECLARATION BY THE REPRESENTATIVES OF THE UNITED STATES OF AMERICA, IN GENERAL CONGRESS ASSEMBLED

When in the course of human events it becomes necessary for one people to dissolve the political bands which have connected them with another, and to assume among the powers of the earth the separate & equal station to which the laws of nature and of nature's God entitle them, a decent respect to the opinions of mankind requires that they should declare the causes which impel them to the separation.

We hold these truths to be self-evident: that all men are created equal; that they are endowed by their creator with *inherent and*[1] inalienable rights; that among these are life, liberty, & the pursuit of happiness: that to secure these rights, governments are instituted among men, deriving their just powers from the consent of the governed; that whenever any form of government becomes destructive of these ends, it is the right of the people to alter or

[1] Certain.

abolish it, & to institute new government, laying it's foundation on such principles, organizing its powers in such form, as to them shall seem most likely to effect their safety & happiness. Prudence, indeed, will dictate that governments long established should not be changed for light & transient causes; and accordingly all experience hath shown that mankind are more disposed to suffer while evils are sufferable, than to right themselves by abolishing the forms to which they are accustomed. But when a long train of abuses & usurpations *begun at a distinguished period and* pursuing invariably the same object, evinces a design to reduce them under absolute despotism, it is their right, it is their duty to throw off such government, & to provide new guards for their future security. Such has been the patient sufferance of these colonies; & such is now the necessity which constrains them to *expunge*[2] their former systems of government. The history of the present king of Great Britain is a history of *unremitting*[3] injuries & usurpations, *among which appears no solitary fact to contradict the uniform tenor of the rest but all have*[4] in direct object the establishment of an absolute tyranny over these states. To prove this, let facts be submitted to a candid world *for the truth of which we pledge a faith yet unsullied by falsehood.*

He has refused his assent to laws the most wholesome & necessary for the public good.

He has forbidden his governors to pass laws of immediate & pressing importance, unless suspended in their operation till his assent should be obtained; & when so suspended, he has utterly neglected to attend to them.

He has refused to pass other laws for the accommodation of large districts of people, unless those people would relinquish the right of representation in the legislature, a right inestimable to them, & formidable to tyrants only.

He has called together legislative bodies at places unusual, uncomfortable, and distant from the depository of their public records, for the sole purpose of fatiguing them into compliance with his measures.

He has dissolved representative houses repeatedly *& continually* for opposing with manly firmness his invasions on the rights of the people.

He has refused for a long time after such dissolutions to cause others to be elected, whereby the legislative powers, incapable of annihilation, have returned to the people at large for their exercise, the state remaining, in the meantime exposed to all the dangers of invasion from without & convulsions within.

He has endeavored to prevent the population of these states; for that purpose obstructing the laws for naturalization of foreigners, refusing to pass others to encourage their migrations hither, & raising the conditions of new appropriations of lands.

He has *suffered*[5] the administration of justice *totally to cease in some of these states*[6] refusing his assent to laws for establishing judiciary powers.

He has made *our* judges dependant on his will alone, for the tenure of their offices, & the amount & payment of their salaries.

He has erected a multitude of new offices *by a self assumed power* and sent hither swarms of new officers to harass our people and eat out their substance.

He has kept among us in times of peace standing armies *and ships of war* without the consent of our legislatures.

He has affected to render the military independant of, and superior to the civil power.

He has combined with others to subject us to a jurisdiction foreign to our

[2] alter.
[3] repeated.
[4] all having.
[5] obstructed.
[6] by.

constitutions & unacknowledged by our laws, giving his assent to their acts of pretended legislation for quartering large bodies of armed troops among us; for protecting them by a mock-trial from punishment for any murders which they should commit on the inhabitants of these states; for cutting off our trade with all parts of the world; for imposing taxes on us without our consent; for depriving us [] [7] of the benefits of trial by jury; for transporting us beyond seas to be tried for pretended offences; for abolishing the free system of English laws in a neighboring province, establishing therein an arbitrary government, and enlarging it's boundaries, so as to render it at once an example and fit instrument for introducing the same absolute rule into these *states;* [8] for taking away our charters, abolishing our most valuable laws, and altering fundamentally the forms of our governments; for suspending our own legislatures, & declaring themselves invested with power to legislate for us in all cases whatsoever.

He has abdicated government here *withdrawing his governors, and declaring us out of his allegiance & protection.*[9]

He has plundered our seas, ravaged our coasts, burnt our towns, & destroyed the lives of our people.

He is at this time transporting large armies of foreign mercenaries to compleat the works of death desolation & tyranny already begun with circumstances of cruelty and perfidy [] [10] unworthy the head of a civilized nation.

He has constrained our fellow citizens taken captive on the high seas, to bear arms against their country to become the executioners of their friends & brethren, or to fall themselves by their hands.

He has [] [11] endeavored to bring on the inhabitants of our frontiers the merciless Indian savages, whose known rule of warfare is an undistinguished destruction of all ages, sexes & conditions *of existence.*

He has incited treasonable insurrections of our fellow-citizens, with the allurements of forfeiture & confiscation of our property.

He has waged cruel war against human nature itself, violating it's most sacred rights of life and liberty in the persons of a distant people who never offended him, captivating & carrying them into slavery in another hemisphere, or to incur miserable death in their transportation thither. This piratical warfare, the opprobium of INFIDEL *powers, is the warfare of the* CHRISTIAN *king of Great Britain. Determined to keep open a market where* MEN *should be bought & sold, he has prostituted his negative for suppressing every legislative attempt to prohibit or to restrain this execrable commerce. And that this assemblage of horrors might want no fact of distinguished die, he is now exciting those very people to rise in arms among us, and to purchase that liberty of which he has deprived them, by murdering the people on whom he also obtruded them: thus paying off former crimes committed against the* LIBERTIES *of one people, with crimes which he urges them to commit against the* LIVES *of another.*

In every stage of these oppressions we have petitioned for redress in the most humble terms: our repeated petitions have been answered only by repeated injuries.

A prince whose character is thus marked by every act which may define a tyrant is unfit to be the ruler of a [] [12]

[7] in many cases.

[8] colonies.

[9] by declaring us out of his protection, and waging war against us.

[10] scarcely paralleled in the most barbarous ages, & totally.

[11] excited domestic insurrection among us, and has.

[12] free.

people *who mean to be free. Future ages will scarcely believe that the hardiness of one man adventured, within the short compass of twelve years only, to lay a foundation so broad & so undisguised for tyranny over a people fostered & fixed in principles of freedom.*

Nor have we been wanting in attentions to our British brethren. We have warned them from time to time of attempts by their legislature to extend *a*[13] jurisdiction over *these our states.*[14] We have reminded them of the circumstances of our emigration & settlement here, *no one of which could warrant so strange a pretension: that these were effected at the expense of our own blood & treasure, unassisted by the wealth or the strength of Great Britain: that in constituting indeed our several forms of government, we had adopted one common king, thereby laying a foundation for perpetual league & amity with them: but that submission to their parliament was no part of our constitution, nor even in idea, if history may be credited: and,* we [][15] appealed to their native justice and magnanimity *as well as to*[16] the ties of our common kindred to disavow these usurpations which *were likely to*[17] interrupt our connection and correspondence. They too have been deaf to the voice of justice & of consanguinity, *and when occasions have been given them, by the regular course of their laws, of removing from their councils the disturbers of our harmony, they have, by their free election, re-established them in power. At this very time too they are permitting their chief magistrate to send over not only soldiers of our common blood, but Scotch & foreign mercenaries to invade & destroy us. These facts have given the last stab to agonizing affection, and manly spirit bids us to renounce forever these unfeeling brethren. We must endeavor to forget our former love for them, and hold them as we hold the rest of mankind, enemies in war, in peace friends. We might have been a free and a great people together; but a communication of grandeur & of freedom it seems is below their dignity. Be it so, since they will have it. The road to happiness & to glory is open to us, too. We will tread it apart from them, and*[18] acquiesce in the necessity which denounces our *eternal* separation [] ! [19]

We therefore the representatives of the United States of America in General Congress assembled do in the name & by the authority of the good people of these *states reject & renounce all allegiance & subjection to the kings of Great Britain & all others who may hereafter claim by, through or under them: we utterly dissolve all political connection which may heretofore have subsisted between us & the people or parliament of Great Britain: & finally we do assert & declare these colonies to be free & independent states,* & that as free & independent states, they have full power to levy war, conclude peace, contract alliances, establish commerce, & to do all other acts & things which independent states may of right do.

And for the support of this declaration we mutually pledge to each other our lives, our fortunes, & our sacred honor.[20]

13 an unwarrantable.

14 us.

15 have.

16 and we have conjured them by.

17 would inevitably.

18 We must therefore.

19 and hold them as we hold the rest of mankind, enemies in war, in peace friends.

20 We therefore the representatives of the United States of America in General Congress assembled, appealing to the supreme judge of the world for the rectitude of our intentions, do in the name, & by the authority of the good people of these colonies, solemnly publish & declare, that these united colonies are & of right ought to be free & independent states; & that they are absolved from all allegiance to the British crown, and that all political connection between them & the state of Great Britain is, & ought to be, totally dis-

The Declaration thus signed on the 4th, on paper, was engrossed on parchment, & signed again on the 2d. of August.

(1775) 1853

From *NOTES ON VIRGINIA*

[INHABITANTS OF THE NEW WORLD]

* * * The Indian of North America being more within our reach, I can speak of him somewhat from my own knowledge, but more from the information of others better acquainted with him, and on whose truth and judgment I can rely. From these sources I am able to say, in contradiction to this representation, that he is neither more defective in ardor, nor more impotent with his female, than the white reduced to the same diet and exercise; that he is brave, when an enterprise depends on bravery; education with him making the point of honor consist in the destruction of an enemy by stratagem, and in the preservation of his own person free from injury; or, perhaps, this is nature, while it is education which teaches us to honor force more than finesse; that he will defend himself against a host of enemies, always choosing to be killed, rather than to surrender, though it be to the whites, who he knows will treat him well; that in other situations, also, he meets death with more deliberation, and endures tortures with a firmness unknown almost to religious enthusiasm with us; that he is affectionate to his children, careful of them, and indulgent in the extreme; that his affections comprehend his other connections, weakening, as with us, from circle to circle, as they recede from the centre; that his friendships are strong and faithful to the uttermost extremity; that his sensibility is keen, even the warriors weeping most bitterly on the loss of their children, though in general they endeavor to appear superior to human events; that his vivacity and activity of mind is equal to ours in the same situation; hence his eagerness for hunting, and for games of chance. The women are submitted to unjust drudgery. This I believe is the case with every barbarous people. With such, force is law. The stronger sex imposes on the weaker. It is civilization alone which replaces women in the enjoyment of their natural equality. That first teaches us to subdue the selfish passions, and to respect those rights in others which we value in ourselves. Were we in equal barbarism, our females would be equal drudges. The man with them is less strong than with us, but their women stronger than ours; and both for the same obvious reason; because our man and their woman is habituated to labor, and formed by it. With both races the sex which is indulged with ease is the least athletic. An Indian man is small in the hand and wrist, for the same reason for which a sailor is large and strong in the arms and shoulders, and a porter in the legs

solved; and that as free & independent states, they have full power to levy war, conclude peace, contract alliances, establish commerce, & to do all other acts & things which independent states may of right do.

And for the support of this declaration, with a firm reliance on the protection of divine providence we mutually pledge to each other our lives, our fortunes, & our sacred honor.

and thighs. They raise fewer children than we do. The causes of this are to be found, not in a difference of nature, but of circumstance. The women very frequently attending the men in their parties of war and of hunting, child-bearing becomes extremely inconvenient to them. It is said, therefore, that they have learned the practice of procuring abortion by the use of some vegetable; and that it even extends to prevent conception for a considerable time after. During these parties they are exposed to numerous hazards, to excessive exertions, to the greatest extremities of hunger. Even at their homes the nation depends for food, through a certain part of every year, on the gleanings of the forest; that is, they experience a famine once in every year. With all animals, if the female be illy fed, or not fed at all, her young perish; and if both male and female be reduced to like want, generation becomes less active, less productive. To the obstacles, then, of want and hazard, which nature has opposed to the multiplication of wild animals, for the purpose of restraining their numbers within certain bounds, those of labour and of voluntary abortion are added with the Indian. No wonder, then, if they multiply less than we do. Where food is regularly supplied, a single farm will show more of cattle, than a whole country of forests can of buffalos. The same Indian women, when married to white traders, who feed them and their children plentifully and regularly, who exempt them from excessive drudgery, who keep them stationary and unexposed to accident, produce and raise as many children as the white women. Instances are known, under these circumstances, of their rearing a dozen children. An inhuman practice once prevailed in this country, of making slaves of the Indians. It is a fact well known with us, that the Indian women so enslaved produced and raised as numerous families as either the whites or blacks among whom they lived. It has been said that Indians have less hair than the whites, except on the head. But this is a fact of which fair proof can scarcely be had. With them it is disgraceful to be hairy on the body. They say it likens them to hogs. They therefore pluck the hair as fast as it appears. But the traders who marry their women, and prevail on them to discontinue this practice, say, that nature is the same with them as with the whites. Nor, if the fact be true, is the consequence necessary which has been drawn from it. Negroes have notoriously less hair than the whites; yet they are more ardent. But if cold and moisture be the agents of nature for diminishing the races of animals, how comes she all at once to suspend their operation as to the physical man of the new world, whom the Count acknowledges to be "à peu près de même stature que l'homme de notre monde," and to let loose their influence on his moral faculties? How has this "combination of the elements and other physical causes, so contrary to the enlargement of animal nature in this new world, these obstacles to the development and formation of great germs," been arrested and suspended, so as to permit the human body to acquire its just dimensions, and by what inconceivable process has their action been directed on his mind alone? To judge of the truth of this, to form a just estimate of their genius and mental powers, more facts are wanting, and great allowance to be made for those circumstances of their situation which call for a display of particular talents only. This done, we shall probably find that they are formed in mind as well as in body, on the same module with the "Homo sapiens Europaeus." The principles of their society forbidding all compulsion, they are to be led to duty and to enterprise by personal influence and persuasion. Hence eloquence in council, bravery and address in war, become the foundations of all consequence with them. To these acquirements all their faculties are directed. Of their bravery and address in war we have multiplied proofs, because we have been the subjects on which they were exercised. Of their eminence in oratory we have fewer examples, because it is displayed chiefly in their own councils. Some, however, we have, of very superior lustre. I may challenge the whole orations of Demosthenes and Cicero, and of any more eminent orator, if Europe has furnished more eminent, to produce a single passage, superior to the speech of Logan, a Mingo chief, to Lord Dunmore, then governor of this State. And as a testimony of their talents in this line, I beg leave to introduce it, first stating the incidents necessary for understanding it. In the spring of the year 1774, a robbery and murder were committed on an inhabitant of the frontier of Virginia, by two Indians of the Shawanee tribe. The neighbouring whites, according to their custom, undertook to punish this outrage in a summary way. Col. Cresap, a man infamous for the many murders he had committed on those much injured people, collected a party and proceeded down the Kanhaway in quest of vengeance. Unfortunately a canoe of women and children, with one man only, was seen coming from the opposite shore, unarmed, and unsuspecting an hostile attack from the whites. Cresap and his party concealed themselves on the bank of the river, and the moment the canoe reached the shore, singled out their objects, and at one fire, killed every person in it. This happened to be the family of Logan, who had long been distinguished as a friend of the whites. This unworthy return provoked his vengeance. He accordingly signalized himself in the war which ensued. In the autumn of the same year a decisive battle was fought at the mouth of the Great Kanhaway, between the collected forces of the Shawanese, Mingoes and Delawares, and a detachment of the Virginia militia. The Indians were defeated and sued for peace. Logan, however, disdained to be seen among the suppliants. But lest the sincerity of a treaty should be disturbed, from which so distinguished a chief absented himself, he sent, by a messenger, the following speech, to be delivered to Lord Dunmore:

"I appeal to any white man to say, if ever he entered Logan's cabin hungry, and he gave him not meat; if ever he came cold and naked, and he clothed him not. During the course of the last long and bloody war Logan remained idle in his cabin, an advocate for peace. Such was my love for the whites, that my countrymen pointed as they passed, and said, 'Logan is the friend of white men.' I had even thought to have lived with you, but for the injuries of one man. Colonel Cresap, the last spring, in cold blood, and unprovoked, murdered all the relations of Logan, not even sparing my women and children. There runs not a drop of my blood in the veins of any living creature. This called on me for revenge. I have sought it: I have killed many: I have fully glutted my vengeance: for my country I rejoice at the beams of peace. But do not harbour a thought that mine is the joy of fear. Logan never felt fear. He will not turn on his heel to save his life. Who is there to mourn for Logan?—Not one."

Before we condemn the Indians of this continent as wanting genius, we must consider that letters have not yet been introduced among them. Were we to compare them in their present state with the Europeans, North of the Alps, when the Roman arms and arts first crossed those mountains, the comparison would be unequal, because, at that time, those parts of Europe were swarming with numbers; because numbers produce emulation, and multiply the chances of improvement, and one improvement begets another. Yet I may safely ask, how many good poets, how many able mathematicians, how many great inventors in arts or sciences, had Europe, North of the Alps, then produced? And it was sixteen centuries after this before a Newton could be formed. I do not mean to deny that there are varieties in the race of man, distinguished by their powers both of body and mind. I believe there are, as I see to be the case in the races of other animals. I only mean to suggest a doubt, whether the bulk and faculties of animals depend on the side of the Atlantic on which their food happens to grow, or which furnishes the elements of which they are compounded? Whether nature has enlisted herself as a Cis or Trans-Atlantic partisan? I am induced to suspect there has been more eloquence than sound reasoning displayed in support of this theory; that it is one of those cases where the judgment has been seduced by a glowing pen; and whilst I render every tribute of honor and esteem to the celebrated Zoologist, who has added, and is still adding, so many precious things to the treasures of science, I must doubt whether in this instance he has not cherished error also, by lending her for a moment his vivid imagination and bewitching language.

So far the Count de Buffon has carried this new theory of the tendency of nature to belittle her productions on this side the Atlantic. Its application to the race of whites transplanted from Europe, remained for the Abbé Raynal. "On doit etre etonné (he says) que l'Amerique n'ait pas encore produit un bon poëte, un habile mathematicien, un homme de genie dans un seul art, ou seule science." 7. Hist. Philos., p. 92, ed. Maestricht, 1774. "America has not yet produced one good poet." When we shall have existed as a people as long as the Greeks did before they produced a Homer, the Romans a Virgil, the French a Racine and Voltaire, the English a Shakespeare and Milton, should this reproach be still true, we will inquire from what unfriendly causes it has proceeded, that the other countries of Europe and quarters of the earth shall not have inscribed any name in the roll of poets. But neither has America produced "one able mathematician, one man of genius in a single art or a single science." In war we have produced a Washington, whose memory will be adored while liberty shall have votaries, whose name will triumph over time, and will in future ages assume its just station among the most celebrated worthies of the world, when that wretched philosophy shall be forgotten which would have arranged him among the degeneracies of nature. In Physics we have produced a Franklin, than whom no one of the present age has made more important discoveries, nor has enriched philosophy with more, or more ingenious solutions of the phænomena of nature. We have supposed Mr. Rittenhouse second to no astronomer living; that in genius he must be the first, because he is self taught. As an artist he has exhibited as great a proof of mechanical genius as the world has ever produced. He has not indeed made a world; but he has by imitation approached nearer its Maker than any man who has lived from the creation to this day. As in philosophy and war, so in government, in oratory, in painting, in the plastic art, we might show that America, though but a child of yesterday, has already given hopeful proofs of genius, as well as of the nobler kinds, which arouse the best feelings of man, which call him into action, which substantiate his freedom, and conduct him to happiness, as of the subordinate, which serve to amuse him only. We therefore suppose, that this reproach is as unjust as it is unkind: and that, of the geniuses which adorn the present age, America contributes its full share. For comparing it with those countries where genius is most cultivated, where are the most excellent models for art, and scaffoldings for the attainment of science, as France and England for instance, we calculate thus: The United States contains three millions of inhabitants; France twenty millions; and the British islands ten. We produce a Washington, a Franklin, a Rittenhouse. France then should have half a dozen in each of these lines, and Great Britain half that number, equally eminent. It may be true that France has; we are but just becoming acquainted with her, and our acquaintance so far gives us high ideas of the genius of her inhabitants. It would be injuring too many of them to name particularly a Voltaire, a Buffon, the constellation of Encyclopedists, the Abbé Raynal himself, &c. &c. We therefore have reason to believe she can produce her full quota of genius. The present war having so long cut off all communication with Great Britain, we are not able to make a fair estimate of the state of science in that country. The spirit in which she wages war, is the only sample before our eyes, and that does not seem the legitimate offspring either of science or of civilization. The sun of her glory is fast descending to the horizon. Her Philosophy has crossed the channel, her freedom the Atlantic, and herself seems passing to that awful dissolution whose issue is not given human foresight to scan. * * *

1784

II. ALEXANDER HAMILTON
(1757–1804)

THE FEDERALIST

NO. XXIII

[AN EFFECTIVE GOVERNMENT]

Dec. 18, 1787.

To the People of the State of New York:

The necessity of a Constitution, at least equally energetic with the one proposed to the preservation of the Union, is the point at the examination of which we are now arrived.

This inquiry will naturally divide itself into three branches: the objects to be provided for by the federal government, the quantity of power necessary to the accomplishment of those objects, the persons upon whom that power ought to operate. Its distribution and organization will more properly claim our attention under the succeeding head.

The principal purposes to be answered by union are these: the common defence of the members; the preservation of the public peace, as well against internal convulsions as external attacks; the regulation of commerce with other nations and between the States; the superintendence of our intercourse, political and commercial, with foreign countries.

The authorities essential to the common defence are these: to raise armies; to build and equip fleets; to prescribe rules for the government of both; to direct their operations; to provide for their support. These powers ought to exist without limitation, *because it is impossible to foresee or define the extent and variety of national exigencies, or the correspondent extent and variety of the means which may be necessary to satisfy them.* The circumstances that endanger the safety of nations are infinite, and for this reason no constitutional shackles can wisely be imposed on the power to which the care of it is committed. This power ought to be co-extensive with all the possible combinations of such circumstances; and ought to be under the direction of the same councils which are appointed to preside over the common defence.

This is one of those truths which, to a correct and unprejudiced mind, carries its own evidence along with it; and may be obscured, but cannot be made plainer by argument or reasoning. It rests upon axioms as simple as they are universal; the *means* ought to be proportioned to the *end;* the persons from whose agency the attainment of any *end* is expected ought to possess the *means* by which it is to be attained.

Whether there ought to be a federal government intrusted with the care of the common defence is a question in the first instance, open for discussion; but the moment it is decided in the affirmative, it will follow, that that government ought to be clothed with all the powers requisite to complete execution of its trust. And unless it can be shown that the circumstances which may affect the public safety are reducible within certain determinate limits; unless the contrary of this position can be fairly and rationally disputed, it must be admitted, as a necessary consequence, that there can be no limitation of that authority which is to provide for the defence and protection of the community, in any matter essential to its efficacy—that is, in any matter essential to the *formation, direction,* or *support* of the NATIONAL FORCES.

Defective as the present Confederation has been proved to be, this principle appears to have been fully recognized by the framers of it; though they have not made proper or adequate provision for its exercise. Congress have an unlimited discretion to make requisitions of men and money; to govern the army and navy; to direct their operations. As their requisitions are made constitutionally binding upon the States, who are in fact under the most solemn obligations to furnish the supplies required of them, the intention evidently was that the United States should command whatever resources were by them judged requisite to the "common defence and general welfare." It was presumed that a sense of their true interests, and a regard to the dictates of good faith, would be found sufficient pledges for the punctual performance of the duty of the members to the federal head.

The experiment has, however, demonstrated that this expectation was ill-founded and illusory; and the observations, made under the last head, will, I imagine, have sufficed to convince the impartial and discerning, that there is an absolute necessity for an entire change in the first principles of the system; that if we are in earnest about giving the Union energy and duration, we must abandon the vain project of legislating upon the States in their collective capacities; we must extend the laws of the federal government to the individual citizens of America; we must discard the fallacious scheme of quotas and requisitions, as equally impracticable and unjust. The result from all this is that the Union ought to be invested with full power to levy troops; to build and equip fleets; and to raise the revenues which will be required for the formation and support of an army and navy, in the customary and ordinary modes practised in other governments.

If the circumstances of our country are such as to demand a compound instead of a simple, a confederate instead of a sole, government, the essential point which will remain to be adjusted will be to discriminate the OBJECTS, as far as it can be done, which shall appertain to the different provinces or departments of power; allowing to each the most ample authority for fulfilling the objects committed to its charge. Shall the Union be constituted the guardian of the common safety? Are fleets and armies and revenues necessary to this purpose? The government of the Union must be empowered to pass all laws, and to make all regulations which have relation to them. The same must be the case in respect to commerce, and to every other matter to which its jurisdiction is permitted to extend. Is the administration of justice between the citizens of the same State the proper department of the local governments? These must possess all the authorities which are connected with this object, and with every other that may be allotted to their particular cognizance and direction. Not to confer in each case a degree of power commensurate to the end would be to violate the most obvious rules of prudence and propriety, and improvidently to trust the great interests of the nation to hands which are disabled from managing them with vigor and success.

Who so likely to make suitable provisions for the public defence, as that body to which the guardianship of the public safety is confided; which, as the centre of information, will best understand the extent and urgency of the dangers that threaten; as the representative of the WHOLE, will feel itself most deeply interested in the preservation of every part; which, from the responsibility implied in the duty assigned to it, will be most sensibly impressed with the necessity of proper exertions; and which, by the extension of its authority throughout the States, can alone establish uniformity and concert in the plans and measures by which the common safety is to be secured? Is there not a manifest inconsistency in devolving upon the federal government the care of the general defence, and leaving in the State governments the *effective* powers by which it is to be provided for? Is not a want of co-operation the infallible consequence of such a system? And will not weakness, disorder, an undue distribution of the burdens and calamities of war, an unnecessary and intolerable increase of expense, be its natural and inevitable concomitants? Have we not had unequivocal experience of its effects in the course of the revolution which we have just accomplished?

Every view we may take of the subject, as candid inquirers after truth, will serve to convince us that it is both unwise and dangerous to deny the federal government an unconfined authority, as to all those objects which are intrusted to its management. It will indeed deserve the most vigilant and careful attention of the people, to see that it be modeled in such a manner as to admit of its being safely vested with the requisite powers. If any plan which has been, or may be, offered to our consideration, should not, upon a dispassionate inspection, be found to answer this description, it ought to be rejected. A government, the constitution of which renders it unfit to be trusted with all the powers which a free people *ought to delegate to any government*, would be an unsafe and improper depositary of the NATIONAL INTERESTS. Wherever THESE can with propriety be confided, the coincident powers may safely accompany them. This is the true result of all just reasoning upon the subject. And the adversaries of the plan promulgated by the convention ought to have confined themselves to showing that the internal structure of the proposed government was such as to render it unworthy of the confidence of the people. They ought not to have wandered into inflammatory declamations and unmeaning cavils about the extent of the powers. The POWERS are not too extensive for the OBJECTS of federal administration, or, in other words, for the management of our NATIONAL INTERESTS; nor can any satisfactory argument be framed to show that they are chargeable with such an excess. If it be true, as has been insinuated by some of the writers on the other side, that the difficulty arises from the nature of the thing, and that the extent of the country will not permit us to form a government in which such ample powers can safely be reposed, it would prove that we ought to contract our views and resort to the expedient of separate confederacies, which will move within more practicable spheres. For the absurdity must continually stare us in the face of confiding to a government the direction of the most essential national interests, without daring to trust to it the authorities which are indispensable to their proper and efficient management. Let us not attempt to reconcile contradictions, but firmly embrace a rational alternative.

I trust, however, that the impracticability of one general system cannot be shown. I am greatly mistaken, if any thing of weight has yet been advanced of this tendency; and I flatter myself that the observations which have been made in the course of these papers have served to place the reverse of that position in as clear a light as any matter still in the womb of time and experience can be susceptible of. This, at all events, must be evident, that the very difficulty itself, drawn from the extent of the country, is the strongest argument in favor of an energetic government; for any other can certainly never preserve the union of so large an empire. If we embrace the tenets of those who oppose the adoption of the proposed Constitution, as the standard of our political creed, we cannot fail to verify the gloomy doctrines which predict the impracticability of a national system pervading the entire limits of the present Confederacy.

PUBLIUS.

1787

THE AWAKENING OF LITERARY CONSCIOUSNESS: POETRY AND ESSAY

I. TIMOTHY DWIGHT (1752–1817)

From *GREENFIELD HILL*

PART II

THE FLOURISHING VILLAGE

Fair Verna! loveliest village of the west;
Of every joy, and every charm, possess'd;
How pleas'd amid thy varied walks I rove,
Sweet, cheerful walks of innocence, and love,
And o'er thy smiling prospects cast my eyes,
And see the seats of peace, and pleasure, rise,
And hear the voice of Industry resound,
And mark the smile of Competence, around!
Hail, happy village! O'er thy cheerful lawns,
With earliest beauty, spring delighted dawns;
The northward sun begins his vernal smile;
The spring-bird carols o'er the cressy rill:
The shower, that patters in the ruffled stream,
The ploughboy's voice, that chides the lingering team,
The bee, industrious, with his busy song,
The woodman's axe, the distant groves among,
The waggon, rattling down the rugged steep,
The light wind, lulling every care to sleep,
All these, with mingled music, from below,
Deceive intruding sorrow, as I go.

How pleas'd, fond Recollection, with a smile,
Surveys the varied round of wintery toil!
How pleas'd, amid the flowers, that scent the plain,
Recalls the vanish'd frost, and sleeted rain;
The chilling damp, the ice-endangering street,
And treacherous earth that slump'd beneath the feet.

Yet even stern winter's glooms could joy inspire:
Then social circles grac'd the nutwood fire;
The axe resounded, at the sunny door;
The swain, industrious, trimm'd his flaxen store;
Or thresh'd, with vigorous flail, the bounding wheat,
His poultry round him pilfering for their meat;
Or slid his firewood on the creaking snow;
Or bore his produce to the main below;
Or o'er his rich returns exulting laugh'd;
Or pledg'd the healthful orchard's sparkling draught:

While, on his board, for friends and neighbours spread,
The turkey smoak'd, his busy housewife fed;
And Hospitality look'd smiling round,
And Leisure told his tale, with gleeful sound.

Then too, the rough road hid beneath the sleigh,
The distant friend despis'd a length of way,
And join'd the warm embrace, and mingling smile,
And told of all his bliss, and all his toil;
And, many a month elaps'd, was pleas'd to view
How well the houshold far'd, the children grew;
While tales of sympathy deceiv'd the hour,
And Sleep, amus'd, resign'd his wonted power.

Yes! let the proud despise, the rich deride,
These humble joys, to Competence allied:
To me, they bloom, all fragrant to my heart,
Nor ask the pomp of wealth, nor gloss of art.
And as a bird, in prison long confin'd,
Springs from his open'd cage, and mounts the wind,
Thro' fields of flowers, and fragrance, gaily flies,
Or re-assumes his birth-right, in the skies:
Unprison'd thus from artificial joys,
Where pomp fatigues, and fussful fashion cloys,
The soul, reviving, loves to wander free
Thro' native scenes of sweet simplicity;
Thro' Peace' low vale, where Pleasure lingers long,
And every songster tunes his sweetest song,
And Zephyr hastes, to breathe his first perfume,
And Autumn stays, to drop his latest bloom:
'Till grown mature, and gathering strength to roam,
She lifts her lengthen'd wings, and seeks her home.

But now the wintery glooms are vanish'd all;
The lingering drift behind the shady wall;
The dark-brown spots, that patch'd the snowy field;
The surly frost, that every bud conceal'd;
The russet veil, the way with slime o'erspread,
And all the saddening scenes of March are fled.

Sweet-smiling village! loveliest of the hills!
How green thy groves! How pure thy glassy rills!
With what new joy, I walk thy verdant streets!
How often pause, to breathe thy gale of sweets;
To mark thy well-built walls! thy budding fields!
And every charm, that rural nature yields;
And every joy, to Competence allied,
And every good, that Virtue gains from Pride!

No griping landlord here alarms the door,
To halve, for rent, the poor man's little store.
No haughty owner drives the humble swain
To some far refuge from his dread domain;
Nor wastes, upon his robe of useless pride,
The wealth, which shivering thousands want beside;

Nor in one palace sinks a hundred cots;
Nor in one manor drowns a thousand lots;
Nor, on one table, spread for death and pain,
Devours what would a village well sustain.

O Competence, thou bless'd by Heaven's decree,
How well exchang'd is empty pride for thee!
Oft to thy cot my feet delighted turn,
To meet thy chearful smile, at peep of morn;
To join thy toils, that bid the earth look gay;
To mark thy sports, that hail the eve of May;
To see thy ruddy children, at thy board,
And share thy temperate meal, and frugal hoard;
And every joy, by winning prattlers giv'n,
And every earnest of a future Heaven.

There the poor wanderer finds a table spread,
The fireside welcome, and the peaceful bed.
The needy neighbour, oft by wealth denied,
There finds the little aids of life supplied;
The horse, that bears to mill the hard-earn'd grain;
The day's work given, to reap the ripen'd plain;
The useful team, to house the precious food,
And all the offices of real good.

There too, divine Religion is a guest,
And all the Virtues join the daily feast.
Kind Hospitality attends the door,
To welcome in the stranger and the poor;
Sweet Chastity, still blushing as she goes;
And Patience smiling at her train of woes;
And meek-eyed Innocence, and Truth refin'd,
And Fortitude, of bold, but gentle mind.

Thou pay'st the tax, the rich man will not pay;
Thou feed'st the poor, the rich man drives away.
Thy sons, for freedom, hazard limbs, and life,
While pride applauds, but shuns the manly strife:
Thou prop'st religion's cause, the world around,
And shew'st thy faith in works, and not in sound.

Say, child of passion! while, with idiot stare,
Thou seest proud grandeur wheel her sunny car;
While kings, and nobles, roll bespangled by,
And the tall palace lessens in the sky;
Say, while with pomp thy giddy brain runs round,
What joys, like these, in splendour can be found?
Ah, yonder turn thy wealth-inchanted eyes,
Where that poor, friendless wretch expiring lies!
Hear his sad partner shriek, beside his bed,
And call down curses on her landlord's head,
Who drove, from yon small cot, her houshold sweet,
To pine with want, and perish in the street.
See the pale tradesman toil, the livelong day,
To deck imperious lords, who never pay!
Who waste, at dice, their boundless breadth of soil,

But grudge the scanty meed of honest toil.
See hounds and horses riot on the store,
By HEAVEN created for the hapless poor!
See half a realm one tyrant scarce sustain,
While meagre thousands round him glean the plain!
See, for his mistress' robe, a village sold,
Whose matrons shrink from nakedness and cold!
See too the Farmer prowl around the shed,
To rob the starving houshold of their bread;
And seize, with cruel fangs, the helpless swain,
While wives, and daughters, plead, and weep, in vain;
Or yield to infamy themselves, to save
Their sire from prison, famine, and the grave.

There too foul luxury taints the putrid mind,
And slavery there imbrutes the reasoning kind:
There humble worth, in damps of deep despair,
Is bound by poverty's eternal bar:
No motives bright the etherial aim impart,
Nor one fair ray of hope allures the heart.

But, O sweet Competence! how chang'd the scene,
Where thy soft footsteps lightly print the green!
Where Freedom walks erect, with manly port,
And all the blessings to his side resort,
In every hamlet, Learning builds her schools,
And beggars, children gain her arts, and rules;
And mild Simplicity o'er manners reigns,
And blameless morals Purity sustains.

From thee the rich enjoyments round me spring,
Where every farmer reigns a little king;
Where all to comfort, none to danger, rise;
Where pride finds few, but nature all supplies;
Where peace and sweet civility are seen,
And meek good-neighbourhood endears the green.
Here every class (if classes those we call,
Where one extended class embraces all,
All mingling, as the rainbow's beauty blends,
Unknown where every hue begins or ends)
Each following, each, with uninvidious strife,
Wears every feature of improving life.
Each gains from other comeliness of dress,
And learns, with gentle mein to win and bless,
With welcome mild the stranger to receive,
And with plain, pleasing decency to live.
Refinement hence even humblest life improves;
Not the loose fair, that form and frippery loves;
But she, whose mansion is the gentle mind,
In thought, and action, virtuously refin'd.
Hence, wives and husbands act a lovelier part,
More just the conduct, and more kind the heart;
Hence brother, sister, parent, child, and friend,

The harmony of life more sweetly blend;
Hence labour brightens every rural scene;
Hence cheerful plenty lives along the green;
Still Prudence eyes her hoard, with watchful care,
And robes of thrift and neatness, all things wear.

But hark! what voice so gaily fills the wind?
Of care oblivious, whose that laughing mind?
'Tis yon poor black, who ceases now his song,
And whistling, drives the cumbrous wain along.
He never, dragg'd, with groans, the galling chain;
Nor hung, suspended, on th' infernal crane;
No dim, white spots deform his face, or hand,
Memorials hellish of the marking brand!
No seams of pincers, scars of scalding oil;
No waste of famine, and no wear of toil.
But kindly fed, and clad, and treated, he
Slides on, thro' life, with more than common glee.
For here mild manners good to all impart,
And stamp with infamy th' unfeeling heart;
Here law, from vengeful rage, the slave defends,
And here the gospel peace on earth extends.

He toils, 'tis true; but shares his master's toil;
With him, he feeds the herd, and trims the soil;
Helps to sustain the house, with clothes, and food,
And takes his portion of the common good:
Lost liberty his sole, peculiar ill,
And fix'd submission to another's will.
Ill, ah, how great! without that cheering sun,
The world is chang'd to one wide, frigid zone;
The mind, a chill'd exotic, cannot grow,
Nor leaf with vigour, nor with promise blow;
Pale, sickly, shrunk, it strives in vain to rise,
Scarce lives, while living, and untimely dies.

See fresh to life the Afric infant spring,
And plume its powers, and spread its little wing!
Firm is it's frame, and vigorous is its mind,
Too young to think, and yet to misery blind.
But soon he sees himself to slavery born;
Soon meets the voice of power, the eye of scorn;
Sighs for the blessings of his peers, in vain;
Condition'd as a brute, tho' form'd a man.
Around he casts his fond, instinctive eyes,
And sees no good, to fill his wishes, rise:
(No motive warms, with animating beam,
Nor praise, nor property, nor kind esteem,
Bless'd independence, on his native ground,
Nor sweet equality with those around;)
Himself, and his, another's shrinks to find,
Levell'd below the lot of human kind.
Thus, shut from honour's paths, he turns to shame,

And filches the small good, he cannot claim.
To sour, and stupid, sinks his active mind;
Finds joy in drink, he cannot elsewhere find;
Rule disobeys; of half his labour cheats;
In some safe cot, the pilfer'd turkey eats;
Rides hard, by night, the steed, his art purloins;
Serene from conscience' bar himself essoins;
Sees from himself his sole redress must flow,
And makes revenge the balsam of his woe.

Thus slavery's blast bids sense and virtue die;
Thus lower'd to dust the sons of Afric lie.
Hence sages grave, to lunar systems given,
Shall ask, why two-legg'd brutes were made by HEAVEN;
HOME seek, what pair first peopled Afric's vales,
And nice MONBODDO calculate their tails.

O thou chief curse, since curses here began;
First guilt, first woe, first infamy of man;
Thou spot of hell, deep smirch'd on human kind,
The uncur'd gangrene of the reasoning mind;
Alike in church, in state, and household all,
Supreme memorial of the world's dread fall;
O slavery! laurel of the Infernal mind,
Proud Satan's triumph over lost mankind! * * *

Behold yon humbler mansion lift its head!
Where infant minds to science door are led.
As now, by kind indulgence loos'd to play,
From place to place, from sport to sport, they stray,
How light their gambols frolic o'er the green!
How their shrill voices cheer the rural scene!
Sweet harmless elves! in Freedom's household born,
Enjoy the raptures of your transient morn;
And let no hour of anxious manhood see
Your minds less innocent, or bless'd, or free!

See too, in every hamlet, round me rise
A central school-house, dress'd in modest guise!
Where every child for useful life prepares,
To business moulded, ere he knows its cares;
In worth matures, to independence grows,
And twines the civic garland o'er his brows.

Mark, how invited by the vernal sky,
Yon cheerful group of females passes by!
Whose hearts, attun'd to social joy, prepare
A friendly visit to some neighbouring fair.
How neatness glistens from the lovely train!
Bright charm! which pomp to rival tries in vain.

Ye Muses! dames of dignified renown,
Rever'd alike in country, and in town,

Your bard the mysteries of a visit show;
For sure your Ladyships those mysteries know:
What is it then, obliging Sisters! say,
The debt of social visiting to pay?

'Tis not to toil before the idol pier;
To shine the first in fashion's lunar sphere;
By sad engagements forc'd, abroad to roam,
And dread to find the expecting fair, at home!
To stop at thirty doors, in half a day,
Drop the gilt card, and proudly roll away;
To alight, and yield the hand, with nice parade;
Up stairs to rustle in the stiff brocade;
Swim thro' the drawing room, with studied air;
Catch the pink'd beau, and shade the rival fair;
To sit, to curb, to toss, with bridled mien,
Mince the scant speech, and lose a glance between;
Unfurl the fan, display the snowy arm,
And ope, with each new motion, some new charm:
Or sit, in silent solitude, to spy
Each little failing, with malignant eye;
Or chatter, with incessancy of tongue,
Careless, if kind, or cruel, right, or wrong;
To trill of us, and ours, of mine, and me,
Our house, our coach, our friends, our family,
While all th' excluded circle sit in pain,
And glance their cool contempt, or keen disdain:
T' inhale, from proud Nanking, a sip of tea,
And wave a curtsey trim, and flirt away:
Or waste, at cards, peace, temper, health and life,
Begin with sullenness, and end in strife,
Lose the rich feast, by friendly converse given,
And backward turn from happiness, and heaven.

It is, in decent habit, plain and neat,
To spend a few choice hours, in converse sweet;
Careless of forms, to act th' unstudied part,
To mix in friendship, and to blend the heart;
To choose those happy themes, which all must feel,
The moral duties, and the houshold weal,
The tale of sympathy, the kind design,
Where rich affections soften, and refine;
T' amuse, to be amus'd, to bless, be bless'd,
And tune to harmony the common breast;
To cheer, with mild good-humour's sprightly ray,
And smooth life's passage, o'er its thorny way;
To circle round the hospitable board,
And taste each good, our generous climes afford;
To court a quick return, with accents kind,
And leave, at parting, some regret behind.

Such, here, the social intercourse is found;
So slides the year, in smooth enjoyment, round.

1794

II. JOHN TRUMBULL
(1750–1831)

From *THE PROGRESS OF DULNESS*

[TOM BRAINLESS AT COLLEGE]

So said, so done, at college now
He enters well, no matter how;
New scenes awhile his fancy please,
But all must yield to love of ease.
In the same round condemn'd each day,
To study, read, recite and pray;
To make his hours of business double—
He can't endure th' increasing trouble;
And finds at length, as times grow pressing,
All plagues are easier than his lesson.
With sleepy eyes and count'nance heavy,
With much excuse of *non paravi,*
Much absence, *tardes* and *egresses,*
The college-evil on him seizes.
Then ev'ry book, which ought to please,
Stirs up the seeds of dire disease;
Greek spoils his eyes, the print's so fine,
Grown dim with study, or with wine;
Of Tully's latin much afraid,
Each page, he calls the doctor's aid;
While geometry, with lines so crooked,
Sprains all his wits to overlook it.
His sickness puts on every name,
Its cause and uses still the same;
'Tis tooth-ache, cholic, gout or stone,
With phases various as the moon;
But though through all the body spread,
Still makes its cap'tal seat, the head.
In all diseases, 'tis expected,
The weakest parts be most infected.
Kind head-ache hail! thou blest disease,
The friend of idleness and ease;
Who mid the still and dreary bound
Where college walls her sons surround,
In spite of fears, in justice' spite,
Assumest o'er laws dispensing right,
Sett'st from his task the blunderer free,
Excused by dulness and by thee.
Thy vot'ries bid a bold defiance
To all the calls and threats of science,
Slight learning human and divine,
And hear no prayers, and fear no fine.
And yet how oft the studious gain,
The dulness of a letter'd brain;
Despising such low things the while,
As English grammar, phrase and style;
Despising ev'ry nicer art,
That aids the tongue, or mends the heart;
Read ancient authors o'er in vain,
Nor taste one beauty they contain;
Humbly on trust accept the sense,
But deal for words at vast expense;
Search well how every term must vary
From Lexicon to Dictionary;
And plodding on in one dull tone,
Gain ancient tongues and lose their own,
Bid every graceful charm defiance,
And woo the skeleton of science.
Come ye, who finer arts despise,
And scoff at verse as heathen lies;
In all the pride of dulness rage
At Pope, or Milton's deathless page;
Or stung by truth's deep-searching line,
Rave ev'n at rhymes as low as mine;
Say ye, who boast the name of wise,
Wherein substantial learning lies.
Is it, superb in classic lore,
To speak what Homer spoke before,
To write the language Tully wrote,
The style, the cadence and the note?
Is there a charm in sounds of Greek,
No language else can learn to speak;
That cures distemper'd brains at once,
Like Pliny's rhymes for broken bones?
Is there a spirit found in Latin,
That must evap'rate in translating?

And say are sense and genius bound
To any vehicle of sound?
Can knowledge never reach the brains,
Unless convey'd in ancient strains?
While Homer sets before your eyes
Achilles' rage, Ulysses' lies,
Th' amours of Jove in masquerade,
And Mars entrapp'd by Phœbus' aid;
While Virgil sings, in verses grave,
His lovers meeting in a cave,
His ships turn'd nymphs, in pagan fables,
And how the Trojans eat their tables;
While half this learning but displays
The follies of the former days;
And for our linguists, fairly try them,
A tutor'd parrot might defy them.
Go to the vulgar—'tis decreed,
There you must preach and write or plead;
Broach every curious Latin phrase
From Tully down to Lily's days:
All this your hearers have no share in,
Bate but their laughing and their staring.
Interpreters must pass between,
To let them know a word you mean.
Yet could you reach that lofty tongue
Which Plato wrote and Homer sung;
Or ape the Latin verse and scanning,
Like Vida, Cowley or Buchanan;
Or bear ten phrase-books in your head;
Yet know, these languages are dead,
And nothing, e'er, by death, was seen
Improved in beauty, strength or mien,
Whether the sexton use his spade,
Or sorcerer wake the parted shade.
Think how would Tully stare or smile
At these wan spectres of his style,
Or Horace in his jovial way
Ask what these babblers mean to say.
Let modern Logic next arise
With newborn light to glad your eyes,
Enthroned on high in Reason's chair,
Usurp her name, assume her air,
Give laws, to think with quaint precision,
And deal out loads of definition.
Sense, in dull syllogisms confined,
Scorns these weak trammels of the mind,
Nor needs t' enquire by logic's leave
What to reject and what receive;
Throws all her trifling bulwarks down,
Expatiates free; while from her frown
Alike the dunce and pedant smart,
The fool of nature, or of art.
On books of Rhetorick turn your hopes,
Unawed by figures or by tropes.
What silly rules in pomp appear!
What mighty nothings stun the ear!
Athroismos, Mesoteleuton,
Symploce and *Paregmenon!*
Thus, in such sounds high rumbling, run
The names of jingle and of pun;
Thus shall your pathos melt the heart,
And shame the Greek and Roman art.
Say then, where solid learning lies
And what the toil that makes us wise!
Is it by mathematic's aid
To count the worlds in light array'd,
To know each star, that lifts its eye,
To sparkle in the midnight sky?
Say ye, who draws the curious line
Between the useful and the fine,
How little can this noble art
Its aid in human things impart,
Or give to life a cheerful ray,
And force our pains, and cares away.
Is it to know whate'er was done
Above the circle of the sun?
Is it to lift the active mind
Beyond the bounds by heaven assign'd;
And leave our little world at home,
Through realms of entity to roam;
Attempt the secrets dark to scan,
Eternal wisdom hid from man;
And make religion but the sign
In din of battle when to join?
Vain man, to madness still a prey,
Thy space a point, thy life a day,

A feeble worm, that aim'st to stride
In all the foppery of pride!
The glimmering lamp of reason's ray
Was given to guide thy darksome way.
Why wilt thou spread thy insect wings,
And strive to reach sublimer things?
Thy doubts confess, thy blindness own,
Nor vex thy thoughts with scenes unknown.
Indulgent heaven to man below,
Hath all explain'd we need to know;
Hath clearly taught enough to prove
Content below, and bliss above.
Thy boastful wish how proud and vain,
While heaven forbids the vaunting strain!
For metaphysics rightly shown
But teach how little can be known:
Though quibbles still maintain their station,
Conjecture serves for demonstration,
Armies of pens draw forth to fight,
And * * * * and * * * * write.
  Oh! might I live to see that day,
When sense shall point to youths their way;
Through every maze of science guide;
O'er education's laws preside;
The good retain, with just discerning
Explode the quackeries of learning;
Give ancient arts their real due,
Explain their faults, and beauties too;
Teach where to imitate, and mend,
And point their uses and their end.
Then bright philosophy would shine,
And ethics teach the laws divine;
Our youths might learn each nobler art,
That shews a passage to the heart;
From ancient languages well known
Transfuse new beauties to our own;
With taste and fancy well refin'd,
Where moral rapture warms the mind,
From schools dismiss'd, with lib'ral hand,
Spread useful learning o'er the land;
And bid the eastern world admire
Our rising worth, and bright'ning fire.
  But while through fancy's realms we roam,
The main concern is left at home;
Return'd, our hero still we find
The same, as blundering and as blind.
  Four years at college dozed away
In sleep, and slothfulness and play,
Too dull for vice, with clearest conscience,
Charged with no fault but that of nonsense,
And nonsense long, with serious air,
Has wander'd unmolested there,
He passes trial, fair and free,
And takes in form his first degree.
  A scholar see him now commence
Without the aid of books or sense;
For passing college cures the brain,
Like mills to grind men young again.
The scholar-dress, that once array'd him,
The charm, *Admitto te ad gradum*,
With touch of parchment can refine,
And make the veriest coxcomb shine,
Confer the gift of tongues at once,
And fill with sense the vacant dunce.
So kingly crowns contain quintessence
Of worship, dignity and presence;
Give learning, genius, virtue, worth,
Wit, valor, wisdom and so forth;
Hide the bald pate and cover o'er
The cap of folly worn before.
  Our hero's wit and learning now may
Be proved by token of diploma,
Of that diploma, which with speed
He learns to construe and to read;
And stalks abroad with conscious stride,
In all the airs of pedant pride,
With passport sign'd for wit and knowledge,
And current under seal of college. * * *

1772–73

M'FINGAL

CANTO III

The Liberty Pole

Now warm with ministerial ire,
Fierce sallied forth our loyal 'Squire,
And on his striding steps attends
His desperate clan of Tory friends.
When sudden met his wrathful eye
A pole ascending through the sky,
Which numerous throngs of whiggish race
Were raising in the market-place.
Not higher school-boy's kites aspire,
Or royal mast, or country spire;
Like spears at Brobdignagian tilting,
Or Satan's walking-staff in Milton.
And on its top, the flag unfurl'd
Waved triumph o'er the gazing world,
Inscribed with inconsistent types
Of *Liberty* and *thirteen stripes.*
Beneath, the crowd without delay
The dedication-rites essay,
And gladly pay, in antient fashion,
The ceremonies of libation;
While briskly to each patriot lip
Walks eager round the inspiring flip:
Delicious draught! whose powers inherit
The quintessence of public spirit;
Which whoso tastes, perceives his mind
To nobler politics refined;
Or roused to martial controversy,
As from transforming cups of Circe;
Or warm'd with Homer's nectar'd liquor,
That fill'd the veins of gods with ichor.
At hand for new supplies in store,
The tavern opes its friendly door,
Whence to and fro the waiters run,
Like bucket-men at fires in town.
Then with three shouts that tore the sky,
'Tis consecrate to Liberty.
To guard it from th' attacks of Tories,
A grand Committee cull'd of four is;
Who foremost on the patriot spot,
Had brought the flip, and paid the shot.
By this, M'Fingal with his train
Advanced upon th' adjacent plain,
And full with loyalty possest,
Pour'd forth the zeal, that fired his breast.
"What mad-brain'd rebel gave commission,
To raise this May-pole of sedition?
Like Babel, rear'd by bawling throngs,
With like confusion too of tongues,
To point at heaven and summon down
The thunders of the British crown?
Say, will this paltry Pole secure
Your forfeit heads from Gage's power?
Attack'd by heroes brave and crafty,
Is this to stand your ark of safety;
Or driven by Scottish laird and laddie,
Think ye to rest beneath its shadow?
When bombs, like fiery serpents, fly,
And balls rush hissing through the sky,
Will this vile Pole, devote to freedom,
Save like the Jewish pole in Edom;
Or like the brazen snake of Moses,
Cure your crackt skulls and batter'd noses?
"Ye dupes to every factious rogue
And tavern-prating demagogue,
Whose tongue but rings, with sound more full,
On th' empty drumhead of his scull;
Behold you not what noisy fools
Use you, worse simpletons, for tools?
For Liberty, in your own by-sense,
Is but for crimes a patent license,
To break of law th' Egyptian yoke,
And throw the world in common stock;
Reduce all grievances and ills
To Magna Charta of your wills;
Establish cheats and frauds and nonsense,
Framed to the model of your conscience;
Cry justice down, as out of fashion,
And fix its scale of depreciation;
Defy all creditors to trouble ye,

And keep new years of Jewish jubilee;
Drive judges out, like Aaron's calves,
By jurisdiction of white staves,
And make the bar and bench and steeple
Submit t' our Sovereign Lord, The People;
By plunder rise to power and glory,
And brand all property, as Tory;
Expose all wares to lawful seizures
By mobbers or monopolizers;
Break heads and windows and the peace,
For your own interest and increase;
Dispute and pray and fight and groan
For public good, and mean your own;
Prevent the law by fierce attacks
From quitting scores upon your backs;
Lay your old dread, the gallows, low,
And seize the stocks, your ancient foe,
And turn them to convenient engines
To wreak your patriotic vengeance;
While all, your rights who understand,
Confess them in their owner's hand;
And when by clamours and confusions,
Your freedom's grown a public nuisance,
Cry "Liberty," with powerful yearning,
As he does "Fire!" whose house is burning;
Though he already has much more
Than he can find occasion for.
While every clown, that tills the plains,
Though bankrupt in estate and brains,
By this new light transform'd to traitor,
Forsakes his plough to turn dictator,
Starts an haranguing chief of Whigs,
And drags you by the ears, like pigs.
All bluster, arm'd with factious licence,
New-born at once to politicians.
Each leather-apron'd dunce, grown wise,
Presents his forward face t' advise,
And tatter'd legislators meet,
From every workshop through the street.
His goose the tailor finds new use in,
To patch and turn the Constitution;
The blacksmith comes with sledge and grate
To iron-bind the wheels of state;
The quack forbears his patients' souse,
To purge the Council and the House;
The tinker quits his moulds and doxies,
To cast assembly-men and proxies.
From dunghills deep of blackest hue,
Your dirt-bred patriots spring to view,
To wealth and power and honors rise,
Like new-wing'd maggots changed to flies,
And fluttering round in high parade,
Strut in the robe, or gay cockade.
See Arnold quits, for ways more certain,
His bankrupt-perj'ries for his fortune,
Brews rum no longer in his store,
Jockey and skipper now no more,
Forsakes his warehouses and docks,
And writs of slander for the pox;
And cleansed by patriotism from shame,
Grows General of the foremost name.
For in this ferment of the stream
The dregs have work'd up to the brim,
And by the rule of topsy-turvies,
The scum stands foaming on the surface.
You've caused your pyramid t' ascend,
And set it on the little end.
Like Hudibras, your empire's made,
Whose crupper had o'ertopp'd his head.
You've push'd and turn'd the whole world up-
Side down, and got yourselves at top,
While all the great ones of your state
Are crush'd beneath the popular weight;
Nor can you boast, this present hour,
The shadow of the form of power.

For what's your Congress or its end?
A power, t' advise and recommend;
To call forth troops, adjust your quotas—
And yet no soul is bound to notice;
To pawn your faith to th' utmost limit,
But cannot bind you to redeem it;
And when in want no more in them lies,
Than begging from your State-Assemblies;
Can utter oracles of dread,
Like friar Bacon's brazen head,
But when a faction dares dispute 'em,
Has ne'er an arm to execute 'em:
As tho' you chose supreme dictators,
And put them under conservators.
You've but pursued the self-same way
With Shakespeare's Trinc'lo in the play;
"You shall be Viceroys here, 'tis true,
But we'll be Viceroys over you."
What wild confusion hence must ensue?
Tho' common danger yet cements you:
So some wreck'd vessel, all in shatters,
Is held up by surrounding waters,
But stranded, when the pressure ceases,
Falls by its rottenness to pieces.
And fall it must! if wars were ended,
You'll ne'er have sense enough to mend it:
But creeping on, by low intrigues,
Like vermin of a thousand legs,
'Twill find as short a life assign'd,
As all things else of reptile kind.
Your Commonwealth's a common harlot,
The property of every varlet;
Which now in taste, and full employ,
All sorts admire, as all enjoy:
But soon a batter'd strumpet grown,
You'll curse and drum her out of town.
Such is the government you chose;
For this you bade the world be foes;
For this, so mark'd for dissolution,
You scorn the British Constitution,
That constitution form'd by sages,
The wonder of all modern ages;
Which owns no failure in reality,
Except corruption and venality;
And merely proves the adage just,
That best things spoil'd corrupt to worst:
So man supreme in earthly station,
And mighty lord of this creation,
When once his corse is dead as herring,
Becomes the most offensive carrion,
And sooner breeds the plague, 'tis found,
Than all beasts rotting on the ground.
Yet with republics to dismay us,
You've call'd up Anarchy from chaos,
With all the followers of her school,
Uproar and Rage and wild Misrule:
For whom this rout of Whigs distracted,
And ravings dire of every crack'd head;
These new-cast legislative engines
Of County-meetings and Conventions;
Committees vile of correspondence,
And mobs, whose tricks have almost undone 's:
While reason fails to check your course,
And Loyalty's kick'd out of doors,
And Folly, like inviting landlord,
Hoists on your poles her royal standard;
While the king's friends, in doleful dumps,
Have worn their courage to the stumps,
And leaving George in sad disaster,
Most sinfully deny their master.
What furies raged when you, in sea,
In shape of Indians, drown'd the tea;
When your gay sparks, fatigued to watch it,
Assumed the moggison and hatchet,
With wampum'd blankets hid their laces,

And like their sweethearts, primed their faces:
While not a red-coat dared oppose,
And scarce a Tory show'd his nose;
While Hutchinson, for sure retreat,
Manœuvred to his country seat,
And thence affrighted, in the suds,
Stole off bareheaded through the woods.
"Have you not roused your mobs to join,
And make Mandamus-men resign,
Call'd forth each duffil-drest curmudgeon,
With dirty trowsers and white bludgeon,
Forced all our Councils through the land,
To yield their necks at your command;
While paleness marks their late disgraces,
Through all their rueful length of faces?
"Have you not caused as woeful work
In our good city of New-York,
When all the rabble, well cockaded,
In triumph through the streets paraded,
And mobb'd the Tories, scared their spouses,
And ransack'd all the custom-houses;
Made such a tumult, bluster, jarring,
That mid the clash of tempests warring,
Smith's weather-cock, in veers forlorn,
Could hardly tell which way to turn?
Burn'd effigies of higher powers,
Contrived in planetary hours;
As witches with clay-images
Destroy or torture whom they please:
Till fired with rage, th' ungrateful club
Spared not your best friend, Beelzebub,
O'erlook'd his favors, and forgot
The reverence due his cloven foot,
And in the selfsame furnace frying,
Stew'd him, and North and Bute and Tryon?
Did you not, in as vile and shallow way,
Fright our poor Philadelphian, Galloway,
Your Congress, when the loyal ribald
Belied, berated and bescribbled?
What ropes and halters did you send,
Terrific emblems of his end,
Till, least he'd hang in more than effigy,
Fled in a fog the trembling refugee?
Now rising in progression fatal,
Have you not ventured to give battle?
When Treason chaced our heroes troubled,
With rusty gun, and leathern doublet;
Turn'd all stone-walls and groves and bushes,
To batteries arm'd with blunderbusses;
And with deep wounds, that fate portend,
Gaul'd many a Briton's latter end;
Drove them to Boston, as in jail,
Confined without mainprize or bail.
Were not these deeds enough betimes,
To heap the measure of your crimes:
But in this loyal town and dwelling,
You raise these ensigns of rebellion?
'Tis done! fair Mercy shuts her door;
And Vengeance now shall sleep no more.
Rise then, my friends, in terror rise,
And sweep this scandal from the skies.
You'll see their Dagon, though well jointed,
Will shrink before the Lord's anointed;
And like old Jericho's proud wall,
Before our ram's horns prostrate fall."
This said, our 'Squire, yet undismay'd,
Call'd forth the Constable to aid,
And bade him read, in nearer station,
The Riot-act and Proclamation.
He swift, advancing to the ring,

Began, "Our Sovereign Lord, the King"—
When thousand clam'rous tongues he hears,
And clubs and stones assail his ears.
To fly was vain; to fight was idle;
By foes encompass'd in the middle,
His hope, in stratagems, he found,
And fell right craftily to ground;
Then crept to seek an hiding place,
'Twas all he could, beneath a brace;
Where soon the conq'ring crew espied him,
And where he lurk'd, they caught and tied him.
At once with resolution fatal,
Both Whigs and Tories rush'd to battle.
Instead of weapons, either band
Seized on such arms as came to hand.
And as famed Ovid paints th' adventures
Of wrangling Lapithæ and Centaurs,
Who at their feast, by Bacchus led,
Threw bottles at each other's head;
And these arms failing in their scuffles,
Attack'd with andirons, tongs and shovels:
So clubs and billets, staves and stones
Met fierce, encountering every sconce,
And cover'd o'er with knobs and pains
Each void receptacle for brains;
Their clamours rend the skies around,
The hills rebellow to the sound;
And many a groan increas'd the din
From batter'd nose and broken shin.
M'Fingal, rising at the word,
Drew forth his old militia-sword;
Thrice cried "King George," as erst in distress,
Knights of romance invoked a mistress;
And brandishing the blade in air,
Struck terror through th' opposing war.
The Whigs, unsafe within the wind
Of such commotion, shrunk behind.
With whirling steel around address'd,
Fierce through their thickest throng he press'd,
(Who roll'd on either side in arch,
Like Red Sea waves in Israel's march)
And like a meteor rushing through,
Struck on their Pole a vengeful blow.
Around, the Whigs, of clubs and stones
Discharged whole vollies, in platoons,
That o'er in whistling fury fly;
But not a foe dares venture nigh.
And now perhaps with glory crown'd
Our 'Squire had fell'd the pole to ground,
Had not some Pow'r, a whig at heart,
Descended down and took their part;
(Whether 'twere Pallas, Mars or Iris,
'Tis scarce worth while to make inquiries)
Who at the nick of time alarming,
Assumed the solemn form of Chairman,
Address'd a Whig, in every scene
The stoutest wrestler on the green,
And pointed where the spade was found,
Late used to set their pole in ground,
And urged, with equal arms and might,
To dare our 'Squire to single fight.
The Whig thus arm'd, untaught to yield,
Advanced tremendous to the field:
Nor did M'Fingal shun the foe,
But stood to brave the desp'rate blow;
While all the party gazed, suspended
To see the deadly combat ended;
And Jove in equal balance weigh'd
The sword against the brandish'd spade,
He weigh'd; but lighter than a dream,
The sword flew up, and kick'd the beam.
Our 'Squire on tiptoe rising fair
Lifts high a noble stroke in air,
Which hung not, but like dreadful engines,
Descended on his foe in vengeance.
But ah! in danger, with dishonor

The sword perfidious fails its owner;
That sword, which oft had stood its ground,
By huge trainbands encircled round;
And on the bench, with blade right loyal,
Had won the day at many a trial,
Of stones and clubs had braved th' alarms,
Shrunk from these new Vulcanian arms.
The spade so temper'd from the sledge,
Nor keen nor solid harm'd its edge,
Now met it, from his arm of might,
Descending with steep force to smite;
The blade snapp'd short—and from his hand,
With rust embrown'd the glittering sand.
Swift turn'd M'FINGAL at the view,
And call'd to aid th' attendant crew,
In vain; the Tories all had run,
When scarce the fight was well begun;
Their setting wigs he saw decreas'd
Far in th' horizon tow'rd the west.
Amazed he view'd the shameful sight,
And saw no refuge, but a flight:
But age unwieldy check'd his pace,
Though fear had wing'd his flying race;
For not a trifling prize at stake;
No less than great M'FINGAL's back.
With legs and arms he work'd his course,
Like rider that outgoes his horse,
And labor'd hard to get away, as
Old Satan struggling on through chaos;
'Till looking back, he spied in rear
The spade-arm'd chief advanced too near:
Then stopp'd and seized a stone, that lay
An ancient landmark near the way;
Nor shall we as old bards have done,
Affirm it weigh'd an hundred ton;
But such a stone, as at a shift
A modern might suffice to lift,
Since men, to credit their enigmas,
Are dwindled down to dwarfs and pigmies,
And giants exiled with their cronies
To Brobdignags and Patagonias.
But while our Hero turn'd him round,
And tugg'd to raise it from the ground,
The fatal spade discharged a blow
Tremendous on his rear below:
His bent knee fail'd, and void of strength
Stretch'd on the ground his manly length.
Like ancient oak o'erturn'd, he lay,
Or tower to tempests fall'n a prey,
Or mountain sunk with all his pines,
Or flow'r the plow to dust consigns,
And more things else—but all men know 'em,
If slightly versed in epic poem.
At once the crew, at this dread crisis,
Fall on, and bind him, ere he rises;
And with loud shouts and joyful soul,
Conduct him prisoner to the pole.
When now the mob in lucky hour
Had got their en'mies in their power,
They first proceed, by grave command,
To take the Constable in hand.
Then from the pole's sublimest top
The active crew let down the rope,
At once its other end in haste bind,
And make it fast upon his waistband;
Till like the earth, as stretch'd on tenter,
He hung self-balanced on his centre.
Then upwards, all hands hoisting sail,
They swung him, like a keg of ale,
Till to the pinnacle in height
He vaulted, like balloon or kite.
As Socrates of old at first did
To aid philosophy get hoisted,
And found his thoughts flow strangely clear,
Swung in a basket in mid air:
Our culprit thus, in purer sky,
With like advantage raised his eye,
And looking forth in prospect wide,
His Tory errors clearly spied,
And from his elevated station,

With bawling voice began addressing.
"Good Gentlemen and friends and kin,
For heaven's sake hear, if not for mine!
I here renounce the Pope, the Turks,
The King, the Devil and all their works;
And will, set me but once at ease,
Turn Whig or Christian, what you please;
And always mind your rules so justly,
Should I live long as old Methus'lah,
I'll never join in British rage,
Nor help Lord North, nor Gen'ral Gage;
Nor lift my gun in future fights,
Nor take away your Charter-rights;
Nor overcome your new-raised levies,
Destroy your towns, nor burn your navies;
Nor cut your poles down while I've breath,
Though raised more thick than hatchel-teeth:
But leave King George and all his elves
To do their conq'ring work themselves."
This said, they lower'd him down in state,
Spread at all points, like falling cat;
But took a vote first on the question,
That they'd accept this full confession,
And to their fellowship and favor,
Restore him on his good behaviour.
Not so our 'Squire submits to rule,
But stood, heroic as a mule.
"You'll find it all in vain, quoth he,
To play your rebel tricks on me.
All punishments, the world can render,
Serve only to provoke th' offender;
The will gains strength from treatment horrid,
As hides grow harder when they're curried.
With good opinion of the law;
No man e'er felt the halter draw,
Or held in method orthodox
His love of justice, in the stocks;
Or fail'd to lose by sheriff's shears
At once his loyalty and ears.
Have you made Murray look less big,
Or smoked old Williams to a Whig?
Did our mobb'd Ol'ver quit his station,
Or heed his vows of resignation?
Has Rivington, in dread of stripes,
Ceased lying since you stole his types?
And can you think my faith will alter,
By tarring, whipping or the halter?
I'll stand the worst; for recompense
I trust King George and Providence.
And when with conquest gain'd I come,
Array'd in law and terror home,
Ye'll rue this inauspicious morn,
And curse the day, when ye were born,
In Job's high style of imprecations,
With all his plagues, without his patience."
Meanwhile beside the pole, the guard
A bench of Justice had prepared,
Where sitting round in awful sort
The grand Committee hold their Court;
While all the crew, in silent awe,
Wait from their lips the lore of law.
Few moments with deliberation
They hold the solemn consultation;
When soon in judgment all agree,
And Clerk proclaims the dread decree;
"That 'Squire M'Fingal having grown
The vilest Tory in the town,
And now in full examination
Convicted by his own confession,
Finding no tokens of repentance,
This Court proceeds to render sentence:
That first the Mob a slip-knot single
Tie round the neck of said M'Fingal,
And in due form do tar him next,
And feather, as the law directs;
Then through the town attendant ride him

In cart with Constable beside him,
And having held him up to shame,
Bring to the pole, from whence he came."
  Forthwith the crowd proceed to deck
With halter'd noose M'Fingal's neck,
While he in peril of his soul
Stood tied half-hanging to the pole;
Then lifting high the ponderous jar,
Pour'd o'er his head the smoaking tar.
With less profusion once was spread
Oil on the Jewish monarch's head,
That down his beard and vestments ran,
And cover'd all his outward man.
As when (so Claudian sings) the Gods
And earth-born Giants fell at odds,
The stout Enceladus in malice
Tore mountains up to throw at Pallas;
And while he held them o'er his head,
The river, from their fountains fed,
Pour'd down his back its copious tide,
And wore its channels in his hide:
So from the high-raised urn the torrents
Spread down his side their various currents;
His flowing wig, as next the brim,
First met and drank the sable stream;
Adown his visage stern and grave
Roll'd and adhered the viscid wave;
With arms depending as he stood,
Each cuff capacious holds the flood;
From nose and chin's remotest end,
The tarry icicles descend;
Till all o'erspread, with colors gay,
He glitter'd to the western ray,
Like sleet-bound trees in wintry skies,
Or Lapland idol carved in ice.
And now the feather-bag display'd
Is waved in triumph o'er his head,
And clouds him o'er with feathers missive,
And down, upon the tar, adhesive:
Not Maia's son, with wings for ears,
Such plumage round his visage wears;
Nor Milton's six-wing'd angel gathers
Such superfluity of feathers.
Now all complete appears our 'Squire,
Like Gorgon or Chimæra dire;
Nor more could boast on Plato's plan
To rank among the race of man,
Or prove his claim to human nature,
As a two-legg'd, unfeather'd creature.
  Then on the fatal cart, in state
They raised our grand Duumvirate.
And as at Rome a like committee,
Who found an owl within their city,
With solemn rites and grave processions
At every shrine perform'd lustrations;
And least infection might take place
From such grim fowl with feather'd face,
All Rome attends him through the street
In triumph to his country seat:
With like devotion all the choir
Paraded round our awful 'Squire;
In front the martial music comes
Of horns and fiddles, fifes and drums,
With jingling sound of carriage bells,
And treble creak of rusted wheels.
Behind, the croud, in lengthen'd row
With proud procession, closed the show.
And at fit periods every throat
Combined in universal shout;
And hail'd great Liberty in chorus,
Or bawl'd 'confusion to the Tories.'
Not louder storm the welkin braves
From clamors of conflicting waves;
Less dire in Lybian wilds the noise
When rav'ning lions lift their voice;
Or triumphs at town-meetings made,
On passing votes to regulate trade.
  Thus having borne them round the town,
Last at the pole they set them down;
And to the tavern take their way
To end in mirth the festal day.
  And now the Mob, dispersed and gone,
Left 'Squire and Constable alone.
The constable with rueful face

Lean'd sad and solemn o'er a brace;
And fast beside him, cheek by jowl,
Stuck 'Squire M'Fingal 'gainst the pole,
Glued by the tar t' his rear applied,
Like barnacle on vessel's side.
But though his body lack'd physician,
His spirit was in worse condition.
He found his fears of whips and ropes
By many a drachm outweigh'd his hopes.
As men in jail without mainprize
View every thing with other eyes,
And all goes wrong in church and state,
Seen through perspective of the grate:
So now M'Fingal's Second-sight
Beheld all things in gloomier light;
His visual nerve, well purged with tar,
Saw all the coming scenes of war.
As his prophetic soul grew stronger,
He found he could hold in no longer.
First from the pole, as fierce he shook,
His wig from pitchy durance broke,
His mouth unglued, his feathers flutter'd,
His tarr'd skirts crack'd, and thus he utter'd.
"Ah, Mr. Constable, in vain
We strive 'gainst wind and tide and rain!
Behold my doom! this feathery omen
Portends what dismal times are coming.
Now future scenes, before my eyes,
And second-sighted forms arise.
I hear a voice, that calls away,
And cries 'The Whigs will win the day.'
My beck'ning Genius gives command,
And bids me fly the fatal land;
Where changing name and constitution,
Rebellion turns to Revolution,
While Loyalty, oppress'd, in tears,
Stands trembling for its neck and ears.
"Go, summon all our brethren, greeting,
To muster at our usual meeting;
There my prophetic voice shall warn 'em
Of all things future that concern 'em,
And scenes disclose on which, my friend,
Their conduct and their lives depend.
There I—but first 'tis more of use,
From this vile pole to set me loose;
Then go with cautious steps and steady,
While I steer home and make all ready.

1775–82

III. JOEL BARLOW
(1754–1812)

THE HASTY-PUDDING

A POEM IN THREE CANTOS

Omne tulit punctum qui miscuit utile dulci.
He makes a good breakfast who mixes pudding with molasses.

PREFACE

A simplicity in diet, whether it be considered with reference to the happiness of individuals or the prosperity of a nation, is of more consequence than we are apt to imagine. In recommending so important an object to the rational part of mankind, I wish it were in my power to do it in such a manner as would be likely to gain their attention. I am sensible that it is one of those subjects in which example has infinitely more power than the most convincing arguments on the highest charms of poetry. Goldsmith's Deserted Village, *though possessing these two advantages in a greater degree than any other work of the kind, has not prevented villages in England from being deserted. The apparent interest of the rich individuals, who form the taste as well as the laws in that country, has been against him; and with that interest it has been vain to contend.*

The vicious habits which in this little piece I endeavor to combat, seem to me not so difficult to cure. No class of people has any interest *in supporting them; unless it be the interest which certain families may feel in vying with each other in sumptuous entertainments. There may indeed be some instances of depraved appetites, which no arguments will conquer; but these may be rare. There are very few persons but what would always prefer a plain dish for themselves, and would prefer it likewise for their guests, if there were no risk of reputation in the case. This difficulty can only be removed by example; and the example should proceed from those whose situation enables them to take the lead in forming the manners of a nation. Persons of this description in America, I should hope, are neither above nor below the influence of truth and reason, when conveyed in language suited to the subject.*

Whether the manner I have chosen to address my arguments to them be such as to promise any success is what I cannot decide. But I certainly had hopes of doing some good, or I should not have taken the pains of putting so many rhymes together.—The example of domestic virtues has doubtless a great effect. I only wish to rank simplicity of diet *among the virtues. In that case I should hope it will be cherished and more esteemed by others than it is at present.*

THE AUTHOR.

THE HASTY-PUDDING: A POEM

CANTO I

Ye Alps audacious, thro' the heav'ns that rise,
To cramp the day and hide me from the skies;
Ye Gallic flags, that o'er their heights unfurl'd,
Bear death to kings, and freedom to the world,
I sing not you. A softer theme I chuse,
A virgin theme, unconscious of the Muse,
But fruitful, rich, well suited to inspire
The purest frenzy of poetic fire.
Despise it not, ye Bards to terror steel'd,
Who hurl your thunders round the epic field;
Nor ye who strain your midnight throats to sing
Joys that the vineyard and the still-house bring;
Or on some distant fair your notes employ,
And speak of raptures that you ne'er enjoy.
I sing the sweets I know, the charms I feel,
My morning incense, and my evening meal,
The sweets of Hasty-Pudding. Come, dear bowl,
Glide o'er my palate, and inspire my soul.
The milk beside thee, smoking from the kine,
Its substance mingled, married in with thine,
Shall cool and temper thy superior heat,

And save the pains of blowing while I eat.

Oh! could the smooth, the emblematic song
Flow like thy genial juices o'er my tongue,
Could those mild morsels in my numbers chime,
And, as they roll in substance, roll in rhyme,
No more thy aukward unpoetic name
Should shun the muse, or prejudice thy fame;
But rising grateful to th' accustom'd ear,
All Bards should catch it, and all realms revere!

Assist me first with pious toil to trace
Thro' wrecks of time thy lineage and thy race;
Declare what lovely squaw, in days of yore,
(Ere great Columbus sought thy native shore)
First gave thee to the world; her works of fame
Have liv'd indeed, but liv'd without a name.
Some tawny Ceres, goddess of her days,
First learn'd with stones to crack the well-dry'd maize,
Thro' the rough seive to shake the golden show'r,
In boiling water stir the yellow flour:
The yellow flour, bestrew'd and stir'd with haste,
Swells in the flood and thickens to a paste,
Then puffs and wallops, rises to the brim,
Drinks the dry knobs that on the surface swim;
The knobs at last the busy ladle breaks,
And the whole mass its true consistence takes.
Could but her sacred name, unknown so long,
Rise like her labors, to the son of song,
To her, to them, I'd consecrate my lays,
And blow her pudding with the breath of praise.
If 'twas Oella whom I sang before,
I here ascribe her one great virtue more.
Not thro' the rich Peruvian realms alone
The fame of Sol's sweet daughter should be known,
But o'er the world's wide clime should live secure,
Far as his rays extend, as long as they endure.

Dear Hasty-Pudding, what unpromis'd joy
Expands my heart, to meet thee in Savoy!
Doom'd o'er the world thro' devious paths to roam,
Each clime my country, and each house my home,
My soul is sooth'd, my cares have found an end,
I greet my long-lost, unforgotten friend.

For thee thro' Paris, that corrupted town,
How long in vain I wandered up and down,
Where shameless Bacchus, with his drenching hoard,
Cold from his cave usurps the morning board.
London is lost in smoke and steep'd in tea;
No Yankee there can lisp the name of thee;
The uncouth word, a libel on the town,
Would call a proclamation from the crown.
For climes oblique, that fear the sun's full rays,
Chilled in their fogs, exclude the generous maize;

A grain whose rich luxuriant growth requires
Short gentle showers, and bright, ethereal fires.

But here, though distant from our native shore,
With mutual glee we meet and laugh once more.
The same! I know thee by that yellow face,
That strong complexion of true Indian race,
Which time can never change, nor soil impair,
Nor Alpine snows, nor Turkey's morbid air;
For endless years, thro' every mild domain,
Where grows the maize, there thou art sure to reign.

But man, more fickle, the bold licence claims,
In different realms to give thee different names.
Thee the soft nations round the warm Levant
Polanta call, the French of course, *Polante;*
E'en in thy native regions, how I blush
To hear the Pennsylvanians call thee *Mush!*
On Hudson's banks, while men of Belgic spawn
Insult and eat thee by the name *Suppawn.*
All spurious appellations, void of truth;
I've better known thee from my earliest youth,
Thy name is *Hasty-Pudding!* thus our sires
Were wont to greet thee fuming from the fires;
And while they argu'd in thy just defence
With logic clear, they thus explained the sense:—
"In *haste* the boiling cauldron, o'er the blaze,
Receives and cooks the ready-powder'd maize;
In *haste* 'tis serv'd, and then in equal *haste,*
With cooling milk, we make the sweet repast.
No carving to be done, no knife to grate
The tender ear, and wound the stony plate;
But the smooth spoon, just fitted to the lip,
And taught with art the yielding mass to dip,
By frequent journeys to the bowl well stor'd,
Performs the hasty honors of the board."
Such is thy name, significant and clear,
A name, a sound to every Yankee dear,
But most to me, whose heart and palate chaste
Preserve my pure hereditary taste.

There are who strive to stamp with disrepute
The luscious food, because it feeds the brute;
In tropes of high-strain'd wit, while gaudy prigs
Compare thy nursling man to pamper'd pigs;
With sovereign scorn I treat the vulgar jest,
Nor fear to share thy bounties with the beast.
What though the generous cow gives me to quaff
The milk nutritious; am I then a calf?
Or can the genius of the noisy swine,
Tho' nursed on pudding, thence lay claim to mine?
Sure the sweet song, I fashion to thy praise,
Runs more melodious than the notes they raise.

My song resounding in its grateful glee,

No merit claims; I praise myself in thee.
My father lov'd thee thro' his length of days!
For thee his fields were shaded o'er with maize;
From thee what health, what vigor he possest,
Ten sturdy freemen sprung from him attest;
Thy constellation ruled my natal morn,
And all my bones were made of Indian corn.
Delicious grain! whatever form it take,
To roast or boil, to smother or to bake,
In every dish 'tis welcome still to me,
But most, my Hasty-Pudding, most in thee.
  Let the green succatash with thee contend,
Let beans and corn their sweetest juices blend,
Let butter drench them in its yellow tide,
And a long slice of bacon grace their side;
Not all the plate, how famed soe'er it be,
Can please my palate like a bowl of thee.
  Some talk of Hoe-Cake, fair Virginia's pride,
Rich Johnny-Cake this mouth has often tri'd;
Both please me well, their virtues much the same;
Alike their fabric, as allied their fame,
Except in dear New England, where the last
Receives a dash of pumpkin in the paste,
To give it sweetness and improve the taste.
But place them all before me, smoaking hot,
The big round dumplin rolling from the pot;
The pudding of the bag, whose quivering breast,
With suet lined leads on the Yankee feast;
The Charlotte brown, within whose crusty sides
A belly soft the pulpy apple hides;
The yellow bread whose face like amber glows,
And all of Indian that the bake-pan knows—
Ye tempt me not—my fav'rite greets my eyes,
To that lov'd bowl my spoon by instinct flies.

CANTO II

TO mix the food by vicious rules of art,
To kill the stomach and to sink the heart,
To make mankind to social virtue sour,
Cram o'er each dish, and be what they devour;
For this the Kitchen Muse first fram'd her book,
Commanding sweats to stream from every cook;
Children no more their antic gambols tri'd,
And friends to physic wonder'd why they died.
  Not so the Yankee—his abundant feast,
With simples furnish'd, and with plainness drest,
A numerous offspring gathers round the board,
And cheers alike the servant and the lord;
Whose well-bought hunger prompts the joyous taste,
And health attends them from the short repast.
  While the full pail rewards the milkmaid's toil,
The mother sees the morning cauldron boil;

To stir the pudding next demands their care,
To spread the table and the bowls prepare;
To feed the children, as their portions cool,
And comb their heads, and send them off to school.
Yet may the simplest dish some rules impart,
For nature scorns not all the aids of art.
E'en Hasty-Pudding, purest of all food,
May still be bad, indifferent, or good,
As sage experience the short process guides,
Or want of skill, or want of care presides.
Whoe'er would form it on the surest plan,
To rear the child and long sustain the man;
To shield the morals while it mends the size,
And all the powers of every food supplies,
Attend the lessons that the Muse shall bring,
Suspend your spoons, and listen while I sing.
But since, O man! thy life and health demand
Not food alone, but labour from thy hand,
First in the field, beneath the sun's strong rays,
Ask of thy Mother Earth the needful maize;
She loves the race that courts her yielding soil,
And gives her bounties to the sons of toil.
When now the ox, obedient to thy call,
Repays the loan that fill'd the winter stall,
Pursue his traces o'er the furrow'd plain,
And plant in measur'd hills the golden grain.
But when the tender germe begins to shoot,
And the green spire declares the sprouting root,
Then guard your nursling from each greedy foe,
Th' insidious worm, the all-devouring crow.
A little ashes, sprinkled round the spire,
Soon steep'd in rain, will bid the worm retire;
The feather'd robber with his hungry maw
Swift flies the field before your man of straw,
A frightful image, such as school-boys bring
When met to burn the Pope, or hang the King.
Thrice in the season, through each verdant row
Wield the strong plow-share and the faithful hoe;
The faithful hoe; a double task that takes,
To till the summer corn, and roast the winter cakes.
Slow springs the blade, while check'd by chilling rains,
Ere yet the sun the seat of Cancer gains;
But when his fiercest fires emblaze the land,
Then start the juices, then the roots expand;
Then, like a column of Corinthian mould,
The stalk struts upward, and the leaves unfold;
The bushy branches all the ridges fill,
Entwine their arms, and kiss from hill to hill.
Here cease to vex them, all your cares are done;
Leave the last labors to the parent sun;

Beneath his genial smiles, the well-drest field,
When autumn calls, a plenteous crop shall yield.
  Now the strong foliage bears the standards high,
And shoots the tall top-gallants to the sky;
The suckling ears their silky fringes bend,
And pregnant grown, their swelling coats distend;
The loaded stalk, while still the burthen grows,
O'erhangs the space that runs between the rows;
High as a hop-field waves the silent grove,
A safe retreat for little thefts of love,
When the pledg'd roasting-ears invite the maid,
To meet her swain beneath the new-form'd shade;
His generous hand unloads the cumbrous hill,
And the green spoils her ready basket fill;
Small compensation for the two-fold bliss,
The promis'd wedding and the present kiss.
  Slight depredations these: but now the moon
Calls from his hollow tree the sly raccoon;
And while by night he bears his prize away,
The bolder squirrel labors thro' the day.
Both thieves alike, but provident of time,
A virtue rare, that almost hides their crime.
Then let them steal the little stores they can,
And fill their grain'ries from the toils of man;
We've one advantage where they take no part,—
With all their wiles they ne'er have found the art
To boil the Hasty-Pudding; here we shine
Superior far to tenants of the pine;
This envy'd boon to man shall still belong,
Unshar'd by them in substance or in song.
  At last the closing season browns the plain,
And ripe October gathers in the grain;
Deep loaded carts the spacious corn-house fill,
The sack distended marches to the mill;
The lab'ring mill beneath the burthen groans,
And show'rs the future pudding from the stones;
Till the glad house-wife greets the powder'd gold,
And the new crop exterminates the old.
[Ah! who can sing what every wight must feel,
The joy that enters with the bag of meal.
A general jubilee pervades the house,
Wakes every child and gladdens every mouse.]

CANTO III

THE days grow short; but though the falling sun
To the glad swain proclaims his day's work done,
Night's pleasing shades his various task prolong,
And yield new subjects to my various song.
For now, the corn-house fill'd, the harvest home,
Th' invited neighbours to the *Husking* come;
A frolic scene, where work, and mirth, and play,
Unite their charms, to chace the hours away.

Where the huge heap lies center'd in the hall,
The lamp suspended from the cheerful wall,
Brown corn-fed nymphs, and strong hard-handed beaux,
Alternate rang'd, extend in circling rows,
Assume their seats, the solid mass attack;
The dry husks rustle, and the corn-cobs crack;
The song, the laugh, alternate notes resound,
And the sweet cider trips in silence round.

The laws of Husking ev'ry wight can tell;
And sure no laws he ever keeps so well:
For each red ear a general kiss he gains,
With each smut ear she smuts the luckless swains;
But when to some sweet maid a prize is cast,
Red as her lips, and taper as her waist,
She walks the round, and culls one favor'd beau,
Who leaps, the luscious tribute to bestow.
Various the sport, as are the wits and brains
Of well pleas'd lasses and contending swains;
Till the vast mound of corn is swept away,
And he that gets the last ear, wins the day.

Meanwhile the house-wife urges all her care,
The well-earn'd feast to hasten and prepare.
The sifted meal already waits her hand,
The milk is strain'd, the bowls in order stand,
The fire flames high; and, as a pool (that takes
The headlong stream that o'er the mill-dam breaks)
Foams, roars and rages with incessant toils,
So the vext cauldron rages, roars and boils.

First with clean salt she seasons well the food,
Then strews the flour, and thickens all the flood.
Long o'er the simmering fire she lets it stand:
To stir it well demands a stronger hand;
The husband takes his turn, and round and round
The ladle flies; at last the toil is crown'd;
When to the board the thronging huskers pour,
And take their seats as at the corn before.

I leave them to their feast. There still belong
More copious matters to my faithful song.
For rules there are, though ne'er unfolded yet,
Nice rules and wise, how pudding should be ate.

Some with molasses line the luscious treat,
And mix, like bards, the useful with the sweet.
A wholesome dish, and well deserving praise,
A great resource in those bleak wintry days,
When the chill'd earth lies buried deep in snow,
And raging Boreas drives the shivering cow.

Blest cow! thy praise shall still my notes employ,
Great source of health, the only source of joy;
Mother of Egypt's god;—but sure, for me,
Were I to leave my God, I'd worship thee.

How oft thy teats these pious hands have prest!
How oft thy bounties prove my only feast!
How oft I've fed thee with my fav'rite grain!
And roar'd like thee, to see thy children slain!
Ye swains who know her various worth to prize,
Ah! house her well from Winter's angry skies.
Potatoes, pumpkins, should her sadness cheer,
Corn from your crib, and mashes from your beer;
When spring returns she'll well acquit the loan,
And nurse at once your infants and her own.
Milk then with pudding I should always chuse;
To this in future I confine my Muse,
Till she in haste some farther hints unfold,
Well for the young, nor useless to the old.
First in your bowl the milk abundant take,
Then drop with care along the silver lake
Your flakes of pudding; these at first will hide
Their little bulk beneath the swelling tide;
But when their growing mass no more can sink,
When the soft island looms above the brink,
Then check your hand; you've got the portion's due,
So taught our sires, and what they taught is true.
There is a choice in spoons. Tho' small appear
The nice distinction, yet to me 'tis clear.
The deep bowl'd Gallic spoon, contriv'd to scoop
In ample draughts the thin diluted soup,
Performs not well in those substantial things,
Whose mass adhesive to the metal clings;
Where the strong labial muscles must embrace,
The gentle curve, and sweep the hollow space.
With ease to enter and discharge the freight,
A bowl less concave but still more dilate,
Becomes the pudding best. The shape, the size,
A secret rests unknown to vulgar eyes.
Experienc'd feeders can alone impart
A rule so much above the lore of art.
These tuneful lips, that thousand spoons have tried,
With just precision could the point decide,
Tho' not in song; the muse but poorly shines
In cones, and cubes, and geometric lines.
Yet the true form, as near as she can tell,
Is that small section of a goose-egg shell,
Which in two equal portions shall divide
The distance from the centre to the side.
Fear not to slaver; 'tis no deadly sin.
Like the free Frenchman, from your joyous chin
Suspend the ready napkin; or, like me,
Poise with one hand your bowl upon your knee;
Just in the zeneth your wise head project,
Your full spoon, rising in a line direct,
Bold as a bucket, heeds no drops that fall,

The wide mouth'd bowl will surely catch them all!
(1793) 1796

IV. FRANCIS HOPKINSON
(1737–1791)

TO MYRTILLA

With sprightly air, and graceful mien,
Easy and ever gay;
Myrtilla trips along the green,
And steals all hearts away.

Good-humour smiling in her face,
Seems sorrow to defy;
Wit lights up ev'ry sprightly grace,
And sparkles in her eye.

Fair is her form, her spotless mind
With ev'ry virtue blest;
And no offence could ever find
A harbour in her breast.

Ye swains, with caution pass this way;
For should you meet the fair,
You must to beauty fall a prey;
Love would your hearts ensnare.
(1766) 1792

THE BATTLE OF THE KEGS

Gallants attend and hear a friend,
Trill forth harmonious ditty,
Strange things I'll tell which late befel
In Philadelphia city.

'Twas early day, as poets say,
Just when the sun was rising,
A soldier stood on a log of wood,
And saw a thing surprising.

As in amaze he stood to gaze,
The truth can't be denied, sir,
He spied a score of kegs or more
Come floating down the tide, sir.

A sailor too in jerkin blue,
This strange appearance viewing,
First damn'd his eyes, in great surprise,
Then said some mischief's brewing.

These kegs, I'm told, the rebels bold,
Pack'd up like pickling herring;
And they're come down t' attack the town,
In this new way of ferrying.

The soldier flew, the sailor too,
And scar'd almost to death, sir,
Wore out their shoes, to spread the news,
And ran till out of breath, sir.

Now up and down throughout the town,
Most frantic scenes were acted;
And some ran here, and others there,
Like men almost distracted.

Some fire cry'd, which some denied,
But said the earth had quaked;
And girls and boys, with hideous noise,
Ran thro' the streets half naked.

Sir William he, snug as a flea,
Lay all this time asnoring,
Nor dream'd of harm as he lay warm,
In bed with Mrs. L—g.

Now in a fright, he starts upright,
Awak'd by such a clatter;
He rubs both eyes, and boldly cries,
For God's sake, what's the matter?

At his bed-side he then espy'd,
Sir Erskine at command, sir,
Upon one foot, he had one boot,
And th' other in his hand, sir.

"Arise, arise, sir Erskine cries,
The rebels—more's the pity,
Without a boat are all afloat,
And rang'd before the city.

"The motley crew, in vessels new,
With Satan for their guide, sir.
Pack'd up in bags, or wooden kegs,
Come driving down the tide, sir.

"Therefore prepare for bloody war,
These kegs must all be routed,
Or surely we despised shall be,
And British courage doubted."

The royal band, now ready stand
All rang'd in dread array, sir,
With stomach stout to see it out,
And make a bloody day, sir.

The cannons roar from shore to shore,
The small arms make a rattle;
Since wars began I'm sure no man
E'er saw so strange a battle.

The rebel dales, the rebel vales,
With rebel trees surrounded;
The distant wood, the hills and floods,
With rebel echoes sounded.

The fish below swam to and fro,
Attack'd from ev'ry quarter;
Why sure, thought they, the devil's to pay,
'Mongst folks above the water.

The kegs, 'tis said, tho' strongly made,
Of rebel staves and hoops, sir,
Could not oppose their powerful foes,
The conqu'ring British troops, sir.

From morn to night these men of might
Display'd amazing courage;
And when the sun was fairly down,
Retir'd to sup their porrage.

An hundred men with each a pen,
Or more upon my word, sir,
It is most true would be too few,
Their valour to record, sir.

Such feats did they perform that day,
Against these wick'd kegs, sir,
That years to come, if they get home,
They'll make their boasts and brags, sir.

1778

THE NEW ROOF: A SONG FOR FEDERAL MECHANICS

I

Come, muster, my lads, your mechanical tools,
Your saws and your axes, your hammers and rules;
Bring your mallets and planes, your level and line,
And plenty of pins of American pine:
For our roof we will raise, and our song still shall be,
Our government firm, and our citizens free.

II

Come, up with *the plates*, lay them firm on the wall,
Like the people at large, they're the ground work of all;
Examine them well, and see that they're sound,
Let no rotten part in our building be found:
For our roof we will raise, and our song still shall be
A government firm, and our citizens free.

III

Now hand up the *girders,* lay each in his place,
Between them the *joists,* must divide all the space;
Like assemblymen *these* should lie level along,
Like *girders,* our senate prove loyal and strong:
For our roof we will raise, and our song still shall be
A government firm over citizens free.

IV

The *rafters* now frame; your *king-posts* and *braces,*
And drive your pins home, to keep all in their places;
Let wisdom and strength in the fabric combine,
And your pins be all made of American pine:
For our roof we will raise, and our song still shall be,
A government firm over citizens free.

V

Our *king-posts* are *judges;* how upright they stand,
Supporting the *braces;* the laws of the land:
The laws of the land, which divide right from wrong,
And strengthen the weak, by weak'ning the strong:
For our roof we will raise, and our song still shall be,
Laws equal and just, for a people that's free.

VI

Up! up! with the *rafters;* each frame is a *state:*
How nobly they rise! their span, too, how great!
From the north to the south, o'er the whole they extend,
And rest on the walls, whilst the walls they defend:
For our roof we will raise, and our song still shall be
Combined in strength, yet as citizens free.

VII

Now enter the *purlins,* and drive your pins through;
And see that your joints are drawn home and all true.
The *purlins* will bind all the rafters together:
The strength of the whole shall defy wind and weather:
For our roof we will raise, and our song still shall be,
United as states, but as citizens free.

VIII

Come, raise up the *turret;* our glory and pride;
In the centre it stands, o'er the whole to *preside:*
The sons of Columbia shall view with delight
Its pillars, and arches, and towering height:
Our roof is now rais'd, and our song still shall be,
A federal head o'er a people that's free.

IX

Huzza! my brave boys, our work is complete;
The world shall admire Columbia's fair seat;
Its strength against tempest and time shall be proof,
And thousands shall come to dwell under our roof:
Whilst we drain the deep bowl, our toast still shall be
Our government firm, and our citizens free.

1788

ON WHITE-WASHING

DEAR SIR,

The peculiar customs of every country appear to strangers awkward and absurd, but the inhabitants consider them as very proper and even necessary. Long habit imposes on the understanding, and reconciles it to any thing that is not manifestly pernicious or immediately destructive.

The religion of a country is scarcely

held in greater veneration than its established customs: and it is almost as difficult to produce an alteration in the one as in the other. Any interference of government for the reformation of natural customs, however trivial and absurd they may be, never fails to produce the greatest discontent, and sometimes dangerous convulsions. Of this there are frequent instances in history. Bad habits are most safely removed by the same means that establish them, viz. by imperceptible gradations, and the constant example and influence of the higher class of the people.

We are apt to conclude that the fashions and manners of our own country are most rational and proper, because the eye and the understanding have long since been reconciled to them, and we ridicule or condemn those of other nations on account of their novelty: yet the foreigner will defend his national habits with at least as much plausibility as we can our own. The truth is, that reason has little to do in the matter. Customs are for the most part arbitrary, and one nation has as good a right to fix its peculiarities as another. It is of no purpose to talk of convenience as a standard: every thing becomes convenient by practice and habit.

I have read somewhere of a nation (in Africa I think) which is governed by twelve counsellors. When these counsellors are to meet on public business, twelve large earthen jars are set in two rows, and filled with water. The counsellors enter the apartment one after another, stark naked, and each leaps into a jar, where he sits up to the chin in water. When the jars are all filled with counsellors, they proceed to deliberate on the great concerns of the nation. This, to be sure, forms a very grotesque scene; but the object is to transact the public business: they have been accustomed to do it in this way, and therefore it appears to them the most rational and convenient way. Indeed, if we consider it impartially, there seems to be no reason why a counsellor may not be as wise in an earthen jar as in an elbow chair; or why the good of the people may not be as maturely considered in the one as in the other.

The established manners of every country are the standards of propriety with the people who have adopted them; and every nation assumes the right of considering all deviations therefrom as barbarisms and absurdities.

The *Chinese* have retained their laws and customs for ages immemorial: and although they have long had a commercial intercourse with European nations, and are well acquainted with their improvements in the arts, and their modes of civilization, yet they are so far from being convinced of any superiority in the European manners, that their government takes the most serious measures to prevent the customs of foreigners taking root amongst them. It employs their utmost vigilance to enjoy the benefits of commerce, and at the same time guard against innovations that might affect the characteristic manners of the people.

Since the discovery of the *Sandwich* islands in the South-Sea, they have been visited by ships from several nations; yet the natives have shewn no inclination to prefer the dress and manners of the visitors to their own.

It is even probable that they pity the ignorance of the Europeans they have seen, as far removed from civilization; and value themselves on the propriety and advantage of their own customs.

There is nothing new in these observations, and I had no intention of making them when I sat down to write, but they obtruded themselves upon me. My intention was to give you some account of the people of these new states; but I am not sufficiently informed for the purpose, having, as yet, seen little more than the cities of *New-York* and *Philadelphia*. I have discovered but few national singularities amongst them. Their customs and manners are nearly the same with those of England, which they have long been used to copy. For, previous to the late revolution, the Americans were taught from their infancy to look up to the English as the patterns of perfection in all things.

I have, however, observed one custom, which, for ought I know, is peculiar to this country. An account of it will serve to fill up the remainder of this sheet, and may afford you some amusement.

When a young couple are about to enter on the matrimonial state, a never failing article in the marriage treaty is, that the lady shall have and enjoy the free and unmolested exercise of the rights of WHITE-WASHING, with all its ceremonials, privileges, and appurtenances. You will wonder what this privilege of *white-washing* is. I will endeavour to give you an idea of the ceremony, as I have seen it performed.

There is no season of the year in which the lady may not, if she pleases, claim her privilege; but the latter end of May is generally fixed upon for the purpose. The attentive husband may judge, by certain prognostics, when the storm is nigh at hand. If the lady grows uncommonly fretful, finds fault with the servants, is discontented with the children, and complains much of the nastiness of every thing about her: these are symptoms which ought not to be neglected, yet they sometimes go off without any further effect. But if, when the husband rises in the morning, he should observe in the yard, a wheelbarrow, with a quantity of lime in it, or should see certain buckets filled with a solution of lime in water, there is no time for hesitation. He immediately locks up the apartment or closet where his papers, and private property are kept, and putting the key in his pocket, betakes himself to flight. A husband. however beloved, becomes a perfect nuisance during this season of female rage. His authority is superseded, his commission suspended, and the very scullion who cleans the brasses in the kitchen becomes of more importance than him. He has nothing for it but to abdicate, for a time, and run from an evil which he can neither prevent nor mollify.

The husband gone, the ceremony begins. The walls are stripped of their furniture—paintings, prints, and looking-glasses lie in huddled heaps about the floors; the curtains are torn from their testers, the beds crammed into windows, chairs and tables, bedsteads and cradles crowd the yard; and the garden fence bends beneath the weight of carpets, blankets, cloth cloaks, old coats, under petticoats, and ragged breeches. *Here* may be seen the lumber of the kitchen, forming a dark and confused mass for the fore-ground of the picture; gridirons and frying-pans, rusty shovels and broken tongs, joint stools, and the fractured remains of rush bottomed chairs. *There* a closet has disgorged its bowels—rivetted plates and dishes, halves of china bowls, cracked tumblers, broken wine-glasses, phials of forgotten physic, papers of unknown powders, seeds and dried herbs, tops of tea-pots, and stoppers of departed decanters—from the rag hole in the garret, to the rat hole in the cellar, no place escapes unrummaged. It would seem as if the day of general doom was come, and the utensils of the house were dragged forth to judgment. In this tempest, the words of king *Lear* unavoidably present, and might with little alteration be made strictly applicable.

Let the great gods
That keep this dreadful pudder o'er our heads
Find out their enemies now. Tremble thou wretch
That hast within thee undivulged crimes
Unwhipt of justice. Close pent up guilt,
Rive your concealing continents, and ask
These dreadful summoners grace.

This ceremony completed, and the house thoroughly evacuated, the next operation is to smear the walls and ceilings with brushes, dipped in a solution of lime called WHITE-WASH; to pour buckets of water over every floor, and scratch all the partitions and wainscots with hard brushes, charged with soft soap and stone-cutter's sand.

The windows by no means escape the general deluge. A servant scrambles out upon the pent-house, at the risk of her neck, and with a mug in her hand, and a bucket within reach, dashes innumerable gallons of water against the glass panes, to the great annoyance of passengers in the street.

I have been told that an action at law, was once brought against one of these water nymphs, by a person who had a new suit of clothes spoiled by this operation: but after long argument it was determined, that no damages could be awarded; inasmuch as the defendant was in the exercise of a legal right, and not answerable for the consequences. And so the poor gentleman was doubly nonsuited; for he lost both his suit of clothes and his suit at law.

These smearings and scratchings, these washings and dashings, being duly performed, the next ceremonial is to cleanse and replace the distracted furniture. You may have seen a house-raising, or a ship-launch—recollect, if you can, the hurry, bustle, confusions, and noise of such a scene, and you will have some idea of this cleansing match. The misfortune is, that the sole object is to make things *clean.* It matters not how many useful, ornamental, or valuable articles suffer mutilation or death under the operation. A mahogany chair and a carved frame undergo the same discipline: they are to be made *clean* at all events; but their preservation is not worthy of attention. For instance: a fine large engraving is laid flat upon the floor; a number of smaller prints are piled upon it, until the super-incumbent weight cracks the lower glass—but this is of no importance. A valuable picture is placed leaning against the sharp corner of a table; others are made to lean against that, till the pressure of the whole forces the corner of the table through the canvas of the first. The frame and glass of a fine print are to be cleaned; the spirit and oil used on this occasion are suffered to leak through and deface the engraving—no matter! If the glass is clean and the frame shines it is sufficient—the rest is not worthy of consideration. An able arithmetician hath made a calculation, founded on long experience, and proved that the losses and destruction incident to two white-washings are equal to one removal and three removals equal to one fire.

This cleansing frolic over, matters begin to resume their pristine appearance: the storm abates, and all would be well again; but it is impossible that so great a convulsion in so small a community should pass over without producing some consequences. For two or three weeks after the operation, the family are usually afflicted with sore eyes, sore throats, or severe colds, occasioned by exhalations from wet floors and damp walls.

I know a gentleman here who is fond of accounting for everything in a philosophical way. He considers this, which I call a *custom,* as a real, periodical disease, peculiar to the climate.—His train of reasoning is whimsical and ingenious, but I am not at leisure to give you the detail. The result was, that he found the distemper to be incurable; but after much study, he thought he had discovered a method to divert the evil he could not subdue. For this purpose, he caused a small building, about twelve feet square, to be erected in his garden, and furnished with some ordinary chairs and tables, and a few prints of the cheapest sort. His hope was, that when the white-washing frenzy seized the females of his family they might repair to this apartment, and scrub, and scour, and smear to their hearts content; and so spend the violence of the disease in this out-post, whilst he enjoyed himself in quiet at head-quarters. But the experiment did not answer his expectation. It was impossible it should, since a principal part of the gratification consists in the lady's having an uncontrolled right to torment her husband, at least once in every year; to turn him out of doors, and take the reins of government into her own hands.

There is a much better contrivance than this of the philosopher's: which is, to cover the walls of the house with paper. This is generally done. And though it does not abolish, it at least shortens the period of female dominion. This paper is decorated with various fancies, and made so ornamental that the women have admitted the fashion without perceiving the design.

There is also another alleviation of the husband's distress. He generally has the sole use of a small room or closet for his books and papers, the key of which he is allowed to keep. This is considered as a privileged place, even in the white-washing season, and stands like the land of *Goshen* amidst the plagues of *Egypt*. But then he must be extremely cautious, and ever upon his guard: for should he inadvertently go abroad, and leave the key in his door, the house maid, who is always on the watch for such an opportunity, immediately enters in triumph with buckets, brooms, and brushes—takes possession of the premises, and forthwith puts all his books and papers *to rights,* to his utter confusion, and sometimes serious detriment. I can give you an instance.

A gentleman was sued at law, by the executors of a mechanic, on a charge found against him in the deceased's books to the amount of £30. The defendant was strongly impressed with a belief that he had discharged the debt and taken a receipt; but as the transaction was of long standing, he knew not where to find the receipt. The suit went on in course, and the time approached when judgment should be obtained against him. He then sat down seriously to examine a large bundle of old papers, which he had untied and displayed on a table for the purpose. In the midst of his search he was suddenly called away on business of importance. He forgot to lock the door of his room. The house maid who had been long looking for such a opportunity, immediately entered with the usual implements, and with great alacrity fell to cleaning the room and *putting things to rights.* One of the first objects that struck her eye was the confused situation of the papers on the table. These, without delay, she huddled together like so many dirty knives and forks; but in the action a small piece of paper fell unnoticed to the floor, which unfortunately happened to be the very receipt in question. As it had no very respectable appearance, it was soon after swept out with the common dirt of the room, and carried in a dust pan to the yard. The tradesman had neglected to enter the credit in his book. The defendant could find nothing to obviate the charge, and so judgment went against him for debt and costs. A fortnight after the whole was settled, and the money paid, one of the children found the receipt amongst the dirt in the yard.

There is also another custom, peculiar to the city of Philadelphia, and nearly allied with the former. I mean that of washing the pavements before the doors every Saturday evening. I at first supposed this to be a regulation of the police; but, on further enquiry, I find it is a religious rite preparatory to the Sabbath: and it is, I believe, the only religious rite in which the numerous sectaries of this large city perfectly agree. The ceremony begins about sunset and continues till ten or eleven at night. It is very difficult for a stranger to walk the streets on those evenings. He runs a continual risk of having a bucket of dirty water dashed against his legs; but a Philadelphian born is so much accustomed to the danger that he avoids it with suprising dexterity. It is from this circumstance that a Philadelphian may be known any where by a certain skip in his gait. The streets of New York are paved with rough stones. These, indeed, are not washed, but the dirt is so thoroughly swept from between them that they stand up sharp and prominent, to the great annoyance of those who are not accustomed to so rough a path. But habit reconciles every thing. It is diverting enough to see a Philadelphian at New York. He walks the street with as much painful caution as if his toes were covered with corns, or his feet lamed by the gout: whilst a New Yorker, as little approving the plain masonry of Philadelphia, shuffles along the pavement like a parrot upon a mahogany table.

It must be acknowledged that the ablutions I have mentioned are attended with no small inconvenience; yet the women would not be induced by consideration to resign their privilege.

NOTWITHSTANDING this singularity, I can give you the strongest assurances that the women of America make the most faithful wives, and the most attentive mothers in the world. And I don't doubt but you will join me in opinion, that if a married man is made miserable only for one week in a whole year, he will have no great cause to complain of the matrimonial bond.

This letter has run on to a length I did not expect; I therefore hasten to assure you that I am as ever,

Your, &c. &c. &c.

1785

V. THOMAS GODFREY
(1736–1763)

SONG

I

When in *Celia's* heav'nly Eye
Soft inviting Love I spy,
Tho' you say 'tis all a cheat,
I must clasp the dear deceit.

II

Why should I more knowledge gain,
When it only gives me pain?
If deceiv'd I'm still at rest,
In the sweet Delusion blest.

1765

VI. JOSEPH DENNIE
(1768–1812)

From *THE LAY PREACHER*

THE MAN OF UNDERSTANDING

> When thou seests a man of understanding, get thee betimes unto him, and let thy feet wear the steps of his door.
>
> —Ecc. vi. 36.

Yes, in a world of weak ones, it is our duty, it will be our pleasure, and, ye selfish generations, it will be for our *interest* too, to yield favours to the wise, and bread to men of understanding. Our patronage will be but rarely exercised, and few will be the loaves for these wise men to devour, for I looked, and lo! they are a solitary and scanty band, unobtrusive, like the hermit of the mountains.

But, though the "man of understanding" is rarely to be seen, and, though it would profit us much under the sun, to gather the honey of his lips, such is our perverseness, our folly, or our fate, that, untrodden by our "feet," we suffer the moss to gather on the "steps of his door."

My study window overlooks the house of an eminent physician: he understands accurately the nice movements of the human machine; he is a botanist, skilled in the properties of plants, the cedar of Libanus, and the "hyssop on the wall;" he has meditated on the system of nature, and he has tried many of the processes of art. I see him turning over the volumes which contain the secrets of medicine, and I hear him describe skillfully, the various modes to blunt, or to extract, the arrows of disease. But, alas! my careless countrymen, "all this availeth him nothing." The blind, the maim, and the halt of our villages, refuse bread to this "man of understanding," and measure their wheat, in brimming bushels, to the quack, who cannot distinguish between a fever and the gout, who applies his nippers to a wart, and thinks he extracts a cancer, who poisons you with antimony, curdles your blood with calomel, drenches you with enfeebling teas, and, as a wit once expressed it, prescribes draughts so *neutral* they declare neither for the patient nor the malady. If the royal preacher, in whose writings I find my text, had seen whole villages, clamorous, at the midnight hour, for a fetid quack, and his powders, and "passing by on the other side," when they see the regular practitioner, he would have forgotten, for a moment, all the wisdom of the east, and, like provoked Peter, in the gospel, would "curse and swear" at such egregious folly.

Those of my readers, who will gladly turn out of the paths of error, when they hear a warning voice behind them, "here is a better path, walk therein," will, I hope, learn the value of "men of understanding." When their value is once known, the "steps of their door" will be hourly ascended. They will teach us how to think, to speak, and to act. If divines, they will not attempt to persuade you, that heaven cannot be taken, but by the violence of Scotch divinity. If lawyers, they will not demand exorbitant fees to support a rotten cause. If physicians, you will hear them utter no words more cramp than "temperance" and "regimen." If moralists, they will mark the difference between wisdom and cunning, they will point out the weakness, as well as wickedness, of those petty frauds, those iniquitous contracts, those tricking arts of *jockeyship,* so frequent and so disgraceful among a rural people, where nought but simplicity should be found. To such divines you will cheerfully vote the amplest salary, and you will receive in exchange that wisdom, which we are assured, in a volume of the highest authority, is better than rubies.

1795–96

ON THE SABBATH

> When will the new moon be gone that we may sell corn? and the sabbath, that we may set forth wheat?
>
> —Amos viii. 5.

In the dissipated cities of London and Edinburgh, the abuse of Sunday has been a common theme of reproach among those weekly guardians of the public virtue, the periodical essayists. Johnson and Hawksworth heard the turbulence of a riot, and the roar of intoxication, from the saloons and taverns of the capital; but their confidence in the innocence, or the piety of the villagers, precluded even the faint inquiry, whether holy days were profaned by rustics. Moralists might repair to the hamlet on week days, and remark vice and folly; but on the Sabbath, the young and the old, the careless and the regular, would be found no where, but in a church.

Though the catholic spirit of the age of reason indulge the latitudinarian with an immunity from Sabbath formalities, still it might be imagined there could be found, both in town and country, men, who if they did not kneel at the altar, would sit decently and seriously at the fire-side. Libertines might be averse to hear a sermon, or make a response, yet not wish a Sunday away, that they might set forth wheat, the bottle, or card table.

This, however, experience proves a vain imagination. The seventh day is observed by multitudes, neither as a season of worship, nor rest. The country and the city are alike neglectful. On Sunday the husbandman often examines his crops, the merchant computes interest, the rake urges his steed, and the attorney draws his declaration.

This impatience of a day, sacred to quiet and piety, is an odd trait in the character of those, who are saluted with the title of rational. Man is such an indolent being, we are not surprised that he declines the exercises of Sunday, but that he loathes its rest. Of many loungers whom I know, I have computed, with mathematical precision, the yawns on every Sunday and Monday, through the year. I find that the aggregate lassitude of the former to the latter is as ten to one.

The watch is fretfully consulted, and its owner querulously asks why tarry its wheels? why does the dial-point so tardily indicate the twilight hour?

Although the custom of going to church is ancient, honourable, and from social and political, as well as moral and religious reasons, laudable; yet, as my liberal scheme never excludes from the pale of charity, one, who prefers retired to ostentatious devotion, I am desirous of convincing the loiterer at home on the Sabbath, that there is no reason for abolishing, or abbreviating that tranquil day. It is better to go up with the Israelites to the temple; but still a domestic Sunday may be useful and pious, if correctly improved; and if we do not absurdly wish it away. The apostle prescribes "milk for babes." The moralist good-naturedly allows some squeamish ones the indulgence of a vitiated devotional taste; and suggests a pleasant and practicable regimen.

It must, however, be peremptorily required, that no immoral querist ask when the Sabbath will be gone that he may sell corn, set forth wheat, or attend to any low and secular cares. If he stay from church, let him not grieve the Sunday. If he will not sing with the organ, let him not play on the violin.

That Sunday may delectably pass, it is not necessary that cocks should fight, bowls be quaffed, or bargains be made. The seventh day is like a hermit, who not only utters the orison, and numbers beads, but loves the "studious nook," and the lonely scene. Nothing militating, therefore, with order and peace should be tolerated. The jovial cry may be raised, and "quips and cranks," uttered at "the time to laugh"; but the grave and the composed style, suits the sobriety of the Sabbath.

Lest the gayer department of my readers should think I envelop the christian day in funeral weeds and tragic pall, I will strive to convince by my conclusion, that pleasure and piety, like the Hermia and Helena of the poet, "may sing one song, both in one key."

The man who has toiled, or idled six days, may, on the morning of the seventh, choose a retired walk, avoiding the highway, and offence to the weaker brother. I will not be so puritanical or unfashionable, as to hint that the vista of this walk should be a fane, or a chapel. The contemplation of the sublime and beautiful of nature, vivified "by the regent of the world," will naturally excite in a good mind, the proper emotion. Of ecstasy or of rant, there is no need. The homage of the heart is better than the nasal twang of a whole conventicle.

The forenoon may be devoted to popular theology and to sermons. My airy pupils need not start nor turn pale. I do not place them in the tutelage of the dozing Gill, or the mystical Behmen. I do not place them among Westminster divines, or on the Saybrook platform. Privileged with the company of Atterbury, Bishop Watson and Laurence Sterne, they may consider themselves not only in a learned and ingenious, but a polite circle. I shall not be called a sour presbyter, by those whom I advise, if I select for their Sunday acquaintance, gentlemen as well as Christians.

A dinner with some liberal clergyman, though "a dinner of herbs," will prove a better refection than a corporation feast.

The afternoon will pass without much tedium, if employed among a well-ordered family, and rational friends. At intervals, serious poetry will yield a high delight. The gospel sonnets of Ersking are not recommended, but the moral Young, and the enthusiastic Gray.

At the close of such a day, the observer of it will not repine that religion and the laws refuse, once a week, to permit the sowing of wheat, or the sale of corn. He will rejoice in this tabernacle of rest, and though delighting, at proper periods, in business and the agitations of life, will not forsake the waters of that Sabbath Siloam which flow softly.

1795–96

OF PRECIPITATION

> And the driving is like the driving of Jehu, the son of Nimshi; for he driveth furiously.
>
> —2 KINGS ix. 20.

Nothing is to be gained by such excessive speed. It is the mark of a giddy, hair-brained charioteer. He generally either breaks his neck, or is distanced in the race, by his very eagerness to reach the goal.

Lord Chesterfield took a distinction between haste and hurry, and, with the precision of a lawyer, marked their dissimilitude. There is positively as much difference between these pretended cousin-germans, as between my sermons and those of the archbishop of Canterbury.

Hurry, or as it is called in the text, "driving," is a mischievous imp, goading us to dash our feet against a stone; to run, with night cap on, into the streets; in fine, to be ever slovenly and imperfect. You may dispatch business, but if you hurry it, I will not ask for the second sight of a Scotchman, that I may discover you approaching bankruptcy.

Young man, I say unto thee, walk gently to riches, to honours, to pleasure. Do not run. Observe the impatient racer. He is breathless; he is fallen; bemired and beluted; like Dr. Slop, overthrown by Obadiah; he is distanced; he is hissed. Walk circumspectly; it is Paul's advice; not like a fool, but like a philosopher. Compare the man of moderation, with the man of impetuosity. The first becomes honoured in king's courts. The second is either in jail, or in "poverty to the very lips."

In my boyhood, I remember that a parent would sometimes repeat lessons of economy as I sat on his knees, and then lift me in his arms, that I might look at Hogarth's plates of Industry and Idleness. On youthful fancy the picture was more impressed than the precept. To relieve that description of my readers, who tire at the didactic and the trite style of morality, I will attempt a sketch or two, perhaps with a little *colouring*.

I will imagine the figure of a stripling, educated for business. Seven years he swept and garnished a counting-house; opened it at five, and did not bar it until nine; sold ropes and boxes for himself, as well as bales for his master; read "The Sure Guide to Love and Esteem," and worked every rule in Hodder's arithmetic. This, all must allow, was a *gentle* pace. No freaks, no starts, discompose the placid life of youth in these habits. Men already look forward, and behold him a bank director, or see him in the largest store in the mart.

One ill-omened day, when the moon was full or the dog star growled, I do not remember which, our sober youth, whose studies were seldom more miscellaneous than an invoice, or bill of lading, unluckily had his eye caught by a land advertisement in a newspaper. It will abridge a tedious process of circumstances, to imagine him in Georgia. How many acres of sand were then bought and sold, and how he dashed about thy falls, St. Anthony, who art more visited than the shrine of Thomas à Becket! Over these sands he already drives in his chariot, with somebody by his side too; a *lady* from *Babylon*. Although the carriage is encumbered with a speculator, and—and imaginary bank-bills in bales, yet how we glide along, not like the son of Ahimaaz bringing good tidings. The driving is like the charioteership of the son of Nimshi; furious, careless, mad.

But his vehicle, like count Basset's in the play, rolls on the four aces, or something as unstable. He drives furiously against a post. He is an overthrown Pharaoh; not as it is vulgarly expressed, in a *peck,* but in a Red Sea of troubles. He has driven so furiously, that he has snapped its traces, lost the linch pin, and broken the axle of his credit.

A quack is a Jehu; he not only drives furiously himself, but he drives his poor patients too. When I see one of these mountebanks, I always consider the sick he attends, as so many coughing dray horses, soon to be driven out of breath. Ye simple farmers, why do you grease his wheels? When ye are diseased, cannot a leaf of mugwort be obtained, without paying for the cropping? When you are wounded, your youngest children may bring you a bit of betony, and it will not be charged.

Of this genus of drivers, the negro driver, and the impetuous Frenchman, are a noted species. But it does not demand the perspicacity of a *watchman* to discover their course. They go on, at a fearful rate; and it may demand a thunderbolt to arrest either in the impious career.

1795–96

VII. BENJAMIN RUSH
(1745–1813)

From *ESSAYS*

[THE PROGRESS OF POPULATION IN PENNSYLVANIA]

An account of the progress of population, agriculture, manners, and government in Pennsylvania, in a letter to a friend in England

DEAR SIR,

Whatever tends to unfold *facts* in the history of the human species, must be interesting to a curious enquirer.—The manner of settling a new country, exhibits a view of the human mind so foreign to the views of it which have been taken for many centuries in Europe, that I flatter myself the following account of the progress of population, agriculture, manners, and government in Pennsylvania will be acceptable to you. I have chosen to confine myself in the present letter to Pennsylvania only, that all the information I shall give you may be derived from my own knowledge and observations.

The *first* settler in the woods is generally a man who has outlived his credit or fortune in the cultivated parts of the State. His time for migrating is in the month of April. His first object is to build a small cabbin of rough logs for himself and family. The floor of this cabbin is of earth, the roof is of split logs—the light is received through the door, and, in some instances, through a small window made of greased paper. A coarser building adjoining this cabbin affords a shelter to a cow and a pair of poor horses. The labor of erecting these buildings is succeeded by killing the trees on a few acres of ground near his cabbin; this is done by cutting a circle round the trees, two or three feet from the ground. The ground around these trees is then ploughed and Indian-corn planted in it. The season for planting this grain is about the 20th of May—. It grows generally on new ground with but little cultivation, and yields in the month of October following, from forty to fifty bushels by the acre. After the first of September it affords a good deal of nourishment to his family, in its green or unripe state, in the form of what is called *roasting ears*. His family is fed during the summer by a small quantity of grain which he carries with him, and by fish and game. His cows and horses feed upon wild grass, or the succulent twigs of the woods. For the first year he endures a great deal of distress from hunger—cold—and a variety of accidental causes, but he seldom complains or sinks under them. As he lives in the neighbourhood of Indians, he soon acquires a strong tincture of their manners. His exertions, while they continue, are violent; but they are succeeded by long intervals of rest. His pleasures consist chiefly in fishing and hunting. He loves spirituous liquors, and he eats, drinks and sleeps in dirt and rags in his little cabbin. In his intercourse with the world he manifests all the arts which characterize the Indians of our country. In this situation he passes two or three years. In proportion as population increases around him, he becomes uneasy and dissatisfied. Formerly his cattle ranged at large, but now his neighbours call upon him to confine them within fences, to prevent their trespassing upon their fields of grain. Formerly he fed his family with wild animals, but these, which fly from the face of man, now cease to afford him an easy subsistence, and he is compelled to raise domestic animals for the support of his family. Above all, he revolts against the operation of laws. He cannot bear to surrender up a single natural right for all the benefits of government,—and therefore he abandons his little settlement, and seeks a retreat in the woods, where he again submits to all the toils which have been mentioned. There are instances of many men who have broken ground on bare creation, not less than four different times in this way, in different and more advanced parts of the State. It has been remarked, that the flight of this class of people is always increased by the preaching of the gospel. This will not surprise us when we consider how opposite its precepts are to their licentious manner of living. If our first settler was the owner of the spot of land which he began to cultivate, he sells it at a considerable profit to his successor; but if (as is oftener the case) he was a tenant to some rich landholder, he abandons it in debt; however, the small improvements he leaves behind him, generally make it an object of immediate demand to a *second* species of settler.

This species of settler is generally a man of some property,—he pays one-third or one-fourth part in case for his plantation, which consists of three or four hundred acres, and the rest in gales or instalments, as it is called here; that is, a certain sum yearly, without interest, 'till the whole is paid. The first object of this settler is to build an addition to his cabbin; this is done with hewed logs: and as saw-mills generally follow settlements, his floors are made of boards; his roof is made of what are called clapboards, which are a kind of coarse shingles, split out of short oak logs. This house is divided by two floors, on each of which are two rooms: under the whole is a cellar walled with stone. The cabbin serves as kitchen to this house. His next object is to clear a little meadow ground, and plant an orchard of two or three hundred apple trees. His stable is likewise enlarged; and, in the course of a year or two, he builds a large log barn, the roof of which is commonly thatched with rye straw: he moreover encreases the quantity of his arable land; and, instead of cultivating Indian-corn alone, he raises a quantity of wheat and rye: the latter is cultivated chiefly for the purpose of being distilled into whiskey. This species of settler by no means extracts all from the earth, which it is capable of giving. His fields yield but a scanty increase, owing to the ground not being sufficiently ploughed. The hopes of the year are often blasted by his cattle breaking through his half-made fences, and destroying his grain. His horses perform but half the labour that might be expected from them, if they were better fed; and his cattle often die in the spring from want of provision, and the delay of grass. His house, as well as his farm, bear many marks of a weak tone of mind. His windows are unglazed, or, if they have had glass in them, the ruins of it are supplied with old hats or pillows. This species of settler is seldom a good member of civil or religious society: with a large portion of a hereditary mechanical kind of religion, he neglects to contribute sufficiently towards building a church, or maintaining a regular administration of the ordinances of the gospel: he is equally indisposed to support civil government: with high ideas of liberty, he refuses to bear his proportion of the debt contracted by its establishment in our country: he delights chiefly in company—sometimes drinks spirituous liquors to excess—will spend a day or two in every week, in attending political meetings; and, thus, he contracts debts which, (if he cannot discharge in a depreciated paper currency) compel him to sell his plantation, generally in the course of a few years, to the *third* and last species of settler.

This species of settler is commonly a man of property and good character—sometimes he is the son of a wealthy farmer in one of the interior and ancient counties of the state. His first object is to convert every spot of ground, over which he is able to draw water, into meadow: where this cannot be done, he selects the most fertile spots on the farm, and devotes it by manure to that purpose. His next object is to build a barn, which he prefers of stone. This building is, in some instances, 100 feet in front, and 40 in depth: it is made very compact, so as to shut out the cold in winter; for our farmers find that their horses and cattle, when kept warm, do not require near as much food, as when they are exposed to the cold. He uses œconomy, likewise, in the consumption of his wood. Hence he keeps himself warm in winter, by means of stoves, which save an immense deal of labour to himself and his horses, in cutting and hawling wood in cold and wet weather. His fences are every where repaired, so as to secure his grain from his own and his neighbour's cattle. But further, he increases the number of the articles of his cultivation, and, instead of raising corn, wheat and rye alone, he raises oats, buckwheat, (the sagopyrum of Linnæus) and spelts. Near his house, he allots an acre or two of ground for a garden, in which he raises a large quantity of cabbage and potatoes. His newly cleared fields afford him every year a large increase of turnips. Over the spring which supplies him with water, he builds a milk-house and over this, in some instances, he builds a smoke-house; he likewise adds to the number, and improves the quality of his fruit trees:— His sons work by his side all the year and his wife and daughters forsake the dairy and the spinning wheel, to share with him in the toils of harvest. The last object of his industry is to build a dwelling house. This business is sometimes effected in the course of his life, but is oftener bequeathed to his son, or the inheritor of his plantation: and hence we have a common saying among our best farmers, "that a son should always begin where his father left off;" that is, he should begin his improvements, by building a commodious dwelling-house, suited to the improvements and value of the plantation. This dwelling-house is generally built of stone—it is large, convenient, and filled with useful and substantial furniture— It sometimes adjoins the house of the second settler, but is frequently placed at a little distance from it. The horses and cattle of this species of settler, bear marks in their strength, fat and fruitfulness—of their being plentifully fed and carefully kept. His table abounds with a variety of the best provisions—his very kitchen flows with milk and honey—beer, cyder, and home-made wine are the usual drinks of his family: the greatest part of the cloathing of his family is manufactured by his wife and daughters: in proportion as he increases in wealth, he values the protection of laws: hence he punctually pays his taxes towards the support of government. Schools and churches likewise, as the means of promoting order and happiness in society, derive a due support from him: for benevolence and public spirit, as to these objects, are the natural offspring of affluence and independence. Of this class of settlers are two-thirds of the farmers of Pennsylvania. These are the men to whom Pennsylvania owes her ancient fame and consequence. If they possess less refinement than their southern neighbours, who cultivate their land with slaves, they possess more republican virtue. It was from the farms cultivated by these men, that the American and French armies were chiefly fed with bread during the late revolution; and it was from the produce of these farms, that those millions of dollars were obtained from the Havanna after the year 1780, which laid the foundation of the bank of North America, and which fed and cloathed the American army, till the Peace of Paris.—This is a short account of the happiness of a Pennsylvania farmer— To this happiness our state invites men of every religion and country.

We do not pretend to offer emigrants the pleasures of Arcadia— It is enough if affluence, independence, and happiness are ensured to patience, industry, and labour. The moderate price of land, the credit which arises from prudence, and the safety from our courts of law, of every species of property, render the blessings which I have described, objects within the reach of every man.

From a review of the three different species of settlers, it appears, that there are certain regular stages which mark the progress from the savage to civilized life. The first settler is nearly related to an Indian in his manners— In the second, the Indian manners are more diluted: It is in the third species of settlers only, that we behold civilization completed — It is to the third species of settlers only, that it is proper to apply the term of *farmers*. While we record the vices of the first and second settlers, it is but just to mention their virtues likewise.— Their mutual wants produce mutual dependence: hence they are kind and friendly to each other—their solitary situation makes visitors agreeable to them;—hence they are hospitable to strangers: their want of money, (for they raise but little more than is necessary to support their families) has made it necessary for them to associate for the purposes of building houses, cutting their grain, and the like:—This they do in turns for each other, without any other pay than the pleasures which usually attend a country frolic— Perhaps what I have called virtues are rather *qualities,* arising from necessity, and the peculiar state of society in which these people live.—Virtue should, in all cases, be the offspring of principle.

I do not pretend to say, that this mode of settling farms in Pennsylvania is universal—I have known some instances where the first settler has performed the improvements of the second, and yielded to the third. I have known a few instances likewise, of men of enterprizing spirits, who have settled in the wilderness, and who, in the course of a single life, have advanced through all the intermediate stages of improvement that I have mentioned and produced all those conveniences which have been ascribed to the third species of settlers; thereby resembling, in their exploits, not only the pioneers and light-infantry, but the main body of an army. There are instances likewise, where the first settlement has been improved by the same family, in hereditary succession, 'till it has reached the third stage of cultivation. There are many spacious stone houses and highly cultivated farms in the neighbouring counties of the city of Philadelphia, which are possessed by the grandsons and great-grandsons of men who accompanied William Penn across the ocean, and who laid the foundation of the present improvements of their posterity, in such cabbins as have been described.

This passion for migration which I have described, will appear strange to an European. To see men turn their backs upon the houses in which they drew their first breath—upon the church in which they were dedicated to God—upon the graves of their ancestors—upon the friends and companions of their youth—and upon all the pleasures of cultivated society, and exposing themselves to all the hardships and accidents of subduing the earth, and thereby establishing settlements in a wilderness, must strike a philosopher on your side the water, as a picture of human nature that runs counter to the usual habits and principles of action in man. But this passion, strange and new as it appears, is wisely calculated for the extension of population in America: and this it does, not only by promoting the increase of the human species in new settlements, but in the old settlements likewise. While the degrees of industry and knowledge in agriculture, in our country, are proportioned to farms of from 75 to 300 acres, there will be a languor in population, as soon as farmers multiply beyond the number of farms of the above dimensions. To remove this languor, which is kept up alike by the increase of the price, and the division of farms, a migration of part of the community becomes absolutely necessary. And as this part of the community often consists of the idle and extravagant, who eat without working, their removal, by increasing the facility of subsistence to the frugal and industrious who remain behind, naturally increases the number of people, just as the cutting off the suckers of an apple-tree increases the size of the tree, and the quantity of fruit.

I have only to add upon this subject, that the migrants from Pennsylvania always travel to the southward. The soil and climate of the western parts of Virginia, North and South Carolina, and Georgia, afford a more easy support to lazy farmers, than the stubborn but durable soil of Pennsylvania.—*Here,* our ground requires deep and repeated plowing to render it fruitful—*there,* scratching the ground once or twice affords tolerable crops. In Pennsylvania, the length and coldness of the winter make it necessary for the farmers to bestow a large share of their labour in providing for and feeding their cattle; but in the southern states, cattle find pasture during the greatest part of the winter, in the fields or woods. For these reasons, the greatest part of the western counties of the States, that have been mentioned, are settled by original inhabitants of Pennsylvania. During the late war, the militia of Orange county, in North Carolina, were enrolled, and their number amounted to 3,500, *every* man of whom had migrated from Pennsylvania. From this you will see that our State is the great outport of the United States for Europeans; and that, after performing the office of a sieve by detaining all those people who possess the stamina of industry and virtue, it allows a passage to the rest, to those States which are accommodated to their habits of indolence.

I shall conclude this letter by remarking, that in the mode of extending population and agriculture, which I have described, we behold a new species of war. The *third* settler may be viewed as a conqueror. The weapons with which he achieves his conquests are the implements of husbandry: and the virtues which direct them are industry and œconomy. Idleness—extravagance—and ignorance fly before him. Happy would it be for mankind, if the kings of Europe would adopt this mode of extending their territories: it would soon put an end to the dreadful connection, which has existed in every age, between war and poverty, and between conquest and desolation.

With great respect,
I have the honor to be,
Sir,
Your most obedient
Humble servant.

1798

PHILIP FRENEAU
(1752–1832)

THE BRITISH PRISON SHIP

CANTO III

THE HOSPITAL PRISON SHIP

Now tow'rd the HUNTER's gloomy sides we came,
A slaughter-house, yet *hospital* in name;
For none came there (to pass through all degrees)
'Till half consum'd, and dying with disease;—
But when too near with labouring oars we ply'd
The *Mate* with curses drove us from the side;
That wretch who, banish'd from the navy crew,
Grown old in blood, did here his trade renew,
His serpent's tongue, when on his *charge* let loose,
Utter'd reproaches, scandal, and abuse,
Gave all to hell who dar'd his *king* disown,
And swore mankind were made for *George* alone:
Ten thousand times, to irritate our woe,
He wish'd us founder'd in the gulph below;
Ten thousand times he brandish'd high his stick,
And swore as often that we were not sick—
And yet so pale!—that we were thought by some
A freight of ghosts from Death's dominions come—
But calm'd at length—for who can always rage,
Or the fierce war of endless passion wage,
He pointed to the stairs that led below
To damps, disease, and varied shapes of woe—
Down to the gloom I took my pensive way,
Along the decks the dying captives lay;
Some struck with madness, some with scurvy pain'd,
But still of putrid fevers most complain'd!
On the hard floors these wasted objects laid,
There toss'd and tumbled in the dismal shade,
There no soft voice their bitter fate bemoan'd,
And Death trode stately, while the victims groan'd;
Of leaky decks I heard them long complain,
Drown'd as they were in deluges of rain,
Deny'd the comforts of a dying bed,
And not a pillow to support the head—
How could they else but pine, and grieve, and sigh,
Detest a wretched life—and wish to die.

SCARCE had I mingled with this dismal band
When a thin spectre seiz'd me by the hand—
"And art thou come, (death heavy on his eyes)

And art thou come to these abodes," he cries;
"Why didst thou leave the *Scorpion's* dark retreat,
And hither haste a surer death to meet?
Why didst thou leave thy damp infected cell,
If *that* was purgatory, this is hell—
We too grown weary of that horrid shade
Petitioned early for the doctor's aid;
His aid denied, more deadly symptoms came,
Weak, and yet weaker, glow'd the vital flame;
And when disease had worn us down so low
That few could tell if we were ghosts, or no,
And all asserted, death would be our fate—
Then to the doctor we were sent—too late.
Here wastes away *Autolycus* the brave,
Here young *Orestes* finds a wat'ry grave,
Here, gay *Alcander* gay, alas! no more,
Dies far sequester'd from his native shore;
He late, perhaps, too eager for the fray,
Chac'd the vile Briton o'er the wat'ry way
'Till fortune jealous, bade her clouds appear,
Turn'd hostile to his fame, and brought him *here*,
Thus do our warriors, thus our heroes fall,
Imprison'd here, base ruin meets them all,
Or, sent afar to Britain's barbarous shore,
There die neglected, and return no more:
Ah rest in peace, poor, injur'd, parted shade,
By cruel hands in death's dark weeds array'd,
But happier climes, where suns unclouded shine,
Light undisturb'd, and endless peace are thine."—

From *Brookland* groves a Hessian doctor came,
Not great his skill, nor greater much his fame;
Fair Science never call'd the wretch her son,
And Art disdain'd the stupid man to own;—
Can you admire that Science was so coy,
Or Art refus'd his genius to employ!—
Do men with brutes an equal dullness share,
Or cuts yon' groveling mole the midway air—
In polar worlds can Eden's blossoms blow,
Do trees of God in barren desarts grow,
Are loaded vines to Etna's summit known,
Or swells the peach beneath the torrid zone—?
Yet still he doom'd his genius to the rack,
And, as you may suppose, was own'd a *quack*.

He on his charge the healing work begun
With antimonial mixtures, by the tun,
Ten minutes was the time he deign'd to stay,
The time of grace allotted once a day—
He drencht us well with bitter draughts, 'tis true,
Nostrums from hell, and *cortex* from Peru—
Some with his pills he sent to Pluto's reign,
And some he blister'd with his flies of Spain;
His cream of Tartar walk'd its deadly round,

Till the lean patient at the potion frown'd,
And swore that hemlock, death, or what you will,
Were nonsense to the drugs that stuff'd his bill.—
On those refusing he bestow'd a kick,
Or menac'd vengeance with his walking stick,
Here uncontroul'd he exercis'd his trade,
And grew experienced by the deaths he made,
By frequent blows we from his cane endur'd
He kill'd at least as many as he cur'd,
On our lost comrades built his future fame,
And scatter'd fate where'er his footsteps came.

Some did not seem obedient to his will,
And swore he mingled poison with his pill,
But I acquit him by a fair confession,
He was no Englishman—he was a Hessian—
Although a dunce, he had some sense of sin
Or else the Lord knows where we now had been;
Perhaps in that far country sent to range
Where never prisoner meets with an exchange—
Then had we all been banish'd out of time
Nor I return'd to plague the world with rhyme.

Fool though he was, yet candour must confess
Not chief Physician was this dog of Hesse—
One master o'er the murdering tribe was plac'd,
By him the rest were honour'd or disgrac'd;—
Once, and but once, by some strange fortune led
He came to see the dying and the dead—
He came—but anger so deform'd his eye,
And such a faulchion glitter'd on his thigh
And such a gloom his visage darken'd o'er,
And two such pistols in his hands he bore!
That, by the gods!—with such a load of steel
He came, we thought, to murder, not to heal—
Hell in his heart, and mischief in his head,
He gloom'd destruction, and had smote us dead,
Had he so dar'd—but fate with-held his hand—
He came — blasphem'd — and turn'd again to land.

From this poor vessel, and her sickly crew
An English ruffian all his titles drew,
Captain, esquire, commander, too, in chief,
And hence he gain'd his bread, and hence his beef,
But, sir, you might have search'd creation round
Ere such another miscreant could be found—
Though unprovok'd, an angry face he bore,
We stood astonish'd at the oaths he swore;
He swore, till every prisoner stood aghast,
And thought him Satan in a brimstone blast;
He wish'd us banish'd from the public light,
He wish'd us shrouded in perpetual night!
That were he king, no mercy would he show,
But drive all *rebels* to the world below;

That if we *scoundrels* did not scrub the decks
His staff should break our damn'd *rebellious* necks;
He swore, besides, that if the ship took fire
We too should in the pitchy flame expire;
And meant it so—this tyrant I engage
Had lost his breath to gratify his rage.—

If where he walk'd a captive carcase lay,
Still dreadful was the language of the day—
He call'd us *dogs,* and would have us'd us so,
But vengeance check'd the meditated blow,
The vengeance from our injur'd nation due
To him, and all the base, unmanly crew.

Such food they sent, to make complete our woes,
It look'd like carrion torn from hungry crows,
Such vermin vile on every joint were seen,
So black, corrupted, mortified, and lean
That once we try'd to move our flinty chief,
And thus address'd him, holding up the beef:

"See, captain, see! what rotten bones we pick,
What kills the healthy cannot cure the sick:
Not dogs on such by *Christian* men are fed,
And see, good master, see, what lousy bread!"

"Your meat and bread (this man of flint replied)
Is not my care to manage or provide—
But this, damn'd rebel dogs, I'd have you know,
That better than you merit we bestow;
Out of my sight!"—nor more he deign'd to say,
But whisk'd about, and frowning, strode away.

Each day, at least three carcases we bore,
And scratch'd them graves along the sandy shore,
By feeble hands the shallow graves were made,
No stone memorial o'er the corpses laid;
In barren sands, and far from home, they lie,
No friend to shed a tear, when passing by;
O'er the mean tombs insulting Britons tread,
Spurn at the sand, and curse the rebel dead.

When to your arms these fatal islands fall,
(For first or last they must be conquer'd all)
Americans! to rites sepulchral just,
With gentlest footstep press this kindred dust,
And o'er the tombs, if tombs can then be found,
Place the green turf, and plant the myrtle round.

Americans! a just resentment shew,
And glut revenge on this detested foe;
While the warm blood exults the glowing vein
Still shall resentment in your bosoms reign,
Can you forget the greedy Briton's ire,
Your fields in ruin, and your domes on fire,
No age, no sex from lust and murder free,
And, black, as night, the hell born refugee!
Must *York* forever your best blood entomb,

And these gorg'd monsters triumph in their doom,
Who leave no art of cruelty untry'd;
Such heavy vengeance, and such hellish pride!
Death has no charms—his realms dejected lie
In the dull climate of a clouded sky,
Death has no charms, except in British eyes,
See, arm'd for death, the infernal miscreants rise,
See how they pant to stain the world with gore,
And millions murder'd, still would murder more;
This selfish race, from all the world disjoin'd,
Perpetual discord spread throughout mankind,
Aim to extend their empire o'er the ball,
Subject, destroy, absorb, and conquer all,
As if the power that form'd us did condemn
All other nations to be slaves to them—
Rouse from your sleep, and crush the thievish band,
Defeat, destroy, and sweep them from the land,
Ally'd like you, what madness to despair,
Attack the ruffians while they linger there;
There *Tryon* sits, a monster all complete
See *Clinton* there with vile *Knyphausen* meet,
And every wretch whom honour should detest
There finds a home—and Arnold with the rest.
Ah! traitors, lost to every sense of shame,
Unjust supporters of a tyrant's claim;
Foes to the rights of freedom and of men,
Flush'd with the blood of thousands you have slain,
To the just doom the righteous skies decree
We leave you, toiling still in cruelty,
Or on dark plans in future herds to meet,
Plans form'd in hell, and projects half complete:
The years approach that shall to ruin bring
Your lords, your chiefs, your miscreant of a king
Whose murderous acts shall stamp his name accurs'd,
And his last triumphs more than damn the first.

(1780) 1781

ON THE MEMORABLE VICTORY

OBTAINED BY THE GALLANT CAPTAIN PAUL JONES, OF "LE BON HOMME RICHARD" (OR FATHER RICHARD) OVER THE "SERAPHIS," OF 44 GUNS, UNDER THE COMMAND OF CAPTAIN PEARSON

O'er the rough main with flowing sheet
The guardian of a numerous fleet,
Seraphis from the Baltic came;
A ship of less tremendous force
Sailed by her side the self-same course,
Countess of Scarborough was her name.

And now their native coasts appear,
Brittannia's hills their summits rear
Above the German main:
Fond to suppose their dangers o'er,
They southward coast along the shore,
Thy waters, gentle Thames, to gain.

Full forty guns Seraphis bore,
And Scarborough's Countess twenty-four,
Manned with Old England's boldest tars—

What flag that rides the Gallic seas
Shall dare attack such piles as these,
Designed for tumults and for wars!

Now from the top-mast's giddy heights
A seaman cried—"Four sail in sight
Approach with favouring gales;"
Pearson, resolved to save the fleet,
Stood off to sea, these ships to meet,
And closely braced his shivering sails.

With him advanc'd the Countess bold,
Like a black tar in wars grown old:
And now these floating piles drew nigh;
But, muse, unfold, what chief of fame
In the other warlike squadron came.
Whose standards at his mast head fly.

'Twas Jones, brave JONES, to battle led
As bold a crew as ever bled
Upon the sky-surrounded main;
The standards of the western world
Were to the willing winds unfurled,
Denying Britain's tyrant reign.

The *Good-Man-Richard* led the line;
The *Alliance* next: with these combine
The Gallic ship they *Pallas* call:
The *Vengeance,* armed with sword and flame,
These to attack the Britons came—
But *two* accomplished all.

Now Phoebus sought his pearly bed:
But who can tell the scenes of dread,
The horrors of that fatal night!
Close up these floating castles came;
The Good Man Richard bursts in flame;
Seraphis trembled at the sight.

She felt the fury of *her* ball:
Down, prostrate down, the Britons fall;
The decks were strewed with slain:
Jones to the foe his vessel lashed;
And, while the black artillery flashed,
Loud thunders shook the main.

Alas! that mortals should employ
Such murdering engines, to destroy
That frame by heaven so nicely joined;
Alas! that e'er the god decreed
That brother should by brother bleed,
And pour'd such madness in the mind.

But thou, brave Jones, no blame shalt bear;
The rights of men demand thy care:
For *these* you dare the greedy waves—
No tyrant, on destruction bent
Has planned thy conquests—thou art sent
To humble tyrants and their slaves.

See!—dread Seraphis flames again—
And art thou, *Jones,* among the slain,
And sunk to Neptune's caves below—
He lives—though crowds around him fall,
Still he, unhurt, survives them all;
Almost alone he fights the foe.

And can thy ship these strokes sustain?
Behold thy brave companions slain,
All clasped in ocean's dark embrace.
"STRIKE OR BE SUNK!"—the Briton cries—
"SINK, IF YOU CAN!"—the chief replies,
Fierce lightnings blazing in his face.

Then to the side three guns he drew,
(Almost deserted by his crew)
And charged them deep with woe:
By *Pearson's* flash he aim'd hot balls;
His main-mast totters—down it falls—
O'erwhelming half below.

Pearson as yet disdained to yield,
But scarce he secret fears concealed,
And thus was heard to cry—
"With hell, not mortals, I contend;
What art thou—human or a fiend,
That dost my force defy?

"Return, my lads, the fight renew!"
So called bold Pearson to his crew;
But called, alas! in vain;
Some on the decks lay maimed and dead;
Some to their deep recesses fled,
And more were shrouded in the main.

Distressed, forsaken, and alone,
He hauled his tattered standard down,
And yielded to his gallant foe;
Bold *Pallas* soon the *Countess* took,—
Thus both their haughty colours struck,
Confessing what the brave can do.

But, Jones, too dearly didst thou buy
These ships possest so gloriously,
Too many deaths disgraced the fray:
Thy barque that bore the conquering flame,
That the proud Briton overcame,
Even she forsook thee on thy way;

For when the morn began to shine,
Fatal to her, the ocean brine
Poured through each spacious wound;
Quick in the deep she disappeared,
But Jones to friendly Belgia steered,
With conquest and with glory crowned.

Go on, great man, to scourge the foe,
And bid the haughty Britons know
They to our *Thirteen Stars* shall bend;
The *Stars* that clad in dark attire,
Long glimmered with a feeble fire,
But radiant now ascend.

Bend to the Stars that flaming rise
On western worlds, more brilliant skies.
Fair Freedom's reign restored.
So when the Magi, come from far,
Beheld the God-attending Star,
They trembled and adored.

1781

TO THE MEMORY

OF THE BRAVE AMERICANS, UNDER GENERAL GREENE, IN SOUTH CAROLINA, WHO FELL IN THE ACTION OF SEPTEMBER 8, 1781

At Eutaw springs the valiant died:
Their limbs with dust are cover'd o'er—
Weep on, ye springs, your tearful tide;
How many heroes are no more!

If in this wreck of ruin, they
Can yet be thought to claim a tear,
O smite thy gentle breast, and say
The friends of freedom slumber here!

Thou, who shalt trace this bloody plain,
If goodness rules thy generous breast,
Sigh for the wasted rural reign;
Sigh for the shepherds, sunk to rest!

Stranger, their humble graves adorn;
You too may fall, and ask a tear:
'Tis not the beauty of the morn
That proves the evening shall be clear—

They saw their injur'd country's woe;
The flaming town, the wasted field;
Then rush'd to meet the insulting foe;
They took the spear—but left the shield,

Let by thy conquering genius, GREENE,
The Britons they compell'd to fly:
None distant view'd the fatal plain,
None griev'd, in such a cause, to die—

But, like the Parthian, fam'd of old,
Who, flying, still their arrows threw;
These routed Britons, full as bold,
Retreated, and retreating slew.

Now rest in peace, our patriot band;
Though far from Nature's limits thrown,
We trust, they find a happier land,
A brighter sun-shine of their own.

1781

TO SHYLOCK AP-SHENKIN

Since the day I attempted to print a gazette,
This Shylock Ap-Shenkin does nothing but fret:
Now preaching and screeching, then nibbling and scribbling,
Remarking and barking, and whining and pining,
And still in a pet,
From morning 'till night, with my humble gazette.

Instead of whole columns our page to abuse,
Your readers would rather be treated with News:
While wars are a-brewing, and kingdoms undoing,
While monarchs are falling, and princesses squalling,
While France is reforming, and Irishmen storming—
In a glare of such splendour, what folly to fret
At so humble a thing as a poet's Gazette!

No favours I ask'd from your friends in the East:
On your wretched soup-meagre I left them to feast;
So many base lies you have sent them in print,
That scarcely a man at our paper will squint:—
And now you begin (with a grunt and a grin,
With the bray of an ass, and a visage of brass,
With a quill in your hand and a Lie in your mouth)
To play the same trick on the men of the South!

One Printer for Congress (some think) is enough,
To flatter, and lie, to palaver, and puff,
To preach up in favour of monarchs and titles,
And garters, and ribbands, to prey on our vitals:
Who knows but Pomposo will give it in fee,
Or make mister Shenkin the Grand Patentee!!!
Then take to your scrapers, ye Republican Papers,
No rogue shall go snacks—and the News-Paper Tax
Shall be puff'd to the skies, as a measure most wise—
So, a spaniel, when master is angry, and kicks it,
Sneaks up to his shoe, and submissively licks it.

1792

ODE

God save the Rights of Man!
Give us a heart to scan
Blessings so dear:
Let them be spread around
Wherever man is found,
And with the welcome sound
Ravish his ear.

Let us with France agree,
And bid the world be free,
While tyrants fall!
Let the rude savage host
Of their vast numbers boast—
Freedom's almighty trust
Laughs at them all!

Though hosts of slaves conspire
To quench fair Gallia's fire,
Still shall they fail:
Though traitors round her rise,
Leagu'd with her enemies,
To war each patriot flies,
And will prevail.

No more is valour's flame
Devoted to a name,
Taught to adore—
Soldiers of LIBERTY
Disdain to bow the knee,
But teach EQUALITY
To every shore.

The world at last will join
To aid thy grand design,
Dear Liberty!
To Russia's frozen lands
The generous flame expands:
On Afric's burning sands
Shall man be free!

In this our western world
Be Freedom's flag unfurl'd
Through all its shores!
May no destructive blast
Our heaven of joy o'ercast,
May Freedom's fabric last
While time endures.

If e'er her cause require!
Should tyrants e'er aspire
To aim their stroke,
May no proud despot daunt—
Should he his standard plant,
Freedom will never want
Her hearts of oak!

(1793) 1795

ON THE ANNIVERSARY

OF THE STORMING OF THE BASTILLE, AT PARIS, JULY 14TH, 1789

The chiefs that bow to Capet's reign,
In mourning, now, their weeds display;
But we, that scorn a monarch's chain,
Combine to celebrate the DAY
Of Freedom's birth that put the seal,
And laid in dust the proud Bastille.

To Gallia's rich and splendid crown,
This mighty *Day* gave such a blow
As Time's recording hand shall own
No former *age* had power to do:
No single gem some Brutus stole,
But instant ruin seiz'd the whole.

Now tyrants rise, once more to bind
In royal chains a nation freed—
Vain hope! for they, to death consign'd,
Shall soon, like perjur'd Louis, bleed:
O'er every king, o'er every queen
Fate hangs the sword, and guillotine.

"Plung'd in a gulf of deep distress
France turns her back—(so traitors say)
Kings, priests, and nobles, round her press,
Resolv'd to seize their destin'd prey:
Thus Europe swears (in arms combin'd)
To Poland's doom is France consign'd."

Yet those, who now are thought so low
From conquests that were *basely* gain'd,
Shall rise tremendous from the blow
And free Two WORLDS, that still are chain'd,
Restrict the Briton to his isle,
And Freedom plant in every soil.

Ye sons of this degenerate clime,
Haste, arm the barque, expand the sail;
Assist to speed that golden time
When Freedom rules, and monarchs fail;

All left to France—*new powers* may join,
And help to crush the cause divine.

Ah! while I write, dear France ALLIED,
My ardent wish I scarce restrain,
To throw these Sybil leaves aside,
And fly to join you on the main:
Unfurl the topsail for the chace
And help to crush the tyrant race!

1793

THE HOUSE OF NIGHT

A VISION

Advertisement—This Poem is founded upon the authority of Scripture, inasmuch as these sacred books assert, that *the last enemy that shall be conquered is Death.* For the purposes of poetry he is here personified, and represented as on his dying bed. The scene is laid at a solitary palace, (the time midnight) which, tho' before beautiful and joyous, is now become sad and gloomy, as being the abode and receptacle of Death. Its owner, an amiable, majestic youth, who had lately lost a beloved consort, nevertheless with a noble philosophical fortitude and humanity, entertains him in a friendly manner, and by employing Physicians, endeavours to restore him to health, altho' an enemy; convinced of the excellence and propriety of that divine precept, *If thine enemy hunger, feed him; if he thirst, give him drink.* He nevertheless, as if by a spirit of prophecy, informs this (fictitiously) wicked being of the certainty of his doom, and represents to him in a pathetic manner the vanity of his expectations, either of a reception into the abodes of the just, or continuing longer to make havock of mankind upon earth. The patient finding his end approaching, composes his epitaph, and orders it to be engraved on his tombstone, hinting to us thereby, that even Death and Distress have vanity; and would be remembered with honour after he is no more, altho' his whole life has been spent in deeds of devastation and murder. He dies at last in the utmost agonies of despair, after agreeing with the avaricious Undertaker to intomb his bones. This reflects upon the inhumanity of those men, who, not to mention an enemy, would scarcely cover a departed friend with a little dust, without the certainty of a reward for so doing. The circumstances of his funeral are then recited, and the visionary and fabulous part of the poem disappears. It concludes with a few reflections on the impropriety of a too great attachment to the present life, and incentives to such moral virtue as may assist in conducting us to a better.

1

Trembling I write my dream, and recollect
A fearful vision at the midnight hour;
So late, Death o'er me spread his sable wings,
Painted with fancies of malignant power! * * *

5

Fancy, I own thy power—when sunk in sleep
Thou play'st thy wild delusive part so well
You lift me into immortality,
Depict new heavens, or draw scenes of hell.

6

By some sad means, when Reason holds no sway,
Lonely I rov'd at midnight o'er a plain
Where murmuring streams and mingling rivers flow,
Far to their springs, or seek the sea again.

7

Sweet vernal May! tho' then thy woods in bloom
Flourish'd, yet nought of this could Fancy see,
No wild pinks bless'd the meads, no green the fields,
And naked seem'd, to stand each lifeless tree:

8

Dark was the sky, and not one friendly star
Shone from the zenith or horizon, clear,
Mist sate upon the woods, and darkness rode

In her black chariot, with a wild career.

9

And from the woods the late resounding note
Issued of the loquacious *Whip-poor-will,*
Hoarse, howling dogs, and nightly roving wolves
Clamour'd from far off clifts invisible.

10

Rude, from the wide extended *Chesapeke*
I heard the winds the dashing waves assail,
And saw from far, by pictures fancy form'd,
The black ship travelling through the noisy gale.

11

At last, by chance and guardian fancy led,
I reach'd a noble dome, rais'd fair and high,
And saw the light from upper windows flame,
Presage of mirth and hospitality.

12

And by that light around the dome appear'd
A mournful garden of autumnal hue,
Its lately pleasing flowers all drooping stood
Amidst high weeds that in rank plenty grew.

13

The Primrose there, the violet darkly blue,
Daisies and fair Narcissus ceas'd to rise,
Gay spotted pinks their charming bloom withdrew,
And Polyanthus quench'd its thousand dyes.

14

No pleasant fruit or blossom gaily smil'd.
Nought but unhappy plants and trees were seen,
The yew, the myrtle, and the church-yard elm,
The cypress, with its melancholy green.

15

There cedars dark, the osier, and the pine,
Shorn tamarisks, and weeping willows grew,
The poplar tall, the lotos, and the lime,
And pyracantha did her leaves renew.

16

The poppy there, companion to repose,
Display'd her blossoms that began to fall,
And here the purple amaranthus rose
With mint strong-scented, for the funeral.

17

And here and there with laurel shrubs between
A tombstone lay, inscrib'd with strains of woe,
And stanzas sad, throughout the dismal green,
Lamented for the dead that slept below. * * *

23

Then up three winding stairs my feet were brought
To a high chamber, hung with mourning sad,
The unsnuff'd candles glar'd with visage dim,
'Midst grief, in ecstacy of woe run mad.

24

A wide leaf'd table stood on either side,
Well fraught with phials, half their liquid spent,
And from a couch, behind the curtain's veil,
I heard a hollow voice of loud lament.

25

Turning to view the object whence it came,
My frighted eyes a horrid form survey'd;
Fancy, I own thy power—Death on the couch,
With fleshless limbs, at rueful length, was laid.

26

And o'er his head flew jealousies and cares,
Ghosts, imps, and half the black Tartarian crew,
Arch-angels damn'd, nor was their Prince remote,
Borne on the vaporous wings of Stygian dew.

27

Around his bed, by the dull flambeaux' glare,
I saw pale phantoms—Rage to madness vext,
Wan, wasting grief, and ever musing care,
Distressful pain, and poverty perplext.

28

Sad was his countenance, if we can call
That *countenance,* where only bones were seen
And eyes sunk in their sockets, dark and low,
And teeth, that only show'd themselves to grin.

29

Reft was his scull of hair, and no fresh bloom
Of cheerful mirth sate on his visage hoar:
Sometimes he rais'd his head, while deep-drawn groans
Were mixt with words that did his fate deplore.

30

Oft did he wish to see the daylight spring,
And often toward the window lean'd to hear,
Fore-runner of the scarlet-mantled morn,
The early note of wakeful *Chanticleer.* * * *

98

"Death in this tomb his weary bones hath laid,
Sick of dominion o'er the human kind—
Behold what devastations he hath made,
Survey the millions by his arm confin'd.

99

"Six thousand years has sovereign sway been mine,
None, but myself, can real glory claim;
Great Regent of the world I reign'd alone,
And princes trembled when my mandate came.

100

"Vast and unmatch'd throughout the world, my fame
Takes place of gods, and asks no mortal date—
No; by myself, and by the heavens, I swear,

Not Alexander's name is half so great.

101

"Nor swords nor darts my prowess could withstand,
All quit their arms, and bow'd to my decree,
Even mighty Julius *died beneath my hand,*
For slaves and Caesars were the same to me!

102

"Traveller, wouldst thou his noblest trophies seek,
Search in no narrow spot obscure for those;
The sea profound, the surface of all land
Is moulded with the myriads of his foes."

103

Scarce had he spoke, when on the lofty dome
Rush'd from the clouds a hoarse resounding blast—
Round the four eaves so loud and sad it play'd
As though all musick were to breathe its last.

104

Warm was the gale, and such as travellers say
Sport with the winds on Zaara's waste;
Black was the sky, a mourning carpet spread,
Its azure blotted, and its stars o'ercast!

105

Lights in the air like burning stars were hurl'd,
Dogs howl'd, heaven mutter'd, and the tempest blew,
The red half-moon peeped from behind a cloud
As if in dread the amazing scene to view.

106

The mournful trees that in the garden stood
Bent to the tempest as it rush'd along,
The elm, the myrtle, and the cypress sad
More melancholy tun'd its bellowing song.

107

No more that elm its noble branches spread,
The yew, the cypress, or the myrtle tree,
Rent from the roots the tempest tore them down,
And all the grove in wild confusion lay.

108

Yet, mindful of his dread command, I part
Glad from the magic dome—nor found relief;
Damps from the dead hung heavier round my heart,
While sad remembrance rous'd her stores of grief.

109

O'er a dark field I held my dubious way
Where Jack-a-lanthorn walk'd his lonely round,
Beneath my feet substantial darkness lay,
And screams were heard from the distemper'd ground.

110

Nor look'd I back, till to a far off wood
Trembling with fear, my weary feet had sped—
Dark was the night, but at the inchanted dome

I saw the infernal windows flaming red.

111

And from within the howls of Death I heard,
Cursing the dismal night that gave him birth,
Damning his ancient sire, and mother sin,
Who at the gates of hell, accursed, brought him forth.

112

(For fancy gave to my enraptur'd soul
An eagle's eye, with keenest glance to see,
And bade those distant sounds distinctly roll,
Which, waking, never had affected me.)

113

Oft his pale breast with cruel hand he smote,
And tearing from his limbs a winding sheet,
Roar'd to the black skies, while the woods around,
As wicked as himself, his words repeat.

114

Thrice tow'rd the skies his meagre arms he rear'd,
Invok'd all hell, and thunders on his head,
Bid light'nings fly, earth yawn, and tempest roar,
And the sea wrap him in its oozy bed. * * *

132

What is this *Death,* ye deep read sophists, say?—
Death is no more than one unceasing change;
New forms arise, while other forms decay,
Yet all is Life throughout creation's range.

133

The towering *Alps,* the haughty *Appenine,*
The *Andes,* wrapt in everlasting snow,
The *Apalachian* and the *Ararat*
Sooner or later must to ruin go.

134

Hills sink to plains, and man returns to dust,
That dust supports a reptile or a flower;
Each changeful atom by some other nurs'd
Takes some new form, to perish in an hour.

135

Too nearly join'd to sickness, toils, and pains,
(Perhaps for former crimes imprison'd here)
True to itself the immortal soul remains,
And seeks new mansions in the starry sphere.

136

When Nature bids thee from the world retire,
With joy thy lodging leave, a fated guest;
In Paradise, the land of thy desire,
Existing always, always to be blest.

1779

THE PYRAMIDS OF EGYPT

A DIALOGUE
WRITTEN IN 1769

Scene. Egypt.
Persons. Traveller, Genius, Time.

Traveller

Where are those far-famed piles of human grandeur,
Those sphinxes, pyramids, and Pompey's pillar,

That bid defiance to the arm of Time—
Tell me, dear Genius, for I long to see them.

Genius

At Alexandria rises Pompey's pillar,
Whose date is but of yesterday, compared
With those prodigious fabricks that you see
O'er yonder distant plain—upon whose breast
Old Nile hath never roll'd his swelling stream,
The only plain so privileged in Egypt;
These pyramids may well excite your wonder;
They are of most remote antiquity,
Almost coeval with those cloud-crown'd hills
That westward from them rise—long ere the age
That saw old Babel's tower aspiring high,
Then first the sage Egyptian architects
These ancient turrets to the heavens rais'd:—
But Babel's tower is gone, and these remain!

Traveller

Old Rome I thought unrival'd in her years,
At least the remnants that we find at Rome,—
Deep are they sunk in dark antiquity;—
But these, you tell me, are of older date.

Genius

Talk not of Rome!—Before they lopt a bush
From the seven hills where Rome, earth's empress, stood,
These pyramids were old—their birthday is
Beyond tradition's reach, or history.

Traveller

Then let us haste toward those piles of wonder
That scorn to bend beneath this weight of years—
Lo! to my view, the aweful mansions rise
The pride of art, the sleeping place of death!
Are these the four prodigious monuments
That so astonish every generation—
Let us examine this, the first and greatest—
A secret horror, chills my breast, dear Genius,
To touch these monuments that are so ancient,
The fearful property of ghosts and death!—
And of such mighty bulk, that I presume
A race of giants were the architects.—
Since these proud fabricks to the heavens were rais'd
How many generations have decay'd,
How many monarchies to ruin pass'd!
How many empires had their rise and fall!
While these remain—and promise to remain
As long as yonder sun, that gilds their summits,
Or moon or stars their wonted circuits run.

Genius

——————The time will come
When these stupendous piles you deem immortal,
Worn out with age, shall moulder on their bases,
And down, down, low to endless ruin verging,

O'erwhelm'd by dust, be seen and known no more!—
Ages ago, in dark oblivion's lap
Had they been shrouded, but the atmosphere
In these parch'd climates, hostile to decay,
Is pregnant with no rain, that by its moisture
Might waste their bulk in such excess of time,
And prove them briefly mortal.—
'Twas on this plain the ancient Memphis stood,
walls encircled these tall pyramids—
But where is Pharaoh's palace, where the domes
Of Egypt's haughty lords? all, all are gone,
And like the phantom snows of a May morning,
Left not a vestige to remember them!

TRAVELLER

How shall I reach the vertex of this pile—
How shall I clamber up its shelving sides?
I scarce endure to glance towards the summit,
It seems among the clouds—When wast thou rais'd
O work of more than mortal majesty—
Was this produced by persevering man,
Or did the gods erect this pyramid?

GENIUS

Nor gods, nor giants rais'd this pyramid—
It was the toil of mortals like yourself,
That swell'd it to the skies—
Seest thou yon' little door? Through that they pass'd,
Who rais'd so high this aggregate of wonders!
What cannot tyrants do,
When they have subject nations at their will,
And the world's wealth to gratify ambition!
Millions of slaves beneath their labours fainted
Who here were doom'd to toil incessantly,
And years elaps'd while groaning myriads strove
To raise this mighty tomb—and but to hide
The worthless bones of an Egyptian king.—
O wretch, might not a humbler tomb have done,
Could nothing but a pyramid inter thee?

TRAVELLER

Perhaps old Israel's race, when here oppress'd,
Rais'd, in their years of bondage, this dread pile.

GENIUS

Before the Jewish patriarchs saw the light,
While yet the globe was in its infancy
These were erected to the pride of man—
Five thousand years have run their tedious round
Since these smooth stones were on each other laid,
Five thousand more may run as dull a round
Ere Egypt sees her pyramids decay'd.

TRAVELLER

But suffer me to enter, and behold
The interior wonders of this edifice.

GENIUS

'Tis darkness all, with hateful silence join'd—
Here drowsy bats enjoy a dull repose,

And marble coffins, vacant of their bones,
Shew where the royal dead in ruin lay!
By every pyramid a temple rose
Where oft, in concert, those of ancient time
Sung to their goddess Isis hymns of praise;
But these are fallen!—their columns too superb
Are levell'd with the dust—nor these alone—
Where is thy vocal statue, *Memnon,* now,
That, once, responsive to the morning beams,
Harmoniously to father Phoebus sung!
Where is the image that in past time stood
High on the summit of yon' pyramid?
Still may you see its polish'd pedestal—
Where art thou ancient Thebes?—all buried low,
All vanish'd! crumbled into mother dust,
And nothing of antiquity remains
But these huge pyramids, and yonder hills.

Time

Old Babel's tower hath felt my potent arm,
I ruin'd *Ecbatan* and *Babylon,*
Thy huge Colossus, *Rhodes,* I tumbled down,
And on these pyramids I smote my scythe;
But they resist its edge—then let them stand.—
But I can boast a greater feat than this,
I long ago have shrouded those in death
Who made these structures rebels to my power—
But, O return!—These piles are not immortal!
This earth, with all its belts of hills and mountains,
Shall perish by my hand—then how can these,
These hoary-headed pyramids of Egypt,
That are but dwindled moates upon her body,
That on a little, little spot of ground
Extinguish the dull radiance of the sun,
Be proof to death and me?—Traveller, return—
There's nought but God immortal—He alone
Exists secure, when Genius, and *Time,*
(Time not immortal, but a viewless point
In the vast circle of eternity)
Are swallowed up, and, like the pyramids,
Leave not an atom for their monument!

(1769) 1786

THE INDIAN BURYING GROUND

In spite of all the learned have said,
I still my old opinion keep;
The *posture,* that *we* give the dead,
Points out the soul's eternal sleep.

Not so the ancients of these lands—
The Indian, when from life released,
Again is seated with his friends,
And shares again the joyous feast.

His imaged birds, and painted bowl,
And venison, for a journey dressed,
Bespeak the nature of the soul,
Activity, that knows no rest.

His bow, for action ready bent,
And arrows, with a head of stone,
Can only mean that life is spent,
And not the old ideas gone.

Thou, stranger, that shalt come this way,

No fraud upon the dead commit—
Observe the swelling turf, and say
They do not *lie*, but here they *sit*.

Here still a lofty rock remains,
On which the curious eye may trace
(Now wasted, half, by wearing rains)
The fancies of a ruder race.

Here still an aged elm aspires,
Beneath whose far-projecting shade
(And which the shepherd still admires)
The children of the forest played!

There oft a restless Indian queen
(Pale *Shebah*, with her braided hair)
And many a barbarous form is seen
To chide the man that lingers there.

By midnight moons, o'er moistening dews,
In habit for the chase arrayed,
The hunter still the deer pursues,
The hunter and the deer, a shade!

And long shall timorous fancy see
The painted chief, and pointed spear,
And Reason's self shall bow the knee
To shadows and delusions here.

1788

THE DYING INDIAN:

Tomo-Chequi

"On yonder lake I spread the sail no more!
Vigour, and youth, and active days are past—
Relentless demons urge me to that shore
On whose black forests all the dead are cast:—
Ye solemn train, prepare the funeral song,
For I must go to shades below,
Where all is strange and all is new;
Companion to the airy throng!—
What solitary streams,
In dull and dreary dreams,
All melancholy, must I rove along!

"To what strange lands must *Chequi* take his way!
Groves of the dead departed mortals trace:
No deer along those gloomy forests stray,
No huntsmen there take pleasure in the chace,
But all are empty unsubstantial shades,
That ramble through those visionary glades;
No spongy fruits from verdant trees depend,
But sickly orchards there
Do fruits as sickly bear,
And apples a consumptive visage shew,
And withered hangs the hurtle-berry blue.

"Ah me! what mischiefs on the dead attend!
Wandering a stranger to the shores below,
Where shall I brook or real fountain find?
Lazy and sad deluding waters flow—
Such is the picture in my boding mind!
Fine tales, indeed, they tell
Of shades and purling rills,
Where our dead fathers dwell
Beyond the western hills,
But when did ghost return his state to shew;
Or who can promise half the tale is true?

"I too must be a fleeting ghost!—no more—
None, none but shadows to those mansions go;
I leave my woods, I leave the Huron shore,
For emptier groves below!

Ye charming solitudes,
Ye tall ascending woods,
Ye glassy lakes and prattling streams,
Whose aspect still was sweet,
Whether the sun did greet,
Or the pale moon embraced you with her beams—
Adieu to all!
To all, that charmed me where I strayed,
The winding stream, the dark sequestered shade;
Adieu all triumphs here!
Adieu the mountain's lofty swell,
Adieu, thou little verdant hill,
And seas, and stars, and skies—farewell,
For some remoter sphere!

"Perplexed with doubts, and tortured with despair,
Why so dejected at this hopeless sleep?
Nature at last these ruins may repair,
When fate's long dream is o'er, and she forgets to weep
Some real world once more may be assigned,
Some new born mansion for the immortal mind!
Farewell, sweet lake; farewell surrounding woods,
To other groves, through midnight glooms, I stray,
Beyond the mountains, and beyond the floods,
Beyond the Huron bay!
Prepare the hollow tomb, and place me low,
My trusty bow and arrows by my side,
The cheerful bottle and the venison store;
For long the journey is that I must go,
Without a partner, and without a guide."
He spoke, and bid the attending mourners weep,
Then closed his eyes, and sunk to endless sleep!

1784

THE INDIAN STUDENT:

OR,

FORCE OF NATURE

FROM Susquehanna's farthest springs
Where savage tribes pursue their game,
(His blanket tied with yellow strings,)
A shepherd of the forest came.

Not long before, a wandering priest
Expressed his wish, with visage sad—
"Ah, why (he cried) in Satan's waste,
Ah, why detain so fine a lad?

"In white-man's land there stands a town
Where learning may be purchased low—
Exchange his blanket for a gown,
And let the lad to college go."—

From long debate the council rose,
And viewing *Shalum's* tricks with joy
To *Cambridge Hall,* o'er wastes of snows,
They sent the copper-coloured boy.

One generous chief a bow supplied,
This gave a shaft, and that a skin;
The feathers, in vermillion dyed,
Himself did from a turkey win:

Thus dressed so gay, he took his way
O'er barren hills, alone, alone!
His guide a star, he wandered far,
His pillow every night a stone.

At last he came, with foot so lame,
Where learned men talk heathen Greek,
And Hebrew lore is gabbled o'er,
To please the Muses,—twice a week.

Awhile he writ, awhile he read,
Awhile he conned their grammar rules—

(An Indian savage so well bred
Great credit promised to the schools.)

Some thought he would in *law* excel,
Some said in *physic* he would shine;
And one that knew him, passing well,
Beheld, in him, a sound Divine.

But those of more discerning eye
Even then could other prospects show,
And saw him lay his *Virgil* by
To wander with his dearer *bow.*

The tedious hours of study spent,
The heavy-moulded lecture done,
He to the woods a hunting went,
Through lonely wastes he walked, he run.

No mystic wonders fired his mind;
He sought to gain no learned degree,
But only sense enough to find
The squirrel in the hollow tree.

The shady bank, the purling stream,
The woody wild his heart possessed,
The dewy lawn, his morning dream
In fancy's gayest colours dressed.

"And why (he cried) did I forsake
My native wood for gloomy walls;
The silver stream, the limpid lake
For musty books and college halls.

"A little could my wants supply—
Can wealth and honour give me more;
Or, will the sylvan god deny
The humble treat he gave before?

"Let seraphs gain the bright abode,
And heaven's sublimest mansions see—
I only bow to Nature's God—
The land of shades will do for me.

"These dreadful secrets of the sky
Alarm my soul with chilling fear—
Do planets in their orbits fly?
And is the earth, indeed, a sphere?

"Let planets still their course pursue,
And comets to the Centre run—
In Him my faithful friend I view,
The image of my God—the Sun.

"Where Nature's ancient forests grow,
And mingled laurel never fades,
My heart is fixed;—and I must go
To die among my native shades."

He spoke and to the western springs,
(His gown discharged, his money spent,
His blanket tied with yellow strings,)
The shepherd of the forest went.
(1778) 1790

THE DESERTED FARM-HOUSE

This antique dome the insatiate tooth of time
  Now level with the dust has almost laid;—
Yet ere 'tis gone, I seize my humble theme
  From these low ruins, that his years have made.

Behold the unsocial hearth! where once the fires
  Blazed high, and soothed the storm-stay'd traveller's woes;
See! the weak roof, that abler props requires,
  Admits the winds, and swift descending snows.

Here, to forget the labours of the day,
  No more the swains at evening hours repair,
But wandering flocks assume the well known way
  To shun the rigours of the midnight air.

In yonder chamber, half to ruin gone,
  Once stood the ancient housewife's curtained bed—
Timely the prudent matron has withdrawn,

And each domestic comfort with her fled.

The trees, the flowers that her own hands had reared,
  The plants, the vines, that were so verdant seen,—
The trees, the flowers, the vines have disappear'd,
  And every plant has vanish'd from the green.

So sits in tears on wide Campania's plain
  Rome, once the mistress of a world enslaved;
That triumph'd o'er the land, subdued the main,
  And Time himself, in her wild transports, braved.

So sits in tears on Palestina's shore
  The Hebrew town, of splendour once divine—
Her kings, her lords, her triumphs are no more;
  Slain are her priests, and ruin'd every shrine.

Once, in the bounds of this deserted room,
  Perhaps some swain nocturnal courtship made,
Perhaps some *Sherlock* mused amidst the gloom;
  Since Love and Death forever seek the shade.

Perhaps some miser, doom'd to discontent,
  Here counted o'er the heaps acquired with pain;
He to the dust—his gold, on traffick sent,
  Shall ne'er disgrace these mouldering walls again.

Nor shall the glow-worm fopling, sunshine bred,
  Seek, at the evening hour this wonted dome—
Time has reduced the fabrick to a shed,
  Scarce fit to be the wandering beggar's home.

And none but I its dismal case lament—
  None, none but I o'er its cold relics mourn,
Sent by the muse—(the time perhaps misspent)—
  To write dull stanzas on this dome forlorn.

1775

THE WILD HONEY SUCKLE

Fair flower, that dost so comely grow,
Hid in this silent, dull retreat,
Untouched thy honied blossoms blow,
Unseen thy little branches greet:
  No roving foot shall crush thee here,
  No busy hand provoke a tear.

By Nature's self in white arrayed,
She bade thee shun the vulgar eye,
And planted here the guardian shade,
And sent soft waters murmuring by;
  Thus quietly thy summer goes,
  Thy days declining to repose.

Smit with those charms, that must decay,
I grieve to see your future doom;
They died—nor were those flowers more gay,
The flowers that did in Eden bloom;
  Unpitying frosts, and Autumn's power
  Shall leave no vestige of this flower.

From morning suns and evening dews
At first thy little being came:
If nothing once, you nothing lose,
For when you die you are the same;
  The space between, is but an hour,
  The frail duration of a flower.

1786

ON A HONEY BEE

DRINKING FROM A GLASS OF WINE, AND DROWNED THEREIN

(By Hezekiah Salem)

Thou, born to sip the lake or spring,
Or quaff the waters of the stream,
Why hither come on vagrant wing?—
Does Bacchus tempting seem—
Did he, for you, this glass prepare?—
Will I admit you to a share?

Did storms harass or foes perplex,
Did wasps or king-birds bring dismay—
Did wars distress, or labours vex,
Or did you miss your way?—
A better seat you could not take
Than on the margin of this lake.

Welcome!—I hail you to my glass:
All welcome, here, you find;
Here, let the cloud of trouble pass,
Here, be all care resigned.—
This fluid never fails to please,
And drown the griefs of men or bees.

What forced you here, we cannot know,
And you can scarcely tell—
But cheery we would have you go
And bid a fond farewell:
On lighter wings we bid you fly,
Your dart will now all foes defy.

Yet take not, oh! too deep a drink,
And in this ocean die;
Here bigger bees than you might sink,
Even bees full six feet high.
Like Pharaoh, then, you would be said
To perish in a sea of red.

Do as you please, your will is mine;
Enjoy it without fear—
And your grave will be this glass of wine,
Your epitaph—a tear—
Go, take your seat in Charon's boat,
We'll tell the hive, you died afloat.

1809

TO A CATY-DID

In a branch of a willow hid
Sings the evening Caty-did:
From the lofty locust bough
Feeding on a drop of dew,
In her suit of green array'd
Hear her singing in the shade
Caty-did, Caty-did, Caty-did!

While upon a leaf you tread,
Or repose your little head,
On your sheet of shadows laid,
All the day you nothing said:
Half the night your cheery tongue
Revell'd out its little song,
Nothing else but Caty-did.

From your lodgings on the leaf
Did you utter joy or grief—?
Did you only mean to say,
I have had my summer's day,
And am passing, soon, away
To the grave of Caty-did;—
Poor, unhappy Caty-did!

But you would have utter'd more
Had you known of nature's power—
From the world when you retreat,
And a leaf's your winding sheet,
Long before your spirit fled,
Who can tell but Nature said,
Live again, my Caty-did!
Live, and chatter Caty-did.

Tell me, what did Caty do?
Did she mean to trouble you?—
Why was Caty not forbid
To trouble little Caty-did?—
Wrong, indeed at you to fling,
Hurting no one while you sing
Caty-did! Caty-did! Caty-did!

Why continue to complain?
Caty tells me, she again
Will not give you plague or pain:—
Caty says you may be hid
Caty will not go to bed
While you sing us Caty-did.
Caty-did! Caty-did! Caty-did!

But, while singing, you forgot
To tell us what did Caty *not:*
Caty-did not think of cold,
Flocks retiring to the fold,
Winter, with his wrinkles old,
Winter, that yourself foretold
When you gave us Caty-did.

Stay securely in your nest;
Caty now, will do her best,
All she can, to make you blest;
But, you want no human aid—
Nature, when she form'd you, said,
"Independent you are made,
My dear little Caty-did:
Soon yourself must disappear
With the verdure of the year,"—
And to go, we know not where,
With your song of Caty-did.

1815

MAN OF NINETY

"To yonder boughs that spread so wide,
Beneath whose shade soft waters glide,
Once more I take the well known way;
With feeble step and tottering knee
I sigh to reach my White Oak tree,
Where rosy health was wont to play.

If to the shades, consuming slow,
The shadow of myself, I go,
When I am gone, wilt thou remain!—
From dust you rose, and grew like me;
I man became, and you a tree,
Both natives of one grassy plain.

How much alike; yet not the same!—
You could no kind protector claim;
Alone you stood, to chance resigned:
When winter came, with blustering sky,
You feared its blasts—and so did I,
And for warm suns in secret pined.

When vernal suns began to glow
You felt returning vigour flow;
Which once a year new leaves supplied;
Like you, fine days I wished to see,
And May was a sweet month to me,
But when November came—I sighed!

If through your bark some ruffian arm
A mark impressed, you took the alarm,
And tears awhile I saw descend;
Till Nature's kind maternal aid
A plaister on your bruises laid,
And bade your trickling sorrows end.

Like you, I feared the lightning's stroke,
Whose flame dissolves the strength of oak,
And ends at once this mortal dream;—
You saw, with grief, the soil decay
That from your roots was torn away;
You sighed—and cursed the stream.

With borrowed earth, and busy spade,
Around your roots new life I laid,
While joy revived in every vein;
(The care of man shall life impart)—
Though *Nature* owns the aid of art,
No art, immortal, makes their reign.

How much alike our fortune—say—
Yet, why must I so soon decay
When thou hast scarcely reached thy prime—
Erect and tall, you joyous stand;
The staff of age has found my hand,
That guides me to the grave of time.

Could I, fair tree, like you, resign,
And banish all those fears of mine,
Grey hairs would be no cause of grief;
Your blossoms die, but you remain,
Your fruit lies scattered o'er the plain—
Learn wisdom from the falling leaf.

As you survive, by heaven's decree,
Let withered flowers be thrown on me
Sad compensation for my doom,
While winter greens and withering pines,
And cedars dark, and barren vines,
Point out the lonely tomb.

The enlivening sun, that burns so bright,
Ne'er had a noon without a night,
So LIFE and DEATH agree;
The joys of man by years are broke"—
'Twas thus the man of ninety spoke,
Then rose, and left his tree.

1788

THE VANITY OF EXISTENCE

TO THYRSIS

IN youth, gay scenes attract our eyes,
And not suspecting their decay
Life's flowery fields before us rise,
Regardless of its winter day.

But vain pursuits, and joys as vain,
Convince us life is but a dream.
Death is to wake, to rise again
To that true life you best esteem.

So nightly on some shallow tide,
Oft have I seen a splendid show;
Reflected stars on either side,
And glittering moons were seen below.

But when the tide had ebbed away,
The scene fantastic with it fled,
A bank of mud around me lay,
And sea-weed on the river's bed.

1781

ON THE RELIGION OF NATURE

THE power, that gives with liberal hand
The blessings man enjoys, while here,
And scatters through a smiling land
Abundant products of the year;
That power of nature, ever bless'd,
Bestow'd religion with the rest.

Born with ourselves, her early sway
Inclines the tender mind to take
The path of right, fair virtue's way
Its own felicity to make.
This universally extends
And leads to no mysterious ends.

Religion, such as nature taught,
With all divine perfection suits;
Had all mankind this system sought
Sophists would cease their vain disputes,
And from this source would nations know
All that can make their heaven below.

This deals not curses on mankind,
Or dooms them to perpetual grief,
If from its aid no joys they find,
It damns them not for unbelief;
Upon a more exalted plan
Creatress nature dealt with man—

Joy to the day, when all agree
On such grand systems to proceed,
From fraud, design, and error free,
And which to truth and goodness lead:
Then persecution will retreat
And man's religion be complete.

1815

ADVICE TO AUTHORS

By the Late Mr. Robert Slender

There are few writers of books in this new world, and amongst these very few that deal in works of imagination, and, I am sorry to say, fewer still that have any success attending their lucubrations. Perhaps, however, the world thinks justly on this subject. The productions of the most brilliant imagination are at best but mere beautiful flowers, that may amuse us in a walk through a garden in a fine afternoon, but can by no means be expected to engage much of that time which God and nature designed to be spent in very different employments. In a country, which two hundred years ago was peopled only by savages, and where the government has ever, in effect, since the first establishment of the white men in these parts, been no other than republican, it is really wonderful there should be any polite original authors at all in any line, especially when it is considered, that according to the common course of things, any particular nation or people must have arrived to, or rather passed, their meridian of opulence and refinement, before they consider the professors of the fine arts in any other light than a nuisance to the community. This is evidently the case at present in our age and country; all you have to do then, my good friends, is to graft your authorship upon some other calling, or support drooping genius by the assistance of some mechanical employment, in the same manner as the helpless ivy takes hold of the vigorous oak, and cleaves to it for support—I mean to say, in plain language, that you may make something by weaving garters, or mending old sails, when an Epic poem would be your utter destruction.

But I see no reason that, because we are all striving to live by the same idle trade, we should suffer ourselves to be imbittered against each other, like a fraternity of rival mechanics in the same street. Authors (such I mean as are not possessed of fortunes) are at present considered as the dregs of the community: their situation and prospects are truly humiliating, and any other sett of men in a similar state of calamitous adversity would unite together for their mutual defence, instead of worrying and lampooning each other for the amusement of the illiberal vulgar. —And I cannot do otherwise than freely declare, that where the whole profits of a company amount to little or nothing at all, there ought not, in the nature of things, to be any quarrelling about shares and dividends.

As to those authors who have lately exported themselves from Britain and Ireland, and boast that they have introduced the Muses among us since the conclusion of the late war, I really believe them to be a very good natured sett of gentlemen, notwithstanding they, in the course of the last winter, called me *poetaster* and *scribbler,* and some other names still more unsavoury. They are, however, excuseable in treating the American authors as inferiors; a political and a literary independence of their nation being two very different things—the first was accomplished in about seven years, the latter will not be completely effected, perhaps, in as many centuries. It is my opinion, nevertheless, that a duty ought to be laid upon all imported authors, the nett proceeds of which should be appropriated to the benefit of real American writers, when become old and helpless, and no longer able to wield the pen to advantage.

If a coach or a chariot constructed in Britain pays an impost of twenty pounds at the custom-house, why should not at least twice that sum be laid upon all imported authors who are able to do twice as much mischief with their rumbling pindaric odes, and gorgeous apparatus of strophes, antistrophes and recitativos? —I, for my own part, am clearly of opinion that these gentlemen should be taxed; not that I would wish to nip their buds of beauty with the untimely frost of excise, but merely to teach them that our own natural manufactures ought to be primarily attended to and encouraged.

I will now, gentlemen, with your leave, lay down a few simple rules, to which, in my opinion, every genuine author will make no difficulty to conform.

1. When you write a book for the public, have nothing to do with *Epistles dedicatory*. They were first invented by slaves, and have been continued by fools and sycophants. I would not give a farthing more for a book on account of its being patronized by all the noblemen or crowned heads in Christendom. If it does not possess intrinsic merit enough to protect itself, and force its way through the world, their supposed protection will be of no avail: besides, by this ridiculous practice you degrade the *dignity authorial,* the honour of authorship, which ought evermore to be uppermost in your thoughts. The silly unthinking author addresses a great man in the stile of a servile dependent, whereas a real author, and a man of true genius, has upon all occasions a bold, disinterested and daring confidence in himself, and considers the common cant of adulation to the sons of fortune as the basest and most abominable of all prostitution.

2. Be particularly careful to avoid all connexion with doctors of law and divinity, masters of arts, professors of colleges, and in general all those that wear square black caps. A mere scholar and an original author are two animals as different from each other as a fresh and salt water sailor. There has been an old rooted enmity between them from the earliest ages, and which it is likely will forever continue. The scholar is not unlike that piddling orator, who, cold and inanimate, not roused into action by the impelling flame of inspiration, can only pronounce the oration he has learned by rote; the real author, on the contrary, is the nervous Demosthenes, who stored with an immensity of ideas, awakened within him he knows not how, has them at command upon every occasion; and must therefore be disregarded as a madman or an enthusiast by the narrow and limited capacity, as well as the natural self-sufficiency of the other.

3. It is risquing a great deal to propose a subscription for an original work. The world will be ready enough to anticipate your best endeavours; and that which has been long and anxiously expected, rarely or never comes up to their expectations at last.

4. If you are so poor that you are compelled to live in some miserable garret or cottage; do not repine, but give thanks to heaven that you are not forced to pass your life in a tub, as was the fate of Diogenes of old. Few authors in any country are rich, because a man must first be reduced to a state of penury before he will commence author. Being poor therefore in externals, take care, gentlemen, that you say or do nothing that may argue a poverty of spirit. Riches, we have often heard, are by no means the standard of the value of a man. This maxim the world allows to be true, and yet contradicts it every hour and minute in the year. Fortune most commonly bestows wealth and abundance upon fools and idiots; and men of the dullest natural parts are, notwithstanding, generally best calculated to acquire large estates, and hoard up immense sums from small beginnings.

5. Never borrow money of any man, for if you should once be mean enough to fall into such a habit you will find yourselves unwelcome guests every where. If upon actual trial you are at length convinced you possess no abilities that will command the esteem, veneration or gratitude of mankind, apply yourselves without loss of time to some of the lower arts, since it is far more honourable to be a good bricklayer or a skilful weaver than an indifferent poet. —If you cannot at all exist without now and then gratifying your itch for scribbling, follow my example who can both weave stockings and write poems. —But, if you really possess that sprightliness of fancy and elevation of soul which alone constitute an author, do not on that account be troublesome to your friends. A little reflection will point out other means to extract money from the hands and pockets of your fellow citizens than by poorly borrowing what, perhaps, you will never be able to repay.

6. Never engage in any business as an inferior or understrapper. I cannot endure to see an author debase his profession so far as to submit to be second or third in any office or employment whatever. If fortune, or the ill taste of the public compels you even to turn shallopman on the Delaware, let it be your first care to have the command of the boat. Beggary itself, with all its hideous apparatus of rags and misery, becomes at once respectable whenever it exhibits the least token of independence of spirit and a single spark of laudable ambition.

7. If you are in low circumstances, do not forget that there is such a thing in the world as a decent pride. They are only cowards and miscreants that poverty can render servile in their behaviour. Your haughtiness should always rise in proportion to the wretchedness and desperation of your circumstances. If you have only a single guinea in the world be complaisant and obliging to every one: if you are absolutely destitute of a shilling, immediately assume the air of a despot, pull off your hat to no one, let your discourse, in every company, turn upon the vanity of riches, the insignificancy of the great men of the earth, the revolution of empires, and the final consummation of all things. —By such means you will at least conceal a secret of some importance to yourself—that you have not

a shilling in the world to pay for your last night's lodging.

8. Should you ever be prevailed upon to dedicate your book to any great man or woman, consider first, whether the tenor and subject of it be such as may in some measure coincide with the age, temper, education, business and general conversation of the person whose patronage is requested. A friend of mine once committed a great error on this score. He wrote a bawdy poem, and dedicated it to the principal in the department of finance.

9. Never make a present of your works to great men. If they do not think them worth purchasing, trust me, they will never think them worth reading.

10. If fortune seems absolutely determined to starve you, and you can by no means whatever make your works sell; to keep up as much as in you lies, the expiring dignity of authorship, do not take to drinking, gambling or bridge-building as some have done, thereby bringing the trade of authorship into disrepute; but retire to some uninhabited island or desert, and there, at your leisure, end your life with decency.

1788

THE SAILOR'S RELIEF

Alexander Dismal, Inn-holder, to the Printer of the *Weekly Gazette*.

Right Worthy!

Since all are for the public good distrest,
And each proposes what he thinks is best—
Why may not I propose, among the rest?—

I am one of that numerous tribe, who, under the smiles of heaven, endeavour to make an honest livelihood by keeping a house of decent entertainment for such as chuse to favour me with their custom:—but I beg leave to observe (I hope without offence) that there is no class of people by which our fraternity, adjacent to the river, so much suffer, at times, as by sea-faring men; though none expend their money with a more liberal hand and heart, as long as they have a single sixpence in their funds to draw upon. —Sunday last, the twenty-third day of January, 1784, was a time of woeful humiliation to us poor publicans. The river opened on a sudden, the sailors went off in triumph, and, for the most part, considerably indebted to those, who had for several weeks preceding found them in victuals and lodging. As I am a sincere and hearty friend to all sea-faring men, having myself been formerly master of a small coasting packet; and notwithstanding I have frequently been a considerable sufferer by the roguery of some individuals, I would nevertheless beg leave to remark, that in a country like this, so remarkable for its public and private charity toward our unfortunate fellow men, it would well become us to provide some resources, either by a general tax, or certain tolls to be paid by every vessel passing and repassing Gloucester Point, to assist, comfort, cherish and support such seafaring men, in needy circumstances, as happen to be detained here during the winter season by the temporary interruption of our navigation; particularly those who are unable, through mere mischance, mishap, old age, or other incapacity, immediately to help themselves.

In pursuance of this plan, I would humbly propose that a three decked ship, of about four hundred tons burthen, should be forthwith built and finished off in a plain manner at the public expence, with commodious and comfortable apartments throughout for poor and distressed seamen, regard being always had, in the distribution of the various apartments, to the known rank and station of the party relieved. I do not mean, however, that this vessel should be launched into the water. Every purpose of accommodation would be much better answered by letting her remain upon dry land, and many disagreeable accidents thereby prevented. It would nevertheless be necessary that her station should be as near as possible to the river, as no true Jacktar can endure to be long out of sight of navigable water. The most applicable name I can at present think of for this humane foundation, is, THE SAILOR'S RELIEF.

It is obvious, at first glance, that such a ship as this would not cost so much to the public as one designed for real sea service. She would not require more than one half of the crooked timber commonly made use of in vessels of the proposed burthen, nor need her planks be more than three fourths of an inch thick, or at most one inch. Sailors are never truly and fully contented except when on shipboard, consequently they would be no where better pleased than in such a situation as this, where they would enjoy all the merriment and good humour of a sea-faring life, without having those bitter gales and mountainous waves to encounter, which, for a great part of the year, are so fatal and terrible to the marine fraternity on these coasts. —I would further propose, that the ship should be kept constantly victualled by contract, or otherwise, with common sea provisions, faithfully laid in, and a cook to be provided by the public, who had not been previously less than seven years at sea in that capacity. —Rigged she should be completely, to the end that the older sailors might be constantly practicing their various manœuvres according to the state of the winds and weather, and the younger ones taught to be ready and dextrous in the art of working a ship when in actual service. Over and above the standing rigging, she should be furnished with a complete sett of running geer, including every article from the topgallant sheets to the jeer falls and clue-garnets: Not a brace, bow-line, top-rope, sheet, halyard, bunt line, clew line or reef takle should be wanting; and the masts, yards, sails, stays, shrouds and tops should be as punctually supplied, and as exactly arranged in their proper places, as if they were really to travel the high seas. —Some distressed or disabled old sea-commander, of good character and sober conversation, might preside here, in the two capacities of master and chaplain, with the proper officers under him, during the hard season, for keeping the crew in order; but whenever the river is clear of ice, I would have all hands discharged (excepting such as should be found absolutely helpless, and a few others) and the skuttles barred down till the navigation should be again obstructed, and these useful men once more seen wandering about the streets to look out a shelter from the unpitying storm.

I leave it to others to point out a proper spot of ground whereon to erect this pile of benevolence; only taking care that the horizon should be as little obstructed as possible, that they might every day have an opportunity of determining the latitude and longitude of the ship with the precision in such cases necessary. As to the manual labour on board, I am of opinion it would not be excessive, especially as the helm, the anchor, and the pump would require little or no attendance,—yet an allowance of weak grog would be absolutely necessary to keep up the spirits of the crew, and it should be a standing rule among them to take in all sail at sunset, for fear of being incommoded with squalls in the night.

A certain sailor went off clandestinely a few days ago, no less than fourteen pounds three shillings and fourpence in my debt, leaving an old sea chest in my possession for security, which, upon the word of a Christian man, contained nothing more than two pair of old frocks and trowsers, a small brown wig (three fourths knawed away by the rats), a sea cap, which by its appearance may, for aught I know, have circumnavigated the globe half a dozen times, and a book called the Seaman's Assistant, which I will adventure to say would not fetch *ninepence,* even if it were to be set up at *Bell's* auction room to be disposed of to the highest bidder, and recommended by all the persuasive oratory of that truly original humourist ——. There is also, among his other trumpery, a sort of strange diary or journal of his proceedings, which seems to have been penned while he lodged in my house. Three or four paragraphs of this elegant performance I shall transcribe for the amusement of yourself and your readers, and therewith conclude this paper. The bad spelling your compositor will be pleased to correct, for I really have not skill enough in language to do it myself.

Decem. 20, 1784. This day I came in from sea in the brig *Ragged Fortune*—settled with the captain—the balance in my favour being four dollars and two thirds. —N.B. The captain, I suspect, cheated me damnably, but upon my taking a cud of tobacco into my mouth, and telling him as much, he gave me a glass of your right stiff grog, true old *stingo,* which squared accounts, and set all to rights again. I then signed a receipt in full.

Decem. 22. Had high fun last night at *Moll Clinker's,* but upon my feeling in my pockets for money to pay the *reckoning,* when I was leaving the house, found not a farthing to bless myself with. —*Mem.* No getting through life without now and then falling in with breakers, and thumping on the shoal grounds—left my new silver buckles in pawn.

January 3, 1785. Find myself woefully in debt already—dream every night of old *Carlisle,* and other pickaroon constables. —*Mem.* to keep a good look out from my tops, and if possible steer clear of those cutter built sons of whores till the river opens. —Jan. 5. At 12 last night, fell in with a watchman, the new building then bearing due west, and Christ church steeple nearly south east. As bad luck would have it he carried no lanthorns, so that he suddenly boarded me in the dark, and at the first shock carried away all the breast hooks of my new blue jacket, the starboard lifts of my half worn castor hat, and nearly two thirds of the after leech of my old great coat. *Note,* he battered my hull severely, but I suspect his main top was somewhat the worse of the judicious and masterly discharges I made upon it with my short oaken cudgel. —After engaging, as near as I could judge, about half a glass, he thought fit to sheer off, with his cut-water in a shattered condition, and his dead lights beaten in; and so left me to pursue my course without further molestation.

January 10. This morning, about eight o'clock, being then in the latitude of *Swede's church,* (the weather cold, with strong gales from the northwest) saw a very ugly fellow, with his jib-boom unrigg'd, steering after me, directly in my wake. —As I judged him to be in chace, I instantly put about and stood to the northward. He pursued me at a great rate; and for a while neared me every minute *hand over hand;* but my manœuvres were so uncommonly excellent and well timed, that I fairly lost sight of him by half past twelve, P.M. the Methodist meeting house then bearing S.S.E. distant one hundred and fifty yards by dead reckoning. —Nothing remarkable this afternoon, except that the wind changed to southwest.

January 15. My landlord begins to look sour at me, and talks of nothing else but scarcity of money and the hardness of the times. —Possibly he means to carry me into dock—I want new sheathing, it's true; but I'll be d—d if they shall lay me ashore at spring tides, however—one has no certainty when they'll float again. —I once lay three long weeks fast aground on my beam ends in Baltimore jail, and, by the diamonds on our *bosen's* nose, did not get off at last till I had thrown overboard the very watch from my pocket, and—ah poor Sue!—thine own ring from my finger, to lighten me!

January 19. Still beating to windward upon a very short allowance—my grog all out, my rigging daily becoming worse and worse, and something every hour giving way. —Yesterday morning at three quarters past four, the wind blowing fresh at east-south-east, half east, with rain and sleet, I carried away the lee strap of my larboard boot hose, back stays and all, in making the best of my way to avoid one of the most active, privateer-built devils of constables that ever cruised in these seas. He rather outwalked me, going large, but by keeping well to windward, that is, by skulking through the narrow allies and by-streets, I had evidently the advantage till sunrise, when I very fortunately got clear of him by favour of a thick fog and heavy rain.

January 21. At 25 minutes past eight, had the misfortune to run foul of a large black double decked transport belonging to the *holy see,* with a grey goose in tow. In less than two minutes I cut away his main spritsail yard, bobstay, topping lifts, quarter cloths, fore-topsail bowlines, and the weather lanyards of his main shrouds. In the conflict, which was very dreadful, they threw overboard a volume of *Ernulphus's* curses, and other contraband Romish commodities, together with a large bundle of certificates, which I picked up and made off with, intending to restore them (at least the certificates) to the right owners, the poor devils of soldiers, upon their paying me *two and sixpence* in the pound.

It would be presuming too much upon the patience of your readers, Mr. Printer, to transcribe any more of this strange animal's remarks. He has writ me a letter from the Delaware capes, however, in which he promises to pay me honourably *when he returns,* even if he should be forced to go to the very centre of the north pole, or to a certain outlandish people he calls the *Hantipods,* to earn the money.

1788

THE AWAKENING OF LITERARY CONSCIOUSNESS: DRAMA AND NOVEL

I. ROYALL TYLER (1757–1826)

THE CONTRAST

PROLOGUE

Written by a Young Gentleman of New-York, and Spoken by Mr. Wignell

Exult each patriot heart!—this night is shewn
A piece, which we may fairly call our own;
Where the proud titles of "My Lord! Your Grace!"
To humble Mr. and plain Sir give place.
Our Author pictures not from foreign climes
The fashions, or the follies of the times;
But has confin'd the subject of his work
To the gay scenes—the circles of New-York.
On native themes his Muse displays her pow'rs;
If ours the faults, the virtues too are ours.
Why should our thoughts to distant countries roam,
When each refinement may be found at home?
Who travels now to ape the rich or great,
To deck an equipage and roll in state;
To court the graces, or to dance with ease,
Or by hypocrisy to strive to please?
Our free-born ancestors such arts despis'd;
Genuine sincerity alone they priz'd;
Their minds, with honest emulation fir'd,
To solid good—not ornament—aspir'd;
Or, if ambition rous'd a bolder flame,
Stern virtue throve, where indolence was shame.

But modern youths, with imitative sense,
Deem taste in dress the proof of excellence;
And spurn the meanness of your homespun arts,
Since homespun habits would obscure their parts;
Whilst all, which aims at splendour and parade,
Must come from Europe, and be ready made.
Strange! we should thus our native worth disclaim,
And check the progress of our rising fame.
Yet one, whilst imitation bears the sway,
Aspires to nobler heights, and points the way,
Be rous'd, my friends! his bold example view;
Let your own Bards be proud to copy you!
Should rigid critics reprobate our play,
At least the patriotic heart will say,
"Glorious our fall, since in a noble cause.
"The bold attempt alone demands applause."
Still may the wisdom of the Comic Muse
Exalt your merits, or your faults accuse.
But think not, 'tis her aim to be severe;—
We all are mortals, and as mortals err.
If candour pleases, we are truly blest;
Vice trembles, when compell'd to stand confess'd.
Let not light Censure on your faults, offend.
Which aims not to expose them, but amend.
Thus does our Author to your candour trust;
Conscious, the free are generous, as just.

ACT FIRST

SCENE 1. *An Apartment at* CHARLOTTE'S.

[CHARLOTTE *and* LETITIA *discovered.*]

LETITIA. And so, Charlotte, you really think the pocket-hoop unbecoming.

CHARLOTTE. No, I don't say so: It may be very becoming to saunter round the house of a rainy day; to visit my grand-mamma, or go to Quakers' meeting: but to swim in a minuet, with the eyes of fifty well-dressed beaux upon me, to trip it in the Mall, or walk on the battery, give me the luxurious, jaunty, flowing, bell-hoop. It would have delighted you to have seen me the last evening, my charming girl! I was dangling o'er the battery with Billy Dimple; a knot of young fellows were upon the platform; as I passed them I faultered with one of the most bewitching false steps you ever saw, and then recovered myself with such a pretty confusion, flirting my hoop to discover a jet black shoe and brilliant buckle. Gad! how my little heart thrilled to hear the confused raptures of—*"Demme, Jack, what a delicate foot!" "Ha! General, what a well-turn'd—"*

LETITIA. Fie! fie! Charlotte [*stopping her mouth*], I protest you are quite a libertine.

CHARLOTTE. Why, my dear little prude, are we not all such libertines? Do you think, when I sat tortured two hours under the hands of my friseur, and an hour more at my toilet, that I had any thoughts of my aunt Susan, or my cousin Betsey? though they are both allowed to be critical judges of dress.

LETITIA. Why, who should we dress to please, but those who are judges of its merit?

CHARLOTTE. Why a creature who does not know *Buffon* from *Souflee*—Man!—my Letitia—Man! for whom we dress, walk, dance, talk, lisp, languish, and smile. Does not the grave Spectator assure us, that even our much bepraised diffidence, modesty, and blushes, are all directed to make ourselves good wives and mothers as fast as we can. Why, I'll undertake with one flirt of this hoop to bring more beaux to my feet in one week, than the grave Maria, and her sentimental circle, can do, by sighing sentiment till their hairs are grey.

LETITIA. Well, I won't argue with you; you always out talk me; let us change the subject. I hear that Mr. Dimple and Maria are soon to be married.

CHARLOTTE. You hear true. I was consulted in the choice of the wedding clothes. She is to be married in a delicate white sattin, and has a monstrous pretty brocaded lutestring for the second day. It would have done you good to have seen with what an affected indifference the dear sentimentalist turned over a thousand pretty things, just as if her heart did not palpitate with her approaching happiness, and at last made her choice, and arranged her dress with such apathy, as if she did not know that plain white sattin, and a simple blond lace, would shew her clear skin, and dark hair, to the greatest advantage.

LETITIA. But they say her indifference to dress, and even to the gentleman himself, is not entirely affected.

CHARLOTTE. How?

LETITIA. It is whispered, that if

Maria gives her hand to Mr. Dimple, it will be without her heart.

CHARLOTTE. Though the giving the heart is one of the last of all laughable considerations in the marriage of a girl of spirit, yet I should like to hear what antiquated notions the dear little piece of old fashioned prudery has got in her head.

LETITIA. Why you know that old Mr. John-Richard-Robert-Jacob-Isaac-Abraham-Cornelius Van Dumpling, Billy Dimple's father, (for he has thought fit to soften his name, as well as manners, during his English tour) was the most intimate friend of Maria's father. The old folks, about a year before Mr. Van Dumpling's death, proposed this match: the young folks were accordingly introduced, and told they must love one another. Billy was then a good natured, decent, dressing young fellow, with a little dash of the coxcomb, such as our young fellows of fortune usually have. At this time, I really believe she thought she loved him; and had they then been married, I doubt not, they might have jogged on, to the end of the chapter, a good kind of a sing-song lack-a-daysaical life, as other honest married folks do.

CHARLOTTE. Why did they not then marry?

LETITIA. Upon the death of his father, Billy went to England to see the world, and rub off a little of the patroon rust. During his absence, Maria like a good girl, to keep herself constant to her *nown true-love,* avoided company, and betook herself, for her amusement, to her books, and her dear Billy's letters. But, alas! how many ways has the mischievous demon of inconstancy of stealing into a woman's heart! Her love was destroyed by the very means she took to support it.

CHARLOTTE. How?—Oh! I have it—some likely young beau found the way to her study.

LETITIA. Be patient, Charlotte—your head so runs upon beaux.— Why she read Sir Charles Grandison, Clarissa Harlow, Shenstone, and the Sentimental Journey; and between whiles, as I said, Billy's letters. But as her taste improved, her love declined. The contrast was so striking betwixt the good sense of her books, and the flimsiness of her love-letters, that she discovered she had unthinkingly engaged her hand without her heart; and then the whole transaction managed by the old folks, now appeared so unsentimental, and looked so like bargaining for a bale of goods, that she found she ought to have rejected, according to every rule of romance, even the man of her choice, if imposed upon her in that manner—Clary Harlow would have scorned such a match.

CHARLOTTE. Well, how was it on Mr. Dimple's return? Did he meet a more favourable reception than his letters?

LETITIA. Much the same. She spoke of him with respect abroad, and with contempt in her closet. She watched his conduct and conversation, and found that he had by travelling acquired the wickedness of Lovelace without his wit, and the politeness of Sir Charles Grandison without his generosity. The ruddy youth who washed his face at the cistern every morning, and swore and looked eternal love and constancy, was now metamorphosed into a flippant, palid, polite beau, who devotes the morning to his toilet, reads a few pages of Chesterfield's letters, and then minces out, to put the infamous principles in practice upon every woman he meets.

Charlotte. But, if she is so apt at conjuring up these sentimental bugbears, why does she not discard him at once?

Letitia. Why, she thinks her word too sacred to be trifled with. Besides, her father, who has a great respect for the memory of his deceased friend, is ever telling her how he shall renew his years in their union, and repeating the dying injunctions of old Van Dumpling.

Charlotte. A mighty pretty story! And so you would make me believe, that the sensible Maria would give up Dumpling manor, and the all-accomplished Dimple as a husband, for the absurd, ridiculous reason, forsooth, because she despises and abhors him. Just as if a lady could not be privileged to spend a man's fortune, ride in his carriage, be called after his name, and call him her *nown dear lovee* when she wants money, without loving and respecting the great he-creature. Oh! my dear girl, you are a monstrous prude.

Letitia. I don't say what I would do; I only intimate how I suppose she wishes to act.

Charlotte. No, no, no! A fig for sentiment. If she breaks, or wishes to break, with Mr. Dimple, depend upon it, she has some other man in her eye. A woman rarely discards one lover, until she is sure of another.— Letitia little thinks what a clue I have to Dimple's conduct. The generous man submits to render himself disgusting to Maria, in order that she may leave him at liberty to address me. I must change the subject. [*Aside, and rings a bell.*]

[*Enter* Servant.]

Frank, order the horses to.— Talking of marriage—did you hear that Sally Bloomsbury is going to be married next week to Mr. Indigo, the rich Carolinian?

Letitia. Sally Bloomsbury married!— Why, she is not yet in her teens.

Charlotte. I do not know how that is, but, you may depend upon it, 't is a done affair. I have it from the best authority. There is my aunt Wyerley's Hannah (you know Hannah —though a black, she is a wench that was never caught in a lie in her life); now Hannah has a brother who courts Sarah, Mrs. Catgut the milliner's girl, and she told Hannah's brother, and Hannah, who, as I said before, is a girl of undoubted veracity, told it directly to me, that Mrs. Catgut was making a new cap for Miss Bloomsbury, which, as it was very dressy, it is very probable is designed for a wedding cap: now, as she is to be married, who can it be to, but to Mr. Indigo? Why, there is no other gentleman that visits at her papa's.

Letitia. Say not a word more, Charlotte. Your intelligence is so direct and well grounded, it is almost a pity that it is not a piece of scandal.

Charlotte. Oh! I am the pink of prudence. Though I cannot charge myself with ever having discredited a tea-party by my silence, yet I take care never to report any thing of my acquaintance, especially if it is to their credit,—*discredit,* I mean—until I have searched to the bottom of it. It is true, there is infinite pleasure in this charitable pursuit. Oh! how delicious to go and condole with the friends of some backsliding sister, or to retire with some old dowager or maiden aunt of the family, who love scandal so well, that they cannot forbear gratifying their appetite at the expence of the reputation of their nearest relations! And then to return full fraught with a rich collection of circumstances, to retail to the next circle of our acquaintance under the strongest injunctions of secrecy,—ha, ha, ha!—interlarding the melancholy tale with so many doleful shakes of the head, and more doleful, "Ah! who would have thought it! so amiable, so prudent a young lady, as we all thought her, what a monstrous pity! well, I have nothing to charge myself with; I acted the part of a friend, I warned her of the principles of that rake, I told her what would be the consequence; I told her so, I told her so."—Ha, ha, ha!

LETITIA. Ha, ha, ha! Well, but Charlotte, you don't tell me what you think of Miss Bloomsbury's match.

CHARLOTTE. Think! why I think it is probable she cried for a plaything, and they have given her a husband. Well, well, well, the puling chit shall not be deprived of her plaything: 't is only exchanging London dolls for American babies— Apropos, of babies, have you heard what Mrs. Affable's high-flying notions of delicacy have come to?

LETITIA. Who, she that was Miss Lovely?

CHARLOTTE. The same; she married Bob Affable of Schenectady. Don't you remember?

[*Enter* SERVANT.]

SERVANT. Madam, the carriage is ready.

LETITIA. Shall we go to the stores first, or visiting?

CHARLOTTE. I should think it rather too early to visit; especially Mrs. Prim: you know she is so particular.

LETITIA. Well, but what of Mrs. Affable?

CHARLOTTE. Oh, I'll tell you as we go; come, come, let us hasten. I hear Mrs. Catgut has some of the prettiest caps arrived, you ever saw. I shall die if I have not the first sight of them. [*Exeunt.*]

SCENE 2. *A Room in* VAN ROUGH'S *House.*

[MARIA *sitting disconsolate at a Table, with Books, etc.*]

SONG

I

The sun sets in night, and the stars shun the day;
But glory remains when their lights fade away!
Begin, ye tormentors! your threats are in vain,
For the son of Alknomook shall never complain.

II

Remember the arrows he shot from his bow;
Remember your chiefs by his hatchet laid low:
Why so slow?—do you wait till I shrink from the pain?
No—the son of Alknomook will never complain.

III

Remember the wood where in ambush we lay;
And the scalps which we bore from your nation away:

Now the flame rises fast, you exult in my pain;
But the son of Alknomook can never complain.

IV

I go to the land where my father is gone;
His ghost shall rejoice in the fame of his son:
Death comes like a friend, he relieves me from pain;
And thy son, Oh Alknomook! has scorn'd to complain.

There is something in this song which ever calls forth my affections. The manly virtue of courage, that fortitude which steels the heart against the keenest misfortunes, which interweaves the laurel of glory amidst the instruments of torture and death, displays something so noble, so exalted, that in despite of the prejudices of education, I cannot but admire it, even in a savage. The prepossession which our sex is supposed to entertain for the character of a soldier, is, I know, a standing piece of raillery among the wits. A cockade, a lapell'd coat, and a feather, they will tell you, are irresistible by a female heart. Let it be so.— Who is it that considers the helpless situation of our sex, that does not see we each moment stand in need of a protector, and that a brave one too. Formed of the more delicate materials of nature, endowed only with the softer passions, incapable, from our ignorance of the world, to guard against the wiles of mankind, our security for happiness often depends upon their generosity and courage:— Alas! how little of the former do we find. How inconsistent! that man should be leagued to destroy that honour, upon which, solely rests his respect and esteem. Ten thousand temptations allure us, ten thousand passions betray us; yet the smallest deviation from the path of rectitude is followed by the contempt and insult of man, and the more remorseless pity of woman: years of penitence and tears cannot wash away the stain, nor a life of virtue obliterate its remembrance. Reputation is the life of woman; yet courage to protect it, is masculine and disgusting; and the only safe asylum a woman of delicacy can find, is in the arms of a man of honour. How naturally then, should we love the brave, and the generous; how gratefully should we bless the arm raised for our protection, when nerv'd by virtue, and directed by honour! Heaven grant that the man with whom I may be connected—may be connected!— Whither has my imagination transported me—whither does it now lead me?— Am I not indissolubly engaged by every obligation of honour, which my own consent, and my father's approbation can give, to a man who can never share my affections, and whom a few days hence, it will be criminal for me to disapprove—to disapprove! would to heaven that were all—to despise. For, can the most frivolous manners, actuated by the most depraved heart, meet, or merit, anything but contempt from every woman of delicacy and sentiment?

[VAN ROUGH, *without*.] Mary!

MARIA. Ha, my father's voice—Sir!—

[*Enter* VAN ROUGH.]

VAN ROUGH. What, Mary, always singing doleful ditties, and moping over these plaguy books.

MARIA. I hope, Sir, that it is not

criminal to improve my mind with books; or to divert my melancholy with singing at my leisure hours.

Van Rough. Why, I don't know that, child; I don't know that. They us'd to say when I was a young man, that if a woman knew how to make a pudding, and to keep herself out of fire and water, she knew enough for a wife. Now, what good have these books done you? have they not made you melancholy? as you call it. Pray, what right has a girl of your age to be in the dumps? hav n't you every thing your heart can wish; ain't you going to be married to a young man of great fortune; ain't you going to have the quit-rent of twenty miles square?

Maria. One hundredth part of the land, and a lease for life of the heart of a man I could love, would satisfy me.

Van Rough. Pho, pho, pho! child; nonsense, downright nonsense, child. This comes of your reading your story-books; your Charles Grandisons, your Sentimental Journals, and your Robinson Crusoes, and such other trumpery. No, no, no! child, it is money makes the mare go; keep your eye upon the main chance, Mary.

Maria. Marriage, Sir, is, indeed, a very serious affair.

Van Rough. You are right, child; you are right. I am sure I found it so to my cost.

Maria. I mean, Sir, that as marriage is a portion for life, and so intimately involves our happiness, we cannot be too considerate in the choice of our companion.

Van Rough. Right, child; very right. A young woman should be very sober when she is making her choice, but when she has once made it, as you have done, I don't see why she should not be as merry as a grig; I am sure she has reason enough to be so— Solomon says, that "there is a time to laugh, and a time to weep"; now a time for a young woman to laugh is when she has made sure of a good rich husband. Now a time to cry, according to you, Mary, is when she is making choice of him: but, I should think, that a young woman's time to cry was, when she despaired of *getting* one.— Why, there was your mother now; to be sure when I popp'd the question to her, she did look a little silly; but when she had once looked down on her apron-strings, as all modest young women us'd to do, and drawled out ye-s, she was as brisk and as merry as a bee.

Maria. My honoured mother, Sir, had no motive to melancholy; she married the man of her choice.

Van Rough. The man of her choice! And pray, Mary, an't you going to marry the man of your choice —what trumpery notion is this?— It is these vile books [*throwing them away*]. I'd have you to know, Mary, if you won't make young Van Dumpling the man of *your* choice, you shall marry him as the man of *my* choice.

Maria. You terrify me, Sir. Indeed, Sir, I am all submission. My will is yours.

Van Rough. Why, that is the way your mother us'd to talk. "My will is yours, my dear Mr. Van Rough, my will is yours": but she took special care to have her own way though for all that.

Maria. Do not reflect upon my mother's memory, Sir—

Van Rough. Why not, Mary, why not? She kept me from speaking my mind all *her* life, and do you think she shall henpeck me now she is *dead* too? Come, come; don't go to snivel-ing: be a good girl, and mind the main chance. I'll see you well settled in the world.

MARIA. I do not doubt your love, Sir; and it is my duty to obey you.— I will endeavor to make my duty and inclination go hand in hand.

VAN ROUGH. Well, well, Mary; do you be a good girl, mind the main chance, and never mind inclination.— Why, do you know that I have been down in the cellar this very morning to examine a pipe of Madeira which I purchased the week you were born, and mean to tap on your wedding day. — That pipe cost me fifty pounds sterling. It was well worth sixty pounds; but I over-reached Ben Bulk-head, the supercargo: I'll tell you the whole story. You must know that—

[*Enter* SERVANT.]

SERVANT. Sir, Mr. Transfer, the broker, is below. [*Exit.*]

VAN ROUGH. Well, Mary, I must go.— Remember, and be a good girl, and mind the main chance. [*Exit.*]

MARIA [*alone*]. How deplorable is my situation! How distressing for a daughter to find her heart militating with her filial duty! I know my father loves me tenderly, why then do I re-luctantly obey him? Heaven knows! with what reluctance I should oppose the will of a parent, or set an example of filial disobedience; at a parent's command I could wed aukwardness and deformity. Were the heart of my husband good, I would so magnify his good qualities with the eye of con-jugal affection, that the defects of his person and manners should be lost in the emanation of his virtues. At a father's command, I could embrace poverty. Were the poor man my hus-band, I would learn resignation to my lot; I would enliven our frugal meal with good humour, and chase away misfortune from our cottage with a smile. At a father's command, I could almost submit, to what every female heart knows to be the most mortify-ing, to marry a weak man, and blush at my husband's folly in every com-pany I visited.— But to marry a de-praved wretch, whose only virtue is a polished exterior; who is actuated by the unmanly ambition of conquering the defenceless; whose heart, insensi-ble to the emotions of patriotism, di-lates at the plaudits of every unthink-ing girl: whose laurels are the sighs and tears of the miserable victims of his specious behaviour.— Can he, who has no regard for the peace and happiness of other families, ever have a due regard for the peace and happi-ness of his own? Would to heaven that my father were not so hasty in his temper! Surely, if I were to state my reasons for declining this match, he would not compel me to marry a man—whom, though my lips may solemnly promise to honour, I find my heart must ever despise. [*Exit.*]

ACT SECOND

SCENE 1

[*Enter* CHARLOTTE *and* LETITIA.]

CHARLOTTE [*at entering*]. Betty, take those things out of the carriage and carry them to my chamber; see that you don't tumble them.— My dear, I protest, I think it was the homeliest of the whole. I declare I was almost tempted to return and change it.

LETITIA. Why would you take it?

CHARLOTTE. Didn't Mrs. Catgut say it was the most fashionable?

LETITIA. But, my dear, it will never sit becomingly on you.

CHARLOTTE. I know that; but did not you hear Mrs. Catgut say it was fashionable?

LETITIA. Did you see that sweet airy cap with the white sprig?

CHARLOTTE. Yes, and I longed to take it; but, my dear, what could I do?— Did not Mrs. Catgut say it was the most fashionable; and if I had not taken it, was not that aukward gawky, Sally Slender, ready to purchase it immediately?

LETITIA. Did you observe how she tumbled over the things at the next shop, and then went off without purchasing any thing, nor even thanking the poor man for his trouble?— But of all the aukward creatures, did you see Miss Blouze, endeavouring to thrust her unmerciful arm into those small kid gloves?

CHARLOTTE. Ha, ha, ha, ha!

LETITIA. Then did you take notice, with what an affected warmth of friendship she and Miss Wasp met? when all their acquaintances know how much pleasure they take in abusing each other in every company?

CHARLOTTE. Lud! Letitia, is that so extraordinary? Why, my dear, I hope you are not going to turn sentimentalist.— Scandal, you know, is but amusing ourselves with the faults, foibles, follies and reputations of our friends;—indeed, I don't know why we should have friends, if we are not at liberty to make use of them. But no person is so ignorant of the world as to suppose, because I amuse myself with a lady's faults, that I am obliged to quarrel with her person, every time we meet; believe me, my dear, we should have very few acquaintances at that rate.

[SERVANT *enters and delivers a letter to* CHARLOTTE, *and exit.*]

CHARLOTTE. You'll excuse me, my dear. [*Opens and reads to herself.*]

LETITIA. Oh, quite excusable.

CHARLOTTE. As I hope to be married, my brother Henry is in the city.

LETITIA. What, your brother, Colonel Manly?

CHARLOTTE. Yes, my dear; the only brother I have in the world.

LETITIA. Was he never in this city?

CHARLOTTE. Never nearer than Harlem Heights, where he lay with his regiment.

LETITIA. What sort of a being is this brother of yours? If he is as chatty, as pretty, as sprightly as you, half the belles in the city will be pulling caps for him.

CHARLOTTE. My brother is the very counterpart and reverse of me: I am gay, he is grave; I am airy, he is solid; I am ever selecting the most pleasing objects for my laughter, he has a tear for every pitiful one. And thus, whilst he is plucking the briars and thorns from the path of the unfortunate, I am strewing my own path with roses.

LETITIA. My sweet friend, not quite so poetical, and little more particular.

CHARLOTTE. Hands off, Letitia. I feel the rage of simile upon me; I can't talk to you in any other way. My brother has a heart replete with the noblest sentiments, but then, it is like—it is like—Oh! you provoking girl, you have deranged all my ideas —it is like—Oh! I have it—his heart is like an old maiden lady's band-box; it contains many costly things, arranged with the most scrupulous nicety, yet the misfortune is, that they are too delicate, costly, and antiquated, for common use.

LETITIA. By what I can pick out of your flowery description, your brother is no beau.

CHARLOTTE. No, indeed; he makes no pretension to the character. He'd ride, or rather fly, an hundred miles to relieve a distressed object, or to do a gallant act in the service of his country: but, should you drop your fan or bouquet in his presence, it is ten to one that some beau at the farther end of the room would have the honour of presenting it to you, before he had observed that it fell. I'll tell you one of his antiquated, anti-gallant notions.— He said once in my presence, in a room full of company—would you believe it—in a large circle of ladies, that the best evidence a gentleman could give a young lady of his respect and affection, was, to endeavour in a friendly manner to rectify her foibles. I protest I was crimson to the eyes, upon reflecting that I was known as his sister.

LETITIA. Insupportable creature! tell a lady of her faults! If he is so grave, I fear I have no chance of captivating him.

CHARLOTTE. His conversation is like a rich old fashioned brocade, it will stand alone; every sentence is a sentiment. Now you may judge what a time I had with him, in my twelve months' visit to my father. He read me such lectures, out of pure brotherly affection, against the extremes of fashion, dress, flirting, and coquetry, and all the other dear things which he knows I doat upon, that, I protest, his conversation made me as melancholy as if I had been at church; and heaven knows, though I never prayed to go there but on one occasion, yet I would have exchanged his conversation for a psalm and a sermon. Church is rather melancholy, to be sure; but then I can ogle the beaux, and be regaled with "here endeth the first lesson"; but his brotherly *here,* you would think had no end. You captivate him! Why, my dear, he would as soon fall in love with a box of Italian flowers. There is Maria now, if she were not engaged, she might do something.— Oh, how I should like to see that pair of pensorosos together, looking as grave as two sailors' wives of a stormy night, with a flow of sentiment meandering through their conversation like purling streams in modern poetry.

LETITIA. Oh! my dear fanciful—

CHARLOTTE. Hush! I hear some person coming through the entry.

[*Enter* SERVANT.]

SERVANT. Madam, there's a gentleman below who calls himself Colonel Manly; do you chuse to be at home?

CHARLOTTE. Shew him in. [*Exit* SERVANT.] Now for a sober face.

[*Enter* COLONEL MANLY.]

MANLY. My dear Charlotte, I am happy that I once more enfold you within the arms of fraternal affection. I know you are going to ask (amiable impatience!) how our parents do,—

the venerable pair transmit you their blessing by me—they totter on the verge of a well-spent life, and wish only to see their children settled in the world, to depart in peace.

CHARLOTTE. I am very happy to hear that they are well. [*Coolly.*] Brother, will you give me leave to introduce you to our uncle's ward, one of my most intimate friends.

MANLY [*saluting* LETITIA]. I ought to regard your friends as my own.

CHARLOTTE. Come, Letitia, do give us a little dash of your vivacity; my brother is so sentimental, and so grave, that I protest he'll give us the vapours.

MANLY. Though sentiment and gravity, I know, are banished the polite world, yet, I hoped, they might find some countenance in the meeting of such near connections as brother and sister.

CHARLOTTE. Positively, brother, if you go one step further in this strain, you will set me crying, and that, you know, would spoil my eyes; and then I should never get the husband which our good papa and mamma have so kindly wished me—never be established in the world.

MANLY. Forgive me, my sister—I am no enemy to mirth; I love your sprightliness; and I hope it will one day enliven the hours of some worthy man; but when I mention the respectable authors of my existence,—the cherishers and protectors of my helpless infancy, whose hearts glow with such fondness and attachment, that they would willingly lay down their lives for my welfare, you will excuse me, if I am so unfashionable as to speak of them with some degree of respect and reverence.

CHARLOTTE. Well, well, brother; if you won't be gay, we'll not differ; I will be as grave as you wish. [*Affects gravity.*] And so, brother, you have come to the city to exchange some of your commutation notes for a little pleasure.

MANLY. Indeed, you are mistaken; my errand is not of amusement, but business; and as I neither drink nor game, my expences will be so trivial, I shall have no occasion to sell my notes.

CHARLOTTE. Then you won't have occasion to do a very good thing. Why, there was the Vermont General—he came down some time since, sold all his musty notes at one stroke, and then laid the cash out in trinkets for his dear Fanny. I want a dozen pretty things myself; have you got the notes with you?

MANLY. I shall be ever willing to contribute as far as it is in my power, to adorn, or in any way to please my sister; yet, I hope, I shall never be obliged for this, to sell my notes. I may be romantic, but I preserve them as a sacred deposit. Their full amount is justly due to me, but as embarrassments, the natural consequences of a long war, disable my country from supporting its credit, I shall wait with patience until it is rich enough to discharge them. If that is not in my day, they shall be transmitted as an honourable certificate to posterity, that I have humbly imitated our illustrious WASHINGTON, in having exposed my health and life in the service of my country, without reaping any other reward than the glory of conquering in so arduous a contest.

CHARLOTTE. Well said heroics. Why, my dear Henry, you have such a lofty way of saying things, that I protest I almost tremble at the thought of introducing you to the polite circles in the city. The belles would think you were a player run mad, with your head filled with old scraps of tragedy: and, as to the beaux, they might admire, because they would not understand you.—But, however, I must, I believe, venture to introduce you to two or three ladies of my acquaintance.

LETITIA. And that will make him acquainted with thirty or forty beaux.

CHARLOTTE. Oh! brother, you don't know what a fund of happiness you have in store.

MANLY. I fear, sister, I have not refinement sufficient to enjoy it.

CHARLOTTE. Oh! you cannot fail being pleased.

LETITIA. Our ladies are so delicate and dressy.

CHARLOTTE. And our beaux so dressy and delicate.

LETITIA. Our ladies chat and flirt so agreeably.

CHARLOTTE. And our beaux simper and bow so gracefully.

LETITIA. With their hair so trim and neat.

CHARLOTTE. And their faces so soft and sleek.

LETITIA. Their buckles so tonish and bright.

CHARLOTTE. And their hands so slender and white.

LETITIA. I vow, Charlotte, we are quite poetical.

CHARLOTTE. And then, brother, the faces of the beaux are of such a lily white hue! None of that horrid robustness of constitution, that vulgar corn-fed glow of health, which can only serve to alarm an unmarried lady with apprehensions, and prove a melancholy memento to a married one, that she can never hope for the happiness of being a widow. I will say this to the credit of our city beaux, that such is the delicacy of their complexion, dress, and address, that, even had I no reliance upon the honour of the dear Adonises, I would trust myself in any possible situation with them, without the least apprehensions of rudeness.

MANLY. Sister Charlotte!

CHARLOTTE. Now, now, now brother [*interrupting him*], now don't go to spoil my mirth with a dash of your gravity; I am so glad to see you, I am in tip-top spirits. Oh! that you could be with us at a little snug party. There is Billy Simper, Jack Chassé, and Colonel Van Titter, Miss Promonade, and the two Miss Tambours, sometimes make a party, with some other ladies, in a side-box at the play. Everything is conducted with such decorum,—first we bow round to the company in general, then to each one in particular, then we have so many inquiries after each other's health, and we are so happy to meet each other, and it is so many ages since we last had that pleasure, and, if a married lady is in company, we have such a sweet dissertation upon her son Bobby's chin-cough, then the curtain rises, then our sensibility is all awake, and then by the mere force of apprehension, we torture some harmless expression into a double meaning, which the poor author never dreamt of, and then we have recourse to our fans, and then we blush, and then the gentlemen jog one another, peep under the fan, and make the prettiest remarks; and then we giggle and they simper, and they giggle and we simper, and then the curtain drops, and then for nuts and oranges, and then we bow, and it's pray Ma'am take it, and pray Sir keep it, and oh! not for the world, Sir: and then the curtain rises again, and then we blush, and giggle, and simper, and bow, all over again. Oh! the sentimental charms of a side-box conversation! [*All laugh.*]

MANLY. Well, sister, I join heartily with you in the laugh; for, in my opinion, it is as justifiable to laugh at folly, as it is reprehensible to ridicule misfortune.

CHARLOTTE. Well, but brother, positively, I can't introduce you in these clothes: why, your coat looks as if it were calculated for the vulgar purpose of keeping yourself comfortable.

MANLY. This coat was my regimental coat in the late war. The public tumults of our state have induced me to buckle on the sword in support of that government which I once fought to establish. I can only say, sister, that there was a time when this coat was respectable, and some people even thought that those men who had endured so many winter campaigns in the service of their country, without bread, clothing, or pay, at least deserved that the poverty of their appearance should not be ridiculed.

CHARLOTTE. We agree in opinion entirely, brother, though it would not have done for me to have said it: it is the coat makes the man respectable. In the time of the war, when we were almost frightened to death, why, your coat was respectable, that is, fashionable; now another kind of coat is fashionable, that is, respectable. And pray direct the taylor to make yours the height of the fashion.

MANLY. Though it is of little consequence to me of what shape my coat is, yet, as to the height of the fashion, there you will please to excuse me, sister. You know my sentiments on that subject. I have often lamented the advantage which the French have over us in that particular. In Paris, the fashions have their dawnings, their routine and declensions, and depend as much upon the caprice of the day as in other countries; but there every lady assumes a right to deviate from the general *ton,* as far as will be of advantage to her own appearance. In America, the cry is, what is the fashion? and we follow it, indiscriminately, because it is so.

CHARLOTTE. Therefore it is, that when large hoops are in fashion, we often see many a plump girl lost in the immensity of a hoop petticoat, whose want of height and *em-bon-point* would never have been remarked in any other dress. When the high head-dress is the mode, how then do we see a lofty cushion, with a profusion of gauze, feathers, and ribband, supported by a face no bigger than an apple; whilst a broad full-faced lady, who really would have appeared tolerably handsome in a large head-dress, looks with her smart *chapeau* as masculine as a soldier.

MANLY. But remember, my dear sister, and I wish all my fair countrywomen would recollect, that the only excuse a young lady can have for going extravagantly into a fashion, is, because it makes her look extravagantly handsome.— Ladies, I must wish you a good morning.

CHARLOTTE. But, brother, you are going to make home with us.

MANLY. Indeed, I cannot. I have seen my uncle, and explained that matter.

CHARLOTTE. Come and dine with us, then. We have a family dinner about half past four o'clock.

MANLY. I am engaged to dine with the Spanish ambassador. I was introduced to him by an old brother officer; and instead of freezing me with a cold card of compliment to dine with him ten days hence, he, with the true old Castilian frankness, in a friendly manner, asked me to dine with him to-day—an honour I could not refuse. Sister, adieu—Madam, your most obedient— [*Exit.*]

CHARLOTTE. I will wait upon you to the door, brother; I have something particular to say to you. [*Exit.*]

LETITIA [*alone*]. What a pair!—She the pink of flirtation, he the essence of everything that is *outré* and gloomy.— I think I have completely deceived Charlotte by my manner of speaking of Mr. Dimple; she's too much the friend of Maria to be confided in. He is certainly rendering himself disagreeable to Maria, in order to break with her and proffer his hand to me. This is what the delicate fellow hinted in our last conversation. [*Exit.*]

SCENE 2. *The Mall.*

[*Enter* JESSAMY.]

JESSAMY. Positively this Mall is a very pretty place. I hope the city won't ruin it by repairs. To be sure, it won't do to speak of in the same day with Ranelagh or Vauxhall; however, it's a fine place for a young fellow to display his person to advantage. Indeed, nothing is lost here; the girls have taste, and I am very happy to find they have adopted the elegant London fashion of looking back, after a genteel fellow like me has passed them. Ah! who comes here? This, by his aukwardness, must be the Yankee colonel's servant. I'll accost him.

[*Enter* JONATHAN.]

Votre très—humble *serviteur,* Monsieur. I understand Colonel Manly, the Yankee officer, has the honour of your services.

JONATHAN. Sir!—

JESSAMY. I say, Sir, I understand that Colonel Manly has the honour of having you for a servant.

JONATHAN. Servant! Sir, do you take me for a neger,—I am Colonel Manly's waiter.

JESSAMY. A true Yankee distinction, egad, without a difference. Why, Sir, do you not perform all the offices of a servant? Do you not even blacken his boots?

JONATHAN. Yes; I do grease them a bit sometimes; but I am a true blue son of liberty, for all that. Father said I should come as Colonel Manly's waiter to see the world, and all that; but no man shall master me: my father has as good a farm as the colonel.

JESSAMY. Well, Sir, we will not quarrel about terms upon the eve of an acquaintance, from which I promise myself so much satisfaction,—therefore *sans ceremonie*—

JONATHAN. What?—

JESSAMY. I say, I am extremely

happy to see Colonel Manly's waiter.

JONATHAN. Well, and I vow, too, I am pretty considerably glad to see you—but what the dogs need of all this outlandish lingo? Who may you be, Sir, if I may be so bold?

JESSAMY. I have the honour to be Mr. Dimple's servant, or, if you please, waiter. We lodge under the same roof, and should be glad of the honour of your acquaintance.

JONATHAN. You a waiter! By the living jingo, you look so topping, I took you for one of the agents to Congress.

JESSAMY. The brute has discernment notwithstanding his appearance. — Give me leave to say I wonder then at your familiarity.

JONATHAN. Why, as to the matter of that, Mr.—pray, what's your name?

JESSAMY. Jessamy, at your service.

JONATHAN. Why, I swear we don't make any great matter of distinction in our state, between quality and other folks.

JESSAMY. This is, indeed, a levelling principle. I hope, Mr. Jonathan, you have not taken part with the insurgents.

JONATHAN. Why, since General Shays has sneaked off, and given us the bag to hold, I don't care to give my opinion; but you'll promise not to tell—put your ear this way—you won't tell?— I vow, I did think the sturgeons were right.

JESSAMY. I thought, Mr. Jonathan, you Massachusetts men always argued with a gun in your hand.— Why didn't you join them?

JONATHAN. Why, the colonel is one of those folks called the Shin—shin—dang it all, I can't speak them *lignum vitæ* words—you know who I mean—there is a company of them—they wear a China goose at their button-hole—a kind of gilt thing.— Now the colonel told father and brother,—you must know there are, let me see—there is Elnathan, Silas, and Barnabas, Tabitha—no, no, she's a she—tarnation, now I have it—there's Elnathan, Silas, Barnabas, Jonathan, that's I—seven of us, six went into the wars, and I staid at home to take care of mother. Colonel said that it was a burning shame for the true blue Bunker-hill sons of liberty, who had fought Governor Hutchinson, Lord North, and the Devil, to have any hand in kicking up a cursed dust against a government, which we had every mother's son of us a hand in making.

JESSAMY. Bravo!— Well, have you been abroad in the city since your arrival? What have you seen that is curious and entertaining?

JONATHAN. Oh! I have seen a power of fine sights. I went to see two marble-stone men and a leaden horse, that stands out in doors in all weathers; and when I came where they was, one had got no head, and t'other wer'nt there. They said as how the leaden man was a damn'd tory, and that he took wit in his anger and rode off in the time of the troubles.

JESSAMY. But this was not the end of your excursion.

JONATHAN. Oh, no; I went to a place they call Holy Ground. Now I counted this was a place where folks go to meeting; so I put my hymn-book in my pocket, and walked softly and grave as a minister; and when I came there, the dogs a bit of a meeting-house could I see. At last I spied a young gentlewoman standing by one of the seats, which they have here at the doors—I took her to be the deacon's daughter, and she looked so kind, and so obliging, that I thought I would go and ask her the way to lecture, and would you think it—she called me dear, and sweeting, and honey, just as if we were married; by the living jingo, I had a month's mind to buss her.

JESSAMY. Well, but how did it end?

JONATHAN. Why, as I was standing talking with her, a parcel of sailor men and boys got round me, the snarl headed curs fell a-kicking and cursing of me at such a tarnal rate, that, I vow, I was glad to take to my heels and split home, right off, tail on end like a stream of chalk.

JESSAMY. Why, my dear friend, you are not acquainted with the city; that girl you saw was a— [*Whispers.*]

JONATHAN. Mercy on my soul! was that young woman a harlot!— Well, if this is New York Holy Ground, what must the Holy-day Ground be!

JESSAMY. Well, you should not judge of the city too rashly. We have a number of elegant fine girls here, that make a man's leisure hours pass very agreeably. I would esteem it an honour to announce you to some of them.— Glad! that announce is a select word; I wonder where I picked it up.

JONATHAN. I don't want to know them.

JESSAMY. Come, come, my dear friend, I see that I must assume the honour of being the director of your amusements. Nature has give us passions, and youth and opportunity stimulate to gratify them. It is no shame, my dear Blueskin, for a man to amuse himself with a little gallantry.

JONATHAN. Girl huntry! I don't altogether understand. I never played at that game. I know how to play hunt the squirrel, but I can't play anything with the girls; I am as good as married.

JESSAMY. Vulgar, horrid brute! Married, and above a hundred miles from his wife, and think that an objection to his making love to every woman he meets! He never can have read, no, he never can have been in a room with a volume of the divine Chesterfield.— So you are married?

JONATHAN. No, I don't say so; I said I was as good as married, a kind of promise.

JESSAMY. As good as married!—

JONATHAN. Why, yes; there's Tabitha Wymen, the deacon's daughter, at home, she and I have been courting a great while, and folks say as how we are to be married; and so I broke a piece of money with her when we parted, and she promised not to spark it with Solomon Dyer while I am gone. You wouldn't have me false to my true love, would you?

JESSAMY. May be you have another reason for constancy; possibly the young lady has a fortune? Ha! Mr. Jonathan, the solid charms; the chains of love are never so binding as when the links are made of gold.

JONATHAN. Why, as to fortune, I must needs say her father is pretty dumb rich; he went representative for our town last year. He will give her—let me see—four times seven is —seven times four—nought and carry one;—he will give her twenty acres of land—somewhat rocky though—a bible, and a cow.

JESSAMY. Twenty acres of rock, a bible, and a cow! Why, my dear Mr. Jonathan, we have servant maids, or, as you would more elegantly express it, wait'resses, in this city, who collect more in one year from their mistress' cast clothes.

JONATHAN. You don't say so!—

JESSAMY. Yes, and I'll introduce you to one of them. There is a little lump of flesh and delicacy that lives at next door, wait'ress to Miss Maria; we often see her on the stoop.

JONATHAN. But are you sure she would be courted by me?

JESSAMY. Never doubt it; remember a faint heart never—blisters of my tongue—I was going to be guilty of a vile proverb; flat against the authority of Chesterfield.— I say there can be no doubt, that the brilliancy of your merit will secure you a favourable reception.

JONATHAN. Well, but what must I say to her?

JESSAMY. Say to her! why, my dear friend, though I admire your profound knowledge on every other subject, yet, you will pardon my saying, that your want of opportunity has made the female heart escape the poignancy of your penetration. Say to her!— Why, when a man goes a-courting, and hopes for success, he must begin with doing, and not saying.

JONATHAN. Well, what must I do?

JESSAMY. Why, when you are introduced you must make five or six elegant bows.

JONATHAN. Six elegant bows! I understand that; six, you say? Well—

JESSAMY. Then you must press and kiss her hand; then press and kiss, and so on to her lips and cheeks; then talk as much as you can about hearts, darts, flames, nectar and ambrosia—the more incoherent the better.

JONATHAN. Well, but suppose she should be angry with I?

JESSAMY. Why, if she should pretend—please to observe, Mr. Jonathan—if she should pretend to be offended, you must— But I'll tell you how my master acted in such a case: He was seated by a young lady of eighteen upon a sopha, plucking with a wanton hand the blooming sweets of youth and beauty. When the lady thought it necessary to check his ardour, she called up a frown upon her lovely face, so irresistably alluring, that it would have warmed the frozen bosom of age: remember, said she, putting her delicate arm upon his, remember your character and my honour. My master instantly dropped upon his knees, with eyes swimming with love, cheeks glowing with desire, and in the gentlest modulation of voice, he said—My dear Caroline, in a few months our hands will be indissolubly united at the altar; our hearts I feel are already so—the favours you now grant as evidence of your affection, are favours indeed; yet when the ceremony is once past, what will now be received with rapture, will then be attributed to duty.

JONATHAN. Well, and what was the consequence?

JESSAMY. The consequence!— Ah! forgive me, my dear friend, but you New England gentlemen have such a laudable curiosity of seeing the bottom of every thing;—why, to be honest, I confess I saw the blooming cherub of a consequence smiling in its angelic mother's arms, about ten months afterwards.

JONATHAN. Well, if I follow all your plans, make them six bows, and all that; shall I have such little cherubim consequences?

JESSAMY. Undoubtedly.— What are you musing upon?

JONATHAN. You say you'll certainly make me acquainted?— Why, I was thinking then how I should contrive to pass this broken piece of silver—won't it buy a sugar-dram?

JESSAMY. What is that, the love-token from the deacon's daughter?— You come on bravely. But I must hasten to my master. Adieu, my dear friend.

JONATHAN. Stay, Mr. Jessamy— must I buss her when I am introduced to her?

JESSAMY. I told you, you must kiss her.

JONATHAN. Well, but must I buss her?

JESSAMY. Why, kiss and buss, and buss and kiss, is all one.

JONATHAN. Oh! my dear friend, though you have a profound knowledge of all, a pugnancy of tribulation, you don't know everything. [*Exit.*]

JESSAMY [*alone*]. Well, certainly I improve; my master could not have insinuated himself with more address into the heart of a man he despised.— Now will this blundering dog sicken Jenny with his nauseous pawings, until she flies into my arms for very ease. How sweet will the contrast be, between the blundering Jonathan, and the courtly and accomplished Jessamy!

ACT THIRD

SCENE 1. DIMPLE'S *Room.*

[DIMPLE *discovered at a Toilet, reading.*]

DIMPLE. "Women have in general but one object, which is their beauty." Very true, my lord; positively very true. "Nature has hardly formed a woman ugly enough to be insensible to flattery upon her person." Extremely just, my lord; every day's delightful experience confirms this. "If her face is so shocking, that she must, in some degree, be conscious of it, her figure and air, she thinks, make ample amends for it." The sallow Miss Wan is a proof of this.— Upon my telling the distasteful wretch, the other day, that her countenance spoke the pensive language of sentiment, and that Lady Wortley Montague declared, that if the ladies were arrayed in the garb of innocence, the face would be the last part which would be admired as Monsieur Milton expresses it, she grin'd horribly a ghastly smile. "If her figure is deformed, she thinks her face counterbalances it."

[*Enter* JESSAMY *with letters.*]

DIMPLE. Where got you these, Jessamy?

JESSAMY. Sir, the English packet is arrived.

[DIMPLE *opens and reads a letter enclosing notes.*]

"Sir,

"I have drawn bills on you in favour of Messrs. Van Cash and Co. as per margin. I have taken up your note to Col. Piquet, and discharged your debts to my

Lord Lurcher and Sir Harry Rook. I herewith enclose you copies of the bills, which I have no doubt will be immediately honoured. On failure, I shall empower some lawyer in your country to recover the amounts.

"I am, Sir,

"Your most humble servant,

"John Hazard."

Now, did not my lord expressly say, that it was unbecoming a well-bred man to be in a passion, I confess I should be ruffled. [*Reads.*] "There is no accident so unfortunate, which a wise man may not turn to his advantage; nor any accident so fortunate, which a fool will not turn to his disadvantage." True, my lord: but how advantage can be derived from this, I can't see. Chesterfield himself, who made, however, the worst practice of the most excellent precepts, was never in so embarrassing a situation. I love the person of Charlotte, and it is necessary I should command the fortune of Letitia. As to Maria!—I doubt not by my *sang-froid* behavior I shall compel her to decline the match; but the blame must not fall upon me. A prudent man, as my lord says, should take all the credit of a good action to himself, and throw the discredit of a bad one upon others. I must break with Maria, marry Letitia, and as for Charlotte—why, Charlotte must be a companion to my wife.—Here, Jessamy!

[*Enter* Jessamy]

[Dimple *folds and seals two letters.*]

Dimple. Here, Jessamy, take this letter to my love. [*Gives one.*]

Jessamy. To which of your honour's loves?— Oh! [*reading*] to Miss Letitia, your honour's rich love.

Dimple. And this [*delivers another*] to Miss Charlotte Manly. See that you deliver them privately.

Jessamy. Yes, your honour. [*Going.*]

Dimple. Jessamy, who are these strange lodgers that came to the house last night?

Jessamy. Why, the master is a Yankee colonel; I have not seen much of him; but the man is the most unpolished animal your honour ever disgraced your eyes by looking upon. I have had one of the most *outré* conversations with him!— He really has a most prodigious effect upon my risibility.

Dimple. I ought, according to every rule of Chesterfield, to wait on him and insinuate myself into his good graces.— Jessamy, wait on the colonel with my compliments, and if he is disengaged, I will do myself the honour of paying him my respects.— Some ignorant unpolished boor—

[Jessamy *goes off and returns.*]

Jessamy. Sir, the colonel is gone out, and Jonathan, his servant, says that he is gone to stretch his legs upon the Mall— Stretch his legs! what an indelicacy of diction!

Dimple. Very well. Reach me my hat and sword. I'll accost him there, in my way to Letitia's, as by accident; pretend to be struck with his person and address, and endeavour to steal into his confidence. Jessamy, I have no business for you at present.

[*Exit.*]

Jessamy [*taking up the book*]. My master and I obtain our knowledge from the same source;—though, gad! I think myself much the prettier fellow of the two. [*Surveying himself in the glass.*] That was a brilliant thought, to insinuate that I folded my master's letters for him; the folding is so neat, that it does honour to the operator. I once intended to have insinuated that I wrote his letters too; but that was before I saw them; it won't do now! no honour there, positively.— "Nothing looks more vulgar [*reading affectedly*], ordinary, and illiberal, than ugly, uneven, and ragged nails; the ends of which should be kept even and clean, not tipped with black, and cut in small segments of circles"— Segments of circles! surely my lord did not consider that he wrote for the beaux. Segments of circles! what a crabbed term! Now I dare answer, that my master, with all his learning, does not know that this means, according to the present mode, to let the nails grow long, and then cut them off even at top. [*Laughing without.*] Ha! that's Jenny's titter. I protest I despair of ever teaching that girl to laugh; she has something so execrably natural in her laugh, that I declare it absolutely discomposes my nerves. How came she into our house!— [*Calls.*] Jenny!

[*Enter* JENNY.]

JESSAMY. Prythee, Jenny, don't spoil your fine face with laughing.

JENNY. Why, mustn't I laugh, Mr. Jessamy?

JESSAMY. You may smile; but, as my lord says, nothing can authorise a laugh.

JENNY. Well, but I can't help laughing— Have you seen him, Mr. Jessamy? Ha, ha, ha!

JESSAMY. Seen whom?—

JENNY. Why, Jonathan, the New-England colonel's servant. Do you know he was at the play last night, and the stupid creature don't know where he has been. He would not go to a play for the world; he thinks it was a show, as he calls it.

JESSAMY. As ignorant and unpolished as he is, do you know, Miss Jenny, that I propose to introduce him to the honour of your acquaintance.

JENNY. Introduce him to me! for what?

JESSAMY. Why, my lovely girl, that you may take him under your protection, as Madam Ramboulliet did young Stanhope; that you may, by your plastic hand, mould this uncouth cub into a gentleman. He is to make love to you.

JENNY. Make love to me!—

JESSAMY. Yes, Mistress Jenny, make love to you; and, I doubt not, when he shall become domesticated in your kitchen, that this boor, under your auspices, will soon become *un aimable petit Jonathan.*

JENNY. I must say, Mr. Jessamy, if he copies after me, he will be vastly monstrously polite.

JESSAMY. Stay here one moment, and I will call him.—Jonathan!—Mr. Jonathan!— [*Calls.*]

JONATHAN [*within*]. Holla! there— [*Enters.*] You promise to stand by me—six bows you say. [*Bows.*]

JESSAMY. Mrs. Jenny, I have the honour of presenting Mr. Jonathan, Colonel Manly's waiter, to you. I am extremely happy that I have it in my power to make two worthy people acquainted with each other's merit.

JENNY. So, Mr. Jonathan, I hear you were at the play last night.

JONATHAN. At the play! why, did

you think I went to the devil's drawing-room!

JENNY. The devil's drawing-room!

JONATHAN. Yes; why an't cards and dice the devil's device; and the play-house the shop where the devil hangs out the vanities of the world, upon the tenterhooks of temptation. I believe you have not heard how they were acting the old boy one night, and the wicked one came among them sure enough; and went right off in a storm, and carried one quarter of the play-house with him. Oh! no, no, no! you won't catch me at a play-house, I warrant you.

JENNY. Well, Mr. Jonathan, though I don't scruple your veracity, I have some reasons for believing you were there; pray, where were you about six o'clock?

JONATHAN. Why, I went to see one Mr. Morrison, the *hocus pocus* man; they said as how he could eat a café knife.

JENNY. Well, and how did you find the place?

JONATHAN. As I was going about here and there, to and again, to find it, I saw a great croud of folks going into a long entry, that had lantherns over the door; so I asked a man, whether that was not the place where they played *hocus pocus?* He was a very civil kind man, though he did speak like the Hessians; he lifted up his eyes and said—"they play *hocus pocus* tricks enough there, Got knows, mine friend."

JENNY. Well—

JONATHAN. So I went right in, and they shewed me away clean up to the garret, just like a meeting-house gallery. And so I saw a power of topping folks, all sitting round in little cabins, just like father's corn-cribs;—and then there was such a squeaking with the fiddles, and such a tarnal blaze with the lights, my head was near turned. At last the people that sat near me set up such a hissing—hiss—like so many mad cats; and then they went thump, thump, thump, just like our Peleg threshing wheat, and stampt away, just like the nation; and called out for one Mr. Langolee,—I suppose he helps act the tricks.

JENNY. Well, and what did you do all this time?

JONATHAN. Gor, I—I liked the fun, and so I thumpt away, and hiss'd as lustily as the best of 'em. One sailor-looking man that sat by me, seeing me stamp, and knowing I was a cute fellow, because I could make a roaring noise, clapt me on the shoulder and said, you are a d——d hearty cock, smite my timbers! I told him so I was, but I thought he need not swear so, and make use of such naughty words.

JESSAMY. The savage!—Well, and did you see the man with his tricks?

JONATHAN. Why, I vow, as I was looking out for him, they lifted up a great green cloth, and let us look right into the next neighbour's house. Have you a good many houses in New York made so in that 'ere way?

JENNY. Not many: but did you see the family?

JONATHAN. Yes, swamp it; I see'd the family.

JENNY. Well, and how did you like them?

JONATHAN. Why, I vow they were pretty much like other families;—there was a poor, good natured, curse of a husband, and a sad rantipole of a wife.

JENNY. But did you see no other folks?

JONATHAN. Yes. There was one youngster, they called him Mr. Joseph; he talked as sober and as pious as a minister; but like some ministers that I know, he was a fly tike in his heart for all that: He was going to ask a young woman to spark it with him, and—the Lord have mercy on my soul!—she was another man's wife.

JESSAMY. The Wabash!

JENNY. And did you see any more folks?

JONATHAN. Why they came on as thick as mustard. For my part, I thought the house was haunted. There was a soldier fellow, who talked about his row de dow dow, and courted a young woman: but of all the cute folk I saw, I liked one little fellow—

JENNY. Aye! who was he?

JONATHAN. Why, he had red hair, and a little round plump face like mine, only not altogether so handsome. His name was Darby:—that was his baptizing name, his other name I forgot. Oh! it was, Wig—Wag—Wag-all, Darby Wag-all;—pray, do you know him?—I should like to take a fling with him, or a drap of cyder with a pepper-pod in it, to make it warm and comfortable.

JENNY. I can't say I have that pleasure.

JONATHAN. I wish you did, he is a cute fellow. But there was one thing I didn't like in that Mr. Darby; and that was, he was afraid of some of them 'ere shooting irons, such as your troopers wear on training days. Now, I'm a true born Yankee American son of liberty, and I never was afraid of a gun yet in all my life.

JENNY. Well, Mr. Jonathan, you were certainly at the play-house.

JONATHAN. I at the play-house!—Why didn't I see the play then?

JENNY. Why, the people you saw were players.

JONATHAN. Mercy on my soul! did I see the wicked players?—Mayhap that 'ere Darby that I liked so, was the old serpent himself, and had his cloven foot in his pocket. Why, I vow, now I come to think on 't, the candles seemed to burn blue, and I am sure where I sat it smelt tarnally of brimstone.

JESSAMY. Well, Mr. Jonathan, from your account, which I confess is very accurate, you must have been at the play-house.

JONATHAN. Why, I vow I began to smell a rat. When I came away, I went to the man for my money again: you want your money, says he; yes, says I; for what, says he; why, says I, no man shall jocky me out of my money; I paid my money to see sights, and the dogs a bit of a sight have I seen, unless you call listening to people's private business a sight. Why, says he, it is the School for Scandalization.—The School for Scandalization—Oh, ho! no wonder you New York folks are so cute at it, when you go to school to learn it: and so I jogged off.

JESSAMY. My dear Jenny, my master's business drags me from you; would to heaven I knew no other servitude than to your charms.

JONATHAN. Well, but don't go; you won't leave me so.—

JESSAMY. Excuse me.—Remember the cash. [*Aside to him, and—Exit.*]

JENNY. Mr. Jonathan, won't you please to sit down. Mr. Jessamy tells me you wanted to have some conversation with me.

[*Having brought forward two chairs, they sit.*]

JONATHAN. Ma'am!—

JENNY. Sir!—

JONATHAN. Ma'am!—

JENNY. Pray, how do you like the city, Sir?

JONATHAN. Ma'am!—

JENNY. I say, Sir, how do you like New York?

JONATHAN. Ma'am!—

JENNY. The stupid creature! but I must pass some little time with him, if it is only to endeavour to learn, whether it was his master that made such an abrupt entrance into our house, and my young mistress's heart, this morning. [*Aside.*] As you don't seem to like to talk, Mr. Jonathan—do you sing?

JONATHAN. Gor, I—I am glad she asked that, for I forgot what Mr. Jessamy bid me say, and I dare as well be hanged as act what he bid me do, I'm so ashamed. [*Aside.*] Yes, Ma'am, I can sing—I can sing Mear, Old Hundred, and Bangor.

JENNY. Oh, I don't mean psalm tunes. Have you no little song to please the ladies; such as Roslin Castle, or the Maid of the Mill?

JONATHAN. Why, all my tunes go to meeting tunes, save one, and I count you won't altogether like that 'ere.

JENNY. What is it called?

JONATHAN. I am sure you have heard folks talk about it, it is called Yankee Doodle.

JENNY. Oh! it is the tune I am fond of; and, if I know anything of my mistress, she would be glad to dance to it. Pray, sing?

JONATHAN [*sings*].

Father and I went to camp,—
Along with Captain Goodwin;
And there we saw the men and boys,
As thick as hasty pudding.
Yankee Doodle do, etc.

And there we saw a swamping gun,
Big as log of maple,
On a little deuced cart,
A load for father's cattle.
Yankee Doodle do, etc.

And every time they fired it off,
It took a horn of powder,
It made a noise—like father's gun,
Only a nation louder.
Yankee Doodle do, etc.

There was a man in our town,
His name was—

No, no, that won't do. Now, if I was with Tabitha Wymen and Jemima Cawley, down at father Chase's, I shouldn't mind singing this all out before them—you would be affronted if I was to sing that, though that's a lucky thought; if you should be affronted, I have something dang'd cute, which Jessamy told me to say to you.

JENNY. Is that all! I assure you I like it of all things.

JONATHAN. No, no; I can sing more, some other time, when you and I are better acquainted, I'll sing the whole of it—no, no—that's a fib—I can't sing but a hundred and ninety verses: our Tabitha at home can sing it all.— [*Sings.*]

Marblehead's a rocky place,
And Cape-Cod is sandy;
Charleston is burnt down,
Boston is the dandy.
Yankee Doodle do, etc.

I vow, my own town song has put me into such topping spirits, that I believe I'll begin to do a little, as Jessamy says we must when we go a courting—[*Runs and kisses her.*] Burning rivers! cooling flames! red hot roses! pig-nuts! hasty-pudding and ambrosia!

JENNY. What means this freedom! you insulting wretch. [*Strikes him.*]

JONATHAN. Are you affronted?

JENNY. Affronted! with what looks shall I express my anger?

JONATHAN. Looks! why, as to the matter of looks, you look as cross as a witch.

JENNY. Have you no feeling for the delicacy of my sex?

JONATHAN. Feeling! Gor, I—I feel the delicacy of your sex pretty smartly [*rubbing his cheek*], though, I vow, I thought when you city ladies courted and married, and all that, you put feeling out of the question. But I want to know whether you are really affronted, or only pretend to be so? 'Cause, if you are certainly right down affronted, I am at the end of my tether;—Jessamy didn't tell me what to say to you.

JENNY. Pretend to be affronted!

JONATHAN. Aye, aye, if you only pretend, you shall hear how I'll go to work to make cherubim consequences. [*Runs up to her.*]

JENNY. Begone, you brute!

JONATHAN. That looks like mad; but I won't lose my speech. My dearest Jenny—your name is Jenny, I think? My dearest Jenny, though I have the highest esteem for the sweet favours you have just now granted me—Gor, that's a fib though, but Jessamy says it is not wicked to tell lies to the women. [*Aside.*] I say, though I have the highest esteem for the favours you have just now granted me, yet, you will consider, that as soon as the dissolvable knot is tied, they will no longer be favours, but only matters of duty, and matters of course.

JENNY. Marry you! you audacious monster! get out of my sight, or rather let me fly from you. [*Exit hastily.*]

JONATHAN. Gor! she's gone off in a swinging passion, before I had time to think of consequences. If this is the way with your city ladies, give me the twenty acres of rocks, the bible, the cow, and Tabitha, and a little peaceable bundling.

SCENE 2. *The Mall.*

[*Enter* MANLY.]

MANLY. It must be so, Montague! and it is not all the tribe of Mandevilles shall convince me, that a nation, to become great, must first become dissipated. Luxury is surely the bane of a nation: Luxury! which enervates both soul and body, by opening a thousand new sources of enjoyment, opens, also, a thousand new sources of contention and want: Luxury! which renders a people weak at home, and accessible to bribery, corruption, and force from abroad. When the Grecian states knew no other tools than the axe and the saw, the Grecians were a great, a free, and a happy people. The kings of Greece devoted their lives to the service of their country, and her senators knew no other superiority over their fellow-citizens than a glorious preëminence in danger and virtue. They exhibited to the world a noble spectacle,—a number of independent states united by a similarity of language, sentiment, manners, common interest, and common consent, in one grand mutual league of protection.—And, thus united, long might they have continued the cherishers of arts and sciences, the protectors of the oppressed, the scourge of tyrants, and the safe asylum of liberty: But when foreign gold, and still more pernicious, foreign luxury, had crept among them, they sapped the vitals of their virtue. The virtues of their ancestors were only found in their writings. Envy and suspicion, the vices of little minds, possessed them. The various states engendered jealousies of each other; and, more unfortunately, growing jealous of their great federal council, the Amphictyons, they forgot that their common safety had existed, and would exist, in giving them an honourable extensive prerogative. The common good was lost in the pursuit of private interest; and that people, who, by uniting, might have stood against the world in arms, by dividing, crumbled into ruin;—their name is now only known in the page of the historian, and what they once were, is all we have left to admire. Oh! that America! Oh! that my country, would in this her day, learn the things which belong to her peace!

[*Enter* DIMPLE.]

DIMPLE. You are Colonel Manly, I presume?

MANLY. At your service, Sir.

DIMPLE. My name is Dimple, Sir. I have the honour to be a lodger in the same house with you, and hearing you were in the Mall, came hither to take the liberty of joining you.

MANLY. You are very obliging, Sir.

DIMPLE. As I understand you are a stranger here, Sir, I have taken the liberty to introduce myself to your acquaintance, as possibly I may have it in my power to point out some things in this city worthy your notice.

MANLY. An attention to strangers is worthy a liberal mind, and must ever be gratefully received. But to a soldier, who has no fixed abode, such attentions are particularly pleasing.

DIMPLE. Sir, there is no character so respectable as that of a soldier. And, indeed, when we reflect how much we owe to those brave men who have suffered so much in the service of their country, and secured to us those inestimable blessings that we now enjoy, our liberty and independence, they demand every attention which gratitude can pay. For my own part, I never meet an officer, but I embrace him as my friend, nor a private in distress, but I insensibly extend my charity to him.—I have hit the Bum[p]kin off very tolerably. [*Aside.*]

MANLY. Give me your hand, Sir! I do not proffer this hand to everybody; but you steal into my heart. I hope I am as insensible to flattery as most men; but I declare (it may be my weak side), that I never hear the name of soldier mentioned with respect, but I experience a thrill of pleasure, which I never feel on any other occasion.

DIMPLE. Will you give me leave, my dear colonel, to confer an obligation on myself, by shewing you some civilities during your stay here, and giving a similar opportunity to some of my friends?

MANLY. Sir, I thank you; but I believe my stay in this city will be very short.

DIMPLE. I can introduce you to some men of excellent sense, in whose company you will esteem yourself happy; and, by way of amusement, to some fine girls, who will listen to your soft things with pleasure.

MANLY. Sir, I should be proud of the honour of being acquainted with those gentlemen;—but, as for the ladies, I don't understand you.

DIMPLE. Why, Sir, I need not tell you, that when a young gentleman is alone with a young lady, he must say some soft things to her fair cheek—indeed the lady will expect it. To be sure, there is not much pleasure, when a man of the world and a finished coquet meet, who perfectly know each other; but how delicious is it to excite the emotions of joy, hope, expectation, and delight, in the bosom of a lovely girl, who believes every tittle of what you say to be serious.

MANLY. Serious, Sir! In my opinion, the man, who, under pretensions of marriage, can plant thorns in the bosom of an innocent, unsuspecting girl, is more detestable than a common robber, in the same proportion, as private violence is more despicable than open force, and money of less value than happiness.

DIMPLE. How he awes me by the superiority of his sentiments. [*Aside.*] As you say, Sir, a gentleman should be cautious how he mentions marriage.

MANLY. Cautious, Sir! No person more approves of an intercourse between the sexes than I do. Female conversation softens our manners, whilst our discourse, from the superiority of our literary advantages, improves their minds. But, in our young country, where there is no such thing as gallantry, when a gentleman speaks of love to a lady, whether he mentions marriage, or not, she ought to conclude, either that he meant to insult her, or, that his intentions are the most serious and honourable. How mean, how cruel, is it, by a thousand tender assiduities, to win the affections of an amiable girl, and though you leave her virtue unspotted, to betray her into the appearance of so many tender partialities, that every man of delicacy would suppress his inclination towards her, by supposing her heart engaged! Can any man, for the trivial gratification of his leisure hours, affect the happiness of a whole life! His not having spoken of marriage, may add to his perfidy, but can be no excuse for his conduct.

DIMPLE. Sir, I admire your sentiments;—they are mine. The light observations that fell from me, were only a principle of the tongue; they came not from the heart—my practice has ever disapproved these principles.

MANLY. I believe you, Sir. I should with reluctance suppose that those pernicious sentiments could find admittance into the heart of a gentleman.

DIMPLE. I am now, Sir, going to visit a family, where, if you please, I will have the honour of introducing you. Mr. Manly's ward, Miss Letitia, is a young lady of immense fortune; and his niece, Miss Charlotte Manly is a young lady of great sprightliness and beauty.

MANLY. That gentleman, Sir, is my uncle, and Miss Manly my sister.

DIMPLE. The devil she is! [*Aside.*] Miss Manly your sister, Sir? I rejoice to hear it, and feel a double pleasure in being known to you.—

Plague on him! I wish he was at Boston again with all my soul. [*Aside.*]

Manly. Come, Sir, will you go?

Dimple. I will follow you in a moment, Sir. [*Exit* Manly.] Plague on it! this is unlucky. A fighting brother is a cursed appendage to a fine girl. Egad! I just stopped in time; had he not discovered himself, in two minutes more I should have told him how well I was with his sister.—Indeed, I cannot see the satisfaction of an intrigue, if one can't have the pleasure of communicating it to our friends. [*Exit.*]

ACT FOURTH

Scene 1. Charlotte's *Apartment.*

[Charlotte *leading in* Maria.]

Charlotte. This is so kind, my sweet friend, to come to see me at this moment. I declare, if I were going to be married in a few days, as you are, I should scarce have found time to visit my friends.

Maria. Do you think then that there is an impropriety in it?—How should you dispose of your time?

Charlotte. Why, I should be shut up in my chamber; and my head would so run upon—upon—upon the solemn ceremony that I was to pass through—I declare it would take me above two hours merely to learn that little monosyllable—*Yes.* Ah! my dear, your sentimental imagination does not conceive what that little tiny word implies.

Maria. Spare me your raillery, my sweet friend; I should love your agreeable vivacity at any other time.

Charlotte. Why this is the very time to amuse you. You grieve me to see you look so unhappy.

Maria. Have I not reason to look so?

Charlotte. What new grief distresses you?

Maria. Oh! how sweet it is, when the heart is borne down with misfortune, to recline and repose on the bosom of friendship! Heaven knows, that, although it is improper for a young lady to praise a gentleman, yet I have ever concealed Mr. Dimple's foibles, and spoke of him as of one whose reputation I expected would be linked with mine: but his late conduct towards me, has turned my coolness into contempt. He behaves as if he meant to insult and disgust me; whilst my father, in the last conversation on the subject of our marriage, spoke of it as a matter which laid near his heart, and in which he would not bear contradiction.

Charlotte. This works well: oh! the generous Dimple. I'll endeavour to excite her to discharge him. [*Aside.*] But, my dear friend, your happiness depends on yourself:—Why don't you discard him? Though the match has been of long standing, I would not be forced to make myself miserable: no parent in the world should oblige me to marry the man I did not like.

Maria. Oh! my dear, you never lived with your parents, and do not know what influence a father's frowns have upon a daughter's heart. Besides, what have I to allege against Mr. Dimple, to justify myself to the world? He carries himself so smoothly, that every one would impute the blame to me, and call me capricious.

Charlotte. And call her capricious! Did ever such an objection start into the heart of woman? For my part, I wish I had fifty lovers to discard, for no other reason, than because I did not fancy them. My dear Maria, you will forgive me; I know your candour and confidence in me; but I have at times, I confess, been led to suppose, that some other gentleman was the cause of your aversion to Mr. Dimple.

Maria. No, my sweet friend, you may be assured, that though I have seen many gentlemen I could prefer to Mr. Dimple, yet I never saw one that I thought I could give my hand to, until this morning.

Charlotte. This morning!

Maria. Yes;—one of the strangest accidents in the world. The odious Dimple, after disgusting me with his conversation, had just left me, when a gentleman, who, it seems, boards in the same house with him, saw him coming out of our door, and the houses looking very much alike, he came into our house instead of his lodgings; nor did he discover his mistake until he got into the parlour, where I was: he then bowed so gracefully; made such a genteel apology, and looked so manly and noble!—

Charlotte. I see some folks, though it is so great an impropriety, can praise a gentleman, when he happens to be the man of their fancy. [*Aside.*]

Maria. I don't know how it was, —I hope he did not think me indelicate—but I asked him, I believe, to sit down, or pointed to a chair. He sat down, and instead of having recourse to observations upon the weather, or hackneyed criticisms upon the theatre, he entered readily into a conversation worthy a man of sense to speak, and a lady of delicacy and sentiment to hear. He was not strictly handsome, but he spoke the language of sentiment, and his eyes looked tenderness and honour.

Charlotte. Oh! [*eagerly*] you sentimental grave girls, when your hearts are once touched, beat us rattles a bar's length. And so, you are quite in love with this he-angel?

Maria. In love with him! How can you rattle so, Charlotte? am I not going to be miserable? [*Sighs.*] In love with a gentleman I never saw but one hour in my life, and don't know his name!—No: I only wished that the man I shall marry, may look, and talk, and act, just like him. Besides, my dear, he is a married man.

Charlotte. Why, that was good natured.—He told you so, I suppose, in mere charity, to prevent your falling in love with him?

Maria. He didn't tell me so [*peevishly*]; he looked as if he was married.

Charlotte. How, my dear, did he look sheepish?

Maria. I am sure he has a susceptible heart, and the ladies of his acquaintance must be very stupid not to—

Charlotte. Hush! I hear some person coming.

[*Enter* Letitia.]

Letitia. My dear Maria, I am happy to see you. Lud! what a pity it is that you have purchased your wedding clothes.

Maria. I think so. [*Sighing.*]

Letitia. Why, my dear, there is the sweetest parcel of silks come over you ever saw. Nancy Brilliant has a full suit come; she sent over her measure, and it fits her to a hair; it is immensely dressy, and made for a court-hoop. I thought they said the large hoops were going out of fashion.

CHARLOTTE. Did you see the hat? —Is it a fact, that the deep laces round the border is still the fashion?

DIMPLE [*within*]. Upon my honour, Sir!

MARIA. Ha! Dimple's voice! My dear, I must take leave of you. There are some things necessary to be done at our house.—Can't I go through the other room?

[*Enter* DIMPLE *and* MANLY.]

DIMPLE. Ladies, your most obedient.

CHARLOTTE. Miss Van Rough, shall I present my brother Henry to you? Colonel Manly, Maria,—Miss Van Rough, brother.

MARIA. Her brother! [*Turns and sees* MANLY.] Oh! my heart! The very gentleman I have been praising.

MANLY. The same amiable girl I saw this morning!

CHARLOTTE. Why, you look as if you were acquainted.

MANLY. I unintentionally intruded into this lady's presence this morning, for which she was so good as to promise me her forgiveness.

CHARLOTTE. Oh! ho! is that the case! Have these two penserosos been together? Were they Henry's eyes that looked so tenderly? [*Aside*.] And so you promised to pardon him? and could you be so good natured? —have you really forgiven him? I beg you would do it for my sake. [*Whispering loud to* MARIA.] But, my dear, as you are in such haste, it would be cruel to detain you: I can show you the way through the other room.

MARIA. Spare me, sprightly friend.

MANLY. The lady does not, I hope, intend to deprive us of the pleasure of her company so soon.

CHARLOTTE. She has only a mantua-maker who waits for her at home. But, as I am to give my opinion of the dress, I think she cannot go yet. We were talking of the fashions when you came in; but I suppose the subject must be changed to something of more importance now.—Mr. Dimple, will you favour us with an account of the public entertainments?

DIMPLE. Why, really, Miss Manly, you could not have asked me a question more *mal-apropos*. For my part, I must confess, that to a man who has travelled, there is nothing that is worthy the name of amusement to be found in this city.

CHARLOTTE. Except visiting the ladies.

DIMPLE. Pardon me, Madam; that is the avocation of a man of taste. But, for amusement, I positively know of nothing that can be called so, unless you dignify with that title the hopping once a fortnight to the sound of two or three squeaking fiddles, and the clattering of the old tavern windows, or sitting to see the miserable mummers, whom you call actors, murder comedy, and make a farce of tragedy.

MANLY. Do you never attend the theatre, Sir?

DIMPLE. I was tortured there once.

CHARLOTTE. Pray, Mr. Dimple, was it a tragedy or a comedy?

DIMPLE. Faith, Madam, I cannot tell; for I sat with my back to the stage all the time, admiring a much better actress than any there;—a lady who played the fine woman to perfection;—though, by the laugh of the horrid creatures around me, I suppose it was comedy. Yet, on second thoughts, it might be some hero in a tragedy, dying so comically as to set the whole house in an uproar.—Colonel, I presume you have been in Europe?

MANLY. Indeed, Sir, I was never ten leagues from the continent.

DIMPLE. Believe me, Colonel, you have an immense pleasure to come; and when you shall have seen the brilliant exhibitions of Europe, you will learn to despise the amusements of this country as much as I do.

MANLY. Therefore I do not wish to see them; for I can never esteem that knowledge valuable, which tends to give me a distaste for my native country.

DIMPLE. Well, Colonel, though you have not travelled, you have read.

MANLY. I have, a little: and by it have discovered that there is a laudable partiality, which ignorant, untravelled men entertain for everything that belongs to their native country. I call it laudable;—it injures no one; adds to their own happiness; and, when extended, becomes the noble principle of patriotism. Travelled gentlemen rise superior, in their own opinion, to this: but, if the contempt which they contract for their country is the most valuable acquisition of their travels, I am far from thinking that their time and money are well spent.

MARIA. What noble sentiments!

CHARLOTTE. Let my brother set out from where he will in the fields of conversation, he is sure to end his tour in the temple of gravity.

MANLY. Forgive me, my sister. I love my country; it has its foibles undoubtedly;—some foreigners will with pleasure remark them—but such remarks fall very ungracefully from the lips of her citizens.

DIMPLE. You are perfectly in the right, Colonel—America has her faults.

MANLY. Yes, Sir; and we, her children, should blush for them in private, and endeavour, as individuals, to reform them. But, if our country has its errors in common with other countries, I am proud to say America, I mean the United States, have displayed virtues and achievements which modern nations may admire, but of which they have seldom set us the example.

CHARLOTTE. But, brother, we must introduce you to some of our gay folks, and let you see the city, such as it is. Mr. Dimple is known to almost every family in town;—he will doubtless take a pleasure in introducing you.

DIMPLE. I shall esteem every service I can render your brother an honour.

MANLY. I fear the business I am upon will take up all my time, and my family will be anxious to hear from me.

MARIA. His family! But what is it to me that he is married! [*Aside.*] Pray, how did you leave your lady, Sir?

CHARLOTTE. My brother is not married [*observing her anxiety*]; it is only an odd way he has of expressing himself.—Pray, brother, is this business, which you make your continual excuse, a secret?

MANLY. No, sister, I came hither to solicit the honourable Congress that a number of my brave old soldiers may be put upon the pension-list, who were, at first, not judged to be so materially wounded as to need the public assistance.—My sister says true: [*To* MARIA.] I call my late soldiers my family.—Those who were not in the field in the late glorious contest, and those who were, have their respective merits; but, I confess, my old brother-soldiers are dearer to me than the former description. Friendships made in adversity are lasting; our countrymen may forget us; but that is no reason why we should forget one another. But I must leave you; my time of engagement approaches.

CHARLOTTE. Well, but brother, if you will go, will you please to conduct my fair friend home? You live in the same street;—I was to have gone with her myself— [*Aside.*] A lucky thought.

MARIA. I am obliged to your sister, Sir, and was just intending to go. [*Going.*]

MANLY. I shall attend her with pleasure.

[*Exit with* MARIA, *followed by* DIMPLE *and* CHARLOTTE.]

MARIA. Now, pray don't betray me to your brother.

CHARLOTTE [*just as she sees him make a motion to take his leave*]. One word with you, brother, if you please. [*Follows them out.*]

[*Manent* DIMPLE *and* LETITIA.]

DIMPLE. You received the billet I sent you, I presume?

LETITIA. Hush!—Yes.

DIMPLE. When shall I pay my respects to you?

LETITIA. At eight I shall be unengaged.

[*Reënter* CHARLOTTE.]

DIMPLE. Did my lovely angel receive my billet? [*To* CHARLOTTE.]

CHARLOTTE. Yes.

DIMPLE. What hour shall I expect with impatience?

CHARLOTTE. At eight I shall be at home, unengaged.

DIMPLE. Unfortunate! I have a horrid engagement of business at that hour.—Can't you finish your visit earlier, and let six be the happy hour?

CHARLOTTE. You know your influence over me. [*Exeunt severally.*]

SCENE 2. VAN ROUGH'S *House.*

[VAN ROUGH, *alone.*]

VAN ROUGH. It cannot possibly be true! The son of my old friend can't have acted so unadvisedly. Seventeen thousand pounds! in bills!—Mr. Transfer must have been mistaken. He always appeared so prudent, and talked so well upon money-matters, and even assured me that he intended to change his dress for a suit of clothes which would not cost so much, and look more substantial, as soon as he married. No, no, no! it can't be; it cannot be.—But, however, I must look out sharp. I did not care what his principles or his actions were, so long as he minded the main chance. Seventeen thousand pounds!—If he had lost it in trade, why the best men may have ill-luck; but to game it away, as Transfer says—why, at this rate, his whole estate may go in one night, and, what is ten times worse, mine into the bargain. No, no; Mary is right. Leave women to look out in these matters; for all they look as if they didn't know a journal from a ledger, when their interest is concerned, they know what's what; they mind the main chance as well as the best of us.—I wonder Mary did not tell me she knew of his spending his money so foolishly. Seventeen thousand pounds! Why, if my daughter was standing up to be married, I would forbid the banns, if I found it was to a man who did not mind the main chance.—Hush! I hear somebody coming. 'T is Mary's voice: a man with her too! I shouldn't be surprized if this should be the other string to her bow.—Aye, aye, let them alone; women understand the main chance.—Though, i' faith, I'll listen a little.

[*Retires into a closet.*]

[MANLY *leading in* MARIA.]

MANLY. I hope you will excuse my speaking upon so important a subject, so abruptly; but the moment I entered your room, you struck me as the lady whom I had long loved in imagination, and never hoped to see.

MARIA. Indeed, Sir, I have been led to hear more upon this subject than I ought.

MANLY. Do you then disapprove my suit, Madam, or the abruptness of my introducing it? If the latter, my peculiar situation, being obliged to leave the city in a few days, will, I hope, be my excuse; if the former, I will retire: for I am sure I would not give a moment's inquietude to her, whom I could devote my life to please. I am not so indelicate as to seek your immediate approbation; permit me only to be near you, and by a thousand tender assiduities to endeavour to excite a grateful return.

MARIA. I have a father, whom I would die to make happy—he will disapprove—

MANLY. Do you think me so ungenerous as to seek a place in your esteem without his consent? You must—you ever ought to consider that man as unworthy of you, who seeks an interest in your heart, contrary to a father's approbation. A young lady should reflect, that the loss of a lover may be supplied, but nothing can compensate for the loss of a parent's affection. Yet, why do you suppose your father would disapprove? In our country, the affections are not sacrificed to riches, or family aggrandizement:—should you approve, my family is decent, and my rank honourable.

MARIA. You distress me, Sir.

MANLY. Then I will sincerely beg your excuse for obtruding so disagreeable a subject and retire. [*Going.*]

MARIA. Stay, Sir! your generosity and good opinion of me deserve a return; but why must I declare what, for these few hours, I have scarce suffered myself to think?—I am—

MANLY. What?—

MARIA. Engaged, Sir;—and, in a few days, to be married to the gentleman you saw at your sister's.

MANLY. Engaged to be married! And have I been basely invading the rights of another? Why have you permitted this?—Is this the return for the partiality I declared for you?

MARIA. You distress me, Sir. What would you have me say? You are too generous to wish the truth: ought I to say that I dared not suffer myself to think of my engagement, and that I am going to give my hand without my heart?—Would you have me confess a partiality for you? If so, your triumph is complete; and can be only more so, when days of misery, with the man I cannot love, will make me think of him whom I could prefer.

MANLY [*after a pause*]. We are both unhappy; but it is your duty to obey your parent,—mine to obey my honour. Let us, therefore, both follow the path of rectitude; and of this we may be assured, that if we are not happy, we shall, at least deserve to be so. Adieu! I dare not trust myself longer with you.

[*Exeunt severally.*]

ACT FIFTH

SCENE 1. DIMPLE'S *Lodgings.*

[JESSAMY *meeting* JONATHAN.]

JESSAMY. Well, Mr. Jonathan, what success with the fair?

JONATHAN. Why, such a tarnal cross tike you never saw!—You would have counted she had lived upon crab-apples and vinegar for a fortnight. But what the rattle makes you look so tarnation glum?

JESSAMY. I was thinking, Mr. Jonathan, what could be the reason of her carrying herself so coolly to you.

JONATHAN. Coolly, do you call it? Why, I vow, she was fire-hot angry: may be it was because I buss'd her.

JESSAMY. No, no, Mr. Jonathan; there must be some other cause: I never yet knew a lady angry at being kissed.

JONATHAN. Well, if it is not the young woman's bashfulness, I vow I can't conceive why she shou'd n't like me.

JESSAMY. May be it is because you have not the Graces, Mr. Jonathan.

JONATHAN. Grace! Why, does the young woman expect I must be converted before I court her?

JESSAMY. I mean graces of person; for instance, my lord tells us that we must cut off our nails even at top, in small segments of circles;—though you won't understand that—In the next place, you must regulate your laugh.

JONATHAN. Maple-log seize it! don't I laugh natural?

JESSAMY. That's the very fault, Mr. Jonathan. Besides, you absolutely misplace it. I was told by a friend of mine that you laughed outright at the play the other night, when you ought only to have tittered.

JONATHAN. Gor! I—what does one go to see fun for if they can't laugh?

JESSAMY. You may laugh;—but you must laugh by rule.

JONATHAN. Swamp it—laugh by rule! Well, I should like that tarnally.

JESSAMY. Why you know, Mr. Jonathan, that to dance, a lady to play with her fan, or a gentleman with his cane, and all other natural motions, are regulated by art. My master has composed an immensely pretty gamut, by which any lady, or gentleman, with a few years' close application, may learn to laugh as gracefully as if they were born and bred to it.

JONATHAN. Mercy on my soul! A gamut for laughing—just like fa, la, sol?

JESSAMY. Yes. It comprises every possible display of jocularity, from an *affetuoso* smile to a *piano* titter, or full chorus *fortissimo* ha, ha, ha! My master employs his leisure-hours in marking out the plays, like a cathedral chanting-book, that the ignorant may know where to laugh; and that pit, box, and gallery may keep time together, and not have a snigger in one part of the house, a broad grin in the other, and a d——d grum look in the third. How delightful to see the audience all smile together, then look on their books, then twist their mouths into an agreeable simper, then altogether shake the house with a general ha, ha, ha! loud as a full chorus of Handel's, at an Abbey-commemoration.

JONATHAN. Ha, ha, ha! that's dang'd cute, I swear.

JESSAMY. The gentlemen, you see, will laugh the tenor; the ladies will play the counter-tenor; the beaux will squeak the treble; and our jolly friends in the gallery a thorough bass, ho, ho, ho!

JONATHAN. Well, can't you let me see that gamut?

JESSAMY. Oh! yes, Mr. Jonathan; here it is. [*Takes out a book.*] Oh! no, this is only a titter with its variations. Ah, here it is. [*Takes out another.*] Now you must know, Mr. Jonathan, this is a piece written by Ben Jonson, which I have set to my master's gamut. The places where you must smile, look grave, or laugh outright, are marked below the line. Now look over me.—"There was a certain man"—now you must smile.

JONATHAN. Well, read it again; I warrant I'll mind my eye.

JESSAMY. "There was a certain man, who had a sad scolding wife,"—now you must laugh.

JONATHAN. Tarnation! That's no laughing matter, though.

JESSAMY. "And she lay sick a-dying;"—now you must titter.

JONATHAN. What, snigger when the good woman's a-dying! Gor, I—

JESSAMY. Yes; the notes say you must—"And she asked her husband leave to make a will,"—now you must begin to look grave;—"and her husband said"—

JONATHAN. Ay, what did her husband say?—Something dang'd cute, I reckon.

JESSAMY. "And her husband said, you have had your will all your life time, and would you have it after you are dead too?"

JONATHAN. Ho, ho, ho! There the old man was even with her; he was up to the notch—ha, ha, ha!

JESSAMY. But, Mr. Jonathan, you must not laugh so. Why, you ought to have tittered *piano*, and you have laughed *fortissimo*. Look here; you see these marks, A. B. C. and so on; these are the references to the other part of the book. Let us turn to it, and you will see the directions how to manage the muscles. This [*turns over*] was note D you blundered at.—"You must purse the mouth into a smile, then titter, discovering the lower part of the three front upper teeth."

JONATHAN. How! read it again.

JESSAMY. "There was a certain man"—very well!—"who had a sad scolding wife,"—why don't you laugh?

JONATHAN. Now, that scolding wife sticks in my gizzard so pluckily, that I can't laugh for the blood and nowns of me. Let me look grave here, and I'll laugh your belly full where the old creature's a-dying.—

JESSAMY. "And she asked her husband"—[*Bell rings.*] My master's bell! he's returned, I fear—Here, Mr. Jonathan, take this gamut; and, I make no doubt but with a few years' close application, you may be able to smile gracefully. [*Exeunt severally.*]

SCENE 2. CHARLOTTE'S *Apartment.*

[*Enter* MANLY.]

MANLY. What, no one at home? How unfortunate to meet the only lady my heart was ever moved by, to find her engaged to another, and confessing her partiality for me! Yet engaged to a man, who, by her intimation, and his libertine conversation with me, I fear, does not merit her. Aye! there's the sting; for, were I assured that Maria was happy, my heart is not so selfish, but that it would dilate in knowing it, even though it were with another.—But to know she is unhappy!—I must drive these thoughts from me. Charlotte has some books; and this is what I believe she calls her little library. [*Enters a closet.*]

[*Enter* DIMPLE *leading* LETITIA.]

LETITIA. And will you pretend to say, now, Mr. Dimple, that you propose to break with Maria? Are not the banns published? Are not the clothes purchased? Are not the friends invited? In short, is it not a done affair?

DIMPLE. Believe me, my dear Letitia, I would not marry her.

LETITIA. Why have you not broke with her before this, as you all along deluded me by saying you would?

DIMPLE. Because I was in hopes she would ere this have broke with me.

LETITIA. You could not expect it.

DIMPLE. Nay, but be calm a moment; 't was from my regard to you that I did not discard her.

LETITIA. Regard to me!

DIMPLE. Yes; I have done everything in my power to break with her, but the foolish girl is so fond of me, that nothing can accomplish it. Besides, how can I offer her my hand, when my heart is indissolubly engaged to you?—

LETITIA. There may be reason in this; but why so attentive to Miss Manly?

DIMPLE. Attentive to Miss Manly! For heaven's sake, if you have no better opinion of my constancy, pay not so ill a compliment to my taste.

LETITIA. Did I not see you whisper her to-day?

DIMPLE. Possibly I might—but something of so very trifling a nature, that I have already forgot what it was.

LETITIA. I believe, she has not forgot it.

DIMPLE. My dear creature, how can you for a moment suppose I should have any serious thoughts of that trifling, gay, flighty coquette, that disagreeable—

[*Enter* CHARLOTTE.]

DIMPLE. My dear Miss Manly, I rejoice to see you; there is a charm in your conversation that always marks your entrance into company as fortunate.

LETITIA. Where have you been, my dear?

CHARLOTTE. Why, I have been

about to twenty shops, turning over pretty things, and so have left twenty visits unpaid. I wish you would step into the carriage and whisk round, make my apology, and leave my cards where our friends are not at home; that you know will serve as a visit. Come, do go.

LETITIA. So anxious to get me out! but I'll watch you. [*Aside.*] Oh! yes, I'll go; I want a little exercise.—Positively [DIMPLE *offering to accompany her*], Mr. Dimple, you shall not go, why, half my visits are cake and caudle visits; it won't do, you know, for you to go.—

[*Exit, but returns to the door in the back scene and listens.*]

DIMPLE. This attachment of your brother to Maria is fortunate.

CHARLOTTE. How did you come to the knowledge of it?

DIMPLE. I read it in their eyes.

CHARLOTTE. And I had it from her mouth. It would have amused you to have seen her! She that thought it so great an impropriety to praise a gentleman, that she could not bring out one word in your favour, found a redundancy to praise him.

DIMPLE. I have done everything in my power to assist his passion there: your delicacy, my dearest girl, would be shocked at half the instances of neglect and misbehaviour.

CHARLOTTE. I don't know how I should bear neglect; but Mr. Dimple must misbehave himself indeed, to forfeit my good opinion.

DIMPLE. Your good opinion, my angel, is the pride and pleasure of my heart; and if the most respectful tenderness for you and an utter indifference for all your sex besides, can make me worthy of your esteem, I shall richly merit it.

CHARLOTTE. All my sex besides, Mr. Dimple—you forgot your *tête-à-tête* with Letitia.

DIMPLE. How can you, my lovely angel, cast a thought on that insipid, wry-mouthed, ugly creature!

CHARLOTTE. But her fortune may have charms?

DIMPLE. Not to a heart like mine. The man who has been blessed with the good opinion of my Charlotte, must despise the allurements of fortune.

CHARLOTTE. I am satisfied.

DIMPLE. Let us think no more on the odious subject, but devote the present hour to happiness.

CHARLOTTE. Can I be happy, when I see the man I prefer going to be married to another?

DIMPLE. Have I not already satisfied my charming angel that I can never think of marrying the puling Maria. But, even if it were so, could that be any bar to our happiness; for, as the poet sings—

Love, free as air, at sight of human ties,
Spreads his light wings, and in a moment flies.

Come then, my charming angel! why delay our bliss! The present moment is ours; the next is in the hand of fate. [*Kissing her.*]

CHARLOTTE. Begone, Sir! By your delusions you had almost lulled my honour asleep.

DIMPLE. Let me lull the demon to sleep again with kisses.

[*He struggles with her; she screams.*]

[*Enter* MANLY.]

MANLY. Turn, villain! and defend yourself.—

[*Draws.* Van Rough *enters and beats down their swords.*]

Van Rough. Is the devil in you? are you going to murder one another? [*Holding* Dimple.]

Dimple. Hold him, hold him,—I can command my passion.

[*Enter* Jonathan.]

Jonathan. What the rattle ails you? Is the old one in you? Let the colonel alone, can't you? I feel chock full of fight,—do you want to kill the colonel?—

Manly. Be still, Jonathan; the gentleman does not want to hurt me.

Jonathan. Gor! I—I wish he did; I'd shew him Yankee boys play, pretty quick—Don't you see you have frightened the young woman into the *hystrikes?*

Van Rough. Pray, some of you explain this; what has been the occasion of all this racket?

Manly. That gentleman can explain it to you; it will be a very diverting story for an intended father-in-law to hear.

Van Rough. How was this matter, Mr. Van Dumpling?

Dimple. Sir, upon my honour—all I know is, that I was talking to this young lady, and this gentleman broke in on us, in a very extraordinary manner.

Van Rough. Why, all this is nothing to the purpose: can you explain it, Miss? [*To* Charlotte.]

[*Enter* Letitia *through the back scene.*]

Letitia. I can explain it to that gentleman's confusion. Though long betrothed to your daughter [*to* Van Rough], yet allured by my fortune, it seems (with shame do I speak it), he has privately paid his addresses to me. I was drawn in to listen to him by his assuring me that the match was made by his father without his consent, and that he proposed to break with Maria, whether he married me or not. But whatever were his intentions respecting your daughter, Sir, even to me he was false; for he has repeated the same story, with some cruel reflections upon my person, to Miss Manly.

Jonathan. What a tarnal curse!

Letitia. Nor is this all, Miss Manly. When he was with me this very morning, he made the same ungenerous reflections upon the weakness of your mind as he has so recently done upon the defects of my person.

Jonathan. What a tarnal curse and damn too!

Dimple. Ha! since I have lost Letitia, I believe I had as good make it up with Maria—Mr. Van Rough, at present I cannot enter into particulars; but, I believe I can explain everything to your satisfaction in private.

Van Rough. There is another matter, Mr. Van Dumpling, which I would have you explain:—pray, Sir, have Messrs. Van Cash and Co. presented you those bills for acceptance?

Dimple. The deuce! Has he heard of those bills! Nay, then, all's up with Maria, too; but an affair of this sort can never prejudice me among the ladies; they will rather long to know what the dear creature possesses to make him so agreeable. [*Aside.*] Sir, you'll hear from me. [*To* Manly.]

MANLY. And you from me, Sir.—

DIMPLE. Sir, you wear a sword.—

MANLY. Yes, Sir:—This sword was presented to me by that brave Gallic hero, the Marquis De La Fayette. I have drawn it in the service of my country, and in private life, on the only occasion where a man is justified in drawing his sword, in defence of a lady's honour. I have fought too many battles in the service of my country to dread the imputation of cowardice.—Death from a man of honour would be a glory you do not merit; you shall live to bear the insult of man, and the contempt of that sex, whose general smiles afforded you all your happiness.

DIMPLE. You won't meet me, Sir? —Then I'll post you for a coward.

MANLY. I'll venture that, Sir.—The reputation of my life does not depend upon the breath of a Mr. Dimple. I would have you to know, however, Sir, that I have a cane to chastise the insolence of a scoundrel, and a sword and the good laws of my country, to protect me from the attempts of an assassin.—

DIMPLE. Mighty well! Very fine, indeed!—ladies and gentlemen, I take my leave, and you will please to observe, in the case of my deportment, the contrast between a gentleman, who has read Chesterfield and received the polish of Europe, and an unpolished, untravelled American.

[*Exit.*]

[*Enter* MARIA.]

MARIA. Is he indeed gone?—

LETITIA. I hope never to return.

VAN ROUGH. I am glad I heard of those bills; though it's plaguy unlucky: I hoped to see Mary married before I died.

MANLY. Will you permit a gentleman, Sir, to offer himself as a suitor to your daughter? Though a stranger to you, he is not altogether so to her, or unknown in this city. You may find a son-in-law of more fortune, but you can never meet with one who is richer in love for her, or respect for you.

VAN ROUGH. Why, Mary, you have not let this gentleman make love to you without my leave?

MANLY. I did not say, Sir—

MARIA. Say, Sir!—I—the gentleman, to be sure, met me accidentally.

VAN ROUGH. Ha, ha, ha! Mark me, Mary; young folks think old folks to be fools; but old folks know young folks to be fools.—Why, I knew all about this affair:—This was only a cunning way I had to bring it about —Hark ye! I was in the closet when you and he were at our house. [*Turns to the company.*] I heard that little baggage say she loved her old father, and would die to make him happy! Oh! how I loved the little baggage!—And you talked very prudently, young man. I have inquired into your character, and find you to be a man of punctuality and mind the main chance. And so, as you love Mary, and Mary loves you, you shall have my consent immediately to be married. I'll settle my fortune on you, and go and live with you the remainder of my life.

MANLY. Sir, I hope—

VAN ROUGH. Come, come, no fine speeches; mind the main chance, young man, and you and I shall always agree.

LETITIA. I sincerely wish you joy

[*advancing to* Maria]; and hope your pardon for my conduct.

Maria. I thank you for your congratulations, and hope we shall at once forget the wretch who has given us so much disquiet, and the trouble that he has occasioned.

Charlotte. And I, my dear Maria,—how shall I look up to you for forgiveness? I, who, in the practice of the meanest arts, have violated the most sacred rights of friendship? I can never forgive myself, or hope charity from the world, but I confess I have much to hope from such a brother! and I am happy that I may soon say, such a sister.—

Maria. My dear, you distress me; you have all my love.

Manly. And mine.

Charlotte. If repentance can entitle me to forgiveness, I have already much merit; for I despise the littleness of my past conduct. I now find, that the heart of any worthy man cannot be gained by invidious attacks upon the rights and characters of others;—by countenancing the addresses of a thousand;—or that the finest assemblage of features, the greatest taste in dress, the genteelest address, or the most brilliant wit, cannot eventually secure a coquette from contempt and ridicule.

Manly. And I have learned that probity, virtue, honour, though they should not have received the polish of Europe, will secure to an honest American the good graces of his fair countrywoman, and, I hope, the applause of The Public.

[curtain]

(1786) 1790

II. HUGH HENRY BRACKENRIDGE (1748–1816)

From *MODERN CHIVALRY*

Volume I, Book I

CHAPTER I

[CAPTAIN FARRAGO]

John Farrago was a man of about fifty-three years of age, of good natural sense, and considerable reading; but in some things whimsical, owing perhaps to his greater knowledge of books than of the world; but, in some degree, also, to his having never married, being what they call an old batchelor, a characteristic of which is, usually, singularity and whim. He had the advantage of having had in early life, an academic education; but having never applied himself to any of the learned professions, he had lived the greater part of his life on a small farm, which he cultivated with servants or hired hands, as he could conveniently supply himself with either. The servant that he had at this time, was an Irishman, whose name was Teague Oregan. I shall say nothing of the character of this man, because the very name imports what he was.

A strange idea came into the head of Captain Farrago about this time; for, by the bye, I had forgot to mention that having been chosen captain of a company of militia in the neighbourhood, he had gone by the name of Captain ever since; for the rule is, once a captain, and always a captain; but, as I was observing, the idea had come in to his head, to saddle an old horse that he had, and ride about the world a little, with his man Teague at his heels, to see how things were going on here and there, and to observe human nature. For it is a mistake to suppose, that a man cannot learn man by reading him in a corner, as well as on the widest space of transaction. At any rate, it may yield amusement. * * *

1792

Volume II, Book I

CHAPTER I

[AN ELECTION]

Rising early next morning, the Captain proceeded, with his man Teague, on his journey, and having breakfasted at an inn, where nothing material happened, we shall pass it over, and come as far down in the day as eleven o'clock; tho', by the bye, it might have been more correct to have said up in the day, because the sun rises until twelve o'clock, and then descends: But waving this nicety, we shall go on to relate what actually took place. A man was seen before them, driving, leisurely, a horse with two kegs upon his back. The Captain took him for what is called a pack-horse man, that was carrying salt or sugar to some place of market. A man of a philosophic turn of mind never hesitates to enter into conversation with any character; because human nature is the field whence he gathers thoughts and expressions. The Captain therefore accosting this man, said, Is it salt or molasses you have in your kegs, countryman? You are going home from some store, I suppose, where you have purchased; or going to set up a small store of your own, and vend goods. No, said the man, with a Scotch-Irish pronunciation, there is an election this day a little way before us, and I am setting up for the legislature, and have these two kegs of whisky to give a dram to the voters. The Captain was thrown into a reverie of thought, and began to reflect with himself on the nature of a republican government, where canvassing by such means as this, can work so great an evil as to elevate the most unqualified persons to the highest deliberative assemblies. But, in the mean time, roused a little from his thought, he had presence of mind to recollect the danger in which he was about to be involved afresh with his man Teague; whom, now looking round, he saw to be about forty yards behind him. It would have been adviseable to have diverted from the road, and taken a circuitous rout, to avoid the election ground. But as the devil, or some worse being, would have it, it was a lane in which they were, with a fence on each side; so that he could not divert without leaping like a fox-hunter, or one of your light-horse men, to which the sober nag on which he rode was not competent. Besides, if Teague did not leap after him he would be left exposed in the lane to the populace, who might solicit him to be their representative. To turn directly back would appear indecorous, and unless he could drive Teague on before him, which was not customary, and to which he might not, all at once submit, his station would of course be the rear, where he might be picked up as a straggler, and sent to some public body.

In this quandary of thought, looking up, he saw the breakers just a-head; that is, the people met for the purpose of electing, and that it was now impossible to avoid them. Depending, therefore, on his own address, to make the best of circumstances, he suffered himself to be carried along towards them, keeping, in the meantime, an eye upon Teague, who was the cause of his concern.

Meeting accidentally with a Scotch gentleman on the ground, whom he knew, he communicated to him the delicacy of his situation, and the apprehensions he had on the part of Teague. Said the Scotch gentleman, Ye need na gie your sel any trouble on that head, man; for I sal warrant the man wi the twa kegs will carry the elaction: there is na resisting guid liquor; it has an unco effec on the judgment in the choice of a representative. The man that has a distillery or twa in our country, canna want suffrages. He has his votaries about him like ane o' the Heathen gods, and because the fluid exhilerates the brain, they think he maun be a deity that makes it; and they fa' down, especially when they have drank ower muckle, and worship him, just as at the shrine of Apollo or Bacchus, among the ancients.

The candidate that opposed the man of the two kegs, was a person of gravity and years, and said to be of good sense and experience in facts. The judgment of the people was in his favour, but their appetite leaned against him.

There is a story of one Manlius, a Roman, who had saved the capitol from the Gauls, by putting his breast to the rampart, and throwing them down as they ascended. When this man afterwards, elated with the honours paid him, forgot the duties of a citizen, wishing to subvert the republic, by usurping the power of a tyrant, the people, jealous of liberty, were incensed; and being convicted of the crime, he was dragged to punishment. It was not the way, at that time, to hang, as you would a dog; or behead, as you would a wild beast: but to throw from a high rock, which they called the Tarpeian. The capitol was just in view, and while they were dragging him along to the place, he would stretch his hand to this; as much as to say, There, O Romans, I saved you: The populace at this would stop a while, irresolute whether to desist or drag him on. While they recollected his offence, they marched a step; but when they cast their eye on the capitol, they stood still; and not until some principal men directed the rout out of the view of the capitol, could he be brought to justice.

So it was with the multitude convened on this occasion, between the man with the two kegs and the grave looking person. When they looked on the one, they felt an inclination to promote him. But when again on the other hand, they saw two kegs which they knew to be replenished with a very chearing liquor, they seemed to be inclined in favour of the other.

But appetite prevailed, and they gave their votes in favour of the man with the two kegs.

Teague in the mean time thinking he had another chance of being a great man, had been busy, but to no purpose; for the people gave their votes to the man of the two kegs. The Captain thought himself fortunate to be thus relieved, and proceeded on his journey.

Volume II, Book IV

CHAPTER I

[ANOTHER ELECTION]

The insuing day, the Captain arrived in a certain city, and put up at the sign of the Indian Queen. Taking a day or two to refresh himself, and get a new pair of breeches made, and his coat mended, which was a little worn at the elbows, he went to look about the city. The fourth day, when he had proposed to set out to perambulate this modern Babylon, and called for Teague to bring him his boots, there was no Teague there. The hostler being called, with whom he used to sleep, informed, that he had disappeared the day before. The Captain was alarmed; and, from the recollection of former incidents, began to enquire if there were any elections going on at that time. As it so happened, there was one that very day. Thinking it probable the bog-trotter, having still a hankering after an appointment might offer himself on that occasion, he set out to the place where the people were convened, to see if he could discover Teague amongst the candidates. He could see nothing of him; and though he made enquiry, he could hear no account. But the circumstance of the election drawing his attention for some time, he forgot Teague.

The candidates were all remarkably pot-bellied; and waddled in their gait. The Captain enquiring what were the pretensions of these men to be elected; he was told, that they had all stock in the funds, and lived in large brick buildings; and some of them entertained fifty people at a time, and eat and drank abundantly; and, living an easy life, and pampering their appetites, they had swollen to this size.

It is a strange thing, said the Captain, that in the country, in my route, they would elect no one but a weaver, or a whisky distiller; and here none but fat swabs, that guzzle wine, and smoke segars. It was not so in Greece, where Phocion came with his plain coat, from his humble dwelling, and directed the counsels of the people; or in Rome, where Cincinnatus was made dictator from the plough. Something must be wrong, where the inflate, and pompous are the objects of choice. Though there is one good arising from it, that there is no danger of my Teague here. He could not afford to give a dinner; and as to funds, he has not a single shilling in them. They will make him neither mayor nor legislator in this city.

Na faith, said Mr. M'Donald, the Scotch gentleman who had been present at the embarrassment of the Captain, on the occasion of the former election; and having, a few days before, come to the city, and observing the Captain in the crowd, had come up to accost him, just as he was uttering these last words to himself: Na faith, said he, there is na danger of Teague here, unless he had his scores o' shares in the bank; and was in league with the brokers, and had a brick house at his hurdies, or a ship or twa on the stocks. A great deal used to be done, by employing advocates with the tradesmen, to listen to the news, and tell them fair stories; but all is now lost in substantial interest, and the funds command every thing. Besides, this city is swarming with Teagues, and O'Regans, and O'Brians, and O'Murphys, and O'Farrels; I see, that they cannot be at a loss without your bog trotter.

The Captain having his fears eased, in this particular, returned home, greatly troubled, nevertheless, that he could not come up with the Irishman.

Volume II, Book V

CHAPTER I

[MODERN PHILOSOPHERS]

Returning to his lodging, he could not help reflecting by the way, that probably poor Teague, mortified by repeated disappointments, in going to Congress, being suffered to preach, or be a member of the Philosophical Society; and what might afflict him still more, the not marrying the rich hostess, who had made him overtures, might, in his despair of ever coming forward in any respectable capacity in life, have suspended himself from a beam, or plunged into the river, and have put an end to his existence; which, should it be the case, being in some measure accessary to this catastrophe of the bog-trotter, by dissuading from these several pretensions, he could not acquit himself of guilt; at all events, he would feel great pain and sorrow.

Such were his reflections for a great part of this day; and had thought of putting an advertisement in the paper, to know if any dead body had been lately discovered; or inquisition held on a young man, with red hair, and a long leg, who had been missing some days, and was supposed to have hung or drowned himself. But in the evening, meditating thus, mention being made by some of the lodgers, of going to hear the annual oration, delivered before the Philosophical Society, by a member; it struck his mind, that possibly Teague, falling in with some of this body, had been induced by them to take a seat, and might be present on that occasion. Not hesitating, therefore, he seconded the proposal of going; and offered to be of the party.

Coming to the hall, the philosophers were seated; but a black member sat with a taper before him, who, it seems, was to deliver the oration.

The fact was this; A gentleman of Maryland of the name of Gorum, had sent to the society, some time before, a curiosity found by one of his negroes in the mud of Wye river, on the banks of which his seat was. It appeared to be a stone, with a cavity sufficient to receive a man's foot, and was adjudged by the society to be an Indian's petrified moccason. The singularity of the discovery, well intitling the gentleman to a seat, he was invited; but sending his compliments, he gave them to understand, that Cuff, (for that was the name of the negro) was more intitled to that honour than he was, being the person who had found the curiosity; and as he made it a point to do his slaves justice in any perquisite of their own, he could not think of robbing one, on this occasion of any honour, to which he might be introduced by this discovery.

The society approved his honesty, and fair dealing; and by unanimous ballot, admitted the negro; who, having been a member some time, had been appointed, to pronounce the annual oration. Cuff, a good deal disconcerted in hearing of the task imposed upon him, had applied to his master to know what to say. Colonel Gorum attending a good deal to literary matters, had heard of an oration delivered before the society, the object of which was to prove that the Africans had been once white, had sharp noses, and long hair; but that by living in sun-burnt climates, the skin had changed colour, the hair become frizzled, and in the course of generation, the imagination of the mother, presenting obtuse objects, had produced an offspring with flat noses. He therefore gave Cuff to understand, that it would be doing no more than justice to his countrymen, for he was a Guinea negro, if he should avail himself of this occasion to prove that men were all once black, and that by living in snowy countries, and being bleached by the weather, the skin had gradually become white, and the hair moist and long, and the imagination presenting prominent objects to the mothers, or the fathers differing among themselves, and pulling one another by this part, had given the long and pointed nose.

Cuff, thus prepared, set out; having arrived, and being on this occasion to harangue, began as follows:

THE ORATION

Massa shentiman; I be cash crab in de Wye riva: found ting in de mud; tone, big a man's foot: hols like to he; fetch Massa: Massa say, it be de Indian moccason.—O! fat de call it; all tone. He say, you be a filasafa, Cuff: I say, O no, Massa; you be de filasafa. Wel; two tree monts afta, Massa call me, and say, You be a filasafa, Cuff, fo' sartan: Getta ready, and go dis city, and make grate peech for shentima filasafa. I say, Fat say? Massa: Massa say, somebody say, dat de first man was de fite man; but you say, dat de first man was de black a-man. Vel, I set out: come along: Massa gi me pass. Some say, where you go, Cuff? I say, dis city, be a filasafa. O no, Cuff, you be no filasafa: call me fool, gi me kick i' de backside; fall down; get up again, and come to dis city.

Now, shentima, I say, dat de first man was de black a man, and de first woman de black a woman; an get two tree children; de rain vasha dese, an de snow pleach, an de coula come brown, yella, coppa coula, and, at de last, quite fite; an de hair long; an da fal out vid van anoda; and van cash by de nose, an pull; so de nose come lang, sharp nose.

Now I go home, Massa shentima; an tel grate Massa, dat make peech, an ibedy body vas da; an den Cuff fin a more tings—cabs, oysta, cat-fish, bones, tones, ibedy ting; sen to you, shentima.

The oration being ended, the Society could do no less than appoint a committee to wait on Mr. Cuff, and request a copy of his oration, that it might be published.

But the Captain, in the mean time, had examined, with great attention, the whole audience; but could not discover Teague. Departing, therefore, with the rest, his thoughts recurred to his first idea, viz. that the unfortunate creature had committed suicide. Drawing up, therefore, an advertisement, he sent it to a daily paper; but, though it appeared next morning, and the day elapsed, there was no word of Teague.

CHAPTER III

[A CONVERSION]

As I have said, the day passed over, and there was no word of Teague. In the evening, as it was usual with the gentlemen at the Indian Queen, to go to some place for the amusement of an hour or two; mention being made of a celebrated preacher, a Universalist, as he was called; that is, one who preaches the doctrine of universal salvation; it was proposed to go to hear him, as he was to hold forth that evening. The Captain readily consented; and it struck him, that, as this was a new fangled doctrine, and the preacher had made a great noise; and as it was a doctrine that, conscious of a good deal of fornication, would naturally please Teague, it was not impossible but the Irishman might have become a disciple of this reformist, and be at his conventicle.

Coming in amongst the crowd, and obtaining seats, they saw the preacher ascend the pulpit, and, after the preliminary exercise of psalms and prayer, take a text, and begin his sermon.

His text was taken from one of those passages of scripture, which speaks of "the lion lying down with the kid, and the tyger with the lamb;" which have been interpreted of the Millenium; but were applied by him, to that period, when, as the sea shall give up her dead, so hell shall give up her damned; and the devil himself shall come to lick salt out of the hand of an angel.

Enlarging on this doctrine, and supporting it with a variety of proofs from scripture, and arguments from reason, he seemed to have brought the matter to a point; answering all objections, and closing in with the hearer. At this stage, using that figure of oratory, which is usual in the pulpit, of asking questions, and pressing for an answer, but expecting none; he would say, Is not this conclusive? Is it not evident? Is there any here can advance an argument against it? Will any of you speak—I pause for an answer?

Mr. M'Donald, in the mean time, (the Scotch gentleman; who happened to be there,) thinking him really serious, and that he wanted an answer; or taking advantage of the pause, and the interrogation, to speak his mind, leaning over the front of a back seat, made reply:

Why, said he, I like the doctrine well enough, and ha' na' disposition to o'er throw it. I dinna muckle care if there ware na' hell ava. If ye could make that out, I wad rather hear it, than o' being smoaked twa' or three thousand years in the devil's nuke, or singed wi' his burnt brimstone, even if we should get out afterwards. Ye need na' put yoursel in a passion, or be flee'd that you'll no get proselytes; for I shall warrant you, as many every night as ye can weel stow awa i' the conventicle.

The preacher giving thanks to God for the success in his ministry, in the remarkable conversion of the man who spoke, the Scotch gentleman said again; Ye need na ca' it a conversion; for I ha' been o' the same opinion a' my life; that it was a rare thing to bide the kiln of hell, and they wad deserve muckle thanks wha could establish that we should na' stay long in it, or that there was na' such place ava.

The preacher commenting upon this,

observed that some were orthodox from their birth, like Jeremiah, who was sanctified in his mother's womb; but others were hardly brought to the truth, with much teaching and instruction. That the present was a happy instance of one who was in the right way from his very early years.

The Captain in the mean time, had been thinking of the doctrine; and thought it reasonable to suppose, that the Almighty might relieve after some time, and let the damned devils go. Just as with himself at present in the case of Teague; if he had got his hands on the bog-trotter, he could not help being very angry, and would be disposed to punish him with great severity; but after some time he knew his passion would subside, and he would forget his delinquencies.

Teague in this manner running in his head, as the people, after some epilogue of prayer and benediction, being dismissed, were retiring, he got up, and raising his voice, begged the audience to detain a little.— Good people, said he, if any of you should come across a young man, a servant of mine, of the name of Teague O'Regan, I shall thank you to send me notice to the Indian Queen, where I lodge. And, according to the advertisement in this day's paper, I will give two dollars reward.

Thinking him deranged in his brain, they proceeded, and took no notice of the proclamation.

CHAPTER IV

CONTAINING OBSERVATIONS

In the infancy of Christianity it was thought a hard matter to get to heaven; and that when once in hell, there was no geting out. A certain father of the church, of the name of Origen, was the first to be more liberal in his sentiments, and thought, that after a certain period, there would be a jail-delivery of the damned. I do not know that he went so far as to let the devils themselves out upon a furlough; but at the present time, we all know very well, that the time will come, when they will be out all together; at least the universalists tell us this, and prove it.

The doctrine was received in some part by the early councils; but in other parts rejected. The matter was compounded by establishing a purgatory; for not consenting to liberate from hell, in order to satisfy the advocates of a temporary punishment, they fixed up a middle place, where all the advantages of penal purgation could be enjoyed, without the necessity of contradicting the eternity of hell torments.

Indeed under the catholic church, the *strait gate,* and *the narrow way,* and the *many called, and few chosen,* was a good deal laid aside, and the road made pretty plain by indulgencies and absolutions. But at the reformation, the matter was brought back to its old bed again, and the cry of their being but a *remnant* saved, was raised in every pulpit. There has been some relaxation of late years with almost every sect of Protestants; and there is not just such a fury of tumbling great crowds into the tolbooth, as there was in the days of John Knox, and the framers of the Westminster confession of faith, and catechisms. Dr. Bellamy, a New-England divine, some years ago, stated in his pamphlet, that the damned would be to the saved, as the malefactors of a country to honest people that came to an untimely end by jail or gibbet. Some now preach boldly, not perhaps a total exemption, from future punishment, but a final restoration from it; so that the matter is now brought nearly to what it was in the days of Origen. I do not know that I would be of opinion with the Scotch gentleman, and wish the matter carried farther, establishing that there is no hell at all; because if the thing should take a turn, it might go to the other extreme, and be all hell; so that none should be saved; and instead of universal salvation, we should then have the doctrine of the damnation of the whole, bodily.

1792

CHAPTER V

[A CONGRESSIONAL DEBATE]

The next day, revolving every thing in his mind, it occurred to the Captain, that the Irishman might have gone out of town, hearing of an election at a district, and have been elected to Congress. As that body was then sitting, he thought it could be no great trouble to go to the house, and cast an eye from the gallery, and see if the raggamuffin had got there. There was one that had a little of the brogue of Teague upon his tongue, but nothing of his physiognomy; others had a good deal of his manner; but there was none that came absolutely up to the physic of his person.

However, being here, the Captain tho't it not amiss to listen a while to the debates upon the carpet. A certain bill was depending, and made, it seems, the order of the day. Mr. Cogan being on the floor, spoke:—Sir, said he, addressing himself to the chair, the bill in contemplation, is, in my opinion, of a dangerous tendency. I will venture to foretel, that, if it goes into a law, the cows will have fewer calves, and the sheep less wool; hens will lay fewer eggs, and cocks forget to crow daylight. The horses will be worse shod, and stumble more; our watches go too slow; corns grow upon our toes; young women have the stomach ach; old men the gout; and middle aged persons fainting fits. The larks will fall dead in the field; the frogs croak till they burst their bags; and the leaves of the trees fall before the autumn. Snow will be found in the heat of harvest, and dog days in winter. The rivers will revert; and the shadows fall to the east in the morning. The moon will be eclipsed; and the equinoxes happen at a wrong season of the year. Was it not such a bill as this, that changed the old stile; that made the eclipse in the time of Julius Cesar; that produced an earthquake at Jamaica, and sunk Port Royal? All history, both ancient and modern, is full of the mischiefs of such a bill. I shall, therefore, vote against it.

Mr. Bogan was now on the floor, and advocated the good effects of the bill.

Sir, said he, addressing himself to the chair, I appear in support of the bill. I say, it will have a good effect on the physical world especially. The ducks will be fatter, the geese heavier, the swans whiter, the red-birds sing better, and partridges come more easily into traps. It will kill rats, muzzle calves, and cut colts; and multiply the breed of oysters, and pickle cod-fish. It will moderate the sun's heat, and the winter's cold; prevent fogs, and cure the ague. It will help the natural brain; brace the nerves, cure sore eyes, and the cholic, and remove rheumatisms. Consult experience, and it will be found, that provisions of the nature proposed by this bill, have an astonishing influence in this respect, where they have been tried. I must take the liberty to say, the gentleman's allegations are totally *unfounded;* and he has *committed* himself, in the matter of his history; the earthquake in Jamaica, not happening in the time of Julius Cesar; and therefore could have nothing to do with the eclipse of the sun. I shall, therefore, vote in favour of the bill.

Mr. Cogan rose to explain; and said, that he did not say, that the earthquake at Jamaica, was at the same time with the eclipse of the sun, which happened at the birth of Julius Cesar.

Mr. Bogan rose to correct the gentleman: it was not at the birth of Julius Cesar, but at his death, that the earthquake happened.

Mr. Hogan was on the floor: Said, he thought he could reconcile the gentlemen on that head. It was well known Julius Cesar lived about the time of the rebellion in Scotland; a little after Nebuchadnezzar, king of the Jews. As to the earthquake, he did not remember what year it happened; and therefore could say nothing about it.

At this period, the question being called, it was put, and carried by a majority of 25.

The Captain, satisfied with this sample of Congressional debates, retired, and came to his lodging.

CHAPTER VI

[GREEK AND IRISH]

It was about three or four o'clock in the afternoon, that some one, who had read the advertisement respecting Teague, came to the Captain, and informed him, that a person, answering the description, had been lately employed to teach Greek in the University. Struck with the idea, that the bog-trotter might have passed himself for a Greek scholar, whereas he understood only Irish, he set out to the University, to make enquiry. Knocking at the door of the principal, he was admitted; and, being seated, addressed him as follows: Said he, sir, a pedeseque of mine, (for talking to the rector of a college, he did not chuse to use the vulgar terms, waiter, or bog-trotter,) a pedeseque of mine, whom I have found useful, save that he is somewhat troublesome in pretending to places of appointment for which he is not qualified; a thing, by the bye, too common in this country; where men, without the aid of academic knowledge, thrust themselves into places requiring great learning and ability: (This he said to flatter the man of letters; as if a man could know but little, that had not been forged or furbished at his school): I say, this pedeseque of mine, has absconded for some days; and I have been able to collect no account of him until last evening, that a person, having read an advertisement of mine in the gazette, came to me, and informed, that one, answering the description I had given, both as to appearance and accomplishments, had been lately employed, as professor of the Greek language, in this University. Now, though I well know this Pady, as I may call him, to understand no Greek; yet, as he speaks Irish, and has much assurance, and little honesty in matters where his ambition is concerned, I did not know, but he might have imposed himself upon you, for a Greek scholar, and obtained a professorship.

The principal made answer, that it was true that a person from Ireland had been lately employed in that capacity; and that should he be discovered to be an impostor, it would be using the university very ill. The Captain thought so too; and taking it for granted that it was Teague, expressed his surprise that they had not examined him, before he was admitted; or at least had such proof by letters as would have had ascertained his being qualified. The principal observed, that as to examination they had no one at hand to examine, as there were none of the trustees or professors of other branches in the university understood Greek; as for himself he did not, having not studied it in early life, and for a series of years, having giving himself to politics and mathematics; so that unless they could send out for a Roman Catholic priest, or a Scotch clergyman, there was none to examine. The improbability of any person passing himself, above all things, for a master of the Greek language on the score of understanding Irish, was such, that it never came into their heads to suspect it, so as to demand letters.

Had you known said the Captain, this bog-trotter of mine, (here he forgot the word pedeseque) as well as I do, you would not be surprised at his attempting any thing; and that he should be now in your academy giving Greek lectures, understanding nothing but the vernacular tongue of his own country. Here he gave an account of his setting up for Congress, &c. as explained in the preceding part of this narrative.

However, wishing to see the ragga-muffin that he might unkennel him, he was accompanied by the principal to the chamber of the pseudo professor, considering as he went along, in what manner he should accost him; whether he should break out upon him with a direct invective, or with ironical words; such as, Mr. Professor, you must be a very learned man, not only to understand Irish, but Greek: but perhaps the Greek and Irish language are much the same. It must be so; for I know that a few days ago, you did not understand a word of this, and to acquire a dead language in such a short time would be impossible, unless the living tongue was a good deal a-kin to it. But I had never understood that Irish had any more affinity to the language of Athens and Sparta, than the Erse, or the German, or the Welch; however, we must live and learn, as the saying is; you have shewn us what we never knew before.

Conning a speech of this sort in his own mind, with a view to divert the principal, and amuse himself with Teague, he entered the chamber of the professor; who sat in an elbow chair with Thucidydes before him.

What was the surprise of the Captain to find that it was not Teague.

In fact, it was a person not wholly unlike him, especially in a hinge of the brogue which he betrayed in his discourse; for though the professor was really a man of education, having been early sent to St. Omer's, where he had studied, being intended for a priest, and understood not only the Greek, and Latin, but spoke French; yet in the pronunciation of the English tongue, he had that prolongation of the sound of a word, and articulation of the vowel O, which constitutes what is vulgarly called the brogue, as being the pronunciation of the native Irish; who being a depressed people, are most of them poor, and wear a kind of mean shoe, which they call a brogue.

After an apology to the professor for mistaking him for a certain Teague O'Regan, whom he had in his employment, at the request of the professor, the principal and the Captain took seats.

The professor said, his name was not O'Regan, being O'Dougherty; but he knew the O'Regans very well in Ireland. There was a Pady O'Regan in the same class with him at St. Omer's, when he read Craike. That he was a good scholar, and understood Craike very well; and he would be glad if he was over in this country to tach Craike here; it appeared to be a very scarce language; but he had become a praste, and was now a missionary to Paraguay, in Sout-America.

The Captain punning on his pronunciation of the word Greek; and willing to amuse himself a little with the professor, could not help observing, that he was under a mistake, as to the scarceness of the Craike language in these States. That there were whole tribes who spoke the Craike language; there was that of the heron, and the raven, and several other fowls. A German professor, who was present, apprehending the Captain to be under a mistake, and willing to correct him, observed—It is, said he, the Creek language, that the professor means. As to that, said the Captain, it is also spoken plentifully in America. There is a whole nation of Indians, on the borders of South Carolina and Georgia, that speak the Creek language; men, women, and children.

The professor knowing more of the classics than of the geography of these United States, and of the heathen gods more than of the aborigines of this country, expressed astonishment. If what you tell me be a trut, said he, it is a crate discovery: perhaps dese may have de fragments o' de books o' de philosophers and poets that are lost, and de professors cannot come acrass in deir own countries; but I have tought dat de Craike language was spoke only in de Morea, and a little in Russia, and Constantinople.

The Captain assured him, the principal favouring the mistake, by a grave face, and bowing as the Captain spoke, that it was absolutely the vernacular language of these people.

Why den, said the other, do dey not get professors from amongst dese, to tache Craike in deir Colleges?

Because, said the Captain, we have been heretofore on hostile terms with these Indians; and it is but of late that we have made a peace. But now, it is to be presumed, we shall have it in our power to procure from them able teachers.

The professor was alarmed at this; as supposing it would supercede the necessity of his services; or, at least, much reduce the price of his tuition. He could have wished he had not come to this quarter of the world; and was almost ready, in his own mind, to bind up what he had, and go back to Clogher.

So ended their visit to the University, and the Captain withdrew.

1792

III. SUSANNA HASWELL ROWSON (1762–1824)

CHARLOTTE TEMPLE

[THE ELOPEMENT OF CHARLOTTE]

Chapter I

A BOARDING SCHOOL

"Are you for a walk," said Montraville to his companion, as they arose from table; "are you for a walk? or shall we order the chaise and proceed to Portsmouth?" Belcour preferred the former; and they sauntered out to view the town, and to make remarks on the inhabitants, as they returned from church.

Montraville was a Lieutenant in the army: Belcour was his brother officer: they had been to take leave of their friends previous to their departure for America, and were now returning to Portsmouth, where the troops waited orders for embarkation. They had stopped at Chichester to dine; and knowing they had sufficient time to reach the place of destination before dark, and yet allow them a walk, had resolved, it being Sunday afternoon, to take a survey of the Chichester ladies as they returned from their devotions.

They had gratified their curiosity, and were preparing to return to the inn without honouring any of the belles with particular notice, when Madame Du Pont, at the head of her school, descended from the church. Such an assemblage of youth and innocence naturally attracted the young soldiers: they stopped; and, as the little cavalcade passed, almost involuntarily pulled off their hats. A tall, elegant girl looked at Montraville and blushed: he instantly recollected the features of Charlotte Temple, whom he had once seen and danced with at a ball at Portsmouth. At that time he thought on her only as a very lovely child, she being then only thirteen; but the improvement two years had made in her person, and the blush of recollection which suffused her cheeks as she passed, awakened in his bosom new and pleasing ideas. Vanity led him to think that pleasure at again beholding him might have occasioned the emotion he had witnessed, and the same vanity led him to wish to see her again.

"She is the sweetest girl in the world," said he, as he entered the inn. Belcour stared. "Did you not notice her?" continued Montraville: "she had on a blue bonnet, and with a pair of lovely eyes of the same colour, has contrived to make me feel devilish odd about the heart."

"Poh," said Belcour, "a musket-ball from our friends, the Americans, may in less than two months make you feel worse."

"I never think of the future," replied Montraville; "but am determined to make the most of the present, and would willingly compound with any kind Familiar who would inform me who the girl is, and how I might be likely to obtain an interview."

But no kind Familiar at that time appearing, and the chaise which they had ordered, driving up to the door, Montraville and his companion were obliged to take leave of Chichester and its fair inhabitant, and proceed on their journey.

But Charlotte had made too great an impression on his mind to be easily eradicated: having therefore spent three whole days in thinking on her and in endeavouring to form some plan for seeing her, he determined to set off for Chichester, and trust to chance either to favour or frustrate his designs. Arriving at the verge of the town, he dismounted, and sending the servant forward with the horses, proceeded toward the place, where, in the midst of an extensive pleasure ground, stood the mansion which contained the lovely Charlotte Temple. Montraville leaned on a broken gate, and looked earnestly at the house. The wall which surrounded it was high, and perhaps the Argus's who guarded the Hesperian fruit within, were more watchful than those famed of old.

" 'Tis a romantic attempt," said he; "and should I even succeed in seeing and conversing with her, it can be productive of no good: I must of necessity leave England in a few days, and probably may never return; why then should I endeavour to engage the affections of this lovely girl, only to leave her a prey to a thousand inquietudes, of which at present she has no idea? I will return to Portsmouth and think no more about her."

The evening now was closed; a serene stillness reigned; and the chaste Queen of Night with her silver crescent faintly illuminated the hemisphere. The mind of Montraville was hushed into composure by the serenity of the surrounding objects. "I will think on her no more," said he, and turned with an intention to leave the place; but as he turned, he saw the gate which led to the pleasure grounds open, and two women come out, who walked arm-in-arm across the field.

"I will at least see who these are," said he. He overtook them, and giving them the compliments of the evening, begged leave to see them into the more frequented parts of the town: but how was he delighted, when, waiting for an answer, he discovered, under the concealment of a large bonnet, the face of Charlotte Temple.

He soon found means to ingratiate himself with her companion, who was a French teacher at the school, and, at parting, slipped a letter he had purposely written, into Charlotte's hand, and five guineas into that of Mademoiselle, who promised she would endeavour to bring her young charge into the field again the next evening.
* * *

Chapter IX

WE KNOW NOT WHAT A DAY MAY BRING FORTH

Various were the sensations which agitated the mind of Charlotte, during the day preceding the evening in which she was to meet Montraville. Several times did she almost resolve to go to her governess, show her the letter, and be guided by her advice: but Charlotte had taken one step in the ways of imprudence; and when that is once done, there are always innumerable obstacles to prevent the erring person returning to the path of rectitude: yet these obstacles, however forcible they may appear in general, exist chiefly in imagination.

Charlotte feared the anger of her governess: she loved her mother, and the very idea of incurring her displeasure, gave her the greatest uneasiness; but there was a more forcible reason still remaining: should she show the letter to Madame Du Pont, she must confess the means by which it came into her possession; and what would be the consequences? Mademoiselle would be turned out of doors.

"I must not be ungrateful," said she, "La Rue is very kind to me; besides I can, when I see Montraville, inform him of the impropriety of our continuing to see or correspond with each other, and request him to come no more to Chichester."

However prudent Charlotte might be in these resolutions, she certainly did not take a proper method to confirm herself in them. Several times in the course of the day, she indulged herself in reading over the letter, and each time she read it, the contents sunk deeper into her heart. As evening drew near, she caught herself frequently consulting her watch. "I wish this foolish meeting was over," said she, by way of apology to her own heart, "I wish it was over; for when I have seen him, and convinced him my resolution is not to be shaken, I shall feel my mind much easier."

The appointed hour arrived. Charlotte and Mademoiselle eluded the eye of vigilance; and Montraville who had waited their coming with impatience, received them with rapturous and unbounded acknowledgements for their condescension: he had wisely brought Belcour with him to entertain Mademoiselle, while he enjoyed an uninterrupted conversation with Charlotte.

Belcour was a man whose character might be comprised in a few words; and as he will make some figure in the ensuing pages, I shall here describe him. He possessed a genteel fortune, and had a liberal education; dissipated, thoughtless, and capricious, he paid little regard to the moral duties, and less to religious ones: eager in the pursuit of pleasure, he minded not the miseries he inflicted on others, provided his own wishes, however, extravagant, were gratified. Self, daring self, was the idol he worshipped, and to that he would have sacrificed the interest and happiness of all mankind. Such was the friend of Montraville: will not the reader be ready to imagine, that the man who could regard such a character, must be actuated by the same feelings, follow the same pursuits, and be equally unworthy with the person to whom he thus gave his confidence?

But Montraville was a different character: generous in his disposition, liberal in his opinions, and good natured almost to a fault; yet eager and impetuous in the pursuit of a favourite object, he staid not to reflect on the consequence which might follow the attainment of his wishes; with a mind ever open to conviction, had he been so fortunate as to possess a friend who would have pointed out the cruelty of endeavouring to gain the heart of an innocent artless girl, when he knew it was utterly impossible for him to marry her, and when the gratification of his passion would be unavoidable infamy and misery to her, and a cause of neverceasing remorse to himself: had these dreadful consequences been placed before him in a proper light, the humanity of his nature would have urged him to give up the pursuit: but Belcour was not this friend; he rather encouraged the growing passion of Montraville; and being pleased with the vivacity of Mademoiselle, resolved to leave no argument untried, which he thought might prevail on her to be the companion of their intended voyage; and he made no doubt but her example, added to the rhetoric of Montraville, would persuade Charlotte to go with them.

Charlotte had, when she went out to meet Montraville, flattered herself that her resolution was not to be shaken, and that, conscious of the impropriety of her conduct in having a clandestine intercourse with a stranger, she would never repeat the indiscretion.

But alas! poor Charlotte, she knew not the deceitfulness of her own heart, or she would have avoided the trial of her stability.

Montraville was tender, eloquent, ardent, and yet respectful. "Shall I not see you once more," said he, "before I leave England? will you not bless me by an assurance that when we are divided by a vast expanse of sea I shall not be forgotten?"

Charlottle sighed.

"Why that sigh, my dear Charlotte? could I flatter myself that a fear for my safety, or a wish for my welfare occasioned it, how happy would it make me."

"I shall ever wish you well, Montraville," said she; "but we must meet no more."

"Oh, say not so, my lovely girl: reflect, that when I leave my native land, perhaps a few short weeks may terminate my existence; the perils of the ocean—the dangers of war—"

"I can hear no more," said Charlotte in a tremulous voice. "I must leave you."

"Say you will see me once again."

"I dare not," said she.

"Only for one half hour to-morrow evening: 'tis my last request, I shall never trouble you again, Charlotte."

"I know not what to say," cried Charlotte, struggling to draw her hands from him: "let me leave you now."

"And you will come to-morrow," said Montraville.

"Perhaps I may," said she.

"Adieu then, I will live upon that hope till we meet again."

He kissed her hand. She sighed an adieu, and catching hold of Mademoiselle's arm, hastily entered the garden gate.

Chapter XI

CONFLICT OF LOVE AND DUTY

Almost a week was now gone, and Charlotte continued every evening to meet Montraville, and in her heart every meeting was resolved to be the last; but alas! when Montraville at parting would earnestly intreat one more interview, that treacherous heart betrayed her; and, forgetful of its resolution, pleaded the cause of the enemy so powerfully, that Charlotte was unable to resist. Another and another meeting succeeded; and so well did Montraville improve each opportunity, that the heedless girl at length confessed no idea could be so painful to her as that of never seeing him again.

"Then we will never be parted," said he.

"Ah, Montraville," replied Charlotte, forcing a smile, "how can it be avoided! My parents would never consent to our union; and even could they be brought to approve it, how could I bear to be separated from my kind, my beloved mother?"

"Then you love your parents more than you do me, Charlotte!"

"I hope I do," said she, blushing and looking down. "I hope my affection for them will ever keep me from infringing the laws of filial duty."

"Well, Charlotte," said Montraville gravely, and letting go her hand, "since that is the case, I find I have deceived myself with fallacious hopes. I had flattered my fond heart, that I was dearer to Charlotte than any thing in the world beside. I thought that you would for my sake have braved the dangers of the ocean, that you would, by your affection and smiles, have softened the hardships of war, and, had it been my fate to fall, that your tenderness would cheer the hour of death, and smooth my passage to another world. But farewell, Charlotte! I see you never loved me. I shall now welcome the friendly ball that deprives me of the sense of my misery."

"Oh stay, unkind Montraville," cried she, catching hold of his arm, as he pretended to leave her, "stay, and to calm your fears, I will here protest that was it not for the fear of giving pain to the best of parents, and returning their kindness with ingratitude, I would follow you through every danger, and, in studying to promote your happiness, insure my own. But I cannot break my mother's heart, Montraville; I must not bring the grey hairs of my doating grand-father with sorrow to the grave, or make my beloved father perhaps curse the hour that gave me birth." She covered her face with her hands, and burst into tears.

"All these distressing scenes, my dear Charlotte," cried Montraville, "are merely the chimeras of a disturbed fancy. Your parents might perhaps grieve at first; but when they heard from your own hand that you was with a man of honour, and that it was to insure your felicity by an union with him, to which you feared they would never have given their assent, that you left their protection, they will, be assured, forgive an error which love alone occasioned, and when we return from America, receive you with open arms and tears of joy."

Belcour and Mademoiselle heard this last speech, and conceiving it a proper time to throw in their advice and persuasions, approached Charlotte, and so well seconded the intreaties of Montraville, that finding Mademoiselle intended going with Belcour, and feeling her own treacherous heart too much inclined to accompany them, the hapless Charlotte, in an evil hour, consented that the next evening they should bring a chaise to the end of the town, and that she would leave her friends, and throw herself entirely on the protection of Montraville. "But should you," said she, looking earnestly at him, her eyes full of tears, "should you, forgetful of your promises, and repenting the engagements you here voluntarily enter into, forsake and leave me on a foreign shore—"

"Judge not so meanly of me," said he. "The moment we reach our place of destination, Hymen shall sanctify our love; and when I shall forget your goodness, may heaven forget me."

"Ah," said Charlotte, leaning on Mademoiselle's arm as they walked up the garden together, "I have forgot all that I ought to have remembered, in consenting to this intended elopement."

"You are a strange girl," said Mademoiselle: "you never know your own mind two minutes at a time. Just now you declared Montraville's happiness was what you prized most in the world; and now I suppose you repent having insured that happiness by agreeing to accompany him abroad."

"Indeed I do repent," replied Charlotte, "from my soul: but while discretion points out the impropriety of my conduct, inclination urges me on to ruin."

"Ruin! fiddlestick!" said Mademoiselle; "am not I going with you? and do I feel any of these qualms?"

"You do not renounce a tender father and mother," said Charlotte.

"But I hazard my dear reputation," replied Mademoiselle, bridling.

"True," replied Charlotte, "but you do not feel what I do." She then bade her good night: but sleep was a stranger to her eyes, and the tear of anguish watered her pillow.

Chapter XII

[The Assignation]

Nature's last, best gift:
Creature in whom excell'd, whatever could
To sight or thought be nam'd!
Holy, divine! good, amiable, and sweet!
How thou art fall'n!—

When Charlotte left her restless bed, her languid eye and pale cheek discovered to Madam Du Pont the little repose she had tasted.

"My dear child," said the affectionate governess, "what is the cause of the langour so apparent in your frame? Are you not well?"

"Yes, my dear Madam, very well," replied Charlotte, attempting to smile, "but I know not how it was; I could not sleep last night, and my spirits are depressed this morning."

"Come, chear up, my love," said the governess; "I believe I have brought a cordial to revive them. I have just received a letter from your good mama, and here is one for yourself."

Charlotte hastily took the letter: it contained these words—

As to-morrow is the anniversary of the happy day that gave my beloved girl to the anxious wishes of a maternal heart, I have requested your governess to let you come home and spend it with us; and as I know you to be a good affectionate child, and make it your study to improve in those branches of education which you know will give most pleasure to your delighted parents, as a reward for your diligence and attention I have prepared an agreeable surprize for your reception. Your grand father, eager to embrace the darling of his aged heart, will come in the chaise for you; so hold yourself in readiness to attend him by nine o'clock. Your dear father joins in every tender wish for your health and future felicity, which warms the heart of my dear Charlotte's affectionate mother.

L. Temple.

"Gracious heaven!" cried Charlotte, forgetting where she was, and raising her streaming eyes as in earnest supplication.

Madame Du Pont was surprised. "Why these tears, my love?" said she. "Why this seeming agitation? I thought the letter would have rejoiced, instead of distressing you."

"It does rejoice me," replied Charlotte, endeavouring at composure, "but I was praying for merit to deserve the unremitted attentions of the best of parents."

"You do right," said Madame Du Pont, "to ask the assistance of heaven that you may continue to deserve their love. Continue, my dear Charlotte, in the course you have ever pursued, and you will insure at once their happiness and your own."

"Oh!" cried Charlotte, as her governess left her, "I have forfeited both for ever! Yet let me reflect:—The irrevocable step is not yet taken: it is not too late to recede from the brink of a precipice, from which I can only behold the dark abyss of ruin, shame, and remorse!"

She arose from her seat, and flew to the apartment of La Rue. "Oh Mademoiselle!" said she. "I am snatched by a miracle from destruction! This letter has saved me: it has opened my eyes to the folly I was so near committing. I will not go, Mademoiselle; I will not wound the hearts of those dear parents who make my happiness the whole study of their lives."

"Well," said Mademoiselle, "do as you please, Miss; but pray understand that my resolution is taken, and it is not in your power to alter it. I shall meet the gentlemen at the appointed hour, and shall not be surprized at any outrage which Montraville may commit, when he finds himself disappointed. Indeed I should not be astonished, was he to come immediately here, and reproach you for your instability in the hearing of the whole school: and what will be the consequence? you will bear the odium of having formed the resolution of eloping, and every girl of spirit will laugh at your want of fortitude to put it in execution, while prudes and fools will load you with reproach and contempt. You will have lost the confidence of your parents, incurred their anger, and the scoffs of the world; and what fruit do you expect to reap from this piece of heroism (for such no doubt you think it is?) you will have the pleasure to reflect, that you have deceived the man who adores you, and whom in your heart you prefer to all other men, and that you are separated from him forever."

This eloquent harangue was given with such volubility, that Charlotte could not find an opportunity to interrupt her, or to offer a single word till the whole was finished, and then found her ideas so confused, that she knew not what to say.

At length she determined that she would go with Mademoiselle to the place of assignation, convince Montraville of the necessity of adhering to the resolution of remaining behind; assure him of her affection, and bid him adieu.

Charlotte formed this plan in her mind, and exulted in the certainty of its success. "How shall I rejoice," said she, "in this triumph of reason over inclination, and, when in the arms of my affectionate parents, lift up my soul in gratitude to heaven as I look back on the dangers I have escaped!"

The hour of assignation arrived: Mademoiselle put what money and valuables she possessed in her pocket, and advised Charlotte to do the same; but she refused; "my resolution is fixed," said she; "I will sacrifice love to duty."

Mademoiselle smiled internally; and they proceeded softly down the back stairs and out of the garden gate. Montraville and Belcour were ready to receive them.

"Now," said Montraville, taking Charlotte in his arms, "you are mine forever."

"No," said she, withdrawing from his embrace, "I am come to take an everlasting farewell."

It would be useless to repeat the conversation that here ensued; suffice it to say, that Montraville used every argument that had formerly been successful, Charlotte's resolution began to waver, and he drew her almost imperceptibly towards the chaise.

"I cannot go," said she: "cease, dear Montraville, to persuade. I must not: religion, duty, forbid."

"Cruel Charlotte," said he, "if you disappoint my ardent hopes, by all that is sacred, this hand shall put a period to my existence. I cannot—will not live without you."

"Alas! my torn heart!" said Charlotte, "how shall I act?"

"Let me direct you," said Montraville, lifting her into the chaise.

"Oh! my dear forsaken parents!" cried Charlotte.

The chaise drove off. She shrieked, and fainted into the arms of her betrayer.

1790

IV. CHARLES BROCKDEN BROWN
(1771–1810)

From *ARTHUR MERVYN*

CHAPTER XIII

[THE YELLOW FEVER]

* * * The city, we were told, was involved in confusion and panick, for a pestilential disease had begun its destructive progress. Magistrates and citizens were flying to the country. The numbers of the sick multiplied beyond all example; even in the pest affected cities of the Levant. The malady was malignant, and unsparing.

The usual occupations and amusements of life were at an end. Terror had exterminated all the sentiments of nature. Wives were deserted by husbands, and children by parents. Some had shut themselves in their houses, and debarred themselves from all communication with the rest of mankind. The consternation of others had destroyed their understanding, and their misguided steps hurried them into the midst of the danger which they had previously laboured to shun. Men were seized by this disease in the streets; passengers fled from them; entrance into their own dwellings was denied to them; they perished in the public ways.

The chambers of disease were deserted, and the sick left to die of negligence. None could be found to remove the lifeless bodies. Their remains, suffered to decay by piecemeal, filled the air with deadly exhalations, and added tenfold to the devastation.

Such was the tale, distorted and diversified a thousand ways, by the credulity and exaggeration of the tellers. At first I listened to the story with indifference or mirth. Methought it was confuted by its own extravagance. The enormity and variety of such an evil made it unworthy to be believed. I expected that every new day would detect the absurdity and fallacy of such representations. Every new day, however, added to the number of witnesses and the consistency of the tale, till, at length, it was not possible to withhold my faith.

CHAPTER XV

[THE STRICKEN CITY]

These meditations did not enfeeble my resolution, or slacken my pace. In proportion as I drew near the city, the tokens of its calamitous condition became more apparent. Every farm-house was filled with supernumerary tenants, fugitives from home; and haunting the skirts of the road, eager to detain every passenger with inquiries after news. The passengers were numerous; for the tide of emigration was by no means exhausted. Some were on foot, bearing in their countenances the tokens of their recent terror, and filled with mournful reflections on the forlornness of their state. Few had secured to themselves an asylum; some were without the means of paying for victuals or lodging for the coming night; others, who were not thus destitute, yet knew not whither to apply for entertainment, every house being already over-stocked with inhabitants, or barring its inhospitable doors at their approach.

Families of weeping mothers, and dismayed children, attended with a few pieces of indispensable furniture, were carried in vehicles of every form. The parent or husband had perished; and the price of some movable, or the pittance handed forth by public charity, had been expended to purchase the means of retiring from this theatre of disasters; though uncertain and hopeless of accommodation in the neighbouring districts.

Between these and the fugitives whom curiosity had led to the road, dialogues frequently took place, to which I was suffered to listen. From every mouth the tale of sorrow was repeated with new aggravations. Pictures of their own distress, or of that of their neighbours, were exhibited in all the hues which imagination can annex to pestilence and poverty.

My preconceptions of the evil now appeared to have fallen short of the truth. The dangers into which I was rushing seemed more numerous and imminent than I had previously imagined. I wavered not in my purpose. A panick crept to my heart, which more vehement exertions were necessary to subdue or control; but I harboured not a momentary doubt that the course which I had taken was prescribed by duty. There was no difficulty or reluctance in proceeding. All for which my efforts were demanded, was to walk in this path without tumult or alarm.

Various circumstances had hindered me from setting out upon this journey as early as was proper. My frequent pauses to listen to the narratives of travellers, contributed likewise to procrastination. The sun had nearly set before I reached the precincts of the city. I pursued the track which I had formerly taken, and entered High-street after nightfall. Instead of equipages and a throng of passengers, the voice of levity and glee, which I had formerly observed, and which the mildness of the season would, at other times, have produced, I found nothing but a dreary solitude.

The market-place, and each side of this magnificent avenue were illuminated, as before, by lamps; but between the verge of Schuylkill and the heart of the city I met not more than a dozen figures; and these were ghost-like, wrapped in cloaks, from behind which they cast upon me glances of wonder and suspicion, and, as I approached, changed their course, to avoid touching me. Their clothes were sprinkled with vinegar; and their nostrils defended from contagion by some powerful perfume.

I cast a look upon the houses, which I recollected to have formerly been, at this hour, brilliant with lights, resounding with lively voices, and thronged with busy faces. Now they were closed, above and below; dark, and without tokens of being inhabited. From the upper windows of some, a gleam sometimes fell upon the pavement I was traversing, and showed that their tenants had not fled, but were secluded or disabled.

These tokens were new, and awakened all my panicks. Death seemed to hover over this scene, and I dreaded that the floating pestilence had already lighted on my frame. I had scarcely overcome these tremors, when I approached an house, the door of which was open, and before which stood a vehicle, which I presently recognized to be an *hearse*.

The driver was seated on it. I stood still to mark his visage, and to observe the course which he proposed to take. Presently a coffin, borne by two men, issued from the house. The driver was a negro; but his companions were white. Their features were marked by ferocious indifference to danger or pity. One of them as he assisted in thrusting the coffin into the cavity provided for it, said, I'll be damned if I think the poor dog was quite dead. It wasn't the *fever* that ailed him, but the sight of the girl and her mother on the floor. I wonder how they all got into that room. What carried them there?

The other surlily muttered, Their legs, to-be-sure.

But what should they hug together in one room for?

To save us trouble, to be sure.

And I thank them with all my heart; but, damn it, it wasn't right to put him in his coffin before the breath was fairly gone. I thought the last look he gave me told me, to stay a few minutes.

Pshaw! He could not live. The sooner dead the better for him; as well as for us. Did you mark how he eyed us, when we carried away his wife and daughter? I never cried in my life, since I was knee-high, but curse me if I ever felt in better tune for the business than just then. Hey! continued he, looking up, and observing me standing a few paces distant, and listening to their discourse; What's wanted? Anybody dead?

I stayed not to answer or parly, but hurried forward. My joints trembled, and cold drops stood on my forehead. I was ashamed of my own infirmity; and by vigorous efforts of my reason, regained some degree of composure. The evening had now advanced, and it behooved me to procure accommodation at some of the inns.

These were easily distinguished by their *signs,* but many were without inhabitants. At length, I lighted upon one, the hall of which was open, and the windows lifted. After knocking for some time, a young girl appeared, with many marks of distress. In answer to my question, she answered that both her parents were sick, and that they could receive no one. I inquired, in vain, for any other tavern at which strangers might be accommodated. She knew of none such; and left me, on some one's calling to her from above, in the midst of my embarrassment. After a moment's pause, I returned, discomforted and perplexed, to the street.

I proceeded, in a considerable degree, at random. At length, I reached a spacious building in Fourth-street, which the sign-post shewed me to be an inn. I knocked loudly and often at the door. At length, a female opened the window of the second story, and, in a tone of peevishness, demanded, what I wanted? I told her that I wanted lodging.

Go hunt for it somewhere else, said she; you'll find none here. I began to expostulate; but she shut the window with quickness, and left me to my own reflections. * * *

1799–1800

WIELAND

[THE LIGHT IN THE TEMPLE]

CHAPTER I

I Feel little reluctance in complying with your request. You know not fully the cause of my sorrows. You are a stranger to the depth of my distresses. Hence your efforts at consolation must necessarily fail. Yet the tale that I am going to tell is not intended as a claim upon your sympathy. In the midst of my despair, I do not disdain to contribute what little I can to the benefit of mankind. I acknowledge your right to be informed of the events that have lately happened in my family. Make what use of the tale you shall think proper. If it be communicated to the world, it will inculcate the duty of avoiding deceit. It will exemplify the force of early impressions, and show the immeasurable evils that flow from an erroneous or imperfect discipline.

My state is not destitute of tranquility. The sentiment that dictates my feelings is not hope. Futurity has no power over my thoughts. To all that is to come I am perfectly indifferent. With regard to myself, I have nothing more to fear. Fate has done its worst. Henceforth, I am callous to misfortune.

I address no supplication to the Deity. The power that governs the course of human affairs has chosen his path. The decree that ascertained the condition of my life, admits of no recal. No doubt it squares with the maxims of eternal equity. That is neither to be questioned nor denied by me. It suffices that the past is exempt from mutation. The storm that tore up our happiness, and changed into dreariness and desert the blooming scene of our existence, is lulled into grim repose; but not until the victim was transfixed and mangled; till every obstacle was dissipated by its rage; till every remnant of good was wrested from our grasp and exterminated.

How will your wonder, and that of your companions, be excited by my story! Every sentiment will yield to your amazement. If my testimony were without corroborations, you would reject it as incredible. The experience of no human being can furnish a parallel: that I, beyond the rest of mankind, should be reserved for a destiny without alleviation and without example! Listen to my narrative, and then say what it is that has made me deserve to be placed on this dreadful eminence, if, indeed, every faculty be not suspended in wonder that I am still alive and am able to relate it.

My father's ancestry was noble on the paternal side; but his mother was the daughter of a merchant. My grand-father was a younger brother, and a native of Saxony. He was placed, when he had reached the suitable age, at a German college. During the vacations, he employed himself in traversing the neighbouring territory. On one occasion it was his fortune to visit Hamburg. He formed an acquaintance with Leonard Weise, a merchant of that city, and was a frequent guest at his house. The merchant had an only daughter, for whom his guest speedily contracted an affection; and, in spite of parental menaces and prohibitions, he, in due season, became her husband.

By this act he mortally offended his relations. Thenceforward he was entirely disowned and rejected by them. They refused to contribute any thing to his support. All intercourse ceased, and he received from them merely that treatment to which an absolute stranger, or detested enemy, would be entitled.

He found an asylum in the house of his new father, whose temper was kind, and whose pride was flattered by this alliance. The nobility of his birth was put in the balance against his poverty. Weise conceived himself, on the whole, to have acted with the highest discretion in thus disposing of his child. My grand-father found it incumbent on him to search out some mode of independent subsistence. His youth had been eagerly devoted to literature and music. These had hitherto been cultivated merely as sources of amusement. They were now converted into the means of gain. At this period there were few works of taste in the Saxon dialect. My ancestor may be considered as the founder of the German Theatre. The modern poet of the same name is sprung from the same family, and, perhaps, surpasses but little, in the fruitfulness of his invention, or the soundness of taste, the elder Wieland. His life was spent in the composition of sonatas and dramatic pieces. They were not unpopular, but merely afforded him a scanty subsistence. He died in the bloom of his life, and was quickly followed to the grave by his wife. Their only child was taken under the protection of the merchant. At an early age he was apprenticed to a London trader, and passed seven years of mercantile servitude.

My father was not fortunate in the character of him under whose care he was now placed. He was treated with rigour, and full employment was provided for every hour of his time. His duties were laborious and mechanical. He had been educated with a view to this profession, and, therefore, was not tormented with unsatisfied desires. He did not hold his present occupations in abhorrence, because they withheld him from paths more flowery and more smooth, but he found in unintermitted labour, and in the sternness of his master, sufficient occasions for discontent. No opportunities of recreation were allowed him. He spent all his time pent up in a gloomy apartment, or traversing narrow and crowded streets. His food was coarse, and his lodging humble.

His heart gradually contracted a habit of morose and gloomy reflection. He could not accurately define what was wanting to his happiness. He was not tortured by comparisons drawn between his own situation and that of others. His state was such as suited his age and his views as to fortune. He did not imagine himself treated with extraordinary or unjustifiable rigor. In this respect he supposed the condition of others, bound like himself to mercantile service, to resemble his own; yet every engagement was irksome, and every hour tedious in its lapse.

In this state of mind he chanced to light upon a book written by one of the teachers of the Albigenses, or French Protestants. He entertained no relish for books, and was wholly unconscious of any power they possessed to delight or instruct. This volume had lain for years in a corner of his garret, half buried in dust and rubbish. He had marked it as it lay; had thrown it, as his occasions required, from one spot to another; but had felt no inclination to examine its contents, or even to inquire what was the subject of which it treated.

One Sunday afternoon, being induced to retire for a few minutes to his garret, his eye was attracted by a page of this book, which, by some accident, had been opened and placed full in his view. He was seated on the edge of his bed, and was employed in repairing a rent in some part of his clothes. His eyes were not confined to his work, but occasionally wandering, lighted at length upon the page. The words "Seek and ye shall find," were those that first offered themselves to his notice. His curiosity was roused by these so far as to prompt him to proceed. As soon as he finished his work, he took up the book and turned to the first page. The further he read, the more inducement he found to continue, and he regretted the decline of the light which obliged him for the present to close it.

The book contained an exposition of the doctrine of the sect of Camissards, and an historical account of its origin. His mind was in a state peculiarly fitted for the reception of devotional sentiments. The craving which had haunted him was now supplied with an object. His mind was at no loss for a theme of meditation. On days of business, he rose at the dawn, and retired to his chamber not till late at night. He now supplied himself with candles, and employed his nocturnal and Sunday hours in studying this book. It, of course, abounded with allusions to the Bible. All its conclusions were deduced from the sacred text. This was the fountain, beyond which it was unnecessary to trace the stream of religious truth; but it was his duty to trace it thus far.

A Bible was easily procured, and he ardently entered on the study of it. His understanding had received a particular direction. All his reveries were fashioned in the same mould. His progress towards the formation of his creed was rapid. Every fact and sentiment in this book were viewed through a medium which the writings of the Camissard apostle had suggested. His constructions of the text were hasty, and formed on a narrow scale. Every thing was viewed in a disconnected position. One action and one precept were not employed to illustrate and restrict the meaning of another. Hence arose a thousand scruples to which he had hitherto been a stranger. He was alternately agitated by fear and by ecstacy. He imagined himself beset by the snares of a spiritual foe, and that his security lay in ceaseless watchfulness and prayer.

His morals, which had never been loose, were now modelled by a stricter standard. The empire of religious duty extended itself to his looks, gestures, and phrases. All levities of speech, and negligences of behaviour, were proscribed. His air was mournful and contemplative. He laboured to keep alive a sentiment of fear, and a belief of the awe creating presence of the Deity. Ideas foreign to this were sedulously excluded. To suffer their intrusion was a crime against the Divine Majesty, inexpiable but by days and weeks of the keenest agonies.

No material variation had occurred in the lapse of two years. Every day confirmed him in his present modes of thinking and acting. It was to be expected that the tide of his emotions would sometimes recede, that intervals of despondency and doubt would occur; but these gradually were more rare, and of shorter duration; and he, at last, arrived at a state considerably uniform in this respect.

His apprenticeship was now almost expired. On his arrival of age he became entitled, by the will of my grandfather, to a small sum. This sum would hardly suffice to set him afloat as a trader in his present situation, and he had nothing to expect from the generosity of his master. Residence in England had, besides, become almost impossible, on account of his religious tenets. In addition to these motives for seeking a new habitation, there was another of the most imperious and irresistible necessity. He had imbibed an opinion that it was his duty to disseminate the truths of the gospel among the unbelieving nations. He was terrified at first by the perils and hardships to which the life of a missionary is exposed. This cowardice made him diligent in the invention of objections and excuses; but he found it impossible wholly to shake off the belief that such was the injunction of his duty. The belief, after every new conflict with his passions, acquired new strength; and, at length, he formed a resolution of complying with what he deemed the will of heaven.

The North-American Indians naturally presented themselves as the first objects for this species of benevolence. As soon as his servitude expired, he converted his little fortune into money, and embarked for Philadelphia. Here his fears were revived, and a nearer survey of savage manners once more shook his resolution. For a while he relinquished his purpose, and purchasing a farm on the Schuylkill, within a few miles of the city, set himself down to the cultivation of it. The cheapness of land, and the service of African slaves, which were then in general use, gave him who was poor in Europe all the advantages of wealth. He passed fourteen years in a thrifty and laborious manner. In this time new objects, new employments, and new associates appeared to have nearly obliterated the devout impressions of his youth. He now became acquainted with a woman of a meek and quiet disposition, and of slender acquirements like himself. He proffered his hand and was accepted.

His previous industry had now enabled him to dispense with personal labour, and direct attention to his own concerns. He enjoyed leisure, and was visited afresh by devotional contemplation. The reading of the scriptures, and other religious books, became once more his favourite employment. His ancient belief relative to the conversion of the savage tribes, was revived with uncommon energy. To the former obstacles were now added the pleadings of parental and conjugal love. The struggle was long and vehement; but his sense of duty would not be stifled or enfeebled, and finally triumphed over every impediment.

His efforts were attended with no permanent success. His exhortations had sometimes a temporary power, but more frequently were repelled with insult and derision. In pursuit of this object he encountered the most imminent perils, and underwent incredible fatigues, hunger, sickness, and solitude. The license of savage passion, and the artifices of his depraved countrymen, all opposed themselves to his progress. His courage did not forsake him till there appeared no reasonable ground to hope for success. He desisted not till his heart was relieved from the supposed obligation to persevere. With a constitution somewhat decayed, he at length returned to his family. An interval of tranquillity succeeded. He was frugal, regular, and strict in the performance of domestic duties. He allied himself with no sect, because he perfectly agreed with none. Social worship is that by which they are all distinguished; but this article found no place in his creed. He rigidly interpreted that precept which enjoins us, when we worship, to retire into solitude, and shut out every species of society. According to him, devotion was not only a silent office, but must be performed alone. An hour at noon, and an hour at midnight were thus appropriated.

At the distance of three hundred yards from his house, on the top of a rock whose sides were steep, rugged, and encumbered with dwarf cedars and stony asperities, he built what to a common eye would have seemed a summer-house. The eastern verge of this precipice was sixty feet above the river which flowed at its foot. The view before it consisted of a transparent current, fluctuating and rippling in a rocky channel, and bounded by a rising scene of cornfields and orchards. The edifice was slight and airy. It was no more than a circular area, twelve feet in diameter, whose flooring was the rock, cleared of moss and shrubs, and exactly levelled, edged by twelve Tuscan columns, and covered by an undulating dome. My father furnished the dimensions, and outlines, but allowed the artist whom he employed to complete the structure on his own plan. It was without seat, table, or ornament of any kind.

This was the temple of his Deity. Twice in twenty-four hours he repaired hither, unaccompanied by any human being. Nothing but physical inability to move was allowed to obstruct or postpone this visit. He did not exact from his family compliance with his example. Few men, equally sincere in their faith, were as sparing in their censures and restrictions, with respect to the conduct of others, as my father. The character of my mother was no less devout; but her education had habituated her to a different mode of worship. The loneliness of their dwelling prevented her from joining any established congregation; but she was punctual in the offices of prayer, and in the performance of hymns to her Saviour, after the manner of the disciples of Zinzendorf. My father refused to interfere in her arrangements. His own system was embraced not, accurately speaking, because it was the best, but because it had been expressly prescribed to him. Other modes, if practised by other persons, might be equally acceptable.

His deportment to others was full of charity and mildness. A sadness perpetually overspread his features, but was unmingled with sternness or discontent. The tones of his voice, his gestures, his steps, were all in tranquil uniform. His conduct was characterized by a certain forbearance and humility, which secured the esteem of those to whom his tenets were most obnoxious. They might call him a fanatic and a dreamer, but they could not deny their veneration to his invincible candour and invariable integrity. His own belief of rectitude was the foundation of his happiness. This, however, was destined to find an end.

Suddenly the sadness that constantly attended him was deepened. Sighs, and even tears, sometimes escaped him. To the expostulations of his wife he seldom answered any thing. When he designed to be communicative, he hinted that his peace of mind was flown, in consequence of deviation from his duty. A command had been laid upon him, which he had delayed to perform. He felt as if a certain period of hesitation and reluctance had been allowed him, but that this period was passed. He was no longer permitted to obey. The duty assigned to him was transferred, in consequence of his disobedience, to another, and all that remained was to endure the penalty.

He did not describe this penalty. It appeared to be nothing more for some time than a sense of wrong. This was sufficiently acute, and was aggravated by the belief that his offence was incapable of expiation. No one could contemplate the agonies which he seemed to suffer without the deepest compassion. Time, instead of lightening the burden, appeared to add to it. At length he hinted to his wife, that his end was near. His imagination did not prefigure the mode or the time of his decease, but was fraught with an incurable persuasion that his death was at hand. He was likewise haunted by the belief that the kind of death that awaited him was strange and terrible. His anticipations were thus far vague and indefinite; but they sufficed to poison every moment of his being and devote him to ceaseless anguish.

CHAPTER II

Early in the morning of a sultry day in August, he left Mettingen, to go to the city. He had seldom passed a day from home since his return from the shores of the Ohio. Some urgent engagements at this time existed, which would not admit of further delay. He returned in the evening, but appeared to be greatly oppressed with fatigue. His silence and dejection were likewise in a more than ordinary degree conspicuous. My mother's brother, whose profession was that of a surgeon, chanced to spend this night at our house. It was from him that I have frequently received an exact account of the mournful catastrophe that followed.

As the evening advanced, my father's inquietudes increased. He sat with his family as usual, but took no part in their conversation. He appeared fully engrossed by his own reflections. Occasionally his countenance exhibited tokens of alarm; he gazed steadfastly and wildly at the ceiling; and the exertions of his companions were scarcely sufficient to interrupt his reverie. On recovering from these fits, he expressed no surprize; but, pressing his hand to his head, complained, in a tremulous and terrified tone, that his brain was scorched to cinders. He would then betray marks of insupportable anxiety.

My uncle perceived, by his pulse, that he was indisposed, but in no alarming degree, and ascribed appearances chiefly to the workings of his mind. He exhorted him to recollection and composure, but in vain. At the hour of repose he readily retired to his chamber. At the persuasion of my mother he even undressed and went to bed. Nothing could abate his restlessness. He checked her tender expostulations with some sternness. "Be silent," said he, "for that which I feel there is but one cure, and that will shortly come. You can help me nothing. Look to your own condition, and pray to God to strengthen you under the calamities that await you." "What am I to fear?" she answered. "What terrible disaster is it that you think of?" "Peace—as yet I know it not myself, but come it will, and shortly." She repeated her inquiries and doubts; but he suddenly put an end to the discourse, by a stern command to be silent.

She had never before known him in this mood. Hitherto all was benign in his deportment. Her heart was pierced with sorrow at the contemplation of this change. She was utterly unable to account for it, or to figure to herself the species of disaster that was menaced.

Contrary to custom, the lamp, instead of being placed on the hearth, was left upon the table. Over it against the wall there hung a small clock, so contrived as to strike a very hard stroke at the end of every sixth hour. That which was now approaching was the signal for retiring to the fane at which he addressed his devotions. Long habit had occasioned him to be always awake at this hour, and the toll was instantly obeyed.

Now frequent and anxious glances were cast at the clock. Not a single movement of the index appeared to escape his notice. As the hour verged towards twelve his anxiety visibly augmented. The trepidations of my mother kept pace with those of her husband; but she was intimidated into silence. All that was left to her was to watch every change of his features, and give vent to her sympathy in tears.

At length the hour was spent, and the clock tolled. The sound appeared to communicate a shock to every part of my father's frame. He rose immediately, and threw over himself a loose gown. Even this office was performed with difficulty, for his joints trembled, and his teeth chattered with dismay. At this hour his duty called him to the rock, and my mother naturally concluded that it was thither he intended to repair. Yet these incidents were so uncommon, as to fill her with astonishment and foreboding. She saw him leave the room, and heard his steps as they hastily descended the stairs. She half resolved to rise and pursue him, but the wildness of the scheme quickly suggested itself. He was going to a place whither no power on earth could induce him to suffer an attendant.

The window of her chamber looked towards the rock. The atmosphere was clear and calm, but the edifice could not be discovered at that distance through the dusk. My mother's anxiety would not allow her to remain where she was. She rose, and seated herself at the window. She strained her sight to get a view of the dome, and of the path that led to it. The first painted itself with sufficient distinctness on her fancy, but was undistinguishable by the eye from the rocky mass on which it was erected. The second could be imperfectly seen; but her husband had already passed, or had taken a different direction.

What was it that she feared? Some disaster impended over her husband or herself. He had predicted evils, but professed himself ignorant of what nature they were. When were they to come? Was this night, or this hour to witness the accomplishment? She was tortured with impatience, and uncertainty. All her fears were at present linked to his person, and she gazed at the clock, with nearly as much eagerness as my father had done, in expectation of the next hour.

An half hour passed away in this state of suspense. Her eyes were fixed upon the rock; suddenly it was illuminated. A light proceeding from the edifice, made every part of the scene visible. A gleam diffused itself over the intermediate space, and instantly a loud report, like the explosion of a mine, followed. She uttered an involuntary shriek, but the new sounds that greeted her ear, quickly conquered her surprise. They were piercing shrieks, and uttered without intermission. The gleams which had diffused themselves far and wide were in a moment withdrawn, but the interior of the edifice was filled with rays.

The first suggestion was that a pistol was discharged, and that the structure was on fire. She did not allow herself time to meditate a second thought, but rushed into the entry and knocked loudly at the door of her brother's chamber. My uncle had been previously roused by the noise, and instantly flew to the window. He also imagined what he saw to be fire. The loud and vehement shrieks which succeeded the first explosion, seemed to be an invocation of succour. The incident was inexplicable; but he could not fail to perceive the propriety of hastening to the spot. He was unbolting the door, when his sister's voice was heard on the outside conjuring him to come forth.

He obeyed the summons with all the speed in his power. He stopped not to question her, but hurried down stairs and across the meadow which lay between the house and the rock. The shrieks were no longer to be heard; but a blazing light was clearly discernible between the columns of the temple. Irregular steps, hewn in the stone, led him to the summit. On three sides, this edifice touched the very verge of the cliff. On the fourth side, which might be regarded as the front, there was an area of small extent, to which the rude staircase conducted you. My uncle speedily gained this spot. His strength was for a moment exhausted by his haste. He paused to rest himself. Meanwhile he bent the most vigilant attention towards the object before him.

Within the columns he beheld what he could no better describe, than by saying that it resembled a cloud impregnated with light. It had the brightness of flame, but was without its upward motion. It did not occupy the whole area, and rose but a few feet above the floor. No part of the building was on fire. This appearance was astonishing. He approached the temple. As he went forward the light retired, and, when he put his feet within the apartment, utterly vanished. The suddenness of this transition increased the darkness that succeeded in a tenfold degree. Fear and wonder rendered him powerless. An occurrence like this, in a place assigned to devotion, was adapted to intimidate the stoutest heart.

His wandering thoughts were recalled by the groans of one near him. His sight gradually recovered its power, and he was able to discern my father stretched on the floor. At that moment my mother and servants arrived with a lanthorn, and enabled my uncle to examine more closely this scene. My father, when he left the house, besides a loose upper vest and slippers, wore a shirt and drawers. Now he was naked, his skin throughout the greater part of his body was scorched and bruised. His right arm exhibited marks as of having been struck by some heavy body. His clothes had been removed, and it was not immediately perceived that they were reduced to ashes. His slippers and his hair were untouched.

He was removed to his chamber, and the requisite attention paid to his wounds, which gradually became more painful. A mortification speedily shewed itself in the arm, which had been most hurt. Soon after, the other wounded parts exhibited the like appearance.

Immediately subsequent to this disaster, my father seemed nearly in a state of insensibility. He was passive under every operation. He scarcely opened his eyes, and was with difficulty prevailed upon to answer the questions that were put to him. By his imperfect account, it appeared, that while engaged in silent orisons, with thoughts full of confusion and anxiety, a faint gleam suddenly shot athwart the apartment. His fancy immediately pictured to itself, a person bearing a lamp. It seemed to come from behind. He was in the act of turning to examine the visitant, when his right arm received a blow from a heavy club. At the same instant, a very bright spark was seen to light upon his clothes. In a moment, the whole was reduced to ashes. This was the sum of the information which he chose to give. There was somewhat in his manner that indicated an imperfect tale. My uncle was inclined to believe that half the truth had been suppressed.

Meanwhile, the disease thus wonderfully generated betrayed more terrible symptoms. Fever and delirium terminated in lethargic slumber, which, in the course of two hours, gave place to death. Yet not till insupportable exhalations and crawling putrefaction had driven from his chamber and the house every one whom their duty did not detain.

Such was the end of my father. None surely was ever more mysterious. When we recollect his gloomy anticipations and unconquerable anxiety; the security from human malice which his character, the place, and the condition of the times might be supposed to confer; the purity and cloudlessness of the atmosphere, which rendered it impossible that lightning was the cause; what are the conclusions that we must form?

The prelusive gleam, the blow upon his arm, the fatal spark, the explosion heard so far, the fiery cloud that environed him, without detriment to the structure, though composed of combustible materials, the sudden vanishing of this cloud at my uncle's approach—what is the inference to be drawn from these facts? Their truth cannot be doubted. My uncle's testimony is peculiarly worthy of credit, because no man's temper is more sceptical, and his belief is unalterably attached to natural causes.

I was at this time a child of six years of age. The impressions that were then made upon me, can never be effaced. I was ill qualified to judge respecting what was then passing; but as I advanced in age, and became more fully acquainted with these facts, they oftener became the subject of my thoughts. Their resemblance to recent events revived them with new force in my memory, and made me more anxious to explain them. Was this the penalty of disobedience? this the stroke of a vindictive and invisible hand? Is it a fresh proof that the Divine Ruler interferes in human affairs, meditates an end, selects, and commissions his agents, and enforces, by unequivocal sanctions, submission to his will? Or, was it merely the irregular expansion of the fluid that imparts warmth to our heart and our blood, caused by the fatigue of the preceding day, or flowing, by established laws, from the condition of his thoughts?

1798

EDGAR HUNTLY

CHAPTER XV

[THE CAVERN AND THE PANTHER]

Here, my friend, thou must permit me to pause. The following incidents are of a kind to which the most ardent invention has never conceived a parallel. Fortune, in her most wayward mood, could scarcely be suspected of an influence like this. The scene was pregnant with astonishment and horror. I cannot, even now, recall it without reviving the dismay and confusion which I then experienced.

Possibly, the period will arrive when I shall look back without agony on the perils I have undergone. That period is still distant. Solitude and sleep are now no more than the signals to summon up a tribe of ugly phantoms. Famine, and blindness, and death, and savage enemies, never fail to be conjured up by silence and darkness of the night. I cannot dissipate them by any efforts of reason. My cowardice requires the perpetual consolation of light. My heart droops when I mark the decline of the sun, and I never sleep but with a candle burning at my pillow. If, by any chance, I should awake and find myself immersed in darkness, I know not what act of desperation I might be suddenly impelled to commit.

I have delayed this narrative, longer than my duty to my friend enjoined. Now that I am able to hold a pen, I will hasten to terminate that uncertainty with regard to my fate, in which my silence has involved thee. I will recall that series of unheard of and disastrous vicissitudes which has constituted the latest portion of my life.

I am not certain, however, that I shall relate them in an intelligible manner. One image runs into another, sensations succeed in so rapid a train, that I fear, I shall be unable to distribute and express them with sufficient perspicuity. As I look back, my heart is sore and aches within my bosom. I am conscious to a kind of complex sentiment of distress and forlornness that cannot be perfectly pourtrayed by words; but I must do as well as I can. In the utmost vigour of my faculties, no eloquence that I possess would do justice to the tale. Now, in my languishing and feeble state, I shall furnish thee with little more than a glimpse of the truth. With these glimpses, transient and faint as they are, thou must be satisfied.

I have said that I slept. My memory assures me of this: It informs me of the previous circumstances of my laying aside my clothes, of placing the light upon a chair within reach of my pillow, of throwing myself upon the bed, and of gazing on the rays of the moon reflected on the wall, and almost obscured by those of the candle. I remember my occasional relapses into fits of incoherent fancies, the harbingers of sleep: I remember, as it were, the instant when my thoughts ceased to flow, and my senses were arrested by the leaden wand of forgetfulness.

My return to sensation and to consciousness took place in no such tranquil scene. I emerged from oblivion by degrees so slow and so faint, that their succession cannot be marked. When enabled at length to attend to the information which my senses afforded, I was conscious, for a time, of nothing but existence. It was unaccompanied with lassitude or pain, but I felt disinclined to stretch my limbs, or raise my eye-lids. My thoughts were wildering and mazy, and though consciousness were present, it was disconnected with the loco-motive or voluntary power.

From this state a transition was speedily effected. I perceived that my posture was supine, and that I lay upon my back. I attempted to open my eyes. The weight that oppressed them was too great for a slight exertion to remove. The exertion which I made cost me a pang more acute than any which I ever experienced. My eyes, however, were opened; but the darkness that environed me was as intense as before.

I attempted to rise, but my limbs were cold, and my joints had almost lost their flexibility. My efforts were repeated, and at length I attained a sitting posture. I was now sensible of pain in my shoulders and back. I was universally in that state to which the frame is reduced by blows of a club, mercilessly and endlessly repeated; my temples throbbed and my face was covered with clamy and cold drops, but that which threw me into the deepest consternation was, my inability to see. I turned my head to different quarters, I stretched my eye-lids, and exerted every visual energy, but in vain. I was wrapped in the murkiest and most impenetrable gloom.

The first effort of reflection was to suggest the belief that I was blind; that disease is known to assail us in a moment and without previous warning. This surely was the misfortune that had now befallen me. Some ray, however fleeting and uncertain, could not fail to be discerned, if the power of vision were not utterly extinguished. In what circumstances could I possibly be placed, from which every particle of light should, by other means, be excluded.

This led my thoughts into a new train. I endeavoured to recall the past, but the past was too much in contradiction to the present, and my intellect was too much shattered by external violence, to allow me accurately to review it.

Since my sight availed nothing to the knowledge of my condition, I betook myself to other instruments. The element which I breathed was stagnant and cold. The spot where I lay was rugged and hard. I was neither naked nor clothed, a shirt and trossers composed my dress, and the shoes and stockings, which always accompanied these, were now wanting. What could I infer from this scanty garb, this chilling atmosphere, this stony bed?

I had awakened as from sleep. What was my condition when I fell asleep? Surely it was different from the present. Then I inhabited a lightsome chamber and was stretched upon a down bed; now I was supine upon a rugged surface and immersed in palpable obscurity. Then I was in perfect health; now my frame was covered with bruises and every joint was racked with pain. What dungeon or den had received me, and by whose command was I transported hither?

After various efforts I stood upon my feet. At first I tottered and staggered. I stretched out my hands on all sides, but met only with vacuity. I advanced forward. At the third step my foot moved something which lay upon the ground, I stooped and took it up, and found, on examination, that it was an Indian Tom-hawk. This incident afforded me no hint from which I might conjecture my state.

Proceeding irresolutely and slowly forward, my hands at length touched a wall. This, like the flooring, was of stone, and was rugged and impenetrable. I followed this wall. An advancing angle occurred at a short distance, which was followed by similar angles. I continued to explore this clue, till the suspicion occurred that I was merely going round the walls of a vast and irregular apartment.

The utter darkness disabled me from comparing directions and distances. This discovery, therefore, was not made on a sudden, and was still entangled with some doubt. My blood recovered some warmth, and my muscles some elasticity, but in proportion as my sensibility returned my pains augmented. Overpowered by my fears and my agonies I desisted from my fruitless search, and sat down, supporting my back against the wall.

My excruciating sensations for a time occupied my attention. These, in combination with other causes, gradually produced a species of delirium. I existed as it were in a wakeful dream. With nothing to correct my erroneous perceptions, the images of the past occurred in capricious combinations, and vivid hues. Methought I was the victim of some tyrant who had thrust me into a dungeon of his fortress, and left me no power to determine whether he intended I should perish with famine, or linger out a long life in hopeless imprisonment: Whether the day was shut out by insuperable walls, or the darkness that surrounded me, was owing to the night and to the smallness of those cranies through which daylight was to be admitted, I conjectured in vain.

Sometimes I imagined myself buried alive. Methought I had fallen into seeming death, and my friends had consigned me to the tomb, from which a resurrection was impossible. That in such a case, my limbs would have been confined to a coffin, and my coffin to a grave, and that I should instantly have been suffocated, did not occur to destroy my supposition: Neither did this supposition overwhelm me with terror or prompt my efforts at deliverance. My state was full of tumult and confusion, and my attention was incessantly divided between my painful sensations and my feverish dreams,

There is no standard by which time can be measured, but the succession of our thoughts, and the changes that take place in the external world. From the latter I was totally excluded. The former made the lapse of some hours appear like the tediousness of weeks and months. At length, a new sensation, recalled my rambling meditations, and gave substance to my fears. I now felt the cravings of hunger, and perceived that unless my deliverance were speedily effected. I must suffer a tedious and lingering death.

I once more tasked my understanding and my senses, to discover the nature of my present situation and the means of escape. I listened to catch some sound. I heard an unequal and varying echo, sometimes near and sometimes distant, sometimes dying away and sometimes swelling into loudness. It was unlike any thing I had before heard, but it was evident that it arose from wind sweeping through spacious halls and winding passages. These tokens were incompatible with the result of the examination I had made. If my hands were true, I was immured between walls through which there was no avenue.

I now exerted my voice, and cried as loud as my wasted strength would admit. Its echoes were sent back to me in broken and confused sounds and from above. This effort was casual, but some part of that uncertainty in which I was involved, was instantly dispelled by it. In passing through the cavern on the former day, I have mentioned the verge of the pit at which I arrived. To acquaint me as far as was possible, with the dimensions of the place, I had hallooed with all my force, knowing that sound is reflected according to the distance and relative positions of the substances from which it is repelled.

The effect produced by my voice on this occasion resembled, with remarkable exactness, the effect which was then produced. Was I then shut up in the same cavern? Had I reached the brink of the same precipice and been thrown headlong into that vacuity? Whence else could arise the bruises which I had received, but from my fall? Yet all remembrance of my journey hither was lost. I had determined to explore this cave on the ensuing day, but my memory informed me not that this intention had been carried into effect. Still it was only possible to conclude that I had come hither on my intended expedition, and had been thrown by another, or had, by some ill chance, fallen, into the pit.

This opinion was conformable to what I had already observed. The pavement and walls were rugged like those of the footing and sides of the cave through which I had formerly passed.

But if this were true, what was the abhorred catastrophe to which I was now reserved? The sides of this pit were inaccessible: human foot-steps would never wander into these recesses. My friends were unapprised of my forlorn state. Here I should continue till wasted by famine. In this grave should I linger out a few days, in unspeakable agonies and then perish forever.

The inroads of hunger were already experienced, and this knowledge of the desperateness of my calamity, urged me to frenzy. I had none but capricious and unseen fate to condemn. The author of my distress and the means he had taken to decoy me hither, were incomprehensible. Surely my senses were fettered or depraved by some spell. I was still asleep, and this was merely a tormenting vision, or madness had seized me, and the darkness that environed and the hunger that afflicted me, existed only in my own distempered imagination.

The consolation of these doubts could not last long. Every hour added to the proof that my perceptions were real. My hunger speedily became ferocious. I tore the linen of my shirt between my teeth and swallowed the fragments. I felt a strong propensity to bite the flesh from my arm. My heart overflowed with cruelty, and I pondered on the delight I should experience in rending some living animal to pieces, and drinking its blood and grinding its quivering fibres between my teeth.

This agony had already passed beyond the limits of endurance. I saw that time, instead of bringing respite or relief, would only aggravate my wants, and that my only remaining hope was to die before I should be assaulted by the last extremes of famine. I now recollected that a Tom-hawk was at hand, and rejoiced in the possession of an instrument by which I could so effectually terminate my sufferings.

I took it in my hand, moved its edge over my fingers, and reflected on the force that was required to make it reach my heart. I investigated the spot where it should enter, and strove to fortify myself with resolution to repeat the stroke a second or third time, if the first should prove insufficient. I was sensible that I might fail to inflict a mortal wound, but delighted to consider that the blood which would be made to flow, would finally release me, and that meanwhile my pains would be alleviated by swallowing this blood.

You will not wonder that I felt some reluctance to employ so fatal though indispensable a remedy. I once more ruminated on the possibility of rescuing myself by other means. I now reflected that the upper termination of the wall could not be an immeasurable distance from the pavement. I had fallen from a height, but if that height had been considerable, instead of being merely bruised, should I not have been dashed into pieces?

Gleams of hope burst anew upon my soul. Was it not possible, I asked, to reach the top of this pit? The sides were rugged and uneven. Would not their projectures and abruptnesses serve me as steps by which I might ascend in safety? This expedient was to be tried without delay. Shortly my strength would fail and my doom would be irrevocably sealed.

I will not enumerate my laborious efforts, my alternations of despondency and confidence, the eager and unwearied scrutiny with which I examined the surface, the attempts which I made, and the failures which, for a time, succeeded each other. An hundred times, when I had ascended some feet from the bottom, I was compelled to relinquish my undertaking by the *untenable* smoothness of the spaces which remained to be gone over. A hundred times I threw myself, exhausted by fatigue and my pains, on the ground. The consciousness was gradually restored that till I had attempted every part of the wall, it was absurd to despair, and I again drew my tottering limbs and aching joints to that part of the wall which had not been surveyed.

At length, as I stretched my hand upward, I found somewhat that seemed like a recession in the wall. It was possible that this was the top of the cavity, and this might be the avenue to liberty. My heart leaped with joy, and I proceeded to climb the wall. No undertaking could be conceived more arduous than this. The space between this verge and the floor was nearly smooth. The verge was higher from the bottom than my head. The only means of ascending that were offered me were by my hands, with which I could draw myself upward so as, at length, to maintain my hold with my feet.

My efforts were indefatigable, and at length I placed myself on the verge when this was accomplished my strength was nearly gone. Had I not found space enough beyond this brink to stretch myself at length, I should unavoidably have fallen backward into the pit, and all my pains had served no other end than to deepen my despair and hasten my destruction.

What impediments and perils remained to be encountered I could not judge. I was now inclined to forbode the worst. The interval of repose which was necessary to be taken, in order to recruit my strength, would accelerate the ravages of famine, and leave me without the power to proceed.

In this state, I once more consoled myself that an instrument of death was at hand. I had drawn up with me the Tom-hawk, being sensible that should this impediment be overcome others might remain that would prove insuperable. Before I employed it, however, I cast my eyes wildly and languidly around. The darkness was no less intense than in the pit below, and yet two objects were distinctly seen.

They resembled a fixed and obscure flame. They were motionless. Though lustrous themselves they created no illumination around them. This circumstance, added to others, which reminded me of similar objects noted on former occasions, immediately explained the nature of what I beheld. These were the eyes of a panther.

Thus had I struggled to obtain a post where a savage was lurking and waited only till my efforts should place me within reach of his fangs. The first impulse was to arm myself against this enemy. The desperateness of my condition was, for a moment, forgotten. The weapon which was so lately lifted against my own bosom, was now raised to defend my life against the assault of another.

There was no time for deliberation and delay. In a moment he might spring from his station and tear me to pieces. My utmost speed might not enable me to reach him where he sat, but merely to encounter his assault. I did not reflect how far my strength was adequate to save me. All the force that remained was mustered up and exerted in a throw.

No one knows the powers that are latent in his constitution. Called forth by imminent dangers, our efforts frequently exceed our most sanguine belief. Though tottering on the verge of dissolution, and apparently unable to crawl from this spot, a force was exerted in this throw, probably greater than I had ever before exerted. It was resistless and unerring. I aimed at the middle space between those glowing orbs. It penetrated the scull and the animal fell, struggling and shrieking, on the ground.

My ears quickly informed me when his pangs were at an end. His cries and his convulsions lasted for a moment and then ceased. The effect of his voice, in these subterranean abodes, was unspeakably rueful.

The abruptness of this incident, and the preternatural exertion of my strength, left me in a state of languor and sinking from which slowly and with difficulty I recovered. The first suggestion that occurred was to feed upon the carcass of this animal. My hunger had arrived at that pitch where all fastidiousness and scruples are at an end. I crept to the spot. . . . I will not shock you by relating the extremes to which dire necessity had driven me. I review this scene with loathing and horror. Now that it is past I look back upon it as on some hideous dream. The whole appears to be some freak of insanity. No alternative was offered, and hunger was capable of being appeased, even by a banquet so detestable.

If this appetite has sometimes subdued the sentiments of nature, and compelled the mother to feed upon the flesh of her offspring, it will not excite amazement that I did not turn from the yet warm blood and reeking fibres of a brute.

One evil was now removed, only to give place to another. The first sensations of fulness had scarcely been felt when my stomach was seized by pangs whose acuteness exceeded all that I ever before experienced. I bitterly lamented my inordinate avidity. The excruciations of famine were better than the agonies which this abhorred meal had produced.

Death was now impending with no less proximity and certainty, though in a different form. Death was a sweet relief for my present miseries, and I vehemently longed for its arrival. I stretched myself on the ground. I threw myself into every posture that promised some alleviation of this evil. I rolled along the pavement of the cavern, wholly inattentive to the dangers that environed me. That I did not fall into the pit, whence I had just emerged, must be ascribed to some miraculous chance.

How long my miseries endured, it is not possible to tell. I cannot even form a plausible conjecture. Judging by the lingering train of my sensations, I should conjecture that some days elapsed in this deplorable condition, but nature could not have so long sustained a conflict like this.

Gradually my pains subsided, and I fell into a deep sleep. I was visited by dreams of a thousand hues. They led me to flowing streams and plenteous banquets, which, though placed within my view, some power forbade me to approach. From this sleep I recovered to the fruition of solitude and darkness, but my frame was in a state less feeble than before. That which I had eaten had produced t[e]mporary distress but on the whole had been of use. If this food had not been provided for me I should scarcely have avoided death. I had reason, therefore, to congratulate myself on the danger that had lately occurred.

I had acted without foresight, and yet no wisdom could have prescribed more salutary measures. The panther was slain, not from a view to the relief of my hunger, but from the self-preserving and involuntary impulse. Had I fore-known the pangs to which my ravenous and bloody meal would give birth, I should have carefully abstained, and yet these pangs were a useful effort of nature to subdue and convert to nourishment the matter I had swallowed.

I was now assailed by the torments of thirst. My invention and my courage were anew bent to obviate this pressing evil. I reflected that there was some recess from this cavern, even from the spot where I now stood. Before, I was doubtful whether in this direction from the pit any avenue could be found; but, since the panther had come hither there was reason to suppose the existence of some such avenue.

I now likewise attended to a sound, which, from its invariable tenour, denoted somewhat different from the whistling of a gale. It seemed like the murmur of a running stream. I now prepared to go forward and endeavour to move along in that direction in which this sound apparently came.

On either side and above my head, there was nothing but vacuity. My steps were to be guided by the pavement, which, though unequal and rugged, appeared, on the whole, to ascend. My safety required that I should employ both hands and feet in exploring my way.

I went on thus for a considerable period. The murmur, instead of becoming more distinct, gradually died away. My progress was arrested by fatigue, and I began once more to despond. My exertions, produced a perspiration, which, while it augmented my thirst, happily supplied me with imperfect means of appeasing it.

This expedient would, perhaps, have been accidentally suggested, but my ingenuity was assisted by remembering the history of certain English prisoners in Bengal, whom their merciless enemy imprisoned in a small room, and some of whom preserved themselves alive merely by swallowing the moisture that flowed from their bodies. This experiment I now performed with no less success.

This was slender and transitory consolation. I knew that, wandering at random, I might never reach the outlet of this cavern, or might be disabled, by hunger and fatigue, from going farther than the outlet. The cravings which had lately been satiated, would speedily return, and my negligence had cut me off from the resource which had recently been furnished. I thought not till now that a second meal might be indispensable.

To return upon my foot-steps to the spot where the dead animal lay was an heartless project. I might thus be placing myself at an hopeless distance from liberty. Besides my track could not be retraced. I had frequently deviated from a straight direction for the sake of avoiding impediments. All of which I was sensible was, that I was travelling up an irregular acclivity. I hoped some time to reach the summit, but had no reason for adhering to one line of ascent in preference to another.

To remain where I was, was manifestly absurd. Whether I mounted or descended, a change of place was most likly to benefit me. I resolved to vary my direction, and, instead of ascending, keep along the side of what I accounted an hill. I had gone some hundred feet when the murmur, before described, once more saluted my ear.

This sound, being imagined to proceed from a running stream, could not but light up joy in the heart of one nearly perishing with thirst. I proceeded with new courage. The sound approached no nearer nor became more distinct; but as long as it died not away, I was satisfied to listen and to hope.

I was eagerly observant if any the least glimmering of light, should visit this recess. At length, on the right hand a gleam, infinitely faint, caught my attention. It was wavering and unequal. I directed my steps towards it. It became more vivid, and permanent. It was that kind, however, which proceeded from a fire, kindled with dry sticks, and not from the sun. I now heard the crackling of flames.

This sound made me pause, or at least to proceed with circumspection. At length, the scene opened, and I found myself at the entrance of a cave. I quickly reached a station when I saw a fire burning. At first no other object was noted, but it was easy to infer that the fire was kindled by men, and that they who kindled it could be at no great distance.

1799

THE NATURALISTS

I. WILLIAM BARTRAM
(1739–1823)

TRAVELS

PART II, CHAPTER V

[THE FIGHT WITH THE CROCODILES]

Being desirous of continuing my travels and observations, higher up the river, and having an invitation from a gentleman who was agent for, and resident at a large plantation, the property of an English gentleman, about sixty miles higher up, I resolved to pursue my researches to that place; and having engaged in my service a young Indian, nephew to the White Captain, he agreed to assist me in working my vessel up as high as a certain bluff, where I was, by agreement, to land him, on the West or Indian shore, whence he designed to go in quest of the camp of the White Trader, his relation.

Provisions and all necessaries being procured, and the morning pleasant, we went on board and stood up the river. We passed for several miles on the left, by islands of high swamp land, exceedingly fertile, their banks for a good distance from the water, much higher than the interior part, and sufficiently so to build upon, and be out of the reach of inundations. They consist of a loose black mould, with a mixture of sand, shells and dissolved vegetables. The opposite Indian coast is a perpendicular bluff, ten or twelve feet high, consisting of a black sandy earth, mixed with a large proportion of shells, chiefly various species of fresh water Cochleae and Mytuli. Near the river, on this high shore, grew Corypha palma, Magnolia grandiflora, Live Oak, Callicarpa, Myrica cerifera, Hibiscus spinifex, and the beautiful evergreen shrub called Wild lime or Tallow nut. This last shrub grows six or eight feet high, many erect stems spring from a root; the leaves are lanciolate and intire, two or three inches in length and one in breadth, of a deep green colour, and polished; at the foot of each leaf grows a stiff, sharp thorn; the flowers are small and in clusters, of a greenish yellow colour, and sweet scented; they are succeeded by a large oval fruit, of the shape and size of an ordinary plumb, of a fine yellow colour when ripe; a soft sweet pulp covers a nut which has a thin shell, enclosing a white kernal somewhat of the consistence and taste of the sweet Almond, but more oily and very much like hard tallow, which induced my father, when he first observed it, to call it the Tallow nut.

At the upper end of this bluff is a fine Orange grove. Here my Indian companion requested me to set him on shore, being already tired of rowing under a fervid sun, and having for some time intimated a dislike to his situation, I readily complied with his desire, knowing the impossibility of compelling an Indian against his own inclinations, or even prevailing upon him by reasonable arguments, when labour is in the question; before my vessel reached the shore, he sprang out of her and landed, when uttering a shrill and terrible whoop, he bounded off like a roebuck, and I lost sight of him. I at first apprehended, that as he took his gun with him, he intended to hunt for some game and return to me in the evening. The day being excessively hot and sultry, I concluded to take up my quarters here until next morning.

The Indian not returning this morning, I sat sail alone. The coasts on each side had much the same appearance as already described. The Palm trees here seem to be of a different species from the Cabbage tree; their straight trunks are sixty, eighty or ninety feet high, with a beautiful taper, of a bright ash colour, until within six or seven feet of the top, where it is a fine green colour, crowned with an orb of rich green plumed leaves: I have measured the stem of these plumes fifteen feet in length, besides the plume, which is nearly of the same length.

The little lake, which is an expansion of the river, now appeared in view; on the East side are extensive marshes, and on the other high forests and Orange groves, and then a bay, lined with vast Cypress swamps, both coasts gradually approaching each other, to the opening of the river again, which is in this place about three hundred yards wide; evening now drawing on, I was anxious to reach some high bank of the river, where I intended to lodge; and agreeably to my wishes, I soon after discovered on the West shore, a little promontory, at the turning of the river, contracting it here to about one hundred and fifty yards in width. This promontory is a peninsula, containing about three acres of high ground, and is one entire Orange grove, with a few Live Oaks, Magnolias, and Palms. Upon doubling the point, I arrived at the landing, which is a circular harbour, at the foot of the bluff, the top of which is about twelve feet high; the back of it is a large Cypress swamp, that spreads each way, the right wing forming the West coast of the little lake, and the left stretching up the river many miles, and encompassing a vast space of low grassy marshes. From this promontory, looking Eastward across the river, we behold a landscape of low country, unparalleled as I think; on the left is the East coast of the little lake, which I had just passed, and from the Orange bluff at the lower end, the high forests begin, and increase in breadth from the shore of the lake, making a circular sweep to the right, and contain many hundred thousand acres of meadow; and this grand sweep of high forests encircles, as I apprehend, at least twenty miles of these green fields, interspersed with hommocks or islets of evergreen trees, where the sovereign Magnolia and lordly Palm stand conspicuous. The islets are high shelly knolls, on the sides of creeks or branches of the river, which wind about and drain off the superabundant waters that cover these meadows, during the winter season.

The evening was temperately cool and calm. The crocodiles began to roar and appear in uncommon numbers along the shores and in the river.

I fixed my camp in an open plain, near the utmost projection of the promontory, under the shelter of a large Live Oak, which stood on the highest part of the ground, and but a few yards from my boat. From this open, high situation, I had a free prospect of the river, which was a matter of no trivial consideration to me, having good reason to dread the subtle attacks of the allegators, who were crowding about my harbour. Having collected a good quantity of wood for the purpose of keeping up a light and smoke during the night, I began to think of preparing my supper, when, upon examining my stores, I found but a scanty provision, I thereupon determined, as the most expeditious way of supplying my necessities, to take my bob and try for some trout. About one hundred yards above my harbour began a cove or bay of the river, out of which opened a large lagoon. The mouth or entrance from the river to it was narrow, but the waters soon after spread and formed a little lake, extending into the marshes, its entrance and shores within I observed to be verged with floating lawns of the Pistia and Nymphea and other aquatic plants; these I knew were excellent haunts for trout.

The verges and islets of the lagoon were elegantly embellished with flowering plants and shrubs; the laughing coots with wings half spread were tripping over the little coves, and hiding themselves in the tufts of grass; young broods of the painted summer teal, skimming the still surface of the waters, and following the watchful parent unconscious of danger, were frequently surprised by the voracious trout; and he, in turn, as often by the subtle greedy alligator. Behold him rushing forth from the flags and reeds. His enormous body swells. His plaited tail brandished high, floats upon the lake. The waters like a cataract descend from his opening jaws. Clouds of smoke issue from his dilated nostrils. The earth trembles with his thunder. When immediately from the opposite coast of the lagoon, emerges from the deep his rival champion. They suddenly dart upon each other. The boiling surface of the lake marks their rapid course, and a terrific conflict commences. They now sink to the bottom folded together in horrid wreaths. The water becomes thick and discoloured. Again they rise, their jaws clap together, re-echoing through the deep surrounding forests. Again they sink, when the contest ends at the muddy bottom of the lake, and the vanquished makes a hazardous escape, hiding himself in the muddy turbulent waters and sedge on a distant shore. The proud victor exulting returns to the place of action. The shores and forests resound his dreadful roar, together with the triumphing shouts of the plaited tribles around, witnesses of the horrid combat.

My apprehensions were highly alarmed after being a spectator of so dreadful a battle; it was obvious that every delay would but tend to encrease my dangers and difficulties, as the sun was near setting, and the alligators gathered around my harbour from all quarters; from these considerations I concluded to be expeditious in my trip to the lagoon, in order to take some fish. Not thinking it prudent to take my fusee with me, lest I might lose it overboard in case of a battle, which I had every reason to dread before my return, I therefore furnished myself with a club for my defence, went on board, and penetrating the first line of those which surrounded my harbour, they gave way; but being pursued by several very large ones, I kept strictly on the watch, and paddled with all my might towards the entrance of the lagoon, hoping to be sheltered there from the multitude of my assailants; but ere I had half-way reached the place, I was attacked on all sides, several endeavouring to overset the canoe. My situation now became precarious to the last degree: two very large ones attacked me closely, at the same instant, rushing up with their heads and part of their bodies above the water, roaring terribly and belching floods of water over me. They struck their jaws together so close to my ears, as almost to stun me, and I expected every moment to be dragged out of the boat and instantly devoured, but I applied my weapons so effectually about me, though at random, that I was so successful as to beat them off a little; when, finding that they designed to renew the battle, I made for the shore, as the only means left me for my preservation, for, by keeping close to it, I should have my enemies on one side of me only, whereas I was before surrounded by them; and there was a probability, if pushed to the last extremity, of saving myself, by jumping out of the canoe on shore, as it is easy to outwalk them on land, although comparatively as swift as lightning in the water. I found this last expedient alone could fully answer my expectations, for as soon as I gained the shore they drew off and kept aloof. This was a happy relief, as my confidence was, in some degree, recovered by it. On recollecting myself, I discovered that I had almost reached the entrance of the lagoon, and determined to venture in, if possible, to take a few fish and then return to my harbour, while day-light continued; for I could now, with caution and resolution, make my way with safety along shore, and indeed there was no other way to regain my camp, without leaving my boat and making my retreat through the marshes and reeds, which, if I could even effect, would have been in a manner throwing myself away, for then there would have been no hopes of ever recovering my bark, and returning in safety to any settlements of men. I accordingly proceeded and made good my entrance into the lagoon, though not without opposition from the alligators, who formed a line across the entrance, but did not pursue me into it, nor was I molested by any there, though there were some very large ones in a cove at the upper end. I soon caught more trout than I had present occasion for, and the air was too hot and sultry to admit of their being kept for many hours, even though salted or barbecued. I now prepared for my return to camp, which I succeeded in with but little trouble, by keeping close to the shore; yet I was opposed upon re-entering the river out of the lagoon, and pursued near to my landing (though not closely attacked) particularly by an old daring one, about twelve feet in length, who kept close after me, and when I stepped on shore and turned about, in order to draw up my canoe, he rushed up near my feet and lay there for some time, looking me in the face, his head and shoulders out of water; I resolved he should pay for his temerity, and having a heavy load in my fusee, I ran to my camp, and returning with my piece, found him with his foot on the gunwale of the boat, in search of fish, on my coming up he withdrew sullenly and slowly into the water, but soon returned and placed himself in his former position, looking at me, and seeming neither fearful nor any way disturbed. I soon dispatched him by lodging the contents of my gun in his head, and then proceeded to cleanse and prepare my fish for supper, and accordingly took them out of the boat, laid them down on the sand close to the water, and began to scale them; when, raising my head, I saw before me, through the clear water, the head and shoulders of a very large alligator, moving slowly towards me. I instantly stepped back, when, with a sweep of his tail, he brushed off several of my fish. It was certainly most providential that I looked up at that instant, as the monster would probably, in less than a minute, have seized and dragged me into the river. This incredible boldness of the animal disturbed me greatly, supposing there could now be no reasonable safety for me during the night, but by keeping continually on the watch: I therefore, as soon as I had prepared the fish, proceeded to secure myself and effects in the best manner I could: in the first place, I hauled my bark upon the shore, almost clear out of the water, to prevent their oversetting or sinking her, after this, every moveable was taken out and carried to my camp, which was but a few yards off; then ranging some dry wood in such order as was the most convenient, cleared the ground round about it, that there might be no impediment in my way, in case of an attack in the night, either from the water or the land; for I discovered by this time, that this small isthmus, from its remote situation and fruitfulness, was resorted to by bears and wolves. Having prepared myself in the best manner I could, I charged my gun, and proceeded to reconnoitre my camp and the adjacent grounds; when I discovered that the peninsula and grove, at the distance of about two hundred yards from my encampment, on the land side, were invested by a Cypress swamp, covered with water, which below was joined to the shore of the little lake, and above to the marshes surrounding the lagoon, so that I was confined to an islet exceedingly circumscribed, and I found there was no other retreat for me, in case of an attack, but by either ascending one of the large Oaks, or pushing off with my boat.

It was by this time dusk, and the alligators had nearly ceased their roar, when I was again alarmed by a tumultuous noise that seemed to be in my harbour, and therefore engaged my immediate attention. Returning to my camp I found it undisturbed, and then continued on to the extreme point of the promontory, where I saw a scene, new and surprising, which at first threw my senses into such a tumult, that it was some time before I could comprehend what was the matter; however, I soon accounted for the prodigious assemblage of crocodiles at this place, which exceeded every thing of the kind I had ever heard of.

How shall I express myself so as to convey an adequate idea of it to the reader, and at the same time avoid raising suspicions of my veracity? Should I say, that the river (in this place) from shore to shore, and perhaps near half a mile above and below me, appeared to be one solid bank of fish, of various kinds, pushing through this narrow pass of St. Juans into the little lake, on their return down the river, and that the alligators were in such incredible numbers, and so close together from shore to shore, that it would have been easy to have walked across on their heads, had the animals been harmless. What expressions can sufficiently declare the shocking scene that for some minutes continued, whilst this mighty army of fish were forcing the pass? During this attempt, thousands I may say hundreds of thousands, of them were caught and swallowed by the devouring alligators. I have seen an alligator take up out of the water several great fish at a time, and just squeeze them betwixt his jaws, while the tails of the great trout flapped about his eyes and lips, ere he had swallowed them. The horrid noise of their closing jaws, their plunging amidst the broken banks of fish, and rising with their prey some feet upright above the water, the floods of water and blood rushing out of their mouths, and the clouds of vapour issuing from their wide nostrils, were truly frightful. This scene continued at intervals during the night, as the fish came to the pass. After this sight, shocking and tremendous as it was, I found myself somewhat easier and more reconciled to my situation, being convinced that their extraordinary assemblage here was owing to the annual feast of fish; and that they were so well employed in their own element, that I had little occasion to fear their paying me a visit.

It being now almost night, I returned to my camp, where I had left my fish broiling, and my kettle of rice stewing, and having with me, oil, pepper and salt, and excellent oranges hanging in abundance over my head (a valuable substitute for vinegar) I sat down and regaled myself chearfully; having finished my repast, I re-kindled my fire for light and whilst I was revising the notes of my past day's journey, I was suddenly roused with a noise behind me toward the main land; I sprang up on my feet, and listening, I distinctly heard some creature wading the water of the isthmus; I seized my gun and went cautiously from my camp, directing my steps towards the noise; when I had advanced about thirty yards, I halted behind a coppice of Orange trees, and soon perceived two very large bears, which had made their way through the water, and had landed in the grove, about one hundred yards distance from me, and were advancing towards me. I waited until they were within thirty yards of me, they there began to snuff and look towards my camp, I snapped my piece, but it flashed, on which they both turned about and galloped off, plunging through the water and swamp, never halting as I suppose, until they reached fast land, as I could hear them leaping and plunging a long time. They did not presume to return again. * * *

1791

II. ST. JOHN DE CRÈVECŒUR (1735–1813)

LETTERS FROM AN AMERICAN FARMER

LETTER III

WHAT IS AN AMERICAN?

I wish I could be acquainted with the feelings and thoughts which must agitate the heart and present themselves to the mind of an enlightened Englishman, when he first lands on this continent. He must greatly rejoice that he lived at a time to see this fair country discovered and settled; he must necessarily feel a share of national pride, when he views the chain of settlements which embellishes these extended shores. When he says to himself, this is the work of my countrymen, who, when convulsed by factions, afflicted by a variety of miseries and wants, restless and impatient, took refuge here. They brought along with them their national genius, to which they principally owe what liberty they enjoy, and what substance they possess. Here he sees the industry of his native country displayed in a new manner, and traces in their works the embrios of all the arts, sciences, and ingenuity which flourish in Europe. Here he beholds fair cities, substantial villages, extensive fields, an immense country filled with decent houses, good roads, orchards, meadows, and bridges, where an hundred years ago all was wild, woody and uncultivated! What a train of pleasing ideas this fair spectacle must suggest; it is a prospect which must inspire a good citizen with the most heartfelt pleasure. The difficulty consists in the manner of viewing so extensive a scene. He is arrived on a new continent; a modern society offers itself to his contemplation, different from what he had hitherto seen. It is not composed, as in Europe, of great lords who possess every thing, and of a herd of people who have nothing. Here are no aristocratical families, no courts, no kings, no bishops, no ecclesiastical dominion, no invisible power giving to a few a very visible one; no great manufacturers employing thousands, no great refinements of luxury. The rich and the poor are not so far removed from each other as they are in Europe. Some few towns excepted, we are all tillers of the earth, from Novia Scotia to West Florida. We are a people of cultivators, scattered over an immense territory, communicating with each other by means of good roads and navigable rivers, united by the silken bands of mild government, all respecting the laws, without dreading their power, because they are equitable. We are all animated with the spirit of an industry which is unfettered and unrestrained, because each person works for himself. If he travels through our rural districts he views not the hostile castle, and the haughty mansion, contrasted with the claybuilt hut and miserable cabbin, where cattle and men help to keep each other warm, and dwell in meanness, smoke, and indigence. A pleasing uniformity of decent competence appears throughout our habitations. The meanest of our log-houses is a dry and comfortable habitation. Lawyer or merchant are the fairest titles our towns afford; that of a farmer is the only appellation of the rural inhabitants of our country. It must take some time ere he can reconcile himself to our dictionary, which is but short in words of dignity, and names of honour. There, on a Sunday, he sees a congregation of respectable farmers and their wives, all clad in neat homespun, well mounted, or riding in their own humble waggons. There is not among them an esquire, saving the unlettered magistrate. There he sees a parson as simple as his flock, a farmer who does not riot on the labour of others. We have no princes, for whom we toil, starve, and bleed: we are the most perfect society now existing in the world. Here man is free as he ought to be; nor is this pleasing equality so transitory as many others are. Many ages will not see the shores of our great lakes replenished with inland nations, nor the unknown bounds of North America entirely peopled. Who can tell how far it extends? Who can tell the millions of men whom it will feed and contain? for no European foot has as yet travelled half the extent of this mighty continent!

The next wish of this traveller will be to know whence came all these people? they are a mixture of English, Scotch, Irish, French, Dutch, Germans, and Swedes. From this promiscuous breed, that race now called Americans have arisen. The eastern provinces must indeed be excepted, as being the unmixed descendants of Englishmen. I have heard many wish that they had been more intermixed also: for my part, I am no wisher, and think it much better as it has happened. They exhibit a most conspicuous figure in this great and variegated picture; they too enter for a great share in the pleasing perspective displayed in these thirteen provinces. I know it is fashionable to reflect on them, but I respect them for what they have done; for the accuracy and wisdom with which they have settled their territory; for the decency of their manners; for their early love of letters; their ancient college, the first in this hemisphere; for their industry; which to me who am but a farmer, is the criterion of everything. There never was a people, situated as they are, who with so ungrateful a soil have done more in so short a time. Do you think that the monarchical ingredients which are more prevalent in other governments, have purged them from all foul stains? Their histories assert the contrary.

In this great American asylum, the poor of Europe have by some means met together, and in consequence of various causes; to what purpose should they ask one another what countrymen they are? Alas, two thirds of them had no country. Can a wretch who wanders about, who works and starves, whose life is a continual scene of sore affliction or pinching penury; can that man call England or any other kingdom his country? A country that had no bread for him, whose fields procured him no harvest, who met with nothing but the frowns of the rich, the severity of the laws, with jails and punishments; who owned not a single foot of the extensive surface of this planet? No! urged by a variety of motives, here they came. Every thing has tended to regenerate them; new laws, a new mode of living, a new social system; here they are become men: in Europe they were as so many useless plants, wanting vegitative mould, and refreshing showers; they withered, and were mowed down by want, hunger, and war; but now by the power of transplantation, like all other plants they have taken root and flourished! Formerly they were not numbered in any civil lists of their country, except in those of the poor; here they rank as citizens. By what invisible power has this surprising metamorphosis been performed? By that of the laws and that of their industry. The laws, the indulgent laws, protect them as they arrive, stamping on them the symbol of adoption; they receive ample rewards for their labours; these accumulated rewards procure them lands; those lands confer on them the title of freemen, and to that title every benefit is affixed which men can possibly require. This is the great operation daily performed by our laws. From whence proceed these laws? From our government. Whence the government? It is derived from the original genius and strong desire of the people ratified and confirmed by the crown. This is the great chain which links us all, this is the picture which every province exhibits, Nova Scotia excepted. There the crown has done all; either there were no people who had genius, or it was not much attended to: the consequence is, that the province is very thinly inhabited indeed; the power of the crown in conjunction with the musketos has prevented men from settling there. Yet some parts of it flourished once, and it contained a mild harmless set of people. But for the fault of a few leaders, the whole were banished. The greatest political error the crown ever committed in America, was to cut off men from a country which wanted nothing but men!

What attachment can a poor European emigrant have for a country where he had nothing? The knowledge of the language, the love of a few kindred as poor as himself, were the only cords that tied him: his country is now that which gives him land, bread, protection, and consequence: *Ubi panis ibi patria,* is the motto of all emigrants. What then is the American, this new man? He is either an European, or the descendant of an European, hence that strange mixture of blood, which you will find in no other country. I could point out to you a family whose grandfather was an Englishman, whose wife was Dutch, whose son married a French woman, and whose present four sons have now four wives of different nations. *He* is an American, who leaving behind him all his ancient prejudices and manners, receives new ones from the new mode of life he has embraced, the new government he obeys, and the new rank he holds. He becomes an American by being received in the broad lap of our great *Alma Mater.* Here individuals of all nations are melted into a new race of men, whose labours and posterity will one day cause great changes in the world. Americans are the western pilgrims, who are carrying along with them that great mass of arts, sciences, vigour, and industry which began long since in the east; they will finish the great circle. The

Americans were once scattered all over Europe; here they are incorporated into one of the finest systems of population which has ever appeared, and which will hereafter become distinct by the power of the different climates they inhabit. The American ought therefore to love this country much better than that wherein either he or his forefathers were born. Here the rewards of his industry followed with equal steps the progress of his labour; his labour is founded on the basis of nature, *self-interest;* can it want a stronger allurement? Wives and children, who before in vain demanded of him a morsel of bread, now, fat and frolicsome, gladly help their father to clear those fields whence exuberant crops are to arise to feed and to clothe them all; without any part being claimed, either by a despotic prince, a rich abbot, or a mighty lord. Here religion demands but little of him; a small voluntary salary to the minister, and gratitude to God; can he refuse these? The American is a new man, who acts upon new principles; he must therefore entertain new ideas, and form new opinions. From involuntary idleness, servile dependence, penury, and useless labour, he has passed to toils of a very different nature, rewarded by ample subsistence.—This is an American. * * *

1782

LETTER VI

MARTHA'S VINEYARD

* * * The vessels most proper for whale fishing, are brigs of about 150 tons burthen, particularly when they are intended for distant latitudes; they always man them with thirteen hands, in order that they may row two whale boats; the crews of which must necessarily consist of six, four at the oars, one standing on the bows with the harpoon, and the other at the helm. It is also necessary that there should be two of these boats, that if one should be destroyed in attacking the whale, the other, which is never engaged at the same time, may be ready to save the hands. Five of the thirteen are always Indians; the last of the complement remains on board to steer the vessel during the action. They have no wages; each draws a certain established share in partnership with the proprietor of the vessel; by which œconomy they are all proportionably concerned in the success of the enterprise, and all equally alert and vigilant. None of these whale-men ever exceed the age of forty: they look on those who are past that period not to be possessed of all that vigour and agility which so adventurous a business requires. Indeed if you attentively consider the immense disproportion between the object assailed and the assailants; if you think on the diminutive size, and weakness of their frail vehicle; if you recollect the treachery of the element on which this scene is transacted; the sudden and unforeseen accidents of winds, &c. you will readily acknowledge, that it must require the most consummate exertion of all the strength, agility, and judgment, of which the bodies and minds of men are capable, to undertake these adventurous encounters.

As soon as they arrive in those latitudes where they expect to meet with whales, a man is sent up to the mast head; if he sees one, he immediately cries out AWAITE PAWANA, *here is a whale;* they all remain still and silent until he repeats PAWANA, *a whale,* when in less than six minutes the two boats are launched, filled with every implement necessary for the attack. They row toward the whale with astonishing velocity; and as the Indians early became their fellow labourers in this new warfare, you can easily conceive, how the Nattick expressions became familiar on board the whale-boats. Formerly it often happened that whale vessels were manned with none but Indians and the Master; recollect also that the Nantucket people understand the Nattick, and that there are always five of these people on board. There are various ways of approaching the whale, according to their peculiar species; and this previous knowledge is of the utmost consequence. When these boats are arrived at a reasonable distance, one of them rests on its oars and stands off, as a witness of the approaching engagement; near the bows of the other the harpooner stands up, and on him principally depends the success of the enterprise. He wears a jacket closely buttoned, and round his head a handkerchief tightly bound: in his hands he holds the dreadful weapon, made of the best steel, marked sometimes with the name of their town, and sometimes with that of their vessel; to the shaft of which the end of a cord of due strength coiled up with the utmost care in the middle of the boat, is firmly tied; the other end is fastened to the bottom of the boat. Thus prepared they row in profound silence, leaving the whole conduct of the enterprise to the harpooner and to the steersman, attentively following their directions. When the former judges himself to be near enough to the whale, that is, at the distance of about fifteen feet, he bids them stop; perhaps she has a calf, whose safety attracts all the attention of the dam, which is a favourable circumstance; perhaps she is of a dangerous species, and it is safest to retire, though their ardour will seldom permit them; perhaps she is asleep, in that case he balances high the harpoon, trying in this important moment to collect all the energy of which he is capable. He launches it forth—she is struck: from her first movements they judge of her temper, as well as of their future success. Sometimes in the immediate impulse of rage, she will attack the boat and demolish it with one stroke of her tail; in an instant the frail vehicle disappears and the assailants are immersed in the dreadful element. Were the whale armed with the jaws of a shark, and as voracious, they never would return home to amuse their listening wives with the interesting tale of the adventure. At other times she will dive and disappear from human sight; and every thing must give way to her velocity, or else all is lost. Sometimes she will swim away as if untouched, and draw the cord with such swiftness that it will set the edge of the boat on fire by the friction. If she rises before she has run out the whole length, she is looked upon as a sure prey. The blood she has lost in her flight, weakens her so much, that if she sinks again, it is but for a short time; the boat follows her course with an almost equal speed. She soon re-appears; tired at last with convulsing the element; which she tinges with her blood, she dies, and floats on the surface. At other times it may happen, that she is not dangerously wounded, though she carries the harpoon fast in her body; when she will alternately dive and rise, and swim on with unabated vigour. She then soon reaches beyond the length of the cord, and carries the boat along with amazing velocity: this sudden impediment sometimes will retard her speed, at other times it only serves to rouse her anger, and to accelerate her progress. The harpooner, with the axe in his hands, stands ready. When he observes that the bows of the boat are greatly pulled down by the diving whale, and that it begins to sink deep and to take much water, he brings the axe almost in contact with the cord; he pauses, still flattering himself that she will relax; but the moment grows critical, unavoidable danger approaches: sometimes men more intent on gain, than on the preservation of their lives, will run great risks; and it is wonderful how far these people have carried their daring courage at this awful moment! But it is vain to hope, their lives must be saved, the cord is cut, the boat rises again. If after thus getting loose, she reappears, they will attack and wound her a second time. She soon dies, and when dead she is towed alongside of their vessel, where she is fastened.

The next operation is to cut with axes and spades, every part of her body which yields oil; the kettles are set a boiling, they fill their barrels as fast as it is made; but as this operation is much slower than that of *cutting up,* they fill the hold of their ship with those fragments, least a storm should arise and oblige them to abandon their prize. It is astonishing what a quantity of oil some of these fish will yield, and what profit it affords to those who are fortunate enough to overtake them. The river St. Laurence whale, which is the only one I am well acquainted with, is seventy-five feet long, sixteen deep, twelve in the length of its bone, which commonly weighs 3000 lb. twenty in the breadth of their tails and produces 180 barrels of oil: I once saw 16 boiled out of the tongue only. After having once vanquished this leviathan, there are two enemies to be dreaded beside the wind; the first of which is the shark: that fierce voracious fish, to which nature has given such dreadful offensive weapons, often comes alongside, and in spite of the people's endeavours, will share with them in their prey; at night particularly. They are very mischievous, but the second enemy is much more terrible and irresistible; it is the killer, sometimes called the thrasher, a species of whales about thirty feet long. They are possessed of such a degree of agility and fierceness, as often to attack the largest spermaceti whales, and not seldom to rob the fisherman of their prey; nor is there any means of defence against so potent an adversary. When all their barrels are full, for every thing is done at sea, or when their limited time is expired and their stores almost expended, they return home, freighted with their valuable cargo; unless they have put it on board a vessel for the European market. Such are, as briefly as I can relate them, the different branches of the œconomy practised by these bold navigators, and the method with which they go such distances from their island to catch this huge game. * * *

1782

ANT-HILL TOWN

I am now sitting under one of the most enchanting groves of Virginia; 'tis the work of art, but executed with so much simplicity as greatly to resemble that of Nature. 'Tis an octagon frame round which vines and honeysuckles have been planted. They have grown with such luxuriancy; their limbs and foliage are so interwoven as to refuse all admittance to the rays of the sun, yet leave a free passage to the air. Round this verdant temple at an equal distance, stands a double row of the mellifluous locusts, the umbrageous catalpas, and the soft magnolias. Alternately planted, they expand their friendly limbs all round, and repel the scorching rays of the sun. 'Tis a grove of Tempé; 'tis a Druidical temple, in point of gloom, shade, and solitude.

From this predilected spot, which is my daily resort, an avenue leads to the house, a second to a private garden, and a third to a bath; while the front expands towards an extensive lawn, a very rare thing here; and opens the view to a variety of luxuriant fields of tobacco, corn, etc., reaching to the very shores of that noble river which is the boundary of this province. By extending [the view] beyond the Potomac, the country rises into a most delightful perspective, composed of plantations, buildings intermixed with copses of trees, peach orchards, etc. There is still something wanting: the pride and principal ornaments of more moist, more northern climates. Here they want the verdant lawns of England, or Ireland, and Normandy; all their art cannot produce that which Nature and the soil seem to refuse. To the South you have an imperfect view of that great and capacious bay, where all the great rivers of this province disembogue themselves. The great number of small gulfs, of bays, islands, and shoals formed by the confluence of so many streams affords food and asylum to an amazing number of ducks, of geese, swans, etc. This is the place where the sport they afford presents itself to all those who care not what fatigues they undergo, provided that pleasure is annexed to it.

This rural scene where I am now, this silvan bower, appears to me so much the more enchanting on account of the cool, the calm, the placid retreat it affords; because I contrast it with the scorching fury of their sun which is now ripening with its fullest energy their extensive harvests. Here it is that I forget the toils of my late journeys; the fatigues it occasioned seem now but a moderate purchase for the ease I feel. I am in that state which conveys the most harmless and indefinable happiness. The feelings of [pleasure] and ease encompass me all around. I am perfectly inactive, yet I am anxious to transmit to you some little memorial of friendship by the ——, which is to sail for England from —— in a few days. I cannot at present be very serious. Harvest and the joys it spreads are themes which ought to inspire me with the rural song. Unfortunately it is not very applicable to this country where the grain is gathered by slaves, and where their daily toils absorb the very idea of joys.

What revolutions do we experience in great as well as in small concerns! Life is but a checkered surface, every step of which is perpetually diversified. 'Tis not two months ago that in the province of Massachusetts I thought myself happy to sit by the comfortable fireside of ——, and I thought his warm room, his clean hearth afforded the greatest felicity, and amply supplied the place of their then heatless sun. 'Tis not two months since his potent Madeira, his enlivening pipe afforded me a fund of cheerfulness that now would be improper. There, reading their provincial newspapers, I beheld with pleasure a fictitious renovation of the spring in the growth of the evergreen which over-ran his mantelpiece. Now, on the contrary, I stand surrounded with these southern blasts, big with igneous particles and ready to inflame one of the most irascible of matters. We had, three days ago, a most solemn trial, one of the most awful thunderstorms ever remembered.

But however agreeable this part of America is in consequence of the hospitality of its inhabitants, the temperate zones of Europe are much superior to it. There it is that mankind enjoy a gentleness of seasons which is much more favourable to the increase of mankind and to the preservation of their health. There husbandry may be displayed in all its perfection and beauty; here one sees and feels nothing but extremes. But exclusive of those primary advantages to be enjoyed, nowhere but in the country is there a great variety of other pleasing sensations which never entered into the head of an inhabitant of cities. I don't mean those belonging to the well-pursued plan of an extensive rural economy, which govern and pursue the useful labours of a large landed estate; much less do I mean those fantastic ones often transplanted from the bosom of cities. No, those I mean are those which indeed I have often felt. They, properly speaking, afford no vulgar enjoyment; 'tis a multitude of pleasing sensations from whence one may collect instruction, morality, rectitude of judgment, motives of gratitude.

Here they have no towns of any note, and I am glad of it. How I hate to dwell in these accumulated and crowded cities! They are but the confined theatre of cupidity, they exhibit nothing but the action and reaction of a variety of passions which, being confined within narrower channels, impel one another with the greatest vigour. The same passions are more rare in the country and, from their greater extent and expansion, they are but necessary gales. I always delighted to live in the country. Have you never felt at the returning of spring a glow of general pleasure, an indiscernible something that pervades our whole frame, an inward involuntary admiration of everything which surrounds us? 'Tis then the beauties of Nature, everywhere spread, seem to swell every sentiment as she swells every juice. She dissolves herself in universal love and seems to lead us to the same sentiments. Did you ever unmoved pass by a large orchard in full bloom without feeling an uncommon ravishment, not only arising from the exquisite perfumes surrounding you on all sides, but from the very splendour of the scene? Who can at this time of the year observe the ushering in of buds, the unfolding of leaves, the appearance of flowers, the whole progress of vegetation, and remain insensible? The well-known industry of bees, that excellent government which pervades their habitations, that never-ceasing industry by which they are actuated, though sung by so many poets, and long since become the subject of so many allusions, metaphors, and the theme of so many orators,—yet 'tis a subject ever new. Set yourself down under some trees in their neighbourhood; see them arriving with the spoils of the fields; observe the digested dews, the concocted ethereal particles of flowers and blossoms converted by them into honey. When these industrious citizens are all out, open one of their hives, and see the wonderful instinct which leads them by the most invariable rules to project and to execute with so much regularity that variety of cells calculated to contain their honey, their coarser food, as well as the eggs from whence new swarms are to arise.

Have not the regular arrival and departure of certain birds ever set you a-thinking whence they came? Have you never reflected on the sublimity of the knowledge they possess, in order to overcome so many difficulties, to steer so invariable a course to other more favourable regions unseen by men, either in their flight or return? When in the spring you happen to revisit some trees of your own planting, have you never felt something of the paternal affection, of that peculiar satisfaction which attends viewing the works of our hands? Have you ever enjoyed as you ought the transcendent pleasure attending that magnificent scene—unheeded, alas, by most men—because it is often repeated? Have you never worshipped the Master of Nature in the most august of all temples, in that extensive one of His own framing where He no doubt presides as the great invisible Pontiff, but where He permits His awful representative to become visible in order to bless mankind with light and life? Have you never observed the sun rising on a calm morning? What majesty pervades, then, all Nature, when the variegated aspect of the heavens, when those mixed tinges of emerging light and vanishing shades, united with that diffusive [pleasure] issuing from the fecundated earth, exhibit the most august spectacle which this transitory life affords!

How often have I viewed with admiration that sublime gradation of objects reaching and filling the whole extent of my perception: from the refulgent luminary to the fainting moon, to the dimmed stars, down to the vocal choir, even to the polygonal cobweb, perpendicularly hung or horizontally suspended,—all bespangled with dew-drops refulgent as the diamond, waving to the raptured eyes! 'Tis not that I would mean to recommend to you the worship of fire in this solar appearance. I am far from believing with the disciples of Zoroaster, that the sun is the true Shekinah of the divine presence, the grand tabernacle, the Keblah where He alone resides. No, but relegated as we are at such a distance from the great Author of all, is not it a consolation to view scenes of this nature, by which we are elevated and permitted in thought to approach nearer to His throne? 'Tis in the country alone that you can follow this rotation of objects which feeds contemplation; which delights, improves, and often assuages the pains of an afflicted mind. Even the approach of a thunderstorm, though so dreaded by the generality of mankind,—how solemn, how awful, what reverence does it not inspire us with! Nature seems angry. Yes, but it is for our good, and she wisely draws from that strife of elements the salubrity of the air we breathe.

As soon as the sea breeze came, I took a walk towards the shores of the river. As I was searching for the most convenient spot to descend to the shores I perceived a large, flat stone lying on the ground. As they are very scarce in this part of the country I stopped to view it, and to consider whether it had not been left there on some peculiar account. On looking at it more attentively, I perceived the marks of ancient sea-shells incrusted on its surface. How could this stone have received these marine impressions? How could it be brought here where stones are so scarce? Hoping to find some of these shell fragments better preserved on the opposite side, I lifted it up with some difficulty, when to my great surprise and amusement I found that it served as a roof to a subterranean structure of a very singular appearance. It covered the upper walks of a town seemingly composed of arches, of vaults, of a multitude of passages intermixed throughout the whole. From these obscure mansions there were a number of apertures leading to the excavated surface which was covered by the stone. It was cut into a great number of streets; some times contiguous and parallel to each other; sometimes receding in various directions. These streets were divided from each other by little banks of earth of a different thickness, as is the case in wintertime in the streets of Quebec. The whole surface was about thirty-five inches long and about twenty-three broad. It contained seventy-one streets and had fourteen subterraneous openings. The first idea it conveyed was that of a labyrinth, but on following with attention any one of the streets, the intricacy vanished.

In order to have a fuller view of this scene of mysterious ingenuity I removed the stone with the utmost care. On the southeast, and northwest sides I perceived two considerable breaches full three inches wide gradually sloping from the surface of the ground to the subterranean avenues. These were, I suppose, the two great communications to fetch their foods and to carry off their unnecessary materials.

Here lived thousands of ants of the pismire class. But no pen can delineate the seeming confusion and affright which my bold intrusion caused among them; it was a whole republic thrown into the most imminent danger. The never-failing impulse of instinct immediately led them to provide for the preservation of their young. They appeared to be as big as small grains of wheat, and seemed to have been brought up from the lower habitations in order to receive more immediately the prolific effects of the sun's heat, and to swell their limbs into life and action. These embryos appeared to be in a different degree of animal advancement. Some seemed quite torpid and lifeless; others showed marks of feeling and pains on being suddenly seized, though by maternal claws. No sooner was the first effect of their panic over than they hurried away their young out of my sight, but as they were more numerous than the parents, more assistance immediately came from below; or else the same individuals returned to the pious office. In about five minutes not the least vestiges were left of that numerous society, and no one could have believed that it had been replenished with so many inhabitants. In this great national dismay no one quitted the mansion or attempted to make his escape, although they knew not what sort of enemy I was. The whole community, bound by the ties of the firmest confederacy, unanimously went down, trusting, perhaps, to their works of defence, or to my inability to pursue them where all appeared so dark and so intricate.

What a situation for this Virginian republic, when the refulgent sun at once pervaded every corner of their habitation, where his rays had never reached before! We may then pronounce that what the stone covered were their paths of life and health, the cradles of their rising generations. Their other and visible recesses must have far exceeded this little insignificant surface; for, no doubt, it must have afforded them convenient rooms for their winter-stores, receptacles for their daily food, besides capacious lodgings for so many thousand inhabitants.

Should I turn up and destroy so fair a monument of industry? Should I overwhelm in death and desolation so many harmless animals? No, I could not permit myself to satisfy so impious a curiosity at the expense of so much evil and to pollute my hands by the commission of so atrocious a deed; on the contrary, I replaced the stone.

A few days afterwards I paid them a second visit, when I observed a great number of ants decorated with wings. But this gaudy attire did not appear to add any celerity to their flight; they never expanded them. Like the preposterous dress of some ladies it served only to render them more conspicuous than the rest. Upon a closer inspection they appeared more inactive and wholly deprived of that quickness of motion for which the unwinged sort are so remarkable. Perhaps they were the matrons of the republic, never departing from that formal gravity appointed to the rank by Nature; perhaps they were young damsels embarrassed by the rule of modesty and decorum; perhaps they were young ones just hatched, not having as yet ventured to traverse the air in order to harden their limbs in the aspect of the sun. How sorry [I am] that I never have read Buffon! I could have explained myself technically, whereas I am now speaking to you in the language of a schoolboy who possesses as yet nothing of knowledge besides curiosity.

Within a few rods and nearer to the river were erected eleven great conical buildings three feet high and two and a half broad at the bottom. They were perforated with an immense number of holes. The whole appeared to be built of slight materials, yet by means of sticks and straws, the ends of which only were visible, they had given it a great degree of stability. The inhabitants of this second colony appeared to be of a much larger size, much stronger, and more capable of lifting heavy burthens. What surprised me was that, although so near this subterranean settlement, yet there appeared no kind of communication between them. Weak and defenseless as the first were, a perfect peace and tranquillity prevailed; a most marvellous thing considering the superiority which the one had over the other species. This harmony must have arisen from their feeding on different things. In this case there could be no room either for contention or competition; no cause that could influence their little passions and produce those sanguinary commotions so frequent among mankind. The circumjacent ground which surrounded these eleven pyramids was perfectly cleaned; neither bush, shrub, nor herbage, or any foliage whatever grew nigh that might conceal or harbour any enemy. They had made considerable paths to the waterside as well as to different fields in which they invariably travelled, but I never followed them in any of their excursions.

The same Pythagorean disposition which prevented me from turning up the bowels of the first republic, in order to satisfy a vain curiosity, made me refrain from tumbling down one of these cones which might have showed me the structure within. Whether these serve them only as summer habitations, and are but a collection of materials excavated from below, I dare not ascertain. Such as it presented itself to my view it seems to answer all their purposes, and to preserve them from the inclemency of the air, wind, and rain. What other casual accidents may happen is no doubt quickly repaired by the mutual assistance of so many alert and vigorous insects.

When some of your friends hear of your having received a letter from North America, they will perhaps expect to hear some learned accounts of natural knowledge, botany, etc. What will they think of your correspondent when instead of useful discoveries, important dissertations, they hear you read this trifling incident not worth its passage over the Atlantic? For your sake make some sort of apology which will palliate their disappointment, without lessening your dignity. And, after all, is it not in the course of a long correspondence sometimes necessary to write as we feel? Premeditated subjects become a laborious task and the communicating of those impulses when they arise is truly pleasurable. Indeed, had I my choice I'd much rather amuse myself with these objects of instinctive economy, knowledge, and industry than to wade over fields of battle strewn with the carcasses of friends and foes, the victims of so many phantoms. Such as this is, pray receive it, agreeable to your ancient custom for better, for worse.—Adieu.

(*c.* 1769) 1925

III. JOHN JAMES AUDUBON (1785–1851)

A FLOOD

Many of our larger streams, such as the Mississippi, the Ohio, the Illinois, the Arkansas and the Red River, exhibit at certain seasons the most extensive overflowings of their waters, to which the name of *floods* is more appropriate than the term *freshets,* usually applied to the sudden risings of smaller streams. If we consider the vast extent of country through which an inland navigation is afforded by the never-failing supply of water furnished by these wonderful rivers, we cannot suppose them exceeded in magnitude by any other in the known world. It will easily be imagined what a wonderful spectacle must present itself to the eye of the traveller, who for the first time views the enormous mass of waters, collected from the vast central regions of our continent, booming along, turbid and swollen to overflowing, in the broad channels of the Mississippi and Ohio, the latter of which has a course of more than a thousand miles, and the former of several thousands.

To give you some idea of a *Booming Flood* of these gigantic streams, it is necessary to state the causes which give rise to it. These are, the sudden melting of the snows on the mountains, and heavy rains continued for several weeks. When it happens that, during a severe winter, the Alleghany Mountains have been covered with snow to the depth of several feet, and the accumulated mass has remained unmelted for a length of time, the materials of a flood are thus prepared. It now and then happens that the winter is hurried off by a sudden increase of temperature, when the accumulated snows melt away simultaneously over the whole country, and the south-easterly wind which then usually blows, brings along with it a continued fall of heavy rain, which, mingling with the dissolving snow, deluges the alluvial portions of the western country, filling up the rivulets, ravines, creeks, and small rivers. These, delivering their waters to the great streams, cause the latter not merely to rise to a surprising height, but to overflow their banks, wherever the land is low. On such occasions, the Ohio itself presents a splendid, and at the same time an appalling spectacle; but when its waters mingle with those of the Mississippi, then, is the time to view an American flood in all its astonishing magnificence.

At the foot of the Falls of the Ohio, the water has been known to rise upwards of sixty feet above its lowest level. The river, at this point, has already run a course of nearly seven hundred miles, from its origin at Pittsburg, in Pennsylvania, during which it has received the waters of its numberless tributaries, and overflowing all the bottom lands or valleys, has swept along the fences and dwellings which have been unable to resist its violence. I could relate hundreds of incidents which might prove to you the dreadful effects of such an inundation, and which have been witnessed by thousands besides myself. I have known, for example, of a cow swimming through a window, elevated at least seven feet from the ground, and sixty-two feet above low-water mark. The house was then surrounded by water from the Ohio, which runs in front of it, while the neighbouring country was overflowed; yet the family did not remove from it, but remained in its upper portion, having previously taken off the sashes of the lower windows, and opened the doors. But let us return to the Mississippi.

There the overflowing is astonishing; for no sooner has the water reached the upper part of the banks, than it rushes out and overspreads the whole of the neighbouring swamps, presenting an ocean overgrown with stupendous forest-trees. So sudden is the calamity, that every individual, whether man or beast, has to exert his utmost ingenuity to enable him to escape from the dreaded element. The Indian quickly removes to the hills of the interior; the cattle and game swim to the different strips of land that remain uncovered in the midst of the flood, or attempt to force their way through the waters until they perish from fatigue. Along the banks of the river, the inhabitants have rafts ready made, on which they remove themselves, their cattle and their provisions, and which they then fasten with ropes or grape-vines to the larger trees, while they contemplate the melancholy spectacle presented by the current, as it carries off their houses and wood-yards piece by piece. Some who have nothing to lose, and are usually known by the name of *Squatters,* take this opportunity of traversing the woods in canoes for the purpose of procuring game, and particularly the skins of animals, such as the deer and bear, which may be converted into money. They resort to the low ridges surrounded by the waters, and destroy thousands of deer, merely for their skins, leaving the flesh to putrefy.

The river itself, rolling its swollen waters along, presents a spectacle of the most imposing nature. Although no large vessel, unless propelled by steam, can now make its way against the current, it is seen covered by boats, laden with produce, which running out from all the smaller streams, float silently towards the City of New Orleans, their owners meanwhile not very well assured of finding a landing-place even there. The water is covered with yellow foam and pumice, the latter having floated from the Rocky Mountains of the north-west. The eddies are larger and more powerful than ever. Here and there tracts of forest are observed undetermined, the trees gradually giving way, and falling into the stream. Cattle, horses, bears and deer are seen at times attempting to swim across the impetuous mass of foaming and boiling water; whilst here and there a Vulture or an Eagle is observed perched on a bloated carcass, tearing it up in pieces, as regardless of the flood, as on former occasions it would have been of the numerous *sawyers* and *planters,* with which the surface of the river is covered, when the water is low. Even the steamer is frequently distressed. The numberless trees and logs that float along break its paddles and retard its progress. Besides, it is on such occasions difficult to procure fuel to maintain its fires; and it is only at very distant intervals that a woodyard can be found which the water has not carried off.

Following the river in your canoe, you reach those parts of the shores that are protected against the overflowing of the waters, and are called *Levees*. There you find the whole population of the district at work repairing and augmenting those artificial barriers, which are several feet above the level of the fields. Every person appears to dread the opening of a *crevasse,* by which the waters may rush into his fields. In spite of all exertions, however, the crevasse opens, the water bursts impetuously over the plantations, and lays waste the crops which so lately were blooming in all the luxuriance of spring. It opens up a new channel, which, for aught I know to the contrary, may carry its waters even to the Mexican Gulf.

I have floated on the Mississippi and Ohio when thus swollen, and have in different places visited the submersed lands of the interior, propelling a light canoe by the aid of a paddle. In this manner I have traversed immense portions of the country overflowed by the waters of these rivers, and, particularly whilst floating over the Mississippi bottom-lands, I have been struck with awe at the sight. Little or no current is met with, unless when the canoe passes over the bed of a bayou. All is silent and melancholy, unless when the mournful bleating of the hemmed in Deer reaches your ear, or the dismal scream of an Eagle or a Raven is heard, as the foul bird rises, disturbed by your approach, from the carcass on which it was allaying its craving appetite. Bears, Cougars, Lynxes, and all other quadrupeds that can ascend the trees, are observed crouched among their top branches. Hungry in the midst of abundance, although they see floating around them the animals on which they usually prey, they dare not venture to swim to them. Fatigued by the exertions which they have made in reaching the dry land, they will there stand the hunter's fire, as if to die by a ball were better than to perish amid the waste of waters. On occasions like this, all these animals are shot by hundreds.

Opposite the City of Natchez, which stands on a bluff of considerable elevation, the extent of inundated lands is immense, the greater portion of the tract lying between the Mississippi and the Red River, which is more than thirty miles in breadth, being under water. The mail-bag has often been carried through the immersed forests, in a canoe, for even a greater distance, in order to be forwarded to Natchitochez.

But now, observe this great flood gradually subsiding, and again see the mighty changes which it has effected. The waters have now been carried into the distant ocean. The earth is everywhere covered by a deep deposit of muddy loam, which in drying splits into deep and narrow chasms, presenting a reticulated appearance, and from which, as the weather becomes warmer, disagreeable, and at times noxious, exhalations arise, and fill the lower stratum of the atmosphere as with a dense fog. The banks of the river have almost everywhere been broken down in a greater or less degree. Large streams are now found to exist, where none were formerly to be seen, having forced their way in direct lines from the upper parts of the bends. These are by the navigator called *short-cuts.* Some of them have proved large enough to produce a change in the navigation of the Mississippi. If I mistake not, one of these, known by the name of the *Grand Cut-off,* and only a few miles in length, has diverted the river from its natural course, and has shortened it by fifty miles. The upper parts of the islands present a bulwark consisting of an enormous mass of floated trees of all kinds, which have lodged there. Large sand-banks have been completely removed by the impetuous whirls of the waters, and have been deposited in other places. Some appear quite new to the eye of the navigator, who has to mark their situation and bearings in his log-book. The trees on the margins of the banks have in many parts given way. They are seen bending over the stream, like the grounded arms of an overwhelmed army of giants. Everywhere are heard the lamentations of the farmer and planter, whilst their servants and themselves are busily employed in repairing the damages occasioned by the floods. At one crevasse an old ship or two, dismantled for the purpose, are sunk, to obstruct the passage opened by the still rushing waters, while new earth is brought to fill up the chasms. The squatter is seen shouldering his rifle, and making his way through the morass, in search of his lost stock, to drive the survivors home, and save the skins of the drowned. New fences have everywhere to be formed; even new houses must be erected, to save which from a like disaster, the settler places them on an elevated platform supported by pillars made of the trunks of trees. The lands must be ploughed anew, and if the season is not too far advanced, a crop of corn and potatoes may yet be raised. But the rich prospects of the planter are blasted. The traveller is impeded in his journey, the creeks and smaller streams having broken up their banks in a degree proportionate to their size. A bank of sand, which seems firm and secure, suddenly gives way beneath the traveller's horse, and the next moment the animal has sunk in the quicksand, either to the chest in front, or over the crupper behind, leaving its master in a situation not to be envied.

Unlike the mountain-torrents and small rivers of other parts of the world, the Mississippi rises but slowly during these floods, continuing for several weeks to increase at the rate of about an inch a day. When at its height, it undergoes little flunctuation for some days, and after this subsides as slowly as it rose. The usual duration of a flood is from four to six weeks, although, on some occasions, it is protracted to two months.

Every one knows how largely the idea of floods and cataclysms enters into the speculations of the geologist. If the streamlets of the European Continent afford illustrations of the formation of strata, how much more must the Mississippi, with its ever-shifting sand-banks, its crumbling shores, its enormous masses of drift timber, the source of future beds of coal, its extensive and varied alluvial deposits, and its mighty mass of waters rolling sullenly along, like the flood of eternity!

1831–39

THE FLORIDA KEYS

I left you abruptly, perhaps uncivilly, reader, at the dawn of day, on Sandy Island, which lies just six miles from the extreme point of South Florida. I did so because I was amazed at the appearance of things around me, which in fact looked so different then from what they seemed at night, that it took some minutes' reflection to account for the change. When we laid ourselves down in the sand to sleep, the waters almost bathed our feet; when we opened our eyes in the morning, they were at an immense distance. Our boat lay on her side, looking not unlike a whale reposing on a mud-bank. The birds in myriads were probing their exposed pasture-ground. There great flocks of Ibises fed apart from equally large collections of Godwits, and thousands of Herons gracefully paced along, ever and anon thrusting their javelin bills into the body of some unfortunate fish confined in a small pool of water. Of Fish-Crows I could not estimate the number, but from the havoc they made among the crabs, I conjecture that these animals must have been scarce by the time of next ebb. Frigate Pelicans chased the Jager, which himself had just robbed a poor Gull of its prize, and all the Gallinules ran with spread wings from the mud-banks to the thickets of the island, so timorous had they become when they perceived us.

Surrounded as we were by so many objects that allured us, not one could we yet attain, so dangerous would it have been to venture on the mud; and our pilot, having assured us that nothing could be lost by waiting, spoke of our eating, and on his hint told us that he would take us to a part of the island where "our breakfast would be abundant although uncooked." Off we went, some of the sailors carrying baskets, others large tin pans and wooden vessels, such as they use for eating their meals in. Entering a thicket of about an acre in extent, we found on every bush several nests of the Ibis, each containing three large and beautiful eggs, and all hands fell to gathering. The birds gave way to us, and ere long we had a heap of eggs that promised delicious food. Nor did we stand long in expectation, for kindling a fire, we soon prepared in one way or other, enough to satisfy the cravings of our hungry maws. Breakfast ended, the pilot looking at the gorgeous sunrise, said, "Gentlemen, prepare yourselves for fun, the tide is acoming."

Over these enormous mud-flats, a foot or two of water is quite sufficient to drive all the birds ashore, even the tallest Heron or Flamingo, and the tide seems to flow at once over the whole expanse. Each of us provided with a gun, posted himself behind a bush, and no sooner had the water forced the winged creatures to approach the shore, than the work of destruction commenced. When it at length ceased, the collected mass of birds of different kinds looked not unlike a small haycock. Who could not with a little industry have helped himself to a few of their skins? Why, reader, surely no one as fond of these things as I am. Everyone assisted in this, and even the sailors themselves tried their hand at the work.

Our pilot, good man, told us he was no hand at such occupations, and would go after something else. So taking Long Tom and his fishing-tackle, he marched off quietly along the shores. About an hour afterwards we saw him returning, when he looked quite exhausted, and on our inquiring the cause, said, "There is a doo-fish yonder and a few balacoudas, but I am not able to bring them, or even to haul them here; please send the sailors after them." The fishes were accordingly brought, and as I had never seen a dew fish, I examined it closely, and took an outline of its form, which some days hence you may perhaps see. It exceeded a hundred pounds in weight, and afforded excellent eating. The balacouda is also a good fish, but at times a dangerous one, for, according to the pilot, on more than one occasion "some of these gentry" had followed him when waist-deep in the water, in pursuit of a more valuable prize, until in self-defence he had to spear them, fearing that "the gentlemen" might at one dart cut off his legs, or some other nice bit, with which he was unwilling to part.

Having filled our cask from a fine well, long since dug in the sand of Cape Sable, either by Seminole Indians or pirates, no matter which, we left Sandy Isle about full tide, and proceeded homewards, giving a call here and there at different keys, with the view of procuring rare birds, and also their nests and eggs. We had twenty miles to go "as the birds fly," but the tortuosity of the channels rendered our course fully a third longer. The sun was descending fast, when a black cloud suddenly obscured the majestic orb. Our sails swelled by a breeze, that was scarcely felt by us, and the pilot, requesting us to sit on the weather gunwale, told us that we were "going to get it." One sail was hauled in and secured, and the other was reefed, although the wind had not increased. A low murmuring noise was heard, and across the cloud that now rolled along in tumultuous masses, shot vivid flashes of lightning. Our experienced guide steered directly across a flat towards the nearest land. The sailors passed their quids from one cheek to the other, and our pilot having covered himself with his oil-jacket, we followed his example: "Blow, sweet breeze," cried he at the tiller, and "we'll reach land before the blast overtakes us, for, gentlemen, it is a furious cloud yon."

A furious cloud indeed was the one which now, like an eagle on outstretched wings, approached so swiftly, that one might have deemed it in haste to destroy us. We were not more than a cable's length from the shore, when, with imperative voice, the pilot calmly said to us, "Sit quite still, Gentlemen, for I should not like to lose you overboard just now; the boat can't upset, my word for that, if you will but sit still—here we have it!"

Reader, persons who have never witnessed a hurricane, such as not infrequently desolates the sultry climates of the south, can scarcely form an idea of their terrific grandeur. One would think that, not content with laying waste all on land, it must needs sweep the waters of the shallows quite dry, to quench its thirst. No respite for an instant does it afford to the objects within the reach of its furious current. Like the scythe of the destroying angel, it cuts every thing by the roots, as it were with the careless ease of the experienced mower. Each of its revolving sweeps collects a heap that might be likened to the full sheaf which the husbandman flings by his side. On it goes with a wildness and fury that are indescribable; and when at last its frightful blasts have ceased, Nature, weeping and disconsolate, is left bereaved of her beauteous offspring. In some instances, even a full century is required, before, with all her powerful energies, she can repair her loss. The planter has not only lost his mansion, his crops, and his flocks, but he has to clear his lands anew, covered and entangled as they are with the trunks and branches of trees that are every where strewn. The bark overtaken by the storm, is cast on the lee-shore, and if any are left to witness the fatal results, they are the "wreckers" alone, who, with inward delight, gaze upon the melancholy spectacle.

Our light bark shivered like a leaf the instant the blast reached her sides. We thought she had gone over; but the next instant she was on the shore. And now in contemplation of the sublime and awful storm, I gazed around me. The waters drifted like snow; the tough mangroves hid their tops amid their roots, and the loud roaring of the waves driven among them blended with the howl of the tempest. It was not rain that fell; the masses of water flew in a horizontal direction, and where a part of my body was exposed, I felt as if a smart blow had been given me on it. But enough!—in half an hour it was over. The pure blue sky once more embellished the heavens, and although it was now quite night, we considered our situation a good one.

The crew and some of the party spent the night in the boat. The pilot, myself, and one of my assistants took to the heart of the mangroves, and having found high land, we made a fire as well as we could, spread a tarpawling, and fixing our insect-bars over us, soon forgot in sleep the horrors that had surrounded us. * * *

1831–39

WILLIAM CULLEN BRYANT
(1794–1878)

[AMERICAN POETRY]

Of the poetry of the United States different opinions have been entertained, and prejudice on the one side, and partiality on the other, have equally prevented a just and rational estimate of its merits. Abroad, our literature has fallen under unmerited contumely, from those who were but slenderly acquainted with the subject on which they professed to decide; and at home, it must be confessed, that the swaggering and pompous pretensions of many have done not a little to provoke and excuse the ridicule of foreigners. Either of these extremes exerts an injurious influence on the cause of letters in our country. To encourage exertion and embolden merit to come forward, it is necessary that they should be acknowledged and rewarded—few will have the confidence to solicit what has been withheld from claims as strong as theirs, or the courage to tread a path which presents no prospect but the melancholy wrecks of those who have gone before them. National gratitude—national pride—every high and generous feeling that attaches us to the land of our birth, or that exalts our characters as individuals, ask of us that we should foster the infant literature of our country, and that genius and industry, employing their efforts to hasten its perfection, should receive, from our hands, that celebrity which reflects as much honour on the nation which confers it as on those to whom it is extended. On the other hand, it is not necessary for these purposes—it is even detrimental to bestow on mediocrity the praise due to excellence, and still more so is the attempt to persuade ourselves and others into an admiration of the faults of favorite writers. We make but a contemptible figure in the eyes of the world, and set ourselves up as objects of pity to our posterity, when we affect to rank the poets of our own country with those mighty masters of song who have flourished in Greece, Italy and Britain. Such extravagant admiration may spring from a praiseworthy and patriotic motive, but it seems to us that it defeats its own object of encouraging our literature, by seducing those, who would aspire to the favour of the public, into an imitation of imperfect models, and leading them to rely too much on the partiality of their countrymen to overlook their deficiencies. Were our rewards to be bestowed only on what is intrinsically meritorious, merit alone would have any apology for appearing before the public. The poetical adventurer should be taught that it is only the productions of genius, taste and diligence that can find favour at the bar of criticism—that his writings are not to be applauded merely because they are written by an American, and are not decidedly bad; and that he must produce some more satisfactory evidence of his claim to celebrity than an extract from the parish register. To show him what we expect of him, it is necessary to point out the faults of his predecessors, and to commend their excellencies. He must be taught, as well what to avoid, as what to imitate. This is the only way of diffusing and preserving a pure taste, both among those who read and those who write, and, in our opinion, the only way of affording merit a proper and effectual encouragement.

It must however be allowed, that the poetry of the United States, though it has not reached that perfection to which some other countries have carried theirs, is yet even better than we could have been expected to produce, considering that our nation has scarcely seen two centuries since the first of its founders erected their cabins on its soil, that our literary institutions are yet in their infancy, and that our citizens are just beginning to find leisure to attend to intellectual refinement and indulge in intellectual luxury, and the means of rewarded intellectual excellence. For the first century after the settlement of this country, the few quaint and unskilful specimens of poetry which yet remain to us, are looked upon merely as objects of curiosity, are preserved only in the cabinet of the antiquary, and give little pleasure, if read without reference to the age and people which produced them. A purer taste began after this period to prevail—the poems of the Rev. John Adams, written in the early part of the eighteenth century, which have been considered as no bad specimen of the poetry of his time, are tolerably free from the faults of the generation that preceded him, and show the dawnings of an ambition of correctness and elegance. The poetical writings of Joseph Green, Esq., who wrote about the middle of the same century, have been admired for their humour and the playful ease of their composition.

But, previous to the contest which terminated in the independence of the United States, we can hardly be said to have had any national poetry. Literary ambition was not then frequent amongst us—there was little motive for it, and few rewards. We were contented with considering ourselves as participating in the literary fame of that nation, of which we were a part, and of which many of us were natives, and aspired to no separate distinction. And indeed we might well lay an equal claim, with those who remained on the British soil, to whatever glory the genius and learning as well as the virtue and bravery of other times reflected on the British name. These were qualities which ennobled our common ancestors; and though their graves were not with us, and we were at a distance from the scenes and haunts which were hallowed by their deeds, their studies, and their contemplations, yet we brought with us, and preserved all the more valuable gifts which they left to their posterity and to mankind—their illumination—their piety—their spirit of liberty—reverence for their memory and example and all the proud tokens of a generous descent.

Yet here was no theatre for the display of literary talent—the worshippers of fame could find no altars erected to that divinity in America, and he who would live by his pen must seek patronage in the parent country. Some men of taste and learning amongst us, might occasionally amuse their leisure with poetical trifles, but a country struggling with the difficulties of colonization, and possessing no superfluous wealth, wanted any other class of men rather than poets. Accordingly we find the specimens of American poetry, before this period, mostly desultory and occasional—rare and delicate exotics, cultivated only by the curious.

On our becoming an independent empire, a different spirit began to manifest itself, and the general ambition to distinguish ourselves as a nation was not without its effect on our literature. It seems to us, that it is from this time only that we can be said to have poets of our own, and from this period it is that we must date the origin of American poetry. About this time, flourished Francis Hopkinson, whose humorous ballad, entitled the Battle of the Kegs, is in most of our memories, and some of whose attempts, though deficient in vigour, are not inelegant. The keen and forcible invectives of Dr. Church, which are still recollected by his contemporaries, received an additional edge and sharpness from the exasperated feelings of the times. A writer in verse of inferior note was Philip Freneau, whose pen seems to have been chiefly employed on political subjects, and whose occasional productions, distinguished by a coarse strength of sarcasm, and abounding with allusions to passing events, which is perhaps their greatest merit, attracted in their time considerable notice, and in the year 1786 were collected into a volume. But the influence of that principle which awoke and animated the exertions of all who participated in the political enthusiasm of that time, was still more strongly exemplified in the Connecticut poets —Trumbull, Dwight, Barlow, Humphreys, and Hopkins—who began to write about this period. In all the productions of these authors, there is a pervading spirit of *nationality* and patriotism—a desire to reflect credit on the country to which they belonged, which seems, as much as individual ambition, to have prompted their efforts, and which at times gives a certain glow and interest to their manner.

McFingal, the most popular of the writings of the former of these poets, first appeared in the year 1782. This pleasant satire on the adherents of Britain in those times, may be pronounced a tolerably successful imitation of the great work of Butler—though, like every other imitation of that author, it wants that varied and inexhaustible fertility of allusion, which made all subjects of thought—the lightest and most abstruse parts of learning—every thing in the physical and moral world—in art or nature, the playthings of his wit. The work of Trumbull cannot be much praised for the purity of its diction. Yet perhaps great scrupulousness in this particular was not consistent with the plan of the author, and, to give the scenes of his poem their full effect, it might have been thought necessary to adopt the familiar dialect of the country and the times. We think his Progress of Dulness a more pleasing poem, as more finished, and more perfect in its kind, and though written in the same manner, more free from the constraint and servility of imitation. The graver poems of Trumbull contain some vigorous and animated declamation.

Of Dr. Dwight we would speak with all the respect due to talents, to learning, to piety, and a long life of virtuous usefulness—but we must be excused from feeling any high admiration of his poetry. It seems to us modelled upon a manner altogether too artificial and mechanical. There is something strained, violent, and out of nature, in all his attempts. His Conquest of Canaan will not secure immortality to its author. In this work the author has been considered by some as by no means happy in the choice of his fable—however this may be, he has certainly failed to avail himself of the advantages it offered him—his epic wants the creations and colourings of an inventive and poetical fancy—the charm, which, in the hands of genius, communicates interest to the simplest incidents, and something of the illusion of reality to the most improbable fictions. The versification is remarkable for its unbroken monotony. Yet it contains splendid passages, which, separated from the body of the work, might be admired, but a few pages pall both on the ear and the imagination. It has been urged in its favor that the writer was young—the poetry of his maturer years does not however seem to possess greater beauties or fewer faults. The late Mr. Dennie at one time exerted his ingenuity to render this poem popular with his countrymen; in the year 1800 he published, in the *Farmer's Museum,* a paper printed at Walpole, of which he was the editor, a series of observations and criticisms on the Conquest of Canaan, after the manner of Addison in those numbers of the *Spectator* which made Milton a favourite with the English people. But this attempt did not meet with success—the work would not sell, and loads of copies yet cumber the shelves of our booksellers. In the other poems of Dr. Dwight, which are generally obnoxious to the same criticisms, he sometimes endeavours to descend to a more familiar style, and entertains his reader with laborious attempts at wit, and here he is still unsuccessful. Parts of his Greenfield Hill, and that most unfortunate of his productions, the Triumph of Infidelity, will confirm the truth of this remark.

Barlow, when he began to write, was a poet of no inconsiderable promise. His Hasty Pudding, one of his earliest productions, is a good specimen of mock-heroic poetry, and his Vision of Columbus, at the time of its first appearance, attracted much attention and was hailed as an earnest of better things. It is no small praise to say, that when appointed by the General Assembly of Churches in Connecticut, to revise Watts' Version of the Psalms, and to versify such as were omitted in that work, he performed the task in a manner which made a near approach to the simplicity and ease of that poet, who, according to Dr. Johnson, "has done better than any body else what nobody has done well." In his maturer years, Barlow became ambitious of distinguishing himself and doing honour to his country, by some more splendid and important exertion of his talents, and, for this purpose, projected a national epic, in which was sung the Discovery of America, the successful struggle of the states in the defence of their liberties, and the exalted prospects which were opening before them. It is to be regretted that a design, so honourable and so generously conceived, should have failed. In 1807 appeared the Columbiad, which was his poem of the Vision of Columbus, much enlarged, and with such variations as the feelings and reflections of his riper age and judgment led him to make. The Columbiad is not, in our opinion, so pleasing a poem, in its present form, as in that in which it was originally written. The plan of the work is utterly destitute of interest, and that, which was at first sufficiently wearisome, has become doubly so by being drawn out to its present length. Nor are the additions of much value, on account of the taste in which they are composed. Barlow, in his later poetry, atempted to invigorate his style, but instead of drawing strength and salubrity, from the pure wells of ancient English, he corrupted and debased it with foreign infusions. The imposing but unchaste glitter, which distinguished the manner of Darwin and his imitators, appears likewise to have taken strong hold on his fancy, and he has not scrupled to bestow on his poem much of this meretricious decoration. But notwithstanding the bad taste in which his principal work is composed—notwithstanding he cannot be said to write with much pathos, or many of the native felicities of fancy, there is yet enough, in the poetry of Mr. Barlow to prove, that, had he fixed his eye on purer models, he might have excelled, not indeed in epic or narrative poetry, nor in the delineation of passion and feeling, but in that calm, lofty, sustained style, which suits best with topics of morality and philosophy, and for which the vigour and spirit of his natural manner, whenever he permits it to appear, shew him to have been well qualified. * * *

With respect to the prevailing style of poetry, at the present day, in our country, we apprehend that it will be found, in too many instances, tinged with a sickly and affected imitation of the peculiar manner of some of the late popular poets of England. We speak not of a disposition to enumerate whatever is beautiful and excellent in their writings,—still less would we be understood as intending to censure that sort of imitation which, exploring all the treasures of English poetry, culls from all a diction, that shall form a natural and becoming dress for the conceptions of the writer,—this is a course of preparation which every one ought to go through before he appears before the public—but we desire to set a mark on that servile habit of copying, which adopts the vocabulary of some favourite author, and apes the fashions of his sentences, and cramps and forces the ideas into a shape, which they would not naturally have taken, and of which the only recommendation is, not that it is most elegant or most striking, but that it bears some resemblance to the manner of him who is proposed as a model. This way of writing has an air of poverty and meanness—it seems to indicate a paucity of reading as well as perversion of taste—it might almost lead us to suspect that the writer had but one or two examples of poetical composition in his hands, and was afraid of expressing himself, except according to some formula which they might contain—and it ever has been, and ever will be, the resort of those who are sensible that their works need some factitious recommendation, to give them even a temporary popularity.

We have now given a brief summary of what we conceived to be the characteristic merits and defects of our most celebrated American poets. Some names, of which we are not at present aware, equally deserving of notice with those whom we have mentioned, may have been omitted—some we have passed over, because we would not willingly disturb their passage to that oblivion, towards which, to the honour of our country, they are hastening—and some elegant productions of later date we have not commented on, because we were unwilling to tire our readers with a discussion which they may think already exhausted.

On the whole there seems to be more good taste among those who read, than those who write poetry in our country. With respect to the poets whom we have enumerated, and whose merits we have discussed, we think the judgment pronounced on their works by the public will be found, generally speaking, just. They hold that station in our literature to which they are entitled, and could hardly be admired more than they are, without danger to the taste of the nation. We know of no instance in which great poetical merit has come forward, and finding its claims unallowed, been obliged to retire to the shade from which it emerged. Whenever splendid talents of this description shall appear, we believe that there will be found a disposition to encourage and reward them. The fondness for literature is fast increasing in our country—and if this were not the case, the patrons of literature have multiplied, of course, and will continue to multiply with the mere growth of our population. The popular English works of the day are reprinted in our country—they are dispersed all over the union—they are to be found in every body's hands—they are made the subject of every body's conversation. What should hinder our native works, if equal in merit, from meeting an equally favourable reception? * * *

1818

From *LECTURES ON POETRY*

LECTURE FIRST

ON THE NATURE OF POETRY

* * * Of the nature of poetry different ideas have been entertained. The ancient critics seemed to suppose that they did something toward giving a tolerable notion of it by calling it a mimetic or imitative art, and classing it with sculpture and painting. Of its affinity with these arts there can be no doubt; but that affinity seems to me to consist almost wholly in the principles by which they all produce their effect, and not in the manner in which those principles are reduced to practice. There is no propriety in applying to poetry the term *imitative* in a literal and philosophical sense, as there is in applying it to painting and sculpture. The latter speak to the senses; poetry speaks directly to the mind.

They reproduce sensible objects, and, by means of these, suggest the feeling or sentiment connected with them; poetry, by the symbols of words, suggests both the sensible object and the association. I should be glad to learn how a poem descriptive of a scene or an event is any more an imitation of that scene or that event than a prose description would be. A prose composition giving an account of the proportions and dimensions of a building, and the materials of which it is constructed, is certainly, so far as mere exactness is concerned, a better imitation of it than the finest poem that could be written about it. Yet who, after all, ever thought of giving such a composition the name of an imitation? The truth is, painting and sculpture are, literally, imitative arts, while poetry is only metaphorically so. The epithet as applied to poetry may be well enough, perhaps, as a figure of speech, but to make a metaphor the foundation of a philosophical classification is putting it to a service in which it is sure to confuse what it professes to make clear.

I would rather call poetry a suggestive art. Its power of affecting the mind by pure suggestion, and employing, instead of a visible or tangible imitation, arbitrary symbols, as unlike as possible to the things with which it deals, is what distinguishes this from its two sister arts. It is owing to its operation by means of suggestion that it affects different minds with such different degrees of force. In a picture or a statue the colors and forms employed by the artist impress the senses with the greatest distinctness. In painting, there is little —in sculpture, there is less—for the imagination to supply. It is true that different minds, according to their several degrees of cultivation, will receive different degrees of pleasure from the productions of these arts, and that the moral associations they suggest will be variously felt, and in some instances variously interpreted. Still, the impression made on the senses is in all cases the same; the same figures, the same lights and shades, are seen by all beholders alike. But the creations of Poetry have in themselves nothing of this precision and fixedness of form, and depend greatly for their vividness and clearness of impression upon the mind to which they are presented. Language, the great machine with which her miracles are wrought, is contrived to have an application to all possible things; and wonderful as this contrivance is, and numerous and varied as are its combinations, it is still limited and imperfect, and, in point of comprehensiveness, distinctness, and variety, falls infinitely short of the mighty and diversified world of matter and mind of which it professes to be the representative. It is, however, to the very limitation of this power of language, as it seems to me, that Poetry owes her magic. The most detailed of her descriptions, which, by the way, are not always the most striking, are composed of a few touches; they are glimpses of things thrown into the mind; here and there a trace of the outline; here a gleam of light, and there a dash of shade. But these very touches act like a spell upon the imagination and awaken it to greater activity, and fill it, perhaps, with greater delight than the best defined objects could do. The imagination is the most active and the least susceptible of fatigue of all the faculties of the human mind; its more intense exercise is tremendous, and sometimes unsettles the reason; its repose is only a gentle sort of activity; nor am I certain that it is ever quite unemployed, for even in our sleep it is still awake and busy, and amuses itself with fabricating our dreams. To this restless faculty—which is unsatisfied when the whole of its work is done to its hands, and which is ever wandering from the combination of ideas directly presented to it to other combinations of its own—it is the office of poetry to furnish the exercise in which it delights. Poetry is that art which selects and arranges the symbols of thought in such a manner as to excite it the most powerfully and delightfully. The imagination of the reader is guided, it is true, by the poet, and it is his business to guide it skilfully and agreeably; but the imagination in the mean time is by no means passive. It pursues the path which the poet only points out, and shapes its visions from the scenes and allusions which he gives. It fills up his sketches of beauty with what suits its own highest conceptions of the beautiful, and completes his outline of grandeur with the noblest images its own stores can furnish. It is obvious that the degree of perfection with which this is done must depend greatly upon the strength and cultivation of that faculty. For example, in the following passage, in which Milton describes the general mother passing to her daily task among the flowers:

"With goddess-like demeanor forth she went
Not unattended, for on her as queen
A pomp of winning graces waited still."

The coldest imagination, on reading it, will figure to itself, in the person of Eve, the finest forms, attitudes, and movements of female loveliness and dignity, which, after all, are not described, but only hinted at by the poet. A warmer fancy, kindling at the delicate allusions in these lines, will not only bestow these attractions on the principal figure, but will fill the air around her with beauty, and people it with the airy forms of the graces; it will see the delicate proportions of their limbs, the lustre of their flowing hair, and the soft light of their eyes. Take, also, the following passage from the same poet, in which, speaking of Satan, he says:

"His face
Deep scars of thunder had entrenched, and care
Sat on his faded cheek—but under brows
Of dauntless courage and considerate pride
Waiting revenge; cruel his eye but cast
Signs of remorse and passion to behold
The fellows of his crime, the followers rather,
(Far other once beheld in bliss), condemned
For evermore to have their lot in pain."

The imagination of the reader is stimulated by the hints in this powerful passage to form to itself an idea of the features in which reside this strong expression of malignity and dejection—the brow, the cheek, the eye of the fallen angel, bespeaking courage, pride, the settled purpose of revenge, anxiety, sorrow for the fate of his followers, and fearfully marked with the wrath of the Almighty. There can be no doubt that the picture which this passage calls up in the minds of different individuals will vary accordingly as the imagination is more or less vivid, or more or less excited in the perusal. It will vary, also, accordingly as the individual is more or less experienced in the visible expression of strong passion, and as he is in the habit of associating the idea of certain emotions with certain configurations of the countenance.

There is no question that one principal office of poetry is to excite the imagination, but this is not its sole, nor perhaps its chief, province; another of its ends is to touch the heart, and, as I expect to show in this lecture, it has something to do with the understanding. I know that some critics have made poetry to consist solely in the exercise of the imagination. They distinguish poetry from pathos. They talk of pure poetry, and by this phrase they mean passages of mere imagery, with the least possible infusion of human emotion. I do not know by what authority these gentlemen take the term poetry from the people, and thus limit its meaning.

In its ordinary acceptation, it has, in all ages and all countries, included something more. When we speak of a poem, we do not mean merely a tissue of striking images. The most beautiful poetry is that which takes the strongest hold of the feelings, and, if it is really the most beautiful, then it is poetry in the highest sense. Poetry is constantly resorting to the language of the passions to heighten the effect of her pictures; and, if this be not enough to entitle that language to the appellation of poetical, I am not aware of the meaning of the term. Is there no poetry in the wrath of Achilles? Is there no poetry in the passage where Lear, in the tent of Cordelia, just recovered from his frenzy, his senses yet infirm and unassured, addresses his daughter as she kneels to ask his blessing?

"Pray do not mock me;
I am a very foolish, fond old man,
Fourscore and upward:
Not an hour more or less, and to deal plainly
I fear I am not in my perfect mind."

Is there no poetry in the remorse of Othello, in the terrible consciousness of guilt which haunts Macbeth, or the lamentations of Antony over the body of his friend, the devoted love of Juliet, and the self-sacrificing affection of Cleopatra? In the immortal work of Milton, is there no poetry in the penitence of Adam, or in the sorrows of Eve at being excluded from Paradise? The truth is, that poetry which does not find its way to the heart is scarcely deserving of the name; it may be brilliant and ingenious, but it soon wearies the attention. The feelings and the imagination, when skilfully touched, act reciprocally on each other. For example, when the poet introduces Ophelia, young, beautiful, and unfortunate, the wildness of frenzy in her eye, dressed with fantastic garlands of wild flowers, and singing snatches of old tunes, there is a picture for the imagination, but it is one which affects the heart. But when, in the midst of her incoherent talk, she utters some simple allusion to her own sorrows, as when she says,

"We know what we are, but know not what we may be,"

this touching sentence, addressed merely to our sympathy, strongly excites the imagination. It sets before us the days when she knew sorrow only by name, before her father was slain by the hand of her lover, and before her lover was estranged, and makes us feel the heaviness of that affliction which crushed a being so gentle and innocent and happy.

Those poems, however, as I have already hinted, which are apparently the most affluent of imagery, are not always those which most kindle the reader's imagination. It is because the ornaments with which they abound are not naturally suggested by the subject, not poured forth from a mind warmed and occupied by it; but a forced fruit of the fancy, produced by labor, without spontaneity or excitement.

The language of passion is naturally figurative, but its figures are only employed to heighten the intensity of the expression; they are never introduced for their own sake. Important, therefore, as may be the office of the imagination in poetry, the great spring of poetry is emotion. It is this power that holds the key of the storehouse where the mind has laid up its images, and that alone can open it without violence. All the forms of fancy stand ever in its sight, ready to execute its bidding. Indeed, I doubt not that most of the offences against good taste in this kind of composition are to be traced to the absence of emotion. A desire to treat agreeably or impressively a subject by which the writer is himself little moved, leads him into great mistakes about the means of effecting his purpose. This is the origin of cold conceits, of prosing reflections, of the minute painting of uninteresting circumstances, and of the opposite extremes of tameness and extravagance. On the other hand, strong feeling is always a sure guide. It rarely offends against good taste, because it instinctively chooses the most effectual means of communicating itself to others. It gives a variety to the composition it inspires, with which the severest taste is delighted. It may sometimes transgress arbitrary rules, or offend against local associations, but it speaks a language which reaches the heart in all countries and all times. Everywhere are the sentiments of fortitude and magnanimity uttered in strains that brace our own nerves, and the dead mourned in accents that draw our tears.

But poetry not only addresses the passions and the imagination; it appeals to the understanding also. So far as this position relates to the principles of taste which lie at the foundation of all poetry, and by which its merits are tried, I believe its truth will not be doubted. These principles have their origin in the reason of things, and are investigated and applied by the judgment. True it is that they may be observed by one who has never speculated about them, but it is no less true that their observance always gratifies the understanding with the fitness, the symmetry, and the congruity it produces. To write fine poetry requires intellectual faculties of the highest order, and among these, not the least important, is the faculty of reason. Poetry is the worst mask in the world behind which folly and stupidity could attempt to hide their features. Fitter, safer, and more congenial to them is the solemn discussion of unprofitable questions. Any obtuseness of apprehension or incapacity for drawing conclusions, which shows a deficiency or want of cultivation of the reasoning power, is sure to expose the unfortunate poet to contempt and ridicule.

But there is another point of view in which poetry may be said to address the understanding—I mean in the direct lessons of wisdom that it delivers. Remember that it does not concern itself with abstract reasonings, nor with any course of investigation that fatigues the mind. Nor is it merely didactic; but this does not prevent it from teaching truths which the mind instinctively acknowledges. The elements of moral truth are few and simple, but their combinations with human actions are as innumerable and diversified as the combinations of language. Thousands of inductions resulting from the application of great principles to human life and conduct lie, as it were, latent in our minds, which we have never drawn for ourselves, but which we admit the moment they are hinted at, and which, though not abstruse, are yet new. Nor are these of less value because they require no laborious research to discover them. The best riches of the earth are produced on its surface, and we need no reasoning to teach us the folly of a people who should leave its harvest ungathered to dig for its ores. The truths of which I have spoken, when possessing any peculiar force or beauty, are properly within the province of the art of which I am treating, and, when recommended by harmony of numbers, become poetry of the highest kind. Accordingly, they abound in the works of the most celebrated poets. When Shakespeare says of mercy,

> "it is twice blessed—
> It blesses him that gives and him that takes,"

does he not utter beautiful poetry as well as unquestionable truth? There are passages also in Milton of the same kind, which sink into the heart like the words of an oracle. For instance:

> "Evil into the mind of God or man
> May come and go so unapproved, and leave
> No spot or blame behind."

Take, also, the following example from Cowper, in which he bears witness against the guilt and folly of princes:

> "War is a game which, were their subjects wise,
> Kings should not play at. Nations would do well
> To extort their truncheons from the puny hands
> Of heroes whose infirm and baby minds
> Are gratified with mischief, and who spoil,
> Because men suffer it, their toy—the world."

I call these passages poetry, because the mind instantly acknowledges their truth and feels their force, and is moved and filled and elevated by them. Nor does poetry refuse to carry on a sort of process of reasoning by deducing one truth from another. Her demonstrations differ, however, from ordinary ones by requiring that each step should be in itself beautiful or striking, and that they all should carry the mind to the final conclusion without the consciousness of labor.

All the ways by which poetry affects the mind are open also to the prose-writer. All that kindles the imagination, all that excites emotion, all those moral truths that find an echo in our bosoms, are his property as well as that of the poet. It is true that in the ornaments of style the poet is allowed a greater license, but there are many excellent poems which are not distinguished by any liberal use of the figures of speech from prose writings composed with the same degree of excitement. What, then, is the ground of the distinction between prose and poetry? This is a question about which there has been much debate, but one which seems to me of easy solution to those who are not too ambitious of distinguishing themselves by profound researches into things already sufficiently clear. I suppose that poetry differs from prose, in the first place, by the employment of metrical harmony. It differs from it, in the next place, by excluding all that disgusts, all that tasks and fatigues the understanding, and all matters which are too trivial and common to excite any emotion whatever. Some of these, verse cannot raise into dignity; to others, verse is an encumbrance: they are, therefore, all unfit for poetry; put them into verse, and they are prose still.

A distinction has been attempted to be made between poetry and eloquence, and I acknowledge that there is one; but it seems to me that it consists solely in metrical arrangement. Eloquence is the poetry of prose; poetry is the eloquence of verse. The maxim that the poet is born and the orator made is a pretty antithesis, but a moment's reflection will convince us that one can become neither without natural gifts improved by cultivation. By eloquence I do not mean mere persuasiveness: there are many processes of argument that are not susceptible of eloquence, because they require close and painful attention. But by eloquence I understand those appeals to our moral perceptions that produce emotion as soon as they are uttered. It is in these that the orator is himself affected with the feelings he would communicate, that his eyes glisten, and his frame seems to dilate, and his voice acquires an unwonted melody, and his sentences arrange themselves into a sort of measure and harmony, and the listener is chained in involuntary and breathless attention. This is the very enthusiasm that is the parent of poetry. Let the same man go to his closet and clothe in numbers conceptions full of the same fire and spirit, and they will be poetry.

In conclusion, I will observe that the elements of poetry make a part of our natures, and that every individual is more or less a poet. In this "bank-note world," as it has been happily denominated, we sometimes meet with individuals who declare that they have no taste for poetry. But by their leave I will assert they are mistaken; they have it, although they may have never cultivated it. Is there any one among them who will confess himself insensible to the beauty of order or to the pleasure of variety—two principles, the happy mingling of which makes the perfection of poetic numbers? Is there any one whose eye is undelighted with beautiful forms and colors, whose ear is not charmed by sweet sounds, and who sees no loveliness in the returns of light and darkness, and the changes of the seasons? Is there any one for whom the works of Nature have no associations but such as relate to his animal wants? Is there any one to whom her great courses and operations show no majesty, to whom they impart no knowledge, and from whom they hide no secrets? Is there any one who is attached by no ties to his fellow-beings, who has no hopes for the future, and no memory of the past? Have they all forgotten the days and the friends of their childhood, and do they all shut their eyes to the advances of age? Have they nothing to desire and nothing to lament, and are their minds never darkened with the shadows of fear? Is it, in short, for these men that life has no pleasures and no pains, the grave no solemnity, and the world to come no mysteries? All these things are the sources of poetry, and they are not only part of ourselves, but of the universe, and will expire only with the last of the creatures of God.

(1825) 1884

THANATOPSIS

To him who in the love of Nature holds
Communion with her visible forms, she speaks
A various language; for his gayer hours
She has a voice of gladness, and a smile
And eloquence of beauty, and she glides
Into his darker musings, with a mild
And healing sympathy, that steals away
Their sharpness ere he is aware. When thoughts
Of the last bitter hour come like a blight
Over thy spirit, and sad images
Of the stern agony, and shroud, and pall,
And breathless darkness, and the narrow house,
Make thee to shudder, and grow sick at heart;—
Go forth, under the open sky, and list
To Nature's teachings, while from all around—
Earth and her waters, and the depths of air—
Comes a still voice—Yet a few days, and thee
The all-beholding sun shall see no more
In all his course; nor yet in the cold ground,
Where thy pale form was laid, with many tears,
Nor in the embrace of ocean, shall exist
Thy image. Earth, that nourished thee, shall claim
Thy growth, to be resolved to earth again,
And, lost each human trace, surrendering up
Thine individual being, shalt thou go
To mix for ever with the elements,
To be a brother to the insensible rock
And to the sluggish clod, which the rude swain
Turns with his share, and treads upon. The oak
Shall send his roots abroad, and pierce thy mould.

Yet not to thine eternal resting-place
Shalt thou retire alone, nor couldst thou wish
Couch more magnificent. Thou shalt lie down

With patriarchs of the infant world—with kings,
The powerful of the earth—the wise, the good,
Fair forms, and hoary seers of ages past,
All in one mighty sepulchre. The hills
Rock-ribbed and ancient as the sun,—the vales
Stretching in pensive quietness between;
The venerable woods,—rivers that move
In majesty, and the complaining brooks
That make the meadows green; and, poured round all,
Old Ocean's gray and melancholy waste,—
Are but the solemn decorations all
Of the great tomb of man. The golden sun,
The planets, all the infinite host of heaven,
Are shining on the sad abodes of death,
Through the still lapse of ages. All that tread
The globe are but a handful to the tribes
That slumber in its bosom.—Take the wings
Of morning, pierce the Barcan wilderness,
Or lose thyself in the continuous woods
Where rolls the Oregon, and hears no sound,
Save his own dashings—yet the dead are there:
And millions in those solitudes, since first
The flight of years began, have laid them down
In their last sleep—the dead reign there alone.
So shalt thou rest, and what if thou withdraw
In silence from the living, and no friend
Take note of thy departure? All that breathe
Will share thy destiny. The gay will laugh
When thou art gone, the solemn brood of care
Plod on, and each one as before will chase
His favorite phantom; yet all these shall leave
Their mirth and their employments, and shall come
And make their bed with thee. As the long train
Of ages glide away, the sons of men,
The youth in life's green spring, and he who goes
In the full strength of years, matron, and maid,
And speechless babe, and the gray-headed man—
Shall one by one be gathered to thy side,
By those, who in their turn shall follow them.

So live, that when thy summons comes to join
The innumerable caravan, which moves
To that mysterious realm, where each shall take
His chamber in the silent halls of death,
Thou go not, like the quarry-slave at night,
Scourged to his dungeon, but, sustained and soothed
By an unfaltering trust, approach thy grave
Like one who wraps the drapery of his couch
About him, and lies down to pleasant dreams.

(1811–17) 1817

INSCRIPTION FOR THE ENTRANCE TO A WOOD

Stranger, if thou has learned a truth which needs
No school of long experience, that the world
Is full of guilt and misery, and hast seen
Enough of all its sorrows, crimes, and cares,
To tire thee of it, enter this wild wood
And view the haunts of Nature. The calm shade
Shall bring a kindred calm, and the sweet breeze
That makes the green leaves dance, shall waft a balm
To thy sick heart. Thou will find nothing here
Of all that pained thee in the haunts of men,
And made thee loathe thy life. The primal curse
Fell, it is true, upon the unsinning earth,
But not in vengeance. God hath yoked to guilt
Her pale tormentor, misery. Hence, these shades
Are still the abodes of gladness; the thick roof
Of green and stirring branches is alive
And musical with birds, that sing and sport
In wantonness of spirit; while below
The squirrel, with raised paws and form erect,
Chirps merrily. Throngs of insects in the shade
Try their thin wings and dance in the warm beam
That waked them into life. Even the green trees
Partake the deep contentment; as they bend
To the soft winds, the sun from the blue sky
Looks in and sheds a blessing on the scene.
Scarce less the cleft-born wild-flower seems to enjoy
Existence, than the wingèd plunderer
That sucks its sweets. The mossy rocks themselves,
And the old and ponderous trunks of prostrate trees
That lead from knoll to knoll a causey rude
Or bridge the sunken brook, and their dark roots,
With all their earth upon them, twisting high,
Breathe fixed tranquillity. The rivulet
Sends forth glad sounds, and tripping o'er its bed
Of pebbly sands, or leaping down the rocks,
Seems, with continuous laughter, to rejoice
In its own being. Softly tread the marge,
Lest from her midway perch thou scare the wren
That dips her bill in water. The cool wind,
That stirs the stream in play, shall come to thee,
Like one that loves thee nor will let thee pass
Ungreeted, and shall give its light embrace.

(1815) 1817

TO A WATERFOWL

Whither, midst falling dew,
While glow the heavens with the last steps of day,
Far, through their rosy depths, dost thou pursue
Thy solitary way?

Vainly the fowler's eye
Might mark thy distant flight to do thee wrong,
As, darkly seen against the crimson sky,
Thy figure floats along.

Seek'st thou the plashy brink
Of weedy lake, or marge of river wide,
Or where the rocking billows rise and sink
On the chafed ocean-side?

There is a Power whose care
Teaches thy way along that pathless coast—
The desert and illimitable air—
Lone wandering, but not lost.

All day thy wings have fanned,
At that far height, the cold, thin atmosphere,
Yet stoop not, weary, to the welcome land,
Though the dark night is near.

And soon that toil shall end;
Soon shalt thou find a summer home, and rest,
And scream among thy fellows; reeds shall bend,
Soon, o'er thy sheltered nest.

Thou'rt gone, the abyss of heaven
Hath swallowed up thy form; yet, on my heart
Deeply has sunk the lesson thou hast given,
And shall not soon depart.

He who, from zone to zone,
Guides through the boundless sky thy certain flight,
In the long way that I must tread alone,
Will lead my steps aright.

(1815) 1818

GREEN RIVER

When breezes are soft and skies are fair,
I steal an hour from study and care,
And hie me away to the woodland scene,
Where wanders the stream with waters of green,
As if the bright fringe of herbs on its brink
Had given their stain to the waves they drink;
And they, whose meadows it murmurs through,
Have named the stream from its own fair hue.

Yet pure its waters—its shallows are bright
With colored pebbles and sparkles of light,
And clear the depths where its eddies play,
And dimples deepen and whirl away,
And the plane-tree's speckled arms o'ershoot
The swifter current that mines its root,
Through whose shifting leaves, as you walk the hill,
The quivering glimmer of sun and rill
With a sudden flash on the eye is thrown,
Like the ray that streams from the diamond-stone.
Oh, loveliest there the spring days come,
With blossoms, and birds, and wild-bees' hum;
The flowers of summer are fairest there,
And freshest the breath of the summer air;
And sweetest the golden autumn day
In silence and sunshine glides away.

Yet, fair as thou art, thou shunnest to glide,
Beautiful stream! by the village side;
But windest away from haunts of men,
To quiet valley and shaded glen;
And forest, and meadow, and slope of hill,
Around thee, are lonely, lovely, and still,
Lonely—save when, by thy rippling tides,

From thicket to thicket the angler glides;
Or the simpler comes, with basket and book,
For herbs of power on thy banks to look;
Or haply, some idle dreamer, like me,
To wander, and muse, and gaze on thee,
Still—save the chirp of birds that feed
On the river cherry and seedy reed,
And thy own wild music gushing out
With mellow murmur of fairy shout,
From dawn to the blush of another day,
Like traveller singing along his way.

That fairy music I never hear,
Nor gaze on those waters so green and clear,
And mark them winding away from sight,
Darkened with shade or flashing with light,
While o'er them the vine to its thicket clings,
And the zephyr stoops to freshen his wings,
But I wish that fate had left me free
To wander these quiet haunts with thee,
Till the eating cares of earth should depart,
And the peace of the scene pass into my heart;
And I envy thy stream, as it glides along
Through its beautiful banks in a trance of song.

Though forced to drudge for the dregs of men,
And scrawl strange words with the barbarous pen,
And mingle among the jostling crowd,
Where the sons of strife are subtle and loud—
I often come to this quiet place,
To breathe the airs that ruffle thy face,
And gaze upon thee in silent dream,
For in thy lonely and lovely stream
An image of that calm life appears
That won my heart in my greener years.

(1819) 1820

A WINTER PIECE

The time has been that these wild solitudes,
Yet beautiful as wild, were trod by me
Oftener than now; and when the ills of life
Had chafed my spirit—when the unsteady pulse
Beat with strange flutterings, I would wander forth
And seek the woods. The sunshine on my path
Was to me as a friend. The swelling hills,
The quiet dells retiring far between,
With gentle invitation to explore
Their windings, were a calm society
That talked with me and soothed me. Then the chant
Of birds, and chime of brooks, and soft caress
Of the fresh sylvan air, made me forget
The thoughts that broke my peace; and I began
To gather simples by the fountain's brink,
And lose myself in day-dreams. While I stood
In Nature's loneliness, I was with one
With whom I early grew familiar, one
Who never had a frown for me, whose voice
Never rebuked me for the hours I stole
From cares I loved not, but of which the world
Deems highest, to converse with her. When shrieked
The bleak November winds, and smote the woods,

And the brown fields were herbless, and the shades,
That met above the merry rivulet,
Were spoiled, I sought, I loved them still; they seemed
Like old companions in adversity.
Still there was beauty in my walks; the brook,
Bordered with sparkling frost-work, was as gay
As with its fringe of summer flowers. Afar,
The village with its spires, the path of streams,
And dim receding valleys, hid before
By interposing trees, lay visible
Through the bare grove, and my familiar haunts
Seemed new to me. Nor was I slow to come
Among them, when the clouds, from their still skirts,
Had shaken down on earth the feathery snow,
And all was white. The pure keen air abroad,
Albeit it breathed no scent of herb, nor heard
Love-call of bird nor merry hum of bee,
Was not the air of death. Bright mosses crept
Over the spotted trunks, and the close buds
That lay along the boughs, instinct with life,
Patient, and waiting the soft breath of Spring,
Feared not the piercing spirit of the North.
The snow-bird twittered on the beechen bough;
And 'neath the hemlock, whose thick branches bent
Beneath its bright cold burden, and kept dry
A circle, on the earth, of withered leaves,
The partridge found a shelter. Through the snow
The rabbit sprang away. The lighter track
Of fox, and the raccoon's broad path, were there,
Crossing each other. From his hollow tree,
The squirrel was abroad, gathering the nuts
Just fallen, that asked the winter cold and sway
Of winter blast, to shake them from their hold.

But Winter has yet brighter scenes,—he boasts
Splendors beyond what gorgeous Summer knows,
Or Autumn, with his many fruits, and woods
All flushed with many hues. Come when the rains
Have glazed the snow and clothed the trees with ice,
While the slant sun of February pours
Into the bowers a flood of light. Approach!
The incrusted surface shall upbear thy steps,
And the broad arching portals of the grove
Welcome thy entering. Look! the massy trunks
Are cased in the pure crystal; each light spray,
Nodding and tinkling in the breath of heaven,
Is studded with its trembling water-drops,
That glimmer with an amethystine light.
But round the parent-stem the long low boughs
Bend, in a glittering ring, and arbors hide
The glassy floor. Oh! you might deem the spot
The spacious cavern of some virgin mine,
Deep in the womb of earth—where the gems grow,

And diamonds put forth radiant rods and bud
With amethyst and topaz—and the place
Lit up, most royally, with the pure beam
That dwells in them. Or haply the vast hall
Of fairy palace, that outlasts the night,
And fades not in the glory of the sun;—
Where crystal columns send forth slender shafts
And crossing arches; and fantastic aisles
Wind from the sight in brightness, and are lost
Among the crowded pillars. Raise thine eye;
Thou seest no cavern roof, no palace vault;
There the blue sky and the white drifting cloud
Look in. Again the wildered fancy dreams
Of spouting fountains, frozen as they rose,
And fixed, with all their branching jets, in air,
And all their sluices sealed. All, all is light;
Light without shade. But all shall pass away
With the next sun. From numberless vast trunks
Loosened, the crashing ice shall make a sound
Like the far roar of rivers, and the eve
Shall close o'er the brown woods as it was wont.

And it is pleasant, when the noisy streams
Are just set free, and milder suns melt off
The plashy snow, save only the firm drift
In the deep glen or the close shade of pines—
'Tis pleasant to behold the wreaths of smoke
Roll up among the maples of the hill,
Where the shrill sound of youthful voices wakes
The shriller echo, as the clear pure lymph,
That from the wounded trees, in twinkling drops,
Falls, 'mid the golden brightness of the morn,
Is gathered in with brimming pails, and oft,
Wielded by sturdy hands, the stroke of axe
Makes the woods ring. Along the quiet air,
Come and float calmly off the soft light clouds,
Such as you see in summer, and the winds
Scarce stir the branches. Lodged in sunny cleft,
Where the cold breezes come not, blooms alone
The little wind-flower, whose just opened eye
Is blue as the spring heaven it gazes at—
Startling the loiterer in the naked groves
With unexpected beauty, for the time
Of blossoms and green leaves is yet afar.
And ere it comes, the encountering winds shall oft
Muster their wrath again, and rapid clouds
Shade heaven, and bounding on the frozen earth
Shall fall their volleyed stores, rounded like hail
And white like snow, and the loud North again
Shall buffet the vexed forest in his rage.

(1820) 1821

THE YELLOW VIOLET

When beechen buds begin to swell,
And woods the blue-bird's warble know,
The yellow violet's modest bell
Peeps from the last year's leaves below.

Ere russet fields their green resume,
Sweet flower, I love, in forest bare,
To meet thee, when thy faint perfume
Alone is in the virgin air.

Of all her train, the hands of Spring
First plant thee in the watery mould,
And I have seen thee blossoming
Beside the snow-bank's edges cold.

Thy parent sun, who bade thee view
Pale skies, and chilling moisture sip,
Has bathed thee in his own bright hue,
And streaked with jet thy glowing lip.

Yet slight thy form, and low thy seat,
And earthward bent thy gentle eye,
Unapt the passing view to meet,
When loftier flowers are flaunting nigh.

Oft, in the sunless April day,
Thy early smile has stayed my walk;
But midst the gorgeous blooms of May,
I passed thee on thy humble stalk.

So they, who climb to wealth, forget
The friends in darker fortunes tried.
I copied them—but I regret
That I should ape the ways of pride.

And when again the genial hour
Awakes the painted tribes of light,
I'll not o'erlook the modest flower
That made the woods of April bright.

(1814) 1821

MONUMENT MOUNTAIN

Thou who wouldst see the lovely and the wild
Mingled in harmony on Nature's face,
Ascend our rocky mountains. Let thy foot
Fail not with weariness, for on their tops
The beauty and the majesty of earth,
Spread wide beneath, shall make thee to forget
The steep and toilsome way. There, as thou stand'st,
The haunts of men below thee, and around
The mountain-summits, thy expanding heart
Shall feel a kindred with that loftier world
To which thou art translated, and partake
The enlargement of thy vision. Thou shalt look
Upon the green and rolling forest-tops,
And down into the secrets of the glens,
And streams that with their bordering thickets strive
To hide their windings. Thou shalt gaze, at once,
Here on white villages, and tilth, and herds,
And swarming roads, and there on solitudes
That only hear the torrent, and the wind,
And eagle's shriek. There is a precipice
That seems a fragment of some mighty wall,
Built by the hand that fashioned the old world,
To separate its nations, and thrown down
When the flood drowned them. To the north, a path
Conducts you up the narrow battlement.

Steep is the western side, shaggy and wild
With mossy trees, and pinnacles of flint,
And many a hanging crag. But, to the east,
Sheer to the vale go down the bare old cliffs—
Huge pillars, that in middle heaven upbear
Their weather-beaten capitals, here dark
With moss, the growth of centuries, and there
Of chalky whiteness where the thunderbolt
Has splintered them. It is a fearful thing
To stand upon the beetling verge, and see
Where storm and lightning, from that huge gray wall,
Have tumbled down vast blocks, and at the base
Dashed them in fragments, and to lay thine ear
Over the dizzy depth, and hear the sound
Of winds, that struggle with the woods below,
Come up like ocean murmurs. But the scene
Is lovely round; a beautiful river there
Wanders amid the fresh and fertile meads,
The paradise he made unto himself,
Mining the soil for ages. On each side
The fields swell upward to the hills; beyond,
Above the hills, in the blue distance, rise
The mountain-columns with which earth props heaven.

There is a tale about these reverend rocks,
A sad tradition of unhappy love,
And sorrows borne and ended, long ago,
When over these fair vales the savage sought
His game in the thick woods. There was a maid,
The fairest of the Indian maids, bright-eyed,
With wealth of raven tresses, a light form,
And a gay heart. About her cabin-door
The wide old woods resounded with her song
And fairy laughter all the summer day.
She loved her cousin; such a love was deemed,
By the morality of those stern tribes,
Incestuous, and she struggled hard and long
Against her love, and reasoned with her heart,
As simple Indian maiden might. In vain.
Then her eye lost its lustre, and her step
Its lightness, and the gray-haired men that passed
Her dwelling, wondered that they heard no more
The accustomed song and laugh of her, whose looks
Were like the cheerful smile of Spring, they said,
Upon the Winter of their age. She went
To weep where no eye saw, and was not found
Where all the merry girls were met to dance,
And all the hunters of the tribe were out;
Nor when they gathered from the rustling husk
The shining ear; nor when, by the river's side,
They pulled the grape and startled the wild shades

With sounds of mirth. The keen-eyed Indian dames
Would whisper to each other, as they saw
Her wasting form, and say, *The girl will die.*

One day into the bosom of a friend,
A playmate of her young and innocent years,
She poured her griefs. "Thou know'st, and thou alone,"
She said, "for I have told thee, all my love,
And guilt, and sorrow. I am sick of life.
All night I weep in darkness, and the morn
Glares on me, as upon a thing accursed,
That has no business on the earth. I hate
The pastimes and the pleasant toils that once
I loved; the cheerful voices of my friends
Sound in my ear like mockings, and, at night,
In dreams, my mother, from the land of souls,
Calls me and chides me. All that look on me
Do seem to know my shame; I cannot bear
Their eyes; I cannot from my heart root out
The love that wrings it so, and I must die."

It was a summer morning, and they went
To this old precipice. About the cliffs
Lay garlands, ears of maize, and shaggy skins
Of wolf and bear, the offerings of the tribe
Here made to the Great Spirit, for they deemed,
Like worshippers of the elder time, that God
Doth walk on the high places and affect
The earth-o'erlooking mountains. She had on
The ornaments with which her father loved
To deck the beauty of his bright-eyed girl,
And bade her wear when stranger warriors came
To be his guests. Here the friends sat them down
And sang, all day, old songs of love and death,
And decked the poor wan victim's hair with flowers,
And prayed that safe and swift might be her way
To the calm world of sunshine, where no grief
Makes the heart heavy and the eyelids red.
Beautiful lay the region of her tribe
Below her—waters resting in the embrace
Of the wide forest, and maize-planted glades
Opening amid the leafy wilderness.
She gazed upon it long, and at the sight
Of her own village peeping through the trees,
And her own dwelling, and the cabin roof
Of him she loved with an unlawful love,
And came to die for, a warm gush of tears
Ran from her eyes. But when the sun grew low
And the hill shadows long, she threw herself
From the steep rock and perished. There was scooped,
Upon the mountain's southern slope, a grave;
And there they laid her, in the very garb
With which the maiden decked herself for death,

With the same withering wild-flowers in her hair,
And o'er the mould that covered her, the tribe
Built up a simple monument, a cone
Of small loose stones. Thenceforword all who passed,
Hunter, and dame, and virgin, laid a stone
In silence on the pile. It stands there yet.
And Indians from the distant West, who come
To visit where their fathers' bones are laid,
Yet tell the sorrowful tale, and to this day
The mountain where the hapless maiden died
Is called the Mountain of the Monument.

1824

A FOREST HYMN

The groves were God's first temples. Ere man learned
To hew the shaft, and lay the architrave,
And spread the roof above them—ere he framed
The lofty vault, to gather and roll back
The sound of anthems; in the darkling wood,
Amid the cool and silence, he knelt down,
And offered to the Mightiest solemn thanks
And supplication. For his simple heart
Might not resist the sacred influences
Which, from the stilly twilight of the place,
And from the gray old trunks that high in heaven
Mingled their mossy boughs, and from the sound
Of the invisible breath that swayed at once
All their green tops, stole over him, and bowed
His spirit with the thought of boundless power
And inaccessible majesty. Ah, why
Should we, in the world's riper years, neglect
God's ancient sanctuaries, and adore
Only among the crowd, and under roofs
That our frail hands have raised? Let me, at least,
Here, in the shadow of this aged wood,
Offer one hymn—thrice happy, if it find
Acceptance in His ear.

Father, thy hand
Hath reared these venerable columns, thou
Didst weave this verdant roof. Thou didst look down
Upon the naked earth, and, forthwith, rose
All these fair ranks of trees. They, in thy sun,
Budded, and shook their green leaves in thy breeze,
And shot toward heaven. The century-living crow
Whose birth was in their tops, grew old and died
Among their branches, till, at last, they stood,
As now they stand, massy, and tall, and dark,
Fit shrine for humble worshipper to hold
Communion with his Maker. These dim vaults,
These winding aisles, of human pomp or pride
Report not. No fantastic carvings show
The boast of our vain race to change the form
Of thy fair works. But thou art here—thou fill'st
The solitude. Thou art in the soft winds

That run along the summit of these trees
In music; thou art in the cooler breath
That from the inmost darkness of the place
Comes, scarcely felt; the barky trunks, the ground,
The fresh moist ground, are all instinct with thee.
Here is continual worship;—Nature, here,
In the tranquillity that thou dost love,
Enjoys thy presence. Noiselessly, around,
From perch to perch, the solitary bird
Passes; and yon clear spring, that, midst its herbs,
Wells softly forth and wandering steeps the roots
Of half the mighty forest, tells no tale
Of all the good it does. Thou hast not left
Thyself without a witness, in the shades,
Of thy perfections. Grandeur, strength, and grace
Are here to speak of thee. This mighty oak—
By whose immovable stem I stand and seem
Almost annihilated—not a prince,
In all that proud old world beyond the deep,
E'er wore his crown as loftily as he
Wears the green coronal of leaves with which
Thy hand has graced him. Nestled at his root
Is beauty, such as blooms not in the glare
Of the broad sun. That delicate forest flower,
With scented breath and look so like a smile,
Seems, as it issues from the shapeless mould,
An emanation of the indwelling Life.
A visible token of the upholding Love,
That are the soul of this great universe.

My heart is awed within me when I think
Of the great miracle that still goes on,
In silence, round me—the perpetual work
Of thy creation, finished, yet renewed
Forever. Written on thy works I read
The lesson of thy own eternity.
Lo! all grow old and die—but see again,
How on the faltering footsteps of decay
Youth presses—ever gay and beautiful youth
In all its beautiful forms. These lofty trees
Wave not less proudly that their ancestors
Moulder beneath them. Oh, there is not lost
One of earth's charms: upon her bosom yet,
After the flight of untold centuries,
The freshness of her far beginning lies
And yet shall lie. Life mocks the idle hate
Of his arch-enemy Death—yea, seats himself
Upon the tyrant's throne—the sepulchre,
And of the triumphs of his ghastly foe
Makes his own nourishment. For he came forth
From thine own bosom, and shall have no end.

There have been holy men who hid themselves
Deep in the woody wilderness, and gave
Their lives to thought and prayer, till they outlived
The generation born with them, nor seemed
Less aged than the hoary trees and rocks

Around them;—and there have been holy men
Who deemed it were not well to pass life thus.
But let me often to these solitudes
Retire, and in thy presence reassure
My feeble virtue. Here its enemies,
The passions, at thy plainer footsteps shrink
And tremble and are still. O God! when thou
Dost scare the world with tempests, set on fire
The heavens with falling thunderbolts, or fill,
With all the waters of the firmament,
The swift dark whirlwind that uproots the woods
And drowns the villages; when, at thy call,
Uprises the great deep and throws himself
Upon the continent, and overwhelms
Its cities—who forgets not, at the sight
Of these tremendous tokens of thy power,
His pride, and lays his strifes and follies by?
Oh, from these sterner aspects of thy face
Spare me and mine, nor let us need the wrath
Of the mad unchained elements to teach
Who rules them. Be it ours to meditate,
In these calm shades, thy milder majesty,
And to the beautiful order of thy works
Learn to conform the order of our lives.

1825

JUNE

I gazed upon the glorious sky
And the green mountains round,
And thought that when I came to lie
At rest within the ground,
'Twere pleasant, that in flowery June,
When brooks send up a cheerful tune,
And groves a joyous sound,
The sexton's hand, my grave to make,
The rich, green mountain-turf should break.

A cell within the frozen mould,
A coffin borne through sleet,
And icy clods above it rolled,
While fierce the tempests beat—
Away!—I will not think of these—
Blue be the sky and soft the breeze,
Earth green beneath the feet,
And be the damp mould gently pressed
Into my narrow place of rest.

There through the long, long summer hours,
The golden light should lie,
And thick young herbs and groups of flowers
Stand in their beauty by.
The oriole should build and tell
His love-tale close beside my cell;
The idle butterfly
Should rest him there, and there be heard
The housewife bee and humming-bird.

And what if cheerful shouts at noon
Come, from the village sent,
Or songs of maids, beneath the moon
With fairy laughter blent?
And what if, in the evening light,
Bethrothèd lovers walk in sight
Of my low monument?
I would the lovely scene around
Might know no sadder sight nor sound.

I know that I no more should see
The season's glorious show,
Nor would its brightness shine for me,
Nor its wild music flow;
But if, around my place of sleep,
The friends I love should come to weep,

They might not haste to go.
Soft airs, and song, and light, and bloom
Should keep them lingering by my tomb.

These to their softened hearts should bear
The thought of what has been,
And speak of one who cannot share
The gladness of the scene;
Whose part, in all the pomp that fills
The circuit of the summer hills,
Is that his grave is green;
And deeply would their hearts rejoice
To hear again his living voice.

1825

I CANNOT FORGET WITH WHAT FERVID DEVOTION

I cannot forget with what fervid devotion
I worshipped the visions of verse and of fame;
Each gaze at the glories of earth, sky, and ocean,
To my kindled emotions, was wind over flame.

And deep were my musings in life's early blossom,
Mid the twilight of mountain-groves wandering long;
How thrilled my young veins, and how throbbed my full bosom,
When o'er me descended the spirit of song!

'Mong the deep-cloven fells that for ages had listened
To the rush of the pebble-paved river between,
Where the kingfisher screamed and gray precipice glistened,
All breathless with awe have I gazed on the scene;

Till I felt the dark power o'er my reveries stealing,
From the gloom of the thicket that over me hung,
And the thoughts that awoke, in that rapture of feeling,
Were formed into verse as they rose to my tongue.

Bright visions! I mixed with the world, and ye faded,
No longer your pure rural worshipper now;
In the haunts your continual presence pervaded,
Ye shrink from the signet of care on my brow.

In the old mossy groves on the breast of the mountains,
In deep lonely glens where the waters complain,
By the shade of the rock, by the gush of the fountain,
I seek your loved footsteps, but seek them in vain.

Oh, leave not forlorn and forever forsaken,
Your pupil and victim to life and its tears!
But sometimes return, and in mercy awaken
The glories ye showed to his earlier years.

(1815–1826) 1826

THE PAST

Thou unrelenting Past!
Strong are the barriers round thy dark domain,
And fetters, sure and fast,
Hold all that enter thy unbreathing reign.

Far in thy realm withdrawn,
Old empires sit in sullenness and gloom,
And glorious ages gone
Lie deep within the shadow of thy womb.

Childhood, with all its mirth,
Youth, Manhood, Age that draws us to the ground,
And last, Man's Life on earth,
Glide to thy dim dominions, and are bound.

Thou hast my better years;
Thou hast my earlier friends, the good, the kind,
Yielded to thee with tears—
The venerable form, the exalted mind.

My spirit yearns to bring
The lost ones back—yearns with desire intense,
And struggles hard to wring
Thy bolts apart, and pluck thy captives thence.

In vain; thy gates deny
All passage save to those who hence depart;
Nor to the streaming eye
Thou giv'st them back—nor to the broken heart.

In thy abysses hide
Beauty and excellence unknown; to thee
Earth's wonder and her pride
Are gathered, as the waters to the sea;

Labors of good to man,
Unpublished charity, unbroken faith,
Love, that midst grief began,
And grew with years, and faltered not in death.

Full many a mighty name
Lurks in thy depths, unuttered, unrevered;
With thee are silent fame,
Forgotten arts, and wisdom disappeared.

Thine for a space are they—
Yet shalt thou yield thy treasures up at last:
Thy gates shall yet give way,
Thy bolts shall fall, inexorable Past!
All that of good and fair
Has gone into thy womb from earliest time,
Shall then come forth to wear
The glory and the beauty of its prime.

They have not perished—no!
Kind words, remembered voices once so sweet,
Smiles, radiant long ago,
And features, the great soul's apparent seat.

All shall come back; each tie
Of pure affection shall be knit again;
Alone shall Evil die,
And Sorrow dwell a prisoner in thy reign.

And then shall I behold
Him, by whose kind paternal side I sprung,
And her, who, still and cold,
Fills the next grave—the beautiful and young.

1828

THE EVENING WIND

Spirit that breathest through my lattice, thou
That cool'st the twilight of the sultry day,
Gratefully flows thy freshness round my brow;
Thou hast been out upon the deep at play,
Riding all day the wild blue waves till now,
Roughening their crests, and scattering high their spray,
And swelling the white sail. I welcome thee
To the scorched land, thou wanderer of the sea!

Nor I alone; a thousand bosoms round
Inhale thee in the fulness of delight;

And languid forms rise up, and pulses bound
Livelier, at coming of the wind of night;
And, languishing to hear thy grateful sound,
Lies the vast inland stretched beyond the sight.
Go forth into the gathering shade; go forth,
God's blessing breathed upon the fainting earth!

Go, rock the little wood-bird in his nest,
Curl the still waters, bright with stars, and rouse
The wide old wood from his majestic rest,
Summoning from the innumerable boughs
The strange, deep harmonies that haunt his breast:
Pleasant shall be thy way where meekly bows
The shutting flower, and darkling waters pass,
And where the o'ershadowing branches sweep the grass.

The faint old man shall lean his silver head
To feel thee; thou shalt kiss the child asleep,
And dry the moistened curls that overspread
His temples, while his breathing grows more deep;
And they who stand about the sick man's bed,
Shall joy to listen to thy distant sweep,
And softly part his curtains to allow
Thy visit, grateful to his burning brow.

Go—but the circle of eternal change,
Which is the life of Nature, shall restore,
With sounds and scents from all thy mighty range,
Thee to thy birthplace of the deep once more;
Sweet odors in the sea-air, sweet and strange,
Shall tell the home-sick mariner of the shore;
And, listening to thy murmur, he shall deem
He hears the rustling leaf and running stream.

1829

SONG OF MARION'S MEN

Our band is few but true and tried,
Our leader frank and bold;
The British soldier trembles
When Marion's name is told.
Our fortress is the good greenwood,
Our tent the cypress-tree;
We know the forest round us,
As seamen know the sea.
We know its walls of thorny vines,
Its glades of reedy grass,
Its safe and silent islands
Within the dark morass.

Woe to the English soldiery
That little dread us near!
On them shall light at midnight
A strange and sudden fear:
When, waking to their tents on fire,
They grasp their arms in vain,
And they who stand to face us
Are beat to earth again;
And they who fly in terror deem
A mighty host behind,
And hear the tramp of thousands
Upon the hollow wind.

Then sweet the hour that brings release
From danger and from toil:
We talk the battle over,
And share the battle's spoil.
The woodland rings with laugh and shout,
As if a hunt were up,
And woodland flowers are gathered
To crown the soldier's cup.

With merry songs we mock the wind
That in the pine-top grieves,
And slumber long and sweetly
On beds of oaken leaves.

Well knows the fair and friendly moon
The band that Marion leads—
The glitter of their rifles,
The scampering of their steeds.
'Tis life to guide the fiery barb
Across the moonlight plain;
'Tis life to feel the night-wind
That lifts the tossing mane.
A moment in the British camp—
A moment—and away
Back to the pathless forest,
Before the peep of day.

Grave men there are by broad Santee,
Grave men with hoary hairs;
Their hearts are all with Marion,
For Marion are their prayers.
And lovely ladies greet our band
With kindliest welcoming,
With smiles like those of summer,
And tears like those of spring.
For them we wear these trusty arms,
And lay them down no more
Till we have driven the Briton,
Forever, from our shore.

1831

OH FAIREST OF THE RURAL MAIDS

Oh fairest of the rural maids!
Thy birth was in the forest shades;
Green boughs, and glimpses of the sky,
Were all that met thine infant eye.

Thy sports, thy wanderings, when a child,
Were ever in the sylvan wild;
And all the beauty of the place
Is in thy heart and on thy face.

The twilight of the trees and rocks
Is in the light shade of thy locks;
Thy step is as the wind, that weaves
Its playful way among the leaves.

Thine eyes are springs, in whose serene
And silent waters heaven is seen;
Their lashes are the herbs that look
On their young figures in the brook.

The forest depths, by foot unpressed,
Are not more sinless than thy breast;
The holy peace, that fills the air
Of those calm solitudes, is there.

(1820) 1832

TO THE FRINGED GENTIAN

Thou blossom bright with autumn dew,
And colored with the heaven's own blue,
That openest when the quiet light
Succeeds the keen and frosty night.

Thou comest not when violets lean
O'er wandering brooks and springs unseen,
Or columbines, in purple dressed,
Nod o'er the ground-bird's hidden nest.

Thou waitest late and com'st alone,
When woods are bare and birds are flown,
And frosts and shortening days portend
The aged year is near his end.

Then doth thy sweet and quiet eye
Look through its fringes to the sky,
Blue—blue—as if that sky let fall
A flower from its cerulean wall.

I would that thus, when I shall see
The hour of death draw near to me,
Hope, blossoming within my heart,
May look to heaven as I depart.

(1829) 1832

THE PRAIRIES

These are the gardens of the Desert, these

The unshorn fields, boundless and beautiful,
For which the speech of England has no name—
The Prairies. I behold them for the first,
And my heart swells while the dilated sight
Takes in the encircling vastness. Lo! they stretch
In airy undulations, far away,
As if the ocean, in his gentlest swell,
Stood still, with all his rounded billows fixed,
And motionless forever.—Motionless?—
No—they are all unchained again. The clouds
Sweep over with their shadows, and, beneath,
The surface rolls and fluctuates to the eye;
Dark hollows seem to glide along and chase
The sunny ridges. Breezes of the South!
Who toss the golden and the flame-like flowers,
And pass the prairie-hawk that, poised on high,
Flaps his broad wings, yet moves not—ye have played
Among the palms of Mexico and vines
Of Texas, and have crisped the limpid brooks
That from the fountains of Sonora glide
Into the calm Pacific—have ye fanned
A nobler or a lovelier scene than this?
Man hath no power in all this glorious work:
The hand that built the firmament hath heaved
And smoothed these verdant swells, and sown their slopes
With herbage, planted them with island groves,
And hedged them round with forests. Fitting floor
For this magnificent temple of the sky—
With flowers whose glory and whose multitude
Rival the constellations! The great heavens
Seem to stoop down upon the scene in love,—
A nearer vault, and of a tenderer blue,
Than that which bends above our eastern hills.

As o'er the verdant waste I guide my steed,
Among the high rank grass that sweeps his sides
The hollow beating of his footstep seems
A sacrilegious sound. I think of those
Upon whose rest he tramples. Are they here—
The dead of other days?—and did the dust
Of these fair solitudes once stir with life
And burn with passion? Let the mighty mounds
That overlook the rivers, or that rise
In the dim forest crowded with old oaks,
Answer. A race, that long has passed away,
Built them;—a disciplined and populous race
Heaped, with long toil, the earth, while yet the Greek
Was hewing the Pentelicus to forms
Of symmetry, and rearing on its rock
The glittering Parthenon. These ample fields
Nourished their harvests, here their herds were fed,
When haply by their stalls the bison lowed,
And bowed his manèd shoulder to the yoke.
All day this desert murmured with their toils,
Till twilight blushed, and lovers walked, and wooed

In a forgotten language, and old tunes,
From instruments of unremembered form,
Gave the soft winds a voice. The red man came—
The roaming hunter tribes, warlike and fierce,
And the mound-builders vanished from the earth.
The solitude of centuries untold
Has settled where they dwelt. The prairie-wolf
Hunts in their meadows; and his fresh-dug den
Yawns by my path. The gopher mines the ground
Where stood their swarming cities. All is gone;
All—save the piles of earth that hold their bones,
The platforms where they worshiped unknown gods,
The barriers which they builded from the soil
To keep the foe at bay—till o'er the walls
The wild beleaguerers broke, and, one by one,
The strongholds of the plain were forced, and heaped
With corpses. The brown vultures of the wood
Flocked to those vast uncovered sepulchres,
And sat unscared and silent at their feast.
Haply some solitary fugitive,
Lurking in marsh and forest, till the sense
Of desolation and of fear became
Bitterer than death, yielded himself to die.
Man's better nature triumphed then. Kind words
Welcomed and soothed him; the rude conquerors
Seated the captive with their chiefs; he chose
A bride among their maidens, and at length
Seemed to forget—yet ne'er forgot—the wife
Of his first love, and her sweet little ones
Butchered amid their shrieks, with all his race.

Thus change the forms of being. Thus arise
Races of living things, glorious in strength,
And perish, as the quickening breath of God
Fills them, or is withdrawn. The red man, too,
Has left the blooming wilds he ranged so long,
And, nearer to the Rocky Mountains, sought
A wilder hunting-ground. The beaver builds
No longer by these streams, but far away,
On waters whose blue surface ne'er gave back
The white man's face—among Missouri's springs,
And pools whose issues swell the Oregon—
He rears his little Venice. In these plains
The bison feeds no more. Twice twenty leagues
Beyond remotest smoke of hunter's camp,
Roams the majestic brute, in herds that shake
The earth with thundering steps—yet here I meet
His ancient footprints stamped beside the pool.

Still this great solitude is quick with life.
Myriads of insects, gaudy as the flowers
They flutter over, gentle quadrupeds,
And birds, that scarce have learned the fear of man,

Are here, and sliding reptiles of the ground,
Startlingly beautiful. The graceful deer
Bounds to the wood at my approach. The bee,
A more adventurous colonist than man,
With whom he came across the eastern deep,
Fills the savannas with his murmurings,
And hides his sweets, as in the golden age,
Within the hollow oak. I listen long
To his domestic hum, and think I hear
The sound of that advancing multitude
Which soon shall fill these deserts. From the ground
Comes up the laugh of children, the soft voice
Of maidens, and the sweet and solemn hymn
Of Sabbath worshippers; the low of herds
Blends with the rustling of the heavy grain
Over the dark brown furrows. All at once
A fresher wind sweeps by, and breaks my dream,
And I am in the wilderness alone.
(1832) 1833

OH MOTHER OF A MIGHTY RACE

Oh mother of a mighty race,
Yet lovely in thy youthful grace!
The elder dames, thy haughty peers,
Admire and hate thy blooming years.
With words of shame
And taunts of scorn they join thy name.

For on thy cheeks the glow is spread
That tints thy morning hills with red;
Thy step—the wild-deer's rustling feet
Within thy woods are not more fleet;
Thy hopeful eye
Is bright as thine own sunny sky.

Ay, let them rail—those haughty ones,
While safe thou dwellest with thy sons.
They do not know how loved thou art,
How many a fond and fearless heart
Would rise to throw
Its life between thee and the foe.

They know not, in their hate and pride,
What virtues with thy children bide;
How true, how good, thy graceful maids
Make bright, like flowers, the valley-shades;
What generous men
Spring, like thine oaks, by hill and glen;—

What cordial welcomes greet the guest
By thy lone rivers of the West;
How faith is kept, and truth revered,
And man is loved, and God is feared,
In woodland homes,
And where the ocean border foams.

There's freedom at thy gates and rest
For Earth's down-trodden and opprest,
A shelter for the hunted head,
For the starved laborer toil and bread.
Power, at thy bounds,
Stops and calls back his baffled hounds.

Oh, fair young mother! on thy brow
Shall sit a nobler grace than now.
Deep in the brightness of the skies
The thronging years in glory rise,
And, as they fleet,
Drop strength and riches at thy feet.

Thine eye, with every coming hour,
Shall brighten, and thy form shall tower;

And when thy sisters, elder born,
Would brand thy name with words of scorn,
Before thine eye,
Upon their lips the taunt shall die.
(1846) 1847

ROBERT OF LINCOLN

Merrily swinging on brier and weed,
Near to the nest of his little dame,
Over the mountain-side or mead,
Robert of Lincoln is telling his name:
Bob-o'-link, bob-o'-link,
Spink, spank, spink;
Snug and safe is that nest of ours,
Hidden among the summer flowers.
Chee, chee, chee.

Robert of Lincoln is gayly drest,
Wearing a bright black wedding-coat;
White are his shoulders and white his crest.
Hear him call in his merry note:
Bob-o'-link, bob-o'-link,
Spink, spank, spink;
Look, what a nice new coat is mine,
Sure there was never a bird so fine.
Chee, chee, chee.

Robert of Lincoln's Quaker wife,
Pretty and quiet, with plain brown wings,
Passing at home a patient life,
Broods in the grass while her husband sings,
Bob-o'-link, bob-o'-link,
Spink, spank, spink;
Brood, kind creature; you need not fear
Thieves and robbers while I am here.
Chee, chee, chee.

Modest and shy as a nun is she;
One weak chirp is her only note.
Braggart and prince of braggarts is he,
Pouring boasts from his little throat:
Bob-o'-link, bob-o'-link,
Spink, spank, spink;
Never was I afraid of man;
Catch me, cowardly knaves, if you can!
Chee, chee, chee.

Six white eggs on a bed of hay,
Flecked with purple, a pretty sight!
There as the mother sits all day,
Robert is singing with all his might:
Bob-o'-link, bob-o'-link,
Spink, spank, spink;
Nice good wife, that never goes out,
Keeping house while I frolic about.
Chee, chee, chee.

Soon as the little ones chip the shell,
Six wide mouths are open for food;
Robert of Lincoln bestirs him well,
Gathering seeds for the hungry brood.
Bob-o'-link, bob-o'-link,
Spink, spank, spink;
This new life is likely to be
Hard for a gay young fellow like me.
Chee, chee, chee.

Robert of Lincoln at length is made
Sober with work, and silent with care;
Off is his holiday garment laid,
Half forgotten that merry air:
Bob-o'-link, bob-o'-link,
Spink, spank, spink;
Nobody knows but my mate and I
Where our nest and our nestlings lie.
Chee, chee, chee.

Summer wanes; the children are grown;
Fun and frolic no more he knows;
Robert of Lincoln's a humdrum crone;
Off he flies, and we sing as he goes:
Bob-o'-link, bob-o'-link,
Spink, spank, spink;
When you can pipe that merry old strain,

Robert of Lincoln, come back again.
Chee, chee, chee.

1855

THE DEATH OF LINCOLN

Oh, slow to smite and swift to spare,
Gentle and merciful and just!
Who, in the fear of God, didst bear
The sword of power, a nation's trust!

In sorrow by thy bier we stand,
Amid the awe that hushes all,
And speak the anguish of a land
That shook with horror at thy fall.

Thy task is done; the bond are free:
We bear thee to an honored grave,
Whose proudest monument shall be
The broken fetters of the slave.

Pure was thy life; its bloody close
Hath placed thee with the sons of light,
Among the noble host of those
Who perished in the cause of Right.

(1865) 1866

THE PROGRESS OF ROMANTICISM

I. JAMES GATES PERCIVAL
(1795–1856)

NEW-ENGLAND

Hail to the land whereon we tread,
Our fondest boast;
The sepulchre of mighty dead,
The truest hearts that ever bled,
Who sleep on glory's brightest bed,
A fearless host:
No slave is here—our unchain'd feet
Walk freely, as the waves that beat
Our coast.

Our fathers cross'd the ocean's wave
To seek this shore;
They left behind the coward slave
To welter in his living grave;
With hearts unbent, high, steady, brave,
They sternly bore
Such toil as meaner souls had quell'd;
But souls like these, such toils impell'd
To soar.

Hail to the morn when first they stood
On Bunker's height;
And fearless stemm'd the invading flood,
And wrote our dearest rights in blood,
And mow'd in ranks .the hireling brood,
In desperate fight:
O, 'twas a proud, exulting day,
For ev'n our fallen fortunes lay
In light.

There is no other land like thee,
No dearer shore;
Thou art the shelter of the free;
The home, the port of liberty
Thou hast been, and shalt ever be,
Till time is o'er.
Ere I forget to think upon
My land, shall mother curse the son
She bore.

Thou art the firm, unshaken rock,
On which we rest;
And rising from thy hardy stock,
Thy sons the tyrant's frown shall mock,
And slavery's galling chains unlock,
And free the oppress'd:
All, who the wreath of freedom twine
Beneath the shadow of the vine
Are blest.

We love thy rude and rocky shore,
And here we stand—
Let foreign navies hasten o'er,
And on our heads their fury pour,
And peal their cannon's loudest roar,
And storm our land:
They still shall find, our lives are giv'n
To die for home;—and leant on heav'n
Our hand.

1822

II. CARLOS WILCOX
(1794–1827)

From *THE AGE OF BENEVOLENCE* *

BOOK II

[A SUMMER NOON]

* * * A sultry noon, not in the summer's prime,

* Inasmuch as only extracts from Book II are preserved in the *Remains of the Rev. Carlos Williams,* Hartford, 1828 (the text here used), the present editor has numbered the lines in this selection without reference to the original.

When all is fresh with life, and youth, and bloom,
But near its close when vegetation stops,
And fruits mature, stand ripening in the sun,
Soothes and enervates with its thousand charms,
Its images of silence and of rest,
The melancholy mind. The fields are still;
The husbandman has gone to his repast,
And, that partaken, on the coolest side
Of his abode, reclines, in sweet repose.
Deep in the shaded stream the cattle stand,
The flocks beside the fence, with heads all prone
And panting quick. The fields, for harvest ripe,
No breezes bend in smooth and graceful waves,
While with their motion, dim and bright by turns,
The sun-shine seems to move; nor e'en a breath
Brushes along the surface with a shade,
Fleeting and thin, like that of flying smoke.
The slender stalks, their heavy bended heads
Support as motionless, as oaks their tops.
O'er all the woods the top-most leaves are still,
E'en the wild poplar leaves, that, pendant hung
By stems elastic, quiver at a breath,
Rest in the general calm. The thistle-down
Seen high and thick, by gazing up beside
Some shading object, in a silver shower
Plumb down, and slower than the slowest snow,
Through all the sleepy atmosphere descends;
And where it lights, though on the steepest roof,
Or smallest spire of grass, remains unmoved.
White as a fleece, as dense and as distinct
From the resplendent sky, a single cloud
On the soft bosom of the air becalmed
Drops a lone shadow, as distinct and still,
On the bare plain, or sunny mountain's side;
Or in the polished mirror of the lake,
In which the deep reflected sky appears
A calm, sublime immensity below.

* * * No sound, nor motion, of a living thing
The stillness breaks, but such as serve to soothe,
Or cause the soul to feel the stillness more.
The yellow-hammer by the way-side picks,
Mutely, the thistle's seed; but in her flight,
So smoothly serpentine, her wings outspread
To rise a little, closed to fall as far,
Moving like sea-fowl o'er the heaving waves,
With each new impulse chimes a feeble note.
The russet grasshopper, at times, is heard,
Snapping his many wings, as half he flies,
Half hovers in the air. Where strikes the sun
With sultriest beams, upon the sandy plain,
Or stony mount, or in the close deep vale,
The harmless locust of this western clime,

At intervals, amid the leaves unseen,
Is heard to sing with one unbroken sound,
As with a long-drawn breath, beginning low,
And rising to the midst with shriller swell,
Then in low cadence dying all away.
Beside the stream, collected in a flock,
The noiseless butterflies, though on the ground,
Continue still to wave their open fans
Powder'd with gold; while on the jutting twigs
The spindling insects that frequent the banks,
Rest, with their thin transparent wings outspread
As when they fly. Oft times, though seldom seen,
The cuckoo, that in summer haunts our groves,
Is heard to moan, as if at every breath
Panting aloud. The hawk, in mid-air high,
On his broad pinions sailing round and round,
With not a flutter, or but now and then,
As if his trembling balance to regain,
Utters a single scream, but faintly heard;
And all again is still. * * *

(1819–22) 1822–28

From THE RELIGION OF TASTE

LXXVI

Ere long the clouds were gone, the moon was set;
When deeply blue without a shade of gray,
The sky was filled with stars that almost met,
Their points prolonged and sharpened to one ray;
Through their transparent air the milky-way
Seemed one broad flame of pure resplendent white,
As if some globe on fire, turned far astray,
Had crossed the wide arch with so swift a flight,
That for a moment shone its whole long track of light.

LXXVII

At length in northern skies, at first but small,
A sheet of light meteorrous begun
To spread on either hand, and rise and fall
In waves, that slowly first, then quickly run
Along its edge, set thick but one by one
With spiry beams, that all at once shot high,
Like those through vapours from the setting sun;
Then sidelong as before the wind they fly,
Like streaking rain from clouds that flit along the sky.

LXXVIII

Now all the mountain-tops and gulfs between
Seemed one dark plain; from forests, caves profound,
And rushing waters far below unseen,
Rose a deep roar in one united sound,
Alike pervading all the air around,
And seeming e'en the azure dome to fill,
And from it through soft ether to resound
In low vibrations, sending a sweet thrill
To every finger's end from rapture deep and still.

(1824) 1828

III. EDWARD COOTE PINKNEY (1802–1828)

THE VOYAGER'S SONG

> A tradition prevailed among the natives of Puerto Rico, that in the Isle of Bimini, one of the Lucayos, there was a fountain of such wonderful virtue, as to renew the youth and recall the vigor of every person who bathed in its salutary waters. In hopes of finding this grand restorative, Ponce de Leon and his followers, ranged through the islands, searching with fruitless solicitude for the fountain, which was the chief object of the expedition.
> —[William] Robertson's [*History of*] *America* [Book III].

I

Sound trumpets, ho!—weigh anchor—loosen sail—
The seaward flying banners chide delay;
As if 'twere heaven that breathes this kindly gale,
Our life-like bark beneath it speeds away.
Flit we, a gliding dream, with troublous motion,
Across the slumbers of uneasy ocean;
And furl our canvass by a happier land,
So fraught with emanations from the sun,
That potable gold streams through the sand
Where element should run.

II

Onward, my friends, to that bright, florid isle,
The jewel of a smooth and silver sea,
With springs on which perennial summers smile
A power of causing immortality.
For Bimini;—in its enchanted ground,
The hallowed fountains we would seek, are found;
Bathed in the waters of those mystic wells,
The frame starts up in renovated truth,
And, freed from Time's deforming spells,
Resumes its proper youth.

III

Hail, better birth!—once more my feelings all
A graven image to themselves shall make,
And, placed upon my heart for pedestal,
That glorious idol long will keep awake
Their natural religion, nor be cast
To earth by Age, the great Iconoclast.
As from Gadara's founts they once could come,
Charm-called, from these Love's genii shall arise,
And build their perdurable home,
Miranda, in thine eyes.

IV

By Nature wisely gifted, not destroyed
With golden presents, like the Roman maid,—
A sublunary paradise enjoyed,
Shall teach thee bliss incapable of shade;—
An Eden ours, nor angry gods, nor men,
Nor star-clad Fates, can take from us again.
Superior to animal decay,
Sun of that perfect heaven, thou'lt calmly see
Stag, raven, phenix, drop away
With *human* transiency.

V

Thus rich in being,—beautiful,—adored,
Fear not exhausting pleasure's precious mine;

The wondrous waters we approach, when poured
On passion's lees, supply the wasted wine:
Then be thy bosom's tenant prodigal,
And confident of termless carnival.
Like idle yellow leaves afloat on time,
Let others lapse to death's pacific sea,—
We'll fade nor fall, but sport sublime
In green eternity.

VI

The envious years, which steal our pleasures, thou
May'st call at once, like magic memory, back,
And, as they pass o'er thine unwithering brow,
Efface their footsteps ere they form a track.
Thy bloom with wilful weeping never stain,
Perpetual life must not belong to pain.
For me,—this world hath not yet been a place
Conscious of joys so great as will be mine,
Because the light has kissed no face
Forever fair as thine.

1825

A SERENADE

Look out upon the stars, my love,
And shame them with thine eyes,
On which, than on the lights above,
There hang more destinies.
Night's beauty is the harmony
Of blending shades and light:
Then, Lady, up,—look out, and be
A sister to the night!—

Sleep not!—thine image wakes for aye,
Within my watching breast:
Sleep not!—from her soft sleep should fly,
Who robs all hearts of rest.
Nay, Lady, from thy slumbers break,
And make this darkness gay,
With looks, whose brightness well might make
Of darker nights a day.

(1822) 1823

A HEALTH

I fill this cup to one made up of loveliness alone,
A woman, of her gentle sex the seeming paragon;
To whom the better elements and kindly stars have given,
A form so fair, that, like the air, 'tis less of earth than heaven.

Her every tone is music's own, like those of morning birds,
And something more than melody dwells ever in her words;
The coinage of her heart are they, and from her lips each flows
As one may see the burthened bee forth issue from the rose.

Affections are as thoughts to her, the measures of her hours;
Her feelings have the fragrancy, the freshness, of young flowers;
And lovely passions, changing oft, so fill her, she appears
The image of themselves by turns,—the idol of past years!

Of her bright face one glance will trace a picture on the brain,
And of her voice in echoing hearts a sound must long remain,
But memory such as mine of her so much endears,
When death is nigh my latest sigh will not be life's but hers.

I filled this cup to one made up of loveliness alone,
A woman, of her gentle sex the seeming paragon—

Her health! and would on earth there stood some more of such a frame,
That life might be all poetry, and weariness a name.
(1824) 1824

IV. RICHARD HENRY WILDE
(1789–1847)

MY LIFE IS LIKE THE SUMMER ROSE

My life is like the summer rose
That opens to the morning sky,
But ere the shades of evening close,
Is scatter'd on the ground—to die!
Yet on the rose's humble bed
The sweetest dews of night are shed,
As if she wept the waste to see—
But none shall weep a tear for me!

My life is like the autumn leaf
That trembles in the moon's pale ray:
Its hold is frail, its date is brief,
Restless—and soon to pass away!
Yet ere that leaf shall fall and fade,
The parent tree will mourn its shade,
The winds bewail the leafless tree,
But none shall breathe a sigh for me!

My life is like the prints, which feet
Have left on Tampa's desert strand;
Soon as the rising tide shall beat,
All trace will vanish from the sand;
Yet, as if grieving to efface
All vestige of the human race,
On that lone shore loud moans the sea,
But none, alas! shall mourn for me!
1815

TO THE MOCKING BIRD

Wing'd mimic of the woods! thou motley fool!
Who shall thy gay buffoonery describe?
Thine ever-ready notes of ridicule
Pursue thy fellows still with jest and gibe:
Wit, sophist, songster, YORICK of thy tribe,
Thou sportive satirist of Nature's school,
To thee the palm of scoffing we ascribe,
Arch-mocker and mad Abbot of Misrule!
For such thou art by day—but all night long
Thou pour'st a soft, sweet, pensive, solemn strain,
As if thou didst in this thy moonlight song
Like to the melancholy JACQUES complain,
Musing on falsehood, folly, vice, and wrong,
And sighing for thy motley coat again.
1847

V. JOHN HOWARD PAYNE
(1791–1852)

HOME, SWEET HOME

'Mid pleasures and palaces though we may roam,
Be it ever so humble, there's no place like Home!
A charm from the skies seems to hallow us there,
(Like the love of a mother,
Surpassing all other,)
Which, seek through the world, is ne'er met with elsewhere.
There's a spell in the shade
Where our infancy play'd,
Even stronger than Time, and more deep than despair!

An exile from Home, splendor dazzles in vain!

Oh, give me my lowly, thatch'd cottage again!
The birds and the lambkins that came at my call,—
Those who nam'd me with pride,—
Those who play'd by my side,—
Give me them! with the innocence dearer than all!
The joys of the palaces through which I roam
Only swell my heart's anguish—
There's no place like Home!

To *us*, in despite of the absence of years,
How sweet the remembrance of *home* still appears;
From allurements abroad, which but flatter the eye,
The unsatisfied heart turns, and says, with a sigh,
"Home, home, sweet, sweet home!
There's no place like home!
There's no place like home!"

Your exile is blest with all fate can bestow;
But *mine* has been checkered with many a woe!
Yet, tho' different our fortunes, our thoughts are the same,
And both, as we think of Columbia, exclaim,
"Home, home, sweet, sweet home!
There's no place like home!
There's no place like home!"

(1823) 1885

VI. FITZ-GREENE HALLECK
(1790–1867)

MARCO BOZZARIS

At midnight, in his guarded tent,
The Turk was dreaming of the hour
When Greece, her knee in suppliance bent,
Should tremble at his power:
In dreams, through camp and court, he bore
The trophies of a conqueror;
In dreams his song of triumph heard;
Then wore his monarch's signet ring:
Then pressed that monarch's throne—a king;
As wild his thoughts, and gay of wing,
As Eden's garden bird.

At midnight, in the forest shades,
Bozzaris ranged his Suliote band,
True as the steel of their tried blades,
Heroes in heart and hand.
There had the Persian's thousands stood,
There had the glad earth drunk their blood
On old Platæa's day;
And now there breathed that haunted air
The sons of sires who conquered there,
With arm to strike and soul to dare,
As quick, as far as they.

An hour passed on—the Turk awoke;
That bright dream was his last;
He woke—to hear his sentries shriek,
"To arms! they come! the Greek! the Greek!"
He woke—to die midst flame, and smoke,
And shout, and groan, and sabre-stroke,
And death-shots falling thick and fast
As lightnings from the mountain-cloud;
And heard, with voice as trumpet loud,
Bozzaris cheer his band:
"Strike—till the last armed foe expires;
Strike—for your altars and your fires;

Strike—for the green graves of your sires;
God—and your native land!"

They fought—like brave men, long and well;
They piled that ground with Moslem slain,
They conquered—but Bozzaris fell,
Bleeding at every vein.
His few surviving comrades saw
His smile when rang their proud hurrah,
And the red field was won;
Then saw in death his eyelids close
Calmly, as to a night's repose,
Like flowers at set of sun.

Come to the bridal-chamber, Death!
Come to the mother's, when she feels,
For the first time, her first-born's breath;
Come when the blessed seals
That close the pestilence are broke,
And crowded cities wail its stroke;
Come in consumption's ghastly form,
The earthquake shock, the ocean-storm;
Come when the heart beats high and warm,
With banquet-song, and dance and wine;
And thou art terrible—the tear,
The groan, the knell, the pall, the bier;
And all we know, or dream, or fear
Of agony, are thine.

But to the hero, when his sword
Has won the battle for the free,
Thy voice sounds like a prophet's word;
And in its hollow tones are heard
The thanks of millions yet to be.
Come, when his task of fame is wrought—
Come, with her laurel-leaf, blood bought—
Come in her crowning hour—and then
Thy sunken eye's unearthly light
To him is welcome as the sight
Of sky and stars to prisoned men:
Thy grasp is welcome as the hand
Of brother in a foreign land;
Thy summons welcome as the cry
That told the Indian isles were nigh
To the world-seeking Genoese.
When the land wind, from woods of palm,
And orange-groves, and fields of balm,
Blew o'er the Haytian seas.

Bozzaris! with the storied brave
Greece nurtured in her glory's time,
Rest thee—there is no prouder grave,
Even in her own proud clime.
She wore no funeral-weeds for thee,
Nor bade the dark hearse wave its plume
Like torn branch from death's leafless tree
In sorrow's pomp and pageantry,
The heartless luxury of the tomb:
But she remembers thee as one
Long loved and for a season gone;
For thee her poet's lyre is wreathed,
Her marble wrought, her music breathed;
For thee she rings the birthday bells;
Of thee her babes' first lisping tells;
For thine her evening prayer is said
At palace-couch and cottage-bed;
Her soldier, closing with the foe,
Gives for thy sake a deadlier blow;
His plighted maiden, when she fears
For him the joy of her young years,
Thinks of thy fate, and checks her tears:
And she, the mother of thy boys,
Though in her eye and faded cheek
Is read the grief she will not speak,
The memory of her buried joys,
And even she who gave thee birth,
Will, by their pilgrim-circled hearth,
Talk of thy doom without a sigh:
For thou art Freedom's now, and Fame's;

One of the few, the immortal names,
That were not born to die.

1825

ON THE DEATH OF JOSEPH RODMAN DRAKE

OF NEW YORK, SEPT., 1820

The good die first,
And they, whose hearts are dry as summer dust,
Burn to the socket.

—WORDSWORTH.

Green be the turf above thee,
Friend of my better days!
None knew thee but to love thee,
Nor named thee but to praise.

Tears fell when thou wert dying,
From eyes unused to weep,
And long, where thou art lying,
Will tears the cold turf steep.

When hearts, whose truth was proven,
Like thine, are laid in earth,
There should a wreath be woven
To tell the world their worth;

And I who woke each morrow
To clasp thy hand in mine,
Who shared thy joy and sorrow,
Whose weal and woe were thine:

It should be mine to braid it
Around thy faded brow,
But I've in vain essayed it,
And feel I cannot now.

While memory bids me weep thee,
Nor thoughts nor words are free,
The grief is fixed too deeply
That mourns a man like thee.

(1820) 1821

From *FANNY*

[YOUNG LADY OF NEW YORK]

CIV

But where is Fanny? She has long been thrown
Where cheeks and roses wither—in the shade.
The age of chivalry, you know, is gone;
And although, as I once before have said,
I love a pretty face to adoration,
Yet, still, I must preserve my reputation,

CV

As a true dandy of the modern schools.
One hates to be old-fashioned; it would be
A violation of the latest rules,
To treat the sex with too much courtesy.
'Tis not to worship beauty, as she glows
In all her diamond lustre, that the beaux

CVI

Of these enlightened days at evening crowd,
Where Fashion welcomes in her rooms of light
That "dignified obedience; that proud
Submission," which, in times of yore, the knight
Gave to his "ladye-love," is now a scandal,
And practised only by your Goth and Vandal.

CVII

To lounge in graceful attitudes—be stared
Upon, the while, by every fair one's eye,
And stare one's self, in turn: to be prepared
To dart upon the trays, as swiftly by
The dexterous Simon bears them, and to take
One's share at least of coffee, cream, and cake,

CVIII

Is now to be "the ton." The pouting lip,
And sad, upbraiding eye of the poor girl,
Who hardly of joy's cup one drop can sip,
Ere in the wild confusion, and the whirl,
And tumult of the hour, its bubbles vanish,
Must now be disregarded. One must banish

CIX

Those antiquated feelings, that belong
To feudal manners and a barbarous age.
Time was—when woman "poured her soul" in song,
That all was hushed around. 'Tis now "the rage"
To deem a song, like bugle-tones in battle,
A signal-note, that bids each tongue's artillery rattle.

CX

And, therefore, I have made Miss Fanny wait
My leisure. She had changed, as you will see, as
Much as her worthy sire, and made as great
Proficiency in taste and high ideas.
The careless smile of other days was gone,
And every gesture spoke *"qu'en dira-t-on?"*

CXI

She long had known that in her father's coffers,
And also to his credit in the banks,
There was some cash; and therefore all the offers
Made her, by gentlemen of the middle ranks,
Of heart and hand, had spurned, as far beneath
One whose high destiny it was to breathe,

CXII

Ere long, the air of Broadway or Park Place,
And reign a fairy queen in fairy land;
Display in the gay dance her form of grace,
Or touch with rounded arm and gloveless hand,
Harp or piano.—Madame Catilani
Forgot awhile, and every eye on Fanny.

CXIII

And in anticipation of that hour,
Her star of hope, her paradise of thought,
She'd had as many masters as the power
Of riches could bestow; and had been taught
The thousand nameless graces that adorn
The daughters of the wealthy and high-born.

CXIV

She had been noticed at some public places
(The Battery, and the balls of Mr. Whale),
For hers was one of those attractive faces,
That when you gaze upon them, never fail
To bid you look again; there was a beam,
A lustre in her eye, that oft would seem

CXV

A little like effrontery; and yet
The lady meant no harm; her only aim
Was but to be admired by all she met,

And the free homage of the heart to claim;
And if she showed too plainly this intention,
Others have done the same—'twas not of her invention.

CXVI

She shone at every concert; where are bought
Tickets by all who wish them, for a dollar;
She patronized the Theatre, and thought
That Wallack looked extremely well in Rolla;
She fell in love, as all the ladies do,
With Mr. Simpson—talked as loudly, too,

CXVII

As any beauty of the highest grade,
To the gay circle in the box beside her;
And when the pit—half vexed and half afraid,
With looks of smothered indignation eyed her,
She calmly met their gaze, and stood before 'em,
Smiling at vulgar taste and mock decorum.

CXVIII

And though by no means a *bas bleu,* she had
For literature a most becoming passion;
Had skimmed the latest novels, good and bad,
And read the Croakers, when they were in fashion;
And Dr. Chalmers' sermons of a Sunday;
And Woodworth's Cabinet, and the new Salmagundi.

CXIX

She was among the first and warmest patrons
Of Griscom's *conversaziones,* where
In rainbow groups, our bright-eyed maids and matrons,
On science bent, assemble; to prepare
Themselves for acting well, in life, their part
As wives and mothers. There she learned by heart

CXX

Words, to the witches in Macbeth unknown.
Hydraulics, hydrostatics, and *pneumatics,*
Dioptrics, optics, katoptrics, carbon,
Chlorine, and *iodine,* and *aërostatics;*
Also,—why frogs, for want of air, expire;
And how to set the Tappan Sea on fire!

CXXI

In all the modern languages she was
Exceedingly well-versed; and had devoted,
To their attainment, far more time than has,
By the best teachers, lately been allotted;
For she had taken lessons, twice a week,
For a full month in each; and she could speak

CXXII

French and Italian, equally as well
As Chinese, Portuguese, or German; and,
What is still more surprising, she could spell
Most of our longest English words off-hand;
Was quite familiar in Low Dutch and Spanish,
And thought of studying modern Greek and Danish.

CXXIII

She sang divinely; and in "Love's young dream"
  And "Fanny dearest," and "The soldier's bride;"
And every song, whose dear delightful theme,
  Is "Love, still love," had oft till midnight tried
Her finest, loftiest "pigeon-wings" of sound,
Waking the very watchmen far around.

CXXIV

For her pure taste in dress, I can appeal to
  Madame Bouquet, and Monsieur Pardessus;
She was, in short, a woman you might kneel to,
  If kneeling were in fashion; or if you
Were wearied of your duns and single life,
And wanted a few thousands and a wife.

1819

VII. JOSEPH RODMAN DRAKE
(1795–1820)

THE CULPRIT FAY

My visual orbs are purged from film, and lo!
  Instead of Anster's turnip-bearing vales
I see old fairy land's miraculous show!
  Her trees of tinsel kissed by freakish gales,
Her Ouphs that, cloaked in leaf-gold, skim the breeze,
  And fairies, swarming. . . .

—TENNANT'S *Anster Fair.*

I

'Tis the middle watch of a summer's night—
The earth is dark, but the heavens are bright;
Naught is seen in the vault on high
But the moon, and the stars, and the cloudless sky,
And the flood which rolls its milky hue,
A river of light on the welkin blue.
The moon looks down on old Cronest,
She mellows the shades on his shaggy breast,
And seems his huge gray form to throw
In a silver cone on the wave below;
His sides are broken by spots of shade,
By the walnut bough and the cedar made,
And through their clustering branches dark
Glimmers and dies the firefly's spark—
Like starry twinkles that momently break
Through the rifts of the gathering tempest's rack.

II

The stars are on the moving stream,
  And fling, as its ripples gently flow,
A burnished length of wavy beam
  In an eel-like, spiral line below;
The winds are whist, and the owl is still,
  The bat in the shelvy rock is hid,
And nought is heard on the lonely hill
But the cricket's chirp and the answer shrill
  Of the gauze-winged katy-did;
And the plaint of the wailing whip-poor-will
  Who mourns unseen, and ceaseless sings,
Ever a note of wail and wo,
  Till morning spreads her rosy wings,
And earth and sky in her glances glow.

III

'Tis the hour of fairy ban and spell:
The wood-tick has kept the minutes well;

He has counted them all with click and stroke,
Deep in the heart of the mountain oak,
And he has awakened the sentry elve
  Who sleeps with him in the haunted tree,
To bid him ring the hour of twelve,
  And call the fays to their revelry;
Twelve small strokes on his tinkling bell—
('Twas made of the white snail's pearly shell:—)
"Midnight comes, and all is well!
Hither, hither, wing your way!
'Tis the dawn of the fairy day."

IV

They come from beds of lichen green,
They creep from the mullen's velvet screen;
  Some on the backs of beetles fly
From the silver tops of moon-touched trees,
  Where they swung in their cobweb hammocks high,
And rock'd about in the evening breeze;
  Some from the hum-bird's downy nest—
They had driven him out by elfin power,
  And pillowed on plumes of his rain-bow breast,
Had slumbered there till the charmed hour;
  Some had lain in the scoop of the rock,
With glittering ising-stars inlaid;
  And some had opened the four-o'clock,
And stole within its purple shade.
  And now they throng the moonlight glade,
Above—below—on every side,
  Their little minim forms arrayed
In the tricksy pomp of fairy pride!

V

They come not now to print the lea,
In freak and dance around the tree,
Or at the mushroom board to sup,
And drink the dew from the butter-cup;—
A scene of sorrow waits them now,
For an Ouphe has broken his vestal vow;
He has loved an earthly maid,
And left for her his woodland shade;
He has lain upon her lip of dew,
And sunned him in her eye of blue,
Fann'd her cheek with his wing of air,
Played with the ringlets of her hair,
And, nestling on her snowy breast,
Forgot the lily-king's behest.
For this the shadowy tribes of air
  To the elfin court must haste away:—
And now they stand expectant there,
  To hear the doom of the Culprit Fay.

VI

The throne was reared upon the grass
Of spice-wood and of sassafras;
On pillars of mottled tortoise-shell
  Hung the burnished canopy—
And o'er it gorgeous curtains fell
  Of the tulip's crimson drapery.
The monarch sat on his judgment-seat,
  On his brow the crown imperial shone,
The prisoner Fay was at his feet,
  And his peers were ranged around the throne.
He waved his sceptre in the air,
  He looked around and calmly spoke;
His brow was grave and his eye severe,
  But his voice in a softened accent broke:

VII

"Fairy! Fairy! list and mark,
  Thou has broke thine elfin chain,
Thy flame-wood lamp is quenched and dark,

And thy wings are dyed with a deadly stain—
Thou hast sullied thine elfin purity
In the glance of a mortal maiden's eye,
Thou has scorned our dread decree,
And thou shouldst pay the forfeit high,
But well I know her sinless mind
Is pure as the angel forms above,
Gentle and meek, and chaste and kind,
Such as a spirit well might love;
Fairy! had she spot or taint,
Bitter had been thy punishment.
Tied to the hornet's shardy wings;
Tossed on the pricks of nettles' stings;
Or seven long ages doomed to dwell
With the lazy worm in the walnut-shell;
Or every night to writhe and bleed
Beneath the tread of the centipede;
Or bound in a cobweb dungeon dim,
Your jailer a spider huge and grim,
Amid the carrion bodies to lie,
Of the worm, and the bug, and the murdered fly:
These it had been your lot to bear,
Had a stain been found on the earthly fair.
Now list, and mark our mild decree—
Fairy, this your doom must be:

VIII

"Thou shalt seek the beach of sand
Where the water bounds the elfin land,
Thou shalt watch the oozy brine
Till the sturgeon leaps in the bright moonshine,
Then dart the glistening arch below,
And catch a drop from his silver bow.
The water-spirits will wield their arms
And dash around, with roar and rave,
And vain are the woodland spirits' charms,
They are the imps that rule the wave.
Yet trust thee in thy single might,
If thy heart be pure and thy spirit right,
Thou shalt win the warlock fight.

IX

"If the spray-bead gem be won,
The stain of thy wing is washed away,
But another errand must be done
Ere thy crime be lost for aye;
Thy flame-wood lamp is quenched and dark,
Thou must re-illume its spark.
Mount thy steed and spur him high
To the heaven's blue canopy;
And when thou seest a shooting star,
Follow it fast, and follow it far—
The last faint spark of its burning train
Shall light the elfin lamp again.
Thou hast heard our sentence, Fay;
Hence! to the water-side, away!"

X

The goblin marked his monarch well;
He spake not, but he bowed him low,
Then plucked a crimson colen-bell,
And turned him round in act to go.
The way is long, he cannot fly,
His soiled wing has lost its power,
And he winds adown the mountain high,
For many a sore and weary hour.
Through dreary beds of tangled fern,
Through groves of nightshade dark and dern,
Over the grass and through the brake,
Where toils the ant and sleeps the snake;
Now o'er the violet's azure flush
He skips along in lightsome mood;
And now he thrids the bramble bush,
Till its points are dyed in fairy blood.
He has leapt the bog, he has pierced the briar,

He has swum the brook and waded the mire,
Till his spirits sank, and his limbs grew weak,
And the red waxed fainter in his cheek.
He had fallen to the ground outright,
For rugged and dim was his onward track,
But there came a spotted toad in sight,
And he laughed as he jumped upon her back;
He bridled her mouth with a silk-weed twist;
He lashed her sides with an osier thong;
And now through evening's dewy mist,
With leap and spring they bound along,
Till the mountain's magic verge is past,
And the beach of sand is reached at last.

XI

Soft and pale is the moony beam,
Moveless still the glassy stream,
The wave is clear, the beach is bright
With snowy shells and sparkling stones;
The shore-surge comes in ripples light,
In murmurings faint and distant moans;
And ever afar in the silence deep
Is heard the splash of the sturgeon's leap,
And the bend of his graceful bow is seen—
A glittering arch of silver sheen,
Spanning the wave of burnished blue,
And dripping with gems of the river dew.

XII

The elfin cast a glance around,
As he lighted down from his courser toad,
Then round his breast his wings he wound,
And close to the river's brink he stood;
He sprang on a rock, he breathed a prayer,
Above his head his arms he threw,
Then tossed a tiny curve in air,
And headlong plunged in the waters blue.

XIII

Up sprung the spirits of the waves,
From sea-silk beds in their coral caves,
With snail-plate armour snatched in haste,
They speed their way through the liquid waste;
Some are rapidly borne along
On the mailed shrimp or the prickly prong,
Some on the blood-red leeches glide,
Some on the stony star-fish ride,
Some on the back of the lancing squab,
Some on the sideling soldier-crab;
And some on the jellied quarl, that flings
At once a thousand streamy stings—
They cut the wave with the living oar
And hurry on to the moonlight shore,
To guard their realms and chase away
The footsteps of the invading Fay.

XIV

Fearlessly he skims along,
His hope is high, and his limbs are strong,
He spreads his arms like the swallow's wing,
And throws his feet with a frog-like fling;
His locks of gold on the waters shine,
At his breast the puny foam-beads rise,
His back gleams bright above the brine,
And the wake-line foam behind him lies.

But the water-sprites are gathering near
To check his course along the tide;
Their warriors come in swift career
And hem him round on every side;
On his thigh the leech has fixed his hold,
The quarl's long arms are round him roll'd,
The prickly prong has pierced his skin,
And the squab has thrown his javelin,
The gritty star has rubbed him raw,
And the crab has struck with his giant claw;
He howls with rage, and he shrieks with pain,
He strikes around, but his blows are vain;
Hopeless is the unequal fight,
Fairy! nought is left but flight.

XV

He turned him round and fled amain
With hurry and dash to the beach again;
He twisted over from side to side,
And laid his cheek to the cleaving tide.
The strokes of his plunging arms are fleet,
And with all his might he flings his feet,
But the water-sprites are round him still,
To cross his path and work him ill.
They bade the wave before him rise;
They flung the sea-fire in his eyes,
And they stunned his ears with the scallop stroke,
With the porpoise heave and the drum-fish croak.
Oh! but a weary wight was he
When he reached the foot of the dog-wood tree;
Gashed and wounded, and stiff and sore,
He laid him down on the sandy shore;
He blessed the force of the charmed line,
And he banned the water-goblins' spite,
For he saw around in the sweet moon-shine,
Their little wee faces above the brine,
Giggling and laughing with all their might
At the piteous hap of the Fairy wight.

XVI

Soon he gathered the balsam dew
From the sorrel leaf and the hen-bane bud;
Over each wound the balm he drew,
And with cobweb lint he staunched the blood.
The mild west wind was soft and low,
It cooled the heat of his burning brow,
And he felt new life in his sinews shoot,
As he drank the juice of the cal'mus root;
And now he treads the fatal shore,
As fresh and vigorous as before.

XVII

Wrapped in musing stands the sprite:
'Tis the middle wane of night,
His task is hard, his way is far,
But he must do his errand right
Ere dawning mounts her beamy car,
And rolls her chariot wheels of light;
And vain are the spells of fairy-land,
He must work with a human hand.

XVIII

He cast a saddened look around,
But he felt new joy his bosom swell,
When, glittering on the shadowed ground,
He saw a purple muscle shell;
Thither he ran, and he bent him low,
He heaved at the stern and he heaved at the bow,
And he pushed her over the yielding sand,

Till he came to the verge of the haunted land.
She was as lovely a pleasure boat
As ever fairy had paddled in,
For she glowed with purple paint without,
And shone with silvery pearl within;
A sculler's notch in the stern he made,
An oar he shaped of the bootle blade;
Then sprung to his seat with a lightsome leap,
And launched afar on the calm blue deep.

XIX

The imps of the river yell and rave;
They had no power above the wave,
But they heaved the billow before the prow,
And they dashed the surge against her side,
And they struck her keel with jerk and blow,
Till the gunwale bent to the rocking tide.
She wimpled about in the pale moonbeam,
Like a feather that floats on a windtossed stream;
And momently athwart her track
The quarl upreared his island back,
And the fluttering scallop behind would float,
And spatter the water about the boat;
But he bailed her out with his colen-bell,
And he kept her trimmed with a wary tread,
While on every side like lightning fell
The heavy strokes of his bootle-blade.

XX

Onward still he held his way,
Till he came where the column of moonshine lay,
And saw beneath the surface dim
The brown-backed sturgeon slowly swim:
Around him were the goblin train—
But he skulled with all his might and main,
And followed wherever the sturgeon led,
Till he saw him upward point his head;
Then he dropped his paddle blade,
And held his colen goblet up
To catch the drop in its crimson cup.

XXI

With sweeping tail and quivering fin,
Through the wave the sturgeon flew,
And, like the heaven-shot javelin,
He sprung above the waters blue.
Instant as the star-fall light,
He plunged him in the deep again,
But left an arch of silver bright
The rainbow of the moony main.
It was a strange and lovely sight
To see the puny goblin there;
He seemed an angel form of light,
With azure wing and sunny hair,
Throned on a cloud of purple fair,
Circled with blue and edged with white,
And sitting at the fall of even
Beneath the bow of summer heaven.

XXII

A moment and its lustre fell,
But ere it met the billow blue,
He caught within his crimson bell,
A droplet of its sparkling dew—
Joy to thee, Fay! thy task is done,
Thy wings are pure, for the gem is won—
Cheerily ply thy dripping oar,
And haste away to the elfin shore.

XXIII

He turns, and lo! on either side
The ripples on his path divide;

And the track o'er which his boat must pass
Is smooth as a sheet of polished glass.
Around, their limbs the sea-nymphs lave,
With snowy arms half swelling out,
While on the glossed and gleamy wave
Their sea-green ringlets loosely float;
They swim around with smile and song;
They press the bark with pearly hand,
And gently urge her course along,
Toward the beach of speckled sand;
And, as he lightly leapt to land,
They bade adieu with nod and bow,
Then gayly kissed each little hand,
And dropped in the chrystal deep below.

XXIV

A moment staied the fairy there;
He kissed the beach and breathed a prayer,
Then he spread his wings of gilded blue,
And on to the elfin court he flew;
As ever ye saw a bubble rise.
And shine with a thousand changing dyes,
Till lessening far through ether driven,
It mingles with the hues of heaven:
As, at the glimpse of morning pale,
The lance-fly spreads his silken sail,
And gleams with blendings soft and bright,
Till lost in the shades of fading night;
So rose from earth the lovely Fay—
So vanished, far in heaven away!

. . . .

Up, Fairy! quit thy chick-weed bower,
The cricket has called the second hour,
Twice again, and the lark will rise
To kiss the streaking of the skies—
Up! thy charmed armour don,
Thou'lt need it ere the night be gone.

XXV

He put his acorn helmet on;
It was plumed of the silk of the thistle down:
The corslet plate that guarded his breast
Was once the wild bee's golden vest;
His cloak, of a thousand mingled dyes,
Was formed of the wings of butterflies;
His shield was the shell of a lady-bug queen,
Studs of gold on a ground of green;
And the quivering lance which he brandished bright,
Was the sting of a wasp he had slain in fight.
Swift he bestrode his fire-fly steed;
He bared his blade of the bent grass blue;
He drove his spurs of the cockle seed,
And away like a glance of thought he flew,
To skim the heavens and follow far
The fiery trail of the rocket-star.

XXVI

The moth-fly, as he shot in air,
Crept under the leaf, and hid her there;
The katy-did forgot its lay,
The prowling gnat fled fast away,
The fell mosqueto checked his drone
And folded his wings till the Fay was gone,
And the wily beetle dropped his head,
And fell on the ground as if he were dead;
They crouched them close in the darksome shade,
They quaked all o'er with awe and fear,
For they had felt the blue-bent blade,
And writhed at the prick of the elfin spear;
Many a time on a summer's night,
When the sky was clear and the moon was bright,

They had been roused from the haunted ground,
By the yelp and bay of the fairy hound;
They had heard the tiny bugle horn,
They had heard the twang of the maize-silk string,
When the vine-twig bows were tightly drawn,
And the nettle shaft through air was borne,
Feathered with down of the hum-bird's wing.
And now they deemed the courier ouphe,
Some hunter sprite of the elfin ground;
And they watched till they saw him mount the roof
That canopies the world around;
Then glad they left their covert lair
And freaked about in the midnight air.

XXVII

Up to the vaulted firmament
His path the fire-fly courser bent,
And at every gallop on the wind,
He flung a glittering spark behind;
He flies like a feather in the blast
Till the first light cloud in heaven is past,
But the shapes of air have begun their work,
And a drizzly mist is round him cast,
He cannot see through the mantle murk,
He shivers with cold, but he urges fast,
Through storm and darkness, sleet and shade,
He lashes his steed and spurs amain,
For shadowy hands have twitched the rein,
And flame-shot tongues around him played,
And near him many a fiendish eye
Glared with a fell malignity,
And yells of rage, and shrieks of fear,
Came screaming on his startled ear.

XXVIII

His wings are wet around his breast,
The plume hangs dripping from his crest,
His eyes are blur'd with the lightning's glare,
And his ears are stunned with the thunder's blare,
But he gave a shout, and his blade he drew,
He thrust before and he struck behind,
Till he pierced their cloudy bodies through,
And gashed their shadowy limbs of wind;
Howling the misty spectres flew,
They rend the air with frightful cries,
For he has gained the welkin blue,
And the land of clouds beneath him lies.

XXIX

Up to the cope careering swift
In breathless motion fast,
Fleet as the swallow cuts the drift,
Or the sea-roc rides the blast,
The sapphire sheet of eve is shot,
The sphered moon is past,
The earth but seems a tiny blot
On a sheet of azure cast.
O! it was sweet in the clear moonlight,
To tread the starry plain of even,
To meet the thousand eyes of night,
And feel the cooling breath of heaven!
But the Elfin made no stop or stay
Till he came to the bank of the milky-way,
Then he checked his courser's foot
And watched for the glimpse of the planet-shoot.

XXX

Sudden along the snowy tide
That swelled to meet their foot-steps' fall,
The sylphs of heaven were seen to glide,
Attired in sunset's crimson pall;
Around the Fay they weave the dance,
They skip before him on the plain,
And one has taken his wasp-sting lance,
And one upholds his bridle-rein;
With warbling wild they lead him on
To where through clouds of amber seen,
Studded with stars, resplendent shone
The palace of the sylphid queen.
Its spiral columns gleaming bright
Were streamers of the northern light;
Its curtain's light and lovely flush
Was of the morning's rosy blush,
And the ceiling fair that rose aboon
The white and feathery fleece of noon.

XXXI

But oh! how fair the shape that lay
Beneath a rainbow bending bright,
She seemed to the entranced Fay
The loveliest of the forms of light;
Her mantle was the purple rolled
At twilight in the west afar;
'Twas tied with threads of dawning gold,
And buttoned with a sparkling star.
Her face was like the lily roon
That veils the vestal planet's hue;
Her eyes, two beamlets from the moon,
Set floating in the welkin blue.
Her hair is like the sunny beam,
And the diamond gems which round it gleam
Are the pure drops of dewy even
That ne'er have left their native heaven.

XXXII

She raised her eyes to the wondering sprite,
And they leapt with smiles, for well I ween
Never before in the bowers of light
Had the form of an earthly Fay been seen.
Long she looked in his tiny face;
Long with his butterfly cloak she played;
She smoothed his wings of azure lace,
And handled the tassel of his blade;
And as he told in accents low
The story of his love and wo,
She felt new pains in her bosom rise,
And the tear-drop started in her eyes.
And 'O sweet spirit of earth,' she cried,
'Return no more to your woodland height,
But ever here with me abide
In the land of everlasting light!
Within the fleecy drift we'll lie,
We'll hang upon the rainbow's rim;
And all the jewels of the sky
Around thy brow shall brightly beam!
And thou shalt bathe thee in the stream
That rolls its whitening foam aboon
And ride upon the lightning's gleam,
And dance upon the orbed moon!
We'll sit within the Pleiad ring,
We'll rest on Orion's starry belt,
And I will bid my sylphs to sing
The song that makes the dew-mist melt;
Their harps are of the umber shade,
That hides the blush of waking day,
And every gleamy string is made
Of silvery moonshine's lengthened ray;
And thou shalt pillow on my breast,
While heavenly breathings float around,
And, with sylphs of ether blest,
Forget the joys of fairy ground.'

XXXIII

She was lovely and fair to see
And the elfin's heart [beat] fitfully;
But lovelier far, and still more fair,
The earthly form imprinted there,
Nought he saw in the heavens above
Was half so dear as his mortal love,
For he thought upon her looks so meek,
And he thought of the light flush on her cheek;
Never again might he bask and lie
On that sweet cheek and moonlight eye,
But in his dreams her form to see,
To clasp her in his reverie,
To think upon his virgin bride,
Was worth all heaven and earth beside.

XXXIV

'Lady,' he cried, 'I have sworn to-night,
On the word of a fairy knight,
To do my sentence-task aright;
My honour scarce is free from stain,
I may not soil its snows again;
Betide me weal, betide me wo,
Its mandate must be answered now.'
Her bosom heaved with many a sigh,
The tear was in her drooping eye;
  But she led him to the palace gate,
And called the sylphs who hovered there,
  And bade them fly and bring him straight
Of clouds condensed a sable car.
With charm and spell she blessed it there,
From all the fiends of upper air;
Then round him cast the shadowy shroud,
And tied his steed behind the cloud;
And pressed his hand as she bade him fly
Far to the verge of the northern sky,
For by its wan and wavering light
There was a star would fall to-night.

XXXV

Borne afar on the wings of the blast,
Northward away, he speeds him fast,
And his courser follows the cloudy wain
Till the hoof-strokes fall like pattering rain.
The clouds roll backward as he flies,
Each flickering star behind him lies,
And he has reached the nothern plain
And backed his fire-fly steed again,
Ready to follow in its flight
The streaming of the rocket-light.

XXXVI

The star is yet in the vault of heaven,
  But it rocks in the summer gale;
And now 'tis fitful and uneven,
  And now 'tis deadly pale;
And now 'tis wrapp'd in sulphur smoke,
  And quenched is its rayless beam,
And now with a rattling thunder-stroke
  It bursts in flash and flame.
As swift as the glance of the arrowy lance
  That the storm-spirit flings from high,
The star-shot flew o'er the welkin blue,
  As it fell from the sheeted sky.
As swift as the wind in its trail behind
  The elfin gallops along,
The fiends of the clouds are bellowing loud,
  But the sylphid charm is strong;
He gallops unhurt in the shower of fire,
  While the cloud-fiends fly from the blaze;
He watches each flake till its sparks expire,
  And rides in the light of its rays.
But he drove his steed to the lightning's speed,
  And caught a glimmering spark;

Then wheeled around to the fairy ground,
And sped through the midnight dark.

. . . .

Ouphe and goblin! imp and sprite!
Elf of eve! and starry Fay!
Ye that love the moon's soft light,
Hither—hither wend your way;
Twine ye in a jocund ring,
Sing and trip it merrily,
Hand to hand, and wing to wing,
Round the wild witch-hazel tree.

Hail the wanderer again,
With dance and song, and lute and lyre,
Pure his wing and strong his chain,
And doubly bright his fairy fire.
Twine ye in an airy round,
Brush the dew and print the lea;
Skip and gambol, hop and bound,
Round the wild witch-hazel tree.

The beetle guards our holy ground,
He flies about the haunted place,
And if mortal there be found,
He hums in his ears and flaps his face;
The leaf-harp sounds our roundelay,
The owlet's eyes our lanterns be;
Thus we sing, and dance, and play,
Round the wild witch-hazel tree.

But hark! from tower on tree-top high,
The sentry elf his call has made,
A streak is in the eastern sky,
Shapes of moonlight! flit and fade!
The hill-tops gleam in morning's spring,
The sky-lark shakes his dappled wing,
The day-glimpse glimmers on the lawn,
The cock has crowed and the Fays are gone.

(1816) 1835

TO A FRIEND

You damn me with faint praise.

I

Yes, faint was my applause and cold my praise,
Though soul was glowing in each polished line;
But nobler subjects claim the poet's lays,
A brighter glory waits a muse like thine.
Let amorous fools in lovesick measure pine;
Let Strangford whimper on, in fancied pain,
And leave to Moore his rose leaves and his vine;
Be thine the task a higher crown to gain,
The envied wreath that decks the patriot's holy strain.

II

Yet not in proud triumphal song alone,
Or martial ode, or sad sepulchral dirge,
There needs no voice to make our glories known;
There needs no voice the warrior's soul to urge
To tread the bounds of nature's stormy verge;
Columbia still shall win the battle's prize;
But be it thine to bid her mind emerge
To strike her harp, until its soul arise
From the neglected shade, where low in dust it lies.

III

Are there no scenes to touch the poet's soul?
No deeds of arms to wake the lordly strain?

Shall Hudson's billows unregarded roll?
Has Warren, has Montgomery died in vain?
Shame! that while every mountain stream and plain
Hath theme for truth's proud voice or fancy's wand,
No native bard the patriot harp hath ta'en,
But left to minstrels of a foreign strand
To sing the beauteous scenes of nature's loveliest land.

IV

Oh! for a seat on Appalachia's brow,
That I might scan the glorious prospect round,
Wild waving woods, and rolling floods below,
Smooth level glades and fields with grain embrown'd,
High heaving hills, with tufted forests crown'd,
Rearing their tall tops to the heaven's blue dome,
And emerald isles, like banners green unwound,
Floating along the lake, while round them roam
Bright helms of billowy blue and plumes of dancing foam.

V

'Tis true no fairies haunt our verdant meads,
No grinning imps deform our blazing hearth;
Beneath the kelpie's fang no traveller bleeds,
Nor gory vampyre taints our holy earth,
Nor spectres stalk to frighten harmless mirth,
Nor tortured demon howls adown the gale;
Fair reason checks these monsters in their birth.
Yet have we lay of love and horrid tale
Would dim the manliest eye and make the bravest pale.

VI

Where is the stony eye that hath not shed
Compassion's heart-drops o'er the sweet McRea?
Through midnight's wilds by savage bandits led,
"Her heart is sad—her love is far away!"
Elate that lover waits the promised day
When he shall clasp his blooming bride again—
Shine on, sweet visions! dreams of rapture, play!
Soon the cold corse of her he loved in vain
Shall blight his withered heart and fire his frenzied brain.

VII

Romantic Wyoming! could none be found
Of all that rove thy Eden groves among,
To wake a native harp's untutored sound,
And give thy tale of woe the voice of song?
Oh! if description's cold and nerveless tongue
From stranger harps such hallowed strains could call,
How doubly sweet the descant wild had rung,
From one who, lingering round thy ruined wall,
Had plucked thy mourning flowers and wept thy timeless fall.

VIII

The Huron chief escaped from foemen nigh,
His frail bark launches on Niagara's tides,

"Pride in his port, defiance in his eye,"
Singing his song of death the warrior glides;
In vain they yell along the river sides,
In vain the arrow from its sheaf is torn,
Calm to his doom the willing victim rides,
And, till adown the roaring torrent borne,
Mocks them with gesture proud, and laughs their rage to scorn.

IX

But if the charms of daisied hill and vale,
And rolling flood, and towering rock sublime,
If warrior deed or peasant's lowly tale
Of love or woe should fail to wake the rhyme,
If to the wildest heights of song you climb,
(Tho' some who know you less, might cry, beware!)
Onward! I say—your strains shall conquer time;
Give your bright genius wing, and hope to share
Imagination's worlds—the ocean, earth, and air.

X

Arouse, my friend—let vivid fancy soar,
Look with creative eye on nature's face,
Bid airy sprites in wild Niagara roar,
And view in every field a fairy race.
Spur thy good Pacolet to speed apace,
And spread a train of nymphs on every shore;
Or if thy muse would woo a ruder grace,
The Indian's evil Manitou's explore,
And rear the wondrous tale of legendary lore.

XI

Away! to Susquehannah's utmost springs,
Where, throned in mountain mist, Areouski reigns,
Shrouding in lurid clouds his plumeless wings,
And sternly sorrowing o'er his tribes remains;
His was the arm, like comet ere it wanes
That tore the streamy lightnings from the skies,
And smote the mammoth of the southern plains;
Wild with dismay the Creek affrighted flies,
While in triumphant pride Kanawa's eagles rise.

XII

Or westward far, where dark Miami wends,
Seek that fair spot as yet to fame unknown;
Where, when the vesper dew of heaven descends,
Soft music breathes in many a melting tone,
At times so sadly sweet it seems the moan
Of some poor Ariel penanced in the rock;
Anon a louder burst—a scream! a groan!
And now amid the tempest's reeling shock,
Gibber, and shriek, and wail—and fiend-like laugh and mock.

XIII

Or climb the Pallisado's lofty brows,
Where dark Omana waged the war of hell,
Till, waked to wrath, the mighty spirit rose

And pent the demons in their prison cell;
Full on their head the uprooted mountain fell,
Enclosing all within its horrid womb
Straight from the teeming earth the waters swell,
And pillared rocks arise in cheerless gloom
Around the drear abode—their last eternal tomb!

XIV

Be these your future themes—no more resign
The soul of song to laud your lady's eyes;
Go! kneel a worshipper at nature's shrine!
For you her fields are green, and fair her skies!
For you her rivers flow, her hills arise!
And will you scorn them all, to pour forth tame
And heartless lays of feigned or fancied sighs?
Still will you cloud the muse? nor blush for shame
To cast away renown, and hide your head from fame?

1835

THE AMERICAN FLAG

I

When Freedom from her mountain height
Unfurled her standard to the air,
She tore the azure robe of night,
And set the stars of glory there.
She mingled with its gorgeous dyes
The milky baldric of the skies,
And striped its pure celestial white,
With streakings of the morning light;
Then from his mansion in the sun
She called her eagle bearer down,
And gave into his mighty hand,
The symbol of her chosen land.

II

Majestic monarch of the cloud,
Who rear'st aloft thy regal form,
To hear the tempest trumpings loud
And see the lightning lances driven,
When strike the warriors of the storm,
And rolls the thunder-drum of heaven,
Child of the sun! to thee 'tis given
To guard the banner of the free,
To hover in the sulphur smoke,
To ward away the battle stroke,
And bid its blendings shine afar,
Like rainbows on the cloud of war,
The harbingers of victory!

III

Flag of the brave! thy folds shall fly,
The sign of hope and triumph high,
When speaks the signal trumpet tone,
And the long line comes gleaming on.
Ere yet the life-blood, warm and wet,
Has dimm'd the glistening bayonet,
Each soldier eye shall brightly turn
To where thy sky-born glories burn;
And as his springing steps advance,
Catch war and vengeance from the glance.
And when the cannon-mouthings loud
Heave in wild wreaths the battle shroud,
And gory sabres rise and fall
Like shoots of flame on midnight's pall;
Then shall thy meteor glances glow,
And cowering foes shall shrink beneath
Each gallant arm that strikes below
That lovely messenger of death.

IV

Flag of the seas! on ocean wave
Thy stars shall glitter o'er the brave;
When death, careering on the gale,
Sweeps darkly round the bellied sail,

And frightened waves rush wildly back
  Before the broadside's reeling rack,
Each dying wanderer of the sea
  Shall look at once to heaven and thee,
  And smile to see thy splendours fly
  In triumph o'er his closing eye.

V

Flag of the free heart's hope and home!
  By angel hands to valour given;
Thy stars have lit the welkin dome,
  And all thy hues were born in heaven.
Forever float that standard sheet!
  Where breathes the foe but falls before us,
With Freedom's soil beneath our feet,
  And Freedom's banner streaming o'er us?

1835

VIII. JAMES KIRKE PAULDING (1778–1860)

THE DUTCHMAN'S FIRESIDE

Book II

[COURTSHIP IN NEW YORK]

CHAPTER II

Which may be skipped over by the gentle Reader, as it contains not a single bloody adventure.

Catalina was received with a welcome kindness by Mrs. Aubineau, the lady with whom she had been invited to spend the winter, and who appeared struck with the improvement of her person since she left boarding-school two or three years before. Our heroine was glad to see Mrs. Aubineau again, having a vivid recollection of her pleasing manners and matronly kindness.

The husband of this lady was a son of one of the Huguenots driven by the bigotry or policy of Louis the Fourteenth to this land of liberty—liberty of action, liberty of speech, and liberty of conscience. These emigrants constituted a portion of the best educated, most enlightened, polite, and wealthy of the early inhabitants of New-York. They laid the foundation of families which still exist in good reputation, and from some of them have descended men who are for ever associated with the history of our country. The father of Mr. Aubineau had occupied a dignified situation under the Dutch government while it held possession of New-York; but lost it when the province was assigned to the Duke of York, whose hungry retainers were portioned off in the new world, there not being loaves and fishes enough in the old to satisfy them all. Both father and son cherished some little resentment on this occasion; and when a legislative body was established, one or other being generally a member, they never failed to be found voting and acting with the popular side, in opposition to the governor. They joined the old Dutch party in all their measures, which were generally favourable to the rights of the colony, and attained to great consideration and respect among them.

Notwithstanding his politics, Mr. Aubineau the younger married a handsome English woman; not a descendant merely of English parents, but a real native, born and educated in London. Her father came over with an appointment, being a younger brother, with a younger brother's portion, which generally consists in the family influence employed on all occasions in quartering the young branches upon the public. The great use of colonies is to provide for younger brothers. What this appointment was I do not recollect; but whatever it was it enabled Mr. Majoribanks to live in style, and carry his head high above the unlucky beings who furnished the means, and whose destiny it had been to be born on the wrong side of the Atlantic Ocean, where it is well known every thing, from men down to dandies, degenerates. To be born at *home,* as the phrase then was, operated as a sort of patent of nobility, and desperate was the ambition of the rich young citizens, and still more desperate that of the city heiresses and their mothers, to unite their fate and fortunes with a real genuine exotic. Many a soldier of fortune, "who spent half-a-crown out of sixpence a-day," was thus provided for; and not a few female adventurers gained excellent establishments, over which they were noted for exercising absolute dominion. For a provincial husband to contradict a wife from the mother country was held equivalent to the enormity of a provincial legislature refusing its assent to a rescript of his majesty's puissant governor. It smacked of flat rebellion.

Mr. Aubineau was, however, tolerably fortunate in his choice. His wife always contradicted him aside when in public, and issued her commands in a whisper. She never got angry with him, and only laughed and took her own way whenever he found fault; or, what was still more discreet, took no notice of his ill-humour, and did just as she pleased. She was fond of gayety, dress, and equipage, and particularly fond of flirting with the officers attached to the governor's family and establishment. These gentlemen, having nothing to do, and no inclination to marry, except they were well paid for it, naturally selected the married ladies as objects for their devoirs; very properly concluding, that whatever might be the case with the ladies, there could be no breach of promise of marriage on their part, and, consequently, no dishonour in being as particular as the lady pleased. As to the provincial husbands, they were out of the question.

Among the most prominent of the foibles of Mrs. Aubineau was an idea at that time very prevalent among both English and American women. This was an undisguised and confirmed conviction, that the whole universe was a nest of barbarians, compared with old England, and that there was as much moral and physical difference between being born there and here, as there was space between the two countries. Though not much of the blue-stocking, that sisterhood not having made its appearance as a distinct class in those days, like all good English folks, she could ring the changes on Shakspeare and Milton, and Bacon and Locke; those four great names on which English poetry, philosophy, and metaphysics seem entirely to depend for their renown; and which form a standard to which every blockhead more or less assimilates his mind, as if the reflected rays of their glory had illuminated in some degree the midnight darkness of his own intellect. This truly John Bull notion she considered so settled and established beyond all reasonable question, that she always spoke of it with an amusing simplicity, arising from a perfect confidence in an undisputed point, upon which all mankind, except her husband, agreed with as much unanimity as that the sun shone in a clear day. In regard to the solitary exception aforesaid, Mrs. Aubineau settled that in her mind, by referring it to that undefinable matrimonial sympathy which impels so many men to agree with every other woman when she is wrong, and oppose their wives whenever they are right. The connexion between this lady and our heroine originated in a marriage between the elder Aubineau and a sister Colonel Vancour. Into the hands of Mrs. Aubineau the colonel consigned his daughter for the winter, at the same time communicating her engagement with Sybrandt Westbrook, at which she laughed not a little in her sleeve. She had already a plan in her head for establishing her rich and beautiful guest in a far more splendid sphere, as she was pleased to imagine. At the end of eight or ten days Colonel Vancour took his departure for home in the good sloop Watervliet, which had made vast despatch in unlading and lading, on account of the lateness of the season.

Catalina was connected in different ways with almost all the really respectable and wealthy inhabitants of New-York and its vicinity; such as, the Philipses, the Stuyvesants, the Van Courtlandts, the Beekmans, Bayards, Delanceys, Gouverneurs, Van Hornes, Rapalyes, Rutgers, Waltons, and a score of others too tedious to enumerate. Of course she could be in no want of visiters or invitations, and there was every prospect of a gay winter. But all these good folks were only secondary in the estimation of Mrs. Aubineau, when compared with —not his majesty's governor and his family, for they were out of the sphere of mortal comparison—but with the families of his majesty's chief justice, his majesty's attorney and solicitor-generals, his majesty's collector of the customs, and, indeed, with the families of any of his majesty's petty officers, however insignificant. These formed the focus of high life in the ancient city of New-York, and nothing upon the face of the earth was more ridiculous in the eyes of a discreet observer than the pretensions of this little knot of dependants over the truly dignified independence of the great body of the wealthy inhabitants, except, perhaps, the docility with which these latter submitted to the petty usurpation.

CHAPTER III

A Knight and an Honourable. The Reader is desired to make his best bow.

The morning after Catalina's arrival she received the visits of several officers, two of whom had the honour of being aids to his excellency the governor and commander-in-chief. They therefore merit a particular introduction. "Gentle Reader, this is Sir Thicknesse Throgmorton; and this is the Honourable Barry Gilfillan, of an ancient and noble Irish family, somewhat poor, but very honest, having suffered divers forfeitures for its loyalty to the Stuarts,—that stupid, worthless race, whose persevering pretensions to a crown they had justly forfeited by their tyranny, drew after them the ruin of thousands of generous and devoted victims. Sir Thicknesse and Colonel Gilfillan, this is the gentle Reader, a beautiful, accomplished lady of great taste, as all our female readers are, thank Heaven!"

Sir Thicknesse Throgmorton was what is now generally designated a "real John Bull," a being combining more of the genuine elements of the ridiculous than perhaps any other extant. Stiff as buckram, and awkward as an ill-contrived automaton; silent, stupid, and ill-mannered, yet at the same time full of pretensions to a certain deference, due only from others in exchange for courtesy and good-breeding. Ignorant of his own country from incapacity to learn, and of the rest of the world from a certain contemptuous stupidity, he exalted the one and contemned the other without knowing exactly why, except that—that it certainly was so, and there was an end of the matter. His bow was both an outrage upon nature and inclination, except when he bent to the lady of the governor, or the governor himself; and his dancing the essence of solemn stupidity, aiming at a dignified nonchalance. Nothing called forth his lofty indignation more than being spoken to by an inferior in rank, dress, or station. This indignation was manifested by a most laughable jumble of insurmountable clumsiness with affected dignity and high aristocratic breeding. There was nothing he so much valued himself upon as the air noble. Independently of the outrage upon his personal, hereditary, and official dignity manifested by an abrupt address from an inferior, Sir Thicknesse had another special cause for disliking to be spoken to by strangers. The fact is he was so long in collecting the materials of an answer to the most common observation, that he seldom forgave a person for putting him to the trouble. He had a most rare and, at that time, original style of making the agreeable, which is now however pretty general among high-bred persons. He placed himself directly opposite the lady, straddling like a gigantic pair of brass tongs, to collect his ideas into one great explosion—such, for instance, as "Don't you find it rather warm, *Mawm?*" Perfectly satisfied with this mighty effort, the knight would strut off in triumph, to repose himself for the rest of the evening under the shade of his laurels. Added to this he was a grumbling, ill-tempered, dissatisfied being, full of pretensions on the score of his personal accomplishments and the interest of his family. There is nothing in fact so dignified in the eyes of "a real John Bull" as possessing a family influence, which renders personal merit and services quite superfluous.

With regard to the person of Sir Thicknesse, it was admirably contrived to set off his exemplary awkwardness to the best advantage. It was a perfect caricature of dignified clumsiness. His limbs struck you as being too large for his body, until you studied the latter, when it seemed perfectly clear that the body was too large for the limbs. Taken by itself, every feature of his face was out of proportion; but examine them in connexion as a whole, and there was an harmonious combination of unfinished magnitude, that constituted a true and just proportion of disproportions. His eyes sent forth a leaden lustre; his nose was equally compounded of the pug and the bottle; his lips would have been too large for his mouth, had not his mouth been large enough to harmonize with them; and his cheeks expanded into sufficient amplitude to accommodate the rest of his face without any of his features being crowded two in a room, which every body knows is the abomination of every "real John Bull" in existence. Sir Thicknesse was of an ancient and honourable family, distinguished in the annals of England. One of his ancestors had committed an assassination in the very precincts of the court, and being obliged to fly in the disguise of a peasant, in order the more effectually to escape detection, was overtaken by the king's pursuivant, sawing wood with one of his companions in a forest. His attendant faltering on the appearance of the pursuivant, for a moment stopped sawing, when the other exclaimed significantly, "Thorough"—or "Through"—tradition is doubtful which. The attendant took the hint, continued his work, and the pursuivant passed them without detection. In memory of this great exploit, the illustrious fugitive from justice adopted this phrase as the motto of his coat of arms; and it descended to his posterity. Another of his illustrious ancestors was distinguished in the wars of York and Lancaster for his inflexible loyalty, being always a most stanch supporter of the king *de facto,* and holding kings *de jure* in great contempt. A third, and the greatest of all the family of Sir Thicknesse, was an illegitimate descendant of a theatrical strumpet and a scoundrel king, who demonstrated the force of blood by afterward marrying an actress of precisely the same stamp as her from whom he sprung. No wonder Sir Thicknesse was proud of his family.

But great as his progenitors were, they could not hold a candle to those of Colonel Barry Fitzgerald Macartney Gilfillan, a genuine Milesian, whose ancestors had been kings of Connaught, princes of Breffny, and lords of Ballyshannon, Ballynamora, Ballynahinch, Ballygruddrey, Ballyknockamora, and several lordships besides. Gilfillan was an Irish Bull, a perfect contrast to an English Bull. He was all life, love, gallantry, whim, wit, humour, and hyperbole. His animal spirits were to him as the wings of a bird, on which he mounted into the regions of imagination and folly. They flew away with him ten times an hour. He learned every thing so fast that he knew nothing perfectly; and such was the impetuosity of his conceptions, that one-half the time they came forth wrong end foremost. His ignorance of a subject never for a moment prevented him from dashing right into it, or stopped the torrent of his ideas, which resembled a stream swelled by the rains, being excessively noisy and not very clear. His ideas, in truth, seemed always turning somersets over the heads of each other, and for the most part presented that precise rhetorical arrangement which is indicated by the phrase of "putting the cart before the horse." He never pleaded guilty to ignorance of any thing, nor was ever known to stop a moment to get hold of the right end of an idea,—maintaining with a humorous obstinacy, that as he always came to the right end at last, it was of no consequence where he began.

Nature had given to Colonel Gilfillan a more than usual share of the truly Irish propensity to falling in love extempore. His heart was quite as hot as his head, and between the two there was a perfect volcano. He was always under high steam pressure. He once acknowledged, or rather boasted—for he never confessed any thing—that he had fallen in love at the Curragh of Kildare with six ladies in one day, and was refused by them all in less than twenty-four hours afterward. "But, faith!" added he, "I killed two horses riding about the country after them; and that was some comfort." "Comfort!" said a friend, "how do you make that out, Gilfillan?" "Why, wasn't it a proof I didn't stand shilly-shally, waiting my own consent any more than that of the ladies, my dear!" It is scarcely necessary to add, that he was generous, uncalculating, brave, and a man of his word, except in love affairs, and sometimes in affairs of business, when he occasionally lost at play the money he had promised to a tradesman. His person exhibited a rich redundancy of manly beauty, luscious with youth, health, and vigour; he sang charmingly; played the fiddle so as to bring tears into your eyes; danced, laughed, chatted, blundered, gallanted, flattered, and made love with a graceful confidence and fearless audacity, that caused him to be a great favourite and rather a dangerous companion for women of warm imaginations and mere ordinary refinement of manners and feelings. Like most men of his profession, his ideas on certain subjects were of the latitudinarian order. Gilfillan swore he was a man of as much honour as ever wore a uniform. He would not pick a pocket; but as for picking a lady's white bosom of a sweet little heart—let him alone for that. A fair exchange was no robbery all the world over; and he always left his own with them, if there were twenty. When his brother officers laughed at him for having so many hearts, "Och, my dears!" would he reply, "what, do you talk about having but one heart? A man with only one heart in his bosom is like a poor divil with only a shilling in his pocket—he is afraid to part with it, and so starves himself just for fear of starving!"

CHAPTER VIII

A Hero in snuff-coloured Breeches.

A few days afterward Sybrandt arrived in his snuff-coloured suit, which of itself was enough to ruin the brightest prospects of the most thriving wooer. Think what a contrast to the splendours of an aid-de-camp! the scarlet, gold-laced coat, the bright spurs, and the gorgeous epaulettes. Poor Sybrandt! what superiority of the inside could weigh against this outside gear? Catalina received him, I cannot tell exactly how. She did not know herself, and how should I? It was an odd, incomprehensible, indescribable compound of affected indifference, and affected welcome; fear of showing too little feeling, and horror of exhibiting too much. In short, it was an awkward business, and Sybrandt made it still more so, by being suddenly seized with an acute fit of his old malady of shyness and embarrassment. Such a meeting has often been a prelude to an eternal separation.

The very next evening after his arrival Sybrandt made his debut in the snuff-coloured suit, at a grand party given by his excellency the governor, in honour of his majesty's birthday. All the aristocracy of the city were collected on this occasion, and, in order to give additional dignity to the ceremony, several people of the first consequence delayed making their appearance till almost seven o'clock. The hoops and heads were prodigious; and it is recorded of more than one lady, that she went to this celebrated party with her head sticking out of one of the coach windows, and her hoop out at the other. Their sleeves it is true were not quite so exuberant as those of the present graceful mode; nor was it possible to mistake a lady's arm for her body, as is sometimes done in these degenerate days by near-sighted dandies; one of whom, I am credibly informed, actually put his arm round the sleeve instead of the waist, in dancing the waltz last winter with a young belle just from Paris. Many a little sharp-toed, high-heeled satin shoe, sparkling in diamond paste buckles, did execution that night; and one old lady in particular displayed, with all the pride of conscious superiority, a pair of gloves her mother had worn at court in the reign of the gallant Charles the Second, who came very near asking her to dance, and publicly declared her to be quite as elegant as Nell Gwyn, and almost as beautiful as the Dutchess of Cleveland. These consecrated relics descended in a direct line from generation to generation in this illustrious family, being considered the most valuable of its possessions, until they were sacrilegiously purloined by a gentleman of colour belonging to the house, and afterward exhibited during several seasons at the African balls. "To what vile uses we may come at last!"

All the dignitaries of the province were present on this occasion, for their absence would have been looked upon as a proof of disloyalty that might have cost them their places. Here were the illustrious members of the governor's council, who represented his majesty in the second degree. Next came the chief justice, and the puisne justices, all in those magnificent wigs which, as Captain Basil Hall asserts, give such superiority to the decisions of the judges of England,—inasmuch as that when the head is so full of law that it can hold no more, a vast superfluity of knowledge may be accommodated in the curls of the wig. Hence it has been gravely doubted whether these profound decisions of my Lord Mansfield and Sir William Scott, which constitute the law and the *profits* in our courts, did actually emanate from the brains or the wigs of the aforesaid oracles. Here too figured his majesty's attorney-general and his majesty's solicitor-general, who also wore wigs, but not so large as those of the judges, for that would have been considered a shrewd indication that they thought themselves equally learned in the law with their betters. Next came the rabble of little vermin that are farmed out upon colonies in all ages and nations, to fatten on the spoils of industry, and tread upon the people who give them bread. Custom and excise officers, commissioners and pay-masters, and every creeping thing which had the honour of serving and cheating his majesty in the most contemptible station, here took precedence of the ancient and present lords of the soil, and looked down upon them as inferior beings. His majesty was the fountain of honour and glory; and his excellency the governor being his direct and immediate representative, all claims to distinction were settled by propinquity to that distinguished functionary. Whoever was nearest to him in dignity of office was the next greatest man; and whatever lady could get nearest the governor's lady at a party was indubitably ennobled for that night, and became an object of envy ever afterward. Previous to the late Revolution more than one of our aristocratic families derived their principal distinction from their grandmothers having once dined with the governor, and sat at the right hand of his lady at dinner.

If Sybrandt, the humble and obscure Sybrandt, who had nothing to recommend him but talents, learning, and intrepidity of soul—if he was awed by the majesty of this illustrious assemblage of dignitaries, almost all of whom tacked honourable to their names, who can blame him? And if, as he contrasted his snuff-coloured dress with the gorgeous military costumes of the aids-de-camp and officers, he felt, in spite of himself, a consciousness of inferiority, who can wonder? And if, as he gazed on the big wigs of the judges, and the vast circumference of those hoops in which the beauties of New-York moved and revolved as in a universe of their own, he trembled to his inmost heart, who shall dare to question his courage?

To the weight of this feeling of inferiority, which pressed upon the modesty of his nature, and, as it were, enveloped his intellects in a fog of awkward embarrassment, were added various other causes of vexation. When it was whispered about that he was the country beau, the accepted one of the belle of New-York, the scrutiny he underwent would have quailed the heart of a roaring lion. The young ladies, who envied Catalina the conquest of the two aids, revenged themselves by tittering at her beau behind their fans.

"Lord," whispered Miss Van Dam to Miss Twentyman, "did you ever see such an old-fashioned creature? I declare, he looks frightened out of his wits."

"And then his snuff-coloured breeches!" said the other. "He is handsome, too; but what is a man without a red coat and epaulettes!"

My readers will excuse the insertion of a certain obnoxious word in the reply of the young lady, when they understand it was uttered in a whisper. I am the last man in the world to commit an outrage upon female decorum, and am not so ignorant of what is due to the delicacy of the sex as not to know that though it is considered allowable for young ladies now-a-days to expose their persons in the streets and at parties in the most generous manner, as well as to permit strangers to take them round the waist in a waltz, it would be indelicate in the highest degree to mention such matters in plain English. In fashionable ethics, indelicacy consists not so much in the thing itself as in the words used in describing it.

While the young ladies were criticising the merits of our hero's snuff-coloured costume, the mothers were investigating his other capabilities.

"They say he will be immensely rich," quoth Mrs. Van Dam.

"You don't say so?" cried Mrs. Van Borsum.

"Yes, he has two old bachelor uncles, as rich as Crœsus."

"Crœsus? who is he? I don't know him."

"A rich merchant in London, I believe."

"Well, but is it certain he will have the fortunes of both the old bachelors?"

"O, certain. One of them has adopted him, and the other made his will and left him all he has."

"What a pity he should marry such a flirt as that Miss Vancour!"

"O, a very great pity. Really I am sorry for the young fellow; he deserves a better wife." And she thought of her daughter.

"Indeed he does—so he does," echoed the other lady; and she thought of *her* daughter. They both began to despair of the aids, and the military and the civil dignitaries; and the next object of their ambition was a rich provincial.

It was not many hours after this conversation before our friend Sybrandt was introduced to these good ladies, at their particular instance, and by them to their daughters.

"Is he rich enough to take me *home?*" whispered Miss Van Borsum to her mother—home being the phrase for Old England at that time, when it was considered vulgar to belong to a colony.—"Is he rich enough to take me home?"

"As rich as Crœsus, the great London merchant."

"Then I am determined to set my cap at him in spite of his snuff-coloured ——," thought Miss Van Borsum. By one of those inextricable manœuvres with which experienced dames contrive arrangements of this sort, Sybrandt was actually forced into dancing a minuet with Miss Van Borsum, although he would almost have preferred dancing a jig upon nothing. The young lady nearly equalled Catalina in this the most graceful and ladylike of all dances; and having a beautiful little foot *et cetera,* many were the keen darts she launched from her pointed satin shoes and diamond buckles at the hearts of the beholders. The dancing of our hero was not altogether despicable; but the snuff-coloured ——! they did his business for that night with all the young ladies and their mothers who did not know he was the heir of two rich old bachelors.

1831

THE DIVERTING HISTORY OF JOHN BULL AND BROTHER JONATHAN

By Hector Bull-us

[JONATHAN AND HIS FARM]

CHAPTER I

How Squire Bull quarrelled with his youngest Son, Brother Jonathan, and forced him out in the woods; and how the Squire, when Jonathan had cleared away the woods, grew to be very fond of him, and undertook to pick his pockets, but got handsomely rib-roasted for his pains.

JOHN BULL was a choleric old fellow, who held a good manor in the middle of a great millpond, and which, by reason of its being quite surrounded by water, was generally called *Bullock Island.* Bull was an ingenious man, an exceeding good blacksmith, a dexterous cutler, and a notable weaver and pot-baker besides. He also brewed capital porter, ale, and small beer, and was, in fact, a sort of jack of all trades, and good at each. In addition to these, he was a hearty fellow, an excellent bottle-companion, and passably honest as times go.

But what tarnished all these qualities was a devilish quarrelsome, overbearing disposition, which was always getting him into some scrape or other. The truth is, he never heard of a quarrel going on among his neighbours, but his fingers itched to be in the thickest of them; so that he was hardly ever seen without a broken head, a black eye, or a bloody nose. Such was Squire Bull, as he was commonly called by the country people his neighbours—one of those odd, testy, grumbling, boasting old codgers, that never get credit for what they are, because they are always pretending to be what they are not.

The squire was as tight a hand to deal with in doors as out; sometimes treating his family as if they were not the same flesh and blood, when they happened to differ with him in certain matters. One day he got into a dispute with his youngest son Jonathan, who was familiarly called BROTHER JONATHAN, about whether churches ought to be called churches or meeting-houses; and whether steeples were not an abomination. The squire, either having the worst of the argument, or being naturally impatient of contradiction (I can't tell which), fell into a great passion, and swore he would physic such notions out of the boy's noddle. So he went to some of his *doctors,* and got them to draw up a prescription, made up of *thirty-nine different articles,* many of them bitter enough to some palates. This he tried to make Jonathan swallow; and finding he made villanous wry faces, and would not do it, fell upon him and beat him like fury. After this, he made the house so disagreeable to him, that Jonathan, though as hard as a pine knot and as tough as leather, could bear it no longer. Taking his gun and his axe, he put himself in a boat, and paddled over the millpond to some new lands to which the squire pretended some sort of claim, intending to settle them, and build a meeting-house without a steeple as soon as he grew rich enough.

When he got over, Jonathan found that the land was quite in a state of nature, covered with wood, and inhabited by nobody but wild beasts. But being a lad of mettle, he took his axe on one shoulder and his gun on the other, marched into the thickest of the wood, and clearing a place, built a log hut. Pursuing his labours, and handling his axe like a notable woodman, he in a few years cleared the land, which he laid out into *thirteen good farms:* and building himself a fine frame house, about half finished, began to be quite snug and comfortable.

But Squire Bull, who was getting old and stingy, and besides, was in great want of money, on account of his having lately been made to pay swinging damages for assaulting his neighbours and breaking their heads —the squire, I say, finding Jonathan was getting well to do in the world, began to be very much troubled about his welfare: so he demanded that Jonathan should pay him a good rent for the land which he had cleared and made good for something. He trumped up I know not what claim against him, and under different pretences managed to pocket all Jonathan's honest gains. In fact, the poor lad had not a shilling left for holyday occasions; and had it not been for the filial respect he felt for the old man, he would certainly have refused to submit to such impositions.

But for all this, in a little time, Jonathan grew up to be very large of his age, and became a tall, stout, double-jointed, broad-footed cub of a fellow, awkward in his gait, and simple in his appearance; but showing a lively, shrewd look, and having the promise of great strength when he should get his full growth. He was rather an odd-looking chap, in truth, and had many queer ways; but everybody that had seen John Bull saw a great likeness between them, and swore he was John's own boy, and a true chip of the old block. Like the old squire, he was apt to be blustering and saucy, but in the main was a peaceable sort of careless fellow, that would quarrel with nobody if you only let him alone. He used to dress in homespun trousers with a huge bagging seat, which seemed to have nothing in it. This made people to say he had no *bottom;* but whoever said so lied, as they found to their cost whenever they put Jonathan in a passion. He always wore a linsey-woolsey coat, that did not above half cover his breech, and the sleeves of which were so short that his hand and wrist came out beyond them, looking like a shoulder of mutton. All which was in consequence of his growing so fast that he outgrew his clothes.

While Jonathan was outgrowing his strength in this way, Bull kept on picking his pockets of every penny he could scrape together; till at last, one day when the squire was even more than usually pressing in his demands, which he accompanied with threats, Jonathan started up in a furious passion, and threw the TEA-KETTLE at the old man's head. The choleric Bull was hereupon exceedingly enraged; and after calling the poor lad an undutiful, ungrateful, rebellious rascal, seized him by the collar, and forthwith a furious scuffle ensued. This lasted a long time; for the squire, though in years, was a capital boxer, and of most excellent bottom. At last, however, Jonathan got him under, and before he would let him up, made him sign a paper giving up all claim to the farms, and acknowledging the fee-simple to be in Jonathan for ever.

CHAPTER XVIII

Touching the farms called Southlands, and what roystering blades the tenants were. Also, those honest, hearty fellows, the boys of the Middlelands.

BROTHER JONATHAN, as I said before, had a great estate in lands, which, that he might be able to tell one farm from another, came to be called by different names, such as the Southlands, the Middlelands, Down East, and Far West. This division, in time, proved a great source of heart-burnings and contentions among the tenants occupying these different farms, who because they had different names, began, like a parcel of blockheads as they are, to fancy themselves a separate people, with separate interests, and to squabble among themselves about nothing or next to nothing. In process of time, these sectional feelings grew into fruitful sources of trouble to Brother Jonathan, who had much ado to keep them from falling together by the ears at town meetings and elections. Many people thought they hated each other worse than they did Squire Bull's tenants, and I believe they were half right.

The tenants of the farms commonly called Southlands, having plenty of negroes to work for them, and nothing to do but amuse themselves, did, as will often happen with country blades, amuse themselves pretty considerably with horseracing, cockfighting, barbecues, and the like. They were also wonderful boys for what they called anti-fog-waters, being certain mint-juleps, which, to say the truth, are exceeding loathsome of a foggy morning, and mighty potent in keeping away chills and agues. They are supposed to make a man somewhat belligerant, which I opine is true, seeing I remember I once felt their effects myself at a training, in the which I charged quite through a numerous phalanx of naughty boys, in despite of old shoes and unseemly maledictions.

But for all this, the Southlanders were a set of frank, jolly, hospitable, high-spirited fellows, with hearts always open and aboveboard. A man might live among them free of expense till the cows came home, if they did not kill him with good living and mint-juleps. For my part, I always did and always shall like them, and I don't care who knows it.

These sturdy roystering blades disliked the tenants Down East, of whom I shall speak anon, because they came among them with little one-horse carts, laden with wooden bowls, tinware, and the like, and made divers good bargains out of them in the way of trade. It would do your heart good to hear some of the stories, true or false, told about these travelling pedlers, who wore high steeple-crowned hats, and were about the 'cutest fellows you ever saw. As there is no error more common than to condemn a whole community for the fault of one, the Southlanders, judging from a few bad samples, came at last to consider the Down Easters no better than they should be. Now the first thing a Southlander thinks of, when he catches himself in a passion, is fighting; so whenever he was taken in in a bargain for a wooden clock, or some such thing, he was pretty sure to pummel the tin-trader, who not unfrequently had scruples of conscience about fighting. When the trader got home, he of course told terrible stories of gouging and the like, so that in time one came to be thought little better than bullies, the other downright rogues, though those who were best acquainted with them knew better.

Those who tenant the flourishing farms of the Middlelands are for the most part steady, sober-minded farmers, expert boatmen belonging to the great landings, and comfortable tradesmen well to do in the world. They agree mighty well together, as also with the tenants of the other farms; or if they chance to quarrel about nothing, the one class balances the other, and the farms don't get into a sweat as they do in other parts of Brother Jonathan's estates.

It will be found by those who take the trouble to inquire, that in all Brother Jonathan's farms where this mixture does not prevail, the tenants are very ignorant and headstrong in their opinions and prejudices. Having but one exclusive road to prosperity, they conclude there is no other way but this in the world, that what is their interest must be everybody's interest, and that whenever that is affected, the whole world must be turned upside down. But on the contrary, where, as in the farms I am treating of, the different orders of men are mingled together, the perpetual collision of interests in time wears away their different asperities, and introduces a reasonable regard for each other's welfare.

And now I am in for it, I will make another sage remark, which will be found equally true with the last. It is this: that those farms which form the extremities of Brother Jonathan's property have always been more easily agitated and set in motion than the others; and in this they have a great analogy to single individuals. The tickling of the soles of the feet will set one kicking at a furious rate; and the touch of a feather at the nose causes the proboscis to be violently agitated, while the rest of the body remains quiescent. So if you meddle with the farms of Southlands, which form, as it were, the legs, or with the farms Down East, which constitute the snout, or proboscis, of Brother Jonathan's domain, you will always find a mighty deal of agitation and grimace in them, while the more noble parts that lie in the vicinity, as it were, of the *heart,* remain undisturbed.

1812

WILLIAM ELLERY CHANNING
(1780–1842)

THE MORAL ARGUMENT AGAINST CALVINISM

* * * The principal argument against Calvinism, in the General View of Christian Doctrines, is the *moral argument,* or that which is drawn from the inconsistency of the system with the divine perfections. It is plain, that a doctrine, which contradicts our best ideas of goodness and justice, cannot come from the just and good God, or be a true representation of his character. This moral argument has always been powerful to the pulling down of the strong-holds of Calvinism. Even in the dark period, when this system was shaped and finished at Geneva, its advocates often writhed under the weight of it; and we cannot but deem it a mark of the progress of society, that Calvinists are more and more troubled with the palpable repugnance of their doctrines to God's nature, and accordingly labor to soften and explain them, until in many cases the name only is retained. If the stern reformer of Geneva could lift up his head, and hear the mitigated tone, in which some of his professed followers dispense his fearful doctrines, we fear, that he could not lie down in peace, until he had poured out his displeasure on their cowardice and degeneracy. He would tell them, with a frown, that *moderate Calvinism* was a solecism, a contradiction in terms, and would bid them in scorn to join their real friend, Arminius. Such is the power of public opinion and of an improved state of society on creeds, that naked, undisguised Calvinism is not very fond of showing itself, and many of consequence know imperfectly what it means. What then is the system against which the view of Christian Doctrines is directed?

Calvinism teaches, that, in consequence of Adam's sin in eating the forbidden fruit, God brings into life all his posterity with a nature wholly corrupt, so that they are utterly indisposed, disabled, and made opposite to all that is spiritually good, and wholly inclined to all evil, and that continually. It teaches, that all mankind, having fallen in Adam, are under God's wrath and curse, and so made liable to all miseries in this life, to death itself, and to the pains of hell for ever. It teaches, that, from this ruined race, God, out of his mere good pleasure, has elected a certain number to be saved by Christ, not induced to this choice by any foresight of their faith or good works, but wholly by his free grace and love; and that, having thus predestinated them to eternal life, he renews and sanctifies them by his almighty and special agency, and brings them into a state of grace, from which they cannot fall and perish. It teaches, that the rest of mankind he is pleased to pass over, and to ordain them to dishonor and wrath for their sins, to the honor of his justice and power; in other words, he leaves the rest to the corruption in which they were born, withholds the grace which is necessary to their recovery, and condemns them to "most grievous torments in soul and body without intermission in hell-fire for ever." Such is Calvinism, as gathered from the most authentic records of the doctrine. Whoever will consult the famous Assembly's Catechisms and Confession, will see the peculiarities of the system in all their length and breadth of deformity. A man of plain sense, whose spirit has not been broken to this creed by education or terror, will think that it is not necessary for us to travel to heathen countries, to learn how mournfully the human mind may misrepresent the Deity.

The moral argument against Calvinism, of which we have spoken, must seem irresistible to common and unperverted minds, after attending to the brief statement now given. It will be asked with astonishment, How is it possible that men can hold these doctrines and yet maintain God's goodness and equity? What principles can be more contradictory?—To remove the objection to Calvinism, which is drawn from its repugnance to the Divine perfections, recourse has been had, as before observed, to the distinction between natural and moral inability, and to other like subtilties. But a more common reply, we conceive, has been drawn from the weakness and imperfection of the human mind, and from its incapacity of comprehending God. Calvinists will tell us, that, because a doctrine opposes our convictions of rectitude, it is not necessarily false; that apparent are not always real inconsistencies; that God is an infinite and incomprehensible being, and not to be tried by *our* ideas of fitness and morality; that we bring their system to an incompetent tribunal, when we submit it to the decision of human reason and conscience; that we are weak judges of what is right and wrong, good and evil, in the Deity; that the happiness of the universe may require an administration of human affairs which is very offensive to limited understandings; that we must follow revelation, not reason or moral feeling, and must consider doctrines, which shock us in revelation, as awful mysteries, which are dark through our ignorance, and which time will enlighten. How little, it is added, can man explain or understand God's ways. How inconsistent the miseries of life appear with goodness in the Creator. How prone, too, have men always been to confound good and evil, to call the just, unjust. How presumptuous is it in such a being, to sit in judgment upon God, and to question the rectitude of the divine administration, because it shocks *his* sense of rectitude. Such we conceive to be a fair statement of the manner in which the Calvinist frequently meets the objection, that his system is at war with God's attributes. Such the reasoning by which the voice of conscience and nature is stifled, and men are reconciled to doctrines, which, if tried by the established principles of morality, would be rejected with horror. On this reasoning we purpose to offer some remarks; and we shall avail ourselves of the opportunity, to give our views of *the confidence which is due to our rational and moral faculties in religion.*

That God is infinite, and that man often errs, we affirm as strongly as our Calvinistic brethren. We desire to think humbly of ourselves, and reverently of our Creator. In the strong language of Scripture, "We now see through a glass darkly." "We cannot by searching find out God unto perfection. Clouds and darkness are round about him. His judgments are a great deep." God is great and good beyond utterance or thought. We have no disposition to idolize our own powers, or to penetrate the secret counsels of the Deity. But, on the other hand, we think it ungrateful to disparage the powers which our Creator has given us, or to question the certainty or importance of the knowledge, which he has seen fit to place within our reach. There is an affected humility, we think, as dangerous as pride. We may rate our faculties too meanly, as well as too boastingly. The worst error in religion, after all, is that of the skeptic, who records triumphantly the weaknesses and wanderings of the human intellect, and maintains, that no trust is due to the decisions of this erring reason. We by no means conceive, that man's greatest danger springs from pride of understanding, though we think as badly of this vice as other Christians. The history of the church proves, that men may trust their faculties too little as well as too much, and that the timidity, which shrinks from investigation, has injured the mind, and betrayed the interests of Christianity, as much as an irreverent boldness of thought.

It is an important truth, which, we apprehend, has not been sufficiently developed, that the ultimate reliance of a human being is and must be on his own mind. To confide in God, we must first confide in the faculties by which He is apprehended, and by which the proofs of his existence are weighed. A trust in our ability to distinguish between truth and falsehood is implied in every act of belief; for to question this ability would of necessity unsettle all belief. We cannot take a step in reasoning or action without a secret reliance on our own minds. Religion in particular implies, that we have understandings endowed and qualified for the highest employments of intellect. In affirming the existence and perfections of God, we suppose and affirm the existence in ourselves of faculties which correspond to these sublime objects, and which are fitted to discern them. Religion is a conviction and an act of the human soul, so that, in denying confidence to the one, we subvert the truth and claims of the other. Nothing is gained to piety by degrading human nature, for in the competency of this nature to know and judge of God all piety has its foundation. Our proneness to err instructs us indeed to use our powers with great caution, but not to contemn and neglect them. The occasional abuse of our faculties, be it ever so enormous, does not prove them unfit for their highest end, which is, to form clear and consistent views of God. Because our eyes sometimes fail or deceive us, would a wise man pluck them out, or cover them with a bandage, and choose to walk and work in the dark? or, because they cannot distinguish distant objects, can they discern nothing clearly in their proper sphere, and is sight to be pronounced a fallacious guide? Men who, to support a creed, would shake our trust in the calm, deliberate, and distinct decisions of our rational and moral powers, endanger religion more than its open foes, and forge the deadliest weapon for the infidel.

It is true that God is an infinite being, and also true, that his powers and perfections, his purposes and operations, his ends and means, being unlimited, are *incomprehensible*. In other words, they cannot be *wholly taken in* or *embraced* by the human mind. In the strong and figurative language of Scripture, we "know nothing" of God's ways; that is, we know *very few* of them. But this is just as true of the most advanced archangel as of man. In comparison with the vastness of God's system, the range of the highest created intellect is narrow; and, in this particular, man's lot does not differ from that of his elder brethren in heaven. We are both confined in our observation and experience to a little spot in the creation. But are an angel's faculties worthy of no trust, or is his knowledge uncertain, because he learns and reasons from a small part of God's works? or are his judgments respecting the Creator to be charged with presumption, because his views do not spread through the whole extent of the universe? We grant that our understandings cannot stretch beyond a very narrow sphere. But still the lessons, which we learn within this sphere, are just as sure, as if it were indefinitely enlarged. Because much is unexplored, we are not to suspect what we have actually discovered. Knowledge is not the less real, because confined. The man, who has never set foot beyond his native village, knows its scenery and inhabitants as undoubtingly, as if he had travelled to the poles. We indeed see very little; but that little is as true, as if every thing else were seen; and our future discoveries must agree with and support it. Should the whole order and purposes of the universe be opened to us, it is certain that nothing would be disclosed, which would in any degree shake our persuasion, that the earth is inhabitanted by rational and moral beings, who are authorized to expect from their Creator the most benevolent and equitable government. No extent of observation can unsettle those primary and fundamental principles of moral truth, which we derive from our highest faculties operating in the relations in which God has fixed us. In every region and period of the universe, it will be as true as it is now on the earth, that knowledge and power are the measures of responsibility, and that natural incapacity absolves from guilt. These and other moral verities, which are among our clearest perceptions, would, if possible, be strengthened, in proportion as our powers should be enlarged; because harmony and consistency are the characters of God's administration, and all our researches into the universe only serve to manifest its unity, and to show a wider operation of the laws which we witness and experience on earth.

We grant that God is *incomprehensible,* in the sense already given. But he is not therefore *unintelligible;* and this distinction we conceive to be important. We do not pretend to know the *whole* nature and properties of God, but still we can form some *clear ideas* of him, and can reason from these ideas as justly as from any other. The truth is, that we cannot be said to comprehend any being whatever, not the simplest plant or animal. All have hidden properties. Our knowledge of all is limited. But have we therefore no distinct ideas of the objects around us, and is all our reasoning about them unworthy of trust? Because God is infinite, his name is not therefore a mere sound. It is a representative of some distinct conceptions of our Creator; and these conceptions are as sure, and important, and as proper materials for the reasoning faculty, as they would be if our views were indefinitely enlarged. We cannot indeed trace God's goodness and rectitude through the whole field of his operations; but we know the essential nature of these attributes, and therefore can often judge what accords with and opposes them. God's goodness, because infinite, does not cease to be goodness, or essentially differ from the same attribute in man; nor does justice change its nature, so that it cannot be understood, because it is seated in an unbounded mind. There have indeed been philosophers, "falsely so called," who have argued from the unlimited nature of God, that we cannot ascribe to him justice and other moral attributes, in any proper or definite sense of those words; and the inference is plain, that all religion or worship, wanting an intelligible object, must be a misplaced, wasted offering. This doctrine from the infidel we reject with abhorrence; but something, not very different, too often reaches us from the mistaken Christian, who, to save his creed, shrouds the Creator in utter darkness. In opposition to both, we maintain that God's attributes are intelligible, and that we can conceive as truly of his goodness and justice, as of these qualities in men. In fact, these qualities are essentially the same in God and man, though differing in degree, in purity, and in extent of operation. We know not and we cannot conceive of any other justice or goodness, than we learn from our own nature; and if God have not these, he is altogether unknown to us as a moral being; he offers nothing for esteem and love to rest upon; the objection of the infidel is just, that worship is wasted; "We worship we know not what."

It is asked, On what authority do we ascribe to God goodness and rectitude, in the sense in which these attributes belong to men, or how can we judge of the nature of attributes in the mind of the Creator? We answer by asking, How is it that we become acquainted with the mind of a fellow-creature? The last is as invisible, as removed from *immediate* inspection, as the first. Still we do not hesitate to speak of the justice and goodness of a neighbour; and how do we gain our knowledge? We answer, by witnessing the effects, operations, and expressions of these attributes. It is a law of our nature to argue from the effect to the cause, from the action to the agent, from the ends proposed and from the means of pursuing them, to the character and disposition of the being in whom we observe them. By these processes, we learn the invisible mind and character of man; and by the same we ascend to the mind of God, whose works, effects, operations, and ends are as expressive and significant of justice and goodness, as the best and most decisive actions of men. If this reasoning be sound (and all religion rests upon it,) then God's justice and goodness are intelligible attributes, agreeing essentially with the same qualities in ourselves. Their operation indeed is infinitely wider, and they are employed in accomplishing not only immediate but remote and unknown ends. Of consequence, we must expect that many parts of the divine administration will be *obscure,* that is, will not produce *immediate* good, and an *immediate* distinction between virtue and vice. But still the unbounded operation of these attributes does not change their nature. They are still the same, as if they acted in the narrowest sphere. We can still determine in many cases what does not accord with them. We are particularly sure that those essential principles of justice, which enter into and even form our conception of this attribute, must pervade every province and every period of the administration of a just being, and that to suppose the Creator in any instance to forsake them, is to charge him directly with unrighteousness, however loudly the lips may compliment his equity.

"But is it not presumptuous in man," it is continually said, "to sit in judgment on God?" We answer, that to "sit in judgment on God" is an ambigious and offensive phrase, conveying to common minds the ideas of irreverence, boldness, familiarity. The question would be better stated thus; —Is it not presumptuous in man to judge concerning God, and concerning what agrees or disagrees with his attributes? We answer confidently, No; for in many cases we are competent and even bound to judge. And we plead first in our defense the Scriptures. How continually does God in his word appeal to the understanding and moral judgment of man. "O inhabitants of Jerusalem and men of Judah, judge, I pray you, between me and my vineyard. What could have been done more to my vineyard, that I have not done in it." We observe, in the next place, that all religion supposes and is built on judgments passed by us on God and on his operations. Is it not, for example, our duty and a leading part of piety to *praise* God: And what is praising a being, but to adjudge and ascribe to him just and generous deeds and motives? And of what value is praise, except from those, who are capable of distinguishing between actions which exalt and actions which degrade the character? Is it presumption to call God *excellent?* And what is this, but to refer his character to a standard of excellence, to try it by the established principles of rectitude, and to pronounce its conformity to them; that is, to judge of God and his operations?

We are presumptuous, we are told, in judging of our Creator. But he himself has made this our duty, in giving us a moral faculty; and to decline it, is to violate the primary law of our nature. Conscience, the sense of right, the power of perceiving moral distinctions, the power of discerning between justice and injustice, excellence and baseness, is the highest faculty given us by God, the whole foundation of our responsibility, and our sole capacity for religion. Now we are forbidden by this faculty to love a being, who wants, or who fails to discover, moral excellence. God, in giving us conscience, has implanted a principle within us, which forbids us to prostrate ourselves before mere power, or to offer praise where we do not discover worth; a principle, which challenges our supreme homage for supreme goodness, and which absolves us from guilt, when we abhor a severe and unjust administration. Our Creator has consequently waved his own claims on our veneration and obedience, any farther than he discovers himself to us in characters of benevolence, equity, and righteousness. He rests his authority on the perfect coincidence of his will and government with those great and fundamental principles of morality written on our souls. He desires no worship, but that which springs from the exercise of our moral faculties upon his character, from our discernment and persuasion of his rectitude and goodness. He asks, he accepts, no love or admiration but from those, who can understand the nature and the proofs and moral excellence. * * *

1820

REMARKS ON THE CHARACTER AND WRITINGS OF JOHN MILTON

* * * In speaking of the *intellectual* qualities of Milton, we may begin with observing, that the very splendor of his poetic fame has tended to obscure or conceal the extent of his mind, and the variety of its energies and attainments. To many he seems only a poet, when in truth he was a profound scholar, a man of vast compass of thought, imbued thoroughly with all ancient and modern learning, and able to master, to mould, to impregnate with his own intellectual power, his great and various acquisitions. He had not learned the superficial doctrine of a later day, that poetry flourishes most in an uncultivated soil, and that imagination shapes its brightest visions from the mists of a superstitious age; and he had no dread of accumulating knowledge, lest it should oppress and smother his genius. He was conscious of that within him, which could quicken all knowledge, and wield it with ease and might; which could give freshness to old truths and harmony to discordant thoughts; which could bind together, by living ties and mysterious affinities, the most remote discoveries, and rear fabrics of glory and beauty from the rude materials, which other minds had collected. Milton had that universality which marks the highest order of intellect. Though accustomed almost from infancy to drink at the fountains of classical literature, he had nothing of the pedantry and fastidiousness, which disdain all other draughts. His healthy mind delighted in genius, on whatever soil, or in whatever age, it burst forth and poured out its fulness. He understood too well the rights, and dignity, and pride of creative imagination, to lay on it the laws of the Greek or Roman school. Parnassus was not to him the only holy ground of genius. He felt, that poetry was as a universal presence. Great minds were everywhere his kindred. He felt the enchantment of Oriental fiction, surrendered himself to the strange creations of "Araby the Blest," and delighted still more in the romantic spirit of chivalry, and in the tales of wonder in which it was embodied. Accordingly his poetry reminds us of the

ocean, which adds to its own boundlessness contributions from all regions under heaven. Nor was it only in the department of imagination, that his acquisitions were vast. He travelled over the whole field of knowledge, as far as it had then been explored. His various philological attainments were used to put him in possession of the wisdom stored in all countries, where the intellect had been cultivated. The natural philosophy, metaphysics, ethics, history, theology, and political science, of his own and former times, were familiar to him. Never was there a more unconfined mind; and we would cite Milton as a practical example of the benefits of that universal culture of intellect, which forms one distinction of our times, but which some dread as unfriendly to original thought. Let such remember, that mind is in its own nature diffusive. Its object is the universe, which is strictly one, or bound together by infinite connexions and correspondences; and accordingly its natural progress is from one to another field of thought; and wherever original power, creative genius exists, the mind, far from being distracted or oppressed by the variety of its acquisitions, will see more and more common bearings and hidden and beautiful analogies in all the objects of knowledge, will see mutual light shed from truth to truth, and will compel, as with a kingly power, whatever it understands, to yield some tribute of proof, or illustration, or splendor, to whatever topic it would unfold.

Milton's fame rests chiefly on his poetry, and to this we naturally give our first attention. By those who are accustomed to speak of poetry as light reading, Milton's eminence in this sphere may be considered only as giving him a high rank among the contributors to public amusement. Not so thought Milton. Of all God's gifts of intellect, he esteemed poetical genius the most transcendent. He esteemed it in himself as a kind of inspiration, and wrote his great works with something of the conscious dignity of a prophet. We agree with Milton in his estimate of poetry. It seems to us the divinest of all arts; for it is the breathing or expression of that principle or sentiment, which is deepest and sublimest in human nature; we mean, of that thirst or aspiration, to which no mind is wholly a stranger, for something purer and lovelier, something more powerful, lofty, and thrilling, than ordinary and real life affords. No doctrine is more common among Christians than that of man's immortality; but it is not so generally understood, that the germs or principles of his whole future being are *now* wrapped up in his soul, as the rudiments of the future plant in the seed. As a necessary result of this constitution, the soul, possessed and moved by these mighty though infant energies, is perpetually stretching beyond what is present and visible, struggling against the bounds of its earthly prison-house, and seeking relief and joy in imaginings of unseen and ideal being. This view of our nature, which has never been fully developed, and which goes farther towards explaining the contradictions of human life than all others, carries us to the very foundation and sources of poetry. He who cannot interpret by his own consciousness what we now have said, wants the true key to works of genius. He has not penetrated those secret recesses of the soul, where poetry is born and nourished, and inhales immortal vigor, and wings herself for her heavenward flight. In an intellectual nature, framed for progress and for higher modes of being, there must be creative energies, powers of original and ever-growing thought; and poetry is the form in which these energies are chiefly manifested. It is the glorious prerogative of this art, that it "makes all things new" for the gratification of a divine instinct. It indeed finds its elements in what it actually sees and experiences, in the worlds of matter and mind; but it combines and blends these into new forms and according to new affinities; breaks down, if we may so say, the distinctions and bounds of nature; imparts to material objects life, and sentiment, and emotion, and invests the mind with the powers and splendors of the outward creation; describes the surrounding universe in the colors which the passions throw over it, and depicts the soul in those modes of repose or agitation, of tenderness or sublime emotion, which manifest its thirst for a more powerful and joyful existence. To a man of a literal and prosaic character, the mind may seem lawless in these workings; but it observes higher laws than it transgresses, the laws of the immortal intellect; it is trying and developing its best faculties; and in the objects which it describes, or in the emotions which it awakens, anticipates those states of progressive power, splendor, beauty, and happiness, for which it was created.

We accordingly believe that poetry, far from injuring society, is one of the great instruments of its refinement and exaltation. It lifts the mind above ordinary life, gives it a respite from depressing cares, and awakens the consciousness of its affinity with what is pure and noble. In its legitimate and highest efforts, it has the same tendency and aim with Christianity; that is, to spiritualize our nature. True, poetry has been made the instrument of vice, the pander of bad passions; but, when genius thus stoops, it dims its fires, and parts with much of its power; and, even when poetry is enslaved to licentiousness or misanthropy, she cannot wholly forget her true vocation. Strains of pure feeling, touches of tenderness, images of innocent happiness, sympathies with suffering virtue, bursts of scorn or indignation at the hollowness of the world, passages true to our moral nature, often escape in an immoral work, and show us how hard it is for a gifted spirit to divorce itself wholly from what is good. Poetry has a natural alliance with our best affections. It delights in the beauty and sublimity of the outward creation and of the soul. It indeed portrays, with terrible energy, the excesses of the passions; but they are passions which show a mighty nature, which are full of power, which command awe, and excite a deep though shuddering sympathy. Its great tendency and purpose is, to carry the mind beyond and above the beaten, dusty, weary walks of ordinary life; to lift it into a purer element; and to breathe into it more profound and generous emotion. It reveals to us the loveliness of nature, brings back the freshness of early feeling, revives the relish of simple pleasures, keeps unquenched the enthusiasm which warmed the spring-time of our being, refines youthful love, strengthens our interest in human nature by vivid delineations of its tenderest and loftiest feelings, spreads our sympathies over all classes of society, knits us by new ties with universal being, and, through the brightness of its prophetic visions, helps faith to lay hold on the future life.

We are aware, that it is objected to poetry, that it gives wrong views and excites false expectations of life, peoples the mind with shadows and illusions, and builds up imagination on the ruins of wisdom. That there is a wisdom, against which poetry wars, the wisdom of the senses, which makes physical comfort and gratification the supreme good, and wealth the chief interest of life, we do not deny; nor do we deem it the least service which poetry renders to mankind, that it redeems them from the thraldom of this earthborn prudence. But, passing over this topic, we would observe, that the complaint against poetry, as abounding in illusion and deception, is in the main groundless. In many poems there is more of truth than in many histories and philosophic theories. The fictions of genius are often the vehicles of the sublimest verities, and its flashes often open new regions of thought, and throw new light on the mysteries of our being. In poetry, when the letter is falsehood, the spirit is often profoundest wisdom. And, if truth thus dwells in the boldest fictions of the poet, much more may it be expected in his delineations of life; for the present life, which is the first stage of the immortal mind, abounds in the materials of poetry, and it is the high office of the bard to detect this divine element among the grosser labors and pleasures of our earthly being. The present life is not wholly prosaic, precise, tame, and finite. To the gifted eye it abounds in the poetic. The affections which spread beyond ourselves and stretch far into futurity; the workings of mighty passions, which seem to arm the soul with an almost superhuman energy; the innocent and irrepressible joy of infancy; the bloom, and buoyancy, and dazzling hopes of youth; the throbbings of the heart, when it first wakes to love, and dreams of a happiness too vast for earth; woman, with her beauty, and grace, and gentleness, and fulness of feeling, and depth of affection, and blushes of purity, and the tones and looks which only a mother's heart can inspire;—these are all poetical. It is not true, that the poet paints a life which does not exist. He only extracts and concentrates, as it were, life's ethereal essence, arrests and condenses its volatile fragrance, brings together its scattered beauties, and prolongs its more refined but evanescent joys. And in this he does well; for it is good to feel that life is not wholly usurped by cares for subsistence, and physical gratifications, but admits, in measures which may be indefinitely enlarged, sentiments and delights worthy of a higher being. This power of poetry to refine our views of life and happiness, is more and more needed as society advances. It is needed to withstand the encroachments of heartless and artificial manners, which make civilization so tame and uninteresting. It is needed to counteract the tendency of physical science, which, being now sought, not, as formerly, for intellectual gratification, but for multiplying bodily comforts, requires a new developement of imagination, taste, and poetry, to preserve men from sinking into an earthly, material, Epicurean life.— Our remarks in vindication of poetry have extended beyond our original design. They have had a higher aim than to assert the dignity of Milton as a poet, and that is, to endear and recommend this divine art to all who reverence and would cultivate and refine their nature.

In delineating Milton's character as a *poet*, we are saved the necessity of looking far for its distinguishing attributes. His name is almost identified with sublimity. He is in truth the sublimest of men. He rises, not by effort or discipline, but by a native tendency and a godlike instinct, to the contemplation of objects of grandeur and awfulness. He always moves with a conscious energy. There is no subject so vast or terrific, as to repel or intimidate him. The overpowering grandeur of a theme kindles and attracts him. He enters on the description of the infernal regions with a fearless tread, as if he felt within himself a power to erect the prison-house of fallen spirits, to encircle them with flames and horrors worthy of their crimes, to call forth from them shouts which should "tear hell's concave," and to embody in their Chief an Archangel's energies, and a Demon's pride and hate. Even the stupendous conception of Satan seems never to oppress his faculties. This character of power runs through all Milton's works. His descriptions of nature show a free and bold hand. He has no need of the minute, graphic skill, which we prize in Cowper or Crabbe. With a few strong or delicate touches, he impresses, as it were, his own mind on the scenes which he would describe, and kindles the imagination of the gifted reader to clothe them with the same radiant hues under which they appeared to his own.

This attribute of power is universally felt to characterize Milton. His sublimity is in every man's mouth. Is it felt that his poetry breathes a sensibility and tenderness hardly surpassed by its sublimity? We apprehend, that the grandeur of Milton's mind has thrown some shade over his milder beauties; and this it has done, not only by being more striking and imposing, but by the tendency of vast mental energy to give a certain calmness to the expression of tenderness and deep feeling. A great mind is the master of its own enthusiasm, and does not often break out into those tumults, which pass with many for the signs of profound emotion. Its sensibility, though more intense and enduring, is more self-possessed, and less perturbed, than that of other men, and is therefore less observed and felt, except by those who understand, through their own consciousness, the workings and utterance of genuine feeling. * * *

From this very imperfect view of the qualities of Milton's poetry, we hasten to his great work, "Paradise Lost," perhaps the noblest monument of human genius. The two first books, by universal consent, stand preëminent in sublimity. Hell and hell's king have a terrible harmony, and dilate into new grandeur and awfulness, the longer we contemplate them. From one element, "solid and liquid fire," the poet has framed a world of horror and suffering, such as imagination had never traversed. But fiercer flames than those which encompass Satan, burn in his own soul. Revenge, exasperated pride, consuming wrath, ambition, though fallen, yet unconquered by the thunders of the Omnipotent, and grasping still at the empire of the universe,—these form a picture more sublime and terrible than hell. Hell yields to the spirit which it imprisons. The intensity of its fires reveals the intenser passions and more vehement will of Satan; and the ruined archangel gathers into himself the sublimity of the scene which surrounds him. This forms the tremendous interest of these wonderful books. We see mind triumphant over the most terrible powers of nature. We see unutterable agony subdued by energy of soul. We have not indeed in Satan those bursts of passion, which rive the soul, as well as shatter the outward frame, of Lear. But we have a depth of passion which only an archangel could manifest. The all-enduring, all-defying pride of Satan, assuming so majestically hell's burning throne, and coveting the diadem which scorches his thunder-blasted brow, is a creation requiring in its author almost the spriritual energy with which he invests the fallen seraph. Some have doubted whether the moral effect of such delineations of the storms and terrible workings of the soul is good; whether the interest felt in a spirit so transcendently evil as Satan, favors our sympathies with virtue. But our interest fastens, in this and like cases, on what is not evil. We gaze on Satan with an awe not unmixed with mysterious pleasure, as on a miraculous manifestation of the *power of mind*. What chains us, as with a resistless spell, in such a character, is spiritual might made visible by the racking pains which it overpowers. There is something kindling and ennobling in the consciousness, however awakened, of the energy which resides in mind; and many a virtuous man has borrowed new strength from the force, constancy, and dauntless courage of evil agents.

Milton's description of Satan attests in various ways the power of his genius. Critics have often observed, that the great difficulty of his work was, to reconcile the spiritual properties of his supernatural beings with the human modes of existence, which he is obliged to ascribe to them. The difficulty is too great for any genius wholly to overcome, and we must acknowledge that our enthusiasm is in some parts of the poem checked by a feeling of incongruity between the spriritual agent, and his sphere and mode of agency. But we are visited with no such chilling doubts and misgivings in the description of Satan in hell. Imagination has here achieved its highest triumph, in imparting a character of reality and truth to its most daring creations. That world of horrors, though material, is yet so remote from our ordinary nature, that a spiritual being, exiled from heaven, finds there an appropriate home. There is, too, an indefiniteness in the description of Satan's person, which excites without shocking the imagination, and aids us to reconcile, in our conception of him, a human form with his superhuman attributes. To the production of this effect, much depends on the first impression given by the poet; for this is apt to follow us through the whole work; and here we think Milton eminently successful. The first glimpse of Satan is given us in the following lines, which, whilst too indefinite to provoke, and too sublime to allow, the scrutiny of the reason, fill the imagination of the reader with a form which can hardly be effaced.

"Thus Satan, talking to his nearest mate
With head uplift above the wave, and eyes
That sparkling blazed; his other parts besides
Prone on the flood, extended long and large,
Lay floating many a rood."

—*Par. Lost, B. I, lines* 192–196.

"Forthwith upright he rears from off the pool
His mighty stature; on each hand the flames,
Driven backward, slope their pointing spires, and, roll'd
In billows, leave i' the midst a horrid vale."

—*Lines* 221–224.

We have more which we would gladly say of the delineation of Satan; especially of the glimpses which are now and then given of his deep anguish and despair, and of the touches of better feelings which are skilfully thrown into the dark picture, both suited and designed to blend, with our admiration, dread, and abhorrence, a measure of that sympathy and interest, with which every living, thinking being ought to be regarded, and without which all other feelings tend to sin and pain. But there is another topic which we cannot leave untouched. From hell we flee to Paradise, a region as lovely as hell is terrible, and which, to those who do not know the universality of true genius, will appear doubly wonderful, when considered as the creation of the same mind, which had painted the infernal world.

Paradise and its inhabitants are in sweet accordance, and together form a scene of tranquil bliss, which calms and soothes, whilst it delights, the imagination. Adam and Eve, just moulded by the hand and quickened by the breath of God, reflect in their countenances and forms, as well as minds, the intelligence, benignity, and happiness of their Author. Their new existence has the freshness and peacefulness of the dewy morning. Their souls, unsated and untainted, find an innocent joy in the youthful creation, which spreads and smiles around them. Their mutual love is deep, for it is the love of young, unworn, unexhausted hearts, which meet in each other the only human objects on whom to pour forth their fulness of affection; and still it is serene, for it is the love of happy beings, who know not suffering even by name, whose innocence excludes not only the tumults but the thought of jealousy and shame, who, "imparadised in one another's arms," scarce dream of futurity, so blessed is their present being. We will not say that we envy our first parents; for we feel that there may be higher happiness than theirs, a happiness won through struggle with inward and outward foes, the happiness of power and moral victory, the happiness of disinterested sacrifices and wide-spread love, the happiness of boundless hope, and of "thoughts which wander through eternity." Still there are times, when the spirit, oppressed with pain, worn with toil, tired of tumult, sick at the sight of guilt, wounded in its love, baffled in its hope, and trembling in its faith, almost longs for the "wings of a dove, that it might fly away" and take refuge amidst the "shady bowers," the "vernal airs," the "roses without thorns," the quiet, the beauty, the loveliness of Eden. It is the contrast of this deep peace of Paradise with the storms of life, which gives to the fourth and fifth books of this poem a charm so irresistible, that not a few would sooner relinquish the two first books, with all their sublimity, than part with these. It has sometimes been said, that the English language has no good pastoral poetry. We would ask, in what age or country has the pastoral reed breathed such sweet strains as are borne to us on "the odoriferous wings of gentle gales" from Milton's Paradise?

We should not fulfil our duty, were we not to say one word on what has been justly celebrated, the harmony of Milton's versification. His numbers have the prime charm of expressiveness. They vary with, and answer to, the depth, or tenderness, or sublimity of his conceptions, and hold intimate alliance with the soul. Like Michael Angelo, in whose hands the marble was said to be flexible, he bends our language, which foreigners reproach with hardness, into whatever forms the subject demands. All the treasures of sweet and solemn sound are at his command. Words, harsh and discordant in the writings of less gifted men, flow through his poetry in a full stream of harmony. This power over language is not to be ascribed to Milton's musical ear. It belongs to the soul. It is a gift or exercise of genius, which has power to impress itself on whatever it touches, and finds or frames, in sounds, motions, and material forms, correspondences and harmonies with its own fervid thoughts and feelings.

We close our remarks on Milton's poetry with observing, that it is characterized by seriousness. Great and various as are its merits, it does not discover all the variety of genius, which we find in Shakspeare, whose imagination revelled equally in regions of mirth, beauty, and terror, now evoking spectres, now sporting with fairies, and now "ascending the highest heaven of invention." Milton was cast on times too solemn and eventful, was called to take part in transactions too perilous, and had too perpetual need of the presence of high thoughts and motives, to indulge himself in light and gay creations, even had his genius been more flexible and sportive. But Milton's poetry, though habitually serious, is always healthful, and bright, and vigorous. It has no gloom. He took no pleasure in drawing dark pictures of life; for he knew by experience, that there is a power in the soul to transmute calamity into an occasion and nutriment of moral power and triumphant virtue. We find nowhere in his writings that whining sensibility and exaggeration of morbid feeling, which makes so much of modern poetry effeminating. If he is not gay, he is not spirit-broken. His "L'Allegro" proves, that he understood thoroughly the bright and joyous aspects of nature; and in his "Penseroso," where he was tempted to accumulate images of gloom, we learn, that the saddest views which he took of creation, are such as inspire only pensive musing or lofty contemplation. * * *

1826

REMARKS ON NATIONAL LITERATURE

* * * Our purpose is to treat of the importance and means of a National Literature. The topic seems to us a great one, and to have intimate connexions with morals and religion, as well as with all our public interests. Our views will be given with great freedom, and, if they serve no other purpose than to recommend the subject to more general attention, one of our principal objects will be accomplished.

We begin with stating what we mean by national literature. We mean the expression of a nation's mind in writing. We mean the production among a people of important works in philosophy, and in the departments of imagination and taste. We mean the contributions of new truths to the stock of human knowledge. We mean the thoughts of profound and original minds, elaborated by the toil of composition, and fixed and made immortal in books. We mean the manifestation of a nation's intellect in the only forms by which it can multiply itself at home, and send itself abroad. We mean that a nation shall take a place, by its authors, among the lights of the world. It will be seen, that we include under literature all the writings of superior minds, be the subjects what they may. We are aware that the term is often confined to compositions which relate to human nature, and human life; that it is not generally extended to physical science; that mind, not matter, is regarded as its main subject and sphere. But the worlds of matter and mind are too intimately connected to admit of exact partition. All the objects of human thought flow into one another. Moral and physical truths have many bonds and analogies, and, whilst the former are the chosen and noblest themes of literature, we are not anxious to divorce them from the latter, or to shut them up in a separate department. The expression of superior mind in writing, we regard, then, as a nation's literature. We regard its gifted men, whether devoted to the exact sciences, to mental and ethical philosophy, to history and legislation, or to fiction and poetry, as forming a noble intellectual brotherhood, and it is for the purpose of quickening all to join their labors for the public good, that we offer the present plea in behalf of a national literature.

To show the importance which we attach to the subject, we begin with some remarks on what we deem the distinction which a nation should most earnestly covet. We believe, that more distinct apprehensions on this point are needed, and that, for want of them, the work of improvement is carried on with less energy, consistency, and wisdom, than may and should be brought to bear upon it. The great distinction of a country, then, is that it produces superior men. Its natural advantages are not to be disdained. But they are of secondary importance. No matter what races of animals a country breeds. The great question is, Does it breed a noble race of men? No matter what its soil may be. The great question is, How far is it prolific of moral and intellectual power? No matter how stern its climate is, if it nourish force of thought and virtuous purpose. These are the products by which a country is to be tried, and institutions have value only by the impulses which they give to the mind. It has sometimes been said, that the noblest men grow where nothing else will grow. This we do not believe, for mind is not the creature of climate or soil. But were it true, we should say, that it were better to live among rocks and sands, than in the most genial and productive region on the face of the earth.

As yet, the great distinction of a nation on which we have insisted, has been scarcely recognized. The idea of forming a superior race of men has entered little into schemes of policy. Invention and effort have been expended on matter, much more than on mind. Lofty piles have been reared; the earth has groaned under pyramids and palaces. The thought of building up a nobler order of intellect and character, has hardly crossed the most adventurous statesman. We beg that we may not be misapprehended. We offer these remarks to correct what we deem a disproportioned attention to physical good, and not at all to condemn the expenditure of ingenuity and strength on the outward world. There is a harmony between all our great interests, between inward and outward improvements; and, by establishing among them a wise order, all will be secured. We have no desire to shut up man in his own spiritual nature. The mind was made to act on matter, and it grows by expressing itself in material forms. We believe, too, that, in proportion as it shall gain intellectual and moral power, it will exert itself with increased energy and delight on the outward creation; will pour itself forth more freely in useful and ornamental arts; will rear more magnificent structures, and will call forth new beauties in nature. An intelligent and resolute spirit in a community, perpetually extends its triumphs over matter. It can even subject to itself the most unpromising region. Holland, diked from the ocean,—Venice, rising amidst the waves,—and New England, bleak and rock-bound New England, converted by a few generations from a wilderness into smiling fields and opulent cities,—point us to the mind as the great source of physical good, and teach us, that, in making the culture of man our highest end, we shall not retard, but advance, the cultivation of nature.

The question which we most solicitously ask about this country is, what race of men it is likely to produce. We consider its liberty of value only as far as it favors the growth of men. What is liberty? The removal of restraint from human powers. Its benefit is, that it opens new fields for action, and a wider range for the mind. The only freedom worth possessing, is that which gives enlargement to a people's energy, intellect, and virtues. The savage makes his boast of freedom. But what is its worth? Free as he is, he continues for ages in the same ignorance, leads the same comfortless life, sees the same untamed wilderness spread around him. He is indeed free from what he calls the yoke of civil institutions. But other and worse chains bind him. The very privation of civil government is in effect a chain; for, by withholding protection from property, it virtually shackles the arm of industry, and forbids exertion for the melioration of his lot. Progress, the growth of power, is the end and boon of liberty; and, without this, a people may have the name, but want the substance and spirit of freedom.

We are the more earnest in enlarging on these views, because we feel that our attachment to our country must be very much proportioned to what we deem its tendency to form a generous race of men. We pretend not to have thrown off national feeling; but we have some stronger feelings. We love our country much, but mankind more. As men and Christians, our first desire is to see the improvement of human nature. We desire to see the soul of man wiser, firmer, nobler, more conscious of its imperishable treasures, more beneficent and powerful, more alive to its connexion with God, more able to use pleasure and prosperity aright, and more victorious over poverty, adversity, and pain. In our survey of our own and other countries, the great question which comes to us is this, Where and under what institutions are men most likely to advance? Where are the soundest minds and the purest hearts formed? What nation possesses, in its history, its traditions, its government, its religion, its manners, its pursuits, its relations to other communities, and especially in its private and public means of education, the instruments and pledges of a more resolute virtue and devotion to truth, than we now witness? Such a nation, be it where it may, will engage our warmest interest. We love our country, but not blindly. In all nations we recognize one great family, and our chief wish for our native land is, that it may take the first rank among the lights and benefactors of the human race.

These views will explain the vast importance which we attach to a national literature. By this, as we have said, we understand the expression of a nation's mind in writing. It is the action of the most gifted understandings on the community. It throws into circulation through a wide sphere the most quickening and beautiful thoughts, which have grown up in men of laborious study or creative genius. It is a much higher work than the communication of a gifted intellect in discourse. It is the mind giving to multitudes whom no voice can reach, its compressed and selected thoughts, in the most lucid order and attractive forms which it is capable of inventing. In other words, literature is the concentration of intellect for the purpose of spreading itself abroad and multiplying its energy.

Such being the nature of literature, it is plainly among the most powerful methods of exalting the character of a nation, of forming a better race of men; in truth, we apprehend that it may claim the first rank among the means of improvement. We know nothing so fitted to the advancement of society, as to bring its higher minds to bear upon the multitude; as to establish close connexions between the more and less gifted; as to spread far and wide the light which springs up in meditative, profound, and sublime understandings. It is the ordinance of God, and one of his most benevolent laws, that the human race should be carried forward by impulses which originate in a few minds, perhaps in an individual; and in this way the most interesting relations and dependencies of life are framed. When a great truth is to be revealed, it does not flash at once on the race, but dawns and brightens on a superior understanding, from which it is to emanate and to illumine future ages. On the faithfulness of great minds to this awful function, the progress and happiness of men chiefly depend. The most illustrious benefactors of the race have been men, who, having risen to great truths, have held them as a sacred trust for their kind, and have borne witness to them amidst general darkness, under scorn and persecution, perhaps in the face of death. Such men, indeed, have not always made contributions to literature, for their condition has not allowed them to be authors; but we owe the transmission, perpetuity, and immortal power of their new and high thoughts, to kindred spirits, which have concentrated and fixed them in books.

The quickening influences of literature need not be urged on those who are familiar with the history of modern Europe, and who of course know the spring given to the human mind by the revival of ancient learning. Through their writings, the great men of antiquity have exercised a sovereignty over these later ages, not enjoyed in their own. It is more important to observe, that the influence of literature is perpetually increasing; for, through the press and the spread of education, its sphere is indefinitely enlarged. Reading, once the privilege of a few, is now the occupation of multitudes, and is to become one of the chief gratifications of all. Books penetrate everywhere, and some of the works of genius find their way to obscure dwellings, which, a little while ago, seemed barred against all intellectual light. Writing is now the mightiest instrument on earth. Through this, the mind has acquired a kind of omnipresence. To literature we then look, as the chief means of forming a better race of human beings. To superior minds, which may act through this, we look for the impulses, by which their country is to be carried forward. We would teach them, that they are the depositaries of the highest power on earth, and that on them the best hopes of society rest. * * *

If we have succeeded in conveying the impressions which we have aimed to make, our readers are now prepared to inquire with interest into the condition and prospects of literature among ourselves. Do we possess, indeed, what may be called a national literature? Have we produced eminent writers in the various departments of intellectual effort? Are our chief resources of instruction and literary enjoyment furnished from ourselves? We regret that the reply to these questions is so obvious. The few standard works which we have produced, and which promise to live, can hardly, by any courtesy, be denominated a national literature. On this point, if marks and proofs of our real condition were needed, we should find them in the current apologies for our deficiencies. Our writers are accustomed to plead in our excuse, our youth, the necessities of a newly settled country, and the direction of our best talents to practical life. Be the pleas sufficient or not, one thing they prove, and that is, our consciousness of having failed to make important contributions to the interests of the intellect. We have few names to place by the side of the great names in science and literature on the other side of the ocean. We want those lights which make a country conspicuous at a distance. Let it not be said, that European envy denies our just claims. In an age like this, when the literary world forms a great family, and the products of the mind are circulated more rapidly than those of machinery, it is a nation's own fault, if its name be not pronounced with honor beyond itself. We have ourselves heard, and delighted to hear, beyond the Alps, our country designated as the land of Franklin. This name had scaled that mighty barrier, and made us known where our institutions and modes of life were hardly better understood than those of the natives of our forests.

We are accustomed to console ourselves for the absence of a commanding literature, by urging our superiority to other nations in our institutions for the diffusion of elementary knowledge through all classes of the community. We have here just cause for boasting, though perhaps less than we imagine. That there are gross deficiencies in our common schools, and that the amount of knowledge which they communicate, when compared with the time spent in its acquisition, is lamentably small, the community begin to feel. There is a crying need for a higher and more quickening kind of instruction than the laboring part of society have yet received, and we rejoice that the cry begins to be heard. But, allowing our elementary institutions to be ever so perfect, we confess that they do not satisfy us. We want something more. A dead level of intellect, even if it should rise above what is common in other nations, would not answer our wishes and hopes for our country. We want great minds to be formed among us, minds which shall be felt afar, and through which we may act on the world. We want the human intellect to do its utmost here. We want this people to obtain a claim on the gratitude of the human race, by adding strength to the foundation, and fulness and splendor to the developement of moral and religious truth; by originality of thought, by discoveries of science, and by contributions to the refining pleasures of taste and imagination.

With these views we do and must lament, that, however we surpass other nations in providing for, and spreading elementary instruction, we fall behind many in provision for the liberal training of the intellect, for forming great scholars, for communicating that profound knowledge, and that thirst for higher truths, which can alone originate a commanding literature. The truth ought to be known. There is among us much superficial knowledge, but little severe, persevering research; little of that consuming passion for new truth, which makes outward things worthless; little resolute devotion to a high intellectual culture. There is nowhere a literary atmosphere, or such an accumulation of literary influence, as determines the whole strength of the mind to its own enlargement, and to the manifestation of itself in enduring forms. Few among us can be said to have followed out any great subject of thought patiently, laboriously, so as to know thoroughly what others have discovered and taught concerning it, and thus to occupy a ground from which new views may be gained. Of course, exceptions are to be found. This country has produced original and profound thinkers. We have named Franklin, and we may name Edwards, one of the greatest men of his age, though unhappily his mind was lost, in a great degree, to literature, and we fear to religion, by vassalage to a false theology. His work on the Will throws, indeed, no light on human nature, and notwithstanding the nobleness of the subject, gives no great or elevated thoughts; but, as a specimen of logical acuteness and controversial power, it certainly ranks in the very highest class of metaphysical writings. We might also name living authors who do honor to their country. Still, we may say, we chiefly prize what has been done among us, as a promise of higher and more extensive effort. Patriotism, as well as virtue, forbids us to burn incense to national vanity. The truth should be seen and felt. In an age of great intellectual activity, we rely chiefly for intellectual excitement and enjoyment on foreign minds, nor is our own mind felt abroad. Whilst clamoring against dependence on European manufactures, we contentedly rely on Europe for the nobler and more important fabrics of the intellect. We boast of our political institutions, and receive our chief teachings, books, impressions, from the school of monarchy. True, we labor under disadvantages. But, if our liberty deserves the praise which it receives, it is more than a balance for these. We believe that it is. We believe that it does open to us an indefinite intellectual progress. Did we not so regard it, we should value it little. If hereditary governments minister most to the growth of the mind, it were better to restore them than to cling to a barren freedom. Let us not expose liberty to this reproach. Let us prove, by more generous provisions for the diffusion of elementary knowledge, for the training of great minds, and for the joint culture of the moral and intellectual powers, that we are more and more instructed, by freedom, in the worth and greatness of human nature, and in the obligation of contributing to its strength and glory.

We have spoken of the condition of our literature. We now proceed to the consideration of the causes which obstruct its advancement; and we are immediately struck by one so prevalent, as to deserve distinct notice. We refer to the common doctrine, that we need, in this country, useful knowledge, rather than profound, extensive, and elegant literature, and that this last, if we covet it, may be imported from abroad in such variety and abundance, as to save us the necessity of producing it among ourselves. How far are these opinions just? This question we purpose to answer.

That useful knowledge should receive our first and chief care, we mean not to dispute. But in our views of utility, we may differ from some who take this position. There are those who confine this term to the necessaries and comforts of life, and to the means of producing them. And is it true, that we need no knowledge, but that which clothes and feeds us? Is it true, that all studies may be dispensed with, but such as teach us to act on matter, and to turn it to our use? Happily, human nature is too stubborn to yield to this narrow utility. It is interesting to observe how the very mechanical arts, which are especially designed to minister to the necessities and comforts of life, are perpetually passing these limits; how they disdain to stop at mere convenience. A large and increasing proportion of mechanical labor is given to the gratification of an elegant taste. How simple would be the art of building, if it limited itself to the construction of a comfortable shelter! How many ships should we dismantle, and how many busy trades put to rest, were dress and furniture reduced to the standard of convenience! This "utility" would work a great change in town and country, would level to the dust the wonders of architecture, would annihilate the fine arts, and blot out innumerable beauties, which the hand of taste has spread over the face of the earth. Happily, human nature is too strong for the utilitarian. It cannot satisfy itself with the convenient. No passion unfolds itself sooner than the love of the ornamental. The savage decorates his person, and the child is more struck with the beauty than the uses of its raiment. So far from limiting ourselves to convenient food and raiment, we enjoy but little a repast which is not arranged with some degree of order and taste; and a man who should consult comfort alone in his wardrobe, would find himself an unwelcome guest in circles which he would very reluctantly forego. We are aware that the propensity to which we have referred, often breaks out in extravagance and ruinous luxury. We know that the love of ornament is often vitiated by vanity, and that, when so perverted, it impairs, sometimes destroys, the soundness and simplicity of the mind and the relish for true glory. Still it teaches, even in its excesses, that the idea of beauty is an indestructible principle of our nature, and this single truth is enough to put us on our guard against vulgar notions of utility.

We have said that we prize, as highly as any, useful knowledge. But by this we mean knowledge which answers and ministers to our complex and various nature; we mean that which is useful, not only to the animal man, but to the intellectual, moral, and religious man; useful to a being of spiritual faculties, whose happiness is to be found in their free and harmonious exercise. We grant, that there is primary necessity for that information and skill by which subsistence is earned, and life is preserved; for it is plain that we must live, in order to act and improve. But life is the means; action and improvement the end; and who will deny that the noblest utility belongs to that knowledge, by which the chief purpose of our creation is accomplished? According to these views, a people should honor and cultivate, as unspeakably useful, that literature which corresponds to, and calls forth, the highest faculties; which expresses and communicates energy of thought, fruitfulness of invention, force of moral purpose, a thirst for the true, and a delight in the beautiful. According to these views, we attach special importance to those branches of literature which relate to human nature, and which give it a consciousness of its own powers. History has a noble use, for it shows us human beings in various and opposite conditions, in their strength and weakness, in their progress and relapses, and thus reveals the causes and means by which the happiness and virtue of the race may be enlarged. Poetry is useful, by touching deep springs in the human soul; by giving voice to its more delicate feelings; by breathing out, and making more intelligible, the sympathy which subsists between the mind and the outward universe; by creating beautiful forms of manifestations for great moral truths. Above all, that higher philosophy, which treats of the intellectual and moral constitution of man, of the foundation of knowledge, of duty, of perfection, of our relations to the spiritual world, and especially to God; this has a usefulness so peculiar as to throw other departments of knowledge into obscurity; and a people, among whom this does not find honor, has little ground to boast of its superiority to uncivilized tribes. It will be seen from these remarks, that utility, with us, has a broad meaning. In truth, we are slow to condemn as useless, any researches or discoveries of original and strong minds, even when we discern in them no bearing on any interests of mankind; for all truth is of a prolific nature, and has connexions not immediately perceived; and it may be, that what we call vain speculations, may, at no distant period, link themselves with some new facts or theories, and guide a profound thinker to the most important results. The ancient mathematician, when absorbed in solitary thought, little imagined that his theorems, after the lapse of ages, were to be applied by the mind of Newton to the solution of the mysteries of the universe, and not only to guide the astronomer through the heavens, but the navigator through the pathless ocean. For ourselves, we incline to hope much from truths, which are particularly decried as useless; for the noblest and most useful truth is of an abstract or universal nature; and yet the abstract, though susceptible of infinite application, is generally, as we know, opposed to the practical.

We maintain, that a people, which has any serious purpose of taking a place among improved communities, should studiously promote within itself every variety of intellectual exertion. It should resolve strenuously to be surpassed by none. It should feel that mind is the creative power, through which all the resources of nature are to be turned to account, and by which a people is to spread its influence, and establish the noblest form of empire. It should train within itself men able to understand and to use whatever is thought and discovered over the whole earth. The whole mass of human knowledge should exist among a people, not in neglected libraries, but in its higher minds. Among its most cherished institutions, should be those, which will ensure to it ripe scholars, explorers of ancient learning, profound historians and mathematicians, intellectual laborers devoted to physical and moral science, and to the creation of a refined and beautiful literature.

Let us not be misunderstood. We have no desire to rear in our country a race of pedants, of solemn triflers, of laborious commentators on the mysteries of a Greek accent or a rusty coin. We would have men explore antiquity, not to bury themselves in its dust, but to learn its spirit, and so to commune with its superior minds, as to accumulate on the present age, the influences of whatever was great and wise in former times. What we want is, that those among us, whom God has gifted to comprehend whatever is now known, and to rise to new truths, may find aids and institutions to fit them for their high calling, and may become at once springs of a higher intellectual life to their own country, and joint workers with the great of all nations and times in carrying forward their race.

We know that it will be said, that foreign scholars, bred under institutions which this country cannot support, may do our intellectual work, and send us books and learning to meet our wants. To this we have much to answer. In the first place, we reply, that, to avail ourselves of the higher literature of other nations, we must place ourselves on a level with them. The products of foreign machinery we can use, without any portion of the skill that produced them. But works of taste and genius, and profound investigations of philosophy, can only be estimated and enjoyed through a culture and power corresponding to that from which they sprung.

In the next place, we maintain, that it is an immense gain to a people, to have in its own bosom, among its own sons, men of distinguished intellect. Such men give a spring and life to a community by their presence, their society, their fame; and what deserves remark, such men are nowhere so felt as in a republic like our own; for here the different classes of society flow together and act powerfully on each other, and a free communication, elsewhere unknown, is established between the gifted few and the many. It is one of the many good fruits of liberty, that it increases the diffusiveness of intellect; and accordingly a free country is, above all others, false to itself, in withholding from its superior minds the means of enlargement.

We next observe, and we think the observation important, that the facility with which we receive the literature of foreign countries, instead of being a reason for neglecting our own, is a strong motive for its cultivation. We mean not to be paradoxical, but we believe that it would be better to admit no books from abroad, than to make them substitutes for our own intellectual activity. The more we receive from other countries, the greater the need of an original literature. A people, into whose minds the thoughts of foreigners are poured perpetually, needs an energy within itself to resist, to modify this mighty influence, and, without it, will inevitably sink under the worst bondage, will become intellectually tame and enslaved. We have certainly no desire to complete our restrictive system, by adding to it a literary non-intercourse law. We rejoice in the increasing intellectual connexion between this country and the old world. But sooner would we rupture it, than see our country sitting passively at the feet of foreign teachers. It were better to have no literature, than form ourselves unresistingly on a foreign one. The true sovereigns of a country are those who determine its mind, its modes of thinking, its tastes, its principles; and we cannot consent to lodge this sovereignty in the hands of strangers. A country, like an individual, has dignity and power only in proportion as it is self-founded. There is a great stir to secure to ourselves the manufacturing of our own clothing. We say, let others spin and weave for us, but let them not think for us. A people, whose government and laws are nothing but the embodying of public opinion, should jealously guard this opinion against foreign dictation. We need a literature to counteract, and to use wisely the literature which we import. We need an inward power proportionate to that which is exerted on us, as the means of self-subsistence. It is particularly true of a people, whose institutions demand for their support a free and bold spirit, that they should be able to subject to a manly and independent criticism, whatever comes from abroad. These views seem to us to deserve serious attention. We are more and more a reading people. Books are already among the most powerful influences here. The question is, shall Europe, through these, fashion us after its pleasure? Shall America be only an echo of what is thought and written under the aristocracies beyond the ocean?

Another view of the subject is this. A foreign literature will always, in a measure, be foreign. It has sprung from the soul of another people, which, however like, is still not our own soul. Every people has much in its own character and feelings, which can only be embodied by its own writers, and which, when transfused through literature, makes it touching and true, like the voice of our earliest friend.

We now proceed to an argument in favor of native literature, which, if less obvious, is, we believe, not less sound than these now already adduced. We have hitherto spoken of literature as the expression, the communication, of the higher minds in a community. We now add, that it does much more than is commonly supposed, to *form* such minds, so that, without it, a people wants one of the chief means of educating or perfecting talent and genius. One of the great laws of our nature, and a law singularly important to social beings, is, that the intellect enlarges and strengthens itself by expressing worthily its best views. In this, as in other respects, it is more blessed to give than to receive. Superior minds are formed, not merely by solitary thought, but almost as much by communication. Great thoughts are never fully possessed, till he who has conceived them has given them fit utterance. One of the noblest and most invigorating labors of genius is, to clothe its conceptions in clear and glorious forms, to give them existence in other souls. Thus literature creates, as well as manifests, intellectual power, and, without it, the highest minds will never be summoned to the most invigorating action.

We doubt whether a man ever brings his faculties to bear with their whole force on a subject, until he writes upon it for the instruction or gratification of others. To place it clearly before others, he feels the necessity of viewing it more vividly himself. By attempting to seize his thoughts, and fix them in an enduring form, he finds them vague and unsatisfactory, to a degree which he did not suspect, and toils for a precision and harmony of views, of which he never before felt the need. He places his subject in new lights; submits it to a searching analysis; compares and connects with it his various knowledge; seeks for it new illustrations and analogies; weighs objections; and, through these processes, often arrives at higher truths than he at first aimed to illustrate. Dim conceptions grow bright. Glorious thoughts, which had darted as meteors through the mind, are arrested, and gradually shine with a sun-like splendor, with prolific energy, on the intellect and heart. It is one of the chief distinctions of a great mind, that it is prone to rush into twilight regions, and to catch faint glimmerings of distant and unbounded prospects; and nothing perhaps aids it more to pierce the shadows which surround it, than the labor to unfold to other minds the indistinct conceptions which have dawned on its own. Even where composition yields no such fruits, it is still a great intellectual help. It always favors comprehensive and systematical views. The laborious distribution of a great subject, so as to assign to each part or topic its just position and due proportion, is singularly fitted to give compass and persevering force of thought.

If we confine ourselves simply to the consideration of style, we shall have reason to think that a people among whom this is neglected, wants one important intellectual aid. In this, great power is exerted, and by exertion increased. To the multitude, indeed, language seems so natural an instrument, that to use it with clearness and energy seems no great effort. It is framed, they think, to the writer's hand, and so continually employed as to need little thought or skill. But in nothing is the creative power of a gifted writer seen more than in his style. True, his words may be found in the dictionary. But here they lie disjointed and dead. What a wonderful life does he breathe into them by compacting them into his sentences! Perhaps he uses no term which has not been hackneyed by ordinary writers; and yet with these vulgar materials what miracles does he achieve! What a world of thought does he condense into a phrase! By new combinations of common words, what delicate hues or what a blaze of light does he pour over his subject! Power of style depends very little on the structure or copiousness of the language which the writer of genius employs, but chiefly, if not wholly, on his own mind. The words, arranged in his dictionary, are no more fitted to depict his thoughts, than the block of marble in the sculptor's shop, to show forth the conceptions which are dawning in his mind. Both are inert materials. The power, which pervades them, comes from the soul; and the same creative energy is manifested in the production of a noble style, as in extracting beautiful forms from lifeless stone. How unfaithful, then, is a nation to its own intellect, in which grace and force of style receive no culture. * * *

We come now to our last, and what

we deem a weighty argument in favor of a native literature. We desire and would cherish it, because we hope from it important aids to the cause of truth and human nature. We believe, that a literature, springing up in this new soil, would bear new fruits, and, in some respects, more precious fruits, than are elsewhere produced. We know that our hopes may be set down to the account of that national vanity, which, with too much reason, is placed by foreigners among our besetting sins. But we speak from calm and deliberate conviction. We are inclined to believe, that, as a people, we occupy a position, from which the great subjects of literature may be viewed more justly than from those which most other nations hold. Undoubtedly we labor under disadvantages. We want the literary apparatus of Europe; her libraries, her universities, her learned institutions, her race of professed scholars, her spots consecrated by the memory of sages, and a thousand stirring associations which hover over ancient nurseries of learning. But the mind is not a local power. Its spring is within itself, and, under the inspiration of liberal and high feeling, it may attain and worthily express nobler truth than outward helps could reveal.

The great distinction of our country is, that we enjoy some peculiar advantages for understanding our own nature. Man is the great subject of literature, and juster and profounder views of man may be expected here, than elsewhere. In Europe, political and artificial distinctions have, more or less, triumphed over and obscured our common nature. In Europe, we meet kings, nobles, priests, peasants. How much rarer is it to meet *men;* by which we mean, human beings conscious of their own nature, and conscious of the utter worthlessness of all outward distinctions, compared with what is treasured up in their own souls. Man does not value himself as man. It is for his blood, his rank, or some artificial distinction, and not for the attributes of humanity, that he holds himself in respect. The institutions of the old world all tend to throw obscurity over what we most need to know, and that is, the worth and claims of a human being. We know that great improvements in this respect are going on abroad. Still the many are too often postponed to the few. The mass of men are regarded as instruments to work with, as materials to be shaped for the use of their superiors. That consciousness of our own nature, which contains, as a germ, all nobler thoughts, which teaches us at once self-respect and respect for others, and which binds us to God by filial sentiment and hope, this has been repressed, kept down by establishments founded in force; and literature, in all its departments, bears, we think, the traces of this inward degradation. We conceive that our position favors a juster and profounder estimate of human nature. We mean not to boast, but there are fewer obstructions to that moral consciousness, that consciousness of humanity, of which we have spoken. Man is not hidden from us by so many disguises as in the old world. The essential equality of all human beings, founded on the possession of a spiritual, progressive, immortal nature, is, we hope, better understood;

and nothing more than this single conviction is needed, to work the mightiest changes in every province of human life and of human thought.

We have stated what seems to us our most important distinction. But our position has other advantages. The mere circumstance of its being a new one, gives reason to hope for some new intellectual activity, some fresher views of nature and life. We are not borne down by the weight of antiquated institutions, time-hallowed abuses, and the remnants of feudal barbarism. The absence of a religious establishment is an immense gain, as far as originality of mind is in question; for an establishment, however advantageous in other respects, is, by its nature, hostile to discovery and progress. To keep the mind where it is, to fasten the notions of one age on all future time, is its aim and proper business; and if it happened, as has generally been the case, to grow up in an age of strife and passion, when, as history demonstrates, the church was overrun with error, it cannot but perpetuate darkness and mental bondage. Among us, intellect, though far from being free, has broken some of the chains of other countries, and is more likely, we conceive, to propose to itself its legitimate object, truth,—everlasting and universal truth.

We have no thought of speaking contemptuously of the literature of the old world. It is our daily nutriment. We feel our debt to be immense to the glorious company of pure and wise minds, which in foreign lands have bequeathed us in writing their choicest thoughts and holiest feelings. Still we feel, that all existing literature has been produced under influences, which have necessarily mixed with it much error and corruption; and that the whole of it ought to pass, and must pass, under rigorous review. For example, we think that the history of the human race is to be re-written. Men imbued with the prejudices which thrive under aristocracies and state religions, cannot understand it. Past ages, with their great events, and great men, are to undergo, we think, a new trial, and to yield new results. It is plain, that history is already viewed under new aspects, and we believe, that the true principles for studying and writing it are to be unfolded here, at least as rapidly as in other countries. It seems to us that in literature an immense work is yet to be done. The most interesting questions to mankind are yet in debate. Great principles are yet to be settled in criticism, in morals, in politics; and, above all, the true character of religion is to be rescued from the disguises and corruptions of ages. We want a reformation. We want a literature, in which genius will pay supreme, if not undivided homage, to truth and virtue; in which the childish admiration of what has been called greatness, will give place to a wise moral judgment; which will breathe reverence for the mind, and elevating thoughts of God. The part which this country is to bear in this great intellectual reform, we presume not to predict. We feel, however, that, if, true to itself, it will have the glory and happiness of giving new impulses to the human mind. This is our cherished hope. We should have no heart to encourage native literature, did we not hope that it would become instinct with a new spirit. We cannot admit the thought, that this country is to be only a repetition of the old world. We delight to believe that God, in the fulness of time, has brought a new continent to light, in order that the human mind should move here with a new freedom, should frame new social institutions, should explore new paths, and reap new harvests. We are accustomed to estimate nations by their creative energies, and we shall blush for our country, if, in circumstances so peculiar, original, and creative, it shall satisfy itself with a passive reception and mechanical reiteration of the thoughts of strangers. * * *

1830

WASHINGTON IRVING
(1783–1859)

KNICKERBOCKER'S HISTORY OF NEW YORK

Book II

[ARRIVAL OF THE DUTCH]

CHAPTER II

Containing an account of a mighty Ark which floated, under the protection of St. Nicholas, from Holland to Gibbet Island—the descent of the strange Animals therefrom—a great victory, and a description of the ancient village of Communipaw.

The delectable accounts given by the great Hudson, and Master Juet, of the country they had discovered, excited not a little talk and speculation among the good people of Holland.—Letters patent were granted by government to an association of merchants, called the West-India company, for the exclusive trade on Hudson river, on which they erected a trading house called Fort Aurania, or Orange, at present the superb and hospitable city of Albany. But I forbear to dwell on the various commercial and colonizing enterprizes which took place; among which was that of Mynheer Adrian Block, who discovered and gave a name to Block Island, since famous for its cheese—and shall barely confine myself to that, which gave birth to this renowned city.

It was some three or four years after the return of the immortal Hendrick, that a crew of honest, well meaning, copper headed, low dutch colonists set sail from the city of Amsterdam, for the shores of America. It is an irreparable loss to history, and a great proof of the darkness of the age, and the lamentable neglect of the noble art of book-making, since so industriously cultivated by knowing sea-captains, and spruce supercargoes, that an expedition so interesting and important in its results, should have been passed over in utter silence. To my great great grandfather am I again indebted, for the few facts, I am enabled to give concerning it—he having once more embarked for this country, with a full determination, as he said, of ending his days here—and of begetting a race of Knickerbockers, that should rise to be great men in the land.

The ship in which these illustrious adventurers set sail was called the *Goede Vrouw,* or Good Woman, in compliment to the wife of the President of the West India Company, who was allowed by every body (except her husband) to be a singularly sweet tempered lady, when not in liquor. It was in truth a gallant vessel, of the most approved dutch construction, and made by the ablest ship carpenters of Amsterdam, who it is well known, always model their ships after the fair forms of their country women. Accordingly it had one hundred feet in the keel, one hundred feet in the beam, and one hundred feet from the bottom of the stern post to the tafforel. Like the beauteous model, who was declared the greatest belle in Amsterdam, it was full in the bows, with a pair of enormous cat-heads, a copper bottom, and withal, a most prodigious poop!

The architect, who was somewhat of a religious man, far from decorating the ship with pagan idols, such as Jupiter, Neptune, or Hercules (which heathenish abominations, I have no doubt, occasion the misfortunes and shipwrack of many a noble vessel) he I say, on the contrary, did laudibly erect for a head, a goodly image of St. Nicholas, equipped with a low, broad brimmed hat, a huge pair of Flemish trunk hose, and a pipe that reached to the end of the bowsprit. Thus gallantly furnished, the staunch ship floated sideways, like a majestic goose, out of the harbour of the great city of Amsterdam, and all the bells, that were not otherwise engaged, rung a triple bob-major on the joyful occasion.

My great great grandfather remarks, that the voyage was uncommonly prosperous, for being under the especial care of the ever-revered St. Nicholas, the Goede Vrouw seemed to be endowed with qualities, unknown to common vessels. Thus she made as much lee-way as head-way, could get along very nearly as fast with the wind a-head, as when it was a-poop —and was particularly great in a calm; in consequence of which singular advantages, she made out to accomplish her voyage in a very few months, and came to anchor at the mouth of the Hudson, a little to the east of Gibbet Island.

Here lifting up their eyes, they beheld, on what is at present called the Jersey shore, a small Indian village, pleasantly embowered in a grove of spreading elms, and the natives all collected on the beach, gazing in stupid admiration at the Goede Vrouw. A boat was immediately dispatched to enter into a treaty with them, and approaching the shore, hailed them through a trumpet, in the most friendly terms; but so horribly confounded were these poor savages at the tremendous and uncouth sound of the low dutch language, that they one and all took to their heels, scampered over the Bergen hills, nor did they stop until they had buried themselves, head and ears, in the marshes, on the other side, where they all miserably perished to a man—and their bones being collected, and decently covered by the Tammany Society of that day, formed that singular mound, called *Rattle-snake-hill,* which rises out of the centre of the salt marshes, a little to the east of the Newark Causeway.

Animated by this unlooked-for victory our valiant heroes sprang ashore in triumph, took possession of the soil as conquerors in the name of their High Mightinesses the lords states general, and marching fearlessly forward, carried the village of *Communipaw* by storm—having nobody to withstand them, but some half a score of old squaws, and poppooses, whom they tortured to death with low dutch. On looking about them they were so transported with the excellencies of the place, that they had very little doubt, the blessed St. Nicholas, had guided them thither, as the very spot whereon to settle their colony. The softness of the soil was wonderfully adapted to the driving of piles; the swamps and marshes around them afforded ample opportunities for the constructing of dykes and dams; the shallowness of the shore was peculiarly favourable to the building of docks—in a word, this spot abounded with all the singular inconveniences, and aquatic obstacles, necessary for the foundation of a great dutch city. On making a faithful report therefore, to the crew of the Goede Vrouw, they one and all determined that this was the destined end of their voyage. Accordingly they descended from the Goede Vrouw, men women and children, in goodly groups, as did the animals of yore from the ark, and formed themselves into a thriving settlement, which they called by the Indian name *Communipaw*. * * *

1809

Book IV

[THE REIGN OF WILLIAM THE TESTY]

CHAPTER IV

Philosophical reflections on the folly of being happy in time of prosperity.—Sunday troubles on the southern Frontiers.—How William the Testy by his great learning had well nigh ruined the province through a Cabalistic word—As also the secret expeditions of Jan Jansen Alpenden, and his astonishing reward.

If we could but get a peep at the tally of dame Fortune, where, like a notable landlady, she regularly chalks up the debtor and creditor accounts of mankind, we should find that, upon the whole, good and evil are pretty nearly balanced in this world; and that though we may for a long while revel in the very lap of prosperity, the time will at length come, when we must ruefully pay off the reckoning. Fortune, in fact, is a pestilent shrew, and withal a most inexorable creditor; for though she may indulge her favourites in long credits, and overwhelm them with her favours; yet sooner or later, she brings up her arrears with the rigour of an experienced publican, and washes out her scores with their tears. "Since," says good old Bœtius in his consolations of philosophy, "since no man can retain her at his pleasure, and since her flight is so deeply lamented, what are her favors but sure prognostications of approaching trouble and calamity."

There is nothing that more moves my contempt at the stupidity and want of reflection in my fellow men, than to behold them rejoicing, and indulging in security and self confidence, in times of prosperity. To a wise man, who is blessed with the light of reason, those are the very moments of anxiety and apprehension; well knowing that according to the system of things, happiness is at best but transient—and that the higher a man is elevated by the capricious breath of fortune, the lower must be his proportionate depression. Whereas, he who is overwhelmed by calamity, has the less chance of encountering fresh disasters, as a man at the bottom of a hill, runs very little risk of breaking his neck by tumbling to the top.

This is the very essence of true wisdom, which consists in knowing when we ought to be miserable; and was discovered much about the same time with that invaluable secret, that "everything is vanity and vexation of spirit;" in consequence of which maxim your wise men have ever been the unhappiest of the human race; esteeming it as an infallible mark of genius to be distressed without reason—since any man may be miserable in time of misfortune, but it is the philosopher alone who can discover cause for grief in the very hour of prosperity.

According to the principle I have just advanced, we find that the colony of New Netherlands, which under the reign of the renowned Van Twiller, had flourished in such alarming and fatal serenity; is now paying for its former welfare, and discharging the enormous debt of comfort which it contracted. Foes harass it from different quarters; the city of New Amsterdam, while yet in its infancy is kept in constant alarm; and its valiant commander little William the Testy answers the vulgar, but expressive idea of "a man in a peck of troubles."

While busily engaged repelling his bitter enemies the Yankees, on one side, we find him suddenly molested in another quarter, and by other assailants. A vagrant colony of Swedes, under the conduct of Peter Minnewits, and professing allegiance to that redoubtable virago, Christina queen of Sweden; had settled themselves and erected a fort on south (or Delaware) river—within the boundaries, claimed by the Government of the New Netherlands. History is mute as to the particulars of their first landing, and their real pretensions to the soil, and this is the more to be lamented; as this same colony of Swedes will hereafter be found most materially to affect, not only the interests of the Nederlanders, but of the world at large!

In whatever manner therefore, this vagabond colony of Swedes first took possession of the country, it is certain that in 1638, they established a fort, and Minnewits, according to the off hand usage of his contemporaries, declared himself governor of all the adjacent country, under the name of the province of New Sweden. No sooner did this reach the ears of the choleric Wilhelmus, than, like a true spirited chieftain, he immediately broke into a violent rage, and calling together his council, belaboured the Swedes most lustily in the longest speech that had ever been heard in the colony, since the memorable dispute of Ten breeches and Tough breeches. Having thus given vent to the first ebullitions of his indignation, he had resort to his favourite measure of proclamation, and dispatched one, piping hot, in the first year of his reign, informing Peter Minnewits that the whole territory, bordering on the south river, had, time out of mind, been in possession of the Dutch colonists, having been "beset with forts, and sealed with their blood."

The latter sanguinary sentence, would convey an idea of direful war and bloodshed; were we not relieved by the information that it merely related to a fray, in which some half a dozen Dutchmen had been killed by the Indians, in their benevolent attempts to establish a colony and promote civilization. By this it will be seen that William Kieft, though a very small man, delighted in big expressions, and was much given to a praiseworthy figure in rhetoric, generally cultivated by your little great men, called hyperbole. A figure which has been found of infinite service among many of his class, and which has helped to swell the grandeur of many a mighty self-important, but windy chief magistrate. Nor can I resist in this place, from observing how much my beloved country is indebted to this same figure of hyperbole, for supporting certain of her greatest characters—statesmen, orators, civilians and divines; who by dint of big words, inflated periods, and windy doctrines, are kept afloat on the surface of society, as ignorant swimmers are buoyed up by blown bladders.

The proclamation against Minnewits concluded by ordering the self-dubbed governor, and his gang of Swedish adventurers, immediately to leave the country under penalty of the high displeasure, and inevitable vengeance of the puissant government of the Nieuw Nederlandts. This "strong measure," however, does not seem to have had a whit more effect than its predecessors, which had been thundered against the Yankees—the Swedes resolutely held on to the territory they had taken possession of—whereupon matters for the present remained in statu quo.

That Wilhelmus Kieft should put up with this insolent obstinacy in the Swedes, would appear incompatible with his valourous temperament; but we find that about this time the little man had his hands full; and what with one annoyance and another, was kept continually on the bounce.

There is a certain description of active legislators, who by shrewd management, contrive always to have a hundred irons on the anvil, every one of which must be immediately attended to; who consequently are ever full of temporary shifts and expedients, patching up the public welfare and cobbling the national affairs, so as to make nine holes where they mend one—stopping chinks and flaws with whatever comes first to hand, like the Yankees I have mentioned stuffing old clothes in broken windows. Of this class of statesmen was William the Testy—and had he only been blessed with powers equal to his zeal, or his zeal been disciplined by a little discretion, there is very little doubt that he would have made the greatest governor of his size on record—the renowned governor of the island of Barataria alone excepted.

The great defect of Wilhelmus Kieft's policy was, that though no man could be more ready to stand forth in an hour of emergency, yet he was so intent upon guarding the national pocket, that he suffered the enemy to break its head—in other words, whatever precaution for public safety he adopted, he was so intent upon rendering it cheap, that he invariably rendered it ineffectual. All this was a remote consequence of his profound education at the Hague—where having acquired a smattering of knowledge, he was ever after a great conner of indexes, continually dipping into books, without ever studying to the bottom of any subject; so that he had the scum of all kinds of authors fermenting in his pericranium. In some of these title page researches he unluckily stumbled over a grand political *cabalistic word,* which, with his customary facility he immediately incorporated into his great scheme of government, to the irretrievable injury and delusion of the honest province of Nieuw Nederlandts, and the eternal misleading, of all experimental rulers.

In vain have I pored over the Theurgia of the Chaldeans, the Cabala of the Jews, the Necromancy of the Arabians—The Magic of the Persians—the Hocus Pocus of the English, the Witch-craft of the Yankees, or the Pow-wowing of the Indians to discover where the little man first laid eyes on this terrible word. Neither the Sephir Jetzirah, that famous cabalistic volume, ascribed to the Patriarch Abraham; nor the pages of the Zohar, containing the mysteries of the cabala, recorded by the learned rabbi Simeon Jochaides, yield any light to my inquiries—Nor am I in the least benefited by my painful researches in the Shem-hamphorah of Benjamin, the wandering Jew, though it enabled Davidus Elm to make a ten days' journey, in twenty four hours. Neither can I perceive the slightest affinity in the Tetragrammaton, or sacred name of four letters, the profoundest word of the Hebrew Cabala; a mystery, sublime, ineffable and incommunicable—and the letters of which Jod-He-Van-He, having been stolen by the Pagans, constituted their great name Jao, or Jove. In short, in all my cabalistic, theurgic, necromantic, magical and astrological researches, from the Tetractys of Pythagoras, to the recondite works of Breslaw and mother Bunch, I have not discovered the least vestige of an origin of this word, nor have I discovered any word of sufficient potency to counteract it.

Not to keep my reader in any suspense, the word which had so wonderfully arrested the attention of William the Testy and which in German characters, had a particularly black and ominous aspect, on being fairly translated into the English is no other than *economy*—a talismanic term, which by constant use and frequent mention, has ceased to be formidable in our eyes, but which has as terrible potency as any in the arcana of necromancy.

When pronounced in a national assembly it has an immediate effect in closing the hearts, beclouding the intellects, drawing the purse strings and buttoning the breeches pockets of all philosophic legislators. Nor are its effects on the eye less wonderful. It produces a contraction of the retina, an obscurity of the christaline lens, a viscidity of the vitreous and an inspiration of the aqueous humours, an induration of the tunica sclerotica and a convexity of the cornea; insomuch that the organ of vision loses its strength and perspicuity, and the unfortunate patient becomes *myopes* or in plain English, purblind; perceiving only the amount of immediate expense without being able to look further, and regard it in connexion with the ultimate object to be effected.—"So that," to quote the words of the eloquent Burke, "a briar at his nose is of greater magnitude than an oak at five hundred yards distance." Such are its instantaneous operations, and the results are still more astonishing. By its magic influence seventy-fours, shrink into frigates—frigates into sloops, and sloops into gun-boats. As the defenceless fleet of Eneas, at the command of the protecting Venus, changed into sea nymphs and protected itself by diving; so the mighty navy of America, by the cabalistic word economy, dwindles into small craft, and shelters itself in a mill-pond!

This all potent word, which served as his touchstone in politics, at once explains the whole system of proclamations, protests, empty threats, windmills trumpeters, and paper war, carried on by Wilhelmus the Testy—and we may trace its operations in an armament which he fitted out in 1642 in a moment of great wrath; consisting of two sloops and *thirty* men, under the command of Mynheer Jan Jansen Alpendam, as admiral of the fleet, and commander in chief of the forces. This formidable expedition, which can only be paralleled by some of the daring cruizes of our infant navy, about the bay and up the Sound; was intended to drive the Marylanders from the Schuylkill, of which they had recently taken possession—and which was claimed as part of the province of New Nederlants—for it appears that at this time our infant colony was in that enviable state, so much coveted by ambitious nations, that is to say, the government had a vast extent of territory; part of which it enjoyed, and the greater part of which it had continually to quarrel about.

Admiral Jan Jansen Alpendam was a man of great mettle and prowess; and no way dismayed at the character of the enemy; who were represented as a gigantic gunpowder race of men, who lived on hoe cakes and bacon, drank mint juleps and brandy toddy, and were exceedingly expert at boxing, biting, gouging, tar and feathering, and a variety of other athletic accomplishments, which they had borrowed from their cousins german and prototypes the Virginians, to whom they have ever borne considerable resemblance—Notwithstanding all these alarming representations, the admiral entered the Schuylkill most undauntedly with his fleet, and arrived without disaster or opposition at the place of destination.

Here he attacked the enemy in a vigorous speech in low dutch, which the wary Kieft had previously put in his pocket; wherein he courteously commenced by calling them a pack of lazy, louting, dram drinking, cock fighting, horse racing, slave driving, tavern haunting, sabbath breaking, mulatto breeding upstarts—and concluded by ordering them to evacuate the country immediately—to which they most laconically replied in plain English (as was very natural for Swedes) "they'd see him d——d first."

Now this was a reply for which neither Jan Jansen Alpendam nor Wilhelmus Kieft had made any calculation—and finding himself totally unprepared to answer so terrible a rebuff with suitable hostility he concluded, like a most worthy admiral of a modern English expedition, that his wisest course was to return home and report progress. He accordingly sailed back to New Amsterdam, where he was received with great honours, and considered as a pattern for all commanders; having achieved a most hazardous enterprize, at a trifling expense of treasure, and without losing a single man to the state!—He was unanimously called the deliverer of his country; (an appellation liberally bestowed on all great men) his two sloops having done their duty, were laid up (or dry docked) in a cove now called the Albany Bason, where they quietly rotted in the mud; and to immortalize his name, they erected, by subscription, a magnificent shingle monument on the top of Flatten barrack Hill, which lasted three whole years; when it fell to pieces, and was burnt for fire-wood.

1809

Book VI

[THE VALIANT PETER STUYVESANT]

CHAPTER VII

Containing the most horrible battle ever recorded in poetry or prose; with the admirable exploits of Peter the Headstrong.

"Now had the Dutchman snatch'd a huge repast," and finding themselves wonderfully encouraged and animated thereby, prepared to take the field. Expectation, says a faithful matter of fact dutch poet, whose works were unfortunately destroyed in the conflagration of the Alexandrian library—Expectation now stood on stilts. The world forgot to turn round, or rather stood still, that it might witness the affray; like a fat round bellied alderman, watching the combat of two chivalric flies upon his jerkin. The eyes of all mankind, as usual in such cases, were turned upon Fort Christina. The sun, like a little man in a crowd, at a puppet shew, scampered about the heavens, popping his head here and there, and endeavouring to get a peep between the unmannerly clouds, that obtruded themselves in his way. The historians filled their ink-horns—the poets went without their dinners, either that they might buy paper and goosequills, or because they could not get any thing to eat—antiquity scowled sulkily out of its grave, to see itself outdone—while even posterity stood mute, gazing in gaping extacy of retrospection, on the eventful field!

The immortal deities, who whilome had seen service at the "affair" of Troy—now mounted their feather-bed clouds, and sailed over the plain, or mingled among the combatants in different disguises, all itching to have a finger in the pie. Jupiter sent off his thunderbolt to a noted coppersmiths, to have it furbished up for the direful occasion. Venus, swore by her chastity she'd patronize the Swedes, and in semblance of a blear eyed trull, paraded the battlements of Fort Christina, accompanied by Diana, as a serjeant's widow, of cracked reputation—The noted bully Mars, stuck two horse pistols into his belt, shouldered a rusty firelock, and gallantly swaggered at their elbow, as a drunken corporal—while Apollo trudged in their rear, as a bandy-legged fifer, playing most villainously out of tune.

On the other side, the ox-eyed Juno, who had won a pair of black eyes over night, in one of her curtain lectures with old Jupiter, displayed her haughty beauties on a baggage waggon—Minerva, as a brawny gin suttler, tucked up her skirts, brandished her fists, and swore most heroically, in exceeding bad dutch, (having but lately studied the language) by way of keeping up the spirits of the soldiers; while Vulcan halted as a club-footed blacksmith, lately promoted to be a captain of militia. All was silent horror, or bustling preparation; war reared his horrid front, gnashed loud his iron fangs, and shook his direful crest of bristling bayonets.

And now the mighty chieftains marshalled out their hosts. Here stood stout Risingh, firm as a thousand rocks——encrusted with stockades, and entrenched to the chin in mud batteries—His artillery consisting of two swivels and a carronade, loaded to the muzzle, the touch holes primed, and a whiskerd bombardier stationed at each, with lighted match in hand, waiting the word. His valiant infantry, that had never turned back upon an enemy (having never seen any before)—lined the breast work in grim array, each having his mustachios fiercely greased, and his hair pomatomed back, and queued so stiffly, that he grinned above the ramparts like a grizly death's head.

There came on the intrepid Hardkoppig Piet,—a second Bayard, without fear or reproach—his brows knit, his teeth clenched, his breath held hard, rushing on like ten thousand bellowing bulls of Bashan. His faithful squire Van Corlear, trudging valiantly at his heels, with his trumpet gorgeously bedecked with red and yellow ribbands, the remembrances of his fair mistresses at the Manhattoes. Then came waddling on his sturdy comrades, swarming like the myrmidons of Achilles. There were the Van Wycks and the Van Dycks and the Ten Eycks—the Van Nesses, the Van Tassels, the Van Grolls; the Van Hoesens, the Van Giesons, and the Van Blarcoms—the Van Warts, the Van Winkles, the Van Dams; the Van Pelts, the Van Rippers, and the Van Brunts. —There were the Van Horns, the Van Borsums, the Van Bunschotens; the Van Gelders, the Van Arsdales, and the Van Bummels—the Vander Belts, the Vander Hoofs, the Vander Voorts, the Vander Lyns, the Vander Pools and the Vander Spiegels.—There came the Hoffmans, the Hooglands, the Hoppers, the Cloppers, the Oothouts, the Quackenbosses, the Roerbacks, the Garrebrantzs, the Onderdonks, the Varra Vangers, the Schermerhorns, the Brinkerhoffs, the Bontecous, the Knickerbockers, the Hockstrassers, the Ten Breecheses and the Tough Breecheses, with a host more of valiant worthies, whose names are too crabbed to be written, or if they could be written, it would be impossible for man to utter—all fortified with a mighty dinner, and to use the words of a great Dutch poet

—"Brimful of wrath and cabbage!"

For an instant the mighty Peter paused in the midst of his career, and mounting on a rotten stump addressed his troops in eloquent low dutch, exhorting them to fight like *duyvels,* and assuring them that if they conquered, they should get plenty of booty—if they fell they should be allowed the unparalleled satisfaction, while dying, of reflecting that it was in the service of their country—and after they were dead, of seeing their names inscribed in the temple of renown and handed down, in company with all the other great men of the year, for the admiration of posterity.—Finally he swore to them, on the word of a governor (and they knew him too well to doubt it for a moment) that if he caught any mother's son of them looking pale, or playing craven, he'd curry his hide till he made him run out of it like a snake in spring time.—Then lugging out his direful snickersnee, he brandished it three times over his head, ordered Van Corlear to sound a tremendous charge, and shouting the word "St. Nicholas and the Manhattoes!" courageously dashed forwards. His warlike followers, who had employed the interval in lighting their pipes, instantly stuck them in their mouths, gave a furious puff, and charged gallantly, under cover of the smoke.

The Swedish garrison, ordered by the cunning Risingh not to fire until they could distinguish the whites of their assailants' eyes, stood in horrid silence on the covert-way; until the eager dutchmen had half ascended the glacis. Then did they pour into them such a tremendous volley, that the very hills quaked around, and were terrified even unto an incontinence of water, insomuch that certain springs burst forth from their sides, which continue to run unto the present day. Not a dutchman but would have bit the dust, beneath that dreadful fire, had not the protecting Minerva kindly taken care, that the Swedes should one and all, observe their usual custom of shutting their eyes and turning away their heads, at the moment of discharge.

But were not the muskets levelled in vain, for the balls, winged with unerring fate, went point blank into a flock of wild geese, which, like geese as they were, happened at that moment to be flying past——and brought down seventy dozen of them—which furnished a luxurious supper to the conquerors, being well seasoned and stuffed with onions.

Neither was the volley useless to the musqueteers, for the hostile wind, commissioned by the implacable Juno, carried the smoke and dust full in the faces of the dutchmen, and would inevitably have blinded them, had their eyes been open. The Swedes followed up their fire, by leaping the counterscarp, and falling tooth and nail upon the foe, with furious outcries. And now might be seen prodigies of valour, of which neither history nor song have ever recorded a parallel. Here was beheld the sturdy Stoffel Brinkerhoff brandishing his lusty quarter staff, like the terrible giant Blanderon his oak tree (for he scorned to carry any other weapon,) and drumming a horrific tune upon the heads of whole squadrons of Swedes. There were the crafty Van Courtlandts, posted at a distance, like the little Locrian archers of yore, and plying it most potently with the long bow, for which they were so justly renowned. At another place were collected on a rising knoll the valiant men of Sing-Sing, who assisted marvellously in the fight, by chaunting forth the great song of St. Nicholas. In a different part of the field might be seen the Van Grolls of Anthony's nose; but they were horribly perplexed in a defile between two little hills, by reason of the length of their noses. There were the Van Bunschotens of Nyack and Kakiat, so renowned for kicking with the left foot, but their skill availed them little at present, being short of wind in consequence of the hearty dinner they had eaten—and they would irretrievably have been put to rout, had they not been reinforced by a gallant corps of *Voltigeurs* composed of the Hoppers, who advanced to their assistance nimbly on one foot. At another place might you see the Van Arsdales, and the Van Blummels, who ever went together, gallantly pressing forward to bombard the fortress—but as to the Gardeniers of Hudson, they were absent from the battle, having been sent out on a marauding party, to lay waste the neighbouring watermelon patches. Nor must I omit to mention the incomparable atchievement of Antony Van Corlear, who, for a good quarter of an hour waged horrid fight with a little pursy Swedish drummer, whose hide he drummed most magnificently; and had he not come into the battle with no other weapon but his trumpet, would infallibly have put him to an untimely end.

But now the combat thickened—on came the mighty Jacobus Varra Vanger and the fighting men of the Wael Bogtig; after them thundered the Van Pelts of Esopus, together with the Van Rippers and the Van Brunts, bearing down all before them—then the Suy Dams and the Van Dams, pressing forward with many a blustering oath, at the head of the warriors of Hell-gate, clad in their thunder and lighting [*sic*] gaberdines; and lastly the standard bearers and body guards of Peter Stuyvesant, bearing the great beaver of the Manhattoes.

And now commenced the horrid din, the desperate struggle, the maddening ferocity, the frantic desperation, the confusion and self abandonment of war. Dutchman and Swede commingled, tugged, panted and blowed. The heavens were darkened with a tempest of missives. Carcasses, fire balls, smoke balls, stink balls and hand grenades, jostling each other, in the air. Bang! went the guns—whack! struck the broad swords—thump! went the cudgels—crash! went the musket stocks—blows—kicks—cuffs——scratches——black eyes and bloody noses swelling the horrors of the scene! Thick-thwack, cut and hack, helter-skelter, higgledy-piggledy, hurley-burley, head over heels, klip-klap, slag op slag, hob over bol, rough and tumble!——Dunder and blixum! swore the dutchmen, splitter and splutter! cried the Swedes—Storm the works! shouted Hard-koppig Piet—fire the mine! roared stout Risingh—Tantara-ra-ra! twang'd the trumpet of Antony Van Corlear—until all voice and sound became unintelligible—grunts of pain, yells of fury, and shouts of triumph commingling in one hideous clamour. The earth shook as if struck with a paralytic stroke—the trees shrunk aghast, and wilted at the sight—the rocks burrowed in the ground like rabbits, and even Christina creek turned from its course, and ran up a mountain in breathless terror!

Nothing, save the dullness of their weapons, the damaged condition of their powder, and the singular accident of one and all striking with the flat instead of the edge of their swords, could have prevented a most horrible carnage—As it was, the sweat prodigiously streaming, ran in rivers on the field, fortunately without drowning a soul, the combatants being to a man, expert swimmers, and furnished with cork jackets for the occasion—but many a valiant head was broken, many a stubborn rib belaboured, and many a broken winded hero drew short breath that day!

Long hung the contest doubtful, for though a heavy shower of rain, sent by the "cloud compelling Jove," in some measure cooled their ardour, as doth a bucket of water thrown on a group of fighting mastiffs, yet did they but pause for a moment, to return with tenfold fury to the charge, belabouring each other with black and bloody bruises. Just at this juncture was seen a vast and dense column of smoke, slowly rolling towards the scene of battle, which for a while made even the furious combatants to stay their arms in mute astonishment—but the wind for a moment dispersing the murky cloud, from the midst thereof emerged the flaunting banner of the immortal Michael Paw. This noble chieftain came fearlessly on, leading a solid phalanx of oyster-fed Pavonians, who had remained behind, partly as a *corps de reserve,* and partly to digest the enormous dinner they had eaten. These sturdy yeomen, nothing daunted, did trudge manfully forward, smoaking their pipes with outrageous vigour, so as to raise the awful cloud that has been mentioned; but marching exceedingly slow, being short of leg and of great rotundity in the belt.

And now the protecting deities of the army of New Amsterdam, having unthinkingly left the field and stept into a neighbouring tavern to refresh themselves with a pot of beer, a direful catastrophe had well nigh chanced to befall the Nederlanders. Scarcely had the myrmidons of the puissant Paw attained the front of battle, before the Swedes, instructed by the cunning Risingh, levelled a shower of blows, full at their tobacco pipes. Astounded at this unexpected assault, and totally discomfited at seeing their pipes broken by this "d——d nonsense," the valiant dutchmen fall in vast confusion—already they begin to fly—like a frightened drove of unwieldy Elephants they throw their own army in an uproar—bearing down a whole legion of little Hoppers—the sacred banner on which is blazoned the gigantic oyster of Communipaw is trampled in the dirt—The Swedes pluck up new spirits and pressing on their rear, apply their feet *a parte poste* with a vigour that prodigiously accelerates their motions—nor doth the renowned Paw himself, fail to receive divers grievous and intolerable visitations of shoe leather!

But what, Oh muse! was the rage of the gallant Peter, when from afar he saw his army yield? With a voice of thunder did he roar after his recreant warriors, putting up such a war whoop, as did the stern Achilles, when the Trojan troops were on the point of burning all his gunboats. The dreadful shout rung in loud echoes through the woods—trees toppled at the noise; bears, wolves, and panthers jumped out of their skins, in pure affright; several wild looking hills bounced clear over the Delaware; and all the small beer in Fort Christina, turned sour at the sound!

The men of the Manhattoes plucked up new courage when they heard their leader——or rather they dreaded his fierce displeasure, of which they stood in more awe than of all the Swedes in Christendom—but the daring Peter, not waiting for their aid, plunged sword in hand, into the thickest of the foe. Then did he display some such incredible atchievements, as have never been known since the miraculous days of the giants. Wherever he went the enemy shrunk before him—with fierce impetuosity he pushed forward, driving the Swedes, like dogs, into their own ditch—but as he fearlessly advanced, the foe, like rushing waves which close upon the scudding bark, thronged in his rear, and hung upon his flank with fearful peril. One desperate Swede, who had a mighty heart, almost as large as a pepper corn, drove his dastard sword full at the hero's heart. But the protecting power that watches over the safety of all great and good men turned aside the hostile blade, and directed it to a large side pocket, where reposed an enormous Iron Tobacco Box, endowed like the shield of Achilles with supernatural powers——no doubt in consequence of its being piously decorated with a portrait of the blessed St. Nicholas. Thus was the dreadful blow repelled, but not without occasioning to the great Peter a fearful loss of wind.

Like as a furious bear, when gored by worrying curs, turns fiercely round, shews his dread teeth, and springs upon the foe, so did our hero turn upon the treacherous Swede. The miserable varlet sought in flight, for safety——but the active Peter, seizing him by an immeasurable queue, that dangled from his head—"Ah Whoreson Caterpillar!" roared he, "here is what shall make dog's meat of thee!" So saying he whirled his trusty sword, and made a blow, that would have decapitated him had he, like Briareus, half a hundred heads, but that the pitying steel struck short and shaved the queue forever from his crown. At this very moment a cunning arquebusier, perched on the summit of a neighbouring mound, levelled his deadly instrument, and would have sent the gallant Stuyvesant, a wailing ghost to haunt the Stygian shore——had not the watchful Minerva, who had just stopped to tie up her garter, saw the great peril of her favourite chief, and dispatched old Boreas with his bellows; who in the very nick of time, just as the direful match descended to the pan, gave such a lucky blast, as blew all the priming from the touch hole!

Thus waged the horried fight——when the stout Risingh, surveying the battle from the top of a little ravelin, perceived his faithful troops, banged, beaten, and kicked by the invincible Peter. Language cannot describe the choler with which he was seized at the sight——he only stopped for a moment to disburthen himself of five thousand anathemas; and then drawing his immeasurable cheese toaster, straddled down to the field of combat, with some such thundering strides, as Jupiter is said by old Hesiod to have taken, when he strode down the spheres, to play off his sky rockets at the Titans.

No sooner did these two rival heroes come face to face, than they each made a prodigious start of fifty feet, (flemish measure) such as is made by your most experienced stage champions. Then did they regard each other for a moment, with bitter aspect, like two furious ram cats, on the very point of a clapper clawing. Then did they throw themselves in one attitude, then in another, striking their swords on the ground, first on the right side, then on the left, at last at it they went, like five hundred houses on fire! Words cannot tell the prodigies of strength and valour, displayed in this direful encounter—an encounter, compared to which the far famed battles of Ajax with Hector, of Eneas with Turnus, Orlando with Rodomont, Guy of Warwick with Colbrand the Dane, or of that renowned Welsh Knight Sir Owen of the mountains with the giant Guylon, were all gentle sports and holliday recreations. At length the valiant Peter watching his opportunity, aimed a fearful blow with the full intention of cleaving his adversary to the very chine; but Risingh nimbly raising his sword, warded it off so narrowly, that glancing on one side, it shaved away a huge canteen full of fourth proof brandy, that he always carried swung on one side; thence pursuing its tranchant course, it severed off a deep coat pocket, stored with bread and cheese—all which dainties rolling among the armies, occasioned a fearful scrambling between the Swedes and Dutchmen, and made the general battle to wax ten times more furious than ever.

Enraged to see his military stores thus wofully laid waste, the stout Risingh collecting all his forces, aimed a mighty blow, full at the hero's crest. In vain did his fierce little cocked hat oppose its course; the biting steel clove through the stubborn ram beaver, and would infallibly have cracked his gallant crown, but that the scull was of such adamantine hardness that the brittle weapon shivered into five and twenty pieces, shedding a thousand sparks, like beams of glory, round his grizly visage.

Stunned with the blow the valiant Peter reeled, turned up his eyes and beheld fifty thousand suns, besides moons and stars, dancing Scotch reels about the firmament—at length, missing his footing, by reason of his wooden leg, down he came, on his seat of honour, with a crash that shook the surrounding hills, and would infallibly have wracked his anatomical system, had he not been received into a cushion softer than velvet, which providence, or Minerva, or St. Nicholas, or some kindly cow, had benevolently prepared for his reception.

The furious Risingh, in despight of that noble maxim, cherished by all true knights, that "fair play is a jewel," hastened to take advantage of the hero's fall; but just as he was stooping to give the fatal blow, the ever vigilant Peter bestowed him a sturdy thwack over the sconce, with his wooden leg, that set some dozen chimes of bells ringing triple bob-majors in his cerebellum. The bewildered Swede staggered with the blow, and in the mean time the wary Peter, espying a pocket pistol lying hard by (which had dropped from the wallet of his faithful squire and trumpeter Van Corlear during his furious encounter with the drummer) discharged it full at the head of the reeling Risingh—Let not my reader mistake—it was not a murderous weapon loaded with powder and ball, but a little sturdy stone pottle, charged to the muzzle with a double dram of true dutch courage, which the knowing Van Corlear always carried about him by way of replenishing his valour. The hideous missive sung through the air, and true to its course, as was the mighty fragment of a rock, discharged at Hector by bully Ajax, encountered the huge head of the gigantic Swede with matchless violence.

This heaven directed blow decided the eventful battle. The ponderous pericranium of general Jan Risingh sunk upon his breast; his knees tottered under under [*sic*] him; a death-like torpor seized upon his Titan frame, and he tumbled to the earth with such tremendous violence, that old Pluto started with affright, lest he should have broken through the roof of his infernal palace.

His fall, like that of Goliah, was the signal for defeat and victory—The Swedes gave way—the Dutch pressed forward; the former took to their heels, the latter hotly pursued—Some entered with them, pell mell, through the sally port—others stormed the bastion and others scrambled over the curtain. Thus in a little while the impregnable fortress of Fort Christina, which like another Troy had stood a siege of full ten *hours*, was finally carried by assault, without the loss of a single man on either side. Victory in the likeness of a gigantic ox fly, sat perched upon the little cocked hat of the gallant Stuyvesant, and it was universally declared, by all the writers, whom he hired to write the history of his expedition, that on this memorable day he gained a sufficient quantity of glory to immortalize a dozen of the greatest heroes in Christendom!

1809

THE SKETCH BOOK OF GEOFFREY CRAYON, GENTN.

THE AUTHOR'S ACCOUNT OF HIMSELF

> I am of this mind with Homer, that as the snaile that crept out of her shel was turned eftsoons into a toad, and thereby was forced to make a stoole to sit on; so the traveller that stragleth from his owne country is in a short time transformed into so monstrous a shape, that he is faine to alter his mansion with his manners, and to live where he can, not where he would.
>
> —Lyly's *Euphues.*

I was always fond of visiting new scenes, and observing strange characters and manners. Even when a mere child I began my travels, and made many tours of discovery into foreign parts and unknown regions of my native city, to the frequent alarm of my parents, and the emolument of the town-crier. As I grew into boyhood, I extended the range of my observations. My holiday afternoons were spent in rambles about the surrounding country. I made myself familiar with all its places famous in history or fable. I knew every spot where a murder or robbery had been committed, or a ghost seen. I visited the neighboring villages, and added greatly to my stock of knowledge, by noting their habits and customs, and conversing with their sages and great men. I even journeyed one long summer's day to the summit of the most distant hill, whence I stretched my eye over many a mile of terra incognita, and was astonished to find how vast a globe I inhabited.

This rambling propensity strengthened with my years. Books of voyages and travels became my passion, and in devouring their contents, I neglected the regular exercises of the school. How wistfully would I wander about the pier-heads in fine weather, and watch the parting ships, bound to distant climes—with what longing eyes would I gaze after their lessening sails, and waft myself in imagination to the ends of the earth!

Further reading and thinking, though they brought this vague inclination into more reasonable bounds, only served to make it more decided. I visited various parts of my own country; and had I been merely a lover of fine scenery, I should have felt little desire to seek elsewhere its gratification: for on no country have the charms of nature been more prodigally lavished. Her mighty lakes, like oceans of liquid silver; her mountains, with their bright aerial tints, her valleys, teeming with wild fertility; her tremendous cataracts, thundering in their solitudes; her boundless plains, waving with spontaneous verdure; her broad deep rivers, rolling in solemn silence to the ocean; her trackless forests, where vegetation puts forth all its magnificence; her skies, kindling with the magic of summer clouds and glorious sunshine;—no, never need an American look beyond his own country for the sublime and beautiful of natural scenery.

But Europe held forth the charms of storied and poetical association. There were to be seen the masterpieces of art, the refinements of highly-cultivated society, the quaint peculiarities of ancient and local custom. My native country was full of youthful promise: Europe was rich in the accumulated treasures of age. Her very ruins told the history of times gone by, and every mouldering stone was a chronicle. I longed to wander over the scenes of renowned achievement—to tread, as it were, in the footsteps of antiquity—to loiter about the ruined castle—to meditate on the falling tower—to escape, in short, from the commonplace realities of the present, and lose myself among the shadowy grandeurs of the past.

I had, beside all this, an earnest desire to see the great men of the earth. We have, it is true, our great men in America: not a city but has an ample share of them. I have mingled among them in my time, and been almost withered by the shade into which they cast me; for there is nothing so baleful to a small man as the shade of a great one, particularly the great man of a city. But I was anxious to see the great men of Europe; for I had read in the works of various philosophers, that all animals degenerated in America, and man among the number. A great man of Europe, thought I, must therefore be as superior to a great man of America, as a peak of the Alps to a highland of the Hudson, and in this idea I was confirmed, by observing the comparative importance and swelling magnitude of many English travelers among us, who, I was assured, were very little people in their own country. I will visit this land of wonders, thought I, and see the gigantic race from which I am degenerated.

It has been either my good or evil lot to have my roving passion gratified. I have wandered through different countries, and witnessed many of the shifting scenes of life. I cannot say that I have studied them with the eye of a philosopher; but rather with the sauntering gaze with which humble lovers of the picturesque stroll from the window of one print-shop to another; caught sometimes by the delineations of beauty, sometimes by the distortions of caricature, and sometimes by the loveliness of landscape. As it is the fashion for modern tourists to travel pencil in hand, and bring home their port-folios filled with sketches, I am disposed to get up a few for the entertainment of my friends. When, however, I look over the hints and memorandums I have taken down for the purpose, my heart almost fails me at finding how my idle humor has led me aside from the great objects studied by every regular traveler who would make a book. I fear I shall give equal disappointment with an unlucky landscape painter, who had traveled on the continent, but, following the bent of his vagrant inclination, had sketched in nooks, and corners, and by-places. His sketch-book was accordingly crowded with cottages, and landscapes, and obscure ruins; but he had neglected to paint St. Peter's, or the Coliseum; the cascade of Terni, or the bay of Naples; and had not a single glacier or volcano in his whole collection.

1819–20

CHRISTMAS EVE

Saint Francis and Saint Benedight
Blesse this house from wicked wight;
From the night-mare and the goblin,
That is hight good fellow Robin;
Keep it from all evil spirits,
Fairies, weezels, rats, and ferrets:
From curfew time
To the next prime.

—CARTWRIGHT.

It was a brilliant moonlight night, but extremely cold; our chaise whirled rapidly over the frozen ground; the postboy smacked his whip incessantly, and a part of the time his horses were on a gallop. "He knows where he is going," said my companion, laughing, "and is eager to arrive in time for some of the merriment and good cheer of the servants' hall. My father, you must know, is a bigoted devotee of the old school, and prides himself upon keeping up something of old English hospitality. He is a tolerable specimen of what you will rarely meet with nowadays in its purity, the old English country gentleman; for our men of fortune spend so much of their time in town, and fashion is carried so much into the country, that the strong rich peculiarities of ancient rural life are almost polished away. My father, however, from early years, took honest Peacham * for his text-book, instead of Chesterfield; he determined in his own mind, that there was no condition more truly honorable and enviable than that of a country gentleman on his paternal lands, and therefore passes the whole of his time on his estate. He is a strenuous advocate for the revival of the old rural games and holiday observances, and is deeply

* Peacham's Complete Gentleman, 1622. [Author's note.]

read in the writers, ancient and modern, who have treated on the subject. Indeed his favorite range of reading is among the authors who flourished at least two centuries since; who, he insists, wrote and thought more like true Englishmen than any of their successors. He even regrets sometimes that he had not been born a few centuries earlier, when England was itself, and had its peculiar manners and customs. As he lives at some distance from the main road, in rather a lonely part of the country, without any rival gentry near him, he has that most enviable of all blessings to an Englishman, an opportunity of indulging the bent of his own humor without molestation. Being representative of the oldest family in the neighborhood, and a great part of the peasantry being his tenants, he is much looked up to, and, in general, is known simply by the appellation of 'The Squire;' a title which has been accorded to the head of the family since time immemorial. I think it best to give you these hints about my worthy old father, to prepare you for any eccentricities that might otherwise appear absurd."

We had passed for some time along the wall of a park, and at length the chaise stopped at the gate. It was in a heavy magnificent old style, of iron bars, fancifully wrought at top into flourishes and flowers. The huge square columns that supported the gate were surmounted by the family crest. Close adjoining was the porter's lodge, sheltered under dark fir-trees, and almost buried in shrubbery.

The postboy rang a large porter's bell, which resounded through the still frosty air, and was answered by the distant barking of dogs, with which the mansion-house seemed garrisoned. An old woman immediately appeared at the gate. As the moonlight fell strongly upon her, I had a full view of a little primitive dame, dressed very much in the antique taste, with a neat kerchief and stomacher, and her silver hair peeping from under a cap of snowy whiteness. She came courtesying forth, with many expressions of simple joy at seeing her young master. Her husband, it seemed, was up at the house keeping Christmas eve in the servants' hall; they could not do without him, as he was the best hand at a song and story in the household.

My friend proposed that we should alight and walk through the park to the hall, which was at no great distance, while the chaise should follow on. Our road wound through a noble avenue of trees, among the naked branches of which the moon glittered, as she rolled through the deep vault of a cloudless sky. The lawn beyond was sheeted with a slight covering of snow, which here and there sparkled as the moonbeams caught a frosty crystal; and at a distance might be seen a thin transparent vapor, stealing up from the low grounds and threatening gradually to shroud the landscape.

My companion looked around him with transport:—"How often," said he, "have I scampered up this avenue, on returning home on school vacations! How often have I played under these trees when a boy! I feel a degree of filial reverence for them, as we look up to those who have cherished us in childhood. My father was always scrupulous in exacting our holidays, and having us around him on family festivals. He used to direct and superintend our games with the strictness that some parents do the studies of their children. He was very particular that we should play the old English games according to their original form; and consulted old books for precedent and authority for every 'merrie disport;' yet I assure you there never was pedantry so delightful. It was the policy of the good old gentleman to make his children feel that home was the happiest place in the world; and I value this delicious home-feeling as one of the choicest gifts a parent could bestow."

We were interrupted by the clamor of a troop of dogs of all sorts and sizes, "mongrel, puppy, whelp and hound, and curs of low degree," that, disturbed by the ring of the porter's bell and the rattling of the chaise, came bounding, open-mouthed, across the lawn.

"——The little dogs and all,
Tray, Blanch, and Sweetheart, see, they bark at me!"

cried Bracebridge, laughing. At the sound of his voice, the bark was changed into a yelp of delight, and in a moment he was surrounded and almost overpowered by the caresses of the faithful animals.

We had now come in full view of the old family mansion, partly thrown in deep shadow, and partly lit up by the cold moonshine. It was an irregular building, of some magnitude, and seemed to be of the architecture of different periods. One wing was evidently very ancient, with heavy stone-shafted bow windows jutting out and overrun with ivy, from among the foliage of which the small diamond-shaped panes of glass glittered with the moonbeams. The rest of the house was in the French taste of Charles the Second's time, having been repaired and altered, as my friend told me, by one of his ancestors, who returned with that monarch at the Restoration. The grounds about the house were laid out in the old formal manner of artificial flower-beds, clipped shrubberies, raised terraces, and heavy stone balustrades, ornamented with urns, a leaden statue or two, and a jet of water. The old gentleman, I was told, was extremely careful to preserve this obsolete finery in all its original state. He admired this fashion in gardening; it had an air of magnificence, was courtly and noble, and befitting good old family style. The boasted imitation of nature in modern gardening had sprung up with modern republican notions, but did not suit a monarchical government; it smacked of the leveling system.—I could not help smiling at this introduction of politics into gardening, though I expressed some apprehension that I should find the old gentleman rather intolerant in his creed.—Frank assured me, however, that it was almost the only instance in which he had ever heard his father meddle with politics; and he believed that he had got this notion from a member of parliament who once passed a few weeks with him. The squire was glad of any argument to defend his clipped yew-trees and formal terraces, which had been occasionally attacked by modern landscape gardeners.

As we approached the house, we

heard the sound of music, and now and then a burst of laughter, from one end of the building. This, Bracebridge said, must proceed from the servants' hall, where a great deal of revelry was permitted, and even encouraged by the squire, throughout the twelve days of Christmas, provided every thing was done conformably to ancient usage. Here were kept up the old games of hoodman blind, shoe the wild mare, hot cockles, steal the white loaf, bob apple, and snap dragon: the Yule clog and Christmas candle were regularly burnt, and the mistletoe, with its white berries, hung up, to the imminent peril of all the pretty housemaids.*

So intent were the servants upon their sports that we had to ring repeatedly before we could make ourselves heard. On our arrival being announced, the squire came out to receive us, accompanied by his two other sons; one a young officer in the army, home on leave of absence; the other an Oxonian, just from the university. The squire was a fine, healthy-looking old gentleman, with silver hair curling lightly round an open florid countenance; in which the physiognomist, with the advantage, like myself, of a previous hint or two, might discover a singular mixture of whim and benevolence.

The family meeting was warm and affectionate: as the evening was far advanced, the squire would not permit us to change our travelling dresses, but ushered us at once to the company, which was assembled in a large old-fashioned hall. It was composed of different branches of a numerous family connection, where there were the usual proportion of old uncles and aunts, comfortable married dames, superannuated spinsters, blooming country cousins, half-fledged striplings, and bright-eyed boarding-school hoydens. They were variously occupied; some at a round game of cards; others conversing around the fireplace; at one end of the hall was a group of the young folks, some nearly grown up, others of a more tender and budding age, fully engrossed by a merry game; and a profusion of wooden horses, penny trumpets, and tattered dolls, about the floor, showed traces of a troop of little fairy beings, who, having frolicked through a happy day, had been carried off to slumber through a peaceful night.

While the mutual greetings were going on between young Bracebridge and his relatives, I had time to scan the apartment. I have called it a hall, for so it had certainly been in old times, and the squire had evidently endeavored to restore it to something of its primitive state. Over the heavy projecting fireplace was suspended a picture of a warrior in armor, standing by a white horse, and on the opposite wall hung a helmet, buckler, and lance. At one end an enormous pair of antlers were inserted in the wall, the branches serving as hooks on which to suspend hats, whips, and spurs; and in the corners of the apartment were fowling-pieces, fishing-rods, and other sporting implements. The furniture was of the cumbrous workmanship of

* The mistletoe is still hung up in farmhouses and kitchens at Christmas; and the young men have the privilege of kissing the girls under it, plucking each time a berry from the bush. When the berries are all plucked, the privilege ceases. [Author's note.]

former days, though some articles of modern convenience had been added, and the oaken floor had been carpeted; so that the whole presented an odd mixture of parlor and hall.

The grate had been removed from the wide overwhelming fireplace, to make way for a fire of wood, in the midst of which was an enormous log glowing and blazing, and sending forth a vast volume of light and heat: this I understood was the Yule clog, which the squire was particular in having brought in and illumined on a Christmas eve, according to ancient custom.*

It was really delightful to see the old squire seated in his hereditary elbow chair, by the hospitable fireside of his ancestors, and looking around him like the sun of a system, beaming warmth and gladness to every heart. Even the very dog that lay stretched at his feet, as he lazily shifted his position and yawned, would look fondly up in his master's face, wag his tail against the floor, and stretch himself again to sleep, confident of kindness and protection. There is an emanation from the heart in genuine hospitality which cannot be described, but is immediately felt, and puts the stranger at once at his ease. I had not been seated many minutes by the comfortable hearth of the worthy old cavalier, before I found myself as much at home as if I had been one of the family.

Supper was announced shortly after our arrival. It was served up in a spacious oaken chamber, the panels of which shone with wax, and around which were several family portraits decorated with holly and ivy. Besides the accustomed lights, two great wax tapers, called Christmas candles, wreathed with greens, were placed on a highly-polished beaufet among the family plate. The table was abundantly spread with substantial fare; but the squire made his supper of frumenty, a dish made of wheat cakes boiled in milk, with rich spices, being a standing dish in old times for Christmas eve. I was happy to find my old friend, minced pie, in the retinue of the feast; and finding him to be perfectly orthodox, and that I need not be ashamed of my predilection, I greeted him with all the warmth wherewith we usually greet an old and very genteel acquaintance.

The mirth of the company was greatly promoted by the humors of an eccentric personage whom Mr. Bracebridge always addressed with the quaint appellation of Master Simon. He was a tight brisk little man, with the air of an arrant old bachelor. His

* The *Yule clog* is a great log of wood, sometimes the root of a tree, brought into the house with great ceremony on Christmas eve, laid in the fireplace, and lighted with the brand of last year's clog. While it lasted, there was great drinking, singing, and telling of tales. Sometimes it was accompanied by Christmas candles; but in the cottages the only light was from the ruddy blaze of the great wood fire. The Yule clog was to burn all night; if it went out, it was considered a sign of ill luck. Herrick mentions it in one of his songs:—

Come bring with a noise,
My merrie, merrie boyes,
The Christmas log to the firing;
While my good dame, she
Bids ye all be free,
And drink to your hearts desiring.

The Yule clog is still burnt in many farmhouses and kitchens in England, particularly in the north, and there are several superstitions connected with it among the peasantry. If a squinting person come to the house while it is burning, or a person barefooted, it is considered an ill omen. The brand remaining from the Yule clog is carefully put away to light the next year's Christmas fire. [Author's note.]

nose was shaped like the bill of a parrot; his face slightly pitted with the small-pox, with a dry perpetual bloom on it, like a frost-bitten leaf in autumn. He had an eye of great quickness and vivacity, with a drollery and lurking waggery of expression that was irresistible. He was evidently the wit of the family, dealing very much in sly jokes and innuendoes with the ladies, and making infinite merriment by harping upon old themes; which, unfortunately, my ignorance of the family chronicles did not permit me to enjoy. It seemed to be his great delight during supper to keep a young girl next him in a continual agony of stifled laughter, in spite of her awe of the reproving looks of her mother, who sat opposite. Indeed, he was the idol of the younger part of the company, who laughed at every thing he said or did, and at every turn of his countenance; I could not wonder at it, for he must have been a miracle of accomplishments in their eyes. He could imitate Punch and Judy; make an old woman of his hand, with the assistance of a burnt cork and pocket-handkerchief; and cut an orange into such a ludicrous caricature, that the young folks were ready to die with laughing.

I was let briefly into his history by Frank Bracebridge. He was an old bachelor, of a small independent income, which, by careful management, was sufficient for all his wants. He revolved through the family system like a vagrant comet in its orbit; sometimes visiting one branch, and sometimes another quite remote; as is often the case with gentlemen of extensive connections and small fortunes in England. He had a chirping buoyant disposition, always enjoying the present moment; and his frequent change of scene and company prevented his acquiring those rusty unaccommodating habits, with which old bachelors are so uncharitably charged. He was a complete family chronicle, being versed in the genealogy, history, and intermarriages of the whole house of Bracebridge, which made him a great favorite with the old folks; he was a beau of all the elder ladies and superannuated spinsters, among whom he was habitually considered rather a young fellow, and he was master of the revels among the children; so that there was not a more popular being in the sphere in which he moved than Mr. Simon Bracebridge. Of late years, he had resided almost entirely with the squire, to whom he had become a factotum, and whom he particularly delighted by jumping with his humor in respect to old times, and by having a scrap of an old song to suit every occasion. We had presently a specimen of his last-mentioned talent, for no sooner was supper removed, and spiced wines and other beverages peculiar to the season introduced, than Master Simon was called on for a good old Christmas song. He bethought himself for a moment, and then, with a sparkle of the eye, and a voice that was by no means bad, excepting that it ran occasionally into a falsetto, like the notes of a split reed, he quavered forth a quaint old ditty.

Now Christmas is come,
Let us beat up the drum,
And call all our neighbors together,
And when they appear,

Let us make them such cheer,
As will keep out the wind and the weather, *etc.*

The supper had disposed every one to gayety, and an old harper was summoned from the servants' hall, where he had been strumming all the evening, and to all appearance comforting himself with some of the squire's home-brewed. He was a kind of hanger-on, I was told, of the establishment, and, though ostensibly a resident of the village, was oftener to be found in the squire's kitchen than his own home, the old gentleman being fond of the sound of "harp in hall."

The dance, like most dances after supper, was a merry one; some of the older folks joined in it, and the squire himself figured down several couple with a partner, with whom he affirmed he had danced at every Christmas for nearly half a century. Master Simon, who seemed to be a kind of connecting link between the old times and the new, and to be withal a little antiquated in the taste of his accomplishments, evidently piqued himself on his dancing, and was endeavoring to gain credit by the heel and toe, rigadoon, and other graces of the ancient school; but he had unluckily assorted himself with a little romping girl from boarding-school, who, by her wild vivacity, kept him continually on the stretch, and defeated all his sober attempts at elegance:—such are the ill-assorted matches to which antique gentlemen are unfortunately prone!

The young Oxonian, on the contrary, had led out one of his maiden aunts, on whom the rogue played a thousand little knaveries with impunity: he was full of practical jokes, and his delight was to tease his aunts and cousins; yet, like all madcap youngsters, he was a universal favorite among the women. The most interesting couple in the dance was the young officer and a ward of the squire's, a beautiful blushing girl of seventeen. From several shy glances which I had noticed in the course of the evening, I suspected there was a little kindness growing up between them; and, indeed, the young soldier was just the hero to captivate a romantic young girl. He was tall, slender, and handsome, and, like most young British officers of late years, had picked up various small accomplishments on the continent—he could talk French and Italian—draw landscapes, sing very tolerably—dance divinely; but, above all, he had been wounded at Waterloo:—what girl of seventeen, well read in poetry and romance, could resist such a mirror of chivalry and perfection!

The moment the dance was over, he caught up a guitar, and, lolling against the old marble fireplace, in an attitude which I am half inclined to suspect was studied, began the little French air of the Troubadour. The squire, however, exclaimed against having any thing on Christmas eve but good old English; upon which the young minstrel, casting up his eye for a moment, as if in an effort of memory, struck into another strain, and, with a charming air of gallantry, gave Herrick's "Night-Piece to Julia:"

Her eyes the glow-worm lend thee,
The shooting stars attend thee,
And the elves also,
Whose little eyes glow
Like the sparks of fire, befriend thee.

No Will o' the Wisp mislight thee;
Nor snake nor slow-worm bite thee;
But on, on thy way,
Not making a stay,
Since ghost there is none to affright thee.

Then let not the dark thee cumber;
What though the moon does slumber,
The stars of the night
Will lend thee their light,
Like tapers clear without number.

Then, Julia, let me woo thee,
Thus, thus to come unto me,
And when I shall meet
Thy silvery feet,
My soul I'll pour into thee.

The song might or might not have been intended in compliment to the fair Julia, for so I found his partner was called; she, however, was certainly unconscious of any such application, for she never looked at the singer, but kept her eyes cast upon the floor. Her face was suffused, it is true, with a beautiful blush, and there was a gentle heaving of the bosom, but all that was doubtless caused by the exercise of the dance; indeed, so great was her indifference, that she amused herself with plucking to pieces a choice bouquet of hothouse flowers, and by the time the song was concluded the nosegay lay in ruins on the floor.

The party now broke up for the night with the kind-hearted old custom of shaking hands. As I passed through the hall, on my way to my chamber, the dying embers of the Yule clog still sent forth a dusky glow, and had it not been the season when "no spirit dares stir abroad," I should have been half tempted to steal from my room at midnight, and peep whether the fairies might not be at their revels about the hearth.

My chamber was in the old part of the mansion, the ponderous furniture of which might have been fabricated in the days of the giants. The room was panelled with cornices of heavy carved work, in which flowers and grotesque faces were strangely intermingled; and a row of black-looking portraits stared mournfully at me from the walls. The bed was of rich, though faded damask, with a lofty tester, and stood in a niche opposite a bow window. I had scarcely got into bed when a strain of music seemed to break forth in the air just below the window. I listened, and found it proceeded from a band, which I concluded to be the waifs from some neighboring village. They went round the house, playing under the windows. I drew aside the curtains to hear them more distinctly. The moonbeams fell through the upper part of the casement, partially lighting up the antiquated apartment. The sounds, as they receded, became more soft and aerial, and seemed to accord with the quiet and moonlight. I listened and listened—they became more and more tender and remote, and, as they gradually died away, my head sunk upon the pillow, and I fell asleep.

1819–20

RIP VAN WINKLE

A POSTHUMOUS WRITING OF DIEDRICH KNICKERBOCKER

By Woden, God of Saxons,
From whence comes Wensday, that is Wodensday,
Truth is a thing that ever I will keep
Unto thylke day in which I creep into
My sepulchre——.

—Cartwright.

(The following Tale was found among the papers of the late Diedrich

Knickerbocker, an old gentleman of New-York, who was very curious in the Dutch history of the province, and the manners of the descendants from its primitive settlers. His historical researches, however, did not lie so much among books as among men; for the former are lamentably scanty on his favorite topics; whereas he found the old burghers, and still more their wives, rich in that legendary lore, so invaluable to true history. Whenever, therefore, he happened upon a genuine Dutch family, snugly shut up in its low-roofed farmhouse, under a spreading sycamore, he looked upon it as a little clasped volume of black-letter, and studied it with the zeal of a book-worm.

The result of all these researches was a history of the province during the reign of the Dutch governors, which he published some years since. There have been various opinions as to the literary character of his work, and, to tell the truth, it is not a whit better than it should be. Its chief merit is its scrupulous accuracy, which indeed was a little questioned on its first appearance, but has since been completely established; and it is now admitted into all historical collections, as a book of unquestionable authority.

The old gentleman died shortly after the publication of his work, and now that he is dead and gone, it cannot do much harm to his memory to say, that his time might have been much better employed in weightier labors. He, however, was apt to ride his hobby his own way; and though it did now and then kick up the dust a little in the eyes of his neighbors, and grieve the spirit of some friends, for whom he felt the truest deference and affection; yet his errors and follies are remembered "more in sorrow than in anger," and it begins to be suspected, that he never intended to injure or offend. But however his memory may be appreciated by critics, it is still held dear by many folks, whose good opinion is well worth having; particularly by certain biscuit-bakers, who have gone so far as to imprint his likeness on their new-year cakes; and have thus given him a chance for immortality, almost equal to the being stamped on a Waterloo Medal, or a Queen Anne's farthing.)

Whoever has made a voyage up the Hudson must remember the Kaatskill mountains. They are a dismembered branch of the great Appalachian family, and are seen away to the west of the river, swelling up to a noble height, and lording it over the surrounding country. Every change of season, every change of weather, indeed every hour of the day, produces some change in the magical hues and shapes of these mountains, and they are regarded by all the good wives, far and near, as perfect barometers. When the weather is fair and settled, they are clothed in blue and purple, and print their bold outlines on the clear evening sky; but, sometimes, when the rest of the landscape is cloudless, they will gather a hood of gray vapors about their summits, which, in the last rays of the setting sun, will glow and light up like a crown of glory.

At the foot of these fairy mountains, the voyager may have descried the light smoke curling up from a village, whose shingle-roofs gleam among the trees, just where the blue tints of the upland melt away into the fresh green of the nearer landscape. It is a little village of great antiquity, having been founded by some of the Dutch colonists, in the early times of the province, just about the beginning of the government of the good Peter Stuyvesant, (may he rest in peace!) and there were some of the houses of the original settlers standing within a few years, built of small yellow bricks brought from Holland, having latticed windows and gable fronts, surmounted with weather-cocks.

In that same village, and in one of these very houses (which, to tell the precise truth, was sadly time-worn and weather-beaten), there lived many years since, while the country was yet a province of Great Britain, a simple good-natured fellow of the name of Rip Van Winkle. He was a descendant of the Van Winkles who figured so gallantly in the chivalrous days of Peter Stuyvesant, and accompanied him to the siege of Fort Christina. He inherited, however, but little of the martial character of his ancestors. I have observed that he was a simple good-natured man; he was, moreover, a kind neighbor, and an obedient hen-pecked husband. Indeed, to the latter circumstance might be owing that meekness of spirit which gained him such universal popularity; for those men are most apt to be obsequious and conciliating abroad, who are under the discipline of shrews at home. Their tempers, doubtless, are rendered pliant and malleable in the fiery furnace of domestic tribulation; and a curtain lecture is worth all the sermons in the world for teaching the virtues of patience and long-suffering. A termagant wife may, therefore, in some respects, be considered a tolerable blessing; and if so, Rip Van Winkle was thrice blessed.

Certain it is, that he was a great favorite among all the good wives of the village, who, as usual, with the amiable sex, took his part in all family squabbles; and never failed, whenever they talked those matters over in their evening gossipings, to lay all the blame on Dame Van Winkle. The children of the village, too, would shout with joy whenever he approached. He assisted at their sports, made their playthings, taught them to fly kites and shoot marbles, and told them long stories of ghosts, witches, and Indians. Whenever he went dodging about the village, he was surrounded by a troop of them, hanging on his skirts, clambering on his back, and playing a thousand tricks on him with impunity; and not a dog would bark at him throughout the neighborhood.

The great error in Rip's composition was an insuperable aversion to all kinds of profitable labor. It could not be from the want of assiduity or perseverance; for he would sit on a wet rock, with a rod as long and heavy as a Tartar's lance, and fish all day without a murmur, even though he should not be encouraged by a single nibble. He would carry a fowling-piece on his shoulder for hours together, trudging through woods and swamps, and up hill and down dale, to shoot a few squirrels or wild pigeons. He would never refuse to assist a neighbor even in the roughest toil, and was a foremost man at all country frolics for husking Indian corn, or building stone-fences; the women of the village, too, used to employ him to run their errands, and to do such little odd jobs as their less obliging husbands would not do for them. In a word Rip was ready to attend to anybody's business but his own; but as to doing family duty, and keeping his farm in order, he found it impossible.

In fact, he declared it was of no use to work on his farm; it was the most pestilent little piece of ground in the whole country; every thing about it went wrong, and would go wrong, in spite of him. His fences were continually falling to pieces; his cow would either go astray, or get among the cabbages; weeds were sure to grow quicker in his fields than anywhere else; the rain always made a point of setting in just as he had some out-door work to do; so that though his patrimonial estate had dwindled away under his management, acre by acre, until there was little more left than a mere patch of Indian corn and potatoes, yet it was the worst conditioned farm in the neighborhood.

His children, too, were as ragged and wild as if they belonged to nobody. His son Rip, an urchin begotten in his own likeness, promised to inherit the habits, with the old clothes of his father. He was generally seen trooping like a colt at his mother's heels, equipped in a pair of his father's cast-off galligaskins, which he had much ado to hold up with one hand, as a fine lady does her train in bad weather.

Rip Van Winkle, however, was one of those happy mortals, of foolish, well-oiled dispositions, who take the world easy, eat white bread or brown, whichever can be got with least thought or trouble, and would rather starve on a penny than work for a pound. If left to himself, he would have whistled life away in perfect contentment; but his wife kept continually dinning in his ears about his idleness, his carelessness, and the ruin he was bringing on his family. Morning, noon, and night, her tongue was incessantly going, and everything he said or did was sure to produce a torrent of household eloquence. Rip had but one way of replying to all lectures of the kind, and that, by frequent use, had grown into a habit. He shrugged his shoulders, shook his head, cast up his eyes, but said nothing. This, however, always provoked a fresh volley from his wife; so that he was fain to draw off his forces, and take to the outside of the house—the only side which, in truth, belongs to a hen-pecked husband.

Rip's sole domestic adherent was his dog Wolf, who was as much henpecked as his master; for Dame Van Winkle regarded them as companions in idleness, and even looked upon Wolf with an evil eye, as the cause of his master's going so often astray. True it is, in all points of spirit befitting an honorable dog, he was as courageous an animal as ever scoured the woods—but what courage can withstand the ever-during and all-besetting terrors of a woman's tongue? The moment Wolf entered the house his crest fell, his tail drooped to the ground, or curled between his legs, he sneaked about with a gallows air, casting many a sidelong glance at Dame Van Winkle, and at the least flourish of a broomstick or ladle, he would fly to the door with yelping precipitation.

Times grew worse and worse with Rip Van Winkle as years of matrimony rolled on; a tart temper never mellows with age, and a sharp tongue is the only edged tool that grows keener with constant use. For a long while he used to console himself, when driven from home, by frequenting a kind of perpetual club of the sages, philosophers, and other idle personages of the village; which held its sessions on a bench before a small inn, designated by a rubicund portrait of His Majesty George the Third. Here they used to sit in the shade through a long lazy summer's day, talking listlessly over village gossip, or telling endless sleepy stories about nothing. But it would have been worth any statesman's money to have heard the profound discussions that sometimes took place, when by chance an old newspaper fell into their hands from some passing traveler. How solemnly they would listen to the contents, as drawled out by Derrick Van Bummel, the schoolmaster, a dapper learned little man, who was not to be daunted by the most gigantic word in the dictionary; and how sagely they would deliberate upon public events some months after they had taken place.

The opinions of this junto were completely controlled by Nicholas Vedder, a patriarch of the village, and landlord of the inn, at the door of which he took his seat from morning till night, just moving sufficiently to avoid the sun and keep in the shade of a large tree; so that the neighbors could tell the hour by his movements as accurately as by a sun-dial. It is true he was rarely heard to speak, but smoked his pipe incessantly. His adherents, however (for every great man has his adherents), perfectly understood him, and knew how to gather his opinions. When any thing that was read or related displeased him, he was observed to smoke his pipe vehemently, and to send forth short, frequent and angry puffs; but when pleased, he would inhale the smoke slowly and tranquilly, and emit it in light and placid clouds; and sometimes, taking the pipe from his mouth, and letting the fragrant vapor curl about his nose, would gravely nod his head in token of perfect approbation.

From even this strong-hold the unlucky Rip was at length routed by his termagant wife, who would suddenly break in upon the tranquillity of the assemblage and call the members all to naught; nor was that august personage, Nicholas Vedder himself, sacred from the daring tongue of this terrible virago, who charged him outright with encouraging her husband in habits of idleness.

Poor Rip was at last reduced almost to despair; and his only alternative, to escape from the labor of the farm and clamor of his wife, was to take gun in hand and stroll away into the woods. Here he would sometimes seat himself at the foot of a tree, and share the contents of his wallet with Wolf, with whom he sympathized as a fellow-sufferer in persecution. "Poor Wolf," he would say, "thy mistress leads thee a dog's life of it; but never mind, my lad, whilst I live thou shalt never want a friend to stand by thee!" Wolf would wag his tail, look wistfully in his master's face, and if dogs can feel pity, I verily believe he reciprocated the sentiment with all his heart.

In a long ramble of the kind on a fine autumnal day, Rip had unconsciously scrambled to one of the highest parts of the Kaatskill mountains. He was after his favorite sport of squirrel shooting, and the still solitudes had echoed and re-echoed with the reports of his gun. Panting and fatigued, he threw himself, late in the afternoon, on a green knoll, covered with mountain herbage, that crowned the brow of a precipice. From an opening between the trees he could overlook all the lower country for many a mile of rich woodland. He saw at a distance the lordly Hudson, far, far below him, moving on its silent but majestic course, with the reflection of a purple cloud, or the sail of a lagging bark, here and there sleeping on its glassy bosom, and at last losing itself in the blue highlands.

On the other side he looked down into a deep mountain glen, wild, lonely, and shagged, the bottom filled with fragments from the impending cliffs, and scarcely lighted by the reflected rays of the setting sun. For some time Rip lay musing on the scene; evening was gradually advancing; the mountains began to throw their long blue shadows over the valleys; he saw that it would be dark long before he could reach the village, and he heaved a heavy sigh when he thought of encountering the terrors of Dame Van Winkle.

As he was about to descend, he heard a voice from a distance, hallooing, "Rip Van Winkle! Rip Van Winkle!" He looked round, but could see nothing but a crow winging its solitary flight across the mountain. He thought his fancy must have deceived him, and turned again to descend, when he heard the same cry ring through the still evening air; "Rip Van Winkle! Rip Van Winkle!"—at the same time Wolf bristled up his back, and giving a low growl, skulked to his master's side, looking fearfully down into the glen. Rip now felt a vague apprehension stealing over him; he looked anxiously in the same direction, and perceived a strange figure slowly toiling up the rocks, and bending under the weight of something he carried on his back. He was surprised to see any human being in this lonely and unfrequented place, but supposing it to be some one of the neighborhood in need of his assistance, he hastened down to yield it.

On nearer approach he was still more surprised at the singularity of the stranger's appearance. He was a short square-built old fellow, with thick bushy hair, and a grizzled beard. His dress was of the antique Dutch fashion—a cloth jerkin strapped round the waist—several pair of breeches, the outer one of ample volume, decorated with rows of buttons down the sides, and bunches at the knees. He bore on his shoulder a stout keg, that seemed full of liquor, and made signs for Rip to approach and assist him with the load. Though rather shy and distrustful of this new acquaintance, Rip complied with his usual alacrity; and mutually relieving each other, they clambered up a narrow gully, apparently the dry bed of a mountain torrent. As they ascended, Rip every now and then heard long rolling peals, like distant thunder, that seemed to issue out of a deep ravine, or rather cleft, between lofty rocks, toward which their rugged path conducted. He paused for an instant, but supposing it to be the muttering of one of those transient thunder-showers which often take place in mountain heights, he proceeded. Passing through the ravine, they came to a hollow, like a small amphitheatre, surrounded by perpendicular precipices, over the brinks of which impending trees shot their branches, so that you only caught glimpses of the azure sky and the bright evening cloud. During the whole time Rip and his companion had labored on in silence; for though the former marvelled greatly what could be the object of carrying a keg of liquor up this wild mountain, yet there was something strange and incomprehensible about the unknown, that inspired awe and checked familiarity.

On entering the amphitheatre, new objects of wonder presented themselves. On a level spot in the centre was a company of odd-looking personages playing at nine-pins. They were dressed in a quaint outlandish fashion; some wore short doublets, others jerkins, with long knives in their belts, and most of them had enormous breeches, of similar style with that of the guide's. Their visages, too, were peculiar: one had a large beard, broad face, and small piggish eyes: the face of another seemed to consist entirely of nose, and was surmounted by a white sugar-loaf hat set off with a little red cock's tail. They all had beards, of various shapes and colors. There was one who seemed to be the commander. He was a stout old gentleman, with a weather-beaten countenance; he wore a laced doublet, broad belt and hanger, high-crowned hat and feather, red stockings, and high-heeled shoes, with roses in them. The whole group reminded Rip of the figures in an old Flemish painting, in the parlor of Dominie Van Shaick, the village parson, and which had been brought over from Holland at the time of the settlement.

What seemed particularly odd to Rip was, that though these folks were evidently amusing themselves, yet they maintained the gravest faces, the most mysterious silence, and were, withal, the most melancholy party of pleasure he had ever witnessed. Nothing interrupted the stillness of the scene but the noise of the balls, which, whenever they were rolled, echoed along the mountains like rumbling peals of thunder.

As Rip and his companion approached them, they suddenly desisted from their play, and stared at him with such fixed statue-like gaze, and such strange, uncouth, lack-lustre countenances, that his heart turned within him, and his knees smote together. His companion now emptied the contents of the keg into large flagons, and made signs to him to wait upon the company. He obeyed with fear and trembling; they quaffed the liquor in profound silence, and then returned to their game.

By degrees Rip's awe and apprehension subsided. He even ventured, when no eye was fixed upon him, to taste the beverage, which he found had much of the flavor of excellent Hollands. He was naturally a thirsty soul, and was soon tempted to repeat the draught. One taste provoked another; and he reiterated his visits to the flagon so often that at length his senses were overpowered, his eyes swam in his head, his head gradually declined, and he fell into a deep sleep.

On waking, he found himself on the green knoll whence he had first seen the old man of the glen. He rubbed his eyes—it was a bright sunny morning. The birds were hopping and twittering among the bushes, and the eagle was wheeling aloft, and breasting the pure mountain breeze. "Surely," thought Rip, "I have not slept here all night." He recalled the occurrences before he fell asleep. The strange man with a keg of liquor—the mountain ravine—the wild retreat among the rocks—the woe-begone party at nine-pins—the flagon—"Oh! that flagon! that wicked flagon!" thought Rip—"what excuse shall I make to Dame Van Winkle!"

He looked round for his gun, but in place of the clean, well-oiled fowling-piece, he found an old firelock lying by him, the barrel incrusted with rust, the lock falling off, and the stock worm-eaten. He now suspected that the grave roysters of the mountain had put a trick upon him, and, having dosed him with liquor, had robbed him of his gun. Wolf, too, had disappeared, but he might have strayed away after a squirrel or partridge. He whistled after him and shouted his name, but all in vain; the echoes repeated his whistle and shout, but no dog was to be seen.

He determined to revisit the scene of the last evening's gambol, and if he met with any of the party, to demand his dog and gun. As he rose to walk, he found himself stiff in the joints, and wanting in his usual activity. "These mountain beds do not agree with me," thought Rip, "and if this frolic should lay me up with a fit of the rheumatism, I shall have a blessed time with Dame Van Winkle." With some difficulty he got down into the glen: he found the gully up which he and his companion had ascended the preceding evening; but to his astonishment a mountain stream was now foaming down it, leaping from rock to rock, and filling the glen with babbling murmurs. He, however, made shift to scramble up its sides, working his toilsome way through thickets of birch, sassafras, and witch-hazel, and sometimes tripped up or entangled by the wild grapevines that twisted their coils or tendrils from tree to tree, and spread a kind of network in his path.

At length he reached to where the ravine had opened through the cliffs to the amphitheatre; but no traces of such opening remained. The rocks presented a high impenetrable wall over which the torrent came tumbling in a sheet of feathery foam, and fell into a broad deep basin, black from the shadows of the surrounding forest. Here, then, poor Rip was brought to a stand. He again called and whistled after his dog; he was only answered by the cawing of a flock of idle crows, sporting high in air about a dry tree that overhung a sunny precipice; and who, secure in their elevation, seemed to look down and scoff at the poor man's perplexities. What was to be done? the morning was passing away, and Rip felt famished for want of his breakfast. He grieved to give up his dog and gun; he dreaded to meet his wife; but it would not do to starve among the mountains. He shook his head, shouldered the rusty firelock, and, with a heart full of trouble and anxiety, turned his steps homeward.

As he approached the village he met a number of people, but none whom he knew, which somewhat surprised him, for he had thought himself acquainted with every one in the country round. Their dress, too, was of a different fashion from that to which he was accustomed. They all stared at him with equal marks of surprise, and whenever they cast their eyes upon him, invariably stroked their chins. The constant recurrence of this gesture induced Rip, involuntarily, to do the same, when, to his astonishment, he found his beard had grown a foot long!

He had now entered the skirts of the village. A troop of strange children ran at his heels, hooting after him, and pointing at his gray beard. The dogs, too, not one of which he recognized for an old acquaintance, barked at him as he passed. The very village was altered; it was larger and more populous. There were rows of houses which he had never seen before, and those which had been his familiar haunts had disappeared. Strange names were over the doors—strange faces at the windows—every thing was strange. His mind now misgave him; he began to doubt whether both he and the world around him were not bewitched. Surely this was his native village, which he had left but the day before. There stood the Kaatskill mountains—there ran the silver Hudson at a distance—there was every hill and dale precisely as it had always been—Rip was sorely perplexed—"That flagon last night," thought he, "has addled my poor head sadly!"

It was with some difficulty that he found the way to his own house, which he approached with silent awe, expecting every moment to hear the shrill voice of Dame Van Winkle. He found the house gone to decay—the roof fallen in, the windows shattered, and the doors off the hinges. A half-starved dog that looked like Wolf was skulking about it. Rip called him by name, but the cur snarled, showed his teeth, and passed on. This was an unkind cut indeed—"My very dog," sighed poor Rip, "has forgotten me!"

He entered the house, which, to tell the truth, Dame Van Winkle had always kept in neat order. It was empty, forlorn, and apparently abandoned. This desolateness overcame all his connubial fears—he called loudly for his wife and children—the lonely chambers rang for a moment with his voice, and then all again was silence. He now hurried forth, and hastened to his old resort, the village inn—but it too was gone. A large rickety wooden building stood in its place, with great gaping windows, some of them broken and mended with old hats and petticoats, and over the door was painted, "the Union Hotel, by Jonathan Doolittle." Instead of the great tree that used to shelter the quiet little Dutch inn of yore, there now was reared a tall naked pole, with something on the top that looked like a red night-cap, and from it was fluttering a flag, on which was a singular assemblage of stars and stripes—all this was strange and incomprehensible. He recognized on the sign, however, the ruby face of King George, under which he had smoked so many a peaceful pipe; but even this was singularly metamorphosed. The red coat was changed for one of blue and buff, a sword was held in the hand instead of a sceptre, the head was decorated with a cocked hat, and underneath was painted in large characters, GENERAL WASHINGTON.

There was, as usual, a crowd of folk

about the door, but none that Rip recollected. The very character of the people seemed changed. There was a busy, bustling, disputatious tone about it, instead of the accustomed phlegm and drowsy tranquillity. He looked in vain for the sage Nicholas Vedder, with his broad face, double chin, and fair long pipe, uttering clouds of tobacco-smoke instead of idle speeches; or Van Bummel, the schoolmaster, doling forth the contents of an ancient newspaper. In place of these, a lean, bilious-looking fellow, with his pockets full of handbills, was haranguing vehemently about rights of citizens—elections—members of congress—liberty—Bunker's Hill—heroes of seventy-six—and other words, which were a perfect Babylonish jargon to the bewildered Van Winkle.

The appearance of Rip, with his long grizzled beard, his rusty fowling-piece, his uncouth dress, and an army of women and children at his heels, soon attracted the attention of the tavern politicians. They crowded round him, eyeing him from head to foot with great curiosity. The orator bustled up to him, and, drawing him partly aside, inquired "on which side he voted?" Rip stared in vacant stupidity. Another short but busy little fellow pulled him by the arm, and, rising on tiptoe, inquired in his ear, "Whether he was Federal or Democrat?" Rip was equally at a loss to comprehend the question; when a knowing, self-important old gentleman, in a sharp cocked hat, made his way through the crowd, putting them to the right and left with his elbows as he passed, and planting himself before Van Winkle, with one arm akimbo, the other resting on his cane, his keen eyes and sharp hat penetrating, as it were, into his very soul, demanded in an austere tone, "what brought him to the election with a gun on his shoulder, and a mob at his heels, and whether he meant to breed a riot in the village?"—"Alas! gentlemen," cried Rip, somewhat dismayed, "I am a poor quiet man, a native of the place, and a loyal subject of the king, God bless him!"

Here a general shout burst from the by-standers—"A tory! a tory! a spy! a refugee! hustle him! away with him!" It was with great difficulty that the self-important man in the cocked hat restored order; and, having assumed a tenfold austerity of brow, demanded again of the unknown culprit, what he came there for, and whom he was seeking? The poor man humbly assured him that he meant no harm, but merely came there in search of some of his neighbors, who used to keep about the tavern.

"Well — who are they? — name them."

Rip bethought himself a moment, and inquired, "Where's Nicholas Vedder?"

There was a silence for a little while, when an old man replied, in a thin piping voice, "Nicholas Vedder! why, he is dead and gone these eighteen years! There was a wooden tombstone in the church-yard that used to tell all about him, but that's rotten and gone too."

"Where's Brom Dutcher?"

"Oh, he went off to the army in the beginning of the war; some say he was killed at the storming of Stony Point—others say he was drowned in a squall at the foot of Antony's Nose.

I don't know—he never came back again."

"Where's Van Bummel, the schoolmaster?"

"He went off to the wars too, was a great militia general, and is now in congress."

Rip's heart died away at hearing of these sad changes in his home and friends, and finding himself thus alone in the world. Every answer puzzled him too, by treating of such enormous lapses of time, and of matters which he could not understand: war—congress—Stony Point;—he had no courage to ask after any more friends, but cried out in despair, "Does nobody here know Rip Van Winkle?"

"Oh, Rip Van Winkle!" exclaimed two or three, "Oh, to be sure! that's Rip Van Winkle yonder, leaning against the tree."

Rip looked, and beheld a precise counterpart of himself, as he went up the mountain: apparently as lazy, and certainly as ragged. The poor fellow was now completely confounded. He doubted his own identity, and whether he was himself or another man. In the midst of his bewilderment, the man in the cocked hat demanded who he was, and what was his name?

"God knows," exclaimed he, at his wit's end; "I'm not myself—I'm somebody else—that's me yonder—no—that's somebody else got into my shoes—I was myself last night, but I fell asleep on the mountain, and they've changed my gun, and every thing's changed, and I'm changed, and I can't tell what's my name, or who I am!"

The by-standers began now to look at each other, nod, wink significantly, and tap their fingers against their foreheads. There was a whisper, also, about securing the gun, and keeping the old fellow from doing mischief, at the very suggestion of which the self-important man in the cocked hat retired with some precipitation. At this critical moment a fresh comely woman pressed through the throng to get a peep at the gray-bearded man. She had a chubby child in her arms, which, frightened at his looks, began to cry. "Hush, Rip," cried she, "hush, you little fool; the old man won't hurt you." The name of the child, the air of the mother, the tone of her voice, all awakened a train of recollections in his mind. "What is your name, my good woman?" asked he.

"Judith Gardenier."

"And your father's name?"

"Ah, poor man, Rip Van Winkle was his name, but it's twenty years since he went away from home with his gun, and never has been heard of since—his dog came home without him; but whether he shot himself, or was carried away by the Indians, nobody can tell. I was then but a little girl."

Rip had but one question more to ask; but he put it with a faltering voice:

"Where's your mother?"

"Oh, she too had died but a short time since; she broke a blood-vessel in a fit of passion at a New-England peddler."

There was a drop of comfort, at least, in this intelligence. The honest man could contain himself no longer. He caught his daughter and her child in his arms. "I am your father!" cried he—"Young Rip Van Winkle once—old Rip Van Winkle now!—

Does nobody know poor Rip Van Winkle?"

All stood amazed, until an old woman, tottering out from among the crowd, put her hand to her brow, and peering under it in his face for a moment, exclaimed, "Sure enough! it is Rip Van Winkle—it is himself! Welcome home again, old neighbor—Why, where have you been these twenty long years?"

Rip's story was soon told, for the whole twenty years had been to him but as one night. The neighbors stared when they heard it; some were seen to wink at each other, and put their tongues in their cheeks: and the self-important man in the cocked hat, who, when the alarm was over, had returned to the field, screwed down the corners of his mouth, and shook his head—upon which there was a general shaking of the head throughout the assemblage.

It was determined, however, to take the opinion of old Peter Vanderdonk, who was seen slowly advancing up the road. He was a descendant of the historian of that name, who wrote one of the earliest accounts of the province. Peter was the most ancient inhabitant of the village, and well versed in all the wonderful events and traditions of the neighborhood. He recollected Rip at once, and corroborated his story in the most satisfactory manner. He assured the company that it was a fact, handed down from his ancestor the historian, that the Kaatskill mountains had always been haunted by strange beings. That it was affirmed that the great Hendrick Hudson, the first discoverer of the river and country, kept a kind of vigil there every twenty years, with his crew of the Half-moon; being permitted in this way to revisit the scenes of his enterprise, and keep a guardian eye upon the river, and the great city called by his name. That his father had once seen them in their old Dutch dresses playing at nine-pins in a hollow of the mountain; and that he himself had heard, one summer afternoon, the sound of their balls, like distant peals of thunder.

To make a long story short, the company broke up, and returned to the more important concerns of the election. Rip's daughter took him home to live with her; she had a snug, well-furnished house, and a stout cheery farmer for a husband, whom Rip recollected for one of the urchins that used to climb upon his back. As to Rip's son and heir, who was the ditto of himself, seen leaning against the tree, he was employed to work on the farm; but evinced an hereditary disposition to attend to any thing else but his business.

Rip now resumed his old walks and habits; he soon found many of his former cronies, though all rather the worse for the wear and tear of time; and preferred making friends among the rising generation, with whom he soon grew into great favor.

Having nothing to do at home, and being arrived at that happy age when a man can be idle with impunity, he took his place once more on the bench at the inn door, and was reverenced as one of the patriarchs of the village, and a chronicle of the old times "before the war." It was some time before he could get into the regular track of gossip, or could be made to comprehend the strange events that had taken place during his torpor.

How that there had been a revolutionary war—that the country had thrown off the yoke of old England—and that, instead of being a subject of his Majesty George the Third, he was now a free citizen of the United States. Rip, in fact, was no politician; the changes of states and empires made but little impression on him; but there was one species of despotism under which he had long groaned, and that was—petticoat government. Happily that was at an end; he had got his neck out of the yoke of matrimony, and could go in and out whenever he pleased, without dreading the tyranny of Dame Van Winkle. Whenever her name was mentioned, however, he shook his head, shrugged his shoulders, and cast up his eyes; which might pass either for an expression of resignation to his fate, or joy at his deliverance.

He used to tell his story to every stranger that arrived at Mr. Doolittle's hotel. He was observed, at first, to vary on some points every time he told it, which was, doubtless, owing to his having so recently awaked. It at last settled down precisely to the tale I have related, and not a man, woman, or child in the neighborhood, but knew it by heart. Some always pretended to doubt the reality of it, and insisted that Rip had been out of his head, and that this was one point on which he always remained flighty. The old Dutch inhabitants, however, almost universally gave it full credit. Even to this day they never hear a thunderstorm of a summer afternoon about the Kaatskill, but they say Hendrick Hudson and his crew are at their game of nine-pins; and it is a common wish of all hen-pecked husbands in the neighborhood, when life hangs heavy on their hands, that they might have a quieting draught out of Rip Van Winkle's flagon.

NOTE

The foregoing Tale, one would suspect, had been suggested to Mr. Knickerbocker by a little German superstition about the Emperor Frederick *der Rothbart*, and the Kypphaüser mountain: the subjoined note, however, which he had appended to the tale, shows that it is an absolute fact, narrated with his usual fidelity:

"The story of Rip Van Winkle may seem incredible to many, but nevertheless I give it my full belief, for I know the vicinity of our old Dutch settlements to have been very subject to marvellous events and appearances. Indeed, I have heard many stranger stories than this, in the villages along the Hudson; all of which were too well authenticated to admit of a doubt. I have even talked with Rip Van Winkle myself, who, when last I saw him, was a very venerable old man, and so perfectly rational and consistent on every other point, that I think no conscientious person could refuse to take this into the bargain; nay, I have seen a certificate on the subject taken before a country justice and signed with a cross, in the justice's own handwriting. The story, therefore, is beyond the possibility of doubt.

D. K."

POSTSCRIPT

The following are travelling notes from a memorandum-book of Mr. Knickerbocker:

The Kaatsberg, or Catskill mountains, have always been a region full of fable. The Indians considered them the abode of spirits, who influenced the weather, spreading sunshine or clouds over the landscape, and sending good or bad hunting seasons. They were ruled by an old squaw spirit, said to be their mother. She dwelt on the highest peak of the Catskills, and had charge of the doors of day and night to open and shut them at the proper hour. She hung up the new moons in the skies, and cut up the old ones into stars. In times of drought, if properly propitiated, she would spin light summer clouds out of cobwebs and morning dew, and send them off from the crest of the mountain, flake after flake, like flakes of carded cotton, to float in the air: until, dissolved by the heat of the sun, they would fall in gentle showers, causing the grass to spring, the fruits to ripen, and the corn to grow an inch an hour. If displeased, however, she would brew up clouds black as ink, sitting in the midst of them like a bottle-bellied spider in the midst of its web; and when these clouds broke, woe betide the valleys!

In old times, say the Indian traditions, there was a kind of Manitou or Spirit, who kept about the wildest recesses of the Catskill Mountains, and took a mischievous pleasure in wreaking all kinds of evils and vexations upon the red men. Sometimes he would assume the form of a bear, a panther, or a deer, lead the bewildered hunter a weary chase through tangled forests and among ragged rocks; and then spring off with a loud ho! ho! leaving him aghast on the brink of a beetling precipice or raging torrent.

The favorite abode of this Manitou is still shown. It is a great rock or cliff on the loneliest part of the mountains, and, from the flowering vines which clamber about it, and the wild flowers which abound in its neighborhood, is known by the name of the Garden Rock. Near the foot of it is a small lake, the haunt of the solitary bittern, with water-snakes basking in the sun on the leaves of the pond-lilies which lie on the surface. This place was held in great awe by the Indians, insomuch that the boldest hunter would not pursue his game within its precincts. Once upon a time, however, a hunter who had lost his way, penetrated to the garden rock, where he beheld a number of gourds placed in the crotches of trees. One of these he seized and made off with it, but in the hurry of his retreat he let it fall among the rocks, when a great stream gushed forth, which washed him away and swept him down precipices, where he was dashed to pieces, and the stream made its way to the Hudson, and continues to flow to the present day; being the identical stream known by the name of the Kaaters-kill.

1819–20

BRACEBRIDGE HALL

THE STOUT GENTLEMAN

A STAGE-COACH ROMANCE

I'll cross it though it blast me!

—Hamlet.

It was a rainy Sunday in the gloomy month of November. I had been detained, in the course of a journey, by a slight indisposition, from which I was recovering; but was still feverish, and obliged to keep within doors all day, in an inn of the small town of Derby. A wet Sunday in a country inn!—whoever has had the luck to experience one can alone judge of my situation. The rain pattered against the casements; the bells tolled for church with a melancholy sound. I went to the windows in quest of something to amuse the eye; but it seemed as if I had been placed completely out of the reach of all amusement. The windows of my bedroom looked out among tiled roofs and stacks of chimneys, while those of my sitting-room commanded a full view of the stable-yard. I know of nothing more calculated to make a man sick of this world than a stable-yard on a rainy day. The place was littered with wet straw that had been kicked about by travelers and stable-boys. In one corner was a stagnant pool of water, surrounding an island of muck; there were several half-drowned fowls crowded together under a cart, among which was a miserable, crestfallen cock, drenched out of all life and spirit; his drooping tail matted, as it were, into a single feather, along which the water trickled from his back; near the cart was a half-dozing cow, chewing the cud, and standing patiently to be rained on, with wreaths of vapor rising from her reeking hide; a wall-eyed horse, tired of the loneliness of the stable, was poking his spectral head out of a window, with the rain dripping on it from the eaves; an unhappy cur, chained to a dog-house hard by, uttered something every now and then, between a bark and a yelp; a drab of a kitchen-wench tramped backwards and forwards through the yard in pattens, looking as sulky as the weather itself; everything, in short, was comfortless and forlorn, excepting a crew of hardened ducks, assembled like boon companions round a puddle, and making a riotous noise over their liquor.

I was lonely and listless, and wanted amusement. My room soon became insupportable. I abandoned it, and sought what is technically called the travelers'-room. This is a public room set apart at most inns for the accommodation of a class of wayfarers called travelers, or riders; a kind of commercial knights-errant, who are incessantly scouring the kingdom in gigs, on horseback, or by coach. They are the only successors that I know of at the present day to the knights-errant of yore. They lead the same kind of roving, adventurous life, only changing the lance for a driving-whip, the buckler for a pattern-card, and the coat of mail for an upper Benjamin. Instead of vindicating the charms of peerless beauty, they rove about, spreading the fame and standing of some substantial tradesman, or manufacturer, and are ready at any time to bargain in his name; it being the fashion nowadays to trade, instead of fight, with one another. As the room of the hostel, in the good old fighting-times, would be hung round at night with the armor of wayworn warriors, such as coats of mail, falchions, and yawning helmets, so the travelers'-room is garnished with the harnessing of their successors, with box-coats, whips of all kinds, spurs, gaiters, and oil-cloth covered hats.

I was in hopes of finding some of these worthies to talk with, but was disappointed. There were, indeed, two or three in the room; but I could make nothing of them. One was just finishing his breakfast, quarrelling with his bread and butter, and huffing the waiter; another buttoned on a pair of gaiters, with many execrations at Boots for not having cleaned his shoes well; a third sat drumming on the table with his fingers and looking at the rain as it streamed down the window-glass; they all appeared infected by the weather, and disappeared, one after the other, without exchanging a word.

I sauntered to the window, and stood gazing at the people, picking their way to church, with petticoats hoisted midleg high, and dripping umbrellas. The bell ceased to toll, and the streets became silent. I then amused myself with watching the daughters of a tradesman opposite; who, being confined to the house for fear of wetting their Sunday finery, played off their charms at the front windows, to fascinate the chance tenants of the inn. They at length were summoned away by a vigilant vinegar-faced mother, and I had nothing further from without to amuse me.

What was I to do to pass away the long-lived day? I was sadly nervous and lonely; and every thing about an inn seems calculated to make a dull day ten times duller. Old newspapers, smelling of beer and tobacco smoke, and which I had already read half a dozen times. Good for nothing books, that were worse than rainy weather. I bored myself to death with an old volume of the Lady's Magazine. I read all the commonplace names of ambitious travelers scrawled on the panes of glass; the eternal families of the Smiths, and the Browns, and the Jacksons, and the Johnsons, and all the other sons; and I deciphered several scraps of fatiguing in[n]-window poetry which I have met with in all parts of the world.

The day continued lowering and gloomy; the slovenly, ragged, spongy clouds drifted heavily along; there was no variety even in the rain: it was one dull, continued, monotonous patter—patter—patter, excepting that now and then I was enlivened by the idea of a brisk shower, from the rattling of the drops upon a passing umbrella.

It was quite *refreshing* (if I may be allowed a hackneyed phrase of the day) when, in the course of the morning, a horn blew, and a stage-coach whirled through the street, with outside passengers stuck all over it, cowering under cotton umbrellas, and seethed together, and reeking with the steams of wet box-coats and upper Benjamins.

The sound brought out from their lurking-places a crew of vagabond boys, and vagabond dogs, and the carroty-headed hostler, and that nondescript animal ycleped Boots, and all the other vagabond race that infest the purlieus of an inn; but the bustle was transient; the coach again whirled on its way; and boy and dog, and hostler and Boots, all slunk back again to their holes; the street again became silent, and the rain continued to rain on. In fact, there was no hope of its clearing up; the barometer pointed to rainy weather; mine hostess' tortoise-shell cat sat by the fire washing her face, and rubbing her paws over her ears; and, on referring to the Almanac, I found a direful prediction stretching from the top of the page to the bottom through the whole month, "expect—much—rain—about—this—time!"

I was dreadfully hipped. The hours seemed as if they would never creep by. The very ticking of the clock became irksome. At length the stillness of the house was interrupted by the ringing of a bell. Shortly after I heard the voice of a waiter at the bar: "The stout gentleman in No. 13 wants his breakfast. Tea and bread and butter, with ham and eggs; the eggs not to be too much done."

In such a situation as mine, every incident is of importance. Here was a subject of speculation presented to my mind, and ample exercise for my imagination. I am prone to paint pictures to myself, and on this occasion I had some materials to work upon. Had the guest upstairs been mentioned as Mr. Smith, or Mr. Brown, or Mr. Jackson, or Mr. Johnson, or merely as "the gentleman in No. 13," it would have been a perfect blank to me. I should have thought nothing of it; but "The stout gentleman!"—the very name had something in it of the picturesque. It at once gave the size; it embodied the personage to my mind's eye, and my fancy did the rest.

He was stout, or, as some term it, lusty; in all probability, therefore, he was advanced in life, some people expanding as they grow old. By his breakfasting rather late, and in his own room, he must be a man accustomed to live at his ease, and above the necessity of early rising; no doubt a round, rosy, lusty old gentleman.

There was another violent ringing. The stout gentleman was impatient for his breakfast. He was evidently a man of importance; "well to do in the world;" accustomed to be promptly waited upon; of a keen appetite, and a little cross when hungry; "perhaps," thought I, "he may be some London Alderman; or who knows but he may be a Member of Parliament?"

The breakfast was sent up, and there was a short interval of silence; he was, doubtless, making the tea. Presently there was a violent ringing; and before it could be answered, another ringing still more violent. "Bless me! what a choleric old gentleman!" The waiter came down in a huff. The butter was rancid, the eggs were overdone, the ham was too salt:—the stout gentleman was evidently nice in his eating; one of those who eat and growl, and keep the waiter on the trot, and live in a state militant with the household.

The hostess got into a fume. I should observe that she was a brisk, coquettish woman; a little of a shrew, and something of a slammerkin, but very pretty withal; with a nincompoop for a husband, as shrews are apt to have. She rated the servants roundly for their negligence in sending up so bad a breakfast, but said not a word against the stout gentleman; by which I clearly perceived that he must be a man of consequence, entitled to make a noise and to give trouble at a country inn. Other eggs, and ham, and bread and butter were sent up. They appeared to be more graciously received; at least there was no further complaint.

I had not made many turns about the travelers'-room, when there was another ringing. Shortly afterwards there was a stir and an inquest about the house. The stout gentleman wanted the Times or the Chronicle newspaper. I set him down, therefore, for a whig; or rather, from his being so absolute and lordly where he had a chance, I suspected him of being a radical. Hunt, I had heard, was a large man; "who knows," thought I, "but it is Hunt himself!"

My curiosity began to be awakened. I inquired of the waiter who was this stout gentleman that was making all this stir; but I could get no information: nobody seemed to know his name. The landlords of bustling inns seldom trouble their heads about the names or occupations of their transient guests. The color of a coat, the shape or size of the person, is enough to suggest a traveling name. It is either the tall gentleman, or the short gentleman, or the gentleman in black, or the gentleman in snuff-color; or, as in the present instance, the stout gentleman. A designation of the kind once hit on, answers every purpose, and saves all further inquiry.

Rain—rain—rain! pitiless, ceaseless rain! No such thing as putting a foot out of doors, and no occupation nor amusement within. By and by I heard some one walking overhead. It was in the stout gentleman's room. He evidently was a large man by the heaviness of his tread; and an old man from his wearing such creaking soles. "He is doubtless," thought I, "some rich old square-toes of regular habits, and is now taking exercise after breakfast."

I now read all the advertisements of coaches and hotels that were stuck about the mantel-piece. The Lady's Magazine had become an abomination to me; it was as tedious as the day itself. I wandered out, not knowing what to do, and ascended again to my room. I had not been there long, when there was a squall from a neighboring bedroom. A door opened and slammed violently; a chamber-maid, that I had remarked for having a ruddy, good-humored face, went down stairs in a violent flurry. The stout gentleman had been rude to her!

This sent a whole host of my deductions to the deuce in a moment. This unknown personage could not be an old gentleman; for old gentlemen are not apt to be so obstreperous to chamber-maids. He could not be a young gentleman; for young gentlemen are not apt to inspire such indignation. He must be a middle-aged man, and confounded ugly into the bargain, or the girl would not have taken the matter in such terrible dudgeon. I confess I was sorely puzzled.

In a few minutes I heard the voice of my landlady. I caught a glance of her as she came tramping up-stairs,—her face glowing, her cap flaring, her tongue wagging the whole way. "She'd have no such doings in her house, she'd warrant. If gentlemen did spend money freely, it was no rule. She'd have no servant-maids of hers treated in that way, when they were about their work, that's what she wouldn't."

As I hate squabbles, particularly with women, and above all with pretty women, I slunk back into my room, and partly closed the door; but my curiosity was too much excited not to listen. The landlady marched intrepidly to the enemy's citadel, and entered it with a storm; the door closed after her. I heard her voice in high windy clamor for a moment or two. Then it gradually subsided, like a gust of wind in a garret; then there was a laugh; then I heard nothing more.

After a little while my landlady came out with an odd smile on her face, adjusting her cap, which was a little on one side. As she went down stairs, I heard the landlord ask her what was the matter; she said, "Nothing at all, only the girl's a fool."—I was more than ever perplexed what to make of this unaccountable personage, who could put a good-natured chamber-maid in a passion, and send away a termagant landlady in smiles. He could not be so old, nor cross, nor ugly either.

I had to go to work at his picture again, and to paint him entirely different. I now set him down for one of those stout gentlemen that are frequently met with swaggering about the doors of country inns. Moist, merry fellows, in Belcher handkerchiefs, whose bulk is a little assisted by malt-liquors. Men who have seen the world, and been sworn at Highgate; who are used to tavern life; up to all the tricks of tapsters, and knowing in the ways of sinful publicans. Free-livers on a small scale; who are prodigal within the compass of a guinea: who call all the waiters by name, touzle the maids, gossip with the landlady at the bar, and prose over a pint of port, or a glass of negus, after dinner.

The morning wore away in forming these and similar surmises. As fast as I wove one system of belief, some movement of the unknown would completely overturn it, and throw all my thoughts again into confusion. Such are the solitary operations of a feverish mind. I was, as I have said, extremely nervous; and the continual meditation on the concerns of this invisible personage began to have its effect:—I was getting a fit of the fidgets.

Dinner-time came. I hoped the stout gentleman might dine in the travelers'-room, and that I might at length get a view of his person; but no—he had dinner served in his own room. What could be the meaning of this solitude and mystery? He could not be a radical; there was something too aristocratical in thus keeping himself apart from the rest of the world, and condemning himself to his own dull company throughout a rainy day. And then, too, he lived too well for a discontented politician. He seemed to expatiate on a variety of dishes, and to sit over his wine like a jolly friend of good living. Indeed, my doubts on this head were soon at an end; for he could not have finished his first bottle before I could faintly hear him humming a tune; and on listening I found it to be "God save the King." 'Twas plain, then, he was no radical, but a faithful subject; one who grew loyal over his bottle, and was ready to stand by king and constitution, when he could stand by nothing else. But who could he be? My conjectures began to run wild. Was he not some personage of distinction travelling incog.? "God knows!" said I, at my wit's end; "it may be one of the royal family for aught I know, for they are all stout gentlemen!"

The weather continued rainy. The mysterious unknown kept his room, and, as far as I could judge, his chair, for I did not hear him move. In the meantime, as the day advanced, the travelers'-room began to be frequented. Some, who had just arrived, came in buttoned up in box-coats; others came home who had been dispersed about the town; some took their dinners, and some their tea. Had I been in a different mood, I should have found entertainment in studying this peculiar class of men. There were two especially, who were regular wags of the road, and up to all the standing jokes of travelers. They had a thousand sly things to say to the waiting-maid, whom they called Louisa, and Ethelinda, and a dozen other fine names, changing the name every time, and chuckling amazingly at their own waggery. My mind, however, had been completely engrossed by the stout gentleman. He had kept my fancy in chase during a long day, and it was not now to be diverted from the scent.

The evening gradually wore away. The travelers read the papers two or three times over. Some drew round the fire and told long stories about their horses, about their adventures, their overturns, and breakings-down. They discussed the credit of different merchants and different inns; and the two wags told several choice anecdotes of pretty chambermaids and kind landladies. All this passed as they were quietly taking what they called their night-caps, that is to say, strong glasses of brandy and water and sugar, or some other mixture of the kind; after which they one after another rang for "Boots" and the chamber-maid, and walked off to bed in old shoes cut down into marvellously uncomfortable slippers.

There was now only one man left: a short-legged, long-bodied, plethoric fellow, with a very large, sandy head. He sat by himself, with a glass of port-wine negus, and a spoon; sipping and stirring, and meditating and sipping, until nothing was left but the spoon. He gradually fell asleep bolt upright in his chair, with the empty glass standing before him; and the candle seemed to fall asleep too, for the wick grew long, and black, and cabbaged at the end, and dimmed the little light that remained in the chamber. The gloom that now prevailed was contagious. Around hung the shapeless, and almost spectral, box-coats of departed travelers, long since buried in deep sleep. I only heard the ticking of the clock, with the deep-drawn breathings of the sleeping topers, and the drippings of the rain, drop—drop—drop, from the eaves of the house. The church-bells chimed midnight. All at once the stout gentleman began to walk overhead, pacing slowly backwards and forwards. There was something extremely awful in all this, especially to one in my state of nerves. These ghastly great-coats, these guttural breathings, and the creaking footsteps of this mysterious being. His steps grew fainter and fainter, and at length died away. I could bear it no longer. I was wound up to the desperation of a hero of romance. "Be he who or what he may," said I to myself, "I'll have a sight of him!" I seized a chamber-candle, and hurried up to No. 13. The door stood ajar. I hesitated—I entered: the room was deserted. There stood a large, broad-bottomed elbow-chair at a table, on which was an empty tumbler, and a "Times," newspaper, and the room smelt powerfully of Stilton cheese.

The mysterious stranger had evidently but just retired. I turned off, sorely disappointed, to my room, which had been changed to the front of the house. As I went along the corridor, I saw a large pair of boots, with dirty, waxed tops, standing at the door of a bedchamber. They doubtless belonged to the unknown; but it would not do to disturb so redoubtable a personage in his den: he might discharge a pistol, or something worse, at my head. I went to bed, therefore, and lay awake half the night in a terribly nervous state; and even when I fell asleep, I was still haunted in my dreams by the idea of the stout gentleman and his wax-topped boots.

I slept rather late the next morning, and was awakened by some stir and bustle in the house, which I could not at first comprehend; until getting more awake, I found there was a mail-coach starting from the door. Suddenly there was a cry from below, "The gentleman has forgot his umbrella! Look for the gentleman's umbrella in No. 13!" I heard an immediate scampering of a chambermaid along the passage, and a shrill reply as she ran, "Here it is! here's the gentleman's umbrella!"

The mysterious stranger then was on the point of setting off. This was the only chance I should ever have of knowing him. I sprang out of bed, scrambled to the window, snatched aside the curtains, and just caught a glimpse of the rear of a person getting in at the coach-door. The skirts of a brown coat parted behind, and gave me a full view of the broad disk of a pair of drab breeches. The door closed—"all right!" was the word—the coach whirled off;—and that was all I ever saw of the stout gentleman!

1822

THE ALHAMBRA

LEGEND OF THE ROSE OF THE ALHAMBRA

For some time after the surrender of Granada by the Moors, that delightful city was a frequent and favorite residence of the Spanish sovereigns, until they were frightened away by successive shocks of earthquakes, which toppled down various houses, and made the old Moslem towers rock to their foundation.

Many, many years then rolled away, during which Granada was rarely honored by a royal guest. The palaces of the nobility remained silent and shut up; and the Alhambra, like a slighted beauty, sat in mournful desolation among her neglected gardens. The tower of the Infantas, once the residence of the three beautiful Moorish princesses, partook of the general desolation; the spider spun her web athwart the gilded vault, and bats and owls nestled in those chambers that had been graced by the presence of Zayda, Zorayda, and Zorahayda. The neglect of this tower may have been partly owing to some superstitious notions of the neighbors. It was rumored that the spirit of the youthful Zorahayda, who had perished in that tower, was often seen by moonlight seated beside the fountain in the hall, or moaning about the battlements, and that the notes of her silver lute would be heard at midnight by wayfarers passing along the glen.

At length the city of Granada was once more welcomed by the royal presence. All the world knows that Philip V. was the first Bourbon that swayed the Spanish sceptre. All the world knows that he married, in second nuptials, Elizabetta or Isabella (for they are the same), the beautiful princess of Parma; and all the world knows that by this chain of contingencies a French prince and an Italian princess were seated together on the Spanish throne. For a visit of this illustrious pair, the Alhambra was repaired and fitted up with all possible expedition. The arrival of the court changed the whole aspect of the lately deserted palace. The clangor of drum and trumpet, the tramp of steed about the avenues and outer court, the glitter of arms and display of banners about barbican and battlement, recalled the ancient and warlike glories of the fortress. A softer spirit, however, reigned within the royal palace. There was the rustling of robes and the cautious tread and murmuring voice of reverential courtiers about the antechambers; a loitering of pages and maids of honor about the gardens, and the sound of music stealing from open casements.

Among those who attended in the train of the monarchs was a favorite page of the queen, named Ruyz de Alarcon. To say that he was a favorite page of the queen was at once to speak his eulogium, for every one in the suite of the stately Elizabetta was chosen for grace, and beauty, and accomplishments. He was just turned of eighteen, light and lithe of form, and graceful as a young Antinous. To the queen he was all deference and respect, yet he was at heart a roguish stripling, petted and spoiled by the ladies about the court, and experienced in the ways of women far beyond his years.

This loitering page was one morning rambling about the groves of the Generalife, which overlook the grounds of the Alhambra. He had taken with him for his amusement a favorite gerfalcon of the queen. In the course of his rambles, seeing a bird rising from a thicket, he unhooded the hawk and let him fly. The falcon towered high in the air, made a swoop at his quarry, but missing it, soared away, regardless of the calls of the page. The latter followed the truant bird with his eye, in its capricious flight, until he saw it alight upon the battlements of a remote and lonely tower, in the outer wall of the Alhambra, built on the edge of a ravine that separated the royal fortress from the grounds of the Generalife. It was in fact the "Tower of the Princesses."

The page descended into the ravine and approached the tower, but it had no entrance from the glen, and its lofty height rendered any attempt to scale it fruitless. Seeking one of the gates of the fortress, therefore, he made a wide circuit to that side of the tower facing within the walls.

A small garden, enclosed by a trellis-work of reeds overhung with myrtle, lay before the tower. Opening a wicket, the page passed between beds of flowers and thickets of roses to the door. It was closed and bolted. A crevice in the door gave him a peep into the interior. There was a small Moorish hall with fretted walls, light marble columns, and an alabaster fountain surrounded with flowers. In the centre hung a gilt cage containing a singing-bird; beneath it, on a chair, lay a tortoise-shell cat among reels of silk and other articles of female labor, and a guitar decorated with ribbons leaned against the fountain.

Ruyz de Alarcon was struck with these traces of female taste and elegance in a lonely, and, as he had supposed, deserted tower. They reminded him of the tales of enchanted halls current in the Alhambra; and the tortoise-shell cat might be some spell-bound princess.

He knocked gently at the door. A beautiful face peeped out from a little window above, but was instantly withdrawn. He waited, expecting that the door would be opened, but he waited in vain; no footstep was to be heard within—all was silent. Had his senses deceived him, or was this beautiful apparition the fairy of the tower? He knocked again, and more loudly. After a little while the beaming face once more peeped forth; it was that of a blooming damsel of fifteen.

The page immediately doffed his plumed bonnet, and entreated in the most courteous accents to be permitted to ascend the tower in pursuit of his falcon.

"I dare not open the door, Señor," replied the little damsel, blushing, "my aunt has forbidden it."

"I do beseech you, fair maid—it is the favorite falcon of the queen: I dare not return to the palace without it."

"Are you then one of the cavaliers of the court?"

"I am, fair maid; but I shall lose the queen's favor and my place, if I lose this hawk."

"Santa Maria! It is against you cavaliers of the court my aunt has charged me especially to bar the door."

"Against wicked cavaliers doubtless, but I am none of these, but a simple, harmless page, who will be ruined and undone if you deny me this small request."

The heart of the little damsel was touched by the distress of the page. It was a thousand pities he should be ruined for the want of so trifling a boon. Surely too he could not be one of those dangerous beings whom her aunt had described as a species of cannibal, ever on the prowl to make prey of thoughtless damsels; he was gentle and modest, and stood so entreatingly with cap in hand, and looked so charming.

The sly page saw that the garrison began to waver, and redoubled his entreaties in such moving terms that it was not in the nature of mortal maiden to deny him; so the blushing little warden of the tower descended, and opened the door with a trembling hand, and if the page had been charmed by a mere glimpse of her countenance from the window, he was ravished by the full-length portrait now revealed to him.

Her Andalusian bodice and trim basquina set off the round but delicate symmetry of her form, which was as yet scarce verging into womanhood. Her glossy hair was parted on her forehead with scrupulous exactness, and decorated with a fresh-plucked rose, according to the universal custom of the country. It is true her complexion was tinged by the ardor of a southern sun, but it served to give richness to the mantling bloom of her cheek, and to heighten the lustre of her melting eyes.

Ruyz de Alarcon beheld all this with a single glance, for it became him not to tarry; he merely murmured his acknowledgments, and then bounded lightly up the spiral staircase in quest of his falcon.

He soon returned with the truant bird upon his fist. The damsel, in the meantime, had seated herself by the fountain in the hall, and was winding silk; but in her agitation she let fall the reel upon the pavement. The page sprang and picked it up, then dropping gracefully on one knee, presented it to her; but, seizing the hand extended to receive it, imprinted on it a kiss more fervent and devout than he had ever imprinted on the fair hand of his sovereign.

"Ave Maria, Señor!" exclaimed the damsel, blushing still deeper with confusion and surprise, for never before had she received such a salutation.

The modest page made a thousand apologies, assuring her it was the way at court of expressing the most profound homage and respect.

Her anger, if anger she felt, was easily pacified, but her agitation and embarrassment continued, and she sat blushing deeper and deeper, with her eyes cast down upon her work, entangling the silk which she attempted to wind.

The cunning page saw the confusion in the opposite camp, and would fain have profited by it, but the fine speeches he would have uttered died upon his lips; his attempts at gallantry were awkward and ineffectual; and to his surprise, the adroit page, who had figured with such grace and effrontery among the most knowing and experienced ladies of the court, found himself awed and abashed in the presence of a simple damsel of fifteen.

In fact, the artless maiden, in her own modesty and innocence, had guardians more effectual than the bolts and bars prescribed by her vigilant aunt. Still, where is the female bosom proof against the first whisperings of love? The little damsel, with all her artlessness, instinctively comprehended all that the faltering tongue of the page failed to express, and her heart was fluttered at beholding for the first time, a lover at her feet—and such a lover!

The diffidence of the page, though genuine, was short-lived, and he was recovering his usual ease and confidence, when a shrill voice was heard at a distance.

"My aunt is returning from mass!" cried the damsel in affright: "I pray you, Señor, depart."

"Not until you grant me that rose from your hair as a remembrance."

She hastily untwisted the rose from her raven locks. "Take it," cried she, agitated and blushing, "but pray begone."

The page took the rose, and at the time covered with kisses the fair hand that gave it. Then, placing the flower in his bonnet, and taking the falcon upon his fist he bounded off through the garden, bearing away with him the heart of the gentle Jacinta.

When the vigilant aunt arrived at the tower, she remarked the agitation of her niece, and an air of confusion in the hall; but a word of explanation sufficed. "A ger-falcon had pursued his prey into the hall."

"Mercy on us! to think of a falcon flying into the tower. Did ever one hear of so saucy a hawk? Why, the very bird in the cage is not safe!"

The vigilant Fredegonda was one of the most wary of ancient spinsters. She had a becoming terror and distrust of what she denominated "the opposite sex," which had gradually increased through a long life of celibacy. Not that the good lady had ever suffered from their wiles, nature having set up a safeguard in her face that forbade all trespass upon her premises; but ladies who have least cause to fear for themselves are most ready to keep a watch over their more tempting neighbors.

The niece was the orphan of an officer who had fallen in the wars. She had been educated in a convent, and had recently been transferred from her sacred asylum to the immediate guardianship of her aunt, under whose overshadowing care she vegetated in obscurity, like an opening rose blooming beneath a brier. Nor indeed is this comparison entirely accidental; for, to tell the truth, her fresh and dawning beauty had caught the public eye, even in her seclusion, and, with that poetical turn common to the people of Andalusia, the peasantry of the neighborhood had given her the appellation of "the Rose of the Alhambra."

The wary aunt continued to keep a faithful watch over her tempting little niece as long as the court continued at Granada, and flattered herself that her vigilance had been successful. It is true the good lady was now and then discomposed by the tinkling of guitars and chanting of love-ditties from the moonlit groves beneath the tower; but she would exhort her niece to shut her ears against such idle minstrelsy, assuring her that it was one of the arts of the opposite sex, by which simple maids were often lured to their undoing. Alas! what chance with a simple maid has a dry lecture against a moonlight serenade?

At length King Philip cut short his sojourn at Granada, and suddenly departed with all his train. The vigilant Fredegonda watched the royal pageant as it issued forth from the Gate of Justice, and descended the great avenue leading to the city. When the last banner disappeared from her sight, she returned exulting to her tower, for all her cares were over. To her surprise, a light Arabian steed pawed the ground at the wicket-gate of the garden;—to her horror she saw through the thickets of roses a youth in gayly embroidered dress, at the feet of her niece. At the sounds of her footsteps he gave a tender adieu, bounded lightly over the barrier of reeds and myrtles, sprang upon his horse, and was out of sight in an instant.

The tender Jacinta, in the agony of her grief, lost all thought of her aunt's displeasure. Throwing herself into her arms, she broke forth into sobs and tears.

"Ay de mi!" cried she; "he's gone!—He's gone!—he's gone! and I shall never see him more!"

"Gone!—who is gone?—what youth is that I saw at your feet?"

"A queen's page, aunt, who came to bid me farewell."

"A queen's page, child!" echoed the vigilant Fredegonda, faintly, "and when did you become acquainted with the queen's page?"

"The morning that the ger-falcon came into the tower. It was the queen's ger-falcon, and he came in pursuit of it."

"Ah silly, silly girl! know that there are no ger-falcons half so dangerous as these young prankling pages, and it is precisely such simple birds as thee that they pounce upon."

The aunt was at first indignant at learning that in despite of her boasted vigilance, a tender intercourse had been carried on by the youthful lovers, almost beneath her eye; but when she found that her simple-hearted niece, though thus exposed, without the protection of bolt or bar, to all the machinations of the opposite sex, had come forth unsinged from the fiery ordeal, she consoled herself with the persuasion that it was owing to the chaste and cautious maxims in which she had, as it were, steeped her to the very lips.

While the aunt laid this soothing unction to her pride, the niece treasured up the oft-repeated vows of fidelity of the page. But what is the love of restless, roving man? A vagrant stream that dallies for a time with each flower upon its bank, then passes on, and leaves them all in tears.

Days, weeks, months elapsed, and nothing more was heard of the page. The pomegranate ripened, the vine yielded up its fruit, the autumnal rains descended in torrents from the mountains; the Sierra Nevada became covered with a snowy mantle, and wintry blasts howled through the halls of the Alhambra—still he came not. The winter passed away. Again the genial spring burst forth with song and blossom and balmy zephyr; the snows melted from the mountains, until none remained but on the lofty summit of Nevada, glistening through the sultry summer air. Still nothing was heard of the forgetful page.

In the meantime the poor little Jacinta grew pale and thoughtful. Her former occupations and amusements were abandoned, her silk lay entangled, her guitar unstrung, her flowers were neglected, the notes of her bird unheeded, and her eyes, once so bright, were dimmed with secret weeping. If any solitude could be devised to foster the passion of a love-lorn damsel it would be such a place as the Alhambra, where everything seems disposed to produce tender and romantic reveries. It is a very paradise for lovers: how hard then to be alone in such a paradise—and not merely alone, but forsaken!

"Alas, silly child!" would the staid and immaculate Fredegonda say, when she found her niece in one of her desponding moods—"did I not warn thee against the wiles and deceptions of these men? What couldst thou expect, too, from one of a haughty and aspiring family—thou an orphan, the descendant of a fallen and impoverished line? Be assured, if the youth were true, his father, who is one of the proudest nobles about the court, would prohibit his union with one so humble and portionless as thou. Pluck up thy resolution, therefore, and drive these idle notions from thy mind."

The words of the immaculate Fredegonda only served to increase the melancholy of her niece, but she sought to indulge it in private. At a late hour one midsummer night, after her aunt had retired to rest, she remained alone in the hall of the tower, seated beside the alabaster fountain. It was here that the faithless page had first knelt and kissed her hand; it was here that he had often vowed eternal fidelity. The poor little damsel's heart was overladen with sad and tender recollections, her tears began to flow, and slowly fell drop by drop into the fountain. By degrees the crystal water became agitated, and—bubble—bubble—bubble—boiled up and was tossed about, until a female figure, richly clad in Moorish robes, slowly rose to view.

Jacinta was so frightened that she fled from the hall, and did not venture to return. The next morning she related what she had seen to her aunt, but the good lady treated it as a fantasy of her troubled mind, or supposed she had fallen asleep and dreamt beside the fountain. "Thou hast been thinking of the story of the three Moorish princesses that once inhabited this tower," continued she, "and it has entered into thy dreams."

"What story, aunt? I know nothing of it."

"Thou hast certainly heard of the three princesses, Zayda, Zorayda, and Zorahayda, who were confined in this tower by the king their father, and agreed to fly with three Christian cavaliers. The two first accomplished their escape, but the third failed in her resolution, and, it is said, died in this tower."

"I now recollect to have heard of it," said Jacinta, "and to have wept over the fate of the gentle Zorahayda."

"Thou mayest well weep over her fate," continued the aunt, "for the lover of Zorahayda was thy ancestor. He long bemoaned his Moorish love: but time cured him of his grief, and he married a Spanish lady, from whom thou art descended."

Jacinta ruminated upon these words. "That what I have seen is no fantasy of the brain," said she to herself, "I am confident. If indeed it be the spirit of the gentle Zorahayda, which I have heard lingers about this tower, of what should I be afraid? I'll watch by the fountain to-night—perhaps the visit will be repeated."

Towards midnight, when everything was quiet, she again took her seat in the hall. As the bell in the distant watch-tower of the Alhambra struck the midnight hour, the fountain was again agitated; and bubble—bubble—bubble—it tossed about the waters until the Moorish female again rose to view. She was young and beautiful; her dress was rich with jewels, and in her hand she held a silver lute. Jacinta trembled and was faint, but was reassured by the soft and plaintive voice of the apparition, and the sweet expression of her pale, melancholy countenance.

"Daughter of mortality," said she, "what aileth thee? Why do thy tears trouble my fountain, and thy sighs and plaints disturb the quiet watches of the night?"

"I weep because of the faithlessness of man, and I bemoan my solitary and forsaken state."

"Take comfort; thy sorrows may yet have an end. Thou beholdest a Moorish princess, who, like thee, was unhappy in her love. A Christian knight, thy ancestor, won my heart, and would have borne me to his native land and to the bosom of his church. I was a convert in my heart, but I lacked courage equal to my faith, and lingered till too late. For this the evil genii are permitted to have power over me, and I remain enchanted in this tower until some pure Christian will deign to break the magic spell. Wilt thou undertake the task?"

"I will," replied the damsel, trembling.

"Come hither then, and fear not; dip thy hand in the fountain, sprinkle the water over me, and baptize me after the manner of thy faith; so shall the enchantment be dispelled, and my troubled spirit have repose."

The damsel advanced with faltering steps, dipped her hand in the fountain, collected water in the palm, and sprinkled it over the pale face of the phantom.

The latter smiled with ineffable benignity. She dropped her silver lute at the feet of Jacinta, crossed her white arms upon her bosom, and melted from sight, so that it seemed merely as if a shower of dewdrops had fallen into the fountain.

Jacinta retired from the hall filled with awe and wonder. She scarcely closed her eyes that night; but when she awoke at daybreak out of a troubled slumber, the whole appeared to her like a distempered dream. On descending into the hall, however, the truth of the vision was established, for beside the fountain she beheld the silver lute glittering in the morning sunshine.

She hastened to her aunt, to relate all that had befallen her, and called her to behold the lute as a testimonial of the reality of her story. If the good lady had any lingering doubts, they were removed when Jacinta touched the instrument, for she drew forth such ravishing tones as to thaw even the frigid bosom of the immaculate Fredegonda, that region of eternal winter, into a genial flow. Nothing but supernatural melody could have produced such an effect.

The extraordinary power of the lute became every day more and more apparent. The wayfarer passing by the tower was detained, and, as it were, spell-bound in breathless ecstasy. The very birds gathered in the neighboring trees, and hushing their own strains, listened in charmed silence.

Rumor soon spread the news abroad. The inhabitants of Granada thronged to the Alhambra to catch a few notes of the transcendent music that floated about the tower of Las Infantas.

The lovely little minstrel was at length drawn forth from her retreat. The rich and powerful of the land contended who should entertain and do honor to her; or rather, who should secure the charms of her lute to draw fashionable throngs to their saloons. Wherever she went her vigilant aunt kept a dragon watch at her elbow, awing the throngs of impassioned admirers who hung in raptures on her strains. The report of her wonderful powers spread from city to city. Malaga, Seville, Cordova, all became successively mad on the theme; nothing was talked of throughout Andalusia but the beautiful minstrel of the Alhambra. How could it be otherwise among a people so musical and gallant as the Andalusians, when the lute was magical in its powers, and the minstrel inspired by love!

While all Andalusia was thus music mad, a different mood prevailed at the court of Spain. Philip V., as is well known, was a miserable hypochondriac, and subject to all kinds of fancies. Sometimes he would keep to his bed for weeks together, groaning under imaginary complaints. At other times he would insist upon abdicating his throne, to the great annoyance of his royal spouse, who had a strong relish for the splendors of a court and the glories of a crown, and guided the sceptre of her imbecile lord with an expert and steady hand.

Nothing was found to be so efficacious in dispelling the royal megrims as the power of music; the queen took care, therefore, to have the best performers, both vocal and instrumental, at hand, and retained the famous Italian singer Farinelli about the court as a kind of royal physician.

At the moment we treat of, however, a freak had come over the mind of this sapient and illustrious Bourbon that surpassed all former vagaries. After a long spell of imaginary illness, which set all the strains of Farinelli and the consultations of a whole orchestra of court fiddlers at defiance, the monarch fairly, in idea, gave up the ghost, and considered himself absolutely dead.

This would have been harmless enough, and even convenient both to his queen and courtiers, had he been content to remain in the quietude befitting a dead man; but to their annoyance he insisted upon having the funeral ceremonies performed over him, and, to their inexpressible perplexity, began to grow impatient, and to revile bitterly at them for negligence and disrespect, in leaving him unburied. What was to be done? To disobey the king's positive commands was monstrous in the eyes of the obsequious courtiers of a punctilious court—but to obey him, and bury him alive would be down-right regicide!

In the midst of his fearful dilemma a rumor reached the court of the female minstrel who was turning the brains of all Andalusia. The queen dispatched missions in all haste to summon her to St. Ildefonso, where the court at that time resided.

Within a few days, as the queen with her maids of honor was walking in those stately gardens, intended, with their avenues and terraces and fountains, to eclipse the glories of Versailles, the far-famed minstrel was conducted into her presence. The imperial Elizabetta gazed with surprise at the youthful and unpretending appearance of the little being that had set the world madding. She was in her picturesque Andalusian dress, her silver lute in hand, and stood with modest and downcast eyes, but with a simplicity and freshness of beauty that still bespoke her "the Rose of the Alhambra."

As usual she was accompanied by the ever-vigilant Fredegona, who gave the whole history of her parentage and descent to the inquiring queen. If the stately Elizabetta had been interested by the appearance of Jacinta, she was still more pleased when she learnt that she was of a meritorious though impoverished line, and that her father had bravely fallen in the service of the crown. "If thy powers equal thy renown," said she, "and thou canst cast forth this evil spirit that possesses thy sovereign, thy fortunes shall henceforth be my care, and honors and wealth attend thee."

Impatient to make trial of her skill, she led the way at once to the apartment of the moody monarch.

Jacinta followed with downcast eyes through files of guards and crowds of courtiers. They arrived at length at a great chamber hung with black. The windows were closed to exclude the light of day: a number of yellow wax tapers in silver sconces diffused a lugubrious light, and dimly revealed the figures of mutes in mourning dresses, and courtiers who glided about with noiseless step and woe-begone visage. In the midst of a funeral bed or bier, his hands folded on his breast, and the tip of his nose just visible, lay extended this would-be-buried monarch.

The queen entered the chamber in silence, and pointing to a footstool in an obscure corner, beckoned to Jacinta to sit down and commence. At first she touched her lute with a faltering hand, but gathering confidence and animation as she proceeded, drew forth such soft aërial harmony, that all present could scarce believe it mortal. As to the monarch, who had already considered himself in the world of spirits, he set it down for some angelic melody or the music of the spheres. By degrees the theme was varied, and the voice of the minstrel accompanied the instrument. She poured forth one of the legendary ballads treating of the ancient glories of the Alhambra and the achievements of the Moors. Her whole soul entered into the theme, for with the recollections of the Alhambra was associated the story of her love. The funeral-chamber resounded with the animating strain. It entered into the gloomy heart of the monarch. He raised his head and gazed around: he sat up on his couch, his eye began to kindle—at length, leaping upon the floor, he called for sword and buckler.

The triumph of music, or rather of the enchanted lute, was complete; the demon of melancholy was cast forth; and, as it were, a dead man brought to life. The windows of the apartment were thrown open; the glorious effulgence of Spanish sunshine burst into the late lugubrious chamber; all eyes sought the lovely enchantress, but the lute had fallen from her hand, she had sunk upon the earth, and the next moment was clasped to the bosom of Ruyz de Alarcon.

The nuptials of the happy couple were celebrated soon afterwards with great splendor, and the rose of the Alhambra became the ornament and delight of the court. "But hold—not so fast"—I hear the reader exclaim; "this is jumping to the end of a story at a furious rate! First let us know how Ruyz de Alarcon managed to account to Jacinta for his long neglect?" Nothing more easy; the venerable, time-honored excuse, the opposition to his wishes by a proud, pragmatical old father: besides, young people who really like one another soon come to an amicable understanding, and bury all past grievances when once they meet.

But how was the proud, pragmatical old father reconciled to the match?

Oh! as to that, his scruples were easily overcome by a word or two from the queen; especially as dignities and rewards were showered upon the blooming favorite of royalty. Besides, the lute of Jacinta, you know, possessed a magic power, and could control the most stubborn head and hardest breast.

And what came of the enchanted lute?

Oh, that is the most curious matter of all, and plainly proves the truth of the whole story. That lute remained for some time in the family, but was purloined and carried off, as was supposed, by the great singer Farinelli, in pure jealousy. At his death it passed into other hands in Italy, who were ignorant of its mystic powers, and melting down the silver, transferred the strings to an old Cremona fiddle. The strings still retain something of their magic virtues. A word in the reader's ear, but let it go no further: that fiddle is now bewitching the whole world,—it is the fiddle of Paganini!

1832

From *ABBOTSFORD AND NEWSTED ABBEY*

[SIR WALTER SCOTT]

* * * Late in the evening of the 29th of August, 1817, I arrived at the ancient little border-town of Selkirk, where I put up for the night. I had come down from Edinburgh, partly to visit Melrose Abbey and its vicinity, but chiefly to get a sight of the "mighty minstrel of the north." I had a letter of introduction to him from Thomas Campbell the poet, and had reason to think, from the interest he had taken in some of my earlier scribblings, that a visit from me would not be deemed an intrusion.

On the following morning, after an early breakfast, I set off in a post-chaise for the Abbey. On the way thither I stopped at the gate of Abbotsford, and sent the postillion to the house with the letter of introduction and my card, on which I had written that I was on my way to the ruins of Melrose Abbey, and wished to know whether it would be agreeable to Mr. Scott (he had not yet been made a Baronet) to receive a visit from me in the course of the morning.

While the postillion was on his errand, I had time to survey the mansion. It stood some short distance below the road, on the side of a hill sweeping down to the Tweed; and was as yet but a snug gentleman's cottage, with something rural and picturesque in its appearance. The whole front was overrun with evergreens, and immediately above the portal was a great pair of elk horns, branching out from beneath the foliage, and giving the cottage the look of a hunting-lodge. The huge baronial pile, to which this modest mansion in a manner gave birth, was just emerging into existence: part of the walls, surrounded by scaffolding, already had risen to the height of the cottage, and the courtyard in front was encumbered by masses of hewn stone.

The noise of the chaise had disturbed the quiet of the establishment. Out sallied the warder of the castle, a black greyhound, and, leaping on one of the blocks of stone, began a furious barking. His alarum brought out the whole garrison of dogs:

"Both mongrel, puppy, whelp, and hound,
And curs of low degree;"

all open-mouthed, and vociferous.—I should correct my quotation; not a cur was to be seen on the premises: Scott was too true a sportsman, and had too high a veneration for pure blood, to tolerate a mongrel.

In a little while the "lord of the castle" himself made his appearance. I knew him at once by the descriptions I had read and heard, and the likenesses that had been published of him. He was tall, and of a large and powerful frame. His dress was simple, and almost rustic: an old green shooting-coat, with a dog-whistle at the button-hole, brown linen pantaloons, stout shoes that tied at the ankles, and a white hat that had evidently seen service. He came limping up the gravel-walk, aiding himself by a stout walking-staff, but moving rapidly and with vigor. By his side jogged along a large iron-gray staghound of most grave demeanor, who took no part in the clamor of the canine rabble, but seemed to consider himself bound, for the dignity of the house, to give me a courteous reception.

Before Scott had reached the gate he called out in a hearty tone, welcoming me to Abbotsford, and asking news of Campbell. Arrived at the door of the chaise, he grasped me warmly by the hand: "Come, drive down, drive down to the house," said he, "ye're just in time for breakfast, and afterwards ye shall see all the wonders of the Abbey."

I would have excused myself, on the plea of having already made my breakfast. "Hout, man," cried he, "a ride in the morning in the keen air of the Scotch hills is warrant enough for a second breakfast."

I was accordingly whirled to the portal of the cottage, and in a few moments found myself seated at the breakfast-table. There was no one present but the family: which consisted of Mrs. Scott; her eldest daughter Sophia, then a fine girl about seventeen; Miss Ann Scott, two or three years younger; Walter, a well-grown stripling; and Charles, a lively boy, eleven or twelve years of age. I soon felt myself quite at home, and my heart in a glow with the cordial welcome I experienced. I had thought to make a mere morning visit, but found I was not to be let off so lightly. "You must not think our neighborhood is to be read in a morning, like a newspaper," said Scott. "It takes several days of study for an observant traveller that has a relish for auld-world trumpery. After breakfast you shall make your visit to Melrose Abbey; I shall not be able to accompany you, as I have some household affairs to attend to, but I will put you in charge of my son Charles, who is very learned in all things touching the old ruin and the neighborhood it stands in, and he and my friend Johnny Bower will tell you the whole truth about it, with a good deal more that you are not called upon to believe—unless you be a true and nothing-doubting antiquary. When you come back, I'll take you out on a ramble about the neighborhood. To-morrow we will take a look at the Yarrow, and the next day we will drive over to Dryburgh Abbey, which is a fine old ruin well worth your seeing;"—in a word, before Scott had got through with his plan, I found myself committed for a visit of several days, and it seemed as if a little realm of romance was suddenly opened before me. * * *

After my return from Melrose Abbey, Scott proposed a ramble to show me something of the surrounding country. As we sallied forth, every dog in the establishment turned out to attend us. There was the old stag-hound Maida, that I have already mentioned, a noble animal, and a great favorite of Scott's; and Hamlet, the black greyhound, a wild thoughtless youngster, not yet arrived to the years of discretion; and Finette, a beautiful setter, with soft silken hair, long pendent ears, and a mild eye, the parlor favorite. When in front of the house, we were joined by a superannuated greyhound, who came from the kitchen wagging his tail, and was cheered by Scott as an old friend and comrade.

In our walks, Scott would frequently pause in conversation to notice his dogs and speak to them, as if rational companions; and indeed there appears to be a vast deal of rationality in these faithful attendants on man, derived from their close intimacy with him. Maida deported himself with a gravity becoming his age and size, and seemed to consider himself called upon to preserve a great degree of dignity and decorum in our society. As he jogged along a little distance ahead of us, the young dogs would gambol about him, leap on his neck, worry at his ears, and endeavor to tease him into a frolic. The old dog would keep on for a long time with imperturbable solemnity, now and then seeming to rebuke the wantonness of his young companions. At length he would make a sudden turn, seize one of them, and tumble him in the dust; then giving a glance at us, as much as to say, "You see, gentlemen, I can't help giving way to this nonsense," would resume his gravity and jog on as before.

Scott amused himself with these peculiarities. "I make no doubt," said he, "when Maida is alone with these young dogs, he throws gravity aside, and plays the boy as much as any of them; but he is ashamed to do so in our company, and seems to say, 'Ha' done with your nonsense, youngsters; what will the laird and that other gentleman think of me if I give way to such foolery?' "

Maida reminded him, he said, of a scene on board an armed yacht in which he made an excursion with his friend Adam Ferguson. They had taken much notice of the boatswain, who was a fine sturdy seaman, and evidently felt flattered by their attention. On one occasion the crew were "piped to fun," and the sailors were dancing and cutting all kinds of capers to the music of the ship's band. The boatswain looked on with a wistful eye, as if he would like to join in; but a glance at Scott and Ferguson showed that there was a struggle with his dignity, fearing to lessen himself in their eyes. At length one of his messmates came up, and seizing him by the arm, challenged him to a jig. The boatswain, continued Scott, after a little hesitation complied, made an awkward gambol or two, like our friend Maida, but soon gave it up. "It's of no use," said he, jerking up his waistband and giving a side-glance at us, "one can't dance always nouther."

Scott amused himself with the peculiarities of another of his dogs, a little shamefaced terrier, with large glassy eyes, one of the most sensitive little bodies to insult and indignity in the world. If ever he whipped him, he said, the little fellow would sneak off and hide himself from the light of day, in a lumber garret, whence there was no drawing him forth but by the sound of the chopping-knife, as if chopping up his victuals, when he would steal forth with humbled and downcast look, but would skulk away again if any one regarded him.

While we were discussing the humors and peculiarities of our canine companions, some object provoked their spleen, and produced a sharp and petulant barking from the smaller fry, but it was some time before Maida was sufficiently aroused to ramp forward two or three bounds and join in the chorus, with a deep-mouthed bow-wow!

It was but a transient outbreak, and he returned instantly, wagging his tail, and looking up dubiously in his master's face; uncertain whether he would censure or applaud.

"Aye, aye, old boy!" cried Scott, "you have done wonders. You have shaken the Eildon hills with your roaring; you may now lay by your artillery for the rest of the day. Maida is like the great gun at Constantinople," continued he; "it takes so long to get it ready, that the small guns can fire off a dozen times first, but when it does go off it plays the very d—l."

These simple anecdotes may serve to show the delightful play of Scott's humors and feelings in private life. His domestic animals were his friends; everything about him seemed to rejoice in the light of his countenance: the face of the humblest dependent brightened at his approach, as if he anticipated a cordial and cheering word. I had occasion to observe this particularly in a visit which we paid to a quarry, whence several men were cutting stone for the new edifice; who all paused from their labor to have a pleasant "crack wi' the laird." One of them was a burgess of Selkirk, with whom Scott had some joke about the old song:

"Up with the Souters o' Selkirk,
And down with the Earl of Home."

Another was precentor at the Kirk, and, beside leading the psalmody on Sunday, taught the lads and lasses of the neighborhood dancing on week-days, in the winter-time, when out-of-door labor was scarce.

Among the rest was a tall, straight old fellow, with a healthful complexion and silver hair, and a small round-crowned white hat. He had been about to shoulder a hod, but paused, and stood looking at Scott, with a slight sparkling of his blue eye, as if waiting his turn; for the old fellow knew himself to be a favorite.

Scott accosted him in an affable tone, and asked for a pinch of snuff. The old man drew forth a horn snuff-box. "Hoot, man," said Scott, "not that old mull: where's the bonny French one that I have brought you from Paris?"—"Troth, your honor," replied the old fellow, "sic a mull as that is nae for week-days."

On leaving the quarry, Scott informed me that when absent at Paris, he had purchased several trifling articles as presents for his dependants, and among others the gay snuff-box in question, which was so carefully reserved for Sundays by the veteran. "It was not so much the value of the gifts," said he, "that pleased them, as the idea that the laird should think of them when so far away."

The old man in question, I found, was a great favorite with Scott. If I recollect right, he had been a soldier in early life, and his straight, erect person, his ruddy yet rugged countenance, his gray hair, and an arch gleam in his blue eye, reminded me of the description of Edie Ochiltree. I find that the old fellow has since been introduced by Wilkie, in his picture of the Scott family. * * *

After dinner we adjourned to the drawing-room, which served also for study and library. Against the wall on one side was a long writing-table, with drawers; surmounted by a small cabinet of polished wood, with folding doors richly studded with brass ornaments, within which Scott kept his most valuable papers. Above the cabinet, in a kind of niche, was a complete corselet of glittering steel, with a closed helmet, and flanked by gauntlets and battle-axes. Around were hung trophies and relics of various kinds: a cimeter of Tippoo Saib; a Highland broadsword from Floddenfield; a pair of Rippon spurs from Bannockburn; and above all, a gun which had belonged to Rob Roy, and bore his initials, R. M. G.,—an object of peculiar interest to me at the time, as it was understood Scott was actually engaged in printing a novel founded on the story of that famous outlaw.

On each side of the cabinet were bookcases, well stored with works of romantic fiction in various languages, many of them rare and antiquated. This, however, was merely his cottage library, the principal part of his books being at Edinburgh.

From this little cabinet of curiosities Scot drew forth a manuscript picked up on the field of Waterloo, containing copies of several songs popular at the time in France. The paper was dabbled with blood—"the very life-blood, very possibly," said Scott, "of some gay young officer, who had cherished these songs as a keepsake from some lady-love in Paris."

He adverted in a mellow and delightful manner to the little half gay, half melancholy campaigning song, said to have been composed by General Wolfe, and sung by him at the mess-table, on the eve of the storming of Quebec, in which he fell so gloriously.

"Why, soldiers, why,
Should we be melancholy, boys?
Why, soldiers, why,
Whose business 'tis to die!
For should next campaign
Send us to him who made us, boys,
We're free from pain:
But should we remain,
A bottle and kind landlady
Makes all well again."

"So," added he, "the poor lad who fell at Waterloo, in all probability, had been singing these songs in his tent the night before the battle, and thinking of the fair dame who had taught him them, and promising himself, should he outlive the campaign, to return to her all glorious from the wars."

I find since that Scott published translations of these songs among some of his smaller poems.

The evening passed away delightfully in this quaint-looking apartment, half study, half drawing-room. Scott read several passages from the old romance of Arthur, with a fine deep sonorous voice, and a gravity of tone that seemed to suit the antiquated, black-letter volume. It was a rich treat to hear such a work, read by such a person, and in such a place; and his appearance as he sat reading, in a large armed chair, with his favorite hound Maida at his feet, and surrounded by books and relics, and border trophies, would have formed an admirable and most characteristic picture.

While Scott was reading, the sage

grimalkin already mentioned had already taken his seat in a chair beside the fire, and remained with fixed eye and grave demeanor, as if listening to the reader. I observed to Scott that his cat seemed to have a black-letter taste in literature.

"Ah," said he, "these cats are a very mysterious kind of folk. There is always more passing in their minds than we are aware of. It comes no doubt from their being so familiar with witches and warlocks." He went on to tell a little story about a gude man who was returning to his cottage one night, when, in a lonely out-of-the-way place, he met with a funeral procession of cats all in mourning, bearing one of their race to the grave in a coffin covered with a black velvet pall. The worthy man, astonished and half frightened at so strange a pageant, hastened home and told what he had seen to his wife and children. Scarce had he finished, when a great black cat that sat beside the fire raised himself up, exclaimed "Then I am king of the cats!" and vanished up the chimney. The funeral seen by the gude man was one of the cat dynasty.

"Our grimalkin here," added Scott, "sometimes reminds me of the story, by the airs of sovereignty which he assumes; and I am apt to treat him with respect from the idea that he may be a great prince incog., and may some time or other come to the throne."

In this way Scott would make the habits and peculiarities of even the dumb animals about him subjects for humorous remark or whimsical story.

Our evening was enlivened also by an occasional song from Sophia Scott, at the request of her father. She never wanted to be asked twice, but complied frankly and cheerfully. Her songs were all Scotch, sung without any accompaniment, in a simple manner, but with great spirit and expression, and in their native dialects, which gave them an additional charm. It was delightful to hear her carol off in sprightly style, and with an animated air, some of those generous-spirited old Jacobite songs, once current among the adherents of the Pretender in Scotland, in which he is designated by the appellation of "The Young Chevalier."

These songs were much relished by Scott, notwithstanding his loyalty; for the unfortunate "Chevalier" has always been a hero of romance with him, as he has with many other stanch adherents to the house of Hanover, now that the Stuart line has lost all its terrors. In speaking on the subject, Scott mentioned as a curious fact, that, among the papers of the "Chevalier," which had been submitted by government to his inspection, he had found a memorial to Charles from some adherents in America, dated 1778, proposing to set up his standard in the back settlements. I regret that, at the time, I did not make more particular inquiries of Scott on the subject; the document in question, however, in all probability, still exists among the Pretender's papers, which are in the possession of the British Government.

In the course of the evening, Scott related the story of a whimsical picture hanging in the room, which had been drawn for him by a lady of his acquaintance. It represented the doleful perplexity of a wealthy and handsome young English knight of the olden time, who, in the course of a border foray, had been captured and carried off to the castle of a hard-headed and high-handed old baron. The unfortunate youth was thrown into a dungeon, and a tall gallows erected before the castle-gate for his execution. When all was ready, he was brought into the castle-hall, where the grim baron was seated in state, with his warriors armed to the teeth around him, and was given his choice, either to swing on the gibbet or to marry the baron's daughter. The last may be thought an easy alternative, but, unfortunately, the baron's young lady was hideously ugly, with a mouth from ear to ear, so that not a suitor was to be had for her, either for love or money, and she was known throughout the border country by the name of Muckle-mouthed Mag!

The picture in question represented the unhappy dilemma of the handsome youth. Before him sat the grim baron, with a face worthy of the father of such a daughter, and looking daggers and rat's-bane. On one side of him was Muckle-mouthed Mag, with an amorous smile across the whole breadth of her countenance, and a leer enough to turn a man to stone; on the other side was the father confessor, a sleek friar, jogging the youth's elbow, and pointing to the gallows, seen in perspective through the open portal.

The story goes, that, after long laboring in mind between the altar and the halter, the love of life prevailed, and the youth resigned himself to the charms of Muckle-mouthed Mag. Contrary to all the probabilities of romance, the match proved a happy one. The baron's daughter, if not beautiful, was a most exemplary wife; her husband was never troubled with any of those doubts and jealousies which sometimes mar the happiness of connubial life, and was made the father of a fair and undoubtedly legitimate line, which still flourishes on the border.

I give but a faint outline of the story from vague recollection; it may, perchance, be more richly related elsewhere, by some one who may retain something of the delightful humor with which Scott recounted it.

When I retired for the night, I found it almost impossible to sleep; the idea of being under the roof of Scott, of being on the borders of the Tweed, in the very centre of that region which had for some time past been the favorite scene of romantic fiction, and above all the recollections of the ramble I had taken, the company in which I had taken it, and the conversation which had passed, all fermented in my mind, and nearly drove sleep from my pillow. * * *

1835

JAMES FENIMORE COOPER
(1789–1851)

THE PIONEERS

CHAPTER XXII

[THE FLIGHT OF THE PIGEONS]

> Men, boys, and girls,
> Desert th' unpeopled village; and wild crowds
> Spread o'er the plain, by the sweet phrensy driven.
>
> —SOMERVILLE.

From this time to the close of April the weather continued to be a succession of great and rapid changes. One day, the soft airs of spring seemed to be stealing along the valley, and in unison with an invigorating sun, attempting covertly to rouse the dormant powers of the vegetable world; while on the next, the surly blasts from the north would sweep across the lake, and erase every impression left by their gentle adversaries. The snow, however, finally disappeared, and the green wheat-fields were seen in every direction, spotted with the dark and charred stumps that had, the preceding season, supported some of the proudest trees of the forest. Ploughs were in motion, wherever those useful implements could be used, and the smokes of the sugar-camps were no longer seen issuing from the woods of maple. The lake had lost the beauty of a field of ice, but still a dark and gloomy covering concealed its waters, for the absence of currents left them yet hidden under a porous crust, which, saturated with the fluid, barely retained enough strength to preserve the contiguity of its parts. Large flocks of wild geese were seen passing over the country, which hovered, for a time, around the hidden sheet of water, apparently searching for a resting-place; and then, on finding themselves excluded by the chill covering, would soar away to the north, filling the air with discordant screams, as if venting their complaints at the tardy operations of nature.

For a week, the dark covering of the Otsego was left to the undisturbed possession of two eagles, who alighted on the centre of its field, and sat eying their undisputed territory. During the presence of these monarchs of the air, the flocks of migrating birds avoided crossing the plain of ice by turning into the hills, apparently seeking the protection of the forests, while the white and bald heads of the tenants of the lake were turned upwards, with a look of contempt. But the time had come, when even these kings of birds were to be dispossessed. An opening had been gradually increasing at the lower extremity of the lake, and around the dark spot where the current of the river prevented the formation of ice, during even the coldest weather; and the fresh southerly winds, that now breathed freely upon the valley, made an impression on the waters. Mimic waves began to curl over the margin of the frozen field, which exhibited an outline of crystallizations that slowly receded towards the north. At each step the power of the winds and the waves increased, until, after a struggle of a few hours, the turbulent little billows succeeded in setting the whole field in motion, when it was driven beyond the reach of the eye, with a rapidity that was as magical as the change produced in the scene by this expulsion of the lingering remnant of winter. Just as the last sheet of agitated ice was disappearing in the distance, the eagles rose, and soared with a wide sweep above the clouds, while the waves tossed their little caps of snow into the air, as if rioting in their release from a thraldom of five months' duration.

The following morning Elizabeth was awakened by the exhilarating sounds of the martins, who were quarrelling and chattering around the little boxes suspended above her windows, and the cries of Richard, who was calling in tones animating as the signs of the season itself,—

"Awake! awake! my fair lady! the gulls are hovering over the lake already, and the heavens are alive with pigeons. You may look an hour before you can find a hole through which to get a peep at the sun. Awake! awake! lazy ones! Benjamin is overhauling the ammunition, and we only wait for our breakfasts, and away for the mountains and pigeon shooting."

There was no resisting this animated appeal, and in a few minutes Miss Temple and her friend descended to the parlor. The doors of the hall were thrown open, and the mild, balmy air of a clear spring morning was ventilating the apartment, where the vigilance of the ex-steward had been so long maintaining an artificial heat with such unremitted diligence. The gentlemen were impatiently waiting for their morning's repast, each equipped in the garb of a sportsman. Mr. Jones made many visits to the southern door, and would cry,—

"See, cousin Bess! see, 'duke, the pigeon-roosts of the south have broken up! They are growing more thick every instant. Here is a flock that the eye cannot see the end of. There is food enough in it to keep the army of Xerxes for a month, and feathers enough to make beds for the whole country. Xerxes, Mr. Edwards, was a Grecian king, who—no, he was a Turk, or a Persian, who wanted to conquer Greece, just the same as these rascals will overrun our wheat-fields, when they come back in the fall. Away! away! Bess; I long to pepper them."

In this wish both Marmaduke and young Edwards seemed equally to participate, for the sight was exhilarating to a sportsman; and the ladies soon dismissed the party after a hasty breakfast.

If the heavens were alive with pigeons, the whole village seemed equally in motion, with men, women, and children. Every species of firearms, from the French ducking-gun with a barrel near six feet in length, to the common horseman's pistol, was to be seen in the hands of the men and boys; while bows and arrows, some made of the simple stick of a walnut sapling, and others in a rude imitation of the ancient cross-bows, were carried by many of the latter.

The houses and the signs of life apparent in the village, drove the alarmed birds from the direct line of their flight towards the mountains, along the sides and near the bases of which they were glancing in dense masses, equally wonderful by the rapidity of their motion, and their incredible numbers.

We have already said, that across the inclined plane which fell from the steep ascent of the mountain to the banks of the Susquehanna, ran the highway, on either side of which a clearing of many acres had been made at a very early day. Over those clearings, and up the eastern mountain, and along the dangerous path that was cut into its side, the different individuals posted themselves, and in a few moments the attack commenced.

Among the sportsmen was the tall, gaunt form of Leather-stocking walking over the field, with his rifle hanging on his arm, his dogs at his heels; the latter now scenting the dead or wounded birds, that were beginning to tumble from the flocks and then crouching under the legs of their master, as if they participated in his feelings at this wasteful and unsportsmanlike execution.

The reports of the fire-arms became rapid, whole volleys rising from the plain, as flocks of more than ordinary numbers darted over the opening, shadowing the field like a cloud; and then the light smoke of a single piece would issue from among the leafless bushes on the mountain, as death was hurled on the retreat of the affrighted birds, who were rising from a volley, in a vain effort to escape. Arrows, and missiles of every kind were in the midst of the flocks; and so numerous were the birds, and so low did they take their flight, that even long poles, in the hands of those on the sides of the mountain, were used to strike them to the earth.

During all this time, Mr. Jones, who disdained the humble and ordinary means of destruction used by his companions, was busily occupied, aided by Benjamin, in making arrangements for an assault of more than ordinarily fatal character. Among the relics of the old military excursions, that occasionally are discovered throughout the different districts of the western part of New York, there had been found in Templeton, at its settlement, a small swivel, which would carry a ball of a pound weight. It was thought to have been deserted by a war party of the whites, in one of their inroads into the Indian settlements, when perhaps, convenience or their necessity induced them to leave such an incumbrance behind them in the woods. This miniature cannon had been released from the rust, and being mounted on little wheels, was now in a state for actual service. For several years, it was the sole organ for extraordinary rejoicings used in those mountains. On the mornings of the Fourths of July, it would be heard ringing among the hills; and even Captain Hollister, who was the highest authority in that part of the country on all such occasions, affirmed that, considering its dimensions, it was no despicable gun for a salute. It was somewhat the worse for the service it had performed, it is true, there being but a trifling difference in size between the touch-hole and the muzzle. Still, the grand conceptions of Richard had suggested the importance of such an instrument in hurling death at his nimble enemies. The swivel was dragged by a horse into a part of the open space that the Sheriff thought most eligible for planting a battery of the kind, and Mr. Pump proceeded to load it. Several handfuls of duck-shot were placed on top of the powder, and the major-domo announced that his piece was ready for service.

The sight of such an implement collected all the idle spectators to the spot, who, being mostly boys, filled the air with cries of exultation and delight. The gun was pointed high, and Richard, holding a coal of fire in a pair of tongs, patiently took his seat on a stump, awaiting the appearance of a flock worthy of his notice.

So prodigious was the number of the birds, that the scattering fire of the guns, with the hurling of missiles, and the cries of the boys, had no other effect than to break off small flocks from the immense masses that continued to dart along the valley, as if the whole of the feathered tribe were pouring through that one pass. None pretended to collect the game, which lay scattered over the fields in such profusion as to cover the very ground with the fluttering victims.

Leather-stocking was a silent, but uneasy spectator of all these proceedings, but was able to keep his sentiments to himself until he saw the introduction of the swivel into the sports.

"This comes of settling a country!" he said; "here have I known the pigeons to fly for forty long years, and, till you made your clearings, there was nobody to skear or to hurt them. I loved to see them come in the woods, for they were company to a body; hurting nothing; being, as it was, as harmless as a garter-snake. But now it gives me sore thoughts when I hear the frighty things whizzing through the air, for I know it's only a motion to bring out all the brats in the village. Well! the Lord won't see the waste of his creatures for nothing, and right will be done to the pigeons, as well as others, by and by. There's Mr. Oliver, as bad as the rest of them, firing into the flocks, as if he was shooting down nothing but Mingo warriors."

Among the sportsmen was Billy Kirby, who, armed with an old musket, was loading, and without even looking into the air, was firing and shouting as his victims fell even on his own person. He heard the speech of Natty, and took upon himself to reply—

"What! old Leather-stocking," he cried, "grumbling at the loss of a few pigeons! If you had to sow your wheat twice, and three times, as I have done, you wouldn't be so massyfully feeling toward the divils.—Hurrah, boys! scatter the feathers! This is better than shooting at a turkey's head and neck, old fellow."

"It's better for you, maybe, Billy Kirby," replied the indignant old hunter, "and all them that don't know how to put a ball down a rifle barrel, or how to bring it up again with a true aim; but it's wicked to be shooting into flocks in this wasty manner; and none do it, who know how to knock over a single bird. If a body has a craving for pigeon's flesh, why, it's made the same as all other creatures, for man's eating; but not to kill twenty and eat one. When I want such a thing I go into the woods till I find one to my liking, and then I shoot him off the branches, without touching the feather of another, though there might be a hundred on the same tree. You couldn't do such a thing, Billy Kirby—you couldn't do it, if you tried."

"What's that, old corn-stalk! you sapless stub!" cried the wood-chopper. "You have grown wordy, since the affair of the turkey; but if you are for a single shot, here goes at that bird which comes on by himself."

The fire from the distant part of the field had driven a single pigeon below the flock to which it belonged, and, frightened with the constant reports of the muskets, it was approaching the spot where the disputants stood, darting first to one side, and then to the other, cutting the air with the swiftness of lightning and making a noise with its wings, not unlike the rushing of a bullet. Unfortunately for the wood-chopper, notwithstanding his vaunt, he did not see this bird until it was too late to fire as it approached, and he pulled his trigger at the unlucky moment when it was darting immediately over his head. The bird continued its course with the usual velocity.

Natty lowered the rifle from his arm when the challenge was made, and waiting for a moment, until the terrified victim had got in a line with his eye, and had dropped near the bank of the lake, he raised it again with uncommon rapidity, and fired. It might have been chance, or it might have been skill, that produced the result; it was probably a union of both; but the pigeon whirled over in the air, and fell into the lake, with a broken wing. At the sound of his rifle, both his dogs started from his feet, and in a few minutes the "slut" brought out the bird still alive.

The wonderful exploit of Leather-stocking was noised through the field with great rapidity, and the sportsmen gathered in, to learn the truth of the report.

"What!" said young Edwards, "have you really killed a pigeon on the wing, Natty, with a single ball?"

"Haven't I killed loons before now, lad, that dive at the flash?" returned the hunter. "It's much better to kill only such as you want, without wasting your powder and lead, than to be firing into God's creatures in this wicked manner. But I came out for a bird, and you know the reason why I like small game, Mr. Oliver, and now I have got one I will go home, for I don't relish to see these wasty ways that you are all practysing, as if the least thing wasn't made for use, and not to destroy."

"Thou sayest well, Leather-stocking," cried Marmaduke, "and I begin to think it time to put an end to this work of destruction."

"Put an ind, Judge, to your clearings. An't the woods His work as well as the pigeons? Use, but don't waste. Wasn't the woods made for the beasts and birds to harbor in? and when man wanted their flesh, their skins, or their feathers, there's the place to seek them. But I'll go to the hut with my own game, for I wouldn't touch one of the harmless things that cover the ground here, looking up with their eyes on me, as if they only wanted tongues to say their thoughts."

With this sentiment in his mouth, Leather-stocking threw his rifle over his arm, and followed by his dogs stepped across the clearing with great caution, taking care not to tread on one of the wounded birds in his path. He soon entered the bushes on the margin of the lake, and was hid from view.

Whatever impression the morality of Natty made on the Judge, it was utterly lost on Richard. He availed himself of the gathering of the sportsmen, to lay a plan for one "fell swoop" of destruction. The musket-men were drawn up in battle array, in a line extending on each side of his artillery, with orders to await the signal of firing from himself.

"Stand by, my lads," said Benjamin, who acted as an aide-de-camp on this occasion, "stand by, my hearties, and when Squire Dickens heaves out the signal to begin firing, d'ye see, you may open upon them in a broadside. Take care and fire low, boys, and you'll be sure to hull the flock."

"Fire low!" shouted Kirby—"hear the old fool! If we fire low, we may hit the stumps, but not ruffle a pigeon."

"How should you know, you lubber?" cried Benjamin, with a very unbecoming heat for an officer on the eve of battle—"how should you know, you grampus? Haven't I sailed aboard of the Boadishy for five years? and wasn't it a standing order to fire low, and to hull your enemy? Keep silence at your guns, boys, and mind the order that is passed."

The loud laughs of the musket men were silenced by the more authoritative voice of Richard, who called for attention and obedience to his signals.

Some millions of pigeons were supposed to have already passed, that morning, over the valley of Templeton; but nothing like the flock that was now approaching had been seen before. It extended from mountain to mountain in one solid blue mass, and the eye looked in vain, over the southern hills, to find its termination. The front of this living column was distinctly marked by a line but very slightly indented, so regular and even was the flight. Even Marmaduke forgot the morality of Leather-stocking as it approached, and, in common with the rest, brought his musket to a poise.

"Fire!" cried the Sheriff, clapping a coal to the priming of the cannon. As half of Benjamin's charge escaped through the touch-hole, the whole volley of the musketry preceded the report of the swivel. On receiving this united discharge of small-arms, the front of the flock darted upwards, while, at the same instant, myriads of those in the rear rushed with amazing rapidity into their places, so that when the column of white smoke gushed from the mouth of the little cannon, an accumulated mass of objects was gliding over its point of direction. The roar of the gun echoed along the mountains, and died away to the north, like distant thunder, while the whole flock of alarmed birds seemed, for a moment, thrown into one disorderly and agitated mass. The air was filled with their irregular flight, layer rising above layer, far above the tops of the highest pines, none daring to advance beyond the dangerous pass; when, suddenly, some of the leaders of the feathered tribe shot across the valley, taking their flight directly over the village, and hundreds of thousands in their rear followed the example, deserting the eastern side of the plain to their persecutors and the slain.

"Victory!" shouted Richard, "victory! we have driven the enemy from the field."

"Not so, Dickon," said Marmaduke: "the field is covered with them; and, like the Leather-stocking, I see nothing but eyes, in every direction, as the innocent sufferers turn their heads in terror. Full one half of those that have fallen are yet alive; and I think it is time to end the sport, if sport it be."

"Sport!" cried the Sheriff; "it is princely sport! There are some thousands of the blue-coated boys on the ground, so that every old woman in the village may have a pot-pie for the asking."

"Well, we have happily frightened the birds from this side of the valley," said Marmaduke, "and the carnage must of necessity end, for the present. Boys, I will give you sixpence a hundred for the pigeons' heads only: so go to work, and bring them into the village."

This expedient produced the desired effect, for every urchin on the ground went industriously to work to wring the necks of the wounded birds. Judge Temple retired towards his dwelling with that kind of feeling that many a man has experienced before him, who discovers, after the excitement of the moment has passed, that he has purchased pleasure at the price of misery to others. Horses were loaded with the dead; and, after this first burst of sporting, the shooting of pigeons became a business, with a few idlers, for the remainder of the season. Richard, however, boasted for many a year, of his shot with the "cricket;" and Benjamin gravely asserted, that he thought they killed nearly as many pigeons on that day, as there were Frenchmen destroyed on the memorable occasion of Rodney's victory.

1823

THE LAST OF THE MOHICANS

CHAPTER III

[LEATHER-STOCKING AND CHINGACHGOOK]

Before these fields were shorn and till'd,
Full to the brim our rivers flow'd;
The melody of waters fill'd
The fresh and boundless wood;
And torrents dash'd, and rivulets play'd,
And fountains spouted in the shade.
—Bryant.

Leaving the unsuspecting Heyward and his confiding companions to penetrate still deeper into a forest that contained such treacherous inmates, we must use an author's privilege and shift the scene a few miles to the westward of the place where we have last seen them.

On that day, two men were lingering on the banks of a small but rapid stream, within an hour's journey of the encampment of Webb, like those who awaited the appearance of an absent person, or the approach of some expected event. The vast canopy of woods spread itself to the margin of the river, overhanging the water and shadowing its dark current with a deeper hue. The rays of the sun were beginning to grow less fierce, and the intense heat of the day was lessened, as the cooler vapors of the springs and fountains rose above their leafy beds and rested in the atmosphere. Still that breathing silence, which marks the drowsy sultriness of an American landscape in July, pervaded the secluded spot, interrupted only by the low voices of the men, the occasional and lazy tap of a woodpecker, the discordant cry of some gaudy jay, or a swelling on the ear from the dull roar of a distant waterfall.

These feeble and broken sounds were, however, too familiar to the foresters to draw their attention from the more interesting matter of their dialogue. While one of these loiterers showed the red skin and wild accoutrements of a native of the woods, the other exhibited, through the mask of his rude and nearly savage equipments, the brighter, though sun-burnt and long-faded complexion of one who might claim descent from a European parentage. The former was seated on the end of a mossy log, in a posture that permitted him to heighten the effect of his earnest language by the calm but expressive gestures of an Indian engaged in debate. His body, which was nearly naked, presented a terrific emblem of death, drawn in intermingled colors of white and black. His closely shaved head, on which no other hair than the well-known and chivalrous scalping tuft * was preserved, was without ornament of any kind, with the exception of a solitary eagle's plume that crossed his crown and depended over the left shoulder. A tomahawk and scalping-knife, of English manufacture, were in his girdle; while a short military rifle, of that sort with which the policy of the whites armed their savage allies, lay carelessly across his bare and sinewy knee. The expanded chest, full-formed limbs, and grave countenance of this warrior would denote that he had reached the vigor of his days, though no symptoms of decay appeared to have yet weakened his manhood.

The frame of the white man, judging by such parts as were not concealed by his clothes, was like that of one who had known hardships and exertion from his earliest youth. His person, though muscular, was rather attenuated than full; but every nerve and muscle appeared strung and indurated by unremitted exposure and toil. He wore a hunting-shirt of forest-green, fringed with faded yellow,† and a summer cap of skins which had been shorn of their fur. He also bore a knife in a girdle of wampum, like that which confined the scanty garments of the Indian, but no tomahawk. His moccasins were ornamented after the gay fashion of the natives; while the only part of his underdress which appeared below the hunting-frock was a pair of buckskin leggings

* The North American warrior caused the hair to be plucked from his whole body; a small tuft, only, was left on the crown of his head, in order that his enemy might avail himself of it, in wrenching off the scalp in the event of his fall. The scalp was the only admissible trophy of victory. Thus, it was deemed more important to obtain the scalp than to kill the man. Some tribes lay great stress on the honor of striking a dead body. These practices have nearly disappeared among the Indians of the Atlantic states. [Author's note.]

† The hunting-shirt is a picturesque smock-frock, being shorter, and ornamented with fringes and tassels. The colors are intended to imitate the hues of the wood, with a view to concealment. Many corps of American riflemen have been thus attired; and the dress is one of the most striking of modern times. The hunting-shirt is frequently white. [Author's note.]

that laced at the sides, and which were gartered above the knees with the sinews of a deer. A pouch and horn completed his personal accoutrements, though a rifle of great length,* which the theory of the more ingenious whites had taught them was the most dangerous of all fire-arms, leaned against a neighboring sapling. The eye of the hunter, or scout, whichever he might be, was small, quick, keen, and restless, roving while he spoke, on every side of him, as if in quest of game, or distrusting the sudden approach of some lurking enemy. Notwithstanding these symptoms of habitual suspicion, his countenance was not only without guile, but at the moment at which he is introduced, it was charged with an expression of sturdy honesty.

"Even your traditions make the case in my favor, Chingachgook," he said, speaking in the tongue which was known to all the natives who formerly inhabited the country between the Hudson and the Potomack, and of which we shall give a free translation for the benefit of the reader; endeavoring, at the same time, to preserve some of the peculiarities, both of the individual and of the language. "Your fathers came from the setting sun, crossed the big river,† fought the people of the country, and took the land; and mine came from the red sky of the morning, over the salt lake, and did their work much after the fashion that had been set them by yours; then let God judge the matter between us, and friends spare their words!"

"My fathers fought with the naked red man!" returned the Indian sternly, in the same language. "Is there no difference, Hawk-eye, between the stone-headed arrow of the warrior and the leaden bullet with which you kill?"

"There is reason in an Indian, though nature has made him with a red skin!" said the white man, shaking his head like one on whom such an appeal to his justice was not thrown away. For a moment he appeared to be conscious of having the worst of the argument; then rallying again, he answered the objection of his antagonist in the best manner his limited information would allow: "I am no scholar, and I care not who knows it; but judging from what I have seen, at deer chases and squirrel hunts, of the sparks below, I should think a rifle in the hands of their grandfathers was not so dangerous as a hickory bow and a good flint-head might be, if drawn with Indian judgment, and sent by an Indian eye."

"You have the story told by your fathers," returned the other, coldly waving his hand. "What say your old men? Do they tell the young warriors that the palefaces met the red men, painted for war and armed with the stone hatchet and wooden gun?"

"I am not a prejudiced man, nor one who vaunts himself on his natural privileges, though the worst enemy I have on earth, and he is an Iroquois, daren't deny that I am genuine white," the scout replied, surveying with secret satisfaction the faded color

* The rifle of the army is short; that of the hunter is always long. [Author's note.]

† The Mississippi. The scout alludes to a tradition which is very popular among the tribes of the Atlantic states. Evidence of their Asiatic origin is deduced from the circumstances, though great uncertainty hangs over the whole history of the Indians. [Author's note.]

of his bony and sinewy hand; "and I am willing to own that my people have many ways of which, as an honest man, I can't approve. It is one of their customs to write in books what they have done and seen, instead of telling them in their villages, where the lie can be given to the face of a cowardly boaster, and the brave soldier can call on his comrades to witness for the truth of his words. In consequence of this bad fashion, a man who is too conscientious to misspend his days among the women, in learning the names of black marks, may never hear of the deeds of his fathers, nor feel a pride in striving to outdo them. For myself, I conclude all the Bumppos could shoot, for I have a natural turn with a rifle, which must have been handed down from generation to generation, as our holy commandments tell us all good and evil gifts are bestowed; though I should be loth to answer for other people in such a matter. But every story has its two sides; so I ask you, Chingachgook, what passed, according to the traditions of the red men, when our fathers first met?"

A silence of a minute succeeded, during which the Indian sat mute; then, full of the dignity of his office, he commenced his brief tale with a solemnity that served to heighten its appearance of truth.

"Listen, Hawk-eye, and your ear shall drink no lie. 'Tis what my fathers have said, and what the Mohicans have done." He hesitated a single instant, and bending a cautious glance towards his companion, he continued in a manner that was divided between interrogation and assertion—"Does not this stream at our feet run towards the summer, until its waters grow salt and the current flows upward?"

"It can't be denied that your traditions tell you true in both these matters," said the white man; "for I have been there, and have seen them; though why water, which is so sweet in the shade, should become bitter in the sun, is an alteration for which I have never been able to account."

"And the current!" demanded the Indian, who expected his reply with that sort of interest that a man feels in the confirmation of testimony at which he marvels even while he respects it; "the fathers of Chingachgook have not lied!"

"The holy Bible is not more true, and that is the truest thing in nature. They call this up-stream current the tide, which is a thing soon explained and clear enough. Six hours the waters run in, and six hours they run out, and the reason is this: when there is higher water in the sea than in the river, they run in until the river gets to be highest, and then it runs out again."

"The waters in the woods, and on the great lakes, run downward until they lie like my hand," said the Indian, stretching the limb horizontally before him, "and then they run no more."

"No honest man will deny it," said the scout, a little nettled at the implied distrust of his explanation of the mystery of the tides; "and I grant that it is true on the small scale, and where the land is level. But everything depends on what scale you look at things. Now, on the small scale, the 'arth is level; but on the large scale it is round. In this manner, pools and ponds, and even the great fresh-water lakes, may be stagnant, as you and I both know they are, having seen them; but when you come to spread water over a great tract, like the sea, where the earth is round, how in reason can the water be quiet? You might as well expect the river to lie still on the brink of those black rocks a mile above us, though your own ears tell you that it is tumbling over them at this very moment!"

If unsatisfied by the philosophy of his companion, the Indian was far too dignified to betray his unbelief. He listened like one who was convinced, and resumed his narrative in his former solemn manner.

"We came from the place where the sun is hid at night, over great plains where the buffaloes live, until we reached the big river. There we fought the Alligewi, till the ground was red with their blood. From the banks of the big river to the shores of the salt lake, there was none to meet us. The Maquas followed at a distance. We said the country should be ours from the place where the water runs up no longer on this stream, to a river twenty suns' journey toward the summer. The land we had taken like warriors we kept like men. We drove the Maquas into the woods with the bears. They only tasted salt at the licks; they drew no fish from the great lake; we threw them the bones."

"All this I have heard and believe," said the white man, observing that the Indian paused: "but it was long before the English came into the country."

"A pine grew then where this chestnut now stands. The first pale-faces who came among us spoke no English. They came in a large canoe, when my fathers had buried the tomahawk with the red men around them. Then, Hawk-eye," he continued, betraying his deep emotion, only by permitting his voice to fall to those low, guttural tones, which render his language, as spoken at times, so very musical; "then, Hawk-eye, we were one people, and we were happy. The salt lake gave us its fish, the wood its deer, and the air its birds. We took wives who bore us children; we worshipped the Great Spirit; and we kept the Maquas beyond the sound of our songs of triumph!"

"Know you anything of your own family at that time?" demanded the white. "But you are a just man for an Indian! and, as I suppose you hold their gifts, your fathers must have been brave warriors, and wise men at the council fire."

"My tribe is the grandfather of nations, but I am an unmixed man. The blood of chiefs is in my veins, where it must stay for ever. The Dutch landed, and gave my people the fire-water; they drank until the heavens and the earth seemed to meet, and they foolishly thought they had found the Great Spirit. Then they parted with their land. Foot by foot, they were driven back from the shores, until I, that am a chief and a Sagamore, have never seen the sun shine but through the trees, and have never visited the graves of my fathers!"

"Graves bring solemn feelings over the mind," returned the scout, a good deal touched at the calm suffering of his companion; "and they often aid a man in his good intentions; though, for myself, I expect to leave my own bones unburied, to bleach in the woods, or to be torn asunder by the wolves. But where are to be found those of your race who came to their kin in the Delaware country, so many summers since?"

"Where are the blossoms of those summers!—fallen, one by one: so all of my family departed, each in his turn, to the land of spirits. I am on the hill-top, and must go down into the valley; and when Uncas follows in my footsteps, there will no longer be any of the blood of the Sagamores, for my boy is the last of the Mohicans."

"Uncas is here!" said another voice, in the same soft, guttural tones, near his elbow; "who speaks to Uncas?"

The white man loosened his knife in his leathern sheath, and made an involuntary movement of the hand towards his rifle, at this sudden interruption; but the Indian sat composed, and without turning his head at the unexpected sounds.

At the next instant, a youthful warrior passed between them, with a noiseless step, and seated himself on the bank of the rapid stream. No exclamation of surprise escaped the father, nor was any question asked, or reply given, for several minutes; each appearing to await the moment when he might speak, without betraying womanish curiosity or childish impatience. The white man seemed to take counsel from their customs, and, relinquishing his grasp of the rifle, he also remained silent and reserved. At length Chingachgook turned his eyes slowly towards his son and demanded—

"Do the Maquas dare to leave the print of their moccasins in these woods?"

"I have been on their trail," replied the young Indian, "and know that they number as many as the fingers of my two hands; but they lie hid like cowards."

"The thieves are out-lying for scalps and plunder!" said the white man, whom, we shall call Hawk-eye, after the manner of his companions. "That busy Frenchman, Montcalm, will send his spies into our very camp, but he will know what road we travel!"

"'Tis enough!" returned the father, glancing his eye towards the setting sun; "they shall be driven like deer from their bushes. Hawk-eye, let us eat tonight, and show the Maquas that we are men to-morrow."

"I am as ready to do the one as the other: but to fight the Iroquois 'tis necessary to find the skulkers; and to eat, 'tis necessary to get the game—talk of the devil and he will come; there is a pair of the biggest antlers I have seen this season, moving the bushes below the hill! Now, Uncas," he continued in a half whisper, and laughing with a kind of inward sound, like one who had learnt to be watchful, "I will bet my charger three times full of powder, against a foot of wampum, that I take him atwixt the eyes and nearer to the right than to the left."

"It cannot be!" said the young Indian, springing to his feet with youthful eagerness; "all but the tips of his horns are hid!"

"He's a boy!" said the white man, shaking his head while he spoke, and addressing the father. "Does he think when a hunter sees a part of the creatur', he can't tell where the rest of him should be?"

Adjusting his rifle, he was about to make an exhibition of that skill on which he so much valued himself, when the warrior struck up the piece with his hand, saying:

"Hawk-eye, will you fight the Maquas?"

"These Indians know the nature of the woods, as it might be by instinct!" returned the scout, dropping his rifle, and turning away like a man who was convinced of his error. "I must leave the buck to your arrow, Uncas, or we may kill a deer for them thieves, the Iroquois, to eat."

The instant the father seconded this intimation by an expressive gesture of the hand, Uncas threw himself on the ground and approached the animal with wary movements. When within a few yards of the cover, he fitted an arrow to his bow with the utmost care, while the antlers moved, as if their owner snuffed an enemy in the tainted air. In another moment the twang of the cord was heard, a white streak was seen glancing into the bushes, and the wounded buck plunged from the cover to the very feet of his hidden enemy. Avoiding the horns of the infuriated animal, Uncas darted to his side, and passed his knife across the throat, when bounding to the edge of the river it fell, dyeing the waters with its blood.

"'Twas done with Indian skill," said the scout, laughing inwardly, but with vast satisfaction; "and 'twas a pretty sight to behold; though an arrow is a near shot, and needs a knife to finish the work."

"Hugh!" ejaculated his companion, turning quickly, like a hound who scented game.

"By the Lord, there is a drove of them!" exclaimed the scout, whose eyes began to glisten with the ardor of his usual occupation; "if they come within range of a bullet, I will drop one, though the whole Six Nations should be lurking within sound! What do you hear, Chingachgook? for to my ears the woods are dumb."

"There is but one deer, and he is dead," said the Indian, bending his body till his ear nearly touched the earth. "I hear the sounds of feet!"

"Perhaps the wolves have driven the buck to shelter, and are following on his trail."

"No. The horses of white men are coming!" returned the other, raising himself with dignity, and resuming his seat on the log with his former composure. "Hawk-eye, they are your brothers; speak to them."

"That will I, and in English that the king needn't be ashamed to answer," returned the hunter, speaking in the language of which he boasted; "but I see nothing, nor do I hear the sounds of man or beast; 'tis strange that an Indian should understand white sounds better than a man who, his very enemies will own, has no cross in his blood, although he may have lived with the red skins long enough to be suspected! Ha! there goes something like the cracking of a dry stick, too—now I hear the bushes move—yes, yes, there is a trampling that I mistook for the falls—and—but here they come themselves; God keep them from the Iroquois!"

1826

From *A HISTORY OF THE NAVY*

CHAPTER IX

[THE ACTION BETWEEN THE *SERAPIS* AND THE *BON HOMME RICHARD*]

* * * Com. Jones having ascertained the character of the fleet in sight, showed a signal for a general chase, another to recall the lieutenant in the pilot boat, and crossed royal yards on board the Richard. These signs of hostility alarmed the nearest English ships, which hurriedly tacked together, fired alarm guns, let fly their top-gallant sheets, and made other signals of the danger they were in, while they now gladly availed themselves of the presence of the ships of war, to run to leeward, or sought shelter closer in with the land. The Serapis, on the contrary, signalled the Scarborough to follow, and hauled boldly out to sea, until she had got far enough to windward, when she tacked and stood in shore again, to cover her convoy.

The Alliance being much the fastest vessel of the American squadron, took the lead in the chase, speaking the Pallas as she passed. It has been proved that Capt. Landais told the commander of the latter vessel on this occasion, that if the stranger proved to be a fifty, they had nothing to do but to endeavour to escape. His subsequent conduct fully confirmed this opinion, for no sooner had he run down near enough to the two English vessels of war, to ascertain their force, than he hauled up, and stood off from the land again. All this was not only contrary to the regular order of battle, but contrary to the positive command of Commodore Jones, who had kept the signal to form a line abroad, which should have brought the Alliance astern of the Richard, and the Pallas in the van. Just at this time, the Pallas spoke the Richard and inquired what station she should take, and was also directed to form the line. But the extraordinary movements of Capt. Landais appear to have produced some indecision in the commander of the Pallas, as he too soon after tacked and stood off from the land. Capt. Cottineau, however, was a brave man, and subsequently did his duty in the action, and this manœuvre has been explained by the Richard's hauling up suddenly for the land, which induced him to think that her crew had mutinied and were running away with the ship. Such was the want of confidence that prevailed in a force so singularly composed, and such were the disadvantages under which this celebrated combat was fought!

So far, however, from meditating retreat or mutiny, the people of the Bon Homme Richard had gone cheerfully to their quarters, although every man on board was conscious of the superiority of the force with which they were about to contend; and the high unconquerable spirit of the commander appears to have communicated itself to the crew.

It was now getting to be dark, and Commodore Jones was compelled to follow the movements of the enemy by the aid of a night glass. It is probable that the obscurity which prevailed added to the indecision of the commander of the Pallas, for from this time until the moon rose, objects at a distance were distinguished with difficulty, and even after the moon appeared, with uncertainty. The Richard, however, stood steadily on, and about half-past seven, she came up with the Serapis, the Scarborough being a short distance to leeward. The American ship was to windward, and as she drew slowly near, Capt. Pearson hailed. The answer was equivocal, and both ships delivered their entire broadsides nearly simultaneously. The water being so smooth, Com. Jones had relied materially on the eighteens that were in the gun-room; but at this discharge two of the six that were fired bursted, blowing up the deck above, and killing or wounding a large proportion of the people that were stationed below. This disaster caused all the heavy guns to be instantly deserted, for the men had no longer sufficient confidence in their goodness to use them. It, at once, reduced the broadside of the Richard to about a third less than that of her opponent, not to include the disadvantage of the manner in which the metal that remained was distributed among light guns. In short, the combat was now between a twelve-pounder and an eighteen-pounder frigate; a species of contest in which, it has been said, we know not with what truth, the former has never been known to prevail. Com. Jones informs us himself, that all his hopes, after this accident, rested on the twelve-pounders that were under the command of his first lieutenant.

The Richard, having backed her topsails, exchanged several broadsides, when she filled again and shot ahead of the Serapis, which ship luffed across her stern and came up on the weather quarter of her antagonist, taking the wind out of her sails, and, in her turn, passing ahead. All this time, which consumed half an hour, the cannonading was close and furious. The Scarborough now drew near, but it is uncertain whether she fired or not. On the side of the Americans it is affirmed that she raked the Richard at least once; but by the report of her own commander, it would appear that, on account of the obscurity and the smoke, he was afraid to discharge his guns, not knowing which ship might be the friend, or which the foe. Unwilling to lie by, and to be exposed to shot uselessly, Capt. Piercy edged away from the combatants, exchanged a broadside or two, at a great distance, with the Alliance, and shortly afterwards was engaged at close quarters by the Pallas, which ship compelled him to strike, after a creditable resistance of about an hour.

Having disposed of the inferior ships, we can confine ourselves to the principal combatants. As the Serapis kept her luff, sailing and working better than the Richard, it was the intention of Capt. Pearson to pay broad off across the latter's forefoot, as soon as he had got far enough ahead; but making the attempt, and finding he had not room, he put his helm hard down, to keep clear of his adversary, when the double movement brought the two ships nearly in a line, the Serapis leading. By these uncertain evolutions, the English ship lost some of her way, while the American, having kept her sails trimmed, not only closed, but actually ran aboard of her antagonist, bows on, a little on her weather quarter. The wind being light, much time was consumed in these different manœuvres, and near an hour had elapsed between the firing of the first guns, and the moment when the vessels got foul of each other in the manner just described.

The English now thought that it was the intention of the Americans to board them, and a few minutes passed in the uncertainty which such an expectation would create; but the positions of the vessels were not favourable for either party to pass into the opposing ship. There being at this moment a perfect cessation of the firing, Capt. Pearson demanded, "Have you struck your colors?" "I have not yet begun to fight," was the answer.

The yards of the Richard were braced aback, and, the sails of the Serapis being full, the ships separated. As soon as far enough asunder, the Serapis put her helm hard down, laid all aback forward, shivered her after-sails, and wore short round on her heel, or was box-hauled, with a view, most probably, of luffing up athwart the bow of her enemy, in order to again rake her. In this position the Richard would have been fighting her starboard, and the Serapis her larboard guns; but Commodore Jones, by this time, was conscious of the hopelessness of success against so much heavier metal, and after having backed astern some distance, he filled on the other tack, luffing up with the intention of meeting the enemy as she came to the wind, and of laying her athwart hause. In the smoke, one party or the other miscalculated the distance, for the two vessels came foul again, the bowsprit of the English ship passing over the poop of the American. As neither had much way, the collision did but little injury, and Com. Jones, with his own hands, immediately lashed the enemy's head-gear to his mizzen-mast. The pressure on the after sails of the Serapis, which vessel was nearly before the wind at the time, brought her hull round, and the two ships gradually fell close alongside of each other, head and stern, the jib-boom of the Serapis giving way with the strain. A spare anchor of the English ship now hooked in the quarter of the American, and additional lashings were got out on board the latter to secure her in this position.

Capt. Pearson, who was as much aware of his advantage in a regular combat as his opponent could be of his own disadvantage, no sooner perceived the vessels foul, than he dropped an anchor, in the hope that the Richard would drift clear of him. But such an expectation was perfectly futile, as the yards were interlocked, the hulls were pressed close against each other, there were lashings fore and aft, and even the ornamental work aided in holding the ships together. When the cable of the Serapis took the strain, the vessels slowly tended, with the bows of the Serapis and the stern of the Richard to the tide. At this instant the English made an attempt to board, but were repulsed without loss.

All this time the battle raged. The lower ports of the Serapis having been closed, as the vessel swung, to prevent boarding, they were now blown off, in order to allow the guns to run out; and cases actually occurred in which the rammers had to be thrust into the ports of the opposite ship in order to be entered into the muzzles of their proper guns. It is evident that such a conflict must have been of short duration. In effect, the heavy metal of the Serapis, in one or two discharges, cleared all before it, and the main-deck guns of the Richard were in a great measure abandoned. Most of the people went on the upper deck, and a great number collected on the forecastle, where they were safe from the fire of the enemy, continuing to fight by throwing grenades and using muskets.

In this stage of the combat, the Serapis was tearing her antagonist to pieces below, almost without resistance from her enemy's batteries, only two guns on the quarter-deck, and three or four of the twelves being worked at all. To the former, by shifting a gun from the larboard side, Com. Jones succeeded in adding a third, all of which were used with effect, under his immediate inspection, to the close of the action. He could not muster force enough to get over a second gun. But the combat would now have soon terminated, had it not been for the courage and activity of the people aloft. Strong parties had been placed in the tops, and, at the end of a short contest, the Americans had driven every man belonging to the enemy below; after which they kept up so animated a fire, on the quarter-deck of the Serapis in particular, as to drive nearly every man off it, that was not shot down.

Thus, while the English had the battle nearly all to themselves below, their enemies had the control above the upper-deck. Having cleared the tops of the Serapis, some American seamen lay out on the Richard's main-yard, and began to throw hand-grenades upon the two upper decks of the English ship; the men on the forecastle of their own vessel seconding these efforts, by casting the same combustibles through the ports of the Serapis. At length one man, in particular, became so hardy as to take his post on the extreme end of the yard, whence, provided with a bucket filled with combustibles, and a match, he dropped the grenades with so much precision that one passed through the main-hatchway. The powder-boys of the Serapis had got more cartridges up than were wanted, and, in their hurry, they had carelessly laid a row of them on the main-deck, in a line with the guns. The grenade just mentioned set fire to some loose powder that was lying near, and the flash passed from cartridge to cartridge, beginning abreast of the main-mast, and running quite aft.

The effect of this explosion was awful. More than twenty men were instantly killed, many of them being left with nothing on them but the collars and wristbands of their shirts, and the waistbands of their duck trousers; while the official returns of the ship, a week after the action, show that there were no less than thirty-eight wounded on board still alive, who had been injured in this manner, and of whom thirty were said to have been then in great danger. Capt. Pearson described this explosion as having destroyed nearly all the men at the five or six aftermost guns. On the whole, near sixty of the Serapis' people must have been instantly disabled by the sudden blow.

The advantage thus obtained by the coolness and intrepidity of the topmen, in a great measure restored the chances of the combat, and, by lessening the fire of the enemy, enabled Com. Jones to increase his. In the same degree that it encouraged the crew of the Richard, it diminished the hopes of the people of the Serapis. One of the guns under the immediate inspection of Com. Jones had been pointed some time against the mainmast of his enemy, while the two others had seconded the fire of the tops, with grape and canister. Kept below decks by this double attack, where a scene of frightful horror was present in the agonies of the wounded, and the effects of the explosion, the spirits of the English began to droop, and there was a moment when a trifle would have induced them to submit. From this despondency they were temporarily raised, by one of those unlooked-for events that ever accompany the vicissitudes of battle.

After exchanging the ineffective and distant broadsides already mentioned with the Scarborough, the Alliance had kept standing off and on, to leeward of the two principal ships, out of the direction of their shot, when, about half-past eight, she appeared crossing the stern of the Serapis and the bow of the Richard, firing at such a distance as to render it impossible to say, which vessel would suffer the most. As soon as she had drawn out of the range of her own guns her helm was put up, and she ran down near a mile to leeward, hovering about, until the firing had ceased between the Pallas and Scarborough, when she came within hail and spoke both of these vessels. Capt. Cottineau, of the Pallas, earnestly entreated Capt. Landais to take possession of his prize, and allow him to go to the assistance of the Richard, or to stretch up to windward in the Alliance himself, and succour the commodore.

After some delay, Capt. Landais took the important duty of assisting his consort, into his own hands, and making two long stretches, under his topsails, he appeared, about the time at which we have arrived in the narration of the combat, directly to windward of the two ships, with the head of the Alliance to the westward. Here the latter ship once more opened her fire, doing equal damage at least, to friend and foe. Keeping away a little, and still continuing her fire, the Alliance was soon on the larboard quarter of the Richard, and, it is even affirmed, that her guns were discharged until she had got nearly abeam.

Fifty voices now hailed to tell the people of the Alliance that they were firing into the wrong ship, and three lanterns were shown, in a line on the off side of the Richard, which was the regular signal of recognition for a night action. An officer was directed to hail, and to order Capt. Landais to lay the enemy aboard, and the question being put whether the order was comprehended, the answer was in the affirmative.

As the moon had been up some time, it was impossible not to distinguish between the vessels, the Richard being all black, while the Serapis had yellow sides; and the impression seems to have been general in the former vessel, that they had been attacked intentionally. At the discharge of the first guns of the Alliance, the people left one or two of the twelves on board the Richard, which they had begun to fight again, saying that the Englishmen in the Alliance had got possession of the ship, and were helping the enemy. It appears that this discharge dismounted a gun or two, extinguished several lanterns on the main-deck, and did a good deal of damage aloft.

The Alliance hauled off to some distance, keeping always on the off side of the Richard, and soon after she re-appeared edging down on the larboard beam of her consort, hauling up athwart the bows of that ship and the stern of her antagonist. On this occasion, it is affirmed that her fire re-commenced, when by possibility, the shot could only reach the Serapis through the Richard. Ten or twelve men appear to have been killed and wounded on the forecastle of the latter ship, which was crowded at the time, and among them was an officer of the name of Caswell, who, with his dying breath, maintained that he had received his wound by the fire of the friendly vessel.

After crossing the bows of the Richard, and the stern of the Serapis, delivering grape as she passed, the Alliance ran off to leeward, again standing off and on, doing nothing, for the remainder of the combat.

The fire of the Alliance added greatly to the leaks of the Richard, which ship, by this time, had received so much water through the shot-holes, as to begin to settle. It is even affirmed by many witnesses, that the most dangerous shot-holes on board the Richard, were under her larboard bow, and larboard counter, in places where they could not have been received from the fire of the Serapis. This evidence, however, is not unanswerable, as it has been seen that the Serapis luffed up on the larboard-quarter of the Richard in the commencement of the action, and, forging ahead, was subsequently on her larboard-bow, endeavouring to cross her fore foot. It is certainly possible that shot may have struck the Richard in the places mentioned, on these occasions, and that, as the ship settled in the water from other leaks, the holes then made may have suddenly increased the danger. On the other hand, if the Alliance did actually fire while on the bow and quarter of the Richard, as appears by a mass of uncontradicted testimony, the dangerous shot-holes may very well have come from that ship.

Let the injuries have been received from what quarter they might, soon after the Alliance had run to leeward, an alarm was spread in the Richard, that the ship was sinking. Both vessels had been on fire several times, and some difficulty had been experienced in extinguishing the flames, but here was a new enemy to contend with, and as the information came from the carpenter, whose duty it was to sound the pump-wells, it produced a good deal of consternation. The Richard had more than a hundred English prisoners on board, and the master at arms, in the hurry of the moment, let them all up from below, in order to save their lives. In the confusion of such a scene at night, the master of a letter of marque, that had been taken off the north of Scotland, passed through a port of the Richard into one of the Serapis, when he reported to Capt. Pearson, that a few minutes would probably decide the battle in his favour, or carry his enemy down, he himself having been liberated in order to save his life. Just at this instant the gunner, who had little to occupy him at his quarters, came on deck, and not perceiving Com. Jones, or Mr. Dale, both of whom were occupied with the liberated prisoners, and believing the master, the only other superior he had in the ship, to be dead, he ran up on the poop to haul down the colours. Fortunately the flag-staff had been shot away, and, the ensign already hanging in the water, he had no other means of letting his intention to submit be known, than by calling out for quarter. Capt. Pearson now hailed, to inquire if the Richard demanded quarter, and was answered by Com. Jones himself, in the negative. It is probable that the reply was not heard, or, if heard, supposed to come from an unauthorized source, for encouraged by what he had learned from the escaped prisoner, by the cry, and by the confusion that prevailed in the Richard, the English captain directed his boarders to be called away, and, as soon as mustered, they were ordered to take possession of the prize. Some of the men actually got on the gunwale of the latter ship, but finding boarders ready to repel boarders, they made a precipitate retreat. All this time, the topmen were not idle, and the enemy were soon driven below again with loss.

In the meanwhile, Mr. Dale, who no longer had a gun that could be fought, mustered the prisoners at the pumps, turning their consternation to account, and probably keeping the Richard afloat by the very blunder that had come so near losing her. The ships were now on fire again, and both parties, with the exception of a few guns on each side, ceased fighting, in order to subdue this dangerous enemy. In the course of the combat, the Serapis is said to have been set on fire no less than twelve times, while, towards its close, as will be seen in the sequel, the Richard was burning all the while.

As soon as order was restored in the Richard, after the call for quarter, her chances of success began to increase, while the English driven under cover, almost to a man, appear to have lost, in a great degree, the hope of victory. Their fire materially slackened, while the Richard again brought a few more guns to bear; the main-mast of the Serapis began to totter, and her resistance, in general, to lessen. About an hour after the explosion, or between three hours and three hours and a half after the first gun was fired, and between two hours and two hours and a half after the ships were lashed together, Capt. Pearson hauled down the colours of the Serapis with his own hands, the men refusing to expose themselves to the fire of the Richard's tops.

As soon as it was known that the colours of the English had been lowered, Mr. Dale got upon the gunwale of the Richard, and laying hold of the main brace pendant, he swung himself on board the Serapis. On the quarter-deck of the latter he found Capt. Pearson, almost alone, that gallant officer having maintained his post throughout the whole of this close and murderous conflict. Just as Mr. Dale addressed the English captain, the first lieutenant of the Serapis came up from below to inquire if the Richard had struck, her fire having entirely ceased. Mr. Dale now gave the English officer to understand that he was mistaken in the position of things, the Serapis having struck to the Richard, and not the Richard to the Serapis. Capt. Pearson confirming this account, his subordinate acquiesced, offering to go below and silence the guns that were still playing upon the American ship. To this Mr. Dale would not consent, but both the English officers were immediately passed on board the Richard. The firing was then stopped below. Mr. Dale had been closely followed to the quarter-deck of the Serapis, by Mr. Mayrant, a midshipman, and a party of boarders, and as the former struck the quarter-deck of the prize, he was run through the thigh, by a boarding pike, in the hands of a man in the waist, who was ignorant of the surrender. Thus did the close of this remarkable combat resemble its other features in singularity, blood being shed and shot fired, while the boarding officer was in amicable discourse with his prisoners!

As soon as Capt. Pearson was on board the Richard, and Mr. Drake had received a proper number of hands in the prize, Com. Jones ordered the lashings to be cut, and the vessels to be separated, hailing the Serapis, as the Richard drifted from alongside of her, and ordering her to follow his own ship. Mr. Dale now had the head sails of the Serapis braced sharp aback, and the wheel put down, but the vessel refused both her helm and her canvass. Surprised and excited at this circumstance, the gallant lieutenant sprang from the binnacle on which he had seated himself, and fell at his length on the deck. He had been severely wounded in the leg, by a splinter, and until this moment had been ignorant of the injury. He was replaced on the binnacle, when the master of the Serapis came up and acquainted him with the fact that the ship was anchored.

By this time, Mr. Lunt, the second lieutenant, who had been absent in the pilot-boat, had got alongside, and was on board the prize. To this officer Mr. Dale now consigned the charge of the Serapis, the cable was cut, and the ship followed the Richard, as ordered.

Although this protracted and bloody combat had now ended, neither the danger nor the labours of the victors were over. The Richard was both sinking and on fire. The flames had got within the ceiling, and extended so far that they menaced the magazine, while all the pumps, in constant use, could barely keep the water at the same level. Had it depended on the exhausted people of the two combatants, the ship must have soon sunk, but the other vessels of the squadron sent hands on board the Richard, to assist at the pumps. So imminent did the danger from the fire become, that all the powder was got on deck, to prevent an explosion. In this manner did the night of the battle pass, with one gang always at the pumps, and another contending with the flames, until about ten o'clock in the forenoon of the 24th, when the latter were got under. After the action, eight or ten Englishmen in the Richard, stole a boat from the Serapis, and ran away with it, landing at Scarborough. Several of the men were so alarmed with the condition of their ship, as to jump overboard and swim to the other vessels.

When the day dawned, an examination was made into the condition of the Richard. Abaft, on a line with the guns of the Serapis that had not been disabled by the explosion, the timbers were found to be nearly all beaten in, or beaten out, for in this respect there was little difference between the two sides of the ship; and it was said that her poop and upper decks would have fallen into the gun-room, but for a few futtocks that had been missed. Indeed, so large was the vacuum, that most of the shot fired from this part of the Serapis, at the close of the action, must have gone through the Richard without touching any thing. The rudder was cut from the sternpost, and the transoms were nearly driven out of her. All the after part of the ship, in particular, that was below the quarter-deck, was torn to pieces, and nothing had saved those stationed on the quarter-deck, but the impossibility of elevating guns that almost touched their object.

The result of this examination was to convince every one of the impossibility of carrying the Richard into port, in the event of its coming on to blow. Com. Jones was advised to remove his wounded while the weather continued moderate, and he reluctantly gave the order to commence. The following night and the morning of the succeeding day were employed in executing this imperious duty, and about nine o'clock, the officer of the Pallas, who was in charge of the ship, with a party at the pumps, finding that the water had reached the lower deck, reluctantly abandoned her. About ten, the Bon Homme Richard wallowed heavily, gave a roll, and settled slowly into the sea, bows foremost.

The Serapis suffered much less than the Richard, the guns of the latter having been so light, and so soon silenced; but no sooner were the ships separated, than her main mast fell, bringing down with it the mizzen-top mast. Though jury-masts were erected, the ship drove about, nearly helpless, in the North Sea, until the 6th of October, when the remains of the squadron, with the two prizes, got into the Texel, the port to which they had been ordered to repair.

In the combat between the Richard and the Serapis, an unusual number of lives was lost, though no regular authentic report appears to have been given by either side. Capt. Pearson states the loss of the Richard at about 300 in killed and wounded; a total that would have included very nearly all hands, and which was certainly a great exaggeration, or, at least, a great mistake. According to a muster-roll of the officers and people of the Richard, excluding the marines, which is still in existence, 42 men were killed, or died of their wounds shortly after the battle, and 41 were wounded. This would make a total of 83; for this portion of the crew, which, on the roll, amounted to 227 souls. But many of the persons named on this list are known not to have been in the action at all; such as neither of the junior lieutenants, and some thirty men that were with them, besides those absent in prizes. As there were a few volunteers on board, however, who were not mustered, if we set down 200 as the number of the portion of the regular crew that was in the action, we shall probably not be far from the truth. By estimating the soldiers that remained on board at 120, and observing the same proportion for their casualties, we shall get 49 as the result, which will make a total of 132, as the entire loss of the Richard. It is known, however, that, in the commencement of the action, the soldiers, or marines, suffered out of proportion to the rest of the crew, and general report having made the gross loss of the Richard 150 men, we are disposed to believe that it was not far from the fact.

Capt. Pearson reported a part of his loss at 117 men, admitting, at the same time, that there were many killed and wounded whose names he could not discover. It is probable that the loss of the two ships, in men, was about equal, and that nearly or quite half of all those who were engaged, were either killed or wounded. Com. Jones, in a private letter, written some time after the occurrence, gives an opinion, however, that the loss of the Richard was less than that of the Serapis. That two vessels of so much force should lie lashed together more than two hours, making use of artillery, musketry, and all the other means of annoyance known to the warfare of the day, and not do even greater injury to the crews, strikes us with astonishment; but the fact must be ascribed to the peculiarities of the combat, which, by driving most of the English under cover so early in the battle, and by driving the Americans above the line of fire of their enemies, in a measure protected each party from the missiles of the other. As it was, it proved a murderous and sanguinary conflict, though its duration would probably have been much shorter, and its character still more bloody, but for these unusual circumstances.

1839

From *SATANSTOE*

CHAPTER II

[NEW YORK SOCIETY]

> I would there were no age between ten and three-and-twenty: or that youth would sleep out the rest.
>
> —WINTER'S TALE.

It is not necessary for me to say much of the first fourteen years of my life. They passed like the childhood and youth of the sons of most gentlemen in our colony, at that day, with this distinction, however. There was a class among us which educated its boys at home. This was not a very numerous class, certainly, nor was it always the highest in point of fortune and rank. Many of the large proprietors were of Dutch origin, as a matter of course; and these seldom, if ever, sent their children to England to be taught any thing, in my boyhood. I understand that a few are getting over their ancient prejudices in this particular, and begin to fancy Oxford or Cambridge may be quite as learned schools as that of Leyden; but no Van, in my boyhood, could have been made to believe this. Many of the Dutch proprietors gave their children very little education, in any way or form, though most of them imparted lessons of probity that were quite as useful as learning, had the two things been really inseparable. For my part, while I admit there is a great deal of knowledge going up and down the land, that is just of a degree to trick a fellow-creature out of his rights, I shall never subscribe to the opinion, which is so prevalent among the Dutch portion of our population, and which holds the doctrine that the schools of the New England provinces are the reason the descendants of the Puritans do not enjoy the best of reputations, in this respect. I believe a boy may be well taught, and made all the honester for it; though I admit there may be, and is, such a thing as training a lad into false notions, as well as training him in those that are true. But we had a class, principally of English extraction, that educated its sons well; usually sending them home to the great English schools, and finishing at the universities. These persons, however, lived principally in town, or, having estates on the Hudson, passed their winters there. To this class the Littlepages did not belong; neither their habits nor their fortunes tempting them to so high a flight. For myself, I was taught enough Latin and Greek to enter college, by the Rev. Thomas Worden, an English divine, who was rector of St. Jude's, the parish to which our family properly belonged. This gentleman was esteemed a good scholar, and was very popular among the gentry of the country; attending all the dinners, clubs, races, balls, and other diversions that were given by them, within ten miles of his residence. His sermons were pithy and short; and he always spoke of your half-hour preachers as illiterate prosers who did not understand how to condense their thoughts. Twenty minutes were his gauge, though I remember to have heard my father say, that he had known him preach all of twenty-two. When he compressed down to fourteen, my grandfather invariably protested he was delightful.

I remained with Mr. Worden until I could translate the two first Æneids, and the whole of the Gospel of St. Matthew, pretty readily; and then my father and grandfather, the last in particular, for the old gentleman had a great idea of learning, began to turn over in their minds, the subject of the college to which I ought to be sent. We had the choice of two, in both of which the learned languages and the sciences are taught, to a degree, and in a perfection, that is surprising for a new country. These colleges are Yale, at New Haven, in Connecticut, and Nassau Hall, which was then at Newark, New Jersey, after having been a short time at Elizabethtown, but which has since been established at Princeton. Mr. Worden laughed at both; said that neither had as much learning as a second-rate English grammar-school; and that a lower-form boy, at Eton or Westminster, could take a master's degree at either, and pass for a prodigy in the bargain. My father, who was born in the colonies, and had a good deal of the right colony feeling, was nettled at this, I remember; while my grandfather, being old-country born, but colony educated, was at a loss how to view the matter. The captain had a great respect for his native land, and evidently considered it the paradise of this earth, though his recollections of it were not very distinct; but, at the same time, he loved Old York, and

Westchester in particular, where he had married and established himself at Satan's Toe; or, as he spelt it, and as we all have spelt it, now, this many a day, Satanstoe. I was present at the conversation which decided the question, as regarded my future education, and which took place in the common parlor, around a blazing fire, about a week before Christmas, the year I was fourteen. There were present Captain Hugh Roger, Major Evans, my mother, the Rev. Mr. Worden, and an old gentleman of Dutch designation and extraction, of the name of Abraham Van Valkenburgh, but who was familiarly called, by his friends, 'Brom Follock, or Colonel Follock, or Volleck, as the last happen to be more or less ceremonious, or more or less Dutch. Follock, I think, however, was the favorite pronunciation. This Colonel Van Valkenburgh was an old brother-soldier of my father's, and, indeed, a relation, a sort of cousin through my great-grandmother, besides being a man of much consideration and substance. He lived in Rockland, just across the Hudson, but never failed to pay a visit to Satanstoe at that season of the year. On the present occasion, he was accompanied by his son, Dirck, who was *my* friend, and just a year my junior.

"Vell, den,"—the colonel commenced the discourse by saying, as he tapped the ashes out of his pipe for the second time that evening, having first taken a draught of hot flip, a beverage much in vogue then, as well as now,—"vell, den, Evans, vat is your intention, as to ter poy? Will he pe college-l'arnt, like as his grant-fa'ter, or only school-l'arnt, like as his own fa'ter?" The allusion to the grandfather being a pleasantry of the colonel's, who insisted that all the old-country born were "college-l'arnt" by instinct.

"To own the truth, 'Brom," my father answered, "this is a point that is not yet entirely settled, for there are different opinions as to the place to which he shall be sent, even admitting that he is to be sent at all."

The colonel fastened his full, projecting, blue eyes on my father, in a way that pretty plainly expressed surprise.

"Vat, den, is dere so many colleges, dat it is hart to choose?" he said.

"There are but two that can be of any use to us, for Cambridge is much too distant to think of sending the boy so far. Cambridge was in our thoughts at one time, but that is given up."

"Vhere, den, ist Cambridge?" demanded the Dutchman, removing his pipe to ask so important a question, a ceremony he usually thought unnecessary.

"It is a New England college—near Boston; not half a day's journey distant, I fancy."

"Don't send Cornelius dere," ejaculated the colonel, contriving to get these words out alongside of the stem of the pipe.

"You think not, Colonel Follock," put in the anxious mother; "may I ask the reason for that opinion?"

"Too much Suntay, Matam Littlepage—the poy will be sp'ilt by ter ministers. He will go away an honest lat, and come pack a rogue. He will l'arn how to bray and to cheat."

"Hoity, toity, my noble colonel!" exclaimed the Rev. Mr. Worden, affecting more resentment than he felt. "Then you fancy the clergy, and too much Sunday, will be apt to convert an honest youth into a knave!"

The colonel made no answer, continuing to smoke very philosophically, though he took occasion, while he drew the pipe out of his mouth, in one of its periodical removals, to make a significant gesture with it toward the rising sun, which all present understood to mean "down east," as it is usual to say, when we mean to designate the colonies of New England. That he was understood by the Rev. Mr. Worden, is highly probable; since that gentleman continued to turn the flip of one vessel into another, by way of more intimately blending the ingredients of the mixture, quite as coolly as if there had been no reflection on his trade.

"What do you think of Yale, friend 'Brom?" asked my father, who understood the dumb-show as well as any of them.

"No tifference, Evans; dey all breaches and brays too much. *Goot* men have no neet of so much religion. Vhen a man is *really* goot, religion only does him harm. I mean Yankee religion."

"I have another objection to Yale," observed Captain Hugh Roger, "which is their English."

"Och!" exclaimed the colonel—"Deir English is horriple! Wuss dan ast to us Tutch."

"Well, I was not aware of that," observed my father. "They are English, sir, as well as ourselves, and why should they not speak the language as well as we!"

"Why toes not a Yorkshire man, or a Cornishman, speak as vell as a Lonnoner? I tell you what, Evans, I'll pet the pest game-cock on ter Neck, against the veriest tunghill the parson hast, ter presitent of Yale calls peen, pen, ant roof, ruff—and so on."

"My birds are all game," put in the divine; "I keep no other breed."

"Surely, Mr. Worden, you do not countenance cockfights by your presence!" my mother said, using as much of reproach in her manner as comported with the holy office of the party she addressed, and with her own gentle nature. The colonel winked at my father, and laughed *through his pipe,* an exploit he might have been said to perform almost hourly. My father smiled in return; for, to own the truth, he *had* been present at such sports on one or two occasions, when the parson's curiosity had tempted him to peep in also; but my grandfather looked grave and much in earnest. As for Mr. Worden himself, he met the imputation like a man. To do him justice, if he were not an ascetic, neither was he a whining hyprocrite, as is the case with too many of those who aspire to be disciples and ministers of our blessed Lord.

"Why not, Madam Littlepage?" Mr. Worden stoutly demanded. "There are worse places than cockpits; for, mark me, I never bet—no, not on a horse-race even; and *that* is an occasion on which any gentleman might venture a few guineas, in a liberal, frank way. There are so few amusements for people of education in this country, Madam Littlepage, that one is not to be too particular. If there were hounds and hunting, now, as there are at home, you should never hear of me at a cock-fight, I can assure you."

"I must say I do not approve of cockfights," rejoined my mother meekly; "and I hope Corny will never be seen at one. No—never—never."

"Dere you're wrong, Matam Littlepage," the colonel remarked, "for ter sight of ter spirit of ter cocks wilt give ter boy spirit himself. My Tirck, dere, goes to all in ter neighborhoot, and he is a game-cock himself, let me tell you. Come, Tirck—come—cock-a-doodle-do!"

This was true all around, as I very well knew, young as I was. Dirck, who was a slow-moving, as dull-seeming, and as anti-mercurial a boy to look at as one could find in a thousand, was thorough game at the bottom, and he had been at many a main, as he had told me himself. How much of his spirit was derived from witnessing such scenes I will not take on me to affirm; for, in these later times, I have heard it questioned whether such exhibitions do really improve the spectator's courage or not. But Dirck had pluck, and plenty of it, and in that particular, at least, his father was not mistaken. The colonel's opinion always carried weight with my mother, both on account of his Dutch extraction, and on account of his well-established probity; for, to own the truth, a text or a sentiment from him had far more weight with her than the same from the clergyman. She was silenced on the subject of cockfighting for the moment, therefore, which gave captain Hugh Roger further opportunity to pursue that of the English language. The grandfather, who was an inveterate lover of the sport, would have cut in to that branch of the discourse, but he had a great tenderness for my mother, whom everybody loved by the way, and he commanded himself, glad to find that so important an interest had fallen into hands as good as those of the colonel. *He* would just as soon be absent from a cockfight, and he was a very good observer of religion.

"I should have sent Evans to Yale, had it not been for the miserable manner of speaking English they have in New England," resumed my grandfather; "and I had no wish to have a son who might pass for a Cornish man. We shall have to send this boy to Newark, in New Jersey. The distance is not so great, and we shall be certain he will not get any of your Roundhead notions of religion, too. Colonel 'Brom, you Dutch are not altogether free from these distressing follies."

"Debble a pit?" growled the colonel, through his pipe; for no devotee of liberalism and latitudinarianism in religion could be more averse to extra-piety than he. The colonel, however, was not of the Dutch Reformed; he was an Episcopalian, like ourselves, his mother having brought this branch of the Follocks into the church; and, consequently, he entered into all our feelings on the subject of religion, heart and hand. Perhaps Mr. Worden was a greater favorite with no member of the four parishes over which he presided, than with Colonel Abraham Van Valkenburgh.

"I should think less of sending Corny to Newark," added my mother, "was it not for crossing the water."

"Crossing the water!" repeated Mr. Worden. "The Newark we mean,

Madam Littlepage, is not at home; the Jersey of which we speak is the adjoining colony of that name."

"I am aware of that, Mr. Worden; but it is not possible to get to Newark, without making that terrible voyage between New York and Powles' Hook. No, sir, it is impossible; and every time the child comes home, that risk will have to be run. It would cause me many a sleepless night!"

"He can go by Tobb's Ferry, Matam Littlepage," quietly observed the colonel.

"Dobb's Ferry can be very little better than that by Powles' Hook," rejoined the tender mother. "A ferry is a ferry; and the Hudson will be the Hudson, from Albany to New York. So water is water."

As these were all self-evident propositions, they produced a pause in the discourse; for men do not deal with new ideas as freely as they deal with the old.

"Dere is a way, Evans, as you and I know py experience," resumed the colonel, winking again at my father, "to go rount the Hudson altoget'er. To pe sure, it is a long way, and a pit in the woots; but petter to untertake dat, than to haf the poy lose his l'arnin'. Ter journey might be made in two mont's, and he none the wuss for ter exercise. Ter major and I were never heartier dan when we were operating on the he't waters of the Hudson. I will tell Corny the roat."

My mother saw that her apprehensions were laughed at, and she had the good sense to be silent. The discussion did not the less proceed, until it was decided, after an hour more of weighing the *pros* and *cons,* that I was to be sent to Nassau Hall, Newark, New Jersey, and was to move from that place with the college, whenever that event might happen.

"You will send Dirck there, too," my father added, as soon as the affair in my case was finally determined. "It would be a pity to separate the boys, after they have been so long together, and have got to be so much used to each other. Their characters are so identical, too, that they are more like brothers than very distant relatives."

"Dey will like one anot'er all de petter for pein' a little tifferent, den," answered the colonel, dryly.

Dirck and I were no more alike than a horse resembles a mule.

"Ay, but Dirck is a lad who will do honor to an education—he is solid and thoughtful, and learning will not be thrown away on such a youth. Was he in England, that sedate lad might get to be a bishop."

"I want no pishops in my family, Major Evans, nor do I want any great l'arnin'. None of us ever saw a college, and we have got on fery vell. I am a colonel and a memper; my fat'er was a colonel and a memper; and my grandfat'er *woult* have peen a colonel and a memper, but dere vast no colonels and no mempers in his time; though Tirck yonter can be a colonel and a memper, wit'out crosting dat terriple ferry that frightens Matam Littlepage so much."

There was usually a little humor in all Colonel Follock said and did, though it must be owned it was humor after a very Dutch model; Dutch-built fun, as Mr. Worden used to call it. Nevertheless, it was humor; and there was enough of Holland in all the junior generation of the Littlepages to enjoy it. My father understood him, and my mother did not hear the last of the "terriple ferry" until not only I, but the college itself, had quitted Newark; for the institution made another remove to Princeton, the place where it is now to be found, some time before I got my degree.

"You have got on very well without a college education, as all must admit, colonel," answered Mr. Worden; "but there is no telling how much *better* you would have got on, had you been an A. M. You might, in the last case, have been a general and a member of the king's council."

"Dere ist no yeneral in ter colony, the commander-in-chief and his majesty's representatif excepted," returned the colonel. "We are no Yankees, to make yenerals of ploughmen."

Hereupon the colonel and my father knocked the ashes out of their pipes at the same instant, and both laughed—a merriment in which the parson, my grandfather, my dear mother, and I myself joined. Even a negro boy, who was about my own age, and whose name was Jacob, or Jaap, but who was commonly called Yaap, grinned at the remark, for he had a sovereign contempt for Yankee-land, and all it contained; almost as sovereign a contempt as that which Yankee-land entertained for York itself, and its Dutch population. Dirck was the only person present who looked grave; but Dirck was habitually as grave and sedate, as if he had been born to become a burgomaster.

"Quite right, Brom," cried my father; "*colonels* are good enough for us; and when we do make a man *that,* even, we are a little particular about his being respectable and fit for the office. Nevertheless learning will not hurt Corny, and to college he shall go, let you do as you please with Dirck. So that matter is settled, and no more need be said about it."

And it was settled, and to college I *did* go, and that by the awful Powles' Hook Ferry, in the bargain. Near as we lived to town, I paid my first visit to the island of Manhattan the day my father and myself started for Newark. I had an aunt, who lived in Queen street, not a very great distance from the fort, and she had kindly invited me and my father to pass a day with her, on our way to New Jersey, which invitation had been accepted. In my youth, the world in general was not so much addicted to gadding about as it is now getting to be, and neither my grandfather nor my father ordinarily went to town, their calls to the legislature excepted, more than twice a year. My mother's visits were still less frequent, although Mrs. Legge, my aunt, was her own sister. Mr. Legge was a lawyer of a good deal of reputation, but he was inclined to be in the opposition, or espoused the popular side in politics; and there could be no great cordiality between one of that frame of mind and our family. I remember we had not been in the house an hour, before a warm discussion took place between my uncle and my father, on the question of the right of the subject to canvass the acts of the government. We had left home immediately after an early breakfast, in order to reach town before dark; but a long detention at the Harlem ferry, compelled us to dine in that village, and it was quite night before we stopped in Queen street. My aunt ordered supper early, in order that we might get early to bed, to recover from our fatigue, and be ready for sight-seeing next day. We sat down to supper, therefore, in less than an hour after our arrival; and it was while we were at table that the discussion I have mentioned took place. It would seem that a party had been got up in town among the disloyal, and I might almost say, the disaffected, which claimed for the subject the right to know in what manner every shilling of the money raised by taxation was expended. This very obviously improper interference with matters that did not belong to them, on the part of the ruled, was resisted by the rulers, and that with energy; inasmuch as such inquiries and investigations would naturally lead to results that might bring authority into discredit, make the governed presuming and prying in their dispositions, and cause much derangement and inconvenience to the regular and salutary action of government. My father took the negative of the proposition, while my uncle maintained its affirmative. I well remember that my poor aunt looked uneasy, and tried to divert the discourse by exciting our curiosity on a new subject.

"Corny has been particularly lucky in having come to town just as he has, since we shall have a sort of gala-day to-morrow, for the blacks and the children."

I was not in the least offended at being thus associated with the negroes, for they mingled in most of the amusements of the young people; but I did not quite so well like to be ranked with the children, now I was fourteen, and on my way to college. Notwithstanding this, I did not fail to betray an interest in what was to come next, by my countenance. As for my father, he did not hesitate about asking an explanation.

"The news came in this morning, by a fast-sailing sloop, that the Patroon of Albany is on his way to New York, in his coach-and-four, and with two outriders, and that he may be expected to reach town in the course of to-morrow. Several of my acquaintances have consented to let their children go out a little way into the country, to see him come in; and as for the blacks, you know, it is just as well to give them *permission* to be of the party, as half of them would otherwise go without asking it."

"This will be a capital opportunity to let Corny see a little of the world," cried my father, "and I would not have him miss it on any account. Besides, it is useful to teach young people early, the profitable lesson of honoring their superiors and seniors."

"In that sense it may do," growled my uncle, who, though so much of a latitudinarian in his political opinions, never failed to inculcate all useful and necessary maxims for private life; the Patroon of Albany being one of the most respectable and affluent of all our gentry. I have no objection to Corny's going to see that sight; and I hope, my dear, you will let both Pompey and Cæsar be of the party. It won't hurt the fellows to see the manner in which the patroon has his carriage kept and horses groomed."

Pompey and Cæsar were of the

party, though the latter did not join us until Pompey had taken me all around the town, to see the principal sights; it being understood that the patroon had slept at Kingsbridge, and would not be likely to reach town until near noon. New York was certainly not the place, in 1751, it is to-day; nevertheless, it was a large and important town, even when I went to college, containing not less than twelve thousand souls, blacks included. The Town Hall is a magnificent structure, standing at the head of Broad street; and thither Pompey led me, even before my aunt had come down to breakfast. I could scarcely admire that fine edifice sufficiently; which, for size, architecture, and position, has scarcely now an equal in all the colonies. It is true, that the town has much improved, within the last twenty years; but York was a noble place, even in the middle of this century! After breakfast, Pompey and I proceeded up Broadway, commencing near the fort, at the Bowling Green, and walking some distance beyond the head of Wall street, or quite a quarter of a mile. Nor did the town stop here; though its principal extent is, or was then, along the margin of the East River. Trinity Church I could hardly admire enough either; for it appeared to me, that it was large enough to contain all the church people in the colony. It was a venerable structure, which had then felt the heats of summer and the snows of winter on its roofs and walls, near half a century, and it still stands a monument of pious zeal and cultivated taste.* There were other churches, belonging to other denominations, of course, that were well worthy of being seen; to say nothing of the markets. I thought I never should tire of gazing at the magnificence of the shops, particularly the silversmiths'; some of which must have had a thousand dollars' worth of plate in their windows, or otherwise in sight. I might say as much of the other shops, too, which attracted a just proportion of my admiration.

About eleven, the number of children and blacks that were seen walking toward the Bowery road, gave us notice that it was time to be moving in that direction. We were in the upper part of Broadway at the time, and Pompey proceeded forthwith to fall into the current, making all the haste he could, as it was thought the traveller might pass down toward the East River, and get into Queen street, before we could reach the point

* The intelligent reader will, of course, properly appreciate the provincial admiration of Mr. Littlepage, who naturally fancied his own best was other people's best. The Trinity of that day was burned down in the great fire of 1776. The edifice that succeeded it at the peace of 1783, has already given place to a successor, that has more claim to be placed on a level with modern English town-church architecture, than any other building in the union. When another shall succeed this, which shall be as much larger and more elaborate than this is, compared to its predecessor, and still another shall succeed, which shall bear the same relation to that, then the country will possess an edifice that is on a level with the first-rate Gothic cathedral architecture of Europe. It would be idle to pretend new Trinity is without faults; some of which are probably the result of circumstances and necessity; but, if the respectable architect who has built it, had no other merit, he would deserve the gratitude of every man of taste in the country, by placing church towers of a proper comparative breadth, dignity, and proportions, before the eyes of its population. The diminutive meanness of American church-towers, has been an eyesore to every *intelligent*, travelled American, since the country was settled.—Editor [Author's note.]

at which he would diverge. It is true, the old town residence of Stephen de Lancey, which stood at the head of Broadway, just above Trinity,* had been converted into a tavern, and we did not know but the patroon might choose to alight there, as it was then the principal inn of the town; still, most people preferred Queen street; and the new City Tavern was so much out of the way, that strangers in particular were not fond of frequenting it. Cæsar came up, much out of breath, just as we got into the country.

Quitting Broadway, we went along the country road that then diverged to the east, but which is now getting to contain a sort of suburb, and passing the road that leads into Queen street, we felt more certain of meeting the traveller, whose carriage we soon learned had not gone by. As there were and are several taverns for country people in this quarter, most of us went quite into the country, proceeding as far as the villas of the Bayards, De Lanceys, and other persons of mark; of which there are several along the Bowery road. Our party stopped under some cherry trees, that were not more than a mile from town, nearly opposite to Lieutenant-Governor de Lancey's country house;† but many boys, etc., went a long, long way into the country, finishing the day by nutting and gathering apples in the grounds of Petersfield and Rosehill, the country residence of the Stuyvesant and Watt, or, as the last is now called, the Watts families. I was desirous of going thus far myself, for I had heard much of both of those grand places; but Pompey told me it would be necessary to be back for dinner by half-past one, his mistress having consented to postpone the hour a little, in order to indulge my natural desire to see all I could while in town.

We were not altogether children and blacks who were out on the Bowery road that day—many tradesmen were among us, the leathern aprons making a goodly parade on the occasion. I saw one or two persons wearing swords, hovering around, in the lanes and in the woods—proof that even gentlemen had some desire to see so great a person as the Patroon of Albany pass. I shall not stop to say much of the *transit* of the *patroon.* He came by about noon, as was expected, and in his coach-and-four, with two outriders, coachmen, etc., in liveries, as is usual in the families of the gentry, and with a team of heavy, black, Dutch-looking horses, that I remember Cæsar pronounced to be of the true Flemish breed. The patroon himself was a sightly, well-dressed gentleman, wearing a scarlet coat, flowing wig, and cocked hat; and I observed that the handle of his sword was of solid silver. But my father wore a sword with a solid silver handle, too, a present from my grandfather when the former first entered the army.* He bowed to the salutations he received in passing, and I thought all the spectators were pleased with the noble sight of seeing such an equipage pass into the town. Such a sight does not occur every day in the colonies, and

* The cite of the present City Hotel.—EDITOR [Author's note.]

† Now Delancey street.—EDITOR [Author's note.]

* This patroon must have been Jeremiah Van Rensselaer * * * [Author's note.]

I felt exceedingly happy that it had been my privilege to witness it. * * *

1845

NOTIONS OF THE AMERICANS

LETTER XXIII

[AMERICAN LITERATURE]

To THE ABBATE GIROMACHI, &c. &c.—

Washington, —.

You ask me to write freely on the subject of the literature and the arts of the United States. The subjects are so meagre as to render it a task that would require no small portion of the talents necessary to figure in either, in order to render them of interest. Still, as the request has come in so urgent a form, I shall endeavour to oblige you.

The Americans have been placed, as respects moral and intellectual advancement, different from all other infant nations. They have never been without the wants of civilization, nor have they ever been entirely without the means of a supply. Thus pictures, and books, and statuary, and every thing else which appertains to elegant life, have always been known to them in an abundance, and of a quality exactly proportioned to their cost. Books, being the cheapest, and the nation having great leisure and prodigious zest for information, are not only the most common, as you will readily suppose, but they are probably more common than among any other people. I scarcely remember ever to have entered an American dwelling, however humble, without finding fewer or more books. As they form the most essential division of the subject, not only on account of their greater frequency, but on account of their far greater importance, I shall give them the first notice in this letter.

Unlike the progress of the two professions in the countries of our hemisphere, in America the printer came into existence before the author. Reprints of English works gave the first employment to the press. Then came almanacs, psalm-books, religious tracts, sermons, journals, political essays, and even rude attempts at poetry. All these preceded the revolution. The first journal was established in Boston at the commencement of the last century. There are several original polemical works of great originality and power that belong to the same period. I do not know that more learning and talents existed at that early day in the States of New-England than in Virginia, Maryland and the Carolinas, but there was certainly a stronger desire to exhibit them. * * *

As respects authorship there is not much to be said. Compared to the books that are printed and read, those of native origin are few indeed. The principal reason of this poverty of original writers, is owing to the circumstance that men are not yet driven to their wits for bread. The United States are the first nation that possessed institutions, and, of course, distinctive opinions of its own, that was ever dependent on a foreign people for its literature. Speaking the same language as the English, and long in the habit of importing their books from the mother country, the revolution effected no immediate change in the nature of their studies, or mental amusements. The works were reprinted, it is true, for the purposes of economy, but they still continued English. Had the latter nation used this powerful engine with tolerable address, I think they would have secured such an ally in this country as would have rendered their own decline not only more secure, but as illustrious as had been their rise. There are many theories entertained as to the effect produced in this country by the falsehoods and jealous calumnies which have been undeniably uttered in the mother country, by means of the press, concerning her republican descendant. It is my own opinion that, like all other ridiculous absurdities, they have defeated themselves, and that they are now more laughed at and derided, even here, than resented. By all that I can learn, twenty years ago, the Americans were, perhaps, far too much disposed to receive the opinions and to adopt the prejudices of their relatives; whereas, I think it is very apparent that they are now beginning to receive them with singular distrust. It is not worth our while to enter further into this subject, except as it has had, or is likely to have, an influence on the national literature.

It is quite obvious, that, so far as taste and forms alone are concerned, the literature of England and that of America must be fashioned after the same models. The authors, previously to the revolution, are common property, and it is quite idle to say that the American has not just as good a right to claim Milton, and Shakespeare, and all the old masters of the language, for his countrymen, as an Englishman. The Americans having continued to cultivate, and to cultivate extensively, an acquaintance with the writers of the mother country, since the separation, it is evident they must have kept pace with the trifling changes of the day. The only peculiarity that can, or ought to be expected in their literature, is that which is connected with the promulgation of their distinctive political opinions. They have not been remiss in this duty, as any one may see, who chooses to examine their books. * * *

The truth is, that public opinion, among its other laws, has imperiously prescribed that, amidst the utmost latitude of discussion, certain limits shall not be passed; and public opinion, which is so completely the offspring of a free press, must be obeyed in this, as well as in other matters.

Leaving the journals, we come to those publications which make their appearance periodically. Of these there are a good many, some few of which are well supported. There are several scientific works, that are printed monthly, or quarterly, of respectable merit, and four or five reviews. Magazines of a more general character are not much encouraged. England, which is teeming with educated men, who are glad to make their bread by writing for these works, still affords too strong a competition for the success of any American attempts, in this species of literature. Though few, perhaps no English magazine is actually republished in America, a vast number are imported and read in the towns, where the support for any similar original production must first be found.

The literature of the United States has, indeed, two powerful obstacles to conquer before (to use a mercantile expression) it can ever enter the markets of its own country on terms of perfect equality with that of England. Solitary and individual works of genius may, indeed, be occasionally brought to light, under the impulses of the high feeling which has conceived them; but, I fear, a good, wholesome, profitable and continued pecuniary support, is the applause that talent most craves. The fact, that an American publisher can get an English work without money, must for a few years longer, (unless legislative protection shall be extended to their own authors,) have a tendency to repress a national literature. No man will pay a writer for an epic, a tragedy, a sonnet, a history, or a romance, when he can get a work of equal merit for nothing. I have conversed with those who are conversant on the subject, and, I confess, I have been astonished at the information they imparted.

A capital American publisher has assured me that there are not a dozen writers in this country, whose works he should feel confidence in publishing at all, while he reprints hundreds of English books without the least hesitation. This preference is by no means so much owing to any difference in merit, as to the fact that, when the price of the original author is to be added to the uniform hazard which accompanies all literary speculations, the risk becomes too great. The general taste of the reading world in this country is better than that of England. The fact is both proved and explained by the circumstances that thousands of works that are printed and read in the mother country, are not printed and read here. The publisher on this side of the Atlantic has the advantage of seeing the reviews of every book he wishes to reprint, and, what is of far more importance, he knows, with the exception of books that he is sure of selling, by means of a name, the decision of the English critics before he makes his choice. Nine times in ten, popularity, which is all he looks for, is a sufficient test of general merit. Thus, while you find every English work of character, or notoriety, on the shelves of an American book-store, you may ask in vain for most of the trash that is so greedily devoured in the circulating libraries of the mother country, and which would be just as eagerly devoured here, had not a better taste been created by a compelled abstinence. That taste must now be overcome before such works could be sold at all.

When I say that books are not rejected here, from any want of talent in the writers, perhaps I ought to explain. I wish to express something a little different. Talent is sure of too many avenues to wealth and honours, in America, to seek, unnecessarily, an unknown and hazardous path. It is better paid in the ordinary pursuits of life, than it would be likely to be paid by an adventure in which an extraordinary and skilful, because practised, foreign competition is certain. Perhaps high talent does not often make the trial with the American bookseller; but it is precisely for the reason I have named.

The second obstacle against which American literature has to contend, is in the poverty of materials. There is scarcely an ore which contributes to the wealth of the author, that is found, here, in veins as rich as in Europe. There are no annals for the historian; no follies (beyond the most vulgar and commonplace) for the satirist; no manners for the dramatist; no obscure fictions for the writer of romance; no gross and hardy offences against decorum for the moralist; nor any of the rich artificial auxiliaries of poetry. The weakest hand can extract a spark from the flint, but it would baffle the strength of a giant to attempt kindling a flame with a pudding-stone. I very well know there are theorists who assume that the society and institutions of this country are, or ought to be, particularly favourable to novelties and variety. But the experience of one month, in these States, is sufficient to show any observant man the falsity of their position. The effect of a promiscuous assemblage any where, is to create a standard of deportment; and great liberty permits every one to aim at its attainment. I have never seen a nation so much alike in my life, as the people of the United States, and what is more, they are not only like each other, but they are remarkably like that which common sense tells them they ought to resemble. No doubt, traits of character that are a little peculiar, without, however, being either very poetical, or very rich, are to be found in remote districts; but they are rare, and not always happy exceptions. In short, it is not possible to conceive a state of society in which more of the attributes of plain good sense, or fewer of the artificial absurdities of life, are to be found, than here. There is no costume for the peasant, (there is scarcely a peasant at all,) no wig for the judge, no baton for the general, no diadem for the chief magistrate. The darkest ages of their history are illuminated by the light of truth; the utmost efforts of their chivalry are limited by the laws of God; and even the deeds of their sages and heroes are to be sung in a language that would differ but little from a version of the ten commandments. However useful and respectable all this may be in actual life, it indicates but one direction to the man of genius.

It is very true there are a few young poets now living in this country, who have known how to extract sweets from even these wholesome, but scentless native plants. They have, however, been compelled to seek their inspiration in the universal laws of nature, and they have succeeded, precisely in proportion as they have been most general in their application. Among these gifted young men, there is one (Halleck) who is remarkable for an exquisite vein of ironical wit, mingled with a fine, poetical, and, frequently, a lofty expression. This gentleman commenced his career as a satirist in one of the journals of New-York. Heaven knows, his materials were none of the richest; and yet the melody of his verse, the quaintness and force of his comparisons, and the exceeding humor of his strong points, brought him instantly into notice. He then attempted a general satire, by giving the history of the early days of a *belle*. He was again successful, though every body, at least every body of any talent, felt that he wrote in leading-strings. But he happened, shortly after the appearance of the little volume just named, (Fanny,) to visit England. Here his spirit was properly excited, and, probably on a rainy day, he was induced to try his hand at a *jeu d'esprit*, in the mother country. The result was one of the finest semi-heroic ironical descriptions to be found in the English language. This simple fact, in itself, proves the truth of a great deal of what I have just been writing, since it shows the effect a superiority of material can produce on the efforts of a man of true genius.

Notwithstanding the difficulties of the subject, talent has even done more than in the instance of Mr. Halleck. I could mention several other young poets of this country of rare merit. By mentioning Bryant, Percival, and Sprague, I shall direct your attention to the names of those whose works would be most likely to give you pleasure. Unfortunately they are not yet known in Italian, but I think even you would not turn in distaste from the task of translation which the best of their effusions will invite.

The next, though certainly an inferior branch of imaginative writing, is fictitious composition. From the facts just named, you cannot expect that the novelists, or romance writers of the United States, should be very successful. The same reason will be likely, for a long time to come, to repress the ardour of dramatic genius. Still, tales and plays are no novelties in the literature of this country. Of the former, there are many as old as soon after the revolution, and a vast number have been published within the last five years. One of their authors of romance, who curbed his talents by as few allusions as possible to actual society, is distinguished for power and comprehensiveness of thought. I remember to have read one of his books (*Wieland*) when a boy, and I take it to be a never-failing evidence of genius that, amid a thousand similar pictures which have succeeded, the images it has left still stand distinct and prominent in my recollection. This author (Mr. Brockden Brown) enjoys a high reputation among his countrymen, whose opinions are sufficiently impartial, since he flattered no particular prejudice of the nation in any of his works.

The reputation of Irving is well known to you. He is an author distinguished for a quality (humor) that has been denied his countrymen; and his merit is the more rare, that it has been shown in a state of society so cold and so restrained. Besides these writers, there are many others of a similar character, who enjoy a greater or less degree of favour in their own country. The works of two or three have even been translated (into French) in Europe, and a great many are reprinted in England. Though every writer of fiction in America has to contend against the difficulties I have named, there is a certain interest in the novelty of the subject, which is not without its charm. I think, however, it will be found that they have all been successful, or the reverse, just as they have drawn warily, or freely, on the distinctive habits of their own country. I now speak of their success purely as writers of romance. It certainly would be impossible for an American to give a description of the manners of his own country, in a book that he might choose to call a romance, which should be read, because the world is curious on the subject, but which would certainly never be read for that nearly indefinable poetical interest which attaches itself to a description of manners less bald and uniform. All the attempts to blend history with romance in America, have been comparatively failures, (and perhaps fortunately,) since the subjects are too familiar to be treated with the freedom that the imagination absolutely requires. Some of the descriptions of the progress of society on the borders, have had a rather better success, since there is a positive, though not very poetical, novelty in the subject; but, on the whole, the books which have been best received, are those in which the authors have trusted most to their own conceptions of character, and to qualities that are common to the rest of the world and to human nature. This fact, if its truth be admitted, will serve to prove that the American writer must seek his renown in the exhibition of qualities that are general, while he is confessedly compelled to limit his observations to a state of society that has a wonderful tendency not only to repress passion, but to equalize humours.

The Americans have always been prolific writers on polemics and politics. Their sermons and fourth of July orations are numberless. Their historians, without being very classical or very profound, are remarkable for truth and good sense. There is not, perhaps, in the language a closer reasoner in metaphysics than Edwards; and their theological writers find great favour among the sectarians of their respective schools.

The stage of the United States is decidedly English. Both plays and players, with few exceptions, are imported. Theatres are numerous, and they are to be found in places where a traveller would little expect to meet them. Of course they are of all sizes, and of every degree of decoration and architectural beauty known in Europe, below the very highest. The façade of the principal theatre in Philadelphia, is a chaste specimen in marble, of the Ionic, if my memory is correct. In New-York, there are two theatres about as large as the Theatre Français (in the interior), and not much inferior in embellishments. Besides these, there is a very pretty little theatre, where lighter pieces are performed, and another with a vast stage for melodramas. There are also one or two other places of dramatic representation in this city, in which horses and men contend for the bays.

The Americans pay well for dramatic talent. Cooke, the greatest English tragedian of our age, died on this side of the Atlantic; and there are few players of eminence in the mother country who are not tempted, at some time or other, to cross the ocean. Shakespeare is, of course, the great author in America, as he is of England, and I think he is quite as well relished here as there. In point of taste, if all the rest of the world be anything against England, that of America is the best, since it unquestionably approaches nearest to that of the continent of Europe. Nearly one-half of the theatrical taste of the English is condemned by their own judgments, since the stage is not much supported by those who have had an opportunity of seeing any other. You will be apt to ask me how it happens, then, that the American taste is better? Because the people, being less exaggerated in their habits, are less disposed to tolerate caricatures, and because the theatres are not yet sufficiently numerous (though that hour is near) to admit of a representation that shall not be subject to the control of a certain degree of intelligence. I have heard an English player complain that he never saw such a dull audience as the one before which he had just been exhibiting; and I heard the same audience complain that they never listened to such dull jokes. Now, there was talent enough in both parties; but the one had formed his taste in a coarse school, and the others had formed theirs under the dominion of common sense. Independently of this peculiarity, there is a vast deal of acquired, travelled taste in this country. English tragedy, and high English comedy, both of which, you know, are excellent, never fail here, if well played; that is, they never fail under the usual limits of all amusement. One will cloy of sweets. But the fact of the taste and judgment of these people, in theatrical exhibitions, is proved by the number of their good theatres, compared to their population.

Of dramatic writers there are none, or next to none. The remarks I have made in respect to novels apply with double force to this species of composition. A witty, and successful American comedy could only proceed from extraordinary talent. There would be less difficulty, certainly, with a tragedy; but still there is rather too much foreign competition, and too much domestic employment in other pursuits, to invite genius to so doubtful an enterprise. The very baldness of ordinary American life is in deadly hostility to scenic representation. The character must be supported solely by its intrinsic power. The judge, the footman, the clown, the lawyer, the belle, or the beau, can receive no great assistance from dress. Melo-dramas, except the scene should be laid in the woods, are out of the question. It would be necessary to seek the great clock, which is to strike the portentous twelve blows, in the nearest church; a vaulted passage should degenerate into a cellar; and, as for ghosts, the country was discovered, since their visitations have ceased. The smallest departure from incidents of ordinary life would do violence to every man's experience; and, as already mentioned, the passions which belong to human nature must be delineated, in America, subject to the influence of that despot —common sense.

Notwithstanding the overwhelming influence of British publications, and all the difficulties I have named, original books are getting to be numerous in the United States. The impulses of talent and intelligence are bearing down a thousand obstacles. I think the new works will increase rapidly, and that they are destined to produce a powerful influence on the world. We will pursue this subject another time. —Adieu.

1828

From *GLEANINGS IN EUROPE* [*FRANCE*]

[A VISIT FROM SCOTT]

We have not only had Mr. Canning in Paris, but Sir Walter Scott has suddenly appeared among us. The arrival of the *Great Unknown,* or, indeed, of any little unknown from England, would be an event to throw all the reading clubs at home into a state of high moral and poetical excitement. We are true village *lionizers.* As the professors of the Catholic religion are notoriously more addicted to yielding faith to miraculous interventions, in the remoter dioceses, than in Rome itself; as loyalty is always more zealous in a colony, than in a court; as fashions are more exaggerated in a province, than in a capital; and men are more prodigious to every one else, than their own valets; so do we throw the haloes of a vast ocean around the honoured heads of the celebrated men of this eastern hemisphere. This, perhaps, is the natural course of things, and is as unavoidable as that the sun shall hold the earth within the influence of its attraction, until matters shall be reversed by the earth's becoming the larger and more glorious orb of the two. Not so in Paris. Here men of every gradation of celebrity, from Napoleon down to the Psalmanazar of the day, are so very common, that one scarcely turns round in the streets to look at them. Delicate and polite attentions, however, fall as much to the share of reputation, here, as in any other country, and perhaps more so, as respects literary men, though there is so little *wonder-mongering.* It would be quite impossible that the presence of Sir Walter Scott should not excite a sensation. He was frequently named in the journals, received a good deal of private, and some public notice, but, on the whole, much less of both, I think, than one would have a right to expect for him, in a place like Paris. I account for the fact, by the French distrusting the forthcoming work on Napoleon, and by a little dissatisfaction which prevails on the subject of the tone of "Paul's Letters to his Kinsfolk." This feeling may surprise you, as coming from a nation as old and as great as France, but, alas! we are all human.

The King spoke to him, in going to his chapel, Sir Walter being in waiting for that purpose, but beyond this I believe he met with no civilities from the court.

As for myself, circumstances that it is needless to recount had brought me, to a slight degree, within the notice of Sir Walter Scott, though we had never met, nor had I ever seen him, even in public, so as to know his person. Still I was not without hopes of being more fortunate now, while I felt a delicacy about obtruding myself any further on his time and attention. Several days after his arrival went by, however, without my good luck bringing me in his way, and I began to give the matter up, though the Princesse [Galitzin], with whom I had the advantage of being on friendly terms, flattered me with an opportunity of seeing the great writer at her house, for she had a fixed resolution of making his acquaintance before he left Paris, *coûte que coûte.*

It might have been ten days after

the arrival of Sir Walter Scott, that I had ordered a carriage, one morning, with an intention of driving over to the other side of the river, and had got as far as the lower flight of steps, on my way to enter it, when, by the tramping of horses in the court, I found that another coach was driving in. It was raining, and, as my own carriage drove from the door, to make way for the new comer, I stopped where I was, until it could return. The carriage-steps rattled, and presently a large, heavy-moulded man appeared in the door of the hotel. He was gray, and limped a little, walking with a cane. His carriage immediately drove round, and was succeeded by mine, again; so I descended. We passed each other on the stairs, bowing as a matter of course. I had got to the door, and was about to enter the carriage, when it flashed on my mind that the visit might be to myself. The two lower floors of the hotel were occupied as a girl's boarding-school; the reason of our dwelling in it, for our own daughters were in the establishment; *au second,* there was nothing but our own *appartement,* and above us, again, dwelt a family whose visitors never came in carriages. The door of the boarding-school was below, and men seldom came to it, at all. Strangers, moreover, sometimes did honour me with calls. Under these impressions I paused, to see if the visitor went as far as our flight of steps. All this time, I had not the slightest suspicion of who he was, though I fancied both the face and form were known to me.

The stranger got up the large stone steps slowly, leaning, with one hand, on the iron railing, and with the other, on his cane. He was on the first landing, as I stopped, and, turning towards the next flight, our eyes met. The idea that I might be the person he wanted seemed then to strike him for the first time. *"Est-ce Monsieur ——, que j'ai l'honneur de voir?"* he asked, in French, and with but an indifferent accent. *"Monsieur, je m'appele ——." "Eh bien, donc— je suis Walter Scott."*

I ran up to the landing, shook him by the hand, which he stood holding out to me cordially, and expressed my sense of the honour he was conferring. He told me, in substance, that the Princesse [Galitzin] had been as good as her word, and having succeeded herself in getting hold of him, she had good-naturedly given him my address. By way of cutting short all ceremony he had driven from his hotel to my lodgings. All this time he was speaking French, while my answers and remarks were in English. Suddenly recollecting himself, he said —"Well, here have I been *parlez-vousing* to you, in a way to surprise you, no doubt; but these Frenchmen have got my tongue so set to their lingo, that I have half forgotten my own language." As we proceeded up the next flight of steps, he accepted my arm, and continued the conversation in English, walking with more difficulty than I had expected to see. You will excuse the vanity of my repeating the next observation he made, which I do in the hope that some of our own *exquisites* in literature may learn in what manner a man of true sentiment and sound feeling regards a trait that they have seen fit to stigmatize as unbecoming. "I'll tell you what I most like," he added abruptly;

"and it is the manner in which you maintain the ascendancy of your own country on all proper occasions, without descending to vulgar abuse of ours. You are obliged to bring the two nations in collision, and I respect your liberal hostility." This will probably be esteemed treason in our own self-constituted mentors of the press, one of whom, I observe, has quite lately had to apologize to his readers for exposing some of the sins of the English writers in reference to ourselves! But these people are not worth our attention, for they have neither the independence which belongs to masculine reason, nor manhood even to prize the quality in others. "I am afraid the mother has not always treated the daughter well," he continued, "feeling a little jealous of her growth, perhaps; for, though we hope England has not yet begun to descend on the evil side, we have a presentiment that she has got to the top of the ladder."

There were two entrances to our apartments; one, the principal, leading by an ante-chamber and *salle à manger* into the *salon,* and thence through other rooms to a terrace; and the other, by a private *corridor,* to the same spot. The door of my *cabinet* opened on this *corridor,* and though it was dark, crooked, and any thing but savoury, as it led by the kitchen, I conducted Sir Walter through it, under an impression that he walked with pain, an idea, of which I could not divest myself, in the hurry of the moment. But for this awkwardness on my part, I believe I should have been the witness of a singular interview. General Lafayette had been with me a few minutes before, and he had gone away by the *salon,* in order to speak to Mrs. ——. Having a note to write, I had left him there, and I think his carriage could not have quitted the court when that of Sir Walter entered. If so, the General must have passed out by the ante-chamber, about the time we came through the *corridor.*

There would be an impropriety in my relating all that passed in this interview; but we talked over a matter of business, and then the conversation was more general. You will remember that Sir Walter was still the *Unknown,* and that he was believed to be in Paris, in search of facts for the life of Napoleon. Notwithstanding the former circumstance, he spoke of his works with great frankness and simplicity, and without the parade of asking any promises of secrecy. In short, as he commenced in this style, his authorship was alluded to by us both, just as if it had never been called in question. He asked me if I had a copy of the —— by me, and on my confessing I did not own a single volume of any thing I had written, he laughed, and said he believed that most authors had the same feeling on the subject: as for himself, he cared not if he never saw a Waverly novel again, as long as he lived. Curious to know whether a writer as great and as practised as he, felt the occasional despondency which invariably attends all my own little efforts of this nature, I remarked that I found the mere composition of a tale a source of pleasure; so much so, that I always invented twice as much as was committed to paper, in my walks, or in bed, and, in my own judgment, much the best parts of the composition never saw the light; for, what was written was usually written at set hours, and was a good deal a matter of chance; and that going over and over the same subject, in proofs, disgusted me so thoroughly with the book, that I supposed every one else would be disposed to view it with the same eyes. To this he answered, that he was spared much of the labour of proof-reading, Scotland, he presumed, being better off than America, in this respect; but, still, he said he "would as soon see his dinner again, after a hearty meal, as to read one of his own tales when he was fairly rid of it."

He sat with me nearly an hour, and he manifested, during the time the conversation was not tied down to business, a strong propensity to humour. Having occasion to mention our common publisher in Paris, he quaintly termed him, with a sort of malicious fun, "our Gosling," adding, that he hoped he, at least, "laid golden eggs."

I hoped that he had found the facilities he desired, in obtaining facts for the forth-coming history. He rather hesitated about admitting this. —"One can hear as much as he pleases, in the way of anecdote," he said, "but then, as a gentleman, he is not always sure how much of it he can, with propriety, relate in a book; —besides," throwing all his latent humour into the expression of his small gray eyes, "one may even doubt how much of what he hears is fit for history, on another account." He paused, and his face assumed an exquisite air of confiding simplicity, as he continued with perfect *bonne foi* and strong Scottish feeling, "I have been to see *my countryman* M'Donald, and I rather think that will be about as much as I can do here, now." This was uttered with so much *naïveté* that I could hardly believe it was the same man, who, a moment before, had shown so much shrewd distrust of oral relations of facts.

I inquired when we might expect the work. "Sometime in the course of the winter," he replied, "though it is likely to prove larger than I, at first, intended. We have got several volumes printed, but I find I must add to the matter, considerably, in order to dispose of the subject. I thought I should get rid of it in seven volumes, which are already written, but it will reach, I think, to nine." "If you have two still to write, I shall not expect to see the book befor spring." "You may. Let me once get back to Abbotsford, and I'll soon knock off those two fellows." To this I had nothing to say, although I thought such a *tour de force* in writing might better suit invention than history.

When he rose to go, I begged him to step into the *salon,* that I might have the gratification of introducing my wife to him. To this he very good naturedly assented, and entering the room, after presenting Mrs. —— and my nephew W[illiam], he took a seat. He sat some little time, and his fit of pleasantry returned, for he illustrated his discourse by one or two apt anecdotes, related with a slightly Scottish accent, that he seemed to drop and assume at will. Mrs. —— observed to him that the *bergère* in which he was seated had been twice honoured that morning, for General

Lafayette had not left it more than half an hour. Sir Walter Scott looked surprised at this, and said, inquiringly, "I thought he had gone to America to pass the rest of his days?" On my explaining the true state of the case, he merely observed, "He is a great man;" and yet, I thought the remark was made coldly, or in complaisance to us. * * *

1837

From *THE AMERICAN DEMOCRAT*

ON DISTINCTIVE AMERICAN PRINCIPLES

Distinctive American principles as properly refer to the institutions of the states as to those of the Union. A correct notion of the first cannot be formed without keeping the latter constantly in view.

The leading distinctive principle of this country, is connected with the fact that all political power is strictly a trust, granted by the constituent to the representative. These representatives possess different duties, and as the greatest check that is imposed on them, while in the exercise of their offices, exists in the manner in which the functions are balanced by each other, it is of the last importance that neither class trespass on the trusts that are not especially committed to its keeping.

The machinery of the state being the same in appearance, in this country and in that from which we are derived, inconsiderate commentators are apt to confound their principles. In England, the institutions have been the result of those circumstances to which time has accidentally given birth. The power of the king was derived from violence, the monarch, before the act of succession, in the reign of Queen Anne, claiming the throne in virtue of the conquest by William, in 1060. In America, the institutions are the result of deliberate consultation, mutual concessions, and design. In England, the people may have gained by diminishing the power of the king, who first obtained it by force; but, in America, to assail the rightful authority of the executive, is attacking a system framed by the constituencies of the states, who are virtually the people, for their own benefit. No assault can be made on any branch of this government, while in the exercise of its constitutional duties, without assaulting the right of the body of the nation, which is the foundation of the whole polity.

In countries, in which executive power is hereditary, and clothed with high prerogatives, it may be struggling for liberty to strive to diminish its influence; but, in this republick, in which the executive is elective, has no absolute authority in framing the laws, serves for a short period, is responsible, and has been created by the people, through the states, for their own purposes, it is assailing the rights of that people, to attempt in any manner to impede its legal and just action.

It is a general law in politics, that the power most to be distrusted, is that which, possessing the greatest force, is the least responsible. Under the constitutional monarchies of Europe, (as they exist in theory, at least,) the king, besides uniting in his single person all the authority of the executive, which includes a power to make war, create peers, and unconditionally to name to all employments, has an equal influence in enacting laws, his veto being absolute; but, in America, the executive, besides being elective, is stripped of most of these high sources of influence, and is obliged to keep constantly in view the justice and legality of his acts, both on account of his direct responsibilities, and on account of the force of public opinion.

In this country, there is far more to apprehend from congress, than from the executive, as is seen in the following reasons:— Congress is composed of many, while the executive is one, bodies of men notoriously acting with less personal responsibilities than individuals; congress has power to enact laws, which it becomes the duty of the executive to see enforced, and the really legislative authority of a country is always its greatest authority; from the decisions and constructions of the executive, the citizen can always appeal to the courts for protection, but no appeal can lie from the acts of congress, except on the ground of unconstitutionality; the executive has direct personal responsibilities under the laws of the land, for any abuses of his authority, but the member of congress, unless guilty of open corruption, is almost beyond personal liabilities.

It follows that the legislature of this country, by the intention of the constitution, wields the highest authority under the least responsibility, and that it is the power most to be distrusted. Still, all who possess trusts, are to be diligently watched, for there is no protection against abuses without responsibility, nor any real responsibility, without vigilance.

Political partisans, who are too apt to mistake the impulses of their own hostilities and friendships for truths, have laid down many false principles on the subject of the duties of the executive. When a law is passed, it goes to the executive for execution, through the executive agents, and, at need, to the courts for interpretation. It would seem that there is no discretion vested in the executive concerning the constitutionality of a law. If he distrust the constitutionality of any law, he can set forth his objections by resorting to the veto; but it is clearly the intention of the system that the whole legislative power, in the last resort, shall abide in congress, while it is necessary to the regular action of the government, that none of its agents, but those who are especially appointed for that purpose, shall pretend to interpret the constitution, in practice. The citizen is differently situated. If he conceive himself oppressed by an unconstitutional law, it is his inalienable privilege to raise the question before the courts, where a final interpretation can be had. By this interpretation the executive and all his agents are equally bound to abide. This obligation arises from the necessity of things, as well as from the nature of the institutions. There must be somewhere a power to decide on the constitutionality of laws, and this power is vested in the supreme court of the United States, on final appeal.

When called on to approve a law, even though its principle should have been already pronounced on by the courts, the executive is independent. He is now a legislator, and can disregard all other constructions of the constitution, but those dictated by his own sense of right. In this character, to the extent of his veto-power, he is superior to the courts, which have cognizance of no more than each case as it is presented for their consideration. The president may approve of a law that the court has decided to be unconstitutional in principle, or he may veto a law that the court has decided to be constitutional in principle. The legislator himself, is compelled to submit to the interpretation of the court, however different his own views of the law may have been in passing it, but as soon as he comes to act again as a legislator, he becomes invested with all his own high duties and rights. The court cannot make the constitution, in any case; it only interprets the law. One court may decide differently from another, and instances often occur in which the same judges see reason to change their own decisions, and it would be, to the last degree, inexpedient, to give the court an authority beyond the necessity of the circumstances.

Although the court can render a law null, its power does not extend beyond the law already passed. Congress may re-enact it, as often as it please, and the court will still exercise its reason in rejecting it. This is the balance of the constitution, which invites inquiry, the constituencies of the states holding a legal authority to render that constitutional which the courts have declared unconstitutional, or vice versa, by amendments to the instrument itself; the supremacy of the court being merely temporary, conditional, and growing out of expediency and necessity.

It has been said that it is a vital principle of this government, that each of its branches should confine itself to the particular duties assigned it by the constitution, and in no manner exceed them. Many grave abuses have already arisen from loosing sight of this truth, and there is danger that the whole system will be perverted from its intention, if not destroyed, unless they are seasonably corrected. Of these, the most prevalent, the one most injurious to the public service, that which has been introduced the most on foreign and the least on American principles, is the practice of using the time and influence of the legislatures, for the purpose of acting on the public mind, with a view to affect the elections. The usage has already gained so much footing, as seriously to impede the course of legislation.

This is one of the cases, in which it is necessary to discriminate between the distinctive principles of our own government, and those of the government of the country from which we are derived. In England, by the mode in which the power of the executive has been curtailed, it is necessary that the ministerial contests should be conducted in the legislative bodies, but, in this country, such a course cannot be imitated, without the legislators' assuming an authority that does not belong to them, and without dispossessing the people, in some measure, of their rights. He who will examine the constitution for the powers of congress, will find no authority to pass resolutions on, or to waste the time, which is the property of the public, in discussing the matters, on which, after all, congress has no power to decide. This is the test of legislative authority. Congress cannot properly even discuss a subject, that congress cannot legally control, unless it be to ascertain its own powers. In cases that do not admit of question, this is one of the grossest abuses of the institutions, and ought to be classed with the usurpations of other systems.

There is a feeling connected with this subject, that it behooves every upright citizen cautiously to watch. He may be opposed to the executive, for instance, as a party-man, and yet have an immediate representative in congress, of his own particular way of thinking; and it is a weakness of humanity, under such circumstances for one to connect himself most directly with his own immediate candidate, and to look on his political opponent with distrust. The jealousy created by this feeling, induces unreflecting men to imagine that curbing their particular representatives, in matters of this nature, is curtailing their own rights, and disposes them to defend what is inherently wrong, on personal motives.

Political systems ought to be, and usually are, framed on certain great and governing principles. These principles cannot be perverted, or lost sight of, without perverting, or rendering nugatory the system itself; and, under a popular government, in an age like this, far more is to be apprehended from indirect attacks on the institutions, than from those which are direct. It is usual to excuse these departures from the right on the plea of human propensities, but human institutions are framed expressly to curb such propensities, and no truth is more salutary than that which is contained in the homely saying, that "law makers should not be law breakers."

It is the duty of the citizen to judge of all political acts on the great principles of the government, and not according to his own political partialities, or prejudices. His own particular representative is no more a representative of the people, than the representative of any other man, and one branch of the government is no more representative than another. All are to keep within their respective spheres, and it may be laid down as a governing maxim of the institutions, *that the representative who exceeds his trusts, trespasses on the rights of the people.*

All comparisons between the powers of the British Parliament and those of congress are more than useless, since they are bodies differently constituted, while one is absolute, and the other is merely a special trustee for limited and defined objects.

In estimating the powers of congress, there is a rule that may be safely confided in, and which has been already hinted at. The powers of congress are express and limited. That body therefore, can have no right *to pass resolutions* other than those which affect their own police, or, in a moral sense, even to make speeches, except on subjects on which *they have a right to pass laws.* The instant they exceed these limits, they exceed the bounds of their delegated authority. By applying this simple test to their proceedings, any citizen may, in ordinary cases, ascertain how far the representatives of the nation abuse their trusts.

Liberty is not a matter of words, but a positive and important condition of society. Its great safeguards, after placing its foundations on a popular base, is in the checks and balances imposed on the public servants, and all its real friends ought to know that the most insidious attacks, are made on it by those who are the largest trustees of authority, in their efforts to increase their power.

The government of the United States has three branches. The executive, the legislative and the judicial. These several branches are independent of each other, though the first is intended to act as a check on the second, no law or resolution being legal that is not first submitted to the president for his approval. This check, however, does not render the first an integral part of the legislature, as laws and resolutions may be passed without his approval, by votes of two thirds.

In most constitutional monarchies, the legislatures, being originally secondary powers, were intended as checks on the action of the crown, which was possessed of the greatest, and, by consequence, of the most dangerous authority; whereas, the case is reversed in America, the executive using his veto as a check on congress. Such is the intention of the constitution, though the tactics of party, and the bitterness of opposition, have endeavored to interpret the instrument differently, by appealing to the ancient prejudices derived from England.

AN ARISTOCRAT AND A DEMOCRAT

We live in an age, when the words aristocrat and democrat are much used, without regard to the real significations. An aristocrat is one of a few, who possess the political power of a country; a democrat, one of the many. The words are also properly applied to those who entertain notions favorable to aristocratical, or democratical forms of government. Such persons are not, necessarily, either aristocrats, or democrats in fact, but merely so in opinion. Thus a member of a democratical government may have an aristocratical bias, and *vice versa*.

To call a man who has the habits and opinions of a gentleman, an aristocrat, from that fact alone, is an abuse of terms, and betrays ignorance of the true principles of government, as well as of the world. It must be an equivocal freedom, under which every one is not the master of his own innocent acts and associations, and he is a sneaking democrat, indeed, who will submit to be dictated to, in those habits over which neither law nor morality assumes a right of control.

Some men fancy that a democrat can only be one who seeks the level, social, mental and moral, of the majority, a rule that would at once exclude all men of refinement, education, and taste from the class. These persons are enemies of democracy, as they at once render it impracticable. They are usually great sticklers for their own associations and habits, too, though unable to comprehend any of a nature that are superior. They are, in truth, aristocrats in principle, though assuming a contrary pretension; the ground work of all their feelings and arguments being self. Such is not the intention of liberty, whose aim is to leave every man to be the master of his own acts; denying hereditary honors, it is true, as unjust and unnecessary, but not denying the inevitable consequences of civilization.

The law of God is the only rule of conduct, in this, as in other matters. Each man should do as he would be done by. Were the question put to the greatest advocate of indiscriminate association, whether he would submit to have his company and habits dictated to him, he would be one of the first to resist the tyranny; for they, who are the most rigid in maintaining their own claims, in such matters, are usually the loudest in decrying those whom they fancy to be better off than themselves. Indeed, it may be taken as a rule in social intercourse, that he who is the most apt to question the pretensions of others, is the most conscious of the doubtful position he himself occupies; thus establishing the very claims he affects to deny, by letting his jealousy of it be seen. Manners, education and refinement, are positive things, and they bring with them innocent tastes which are productive of high enjoyments; and it is as unjust to deny their possessors their indulgence, as it would be to insist on the less fortunate's passing the time they would rather devote to athletic amusements, in listening to operas for which they have no relish, sung in a language they do not understand.

All that democracy means, is as equal a participation in rights as is practicable; and to pretend that social equality is a condition of popular institutions, is to assume that the latter are destructive of civilization, for, as nothing is more self-evident than the impossibility of raising all men to the highest standard of tastes and refinement, the alternative would be to reduce the entire community to the lowest. The whole embarrassment on this point exists in the difficulty of making men comprehend qualities they do not themselves possess. We can all perceive the difference between ourselves and our inferiors, but when it comes to a question of the difference between us and our superiors, we fail to appreciate merits of which we have no proper conceptions. In face of this obvious difficulty, there is the safe and just governing rule, already mentioned, or that of permitting every one to be the undisturbed judge of his own habits and associations, so long as they are innocent, and do not impair the rights of others to be equally judges for themselves. It follows, that social intercourse must regulate itself, independently of institutions, with the exception that the latter, while they withold no natural, bestow no factitious advantages beyond those which are inseparable from the rights of property, and general civilization.

In a democracy, men are just as free to aim at the highest attainable places in society, as to obtain the largest fortunes; and it would be clearly unworthy of all noble sentiment to say, that the grovelling competition for money shall alone be free, while that which enlists all the liberal acquirements and elevated sentiments of the race, is denied the democrat. Such an avowal would be at once, a declaration of the inferiority of the system, since nothing but ignorance and vulgarity could be its fruits.

The democratic gentleman must differ in many essential particulars, from the aristocratical gentleman, though in their ordinary habits and tastes they are virtually identical. Their principles vary; and, to a slight degree, their deportment accordingly. The democrat, recognizing the right of all to participate in power, will be more liberal in his general sentiments, a quality of superiority in itself; but, in conceding this much to his fellow man, he will proudly maintain his own independence of vulgar domination, as indispensable to his personal habits. The same principles and manliness that would induce him to depose a royal despot, would induce him to resist a vulgar tyrant.

There is no more capital, though more common error, than to suppose him an aristocrat who maintains his independence of habits; for democracy asserts the control of the majority, only, in matters of law, and not in matters of custom. The very object of the institution is the utmost practicable personal liberty, and to affirm the contrary, would be sacrificing the end to the means.

An aristocrat, therefore, is merely one who fortifies his exclusive privileges by positive institutions, and a democrat, one who is willing to admit of a free competition, in all things. To say, however, that the last supposes this competition will lead to nothing, is an assumption that means are employed without any reference to an end. He is the purest democrat who best maintains his rights, and no rights can be dearer to a man of cultivation, than exemptions from unseasonable invasions on his time, by the coarse-minded and ignorant.

1838

FOLK LITERATURE

INDIAN SONGS AND LEGENDS

I

HIAWATHA, OR, THE ORIGIN OF THE ONONDAGA COUNCIL-FIRE

[Henry Rowe Schoolcraft]

Tarenyawago taught the Six Nations arts and knowledge. He had a canoe which would move without paddles. It was only necessary to will it, to compel it to go. With this he ascended the streams and lakes. He taught the people to raise corn and beans, removed obstructions from their water-courses, and made their fishing-grounds clear. He helped them to get the mastery over the great monsters which overran the country, and thus prepared the forests for their hunters. His wisdom was as great as his power. The people listened to him with admiration, and followed his advice gladly. There was nothing in which he did not excel good hunters, brave warriors, and eloquent orators.

He gave them wise instructions for observing the laws and maxims of the Great Spirit. Having done these things, he laid aside the high powers of his public mission, and resolved to set them an example of how they should live.

For this purpose, he selected a beautiful spot on the southern shore of one of the lesser and minuter lakes, which is called Tioto (Cross lake) by the natives, to this day. Here he erected his lodge, planted his field of corn, kept by him his magic canoe, and selected a wife. In relinquishing his former position, as a subordinate power to the Great Spirit, he also dropped his name, and, according to his present situation, took that of Hiawatha, meaning a person of very great wisdom, which the people spontaneously bestowed on him.

He now lived in a degree of respect scarcely inferior to that which he before possessed. His words and counsels were implicitly obeyed. The people flocked to him from all quarters, for advice and instruction. Such persons as had been prominent in following his precepts, he favored, and they became eminent on the war-path and in the council-room.

When Hiawatha assumed the duties of an individual, at Tioto, he carefully drew out from the water his beautiful talismanic canoe, which had served for horses and chariot, in his initial excursions through the Iroquois territories, and it was carefully secured on land, and never used except in his journeys to attend the general councils. He had elected to become a member of the Onondaga tribe, and chose the residence of this people, in the shady recesses of their fruitful valley, as the central point of their government.

After the termination of his higher mission from above, years passed away in prosperity, and the Onondagas assumed an elevated rank, for their wisdom and learning, among the other tribes, and there was not one of these which did not yield its assent to their high privilege of lighting the general council-fire.

Suddenly there arose a great alarm at the invasion of a ferocious band of warriors from the north of the Great Lakes. As they advanced, an indiscriminate slaughter was made of men, women, and children. Destruction threatened to be alike the fate of those who boldly resisted, or quietly submitted. The public alarm was extreme. Hiawatha advised them not to waste their efforts in a desultory manner, but to call a general council of all the tribes that could be gathered together from the east to the west; and he appointed the meeting to take place on an eminence on the banks of Onondaga lake.

Accordingly all the chief men assembled at this spot. The occasion brought together vast multitudes of men, women, and children; for there was an expectation of some great deliverance. Three days had already elapsed, and there began to be a general anxiety lest Hiawatha should not arrive. Messengers were despatched for him to Tioto, who found him in a pensive mood, to whom he communicated his strong presentiments that evil betided his attendance. These were overruled by the strong representations of the messengers, and he again put his wonderful vessel in its element, and set out for the council, taking his only daughter with him. She timidly took her seat in the stern, with a light paddle, to give direction to the vessel; for the strength of the current of the Seneca river was sufficient to give velocity to the motion till arriving at So-hah-hi, the Onondaga outlet. At this point the powerful exertions of the aged chief were required, till they entered on the bright bosom of the Onondaga.

The grand council, that was to avert the threatened danger, was quickly in sight, and sent up its shouts of welcome, as the venerated man approached, and landed in front of the assemblage. An ascent led up the banks of the lake to the place occupied by the council. As he walked up this, a loud sound was heard in the air above, as if caused by some rushing current of wind. Instantly the eyes of all were directed upward to the sky, where a spot of matter was discovered descending rapidly, and every instant enlarging in its size and velocity. Terror and alarm were the first impulses, for it appeared to be descending into their midst, and they scattered in confusion.

Hiawatha, as soon as he had gained the eminence, stood still, and caused his daughter to do the same; deeming it cowardly to fly, and impossible, if it were attempted, to divert the designs of the Great Spirit. The descending object had now assumed a more definite aspect, and as it came down, revealed the shape of a gigantic white bird, with wide extended and pointed wings, which came down, swifter and swifter, with a mighty swoop, and crushed the girl to the earth. Not a muscle was moved in the face of Hiawatha. His daughter lay dead before him, but the great and mysterious white bird was also destroyed by the shock. Such had been the violence of the concussion, that it had completely buried its beak and head in the ground. But the most wonderful sight was the carcase of the prostrated bird, which was covered with beautiful plumes of snow-white shining feathers. Each warrior stepped up, and decorated himself with a plume. And it hence became a custom to assume this kind of feathers on the war-path. Succeeding generations substituted the plumes of the white heron, which led this bird to be greatly esteemed.

But yet a greater wonder ensued. On removing the carcase of the bird, not a human trace could be discovered of the daughter. She had completely vanished. At this the father was greatly afflicted in spirits, and disconsolate. But he roused himself, as from a lethargy, and walked to the head of the council with a dignified air, covered with his simple robe of wolf-skins; taking his seat with the chief warriors and counsellors, and listening with attentive gravity to the plans of the different speakers. One day was given to these discussions; on the next day, he arose and said:

"My friends and brothers; you are members of many tribes, and have come from a great distance. We have met to promote the common interest, and our mutual safety. How shall it be accomplished? To oppose these northern hordes in tribes singly, while we are at variance often with each other, is impossible. By uniting in a common band of brotherhood, we may hope to succeed. Let this be done, and we shall drive the enemy from our land. Listen to me by tribes.

"You (the Mohawks), who are sitting under the shadow of the Great Tree, whose roots sink deep in the earth, and whose branches spread wide around, shall be the first nation, because you are warlike and mighty.

"You (the Oneidas), who recline your bodies against the Everlasting Stone, that cannot be moved, shall be the second nation, because you always give wise counsel.

"You (the Onondagas), who have your habitation at the foot of the Great Hills, and are overshadowed by their crags, shall be the third nation, because you are all greatly gifted in speech.

"You (the Senecas), whose dwelling is in the Dark Forest, and whose home is everywhere, shall be the fourth nation, because of your superior cunning in hunting.

"And you (the Cayugas), the people who live in the Open Country, and possess much wisdom, shall be the fifth nation, because you understand better the art of raising corn and beans, and making houses.

"Unite, you five nations, and have one common interest, and no foe shall disturb and subdue you. You, the people who are as the feeble bushes, and you, who are a fishing people, may place yourselves under our protection, and we will defend you. And you of the south and of the west may do the same, and we will protect you. We earnestly desire the alliance and friendship of you all.

"Brothers, if we unite in this great bond, the Great Spirit will smile upon us, and we shall be free, prosperous, and happy. But if we remain as we are, we shall be subject to his frown. We shall be enslaved, ruined, perhaps annihilated. We may perish under the war-storm, and our names be no longer remembered by good men, nor be repeated in the dance and song.

"Brothers, these are the words of Hiawatha. I have said it. I am done."

The next day the plan of union was again considered, and adopted by the council. Conceiving this to be the accomplishment of his mission to the Iroquois, the tutelar patron of this rising confederacy addressed them in a speech elaborate with wise counsels, and then announced his withdrawal to the skies. At its conclusion, he went down to the shore, and assumed his seat in his mystical vessel. Sweet music was heard in the air, at the same moment, and as its cadence floated in the ears of the wondering multitude, it rose in the air, higher and higher, till it vanished from the sight, and disappeared in the celestial regions inhabited only by Owayneo and his hosts.

1851–57

II

HUNTING THE MOOSE

[Natalie Curtis]

The Great Spirit made all things; all men are his children. He made the Indians last of all, and so, since they are his youngest children, they are not as wise as the white men. But the Great Spirit said, "In time you shall know me." And he placed in the hands of the Indian the bow and said, "This shall find for you both food and clothing."

The Great Spirit is in all things; he is the air we breathe. The Great Spirit is our father, but the earth is our mother. She nourishes us; that which we put into the ground she returns to us, and healing plants she gives us likewise. If we are wounded, we go to our mother and seek to lay the wounded part against her, to be healed. Animals, too, do thus, they lay their wounds to the earth. When we go hunting, it is not our arrow that kills the moose, however powerful be the bow; it is nature that kills him. The arrow sticks in his hide; and, like all living things, the moose goes to our mother to be healed. He seeks to lay his wound against the earth, and thus he drives the arrow farther in. Meanwhile I follow. He is out of sight, but I put my ear to a tree in the forest, and that brings me the sound, and I hear when the moose makes his next leap, and I follow. The moose stops again for the pain of the arrow, and he rubs his side upon the earth and drives the arrow farther in. I follow always, listening now and then with my ear against a tree. Every time he stops to rub his side he drives the arrow farther in, till at last when he is nearly exhausted and I come up with him, the arrow may be driven clean through his body. Then I can kill him easily with my knife.

The moose comes when he is called. We call him with a horn made of bark; or we stand in the water and scoop it up and then let it slowly drip as if a moose were drinking. The moose comes to the sound because he thinks to find his mate.

Now follows the story of the moose:

STORY OF THE MOOSE

In olden days the moose was so large that he used to browse on the tops of trees; also he destroyed the people. So the Great Spirit sent Ksiwhambeh to the people, and when he had come he called us all together and said, "I have come to change that animal, the moose, so that you can take comfort in him."

Then Ksiwhambeh called for a strip of birch-bark, three hands long, and when it was brought him he set one hand upon an end of it, and two fingers upon the other end, and he rolled the bark into a horn and began to call the moose. The first time he called, the people could only faintly hear the sound of the answer far in the distance; then he called again, and the answer was nearer and nearer till at last a moose appeared. And Ksiwhambeh spoke to the moose and said: "I have come to make you smaller so that my children can take comfort in you. Come here to me."

The moose came and held down his head, and Ksiwhambeh took him between the horns and pushed him down to the size that he now has. Then Ksiwhambeh said to him, "Henceforth look that you never come till you are called."

Thus Ksiwhambeh changed the moose; and to this day the hunter calls him with a horn of birch-bark.

1907

III

T'ÄPK'O DAAGYA

SONG OF THE ANTELOPE CEREMONY

[NATALIE CURTIS]

There was once a little boy who lived with his old grandmother. One day he happened to lose her spoon—a wooden spoon—for this was long ago, when the people had no iron or other metals. His grandmother was angry and whipped him, and so the boy threw himself upon the ground, crying, beside the wall of the tipi. There he lay, sobbing, until he fell asleep; and in his sleep he dreamed a wonderful dream which gave him mysterious power, so that he would always be able to kill game in plenty.

Time passed, and at length there came a famine upon the people; for many days they could get no meat, and they were hungry. The boy had grown to be a man, yet had he not forgotten the secret power that he had learned in a dream. So he spoke to his grandmother and said: "Call all the people to my tipi. Bid them all come."

"Why," said the grandmother, "we are poor, and we have neither wisdom nor power. The people will be angry if we call them here, for there is no help in us."

The young man himself went out and summoned all the people, and when they were come he took his seat opposite the door of the tipi, and the people sat around in a circle, as many as could find room within the tipi, and the rest waited outside. The man made two arrows, one of wild-cherry, and the other of plum-tree wood.* When they were finished he stood them in the ground before him and began to sing:

"My grandmother punished me,
I wept until I fell asleep,
In dream came a holy power, wonderful,
Mighty to win food."

* The wild-cherry tree and the plum-tree are symbols of spring and autumn fruitfulness, and are thus symbols of plenty. Other details of the ceremony also are probably emblematic. [Collector's note.]

He waved the arrows in time to the song, and at the end of each verse he shook them, and blew upon his whistle of eagle-bone, "Whew!" Down from the arrows fell a shower of antelope-fur! He did this wonder in order to prove to the people his power. When he had finished singing he took his bow in his hands and reached down to the edge of the tipi wall where he had thrown himself when a child. There was nothing there that any man could see, yet the wonderful power that had visited the sleeping boy was still present; and so when he drew back his bow, behold an antelope was caught in it by the horns, and the man dragged him forth into the light of the fire and showed him to the astonished people. All night long they sat in the tipi, singing together in mystic ceremony.

When morning came the man went out on the prairie and walked to the top of a high hill. There he sat down, and the people sat on each side of him, forming a circle as before; and those who had come on horseback gathered outside the circle. The man planted his arrows in the ground and sang again and did his mystic work. Then he gave the two arrows to the two men who sat opposite to him, and they set off in opposite directions, carrying the arrows. The people followed them on foot, gradually separating from one another until they had formed the half of a large circle. Then the two leaders stopped and delivered the arrows to two horsemen, and the horsemen rode on, and other horsemen followed them, gradually separating from one another just as the people afoot had done until they had completed the great circle. And when the arrow-bearers met at the far side of the circle they turned and rode back through the centre of the circle till they came again to the starting-point and delivered up their mystic arrows. Then all the horsemen forming the farther side of the great circle began to gallop here and there, whooping and shouting, to rouse the game; and the horsemen gradually drew nearer, driving the game towards the men on foot; and when the animals were gathered together the people on foot closed in around them, and kept closing in until the circle was small enough for the people to join hands. The frightened antelopes ran around inside the circle until they became dizzy and exhausted; then the people killed them easily with tomahawks and knives, or if any broke through the circle the horsemen outside caught and killed them.

So the people had meat in plenty through the miraculous wisdom taught the boy in a dream. Thus originated this rite, which was performed only when the people were in great need. It came down from father to son for many years—none know how many. It is now no longer used, for all is changed, and there is little game to hunt. But some of the old men saw the ceremony in their youth, and it is well remembered by the aged Eagle Chief.

To*n*-k'a*n* giapowitzep no
Tai*n*kyowitte tai*n* hol
Komdombe to*n*ok'o
Tsai*n*iya ode domgya.

1907

IV

THE STORY OF WAKIASH AND THE FIRST TOTEM POLE

[Natalie Curtis]

There was once a chief named Wakiash, and he was named after the river Wakiash because he was open-handed, flowing with gifts even as the river flowed with fish. It happened on a time that all the tribe were having a big dance. Wakiash had never had any kind of dance of his own, and he was unhappy because all the other chiefs of the tribe had fine dances. So he thought to himself, "I will go up into the mountains to fast." And he made himself ready, and went up into the mountains and stayed there four days, fasting and bathing. On the fourth day, early in the morning, he grew so weary that he lay upon his back and fell asleep; and then he felt something that came upon his breast and woke him. It was a little green frog. The frog said, "Wake up, that you may see where you are going."

Wakiash opened his eyes and saw that the frog was on his breast. The frog said, "Lie still as you are, because you are on the back of a raven that is going to fly with you around the world, so that you may see what you want, and take it." And the frog said that he would stay with the man till they came back again to the same place. Then the frog told the man to get ready, and bade the raven to start.

The raven flew and carried the man around the world and showed him all the things of the world. They flew four days, and when they were on their way back Wakiash saw a house with a beautiful totem-pole in front, and heard a noise of singing inside the house. He thought to himself that these were fine things, and he wished that he might take them with him. Now the frog knew his thoughts and told the raven to stop. So the raven stopped and the frog told the man to hide himself behind the door. The man did as the frog told him, and the frog said, "Stay here, and when they begin to dance, leap out into the room."

The people tried to begin a dance, but could do nothing—they could neither dance nor sing. One of them stood up and said, "There is something the matter with us; there must be something near us that makes us feel like this." And the chief said, "Let one of us, who can run faster than the flames of the fire, go around the house and see." So the little mouse came and said that she would go, for she could go anywhere, even into a box, and if any one were hiding she could find him. The mouse was in the form of a woman, because she had taken off her mouse-skin clothes; indeed, all the people in the house were animals, and their chief was the beaver, but they had taken off their animal-skin clothes to dance, and so they looked like men.

The mouse ran out, and Wakiash caught her and said, "Ha, my friend, wait here and I will make you a gift." And he gave the mouse a piece of mountain-goat's fat. Now this mouse was so pleased with Wakiash that she talked with him and asked him what he wanted, and Wakiash said that he wanted the totem-pole, the house, and the kind of dances and songs that belonged to them. The mouse said, "Stay here, and wait till I come again."

Wakiash stayed, and the mouse went in and said to the people, "I have been everywhere to find if there were a man about, but I could find nobody." And the chief said, "Now let us try again to dance." They tried three times before they could do anything, and they sent out the mouse each time to see what she could find. But each time the mouse was sent out she talked with Wakiash; and the third time that she went out she said, "Now make ready, and when they begin to dance, leap into the room."

Then the mouse went back to the animals and told them that she could find no one, and so they began to dance, and just then Wakiash sprang in. At once the dancers dropped their heads for shame, because a man had seen them looking like men, whereas they were really animals. And they stood silent for some time, till at last the mouse began to speak and said: "Let us not wait thus; let us ask our friend what he wants. He must want something or he would not come here." So they all lifted up their heads, and the chief asked the man what he wanted. Wakiash thought to himself that he would like to have the dance, because he had never had one of his own, though all the other chiefs had dances. Also he wanted the house, and the totem-pole that he had seen outside. Though the man did not speak, the mouse heard his thoughts and told the people. And the chief said, "Let our friend sit down and we will show him how we dance, and he can pick out whatsoever kind of dance he wants."

So they began to dance, and when they had ended the chief asked Wakiash what kind of dance he would like. They were using all sorts of masks. Wakiash wanted most of all the Echo mask, and the mask of the Little Man that goes about the house talking, talking, and trying to quarrel with others. Wakiash only thought to himself; the mouse told the chief his thoughts. So the animals taught Wakiash all their dances, and the chief told him that he might take as many dances and masks as he wished, also the house and the totem-pole. The chief said to Wakiash that these things would all go with him when he went home, and that he should use them all in one dance; also that he should thenceforth have, for his own, the name of the totem-pole, Kalakuyuwish, meaning sky-pole, because the pole was so tall. So the chief took the house and folded it up in a little bundle. He put it in the headdress of one of the dancers, and this he gave to Wakiash, saying, "When you reach home, throw down this bundle; the house will become as it was when you first saw it, and then you can begin to give a dance."

Wakiash went back to the raven, and the raven flew away with him towards the mountain from which they had set out; but before they arrived there Wakiash fell asleep, and when he awoke the raven and the frog were gone and he was all alone. Then he started for home, and when he got there it was night, and he threw down the bundle that was in the headdress, and there was the house with its totem-pole! The whale painted on the house was blowing, the animals carved on the totem-pole were making their noises, and all the masks inside the house were talking and crying aloud. At once Wakiash's people awoke and came out to see what was happening, and Wakiash found that instead of four days he had been away four years. They went into the house, and Wakiash began to make a dance; he taught the people the songs, and they sang, and Wakiash danced, and then the Echo came, and whosoever made a noise the Echo made the same, changing its mouths. When they had finished dancing the house was gone; it went back to the animals. And all the chiefs were ashamed because Wakiash now had the best dance.

Then Wakiash made, out of wood, a house and masks and a totem-pole; and when the totem-pole was finished the people made a song for it. This totem-pole was the first that this tribe had ever had; the animals had named it *Kalakuyuwish*, "the pole that holds up the sky," and they said that it made a creaking noise because the sky was so heavy. And Wakiash took for his own the name of the totem-pole, Kalakuyuwish.

KLAWULA*CHA*

SONG OF THE TOTEM-POLE. IN PRAISE OF WAKIASH KALAKUYUWISH

SUNG BY KLALISH (CHARLES JAMES NOWELL)

KLAWULA*cha*

Waw haw le
Pulnakwila kiash ila koi
Wakiash kiash o wa
  Ya *ch*oi
Waw haw le
Hitlpalkwala kyilish
  Kiash ila koi
Kalakuyuwish kiash o wa
La*ch*nahkwulla
  Ya *ch*oi

SONG OF THE TOTEM-POLE

Now doth it rise, our river;
Our river is Wakiash, good is he.
Now doth it creak, this totem-pole,
  Clouds rest on its top.
Kalakuyuwish, great as the sky-pole is he!

1907

V

MOUNTAIN-SONGS *

[NATALIE CURTIS]

I

Swift and far I journey,
Swift upon the rainbow.
Swift and far I journey,
Lo, yonder, the Holy Place!
  Yea, swift and far I journey.
To Sisnajinni, and beyond it,
  Yea, swift and far I journey;
The Chief of Mountains, and beyond it,
  Yea, swift and far I journey;
To Life Unending, and beyond it,
  Yea, swift and far I journey;
To Joy Unchanging, and beyond it,
  Yea, swift and far I journey.

II

Homeward now shall I journey,
Homeward upon the rainbow;
Homeward now shall I journey,
Lo, yonder, the Holy Place!
  Yea, homeward now shall I journey.
To Sisnajinni, and beyond it,

* Each song sung four times, with substitution, in the sixth line, of the name of another mountain. [Collector's note.]

Yea, homeward now shall I journey;
The Chief of Mountains, and beyond it,
Yea, homeward now shall I journey;
To Life Unending, and beyond it,
Yea, homeward now shall I journey;
To Joy Unchanging, and beyond it,
Yea, homeward now shall I journey.

III

Homeward behold me starting,
Homeward upon the rainbow;
Homeward behold me starting.
Lo, yonder, the Holy Place!
Yea, homeward behold me starting,
To Sisnajinni, and beyond it,
Yea, homeward behold me starting;
The Chief of Mountains, and beyond it,
Yea, homeward behold me starting;
To Life Unending, and beyond it,
Yea, homeward behold me starting;
To Joy Unchanging, and beyond it,
Yea, homeward, behold me starting.

IV

Homeward behold me faring,
Homeward upon the rainbow;
Homeward behold me faring.
Lo, yonder, the Holy Place!
Yea, homeward behold me faring,
To Sisnajinni, and beyond it,
Yea, homeward behold me faring;
The Chief of Mountains, and beyond it,
Yea, homeward behold me faring;
To Life Unending, and beyond it,
Yea, homeward behold me faring;
To Joy Unchanging, and beyond it,
Yea, homeward behold me faring.

V

Now arrived home behold me,
Now arrived upon the rainbow;
Now arrived home behold me,
Lo, here, the Holy Place!
Yea, now arrived home behold me.
At Sisnajinni, and beyond it,
Yea, now arrived home behold me;
The Chief of Mountains, and beyond it,
Yea, now arrived home behold me;
In Life Unending, and beyond it,
Yea, now arrived home behold me;
In Joy Unchanging, and beyond it,
Yea, now arrived home behold me.

VI

Seated at home behold me,
Seated amid the rainbow;
Seated at home behold me,
Lo, here, the Holy Place!
Yea, seated at home behold me;
At Sisnajinni, and beyond it,
Yea, seated at home behold me;
The Chief of Mountains, and beyond it,
Yea, seated at home behold me;
In Life Unending, and beyond it,
Yea, seated at home behold me;
In Joy Unchanging, and beyond it,
Yea, seated at home behold me.

1907

NOTES

In these Notes a concise biographical and critical sketch of each author is provided, with selected, annotated bibliographies. For each specimen full details of publication are given, as is also the source of the text. The more difficult allusions are annotated.

Christopher Columbus (*c. 1451–1506*)

The letter of a Genoese sailor in the temporary service of the Spanish king is the first written record to be dated from the New World. It was published in Spanish at Barcelona in April, 1493, but was immediately translated into Latin and published in Rome in the same year. The voyage which it describes lasted 224 days, from Aug. 3, 1492 to Mar. 15, 1493. Columbus, under the impression that he had reached the eastern coast of Asia, took possession of the islands which he discovered in the name of Christ and his adopted king. The earliest biographical studies of Columbus are by his son Fernando (written before 1539), and Bartolomé de las Casas (written 1527–1561). That by Washington Irving (1827–28) is entirely uncritical; more reliable are those by J. B. Thacher (1903–04) and Filson Young (1906). The Hakluyt Society published *Select Documents Illustrating the Four Voyages of Columbus* (1930), superseding their earlier collection. The Columbus letter, as well as many of the succeeding selections in this volume, may conveniently be found in *Original Narratives of Early American History*, edited by J. F. Jameson.

23. The Discovered Islands is the famous "Columbus Letter," an official report of his exploits, prepared either on the homeward voyage or immediately upon landing, and indorsed to Gabriel Sanchez (not Raphael Sanxis, as it was printed), the Treasurer of Aragon. The text is the translation of Wilberforce Eames from the Latin illustrated edition of 1493, published in facsimile by the Lenox Library (1893). ¶23. "*Concerning the islands,*" in other editions reads, "concerning the islands of India beyond the Ganges, recently discovered." ¶23. "*Ferdinand, king of Spain.*" The name of Isabella as well occurs in the other two Latin editions. ¶23. "*The third of the kalends of May.*" April 29. ¶23. "*Alexander the Sixth.*" Roderigo Borgia (1431–1503); his papacy began in 1492. ¶23. "*Departed from Cadiz.*" A mistake of the Latin translator. Columbus sailed from Palos on Aug. 3, 1492. ¶23. "*The name of the blessed Saviour,*" San Salvador. Probably Watling's Island. ¶23. "*Santa Maria . . .*" Either Crooked Island or North Caico. ¶23. "*Ferdinanda.*" Either Long Island or Little Inagua. ¶23. "*Isabella.*" Either Fortune Island or Great Inagua. ¶23. "*Juana,*" Cuba. ¶23. "*Cathay,*" China. ¶24. "*Hispania,*" Haiti. ¶26. "*From Colonia to Fontarabia.*" From Catalonia by the sea-coast to Fontarabia in Biscay. ¶27. "*Charis,*" Dominica. ¶27. "*Mateunin,*" Martinique. ¶27. "*Chios,*" Greek island off the West Coast of Asia Minor. ¶28. "*Betica.*" One of the provinces into which Rome divided Spain; hence, Spain itself.

Thomas Hariot (*1560–1621*)

Richard Hakluyt, Rector of Gedney, Lincolnshire, published, in 1599, *The Principal Navigations, Voyages, Traffiques & Discoveries of the English Nation Made by Sea or Over-land to the Remote and Farthest Distant Quarters of the Earth at any time within the compasse of these 1600 Yeeres.* Among the documents which he included was a description of Virginia by a young mathematician and astronomer from Oxford named Thomas Hariot. Hariot had been employed by his friend, Sir Walter Raleigh, as technical adviser and surveyor for his third attempt, in 1586–87, to settle the Virginia colony. The settlement, in Wingandacoa, now North Carolina, was almost as unsuccessful as the two previous ones, and Raleigh abandoned his efforts at colonization in 1588.

28. The New Found Land of Virginia, better known perhaps merely as Hariot's *Virginia*, carries the following title on the first edition, the London 1588 quarto: "A

Briefe and true report of the new found land of Virginia: of *the commodities there found and to be raysed, as well mar*chantable, as others for victuall, building and other necess*arie uses for those that are and shalbe the planters there; and of the na*ture and manners of the naturall inhabitants: Discovered by the *English Colony there seated by* Sir Richard Greinvile *Knight in the* yeere 1585. which remained under the government of Rafe Lane Esqui*er, one of her Maiesties Equieres, during the Space of twelve monethes; as* the speciall charge of the Honourable SIR WALTER RALEIGH Knight, Lord Warden of the stanneries; who therein hath beene favoured and authorised by her Maiestie and her letters patents: Directed to the Adventurers, Favourers, *and Welwillers of the action, for the inhabiting and planting* there: By *Thomas Hariot;* servant to the above named *Sir Walter, a member of the Colony, and there imployed in discovering.*" Hakluyt reprinted it complete in *The Principal Navigations, Voyages, Traffiques, & Discoveries of the English Nation*, 1598–1600, including the preface of the Governor, Ralph Lane; he made numerous changes in spelling and punctuation, but otherwise did not amend it. The present text is from the Hakluyt Society edition, VIII, 1904. ¶28. "*The first undertaking by Sir Walter Raleigh.*" Raleigh succeeded to the patent of his half-brother, Sir Humphrey Gilbert, in March, 1584, and sent out an unsuccessful expedition to explore the coast of Virginia. ¶29. "*The Colony transported by . . . Grinvile.*" In 1585, aided by Queen Elizabeth, Raleigh sent out seven vessels commanded by Sir Richard Grenville and 108 colonists under Ralph Lane to Roanoke Island. The colonists became homesick and successfully prevailed upon Sir Francis Drake, in June, 1586, to take them back to England. ¶31. "*Pagatowr.*" Corn; still called maize in England. ¶31. "*Okingier,*" a variety of bean. ¶31. "*Herbe, in forme of a Marigolde.*" The sunflower (*Planta Solis*). ¶32. "*Macocquer,*" Maycock, a sort of squash. ¶32. "*Melden,*" probably melder, or grain. ¶33. "*Uppowoc,*" tobacco.

Samuel de Champlain (1567–1635)

Champlain's various accounts of his voyages and of the settlement of French Canada, 1603–1635, constitute the most complete and vivid record of the early history of New France which has come down to us from a contemporary source. He told the story of his first voyage in *Des Sauvages* (1603), translated into English and included by Samuel Purchas in *Purchas, His Pilgrimes* (1625), the successor to Hakluyt's *Voyages*. Between 1604 and 1607, Champlain was engaged in exploring and mapping the Acadian and New England coasts as far south as Nantucket Sound. His second description of Canada, *Les Voyages* (1613), contains the story of these explorations, of the founding of Quebec, of the fight with the Iroquois Indians on Lake Champlain in July, 1609, of his visits to the St. Lawrence in 1610–11, and of his journey up the Ottawa River in 1613. Champlain has justly been called "The Father of New France," in spite of the fact that Jacques Cartier and others preceded him, because of the extent of his explorations, the accuracy of his written and pictorial descriptions, and the genius of leadership which he displayed. His account of the Indians is particularly valuable as it reveals the French method of dealing with them by using their own mixture of friendliness, craft, and brutality, as the occasion required. Most of his writings were published in French during his lifetime and were edited by the Abbé C. H. Laverdière (1870). They were translated by C. P. Otis for the Prince Society (1878–1882). The first complete edition with both French and English texts is that of the Champlain Society (1922–27). Biographies (in French) by G. Gravier (1900); (in English) by N. E. Dionne (1905) and R. Flenly (1924).

33. [A BATTLE WITH THE IROQUOIS] is Chapter IX of Book II of *Les Voyages* (1613), translated by John Squair and published by The Champlain Society, 1925. It describes an episode of the 1608–1612 voyage, on which Champlain explored the St. Lawrence and penetrated down into New York State. ¶33. "*The river of the Iroquois.*" Also called "St. John's" and "Richelieu." Fort Richelieu was erected at its mouth in 1641. ¶33. "*The second of July,*" July 12. ¶34. "*An island,*" Ste. Theresa Island. ¶35. "*Pilotois or Ostemoy,*" soothsayers or medicine-men. ¶36. "*The entrance to the lake.*" Lake Champlain, some 125 miles in length; Champlain greatly overestimates his distances. The islands are probably Contrecœur, La Motte, and Valcour islands. ¶36. "*Chaousarou,*" probably the garfish. ¶37. "*High mountains,*" the Green Mountains. ¶37. "*Others,*" the Adirondack Mountains. ¶37. "*A rapid,*" Ticonderoga. ¶37. "*Another lake,*" Lake George. ¶37. "*Cross a river,*" the Hudson River. ¶37. "*Norumbega,*" Champlain's geography at

this point becomes somewhat mythical. ¶37. "*The twenty-ninth of the month,*" July 29. ¶37. "*A cape,*" Crown Point. ¶39. "*Arquebus,*" Harquebus, an early form of portable gun.

John Smith (c. 1580–1631)

The first permanent English colony in America was established at Jamestown, Va., on May 14, 1607. One member of the Council, by sealed royal order, was Captain John Smith. He had commenced his travels at about the age of sixteen as a soldier in the Low Countries. He then enlisted in the Austrian service and took part in the campaign of 1600 against the Turks. After receiving a coat-of-arms for service to the Prince of Transylvania, he joined the Virginia Company and sailed for America. Part of the voyage he spent in chains because of arguments with the Captain. Later the same disposition led him to join in deposing President Wingfield and undertaking an expedition to the source of the Chickahominy River to trade with the Indians for corn. The famous meeting with Powhatan was its outcome. His first account of Virginia, *A True Relation* (1608), was superseded by *The Generall Historie of Virginia* (1624), written after Smith had explored New England and retired to his Old World home. *The True Travels* (1630), also written in his retirement, contains most of the information we have of his early life. Henry Adams, in his *Historical Essays* (1891) has examined the evidence for Smith's veracity, and has proved his powers of imagination rather than his historical accuracy. Nevertheless, where it has been possible to check his statements of fact, most of them have been found to be substantially correct. His *Travels and Works* were edited by Edward Arber (1884), and reëdited by A. G. Bradley (1910). Biographies by A. G. Bradley (1905) and E. K. Chatterton (1927).

40. [Combats with the Turks] is from *The True Travels, Adventures, and Observations of Captaine John Smith* (London, 1630). The text is that of A. G. Bradley (1910), which is based upon the edition of Arber. Smith's marginal comments in this and the following passage are here set in parentheses and incorporated in the text. The scene of Smith's exploits is laid before Caniza in Transylvania in the winter of 1601–1602. ¶40. "*Turbashaw.*" It is probable that Smith invented the names of his opponents. ¶40. "*In Battalio,*" formed in battalions. ¶40. "*Howboyes,*" hautboys, a double-reed musical instrument. ¶40. "*A Ianizary,*" a janizary, or member of the Turkish infantry. ¶40. "*Lord Moses.*" For a discussion of the identity of this nobleman see *Am. Hist. Rev.*, III, 737. ¶41. "*Faulchion,*" falchion, a curved broad sword. ¶41. "*Cutlets,*" a part of the armor below the waist.

41. [Captivity] is from the third book of *The Generall Historie of Virginia, New-England, and the Summer Isles* (London, 1624). Smith's first account of this adventure, in *A True Relation of Such Occurrences and Accidents of Noate as Hath Hapned in Virginia since the first Planting of that Collony* (London, 1608), omits the Pocahontas incident, and critics have ever since been debating whether to give him credit more as an historian or as a writer of fiction. President Wingfield had been deposed on Sept. 10, 1607, and the colony was in desperate straits because of sickness and starvation. Radcliffe, the new president, sent Smith to the interior to trade with the Indians for corn and to try the rivers for fish. ¶41. "*Chickahamania.*" Chickahominy River in Virginia, flowing into the James River. ¶42. "*Sixe or seven weekes.*" Rather about three weeks, Dec. 16, 1607 to Jan. 8, 1608. ¶42. "*Pamaunkee.*" The territory presided over by Chief Opechankanough. See *A True Relation.* ¶42. "*Within an houre after they tyed him . . . prepared to shoot him.*" This incident added in 1624 version. ¶42. "*Orapaks,*" located at the source of the Chickahominy on Smith's map; twelve miles from the Falls near Richmond. ¶43. "*With their Arrowes nocked,*" arrows fitted to the bowstring, ready for shooting. ¶43. "*A Bissone.*" In *A True Relation* this is "a bishion," a military formation. ¶43. "*Pocones,*" a swamp berry. ¶43. "*Thirtie or fortie tall fellowes,*" eight in the 1608 version. ¶44. "*Youthtanunds,*" etc. "Youghtanund flu." is a tributary "Pammuk flu." on Smith's map. "Patawomek flu." lies to the north of this river. It is, of course, possible that Smith was taken from this point further north to the banks of the Rappahanock, as he asserts. ¶44. "*Like Mutchatos,*" like mustachios. ¶45. "*Opechancanoughs.*" Below Meronocomoco. ¶45. "*They brought him to Meronocomoco,*" Jan. 5, 1608; Powhatan's favorite residence, on the north side of York River, at a place now called "Powhatan's Chimney." It is spelled "Weronocomoco" on Smith's map. ¶45. "*Appamatuck,*" a small town on a tributary of the James River of the same name. ¶45. "*Having feasted him . . . bells, beads, and copper.*"

Added in the 1624 version. ¶45. "*Pocahontas*," (1595–1617), daughter of Powhatan, married John Rolfe. ¶45. "*Two days after*," Jan. 7, 1608. ¶46. "*So to James towne*." The element of fear is added in the later version. ¶46. "*That night*," Jan. 7. For place names see Smith's celebrated map, "Virginia, Discovered and Disscribed by Captayn John Smith. Graven by William Hole. 1612." in *A Book of Old Maps*, edited by Emerson D. Fite & Archibald Freeman, 1926.

William Bradford (1590–1657)

For the decade 1620–1630, the history of the Plymouth Colony is the history of New England, and it is told "in plaine stile; with singuler regard unto simple truth in all things" by William Bradford. The little group of Separatists that emigrated from England to Holland under the leadership of the Rev. John Robinson in 1609 formed the nucleus of that band which landed from the *Mayflower* on Cape Cod in Nov., 1620, and almost immediately moved to the mainland, spreading rapidly up and down the coast from Plymouth as a center. Bradford had joined them in England as a boy of sixteen, and, on the death of John Carver in 1621, became their governor. He held this post continually, with the exception of five years when he refused it, until his death. To his liberal views and firm character the colonists owed much of their endurance in the face of hardships even greater than those which caused the failures of Raleigh's attempts to settle Virginia more than a half century earlier. His beliefs were Calvinistic in theology and Congregational in polity, but both he and his fellows were far less dogmatic than were their later neighbors of Massachusetts Bay. His history, *Of Plimmoth Plantation,* which was undertaken in 1630, begins with the persecutions of the band in England, and continues the record of the colony to 1646. For two centuries it remained in manuscript, although it was evidently used as a source by Nathaniel Morton for his *New England's Memorial* (1669), as well as by Thomas Prince and Cotton Mather. The manuscript was rediscovered and printed for the first time in 1856 by the Mass. Hist. Soc., with notes by Charles Deane, and again, in facsimile, in 1895. The first complete edition is that edited by W. C. Ford (1912). Other writings of Bradford have been published by the Mass. Hist. Soc. and in other colonial records. The best, though brief, biography and bibliography are by S. E. Morison, in the *D.A.B.*

46. [THE MAYFLOWER COMPACT] is the opening passage of the second book of Bradford's *Of Plimmoth Plantation,* in which the author changes his style from that of narrative history to that of annals, and recapitulates in order to sum up the events of the year 1620. The text of this and the following passage is that of W. C. Ford, published for the Mass. Hist. Soc. (1912). ¶46. "*The patente*." Through the influence of Sir William Sandys, the Virginia Company granted the Pilgrims a patent to settle in its territory; the actual settlement was made, however, in the domain of the Council for New England. The Pilgrims never had a crown charter. See E. B. Greene, *The Foundations of American Nationality,* 1922. ¶47. "*John Carver*," (*c.* 1576–1621), first Governor of Plymouth. ¶47. "*William Brewster*," (1567–1644), the only church officer in the colony until 1629. ¶47. "*Myles Standish*," (*c.* 1584–1657), "Captain" of the small Plymouth Colony army. ¶49. "*Massasoyt*," (1580–1661), chief of the Wampanoag Indians, and a friend of the colonists.

49. [HARDSHIPS OF THE WILDERNESS] is from the account of the year 1633, when Edward Winslow was Governor. ¶49. "*Roger Williams*" came to Plymouth in the summer of 1631; went to Salem in Aug., 1633. ¶50. "*Pequents*," the Pequod Indians, a tribe occupying the lower Connecticut valley. ¶51. "*The Dutch . . . gott in a litle before them;*" they established their fort at Hartford in 1633; the first English settlement (here described) was at Windsor, in 1635. ¶51. "*The Monhatas*," the Manhattan Dutch. ¶51. "*Samuell Fuller*," physician to the Colony, was called at one time to Massachusetts Bay, so valuable were his services.

John Winthrop (1588–1649)

The spirit of the Massachusetts Bay Colony is perhaps best expressed by the Rev. Francis Higginson in his sermon on leaving England: "We do not go to New England as separatists from the church of England, though we cannot but separate from the corruptions in it, but we go to practise the positive part of church reformation, and propagate the gospel in America." John Winthrop, who was elected the first governor of the colony at a preliminary meeting in Cambridge, England, on Aug. 26, 1629, was both positive and zealous in his beliefs, and steadfast in his character. He was a leader of that group within the church which opposed the Romish tendencies of the court, and was in no way associated with the

Dissenters who had settled Plymouth. His journal is the unadorned chronicle of the years 1630–1649. The first two volumes, which carry the narrative up to 1644, were published at Hartford in 1690. The first complete edition is that of James Savage, with a faithful but somewhat modernized text, (1825–26), reprinted with further editing by the same hand (1853). As much of the manuscript has since been burned, no complete type facsimile of the manuscript will ever be published. J. K. Hosmer edited an edition in 1908. The standard biography is that by R. C. Winthrop (1864–67). Letters and other writings of Winthrop were published by the Mass. Hist. Soc. (1863–1872), and a newly edited text of all of Winthrop's extant writings is now in process of publication by the same Society (1929–).

52. LETTERS of John and Margaret Winthrop are quoted from *Some Old Puritan Love Letters, 1618–1638*, edited by J. H. Twichell (1894). Margaret Tyndale was Winthrop's third wife. ¶52. Letter II: from John to Margaret before their marriage, dated from Groton, April 4, 1618. ¶53. "*His sweet love feast*," the sacrament of Holy Communion. ¶54. "*First cast out the beame . . .* ": Matt. vii. 5; Luke vi. 42. ¶55. Letter XXII: When Winthrop decided to attempt the voyage to America, he left his wife and children at home. This letter was written from Groton, to which Margaret had returned because of the sickness of her son Stephen. ¶55. "*Ayme*," the maidservant who had accompanied her to London. ¶55. "*The hard condishtion of Rochell*." After an abortive attempt to relieve the French Huguenots at La Rochelle, the English abandoned them to their fate, in 1627. ¶55. Letter XLVII: Winthrop was now on board the *Arbella* waiting for favorable conditions for sailing. ¶56. Letter XLVIII: The first letter from New England. The hardships of sickness and want had been intensified by the drowning of Winthrop's son Henry who had accompanied him. ¶57. "*My deare daughter*," Henry's wife. ¶57. Letter LII: Written when Margaret and Stephen were expected soon to sail for New England.

58. [ON LIBERTY] is from the third (manuscript) volume of Winthrop's *Journal*, which was not included in the Hartford (1790) edition. The textual problem is fully discussed by S. E. Morison in his introduction to the newly edited text in *Winthrop Papers*, Mass. Hist. Soc., II, 1931. As this new edition does not yet include the entry for the year 1645, the present text is from the second edition of Savage (1853). The narrative of the circumstances which called forth Winthrop's "little speech" begins with the entry for Mar. 14, 1645, when Thomas Dudley was governor and Winthrop deputy governor. Soon after, the town of Hingham was split between two factions, one of which wanted Anthony Eames as Captain of their militia company, and the other, Bozoun Allen. The magistrates ruled in favor of Eames, but the people again voted for Allen. The leaders of the Allen faction, being summoned to appear and give bond, demanded their right to know their accusers and the charge against them. Winthrop ruled that they had no special right to this knowledge, whereupon he was singled out for prosecution. His "impeachment" trial was a test case in which were tried the relative liberties of the people and of their magistrates. Winthrop was "legally and publickly acquit of all that was laid to his charge," after which he delivered his "little speech." Mr. Steward Mitchell, of the Mass. Hist. Soc., has edited the opening passage of "The Deptys Speach," in the style in which it will eventually appear in his edition, as follows: "I suppose somethinge [will *cancelled*] may be expected from me vpon this charge that is befalle [*sic*] me, which moves me to speake [*two words cancelled*] now to you; yet i intend not to intermeddle in the proceedinges of the Court, or with any of the persons concerned therein: onely I blesse God, that I see an Issue of this troublesome bysinesse, I also acknowledge the Justice of the Court, &, for mine owne parte, I am well satisfied." ¶59. "*Miriam*," Num. xii. 14.

Thomas Morton (c. 1590–1646)

The motives of the little band of settlers at Merrymount (Braintree, Mass.) in 1625 were very different from those of their neighbors at Plymouth. They came primarily to trade with the Indians, and the problems of religious toleration and its contrary were very far from their thoughts. It was whispered that Morton himself (not to be confused with Nathaniel Morton) was at least under suspicion for murder in England; at all events, he was an adventurous spirit, and he had probably visited New England some three years before the date of his settlement. One winter was enough for his partner, Captain Wollaston, after whom the colony had first been named, and in the spring he moved to Virginia, leaving Morton, with not more than a half-dozen companions, to his own pleasures and profits. The Plymouth colonists did not look with favor on the revels which resulted, although the Indians were friendly, because Morton had been trading firearms for furs with them. Bradford tells us one side of the story in his *History;* Morton the other in *The New English Canaan* (1637), a queer mixture of half-learning, arrogant defiance, and good sense. The historical fact is that virtue triumphed in the person of "Captain Shrimp" (Miles Standish) and his miniature army. Morton was imprisoned and twice banished to England, but each time he returned, and finally died at Agamenticus, Me., in 1646.

62. OF THE REVELLS OF NEW CANAAN (Book III, Chapter XIV, of *The New English Canaan*) was published in Amsterdam (1637) and edited with an introduction by C. F. Adams for the Prince Society (1883). In the first edition, Morton's eccentricities of style are further obscured by random punctuation; the Adams text, which is otherwise an accurate transcription, is here reprinted. ¶62. "*Pasonagessit,*" Mount Wollaston. Note that "Wessguscus" and "Mount Wollaston" are not the same, as is often claimed. See William Woods' map, "The South Part of New England, London, 1635," in *A Book of Old Maps.* ¶62. "*Oedipus,*" king of Thebes, solved the riddle of the Sphinx. ¶62. "*Caribdis . . . Scilla.*" Scylla and Charybdis were two rocks near Sicily, between which Odysseus passed. ¶62. "*Niobe.*" Artemis slew the children of Niobe because the latter had the presumption to think herself superior to Leto. She is usually represented as in tears. ¶62. "*Amphitrites Darling.*" Amphitrite was the wife of Neptune and the mother of Triton. ¶62. "*Triton,*" a god of the sea with dolphin tail and a shell horn on which he blew to raise or calm the waves. ¶62. "*Protean formes.*" Proteus was an old man of the sea who had the power of assuming many forms, as well as the power of prophecy. ¶62. "*Scogans choise.*" The reference is not clear. John Scogan was court fool to Edward IV. ¶62. "*Esculapius,*" the son of Apollo, was a skilled physician whose feat of restoring the dead to life is referred to here. ¶63. "*Cithareas powre,*" the power of love. "Cytharea" was a name given Aphrodite. ¶63. "*Calfe of Horeb.*" "They made a calf in Horeb and worshipped." Ps. cvi. 19. ¶63. "*Mount Dagon.*" Dagon was the national god of the Philistines. ¶63. "*Gammedes and Iupiter.*" Ganymedes was the Greek cupbearer to the gods. ¶63. "*Iô,*" hail. ¶63. "*Hymen,*" god of marriage. ¶63. "*Precise Seperatists,*" the Plymouth colonists. ¶63. "*Muit and Cummin,*" a mistake for "mint and cummin": "Pay tithe of mint and anise and cummin." Matt. xxiii. 23. ¶64. "*Phaos box.*" The reference is not clear. ¶64. "*Penellope of Greece,*" wife of Odysseus, ruled Ithaca in his absence and was sought after by many suitors, all of whom she resisted according to Homer. ¶64. "*Priapus*" personifies male generative power. ¶64. "*Maja.*" Maia was the Roman goddess of spring.

Roger Williams (c. 1604–1683)

The protest of Roger Williams against religious intolerance has its narrow dogmatic significance, but it led him to a statement of his broader belief in the liberty of human conscience and the compact theory of the state, and is therefore a part of the foundations of American democratic theory. He emigrated to New England in 1631, and was co-pastor of the churches at Salem and, for a briefer period, at Plymouth. In 1635 he was summoned to appear in Boston before the governors and assistants to answer charges of preaching toleration in the administering of oaths, and of denouncing the law which required public worship. These were only a few of his many radical beliefs. He was banished from the colony and imprisoned prior to being returned to England; but he finally left Massachusetts and founded, in 1636, the colony of Providence, now Rhode Island. There he could preach his doctrines unmolested. His later life was divided between work with his congregation and with the Indians. In 1643–44, he attacked the doctrine which had caused his banishment in an open letter to John Cotton, *The Bloudy Tenent of Persecution.* Cotton replied with *The Bloudy Tenent, Washed, and made white in the bloud of the Lamb* (1647), and received for answer, *The Bloody Tenent yet more Bloody: by Mr. Cotton's endeavor to wash it white in the Blood of the Lambe* (1652). Williams's excited and figurative style sometimes interferes with the clear statement of his beliefs, but there was in early New England no more intrepid warrior in the cause of democracy. His writings were published by the Narragansett Club (1866–1874). For criticism and biography, see E. J. Carpenter (1909) and J. E. Ernst (1932).

64. [ON PERSECUTION] is Chapter II of *The Bloudy Tenent of Persecution, for cause of*

Conscience, discussed, in a Conference betweene Truth and Peace (London, 1643–44). The text is from the transcript of the first edition, edited by S. L. Caldwell and published by the Narragansett Club (Providence, R. I., III, 1867). Williams incorporated in this volume the earlier exchange of letters between himself and John Cotton, and then attempted to answer the arguments of the latter at length. ¶64. "*Peace*" has just expressed her desire that Truth revive her with her words "which are sweeter than honey and the honey-combe." ¶65. "*Blurs of troublers of Israel.*" The disfigurements by enemies; a euphuistic pun. ¶65. "*Salomon.*" Prov. xvii. 14. ¶65. "*Nimrods.*" Nimrod was "a mighty hunter before the Lord." Gen. x. 8, 9. ¶65. "*One hundred forty foure thousand Virgins,*" the souls of Christians. ¶65. "*Absaloms.*" II Sam. xvii. 22. ¶65. "*Soules under the Altar,*" the ministers of Christ. ¶66. "*Arguments (against persecution),*" the arguments in the controversy. ¶66. "*Newgate,*" the celebrated London prison.

"The Bay Psalm Book" (1640)

"*The Bay Psalm Book,*" as it is popularly called, was a product of the press of Stephen Day and the first book to be printed in the colonies; as such, it is a literary curiosity rather than artistic effort. The preface was probably written by Richard Mather (1596–1669), and the poetical versions of the Psalms were by Mather, Thomas Welde, and John Eliot. Richard Mather, who settled at Massachusetts Bay in 1635, was the father of Increase Mather, and the founder of the so-called "Mather Dynasty." For biography, criticism, and bibliography, see K. B. Murdock's *Increase Mather* (1925).

67. PREFACE, PSALME I, and (68) 23. A PSALME OF DAVID are from *The Whole Booke of Psalmes Faithfully Translated into English Metre* (Cambridge, 1640). The text is from the facsimile edition of the New England Society of N. Y. (1903).

Anne Bradstreet (c. 1612–1672)

The god Apollo, according to Nathaniel Ward's dedicatory verses, remarked when Minerva showed him a copy of *The Tenth Muse:*

> It half revives my chil frest-bitten blood,
> To see a Woman once, do ought that's good.

Others held similar views, for the writings of this first genuine poet in America immediately received the praise that was due to their simplicity and sincerity, in spite of their imperfect meter and their imitative forms. Anne was the wife of Simon Bradstreet and the daughter of Thomas Dudley, both distinguished colonial officials. She was brought up in an English home among books and tutors in language, music, and other feminine arts. When she came to America in 1630 at the age of eighteen, she was already a wife, and she became the mother of eight children. Domestic and social responsibilities do not seem to have interfered with her reading, for her poetry reflects a knowledge of Sidney, Spenser, Quarles, and Du Bartas, and of Raleigh's *History of the World*. The first edition of her poems was published anonymously in London by her brother-in-law, the Rev. John Woodbridge, as *The Tenth Muse, lately sprung up in America; or, Several Poems, compiled with great variety of Wit and Learning, full of delight* (1650). A second edition, apparently revised by Mrs. Bradstreet, was published posthumously in 1678; it contains "Contemplations" and other new poems. The best modern edition is that edited and annotated by J. H. Ellis (1867, reprinted 1932). It is based on the text of the second, but contains much not included in the two early editions. There is also an edition with an introduction by C. E. Norton (1897) and a biography by H. Campbell (1891). The *D.A.B.* article and bibliography are by L. N. Richardson.

68. TO MY DEAR CHILDREN, printed first in the edition of J. H. Ellis (1867, 1932), refers to *The Tenth Muse*. The text of this and the following poems is from the Ellis edition.

68. THE PROLOGUE to *The Tenth Muse*. ¶68. "*Great Bartas sugar'd lines.*" Guillaume de S. Du Bartas (1544–1590), a French religious poet and her favorite author; translated by Joshua Sylvester. ¶68. "*Sweet tongu'd Greek,*" Demosthenes. ¶69. "*Calliope,*" the muse of epic poetry. ¶69. "*Give Thyme or Parsley wreath, I ask no bayes;*" symbols of a victory more humble than that rewarded by the laurel.

69. TO MY DEAR AND LOVING HUSBAND appeared first in the posthumous volume of 1678.

69. THE FOUR SEASONS OF THE YEAR, SPRING, is a part of a series of "quaternions," poems on the four elements, the four humors of man, the four ages of man, the four seasons, and the four monarchies, published in *The Tenth Muse*. "Spring" is the first part of "The Four Seasons." ¶70. "*Sol into Aries enters.*"

The sun enters the first sign of the zodiac, Aries, about Mar. 21. ¶70. "*The Pleiades their influence now give.*" The rising of the Pleiades, a constellation, occurs in May. ¶70. "*Taurus.*" The sun enters the second sign of the zodiac about Apr. 20, and the third, "*Gemini*" (71), about May 20.

71. CONTEMPLATIONS is from the edition of 1678. ¶71. "*Phoebus,*" the sun. ¶73. "*Methuselah,*" one of the patriarchs in the Bible, Gen. v. 27, said to have lived 969 years. ¶73. "*Our Grandame,*" Eve; Gen. chaps. ii–iv. ¶73. "*A Vagabond to Land of Nod,*" Gen. v. 16. ¶75. "*Thetis house,*" the sea; Thetis, a nereid, dwelt there.

75. THE AUTHOR TO HER BOOK is from the edition of 1678.

Michael Wigglesworth (1631–1705)

Michael Wigglesworth was brought by his father from England in 1638 at the age of seven, graduated from Harvard College in 1651, and became a tutor while completing his preparation for the ministry. Among his students was Increase Mather. From the date of his ordination in 1656 to that of his death, he was minister at Malden, Mass., but ill health prevented him from taking active charge during the earlier years. In his verse preface to *The Day of Doom; or, A poetical description of the great and last Judgment* (1662), he explains how he turned his disability to the service of Jehovah by substituting the pen for the pulpit. In his confession, the modern reader may discover the broodings of a mind cut off from activity by illness, but Wigglesworth's contemporaries accepted the poem as a memorable expression of their daily thought. It attained an amazing popularity and was taught for many generations to the youth of New England as a part of their religious training. There have been many modern editions, the most recent of which is that printed, from the edition of 1701, by Bruce Rogers, with an introduction by K. B. Murdock (1929). Biography by J. W. Dean (1871).

75. TO THE CHRISTIAN READER, (76) [THE APPEARANCE OF CHRIST] and (78) [THE JUDGMENT], are from *The Day of Doom.* No copy of the first edition (Cambridge, Mass., *c.* 1662) is said to exist. The text is that of the earliest known American edition (Boston, 1702). ¶80. "*Easiest room in Hell.*" This was a great concession on Wigglesworth's part, as there is no theological justification for it.

Nathaniel Ward (c. 1579–c. 1652)

In the year that Shakespeare's Globe Theatre was opened on the Bankside, Nathaniel Ward took his A.B. degree from Emmanuel College, Cambridge. These two unrelated facts may help to explain the curious mixture of Elizabethan eccentricity of expression and Puritan rigidity of opinion in *The Simple Cobler of Aggawamm in America* (1647) by "Theodore de la Guard," of Ipswich, Mass. After travels on the continent, Ward had received the living of Stondon Massey, in Essex, only to be excommunicated for his views by Archbishop Laud in 1633. Many of his friends had already emigrated to America, and the next year he followed them. In 1645, he began his *Simple Cobler,* a catch-all for his whimsies and his prejudices, with the serious purpose of stemming what he believed to be religious heresies and civil disobedience. It appeared in London in 1647, about the time that its author returned to his native land after a twelve-year absence. It was reprinted in Boston (1843), and, in facsimile, by the Ipswich Hist. Soc. (1906). Biography by J. W. Dean (1868).

82. [ON TOLERANCE] is from the opening passages of *The Simple Cobler of Aggawamm in America. Willing to help 'mend his Native Country, lamentably tattered, both in the upper-Leather and sole, with all the honest stitches he can take,'* [etc.] (London, 1647). The text is from the facsimile of this edition, published by the Ipswich Hist. Soc. (1906). ¶82. "*Moon into blood.*" Joel ii. 31; Rev. vi. 12. ¶82. "*Laborare varicibus*": walk haltingly. ¶82. "*Paracelsian parts,*" supernatural powers. Paracelsus (Theophrastus von Hohenheim, 1493–1541) was a Swiss alchemist and physician. ¶83. "*Familists, Antinomians, Anabaptists,*" sects regarded as heretical by the strict Calvinists.

Increase Mather (1639–1723)

Increase, the son of Richard and the father of Cotton Mather, was the greatest of his name and the dominant figure of his age and country. No better means for an appreciation of what is generally known as the "Puritan" background of American thought could be found than a thorough study of his life. An extreme Calvinist in doctrine and polity, he may be taken as the personification of the church-state ideal, inherited from the Hebrew law-givers and prophets, and transplanted to American soil by the settlers in Massachusetts Bay. Priest, scholar, and statesman, he touched every aspect of the life of Boston from 1664, when he was formally installed at the Second Church, to 1723, when he died; and where he touched, he shaped with no uncertain hand. With his marriage to his step-sister, Maria Cotton, the families of the two founders of the Massachusetts oligarchy were joined for the second time, Richard Mather having taken the widow of John Cotton for his second wife. The power of Increase Mather in shaping public opinion to his will was first felt when he was elected Moderator of the "Reforming" Synod of 1679; and when the king announced his decision a few years later to revoke the charter of the colony, Mather's defiance reversed the attitude of a conciliatory people. This act was followed by his mission to England, and his return in 1692 with a new charter and his personal choice for governor, Sir William Phipps. But there was another enemy at home with whom to do battle. In his absence the "witchcraft delusion" had developed its full force, and Mather, convinced that the fearful manifestations were the work of Satan, turned all the power of his convictions and his personality to the extermination of the evil and its causes. The foundations of his views had been laid in his *Essay for the Recording of Illustrious Providences* (1684), and his faith had grown with the years. To understand the causes and the full force of this fanaticism, one must remember that it is entirely consistent with the theology of the New England churches of the day, and one must also recall other fanaticisms which general public fears such as war and plague give rise to periodically in human experience. Before his death, Mather had written 175 separate works on religion, politics, and science. His life, by K. B. Murdock (1925), presents a sympathetic picture of the man and his times, and contains a check-list of his writings. There is an exhaustive bibliography by T. J. Holmes (1933), with an introduction by G. P. Winship.

83. [THE HOUSE OF WILLIAM MORSE] is from Chapter V of *An Essay For the Recording of Illustrious Providences, Wherein an Account is given of many Remarkable and very Memorable Events, which have hapned in this last Age; Especially in New-England* (Boston, 1684). The running heads on this edition carry the caption "Remarkable Providences," and the book sometimes is thus titled. The text is from the first issue of the first edition. ¶86. "*The Boy.*" Our modern knowledge of behaviour problems in children may perhaps provide a clue to some of the strange manifestations which Mather records. ¶87. "*Powel,*" Satan.

Cotton Mather (1663–1728)

Cotton Mather was the scholar and historian of the movement in which his father had demonstrated political and theological leadership. During his lifetime the Church Synods determined the political and religious life of the colony. He saw their power complete its rise; and he saw it begin to fall. The fact that he was the author of almost 500 writings, most of which were sermons, histories, and scientific tracts, rather than directly controversial documents like most Puritan prose, is evidence of his sense of security in his world. His private library was probably the largest in the colonies, and he was the most prolific writer, as well as one of the most omniverous readers, of early New England. His greatest book, the *Magnalia Christi Americana* (1702), is the Bible of New England Puritanism. Primarily an ecclesiastical history, it is in effect a monument to the faith of a "chosen" people, as is the Old Testament. His personal life, however, does not reflect the same sense of security as do his more formal activities. He inherited his father's zeal and intellect, but not all of his strength of character. His prose style is more eccentric; it lacks the firmness and directness of that of the elder Mather. A precocious boyhood was followed by the best education afforded by the colony. In 1671, he became assistant to his father in the Second Church, and seven years later, the active head of the parish, a position which he held until his death. His influence in the life of Boston was great, but he spent many more hours in his study than in the world of affairs. His advocacy of smallpox inoculation and his membership in the Royal Society of London have been cited as evidences of his scientific interests. In spite of his fanatical belief that witchcraft was the personal work of Satan, he urged moderation in the persecution of witches. His *Memorable Providences* (1689) and *The Wonders of the Invisible World* (1693) are chapters in the history of a public obsession. In his diary, however, we discover the mental and emotional struggles through which he passed. His later years were saddened by the death of his father and of most of the members of his immediate family, as well as by a recognition of the decline of the power of the church to which he had devoted his life. There is no complete edition of his works, most of which have not been republished during the past century. His diary was edited for the Mass. Hist. Soc. by W. C. Ford (1911–12). A book of selections edited by K. B. Murdock (1926) is representative of his most enduring work. Biography by Barrett Wendell (1891, 1925). For other references, see above, "Increase Mather."

89. INTRODUCTION to *Magnalia Christi Americana* is the introduction to Book I, in which Mather outlines the purpose and scope of his work. The text is from the volume of selections from Mather, edited by K. B. Murdock (1926), and reproduces the text of the first edition (London, 1702). ¶89. "*The only Protestant University*," Harvard College. ¶89. "*Of Criolians*," or Creolians, persons born or naturalized in America but of European stock.

90. [ENCHANTMENTS ENCOUNTERED], and (92) THE TRYAL OF BRIDGET BISHOP are parts of the prefatory discussion of individual cases and of one of the case histories in *The Wonders of the Invisible World. Observations As well Historical as Theological, upon the Nature, The Number, and the Operations of the Devils*, [etc.] (Boston, 1693). The text is from the first edition. ¶90. "*Devils Territories*," lands inhabited by non-Christians. ¶90. "*The Powers of the Air* (*after whom those Ephesians walked*)." Eph. ii. 2. ¶92. "*Bridget Bishop*," servant of the Rev. Parris of Salem, was executed in June, 1692.

95. MERCURY'S NEGOTIATION is one of the allegories in *Political Fables* (first printed by the Mass. Hist. Soc , Ser. III, I, 1825), written to defend Increase Mather's acceptance of the new charter against those who believed he had sacrificed the old rights of New England. The text is from Murdock's volume of selections and is a reprint of that published by the Prince Society in *The Andros Tracts*, Vol. II (Boston, 1868–1874). ¶95. "*Mercury*," Increase Mather. ¶95. "*The Sheep*," the New Englanders. ¶95. "*The Foxes*," their enemies. ¶95. "*Jupiter*," William III., king of England. ¶95. "*Janus*," one of the English politicians who drew up the new charter. ¶95. "*Orpheus*," Cotton Mather himself. ¶96. "*Sysiphus*," king of Corinth, who betrayed one of Jupiter's intrigues and had to roll a stone eternally up hill in hell.

Samuel Sewall (1652–1730)

Judge Sewall was, in the civic affairs of the Bay Colony, as distinguished a figure as was his friend, Cotton Mather, in the religious. As a diarist, he is often compared to his English contemporary, Samuel Pepys. Like Pepys, he reveals his times by recording the details of his own private life, and the "good and wise" Judge of Whittier's poem, who "wears the look of a man unbought," becomes the good neighbor and man of practical affairs in his own very small community. Sewall's first entry in his diary was made in 1673, two years after his graduation from Harvard, and we may follow his career of business man, judge, and prominent citizen, as well as his private life as husband, father, and friend, almost continuously to within a year of his death. The only gap, 1677–1685, is probably accounted for by the loss of one or more of his manuscript notebooks. The purchase of a penknife, the accession of an English king, a sermon by Cotton Mather, the loss of a cow, a courtship, an illness, all receive equal attention. Sewall was also the author of *The Selling of Joseph* (1700), one of the earliest anti-slavery documents to be published in America. The *Diary* was published (1878–1882) and his letter book (1886–88) by the Mass. Hist. Soc.; and the former was edited in an abridged form by Mark Van Doren (1927). Biography by N. H. Chamberlain (1897)

97. [THE COURTSHIP OF MADAM WINTHROP] is from *The Diary of Samuel Sewall*, which was printed first in a literal transcription of the manuscript by the Mass. Hist. Soc., 1878–1882. The text is from this edition (*Collections*, Ser. V, VII). It is somewhat unfair to Sewall that this passage is more often quoted than the earlier and more diversified entries. Madam Katherine (Brattle) Winthrop had been widowed in 1717 by the death of her second husband, Wait Still Winthrop, and Sewall's second wife, Abigail (Melyen) had survived two husbands, but was outlived by the third. Madam Winthrop died a widow, but Sewall was married for the third time on May 29, 1722, to the widow, Mary Gibbs. The courtship of elderly people was apparently more common in those days than it is in these. ¶97. "*My dear Wife*," Abigail (Melyen) Sewall. ¶97. "*What befell . . . Ezekiel.*" The wife of the Hebrew prophet died in 587 B.C. ¶97. "*South, Old, and Mr. Colman's*" were the three principal churches of Boston in Sewall's day. ¶98. "*Mr. Colman's Lecture.*" Benjamin Colman (1673–1747), minister of the Brattle Street Church, and Fellow of Harvard 1717–1728. ¶98. "*Mr. Willard's Fountain.*" Samuel

Willard (1640–1707), was minister of Old South Church, Boston. ¶99. *"Her Sister."* Mary (Brattle) Mico, widow of John Mico. ¶99. *"Mr. Mayhew's Sermon."* Experience Mayhew (1673–1758), father of Jonathan Mayhew and missionary to the Indians at Martha's Vineyard. ¶100. *"Dr. Preston."* Probably John Preston (1587–1628), British Puritan divine and friend of John Cotton. ¶101. *"Mr. Appleton,"* Nathaniel Appleton (1695–1784). Increase Mather preached at his ordination on Oct. 9, 1717. ¶102. *"Dr. Sibb's Bowels." Bowels Opened; or a Discovery of the neere and deere Love . . . between Christ and the Church* (1639), by Richard Sibbes (1577–1635), a Puritan divine. ¶103. *"Mr. Wendell,"* Jacob Wendell, husband of Madam Winthrop's grandniece.

Mary Rowlandson (c. 1636–1678)

Mary (White) Rowlandson, wife of the Rev. Joseph Rowlandson, was a resident of Lancaster, Mass., a frontier town of about fifty families, organized into five or six garrisons. On Jan. 24, 1675, word was brought by a friendly Indian that, in twenty days, hostile Indians would attack the town. The Rev. Rowlandson went, with some others, to the Bay to beg assistance, but during his absence the garrisons were attacked. *The Soveraignty & Goodness of God Together, With the Faithfulness of His Promises Displayed; Being a Narrative Of the Captivity and Restauration of Mrs. Mary Rowlandson* tells the story and recounts the subsequent hardships endured by herself and her six-year-old child Sarah when they were taken by the Indians northwest into Vermont and back to the neighborhood of Lancaster, and held captive for nearly twelve weeks. The earliest surviving edition is the second (1682), which was reprinted in facsimile at Lancaster (1903), with full biographical, textual, and bibliographical notes, by H. S. Nourse and J. E. Thayer. There were many reprints in the 18th and 19th centuries.

105. NARRATIVE OF CAPTIVITY is from *The Soveraignty & Goodness of God Together, With the Faithfulness of His Promises Displayed; Being a Narrative Of the Captivity and Restauration of Mrs. Mary Rowlandson.* The text is from facsimile, published at Lancaster, Mass. (1903), of the "second Addition Corrected and amended" (Cambridge, Mass., 1682); the first edition is unknown. ¶105. *"Lancaster,"* on the Nashua River, near Clinton, Mass. ¶106. *"Come, behold the works of the Lord."* Ps. xlvi. 8. ¶107. *"Marlborough's Praying Indians."* Indians who had been converted to Christianity were known as "praying Indians." They were often treacherous to their own people in the cause of the whites. ¶108. *"King Philip,"* (d. 1676), chief of the Wampanoag Indians, but, unlike his father, Massasoit, hostile to the whites. ¶108. *"Naked came I out of my Mothers Womb."* Job. i. 21. ¶109. *"North-Hampton,"* Northampton, on the Connecticut River, in west-central Massachusetts. ¶110. *"Medfield,"* fifteen miles southwest of Boston.

Sarah Kemble Knight (1666–1727)

Madam Knight spent her childhood in Boston where her father was a shop-keeper, and there she married Capt. Richard Knight, an elderly widower and shipmaster. During her husband's long absences and after his death, she earned her living by teaching the children of the neighborhood, among whom tradition names Franklin and the Mathers, by the task of court scrivener, and by keeping a shop and boarding-house of her own near North Square. Early in Sept., 1704, her kinsman, Caleb Trowbridge, died, leaving a widow and an estate to be settled, and Madam Knight turned her knowledge of the law to good account by undertaking the journey to New York to attend to the settlement. Her *Private Journal of a Journey from Boston to New-York* tells how she set out on horseback, Oct. 2, for the difficult and hazardous journey, which was not completed until her return to Boston on Mar. 3 of the next year. During this adventure she kept what was probably a shorthand record, but the manuscript and all copies of it have been lost. An expanded narrative was published, with an introduction by Theodore Dwight, in 1825, and was reprinted several times during the century. G. P. Winship edited it for a reprint by Bruce Rogers in 1920. The introductions to these editions and the article by Sidney Gunn in the *D. A. B.* contain what biographical information we have.

111. [SETTING OUT], (113) [THE PEOPLE OF CONNECTICUT], (117) [NEW YORK], and (118) [THE RETURN] are from Mrs. Knight's *The Private Journal of a Journey from Boston to New York.* The present text is from the edition of G. P. Winship for Bruce Rogers (Cambridge, Mass., 1920). ¶111. *"Kingston,"* Rhode Island. ¶112. *"Paukataug River,"* Pawcatuk River,

at the Connecticut border. ¶114. *"Stomany,"* understand. ¶114. *"Lecture days and Training days,"* days appointed for periodical lectures and for military drill, respectively. ¶115. *"Pieces of Eight, Ryalls, or Boston or Bay shillings."* The Spanish dollar contains eight reals; the "pine-tree" money of 17th century Massachusetts was known also as "Boston or Bay shillings." ¶116. *"Lex Mercatoria."* Law Merchant, body of commercial law. ¶116. *"The creature Balaam Rode,"* the ass. Num. xxii. 28–30. 117. *"Commodius River,"* Hudson River. ¶117. *"Vendue,"* auction sale. ¶117. *"Their Governor, Lord Cornbury,"* Viscount Edward Hyde Cornbury (1661–1723), Royal Governor of New York and New Jersey (1702–1708).

William Penn (1644–1718)

Although Penn spent only four years in America, 1682–84 and 1699–1701, his influence on the progress of the settlement was great. The son of Admiral Sir William Penn, he disappointed his father's hopes for courtly favor when he became interested in Independency while a gentleman commoner at Christ Church, Oxford, in 1660. Trips to France and Holland proved to be only temporary distractions, for by 1668 he had met Thomas Loe, the Quaker, and become a professed minister of that faith himself. Confined to the Tower for publishing controversial pamphlets, he wrote his most famous work, *No Cross, No Crown* (1669). West New Jersey had already been settled by Quakers when he petitioned, in 1680, for the land beyond the Delaware River as settlement of an inherited claim against the Crown. Two years later he landed from the *Welcome* with his band of colonists at New Castle, Delaware, and proceeded up the river. In his settlement of Pennsylvania as a haven of religious toleration and democratic principles of government, he won fame for himself by his fair treatment of the Indians and by his liberal *Frame of Government* (1682). His accounts of the province (1681, 1683, and 1685) were written primarily to encourage immigration. Much of his writing turns upon religious and political controversy and has little claim to literary excellence. In 1693, he wrote his temperate and prophetic *Essay towards the Present and Future Peace of Europe,* and in the same year, the first of his *Fruits of Solitude,* maxims learned in the school of experience. His *Brief Account of the Rise and Progress of the People called Quakers* (1694) and his *Fruits of a Father's Love* (1726) are expressions of his unswerving religious faith. There is no complete edition of his works; of the four early editions (1726, 1771, 1782, and 1825), the first is the most inclusive. Most of his individual works are listed in J. Smith's *Descriptive Catalogue of Friends' Books* (1867); a more nearly complete check-list is that of M. K. Spence (1932). A. C. Myers has been collecting since 1910 materials for a fifth and definitive edition of his works. Selections were edited by T. P. Cope (1882), Isaac Sharpless (1909), and in *Everyman's Library* (n.d.). Biographies by S. M. Janney (1852), W. J. Buck (1888), J. W. Graham (1916), A. Pound (1932), and others.

119. [THE INDIANS] is from Penn's second and fullest account of the Province of Pennsylvania, 1683. The text is that of the first edition. ¶119. *"Octorockon, Rancocas, Oricton, Shakamaxon, Poquessin."* Most of these place names are still in use. ¶120. *"Duffils,"* obsolete spelling of "duffle," a coarse woollen cloth. ¶121. *"Bills of Lading and Exchange."* Legal forms giving evidence of shipment of goods (lading), and means of making payment (exchange). ¶122. *"Antick,"* a corruption of "antique," which, with this spelling, usually means "strange" or "grotesque." ¶123. *"They do speak little, but fervently."* *Cf.* Logan's speech (p. 282), and Hiawatha's (pp. 680–83). ¶124. *"Ten Tribes."* The tribes of Israel.

124. [MEDITATIONS] are from *Some Fruits of Solitude, in Reflections and Maxims, Relating to the Conduct of Human Life,* the first edition of which appeared anonymously in 1693. The seventh edition (1718), from which the present text is taken, is much fuller than any previous one, and there is reason to believe that it was printed from a manuscript revised by the author. ¶124. *"It were happy if we studied Nature."* Penn's views are common today among "progressive" educators. ¶126. *"The King's Daughter is all glorious within."* Ps. xlv. 13. ¶128. *"Socrates"* (*c.* 470 B.C.–399 B.C.), the Greek philosopher; wrote nothing, and is known chiefly for his influence on others. ¶129. *"Maxima Bella ex levissimis Causis":* "the greatest wars from the least causes." ¶130. *"If you love me keep my Commandments."* John xiv. 15.

William Byrd (1674–1744)

William Byrd, the second Virginia gentleman of that name, succeeded his father as landed proprietor and Receiver General of the Royal Revenues, after an education in the Middle

Temple, in which he attained a "happy proficiency in polite and various learning" in addition to a knowledge of the law. The variety and urbanity of his tastes were reflected in his library, a catalogue of which is still preserved, as well as in the quiet irony of his literary style. In 1728–29, he was appointed one of three commissioners in charge of a party to fix the dividing line between Virginia and Carolina. This line was run from the coast, through the Dismal Swamp, and six hundred miles west. His journal of this adventure was later transcribed by another hand, corrected by him, and published, together with two later journals, "A Progress to the Mines" (1732) and "A Journey to the Land of Eden" (1733), as *The Westover Manuscripts* (1841). A better version was edited by T. H. Wynne (1866). The definitive edition is that of J. S. Bassett (1901), which was reprinted (1928) in popular form by Mark Van Doren. For biography, etc., see the Bassett edition, and R. C. Beatty (1932).

130. [THE DISMAL SWAMP] is an excerpt from *The History of the Dividing Line betwixt Virginia and North Carolina*, which was printed first in German in 1737, and in English at Petersburg, Va., in 1841. The text is from *The Writings of Colonel William Byrd of Westover in Virginia, Esqr.*, ed. by J. S. Bassett, 1901. ¶131. "*Peruvian-Bark, Rhubarb and Hipocoacanah,*" herb remedies. Peruvian-Bark comes from the cinchona tree, the source of quinine. The roots of the rhubarb plant act as a cathartic. Hipocoacanah (one of the various spellings of Ipecacuanha) is a general name for various purgative herbs. ¶131. "*Gall-Bushes,*" bushes or trees, especially oaks, which have an excrescence caused by the action of insects. ¶131. "*Bamboe-briars,*" bamboo-briers, a prickly species of bamboo found especially in the southern part of the U. S. ¶131. "*Terra Australis Incognita.*" Australia is thus marked on many 18th cent. maps. ¶131. "*A Canterbury Tale,*" the title of Chaucer's tales, meaning a good yarn. ¶132. "*Patentees,*" a common term for holders of land by government or royal patent. ¶132. "*Finland Down,*" a particularly soft down. ¶132. "*Desarts of Affrica,*" the Sahara. ¶132. "*Edenton,*" Chowan Co., N. C. ¶133. "*Mast,*" nuts or acorns which serve as food for animals. ¶133. "*Norfolk,*" Va. ¶133. "*Nansimond,*" Nansemond Co., Va. ¶133. "*Burn the Cordage.*" "Cordage" refers to twisted roots or vines, or wood generally; hence the tar is impure. ¶133. "*Solomon's Sluggard,*" "How long wilt thou sleep, O sluggard?" Prov. vi. 9. ¶134. "*Bombo,*" named for Admiral John Benbow (1653–1702). ¶134. "*Balsam of life.*" "Balsam" is any aromatic exudation from trees or shrubs; here used figuratively to mean "good spirits." ¶134. "*Landgraves nor Cassicks,*" men of high rank and influence. The "landgrave" was a judicial official of considerable importance in the Middle Ages. "Cassick" is evidently a corruption of "Cassock," and usually means a military man, ¶134. "*Paraqueets,*" "parrakeets," parrots, especially small parrots. ¶134. "*Mawkins,*" scarecrows. ¶134. "*Thuckleberry Slashes,*" gaps or openings in a wood where huckleberries grow. ¶135. "*Society for propagating the Gospel,*" a British missionary society.

John Woolman (1720–1772)

"The only American book I ever read twice was the Journal of Woolman," Charles Lamb told his visitor, N. P. Willis, at breakfast one morning in London. "His character is one of the finest I ever met with." Little more can be said; Woolman's life and writings—for they are the same, one unified whole—represent the best of the Friendly philosophy, that mysticism, combined with practical common sense, which was characteristic of so many early Americans, whatever their faiths. Most of his life was spent in the little New Jersey town of Mount Holly, eighteen miles from Philadelphia, first as a baker's apprentice, then as a tailor, keeper of a notions shop, and schoolmaster. As Quaker preacher, his journey to western Pennsylvania brought him into immediate contact with the Indian problem, and at home he did not hesitate to advise his neighbors in their private affairs. He died of small-pox on a missionary journey to England, having made the trip from London to York on foot because he disapproved of the treatment of post-boys. Firm in his beliefs and principles, he combined assurance with humility; and he wrote the story of his life in the traditional English of the King James Bible. His *Journal* was rewritten twice, and all three manuscripts are preserved. The first edition appeared in 1774; it was edited by J. G. Whittier in 1871; the best modern edition, which includes some essays, was edited with a biographical introduction by A. M. Gummere (1922).

137. [EARLY LIFE], and (141) [LOVE OF MAN] are early passages of the *Journal*, which was printed first in Woolman's works (1774).

The text of these and the following passages is from the edition of A. M. Gummere (1922), which is based on a careful collation of all extant versions. ¶137. "*West Jersey.*" The colony was originally divided into two parts, East and West Jersey. ¶137. "*Seventh-day,*" Saturday. The Friends number rather than name the days of the week and the months. ¶137. "*He showed me a pure River.*" Rev. xxii. 1. ¶137. "*Our Meridian,*" the highest point reached by the sun in its course; the apparent local noon. ¶138. "*The tender mercies of the wicked are Cruel.*" Prov. xii. 10. ¶139. "*Wanton,*" wandering from moral rectitude; in Woolman's view, young people interested in any worldly pleasures. ¶139. "*We lie down in our shame, and our confusion covers us.*" Jer. iii. 25. ¶140. "*Bear the Cross,*" to endure hardship. ¶140. "*Meetings,*" Quaker equivalent of church services. ¶140. "*Inward Principle,*" Quaker doctrine of the "inner light." *Cf.* Jonathan Edwards' account of his religious experiences, pp. 171–178. ¶141. "*Ministers of Jesus Christ.*" The Quakers have no ordained ministers or pastors as do other Protestant sects. ¶141. "*Ezekiel.*" "Son of man, I have made thee a watchman unto the house of Israel." Ezek. iii. 17.

142. [THE INDIAN MISSION], and (146) [EXPERIENCES IN ENGLAND], are later passages from the *Journal.* A marginal note by Woolman states: "At our Yearly Meeting 1767. Information was given in our meeting of Ministers and Elders that Some Indians far back had sent a Message in which they desired that some of the Quakers would come and pay them a religious Visit. And in the year 1771 a message came to the governor of pensylva part to that import." Woolman's route was the Wyalusing Trail, the present route of the Lehigh Valley Railroad. ¶142. "*The Moravian,*" David Zeisberger. The Moravian sect is now called the United Brethren, an offshoot of the Hussites in Bohemia. ¶143. "*Delaware.*" The Delaware tribe proper occupied the Delaware River basin, but there were many related tribes, with varying dialects. ¶143. "*Papoonal,*" Chief Papunahung, a convert to Christianity. ¶143. "*This place,*" Wahalowsing, or Wyalusing, Bradford Co., Pa. ¶144. "*Bethlehem,*" Lehigh Co., Pa. ¶144. "*Tankhannah,*" Tunkhannock. ¶144. "*Wioming,*" Lucerne Co., Pa. ¶145. "*Fort Allen,*" Allentown, Lehigh Co., Pa. ¶145. "*Blue Mountains,*" the Appalachians. ¶145. "*Richland,*" a town in Lebanon Co., Pa. ¶145. "*Comfortable,*" a common Quaker term for "satisfactory." ¶145. "*Companion,*" not a member of the Society of Friends.

John Wise (1652–1725)

The attempts of the Mathers to establish an oligarchic form of church government in New England were vigorously opposed by the Rev. John Wise, minister of Ipswich, Mass. His thorough study of Pufendorf, Locke, and other writers of the natural-rights school, provided him with a foundation in political theory which made his two tracts, *The Church's Quarrel Espoused* (1710) and *A Vindication of the Government of New England Churches* (1717) unique in their time. So vigorous and so logical was his defense of the democratic principle of government that, when the nation at large was debating a similar issue just before the Revolution, a reprint of his essays (1772) had a wide influence. There has been no reprint since 1860; critical estimates may be found in M. C. Tyler's *History* (1880) and V. L. Parrington's *The Colonial Mind* (1927); biographical sketch by J. N. Mackaye (*N. E. Magazine*, Sept., 1903).

149. [THE FREEDOM OF MAN] is from Chapter II of *A Vindication of the Government of New England Churches.* The text is that of the first edition (1717). Wise here develops his theory of natural and civil liberty, and later applies it to church government in New England. ¶149. "*Baron Puffendorff,*" Samuel von Pufendorf (1632–1694), author of *De Jure Naturae et Gentium* (1672), a source of Locke's conception of the law of nature. ¶149. "*Molloy, De Mao, Pref.*" The reference is probably to the *De Jure Maritimo* (1676), by Charles Molloy (1646–1690). ¶150. "*Plutarch,*" Greek historian and moralist of the first century A.D., author of the famous *Lives.* ¶151. "*Says my Author,*" Puffendorff. ¶152. "*Bœthius.*" The quotation is from the *Consolat. Philosoph.*, III, vi, of Anicius Manlius Severinus, or Bœthius (*c.* 475–*c.* 525). The Latin is extremely incorrect. ¶152. "*Charactacus.*" Caractacus (*c.* 50 A.D.) resisted the Roman invasion for nine years, but was finally overcome. ¶152. "*Hensius.*" Daniel Hensius (1580–1655) was a Dutch classical scholar and philologist. ¶152. "*Ulpian,*" a Roman jurist (*c.* 200 A.D.). ¶153. "*The Eastern Country of the Mogul,*" India, where the Mongolian (or Mogul) dynasty ruled until the advent of the British. ¶153. "*Interregnum,*" the period between the death of a ruler and the accession

of his successor. ¶154. "*Fiat*," command, will. ¶155. "*Plato*," in *The Republic*. ¶155. "*Justin*," Justinian, Emperor of the East (527–565), famed for his Code, a compilation of Roman laws (529, 534). ¶156. "*Elisium*," Elysium; Greek name for paradise or heaven.

Ethan Allen (1738–1789)

While America was still waiting for the treaty with England to be signed, the leader of the Green Mountain Boys and the hero of Ticonderoga turned from sword to pen and prepared an attack on Calvinistic dogma. A scattered reading in Rationalistic philosophy and pseudo-philosophy was brought together in *Reason the Only Oracle of Man* (1784). It seemed important enough to Allen's contemporaries to call out answers, in pulpit and press, from such men as Ezra Stiles, Timothy Dwight, and Lemuel Hopkins, but it has apparently never since been reprinted. Biography by John Pell (1929). Bibliography in M. D. Gilman, *Bibliog. of Vt.* (1897).

157. [SUPERSTITION *vs.* REASON] is from *Reason the Only Oracle of Man; Or, a Compendious System of Natural Religion*, published at Bennington (1784). The book is a great rarity, for most of the copies were destroyed by fire at the printer's, and "practically all of the remainder" were burned by the printer because of their "atheistic" content. ¶157. "*None by searching* . . .," a paraphrase of Job xi. 7.

Samuel Johnson (1696–1772)

The revolt from the "Congregational way," which was led by the Rev. Samuel Johnson in 1722, caused little sensation at the time, but it had lasting consequences. He confesses in his *Autobiography* that he had long disliked Calvinism because of what seemed to him the false pride of its leaders, and because he thought it led to "endless feuds, censoriousness and uncharitableness." A reading of the liturgy broke down his prejudices against the Church of England, and he was ordained a priest of that faith, and pastor of its only church in Connecticut, at Stratford, in 1724. He devoted his life to preaching his new-found gospel, and to developing an idealistic philosophy similar to that of Bishop Berkeley, with whom he became intimate during the latter's stay at Newport, R. I., in 1729. After refusing the presidency of the new college in Philadelphia because he did not wish to abandon what to him was missionary work, he was prevailed upon, in 1753, to accept that of King's College (later Columbia). His *Elementa Philosophica* (1752) contains the most complete statement of his beliefs, and ranks him as the leading exponent of the philosophy of idealism in the America of his day. Most of his writings, which are chiefly letters and controversial tracts, remained in manuscript until a selection of them, in four volumes, was edited by H. and C. Schneider (1929). Biographies by T. B. Chandler (1805), and E. E. Beardsley (1874).

162. [THE LOVE OF TRUTH] is from *Raphael, or The Genius of English America*, which Johnson describes as "a rhapsody." It remained unprinted until the appearance of his collected works, ed. by H. and C. Schneider, in 1929, from which the present text is taken. It consists of two parts: the first, a letter from Aristocles to Crito, in which the Archangel Raphael appears to the writer and expounds the life of reason; the second, another letter to Crito, in which is described a walk with Publicola. Raphael is again encountered, and the talk turns upon the topic of the education of youth. Throughout, Johnson maintains his principle that the free use of the reason is the only means to happiness. ¶162. "*Raphael*." In Milton's *Paradise Lost*, the Archangel Raphael is sent by God to instruct Adam. ¶162. "*Aristocles to Crito*." Johnson apparently has no particular Greek originals in mind. ¶166. "*Is so far from neglecting*." Where hiatus comes in text two pages of MS. are missing.

Jonathan Edwards (1703–1758)

One may mark three stages in the mental development of this last of the Puritan theocrats: that of his youth and education, that of his residence at Northampton, and that of his exile at Stockbridge. During the first he was a boy of sensitive spirit and speculative mind; during the second he was the leader of a religious revival, a preacher of hell-fire; in the last he became the dogmatic theologian of firm convictions and cool logic. His ancestry may partially explain the strong contrasts in his personality. One grandparent was the liberal preacher, Solomon Stoddard, whom Edwards later succeeded in the church at Northampton; another was an intelligent and attractive New Haven girl, Elizabeth Tuttle, whose temperament probably accounts for the mixture of genius and eccentricity in her descendants. His father was a clergyman, and his mother an unusually well-educated and intellectual woman. Edwards' inherited tendencies toward study and introspection were encouraged by early influences and by his life at Yale, where he read Newton and Locke, and studied with Samuel Johnson. When he graduated, his bent was more toward speculative philosophy and science than toward theology. Such essays as "The Flying Spider" and the "Personal Narrative" suggest a career more like that of Emerson than that of Cotton Mather; and the connection between his thought and that of Channing and the Concord Transcendentalists is obvious. The second period in his development extends from 1727, when he was ordained at Northampton, to 1750, when he was dismissed from his charge. Putting rationalistic speculation behind him, he turned wholeheartedly to Calvinistic theology, preached sermons on the wrath of God, and inspired the "Great Awakening," a revival of Evangelical enthusiasm which brought new life into old dogma; and the spirit of the Mathers returned. Finally, as an exile in his missionary church at Stockbridge, in western Massachusetts, he set himself to a justification of the theological position which had caused his dismissal: his insistence that "a credible profession of godliness or sanctifying faith" is essential to church membership. The result was a series of tracts in which his convictions are stated in clear scholastic logic, and the Antinomians and other liberals are attacked as enemies of the true faith. Nevertheless, he was to the end an idealist who never formed a systematic philosophy because he was prevented by a temperamental inclination toward mystical experience and a conviction of the primary importance of theology over metaphysics. A fourth stage in his development was opened by the offer of the presidency of Princeton, but it was checked in its fulfillment by his death from small-pox inoculation in 1758, two months after he had taken up his new responsibilities.

The most important of the works published during Edwards' lifetime are: *A Divine and Supernatural Light* (1734); *A Faithful Narrative of the Surprising Work of God in the Conversion of Many Hundred Souls in Northampton* (1737); *Discourses on Various Important Subjects* (1738); *Sinners in the Hands of an Angry God* (1741); *Some Thoughts Concerning the present Revival of Religion in New-England* (1742); *A Treatise concerning Religious Affections* (1746); *An Account of the Life of the Late Reverend Mr. David Brainerd* (1749); *A Farewell Sermon Preached in Northampton* (1751); *A careful and strict Enquiry into the modern prevailing Notions of that Freedom of the Will, Which is Supposed to be essential to Moral Agency, Vertue and Vice, Reward and Punishment, Praise and Blame* (1754); *The Great Doctrine of Original Sin Defended* (1758); and *Remarks on the Principles of Morality and Natural Religion* (1758). *A History of the Work of Redemption* appeared in 1774, and some of his sermons were collected in 1765, together with a biography by Samuel Hopkins, which quoted the "Personal Narrative," some of the "Resolutions," and other unpublished sources. This biography was reprinted in an "improved and enlarged" form in the first volume of the earliest collection of his writings, published in Leeds, London, and Philadelphia (1806–11). The "first American edition," with a revision of the Hopkins memoir, was edited by Samuel Austin and published in Worcester (1808). The Leeds edition was reprinted in London (1817) with a preface signed by E. Williams and E. Parsons. A more inclusive edition, with a new memoir based on that of Hopkins and on manuscript sources, was edited by Sereno E. Dwight (1829, 1830). Later editions are based on one or another of these. Some *Unpublished Writings* appeared in 1865; and a selection from the sermons, edited by H. N. Gardiner in 1904. Later biographies and critical studies by A. G. V. Allen (1889, 1890), H. B. Parkes (1930), T. H. Johnson (1932), and A. C. McGiffert, Jr. (1932). A bibliography is being prepared by J. T. Gerould. The largest collections of manuscripts, many of them unpublished and all of them in need of reëditing, are at Yale and the Andover Theological Seminary.

168. [THE FLYING SPIDER] was written when Edwards was about twelve years old, and was addressed to an English friend of his father's. It was printed from the manuscript by E. C. Smyth in *The Andover Review* (Jan. 1890), together with what seems to be an earlier version of the same essay. It is here reprinted, as are the other selections from Edwards, from the edition of S. E. Dwight (New York, 1829). Dwight quotes it in his prefatory "Memoir," and alters the text, not only in punctuation and spelling, but occasionally in sentence structure and phrasing. Collation with the Smyth text reveals the following major changes: ¶168. "*It is wonderful at what a distance, these webs may plainly be seen* [in such a Position, to the Sunbeams, which are so fine that they Cannot be seen

without such a position near the eyes]." ¶170. "*And in this way, Sir, I have multitude of times seen spiders mount away into the air,* [with a vast train of this silver web before from a stick in my hand and have also shewed it to others]." ¶171. "*For a new stock the next year.* [Corroll. hence the wisdom of the Creatour in Providing of the Spider with that wonderfull liquor with which their bottle tails are fill'd, that may easily be Drawn Out so exceeding fine and will so immediately in this way exposed to the Air Convert to a Dry substance that shall be very Rare and will so Excellently serve to aid their Progress.]" Collation of other parts of Dwight's text with those of Hopkins and Austin indicates a similarly liberal editorial policy, but until there is a new edition from the manuscripts, that of Dwight must be accepted as standard because it is the most thorough and consistent of existing editions.

171. [PERSONAL NARRATIVE] was written about 1740 and was found among Edwards' manuscripts at his death. It was published in the Hopkins "Memoir" as, "An Account of his Conversion, Experiences, and Religious Exercises, given by himself." Dwight divided it into parts and incorporated it in his "Memoir." The parts are here reassembled, with the exception of the last. ¶172. "*The doctrine of God's sovereignty.*" *Cf.* Wigglesworth's *Day of Doom*, pp. 75 ff. ¶173. "*Cant.*," The Song of Solomon. ¶175. "*I went to preach at New-York,*" Aug., 1722. ¶177. "*Westchester*" County, north of New York City. ¶177. "*Saybrook,*" Conn. ¶177. "*Windsor,*" Conn.

178. [SARAH PIERREPONT]. On July 28, 1727, Edwards married Sarah Pierrepont, of New Haven. This fragment, written in 1723 soon after he had met her, was found on the blank leaf of a book. What we know of her life confirms his first impression of her gentleness and goodness. The note was apparently printed first by Dwight.

178. RESOLUTIONS. The first twenty-one of these resolutions were written early in Edwards' preparation for the ministry, and by 1722, there were thirty-four of them. Others were added from time to time during his residence in New York and after he had returned to his father's home. The last are of Aug., 1723. Some of them were printed by Hopkins, but Dwight was the first to publish the entire series.

179. [THE GREAT AWAKENING AT NORTHAMPTON]. The first of these letters was included in *Some Thoughts Concerning the present Revival of Religion in New-England* (Boston, 1743): the second, which was addressed to the Rev. Mr. Prince, of Boston, was first printed in *Christian History* (Boston, June 11 and 18, 1743). Although they treat of the same circumstances, they are not to be confused with *A Faithful Narrative of the Surprising Work of God in the Conversion of Many Hundred Souls in Northampton, and the Neighboring Towns and Villages* . . . (London, 1737). ¶179. "*Meeting-house,*" church. ¶181. "*George Whitefield,*" (1714–1770); see Introduction, p. 8. ¶182. "*Professors,*" believers.

186. [A DEFINITION OF THE WILL] is from the opening passages of *A careful and strict Enquiry into the modern prevailing Notions of that Freedom of the Will, Which is Supposed to be essential to Moral Agency, Vertue and Vice, Reward and Punishment, Praise and Blame* (Boston, 1754). Written in virtual retirement at Stockbridge, it is his most ambitious statement of his theological position, and a challenge to the revolting Antinomians and others. ¶189. "*Mr. Locke,*" John Locke (1632–1704), English philosopher whom Edwards had read while a student at Yale. ¶190. "*Arminians,*" believers in the doctrines of Arminius (1560–1609), a Dutch Protestant theologian, represented by the Wesleyans in Great Britain and the Methodists in America. ¶190. "*Pelagians,*" followers of Pelagius (d. 418), a British monk, who denied original sin and baptismal regeneration and contended for perfect freedom of man's will. ¶190. "*In equilibrio*": "in equilibrium," in even balance between opposing forces.

Benjamin Franklin (1706–1790)

Franklin tells the story of his own childhood and early manhood in his autobiography, written chiefly in Europe when he was an old man. From these distances of time and space, he saw himself as deliberate and cautious, with much common sense and an eye to the main chance. But as with Sewall, his very frankness has led to a fundamental misconception of his character. The facts themselves, if distinguished from his interpretation of them, reveal a boy of much courage, love of adventure, sense of humor, and ability to take life as it comes. Born in Boston on Jan. 6, 1706, the son of a candle-maker, he was apprenticed to his brother James, a printer, but soon ran away and went to Philadelphia. His first trip to London, 1724–26, was commercial in motive, and on his return, he set up his own printing establishment. Little by little he was drawn from the life of business into that of politics. He became clerk of the Assembly of Pennsylvania in 1736; postmaster of Philadelphia in 1737; deputy postmaster-general of the colonies in 1753; commissioner to the Albany Congress in 1754; colonial agent in London for Pennsylvania in 1757 and 1764, and for Massachusetts in 1770; minister to France for the United States in 1778; and President of the Commonwealth of Pennsylvania in 1785–87. In addition, he represented the people of Pennsylvania in their war with the Proprietors; he presented the cause of the colonies in the English parliament on the eve of the Revolution; he took part in the framing of the Declaration of Independence; he helped to negotiate and he signed the Peace Treaty of 1783; and he contributed to the drafting of the Constitution of the new nation. In our transition period from the status of colonies to that of a united nation, Franklin was our principal spokesman abroad. During this period, his writing was naturally devoted to political topics, but his background of reading in Defoe, Addison, and Swift gave it a literary form and quality which rank it with the better English prose of the day. Similarly, his essays and letters on scientific and practical affairs led to his international recognition as an authority in these fields, while adding incidentally to his literary reputation as well. But he must ultimately be judged as a literary man by the writing of his later years when he turned from constructing his career to playing with it. His informal letters to Madam Brillon and others (notably "The Whistle"), as well as his *Autobiography*, have the detachment, simplicity, sincerity, and pure style which are accounted the chief values of 18th century literature in English. His residence at Passy (Paris), and his final years in America, are characterized by the mellow assurance of a man, rich in experience, who has learned to appreciate the amenities as well as the necessities of life.

The most important of the works published during Franklin's lifetime are: *A Dissertation on Liberty and Necessity, Pleasure and Pain* (1725); *Articles of Belief and Acts of Religion* (1728); *A Proposal for Promoting Useful Knowledge* (1743); *Reflections on Courtship and Marriage* (1746); *Plain Truth, or Serious Considerations on the Present State of the City of Philadelphia, and Province of Pennsylvania* (1747); *Proposals Relating to the Education of Youth in Pensilvania* (1749); *Experiments and Observations on Electricity . . . in several letters to P. Collinson* (1751); *Idea of an English School* (1751); *Poor Richard Improved* (1757); *The Interest of Great Britain Considered* (1760); *The Examination of Dr. Benjamin Franklin* (1766); *The True Sentiments of America* (1768); *Experiments and Observations on Electricity* (1769); *Information to those who would Remove to America* (1784); and *Observations on the Causes and Cure of Smoky Chimneys* (1785). The *Autobiography*, written between 1771 and 1789, was published in parts, the first appearing in French translation at Paris in 1791; the last in 1818, in English. "The Bagatelles" were printed on Franklin's own press at Passy as they were written, between 1778 and 1781; their first publication was in the W. T. Franklin edition (1818). *Poor Richard's Almanac* (1732–1764) contained prefaces by him. He also contributed to *The New-England Courant, The Pennsylvania Gazette, The Gentleman's Magazine, The Public Advertiser*, and other periodicals, several of which were edited by him. The Franklin manuscripts have passed through many hands, and many of them have been destroyed or lost. The principal public collections are those of the Amer. Phil. Soc., the Hist. Soc. of Pa., the U. of Pa., the Library of Congress, and the Huntington and Clements Libraries. The early collected editions of his works are far from complete (1779, 1793, 1806), having been published during the time that William Temple Franklin was scissoring and pasting the manuscripts for his garbled edition of 1818; that edited by Jared Sparks (1840) is inclusive but textually unreliable. The first satisfactory edition was that of John Bigelow (1889); but the edition of A. H. Smyth is the best for modern use. *Benjamin Franklin Self-Revealed*, by W. C. Bruce (1918), quotes the principal autobiographical sources. Biographies by J. Parton (1864), J. B. McMaster (1887), J. T. Morse, Jr. (1889) and A. H. Smyth (*Writings*, Vol. X). Much of the recent work on Franklin has been influenced by special pleading, notably the inclusive biography by Bernard Fäy (1929), and that by Phillips Russell (1926). For bibliography, see *CHAL;* also W. J. Campbell, *The Collection of Franklin Imprints* [etc.], 1918.

192. [Boyhood], (201) [Entering Philadelphia], (203) [First Visit to England], and (206) [Moral Reflections] are from the first part of the *Autobiography*, which brought the narrative up to 1731. It was written at Twyford, near Winchester, in 1771, while

Franklin was visiting his friend, the Rev. Jonathan Shipley, Bishop of St. Asaph's. A bad translation into French, from the manuscript, was published at Paris (1791). The first publication in English direct from the manuscript is that in W. T. Franklin's edition of the *Writings* (London, 1818). The text of all Franklin selections is that of A. H. Smyth (1907). ¶192. "*When you were with me in England.*" When Franklin went to England in 1757 as agent for Pa. and N. J., his son William accompanied him. ¶193. "*Conventicles,*" secret, sometimes illegal, assemblies for religious worship. ¶193. "*Peter Folger,*" (1617–1690), author of *A Looking Glass for the Times* (1676), the "home-spun verse" referred to. ¶193. "*Sherburne town,*" Sherborn, Mass. ¶194. "*My uncle Benjamin,*" a silk-dyer in London, who invented a system of shorthand. ¶195. "*R. Burton's Historical Collections.*" Nathaniel Crouch (1632?–1725?), who called himself "R. Burton," published a series of twelve penny histories, filled, according to Dunton, with "wonders, rarities, and curiosities." ¶195. "*Plutarch's Lives,*" parallel lives of Greek and Roman celebrities. ¶195. "*Essay on Projects,*" (1698), by Daniel Defoe (1661?–1731). This, Defoe's first important work, was a shrewd comment on social conditions in England. ¶195. "*Essays to do Good,*" *Bonifacius, An Essay Upon the Good, That is to be Devised and Designed*, etc. (Boston, 1710); often reprinted as *Essays to do Good.* ¶196. "*Edinborough.*" The University of Edinburgh was, at this time, one of the principal seats of learning in Europe, particularly in the sciences. ¶197. "*The Spectator,*" a series of periodical essays by Joseph Addison (1672–1719) and Sir Richard Steele (1672–1729), published in London (1711–12, 1714). ¶197. "*Tryon,*" Thomas Tryon (1634–1705), author of *The Way to Health, Long Life and Happiness* (2d ed., 1691). ¶198. "*Cocker's book of Arithmetick,*" *Cocker's Arithmetick, being a plain and easy method . . . composed by Edward Cocker* (1678). ¶198. "*Seller's . . . Navigation.*" *The Sea Pilot,* by John Seller (1671). ¶198. "*Locke on Human Understanding,*" *An Essay concerning Humane Understanding* (1690) by John Locke (1632–1704). ¶198. "*The Art of Thinking, by Messrs. du Port Royal,*" *La Logique, ou l'art de penser* (1662), by Antoine Arnauld and Pierre Nicole, members of a school of philosophers at Port Royal, France. ¶198. "*Xenophon's Memorable Things of Socrates.*" The *Memorabilia,* by Xenophon, Greek historian of the 4th century B.C., was written after the death of Socrates to defend his memory from the charges brought against him. ¶198. "*Shaftesbury,*" Anthony Ashley Cooper, third Earl of Shaftesbury (1671–1713), author of *Characteristics of Men, Manners,* etc. (1711). ¶198. "*Collins,*" Anthony Collins (1676–1729), author of an *Essay concerning the Use of Reason* (1707). ¶199. "*Men should be taught . . .*" is from Pope's *Essay on Criticism.* ¶199. "*The only one before it was the Boston News-Letter.*" See Introduction, p. 12. ¶201. "*Dutch dollar,*" a Dutch coin similar to the German *thaler.* ¶202. "*Andrew Bradford,*" son of William Bradford (1658–1752), who set up the first printing press in Philadelphia, in 1685. Franklin was referred to the son by the father, to whom he had applied in New York for employment. ¶202. "*One Keimer,*" Samuel Keimer (1688–*c.* 1739), eccentric and radical printer, who emigrated to Philadelphia and set up his shop in 1721. ¶203. "*Aquila Rose,*" poet (1695–1723), author of *Poems on Several Occasions*, Phila., 1740. ¶203. "*The Governor,*" Sir William Keith (1680–1749) was governor of Pa., 1717–1726. In spite of his misleading promises to Franklin, he seems to have been generally popular because of his liberal views. ¶203. "*Newcastle,*" Del. ¶203. "*Ralph,*" James Ralph (*c.* 1705–62), a minor poet, satirized by Pope in *The Dunciad* as follows:

Silence, ye wolves! while Ralph to Cynthia howls,
And makes Night hideous—answer him, ye owls.

¶204. "*Little Britain.*" *Cf.* Irving's essay on Little Britain in *The Sketch Book.* ¶204. "*Wilkes,*" a comedian. ¶204. "*The Temple,*" the general term applied to the Inner Temple, the Middle Temple, and the other law courts of London. ¶204. "*Wollaston's 'Religion of Nature,'*" *The Religion of Nature Delineated* (1722) by William Wollaston (1660–1724). The book upon which Franklin worked was a reprint of this privately printed edition. ¶204. "*A Dissertation on Liberty and Necessity, Pleasure and Pain.*" See bibliographical note above. ¶205. "*Mandeville,*" Bernard Mandeville (1670?–1733), a Dutch physician who settled in London and was known for his conversational powers. ¶205. "*Dr. Pemberton,*" Henry Pemberton (1694–1771), employed by Newton to superintend the third edition of the *Principia* (1726). ¶205. "*Sir Isaac Newton,*" (1642–1727), leading inventor of the day and discoverer of the law of gravitation. ¶205.

"*Sir Hans Sloane,*" (1660–1753), secretary and president of the Royal Society, had a large private collection of the curiosities of science and art. ¶205. "*Young's Satires,*" *The Universal Passion* (1725), by Edward Young (1683–1765), author also of *The Complaint, or Night Thoughts on Life, Death and Immortality* (1742). ¶206. "*The Dissenting way,*" the term applied to all sects dissenting from the Church of England. ¶206. "*Boyle's Lectures,*" a series of lectures at the Royal Society, endowed by Robert Boyle (1627–1691), whose interests were divided between theology and experimental science. ¶207. "*Whatever is, is right.*" *Cf.* Pope's *Epistle I*, l. 289.

208. [A Rule of Life] is from the part of the *Autobiography* which was written at Passy 1784–85 and was first published in a French translation in 1798. ¶209. "*Seest thou a man,*" etc. Prov. xxii. 29. ¶210. "*Finally, brethren,*" etc. Phil. iv. 8. ¶210. "*Liturgy,*" a form of service for the Holy Communion. ¶211. "*Articles of Belief and Acts of Religion.*" See bibliographical note above. ¶212. "*The advice of Pythagoras.*" *The Golden Verses*, a spurious ethical code of the followers of Pythagoras, Greek philosopher of the 6th century B.C., required members of the society to make an examination of conscience every morning and evening. ¶213. "*Addison's Cato,*" a classical tragedy by Joseph Addison (1672–1719), acted in 1713. ¶213. "*Thomson's Poems.*" James Thomson (1700–1748), author of *The Seasons* (1726–1730)

217. [On Education], the fourth of the letters from "Silence Dogood," appeared first in *The New-England Courant*, May 7–14, 1722. ¶217. "*An sum etiam nunc vel Græcè loqui vel Latinè docendus?*": For am I at this time of life to start teaching the speaking of Greek or Latin? ¶217. "*Clericus*": clerk. ¶219. "*Pecunia,*" the goddess of gain, from the Latin word *pecunia*, wealth. ¶219. "*Plagius,*" from the Latin *plagiarius*, a literary thief. ¶219. "*Tillotson's Works,*" John Tillotson (1630–1694), Archbishop of Canterbury and writer of many religious works.

220. The Way to Wealth, preface to *Poor Richard* for 1758. It was dated July 7, 1757; and is sometimes referred to as "Father Abraham's Speech." The accumulated wisdom of Poor Richard is here offered, perhaps as much to promote the sale of the almanacs as to formulate a working philosophy of life.

226. An Edict by the King of Prussia appeared first in *The Gentleman's Magazine*, Oct., 1773. It is one of a number of such political satires in the manner of Defoe and Swift, aimed at the stupidity of British polity. Here England is placed in the reverse of her actual position with relation to the colonies. ¶226. "*A tous présens et à venir*": to all those present and to come. ¶226. "*Hengist, Horsa, Hella, Uff, Cerdicus, Ida,*" early Germanic leaders who took part in the conquest of Britain. ¶229. "*Rechtmaessig,*" German for "legal."

229. Rules by Which a Great Empire May Be Reduced to a Small One; *Presented to a Late Minister* [the Earl of Huntington], *when he Entered upon his Administration*, appeared first in *The Gentleman's Magazine* for Sept., 1773. Barring considerable exaggeration, Franklin is here merely outlining the policy which England had already pursued in dealing with the colonies. ¶230. "*Newgate solicitors,*" lawyers of low rank. ¶231. "*Habeas Corpus,*" right to trial by jury of fellow-citizens. ¶233. "*Crown cases,*" equity cases in law, which formerly were appealed directly to the King. ¶235. "*Q. E. D.,*" *Quod Erat Demonstrandum:* "which was to be demonstrated"; the usual conclusion to a problem in geometry.

235. The Whistle and (236) The Ephemera are among the many personal letters addressed by Franklin to Madame Brillon during his residence in Passy (then a suburb, now a part, of Paris), and known as "The Bagatelles." "The Whistle" is dated Nov. 10, 1779, and was first printed in W. T. Franklin's edition of the *Writings* (1818). "The Ephemera" was written in 1778 and is the first of these essays. ¶236. "*Moulin Joly,*" Madame Brillon's home. ¶236. "*Cousin . . . Moscheto,*" gnat . . . mosquito. ¶237. "*Brillante,*" a pun on Madame Brillon's name.

John Dickinson (1732–1808)

Born on the plantation of Crosia-doré on the Eastern Shore of Maryland and educated in the law at the Inns of Court, John Dickinson sympathized with the proprietors in their war with the people of Pennsylvania, and, after the Revolutionary War, he was strongly Federalist. In spite of this conservatism, however, he took a leading part in the Stamp Act Congress and taught the rebels the distinction between internal and external taxation in terms of justice. His counsels were influential in all the problems of the construction of the new nation. His twelve "Letters from a Farmer in Pennsylvania" appeared, between Dec. 2, 1767, and Feb. 15, 1768, in *The Pennsylvania Chronicle and Universal Advertiser* and were immediately reprinted in *The Pennsylvania Journal* and *The Pennsylvania Gazette.* They were also printed separately, and in a collected volume in Mar. 1768. There were a half-dozen American editions within the next year, four English, and one French translation published in Amsterdam. Although distinctly rebel documents, they must be clearly distinguished from the protests of radicals like Tom Paine and Samuel Adams against what they believed to be the usurpation of power by the British Parliament. Into the midst of a debate determined by just indignation and ill-founded opinion, Dickinson threw the measured judgment of a man of conservative mind and a knowledge of the law. His *Political Writings* were collected in 1801; and the *Letters* were edited by P. L. Ford (1895) for the Hist. Soc. of Pa., with a biographical introduction by C. J. Stillé (first pub. 1891).

238. LETTERS I and (241) III from Dickinson's *Letters from a Farmer in Pennsylvania to the Inhabitants of the British Colonies,* appeared respectively in the issues for Nov. 30–Dec. 3, and Dec. 7–14, 1767, of *The Pennsylvania Chronicle and Universal Advertiser,* from which the present text is taken. This series was among the most influential of rebel documents in the controversy which led up to the war. His "Letters" continued in *The Chronicle* until February, and were immediately reprinted in pamphlet form. There were ten editions within two years. ¶239. "*The Stamp Act,*" passed in 1765 by Parliament imposing taxes on the colonists without their consent. ¶240. "*Mr. Hampden's ship-money,*" John Hampden (1594–1643), leader in opposing the demand of Charles I for levies from the seaboard counties for defense purposes, known as "ship-money." ¶241. "*Concordia res parvae crescunt*": "In peace little things grow." ¶242. "*Spartans,*" one of the principal peoples of ancient Greece, noted for their bravery and hardihood. ¶243. "*House of Brunswick,*" same as House of Hanover, the present line of British rulers, starting in 1714 with George I. ¶243. "*The reigns of the Stuarts,*" James I (1603)–Anne (1714). ¶243. "*Lord Clarendon,*" Thomas Villiers (1709–1786). ¶243. "*Cleons.*" Cleon was an Athenian demagogue of great influence shortly after the death of Pericles (429 B.C.). ¶243. "*Clodius's.*" Clodius, or Claudius, Roman patrician (*c.* 500 B.C.), unscrupulous and designing. ¶244. "*Nil desperandum*": "Nothing is to be despaired of."

244. A [LIBERTY] SONG was published in *The Pennsylvania Chronicle,* July 4, 1768. A variant, with eight lines by Arthur Lee, appeared in *The Boston Gazette,* July 18, 1768. It was then issued as a ballad sheet, set to the tune of "Hearts of Oak," and was sung and parodied throughout the colonies.

Thomas Paine (1737–1809)

Tom Paine was a specialist in revolutions. Born at Thetford, England, he had been unsuccessful in almost everything he attempted when Franklin met him in London in 1774 and gave him a letter of introduction to Richard Bache of Philadelphia. Robert Aitken had just started a new periodical, *The Pennsylvania Magazine or American Museum,* and Paine was made its editor. His ideas were so original, his point of view so radical, and his style so vigorous that the venture was a great success. The war was already a certainty when his pamphlet, *Common Sense,* which appeared on Jan. 10, 1776, cut the issue clear between the policies of separation and conciliation, and swayed many doubters to the rebel cause. Paine enlisted in the Continental Army and continued his work of inspiring the hesitant by his series of sixteen essays, *The Crisis* (1776–1783), the first of which was written in camp before the Battle of Trenton. After the war, he returned to England and wrote his *Rights of Man* (1791–92), in which he summed up his mature thought on natural rights and democracy. Meanwhile France had been preparing for a revolution, and Paine, finding that the British government was suspicious of his radicalism, crossed the Channel in time for the fall of the Bastille and the Reign of Terror. He allied himself with the moderate Girondist party, was imprisoned, and almost guillotined. He sailed once more for America in 1802, and died seven years later in New York City. *The Age of Reason* (1793–95) is his statement of his deistic creed and his philosophical defense of the theories of man and nature which had motivated all his actions. His biography was written (1892) and his writings edited by M. D. Conway (1894–96). See also, *Selections,* edited by A. W. Peach (1928); the biographies by Ellery Sedgwick (1899) and M. A. Best (1927); and the later editions of his works (1908, 1925). H. H. Clark is preparing a book on his philosophical and political ideas.

245. COMMON SENSE. The section entitled, "Thoughts, on the present State of American Affairs," is here reprinted in full from the text of the second Bell (Phila., 1776) edition. This varies from the first edition, of the same year, only in minor respects, and a few typographical errors have here been restored by collation to their earlier and obviously correct form. The passage in square brackets, which occurs in most modern reprints but is not in the Bell texts, is here quoted from the Bradford edition (Phila., n. d.). ¶245. "*The late Mr. Pelham,*" Thomas Pelham (1693–1768). ¶247. "*Hanover,*" formerly an independent kingdom, now a province of Germany, the scene of part of the Seven Years' War (1756–1763), especially the campaigns of 1757. ¶248. "*The first king of England . . . was a Frenchman.*" William (*c.* 1027–1087) was Duke of Normandy, a territory only loosely allied with the kingdom which was to become the nucleus of modern France. ¶251. "*The removal of North.*" Lord North was held responsible by the colonists for the British policy of taxation, with regard to the principle rather than the burden. ¶251. "*Junto,*" an intriguing political group; a term applied to various factions in British history. Compare Franklin's use of it for his club. ¶251. "*The fatal 19th of April 1775,*" the date of the British march on Concord. ¶251. "*Pharaoh of England,*" George III. ¶255. "*Dragonetti,*" Giacinto Dragonetti (1738–1818), author of *Le Virtù ed i Premi* (1767).

256. THE AMERICAN CRISIS. The first letter in this series was written in the American camp during Washington's retreat through New Jersey before the Battle of Trenton, the eve of Dec. 25, 1776. It was pub. in *The Pennsylvania Journal*, Dec. 19, 1776, and was immediately reprinted, as were the subsequent letters, as a pamphlet (Dec. 23), from which the present text has been taken. These letters are filled with the excitement of action, and they did much to revive the dismayed American forces. ¶257. "*The Jerseys,*" East and West Jersey. ¶257. "*Joan of Arc,*" (1412–1431) led the French troops in the defeat of the British at Orléans, 1429. ¶257. "*The troops at fort Lee,*" New Jersey, on the Hudson River, opposite Manhattan Island. Greene was surprised by Cornwallis on Nov. 20, 1776, and was forced to retire hastily, losing many stores and a few men. ¶257. "*A narrow neck of land,*" between the Hackensack and Hudson Rivers. ¶258. "*Howe,*" General William Howe, commander of the British forces during the first three years of the American Revolution. ¶258. "*Major General* [*Nathanael*] *Greene,*" (1742–1786), was the leader of the Rhode Island militia in 1775; was made a brigadier-general in the Continental army June 22, 1775, and a major-general in Aug., 1776. He commanded the left-wing at Trenton, was active in New Jersey, at Brandywine, Germantown, and Springfield; in Oct., 1780, he took command of the Southern army, and eventually expelled the British from the South. ¶258. "*Voltaire.*" François Arouet (1694–1778), used the *nom de plume* "Voltaire"; French writer and satirist, who wrote *Lettres sur les anglais.* ¶259. "*Tory . . . Whigs.*" The terms then applied in England to the conservative and liberal parties respectively came in America to connote "Loyalist" and "Rebel." ¶261. "*A peace which passeth all understanding,*" Phil. iv. 7. ¶261. "*Army of Britons and Hessians.*" Great Britain hired about 30,000 "mercenaries" in the course of the Revolution, most of them from Hesse-Cassel, Hesse-Hanau, and Brunswick (German principalities). The act aroused the wrath of the Americans and was denounced by Frederick the Great of Prussia, but the "Hessians," as they were popularly called, were necessary and valuable to the British cause. ¶262. "*The White Plains,*" north of New York City, between the Hudson River and Long Island Sound. The British under Howe encountered Washington in an indecisive battle at White Plains on Oct. 28, 1776.

262. LIBERTY TREE, a "New Song" to the tune of "The Gods of the Greeks," was first published in *The Pennsylvania Magazine*, July, 1775, from which the present text has been taken. It celebrated an elm in front of a house opposite the Boylston Market, Boston. On Aug. 14, there was found hanging on this tree an effigy of Andrew Oliver, the stamp distributor, and a boot to symbolize the Earl of Bute. The Chief Justice ordered their removal, but excitement ran too high to allow this action. After a parade, Oliver was induced to go to the tree and publicly resign his commission. The Liberty Tree was thereafter a center for popular demonstrations, and similar trees were consecrated to the cause in other cities. ¶263. "*Atlanticus.*" It was the custom in both England and America at this time to sign anonymous contributions to periodicals with a pseudonym.

263. [A CREED] is the opening chapter of *The Age of Reason, Being an Investigation of*

True and Fabulous Theology, written in prison in Paris while its author was daily anticipating the guillotine. The present text is taken from the edition published in Paris (1794). It was widely reprinted, and its frank deism made enemies for Paine wherever it was read.

Anne Hulton (? –1779)

During her short residence in America, Anne Hulton lived with her brother, Henry Hulton, Commissioner of Customs for Boston, and his family, in Brookline, Mass. The family was, of course, Loyalist in its sympathies. The first of her letters from America, all of which are addressed to Mrs. Adam Lightbody, wife of a merchant in Liverpool, is dated from Castle William, Boston Harbor, June 30, 1768; and the last was written about April, 1775, just before she returned to England. They were published as *Letters from a Loyalist Lady* (1927). A few of those written in England had previously appeared in *The Gentleman's Magazine* for Aug., 1904.

264. [THE CONSEQUENCES OF THE TEA PARTY] and (267) [CONCORD AND LEXINGTON] are from *Letters of a Loyalist Lady* (1927), which were addressed by Miss Hulton to Mrs. Adam Lightbody, the wife of a merchant in Liverpool. ¶264. "*B——*," Boston. ¶264. "*Col. Lessley*," probably Alexander Leslie (*c.* 1740–1794), commander of one of the ships guarding the Port of Boston. ¶265. "*Mr. Paxton*," Charles Paxton, a Commissioner of Customs for the Port of Boston, who went to England in 1768 to encourage Townshend to appoint American revenue commissioners. ¶265. "*Mr. Haliwell*," Benjamin Hallowell, Esq., Controller of His Majesty's Customs for the Port of Boston just before the Revolution. ¶265. "*Mr. Hutchinson*," Thomas Hutchinson (1711–1780), governor of Mass. (1769–1774). His enforcement of the Parliamentary acts aroused great dissatisfaction, resulting in the sacking of his house and his eventual departure for England. ¶265. "*Colo Watson*," probably Robert Watson (1746–1838), an adventurer. ¶265. "*K*," the King of England, George III. ¶266. "*Govr Tryon*," William Tryon (1725–1788), governor of New York (1771–1778). He was a loyalist leader and served as "major-general in America" during the latter part of the Revolution. ¶267. "*Committee of Correspondence*," organized in 1774 by the Boston Town Meeting, on the motion of Samuel Adams, to communicate with other towns and colonies on the "rights of the Colonists." ¶267. "*Genl Gage*," Thomas Gage (1721–1787), last royal governor of Mass., succeeding Hutchinson in 1774. ¶267. "*Marlborough*," Middlesex Co., Mass., about twenty-five miles west of Boston. ¶267. "*Popery*," the Roman Catholic religion. ¶267. "*Lord Percy*," Hugh Percy (1742–1817), British general during the Revolution, who led a brigade of troops out of Boston to protect the retreat of General Gage from Concord, April 19, 1775.

Jonathan Boucher (1738–1804)

Born in England, which he revisited in 1762 to take orders in the Anglican Church, Boucher was never in full sympathy with his fellow-citizens of Maryland, although he rose to a position of great influence before the revolutionary issue became acute. His views on all matters were authoritarian and aristocratic. On the eve of the war he preached a series of sermons against the rebel cause, which were later collected as *A View of the Causes and Consequences of the American Revolution* (1797), and was otherwise so active in opposing colonial resistance that he was forced by popular opinion to return to England in 1775. Many of his sermons were reinforced by a brace of pistols on the pulpit cushion. His autobiography was published (1925) as *Reminiscences of an American Loyalist, 1738–1789*.

269. ON CIVIL LIBERTY; PASSIVE OBEDIENCE, AND NON-RESISTANCE is the twelfth of a series of sermons preached by Boucher in America between 1765 and 1775 and published as *A View of the Causes and Consequences of the American Revolution in Thirteen Discourses* (London, 1797). This sermon is an answer to the Rev. Mr. Duché, who had preached and printed in Philadelphia a sermon on the same text: "Stand fast, therefore, in the liberty wherewith Christ hath made us free." (Gal. v. 1.) The issue is essentially that of the debate between Winthrop and Williams, and that between the Mathers and John Wise. It was soon to become, in a new form, the central issue of that between Jefferson and Hamilton. ¶271. "*Mr. Locke*," John Locke (1632–1704). The quotation is from Chap. VIII, par. 97, of the *Second Treatise on Government*. It is in Chap. XIX that Locke writes concerning the "Dissolution of Government" and the "right of resistance." ¶272. "*Ishmael's*." Ishmael was the son of Abraham by Hagar, Sarah's maid, and was expelled from Abraham's house through Sarah's jealousy. Gen. xvi. 11 ff. He is the literary

prototype for the social outcast and wanderer. *Cf.* Melville's use of this tradition in *Moby Dick.* ¶273. "*Filmer,*" Sir Robert Filmer (d. 1653), an English political writer with monarchist sympathies, criticized by Locke. ¶274. "*Ignes fatui,*" illusions, fancies. ¶274. "*The words of Plato.*" *Cf.* Plato's *Republic,* Bk. II. ¶275. "*Vitruvius,*" Marcus (85–26 B.C.), Latin architect who had a renewed influence during the Renaissance. ¶275. "*Aristotle.*" The reference is to the *Politics,* especially Bk. I.

Thomas Jefferson (1743–1826)

Although he did more than any other American statesman of his time to formulate the democratic theory of government, Jefferson was himself a Virginia gentleman and an aristocrat. His theory that the common man is innately capable of self-government was prompted by his social idealism and was balanced by a reverence for traditional cultures. Born in Virginia, he early built Monticello, and spent all of his life, except that part which he devoted to practical politics, in the midst of his plantation acres and his slaves. His most important services to his country were rendered in his capacities as governor of his state, envoy to France, and president of the United States. His contributions to our national expansion, our foreign policy, our architecture, our agriculture and horticulture, and our higher education did much to determine the national character. The greater part of his writings took the forms of personal and official letters, notably those to Adams and Madison, and of state papers, tracts, and other documents of the kind; but the personality and consistent idealism of the man are evident in even his most formal statements. The largest collections of Jefferson manuscripts are in the Library of Congress and the Mass. Hist. Soc. His writings were edited by P. L. Ford (1892–99); and A. A. Lipscomb and others (1903–04). Biographies by J. T. Morse, Jr. (1883), G. Chinard (1929), and others. See also, *Thomas Jefferson as Architect,* by F. Kimball (1916), and *Jefferson and Hamilton,* by C. Bowers (1925).

276. [The Declaration of Independence] is here printed in the form in which Jefferson left it in his *Autobiography,* unpublished at the time of his death. This is neither the text which was submitted to Congress nor that which was amended and adopted, although the two versions here given conform fairly closely to these two versions. It is expressive of Jefferson's ability to guide the opinions of others into a position with which he could agree rather than to insist upon his own ideas. It was the work of a committee of which he was the chairman; but it is written in his own scholarly and felicitous English. Like his two *Inaugural Addresses* (1801, 1805) it contains a clear statement of his theory of the rights of man as applied to the immediate problem of the nation. The text of this passage and the following is from the edition of P. L. Ford (1892–99). ¶276. "*The same day,*" Thursday, July 4, 1776. ¶276. "*Mr. Dickinson,*" John Dickinson, *q. v.,* pp. 238–245.

280. [Inhabitants of the New World], from his *Notes on Virginia* (1784), is the latter part of Jefferson's answer to the sixth query addressed to him, in a series of twenty-three, by the Marquis de Barbé-Marbois, secretary of the French Legation at Philadelphia, in 1781, and designed to inform the French government of the real character of the American race and nation. In this section, Jefferson discusses his state from the point of view of "the mines and other subterraneous riches; its trees, plants, fruits, &c." The *Notes,* written in retirement, when personal sorrows had sobered Jefferson's views, contains his careful observations and measured opinions, and is perhaps the best example of his sincerity and clarity of mind, as well as of his command of pure English. It was privately printed and circulated in America and France (1784) before its first English publication (1787). The first complete edition is that of 1800. This section is in answer to the theory of the Count de Buffon and others that human life degenerates in the Western Hemisphere. Buffon (1707–1788) was a French naturalistic philosopher and "popularizer" of scientific knowledge. His theory of the degeneration of man is found in *L'Histoire naturelle,* (1749), esp. vol. II. ¶282. "*Homo sapiens Europaeus*": "the European man." ¶282. "*Demosthenes,*" (384–322 B.C.), greatest Athenian orator. ¶282. "*Cicero,*" (106–43 B.C.), Roman orator. ¶282. "*The speech of Logan.*" Jefferson's accuracy in narrating this incident was vigorously questioned and he went to some trouble in verifying the facts. Although he left the passage unchanged at his death, H. A. Washington substituted the following passage, a change which is adopted also in the 1905 edition of his *Writings:* "In the spring of the year 1774, a robbery was committed by some Indians on certain land

adventurers on the river Ohio. The whites in that quarter, according to their custom, undertook to punish this outrage in a summary way. Captain Michael Cresap, and a certain Daniel Greathouse, leading on these parties, surprised at different times, travelling and hunting, parties of the Indians, having their women and children with them, and murdered many. Among these were unfortunately the family of Logan, a chief celebrated in peace and war, and long distinguished as a friend of the whites." ¶282. "*Kanhaway,*" Kanawha River in West Virginia. ¶283. "*Newton,*" Sir Isaac Newton (1642–1727), English natural scientist. ¶283. "*Cis or Trans-Atlantic partisan,*" a partisan of England or of America. ¶283. "*Abbé Raynal,*" (1713–1796), French philosopher and historian. ¶284. "*Mr. Rittenhouse,*" David Rittenhouse (1732–1796), Philadelphia astronomer and scientist. ¶284. "*Encyclopedists.*" A group of French scholars, led by Diderot, whose *Encyclopedie,* probably the most famous in history, was published between 1751 and 1765.

Alexander Hamilton (1757–1804)

The first fifteen years of Hamilton's life were spent in the British West Indies, where he had been born. His friends sent him, an orphan, to Elizabethtown, N. J., where he went to school. During the War, he was Washington's confidential aide, and he early became convinced of the dangers of too loose a union among the colonies. His influence on the national mind was first strongly felt in 1787, when, as a delegate from New York to the Continental Convention, he urged the adoption of a constitution in which power was to be centralized as far as possible in a strong federal government. This doctrine distinguishes the Federalist Party from the "states-rights" Republican Party of Jefferson and his followers. As Secretary of the Treasury in Washington's cabinet, Hamilton developed a financial policy which did much to stabilize the new government. Not only his doctrine, but his personality contrasts him sharply with Jefferson. He was more often hated than loved, and a life-long hostility toward Aaron Burr led to his death after a duel on July 11, 1804. The Hamilton manuscripts are in the Library of Congress. His works were edited by H. C. Lodge (1885–88, 1904), who also wrote a biography (1882, 1898). See also the biography by J. T. Morse, Jr. (1876). *The Federalist* was separately edited by P. L. Ford (1898).

285. [AN EFFECTIVE GOVERNMENT] is the twenty-third number of *The Federalist*, a series of tracts written by Hamilton, Madison, and Jay in defence of the Constitution and in exposition of the Federalist position. It appeared in several newspapers, and has been reprinted many times. There are three texts upon which most of these editions are based: that revised by Hamilton in 1788; that authorized by Madison, with some editing of his own essays, in 1818; and the original newspaper versions to which Dawson returned in 1863, and P.L. Ford in 1898. Lodge used the Dawson text in his edition (1885–88, 1904). The Ford text has been adopted here, although it is practically identical in this passage with that of Lodge.

Timothy Dwight (1752–1817)

The "Connecticut" or "Hartford Wits," of whom Timothy Dwight, John Trumbull, and Joel Barlow wrote the most enduring poetry, were among the first Americans to deal with native subjects in traditional literary forms. When Trumbull and Dwight became tutors at Yale in the 'sixties, their interest in contemporary English literature led them to urge the modernizing of the curriculum. Addison and Pope still dominated the English literary horizon, and the American writings which resulted from this new interest were on such Augustan models as the periodical essay and the mock epic. But the colonials of that day were too much concerned with political and religious controversy to find much vitality in the themes of social satire which interested the elder school. Instead, they turned their attention to those issues which had undermined religious oligarchy and which were already promising a revolutionary war.

Timothy Dwight inherited the religious conviction but not the restless mind of his grandfather, Jonathan Edwards. Rather, his temperament suggests that of Increase Mather in conservatism and vigor. The belief in a church-state had, in this later day, been metamorphosed into a staunch Federalism in politics, linked to Congregationalism in religion. Dwight's work, totaling fourteen volumes in verse and prose, includes poems on theological themes like his ambitious epic, *The Conquest of Canaan* (1785), and *The Triumph of Infidelity* (written 1788); patriotic poems like "Columbia" (written *c.* 1777–78); tracts and addresses in both these fields of interest; many sermons, two volumes of which were collected in 1828; and some uncollected essays in the Addisonian style. There are several early memoirs of Dwight, but the best biographical, critical, and bibliographical sources for him, as well as for the other members of the group, are V. L. Parrington's *The Connecticut Wits* (1926); M. C. Tyler's *Three Men of Letters* (1895); R. J. Purcell's *Connecticut in Transition 1775–1818* (1918); and H. A. Beers' *The Connecticut Wits, and other Essays* (1920).

289. GREENFIELD HILL (pub. 1794) was a casual production, written, its author tells us, "to contribute to the innocent amusement of his countrymen, and to their improvement in manners, and in economical, political, and moral sentiments." It is a deliberate imitation of the styles of various English poets, notably Goldsmith. The poet stands on a hill in his native parish of Greenfield, Conn., overlooking the town of Fairfield and Long Island Sound, three miles away. The first section describes this view; the second discusses the life of the villagers and compares their happiness with the oppressions of Europe; the poem then contains an account of the burning of Fairfield by the British in 1779, and of the attack by Pequod Indians; in the next two parts respectively the village minister and a farmer preach the joys of life in the world to come and the world that is; and in the final section Dwight adopts an epic strain, and prophesies, as did Barlow, the future glories of America. The poem is in various meters, and is of uneven quality, the several parts being virtually independent poems, bound together by a vaguely common theme. The text is from the first edition. ¶289. "*Fair Verna,*" a poetic name for the village. *Cf.* the opening line of Goldsmith's poem: "Sweet Auburn! Loveliest village of the plain." ¶290. "*Zephyr,*" the west wind, or any gentle breeze. ¶293. "*The Afric infant,*" the negro. ¶294. "*Essoins,*" excuses, especially for not appearing in court. ¶294, "*Monboddo,*" Lord, James Burnet (1714–1799). Scottish judge and author. The reference here is to *Of the Origin and Progress of Language* (1774–1792). ¶295. "*Nanking,*" the chief city of the province of Kiangsu, in southern China.

John Trumbull (1750–1831)

In poetic worth, Trumbull should probably be ranked highest in the Hartford group. He was descended from Solomon Stoddard, grandfather of Jonathan Edwards, and his family has included ministers, educators, statesmen, and painters through many generations. He was a precocious youth, who read widely in Greek, Latin, and English authors, and passed the examinations for Yale at the age of seven, entering six years later and finally becoming a tutor. In 1773, he began the study of law in the office of John Adams, but his tastes were academic and literary. The result was a life devoted primarily to the writing of poetry and prose, in support, first of the patriotic, and later of the Federalist party. His *Poetical Works* (1820) were reprinted (1922) by the Andiron Club of N. Y. Biography by A. Cowie (Yale, 1930; unpublished).

296. [TOM BRAINLESS AT COLLEGE] is from Part I of *The Progress of Dulness* (1772–73). By recounting the careers of several typical undergraduates, Trumbull satirizes, in merciless but good-humored vein, the academic life which he had observed. The text of this and the selection from *M'Fingal* are from the edition published by the Andiron Club of New York (1922), and based on the revised text of *The Poetical Works of John Trumbull*, 2 vols., Hartford, 1820. The revisions in the 1820 text are many, but as the volumes are carefully printed, it may be assumed that there was at least a degree of authorization. Changes in words as well as in punctuation suggest the work of the author. ¶296. "*Non paravi*": "I have not prepared for recitation." ¶296. "*Tardes,*" a term used at college upon coming to class late. ¶296. "*Egresses,*" a term used upon leaving before the conclusion of the class. ¶296. "*Tully's.*" Marcus Tullius Cicero (106–43 B.C.), Roman orator, writer, and statesman. ¶296. "*Pliny's,*" Pliny the Younger (62–114), Roman poet. ¶297. "*Achilles' rage, Ulysses' lies, Th'amours of Jove.*" Homer tells in the first book of the *Iliad* of the wrath of Achilles when the beautiful captive Chryseïs was given to Agamemnon after the fall of Thebes; Ulysses, in the second book, prevents the flight of the Greeks by subtlety; the amours of Jove (or Jupiter) furnish a constant theme throughout the poem. ¶297. "*And Mars entrapp'd by Phoebus' aid.*" In the fifth book, when the gods are at war with each other, Phoebus Apollo tricks Mars by a ruse. ¶297. "*Virgil . . . his lovers.*" The references are to incidents in the *Æneid*. ¶297. "*Lily's days,*" John Lyly, a contemporary of Shakespeare. ¶297. "*Vida, Cowley or Buchanan.*" Marco Girolamo Vida (1485–1566); Abraham Cowley (1618–1667); George Buchanan (1506–1582); poets

who studied or imitated the classics. ¶297. "*Horace.*" Quintus Horatius Flaccus, Roman poet of the first century B.C. ¶297. "*Syllogisms,*" forms for arranging judgments to test their logical validity. ¶297. "*Athroismos, Mesoteleuton, Symploce and Paregmenon,*" technical terms in the old books of rhetoric. ¶298 " * * * * *and* * * * * ." The asterisks are in the original. ¶298. "*Admitto te ad gradum*": "I admit you to a degree"; part of the words used in conferring the honors of college.

299. THE LIBERTY POLE is Canto III of *M'Fingal,* Trumbull's most ambitious poem, which was published in Philadelphia (1775), in a form that included only what was later divided into the first two cantos. The first complete edition (Hartford, 1782) was frequently reprinted. The revisions in the 1820 edition may be illustrated by comparison with the first six lines of the 1782 text:

> Now arm'd with ministerial ire,
> Fierce sallied forth our loyal Squire,
> And on his striding steps attends,
> His desp'rate clan of Tory friends.
> When sudden met his angry eye
> A pole, ascending through the sky, . . .

The poem tells of the events in a small Massachusetts village immediately after the Revolution when the patriotic inhabitants came into conflict with the blundering Tory squire, M'Fingal. John Adams may have served as the model for Honorius, the champion of the popular cause. ¶299. "*Brobdignagian,*" a giant race in the second book of *Gulliver's Travels,* by Jonathan Swift (1667–1745). ¶299. "*Cups of Circe,*" the companions of Ulysses were changed into swine by drinking the magic cup of Circe. ¶299. "*Ichor,*" the ethereal fluid supposed to flow like blood in the veins of the gods. ¶299. "*Flip,*" a New England country drink composed of beer, rum, and sugar. ¶299. "*Edom,*" Idumæa, the mountainous tract south of the Dead Sea. ¶299. "*Magna Charta.*" The document granting certain rights to English lords, signed by King John in 1215. ¶299. "*Fix its scale of depreciation.*" Congress fixed a "scale" to measure the declining values of Continental paper currency. ¶300. "*Drive judges out,*" the closing of the courts after popular protests in the early days of the war. ¶300. "*Aaron's calves.*" In the absence of Moses, Aaron permitted the making and worshipping of idols. ¶300. "*See Arnold quits.*" The 1820 edition has an ironic note on this passage: "Arnold's perjuries at the time of his pretended bankruptcy, which was the first rise of his fortune and his curious lawsuit against a brother skipper, who had charged him with having caught the above-mentioned disease, by his connection with a certain African princess in the West-Indies, were among the early promises of his future greatness, and honors." ¶300. "*Hudibras*" (1663–1668), a satirical poem by Samuel Butler (1612–1680). ¶301. "*Friar Bacon's brazen head.*" According to tradition, a head made of brass by the alchemist, Roger Bacon. It could speak and was omniscient. *Cf.* Byron's *Don Juan,* i, 217. ¶301. "*Trinc'lo,*" Trinculo, the drunken jester in Shakespeare's play *The Tempest,* proposed, with Stephano and Caliban, to govern the island: "The folly of this island! They say there's but five upon this isle: we are three of them; if the other two be brained like us, the state totters" (III, ii). ¶301. "*Committees vile of correspondence,*" the committees organized in the various colonies for the spreading of revolutionary propaganda. ¶301. "*Moggison,*" moccasin. ¶302. "*Primed,*" painted. ¶302. "*White Hutchinson . . . Manœuvred to his country seat.*" Thomas Hutchinson (1711–1780), royal governor of Mass., alarmed at the demonstration, retired to his country seat at Milton, from which he escaped when informed that the mob was coming to pull down his house. ¶302. "*Mandamus-men,*" judges who issue writs of mandamus, directing a person to do or not to do something. ¶302. "*Ransack'd all the custom-houses.*" The custom-house in New York was broken open and all the public monies seized. ¶302. "*Smith's weather-cock.*" William Smith, a prominent lawyer of New York. ¶302. "*Beelzebub,*" the devil, or the prince of the devils. ¶302. "*North and Bute and Tryon,*" Lord North, the Earl of Bute (*cf.* Paine's *Liberty Tree*), and William Tryon, governor of New York, all of them staunch royalists. ¶302. "*Galloway.*" Joseph Galloway (1731–1803), a moderate loyalist who unsuccessfully tried to maintain a neutıal position in the war. ¶302. "*Rusty gun,*" at the Battle of Lexington. ¶302. "*Dagon,*" the deity of the ancient Philistines, represented with the head, chest, and arms of a man and the tail of a fish. ¶302. "*Lord's anointed,*" the King. ¶302. "*Jericho's proud wall.*" Jos. vi. 1 ff. ¶303. "*Ovid,*" *Metamorphoses,* XII. ¶303. "*Lapithæ and Centaurs.*" The Lapithæ were a mythical people inhabiting the mountains of Thessaly; the Centauri were the mythological inhabitants of Mount Pelion in Thessaly.

¶303. *"Pallas, Mars, or Iris."* In the following episode Trumbull has in mind the single combats in Homer, Virgil, and Milton. ¶304. *"Old Satan struggling on through chaos."* *Cf.* Milton's *Paradise Lost*, Bk. II, l. 891 ff. Satan decides upon the temptation of man, and, leaving his host of fallen angels in hell, struggles up through chaos alone. ¶304. *"As Socrates of old at first did . . . get hoisted."* In Aristophanes' *Clouds*, Socrates is represented as hoisted in a basket in order to aid contemplation. ¶305. *"Methus'lah,"* biblical character who lived 969 years, supposedly. Gen. v. 27. ¶305. *"Lord North,"* Frederick North, second Earl of Guilford (1732–1792), agent of George III in the ministry and the House of Commons and a particular enemy of the colonists. ¶305. *"Gen'ral Gage."* Thomas Gage (1721–1787), British general, military governor of Mass. Bay following Hutchinson's departure in 1774. ¶305. *"Murray."* James Murray (1719?–1794), governor of Quebec, court-martialed but acquitted (1783). ¶305. *"Williams,"* probably John Williams (1727–1798). ¶305. *"Ol'ver,"* Andrew Oliver (1706–1774), lieut.-gov. of Mass. ¶305. *"Rivington,"* James Rivington (1724–1803), publisher. ¶306. *"So Claudian sings,"* Claudianus (d. *c.* 408), Latin classic poet. ¶306. *"Enceladus,"* one of the hundred-armed giants who made war upon the gods. ¶306. *"Pallas,"* Athena. ¶306. *"Lapland,"* the northern region of Europe including Norway, Sweden, Russia, etc. ¶306. *"Maia's son,"* Hermes, or Mercury. ¶306. *"Gorgon or Chimæra;"* Gorgones, three mythological monsters; Chimæra, a fire-eating monster with the head of a lion and the body of a dragon. ¶306. *"Duumvirate,"* probably a pun on the Triumvirate of Rome, formed by Pompey, Julius Cæsar, and Crassus (60 B.C.). ¶306. *"In Lybian wilds."* Africa was called Lybia by the ancient Greeks. ¶307. *"Drachm,"* or "drachma," an ancient Greek weight of various values.

Joel Barlow (1754–1812)

Barlow was the most radical member of the Hartford group, as well as the most ambitious poet. Until 1788, he accepted the opinions native to his Yankee stock and his Yale environment, although his energy and restlessness were exhibited in a variety of professions. As agent for the Ohio Land Company, he arrived in France at a time when revolutionary doctrines were in a ferment. Speculation in western lands soon gave way to that in democratic political theory and French finance. In the eighteen years of his foreign residence, he left his Connecticut background far behind, and became, like Tom Paine, a cosmopolitan spokesman for the rights of man. When he returned to America in 1805, he set up a *salon* for liberals in his home outside of Washington, and became prominent in domestic political affairs. He died of pneumonia in Poland, where he had been sent on a diplomatic mission in the wake of Napoleon's army. His *Advice to the Privileged Orders in the Several States of Europe* (1792) is, like his other tracts, a statement of his political and social creed. *The Vision of Columbus* (1787), a patriotic poem in nine books, is superior to the ambitious epic for which it furnished the foundation, *The Columbiad* (1807). Although passages in the latter contain glimmerings of poetic light, it was criticized even in its own day as too ambitious an effort for its theme. Barlow explains in his preface that his purposes are two: the poetical, which attempts to "soothe and satisfy the desponding mind of Columbus"; and the moral and political, which attempts to inculcate the belief that the republican form of government and the love of peace are superior to feudal strife. Its appearance in a monumental volume with steel engravings is more significant to the history of American printing than to that of literature. See Bryant's essay on "American Poetry" (page 470). Biographies by C. B. Todd (1886) and T. A. Zunder (Yale, 1927; published only as articles).

308. THE HASTY-PUDDING (pub. 1796) was written in Chambrey, Savoy, three years before its date of publication. Lighter in vein and expressive of a more urbane spirit, it has a homely worth which his other works do not possess. Long acquaintance with the French cookery gave the expatriate a whimsical feeling of homesickness for the characteristic dish of his native state. The text is from the first edition. ¶308. *"Ye Gallic flags."* France was called Gaul in Roman times; the reference is to the French Revolution, the conquest of Europe, and the execution of Louis XVI in 1793. ¶309. *"Ceres,"* the goddess of grain. ¶309. *"Oella."* The reference is probably to *The Columbiad.* Barlow's meaning seems to be that hasty-pudding will carry America's fame through the world. ¶309. *"Bacchus,"* god of wine. ¶310. *"Levant,"* the Orient. ¶310. *"Polanta . . . Polante,"* "polenta" or "polente," cooked wheat cereal, mush (Latin, *polenta*). ¶310. *"Belgic spawn,"* the Dutch. ¶311. *"Hoe-*

Cake," a cake of Indian meal, water, and salt, so-called because originally baked on a hoe over a fire or in ashes. ¶311. "*Johnny-Cake,*" a kind of bread made of Indian meal, flour, eggs, and milk. ¶312. "*Cancer,*" the fourth sign of the zodiac, whose first point is the summer solstice, or the northern limit of the sun's course in its declination. ¶312. "*Corinthian,*" a type of stone column originally used in buildings in Corinth, Greece. ¶313. "*Husking,*" a meeting, often festive, of neighbors or friends for husking Indian corn; also, a "husking bee." ¶314. "*Boreas,*" the north wind. ¶314. "*Mother of Egypt's god,*" the cow, celebrated here as the mother of the bull Apis, worshipped in Egypt as a god of the dead.

Francis Hopkinson (1737–1791)

In versatility, if not in genius, Hopkinson was the Leonardo of his immediate circle. A member of one of Philadelphia's most distinguished families, he was equally proficient in literature, music, law, invention, and politics. While a student at the college in Philadelphia, from which he received in 1757 its first diploma, he wrote the incidental music for *The Masque of Alfred* which was presented at his commencement. Between 1772 and 1789, he was successively collector of customs at Newcastle, Del., signer of the Declaration of Independence, member of the Continental Congress, Chairman of the Navy Board, Treasurer of Loans, and Judge of Admiralty for Pennsylvania. Meanwhile he had contributed essays and poems, on contemporary English models but chiefly of native American spirit and theme, to *The Pennsylvania Magazine* (1775) and other periodicals. *The Miscellaneous Essays* (1792) contain only a small part of his writings in verse and prose; the remainder are preserved in the periodicals in which they first appeared and in manuscript at the Huntington Library and elsewhere. Biography and bibliography by G. E. Hastings (1926).

316. TO MYRTILLA was written at Hartlebury Castle, Berkshire, in 1766. The subject was the niece of the Bishop of Worcester. The text of this and the other Hopkinson selections is that of *The Miscellaneous Essays* (1792).

316. THE BATTLE OF THE KEGS was first published in *The Pennsylvania Packet* of Mar. 4, 1778. During the winter of 1777–78, the American troops were at Valley Forge, while Howe, with the British forces, was comfortably quartered in Philadelphia. On New Year's Day, the river was seen to be full of kegs loaded with gunpowder and intended to annoy the British shipping. Not realizing their purpose, the British fired on them and on everything else floating in the river, including a keg of butter, much to the amusement of Hopkinson and others. This ballad, one of the most popular of the period, seems to have been the most notable result of the experiment. ¶316. "*Sir William.*" General William Howe angered the Colonists and eventually led to his own recall as commander of the British forces by the festivities which he allowed himself and his soldiers during their occupancy of Philadelphia. ¶316. "*Sir Erskine,*" William Erskine, quartermaster of the British forces.

317. THE NEW ROOF: A SONG FOR FEDERAL MECHANICS appeared first in *The American Museum* for July, 1788. It is a celebration in verse of the ratification of the Constitution by the Pennsylvania Convention. Hopkinson also wrote a prose satire of the same title, which shows equally well his strong federalistic sympathies. ¶318. "*Purlins,*" the horizontal members of a roof, supported on the principals and supporting the common rafters.

318. ON WHITE-WASHING, the full title of which is, "A Letter from a Gentleman in in America to his Friend in Europe, on White-washing," appeared first in *The Pennsylvania Packet* for June 18, 1785. It is representative of the Addisonian essay on an American theme, popular in the journals of the period. ¶319. "*The discovery of the Sandwich islands.*" The Hawaiian Islands were called the Sandwich Islands by Capt. James Cook, when he discovered them in 1778, in honor of John Montague, Earl of Sandwich (1718–1792). ¶320. "*White-washing,*" early term for "house-cleaning." ¶321. "*The words of king Lear.*" III, ii, 49–59. Three lines of the passage are here omitted. ¶322. "*The land of Goshen . . . the plagues of Egypt.*" Goshen was that district in Egypt where Jacob and the Israelites lived, in the midst of, but apart from, the Egyptians.

Thomas Godfrey (1736–1763)

Son of a Philadelphia glazier and inventor of the sea-quadrant, Godfrey was among the earliest laureates of his city and dramatists of his country. His schooling in England doubtless contributed to a reverence for the English classics which gave his work technical skill but left it wholly imitative. He was with Hopkinson at the college in Philadelphia, but he died before such literary promise as he had could be realized. He is known chiefly for *The Prince of Parthia* (produced 1767), a bombastic tragedy on an Elizabethan pattern which has the distinction of marking the beginning of native American drama. His works were published in a handsome volume in 1765, with a biographical memoir by Nathaniel Evans and a subscription list which includes all the prominent Philadelphians of the time. See also A. H. Quinn's *History of the American Drama . . . to the Civil War* (1923).

324. SONG, a typical imitation of the Elizabethan lyric, was first published in Godfrey's collected works.

Joseph Dennie (1768–1812)

Dennie was born into the Boston merchant aristocracy which became dominant after the decline of the theological power. When he graduated from Harvard in 1790, his classmate, Josiah Quincy, 3d, commented that, of the members of his class, he was "the most talented, taking light literature as a standard, . . . whose acquaintance with the best English classics was uncommon at that period. His imagination was vivid and he wrote with great ease and facility." While reading law in Charlestown, N. H., he continued his writing, and, in 1792, contributed the first of his "Farrago" papers in the Addisonian manner to *The Morning Ray, or Impartial Observer*, of Windsor, Vt. In 1793–94, he joined in a literary partnership with Royall Tyler and contributed articles from "The Shop of Colon and Spondee" to *The Eagle; or Dartmouth Sentinel*, of Hanover, N. H. So successful were these and other similar efforts, such as *The Lay Preacher*, that, when in Philadelphia, he was encouraged to found a literary journal, the first in this country to maintain a long run. The first number of *The Port Folio*, then a weekly, but later a monthly, appeared Jan. 3, 1801, and Dennie retained its editorship under the pseudonym of "Oliver Oldschool" until his death. He thus became the leader for a literary group which included Charles Brockden Brown, Philip Freneau, C. J. Ingersoll, Joseph Hopkinson, Richard Rush, Alexander Wilson, William B. Wood, and others. Biography by H. M. Ellis (1915).

324. THE MAN OF UNDERSTANDING, (325) ON THE SABBATH, and (327) OF PRECIPITATION, are from the earliest collection of *The Lay Preacher* (1796). The series began in *The New Hampshire Journal; or Farmer's Weekly Museum*, of Walpole, N. H., for Oct. 12, 1795. Its purpose was, in Dennie's own words, to exhibit truths in a plain dress to the common people. The papers appeared weekly thereafter until May 24, 1796. A sequel, "The Lay Preacher of Pennsylvania," was published in *The Gazette of the United States*, in Philadelphia, beginning Nov. 8, 1799, many of which papers were reprints of those in the first series. Cobbett's intended edition in two royal octavo volumes in 1799 never appeared, and there was no later collection. The essays are less American in theme than those of Hopkinson and Freneau. ¶324. "*The cedar of Libanus.*" The cedars of Lebanon, constantly referred to in the Old Testament for their size and beauty. ¶325. "*Provoked Peter.*" In denying Christ the third time, Peter "began to curse, and to swear." Mark xiv. 71. ¶325. "*Arts of jockeyship.*" "To jockey" is to outwit by trickery. ¶325. "*Johnson and Hawksworth.*" Dr. Samuel Johnson (1709–1784) was the author of *The Rambler* (1750–52) and other essays. By Hawksworth, Dennie may mean Sir John Hawkins (1719–89), Johnson's friend and biographer. ¶326. "*Hermia and Helena,*" in Shakespeare's *Love's Labour's Lost.* ¶326. "*Gill,*" Alexander Gill (1565–1635), high-master of St. Paul's School. ¶327. "*Behmen,*" Jacob Böhme (1575–1624), German mystic. His works, published in 1682, had a wide influence. ¶327. "*Saybrook platform.*" The synod of May 13, 1708, at Saybrook, Conn., adopted a stricter form of church government. ¶327. "*Atterbury.*" Francis Atterbury (1662–1732), Bishop of Rochester, mixed politics with religion in a very active life. ¶327. "*Bishop Watson.*" Thomas Watson (1513–1584), Bishop of Lincoln, was a humanist. ¶327. "*Laurence Sterne,*" (1713–1768), humorist and clergyman; author of *Tristram Shandy* (1759–1765). ¶327. "*Ersking.*" *Gospel Sonnets*, by Ralph Erskine (1685–1752), Scottish divine and poet. ¶327. "*Young,*" Edward Young (1683–1765), author of *The Complaint; or Night Thoughts on Life, Death and Immortality* (1742). ¶327. "*Gray,*" Thomas Gray (1716–1771), author of *Elegy written in a Country Churchyard* (1751). ¶327. "*Siloam,*" the underground conduit from Gihon to the pool of Siloam. ¶327. "*Lord Chesterfield,*" Philip Dormer Stanhope, fourth Earl of Chesterfield (1694–1773). His *Letters* to his son provided a code of polite manners for the age. ¶328. "*Dr. Slop, overthrown by Obadiah.*" The reference is to

Sterne's *Tristram Shandy*. ¶328. "*Hogarth's plates.*" William Hogarth (1697–1764), painter and engraver, made many plates illustrating 18th century London life. ¶328. "*Hodder's arithmetic*," a popular textbook by James Hodder, pub. 1661. ¶328. "*A lady from Babylon*," a woman of the street. ¶328. "*The son of Ahimaaz.*" After the battle with Absalom, Ahimaaz outran others and brought the news first to David. II Sam. xviii. 27. ¶328. "*The son of Nimshi*," "for he driveth furiously." II Kings ix. 20. ¶328. "*His vehicle, like count Basset's*," a swindler and bogus count in *The Provoked Husband* (1728), by Colley Cibber (1671–1757). ¶328. "*Pharaoh . . . Red Sea of troubles.*" Pharaoh, king of Egypt, was swallowed up with his army by the Red Sea when in pursuit of the Israelites. ¶328. "*A Jehu*," a son of Nimshi (see note above).

Benjamin Rush (1745–1813)

Rush was among the first of those literary physicians who have always been characteristic of Philadelphia. When he returned from his studies at Edinburgh in 1769, he at once became a leader in the medical circles of the city, and his interest in education, literature, and philanthropy increased his social influence. He is the author of many medical papers in addition to his *Essays, Literary, Moral, and Philosophical* (1798), which combine, as did Franklin's Junto, the literary with other intellectual interests.

329. [THE PROGRESS OF POPULATION IN PENNSYLVANIA], the full title of which is "An account of the progress of population, agriculture, manners, and government in Pennsylvania, in a letter to a friend in England," is included in the *Essays* (1798). It is representative of the formal (as distinguished from the familiar, or periodical) essay, as written by men in all walks of life in England and America during this period. Noah Webster wrote many essays of this type. In this paper, Rush anticipates by many years a part of F. J. Turner's theory of the frontier as a motivating factor in the development of American civilization. ¶331. "*The sagopyrum of Linnæus*," the technical name given barley by Linnæus (1707–1778), Swedish botanist, in his classification of plants. ¶332. "*Dollars were obtained from the Havanna.*" Their extensive trade with the non-British West Indies was for a long time a source of profit and the principal source of metallic coins for the colonists. ¶332. "*Peace of Paris*," 1783. ¶332. "*Arcadia*," the central district of the Grecian Peloponnesus. Rush evidently uses the term to indicate a land of "milk and honey," but its history since 500 B.C. has been one of constant strife and turmoil. ¶334. "*The late war*," the Revolution.

Philip Freneau (1752–1832)

Freneau was known in his own day as the "poet of the American Revolution," and his reputation was restricted almost to the limits of that phrase. Only recently has his work come to be recognized as the beginning of a native American romantic movement in poetry, and its range and originality appreciated. He even anticipated some of the English romantic poets in his observation of nature, his metaphysical perception, his feeling for the supernatural, his experimentation in verse forms, and a nationalism which underlies romantic movements in all literatures. He was born in New York, of French Huguenot stock, on Jan. 2, 1752. His father had inherited a shipping business and a sandy plantation, "Mount Pleasant," near the present Matawan, N. J. From the age of ten, Freneau spent his vacation from New York boarding school in the old colonial house with its acres and its slaves. He was well prepared in both the classics and the English poets when he met H. H. Brackenridge and James Madison at Princeton. Like the Hartford Wits and the Philadelphia group, these undergraduates attacked the current thought in politics, religion, and "belles lettres" with a sudden zest which can be attributed only to the spirit of the times. Their political idealism led to the founding, in 1769, of the American Whig Society, a rival of the more conservative Cliosophic Society. Literary collaboration with Brackenridge produced the commencement poem on "The Rising Glory of America," which the latter read; but Freneau had written most of it, as well as "The Pyramids of Egypt" and "The Power of Fancy." Experiments in school teaching and a visit to Santa Cruz mark the period 1772–78. His voice as poet of the Revolution had already been heard, as from an observer, but his own experience now produced "The British Prison Ship," and his poems in *The Freeman's Journal* (1781–84) express the nationalistic zeal which brought him his first fame. Then followed his marriage, the editorship of the New York *Daily Advertiser*, and a clerkship of foreign languages in the Department of State as a recognition of his services to the cause of Jeffersonian democracy. On Oct. 31, 1791, appeared the first number of *The National Gazette*, a frankly partisan journal, with Freneau's name as editor. It lasted until 1793, when Freneau retired to what was left of his patrimony at "Mount Pleasant." From there he contributed essays to various periodicals, and experimented with several journals of his own, meanwhile writing some of his best poems and revising the old ones. Poverty and the burning of his home saddened his later years. He died of exposure, having lost his way in a snowstorm just before Christmas of 1832.

The first collection of Freneau's poems appeared in 1786, and was followed by a volume of *The Miscellaneous Works . . . containing his Essays and Additional Poems* (1788) and one of *Poems Written between the Years 1768 & 1794* (1795). The last was the first edition to be carefully supervised by its author. Other editions appeared in 1809 and 1815, each of which contained revisions and new poems. A selection from his prose is contained in the 1788 volume, but much of it is still scattered in the journals in which it first appeared. The first inclusive edition of the poems was edited by F. L. Pattee (1902–07), with a biographical introduction. See also the biography by M. S. Austin (1901) and the bibliography by V. H. Paltsits (1903). H. H. Clark reëdited the poems from the early editions in 1929, with an introductory essay, principally on Freneau's place in the romantic movement. His promised volume of selections from the prose has not yet appeared.

335. The British Prison Ship was written in 1780 just after its author's release. It is a record of his impressions after the capture of the American ship *Aurora*, on which he was returning from the West Indies, by the British *Iris*. He was confined first in New York Harbor on the prison ship *Scorpion*, but was transferred later to the hospital ship *Hunter*, of which he writes in this canto. The text of this and the other of Freneau's poems is from the edition of H. H. Clark (1929); that of this poem is based on the edition of 1786. ¶336. "*Autolycus*," son of Hermes, and renowned as the master-thief of antiquity. ¶336. "*Orestes*," son of Agamemnon, who avenged the murder of his father and eventually took possession of his father's kingdom. ¶336. "*Alcander*," probably a character in Mlle. de Scudéry's romance *Clélie* (1656); a picture of Louis XIV as an adventurous youth. ¶336. "*Brookland*," probably in Maryland not far from the present site of Washington, D. C.; or Brooklyn, N. Y. ¶336. "*A Hessian doctor*," the doctor of the hospital ship *Hunter*. ¶336. "*Etna's*." Ætna, a volcanic mountain in Sicily. ¶336. "*Nostrums*," quack medicines. ¶336. "*Cortex from Peru*," Peruvian bark or cinchona, used for fever. ¶336. "*Pluto's reign*." Pluto, god of the underworld; hence "to death." ¶336. "*Flies of Spain*," Spanish fly, a green blister beetle, common to the south of Europe, used when dried and powdered for raising blisters. ¶336. "*Cream of Tartar*," from an Australian desert tree, used as a cathartic. ¶337. "*Hemlock*," poisonous herb; Socrates died by drinking hemlock, following his condemnation by the Athenians (399 B.C.). ¶338. "*York*," probably refers to New York Harbor. ¶339. "*Tryon*," William Tryon (1725–1788), Tory gov. of N. Y. (1771–1778). ¶339. "*Clinton*," Gen. Henry Clinton (*c.* 1738–1795), successor to Howe as commander-in-chief of the British forces, 1778. ¶339. "*Knyphausen*," Wilhelm von Knyphausen (1716–1800), German General, in command of the Hessian troops in America after the recall of Gen. Von Heister (1777).

339. On the Memorable Victory, "Obtained by the gallant Captain Paul Jones, of *Le Bon Homme Richard* (or Father Richard), over the *Seraphis*, of 44 guns, under the command of Captain Pearson," was first published in Francis Bailey's *Freeman's Journal* (Philadelphia, 1781), and was included in the 1781 volume, on which the Clark text is based. On Sept. 23, 1779, Paul Jones sighted forty British merchantmen convoyed by the *Serapis* and one other ship, off Hull, England. His ship, *Le Bon Homme Richard*, closed and boarded the enemy. A hand-to-hand fight resulted in the first great American naval victory. Compare Cooper's account of the same engagement (pp. 643–652). ¶339. "*The German main*," the North Sea. ¶340. "*The Gallic seas*," the seas bordering France. ¶340. "*Phoebus sought his pearly bed*," Phoebus Apollo, god of the sun; "the sun sank into the sea." ¶340. "*Sunk to Neptune's caves*." Neptune was the chief marine divinity of the Romans; hence, to the bottom of the ocean. ¶340. "*Pearson's flash*," Sir Richard Pearson (1731–1806), capt. in British navy, commander of the *Serapis*. ¶341. "*Our Thirteen Stars*." The first U. S. flag had thirteen stars and thirteen stripes by action of the Continental Congress, June 14, 1777.

341. To the Memory "Of the Brave Americans, under General Greene, in *South Carolina*, who fell in the action of September 8, 1781," was written in the year of the action which it celebrates, and was included in the edition of 1795, upon which the Clark text is based. Gen. Greene had succeeded Gates as commander of the American Army in the South on Dec. 2, 1780. His engagements with Cornwallis during the following year did much to end the war, although that at Eutaw Springs, S. C., on Sept. 8, 1781, resulted in a defeat with a loss of 700 men. ¶342. "*The Parthian.*" The Parthians (Parthia, a country in Asia, southeast of the Caspian Sea) were a very warlike people, famous in Greek and Persian times for their use of arrows in cavalry attacks.

342. To Shylock Ap-Shenkin "(In Reply To Big Looks and Menaces)," is a document in the war between Hamilton and Jefferson. When Freneau started his *National Gazette* (1791) in Phila. as a Republican organ, he was charged by John Fenno, editor of the Federalist *Gazette of the United States,* with being a hireling of Jefferson's. This satirical verse is a part of his retort. The Clark text is from the edition of 1795. ¶342. "*Shylock,*" the traditional usurer, hence "close." The "*Ap-Shenkin*" does not seem to have any particular significance. ¶342. "*France is reforming,*" the French Revolution (1789–1799). ¶342. "*Irishmen storming,*" the Irish uprising from 1793–1798, spurred by French sympathy, which led, however, to the Act of Union (with England) in 1800. ¶342. "*Pomposo,*" evidently the personification of "pompous"; probably refers to Hamilton or Adams.

342. Ode, and (343) On the Anniversary "of the Storming of the Bastille, at Paris, July 14th, 1789," both written in 1793, are from the ed. of 1795. ¶343. "*Fair Gallia's fire,*" the French Revolution. ¶343. "*To Russia's frozen lands,*" etc. The Jacobin radicals of the early part of the Revolution offered to help any people throw off their monarchical yoke. ¶343. "*Hearts of oak!*" quoted from a popular song of this title by David Garrick (1717–1779), British actor and dramatist. ¶343. "*Capet's reign,*" Louis XVI, king of France 1774–1793. ¶343. "*Perjur'd Louis.*" Louis had violated his oath to support the Constitution of 1791. ¶343. "*To Poland's doom is France consign'd.*" By the Brunswick Manifesto (1792), the first coalition threatened to partition France as Poland had been divided in 1772. ¶344. "*Sybil leaves,*" prophetic writings. "Sybil" or "Sibyl" was a woman of antiquity reputed to possess powers of prophecy.

344. The House of Night, "A Vision," was written at Santa Cruz in 1777, and appeared in *The United States Magazine* in 1779. The Clark text is from the edition of 1786. It is in that mood of "grave-yard" horror so suggestive of the English poets, Gray, Young, and Blair; and of the American, Poe. The fact that Freneau omitted it in his edition of 1795 is indicative of his more realistic turn of mind, developed after his journalistic experiences. ¶344. "*The last enemy . . . is Death.*" I Cor. xv. 26. ¶344. "*If thine enemy hunger, feed him.*" Romans xii. 20. ¶345. "*Chesapeke,*" the Chesapeake Bay. ¶345. "*The yew,*" etc., traditional graveyard plants and trees. ¶346. "*The black Tartarian crew,*" occupants of Hades. Tartarus was the deep and sunless abyss, often synonymous with Hades. ¶346. "*Stygian dew,*" from the River Styx, the principal river of the underworld. ¶346. "*Chanticleer,*" the name of the cock in the epic of *Reynard the Fox.* ¶347. "*Mighty Julius,*" Julius Cæsar (100–44 B.C.). ¶347. "*Zaara's waste,*" the Sahara Desert. ¶347. "*Jack-a-lanthorn walk'd,*" "Jack-o'-lantern," a night watchman; here evidently in the "land of death." ¶348. "*Alps,*" etc., the famous mountains of Switzerland, Italy, South America, eastern U. S., and Armenia.

348. The Pyramids of Egypt, "A Dialogue Written in 1769," was composed in college, and is one of the earliest expressions of Freneau's naturalistic fatalism. The Clark text is from the edition of 1786. ¶348. "*Pompey's pillar,*" a Corinthian column of red granite at Alexandria, Egypt, erected in 302 A.D. in honor of Diocletian (245–313), Roman emperor 284–305. There is no reason for the name. ¶349. "*Alexandria,*" city near the mouth of the Nile, in Egypt, founded in 332 B.C. by Alexander the Great. ¶349. "*The seven hills.*" Rome was originally built on seven hills, included within the Servian Wall. ¶350. "*The ancient Memphis,*" the early capital of Egypt. ¶350. "*Pharaoh's palace,*" palace of the rulers of Egypt. ¶351. "*Memnon,*" a large statue at Thebes, Egypt, of Memnon, a hero of the Trojan War, slain by Achilles. ¶351. "*Ancient Thebes,*" ancient city of Egypt, sit. on the Nile. ¶351. "*Ecbatan,*" the capital of Media, Persia, plundered by Cyrus, 550 B.C. ¶351. "*Babylon,*" city of antiquity, located on the Euphrates River, in Mesopotamia. ¶351. "*Thy huge Colossus, Rhodes,*" the giant statue of Apollo at Rhodes (an island in the Aegean Sea), made

by Chares in 280 B.C., one of the "Seven Wonders of the Ancient World."

351. THE INDIAN BURYING GROUND (pub. 1788), (352) THE DYING INDIAN (pub. 1784), and (353) THE INDIAN STUDENT: "or, FORCE OF NATURE" (pub. 1788), are all from the edition of 1809. Freneau took the typically romantic attitude toward the Indian, seeing him as a child of nature who can distinguish truth more clearly because he is closer to earth than the civilized white man. The first of these poems refers to the custom of burying in an upright posture, fully equipped for the chase. ¶352. "*Shebah,*" the Queen of Shebah, I Kings, II Chron. ¶353. "*Susquehanna's farthest springs,*" the source of the Susquehanna River, which is Otsego Lake, N. Y. ¶353. "*Shalum's tricks.*" The reference is obscure. ¶353. "*Cambridge Hall,*" Harvard College. ¶354. "*Virgil*" (70–19 B.C.), Roman poet, author of the Æneid.

354. THE DESERTED FARM-HOUSE (pub. 1775) expresses another aspect of the theme of the decay of man and his works. The Clark text is from the edition of 1809. ¶355. "*Campania's plain,*" an especially fertile region in Italy. ¶355. "*Palestina's shore,*" the land of the Hebrews, of which Jerusalem was the capital. ¶355. "*Sherlock,*" William Sherlock (1641?–1707), author of *Practical Discourse concerning Death* (1689).

355. THE WILD HONEY SUCKLE (pub. 1786), and (356) ON A HONEY BEE (pub. 1809) are from the edition of 1809; (356) TO A CATY-DID (pub. 1815) from that of 1815. Like Burns, Freneau found another expression of his idea that nature holds the final truth in the whimsical observation of the more humble aspects of her life. ¶356. "*Hezekiah Salem,*" a *nom de plume.* ¶356. "*Charon's boat.*" In Greek mythology Charon was the ferryman who transported the souls of the dead over the the rivers of the underworld.

357. MAN OF NINETY was written in 1788. The Clark text is from the 1809 edition.

358. THE VANITY OF EXISTENCE, and ON THE RELIGION OF NATURE, the one written almost at the beginning (1781) and the other almost at the end (1815) of Freneau's poetic career, show how consistently he maintained his romantic speculation on the enduring power of nature. Texts are from the 1809 and 1815 editions respectively. ¶358. "*To Thyrsis,*" a herdsman in the "Idylls" of Theocritus; a rustic or shepherd; a favorite character in English pastoral poetry.

359. ADVICE TO AUTHORS, and (362) THE SAILOR'S RELIEF are taken direct from the text of the 1788 volume. They are representative of Freneau's use of the Addisonian essay to express American themes, and, in their particular kind of ironical humor, they are characteristic of his lighter vein, in contrast to "The Philosopher of the Forest" papers (*The Freeman's Journal,* 1786–88), which give a prose expression to his naturalistic philosophy. "Advice to Authors" is one of a long series of pleas, by various hands, for a truly American literature, of which we have, in this volume, the essays of Bryant, Channing, and Cooper. Compare also Webster, Ingersoll, and many others. ¶359. "*Mr. Robert Slender,*" a *nom de plume.* ¶359. "*Polite . . . authors,*" literary authors, as opposed to religious or controversial writers. ¶360. "*A subscription for an original work.*" Godfrey's poems and many other books of this day were published by private subscription. ¶361. "*The fate of Diogenes,*" a Greek Cynic philosopher (412–323 B.C.), who lived in a tub, according to Seneca. ¶361. "*Shallopman,*" the man who runs a "shallop," a light, open boat used usually on rivers. ¶362. "*Gloucester Point,*" below Phila. on the Delaware River. ¶363. "*The skuttles barred down,*" "shuttle," a sluiceway, or artificial water passage fitted with a gate. ¶364. "*Grog,*" a mixture of rum and water. ¶364. "*Bell's auction room,*" Phila. ¶364. "*Old Carlisle,*" in Scotland. ¶364. "*Christchurch steeple,*" in Phila. The steeple was in part designed by Benjamin Franklin, and contains a famous set of bells; it served as a landmark after its completion in 1754. ¶365. "*Swede's church,*" Old Swedes' Church, in So. Phila., built 1698–1700. ¶365. "*Black double decked transport . . . the holy see.*" The sailor is using nautical language to describe a large clergyman in black. A "see," in this sense, means a bishop's chair; the "holy see," Rome. ¶365. "*A grey goose,*" probably means a woman, in the sailor's jargon. ¶365. "*Ernulphus's curses,*" Ernulf (1040–1124), English prelate. His *Textus Roffensis* is his most famous work. ¶365. "*Hantipodes,*" "antipodes," the country of those who live diametrically opposite any particular point on the earth's surface.

Royall Tyler (1757–1826)

Tyler is distinguished in the history of American literature by his authorship of the first social comedy written by an American to be produced in America by a professional company. His introduction to drama was

quite accidental. As a young lawyer and army officer, he visited New York City, where he became acquainted with Thomas Wignell, the comedian. *The Contrast*, in which Wignell took the part of Jonathan, was produced at the John Street Theatre on Apr. 16, 1787, and was published in Phila. in 1790. Although he thus originated the stage Yankee and wrote several other plays, Tyler was more versatile than sustained in his literary art. He wrote essays from "The Shop of Colon and Spondee," in association with Joseph Dennie, for *The Eagle; or Dartmouth Sentinel* (1794); he is the author of one of the earliest American novels, *The Algerine Captive* (1797); and he published, in 1809, the mock travelogue, *A Yankey in London*. Most of his work is of the "belles lettres" kind, but he contributed also to the legal profession by his writings and by his services as Chief Justice of the Supreme Court of Vermont (1807–1813) and as professor of jurisprudence in the university of that state (1811–1814). For biography, see A. H. Quinn's *Hist. of Amer. Drama . . . to the Civil War* (1923); H. M. Ellis' *Joseph Dennie* (1915); and *Grandmother Tyler's Book*, ed. by F. Tupper and H. T. Brown (1925).

366. The Contrast was printed first in 1790, and was reprinted by The Dunlap Society (1887) and in *Representative American Plays*, ed. by A. H. Quinn (1917), from which last edition the present text has been taken, with minor alterations in captions, etc., to conform to the style of this series. It is notable as the first American social comedy on the pattern of Goldsmith and Sheridan, but, like Freneau's essays, thoroughly American in theme and spirit. It has been revived several times in recent years. ¶367. "*Pocket-hoop.*" Hoop-skirts were fashionable in America from about 1700. The pocket-hoop, confined to the hips, was introduced about 1750; the bell-hoop about 1730. ¶367. "*The battery,*" a park at the southern tip of Manhattan, fashionable at that time as a promenade. ¶367. "*Buffon . . . Souflee,*" " . . . cannot tell a bit of gauze worn at a woman's neck from a bit of light pastry." ¶367. "*The grave Spectator,*" Addison. ¶368. "*Sir Charles Grandison*" (1753), a novel by Samuel Richardson (1689–1761). ¶368. "*Clarissa Harlow*" (1740), Richardson's most popular novel. ¶368. "*Shenstone,*" William Shenstone (1714–1763), author of *The Schoolmistress* (1742). ¶368. "*The Sentimental Journey*" (1768), by Laurence Sterne (1713–1768). ¶368. "*Lovelace,*" principal male character in *Clarissa Harlow*, a fashionable villain. ¶369. "*Chesterfield's letters,*" the letters of Lord Chesterfield (1694–1773) to his son, pub. in 1774, as a handbook of fashionable etiquette. ¶372. "*Robinson Crusoes*" (1719), by Daniel Defoe (1661–1731). The reading of novels was considered, in the 18th cent., a suitable occupation for sentimental women. ¶373. "*A pipe of Madeira,*" a large cask of Madeira wine. ¶375. "*An old maiden lady's bandbox,*" a cardboard box, originally made for ruffs, but later put to a variety of uses. ¶377. "*The dear Adonises,*" handsome young men. In mythology, Adonis was a beautiful youth, beloved by Venus. ¶377. "*A side-box at the play,*" the fashionable stage box, still seen in older theatres. ¶379. "*Castilian,*" old-fashioned courtly manners. Castile was a kingdom in Spain. ¶379. "*Outré*": unfashionable. ¶379. "*Mall,*" a promenade in New York City. ¶379. "*Ranelagh or Vauxhall,*" pleasure-gardens in London. ¶379. "*Waiter,*" valet. ¶379. "*Sans ceremonie*": without ceremony. ¶380. "*General Shays has sneaked off.*" Daniel Shays (1747–1825), with a small party, took possession of Worcester, and raided Springfield, Mass., in 1786. He was soon overcome, and was pardoned. ¶380. "*Lignum vitæ*": lit. "staff of life." Jonathan refers to the very tough wood of a tropical tree introduced into N. Eng. ¶381. "*Buss,*" kiss; evidently in Jonathan's vocabulary an emphatic form. ¶381. "*New-York Holy Ground,*" slang for the contrary. ¶381. "*Blueskin,*" a mulatto. ¶383. "*Sugar-dram,*" a dram, or a small amount of sugar. ¶385. "*As Madam Ramboulliet did young Stanhope.*" Catherine de Vivonne, Marquise de Rambouillet (1588–1665) founded the salon which later developed into the French Academy. "Young Stanhope" is probably Philip, second Earl of Chesterfield (1633–1713). ¶385. "*Un aimable petit Jonathan*": "a well-behaved little Jonathan," a term applied to a household pet. ¶386. "*The hocus pocus man,*" the magician. ¶387. "*Mr. Joseph,*" Joseph Surface, a character in Sheridan's *School for Scandal* (1777). ¶388. "*Mear, Old Hundred, and Bangor,*" popular names for hymn tunes: "Mear" is probably "Meae animae Amator," "Jesus, lover of my soul;" "Bangor" is "Eternal God, we look to thee;" "Old Hundred" is "All people that on earth do dwell." ¶388. "*Roslin Castle.*" "'Twas in that season of the year," by R. Hewitt, a popular song. ¶388. "*Maid of the Mill,*" a popular song by H. Aïdé. ¶389. "*Little peaceable bundling,*" an

early American method of courting, much criticized by English visitors. ¶390. "*Bumpkin*," slang term for "rustic." ¶394. "*Two penserosos*," meditative people. ¶394. "*Malapropos*," unfitting. ¶396. "*Billet*," letter. ¶398. "*Affetuoso . . . piano . . . fortissimo*," "passionate, soft, very loud;" terms in music. ¶399. "*Chorus of Handel's, at any Abbey-commemoration*" George Frederick Handel (1685–1759) composed many oratorios, and carried choral music to a high point; an abbey is a monastery church. ¶399. "*Gamut*," scale. ¶401. "*Caudle*," a warm drink, made of wine or ale and bread. ¶401. "*Tête-à-tête*," intimate conversation.

Hugh Henry Brackenridge *(1748–1816)*

Brackenridge came to Pennsylvania from Kintyre, Scotland, at the age of five and began his life on the banks of the Susquehanna, at that time the frontier. An education at Princeton, however, turned his eyes eastward, and we think of him now as a judge and an eighteenth-century gentleman rather than as a hardy pioneer. His undergraduate association with Freneau led to the writing of "The Rising Glory of America" (1772), but a far more characteristic product of this friendship, as far as Brackenridge was concerned, is a fragment of a novel in the manner of Smollett and Fielding, entitled "Father Bumbo's Pilgrimage." His first important work was a verse drama, *The Battle of Bunkers-Hill* (1776). The political activities of his undergraduate days bore fruit in the *United States Magazine*, in the first issue of which (Jan., 1779) he expresses his editorial interest in providing a medium for Whig doctrine and for literary effort. After the failure of the magazine in 1780, his pioneer blood asserted itself once more, and he migrated to Pittsburg, where he saw less competition and greater opportunity for distinction in law and politics than in the capital, already crowded with the great. Although he was never a radical member of the new Republican Party, the essays and poems of his middle years, of which there are many in the style of Butler, Swift, and Fielding, reveal the gradual growth of his democratic political sympathies to a full support of Jefferson in 1799. Previously defeated for Congress, he became, in that year, a justice of the Supreme Court of Pennsylvania. Biography and bibliography by C. M. Newlin (1932).

404. [CAPTAIN FARRAGO], (405) [AN ELECTION], (407) [ANOTHER ELECTION], (408) [MODERN PHILOSOPHERS], (410) [A CONVERSION], (411) CONTAINING OBSERVATIONS, (412) [A CONGRESSIONAL DEBATE], and (413) [GREEK AND IRISH] are all from the first volume of *Modern Chivalry*, the central work of Brackenridge's literary career. The text is from the first edition of Part II, which appeared in 1790. This picaresque political satire grew out of the Hudibrastic attacks on demagogues and popular stupidity which Brackenridge had contributed to the newspapers while urging the adoption of the Federal Constitution. It took the form, however, of a narrative satire in the *Don Quixote* tradition, with a Swiftean addiction to digressions. Captain Farrago is an American knight errant, who, with his Irish squire, Teague O'Regan, wanders from the frontier to the seaboard. Celtic wit is mixed with political doctrine in recounting their adventures with the institutions of the East in the first two volumes, which appeared in Philadelphia (1792), and in the third volume, (Pittsburg, 1793). In the fourth (1798), Captain Farrago returns to the West with a new squire, a Scotchman named Duncan. The attack on stupidity in politics is continued, with the Whiskey Rebellion as the central theme. Part II (2 vols., 1804–05) followed a reprint of the earlier narratives in the same year, and centers its attack upon the extremes of Jeffersonianism and the opposition to the judiciary. The whole work was collected and republished in 1815, with a volume of new matter. Throughout, Brackenridge holds the position of a liberal, midway between the extremes of the two parties, and, although defending democratic polity, he is primarily concerned with the ridicule of stupidity in human nature. His work is therefore satire rather than partisan propaganda. ¶404. "*Fifty-three years of age*," "forty-five" in the later revision. ¶405. "*Two kegs of whisky*." It was common, both in England and America at this time, for candidates to offer free drinks to their constituents during election campaigns. ¶405. "*Light-horse men*," soldiers of light cavalry. ¶406. "*Apollo*," Greek god, renowned for manly youth and beauty. ¶406. "*Bacchus*," god of wine. ¶406. "*Manlius*," Marcus Manlius Capitolinus (d. 384 B.C.), deliverer of the Capitol at Rome from the Gauls (390 B.C.). ¶406. "*The Tarpeian*," the Tarpeian Rock, originally the name of the entire Capitoline Hill in Rome, so called in memory of the treason

of the maid Tarpeia during the Sabine siege; later, the part of the cliff from which criminals were thrown. ¶407. "*Babylon,*" the great ancient city of the Euphrates valley, which flourished 2500–500 B.C.; hence any large and prosperous city. ¶407. "*The bog-trotter,*" one who travels over boggy land; used also for the lowest type of Irishman as a term of derision. ¶407. "*Where Phocion came with his plain coat.*" Phocion (402–317 B.C.) was a celebrated Athenian statesman and general of lowly birth, executed in 317 B.C. on a false charge of treason. ¶407. "*Cincinnatus*" (*c.* 519–*c.* 439 B.C.), when appointed dictator of Rome in 458 B.C., was at work in his field. ¶408. "*The Philosophical Society,*" Amer. Phil. Soc., founded in 1744 by Benjamin Franklin in Phila. ¶408. "*Gorum.*" Brackenridge probably has no one original in mind. ¶408. "*Wye river,*" a small river in Md., flowing into Chesapeake Bay. ¶409. "*A Guinea negro,*" negro from the Guinea district, west coast of Africa. ¶409. "*Massa shentiman,*" etc. This was perhaps the earliest attempt to reproduce the negro dialect in fiction. ¶410. "*A Universalist,*" an adherent to Universalism, the theological doctrine that all men will eventually be saved. ¶410. "*The lion . . . the lamb,*" corruption of Isa. xi. 6, "The wolf shall dwell with the lamb, and the leopard shall lie down with the kid; and the calf and the young lion and the fatling together; and a little child shall lead them." ¶410. "*Millenium,*" the period of a thousand years, mentioned in Rev. xx, when goodness is supposed to prevail throughout the world; Christ's second coming; a period when all evil is banished. ¶410. "*The conventicle,*" a meeting or place of meeting for religious purposes, usually secret. ¶411. "*Jeremiah,*" the biblical prophet, was born of a priestly family. ¶411. "*Origen*" (*c.* 185–253 A.D.), one of the Greek fathers of the Church, a prolific writer on theological subjects; his liberal writings caused him to be degraded from a presbyter to a layman in 232 A.D. ¶411. "*Strait gate,*" in Matt. vii. 13, "Enter ye in at the strait gate," etc.; in Luke xiii. 24, "Strive to enter in at the strait gate." ¶411. "*John Knox*" (1505–1572), a great Scottish reformer, founder of the Presbyterian Church in Scotland. ¶411. "*Westminster confession,*" the "Confession of Faith," written by John Knox, approved by Parliament, Aug. 17, 1560, abolishing Roman Catholicism in Scotland. ¶411. "*Dr. Bellamy,*" Joseph Bellamy (1719–1790), Conn. Congregationalist clergyman and author of *True Religion Delineated* (1750). ¶412. "*Congress,*" then meeting in Phila. ¶412. "*The eclipse in the time of Julius Cæsar.*" Cæsar's death, as well as many other great historical events, is associated in tradition with a total eclipse of the sun. ¶412. "*Earthquake at Jamaica.*" A very severe earthquake shook the island of Jamaica in 1692, destroying Port Royal. ¶413. "*The rebellion in Scotland,*" in the reign of Edward I of England (1272–1307), when the great Scottish heroes Wallace and Bruce distinguished themselves. ¶413. "*Nebuchadnezzar,*" king of Babylonia 605–562 B.C. ¶413. "*The University*" of Pennsylvania. ¶413. "*Pedeseque*": Latin *pedes,* a foot-soldier; French *pêdestre,* one who goes on foot. ¶414. "*Erse,*" in 18th cent. literary English, used to mean the Gaelic language of Scotland, or sometimes also of Ireland. ¶415. "*Thucidydes,*" Thucydides (471–401 B.C.), author of the *History of the Peloponnesian War.* ¶415. "*St. Omer's,*" Pas-de-Calais, France; formerly had a Roman Catholic college for British youths. ¶415. "*Craike,*" Greek. ¶415. "*The Creek language,*" the language of the Creek Indians, a branch of the Muskhogean family, originally settled in Alabama and Georgia. ¶415. "*Morea,*" the modern name for the Peloponnesus.

Susanna Haswell Rowson (1762–1824)

The eight years which Susanna Haswell spent as a girl in British army circles in Boston served as her introduction to American society. She married, in 1786, William Rowson, a hardware merchant and a trumpeter in the Royal Horse Guards. In 1793, she returned to this country as a member of a dramatic company and acted for the next three years in Philadelphia, Boston, New York, and Baltimore. Retiring from the stage at the close of her tour, she settled in Boston, where for many years she maintained a school. A weekly magazine, school textbooks, and many poems, plays, and novels are included in her output of these years. Biographies by the Rev. Elias Nason (1859, 1870) and F. W. Halsey, in his edition of *Charlotte Temple* (1905).

416. [The Elopement of Charlotte] is the opening episode of *Charlotte Temple,* or, *Charlotte; a Tale of Truth,* as it was originally called. It appeared in England (1790), and within a few years had sold 25,000 copies. The first American edition, from which the text of this selection has been taken, followed

in 1794. Its innumerable reprints during the next half-century attest its popularity; not even the novels of Scott or Maria Edgeworth could rival it. There seems to be little doubt that it was a "tale of truth": Charlotte has been identified with reasonable certainty as the daughter of an English clergyman, the younger son of the Earl of Derby, and Montraville as a lieutenant in the British army, who brought her to America with him in 1774. Mrs. Rowson states that she heard the story from a Mrs. Beauchamp, and that she knew Montraville personally, although she throws over the story "a slight veil of fiction." A grave in Trinity Churchyard, New York City, is said to be that of the original Charlotte. ¶416. *"Portsmouth,"* seaport in Hampshire, Eng. ¶416. *"Their departure for America."* They were soldiers in the army sent to suppress the revolution in America. ¶416. *"Chichester,"* a city in Sussex, Eng., 14 miles n.e. of Portsmouth. ¶417. *"The Argus's who guarded the Hesperian fruit."* Argus, in Greek mythology, had one hundred eyes and was guardian of the cow into which Io had been metamorphosed. The Hesperides were maidens who guarded the golden apples which Ge (Earth) had given to Hera upon her marriage to Zeus.

Charles Brockden Brown (1771–1810)

Brown was the first American to attempt to make his living by his pen. To his ill-health, he added the other ingredients of the morbidly romantic: a vivid imagination, a consuming zeal, a predilection for the supernatural and the horrible, a semblance of analytical reasoning, and a brooding mind. Of the many Gothic novels and other books which he read as a boy, William Godwin's *Caleb Williams*, a romantic novel of social purpose, seems to have left the most profound impression, providing the theme and the mood for his best work. His Godwinian social ideas were embodied in his first production, *Alcuin* (1798), a dialogue on the rights of women, published after he had abandoned his legal studies and, through the influence of Dr. Elihu Hubbard Smith, moved temporarily from Philadelphia to New York. The Belles Lettres Club in his native city and the Friendly Club of New York, to which Dr. Smith introduced him, provided him with companions of literary interests during these years. *Wieland* (1798), his most unified and powerful novel, was announced as "the first of a series of performances, which the favourable reception of this will induce the author to publish." His literary purpose is briefly stated in the "Advertisement" as "the illustration of some important branches of the moral condition of man," a social aim which is soon lost in the horror of the narrative. The incidents, which are "extraordinary and rare," are justified in that they "will be found to correspond to the known principles of human nature." This acceptance of possible improbability as the root of his art stamps Brown as the immediate precursor of Poe. His pretense at literal authenticity gives the effect of realism in only a few cases, notably in the description of the 1793 yellow fever epidemic in Philadelphia, in *Arthur Mervyn* (1799–1800). Two other novels appeared in 1799, *Ormond* and *Edgar Huntly*, in the latter of which Brown deliberately substitutes "the incidents of Indian hostility, and the perils of the Western wilderness," for the "puerile superstitions and exploded manners, Gothic castles and chimeras" of the English tales he had read. *Jane Talbot* and *Clara Howard*, which followed in 1801, brought his career as a novelist to an end, and he devoted the remainder of his short life to journalism. He had already contributed a series of essays, signed "The Rhapsodist," to *The Columbian Magazine* (Phila., 1789): *The Monthly Magazine and American Review*, published by the Friendly Club (N. Y., 1799–1800), had occupied his attention while he was still experimenting with fiction; and in 1803 he became editor of *The Literary Magazine and American Register* (Phila., 1803–07), which was followed by *The American Register or General Repository of History, Politics, and Science* (1807–1810). *The Literary Magazine* carried, from Nov., 1803, to May, 1804, a tale called *Carwin the Biloquist*, which was never finished. Brown's novels were reprinted in a uniform edition in Boston (1827), and in Phila. (1857 and 1887). *Wieland* was edited by F. L. Pattee (1926), with a critical introduction and bibliography; and *Edgar Huntly* (1928) with an introduction by D. L. Clark. Biography by W. Dunlap (1815). D. L. Clark issued in 1923 an abstract of a projected biography which has not yet appeared. For bibliography, see *CHAL*.

423. [THE YELLOW FEVER] and (424) [THE STRICKEN CITY] are from the first edition (Phila., 1799) of *Arthur Mervyn*. Arthur, a sensitive boy, who, like Brown himself, is not physically strong, arrives in Philadelphia at nightfall on a mission which involves him in subsequent horrors and mental tortures,

and finds the city in the grip of the plague. Compare the realistic horror of Poe's "The Masque of the Red Death." ¶423. "*The Levant,*" the Orient. ¶425. "*Highstreet,*" now Market St. ¶425. "*Schuylkill,*" the Schuylkill River, west of the old city.

426. [THE LIGHT IN THE TEMPLE] includes the whole of the two opening chapters of *Wieland*, from the first edition (N. Y., 1798). Following *Alcuin*, it was Brown's first published novel. For sources, see: C. Van Doren, "Early American Realism," *Nation*, Nov. 12, 1914. The themes of religious fanaticism, cold-blooded malice, and ventriloquism combine to create an involved and mysterious plot. Brown's effort to assign natural causes to supernatural appearances is here illustrated by his explanation that the destroying fire in the temple was caused by spontaneous combustion. The book is written in his usual autobiographical method, here in the form of a long letter. Compare Poe's "The Fall of the House of Usher." ¶427. "*Saxony,*" a German province, formerly an independent kingdom. ¶427. "*The modern poet of the same name,*" Christopher Martin Wieland (1733–1813), German poet and author. ¶428. "*The Albigenses,*" sects in the south of France in the 12th and 13th centuries who dissented from the doctrines of the Church of Rome and were persecuted ruthlessly. ¶428. "*The sect of Camissards,*" French Protestants of the early 18th cent. who figured in an insurrection; so called from their white blouses. ¶431. "*Tuscan columns,*" columns of late Roman origin and quite plain style. ¶431. "*The disciples of Zinzendorf,*" Nikolaus Ludwig Zinzendorf und Pottendorf (1700–1760), German religious reformer, reviver, and organizer of the Moravian Church. ¶432. "*Mettingen,*" Metzingen, a town in the Black Forest, Würtemberg, Germany.

435. [THE CAVERN AND THE PANTHER] is Chapter XV of *Edgar Huntly*, from the first ed. (N. Y., 1799). It is one of the many crises in this swift-moving but somewhat inconsistent tale of horror built about the themes of revenge and sleep-walking. On one of his mysterious nocturnal adventures, Edgar wakes to find himself in a cavern. The suspended dread of unknown forces gives the incident a unity similar to that of Poe's "The Pit and the Pendulum." ¶443. "*English prisoners in Bengal.*" On June 21, 1756, the Nawab of Bengal descended upon the British in Calcutta, India, and took 146 prisoners. He kept them during the night in a cell only 20 ft. sq. (known as "The Black Hole of Calcutta"); in the morning only 23 were alive.

William Bartram (1739–1823)

William Bartram is somewhat less distinguished as a botanist than his father, John Bartram (1699–1777), native of Phila., Quaker, and correspondent of Peter Collinson, the English scientist. But it was the son's description of the Florida crocodiles which stimulated Coleridge's imagination (see J. L. Lowes' *The Road to Xanadu*, 1927), as well as those of Chateaubriand, Wordsworth, and many others. Between 1773 and 1777, he was enabled by Dr. John Fothergill, an English Quaker and botanist, to study the wild life of the southeastern part of the United States. The result of this trip was his *Travels through North and South Carolina, Georgia, East and West Florida, the Cherokee Country, the extensive territories of the Muscogulges, or Creek Confederacy, and the Country of the Chactaws* (1791). Biography by N. B. Fagin (1933); bibliography by J. H. Barnhart in the supplement to *Bartonia*, XII (Dec. 31, 1931). See also W. Darlington's *Memoir of John Bartram and Humphrey Marshall* (1849), and the bibliographical note by Lane Cooper in the *D.A.B.* The *Travels* were edited by Mark Van Doren (1928).

445. [THE FIGHT WITH THE CROCODILES] is the famous passage from Part II, Chapter V, of Bartram's *Travels* (first ed., Phila., 1791). Proceeding up the St. Juan River, in East Florida, the explorer has passed Lake George and is penetrating further inland. ¶445. "*Corypha palma,*" a genus of gigantic East Indian fan palms. ¶445. "*Magnolia grandiflora,*" a genus of trees having aromatic bark and large, fragrant, white, pink, or purple flowers. ¶445. "*Live Oak,*" an evergreen oak in southern U. S., used much in shipbuilding. ¶445. "*Callicarpa,*" a large genus of shrubs, having berries; some are called mulberries. ¶445. "*Myrica cerifera,*" a large genus of aromatic shrubs. ¶445. "*Hibiscus spinifex,*" widely distributed shrubs with showy flowers. ¶445. "*Wild lime,*" a tree found in southern U. S., valued for its fruit. ¶446. "*The Cabbage tree,*" any of several trees, the heart of which is eaten like a cabbage by the natives of Australia. ¶447. "*The Pistia,*" a kind of water lily. ¶447. "*Nymphea,*" small plants widely distributed in temperate regions; yellow pond lilies. ¶447. "*Clouds of smoke,*" the steamy breath of the alligator, suggesting an expla-

nation of the medieval dragon. ¶450. "*Pass of St. Juans,*" along St. John's River, in Fla., near Lake George.

St. John de Crèvecœur (1735–1813)

The description "an American farmer," which Crèvecœur (Hector St. John, or Michel-Guillaume Jean de Crèvecœur) applies to himself, tells only a small part of the story of his varied life. He lived on a farm, "Pine Hill," in Orange County, N. Y., only for the few years immediately before and after the Revolutionary War, and even then he was far from being a typical inhabitant of the rural community of which he was a part. He had early emigrated from his native France to Canada, and before he finally settled in the English colonies about 1759, he had explored the wilderness beyond the Great Lakes, been a lieutenant under Montcalm at Quebec, learned the habits of the Indians by living with them, and drawn a map of New France. Ten years later (1769) he married and bought his acres in the region dominated by the Dutch and English land-holders. Although a small farmer, his aristocratic sympathies led him, unlike most of his compatriots of French blood, to join the Loyalist cause. For this he was forced finally to seek the protection of the British Army in New York, only to be imprisoned under the suspicion of being an American spy. He returned to France in 1780, and published in London his *Letters from an American Farmer* (1782), which Hazlitt praised in *The Edinburgh Review* (Oct., 1829), for its vivid representation of "not only the objects, but the feelings of the new country." American and French editions followed, and the work had wide influence. It finds its place in American literary history as a collection of familiar essays in the tradition of Montaigne, as a part of the revival of interest in nature which contributed to our romantic movement, and as an interpretation of the life and thought of the Revolutionary period. In 1783, its author came to America as French consul to New York, New Jersey, and Connecticut, only to find that his wife was dead, that an Indian raid had devastated his old home, and that his two children had been adopted by a gentleman in Boston. In 1790, he returned once more to France, where he published his *Voyage dans la haute Pennsylvanie et dans l'état de New York* (1801). Many of his *Letters* had been prepared for publication in a later volume, but remained in manuscript in the family archives in France until their discovery by H. L. Bourdin, and their publication, under the editorship of M. Bourdin, R. H. Gabriel, and S. T. Williams, as *Sketches of Eighteenth Century America* (1925). Biographies (in French) by R. de Crèvecœur (1883), and (in English) by J. P. Mitchell (1916). See also the introductions to *Sketches*, and to modern editions of the *Letters* (1902, etc.).

451. WHAT IS AN AMERICAN? is the first part of Letter III of *Letters from an American Farmer* (first ed., London, 1782). It was written before its author's hardships had dimmed his idealism, and it expresses the Jeffersonian dream of an agrarian civilization in which individual liberty is unhampered by social or political restraints, and in which every man is a gentleman. ¶453. "*Ubi panis ibi patria*": "Where the bread is, there is the fatherland." ¶453. "*Alma Mater*": "dear mother," usually applied to a school, but in this case to a country.

454. MARTHA'S VINEYARD is the latter part of Letter VI (same edition). The island was a center of the whaling industry, even in Crèvecœur's day, and his essay furnishes an interesting background for Melville's *Moby Dick*, written seventy or more years later. ¶455. "*Nattick,*" of Nantucket. ¶456. "*Spermaceti whales,*" yield spermaceti, a waxy substance which separates from the oil.

457. ANT-HILL TOWN was written from Va. in 1769, and is included in *Sketches* (1925), from which this text is taken. In it Crèvecœur is more strictly the natural history essayist and less the commentator on men and ideas. This is perhaps his most charming and characteristic mood. ¶457. "*'Tis a grove of Tempé,*" a valley in eastern Thessaly, Greece, celebrated in ancient times for its beauty. ¶457. "*A Druidical temple.*" The Druids were the priests of the ancient Celts, whose temples were oak-groves, the oak being the symbol of the one Supreme God to them. ¶458. "*Potent Madeira,*" strong wine; an important product of the island of Madeira, off the coast of Africa. ¶459. "*Zoroaster,*" founder of the Perso-Iranian national religion, which prevailed from about 500 B.C. to 600 A.D. ¶459. "*The true Shekinah,*" the visible manifestation of the Divine Majesty. ¶459. "*The Keblah,*" the Kiblah, the point toward which the Mohammedans turn in prayer. ¶461. "*Buffon.*" *Cf.* Jefferson's *Notes on Virginia*, p. 280. ¶462. "*Pythagorean disposition.*" The followers of Pythagoras had great respect for animal life because of their belief in reincarnation.

John James Audubon (1785–1851)

Audubon has a greater claim to distinction as an ornithologist and artist than as a writer, but the incidental prose which he wrote in connection with his studies and pictures of bird life in North America, as well as his journals and letters, accord him a place as an essayist in American literary history. Son of a French merchant planter and a Creole woman, Audubon was born at Les Cayes, Santo Domingo; he studied drawing under David in Paris, and came to America in 1803. After a time spent near Phila., he settled in Louisville, Ky. When his business failed in 1819, he turned to art for a livelihood, and the idea of studying and drawing birds occurred to him. The next years were spent in exploring the Ohio and Mississippi valleys, and in a journey to England and Scotland in quest of a publisher. His *Birds of America*, of which his *Ornithological Biography* (1831–39) is the text, began to appear in 1827, and was completed in 1839. After his return to America, he settled on the lower Hudson, and prepared, in collaboration with John Bachman, his *Viviparous Quadrupeds of North America*. His journals, which include the essays in his other works, were pub. in 1897, and a selection from the sixty essays scattered through the first three volumes of the *Orn. Biog.* were reprinted in 1926 as *Delineations of American Scenery and Character*. Biography by F. H. Herrick (1917).

463. A Flood, and (467) The Florida Keys are representative of the informal essays with which the *Orn. Biog.* (1831–39) is interlarded. They are respectively from Vols. I and II of the first ed., pub. in Phila. ¶463. "*The Red River*," enters the Mississippi about 40 mi. below Natchez, Miss. ¶463. "*The Falls of the Ohio*," near Louisville, Ky. ¶464. "*Sawyers and planters*," trees which have fallen into a stream with their branches projecting so that they rise and fall with changes in the level of the stream. ¶465. "*Levees*," mud banks along a river to prevent floods. ¶465. "*Crevasse*," a deep crevice or opening in an embankment or levee along a river. ¶465. "*The City of Natchez*," in Miss. ¶465. "*Natchitochez*," Natchitoches, La., situated on the Red River, 103 miles w. of Natchez, Miss. ¶466. "*Short-cuts*." *Cf.* Mark Twain's account in *Life on the Mississippi*. ¶467. "*Ibises*," wading birds related to the herons. ¶467. "*Godwits*," any of several species of long-billed wading birds of the snipe family. ¶467. "*Herons*," wading birds with long necks and long tapering bills. ¶467. "*Fish-Crows*," a species of crow found in southeastern U. S. which feeds principally on fish. ¶467. "*Frigate Pelicans*," long-winged birds noted for their capacity for long flights and rapacious habits, found mainly in the West Indies. ¶467. "*Gallinules*," common aquatic birds found in Florida. ¶467. "*Flamingo*," an aquatic bird having very long legs and neck, web feet, and a broad bill. ¶468. "*Doo-fish*." The variation in the spelling is the author's. ¶468. "*Balacoudas*," possibly "barracudas," pike-like fish found off Florida coast. ¶468. "*Seminole Indians*," a tribe of Indians, former members of the Creek Confederacy, who emigrated into Florida in the late 18th century.

William Cullen Bryant (1794–1878)

In his own day, Bryant was regarded as America's first poet and as one of her greatest editors. Part, at least, of this influence may be attributed to the commanding dignity of his personality and to circumstances of his environment which called him to fill the demands of a young nation for a culture of her own. His youth was spent in the wooded Berkshire hills, at Cummington, in western Massachusetts, where he had been born, Nov. 3, 1794, of a race of sturdy farmers with ancestry leading directly back to the Plymouth settlers. Calvinism had become milder in these later days, but the Bible, a stern ideal for personal conduct, and a belief in hardy manhood disciplined the somewhat frail boy to the vigorous living of his ancestry and of his parents. The concentrated intensity of his mind dwelt, in these formative years, upon the beauties of the woods and fields and streams around him, and made nature the central emotional experience of his youth. His tendency toward contemplation was further fostered by a reading of Kirke White, Blair, Bishop Porteus, Cowper, and Wordsworth, and by an early ambition to become a poet himself. In "Thanatopsis" (1817), we find an impassioned expression of this mood, grown from deep roots in the native soil, but mellowed by the broodings of the English "grave-yard" poets. Except for *The Embargo* (1808), a Federalistic satire which its author later repudiated, this was his earliest ambitious work. It is a pronouncement of the mood and message which shaped and limited most of his subsequent poetry. The years 1817–1826 produced other poems and critical prose in *The United States Literary Gazette*, and other periodicals, notably the essay on American poets (1818). He was now acknowledged to be America's leading poet, and was asked to read a course of four lectures on poetry before the New York Athenæum [and Society Library] (1825). These lectures, which William Charvat considers to be central documents in the history of American literary criticism of the period 1810–1835 [forthcoming study], express not only Bryant's own theory of poetry, but that of his many lesser contemporaries, and, to some extent, that of Longfellow and the Cambridge group. In 1826, Bryant became assistant editor of *The New York Evening Post*, and three years later assumed full editorial responsibility and part ownership. For almost half a century he was one of America's leading journalists, liberal in views and conservative in methods; and he gave to his paper an influence and a financial stability which were the envy of his competitors. Founded by Hamilton, the *Post* had a strong Federalistic tradition, for which Bryant substituted a policy of Jacksonian democracy and anti-Whiggism. In later years, he became "black Republican," supported Lincoln in his more extreme policies, and fought for abolition. On the deaths of Irving and of Cooper, he was asked to deliver memorial addresses, a testimony to the respect in which he was held as a man of letters, even after poetry had become to him little more than an avocation. He found relaxation in Roslyn, his home on Long Island, and in pleasure trips to Europe, his impressions of which are reflected in his journalistic travel letters, collected and pub. in 1851, 1859, 1869. His last ambitious undertaking in poetry was a blank verse translation of Homer (1870–73). His volume of *Poems* (1821) was enlarged, rearranged, and republished in 1832, at the same time as an English edition with an introduction by Washington Irving. Later volumes of poetry were: *The Fountain and other Poems* (1842); *The White-Footed Deer and Other Poems* (1844); *Thirty Poems* (1864); *Hymns* (1864); *The Iliad* (1870–71); *The Odyssey* (1871–73); and *The Flood of Years* (1878). Other volumes, which appeared in 1860, 1863, 1865, 1871, 1872, 1873, and 1874, contain no new work. In addition to his orations and travel letters, his principal prose work is *Reminiscences of The Evening Post* (1851). Much of his prose has never been republished from the columns of the *Post* and the many literary collections which he edited or to which he contributed. His writings in prose and verse were collected and edited, with a two-volume biography, by his son-in-law, Parke Godwin (1883–89). See also the shorter biographies by J. Bigelow (1890) and W. A. Bradley (1905); J. G. Wilson's *Bryant and His Friends* (1886); Allen Nevins' *The Evening Post* (1922); various recent articles by Tremaine McDowell and others; and the bibliography in the "Roslyn Edition" of the poems.

470. [American Poetry] is from the first appearance of the essay in the *N. Am. Rev.* for July, 1818. It is included in Vol. I of the collected *Prose* (1884). ¶470. *"Our literature has fallen under unmerited contumely."* See Sydney Smith's article in *The Edinburgh Rev.* (Dec., 1818). ¶471. *"Rev. John Adams,"* (1704–1740), New England clergyman, poet, and "master of nine languages." ¶471. *"Joseph Green, Esq.,"* (1706–1780), Boston poet and revolutionary. ¶472. *"Francis Hopkinson,"* see pp. 316–324. ¶472. *"Dr. Church,"* Benjamin Church (1734–1776), physician, author, traitor, poet. ¶472. *"Philip Freneau,"* see pp. 335–365. ¶472. *"The Connecticut poets,"* see pp. 289–316. ¶472. *"Humphreys,"* David Humphreys (1752–1818), Conn. poet, soldier, and diplomat, one of the "wits." ¶472. *"Hopkins,"* Lemuel Hopkins (1750–1801), Conn. poet, physician, and soldier; another of the "wits." ¶472. *"Butler." Hudibras* (1663–68), by Samuel Butler (1612–1680). ¶473. *"His fable,"* his theme, or story, is that of the Bible. ¶473. *"Mr. Dennie,"* see pp. 324–29. ¶473. *"Watts' Version of the Psalms."* Sir Isaac Watts (1674–1748), author of the *Psalms of David* (1719), which went through many editions. ¶473. *"Dr. Johnson,"* Samuel Johnson (1709–1784); the quotation is from the "Life of Watts," *Lives of the English Poets* (1779–1781). ¶474. *"Darwin,"* Erasmus Darwin (1731–1802), English naturalist and poet, grandfather of Charles Darwin. ¶474. *"The late popular poets of England."* Bryant probably has Pope and his followers in mind.

475. On the Nature of Poetry is from the first of the *Lectures on Poetry*, delivered in Apr., 1825, before the N. Y. Athenæum, and published in the *Prose* (1884) from notes. The text is from this ed. ¶475. *"The ancient critics,"* particularly Aristotle in the *Poetics.* ¶477. *"Milton describes the general mother," Paradise Lost*, VIII, 59. ¶477. *"The same poet . . . speaking of Satan," Paradise Lost*, I, 601 ff. ¶478. *"The wrath of Achilles,"* the opening theme of Homer's *Iliad.* ¶478.

"*Lear . . . addresses his daughter*," *King Lear*, IV, vii, 59 ff. ¶478. "*The remorse of Othello*," after he has discovered the innocence of Desdemona; in *Othello*, V, ii, 259 ff. ¶478. "*The terrible consciousness of guilt which haunts Macbeth*," following the murders which he has plotted and committed; in *Macbeth*, esp. V. ¶478. "*The lamentations of Antony*," after the death of Cæsar; in *Julius Cæsar*, III, i, 253 ff. ¶478. "*The devoted love of Juliet*," for Romeo, *Romeo and Juliet*, II, ii, 84 ff. ¶478. "*The self-sacrificing affection of Cleopatra*," to Antony, in *Antony and Cleopatra*, esp. I, iii. ¶478. "*The penitence of Adam*," *Paradise Lost*, esp. XI. ¶478. "*The sorrows of Eve*," *Paradise Lost*, esp. XI. ¶478. "*When the poet introduces Ophelia*," *Hamlet*, IV, v, 42. ¶480. "*When Shakespeare says of mercy*," *Merchant of Venice*, IV, i, 184–85. ¶480. "*Passages also in Milton*," *Paradise Lost*, V, 117–19. ¶480. "*Example from Cowper*," *The Task*, V, 187 ff.

482. THANATOPSIS. A somewhat shorter version of this poem, prefaced by a separate poem on death, appeared in the *N. Am. Rev.* for Sept., 1817. It was revised in *Poems* (1821), reprinted many times, and pub. separately in 1874. It is Bryant's most popular and characteristic poem, and was written in its first form in 1811. This text, and that of the subsequent selections, is from the "Roslyn Edition" of the *Poems* (1903). ¶483. "*Barcan*," refers to the region of Barca, in northern Africa, most of which is a barren desert. ¶483. "*The Oregon*," the Indian name for the river now called the Columbia.

484. INSCRIPTION FOR THE ENTRANCE TO A WOOD, written in 1815, appeared as "A Fragment" in the *N. Am. Rev.* for Sept., 1817.

484. TO A WATERFOWL, written in 1815, appeared in the *N. Am. Rev.* for Mar., 1818.

485. GREEN RIVER and (486) A WINTER PIECE were published in 1821 in *The Idle Man*, a periodical edited by R. H. Dana. ¶486. "*The zephyr*," the west wind, or any gentle breeze. ¶486. "*Sylvan air*," air from the forest. ¶488. "*Their sluices sealed.*" "Sluice" means a "water-gate," or any door or covering.

489. THE YELLOW VIOLET was first pub. in the 1821 volume.

489. MONUMENT MOUNTAIN was contributed to *The U. S. Literary Gazette*, Sept. 15, 1824. The legend of the Indian maid who, for unrequited or forbidden love, throws herself from a high mountain is found, in different versions, in many parts of U. S. The scene is a cliff near Great Barrington, Mass. ¶490. "*The beetling verge*," overhanging cliff. ¶491. "*Ears of maize*," ears of Indian corn. ¶492. "*Indians from the distant West*." The Indians of N. Y. and N. Eng. retreated westward to Michigan and northward to Canada.

492. A FOREST HYMN was written at Great Barrington just before Bryant left to assume his first editorial duties in New York. It was published in *The Literary Gazette* for Apr. 1, 1825.

494. JUNE appeared in *The Atlantic Souvenir* for 1826. The actual publication date of such annuals is always the year previous.

495. I CANNOT FORGET WITH WHAT FERVID DEVOTION was an earlier poem published in *The N. Y. Rev.*, of which Bryant was one of the editors, in Feb., 1826. It is addressed to the spirit of passing youth rather than to any particular person. ¶495. "*Deep-cloven fells*," mountains with deep gorges.

495. THE PAST appeared in *The Talisman* for 1829 (1828), and (496) THE EVENING WIND in the same annual for 1830 (1829).

497. SONG OF MARION'S MEN was published in *The N. Y. Mirror*, Nov., 1831. Marion was the leader of a small band which harassed the British army in the South, 1778–79. ¶498. "*Santee*," a river in S. Car., southeast of Columbia.

498. OH FAIREST OF THE RURAL MAIDS was addressed to Fanny Fairchild, his wife, and is the only one that Bryant has cared to print of the several poems he wrote to the girl whom he met at a village sociable at Great Barrington. It was first included in the 1832 volume.

498. TO THE FRINGED GENTIAN in the 1832 volume. ¶498. "*The ground-bird's*," any of several thrush-like birds.

498. THE PRAIRIES was written in 1832 after a trip to Illinois, and was published in *The Knickerbocker Mag.*, Dec., 1833. ¶499. "*The prairie-hawk*," a fairly large bird, found in western U. S. ¶499. "*The fountains of Sonora*." Sonora is a state in northwestern Mexico. ¶499. "*Pentelicus*," a mountain in Attica, Greece, famous for its marble. ¶499. "*Parthenon*," the temple of Pallas, at Athens, Greece, begun about 450 B.C. ¶500. "*The mound-builders*," the North American aborigines who built extensive burial and fortification mounds in the Ohio and Miss. valleys. ¶500. "*The prairie-wolf*," the coyote. ¶500. "*The gopher*," any of several burrowing rodents about the size of a rat. ¶500. "*Missouri's springs*," the source of the Missouri River in Montana. ¶500. "*The Oregon*," the Columbia

River. ¶500. "*The bison,*" the buffalo. ¶501. "*The savannas,*" treeless plains, open spaces.

501. OH MOTHER OF A MIGHTY RACE was written after a visit to the West in 1846 and was first pub. in *Graham's Mag.*, July, 1847, when its author was in the midst of the slavery and Free Soil controversies.

502. ROBERT OF LINCOLN was written at Roslyn, Bryant's home on Long Island, in 1855, and was pub. in *Putnam's Mag.* in March of that year. ¶502. "*Quaker wife,*" the female bobolink, so called because of her plain yellowish-brown plumage.

503. THE DEATH OF LINCOLN is Bryant's tribute to the man whom he had introduced at Cooper Union, N. Y., when Lincoln was campaigning for the presidency. It was published in the *Atlantic*, Jan., 1866.

James Gates Percival (1795–1856)

"The son of a Kensington, Conn., physician, Percival was a scholarly recluse who believed that 'poetry should be a sacred thing, not to be thrown away on the dull and low realities of this life' [*Clio No. I*, p. vi.]. He graduated with distinction from Yale Medical Institution in 1820. After failing as a physician, he became a professional poet, publishing *Poems* (1821), *Clio No. I* (1822), *Prometheus Part II* (1822), *Clio No. II* (1822), *Poems* (1823, 1824), and *Clio No. III* (1827). Having become engrossed in botanical, geological, and philological studies, he surrendered his poetical ambitions, publishing before his death only *The Dream of a Day* (1843), translations from almost every known European language. He edited Vicesimus Knox's *Elegant Extracts* (1826), corrected Malte Brun's geography (1834), and made the first geological survey of Connecticut, laying down in his *Report* (1842) the theory of the curvilinear arrangement of trap. As assistant to Noah Webster, he contributed much that was valuable in scientific and etymological lore to the *American Dictionary* (1828). He died while engaged as State Geologist of Wisconsin. His poetry was highly regarded by Willis, Bryant, and Whittier, and was popular in in its day." (Note by Harry R. Warfel.)

504. NEW-ENGLAND first appeared in *Clio No. I* (1822). Its description of nature, in contrast to Bryant's, is Byronic in its lack of detail. ¶504. "*Bunker's height,*" Bunker Hill, near Boston, the scene of a battle in the American Revolution, June 17, 1775.

Carlos Wilcox (1794–1827)

The Rev. Carlos Wilcox, minister of Congregational churches in Hartford and Danbury, Conn., showed perhaps more promise as a poet of nature than any of his contemporaries except Bryant. The son of a farmer, he graduated from Middlebury College in 1813, and immediately entered the ministry. A sincere religious feeling is reflected in his only volume of verse, *The Age of Benevolence*, the first part of which appeared in 1822. Extracts from later books of this poem and of another, *The Religion of Taste*, were included in the *Remains*, which was published the year after his early death in 1827. This latter volume contains also many of his sermons and a memoir.

504. THE AGE OF BENEVOLENCE, and (506) THE RELIGION OF TASTE are selections from the fragments in *Remains* (1827), from which this text is taken. ¶505. "*The Yellow-hammer,*" a bright yellow bird, sometimes called the "flicker."

Edward Coote Pinkney (1802–1828)

Pinkney's short and adventurous life provides a suitable background for his romantic poetry, among the best produced in America at this period. He was born of American parents in London, where his father, William Pinkney of Maryland, was United States agent for the adjustment of claims under the Jay Treaty of 1794; and he was a boy of eight when he was first brought to this country. The period 1815–1824 was spent in the Navy, most of it at sea, but he seems to have found time for both love and poetry. A short and unsuccessful legal career ended in a reënlistment in the Navy and a trip to Mexican waters, from which he returned broken in health. When *The Marylander* was started on Dec. 5, 1827, Pinkney was announced as its editor, and to it he contributed a number of his poems. His fiery temperament led him to interpret a statement in the Jacksonian *Philadelphia Mercury* as a personal insult, and he challenged its editor, Stephen Simpson, to a duel, the outcome of which act was an appearance in a Philadelphia police court two months before his death. A fragment of a long poem, *Rodolph*, appeared in 1823, and the most widely known of his poems were collected and pub. in 1825. To these were added many others reprinted from periodicals, together with some prose, and a biographical and critical introduction, in a volume edited by T. O. Mabbott and F. L. Pleadwell (1926).

507. THE VOYAGER'S SONG appeared in the 1825 volume. The present text is from the ed. of 1926. The theme is based on Ponce de Leon's quest for the Fountain of Youth. ¶507. "*Isle of Bimini*," the name given to Florida on the early maps; to the West Indians, an island or region to the north, location uncertain. The "fountain of youth" was reported to be in this mythical island. ¶507. "*Ponce de Leon*" (1460–1521), Spanish soldier, conqueror of Porto Rico and discoverer of Florida. He died in his quest for the Island of Bimini. ¶507. "[*William*] *Robertson's* [*History of*] *America*," William Robertson (1721–1793), Scottish historian. ¶507. "*Potable gold streams*," "aurum potable," the alchemist's elixir of life. ¶507. "*Gadara's founts*," from which Eros and Anteros (true and false love) were raised by the philosopher Iamblicus (*cf.* Byron's *Manfred*, II, ii, 92–93). ¶507. "*Love's genii*," spirits of love. ¶507. "*Miranda*," the admired one (*cf.* Shakespeare's *The Tempest*). ¶507. "*Roman maid*," Tarpeia, who, bargaining for their golden bracelets, was crushed by the shields of the Sabine soldiers (Livy I, xi). ¶508. "*Passion's lees*," the sediment, the remainder, as the "lees of wine."

508. A SERENADE and A HEALTH are among the love poems of the 1825 volume, and are probably addressed to Georgiana McCausland, whom he married in 1824, although there are other claimants for the distinction. The text is from the 1926 edition.

Richard Henry Wilde (1789–1847)

Like Percival, Wilde was something of a scholar and a man of affairs as well as a writer of lyric poetry. Born in Dublin, he was brought to America in 1797 by his father, a hardware merchant, who died in 1802. The mother, from whom Wilde apparently inherited his poetic gift, moved to Georgia, and the boy studied law and was admitted to the bar of South Carolina in 1809. A political career which placed him in the House of Representatives, a trip to Europe in 1835–1840, and a professorship in the University of Louisiana are the principal facts of his life. While abroad, he conducted researches on Tasso and Dante in the libraries of Italy, the results of which he published in 1842. His poetry, which appears to have been very popular when it was printed in numerous journals, has never been collected; his only pub. volume being a long poem, *Hesperia*, ed. by his son (1867). There is a brief monograph by C. C. Jones, Jr. (1885), and much incidental information about his life in Anthony Barclay's *Wilde's Summer Rose* (1871).

509. MY LIFE IS LIKE THE SUMMER ROSE. The story of "The Lament of the Captive," as this poem was first called, is almost as romantic as the poem itself. It was written as the beginning of a longer work inspired by the exploits of Wilde's brother James, just returned from Florida; but the death of the latter in a duel prevented its completion. It was set to music without its author's permission, and became one of the most popular songs of the day. Anthony Barclay, a friend of Wilde's, tells, in a monograph pub. by the Ga. Hist. Soc. (Savannah, 1871), of the curious results of a practical joke which he played on the author. An Irish poet had already claimed priority for the lyric, and Barclay, to make the controversy seem more absurd, translated the verses into Greek and attributed them to Alcæus. The joke was taken seriously, and it was many years before Wilde was exonerated from the charge of plagiarism. The present text, from Griswold, is that most frequently quoted and sung. The text printed by Jones (1885) varies in minor respects and in the last line, which reads: "But none shall e'er lament for me." ¶509. "*Tampa's desert strand*," Tampa, Fla.

509. TO THE MOCKING BIRD. The text of this popular poem is from Griswold. ¶509. "*Yorick*," the king's jester, whose skull prompts Hamlet's soliloquy in the grave scene, *Hamlet*, V, i, 202 ff. ¶509. "*Abbot of Mis-rule*," a mock character in old English revels. ¶509. "*The melancholy Jacques*," a meditative or "melancholy" character in *As You Like It*.

John Howard Payne (1791–1852)

The close personal friend of Washington Irving, and a collaborator with him in two plays, *Richelieu* and *Charles the Second*, Payne is better remembered as an actor and dramatist than as a poet. Born in New York, he was early lured by the theatre away from the business interests of his father. In 1805–06, he edited *The Thespian Mirror*, and was introduced to the literary group of the city, of which Brockden Brown was then a member. His début on the stage in 1809 was in the character of "Young Norval" in the tragedy of *Douglas*, a part for which his attractive personality made him particularly suited. His success was so great that he never again equalled it, and he was known as "Young Norval" for the rest of his life. On Friday, June 4, 1813, he acted the part again at the Theatre Royal, Drury Lane; but after appearing in twenty-two parts in five years, he left the stage, and turned to the adaptation and writing of plays. His tragedy of *Brutus* (1818) held the stage for many years, and he wrote many other popular successes, among them the opera *Clari* (1823) which contained his famous song, "Home, Sweet Home." Much of his time was spent in Paris, and he was intimate with Irving during the period of their collaboration, the latter for a time occupying his apartment while he was away in London. Editorial activities after his return to America in 1832 took him to Washington, and in 1842, he was appointed consul at Tunis, where he died. Biographies by G. Harrison (1885); and W. T. Hanson (1913).

509. HOME, SWEET HOME is here printed, from Harrison, in the form in which it was originally written, and not as the song in the opera *Clari*. The third and fourth stanzas were added when he made a copy of the poem for a relative in London, Mrs. Bates.

Fitz-Greene Halleck (1790–1867)

When William Godwin asked Fenimore Cooper what America had produced so far in poetry, the latter quoted "something of Bryant's and a little of 'Alnwick Castle'" by Halleck. These two were America's leading poets in 1828, the first to carry her fame abroad; and yet Halleck's name does not appear in a recent anthology of American poetry. Neither circumstance gauges the actual worth of his verse. Born in Guilford, Conn., of English pioneer stock, he went down to New York in 1811 in search of employment, and there became friendly with Joseph Rodman Drake. Miscellaneous verse contributed chiefly to newspapers left the two still unknown outside of a small circle until 1819 when they began their "Croaker" verses in *The New York Evening Post* and *The National Advocate*. Satire—spicy, personal, and fearless—in memorable jingles took the fancy of the town, and Croaker and Co. was famous overnight. It was only a step to the more ambitious *Fanny* (1819); but Drake died the next year, and Croaker, Junior, dropped the name and went abroad. "Marco Bozzaris" (1825) was the result; for Halleck, like Irving, was civilized by Europe to the cost of much of his humor. The 1827 edition of his poems bore witness to his theory that "a poet has nothing to do with the facts of things, for he must continually deny them." Instead of New York society, he sang of Scottish castles and Greek heroes. Of his later poems, "The Field of the Grounded Arms" (in *The Legendary*, 1828) and "Red Jacket," (in *The Talisman*, 1829) brought him the most fame. From 1832 until his death, he was, next to Bryant, the most renowned of our poets, and one of the most popular lions of Knickerbocker society. In 1877, his statue, the first to be erected to an American poet, was unveiled in Central Park. His poems were edited by J. G. Wilson (1869); and his life written by Wilson in the same year. Biography and bibliography by N. F. Adkins (1930).

510. MARCO BOZZARIS is in celebration of the leader of the Greek forces (born *c.* 1788), who fell, Aug. 20, 1823, in the war for Greek independence against the Turks. American sympathy with the cause found immediate expression in popular plays and poems. Halleck's poem was probably written as early as 1824, and was pub. in the first issue (June, 1825) of *The New York Review and Athenæum Magazine*, edited by W. C. Bryant and H. J. Anderson. The text of this and the other Halleck poems are from the collected ed. of 1869. ¶510. "*His Suliote band.*" The Suliotes are a Greco-Albanian people who settled in Suli and fought the Turks in the 18th century; they were subdued in 1822. ¶510. "*Old Platæa's day.*" Platæa was a city in ancient Greece; engaged in many wars, including Marathon in 490 B.C. ¶511. "*Moslem,*" the Turks. ¶511. "*The world-seeking Genoese,*" Columbus.

512. ON THE DEATH OF JOSEPH RODMAN DRAKE was written soon after the event, Sept. 21, 1820; Wilson states that it was written the same day on a blank leaf of a manuscript collection of Drake's poems. Halleck is said to have remarked to De Kay, when they were returning from the funeral, "There will be less sunshine for me hereafter, now that Joe is gone." The poem was first pub. in *The Literary and Scientific Repository and Critical Review*, Jan., 1821.

512. FANNY, a longer poem in the manner of the "Croaker" verses, appeared anonymously in 1819, but was immediately recognized as the work of a member of the firm. It at once reflects Halleck's serio-comic Knickerbocker

mood, his literary kinship with Irving, and Byron's *Beppo*. A new edition, with some additional verses, appeared in 1821. ¶512. "*Your Goth and Vandal.*" Germanic tribes which invaded Rome; here, social barbarians. ¶513. "*Qu'en dira-t-on?*": "What will they (people) say (or do) about it?" ¶513. "*Broadway or Park Place,*" New York's then fashionable streets. ¶513. "*Madame Catilani,*" Angelica Catalani (1780–1849), Italian soprano stage-singer. ¶513. "*The Battery,*" a park of about twenty acres at the southern extremity of New York City, near the site of an old Dutch fort, at one time a fashionable quarter. ¶514. "*Wallack looked extremely well in Rolla.*" James William Wallack (1795–1864), Anglo-American actor, played a wide range of parts, especially in romantic drama and refined comedy. "*Rolla*" was a character in Kotzebue's play, *The Spaniards of Peru*, known in English as Sheridan's *Pizarro*. ¶514. "*Mr. Simpson,*" Edmund Simpson (1784–1848), Anglo-American theatre-manager and actor. ¶514. "*Bas bleu*": literally, "deep blue"; here means a person of genuine intellectual interests. ¶514. "*The Croakers,*" Halleck and Drake. ¶514. "*Dr. Chalmers',*" Thomas Chalmers (1780–1847), Glasgow (Scotland) theologian, preacher, and philanthropist; author of many books. ¶514. "*Woodworth's Cabinet,*" Samuel Woodworth (1785–1842), American poet. ¶514. "*Salmagundi,*" a humorous periodical, pub. in 1807 by Washington Irving, William Irving, and J. K. Paulding, later pub. (1819) by Paulding alone. ¶514. "*Griscom's conversaziones,*" John Griscom (1774–1852), American educator and author; for a time a member of Halleck's group in New York City. ¶514. "*Words, to the witches in Macbeth unknown. Hydraulics,*" etc., not included among the strange words and phrases used by the witches in Macbeth (esp. I, i), but new to science in the late 18th century. ¶514. "*Tappan Sea,*" an expansion of the Hudson River near Tarrytown, N. Y. ¶515. "*Love's young dream . . . Fanny dearest . . . The soldier's bride,*" popular songs. ¶515. "*Madame Bouquet, and Monsieur Pardessus,*" fictitious monitors of fashion in that day.

Joseph Rodman Drake (*1795–1820*)

Although five years Halleck's junior, Drake was the senior partner in the firm of Croaker and Co., and contributed at least his share to the wit and facility of the product. He died of consumption, in spite of trips to Europe and to the South, only five years after he had been licensed to practice medicine in New York. His fame rests on a slim volume, *The Culprit Fay and Other Poems* (1835), which was assembled by his friend Dr. De Kay, in spite of the injunction, prompted by his humility, that his poems be burned. See references for Halleck; J. G. Wilson's *Bryant and His Friends;* and *Papers and Proceedings of the Drake Memorial Celebration, May 29, 1915*, with a bibliography by V. H. Paltsits (1919).

¶515. THE CULPRIT FAY was the result of a debate, in 1816, in which Cooper and Halleck maintained that our native streams furnished no such romantic associations for the uses of poetry as do those of Scotland. Drake composed this poem to refute them, in three days, and laid its scene in the Highlands of the Hudson. It was not printed until N. P. Willis gave a part of it to *The Athenæum* (London), where it appeared on Feb. 7, 1835. It is the title poem of the only collection of Drake's work; and it was orchestrated in a rhapsody by Henry Hadley in 1910. The text of this and the other poems by Drake is that of the 1835 volume. ¶515. "*Anster's,*" *Anster Fair* (1812), mock-heroic poem by William Tenant (1784–1848), Scottish poet. ¶515. "*Ouphs,*" "ouphes," elfs or goblins. ¶515. "*Old Cronest,*" probably a local name for a mountain. ¶515. "*Whist,*" silent, mute, still. ¶516. "*Ising-stars,*" a piece of mica. ¶516. "*Minim forms,*" minute, small forms. ¶517. "*The hornet's shardy wings,*" brittle, shell-like wings. ¶517. "*The warlock fight,*" a fight of monsters. ¶517. "*Colon-bell,*" columbine, a flower; the word was coined by Drake. ¶517. "*Night shade,*" any of several species of Solanum, a weed. ¶517. "*Thrids,*" a variation of "threads." ¶518. "*A Silk-weed twist,*" milk-weed; alluding especially to the slender filaments which are silk-like. ¶518. "*An osier thong,*" a strip of the branch of a willow tree. ¶518. "*The mailed shrimp,*" the shrimp with a heavy shell. ¶518. "*The prickly prong,*" the "stickleback," any of numerous small fishes having "free spines" in front of the dorsal fin. ¶518. "*The blood-red leeches,*" small blood-sucking water animals. ¶518. "*The lancing squab,*" probably the "sand launce," a small marine fish. ¶518. "*The sideling soldier-crab,*" the hermit crab. ¶518. "*The jellied quarl,*" a medusa, or jelly-fish. ¶519. "*The scallop stroke.*" The scallop, a marine mollusk, "strokes," or swims, by opening and closing valves. ¶519. "*The porpoise heave,*" the rhythmical motion of the porpoise, an ocean-fish of considerable size. ¶519. "*The drum-fish croak,*" the drum-like noise of this ocean fish, which grows to about 100 lbs. wt. ¶519. "*The dogwood tree,*" any of several trees of the genus *Cornus*, some of which have flowers. ¶519. "*The balsam dew,*" the aromatic substance flowing from certain plants or trees. ¶519. "*The sorrel leaf,*" the leaf of the sorrel shrub, a plant having a sour juice. ¶519. "*The henbane bud,*" the flower bud of the henbane shrub, the extract of the leaves of which is used as a medicine. ¶519. "*Cobweb lint,*" the fine thread spun by the spider. ¶519. "*The cal'mus root,*" root of the calamus tree, a large genus of palms. ¶519. "*A purple muscle shell,*" the shell of the mollusk. ¶520. "*A sculler's notch,*" an indentation in the stern of a scull, a small boat, for securing an oar. ¶520. "*Bootle-blade,*" a word of uncertain meaning coined by Drake. ¶521. "*Thy chick-weed bower,*" a sheltered place where there is chickweed, any plants relished by fowls. ¶521. "*The cockle seed,*" the hard shell of the mollusk. ¶521. "*The rocket-star,*" a shooting star. ¶521. "*The moth-fly,*" a gnat. ¶522. "*The nettle shaft,*" a stem having pricklers on it. ¶522. "*The welkin blue,*" sky blue. ¶522. "*Up to the cope*": "up to the heavens." ¶522. "*The sphered moon is past,*" the waning moon. ¶522. "*The planet-shoot,*" the planet-fall, the disappearance of the planets. ¶523. "*The sylphid queen.*" The sylphs are imaginary beings inhabiting the air; "sylphid" is a diminutive. ¶523. "*The Pleiad ring,*" a conspicuous loose cluster of stars in the constellation of Taurus. ¶523. "*Orion's starry belt,*" a large, bright constellation on the equator, the row of three stars forming Orion's "belt." ¶524. "*A sable car,*" a dark-colored carriage, used figuratively of the cloud. ¶525. "*The wild witch-hazel tree,*" a shrub having hazel-like leaves and yellow flowers, found especially in eastern U. S.; extract of bark used for bruises. ¶525. "*The leaf-harp.*" The rustling and stirring of the leaves serve as the music for their dance.

525. To a Friend is, like "The Culprit Fay," the result of a debate over the value of American materials; pub. *N. Y. Mirror*, Mar. 3, 1832. The poem is addressed to Fitz-Greene Halleck. ¶525. "*Strangford,*" Percy Smythe, sixth Viscount Strangford (1780–1855), diplomat and poet, friend of Thomas Moore and translator of *Poems from the Portuguese of Camoëns* (1803), satirized by Byron. ¶525. "*Moore,*" Thomas Moore (1779–1852), Irish poet and writer of sentimental songs. ¶526. "*Warren,*" Joseph Warren (b. 1741), Boston revolutionary leader, killed in Battle of Bunker Hill, June 17, 1775. ¶526. "*Montgomery,*" Richard Montgomery (1736–1775), American major-general, killed in attack on Quebec. ¶526. "*Appalachia's brow,*" the mountain range running through the eastern seaboard states. ¶526. "*The kelpie's fang.*" The kelpie is a water spirit, believed to warn those about to be drowned and to assist in their drowning. ¶526. "*McRea,*" Jane M'Crea, Tory heroine, who was slain for scalp bounty. ¶526. "*Romantic Wyoming,*" the Wyoming Valley, Pa. The "stranger harp" is a reference to *Gertrude of Wyoming* by Thomas Campbell (1777–1844), English poet. ¶526. "*The Huron chief,*" a variation of the legend associated with cliffs and waterfalls in many parts of the U. S. *Cf.* Bryant's "Monument Mountain." ¶526. "*Niagara's tides,*" Niagara River. ¶527. "*Pacolet,*" a dwarf in the old romance of Valentine and Arson, said to have made a magic horse of wood by which he could instantly convey himself anywhere. ¶527. "*The Indian's evil Manitou's,*" spirits, in the religion of the American Indians. ¶527. "*Susquehannah's utmost springs,*" Lake Otsego, N. Y., the source of the Susquehanna River. ¶527. "*Areouski,*" possibly a god of the Iroquois Indians. ¶527. "*The Creek,*" the Creek Indians, in southern U. S. ¶527. "*Kanawa's,*" the Kanawha River, flowing from N. Car. north into the Ohio in W. Va. ¶527. "*Miami,*" river in S. W. Ohio. ¶527. "*Ariel.*" The reference is to the character in Shakespeare's *The Tempest*, who was in the power of Prospero. ¶527. "*The Pallisado's lofty brows,*" the Palisades of the Hudson River. ¶527. "*Omana,*" apparently refers to a local legend.

528. The American Flag appeared first in *The New York Evening Post*, May 29, 1819, and was reprinted in the 1835 volume. ¶529. "*The welkin dome,*" the sky.

James Kirke Paulding (1778–1860)

No member of the "Knickerbocker" group more deserved the term than Paulding. By inheritance and by personal association he belonged to that Dutch-English stock of which Irving wrote. His youth was spent in Tarrytown on the lower Hudson, and his early manhood in the energetic mercantile circles of New York society. Patriotic in the narrow sense, as Irving never was, he wrote novels, short stories, plays, poems, and critical prose which express the temper of his time and town, both by their limitations and by their distinguishing virtues. His sister married Irving's brother, and the friends and ideals of Irving's youth were his during his entire life. Even as secretary of the Board of Naval Commissioners under Madison, or as Secretary of the Navy under Van Buren, he seems to belong more to New York than to Washington. Although he never relied upon literature exclusively for his livelihood, it was his real vocation. From the date of his first contribution to Peter Irving's *Morning Chronicle* (1802) to that of the appearance of the first *Salmagundi* (Jan. 24, 1807) Paulding and Irving were Knickerbocker wits, writing about and for their fellow citizens in essays, Addisonian in style, but frontier American in vigorous humor. When Irving's mind turned to England, Paulding's turned against her, and the period from 1812 to 1825 was devoted to a satirical defence of American ideals and manners, starting with *The Diverting History of John Bull and Brother Jonathan* (1812) and closing with *John Bull in America; or The New Munchausen* (1825). Joining in the war against the systematic detractions of the English travelers and *The Quarterly Review*, Paulding became the leading spokesman for the enraged stay-at-home Americans. *A Sketch of Old England by a New England Man* (1822) is, like Cooper's *Notions of the Americans* (1828), a comparative survey of American and English civilizations, written as from the pen of a traveler of strong pro-American sympathies. With the appearance of the second *Salmagundi* series (1820), on Paulding's initiative alone, he became a narrative writer once more, and between 1823 and 1828, he contributed fifty tales and sketches to *The Atlantic Souvenir*, *The New York Mirror*, and other annuals and periodicals. The same period saw the publication of three novels, *Koningsmarke* (1823), *The Dutchman's Fireside* (1831), and *Westward Ho!* (1832), which were followed by *The Old Continental* (1846) and *The Puritan and His Daughter* (1849). Nationalistic in all things, Paulding chose to set his stories in American scenes of the recent past, and gave in these five books a panoramic picture of the last days of the colonies from New York to Kentucky. Fielding was his model for realistic fiction, with the result that his Indians are less heroic than Cooper's and his Dutchmen less grotesque than Irving's. A collection of *American Comedies* (1847), written in collaboration with his son William, and a series of lives of naval officers, contributed to *The Analectic Magazine* (1813–19), complete the list of his principal writings. Biographies by W. I. Paulding (1867) and A. L. Herold (1926). See also references for Irving.

529. [Courtship in New York] is from the middle of *The Dutchman's Fireside* (1831), a leisurely novel in the manner of Fielding, with its scene laid in Albany, N. Y., and New York City. The action takes place during the French and Indian Wars; and in its Dutch characters, its background, its social interest, and even in its fighting at Lake Champlain, the novel provides an interesting parallel to Cooper's *Satanstoe* (1845). The plot centers about the adventures of Sybrandt Westbook, an awkward but worthy young man of mixed English and Dutch heritage, who in some respects is a self-portrait of the author. The scenes here selected recount an episode in the story of his courtship of Catalina Vancour, a capricious New York beauty with social aspirations, not unlike Halleck's Fanny. The text is from the first ed. ¶529. "*The Huguenots*," the Puritans of France. After the massacre of St. Bartholomew (Aug. 24, 1572), many of them emigrated. Their descendants were prominent in the New York society of this period. ¶529. "*The Dutch government*." The State of New York was settled first by the Dutch on a patroon (landed proprietor) plan. Even after the English occupation, the descendants of the Dutch patroons were social aristocrats. ¶529. "*Loaves and fishes*." A reference to Mark vi. 35–41. ¶530. "*A younger brother's portion*": Many early emigrants to America were younger brothers of landed families. The law of primogeniture leaves younger brothers without inherited property. ¶530. "*Degenerates*." See Jefferson's refutation of this theory, pp. 280–84. ¶531. "*Watervliet*," literally, "*water-creek*." ¶531. "*Philipses*," etc., the aristocratic families of New York State, most of them descended from the Dutch patroons and French Huguenots. ¶532. "*Loyalty to the Stuarts*." The Stuart kings found adherents in Ireland and France during Cromwell's Protectorate. ¶532. "*Buckram*," a coarse linen or cotton cloth stiffened with size or glue. ¶533. "*The wars of York and Lancaster*," the Wars of the Roses, 1455–1485. ¶533. "*De facto . . . de jure*": "in fact . . . in law." ¶533. "*Milesian*," Irishman; so called from the traditional con-

quest of the country by the two sons of Milesius, a fabulous king of Spain. ¶534. "*Curragh,*" a plain in County Kildare, Ireland, 27 mi. s. w. of Dublin. ¶535. "*Hoops and heads were prodigious,*" large hoop-skirts and high head-dresses were fashionable at this time. ¶535. "*The reign of the gallant Charles the Second,*" king of England (1660–1685), the first of the restored Stuart kings after the Puritan Revolution. ¶535. "*Nell Gwyn,*" (1650–1687), an English actress, mistress of Charles II. ¶535. "*Dutchess of Cleveland,*" Barbara Villiers (1640–1709), also a mistress of Charles II. ¶535. "*The African balls,*" negro balls. ¶535. "*Captain Basil Hall,*" (1788–1844), British naval officer and traveler. His *Travels in North America* (1829) was widely read and criticized in this country, but was accepted abroad as an authority on the state of American civilization at that time. ¶535. "*My Lord Mansfield,*" William Murray, first Earl of Mansfield (1705–1793), Chief Justice of the King's Bench (1756–1788), and "founder of English commercial law." ¶535. "*Sir William Scott,*" Baron Stowell (1745–1836), Judge of the High Court of the Admiralty (1798–1827); noted in international law. ¶537. "*Crœsus,*" King of Lydia (560 B.C.), famed for his treasures, and cited as the traditional man of wealth.

537. [JONATHAN AND HIS FARM] is a selection of two chapters from *The Diverting History of John Bull and Brother Jonathan,* "by Hector Bull-Us," the first edition of which appeared in 1812. It was several times reprinted, revised and enlarged in 1827, and included in a collection of Paulding's works in 1835. It is the earliest of Paulding's many attacks upon the British criticism of the American character and culture, particularly as expressed by English travelers in America and by *The* [*London*] *Quarterly Review.* In Chapter I, Paulding has in mind, of course, the main issues of the Revolutionary War; and in Chapter XVIII, he prophesies with uncanny foresight those of the Civil War, still almost a quarter century in the future. The text is from the revised ed. of 1835. ¶538. "*Cutler,*" a maker or dealer in cutlery. ¶538. "*Pot-baker,*" one who bakes or fires clay pots, a potter. ¶538. "*Whether churches ought to be called churches.*" Reference is made here to the Puritan movement in the Church of England. ¶538. "*Thirty-nine different articles.*" The articles of faith of the Church of England, the acceptance of which is obligatory upon its clergy; reduced in 1563 from forty-two to thirty-nine. ¶538. "*Thirteen good farms,*" the original colonies. ¶539. "*Linsey-woolsey coat,*" coarse cloth made of linen and wool. ¶539. "*Threw the tea-kettle,*" the Boston Tea Party. ¶540. "*Barbecues,*" originally a picnic or other outdoor gathering at which an ox or hog was roasted whole. ¶540. "*They came among them.*" The Yankee peddlers who traveled through the South gained a reputation for being shrewd at a trade, and clever at a tall tale. ¶541. "*Proboscis,*" the trunk of an elephant.

William Ellery Channing (*1780–1842*)

When Channing defined literature as "the expression of superior mind in writing," he was calling for the quality of prose which he at the moment was supplying. The quarterly reviews, both in this country and in England, had done much to break down the traditional distinction between literary and other kinds of writing. To Jeffrey or Macaulay, an essay on a specific political or religious issue, if well written, was as much literature as a novel or a lyric poem. The day of "belles lettres" was passing, and with it, imitation of traditional literary forms. To Channing and Emerson, writing was the agent of thought, the expression of idealistic principles. A native of Rhode Island and a graduate of Harvard, this high tempered young minister became the leader of the most effective revolt against Calvinism in his sermon at the ordination of Jared Sparks in Baltimore in 1819. There the growing Unitarian movement found its first clear definition, and "the moral argument against Calvinism" its positive statement in a faith in which it was important only that the individual should be "alive to God." The ghost of Edwards' early liberalism could now rest, and the way was prepared for the Transcendentalists and Emerson. Soon, reviews of Milton's *Christian Doctrine* (1826) and essays on Napoleon (1827–28) in *The Christian Examiner* proved that the new thought had application to other than theological problems, and Channing was hailed by the London *Athenæum* (Jan., 1835) as "the most powerful writer of his time." On these few essays, and on a great many sermons, Channing made for himself a reputation for "truth and loftiness of mind" and formal beauty of expression which ranked him, with Irving and Cooper, as a founder of the new national literature for which he pleaded.

His place is in the tradition of lecturer-essayists which gave England Carlyle and Matthew Arnold, and gave us Emerson and Lowell. That tradition, closely allied to the prose of opinion on the one hand, and to oratory and homiletics on the other, has an undefined place in literary history, but in the history of American thought, Channing's position is secure. The first complete American edition of his works appeared in 1841–45; his correspondence with Lucy Aikin in 1874; and his notebook in 1887. Biographies by W. H. Channing (1848, 1880) and J. W. Chadwick (1903).

542. THE MORAL ARGUMENT AGAINST CALVINISM appeared first in *The Christian Disciple* in 1820, as a review of a work entitled: *A General View of the Doctrines of Christianity, designed more especially for the Edification and Instruction of Families* (Boston, 1809), and was republished in the collected *Works* (1841–45), from which the text of this and other Channing selections has been taken. In it, Channing presents, in his customary style of careful logic, the arguments which gave Unitarianism its place as a liberal offshoot of the Calvinistic New England heritage. ¶542. "*The dark period.*" John Calvin (1509–1564), banished from Paris, formulated his doctrine chiefly at Geneva, Switzerland, and founded the Academy of Geneva in 1559. ¶542. "*Arminius,*" Jacobus Harmensen (1560–1609), Protestant leader who was more liberal than Calvin. ¶543. "*The famous Assembly's Catechisms and Confession.*" The Long Parliament summoned an assembly of divines at Westminster (1643–1649). The Westminster Confession, adopted by the Church of Scotland (Presbyterian), but not by the Church of England, was the principal result of its deliberations. ¶545. "*We 'know nothing' of God's ways;*" "For we are but of yesterday, and know nothing," Job viii. 9. ¶546. "*Philosophers . . . who have argued.*" The reference is probably to Spinoza (1632–1677), whose *Ethica*, published in 1674, contains his metaphysical system. ¶547. "*O inhabitants of Jerusalem.*" Isa. v. 3, 4.

548. REMARKS ON THE CHARACTER AND WRITINGS OF JOHN MILTON is a review of *A Treatise on Christian Doctrine, compiled from the Holy Scriptures alone*, by John Milton. It appeared in two parts in *The Christian Examiner* for Jan. and Feb., 1826. Milton had worked on this statement of his theological beliefs from early youth, but the manuscript was not completed until about 1661. The return of the Stuart kings made its publication untimely, and it remained in manuscript until it was rediscovered in 1823, translated from the Latin by Bishop Charles Sumner, and published in London (1825). To a man of Channing's theological and poetical interests the discovery was one of major importance, and he made it the occasion of one of his best critical essays. Milton was to him the personification of his ideal of a poet who combined intellectual with spiritual qualities. ¶548. "*Parnassus,*" a mountain-ridge in Greece, reputed to have been the haunt of Apollo and the muses; hence traditionally the home of inspiration in the arts. ¶548. "*Araby the Blest,*" Arabia. ¶550. "*Makes all things new,*" "Behold, all things are become new," II Cor. v. 17. ¶552. "*Tear hell's concave,*" "A shout that tore Hell's concave," *Paradise Lost*, I, 542. ¶552. "*Cowper,*" William Cowper (1731–1800), author of *The Task* (1785), a poem descriptive of the details of the English countryside. ¶552. "*Crabbe,*" George Crabbe (1754–1832), English poet, author of *The Village* (1783), descriptive of details of English village life. ¶552. "*Solid and liquid fire,*" the element from which God created the universe. ¶554. "*Imparadised in one another's arms,*" *Paradise Lost*, IV, 506. ¶554. "*Thoughts which wander through eternity,*" *Paradise Lost*, II, 147. ¶555. "*Wings of a dove, that it might fly away,*" Ps. lv. 6. ¶555. "*The odoriferous wings of gentle gales,*" "Now gentle gales, Fanning their odoriferous wings," etc., *Paradise Lost*, IV, 157–158. ¶555. "*Michael Angelo,*" (1475–1564), Italian poet sculptor, painter, and architect.

556. REMARKS ON NATIONAL LITERATURE, or, "The Importance and Means of a National Literature," as it was called when it first appeared in *The Christian Examiner* for Jan., 1830, is Channing's literary testament. It was a review of *A Discourse concerning the Influence of America on the Mind*, the annual oration before the American Philosophical Society, delivered by Charles J. Ingersoll in Philadelphia on Oct. 18, 1823. Ingersoll had discussed the practical and utilitarian mind of America and had stressed the desirability of having a national literature in these terms. To Channing, such an ideal was intolerable. Literature, in his view, could not be put into a separate category like "belles lettres" and so divorced from life, but it must do more than accept and give adequate expression to the circumstances of material life. He thus went one step beyond such critics as Webster,

Freneau, and Cooper in his plea for a national literature: and he prepared the way for Emerson's more famous essay on "The American Scholar." ¶561. *"A false theology,"* Calvinism. ¶563. *"Newton,"* Sir Isaac Newton (1642–1727), English scientist, here mentioned as an example of the empirical philosopher.

Washington Irving (1783–1859)

The creator of Diedrich Knickerbocker was the outstanding member of that group of American authors who are usually associated with the old gentleman's name. Halleck, Drake, Paulding, William and Peter Irving, Verplanck, Brevoort and Kemble are, strictly speaking, the "Knickerbockers"; Cooper, Bryant, Dr. J. W. Francis, Charles King, and many others who were contemporary with them in New York, as well as other friends of Irving, like Allston and Leslie, the artists, and Dunlap and Payne, the dramatists, are often included. There is a common spirit of mischievous youth in their comment on their times, which is not unlike that of the humorists of the later frontier, Mark Twain and his fellows; and there is a mixture of Dutch and English strains in their blood. In their writings, the spirit of nationalism which had asserted itself in the Hartford and Philadelphia groups overcame that of imitation; and a national literature began to define itself in a strong, though sometimes crude, provincialism. Irving dominated the group from 1807 to 1820, but thereafter Halleck and Paulding took the leadership. Through their humor, their realism, their interest in folk and other native materials, their journalistic facility, and their unity of purpose, they made a distinctive contribution to American literary history as a group, as well as in their individual work.

Washington Irving, the youngest of the eleven children of Deacon William Irving and his wife Sarah (Sanders), was born in New York City on Apr. 3, 1783. Friendly, romantic, precocious, and somewhat undersized, the boy grew up in a society which was only one step ahead of him in maturity. His brothers, William, seventeen years older than he, and Peter, were leaders in "The Calliopean Society"; and at William's house on Vesey Street, Washington met the intellectuals and artists of New York's somewhat callow mercantile aristocracy. By 1808, Irving was an attorney-at-law, but, more important to him and to posterity, he had published, with the aid of Paulding and his two brothers, the first *Salmagundi*, a series of papers which bore certain resemblances to the English periodical essay of the 18th century. Meanwhile, he had been to Montreal, Bordeaux, Genoa, and Washington. He had experienced the bumping ox-carts of Canadian roads; he had met Washington Allston in Rome and had almost turned painter himself; he had contributed to Peter Irving's *Morning Chronicle* (1802) his "Letters from Jonathan Oldstyle, Gent."; and he had been captured by pirates off Sicily. But his gay quest of health and amusement was interrupted in 1809 by the death of Matilda Hoffman, his betrothed; and he struggled through the concluding chapters of "Diedrich Knickerbocker's" *A History of New York* (1809) in a more serious, but perhaps even more strikingly satirical, vein. Before he sailed for Europe again in 1814, as foreign agent, with the now invalided Peter, of the family hardware business, he had edited a literary magazine, *The Analectic*, in Philadelphia, and he had mingled in Washington society and politics. Irving's second and longest European residence was divided between England, the central continent, and Spain. *The Sketch Book* (1819–1820), *Bracebridge Hall* (1822), and *The Crayon Miscellany* (1835) contain his best work in celebration of a romantic old England for country squires and mellowed traditions; his association with Payne and his interest in German lore took him to Paris and Dresden in 1822–24 and produced a few plays and the *Tales of a Traveller* (1824); and his two diplomatic journeys to Spain, 1826–29 as attaché to the legation of Alexander Everett, and 1842–45 as Envoy Extraordinary, led to a brief residence in the Moorish palace of the Alhambra and to the study of the life of Columbus and of Spanish history. The literary results of these later experiences were his *Life of Columbus* (1828), *The Conquest of Granada* (1829), *The Companions of Columbus* (1831), and his Spanish sketch book, *The Alhambra* (1831), all of which grew out of his effort to translate a Spanish life of Columbus. When he returned to New York in 1832, after a brief period as Chargé d'Affaires at London, he was greeted with a great dinner in his honor by a group of literary and social leaders of New York, and, with the exception of his embassy to Spain, the remainder of his life was spent in his own country, first in New York City and later at Sunnyside, where he wrote, in his old manner but not with his old gusto, lives of Goldsmith, Mahomet, and Washington, a collection of papers, *Wolfert's Roost* (1855), and some miscellaneous works.

The most important of the works published during Irving's lifetime are: *Salmagundi* (1807–08); *A History of New York* (1809; revised 1812 and in subsequent editions); "A Biographical Sketch of Thomas Campbell," in *The Poetical Works of Thomas Campbell* (1810; revised 1815); *Biography of James Lawrence* (1813); *The Sketch Book* (1819–20); *Bracebridge Hall* (1822); *Tales of a Traveler* (1824); *Letters of Jonathan Oldstyle, Gent.* (1824); *A History of the Life and Voyages of Christopher Columbus* (1828; abridged 1829); *A Chronicle of the Conquest of Granada* (1829); *Voyages and Discoveries of the Companions of Columbus* (1831); *The Alhambra* (1832); *The Crayon Miscellany* [containing: (1) "A Tour of the Prairies"; (2) "Abbotsford and Newsted Abbey"; and (3) "Legends of the Conquests of Spain"] (1835); *Astoria* (1836); *The Rocky Mountains* (1837); *The Life of Oliver Goldsmith* (1840; expanded 1849); *Biography and Poetical Remains of Margaret Miller Davidson* (1841); *A Book of the Hudson* (1849); *Mahomet and His Successors* (1850); *Wolfert's Roost* (1855); and *The Life of George Washington* (1855–59). Many of his essays, journals, and letters have been collected and pub. since his death; chief among them are: *Spanish Papers* (ed. by P. M. Irving, 1866); *The Letters of Washington Irving to Henry Brevoort* (ed. by G. S. Hellman, 1915); *The Journals of Washington Irving* (ed. by W. P. Trent and G. S. Hellman, 1919); *Notes and Journals of Travel in Europe, 1804–05* (ed. by W. P. Trent, 1921); *Abu Hassan* (1924) and *The Wild Huntsman* (1925; both with intro. by G. S. Hellman); *An Unwritten Drama of Lord Byron* (1925; with an intro. by T. O. Mabbott); *Washington Irving Diary, Spain, 1828–29* (ed. by C. L. Penny, 1926); *Notes While Preparing The Sketch Book, &c.* (1927) and *Tour in Scotland, 1817* (1927; both ed. with critical intro. by S. T. Williams); *Letters from Sunnyside and Spain* (ed. by S. T. Williams, 1928); *The Poems of Washington Irving* (ed. by W. R. Langfeld, 1931); *Journal of Washington Irving, 1823–24* (ed. by S. T. Williams, 1931); and *Letters of Washington Irving to Mrs. William Renwick* (n. d.). The standard edition of Irving's works is the "Author's Revised Edition," which Irving undertook for Putnam in 1848, and which was continued by the addition of the *Life of Washington*, and repub. (1860–61). The Irving manuscripts are widely scattered, the most important collection of them being in the New York Public Library. At his death, his nephew Pierre first collected his papers and wrote his biography (1862–64). The personal bias and lack of editorial skill shown in this work has been somewhat corrected by the later publication of its sources and by the shorter biographies of H. W. Boynton (1901) and G. S. Hellman (1925). A definitive biography by S. T. Williams is promised; and a descriptive bibliography by W. R. Langfeld and P. C. Blackburn is shortly to appear.

570. [Arrival of the Dutch] is from the second book of "Diedrich Knickerbocker's" *A History of New York*, the first edition of which appeared in 1809. Not counting Irving's contributions to *Salmagundi*, this book is his first important work, the best expression of that youthful insolence and keen wit which we have come to associate with the word "Knickerbocker." It is, to the literature of our first frontier, what Mark Twain's *Innocents Abroad* and *A Yankee in King Arthur's Court* are to that of the later frontier. Father Knickerbocker was an antiquarian, but there was a twinkle in his eye: he did not take the past too seriously. He was, as Irving tells us, "a very worthy good sort of an old gentleman, though a little queer in his ways." The fictitious MS which he left behind him in the Independent Columbian Hotel begins with a grandiose history of the world, but soon, in the second book gets down to the real business in hand, an account of the Dutch settlement and occupancy of New Amsterdam. Irving knew the Dutch character at first hand, but he was at pains to investigate Dutch history from many learned volumes. He tells the story of the first settlement of the "Province of Nieuw Nederlants" (Book II); of "the golden reign of Wouter Van Twiller" (Book III); of the reign of "William the Testy," or "Wilhelmus Kieft" (Book IV); and of the reign of "Peter the Headstrong," or Peter Stuyvesant, and of his battles with the Swedes on the Delaware (Books V, VI, and VII). The work was reprinted in 1812, 1815, and many times thereafter. As its author grew older, he gradually took out of it most of the broadest humor and materially changed its original character. The text of this and other selections is from that ed. by S. T. Williams and T. McDowell (1927), a verbatim reprint of the 1809 ed. ¶570. "*The great Hudson,*" Henry Hudson (d. 1611), English navigator in the employ of the Dutch East India Company, discoverer of the Hudson River (1609). ¶570. "*Master Juet,*" Robert Juet, author of a journal in *Purchas his Pilgrimes* (1625), an early collection of voyages and discoveries. ¶570.

"*Block Island,*" in the Atlantic Ocean, 10 mi. off the coast of R. I. ¶570. "*Knickerbockers.*" Irving seems to have originated this name, originally applied to descendants of the Dutch settlers of New York, but soon extended to include any native of the city. ¶571. "*Taf-forel,*" taffrail, the rail across the stern of a vessel. ¶571. "*Cat-heads,*" beams projecting on each side of a ship for raising and carrying the anchor. ¶571. "*Poop,*" the aftermost part of a ship, the stern. ¶571. "*Jupiter,*" in Rom. myth., the supreme deity. ¶571. "*Neptune,*" god of the sea in Rom. myth. ¶571. "*Hercules,*" god of physical strength and courage, in Rom. myth. ¶571. "*St. Nicholas,*" patron saint of boys (Santa Claus). ¶571. "*Bob-major,*" a term used by bell-ringers to denote a long peal, rung on eight bells; a "bob minor" on six. ¶571. "*Lee-way,*" lateral deviation from the course of a ship. ¶571. "*Gibbet Island,*" probably a small island in New York harbor. ¶571. "*Goede Vrouw*": "good woman" (Dutch). ¶571. "*The Bergen hills,*" in Bergen Co., north-eastern N. J., west of the Hudson. ¶571. "*The Tammany Society of that day.*" In Irving's time Tammany Hall, now a political instrument of the state Democratic Party, was a benevolent and fraternal society, whose members assisted at funerals as one of their fraternal duties. ¶571. "*The Newark Cause-way,*" the road, raised above the marshes, out of Newark, N. J. ¶571. "*Communipaw,*" one of the early Dutch settlements in N. J., opposite Manhattan Isl.

572. [The Reign of William the Testy]. As early as 1850, the fourth book of the *History* was referred to (*Frazer's Mag.*, July) as "a palpable satire of the administration of Thomas Jefferson." The Dutch flavor is maintained, but the characters and actions of Kieft and Jefferson are too nearly parallel to allow us to avoid the conclusion that Irving was satirizing the present as well as the past. In General Poffenburgh's expedition against the Swedes, there is probably a satirical account of General James Wilkinson's betrayal of Burr and of his expedition to the Texan frontier. ¶572. "*A Cabalistic word.*" "Cabal" signifies a secret group; here it means a secret or magic word, "economy." ¶572. "*Boetius,*" Boethius (*c.* 475–*c.* 524 A.D.), Roman philosopher, author of *The Consolations of Philosophy* (*c.* 520). ¶573. "*Van Twiller,*" Wouter Van Twiller (*c.* 1580–1646), Dutch governor of New Netherlands (1633–1637). ¶573. "*The Yankees,*" English inhabitants of Conn. ¶573. "*A vagrant colony of Swedes,*" the Swedes who settled on the Delaware in 1638. ¶573. "*Minnewits,*" Peter Minuit, first governor of the Swedish colony. ¶573. "*The memorable dispute of Ten breeches and Tough breeches,*" probably the dispute between Mass. and New Netherlands regarding Conn. in 1636. ¶574. "*In statu quo*": "in the present condition." ¶574. "*Cobbling the national affairs,*" "patching" or "mending" in a haphazard manner. ¶574. "*The Island of Barataria,*" in *Don Quixote* (1605, 1615), by the Spaniard, Cervantes (1547–1616), the island city of which Sancho Panza was made governor. ¶574. "*The Hague,*" capital city of the Netherlands and site of the royal library. ¶575. "*The Theurgia of the Chaldeans,*" the system of magic practiced by the Egyptians to procure communication with beneficent spirits. ¶575. "*The Cabala of the Jews,*" the pretended mystical interpretation of the Old Testament, based on the oral tradition handed down from Moses. ¶575. "*The necromancy of the Arabians,*" the pretended art of revealing future events by communication with the dead. ¶575. "*The Magic of the Persians,*" similar to the arts of the Egyptians and Arabians. ¶575. "*The Hocus Pocus of the English,*" a conjuror's formula. Irving's humor at this point changes from the mock-heroic to direct satire. ¶575. "*The Witch-craft of the Yankees,*" referring to the Salem witchcraft trials in the late 17th century. ¶575. "*The Pow-wowing of the Indians.*" The "pow-wow" of the North American Indians was a ceremony where magic was practiced under the direction of the "medicine-man." ¶575. "*The Sephir Jetzirah,*" presumably the *Sephiroth*, in the philosophy of the Cabala, the ten hypostatized attributes by which the Infinite enters into relation with the finite. ¶575. "*The pages of the Zohar.*" The "Zohar" is a cabalistic book in the form of a commentary on the Pentateuch, written about 200 A.D. ¶575. "*The Shem-hamphorah of Benjamin . . . Davidus Elm.*" The references here may be fictitious. The wandering Jew is a popular figure in medieval legend. Eugène Sue's novel did not appear until 1844. ¶575. "*Tetragrammaton,*" referring to the Hebrew word "JHVH," or "Jehovah," meaning the ineffable. ¶575. "*Tetractys of Pythagoras,*" the Pythagorean name for the sum of the first four numbers (1, 2, 3, 4), regarded as the source of all things. ¶575. "*Breslaw,*" probably an author here mentioned because of his insignificance. ¶575. "*Mother Bunch,*" a

derisive name used for the hypothetical author of various books of jests, esp. 1604 and 1760: *Mother Bunch's Fairy Tales.* ¶575. "*Viscidity of the vitreous . . . humours,*" etc., a burlesque of medical terms. The entire ten lines mean little more than "blind." ¶575. "*Myopes,*" short-sighted. ¶575. "*The eloquent Burke,*" Edmund Burke (1729–1797), British statesman, orator, and writer. ¶576. "*The defenceless fleet of Eneas.*" Æneas was protected by his mother Venus on his voyage to Italy after the fall of Troy.

577. [The Valiant Peter Stuyvesant]. In the character of Peter Stuyvesant, the last Dutch governor of New Netherlands, Irving gives us a full-length portrait in caricature. Three books are devoted to his reign, and the Thirty Years' War in Europe is mirrored in the conflicts between the Dutch colonists and their neighbors, the Swedes to the South and the English in Conn. With the taking of Fort Good Hope by the British in 1654, the end of the Dutch rule, ten years later, was assured. ¶577. "*Alexandrian library,*" the great library at Alexandria, Egypt, of about 700,000 volumes, which flourished from about 300 B.C. to 640 A.D., when the conquering Saracens burned it. ¶577. "*Fort Christina,*" the Swedish settlement on the Delaware near the present site of Wilmington, Del. The Swedes settled it in 1638 and lost it to the Dutch under Stuyvesant in 1655. ¶577. "*The 'affair' of Troy.*" Throughout the succeeding passage Irving has adopted the mock-heroic manner in a burlesque of Homer's *Iliad.* In the entire epic, but particularly in the fourth book, the gods are constantly brought into conflict with each other because of their partisan interests in the Greeks and Trojans. ¶578. "*Gin suttler,*" a peddler of liquor to soldiers. ¶578. "*Swivels,*" guns with a device to permit turning them around. ¶578. "*Carronade,*" a short gun, usually of large caliber, used principally on ships. ¶578. "*Bayard,*" Pierre du Terrail, Chevalier de Bayard (1475–1525), a French national hero, called "the knight without fear and without reproach." ¶578. "*Bulls of Bashan.*" Bashan is a district of Palestine, east of the Jordan; Ps. xxii. 12 for "Bulls of Bashan." ¶578. "*Duyvels*": "devils" (Dutch). ¶579. "*Snickersnee,*" a knife used in fighting. ¶579. "*Glacis,*" a gently sloping bank leading up to a rampart. ¶579. "*Counterscarp,*" the wall of the trench or ditch. ¶579. "*The little Locrian archers.*" The Locrians were the people of Locri Opuntii, in ancient Greece. ¶580. "*Voltigeurs*": skirmishers; in the French army there was formerly a special company of them. ¶580. "*Hell-gate,*" the narrow channel connecting New York harbor with Long Island Sound. ¶580. "*The great beaver of the Manhattoes.*" The beaver is a part of the seal of the State of New York. ¶581. "*Pavonians.*" Pavonia is the name formerly given to the district of N. J. near N. Y. City. ¶581. "*A parte poste*": "to the rear part." ¶582. "*A pepper corn,*" the dried berry of black pepper. ¶582. "*Like Briareus,*" in Grk. myth., a monster with one hundred arms. ¶582. "*Arquebusier,*" sharpshooter, rifleman. ¶582. "*The Stygian shore,*" the shore of the River Styx, the main stream in Hades. ¶582. "*Boreas,*" in Grk. myth., the personification of the north wind. ¶582. "*Hesiod,*" a celebrated Greek poet (*c.* 700 B.C.). ¶583. "*The far famed battles of Ajaz with Hector,*" the single combat between Ajax, the Greek, and Hector, the Trojan (*Iliad,* VII). ¶583. "*Of Eneas with Turnus,*" the fight between Æneas, the Trojan, and Turnus, king of the Rutulians, in Italy (*Æneid,* XII). ¶583. "*Orlando with Rodomont.*" Orlando and Rodomont are characters in a metrical romance, *Orlando Innamorato,* by Boiardo (d. 1494). ¶583. "*Guy of Warwick with Colbrand the Dane.*" Guy of Warwick is a legendary hero of English romance whose most striking feat was killing the giant Dane, Colbrand, in a duel to decide the war between Athelstane and the Danes. ¶583. "*Of that renowned Welsh Knight Sir Owen of the mountains with the giant Guylon,*" legend from pre-Norman times.

584. The Author's Account of Himself is a portrait of Geoffrey Crayon, Gent., the fictitious author of *The Sketch Book* (1819–20). The comparison of his character with that of Father Knickerbocker is a sure index to the changes which had come over Irving after his contact with English life. He had become respectable, without losing his whimsical outlook. Later revisions of this and Irving's subsequent works did not alter their essential character. The middle-aged mellowness of this essay is characteristic of the later Irving. The text of this and other selections from *The Sketch Book* are from the "Author's Revised Edition" (N. Y., 1848). ¶584. "*Geoffrey Crayon, Gentn.,*" the pseudonym taken by Irving in *The Sketch Book,* and later volumes of essays. ¶584. "*Lyly's Euphues.*" *Euphues, or the Anatomy of Wit,* by John Lyly (1554–1606), English dramatist and novelist. ¶586. "*St. Peter's,*" metropolitan church in Rome, started in 1506, completed in 1626. ¶586.

"*The Coliseum*," the arena, or stadium, for games in ancient Rome. ¶586. "*The cascade of Terni*," the falls of the Veliono River near Terni, Italy. ¶586. "*The bay of Naples*," an arm of the Mediterranean, celebrated for the beauty of its shores.

586. Christmas Eve is from a handful of essays in *The Sketch Book*, the scene of which is Bracebridge Hall, a typical country house of a typical English squire. There seems to have been no one original, but Irving was entertained at so many establishments of the kind that the picture is an authentic, though glamorous, record of the English country life of the day. It was in these essays that the theme of *Bracebridge Hall* (1822) originated. ¶586. "*Saint Francis and Saint Benedight*," St. Francis of Assisi and St. Benedict, founders of the medieval monastic orders bearing their names. ¶586. "*Good fellow Robin*," one of many names for the devil. ¶586. "*Cartwright*," William Cartwright (1611–1643), English divine, dramatist, and poet. ¶588. "*French taste of Charles the Second's time*," the ornate style of the time of Louis XIV (1643–1715). ¶588. "*The Restoration*," the return of Charles II (Stuart) to the English throne in 1660 after the Puritan-Cromwellian interlude. ¶589. "*The twelve days of Christmas*," the period of merry-making of the Christmas season, brought to a close by the feast of the Epiphany on Jan. 6. ¶589. "*Hoodman blind*," etc., old English games. ¶589. "*An Oxonian*," of Oxford University, Eng. ¶590. "*Herrick*," Robert Herrick (1591–1674), English poet, author of *Hesperides* (1648). ¶590. "*Beaufet*," "buffet," serving table, "side-board." ¶591. "*Punch and Judy*," comical characters in an old street puppet-show. ¶591. "*Factotum*," a man of all work, manager of his master's affairs. ¶592. "*The heel and toe*," an old dance of very fast movements of the feet. ¶592. "*Rigadoon*," a lively and rather complicated old dance for two persons. ¶592. "*Waterloo*," in Belgium, the scene of the final overthrow of Napoleon, June 18, 1815. ¶592. "*Troubadour*," minstrel of Provence, southern France. ¶593. "*Will o' the Wisp*," a fancy, an illusion.

593. Rip Van Winkle, also from *The Sketch Book*, marks the beginning of the American short story, although the prose tale and the narrative essay were as common in America as in England before this time. The originality of Irving's method lay in his use of the short narrative to concentrate attention upon a single character, and to develop it in a single incident. His is the structural formula for the short story as we know it today, but as it was not known before his time. "Rip Van Winkle" has never lessened in popularity since the day of its first appearance, and a dramatic version made a reputation for the actor, Joseph Jefferson. ¶593. "*Woden*," "Wodan," or "Odin," Norse deity. ¶594. "A history of the province," see above, pp. 570 ff. ¶594. "*A Queen Anne's farthing*." A farthing is one-fourth of a penny, hence worth very little when full weight, so the currency disturbances of the early 18th century, caused by the fluctuating market and mint ratios of gold and silver, served as good basis for the expression, which is comparable to the American, "not worth a Continental." ¶594. "*The Kaatskill mountains*," the Catskill mountains, in N. Y. State. ¶595. "*The siege of Fort Christina*," see above, p. 577. ¶595. "*A Tartar's lance*." The Tartars were wild nomadic tribes of central Asia who plundered eastern Europe in the 13th century. ¶597. "*Virago*," a man-like woman, a female warrior. ¶602. "*Federal or Democrat*." The Federalists, led by Washington, Hamilton, Marshall, etc., and the Republicans or Democrats, led by Jefferson, Madison, etc., were the political factions which formed in the U. S. shortly after the new government was established in 1789. ¶602. "*A tory*," here means a "loyalist." ¶602. "*Antony's Nose*," a promontory on the east bank of the Hudson River. ¶602. "*Stony Point*," a promontory on the west bank of the Hudson 35 mi. n. of N. Y. City, the site of a battle in the Rev. War. ¶604. "*The Half-moon*," the ship of Henry Hudson, who discovered the river bearing his name, 1609. ¶605. "*Frederick de Rothbart . . . Kypphaüser mountain*." Frederick Barbarossa, Holy Roman emperor, 1152–1189, sleeps on the Kyffhäuser mountain near Weimar, Germany, according to tradition. ¶606. "*Manitou*," a spirit, either good or evil, among the American Indians.

606. The Stout Gentleman is a typical character essay from *Bracebridge Hall* (1822). The text is from the "Author's Revised Edition," (1849). ¶606. "*I'll cross it though it blast me!*" *Hamlet*, I, i, 127. ¶606. "*Derby*," town in north central England. ¶607. "*An upper Benjamin*," an overcoat formerly worn by men, named after a tailor. ¶608. "*The Lady's Magazine*," a popular 18th cent. magazine, edited at one time by Oliver Goldsmith. ¶608. "*Ycleped*," called, named. ¶609. "*Slammerkin*," a slovenly woman, untidy, shabby. ¶609. "*Nincompoop*," slang for a

silly or stupid person. ¶609. "*The Times,*" *The London Times.* ¶609. "*The Chronicle,*" *The Morning Chronicle* (London). ¶611. "*Belcher handkerchiefs,*" large blue neckerchiefs having white spots with blue spots inside; named after Jim Belcher, English pugilist. ¶612. "*Stilton cheese,*" one of the principal English cheeses, rich, unpressed, and of waxy texture.

613. LEGEND OF THE ROSE OF THE ALHAMBRA is one of the tales which Irving learned during his residence in the Moorish palace of the Alhambra, from Apr. to July, 1829. It was one of the most romantic periods of writing, strolling, and reading old legends in his career. The tale was included in *The Alhambra,* a Spanish "Sketch Book" (1832). The text is from the "Author's Revised Edition" (1851). ¶613. "*The surrender of Granada.*" The Moors were finally driven out of Spain in 1492. ¶613. "*Moslem,*" Islamic, Moorish. ¶613. "*The Alhambra,*" a great citadel and palace founded in the 13th century above the city of Granada, Spain, by the Moorish kings. ¶613. "*Infantas,*" princesses; legitimate daughters of a king of Spain or Portugal. ¶613. "*Philip V*" (1683–1746), king of Spain 1700–1746, grandson of Louis XIV of France; Philip's succession to the Spanish throne precipitated the War of the Spanish Succession (1702–1714). ¶613. "*Isabella . . . princess of Parma,*" Elizabeth Farnese (1692–1766), queen of Spain, daughter of Edward III, Prince of Parma (Italy). ¶614. "*Antinous,*" a page, attendant, and favorite of the emperor Hadrian (117–138 A.D.). ¶614. "*The Generalife,*" an old palace of the Moors, in the city of Granada. ¶615. "*Señor*": "Sir." ¶615. "*Andalusian,*" referring to the district of Andalusia, in southern Spain. ¶616. "*Ger-falcon,*" gyrfalcon, a kind of falcon, or hawk-like bird. ¶617. "*Ay de mi!*": "Alas!" an exclamation. ¶618. "*The Sierra Nevada,*" the highest range of mts. in Spain, s. e. of Granada. ¶618. "*Alabaster,*" a compact variety of gypsum, of fine texture and usually translucent. ¶620. "*Malaga,*" capital of the province of Malaga, in Andalusia, Spain. ¶620. "*Seville,*" capital of the province of Seville, in southern Spain. ¶620. "*Cordova,*" capital of the province of Cordova, situated on the Guadalquivir River in southern Spain. ¶621. "*Farinelli,*" Carlo Farinelli (1705–1782), Italian male soprano, who was a great favorite at the Spanish court. ¶621. "*St. Ildefonso,*" near Segovia, Spain, palace of the Spanish rulers, modelled after Versailles through the efforts of Philip V. ¶621. "*Versailles,*" the great palace near Paris, built by Louis XIV (1643–1715). ¶623. "*Paganini,*" Nicolo Paganini (1782–1840), celebrated Italian violinist.

623. [SIR WALTER SCOTT] is from *Abbotsford and Newsted Abbey,* the second part of *The Crayon Miscellany* (1835). The text is from the "Author's Revised Edition" (N. Y., 1849). Scott had read and enjoyed the Knickerbocker *History* several years before, and when Irving stopped at the baronial castle on the Tweed in Aug., 1817, with a letter of introduction from Thomas Campbell, he received a cordial welcome. His appreciation of the aristocratic qualities in Scott's life and thought provides a sharp contrast to Cooper's attitude of critical skepticism (*cf.* pp. 669 ff.). ¶623. "*Selkirk,*" a town about 30 mi. s. of Edinburgh. ¶623. "*Thomas Campbell*" (1777–1844), British poet and critic. ¶623. "*Abbotsford,*" the residence of Sir Walter Scott, on the Tweed, about 3 mi. above Melrose, Scotland. ¶623. "*Melrose Abbey,*" the finest ruin in Scotland, founded by David I (d. 1153) of Scotland, but repaired in the 15th century. ¶624. "*Sophia,*" Scott's elder daughter; later married his biographer, John Lockhart. ¶624. "*Miss Ann Scott,*" second daughter of Scott; devoted to him throughout her life. ¶624. "*Walter,*" the eldest son, lieut.-col. and commander of the 15th Huzzars at Madras. ¶624. "*Charles,*" second son. ¶624. "*Dryburgh Abbey,*" a picturesque ruin near Melrose, Scotland, dating from early Norman times; burial place of Scott. ¶625. "*Adam Ferguson,*" Scottish philosopher and historian (1723–1816). ¶626. "*The Eildon hills,*" three peaks near Melrose, famous in Scottish legend. ¶626. "*Precentor,*" leader of the choir, or of the singing of the congregation. ¶626. "*Edie Ochiltree,*" in Scott's novel *The Antiquary,* a king's beadsman or licensed beggar, called "Blue gown" for his costume. ¶626. "*Wilkie,*" David Wilkie (1775–1841), noted Scottish painter. ¶627. "*Tippoo Saib,*" Sultan of Mysore (1749–1799), son of Hyder Ali, killed in battle with the British at Seringapatim, India. ¶627. "*Rob Roy,*" Robert McGregor, or Campbell, (1671–1734), Scottish outlaw, the subject of a novel by Scott. ¶627. "*General Wolfe,*" James Wolfe (1727–1759), commander of the British expedition against Quebec (1759) in the Seven Years' War. ¶627. "*The old romance of Arthur,*" Malory's *Morte d' Arthur.* ¶628. "*Grimalkin,*" a cat, esp. a she-cat. ¶628. "*The Pretender,*" "The

Young Pretender" to the English throne, Charles Edward Casimir (1720–1788), a Stuart, who led a band of Scots in a brief rebellion in 1745–1746. ¶628. "*The house of Hanover*," the present line of British rulers, beginning in 1714 with George I, so called from their family province of Hanover, Germany. ¶629. "*Rat's-bane*," rat poison, esp. white arsenic.

James Fenimore Cooper (1789–1851)

Cooper was the first American to succeed in the profession which Brockden Brown had attempted, that of making his living by writing novels; and, with Irving and perhaps Channing, he was the first American author to find a place abroad on a par with the popular authors of other nations. His literary career, which began when the success of the *Waverley* novels was at its height and romance was the current vogue, was strongly influenced throughout by his interest in people in social rather than individual relationships. His first novel was a direct imitation of the 18th cent. English novel of manners, and, in spite of his turn to American themes and the romantic formula, this pattern was always present in his work and vied with the long chase and capture as the principal motivation for his narratives. The "Leather-Stocking" series, many of the sea tales, and some of his historical narratives remained pure romance, but most of his other work took the form of the novel of manners or of social purpose. The popularity of his romantic stories and the neglect of the others has led to the conception that he wrote only romances, whereas a good half of his work is in the other mode. This latter interest also asserted itself in his travel letters, his controversial pamphlets, and his naval history and biographies. Nevertheless, his powers in the description of American scenes, in sustaining action through a long succession of events, in creating a romantic atmosphere for his stories, and in drawing vivid though stereotyped characters, have made a place for him as a writer of romantic fiction, second perhaps only to Scott.

Born in Burlington, N. J., Sept. 15, 1789, he was christened "James Cooper," adding himself his mother's family name "Fenimore" many years later. He was the eleventh of twelve children of William Cooper and Elizabeth Fenimore, both descendants of early settlers, the one of English Quaker and the other of Swedish stock. William Cooper who already owned much land in New Jersey, acquired by default, in 1785, a large patent in central New York State. There he built a mansion on the southern shore of Lake Otsego, founded Cooperstown, and moved his family when James was less than a year old. The boy grew up in a small town settled by immigrants from neighboring states, to whom his father was both judge and baronial lord, surrounded by the wilderness estates of Dutch patroons and English patentees. The Indians had migrated north to Canada by this time, but the pathless forests were on all sides. Expelled from Yale in 1806 for a boyish prank, Cooper sailed on a merchant vessel to England and Spain, and two years later enlisted in the U. S. Navy. That winter was spent at Otsego, on Lake Ontario, where the government was building a miniature navy to protect its northern frontier. His father died in 1809, and Cooper married Susan Augusta DeLancey in 1811, resigned from the Navy, and settled at Mamaroneck on the north shore of Long Island Sound. The DeLanceys had been Tories in the Revolution and had lost their lands, but their connections, the Heathcotes, continued the aristocratic tradition, and the young seaman became a landed proprietor, an officer in the local militia, an attendant though not a member of the Episcopal Church, and the owner of a fine horse and a whaling vessel. In 1820, he published his first novel, *Precaution*, an attempt to better an English tale which he had been reading to his wife. His next novel, *The Spy* (1821), an acknowledgment of his error in attempting an English rather than an American theme, was suggested by an anecdote of a spy in the neutral ground about New York City during Revolutionary War, told by his neighbor, Judge Jay. With *The Pioneers* (1823), he turned to his boyhood scenes and began the "Leather-Stocking" series upon which his fame chiefly rests; and with *The Pilot* (1823), he attempted to write a more realistic tale of the sea than Scott's *The Pirate*. By this time his reputation as a novelist had reached Europe and his career was settled. He moved his growing family of daughters to New York City where he became the center of a literary and social group; and in 1826, he set out for Europe with his wife, his daughters, and his infant son, to settle the perplexing business of the foreign publication of his writings and to provide his children with the cultural background of which he so strongly felt the lack in himself. The next seven years were spent chiefly in Paris, with shorter residences in London, Italy, Germany, and Switzerland, of which six novels and the *Gleanings in Europe* (1836–38) were the principal literary products. His friendship with Lafayette and the French liberals led to an involvement in a controversy on the relative expenses of the French and American governments, which aroused considerable enmity at home. Cooper made the mistake of becoming angry at his critics, and the rest of his life was colored by a war with the press, which centered about various issues, but which was actually a social war between a liberal aristocrat of the Lafayette pattern and a people rapidly becoming more and more leveled to a democratic equality in all things, including culture. After his return, he wrote with amazing rapidity a series of historical, Indian, and sea tales, at least parts of which are superior to his early work; but his chief interest had now become social criticism, and the novels into which he threw the greatest effort were those dealing with manners and social problems. In addition, he published his *History of the Navy* (1839), which immediately involved him in another controversy, and many tracts, the most important of which was *The American Democrat* (1838). He remodeled Otsego Hall, his father's second and larger home at Cooperstown, and in 1834 took up the same sort of life that his father had lived before him, with the important difference that he was feared rather than respected by his fellow-townsmen. His popularity grew steadily less, and with it the income from his novels, while he fought with the Whig press for a law of libel which would protect an author from personal criticism; but his legal successes did him little practical good. He wrote steadily almost up to the day of his death, Sept. 14, 1851. The most significant of his social novels are perhaps the three "Littlepage Manuscripts": *Satanstoe* (1845), *The Chainbearer* (1846), and *The Redskins* (1846), a trilogy dealing with the Anti-Rent War in New York State, but providing a thorough study of the decline of the New York aristocracy through three generations.

The most important of the works published during Cooper's lifetime are: *Precaution* (1820); *The Spy* (1821); *The Pioneers* (1823); *Tales for Fifteen* (1823); *The Pilot* (1823); *Lionel Lincoln* (1824–25); *The Last of the Mohicans* (1826); *The Prairie* (1827); *The Red Rover* (1828); *Notions of the Americans, Picked up by a Traveling Bachelor* (1828); *The Wept of Wish-ton-Wish* (1829); *The Water Witch* (1830); *The Bravo* (1831); *Letter to Gen. Lafayette* (1831); *The Heidenmauer* (1832); *The Headsman* (1833); *A Letter to His Countrymen* (1834); *The Monikins* (1835); *Sketches of Switzerland* (1836); *Sketches of Switzerland, Part II* (1836); *Gleanings in Europe* [*France*] (1837); *Gleanings in Europe, England* (1837); *Gleanings in Europe, Italy* (1838); *The American Democrat* (1838); *The Chronicles of Cooperstown* (1838); *Homeward Bound* (1838); *Home as Found* (1838); *The History of the Navy of the United States of America* (1839); *The Pathfinder* (1840); *Mercedes of Castile* (1840); *The Deerslayer* (1841); *The Two Admirals* (1842); *The Wing-and-Wing* (1842); *Le Mouchoir* [*The Autobiography of a Pocket Handkerchief*] (1843); *The Battle of Lake Erie* (1843); *Wyandotté* (1843); *Ned Myers* (1843); *Afloat and Ashore* (1844); *Afloat and Ashore, Part II* [*Miles Wallingford*] (1844); *Satanstoe* (1845); *The Chainbearer* (1846); *Lives of Distinguished Naval Officials* (1846); *The Redskins* (1846); *Jack Tier* [*The Islets of the Gulf*] (1848; published in *Graham's Magazine*, 1846–48); *The Crater* (1847); *The Oak Openings* (1848); *The Sea Lions* (1849); and *The Ways of the Hour* (1849). In addition, there were many contributions to periodicals and collections, only one of which has been separately published, *The Lake Gun* (1932); and a part of a manuscript left unfinished at his death and published as *New York* (1930). The standard edition of Cooper's novels is that published by W. A. Townsend, with illustrations by F. O. C. Darley (1859–61). The critical prose, with the exception of two volumes of the *Gleanings in Europe* (ed. by R. E. Spiller 1928–1930) and *The American Democrat* (1931), has not been republished. Many of the Cooper manuscripts were destroyed, at his own direction; the most important collection of those remaining was recently donated by James Fenimore Cooper, his grandson, to Yale University. Letters have been published in a variety of places, and in the *Correspondence*, edited by J. F. Cooper (1922). For biography, see W. C. Bryant's "Discourse" in *Memorial of James Fenimore Cooper* (1852); T. R. Lounsbury (1883); M. E. Phillips (1913); W. S. B. Clymer (1918); H. W. Boynton (1931); and R. E. Spiller (1931). A descriptive bibliography by R. E. Spiller and P. C. Blackburn is in preparation.

630. THE FLIGHT OF THE PIGEONS is Chapter XXII of *The Pioneers* (1823), the first of the

"Leather-Stocking" series, and the most nearly autobiographical of all of Cooper's novels. In it, he paints a vivid picture of the wooded hills about Cooperstown and of the local characters he had known best in his boyhood. Natty Bumppo is introduced in the early pages as the man of the woods who has learned from nature a complete self-reliance and a homely wisdom. Both qualities are apparent in the narrative of this incident, probably the memory of an actual occurrence. The texts of this and other selections from Cooper's novels are from the revised ed. collected by W. A. Townsend and illustrated F. O. C. Darley (1859–61). ¶630. "*Somerville,*" William Somerville (1677–1742), an English poet. ¶630. "*Otsego,*" the lake formed in the low mountains at the head-waters of the Susquehanna River in central N. Y. State. Cooperstown is at its foot. ¶631. "*Elizabeth,*" Elizabeth Temple, heroine of the novel. ¶631. "*Richard,*" Richard Jones. ¶631. "*The army of Xerxes.*" Xerxes (*c.* 519–*c.* 464 B.C.), king of Persia, assembled a large army for the conquest of Greece, bridged the Hellespont, burned Athens, but was defeated at Salamis (480 B.C.) and returned to Asia Minor. ¶631. "*Marmaduke*" Temple, father of Elizabeth, said to have been patterned after Cooper's father. ¶632. "*Leather-stocking,*" Natty Bumppo, the huntsman hero who under different names figures in all the novels of the series. ¶632. "*Templeton,*" Cooperstown. ¶633. "*Mingo,*" a tribe of Indians. ¶636. "*Rodney's victory.*" Baron George Rodney (1718–1792), English admiral, gained a decisive victory over the French under De Grasse off Dominica, Apr. 12, 1782.

636. [LEATHER-STOCKING AND CHINGACHGOOK] is Chapter III of *The Last of the Mohicans* (1826). The hunter and the Indian about whom the "Leather-Stocking" series is written are here introduced in a typical colloquy. In their discussion of values in human conduct, they express Cooper's personal ideals while revealing his romantic conception of character. ¶636. "*Before these fields,*" etc. is quoted from "An Indian at the Burial-Place of His Fathers," by William Cullen Bryant. ¶638. "*Chingachgook,*" a Mohican, father of Uncas, and long a friend of Leather-Stocking and the whites. ¶638. "*Hawk-eye,*" Natty Bumppo. ¶640 "*Alligewi,*" perhaps the Alleghanies, a group comprised of Delawares and Shawnee. ¶640. "*Maquas,*" "Makwa," a branch of the Mohican. ¶640. "*Sagomore,*" the Abnaki (Algonquins of Maine) name for a chief. ¶641. "*The Delaware country,*" principally the valley of the Delaware River, in Pa., N. J., and Del., the country of the Delaware Indian Tribe. ¶641. "*Montcalm,*" Louis Joseph Montcalm (1712–1759), French general, defeated by Wolfe and killed in battle of Quebec (Sept. 13, 1759). ¶642. "*The whole Six Nations,*" the Iroquois.

643. [THE ACTION BETWEEN THE SERAPIS AND THE BON HOMME RICHARD] is from *A History of the Navy* (1839). Better even than his many novels of the sea, it illustrates his narrative power and his ability to deal with ships as characters in his action. Compare Freneau's poem on the same subject (p.339). ¶643. "*Com. Jones,*" John Paul Jones, commander of the American ship, the *Bon Homme Richard*. ¶643. "*Capt. Landais,*" Pierre Landais (1731–1820), Frenchman, officer in American Navy, commander of the *Alliance* under John Paul Jones in 1779. ¶644. "*Capt. Pearson,*" Sir Richard Pearson (1731–1806), captain of the *Serapis*, British ship captured by John Paul Jones (1779). ¶647. "*Grape and canister,*" military terms denoting types of cannon ammunition, usually a case or bag containing a number of small iron balls. ¶648. "*A Letter of marque,*" a letter given by a sovereign to a subject authorizing him to "privateer" or make raids on foreigners; exempted from piracy charges; the term is also applied to the ship itself. ¶649. "*Mr. Dale,*" Richard Dale (1756–1826), first lieut. of the *Bon Homme Richard*, later a commodore in the American Navy.

652. [NEW YORK SOCIETY] is Chapter II of *Satanstoe* (1845), the first of the "Littlepage" trilogy. It was written primarily as a document in the so-called "Anti-Rent War," of the '40's and '50's in northern N. Y. State. The Dutch patroons, of whom the Van Rensselaers were the most powerful, had maintained their feudal power over the tenants of the vast tracts which they owned since the earliest days. With the death of the last of them, Stephen Van Rensselaer, in 1839, the tenants rose in opposition to the system and conducted a series of raiding parties. Cooper's aristocratic temperament and his feeling for personal property rights led him to take the side of the patroon system against that of the people, and he wrote his novels, *Satanstoe*, *The Chainbearer*, and *The Redskins* as a defense of property against a form of communism. The series has significance as a social document because it carries its story back to pre-Revolutionary days and gives a connected social

history of N. Y. State through three generations. Furthermore, *Satanstoe*, and to a lesser degree *The Chainbearer*, are among the best novels that he ever wrote. Corny Littlepage, the founder of the family, was born in Westchester Co., N. Y., near the DeLancey home. The action of the novel takes place in this section, up the Hudson valley, and in the country n. w. of Cooperstown. Compare Paulding's *The Dutchman's Fireside* (p. 529). ¶652. "*I would there were no age*," etc., *Winter's Tale*, III, iii, 59. ¶652. "*Leyden*," the University of Leyden, founded in 1575, in the city of Leyden, Holland. ¶653. "*The two first Æneids*," probably the first two of the twelve books of Virgil's *Æneid*. ¶653. "*Nassau Hall*," Princeton University. ¶653. "*Eton or Westminster*," schools in Eng. ¶653. "*Old York*," Eng. ¶654. "*Westchester*" Co., N. Y. State. ¶654. "*Satanstoe*," a small peninsula in Long Island Sound above N. Y., shaped like a toe. ¶654. "*Rockland*" County, in southeastern N. Y. State. ¶655. "*Yorkshire man, or a Cornishman*," inhabitants of York or Cornwall, Eng. ¶656. "*Roundhead*," Puritan, esp. the followers of Cromwell. ¶658. "*The fort*," now the aquarium at the Battery. ¶658. "*Harlem ferry*." The Harlem River makes N. Y. City an island by joining the Hudson and East Rivers. ¶659. "*The Patroon of Albany*," Stephen Van Rensselaer (1765–1839), the eighth patroon of Rensselaerwick, in N. Y. State. ¶660. "*Kingsbridge*," now a part of the Bronx, N. Y. City. ¶661. "*Stephen de Lancey*" (*c.* 1740–1801), lawyer, politician, and loyalist; left New York for Nova Scotia in 1783; Mrs. Cooper's cousin.

662. [AMERICAN LITERATURE] is Letter XXIII of *Notions of the Americans, Picked Up by a Travelling Bachelor* (1828). This work is his first sustained defense of the American character, ideals, and institutions against the detraction of British critics and travelers. It is built upon the fiction of a club of traveling gentlemen of all nationalities whose aim in life is studying the varieties of social experience in all parts of the world. The British member of the club comes to America with this intent and is guided by John Cadwalader, an American gentlemen representative of Cooper's social ideal. The work deals with all aspects of American life in an urbane spirit, and, although strongly pro-American in its comments, it is a faithful account in so far as the facts are concerned. ¶662. "*Abbate Giromachi*," an invented character, the Italian member of the club of traveling gentlemen. ¶662. "*The first journal*," see Intro., p. 12. ¶664. "*A capital American publisher*," probably Matthew Carey. ¶665. "*Halleck*," Fitz-Greene Halleck, see pp. 510–515. ¶665. "*One of the journals of New-York*," "The Croaker Papers." ¶666. "*A jeu d'esprit*": "play of mind," a witticism. ¶666. "*Bryant*," see pp. 470–503. ¶666. "*Percival*," see p. 504. ¶666. "*Sprague*," Charles Sprague (1791–1875), American poet. ¶666. "*Their success purely as writers of romance*." Cooper here discusses the problems which confronted him personally. ¶667. "*Edwards*," Jonathan Edwards, see pp. 168–191. ¶667. "*Ionic*," one of the three Greek orders of architecture, distinguished by the spiral volutes of the capital of the columns. ¶667. "*Théâtre Français*," in Paris. ¶667. "*Cooke*," George Frederick Cooke (1756–1811), English actor, esp. Shakespearean rôles.

669. [A VISIT FROM SCOTT] is from *Gleanings in Europe* (1837), the first of Cooper's five volumes of travel letters dealing with his residence in Europe, 1826–33. He had put his daughters in a Paris school and had taken an apartment in the same building. He had never been sympathetic with Scott's social philosophy, and had written many novels to prove that the latter's material was subject to interpretations quite opposite to the feudal ideals of his contemporary, but when Scott presented himself, he immediately welcomed him. The topic of their conversation was the problem of international copyright. Cooper met Scott later in London, but their relationship was never more than superficially courteous. The ideals and personalities of the two men were in sharp opposition, even though their literary interests and methods were similar. ¶669. "*Mr. Canning*," George Canning (1770–1827), English statesman. ¶669. "*Sir Walter Scott*," see pp. 623–29. ¶669. "*Psalmanazar*," "Psalmister," one appointed to sing psalms. ¶669. "*Paul's Letters to his Kinsfolk*," by Sir Walter Scott; a record of his trip to the continent in 1815. ¶669. "*Princesse [Galitzin]*" (1748–1806), Russian emigrée, wife of Dmitri Galitzin (1738–1803), noted pietist. ¶669. "*Coûte que coûte*": "Let it cost what it may." ¶670. "*Au second*": "on the second floor." ¶670. "*Est-ce Monsieur——, que ja'ai l'honneur de voir?*": "Is this Mr. Cooper whom I have the honor to see?" ¶670. "*Monsieur, je m'appele ——.*" "*Eh bien, donc—je suis Walter Scott.*": "Sir, my name is Cooper." "Good, I am Walter Scott." ¶670. "*Exquisites*," overnice in tastes or manners. ¶671. "*Salle à manger*": dining room. ¶671. "*Salon*": living room.

¶671. *"Cabinet"*: study. ¶671. *"Corridor"*: hall. ¶671. *"General Lafayette"* was at this time living in his Paris home in the rue d'Anjou. ¶672. *"Gosling,"* Gosselin, publisher of French translations of the works of Cooper and Scott. ¶672. *"Bonne foi"*: "good faith." ¶672. *"M'Donald,"* John MacDonald (1779–1849), Scottish Presbyterian clergyman. ¶672. *"Tour de force"*: "feat of strength," something requiring great effort. ¶672. *"W[illiam]"* Cooper, his secretary, died a few years later in Paris. ¶672. *"Bergère"*: arm chair.

673. ON DISTINCTIVE AMERICAN PRINCIPLES and (677) AN ARISTOCRAT AND A DEMOCRAT are from *The American Democrat* (1838). In this, the most succinct statement of his social and political creeds, Cooper attempts to prove that an aristocracy of social worth and private property is essential in a political democracy if literature and the other amenities are to thrive. He does so by outlining what he believes to be typical American principles, arguing the advantages of a democratic over other forms of government, and discussing the bearing of his ideals upon such problems as slavery and private property. ¶673. *"The act of succession,"* the Act of Settlement (1701), passed by the British Parliament, deciding that after Anne the British crown should go the Protestant heirs of Sophia of Hanover; George I (1714–1727) was the first of the line.

Indian Songs and Legends

The early Indian missionaries, from John Eliot down, were interested in reforming and converting the aborigines rather than in studying their culture. The literature of the Indians has been preserved to us in its remnants only because American scholars have, in recent years, come to a tardy appreciation of its beauty and importance. When Henry Rowe Schoolcraft (1793–1864) was appointed, in 1822, the government agent for Indian affairs on the northwestern frontiers, he initiated the broader study of Indian culture which led to his *Algic Researches* (1839) and his monumental work on the *History, Conditions and Prospects of the Indian Tribes of the United States* (1851–57). Many of his conclusions have since been proved erroneous; for example, his confusion of the Iroquoian reformer and statesman Hiawatha with the Chippewa deity Manabozho, but he provided a broad foundation for later researches. During the past three decades, with the Indians safely isolated on reservations, the study which he began has been continued by anthropologists, ethnologists, musicians, and literary scholars in great numbers. Representative of this work are Alice C. Fletcher's *Omaha Music* (1899), her *Indian Song and Story* (1900), the various bulletins on Indian music, by Frances Densmore, issued by the Bureau of American Ethnology, and *The Indians' Book*, by Natalie Curtis Burlin (1907). The essays, songs, and stories in this latter book are all taken down in writing from recitation of descendants of the earlier tribes. They are doubtless influenced by contact with the civilization of the white man, but their essential spirit is unquestionably preserved. In them we find the religion of nature, the symbolism, the superstition, the personification of animals, the solemnity, the loyalty, and the love of the open which are associated with all Indians, even those of as different origins as the Algonquins and the Navajos. Mary Austin, in *The American Rhythm* (1923), has presented the thesis that this uniformity of feeling creates a rhythm which is characteristic not only of the literature of the American aborigines, but of that of the white man who has settled the same territory, and is therefore fundamental in all American literature. The Department of the Interior publishes a *Bibliography of Indian Legends*, as well as many other bulletins on various aspects of Indian life.

680. HIAWATHA, OR, THE ORIGIN OF THE ONONDAGA COUNCIL-FIRE is from Schoolcraft's *History* (1851–57). This tale was "derived from the verbal narratives of the late Abraham Le Fort, an Onondaga chief, who was a graduate, it is believed, of Geneva College." Longfellow's version differs in important particulars, and neither he nor Schoolcraft was correct in the identification of Hiawatha. ¶680. *"Onondaga tribe,"* N. A. Indians of the Iroquois Confederacy. ¶681. *"Onondaga lake,"* near Syracuse, N. Y., formerly the center of the Onondaga territory.

683. HUNTING THE MOOSE is from Natalie Curtis' *The Indians' Book* (1907). The legend was told by Bedagi [Big Thunder] of the Wabanaki [Algonquin] Indians. ¶684. *"Ksiwhambeh,"* the cultured hero of the eastern Algonquins.

684. T'ÄPK'O DAAGYA is from *The Indians' Book*. It was sung and told by T'e-ne-t'e [Eagle Chief] of the Kiowa Indians of the southwest plains. These Indians originally came from the sources of the Missouri and

Yellowstone Rivers. A quarrel over an antelope early caused them to divide and migrate.

686. The Story of Wakiash and the First Totem Pole is from *The Indians' Book.* Told by Klalish [Charles James Nowell] of the Kwakiutl Indians, a branch of the Wakashans of the northwest coast near Yakutat Bay.

688. Mountain-Songs are from *The Indians' Book.* They were sung by Navajos near Fort Defiance, Ariz.

INDEX

Non-italic numbers refer to pages in text; italic numbers to pages in notes.

Abbotsford and Newstead Abbey 623, *747*
Action Between the *Serapis* and *Bon Homme Richard* 643, *750*
Advice to Authors 359, *724*
Age of Benevolence, The 504, *734*
Age of Reason, The 263, *712*
Alhambra, The 613, *747*
ALLEN, ETHAN 157, *705*
American Crisis, The 256, *712*
American Democrat, The 673, *752*
American Flag, The 528, *738*
American Literature 662, *751*
American Poetry 470, *732*
Another Election 407, *726*
Ant-Hill Town 457, *730*
Appearance of Christ, The 76, *698*
Aristocrat and a Democrat, An .677, *752*
Arrival of the Dutch 570, *743*
Arthur Mervyn 423, *728*
AUDUBON, JOHN JAMES 463, *731*
Author to Her Book, The 75, *698*
Author's Account of Himself, The 584, *745*
Autobiography, Jefferson 276, *714*
Autobiography, The (Franklin)..192, *708*

BARLOW, JOEL 307, *718*
BARTRAM, WILLIAM 445, *729*
Battle of the Kegs, The 316, *719*
Battle with the Iroquois, A 33, *692*
"Bay Psalm Book, The" 67, *697*
Bloudy Tenent, The 64, *696*
BOUCHER, JONATHAN 269, *713*
Boyhood 192, *708*
Bracebridge Hall 606, *746*
BRACKENRIDGE, HUGH HENRY...404, *726*
BRADFORD, WILLIAM 46, *694*
BRADSTREET, ANNE 68, *697*
BRYANT, WILLIAM CULLEN 470, *731*
British Prison Ship, The 335, *722*
BROWN, CHARLES BROCKDEN ...423, *728*
BYRD, WILLIAM 130, *702*

Captain Farrago 404, *726*
Captivity 41, *693*
Cavern and the Panther, The...435, *729*
CHAMPLAIN, SAMUEL DE 33, *692*
CHANNING, WILLIAM ELLERY ..542, *740*
Charlotte Temple 416, *727*
Christmas Eve 586, *746*
COLUMBUS, CHRISTOPHER 23, *691*
Combats with the Turks 40, *693*
Common Sense 245, *712*
Concord and Lexington 267, *713*
Congressional Debate, A 412, *726*
Consequences of the Tea Party, The 264, *713*
Contemplations 71, *698*
Containing Observations 411, *726*
Contrast, The 366, *725*
Conversion, A 410, *726*
COOPER, JAMES FENIMORE 630, *748*
Courtship in New York 529, *739*
Courtship of Madam Winthrop, The 97, *700*
Creed, A 263, *712*
CRÈVECŒUR, ST. JOHN DE 451, *730*
Culprit Fay, The 515, *737*

Day of Doom, The 75, *698*
Declaration of Independence ...276, *714*
Death of Lincoln, The 503, *734*
DENNIE, JOSEPH 324, *720*
Definition of the Will, A 186, *707*
Deserted Farm-House, The 354, *724*
Diary (Sewall) 97, *700*
DICKINSON, JOHN 238, *710*
Discovered Islands, The 23, *691*
Dismal Swamp, The 130, *703*
Diverting History of John Bull and Brother Jonathan, The ..537, *740*

Dogood Papers 217, *710*
DRAKE, JOSEPH RODMAN 515, *737*
Dutchman's Fireside, The 529, *739*
DWIGHT, TIMOTHY 289, *715*
Dying Indian, The 352, *724*

Early Life 137, *703*
Edgar Huntly 435, *729*
Edict by the King of Prussia, An 226, *710*
EDWARDS, JONATHAN 168, *705*
Effective Government, An 285, *715*
Election, An 405, *726*
Elopement of Charlotte, The ..416, *727*
Enchantments Encountered 90, *700*
Entering Philadelphia 201, *708*
Ephemera, The 236, *710*
Essay for the Recording of Illustrious Providences, An ...83, *699*
Essays (Rush) 329, *721*
Evening Wind, The 496, *733*
Experiences in England 146, *704*

Fanny 512, *736*
Federalist, The 285, *715*
Fight with the Crocodiles, The..445, *729*
First Visit to England 203, *708*
Flight of the Pigeons, The 630, *749*
Flood, A 463, *731*
Florida Keys, The 467, *731*
Flourishing Village, The 289, *716*
Flying Spider, The 168, *706*
FOLK LITERATURE 680, *752*
Forest Hymn, A 492, *733*
Four Seasons of the Year, The ..69, *697*
FRANKLIN, BENJAMIN 192, *707*
Freedom of Man, The 149, *704*
Freedom of the Will 186, *707*
FRENEAU, PHILIP 335, *721*
Fruits of Solitude 124, *702*

General Description of Pennsylvania, A 119, *702*
General Introduction, A (*Magnalia*) 89, *700*
Generalle Historie of Virginia ...41, *693*
Gleanings in Europe 669, *751*
GODFREY, THOMAS 324, *719*
Great Awakening at Northampton, The 179, *707*
Greek and Irish 413, *726*
Greenfield Hill 289, *716*
Green River 485, *733*

HALLECK, FITZ-GREENE 510, *736*
HAMILTON, ALEXANDER 285, *715*
Hardships of the Wilderness 49, *694*
HARIOT, THOMAS 28, *691*
Hasty Pudding, The 307, *718*
HAKLUYT, RICHARD 28, *691*
Health, A 508, *735*
Hiawatha, or, the Origin of the Onondaga Council-fire 680, *752*
History of the Dividing Line ..130, *703*
History of the Navy, A 643, *750*
Home, Sweet Home 509, *736*
HOPKINSON, FRANCIS 316, *719*
House of Night, The 344, *723*
House of William Morse, The ...83, *699*
HULTON, ANNE 264, *713*
Hunting the Moose 683, *752*

I Cannot Forget with What Fervent Devotion 495, *733*
Indian Burying Ground, The ..351, *724*
Indian Mission, The 142, *704*
Indians, The 119, *702*
Indian Student, The 353, *724*
Inhabitants of the New World 280, *714*
Inscription for the Entrance to a Wood 484, *733*
IRVING, WASHINGTON 570, *742*

JEFFERSON, THOMAS 276, *714*
JOHNSON, SAMUEL 162, *705*
Jonathan and His Farm 537, *740*
Journal, The (Woolman) 137, *704*
Judgment, The 78, *698*
June 494, *733*

Knickerbocker's History of New York 570, *743*
KNIGHT, SARAH KEMBLE 111, *701*

Last of the Mohicans, The 636, *750*
Lay Preacher, The 324, *720*
Leather Stocking and Chingachgook 636, *750*
Lectures on Poetry 475, *732*
Legend of the Rose of the Alhambra 613, *747*

Les Voyages 33, *692*
Letters (Hulton) 264, *713*
Letters (Winthrop) 52, *695*
Letters from a Farmer in Pennsylvania 238, *711*
Letters from an American Farmer 451, *730*
Liberty Pole, The 299, *717*
Liberty Song, A 244, *711*
Liberty Tree 262, *712*
Light in the Temple, The 426, *729*
Love of Man 141, *703*
Love of Truth, The 162, *705*

Magnalia Christi Americana 89, *700*
Man of Ninety 357, *724*
Man of Understanding, The 324, *720*
Marco Bozzaris 510, *736*
Martha's Vineyard 454, *730*
MATHER, COTTON 89, *699*
MATHER, INCREASE 83, *698*
MATHER, RICHARD 67, *697*
Mayflower Compact, The 46, *694*
Meditations 124, *702*
Mercury's Negotiation 95, *700*
M'Fingal 299, *717*
Modern Chivalry 404, *726*
Modern Philosophers 408, *726*
Monument Mountain 489, *733*
MORTON, THOMAS 62, *695*
Moral Argument Against Calvinism, The 542, *741*
Moral Reflections 206, *708*
Mountain-Songs 688, *753*
My Life Is Like the Summer Rose 509, *735*

Narrative of Captivity 105, *701*
New-England 504, *734*
New English Canaan, The 62, *696*
New Found Land of Virginia, The 28, *691*
New Roof, The: A Song for Federal Mechanics 317, *719*
New York 117, *701*
New York Society 652, *750*
Notes on Virginia 280, *714*
Notions of the Americans 662, *751*

Ode (Freneau) 342, *723*
Of Plimmoth Plantation 46, *694*
Of Precipitation 327, *720*
Of the Revells of New Canaan ..62, *696*
Oh Fairest of the Rural Maids 498, *733*
Oh Mother of a Mighty Race 501, *734*
On a Honey Bee 356, *724*
On Civil Liberty 269, *713*
On Distinctive American Principles 673, *752*
On Education 217, *710*
On Liberty 58, *695*
On Persecution 64, *696*
On the Anniversary 343, *723*
On the Death of Joseph Rodman Drake 512, *736*
On the Memorable Victory 339, *722*
On the Nature of Poetry 475, *732*
On the Religion of Nature 358, *724*
On the Sabbath 325, *720*
On Tolerance 82, *698*
On White-Washing 318, *719*

PAINE, THOMAS 245, *711*
Past, The 495, *733*
PAULDING, JAMES KIRKE 529, *738*
PAYNE, JOHN HOWARD 509, *735*
PENN, WILLIAM 119, *702*
People of Connecticut, The 113, *701*
PERCIVAL, JAMES GATES 504, *734*
Personal Narrative 171, *707*
PINKNEY, EDWARD COOTE 507, *734*
Pioneers, The 630, *749*
Political Fables 95, *700*
Prairies, The 498, *733*
Preface (to *"Bay Psalm Book"*) 67, *697*
Principal Navigations, Voyages, etc., The 28, *691*
Private Journal on a Journey from Boston to New York, The 111, *701*
Progress of Dulness, The 296, *716*
Progress of Population in Virginia, The 329, *721*
Prologue, The 68, *697*
Psalme I 67, *697*
Psalme of David 68, *697*
Pyramids of Egypt, The 348, *723*

Raphael, or The Genius of English America 162, *705*
Reason, the Only Oracle of Man 157, *705*

Reign of William the Testy, The 572, *744*
Religion of Taste, The 506, *734*
Remarks on National Literature 556, *741*
Remarks on the Character and Writing of John Milton 548, *741*
Resolutions 178, *707*
Return, The 118, *701*
Rip Van Winkle 593, *746*
Robert of Lincoln 502, *734*
ROWLANDSON, MARY 105, *701*
ROWSON, SUSANNA HASWELL ..416, *727*
Rule of Life, A 208, *710*
Rules by which a Great Empire may be Reduced to a Small One 229, *710*
RUSH, BENJAMIN 329, *721*

Sailor's Relief, The 362, *724*
Sarah Pierrepont 178, *707*
Satanstoe 652, *750*
Scott, Sir Walter 623, *747*
Serenade, A 508, *735*
Setting Out 111, *701*
SEWALL, SAMUEL 97, *700*
Simple Cobler of Aggawam, The 82, *698*
Sketch book of Geoffrey Crayon, Gentn, The 584, *745*
SMITH, JOHN 40, *693*
Song (Godfrey) 324, *720*
Song of Marion's Men 497, *733*
Spring 69, *697*
Story of Wakiash and First Totem Pole, The 686, *753*
Stout Gentleman, The 606, *746*
Stricken City, The 424, *728*
Summer Noon, A 504, *734*
Superstition *vs.* Reason 157, *705*

T'Äpk'o Daagya 684, *752*
Thanatopsis 482, *733*
To a Caty-did 356, *724*
To a Friend 525, *738*
To a Waterfowl 484, *733*
Tom Brainless at College 296, *716*
To My Dear and Loving Husband 69, *697*
To My Dear Children 68, *697*
To Myrtilla 316, *719*
To Shylock Ap-Shenkin 342, *723*
To the Christian Reader 75, *698*
To the Fringed Gentian 498, *733*
To the Memory 341, *723*
To the Mocking Bird 509, *735*
Travels 445, *729*
True Travels, The 40, *693*
TRUMBULL, JOHN 296, *716*
Tryal of Bridget Bishop, The ...92, *700*
TYLER, ROYALL 366, *724*

Valiant Peter Stuyvesant, The .577, *745*
Vanity of Existence, The 358, *724*
View of the Causes and Consequences of the American Revolution, A 269, *713*
Vindication of the Government of New England Churches, A 149, *704*
Visit from Scott, A 669, *751*
Voyager's Song, The 507, *735*

WARD, NATHANIEL 82, *698*
Way to Wealth, The 220, *710*
What Is an American 451, *730*
Whistle, The 235, *710*
Wieland 426, *729*
WIGGLESWORTH, MICHAEL 75, *698*
WILCOX, CARLOS 504, *734*
Wild Honey Suckle, The 355, *724*
WILDE, RICHARD HENRY 509, *735*
WILLIAMS, ROGER 64, *696*
Winter Piece, A 486, *733*
WINTHROP, JOHN 52, *694*
WISE, JOHN 149, *704*
Wonders of the Invisible World, The 90, *700*
WOOLMAN, JOHN 137, *703*

Yellow Fever, The 423, *728*
Yellow Violet, The 489, *733*
Young Lady of New York 512, *736*